Sixteenth Edition

College Accounting

Chapters 1–30

JOHN ELLIS PRICE, Ph.D., CPA
Professor of Accounting (Retired)
University of North Texas
Denton, Texas

M. DAVID HADDOCK JR., Ed.D., CPA
Professor of Accounting (Retired)
Chattanooga State Community College
Chattanooga, Tennessee

MICHAEL J. FARINA, MBA, CPA, CGMA
Professor of Accounting
Cerritos College
Norwalk, California

COLLEGE ACCOUNTING, SIXTEENTH EDITION

Chapters 1–30

Published by McGraw-Hill Education, 2 Penn Plaza, New York, NY 10121. Copyright © 2021 by McGraw-Hill Education. All rights reserved. Printed in the United States of America. Previous editions © 2017, 2015, and 2012. No part of this publication may be reproduced or distributed in any form or by any means, or stored in a database or retrieval system, without the prior written consent of McGraw-Hill Education, including, but not limited to, in any network or other electronic storage or transmission, or broadcast for distance learning.

Some ancillaries, including electronic and print components, may not be available to customers outside the United States.

This book is printed on acid-free paper.

1 2 3 4 5 6 7 8 9 LWI 24 23 22 21 20

ISBN 978-1-260-24790-9 (chapters 1–30) (bound edition)
MHID 1-260-24790-2 (chapters 1–30) (bound edition)
ISBN 978-1-260-78027-7 (chapters 1–30) (loose-leaf edition)
MHID 1-260-78027-9 (chapters 1–30) (loose-leaf edition)
ISBN 978-1-260-78041-3 (chapters 1–13) (bound edition)
MHID 1-260-78041-4 (chapters 1–13) (bound edition)
ISBN 978-1-260-78023-9 (chapters 1–13) (loose-leaf edition)
MHID 1-260-78023-6 (chapters 1–13) (loose-leaf edition)

Executive Portfolio Manager: *Steve Schuetz*
Product Developer: *Michael McCormick*
Marketing Manager: *Claire McLemore*
Content Project Managers: *Lori Koetters, Angela Norris*
Senior Buyer: *Laura Fuller*
Design: *Matt Diamond*
Content Licensing Specialist: *Sarah Flynn*
Cover Image: ©*Lixiang/Shutterstock*
Compositor: *SPi Global*

All credits appearing on page or at the end of the book are considered to be an extension of the copyright page.

Library of Congress Control Number: 2019948192

The Internet addresses listed in the text were accurate at the time of publication. The inclusion of a website does not indicate an endorsement by the authors or McGraw-Hill Education, and McGraw-Hill Education does not guarantee the accuracy of the information presented at these sites.

mheducation.com/highered

About the Authors

Courtesy of John Ellis Price

JOHN ELLIS PRICE is a retired professor of accounting at the University of North Texas. Dr. Price has more than 36 years of experience in higher education with over half of those years serving in key leadership positions including as founding president and professor of accounting at the University of North Texas at Dallas. Dr. Price has previously held positions of professor and assistant professor, as well as chair and dean, at the University of North Texas, Jackson State University, and the University of Southern Mississippi. Dr. Price has also been active in the Internal Revenue Service as a member of the Commissioner's Advisory Group for two terms and as an Internal Revenue Agent.

Dr. Price is a certified public accountant who has twice received the UNT College of Business Administration's Outstanding Teaching Award and the university's President's Council Award. Majoring in accounting, he received his BBA and MS degrees from the University of Southern Mississippi and his PhD in accounting from the University of North Texas.

Dr. Price is a member of the Mississippi Society of Certified Public Accountants, the American Accounting Association, and the American Taxation Association (serving as past chair of the Subcommittee on Relations with the IRS and Treasury). Dr. Price has also served as chair of the American Institute of Certified Public Accountants Minority Initiatives Committee and as a member of the Foundation Trustees.

Courtesy of M. David Haddock Jr.

M. DAVID HADDOCK JR. serves as Chief Leadership Officer for a regional operator of senior living communities. He previously led the training efforts for one of the top 50 CPA firms in the United States. In a 35-year career in higher education, Dr. Haddock served in faculty and administrative roles at Auburn University at Montgomery, the University of Alabama in Birmingham, the University of West Georgia, and Chattanooga State Community College. At his retirement from higher education, he was professor of accounting and associate vice president for academic affairs at Chattanooga State Community College in Tennessee. In addition to his teaching, he also maintained a sole proprietorship accounting and tax practice for more than 20 years.

He received his BS in accounting and MS in adult education from the University of Tennessee and the EdD degree in administration of higher education from Auburn University. He is a licensed CPA in Tennessee.

Dr. Haddock served as chair of the Tennessee Society of CPAs and the Educational & Memorial Foundation of the TSCPAs for 2012–2013 and a member of AICPA Council. He is a frequent speaker for Continuing Professional Education programs.

Courtesy of Michael J. Farina

MICHAEL J. FARINA retired as professor of accounting and finance at Cerritos College in California June 2018, after 30 years of service to the college. He continues to teach college accounting and other courses as an adjunct professor at Cerritos College. Professor Farina is currently a member of an advisory committee at a credit union serving the educational community in California.

Prior to joining Cerritos College, Professor Farina was a manager in the audit department at a large multinational firm of certified public accountants and held management positions with other companies in private industry.

He received an AA in business administration from Cerritos College; a BA in business administration from California State University, Fullerton; and an MBA from the University of California, Irvine. Professor Farina is a member of Beta Gamma Sigma, an honorary fraternity for graduate business students. He is a licensed certified public accountant in California and a member of the American Institute of Certified Public Accountants and the California Society of Certified Public Accountants. Professor Farina is also a Chartered Global Management Accountant, a designation bestowed by a joint venture of the American Institute of Certified Public Accountants and the Chartered Institute of Management Accountants.

Professor Farina has received three Outstanding Faculty awards from Cerritos College. He was the co-chair of the Accounting and Finance Department at Cerritos College for over 20 years.

Price/Haddock/Farina

©Lixiang/Shutterstock

For students just embarking on a college career, an accounting course can seem daunting, like a rushing river with no clear path to the other side. As the most trusted and readable text on the market, *College Accounting* by Price, Haddock, and Farina presents material in a way that will help students understand the content better and more quickly. Through proven pedagogy, time-tested and accurate problem material, and a straightforward approach to the basics of accounting, Price/Haddock/Farina **bridges the rushing river,** offering first-time accounting students a path to understanding and mastery.

Whether a student is taking the course in preparation for a four-year degree or as the first step to a career in business, Price/Haddock/Farina guides him or her over the bridge to success. The authors represent the breadth of educational environments—a community college, a career school, and a four-year university—ensuring that the text is appropriate for all student populations. Throughout, they have adhered to a common philosophy about textbooks: They should be readable, contain many opportunities for practice, and be able to make accounting relevant for all.

How Does Price/Haddock/Farina Bridge the Gap from Learning to Mastery?

College Accounting is designed to help students learn and master the material.

Chapter Opener

Brief features about **real-world companies**—like **Uber, H&R Block, Starbucks,** and **Carnival Cruise Lines**—allow students to see how the chapter's information and insights apply to the world outside the classroom. Thinking Critically questions stimulate thought on the topics to be explored in the chapter.

Chapter 1: Accounting: The Language of Business

www.uber.com

How do you get from the airport to your hotel when traveling on business? How do you get home from a party when it is not safe for you to drive? How do you get into the downtown business district for a meeting when parking is difficult and expensive? How do you get to any destination when taking your own vehicle is not convenient or possible? Taxis are not always available or affordable, and public transportation is difficult when in an unfamiliar city. Uber is a viable alternative to taxis and other forms of public transportation.

Uber was created in 2009 as a private company in San Francisco, California, on a smartphone app used to summon personal transportation from Uber drivers who use their own vehicles to transport customers. Uber's initial business model as a personal transportation company has transformed to a multifaceted company that provides transportation, food delivery, bicycle-sharing, and a transfer network company that operates in over 785 metropolitan areas worldwide.

Although Uber has had a turbulent history since its founding as a private company, it has raised a massive amount of investment capital to fund its operations. In January 2018, Uber raised $1.25 billion in cash from an investment group through a financing arrangement that valued the company at $48 billion. In May 2018, Uber announced plans to have an initial public offering in 2019 that would change the company to a publicly traded company.

As Uber continues to grow and seek additional investment funding, accountants are pivotal in tracking and reporting the company's financial results and position in terms of revenues earned, expenses used, assets owned, and liabilities owed as well as calculating the company's net income (revenues − expenses) and net worth (assets − liabilities). Accountants are essential to the company's continued growth and success by providing financial information necessary for decision making.

thinking critically
Can you think of any organizations that would be interested in how Uber is performing?

Learning Objectives

Appearing in the chapter opener, section opener, and within the margins of the text, learning objectives alert students to what they should expect as they progress through the chapter. Many students question the relevance of what they're learning, which is why we explain **"Why It's Important"** at the beginning of each section within the chapter.

About Accounting

These notes contain interesting examples of how accounting is used in the real world, providing relevance to students who might not be going on to a career in accounting.

ABOUT ACCOUNTING
Accounting Software
The use of accounting software eliminates the need to prepare a worksheet. However, adjusting entries must always be made to properly reflect account balances at the end of a reporting period.

Recall and Important!

Recall is a series of brief reinforcements that serve as reminders of material covered in *previous* chapters that are relevant to the new information being presented. **Important!** draws students' attention to critical materials introduced in the *current* chapter.

recall

Expense
An expense is an outflow of cash, the use of other assets, or the incurring of a liability.

important!

Balance Sheet Accounts
The amounts on the balance sheet are carried forward to the next accounting period.

Business Transaction Analysis Models

Instructors say mastering the ability to properly analyze transactions is critical to success in this course. Price/Haddock/Farina's step-by-step transaction analysis illustrations show how to identify the appropriate general ledger accounts affected, determine debit or credit activity, present the transaction in T-account form, and record the entry in the general journal.

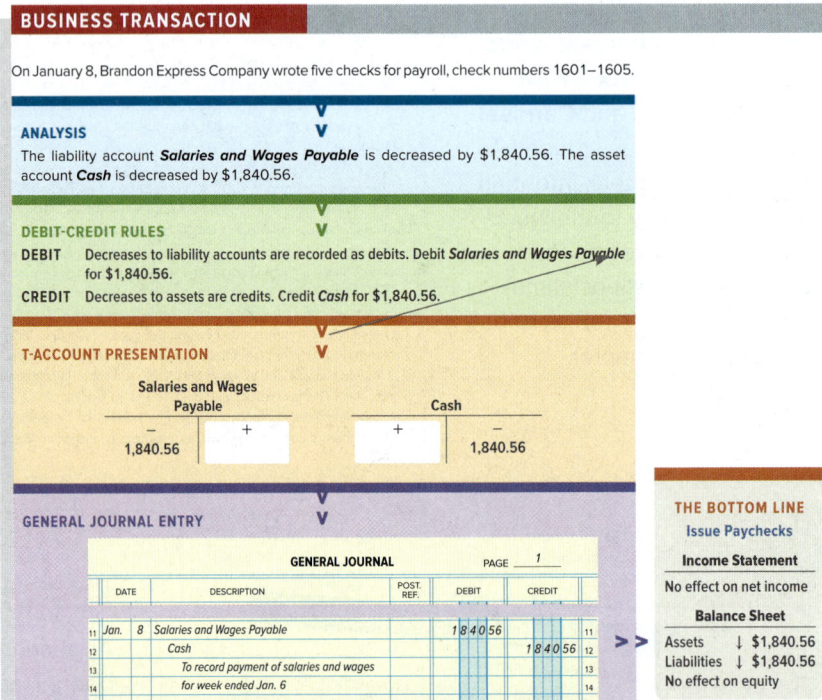

The Bottom Line

Appears in the margins alongside select transactions and concepts in the text. These visuals offer a summary of the effects of these transactions—the end result—on the financial statements of a business.

Managerial Implications

Puts your students in the role of managers and asks them to apply the concepts learned in the chapter.

MANAGERIAL IMPLICATIONS

FINANCIAL INFORMATION
- Managers of a business make sure that the firm's accounting system produces financial information that is timely, accurate, and fair.
- Financial statements should be based on generally accepted accounting principles.
- Each year a publicly traded company must submit financial statements, including an independent auditor's report, to the SEC.
- Internal reports for management need not follow generally accepted accounting principles but should provide useful information that will aid in monitoring and controlling operations.
- Financial information can help managers to control present operations, make decisions, and plan for the future.
- The sound use of financial information is essential to good management.

THINKING CRITICALLY
If you were a manager, how would you use financial information to make decisions?

Section Reviews—Now in Connect!

Each section concludes with a Self Review consisting of multiple-choice questions that are also available in Connect. A Comprehensive Self Review appears at the end of each chapter. Answers to the Comprehensive Self Review are provided at the end of the chapter.

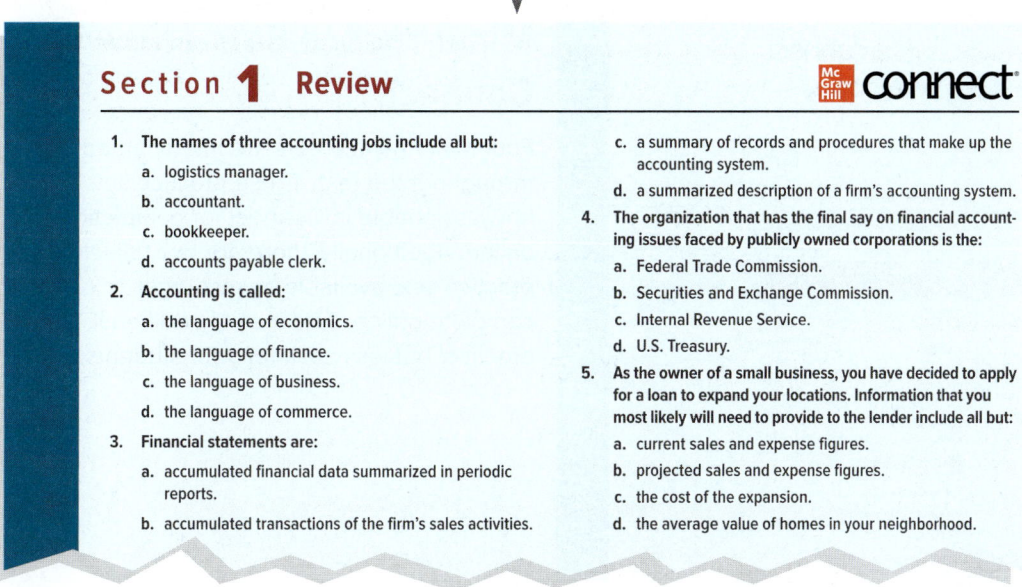

End of Chapter Material

Price/Haddock/Farina includes robust end-of-chapter material to reinforce the content of the chapter, including Discussion Questions, Exercises, Problem Sets A and B, and Critical Thinking Problems. Problem Sets A and B and Critical Thinking Problems conclude with an **Analyze** question asking the student to evaluate each problem critically.

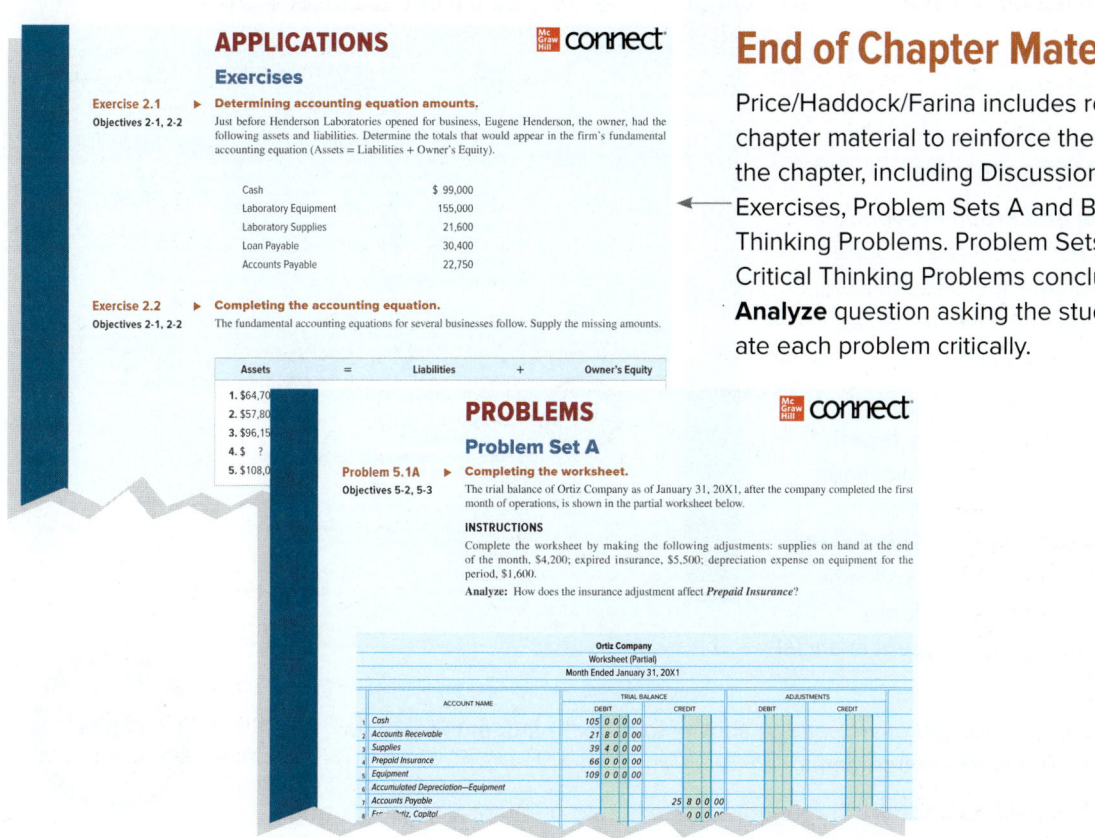

How Can Price/Haddock/Farina Bridge the Gap from Learning to "Doing"?

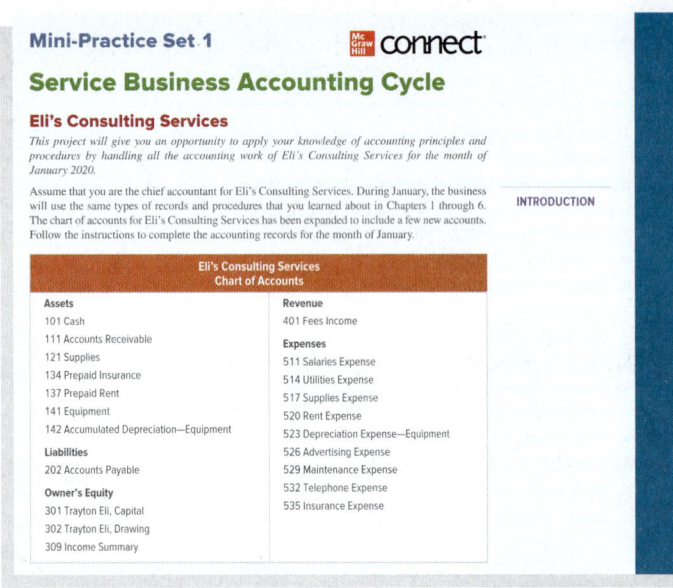

Mini-Practice Sets—Now in Connect!

Four Mini-Practice Sets are interspersed throughout the text. These practice sets are now assignable in Connect for completion online. Additionally, there are two full-length practice sets available as resources to complete offline. This means additional practice, but less cost, for your students.

Business Connections

Reinforces chapter materials from practical and real-world perspectives:

Managerial Focus: Applies accounting concepts to business situations.

Internal Control and Fraud Prevention: Applies techniques discussed throughout the text for different classes of assets including cash, payroll, inventories, and property, plant, and equipment.

Financial Statement Analysis: Uses excerpts from real-world annual reports to illustrate actual business applications of chapter concepts. Excerpts from the **2018 Home Depot Financial Statements** are included in Appendix A for use with some exercises. In others, students research a company's most recent financial reports on the Internet.

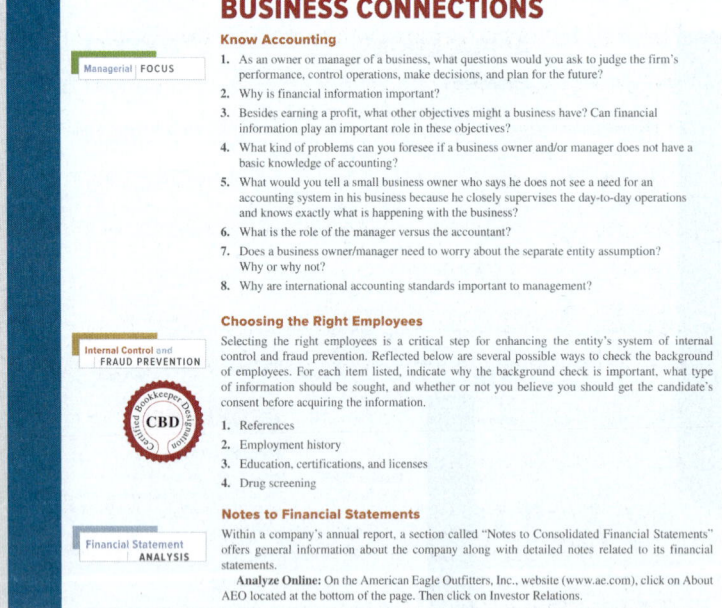

TeamWork: Provides a collaborative learning activity to prepare students for team-oriented projects and work environments.

Certified Bookkeeper Designation: Throughout the text, end-of-chapter materials now include questions that will help aspiring bookkeepers to achieve the Certified Bookkeeper Designation.

New to the Sixteenth Edition

- **NEW** Many bookkeepers aspire to become *Certified Bookkeepers (CB)*, a designation that assures an individual possesses the level of knowledge and skills needed to carry out all key accounting functions through the adjusted trial balance, including payroll. Throughout the text, end-of-chapter materials now include questions that will help aspiring bookkeepers to achieve the Certified Bookkeeper Designation.
- **NEW** Throughout the text, internal control and fraud prevention techniques are discussed for different classes of assets including cash, payroll, inventories, and property, plant, and equipment. **Internal Control and Fraud Prevention** problems are included in every chapter.
- **Chapter openers** have been revised, featuring companies such as Apple, Boeing, Costco, Deloitte, Dr Pepper Snapple, Facebook, Ford, Southwest, Starbucks, Uber, and UPS, and the Financial Accounting Standards Board.
- **Real-world examples** throughout the text have been updated.
- **End-of-chapter** exercises, problems, and critical thinking problems have been revised and updated throughout the text.
- **Section Reviews** have been updated throughout and are now available in Connect.
- **Chapter 1**: New coverage on Internal Control, Fraud, and Certified Bookkeeper added.
- **Chapter 4**: Section on Correcting Journal and Ledger Errors rewritten to reflect current practice.
- **Chapter 9**: Updated and expanded the section Using Online Banking.
- **Chapter 10**: Updated and revised with the 2019 maximum earnings taxable for social security taxes throughout.
- **Chapter 11**: Examples updated throughout text, including social security amounts per new limits of taxable amount. Auto-graded tax form problems are now in Connect.
- **Chapter 13**: New real-world example focused on the inventory turnover, using Amazon's financial data.
- **Chapter 14**: Chapter content updated for IASB Conceptual Framework, and Revenue Recognition discussion updated and expanded.
- **Chapter 20**: Clarification of LLC entities added.
- **Chapter 21**: Content updated to include the corporate income tax rate change and all cumulative effects of that change. The corporate income tax rate change from new tax law to a flat 21% rate on taxable income has a major impact, not just on this chapter, but on all the corporate chapters.
- **Chapter 29**: Real-world examples updated and now include focus on injury prevention programs and workers' compensation.

FOR INSTRUCTORS

You're in the driver's seat.

Want to build your own course? No problem. Prefer to use our turnkey, prebuilt course? Easy. Want to make changes throughout the semester? Sure. And you'll save time with Connect's auto-grading too.

65%
Less Time Grading

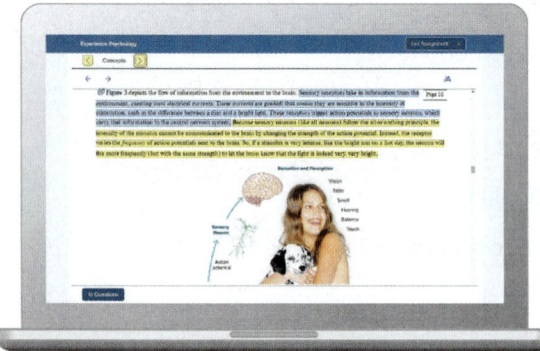

Laptop: McGraw-Hill; Woman/dog: George Doyle/Getty Images

They'll thank you for it.

Adaptive study resources like SmartBook® 2.0 help your students be better prepared in less time. You can transform your class time from dull definitions to dynamic debates. Find out more about the powerful personalized learning experience available in SmartBook 2.0 at **www.mheducation.com/highered/connect/smartbook**

Make it simple, make it affordable.

Connect makes it easy with seamless integration using any of the major Learning Management Systems—Blackboard®, Canvas, and D2L, among others—to let you organize your course in one convenient location. Give your students access to digital materials at a discount with our inclusive access program. Ask your McGraw-Hill representative for more information.

Padlock: Jobalou/Getty Images

Solutions for your challenges.

A product isn't a solution. Real solutions are affordable, reliable, and come with training and ongoing support when you need it and how you want it. Our Customer Experience Group can also help you troubleshoot tech problems—although Connect's 99% uptime means you might not need to call them. See for yourself at **status.mheducation.com**

Checkmark: Jobalou/Getty Images

FOR STUDENTS

Effective, efficient studying.

Connect helps you be more productive with your study time and get better grades using tools like SmartBook 2.0, which highlights key concepts and creates a personalized study plan. Connect sets you up for success, so you walk into class with confidence and walk out with better grades.

Study anytime, anywhere.

Download the free ReadAnywhere app and access your online eBook or SmartBook 2.0 assignments when it's convenient, even if you're offline. And since the app automatically syncs with your eBook and SmartBook 2.0 assignments in Connect, all of your work is available every time you open it. Find out more at **www.mheducation.com/readanywhere**

> *"I really liked this app—it made it easy to study when you don't have your textbook in front of you."*
>
> - Jordan Cunningham, Eastern Washington University

No surprises.

The Connect Calendar and Reports tools keep you on track with the work you need to get done and your assignment scores. Life gets busy; Connect tools help you keep learning through it all.

Calendar: owattaphotos/Getty Images

Learning for everyone.

McGraw-Hill works directly with Accessibility Services Departments and faculty to meet the learning needs of all students. Please contact your Accessibility Services office and ask them to email accessibility@mheducation.com, or visit **www.mheducation.com/about/accessibility** for more information.

Top: Jenner Images/Getty Images, Left: Hero Images/Getty Images, Right: Hero Images/Getty Images

Within Connect, instructors and students have a wealth of material at their fingertips to help make the most of a course in accounting.

Student Resources

SmartBook 2.0®
A personalized and adaptive learning tool used to maximize the learning experience by helping students study more efficiently and effectively. Smartbook 2.0 highlights where in the chapter to focus, asks review questions on the materials covered, and tracks the most challenging content for later review recharge. Smartbook 2.0 is available both online and offline.

Narrated PowerPoint Presentations
For students, the additional student resources include PowerPoint presentations for each chapter, in both narrated and non-narrated versions.

General Ledger Problems
General Ledger Problems expose students to general ledger software similar to that in practice, without the expense and hassle of downloading additional software. They offer students the ability to record financial transactions and see how these transactions flow into financial statements. Easy minimal-scroll navigation, instant "Check My Work" feedback, and fully integrated hyperlinking across tabs show how input data affect each stage of the accounting process. Algorithmic versions are available. All are auto-gradable.

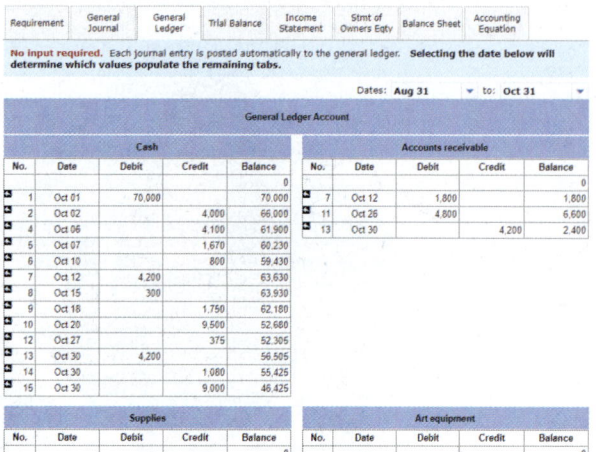

Guided Examples
Guided Examples provide a narrated, animated, step-by-step walk-through of Exercises similar to those assigned. These short presentations, which can be turned on or off by instructors, provide reinforcement when students need it most.

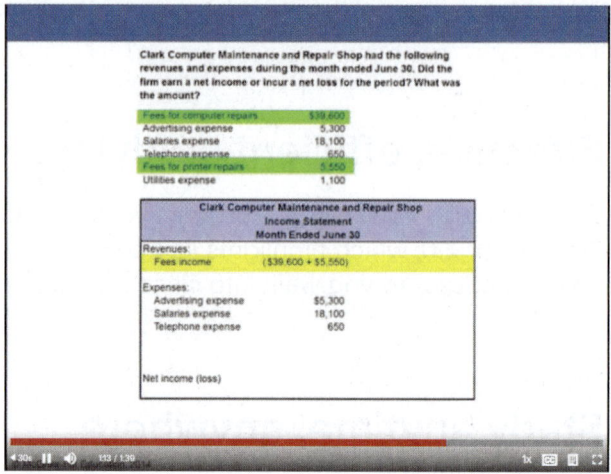

Instructor Resources

Instructor's Resource Manual
This manual provides for each chapter a map of related assignment materials; teaching objectives; a chapter overview and learning objectives; and a topical outline.

Solutions Manual
The Solutions Manual includes detailed solutions for every question, exercise, problem, and case in the text.

Test Bank / Test Builder
The Test Bank for each chapter has been updated to stay current with new and revised chapter material, with all questions available for assignment through Connect. Available within Connect, Test Builder is a cloud-based tool that enables instructors to format tests that can be printed or administered within an LMS. Test Builder offers a modern, streamlined interface for easy content configuration that matches course needs, without requiring a download. Test Builder provides a secure interface for better protection of content and allows for just-in-time updates to flow directly into assessments.

Acknowledgments

The authors are deeply grateful to the following accounting educators for their input during development of *College Accounting*. The feedback from these knowledgeable instructors provided the authors with valuable assistance in meeting the changing needs of the college accounting classroom.

Shawn Abbot
College of the Siskiyous

Cornelia Alsheimer
Santa Barbara City College

Julia Angel
North Arkansas College

James R. Armbrester
Lawson State Community College–Bessemer Campus

Laura Bantz
McHenry County College

Victoria Bentz
Yavapai College

Anne Bikofsky
College of Westchester

David Bland
Cape Fear Community College

Candace M. Boesiger
College of Southern Idaho

Patrick Borja
Citrus College

Kathy Bowen
Murray State College

Lisa Briggs
Columbus State Community College

Tony Cardinalli
Truckee Meadows Community College

Gerald Caton
Yavapai College

Steven L. Christian
Jackson Community College

Marilyn Ciolino
Delgado Community College

Jean Condon
Mid-Plains Community College Area (Nebraska)

Joan Cook
Milwaukee Area Technical College

Susan Snow Davis
Green River College

Gisela Dicklin
Edmonds Community College

Michael Discello
Pittsburgh Technical Institute

Sid Downey
Cochise College

Steven Ernest
Baton Rouge Community College

Ann Esarco
McHenry County College

Brian Fink
Danville Community College

Paul Fisher
Rogue Community College

Allen Ford
Institute for the Deaf, Rochester Institute of Technology

Jeff Forrest
Saint Louis Community College

David Forsyth
Palomar College

Mark Fronke
Cerritos College

Stephanie Gaspard
Central Louisiana Technical Community College

Nancy Goehring
Monterey Peninsula College

Renee Goffinet
Spokane Community College

Jane Goforth
North Seattle Community College

Lori Grady
Buck County Community College

Gretchen Graham
Community College of Allegheny County

Marina Grau
Houston Community College

Chad Grooms
Gateway Community and Technical College

David Grooms
Maui Community College

Sue Gudmunson
Lewis-Clark State College

Rebecca Hancock
El Paso Community College

Christina Hata
Miracosta College

Scott Hays
Central Oregon Community College

Mary Jane Hollars
Vincennes University

R. Stephen Holman
Elizabethtown Community and Technical College

Ray Ingram
Southwest Georgia Technical College

Dennis Jirkovsky
Indiana Business College

Stacy Johnson
Iowa Central Community College

Jane Jones
Mountain Empire Community College

Dmitriy Kalyagin
Chabot College

Norm Katz
National College–Stow

Sandra Kemper
Front Range Community College

Michael Kingsbury
College of the Desert

Patty Kolarik
Hutchinson Community College

Elida Kraja
Saint Louis Community College–Flors Valley

Greg Lauer
North Iowa Area Community College

David Laurel
South Texas College

Thomas E. Lynch
Hocking College

Kara Mahon
Piedmont Technical College

Josephine Mathias
Mercer County Community College

Roger McMillian
Mineral Area College

Angela Medlock
Arkansas Tech University Ozark Campus

Jim Meir
Cleveland State Community College

Michelle Meyer
Joliet Junior College

John Miller
Metropolitan Community College

Lora Miller
Centura College

Peter Neshwat
Brookline College

Marc Newman
Hocking Technical College

Anthony Newton
Highline Community College

Kenneth Newton
Cleveland State Community College

Jon Nitschke
Montana State University

Lizz Ott
Casper College

Angela Payne
Collin College

Joel Peralto
University of Hawaii–Hawaii Community College

Shirley Powell
Arkansas State University

LaNita Ray
Cedar Valley College

Carol Reinke
Empire College

Barbara Rice
KCTCS Gateway Community and Technical College

Reynold Robles
Texas State Technical College–Harlingen

Morgan Rockett
Moberly Area Community College

Joan Ryan
Clackamas Community College

Patricia Scales
Brookstone College

Michael Schaub
Shasta College

Brian D. Schmoldt
Madison College

Angela Seidel
Saint Francis University

Tom Snavely
Yavapai College

Vicky Splawn
Mid-America Christian University

Rick Street
Spokane Community College

Domenico Tavella
Pittsburgh Technical Institute

Judy Toland
Bucks County Community College

Donald Townsend
Forsyth Technical Community College

Yvette Travis
Bishop State Community College

Donna Viens
New England College of Business

Patricia Walczak
Lansing Community College

Linda Whitten
Skyline College

Helen Zhang
Skyline College

Thank You . . .

WE ARE GRATEFUL for the outstanding support from McGraw-Hill Education. In particular, we would like to thank Tim Vertovec, managing director; Steve Schuetz, executive portfolio manager; Michele Janicek, lead product developer; Sarah Wood, freelance product developer (Core); Michael McCormick, product developer (Assessment); Lori Koetters and Angela Norris, content project managers; Laura Fuller, buyer; Matt Diamond, designer; and Sarah Flynn, content licensing specialist.

Finally, we would like to thank our supplement authors and accuracy checkers for their significant contributions: Eric Weinstein, Suffolk County Community College; Teresa Alenikov, Cerritos College; Debra Johnson, Cerritos College; Mark McCarthy, East Carolina University; M. Jeff Quinlan, Madison Area Technical College; Brian Schmoldt, Madison College; April Mohr, Jefferson Community and Technical College, SW; and Helen Roybark, Radford University.

John Price • David Haddock • Michael Farina

Brief Contents

1	Accounting: The Language of Business	1
2	Analyzing Business Transactions	23
3	Analyzing Business Transactions Using T Accounts	55
4	The General Journal and the General Ledger	91
5	Adjustments and the Worksheet	125
6	Closing Entries and the Postclosing Trial Balance	165
7	Accounting for Sales and Accounts Receivable	197
8	Accounting for Purchases and Accounts Payable	243
9	Cash Receipts, Cash Payments, and Banking Procedures	279
10	Payroll Computations, Records, and Payment	349
11	Payroll Taxes, Deposits, and Reports	385
12	Accruals, Deferrals, and the Worksheet	419
13	Financial Statements and Closing Procedure	459
14	Accounting Principles and Reporting Standards	511
15	Accounts Receivable and Uncollectible Accounts	545
16	Notes Payable and Notes Receivable	575
17	Merchandise Inventory	599
18	Property, Plant, and Equipment	623
19	Accounting for Partnerships	665
20	Corporations: Formation and Capital Stock Transactions	707
21	Corporate Earnings and Capital Transactions	745
22	Long-Term Bonds	783
23	Financial Statement Analysis	815
24	The Statement of Cash Flows	859
25	Departmentalized Profit and Cost Centers	891
26	Accounting for Manufacturing Activities	913
27	Job Order Cost Accounting	941
28	Process Cost Accounting	965
29	Controlling Manufacturing Costs: Standard Costs	991
30	Cost-Revenue Analysis for Decision Making	1019

Contents

Preface		**iv**

Chapter 1 — Accounting: The Language of Business — 1

Section 1 What Is Accounting? — 2
- The Need for Financial Information — 2
- Accounting Defined — 2
- Accounting Careers — 3
- Users of Financial Information — 5
- **Section 1 Review** — 8

Section 2 Business and Accounting — 10
- Types of Business Entities — 10
- Generally Accepted Accounting Principles — 12
- **Section 2 Review** — 14

Chapter Review and Applications — 16
- Chapter Summary — 16
- Learning Objectives — 16
- Glossary — 17
- Comprehensive Self Review — 18
- Discussion Questions — 18
- Problem — 19
- Business Connections — 20
- Answers to Comprehensive Self Review — 21

Chapter 2 — Analyzing Business Transactions — 23

Section 1 Property and Financial Interest — 24
- Beginning with Analysis — 24
- Assets, Liabilities, and Owner's Equity — 29
- **Section 1 Review** — 30

Section 2 The Accounting Equation and Financial Statements — 31
- The Fundamental Accounting Equation — 31
- The Income Statement — 36
- The Statement of Owner's Equity and the Balance Sheet — 37
- The Importance of Financial Statements — 40
- **Section 2 Review** — 40

Chapter Review and Applications — 42
- Chapter Summary — 42
- Learning Objectives — 42
- Glossary — 43
- Comprehensive Self Review — 43
- Discussion Questions — 43
- Exercises — 44
- Problems — 47
- Business Connections — 52
- Answers to Comprehensive Self Review — 53

Chapter 3 — Analyzing Business Transactions Using T Accounts — 55

Section 1 Transactions That Affect Assets, Liabilities, and Owner's Equity — 56
- Asset, Liability, and Owner's Equity Accounts — 56
- Account Balances — 62
- **Section 1 Review** — 64

Section 2 Transactions That Affect Revenue, Expenses, and Withdrawals — 65
- Revenue and Expense Accounts — 65
- The Drawing Account — 69
- The Rules of Debit and Credit — 70

The Trial Balance	72
Financial Statements	73
Chart of Accounts	73
Permanent and Temporary Accounts	74
Section 2 Review	**75**
Chapter Review and Applications	**77**

Chapter Summary	77	Exercises	79
Learning Objectives	77	Problems	81
Glossary	77	Business Connections	88
Comprehensive Self Review	78	Answers to Comprehensive Self Review	89
Discussion Questions	78		

Chapter 4

The General Journal and the General Ledger	**91**
Section 1 The General Journal	**92**
Journals	92
The General Journal	92
Section 1 Review	**100**
Section 2 The General Ledger	**101**
Ledgers	101
Correcting Journal and Ledger Errors	105
Section 2 Review	**106**
Chapter Review and Applications	**108**

Chapter Summary	108	Exercises	110
Learning Objectives	108	Problems	112
Glossary	109	Business Connections	122
Comprehensive Self Review	109	Answers to Comprehensive Self Review	123
Discussion Questions	109		

Chapter 5

Adjustments and the Worksheet	**125**
Section 1 The Worksheet	**126**
The Trial Balance Section	126
The Adjustments Section	127
Section 1 Review	**132**
Section 2 Financial Statements	**133**
The Adjusted Trial Balance Section	133
The Income Statement and Balance Sheet Sections	134
Preparing Financial Statements	136
Summary of Financial Statements	146
Journalizing and Posting Adjusting Entries	147
Section 2 Review	**149**
Chapter Review and Applications	**150**

Chapter Summary	150	Exercises	152
Learning Objectives	150	Problems	154
Glossary	151	Business Connections	162
Comprehensive Self Review	151	Answers to Comprehensive Self Review	163
Discussion Questions	151		

Chapter 6

Closing Entries and the Postclosing Trial Balance	**165**
Section 1 Closing Entries	**166**
The Closing Process	166
Section 1 Review	**174**

Section 2 Using Accounting Information					**175**
Preparing the Postclosing Trial Balance					175
Interpreting the Financial Statements					176
The Accounting Cycle					178
Section 2 Review					**180**
Chapter Review and Applications					**181**
Chapter Summary	181	Exercises			182
Learning Objectives	181	Problems			185
Glossary	182	Business Connections			193
Comprehensive Self Review	182	Answers to Comprehensive Self Review			194
Discussion Questions	182				

Mini-Practice Set 1

Service Business Accounting Cycle — **195**

Eli's Consulting Services — 195

Chapter 7

Accounting for Sales and Accounts Receivable — **197**

Section 1 Merchandise Sales — **198**
- Special Journals and Subsidiary Ledgers — 198
- The Sales Journal — 199
- **Section 1 Review** — **204**

Section 2 Accounts Receivable — **205**
- The Accounts Receivable Ledger — 205
- Sales Returns and Allowances — 206
- Schedule of Accounts Receivable — 211
- **Section 2 Review** — **212**

Section 3 Special Topics in Merchandising — **214**
- Credit Sales for a Wholesale Business — 214
- Credit Policies — 216
- Sales Taxes — 220
- **Section 3 Review** — **224**

Chapter Review and Applications — **225**

Chapter Summary	225	Exercises			227
Learning Objectives	225	Problems			231
Glossary	225	Business Connections			240
Comprehensive Self Review	226	Answers to Comprehensive Self Review			241
Discussion Questions	227				

Chapter 8

Accounting for Purchases and Accounts Payable — **243**

Section 1 Merchandise Purchases — **244**
- Accounting for Purchases — 244
- **Section 1 Review** — **250**

Section 2 Accounts Payable — **252**
- The Accounts Payable Ledger — 252
- Purchases Returns and Allowances — 253
- Schedule of Accounts Payable — 255
- Determining the Cost of Purchases — 257
- Internal Control of Purchases — 258
- **Section 2 Review** — **259**

Chapter Review and Applications			261
Chapter Summary	261	Exercises	263
Learning Objectives	261	Problems	265
Glossary	261	Business Connections	275
Comprehensive Self Review	262	Answers to Comprehensive Self Review	277
Discussion Questions	262		

Chapter 9

Cash Receipts, Cash Payments, and Banking Procedures — 279

Section 1 Cash Receipts — 280
- Cash Transactions — 280
- The Cash Receipts Journal — 280
- **Section 1 Review** — 286

Section 2 Cash Payments — 287
- The Cash Payments Journal — 287
- The Petty Cash Fund — 293
- Internal Control over Cash — 295
- **Section 2 Review** — 296

Section 3 Banking Procedures — 298
- Writing Checks — 298
- Endorsing Checks — 299
- Preparing the Deposit Slip — 299
- Handling Postdated Checks — 300
- Reconciling the Bank Statement — 301
- Adjusting the Financial Records — 304
- Internal Control of Banking Activities — 306
- Using Online Banking — 307
- **Section 3 Review** — 308

Appendix to Chapter 9: The Perpetual Inventory System — 310

Chapter Review and Applications			318
Chapter Summary	318	Exercises	321
Learning Objectives	318	Problems	326
Glossary	319	Business Connections	346
Comprehensive Self Review	320	Answers to Comprehensive Self Review	348
Discussion Questions	320		

Chapter 10

Payroll Computations, Records, and Payment — 349

Section 1 Payroll Laws and Taxes — 350
- Who Is an Employee? — 350
- Federal Employee Earnings and Withholding Laws — 350
- State and Local Taxes — 352
- Employer's Payroll Taxes and Insurance Costs — 352
- Employee Records Required by Law — 353
- **Section 1 Review** — 354

Section 2 Calculating Earnings and Taxes — 355
- Computing Total Earnings of Employees — 355
- Determining Pay for Hourly Employees — 356
- Determining Pay for Salaried Employees — 362
- Recording Payroll Information for Employees — 362
- **Section 2 Review** — 364

Section 3 Recording Payroll Information					**365**
Recording Payroll					365
Paying Employees					366
Individual Earnings Records					368
Completing January Payrolls					369
Section 3 Review					**371**
Chapter Review and Applications					**372**
Chapter Summary	372	Exercises			374
Learning Objectives	372	Problems			376
Glossary	372	Business Connections			382
Comprehensive Self Review	373	Answers to Comprehensive Self Review			383
Discussion Questions	373				

Chapter 11 — Payroll Taxes, Deposits, and Reports — 385

Section 1 Social Security, Medicare, and Employee Income Tax			**386**
Payment of Payroll Taxes			386
Wage and Tax Statement, Form W-2			394
Annual Transmittal of Wage and Tax Statements, Form W-3			395
Section 1 Review			**396**
Section 2 Unemployment Tax and Workers' Compensation			**397**
Unemployment Compensation Insurance Taxes			397
Internal Control over Payroll Operations			404
Section 2 Review			**405**
Chapter Review and Applications			**406**
Chapter Summary	406	Exercises	408
Learning Objectives	406	Problems	409
Glossary	407	Business Connections	417
Comprehensive Self Review	407	Answers to Comprehensive Self Review	418
Discussion Questions	407		

Chapter 12 — Accruals, Deferrals, and the Worksheet — 419

Section 1 Calculating and Recording Adjustments			**420**
The Accrual Basis of Accounting			420
Using the Worksheet to Record Adjustments			421
Section 1 Review			**430**
Section 2 Completing the Worksheet			**431**
Preparing the Adjusted Trial Balance Section			431
Preparing Income Statement and Balance Sheet Sections			434
Calculating Net Income or Net Loss			434
Section 2 Review			**436**
Chapter Review and Applications			**437**
Chapter Summary	437	Exercises	439
Learning Objectives	437	Problems	440
Glossary	437	Business Connections	456
Comprehensive Self Review	438	Answers to Comprehensive Self Review	457
Discussion Questions	438		

Chapter 13 — Financial Statements and Closing Procedure — 459

Section 1 Preparing the Financial Statements	**460**
The Classified Income Statement	460
The Statement of Owner's Equity	463

The Classified Balance Sheet	463
Section 1 Review	**465**
Section 2 Completing the Accounting Cycle	**467**
Journalizing and Posting the Adjusting Entries	467
Journalizing and Posting the Closing Entries	470
Preparing a Postclosing Trial Balance	472
Interpreting the Financial Statements	473
Journalizing and Posting Reversing Entries	475
Review of the Accounting Cycle	479
Section 2 Review	**481**
Chapter Review and Applications	**483**

Chapter Summary	483	Exercises	486
Learning Objectives	483	Problems	493
Glossary	483	Business Connections	504
Comprehensive Self Review	484	Answers to Comprehensive Self Review	505
Discussion Questions	485		

Mini-Practice Set 2

Merchandising Business Accounting Cycle	**506**
The Fashion Rack	506

Chapter 14

Accounting Principles and Reporting Standards	**511**
Section 1 Generally Accepted Accounting Principles	**512**
The Need for Generally Accepted Accounting Principles	512
The Development of Generally Accepted Accounting Principles	512
Users and Uses of Financial Reports	516
Section 1 Review	**517**
Section 2 The IASB's Conceptual Framework of Accounting	**518**
Qualitative Characteristics of Financial Reports	519
Underlying Assumptions	521
General Principles	522
Modifying Constraints	525
The Impact of Generally Accepted Accounting Principles	526
Section 2 Review	**527**
Chapter Review and Applications	**529**

Chapter Summary	529	Exercises	532
Learning Objectives	529	Problems	533
Glossary	530	Business Connections	543
Comprehensive Self Review	531	Answers to Comprehensive Self Review	543
Discussion Questions	531		

Chapter 15

Accounts Receivable and Uncollectible Accounts	**545**
Section 1 The Allowance Method of Accounting for Uncollectible Accounts	**546**
Methods of Accounting for Uncollectible Accounts	547
Applying the Allowance Method	547
Section 1 Review	**554**
Section 2 Applying the Direct Charge-Off Method; Internal Control of Accounts Receivable	**556**

	Recording Uncollectible Accounts When the Direct Charge-Off Method Is Used				556
	Collecting an Account Previously Written Off When the Direct Charge-Off Method Is Used				557
	Accounting for Other Receivables and Bad Debt Losses				558
	Internal Control of Accounts Receivable				559
	Section 2 Review				**559**
	Chapter Review and Applications				**561**
	Chapter Summary	561	Exercises		563
	Learning Objectives	561	Problems		565
	Glossary	562	Business Connections		572
	Comprehensive Self Review	562	Answers to Comprehensive Self Review		573
	Discussion Questions	562			

Chapter 16

Notes Payable and Notes Receivable		**575**
Section 1 Accounting for Notes Payable		**576**
Negotiable Instruments		576
Notes Payable		577
Section 1 Review		**581**
Section 2 Accounting for Notes Receivable		**582**
Notes Receivable		582
Drafts and Acceptances		588
Internal Control of Notes Payable, Notes Receivable, and Drafts		589
Section 2 Review		**590**
Chapter Review and Applications		**591**

Chapter Summary	591	Exercises	593
Learning Objectives	591	Problems	594
Glossary	592	Business Connections	597
Comprehensive Self Review	592	Answers to Comprehensive Self Review	598
Discussion Questions	592		

Chapter 17

Merchandise Inventory		**599**
Section 1 Inventory Costing Methods		**600**
Importance of Inventory Valuation		600
Assigning Costs to Inventory		601
Comparing Results of Inventory Costing Methods		603
LIFO Use Internationally		604
Section 1 Review		**604**
Section 2 Inventory Valuation and Control		**605**
Lower of Cost or Net Realizable Value Rule		605
Inventory Estimation Procedures		607
Internal Control of Inventories		610
New Technology in Inventory Control		610
Section 2 Review		**611**
Chapter Review and Applications		**612**

Chapter Summary	612	Exercises	614
Learning Objectives	612	Problems	615
Glossary	612	Business Connections	621
Comprehensive Self Review	613	Answers to Comprehensive Self Review	622
Discussion Questions	613		

Chapter 18 — Property, Plant, and Equipment — 623

Section 1 Acquisition and Depreciation — 624
- Property, Plant, and Equipment Classifications — 624
- Acquisition of Property, Plant, and Equipment — 624
- Depreciation of Property, Plant, and Equipment — 625
- Federal Income Tax Requirements for "Cost Recovery" (Depreciation) of Property, Plant, and Equipment — 630
- **Section 1 Review** — 631

Section 2 Disposition of Assets — 633
- Method of Disposition — 633
- **Section 2 Review** — 638

Section 3 Special Topics in Long-Term Assets — 640
- Depletion — 640
- Impairment of Property, Plant, and Equipment — 641
- Intangible Assets — 643
- Internal Control of Property, Plant, and Equipment — 646
- **Section 3 Review** — 646

Chapter Review and Applications — 647
Chapter Summary	647	Exercises	650
Learning Objectives	647	Problems	652
Glossary	648	Business Connections	663
Comprehensive Self Review	649	Answers to Comprehensive Self Review	664
Discussion Questions	649		

Chapter 19 — Accounting for Partnerships — 665

Section 1 Forming a Partnership — 666
- The Characteristics of a Partnership — 666
- Accounting for the Formation of a Partnership — 667
- **Section 1 Review** — 671

Section 2 Allocating Income or Loss — 672
- Allocating Partnership Income or Loss — 672
- Partnership Financial Statements — 680
- **Section 2 Review** — 682

Section 3 Partnership Changes — 683
- Changes in Partners — 683
- **Section 3 Review** — 689

Chapter Review and Applications — 691
Chapter Summary	691	Exercises	693
Learning Objectives	691	Problems	695
Glossary	692	Business Connections	704
Comprehensive Self Review	692	Answers to Comprehensive Self Review	705
Discussion Questions	692		

Chapter 20 — Corporations: Formation and Capital Stock Transactions — 707

Section 1 Forming a Corporation — 708
- Characteristics of a Corporation — 708
- Formation of a Corporation — 710
- Structure of a Corporation — 710
- **Section 1 Review** — 711

Section 2 Types of Capital Stock		**712**
Capital Stock		712
Dividends on Stock		714
Section 2 Review		**717**
Section 3 Recording Capital Stock Transactions		**718**
Recording the Issuance of Stock		718
Subscriptions for Capital Stock		724
Special Corporation Records and Agents		727
Section 3 Review		**729**
Chapter Review and Applications		**730**

Chapter Summary	730	Exercises	733
Learning Objectives	730	Problems	734
Glossary	731	Business Connections	742
Comprehensive Self Review	732	Answers to Comprehensive Self Review	743
Discussion Questions	732		

Chapter 21

Corporate Earnings and Capital Transactions	**745**
Section 1 Accounting for Corporate Earnings	**746**
Corporate Income Tax	746
Completing the Corporate Worksheet	749
Adjusting and Closing Entries	752
The Corporate Income Statement	752
Section 1 Review	**754**
Section 2 Accounting for Retained Earnings	**755**
Retained Earnings	755
Section 2 Review	**760**
Section 3 Other Capital Transactions and Financial Statements	**761**
Other Capital Transactions	761
Financial Statements for a Corporation	763
Section 3 Review	**766**
Chapter Review and Applications	**767**

Chapter Summary	767	Exercises	769
Learning Objectives	767	Problems	771
Glossary	768	Business Connections	780
Comprehensive Self Review	768	Answers to Comprehensive Self Review	781
Discussion Questions	769		

Chapter 22

Long-Term Bonds	**783**
Section 1 Financing Through Bonds	**784**
Types of Bonds	784
Stock versus Bonds as a Financing Method	786
Section 1 Review	**787**
Section 2 Bond Issue and Interest	**788**
Bonds Issued at Face Value	788
Bonds Issued at a Premium	791
Bonds Issued at a Discount	792
Balance Sheet Presentation of Bond Premium and Discount	793
Accounting for Bond Issue Costs	793
Section 2 Review	**794**

Section 3 Bond Retirement — 795
Accumulating Funds to Retire Bonds — 795
Retirement of Bonds — 797
Section 3 Review — 799
Chapter Review and Applications — 800
Chapter Summary	800	Exercises	802
Learning Objectives	800	Problems	803
Glossary	801	Business Connections	810
Comprehensive Self Review	801	Answers to Comprehensive Self Review	810
Discussion Questions	802		

Mini-Practice Set 3

Corporation Accounting Cycle — 811
The Purple Company — 811

Chapter 23

Financial Statement Analysis — 815

Section 1 Vertical Analysis — 816
The Phases of Statement Analysis — 816
Vertical Analysis of Financial Statements — 816
Section 1 Review — 820

Section 2 Horizontal Analysis — 821
Horizontal Analysis of Financial Statements — 821
Trend Analysis of Financial Statements — 823
Comparison with Industry Averages — 825
Section 2 Review — 826

Section 3 Ratios — 827
Profitability Ratios — 827
Financial Strength Ratios — 831
Liquidity Ratios — 833
Summary of Ratios — 836
Section 3 Review — 838

Chapter Review and Applications — 839
Chapter Summary	839	Exercises	842
Learning Objectives	839	Problems	844
Glossary	840	Business Connections	854
Comprehensive Self Review	841	Answers to Comprehensive Self Review	855
Discussion Questions	841		

Mini-Practice Set 4

Financial Analysis and Decision Making — 856
Home Suppliers, Inc. — 856

Chapter 24

The Statement of Cash Flows — 859

Section 1 Sources and Uses of Cash — 860
The Importance of a Statement of Cash Flows — 860
The Meaning of Cash — 860
Sources and Uses of Cash — 860
Section 1 Review — 861

Section 2 Cash Flows from Operating Activities				862
Statement of Cash Flows				865
Cash Flows from Operating Activities				865
Section 2 Review				**869**
Section 3 Cash Flows from Investing and Financing Activities				**870**
Cash Flows from Investing Activities				870
Cash Flows from Financing Activities				871
Preparing a Statement of Cash Flows				872
Section 3 Review				**874**
Chapter Review and Applications				**875**
Chapter Summary	875	Exercises		877
Learning Objectives	875	Problems		880
Glossary	876	Business Connections		889
Comprehensive Self Review	876	Answers to Comprehensive Self Review		890
Discussion Questions	876			

Chapter 25 Departmentalized Profit and Cost Centers — 891

Section 1 Profit and Cost Centers and Departmental Accounting — 892

Managerial Accounting				892
Profit Centers and Cost Centers				893
Responsibility Accounting				893
Departmentalized Operations				893
Section 1 Review				**897**
Section 2 Departmental Income Statements				**899**
Preparing the Departmental Income Statement				899
Section 2 Review				**902**
Chapter Review and Applications				**903**
Chapter Summary	903	Exercises		905
Learning Objectives	903	Problems		907
Glossary	904	Business Connections		912
Comprehensive Self Review	904	Answers to Comprehensive Self Review		912
Discussion Questions	904			

Chapter 26 Accounting for Manufacturing Activities — 913

Section 1 Accounting for Manufacturing Costs — 914

Cost of Goods Manufactured				914
Statement of Cost of Goods Manufactured				915
Income Statement for a Manufacturing Concern				917
Balance Sheet for a Manufacturing Concern				917
Section 1 Review				**919**
Section 2 Completing the Accounting Cycle				**920**
The Worksheet and Financial Statements				920
Completing the Accounting Cycle				924
Section 2 Review				**927**
Chapter Review and Applications				**929**
Chapter Summary	929	Exercises		931
Learning Objectives	929	Problems		933
Glossary	930	Business Connections		940
Comprehensive Self Review	930	Answers to Comprehensive Self Review		940
Discussion Questions	930			

Chapter 27   Job Order Cost Accounting   941

Section 1   Cost Accounting   942
- Types of Cost Accounting Systems   942
- Cost Flows in a Job Order Cost System   943
- **Section 1 Review**   945

Section 2   Job Order Cost Accounting System   946
- A Job Order Cost Accounting System   946
- **Section 2 Review**   951

Section 3   Accounting for Job Orders   952
- The Job Order Cost Sheet   952
- Summary of Cost Flow Through Inventory Accounts   954
- **Section 3 Review**   955

Chapter Review and Applications   956
Chapter Summary	956	Exercises	958
Learning Objectives	956	Problems	959
Glossary	957	Business Connections	963
Comprehensive Self Review	957	Answers to Comprehensive Self Review	964
Discussion Questions	957		

Chapter 28   Process Cost Accounting   965

Section 1   Process Cost Accounting System   966
- The Process Cost Accounting System   966
- **Section 1 Review**   974

Section 2   Work in Process Inventory   975
- The Beginning Work in Process Inventory   975
- **Section 2 Review**   980

Chapter Review and Applications   981
Chapter Summary	981	Exercises	983
Learning Objectives	981	Problems	985
Glossary	982	Business Connections	989
Comprehensive Self Review	982	Answers to Comprehensive Self Review	990
Discussion Questions	982		

Chapter 29   Controlling Manufacturing Costs: Standard Costs   991

Section 1   Cost Behavior and the Budget   992
- Cost Behavior   992
- Preparation of the Fixed Budget   994
- Preparation of the Flexible Budget   996
- **Section 1 Review**   997

Section 2   Standard Costs as a Control Tool   998
- Developing Standard Costs   998
- Using Standard Costs   999
- **Section 2 Review**   1004

Chapter Review and Applications   1006
Chapter Summary	1006	Exercises	1008
Learning Objectives	1006	Problems	1010
Glossary	1007	Business Connections	1016
Comprehensive Self Review	1007	Answers to Comprehensive Self Review	1017
Discussion Questions	1007		

Chapter 30   Cost-Revenue Analysis for Decision Making   1019

Section 1   The Decision Process   1020
Exploring the Decision Process   1020
Section 1 Review   1023

Section 2   Cost-Revenue Analysis   1025
Product Pricing in Special Situations   1025
Purchasing New Equipment   1026
Making or Buying a Part   1026
Section 2 Review   1028

Chapter Review and Applications   1029

Chapter Summary	1029	Exercises	1031
Learning Objectives	1029	Problems	1033
Glossary	1030	Business Connections	1039
Comprehensive Self Review	1030	Answers to Comprehensive Self Review	1040
Discussion Questions	1030		

Appendix A The Home Depot 2018 Financial Statements   A-1
Appendix B Combined Journal   B-1
Glossary   G-1
Index   I-1
Sample General Ledger Accounts
Rules of Debit and Credit

Accounting: The Language of Business

Chapter 1

©MikeDotta/Shutterstock

www.uber.com

How do you get from the airport to your hotel when traveling on business? How do you get home from a party when it is not safe for you to drive? How do you get into the downtown business district for a meeting when parking is difficult and expensive? How do you get to any destination when taking your own vehicle is not convenient or possible? Taxis are not always available or affordable, and public transportation is difficult when in an unfamiliar city. Uber is a viable alternative to taxis and other forms of public transportation.

Uber was created in 2009 as a private company in San Francisco, California, on a smartphone app used to summon personal transportation from Uber drivers who use their own vehicles to transport customers. Uber's initial business model as a personal transportation company has transformed to a multifaceted company that provides transportation, food delivery, bicycle-sharing, and a transfer network company that operates in over 785 metropolitan areas worldwide.

Although Uber has had a turbulent history since its founding as a private company, it has raised a massive amount of investment capital to fund its operations. In January 2018, Uber raised $1.25 billion in cash from an investment group through a financing arrangement that valued the company at $48 billion. In May 2018, Uber announced plans to have an initial public offering in 2019 that would change the company to a publicly traded company.

As Uber continues to grow and seek additional investment funding, accountants are pivotal in tracking and reporting the company's financial results and position in terms of revenues earned, expenses used, assets owned, and liabilities owed as well as calculating the company's net income (revenues − expenses) and net worth (assets − liabilities). Accountants are essential to the company's continued growth and success by providing financial information necessary for decision making.

thinking critically

Can you think of any organizations that would be interested in how Uber is performing?

LEARNING OBJECTIVES

1-1 Define accounting.
1-2 Identify and discuss career opportunities in accounting.
1-3 Identify the users of financial information.
1-4 Compare and contrast the three types of business entities.
1-5 Describe the process used to develop generally accepted accounting principles.
1-6 Define the accounting terms new to this chapter.

NEW TERMS

accounting
Accounting Standards Codification
Accounting Standards Update
accounting system
auditing
auditor's report
Certified Bookkeeper (CB)
certified public accountant (CPA)
corporation
creditor
discussion memorandum
economic entity
entity
exposure draft
financial statements
fraud
generally accepted accounting principles (GAAP)
governmental accounting
internal control
international accounting
management advisory services
managerial accounting
partnership
public accountants
separate entity assumption
social entity
sole proprietorship
Statements of Financial Accounting Standards
stock
stockholders
tax accounting

Section 1

SECTION OBJECTIVES

>> 1-1 Define accounting.
   WHY IT'S IMPORTANT
   Business transactions affect many aspects of our lives.

>> 1-2 Identify and discuss career opportunities in accounting.
   WHY IT'S IMPORTANT
   There's something for everyone in the field of accounting. Accounting professionals are found in every workplace from public accounting firms to government agencies, from corporations to nonprofit organizations.

>> 1-3 Identify the users of financial information.
   WHY IT'S IMPORTANT
   A wide variety of individuals and businesses depend on financial information to make decisions.

TERMS TO LEARN

accounting
accounting system
auditing
Certified Bookkeeper (CB)
certified public accountant (CPA)
financial statements
fraud
governmental accounting
internal control
management advisory services
managerial accounting
public accountants
tax accounting

What Is Accounting?

Accounting provides financial information about a business or a nonprofit organization. Owners, managers, investors, and other interested parties need financial information in order to make decisions. Because accounting is used to communicate financial information, it is often called the "language of business."

The Need for Financial Information

Suppose a relative leaves you a substantial sum of money and you decide to carry out your lifelong dream of opening a small sportswear shop. You rent space in a local shopping center, purchase fixtures and equipment, purchase goods to sell, hire salespeople, and open the store to customers. Before long you realize that, to run your business successfully, you need financial information about the business. You probably need information that provides answers to the following questions:

- How much cash does the business have?
- How much money do customers owe the business?
- What is the cost of the merchandise sold?
- What is the change in sales volume?
- How much money is owed to suppliers?
- What is the profit or loss?

As your business grows, you will need even more financial information to evaluate the firm's performance and make decisions about the future. An efficient accounting system allows owners and managers to quickly obtain a wide range of useful information. The need for timely information is one reason that businesses have an accounting system directed by a professional staff.

>> **1-1 OBJECTIVE**
Define accounting.

Accounting Defined

Accounting is the process by which financial information about a business is recorded, classified, summarized, interpreted, and communicated to owners, managers, and other interested parties. An **accounting system** is designed to accumulate data about a firm's financial affairs, classify the data in a meaningful way, and summarize it in periodic reports called **financial statements.** Owners and managers obtain a lot of information from financial statements. The accountant

- establishes the records and procedures that make up the accounting system,
- supervises the operations of the system, and
- interprets the resulting financial information.

Most owners and managers rely heavily on the accountant's judgment and knowledge when making financial decisions.

Accounting Careers

Many jobs are available in the accounting profession, and they require varying amounts of education and experience. Bookkeepers and accountants are responsible for keeping records and providing financial information about the business. Generally, bookkeepers are responsible for recording business transactions. In large firms, bookkeepers may also supervise the work of accounting clerks. Many bookkeepers are **Certified Bookkeepers (CB),** a designation that assures an individual possesses the level of knowledge and skills needed to carry out all key accounting functions through the adjusted trial balance, including payroll. To become a CB, one must meet three requirements: you must (1) pass the national certified bookkeepers exam, (2) sign a code of ethics, and (3) submit evidence of at least two years of full-time bookkeeping experience or 3,000 hours of part-time or freelance experience. Accounting clerks are responsible for the recordkeeping part of the accounting system—perhaps payroll, accounts receivable, or accounts payable. Accountants usually supervise bookkeepers and prepare the financial statements and reports of the business.

Newspapers and websites often have job listings for accounting clerks, bookkeepers, and accountants:

- Accounting clerk positions usually require one to two accounting courses and little or no experience.
- Bookkeeper positions usually require one to two years of accounting education plus experience as an accounting clerk.
- Accountant positions usually require a bachelor's degree but are sometimes filled by experienced bookkeepers or individuals with a two-year college degree. Most entry-level accountant positions do not have an experience requirement. Both the education and experience requirements for accountant positions vary according to the size of the firm.

Accountants usually choose to practice in one of three areas:

- public accounting
- managerial accounting
- governmental accounting

Table 1.1 shows a list of occupations with job duties that are similar to those of accountants and auditors.

Public Accounting

Public accountants work for public accounting firms. Public accounting firms provide accounting services for other companies. Usually they offer three services:

- auditing
- tax accounting
- management advisory services

The largest public accounting firms in the United States are called the "Big Four." The Big Four are Deloitte & Touche, Ernst & Young, KPMG, and PricewaterhouseCoopers.

Many public accountants are **certified public accountants (CPAs).** To become a CPA, an individual must have a certain number of college credits in accounting courses, demonstrate good personal character, pass the Uniform CPA Examination, and fulfill the experience requirements of the state of practice. CPAs must follow the professional code of ethics.

>> 1-2 OBJECTIVE
Identify and discuss career opportunities in accounting.

ABOUT ACCOUNTING

Certified Bookkeeper Exam
The Certified Bookkeeper exam consist of four parts. Part one deals with Adjustments and Error Corrections. Part two covers Payroll and Depreciation. Part three covers Inventory, and part four covers Internal Control and Fraud Prevention. To pass the exam, you must score 75% or higher on parts one and two (which are closed-book exams administered by computer), and you must score 70% or higher on parts three and four (which are open-workbook exams). In addition to passing the exam, you must also sign a Code of Ethics and meet either a full-time or part-time experience requirement.

TABLE 1.1 Occupations with Similar Job Duties to Accountants and Auditors

Occupation	Job Duties	Entry-Level Education
Bookkeeping, Accounting, and Auditing Clerks	Bookkeeping, accounting, and auditing clerks produce financial records for organizations. They record financial transactions, update statements, and check financial records for accuracy.	Some college, no degree
Budget Analysts	Budget analysts help public and private institutions organize their finances. They prepare budget reports and monitor institutional spending.	Bachelor's degree
Cost Estimators	Cost estimators collect and analyze data to estimate the time, money, resources, and labor required for product manufacturing, construction projects, or services. Some specialize in a particular industry or product type.	Bachelor's degree
Financial Analysts	Financial analysts provide guidance to businesses and individuals making investment decisions. They assess the performance of stocks, bonds, and other types of investments.	Bachelor's degree
Financial Managers	Financial managers are responsible for the financial health of an organization. They produce financial reports, direct investment activities, and develop strategies and plans for the long-term financial goals of their organization.	Bachelor's degree
Management Analysts	Management analysts, often called management consultants, propose ways to improve an organization's efficiency. They advise managers on how to make organizations more profitable through reduced costs and increased revenues.	Bachelor's degree
Personal Financial Advisors	Personal financial advisors give financial advice to people. They help with investments, taxes, and insurance decisions.	Bachelor's degree
Postsecondary Teachers	Postsecondary teachers instruct students in a wide variety of academic and vocational subjects beyond the high school level. They also conduct research and publish scholarly papers and books.	Doctoral or professional degree
Tax Examiners and Collectors, and Revenue Agents	Tax examiners and collectors and revenue agents ensure that governments get their tax money from businesses and citizens. They review tax returns, conduct audits, identify taxes owed, and collect overdue tax payments.	Bachelor's degree
Top Executives	Top executives devise strategies and policies to ensure that an organization meets its goals. They plan, direct, and coordinate operational activities of companies and public or private-sector organizations.	Bachelor's degree

Source: Bureau of Labor Statistics, U.S. Department of Labor, Occupational Outlook Handbook, 2017–18 Edition, Accountants and Auditors, on the Internet at http://www.bls.gov/ooh/business-and-financial/accountants-and-auditors.htm (visited September 29, 2018).

Auditing is the review of financial statements to assess their fairness and adherence to generally accepted accounting principles. Accountants who are CPAs perform financial audits.

Tax accounting involves tax compliance and tax planning. *Tax compliance* deals with the preparation of tax returns and the audit of those returns. *Tax planning* involves giving advice to clients on how to structure their financial affairs in order to reduce their tax liability.

Management advisory services involve helping clients improve their information systems or their business performance.

Managerial Accounting

Managerial accounting, also referred to as *private accounting,* involves working for a single business in industry. Managerial accountants perform a wide range of activities, including

- establishing accounting policies,
- managing the accounting system,
- preparing financial statements,
- interpreting financial information,
- providing financial advice to management,
- preparing tax forms,
- performing tax planning services, and
- preparing internal reports for management.

Governmental Accounting

Governmental accounting involves keeping financial records and preparing financial reports as part of the staff of federal, state, or local governmental units. Governmental units do not earn profits. However, governmental units receive and pay out huge amounts of money and need procedures for recording and managing this money.

Some governmental agencies hire accountants to audit the financial statements and records of the businesses under their jurisdiction and to uncover possible violations of the law. The Securities and Exchange Commission, the Internal Revenue Service, the Federal Bureau of Investigation, and Homeland Security employ a large number of accountants.

Users of Financial Information

The results of the accounting process are communicated to many individuals and organizations. Who are these individuals and organizations, and why do they want financial information about a particular firm?

Owners and Managers

Assume your sportswear shop is in full operation. One user of financial information about the business is you, the owner. You need information that will help you evaluate the results of your operations as well as plan and make decisions for the future. Questions such as the following are difficult to answer without financial information:

- Should you drop from the product line the long-sleeved pullover that is not selling well, or should you just reduce the price?
- How much should you charge for the denim jacket that you are adding to the product line?
- How much should you spend on advertising?
- How does this month's profit compare with last month's profit?
- Should you open a new store?

A major responsibility of owners and managers of an entity is **internal control** and the prevention of **fraud.** Internal controls are the company's policies and procedures in place to

---

ABOUT ACCOUNTING

Accounting Services
The role of the CPA is expanding. In the past, accounting firms handled audits and taxes. Today accountants provide a wide range of services, including financial planning, investment advice, accounting and tax software advice, and profitability consulting. Accountants provide clients with information and advice on electronic business, health care performance measurement, risk assessment, business performance measurement, and information system reliability.

>> 1-3 OBJECTIVE
Identify the users of financial information.

safeguard assets, ensure reliability of accounting data, and promote compliance with management policies and applicable laws. The goal of internal control policies and procedures is the prevention of fraud, which is intentional or reckless acts that result in the confiscation of a firm's assets or the misrepresentation of the firm's accounting data. Common internal control and fraud prevention policies and procedures include written proof that transactions and payments are authorized and separating duties among employees. Throughout this text and end-of-chapter problems, internal control and fraud prevention techniques are discussed for different classes of assets including cash, payroll, inventories, and property, plant, and equipment.

Suppliers

A number of other people are interested in the financial information about your business. For example, businesses that supply you with sportswear need to assess the ability of your firm to pay its bills. They also need to set a credit limit for your firm.

Banks

What if you decide to ask your bank for a loan so that you can open a new store? The bank needs to be sure that your firm will repay the loan on time. The bank will ask for financial information prepared by your accountant. Based on this information, the bank will decide whether to make the loan and the terms of the loan.

Tax Authorities

The Internal Revenue Service (IRS) and other state and local tax authorities are interested in financial information about your firm. This information is used to determine the tax base:

- Income taxes are based on taxable income.
- Sales taxes are based on sales income.
- Property taxes are based on the assessed value of buildings, equipment, and inventory (the goods available for sale).

The accounting process provides all of this information.

Regulatory Agencies and Investors

If an industry is regulated by a governmental agency, businesses in that industry have to supply financial information to the regulating agency. For example, the Federal Communications Commission receives financial information from radio and television stations. The Securities and Exchange Commission (SEC) oversees the financial information provided by publicly owned corporations to their investors and potential investors. Publicly owned corporations trade their shares on stock exchanges and in over-the-counter markets. Congress passed the Securities Act of 1933 and the Securities Exchange Act of 1934 in order to protect those who invest in publicly owned corporations.

The SEC is responsible for reviewing the accounting methods used by publicly owned corporations. The SEC has delegated this review to the accounting profession but still has the final say on any financial accounting issue faced by publicly owned corporations. If the SEC does not agree with the reporting that results from an accounting method, the SEC can suspend trading of a company's shares on the stock exchanges.

> Major changes were made to the regulatory environment in the accounting profession with the passage of the Public Company Accounting Reform and Investor Protection Act of 2002 (also known as the Sarbanes-Oxley Act) that was signed into law by President George W. Bush on August 2, 2002. The Act was the most far-reaching regulatory crackdown on corporate fraud and corruption since the creation of the Securities and Exchange Commission in 1934.

The Sarbanes-Oxley Act was passed in response to the wave of corporate accounting scandals starting with the demise of Enron Corporation in 2001, the arrest of top executives at WorldCom and Adelphia Communications Corporation, and ultimately the demise of Arthur Andersen, an international public accounting firm formerly a member of the "Big Five." Arthur Andersen was found guilty of an obstruction of justice charge after admitting that the firm destroyed thousands of documents and electronic files related to the Enron audit engagement. Although on May 31, 2008, the Supreme Court of the United States reversed the Andersen guilty verdict, Arthur Andersen has not returned as a viable business. As a result of the demise of Arthur Andersen, the "Big Five" are now the "Big Four."

The Act significantly tightens regulation of financial reporting by publicly held companies and their accountants and auditors. The Sarbanes-Oxley Act created a five-member Public Company Accounting Oversight Board. The Board has investigative and enforcement powers to oversee the accounting profession and to discipline corrupt accountants and auditors. The Securities and Exchange Commission oversees the Board. Two members of the Board are certified public accountants, to regulate the accountants who audit public companies, and the remaining three must not be and cannot have been CPAs. The chair of the Board may be held by one of the CPA members, provided that the individual has not been engaged as a practicing CPA for five years.

Major provisions of the Act include rules on consulting services, auditor rotation, criminal penalties, corporate governance, and securities regulation. The Act prohibits accountants from offering a broad range of consulting services to publicly traded companies that they audit and requires accounting firms to change the lead audit or coordinating partner and the reviewing partner for a company every five years. Additionally, it is a felony to "knowingly" destroy or create documents to "impede, obstruct or influence" any existing or contemplated federal investigation. Auditors are also required to maintain all audit or review work papers for seven years. Criminal penalties, up to 20 years in prison, are imposed for obstruction of justice, and the Act raises the maximum sentence for defrauding pension funds to 10 years.

Chief executives and chief financial officers of publicly traded corporations are now required to certify their financial statements and these executives will face up to 20 years in prison if they "knowingly or willfully" allow materially misleading information into their financial statements. Companies must also disclose, as quickly as possible, material changes in their financial position. Wall Street investment firms are prohibited from retaliating against analysts who criticize investment-banking clients of the firm. The Act contains a provision with broad new protection for whistle-blowers and lengthens the time that investors have to file lawsuits against corporations for securities fraud.

By narrowing the type of consulting services that accountants can provide to companies that they audit, requiring auditor rotation, and imposing stiff criminal penalties for violation of the Act, it appears that this legislation will significantly help to restore public confidence in financial statements and markets and change the regulatory environment in which accountants operate.

Customers

Customers pay special attention to financial information about the firms with which they do business. For example, before a business spends a lot of money on a new computer system, the business wants to know that the computer manufacturer will be around for the next several years in order to service the computer, replace parts, and provide additional components. The business analyzes the financial information about the computer manufacturer in order to determine its economic health and the likelihood that it will remain in business.

Employees and Unions

Often employees are interested in the financial information of the business that employs them. Employees who are members of a profit-sharing plan pay close attention to the financial results because they affect employee income. Employees who are members of a labor union use financial information about the firm to negotiate wages and benefits.

FIGURE 1.1

Users of Financial Information

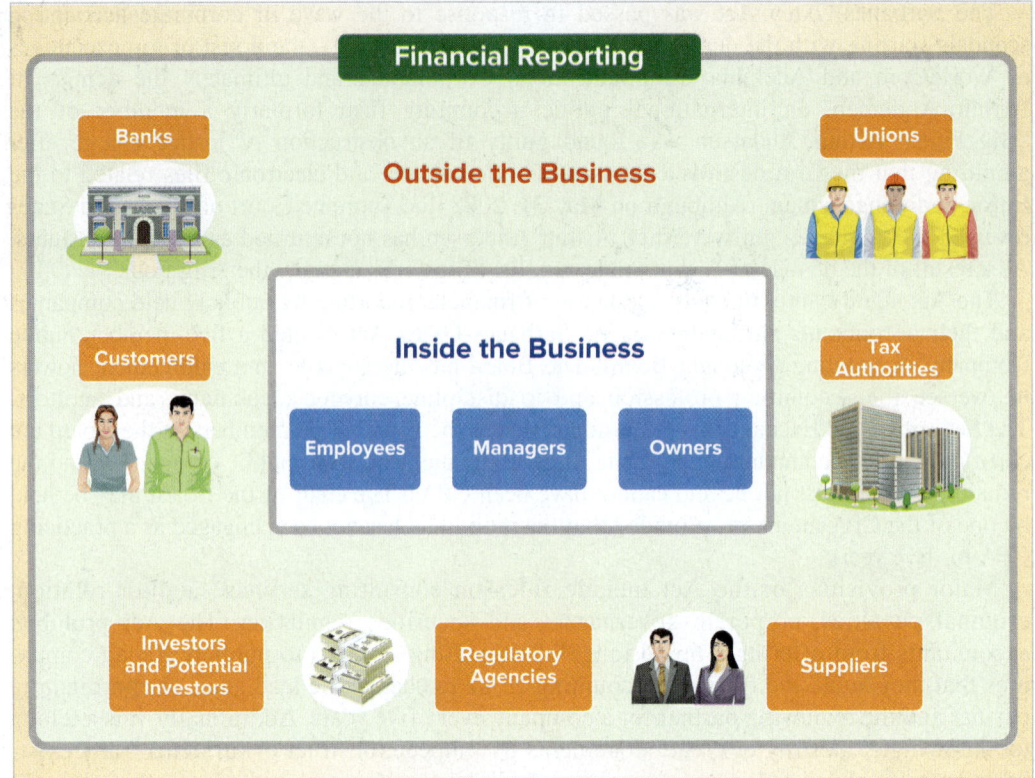

Figure 1.1 illustrates different financial information users. As you learn about the accounting process, you will appreciate why financial information is so important to these individuals and organizations. You will learn how financial information meets users' needs.

Section 1 Review

1. The names of three accounting jobs include all but:
   a. logistics manager.
   b. accountant.
   c. bookkeeper.
   d. accounts payable clerk.

2. Accounting is called:
   a. the language of economics.
   b. the language of finance.
   c. the language of business.
   d. the language of commerce.

3. Financial statements are:
   a. accumulated financial data summarized in periodic reports.
   b. accumulated transactions of the firm's sales activities.
   c. a summary of records and procedures that make up the accounting system.
   d. a summarized description of a firm's accounting system.

4. The organization that has the final say on financial accounting issues faced by publicly owned corporations is the:
   a. Federal Trade Commission.
   b. Securities and Exchange Commission.
   c. Internal Revenue Service.
   d. U.S. Treasury.

5. As the owner of a small business, you have decided to apply for a loan to expand your locations. Information that you most likely will need to provide to the lender include all but:
   a. current sales and expense figures.
   b. projected sales and expense figures.
   c. the cost of the expansion.
   d. the average value of homes in your neighborhood.

6. One requirement for becoming a CPA is to pass the:
   a. Final CPA Examination.
   b. SEC Accounting Examination.
   c. Uniform CPA Exam.
   d. State Board Examination.

7. The CPA designation stands for:
   a. Certified Public Analyst.
   b. Certified Public Appraiser.
   c. Certified Public Accountant.
   d. Certified Public Associate.

8. The Certified Bookkeeper exam includes all of the parts below except:
   a. Business Law.
   b. Adjustments and Error Corrections.
   c. Inventory.
   d. Payroll and Depreciation.

9. To become a Certified Bookkeeper, one must meet all requirements below except:
   a. Pass the national certified bookkeeper exam.
   b. Sign a code of ethics.
   c. Pass a criminal background check.
   d. Submit evidence that you satisfy the experience requirements for the designation.

10. All of the following are users of accounting information except:
    a. owners and managers.
    b. banks and suppliers.
    c. search engines on a website.
    d. tax authorities and regulatory agencies.

11. All of the following are goals of internal control except:
    a. policies and procedures to safeguard assets.
    b. ensuring reliability of accounting data.
    c. fraud prevention.
    d. encouraging noncompliance with management policies and applicable laws.

12. Fraud is intentional or reckless acts that result in the confiscation of a firm's assets or the misrepresentation of the firm's accounting data.
    a. True
    b. False

Section 2

SECTION OBJECTIVES

>> 1-4 Compare and contrast the three types of business entities.

WHY IT'S IMPORTANT
Each type of business entity requires unique legal and accounting considerations.

>> 1-5 Describe the process used to develop generally accepted accounting principles.

WHY IT'S IMPORTANT
Accounting professionals are required to use common standards and principles in order to produce reliable financial information.

TERMS TO LEARN

Accounting Standards Codification
Accounting Standards Update
auditor's report
corporation
creditor
discussion memorandum
economic entity
entity
exposure draft
generally accepted accounting principles (GAAP)
international accounting
partnership
separate entity assumption
social entity
sole proprietorship
Statements of Financial Accounting Standards
stock
stockholders

Business and Accounting

The accounting process involves recording, classifying, summarizing, interpreting, and communicating financial information about an economic or social entity. An **entity** is recognized as having its own separate identity. An entity may be an individual, a town, a university, or a business. The term **economic entity** usually refers to a business or organization whose major purpose is to produce a profit for its owners. **Social entities** are nonprofit organizations, such as cities, public schools, and public hospitals. This book focuses on the accounting process for businesses, but keep in mind that nonprofit organizations also need financial information.

>> **1-4 OBJECTIVE**
Compare and contrast the three types of business entities.

Types of Business Entities

The three major legal forms of business entity are the sole proprietorship, the partnership, and the corporation. In general, the accounting process is the same for all three forms of business. Later in the book you will study the different ways certain transactions are handled depending on the type of business entity. For now, however, you will learn about the different types of business entities.

Sole Proprietorships

A **sole proprietorship** is a business entity owned by one person. The life of the business ends when the owner is no longer willing or able to keep the business going. Many small businesses are operated as sole proprietorships.

The owner of a sole proprietorship is legally responsible for the debts and taxes of the business. If the business is unable to pay its debts, the **creditors** (those people, companies, or government agencies to whom the business owes money) can turn to the owner for payment. The owner may have to pay the debts of the business from personal resources, including personal savings. When the time comes to pay income taxes, the owner's income and the income of the business are combined to compute the total tax responsibility of the owner.

It is important that the business transactions be kept separate from the owner's personal transactions. If the owner's personal transactions are mixed with those of the business, it will be difficult to measure the performance of the business. The term **separate entity assumption** describes the concept of keeping the firm's financial records separate from the owner's personal financial records.

Partnerships

A **partnership** is a business entity owned by two or more people. The partnership structure is common in businesses that offer professional services, such as law firms, accounting firms, architectural firms, medical practices, and dental practices. At the beginning of the partnership, two or more individuals enter into a contract that details the rights, obligations, and limitations of each partner, including

- the amount each partner will contribute to the business,
- each partner's percentage of ownership,
- each partner's share of the profits,
- the duties each partner will perform, and
- the responsibility each partner has for the amounts owed by the business to creditors and tax authorities.

The partners choose how to share the ownership and profits of the business. They may share equally or in any proportion agreed upon in the contract. When a partner leaves, the partnership is dissolved and a new partnership may be formed with the remaining partners.

Partners are individually, and as a group, responsible for the debts and taxes of the partnership. If the partnership is unable to pay its debts or taxes, the partners' personal property, including personal bank accounts, may be used to provide payment. It is important that partnership transactions be kept separate from the personal financial transactions of the partners.

> Under the Limited Liability Partnership Act of most states, a Limited Liability Partnership (LLP) may be formed. An LLP is a general partnership that provides some limited liability for all partners. LLP partners are responsible and have liability for their own actions and the actions of those under their control or supervision. They are not liable for the actions or malfeasance of another partner. Except for the limited liability aspect, LLPs generally have the same characteristics, advantages, and disadvantages as any other partnership.

Corporations

A **corporation** is a business entity that is separate from its owners. A corporation has a legal right to own property and do business in its own name. Corporations are very different from sole proprietorships and partnerships.

Stock, issued in the form of stock certificates, represents the ownership of the corporation. Corporations may be *privately* or *publicly* owned. Privately owned corporations are also called *closely held* corporations. The ownership of privately owned corporations is limited to specific individuals, usually family members. Stock of closely held corporations is not traded on an exchange. In contrast, stock of publicly owned corporations is bought and sold on stock exchanges and in over-the-counter markets. Most large corporations have issued (sold) thousands of shares of stock.

An owner's share of the corporation is determined by the number of shares of stock held by the owner compared to the total number of shares issued by the corporation. Assume that

important!

Separate Entity Assumption

For *accounting* purposes, all forms of business are considered separate entities from their owners. However, the corporation is the only form of business that is a separate *legal* entity.

Hector Flores owns 600 shares of Sample Corporation. If Sample Corporation has issued 2,000 shares of stock, Flores owns 30 percent of the corporation (600 shares ÷ 2,000 shares = 0.30 *or* 30%). Some corporate decisions require a vote by the owners. For Sample Corporation, Flores has 600 votes, one for each share of stock that he owns. The other owners have 1,400 votes.

> Subchapter S corporations, also known as S corporations, are entities formed as corporations that meet the requirements of Subchapter S of the Internal Revenue Code to be treated essentially as a partnership so the corporation pays no income tax. Instead, shareholders include their share of corporate profits, and any items that require special tax treatment, on their individual income tax returns. Otherwise, S corporations have all of the characteristics of regular corporations. The advantage of the S corporation is that the owners have limited liability and avoid double taxation.

One of the advantages of the corporate form of business is the indefinite life of the corporation. A sole proprietorship ends when the owner dies or discontinues the business. A partnership ends on the death or withdrawal of a partner. In contrast, a corporation does not end when ownership changes. Some corporations have new owners daily because their shares are actively traded (sold) on stock exchanges.

Corporate owners, called **stockholders** or *shareholders*, are not personally responsible for the debts or taxes of the corporation. If the corporation is unable to pay its bills, the most stockholders can lose is their investment in the corporation. In other words, the stockholders will not lose more than the cost of the shares of stock.

The accounting process for the corporate entity, like that of the sole proprietorship and the partnership, is separate from the financial affairs of its owners. Usually this separation is easy to maintain. Most stockholders do not participate in the day-to-day operations of the business.

> A limited liability company (LLC) combines the best features of a partnership with those of a corporation even though, from a legal perspective, it is neither. While offering its owners the limited liability of a corporation, an LLC with more than one owner generally is treated as a partnership for tax purposes. The limited liability extends to all the LLC's owners. So the LLC is similar to a limited partnership with no general partners. Unlike an S corporation, an LLC may have an unlimited number of owners who can be almost any type of entity. Under special IRS regulations, an LLC may elect to be taxed as a corporation or as a partnership. If the LLC elects to be treated as a partnership, it should file a Form 1065, U.S. Return of Partnership Income. If the LLC elects to be treated as a corporation, it should file a Form 1120, U.S. Corporation Income Tax Return. If the LLC elects to be treated as an S corporation, it should file a Form 1120S, U.S. Income Tax Return for an S Corporation.

Table 1.2 summarizes the business characteristics for sole proprietorships, partnerships, and corporations.

Generally Accepted Accounting Principles

The Securities and Exchange Commission has the final say on matters of financial reporting by publicly owned corporations. The SEC has delegated the job of determining proper accounting standards to the accounting profession. However, the SEC sometimes overrides decisions the accounting profession makes. To fulfill its responsibility, the accounting profession has developed, and continues to develop, **generally accepted accounting principles (GAAP).** Generally accepted accounting principles must be followed by publicly owned companies unless they can show that doing so would produce information that is misleading.

TABLE 1.2 Major Characteristics of Business Entities

Characteristic	Type of Business Entity		
	Sole Proprietorship	Partnership	Corporation
Ownership	One owner	Two or more owners	One or more owners, even thousands
Life of the business	Ends when the owner dies, is unable to carry on operations, or decides to close the firm	Ends when one or more partners withdraw, when a partner dies, or when the partners decide to close the firm	Can continue indefinitely; ends only when the business goes bankrupt or when the stockholders vote to liquidate
Responsibility for debts of the business	Owner is responsible for the firm's debt when the firm is unable to pay	Partners are responsible individually and jointly for the firm's debts when the firm is unable to pay	Stockholders are not responsible for the firm's debts; they can lose only the amount they invested

The Development of Generally Accepted Accounting Principles

>> 1-5 OBJECTIVE
Describe the process used to develop generally accepted accounting principles.

Generally accepted accounting principles are developed by the Financial Accounting Standards Board (FASB), which is composed of five full-time members. Prior to 2009, the FASB issued 168 **Statements of Financial Accounting Standards.** The FASB developed these statements and, before issuing them, obtained feedback from interested people and organizations.

First, the FASB wrote a **discussion memorandum** to explain the topic being considered. Then public hearings were held where interested parties could express their opinions, either orally or in writing. The groups that consistently expressed opinions about proposed FASB statements were the SEC, the American Institute of Certified Public Accountants (AICPA), public accounting firms, the American Accounting Association (AAA), and businesses with a direct interest in a particular statement.

The AICPA is a national association for certified public accountants. The AAA is a group of accounting educators. AAA members research possible effects of a proposed FASB statement and offer their opinions to the FASB.

After public hearings, the FASB released an **exposure draft,** which described the proposed statement. Then the FASB received and evaluated public comment about the exposure draft. Finally, FASB members voted on the statement. If at least four members approved, the statement was issued.

The above process was used until 2009. Effective July 1, 2009, the source of authoritative U.S. GAAP is the FASB **Accounting Standards Codification,** which is communicated through an **Accounting Standards Update (Update).** The Codification reorganizes U.S. GAAP pronouncements into approximately 90 accounting topics. It also includes relevant U.S. Securities and Exchange Commission guidance that follows the same topical structure in separate sections in the Codification.

Updates are now published on these accounting topics for all authoritative U.S. GAAP promulgated by the FASB, regardless of the form in which such guidance may have been issued prior to the release of the FASB Codification. An Update summarizes the key provisions of the project that led to the Update, details the specific amendments to the FASB Codification, and explains the basis for the Board's decision.

Accounting principles vary from country to country. **International accounting** is the study of the accounting principles used by different countries. In 1973, the International Accounting Standards Committee (IASC) was formed. Recently, the IASC's name was changed to the International Accounting Standards Board (IASB). The IASB deals with issues caused by the lack of uniform accounting principles. The IASB also makes recommendations to enhance comparability of reporting practices.

important!

GAAP
The SEC requires all publicly owned companies to follow generally accepted accounting principles. As new standards are developed or refined, accountants interpret the standards and adapt accounting practices to the new standards.

MANAGERIAL IMPLICATIONS

FINANCIAL INFORMATION

- Managers of a business make sure that the firm's accounting system produces financial information that is timely, accurate, and fair.
- Financial statements should be based on generally accepted accounting principles.
- Each year a publicly traded company must submit financial statements, including an independent auditor's report, to the SEC.
- Internal reports for management need not follow generally accepted accounting principles but should provide useful information that will aid in monitoring and controlling operations.
- Financial information can help managers to control present operations, make decisions, and plan for the future.
- The sound use of financial information is essential to good management.

THINKING CRITICALLY

If you were a manager, how would you use financial information to make decisions?

The Use of Generally Accepted Accounting Principles

Every year, publicly traded companies submit financial statements to the SEC. The financial statements are audited by independent certified public accountants. The CPAs are called *independent* because they are not employees of the company being audited and they do not have a financial interest in the company. The financial statements include the auditor's report. The **auditor's report** contains the auditor's opinion about the fair presentation of the operating results and financial position of the business. The auditor's report also confirms that the financial information is prepared in conformity with generally accepted accounting principles. The financial statements and the auditor's report are made available to the public, including existing and potential stockholders.

Businesses and the environment in which they operate are constantly changing. The economy, technology, and laws change. Generally accepted accounting principles are changed and refined as accountants respond to the changing environment.

Section 2 Review

1. Generally accepted accounting principles are accounting standards that are changed and refined in response to changes in the environment in which businesses operate.
   a. True
   b. False

2. Generally accepted accounting principles are not needed to ensure that financial information is fairly presented in the operating results and financial positions of firms.
   a. True
   b. False

3. Generally accepted accounting principles are developed by the Financial Accounting Standards Board (FASB) through proposed statements and solicitation of feedback from interested individuals, groups, and companies. Subsequently, the FASB evaluates the opinions received and votes on the statements.
   a. True
   b. False

4. A nonprofit organization such as a public school is a(n):
   a. social unit.
   b. economic unit.
   c. economic entity.
   d. social entity.

5. You plan to open a business with two of your friends. You would like to form a corporation, but your friends prefer the partnership form of business. All of the following are advantages of the corporation except:

a. a corporation is a separate, distinct, legal entity.
   b. the corporation's earnings are only taxed once.
   c. a corporation has limited liability.
   d. ease of raising capital.

6. **An organization that has two or more owners who are legally responsible for the debts and taxes of the business is a:**
   a. social entity.
   b. partnership.
   c. sole proprietorship.
   d. corporation.

7. **A limited liability company may choose to be taxed as a partnership or corporation.**
   a. True
   b. False

Chapter REVIEW — Chapter Summary

Accounting is often called the "language of business." The financial information about a business is communicated to interested parties in financial statements.

Learning Objectives

1-1 Define accounting.

Accounting is the process by which financial information about a business is recorded, classified, summarized, interpreted, and communicated to owners, managers, and other interested parties. Accurate accounting information is essential for making business decisions.

1-2 Identify and discuss career opportunities in accounting.

- There are many job opportunities in accounting.
- Accounting clerk positions, such as accounts receivable clerk, accounts payable clerk, and payroll clerk, require the least education and experience.
- Bookkeepers usually have experience as accounting clerks and a minimum of one to two years of accounting education. Certified Bookkeepers (CB) are individuals who have passed a three-part exam that aims to assure the level of knowledge and skills needed to carry out all key accounting functions through the adjusted trial balance, including payroll.
- Most entry-level accounting positions require a college degree or significant experience as a bookkeeper.
- Accountants usually specialize in one of three major areas: public, managerial, or governmental accounting.
  - Some accountants work for public accounting firms and perform auditing, tax accounting, or management advisory functions.
  - Other accountants work in private industry where they set up and supervise accounting systems, prepare financial reports, prepare internal reports, or assist in determining the prices to charge for the firm's products.
  - Still other accountants work for government agencies. They keep track of public funds and expenditures, or they audit the financial records of businesses and individuals to determine whether the records are in compliance with regulatory laws, tax laws, and other laws. The Securities and Exchange Commission, the Internal Revenue Service, the Federal Bureau of Investigation, and Homeland Security employ many accountants.

1-3 Identify the users of financial information.

All types of businesses need and use financial information. Users of financial information include owners and managers, employees, suppliers, banks, tax authorities, regulatory agencies, and investors. Nonprofit organizations need similar financial information.

A major responsibility of owners and managers of an entity is internal control and the prevention of fraud. Internal controls are the company's policies and procedures to safeguard assets, ensure reliability of accounting data, and promote compliance with management policies and applicable laws.

1-4 Compare and contrast the three types of business entities.

- A sole proprietorship is a business entity owned by one person. The life of the business ends when the owner is no longer willing or able to keep the business going.
- A partnership is owned by two or more people. The owners are legally responsible for the debts and taxes of the business. Limited liability companies (LLC) are recognized by most states. LLCs can elect to be taxed as a partnership or corporation.
- A corporation is a separate legal entity from its owners.

Note that all three types of business entities are considered separate entities for accounting purposes.

1-5 Describe the process used to develop generally accepted accounting principles.

- The SEC has delegated the authority to develop generally accepted accounting principles to the accounting profession. The Financial Accounting Standards Board handles this task. A series of steps used by the FASB includes issuing a discussion memorandum, an exposure draft, and a statement of principle.
- The SEC oversees the Public Company Accounting Oversight Board that was created by the Sarbanes-Oxley Act. The Board regulates

- financial reporting by accountants and auditors of publicly held companies.
- Each year, firms that sell stock on stock exchanges or in over-the-counter markets must publish audited financial reports that follow generally accepted accounting principles. They must submit their reports to the SEC. They must also make the reports available to stockholders.

1-6 Define the accounting terms new to this chapter.

Glossary

Accounting (p. 2) The process by which financial information about a business is recorded, classified, summarized, interpreted, and communicated to owners, managers, and other interested parties

Accounting Standards Codification (p. 13) The source of authoritative U.S. GAAP

Accounting Standards Update (p. 13) Changes to Accounting Standards Codification are communicated through Accounting Standards Update covering approximately 90 topics

Accounting system (p. 2) A process designed to accumulate, classify, and summarize financial data

Auditing (p. 5) The review of financial statements to assess their fairness and adherence to generally accepted accounting principles

Auditor's report (p. 14) An independent accountant's review of a firm's financial statements

Certified Bookkeeper (CB) (p. 3) A designation that assures an individual possesses the level of knowledge and skill needed to carry out all key functions through the adjusted trial balance, including payroll

Certified public accountant (CPA) (p. 3) An independent accountant who provides accounting services to the public for a fee

Corporation (p. 11) A publicly or privately owned business entity that is separate from its owners and has a legal right to own property and do business in its own name; stockholders are not responsible for the debts or taxes of the business

Creditor (p. 10) One to whom money is owed

Discussion memorandum (p. 13) An explanation of a topic under consideration by the Financial Accounting Standards Board

Economic entity (p. 10) A business or organization whose major purpose is to produce a profit for its owners

Entity (p. 10) Anything having its own separate identity, such as an individual, a town, a university, or a business

Exposure draft (p. 13) A proposed solution to a problem being considered by the Financial Accounting Standards Board

Financial statements (p. 3) Periodic reports of a firm's financial position or operating results

Fraud (p. 5) Intentional or reckless acts that result in confiscation of a firm's assets or the misrepresentation of the firm's accounting data

Generally accepted accounting principles (GAAP) (p. 12) Accounting standards developed and applied by professional accountants

Governmental accounting (p. 5) Accounting work performed for a federal, state, or local governmental unit

Internal control (p. 5) A company's policies and procedures to safeguard assets, ensure reliability of accounting data, and promote compliance with management policies and applicable laws

International accounting (p. 13) The study of accounting principles used by different countries

Management advisory services (p. 5) Services designed to help clients improve their information systems or their business performance

Managerial accounting (p. 5) Accounting work carried on by an accountant employed by a single business in industry; the branch of accounting that provides financial information about business segments, activities, or products

Partnership (p. 11) A business entity owned by two or more people who carry on a business for profit and who are legally responsible for the debts and taxes of the business

Public accountants (p. 3) Members of firms that perform accounting services for other companies

Separate entity assumption (p. 11) The concept that a business is separate from its owners; the concept of keeping a firm's financial records separate from the owner's personal financial records

Social entity (p. 10) A nonprofit organization, such as a city, public school, or public hospital

Sole proprietorship (p. 10) A business entity owned by one person, who is legally responsible for the debts and taxes of the business

Statements of Financial Accounting Standards (p. 13) Accounting principles established by the Financial Accounting Standards Board

Stock (p. 11) Certificates that represent ownership of a corporation

Stockholders (p. 12) The owners of a corporation; also called shareholders

Tax accounting (p. 5) A service that involves tax compliance and tax planning

Comprehensive Self Review

1. What is the purpose of accounting?
2. What does the accounting process involve?
3. What is the purpose of the auditor's report?
4. What are the three major types of business entities?
5. How is the ownership of a corporation different from that of a sole proprietorship?

(Answers to Comprehensive Self Review are at the end of the chapter.)

Discussion Questions

1. What types of people or organizations are interested in financial information about a firm, and why are they interested in this information?
2. Why is it important for business records to be separate from the records of the business's owner or owners? What is the term accountants use to describe this separation of personal and business records?
3. What are the three types of business entities, and how do they differ?
4. What are the major functions or activities performed by accountants in private industry?
5. What is tax planning?
6. What types of services do public accountants provide?
7. What are the three major areas of accounting?
8. What is the purpose of the Financial Accounting Standards Board?
9. What groups consistently offer opinions about proposed FASB statements?
10. What is the function of the Securities and Exchange Commission?
11. What led to the passage of the Public Company Accounting Reform and Investor Protection Act of 2002?
12. What is the purpose of the Public Company Accounting Oversight Board?
13. What does the Certified Bookkeeper (CB) designation imply?
14. How does one become a Certified Bookkeeper (CB)?
15. What is a limited liability company (LLC)?
16. Define internal control.

17. Define fraud.
18. What is the goal of internal control?
19. Name two common internal control and fraud prevention procedures.
20. Employees sometimes make mistakes and errors in recording accounting transactions. Is this considered fraud?

PROBLEM

Critical Thinking Problem

Which Type of Business Entity?

Since graduating from college five years ago, you have worked for a national chain of men's clothing stores. You have held several positions within the company and are currently manager of a local branch store.

Over the past three years, you have observed a pattern in the purchases of men's suits. You establish that the majority of men's suit purchases are black, brown, blue, gray, and olive. You also noticed that French cuff shirts are now fashionable, but few stores carry a wide color selection. Because you have always wanted to be in business for yourself, you decide to open a shop that will sell suits that are black, brown, blue, gray, and olive and to carry a wide array of colors of French cuff shirts. Your store will also sell fashionable ties and cuff links. You have decided that your store will brand itself for focusing on men's fashion; therefore, the name for your store will be "The Style Shop." You have discussed your plan with a number of people in the industry, and they believe your idea is a viable one and have encouraged you to pursue your dream of becoming an entrepreneur.

A new upscale outdoor shopping mall is opening nearby, and you have decided that now is the time to take the plunge and go into business for yourself. After developing a comprehensive business plan that includes marketing strategies and financial projections, you decide to open The Style Shop in the new mall.

One of the things you must decide in the process of transforming your idea into reality is the form of ownership for your new business. Should it be organized as a sole proprietorship, a partnership, or a corporation?

What advantages or disadvantages are there to each choice? What do you think of the proposed name for the business, The Style Shop? Use the chart below to organize your thoughts.

Business Entity	Advantages	Disadvantages
Sole Proprietorship		
Partnership		
Limited Liability Partnership		
Limited Liability Company		
Corporation		
S Corporation		

BUSINESS CONNECTIONS

Managerial FOCUS

Know Accounting

1. As an owner or manager of a business, what questions would you ask to judge the firm's performance, control operations, make decisions, and plan for the future?
2. Why is financial information important?
3. Besides earning a profit, what other objectives might a business have? Can financial information play an important role in these objectives?
4. What kind of problems can you foresee if a business owner and/or manager does not have a basic knowledge of accounting?
5. What would you tell a small business owner who says he does not see a need for an accounting system in his business because he closely supervises the day-to-day operations and knows exactly what is happening with the business?
6. What is the role of the manager versus the accountant?
7. Does a business owner/manager need to worry about the separate entity assumption? Why or why not?
8. Why are international accounting standards important to management?

Internal Control and FRAUD PREVENTION

Choosing the Right Employees

Selecting the right employees is a critical step for enhancing the entity's system of internal control and fraud prevention. Reflected below are several possible ways to check the background of employees. For each item listed, indicate why the background check is important, what type of information should be sought, and whether or not you believe you should get the candidate's consent before acquiring the information.

1. References
2. Employment history
3. Education, certifications, and licenses
4. Drug screening

Financial Statement ANALYSIS

Notes to Financial Statements

Within a company's annual report, a section called "Notes to Consolidated Financial Statements" offers general information about the company along with detailed notes related to its financial statements.

Analyze Online: On the American Eagle Outfitters, Inc., website (www.ae.com), click on About AEO located at the bottom of the page. Then click on Investor Relations.

Analyze:

1. What types of merchandise does this company sell?
2. Who are the potential users of the information presented? Why would this information be helpful to these users?
3. How many AE company-owned stores are there, and what are their worldwide locations?
4. Would American Eagle Outfitters, Inc., be considered an economic entity or a social entity? Why?

TEAMWORK

Determining Information

Restful Sleep Mattress company is planning to expand into selling bedroom furniture. This expansion will require a loan from the bank. The bank has requested financial information. In a group, discuss the information the bank would require. What information, if any, would you provide to the bank?

Answers to Comprehensive Self Review

1. To gather and communicate financial information about a business.
2. Recording, classifying, summarizing, interpreting, and communicating financial information about a business.
3. To obtain the objective opinion of a professional accountant from outside the company that the statements fairly present the operating results and financial position of the business and that the information was prepared according to GAAP.
4. Sole proprietorship, partnership, and corporation.
5. A sole proprietorship is a business entity owned by one person. A corporation is a separate legal entity that has a legal right to own property and do business in its own name.

Analyzing Business Transactions — Chapter 2

VIAVAL/Shutterstock

www.aa.com

The first American Airlines flight was flown on March 15, 1926, when Charles Lindbergh flew an American aircraft carrying U.S. mail from St. Louis, Missouri, to Chicago, Illinois. With a 90-year-plus history, American Airlines Group is the world's largest airlines measured by fleet size, profit, revenue, passengers transported, and revenue per passenger mile. American Airlines Group was formed on December 9, 2013, with the closing of the merger between American Airlines and US Airways Group. The company is listed on the NASDAQ Global Select Marker under the ticker symbol AAL.

American Airlines and American Eagle fly an average of nearly 6,700 flights per day to more than 50 countries with approximately 350 destinations. After moving its headquarters from New York to Dallas/Fort Worth, Texas, in 1979, American Airlines changed to a hub-and-spoke system. American offers hubs in Charlotte, North Carolina; Chicago, Illinois; Dallas/Fort Worth, Texas; Los Angeles, California; Miami, Florida; New York, New York; Philadelphia, Pennsylvania; Phoenix, Arizona; and Washington, D.C. In 1999, American Airlines, British Airways, Cathay Pacific, Canadian Airlines, and Qantas founded the global airline alliance Oneworld. Alliance members serve more than 1,000 destinations with more than 14,000 daily flights to over 150 countries.

Running an airline is no easy task, and over the years American has had a turbulent history; from employee strikes, to bankruptcy, to mergers, the airline has survived every threat of demise to emerge stronger and better after every challenge. Think of all of the things that could go wrong and all of the financial transactions that take place on a daily basis. The airline has to buy planes, equipment, and supplies and keep all of its customers safe to their final destinations. It also has to pay employees, pay for repairs on its equipment, and buy insurance, just to name a few expenses. Then, it has to sell enough tickets in order to be able to generate money to pay for all of these things. Yikes! That is a lot of cash coming in and going out. American Airlines is uniquely American, proud, innovative, strong, and forward thinking. Today's American Airlines prides itself on providing its customers with a memorable flying experience that triggers thoughts of a world of possibilities for future travel opportunities.

thinking critically

How does American keep track of all of these transactions so that it can continue to run its airline profitably?

LEARNING OBJECTIVES

- **2-1** Record in equation form the financial effects of a business transaction.
- **2-2** Define, identify, and understand the relationship between asset, liability, and owner's equity accounts.
- **2-3** Analyze the effects of business transactions on a firm's assets, liabilities, and owner's equity and record these effects in accounting equation form.
- **2-4** Prepare an income statement.
- **2-5** Prepare a statement of owner's equity and a balance sheet.
- **2-6** Define the accounting terms new to this chapter.

NEW TERMS

accounts payable
accounts receivable
assets
balance sheet
break even
business transaction
capital
equity
expense
fair market value
fundamental accounting equation
income statement
liabilities
net income
net loss
on account
owner's equity
revenue
statement of owner's equity
withdrawals

Section 1

SECTION OBJECTIVES

>> 2-1 Record in equation form the financial effects of a business transaction.

WHY IT'S IMPORTANT
Learning the fundamental accounting equation is a basis for understanding business transactions.

>> 2-2 Define, identify, and understand the relationship between asset, liability, and owner's equity accounts.

WHY IT'S IMPORTANT
The relationship between assets, liabilities, and owner's equity is the basis for the entire accounting system.

TERMS TO LEARN

accounts payable
assets
balance sheet
business transaction
capital
equity
liabilities
on account
owner's equity

Property and Financial Interest

The accounting process starts with the analysis of business transactions. A **business transaction** is any financial event that changes the resources of a firm. For example, purchases, sales, payments, and receipts of cash are all business transactions. The accountant analyzes each business transaction to decide what information to record and where to record it.

>> **2-1 OBJECTIVE**
Record in equation form the financial effects of a business transaction.

Beginning with Analysis

Let's analyze the transactions of Eli's Consulting Services, a firm that provides a wide range of accounting and consulting services. Trayton Eli, CPA, has a master's degree in accounting. He is the sole proprietor of Eli's Consulting Services. Sergio Sanchez, the office manager, has an associate's degree in business and has taken 12 semester hours of accounting. The firm is located in a large office complex.

Every month, Eli's Consulting Services bills clients for the accounting and consulting services provided that month. Customers can also pay in cash when the services are rendered.

Starting a Business

Let's start from the beginning. Trayton Eli obtained the funds to start the business by withdrawing $100,000 from his personal savings account. The first transaction of the new business was opening a checking account in the name of Eli's Consulting Services. The separate bank account helps Eli keep his financial interest in the business separate from his personal funds.

When a business transaction occurs, it is analyzed to identify how it affects the equation *property equals financial interest*. This equation reflects the fact that in a free enterprise system, all property is owned by someone. In this case, Eli owns the business because he supplied the property (cash).

Use these steps to analyze the effect of a business transaction:

1. Describe the financial event.
   - Identify the property.
   - Identify who owns the property.
   - Determine the amount of increase or decrease.

2. Make sure the equation is in balance.

| Property | = | Financial Interest |

BUSINESS TRANSACTION

Trayton Eli withdrew $100,000 from personal savings and deposited it in a new checking account in the name of Eli's Consulting Services.

ANALYSIS
a. The business received $100,000 of *property* in the form of cash.
a. Eli had a $100,000 *financial interest* in the business.
Note that the equation *property* equals *financial interest* remains in balance. The total of one side of the equation must always equal the total of the other side.

Property		=	Financial Interest
	Cash	=	Trayton Eli, Capital
(a) Invested cash	+$100,000		
(a) Increased equity			+$100,000
New balances	$100,000	=	$100,000

An owner's financial interest in the business is called **equity,** or **capital.** Trayton Eli has $100,000 equity in Eli's Consulting Services.

Purchasing Equipment for Cash

The first priority for office manager Sergio Sanchez was to get the business ready for opening day on December 1.

BUSINESS TRANSACTION

Eli's Consulting Services issued a $5,000 check to purchase a computer and other equipment.

ANALYSIS
b. The firm purchased new property (equipment) for $5,000.
b. The firm paid out $5,000 in cash.
The equation remains in balance.

	Property			=	Financial Interest
	Cash	+	Equipment	=	Trayton Eli, Capital
Previous balances	$100,000			=	$100,000
(b) Purchased equipment		+	$5,000		
(b) Paid cash	−5,000				
New balances	$95,000	+	$5,000	=	$100,000

Notice that there is a change in the composition of the firm's property. Now the firm has cash and equipment. The equation shows that the total value of the property remains the same, $100,000. Trayton Eli's financial interest, or equity, is also unchanged. Note that property (Cash and Equipment) is equal to financial interest (Trayton Eli, Capital).

These activities are recorded for the business entity Eli's Consulting Services. Trayton Eli's personal assets, such as his personal bank account, house, furniture, and automobile, are kept separate from the property of the firm. Nonbusiness property is not included in the accounting records of the business entity.

Purchasing Equipment on Credit

Sanchez purchased additional office equipment. Office Plus, the store selling the equipment, allows Eli's Consulting Services 60 days to pay the bill. This arrangement is called buying **on account.** The business has a *charge account,* or *open-account credit,* with its suppliers. Amounts that a business must pay in the future are known as **accounts payable.** The companies or individuals to whom the amounts are owed are called *creditors.*

BUSINESS TRANSACTION

Eli's Consulting Services purchased office equipment on account from Office Plus for $6,000.

ANALYSIS
c. The firm purchased new property (equipment) that cost $6,000.
c. The firm owes $6,000 to Office Plus.
The equation remains in balance.

	Property			=	Financial Interest		
	Cash	+	Equipment	=	Accounts Payable	+	Trayton Eli, Capital
Previous balances	$95,000	+	$ 5,000	=			$100,000
(c) Purchased equip.		+	6,000	=			
(c) Incurred debt				=	+$6,000		
New balances	$95,000	+	$11,000	=	$6,000	+	$100,000

Office Plus is willing to accept a claim against Eli's Consulting Services until the bill is paid. Now there are two different financial interests or claims against the firm's property—the creditor's claim (Accounts Payable) and the owner's claim (Trayton Eli, Capital). Notice that the total property increases to $106,000. Cash is $95,000 and equipment is $11,000. Trayton Eli, Capital stays the same, but the creditor's claim increases to $6,000. After this transaction is recorded, the left side of the equation still equals the right side.

> When Ben Cohen and Jerry Greenfield founded Ben & Jerry's Homemade Ice Cream, Inc., in 1978, they invested $8,000 of their own funds and borrowed funds of $4,000. The equation *property equals financial interest* is expressed as
>
> | Property | = | Financial Interest |
> |---|---|---|
> | cash | = | creditors' claims + owners' claims |
> | $12,000 | = | $ 4,000 |
> | | | +8,000 |
> | | | $12,000 |

ABOUT ACCOUNTING

History

For as long as people have been involved in business, there has been a need for accounting. The system of accounting we use is based upon the works of Luca Pacioli, a Franciscan monk in Italy. In 1494, Pacioli wrote about the bookkeeping techniques in practice during his time.

Purchasing Supplies

Sanchez purchased supplies so that Eli's Consulting Services could start operations. The company that sold the items requires cash payments from companies that have been in business less than six months.

BUSINESS TRANSACTION

Eli's Consulting Services issued a check for $1,500 to Office Delux, Inc., to purchase office supplies.

ANALYSIS
d. The firm purchased office supplies that cost $1,500.
d. The firm paid $1,500 in cash.
The equation remains in balance.

	Property						=	Financial Interest		
	Cash	+	Supplies	+	Equipment	=	Accounts Payable	+	Trayton Eli, Capital
Previous balances	$95,000			+	$11,000	=	$6,000	+	$100,000
(d) Purchased supplies		+	$1,500						
(d) Paid cash	−$1,500								
New balances	$93,500	+	$1,500	+	$11,000	=	$6,000	+	$100,000

Notice that total property remains the same, even though the form of the property has changed. Also note that all of the property (left side) equals all of the financial interests (right side).

Paying a Creditor

Sanchez decided to reduce the firm's debt to Office Plus by $2,500.

CHAPTER 2 Analyzing Business Transactions

BUSINESS TRANSACTION

Eli's Consulting Services issued a check for $2,500 to Office Plus.

ANALYSIS
e. The firm paid $2,500 in cash.
e. The claim of Office Plus against the firm decreased by $2,500.
The equation remains in balance.

	Property						=	Financial Interest		
	Cash	+	Supplies	+	Equipment	=	Accounts Payable	+	Trayton Eli, Capital
Previous balances	$93,500	+	$1,500	+	$11,000	=	$6,000	+	$100,000
(e) Paid cash	−$ 2,500								
(e) Decreased debt							−$2,500		
New balances	$91,000	+	$1,500	+	$11,000	=	$3,500	+	$100,000

Renting Facilities

In November, Sanchez arranged to rent facilities for $4,000 per month, beginning in December. The landlord required that rent for the first two months—December and January—be paid in advance. The firm prepaid (paid in advance) the rent for two months. As a result, the firm obtained the right to occupy facilities for a two-month period. In accounting, this right is considered a form of property.

BUSINESS TRANSACTION

Eli's Consulting Services issued a check for $8,000 to pay for rent for the months of December and January.

ANALYSIS
f. The firm prepaid the rent for the next two months in the amount of $8,000.
f. The firm decreased its cash balance by $8,000.
The equation remains in balance.

	Property								=	Financial Interest		
	Cash	+	Supplies	+	Prepaid Rent	+	Equipment	=	Accounts Payable	+	Trayton Eli, Capital
Previous balances	$91,000	+	$1,500			+	$11,000	=	$3,500	+	$100,000
(f) Paid cash	−$8,000										
(f) Prepaid rent					+$8,000						
New balances	$83,000	+	$1,500	+	$8,000	+	$11,000	=	$3,500	+	$100,000

Notice that when property values and financial interests increase or decrease, the total of the items on one side of the equation still equals the total on the other side.

Property		=	Financial Interest	
Cash	$ 83,000		Accounts Payable	$ 3,500
Supplies	1,500		Trayton Eli, Capital	100,000
Prepaid Rent	8,000			
Equipment	11,000			
Total	$103,500		Total	$103,500

> The balance sheet is also called the *statement of financial position.* Caterpillar Inc., reported assets of $78.5 billion, liabilities of $64.4 billion, and owners' equity of $14.1 billion on its statement of financial position at December 31, 2018.

Assets, Liabilities, and Owner's Equity

Accountants use special accounting terms when they refer to property and financial interests. For example, they refer to the property that a business owns as **assets** and to the debts or obligations of the business as **liabilities.** The owner's financial interest is called **owner's equity.** (Sometimes owner's equity is called *proprietorship* or *net worth.* Owner's equity is the preferred term and is used throughout this book.) At regular intervals, Trayton Eli reviews the status of the firm's assets, liabilities, and owner's equity in a financial statement called a **balance sheet.** The balance sheet shows the firm's financial position on a given date. Figure 2.1 shows the firm's balance sheet on November 30, the day before the company opened for business.

The assets are listed on the left side of the balance sheet and the liabilities and owner's equity are on the right side. This arrangement is similar to the equation *property equals financial interest.* Property is shown on the left side of the equation, and financial interest appears on the right side.

The balance sheet in Figure 2.1 shows

- the amount and types of property the business owns,
- the amount owed to creditors, and
- the owner's interest.

This statement gives Trayton Eli a complete picture of the financial position of his business on November 30.

>> 2-2 OBJECTIVE
Define, identify, and understand the relationship between asset, liability, and owner's equity accounts.

FIGURE 2.1 Balance Sheet for Eli's Consulting Services

Assets		Liabilities	
Cash	83 000 00	Accounts Payable	3 500 00
Supplies	1 500 00		
Prepaid Rent	8 000 00	Owner's Equity	
Equipment	11 000 00	Trayton Eli, Capital	100 000 00
Total Assets	103 500 00	Total Liabilities and Owner's Equity	103 500 00

Eli's Consulting Services
Balance Sheet
November 30, 20X1

Section 1 Review

1. A business transaction is:
   a. any financial event that changes the resources of the firm.
   b. any financial event that changes the ownership of the firm.
   c. any nonfinancial event that changes the resources of the firm.
   d. any nonfinancial event that changes the ownership of the firm.

2. Which transaction below increases an asset and the owner's equity?
   a. a purchase of equipment on credit
   b. a purchase of equipment with cash
   c. payment of rent with cash
   d. a sale of merchandise on credit

3. Amounts that a business must pay in the future are known as:
   a. accounts receivable.
   b. revenue.
   c. expense.
   d. accounts payable.

4. Elizabeth Tolliver purchased a computer for $6,700 on account for her business. What is the effect of this transaction?
   a. *Equipment* decrease of $6,700 and *Accounts Payable* increase of $6,700
   b. *Equipment* increase of $6,700 and *Accounts Payable* increase of $6,700
   c. *Equipment* increase of $6,700 and *Cash* increase of $6,700
   d. *Cash* decrease of $6,700 and *Owner's Equity* increase of $6,700

5. Pauline Palmer began a new business by depositing $100,000 in the business bank account. She wrote two checks from the business account: $20,000 for office furniture and $5,000 for office supplies. What is her financial interest in the company?
   a. $75,000
   b. $100,000
   c. $80,000
   d. $125,000

6. Oriental Rugs has no liabilities. The assets and owner's equity balances are as follows. What is the balance of *Supplies*?

Cash	$150,000
Office Equipment	$ 50,000
Supplies	????
Johnny Johnson, Capital	$230,000

   a. $15,000
   b. $20,000
   c. $30,000
   d. $40,000

7. Precision Drilling has the following balances in its assets and liability accounts. What is the balance of *Avion Canada, Capital*?

Cash	$175,000
Office Equipment	$ 53,500
Accounts Payable	$ 27,900
Avion Canada, Capital	????

   a. $206,200
   b. $200,600
   c. $212,400
   d. $216,200

8. Zena Brown has the following balances in its assets, liability, and owner's equity accounts. What is the balance of *Cash*?

Cash	????
Office Equipment	$ 26,500
Accounts Payable	$ 30,300
Zena Brown, Capital	$115,700

   a. $119,500
   b. $146,000
   c. $122,500
   d. $156,000

Section 2

SECTION OBJECTIVES	TERMS TO LEARN
>> 2-3 Analyze the effects of business transactions on a firm's assets, liabilities, and owner's equity and record these effects in accounting equation form. **WHY IT'S IMPORTANT** Property will always equal financial interest. >> 2-4 Prepare an income statement. **WHY IT'S IMPORTANT** The income statement shows the results of operations. >> 2-5 Prepare a statement of owner's equity and a balance sheet. **WHY IT'S IMPORTANT** These financial statements show the financial condition of a business.	accounts receivable break even expense fair market value fundamental accounting equation income statement net income net loss revenue statement of owner's equity withdrawals

The Accounting Equation and Financial Statements

The word *balance* in the title "balance sheet" has a special meaning. It emphasizes that the total on the left side of the report must equal, or balance, the total on the right side.

The Fundamental Accounting Equation

In accounting terms, the firm's assets must equal the total of its liabilities and owner's equity. This equality can be expressed in equation form, as illustrated here. The amounts are for Eli's Consulting Services on November 30.

Assets	=	Liabilities	+	Owner's Equity
$103,500	=	$3,500	+	$100,000

The relationship between assets and liabilities plus owner's equity is called the **fundamental accounting equation.** The entire accounting process of analyzing, recording, and reporting business transactions is based on the fundamental accounting equation.

If any two parts of the equation are known, the third part can be determined. For example, consider the basic accounting equation for Eli's Consulting Services on November 30, with some information missing.

	Assets	=	Liabilities	+	Owner's Equity
1.	?	=	$3,500	+	$100,000
2.	$103,500	=	?	+	$100,000
3.	$103,000	=	$3,500	+	?

In the first case, we can solve for assets by adding liabilities to owner's equity ($3,500 + $100,000) to determine that assets are $103,500. In the second case, we can solve for liabilities by subtracting owner's equity from assets ($103,500 − $100,000) to determine that liabilities are $3,500. In the third case, we can solve for owner's equity by subtracting liabilities from assets ($103,500 − $3,500) to determine that owner's equity is $100,000.

>> 2-3 OBJECTIVE
Analyze the effects of business transactions on a firm's assets, liabilities, and owner's equity and record these effects in accounting equation form.

important!

Revenues increase owner's equity. Expenses decrease owner's equity.

Earning Revenue and Incurring Expenses

Eli's Consulting Services opened for business on December 1. Some of the other businesses in the office complex became the firm's first clients. Eli also used his contacts in the community to identify other clients. Providing services to clients started a stream of revenue for the business. **Revenue,** or *income,* is the inflow of money or other assets that results from the sales of goods or services or from the use of money or property. A sale on account does not increase money, but it does create a claim to money. When a sale occurs, the revenue increases assets and also increases owner's equity.

An **expense,** on the other hand, involves the outflow of money, the use of other assets, or the incurring of a liability. Expenses include the costs of any materials, labor, supplies, and services used to produce revenue. Expenses cause a decrease in owner's equity.

A firm's accounting records show increases and decreases in assets, liabilities, and owner's equity as well as details of all transactions involving revenue and expenses. Let's use the fundamental accounting equation to show how revenue and expenses affect the business.

Selling Services for Cash

During the month of December, Eli's Consulting Services earned a total of $36,000 in revenue from clients who paid cash for accounting and bookkeeping services. This involved several transactions throughout the month. The total effect of these transactions is analyzed below.

> **ANALYSIS**
> g. The firm received $36,000 in cash for services provided to clients.
> g. Revenue increased by $36,000, which results in a $36,000 increase in owner's equity.
> The fundamental accounting equation remains in balance.

	Assets								=	Liabilities	+	Owner's Equity		
	Cash	+	Supplies	+	Prepaid Rent	+	Equipment	=	Accounts Payable	+	Trayton Eli, Capital	+	Revenue
Previous balances	$83,000	+	$1,500	+	$8,000	+	$11,000	=	$3,500	+	$100,000		
(g) Received cash	+$36,000												
(g) Increased owner's equity by earning revenue												+	$36,000
New balances	$119,000	+	$1,500	+	$8,000	+	$11,000	=	$3,500	+	$100,000	+	$36,000
	$139,500										$139,500		

Notice that revenue amounts are recorded in a separate column under owner's equity. Keeping revenue separate from the owner's equity will help the firm compute total revenue more easily when the financial statements are prepared.

Selling Services on Credit

Eli's Consulting Services has some charge account clients. These clients are allowed 30 days to pay. Amounts owed by these clients are known as **accounts receivable.** This is a new form of asset for the firm—claims for future collection from customers. During December, Eli's Consulting Services earned $11,000 of revenue from charge account clients. The effect of these transactions is analyzed as follows:

ANALYSIS

h. The firm acquired a new asset, accounts receivable, of $11,000.
h. Revenues increased by $11,000, which results in an $11,000 increase in owner's equity.
The fundamental accounting equation remains in balance.

	Assets									=	Liab.	+	Owner's Equity		
	Cash	+	Accts. Rec.	+	Supp.	+	Prepaid Rent	+	Equip.	=	Accts. Pay.	+	Trayton Eli, Capital	+	Rev.
Previous balances	$119,000			+	$1,500	+	$8,000	+	$11,000	=	$3,500	+	$100,000	+	$36,000
(h) Received new asset—accts. rec.			+$11,000												
(h) Increased owner's equity by earning revenue														+	$11,000
New balances	$119,000	+	$11,000	+	$1,500	+	$8,000	+	$11,000	=	$3,500	+	$100,000	+	$47,000
				$150,500									$150,500		

Collecting Receivables

During December, Eli's Consulting Services received $6,000 on account from clients who owed money for services previously billed. The effect of these transactions is analyzed below.

ANALYSIS

i. The firm received $6,000 in cash.
i. Accounts receivable decreased by $6,000.
The fundamental accounting equation remains in balance.

	Assets									=	Liab.	+	Owner's Equity	
	Cash	+	Accts. Rec.	+	Supp.	+	Prepaid Rent	+	Equip.	=	Accts. Pay.	+	Trayton Eli, Capital	+ Rev.
Previous balances	$119,000	+	$11,000	+	$1,500	+	$8,000	+	$11,000	=	$3,500	+	$100,000	+ $47,000
(i) Received cash	+$6,000													
(i) Decreased accounts receivable			−$6,000											
New balances	$125,000	+	$5,000	+	$1,500	+	$8,000	+	$11,000	=	$3,500	+	$100,000	+ $47,000
				$150,500									$150,500	

In this type of transaction, one asset is changed for another asset (accounts receivable for cash). Notice that revenue is not increased when cash is collected from charge account clients. The revenue was recorded when the sale on account took place (see entry (**h**)). Notice that the fundamental accounting equation, *assets equal liabilities plus owner's equity,* stays in balance regardless of the changes arising from individual transactions.

Paying Employees' Salaries

So far Eli has done very well. His equity has increased by the revenues earned. However, running a business costs money, and these expenses reduce owner's equity.

During the first month of operations, Eli's Consulting Services hired an accounting clerk. The salaries for the new accounting clerk and the office manager are considered an expense to the firm.

BUSINESS TRANSACTION

In December, Eli's Consulting Services paid $8,000 in salaries for the accounting clerk and Sergio Sanchez.

ANALYSIS
j. The firm decreased its cash balance by $8,000.
j. The firm paid salaries expense in the amount of $8,000, which decreased owner's equity.
The fundamental accounting equation remains in balance.

	Assets					=	Liab.	+	Owner's Equity		
	Cash	Accts. Rec.	Supp.	Prepaid Rent	Equip.	=	Accts. Pay.	Trayton Eli, Capital		Rev.	Exp.
Previous balances	$125,000 +	$5,000 +	$1,500 +	$8,000 +	$11,000 =		$3,500 +	$100,000 +		$47,000	
(j) Paid cash	−$8,000										
(j) Decreased owner's equity by incurring salaries exp.											+ $8,000
New balances	$117,000 +	$5,000 +	$1,500 +	$8,000 +	$11,000 =		$3,500 +	$100,000 +		$47,000 −	$8,000
	$142,500						$142,500				

Notice that expenses are recorded in a separate column under owner's equity. The separate record of expenses is kept for the same reason that the separate record of revenue is kept—to analyze operations for the period.

Paying Utilities Expense

At the end of December, the firm received a $650 utilities bill.

BUSINESS TRANSACTION

Eli's Consulting Services issued a check for $650 to pay the utilities bill.

ANALYSIS
k. The firm decreased its cash balance by $650.
k. The firm paid utilities expense of $650, which decreased owner's equity.
The fundamental accounting equation remains in balance.

	Assets					=	Liab.	+	Owner's Equity		
	Cash +	Accts. Rec. +	Supp. +	Prepaid Rent +	Equip.	=	Accts. Pay. +	T. Eli, Capital +	Rev.	−	Exp.
Previous balances	$117,000 +	$5,000 +	$1,500 +	$8,000 +	$11,000	=	$3,500 +	$100,000 +	$47,000	−	$8,000
(k) Paid cash	−$650										
(k) Decreased owner's equity by utilities exp.										+	$650
New balances	$116,350 +	$5,000 +	$1,500 +	$8,000 +	$11,000	=	$3,500 +	$100,000 +	$47,000	−	$8,650

$141,850 = $141,850

Effect of Owner'S Withdrawals

On December 30, Eli withdrew $5,000 in cash for personal expenses. **Withdrawals** are funds taken from the business by the owner for personal use. Withdrawals are not a business expense but a decrease in the owner's equity.

BUSINESS TRANSACTION

Trayton Eli wrote a check to withdraw $5,000 cash for personal use.

ANALYSIS
1. The firm decreased its cash balance by $5,000.
1. Owner's equity decreased by $5,000.

The fundamental accounting equation remains in balance.

	Assets					=	Liab.	+	Owner's Equity		
	Cash +	Accts. Rec. +	Supp. +	Prepaid Rent +	Equip.	=	Accts. Pay. +	Trayton Eli, Capital +	Rev.	−	Exp.
Previous balances	$116,350 +	$5,000 +	$1,500 +	$8,000 +	$11,000	=	$3,500 +	$100,000 +	$47,000	−	$8,650
(l) Withdrew cash	−$5,000										
(l) Decreased owner's equity								− $ 5,000			
New balances	$111,350 +	$5,000 +	$1,500 +	$8,000 +	$11,000	=	$3,500 +	$95,000 +	$47,000	−	$8,650

$136,850 = $136,850

Summary of Transactions

Figure 2.2 summarizes the transactions of Eli's Consulting Services through December 31. Notice that after each transaction, the fundamental accounting equation is in balance. Test your understanding by describing the nature of each transaction. Then check your results by referring to the discussion of each transaction.

FIGURE 2.2 Transactions of Eli's Consulting Services Through December 31, 20X1

	Assets						=	Liab.	+	Owner's Equity		
	Cash	+ Accts. Rec.	+ Supp.	+ Prepaid Rent	+ Equip.	=		Accts. Pay.	+	T. Eli, Capital	+ Rev.	− Exp.
(a)	+$100,000									+$100,000		
Balances	100,000					=				100,000		
(b)	−5,000			+$5,000								
Balances	95,000			5,000		=				100,000		
(c)					+6,000			+$6,000				
Balances	95,000			5,000	+11,000	=		6,000	+	100,000		
(d)	−1,500		+$1,500									
Balances	93,500		+1,500		+11,000	=		6,000	+	100,000		
(e)	−2,500							−2,500				
Balances	91,000		+1,500		+11,000	=		3,500	+	100,000		
(f)	−8,000			+$8,000								
Balances	83,000		+1,500	+8,000	+11,000	=		3,500	+	100,000		
(g)	+36,000										+$36,000	
Balances	119,000		+1,500	+8,000	+11,000	=		3,500	+	100,000	+ 36,000	
(h)		+$11,000									+11,000	
Balances	119,000 +	11,000	+1,500	+8,000	+11,000	=		3,500	+	100,000	+ 47,000	
(i)	+6,000	−6,000										
Balances	125,000 +	5,000	+1,500	+8,000	+11,000	=		3,500	+	100,000	+ 47,000	
(j)	−8,000											+$8,000
Balances	117,000 +	5,000	+1,500	+8,000	+11,000	=		3,500	+	100,000	+ 47,000	− 8,000
(k)	−650											+650
Balances	116,350 +	5,000	+1,500	+8,000	+11,000	=		3,500	+	100,000	+ 47,000	− 8,650
(l)	−5,000									−5,000		
Balances	$111,350 +	$5,000	+$1,500	+$8,000	+$11,000	=		$3,500	+	$95,000	+$47,000	−$8,650

$136,850 = $136,850

>> 2-4 OBJECTIVE
Prepare an income statement.

The Income Statement

To be meaningful to owners, managers, and other interested parties, financial statements should provide information about revenue and expenses, assets and claims on the assets, and owner's equity.

The **income statement** shows the results of business operations for a specific period of time such as a month, a quarter, or a year. The income statement shows the revenue earned and the expenses of doing business. (The income statement is sometimes called a *profit and loss statement* or a *statement of income and expenses*. The most common term, income statement, is used throughout this text.) Figure 2.3 shows the income statement for Eli's Consulting Services for its first month of operation.

The income statement shows the difference between revenue from services provided or goods sold and the amount spent to operate the business. **Net income** results when revenue is greater than the expenses for the period. When expenses are greater than revenue, the result is a **net loss.** In the rare case when revenue and expenses are equal, the firm is said to **break even.** The income statement in Figure 2.3 shows a net income; revenue is greater than expenses.

recall

Financial Statements
Financial statements are reports that summarize a firm's financial affairs.

FIGURE 2.3

Income Statement for Eli's Consulting Services

Eli's Consulting Services		
Income Statement		
Month Ended December 31, 20X1		
Revenue		
Fees Income		47 000 00
Expenses		
Salaries Expense	8 000 00	
Utilities Expense	650 00	
Total Expenses		8 650 00
Net Income		38 350 00

The three-line heading of the income statement shows *who*, *what*, and *when*.

- Who—the business name appears on the first line.
- What—the report title appears on the second line.
- When—the period covered appears on the third line.

The third line of the income statement heading in Figure 2.3 indicates that the report covers operations for the "Month Ended December 31, 20X1." Review how other time periods are reported on the third line of the income statement heading.

Period Covered	Third Line of Heading
Jan., Feb., Mar.	Three-Month Period Ended March 31, 20X1
Jan. to Dec.	Year Ended December 31, 20X1
July 1 to June 30	Fiscal Year Ended June 30, 20X1

Note the use of single and double rules in amount columns. A single line is used to show that the amounts above it are being added or subtracted. Double lines are used under the final amount in a column or section of a report to show that the amount is complete. Nothing is added to or subtracted from an amount with a double line.

> Some companies refer to the income statement as the *statement of operations*. American Eagle Outfitters, Inc., reported $4,036 billion in sales on consolidated statements of operations for the fiscal year ended February 2, 2019.

The income statement for Eli's Consulting Services does not have dollar signs because it was prepared on accounting paper with ruled columns. However, dollar signs are used on income statements that are prepared on plain paper, that is, not on a ruled form.

The Statement of Owner's Equity and the Balance Sheet

>> **2-5 OBJECTIVE**
Prepare a statement of owner's equity and a balance sheet.

The **statement of owner's equity** reports the changes that occurred in the owner's financial interest during the reporting period. This statement is prepared before the balance sheet so that the amount of the ending capital balance is available for presentation on the balance sheet. Figure 2.4 shows the statement of owner's equity for Eli's Consulting Services. Note that the statement of owner's equity has a three-line heading: *who, what,* and *when*.

- The first line of the statement of owner's equity is the capital balance at the beginning of the period.
- Net income is an increase to owner's equity; net loss is a decrease to owner's equity.
- Withdrawals by the owner are a decrease to owner's equity.

FIGURE 2.4

Statement of Owner's Equity for Eli's Consulting Services

Eli's Consulting Services		
Statement of Owner's Equity		
Month Ended December 31, 20X1		
Trayton Eli, Capital, December 1, 20X1		100 000 00
Net Income for December	38 350 00	
Less Withdrawals for December	5 000 00	
Increase in Capital		33 350 00
Trayton Eli, Capital, December 31, 20X1		133 350 00

- Additional investments by the owner are an increase to owner's equity.
- The total of changes in equity is reported on the line "Increase in Capital" (or "Decrease in Capital").
- The last line of the statement of owner's equity is the capital balance at the end of the period.

If Trayton Eli had made any additional investments during December, this would appear as a separate line on Figure 2.4. Additional investments can be cash or other assets such as equipment. If an investment is made in a form other than cash, the investment is recorded at its fair market value. **Fair market value** is the current worth of an asset or the price the asset would bring if sold on the open market.

The ending balances in the asset and liability accounts are used to prepare the balance sheet.

	Assets					=	Liab.	+	Owner's Equity		
	Cash	+ Accts. Rec.	+ Supp.	+ Prepaid Rent	+ Equip.	=	Accts. Pay.	+	T. Eli, Capital	+ Rev.	− Exp.
New balances	$111,350	+ $5,000	+ $1,500	+ $8,000	+ $11,000	=	$3,500	+	$95,000	+ $47,000	− $8,650
	$136,850								$136,850		

important!

Financial Statements

The balance sheet is a snapshot of the firm's financial position on a specific date. The income statement, like a movie or video, shows the results of business operations over a period of time.

The ending capital balance from the statement of owner's equity is also used to prepare the balance sheet. Figure 2.5 shows the balance sheet for Eli's Consulting Services on December 31, 20X1.

The balance sheet shows:

- Assets—the types and amounts of property that the business owns.
- Liabilities—the amounts owed to creditors.
- Owner's Equity—the owner's equity on the reporting date.

In preparing a balance sheet, remember the following:

- The three-line heading gives the firm's name (who), the title of the report (what), and the date of the report (when).
- Balance sheets prepared using the account form (as in Figure 2.5) show total assets on the same horizontal line as the total liabilities and owner's equity.
- Dollar signs are omitted when financial statements are prepared on paper with ruled columns. Statements that are prepared on plain paper, not ruled forms, show dollar signs with the first amount in each column and with each total.
- A single line shows that the amounts above it are being added or subtracted. Double lines indicate that the amount is the final amount in a column or section of a report.

Figure 2.6 shows the connections among the financial statements. Financial statements are prepared in a specific order:

- income statement
- statement of owner's equity
- balance sheet

FIGURE 2.5 Balance Sheet for Eli's Consulting Services

Eli's Consulting Services
Balance Sheet
December 31, 20X1

Assets		Liabilities	
Cash	11 135 00	Accounts Payable	3 500 00
Accounts Receivable	5 000 00		
Supplies	1 500 00		
Prepaid Rent	8 000 00	Owner's Equity	
Equipment	11 000 00	Trayton Eli, Capital	133 350 00
Total Assets	136 850 00	Total Liabilities and Owner's Equity	136 850 00

Step 1: Prepare the Income Statement

Eli's Consulting Services
Income Statement
Month Ended December 31, 20X1

Revenue		
Fees Income		47 000 00
Expenses		
Salaries Expense	8 000 00	
Utilities Expense	650 00	
Total Expenses		8 650 00
Net Income		38 350 00

Step 2: Prepare the Statement of Owner's Equity

Eli's Consulting Services
Statement of Owner's Equity
Month Ended December 31, 20X1

Trayton Eli, Capital, December 1, 20X1		100 000 00
Net Income for December	38 350 00	
Less Withdrawals for December	5 000 00	
Increase in Capital		33 350 00
Trayton Eli, Capital, December 31, 20X1		133 350 00

Step 3: Prepare the Balance Sheet

Eli's Consulting Services
Balance Sheet
December 31, 20X1

Assets		Liabilities	
Cash	11 135 00	Accounts Payable	3 500 00
Accounts Receivable	5 000 00		
Supplies	1 500 00		
Prepaid Rent	8 000 00	Owner's Equity	
Equipment	11 000 00	Trayton Eli, Capital	133 350 00
Total Assets	136 850 00	Total Liabilities and Owner's Equity	136 850 00

FIGURE 2.6

Process for Preparing Financial Statements

Net income (or loss) is transferred to the statement of owner's equity.

The ending capital balance is transferred to the balance sheet.

MANAGERIAL IMPLICATIONS

ACCOUNTING SYSTEMS

- Sound financial records and statements are necessary so that businesspeople can make good decisions.
- Financial statements show:
  - the amount of profit or loss,
  - the assets on hand,
  - the amount owed to creditors, and
  - the amount of owner's equity.
- Well-run and efficiently managed businesses have good accounting systems that provide timely and useful information.
- Transactions involving revenue and expenses are recorded separately from owner's equity in order to analyze operations for the period.

THINKING CRITICALLY

If you were buying a business, what would you look for in the company's financial statements?

Net income from the income statement is used to prepare the statement of owner's equity. The ending capital balance from the statement of owner's equity is used to prepare the balance sheet.

The Importance of Financial Statements

Preparing financial statements is one of the accountant's most important jobs. Each day millions of business decisions are made based on the information in financial statements.

Business managers and owners use the balance sheet and the income statement to control current operations and plan for the future. Creditors, prospective investors, governmental agencies, and others are interested in the profits of the business and in the asset and equity structure.

Section 2 Review

1. What affect do withdrawals have on the basic account equation?
   a. increase the owner's equity in the business
   b. decrease the owner's equity in the business
   c. increase the liabilities of the business
   d. have no effect on the basic accounting equation

2. If an owner gives personal tools to the business, how is the transaction recorded?
   a. This is not a transaction and is not recorded.
   b. This is a decrease in the owner's equity in the business.
   c. This is an additional investment by the owner recorded at the cost of the tools to the owner.
   d. This is an additional investment by the owner recorded at the fair market value of the tools.

3. What information is included in the financial statement headings?
   a. the owner's name (who); title of the statement (what); time period covered (when)
   b. the firm's name (who); type of business (what); time period covered (when)
   c. the firm's name (who); title of the statement (what); time period covered (when)
   d. the firm's name (who); the industry of the business (what); time period covered (when)

4. Home Interiors has assets of $120,000 and liabilities of $45,000. What is the owner's equity?
   a. $25,000
   b. $15,000
   c. $75,000
   d. $55,000

5. U Fix It Hardware had revenues of $105,000 and expenses of $60,000. How does this affect owner's equity?
   a. $90,000 increase
   b. $45,000 increase
   c. $165,000 decrease
   d. $40,000 decrease

6. **What information is contained in the income statement?**
   a. revenues and expenses for a period of time
   b. assets, liabilities, and owner's equity for a period of time
   c. revenue and expenses on a specific date
   d. assets, liabilities, and owner's equity on a specific date
7. **What information is contained on the balance sheet?**
   a. revenues and expenses for a period of time
   b. assets, liabilities, and owner's equity for a period of time
   c. revenue and expenses on a specific date
   d. assets, liabilities, and owner's equity on a specific date
8. **All of the following information is contained on the statement of owner's equity except:**
   a. net income or net loss for the period.
   b. owner's equity at the beginning and end of the period.
   c. withdrawals and additional investments for the period.
   d. liabilities at the beginning and end of the period.

Chapter 2 REVIEW — Chapter Summary

Accounting begins with the analysis of business transactions. Each transaction changes the financial position of a business. In this chapter, you have learned how to analyze business transactions and how they affect assets, liabilities, and owner's equity. After transactions are analyzed and recorded, financial statements reflect the summarized changes to and results of business operations.

Learning Objectives

2-1 Record in equation form the financial effects of a business transaction.

The equation *property equals financial interest* reflects the fact that in a free enterprise system all property is owned by someone. This equation remains in balance after each business transaction.

2-2 Define, identify, and understand the relationship between asset, liability, and owner's equity accounts.

The term *assets* refers to property. The terms *liabilities* and *owner's equity* refer to financial interest. The relationship between assets, liabilities, and owner's equity is shown in equation form.

Assets	=	Liabilities	+	Owner's Equity
Owner's Equity	=	Assets	−	Liabilities
Liabilities	=	Assets	−	Owner's Equity

2-3 Analyze the effects of business transactions on a firm's assets, liabilities, and owner's equity and record these effects in accounting equation form.

1. Describe the financial event.
   - Identify the property.
   - Identify who owns the property.
   - Determine the amount of the increase or decrease.
2. Make sure the equation is in balance.

2-4 Prepare an income statement.

The income statement summarizes changes in owner's equity that result from revenue and expenses. The difference between revenue and expenses is the net income or net loss of the business for the period.

An income statement has a three-line heading:
- who
- what
- when

For the income statement, "when" refers to a period of time.

2-5 Prepare a statement of owner's equity and a balance sheet.

Changes in owner's equity for the period are summarized on the statement of owner's equity.
- Net income increases owner's equity.
- Added investments increase owner's equity.
- A net loss for the period decreases owner's equity.
- Withdrawals by the owner decrease owner's equity.

A statement of owner's equity has a three-line heading:
- who
- what
- when

For the statement of owner's equity, "when" refers to a period of time.

The balance sheet shows the assets, liabilities, and owner's equity on a given date.

A balance sheet has a three-line heading:
- who
- what
- when

For the balance sheet, "when" refers to a single date.

The financial statements are prepared in the following order.

1. Income Statement
2. Statement of Owner's Equity
3. Balance Sheet

2-6 Define the accounting terms new to this chapter.

Glossary

Accounts payable (p. 26) Amounts a business must pay in the future

Accounts receivable (p. 32) Claims for future collection from customers

Assets (p. 29) Property owned by a business

Balance sheet (p. 29) A formal report of a business's financial condition on a certain date; reports the assets, liabilities, and owner's equity of the business

Break even (p. 36) A point at which revenue equals expenses

Business transaction (p. 24) A financial event that changes the resources of a firm

Capital (p. 25) Financial investment in a business; equity

Equity (p. 25) An owner's financial interest in a business

Expense (p. 32) An outflow of cash, use of other assets, or incurring of a liability

Fair market value (p. 38) The current worth of an asset or the price the asset would bring if sold on the open market

Fundamental accounting equation (p. 31) The relationship between assets and liabilities plus owner's equity

Income statement (p. 36) A formal report of business operations covering a specific period of time; also called a profit and loss statement or a statement of income and expenses

Liabilities (p. 29) Debts or obligations of a business

Net income (p. 36) The result of an excess of revenue over expenses

Net loss (p. 36) The result of an excess of expenses over revenue

On account (p. 26) An arrangement to allow payment at a later date; also called a charge account or open-account credit

Owner's equity (p. 29) The financial interest of the owner of a business; also called proprietorship or net worth

Revenue (p. 32) An inflow of money or other assets that results from the sales of goods or services or from the use of money or property; also called income

Statement of owner's equity (p. 37) A formal report of changes that occurred in the owner's financial interest during a reporting period

Withdrawals (p. 35) Funds taken from the business by the owner for personal use

Comprehensive Self Review

1. What is the difference between buying for cash and buying on account?
2. If one side of the fundamental accounting equation increases, what will happen to the other side? Why?
3. Describe a transaction that will cause Accounts Receivable to decrease and Cash to increase by $2,800.
4. What effect does revenue and expenses have on owner's equity?
5. In what order are the financial statements prepared? Why?

(Answers to Comprehensive Self Review are at the end of the chapter.)

Discussion Questions

1. What is the fundamental accounting equation?
2. What are assets, liabilities, and owner's equity?

3. What information does the balance sheet contain?
4. What information does the income statement contain?
5. What information does the statement of owner's equity contain?
6. What information is shown in the heading of a financial statement?
7. Why does the third line of the headings differ on the balance sheet and the income statement?
8. What is revenue?
9. What are expenses?
10. How is net income or net loss determined?
11. How does net income affect owner's equity?
12. Describe the effects of each of the following business transactions on assets, liabilities, and owner's equity.

   a. Bought equipment on credit.
   b. Paid salaries to employees.
   c. Sold services for cash.
   d. Paid cash to a creditor.
   e. Bought furniture for cash.
   f. Sold services on credit.

APPLICATIONS

Exercises

Exercise 2.1
Objectives 2-1, 2-2

▶ **Determining accounting equation amounts.**

Just before Henderson Laboratories opened for business, Eugene Henderson, the owner, had the following assets and liabilities. Determine the totals that would appear in the firm's fundamental accounting equation (Assets = Liabilities + Owner's Equity).

Cash	$ 99,000
Laboratory Equipment	155,000
Laboratory Supplies	21,600
Loan Payable	30,400
Accounts Payable	22,750

Exercise 2.2
Objectives 2-1, 2-2

▶ **Completing the accounting equation.**

The fundamental accounting equations for several businesses follow. Supply the missing amounts.

Assets	=	Liabilities	+	Owner's Equity
1. $64,700	=	$13,440	+	$?
2. $57,800	=	$12,760	+	$?
3. $96,150	=	$?	+	$24,600
4. $?	=	$11,400	+	$67,752
5. $108,000	=	$?	+	$58,400

Determining the effects of transactions on the accounting equation.

◀ **Exercise 2.3**

Indicate the impact of each of the transactions below on the fundamental accounting equation (Assets = Liabilities + Owner's Equity) by placing an "I" to indicate an increase and a "D" to indicate a decrease. The first transaction is entered as an example.

Objectives 2-1, 2-2, 2-3

	Assets	=	Liabilities	+	Owner's Equity
Transaction 1	D				D

TRANSACTIONS

1. Paid $4,200 for utilities.
2. Performed services for $21,000 on account.
3. Received $13,000 from charge account customers.
4. Paid salaries of $9,000 to employees.
5. Paid $16,000 to a creditor on account.
6. Owner invested $180,000 in the business.
7. Purchased $53,400 of supplies on account.
8. Purchased equipment for $42,000 cash.
9. Paid $12,000 for rent (in advance).
10. Performed services for $15,600 cash.

Determining balance sheet amounts.

◀ **Exercise 2.4**

The following financial data are for the dental practice of Dr. Jose Ortiz when he began operations in July. Determine the amounts that would appear in Dr. Ortiz's balance sheet.

Objectives 2-1, 2-2, 2-3

1. Owes $42,000 to the Sanderson Equipment Company.
2. Has cash balance of $31,000.
3. Has dental supplies of $11,300.
4. Owes $12,360 to Galaxy Furniture Supply.
5. Has dental equipment of $57,100.
6. Has office furniture of $20,000.

Determining the effects of transactions on the accounting equation.

◀ **Exercise 2.5**

The Business Center had the transactions listed below during the month of June. Show how each transaction would be recorded in the accounting equation. Compute the totals at the end of the month. The headings to be used in the equation follow.

Objectives 2-1, 2-2, 2-3

Assets			=	Liabilities	+	Owner's Equity			
Cash	+ Accounts Receivable	+ Equipment	=	Accounts Payable	+	Jesse Campbell, Capital	+ Revenue	− Expenses

TRANSACTIONS

1. Jesse Campbell started the business with a cash investment of $120,000.
2. Purchased equipment for $44,000 on credit.
3. Performed services for $6,200 in cash.
4. Purchased additional equipment for $9,200 in cash.
5. Performed services for $10,100 on credit.
6. Paid salaries of $8,900 to employees.

7. Received $6,400 cash from charge account customers.
8. Paid $26,000 to a creditor on account.

Exercise 2.6
Objective 2-4

▶ **Computing net income or net loss.**

Technology World had the following revenue and expenses during the month ended July 31. Did the firm earn a net income or incur a net loss for the period? What was the amount?

Fees for computer repairs	$93,600
Advertising expense	16,200
Salaries expense	41,000
Telephone expense	2,160
Fees for printer repairs	13,460
Utilities expense	3,420

Exercise 2.7
Objectives 2-1, 2-2, 2-3

▶ **Identifying transactions.**

The following equation shows the effects of a number of transactions that took place at Cantu Auto Repair Company during the month of July. Describe each transaction.

	Assets					=	Liabilities	+	Owner's Equity				
	Cash	+	Accounts Receivable	+	Equipment	=	Accounts Payable	+	Marie Cantu, Capital	+	Revenue	−	Expenses
Bal.	$41,000	+	$4,000	+	$30,000	=	$20,000	+	$55,000	+	$ 0	−	$ 0
1.	+6,000										+6,000		
2.	−3,900				+3,900								
3.	−2,100						−2,100						
4.	−3,455												+3,455
5.	+900		−900										
6.			+6,690								+6,690		
7.	−2,160												+2,160

Exercise 2.8
Objective 2-4

▶ **Preparing an income statement.**

At the beginning of September, Helen Rojas started Rojas Wealth Management Consulting, a firm that offers financial planning and advice about investing and managing money. On September 30, the accounting records of the business showed the following information. Prepare an income statement for the month of September 20X1.

Cash	$132,400		Fees Income	311,600
Accounts Receivable	16,000		Advertising Expense	26,000
Office Supplies	13,600		Salaries Expense	64,000
Office Equipment	150,000		Telephone Expense	3,200
Accounts Payable	22,800		Withdrawals	36,000
Helen Rojas, Capital, September 1, 20X1	106,800			

Exercise 2.9
Objective 2-4

▶ **Computing net income or net loss.**

On December 1, Karl Zant opened a speech and hearing clinic. During December, his firm had the following transactions involving revenue and expenses. Did the firm earn a net income or incur a net loss for the period? What was the amount?

Paid $6,200 for advertising.

Provided services for $20,800 in cash.

Paid $1,920 for telephone service.

Paid salaries of $5,200 to employees.

Provided services for $6,000 on credit.

Paid $1,800 for office cleaning service.

Preparing a statement of owner's equity and a balance sheet.

◀ **Exercise 2.10**

Using the information provided in Exercise 2.8, prepare a statement of owner's equity for the month of September and a balance sheet for Rojas Wealth Management Consulting as of September 30, 20X1.

Objective 2-5

PROBLEMS

Problem Set A

Analyzing the effects of transactions on the accounting equation.

◀ **Problem 2.1A**

On July 1, Alfred Herron established Herron Commercial Appraisal Services, a firm that provides expert commercial appraisals and represents clients in commercial appraisal hearings.

Objectives 2-1, 2-2, 2-3

INSTRUCTIONS

Analyze the following transactions. Record in equation form the changes that occur in assets, liabilities, and owner's equity. (Use plus, minus, and equals signs.)

TRANSACTIONS

1. The owner invested $200,000 in cash to begin the business.
2. Paid $40,500 in cash for the purchase of equipment.
3. Purchased additional equipment for $30,400 on credit.
4. Paid $25,000 in cash to creditors.
5. The owner made an additional investment of $50,000 in cash.
6. Performed services for $19,500 in cash.
7. Performed services for $15,600 on account.
8. Paid $12,000 for rent expense.
9. Received $11,000 in cash from credit clients.
10. Paid $15,100 in cash for office supplies.
11. The owner withdrew $24,000 in cash for personal expenses.

Analyze: What is the ending balance of cash after all transactions have been recorded?

Analyzing the effects of transactions on the accounting equation.

◀ **Problem 2.2A**

Carter Wilson is a painting contractor who specializes in painting commercial buildings. At the beginning of June, his firm's financial records showed the following assets, liabilities, and owner's equity.

Objectives 2-1, 2-2, 2-3

Cash	$144,000	Accounts Payable	30,600
Accounts Receivable	37,000	Carter Wilson, Capital	214,500
Office Furniture	85,000	Revenue	131,600
Auto	55,000	Expenses	55,700

INSTRUCTIONS

Set up an accounting equation using the balances given above. Record the effects of the following transactions in the equation. (Use plus, minus, and equals signs.) Record new balances after each transaction has been entered. Prove the equality of the two sides of the final equation on a separate sheet of paper.

TRANSACTIONS

1. Performed services for $14,400 on credit.
2. Paid $3,640 in cash for new office chairs.
3. Received $27,600 in cash from credit clients.
4. Paid $1,820 in cash for telephone service.
5. Sent a check for $10,400 in partial payment of the amount due creditors.
6. Paid salaries of $21,160 in cash.
7. Sent a check for $2,570 to pay electric bill.
8. Performed services for $25,800 in cash.
9. Paid $5,320 in cash for auto repairs.
10. Performed services for $27,600 on account.

Analyze: What is the amount of total assets after all transactions have been recorded?

Problem 2.3A
Objective 2-5

▶ **Preparing a balance sheet.**

Oil Field Equipment Repair Service is owned by Jack Phillips.

INSTRUCTIONS

Use the following figures to prepare a balance sheet dated February 28, 20X1. (You will need to compute the owner's equity.)

Cash	$137,200	Equipment	312,000
Supplies	25,520	Accounts Payable	96,000
Accounts Receivable	52,800		

Analyze: What is the net worth, or owner's equity, at February 28, 20X1, for Oil Field Equipment Repair Service?

Problem 2.4A
Objectives 2-4, 2-5

▶ **Preparing an income statement, a statement of owner's equity, and a balance sheet.**

The following equation shows the transactions of Cotton Cleaning Service during May. The business is owned by Taylor Cotton.

	Assets					=	Liab.	+	Owner's Equity				
	Cash	+	Accts. Rec.	+ Supp. +	Equip.	=	Accts. Pay.	+	T. Cotton, Capital	+	Rev.	−	Exp.
Balances, May 1	15,000	+	3,000	+ 5,800 +	33,800	=	7,000	+	50,600	+	0	−	0
Paid for utilities	−980												+980
New balances	14,020	+	3,000	+ 5,800 +	33,800	=	7,000	+	50,600	+	0	−	980
Sold services for cash	+4,980										+4,980		
New balances	19,000	+	3,000	+ 5,800 +	33,800	=	7,000	+	50,600	+	4,980	−	980
Paid a creditor	−2,100						−2,100						
New balances	16,900	+	3,000	+ 5,800 +	33,800	=	4,900	+	50,600	+	4,980	−	980
Sold services on credit			+2,900								+2,900		
New balances	16,900	+	5,900	+ 5,800 +	33,800	=	4,900	+	50,600	+	7,880	−	980
Paid salaries	−8,900												+8,900
New balances	8,000	+	5,900	+ 5,800 +	33,800	=	4,900	+	50,600	+	7,880	−	9,880
Paid telephone bill	−314												+314
New balances	7,686	+	5,900	+ 5,800 +	33,800	=	4,900	+	50,600	+	7,880	−	10,194
Withdrew cash for personal expenses	−3,000								−3,000				
New balances	4,686	+	5,900	+ 5,800 +	33,800	=	4,900	+	47,600	+	7,880	−	10,194

INSTRUCTIONS

Analyze each transaction carefully. Prepare an income statement and a statement of owner's equity for the month. Prepare a balance sheet for May 31, 20X1. List the expenses in detail on the income statement.

Analyze: In order to complete the balance sheet, which amount was transferred from the statement of owner's equity?

Problem Set B

Analyzing the effects of transactions on the accounting equation.

◀ **Problem 2.1B**
Objectives 2-1, 2-2, 2-3

On September 1, Takka Myers opened Takka Myers Tutoring Service.

INSTRUCTIONS

Analyze the following transactions. Use the fundamental accounting equation form to record the changes in property, claims of creditors, and owner's equity. (Use plus, minus, and equals signs.)

TRANSACTIONS

1. The owner invested $72,000 in cash to begin the business.
2. Purchased equipment for $32,000 in cash.
3. Purchased $12,000 of additional equipment on credit.
4. Paid $6,000 in cash to creditors.
5. The owner made an additional investment of $12,000 in cash.
6. Performed services for $8,400 in cash.
7. Performed services for $7,300 on account.
8. Paid $5,200 for rent expense.
9. Received $5,000 in cash from credit clients.
10. Paid $6,300 in cash for office supplies.
11. The owner withdrew $10,000 in cash for personal expenses.

Analyze: Which transactions increased the company's debt? By what amount?

Analyzing the effects of transactions on the accounting equation.

◀ **Problem 2.2B**
Objectives 2-1, 2-2, 2-3

Royce Alexander owns Alexander's Consulting Service. At the beginning of September, his firm's financial records showed the following assets, liabilities, and owner's equity.

Cash	$152,000	Accounts Payable	40,000
Accounts Receivable	48,000	Royce Alexander, Capital	199,200
Supplies	51,200	Revenue	208,000
Office Furniture	96,000	Expenses	100,000

INSTRUCTIONS

Set up an equation using the balances given above. Record the effects of the following transactions in the equation. (Use plus, minus, and equals signs.) Record new balances after each transaction has been entered. Prove the equality of the two sides of the final equation on a separate sheet of paper.

TRANSACTIONS

1. Performed services for $32,000 on credit.
2. Paid $11,520 in cash for utilities.
3. Performed services for $40,000 in cash.
4. Paid $6,400 in cash for office cleaning service.
5. Sent a check for $19,200 to a creditor.

6. Paid $7,680 in cash for the telephone bill.
7. Issued checks for $56,000 to pay salaries.
8. Performed services for $44,800 in cash.
9. Purchased additional supplies for $8,000 on credit.
10. Received $24,000 in cash from credit clients.

Analyze: What is the ending balance for owner's equity after all transactions have been recorded?

Problem 2.3B
Objective 2-5

▶ **Preparing a balance sheet.**

Rayshanti Williamson is opening a tax preparation service on December 1, which will be called Williamson's Tax Service. Williamson plans to open the business by depositing $50,000 cash into a business checking account. The following assets will also be owned by the business: furniture (fair market value of $15,000) and computers and printers (fair market value of $17,000). There will be no outstanding debts of the business when it is formed.

INSTRUCTIONS

Prepare a balance sheet for December 1, 20X1, for Williamson's Tax Service by entering the correct balances in the appropriate accounts. (You will need to use the accounting equation to compute owner's equity.)

Analyze: If Williamson's Tax Service had an outstanding debt of $16,000 when the business was formed, what amount should be reported on the balance sheet for owner's equity?

Problem 2.4B
Objectives 2-4, 2-5

▶ **Preparing an income statement, a statement of owner's equity, and a balance sheet.**

The equation below shows the transactions of Kathryn Proctor, Attorney and Counselor at Law, during August. This law firm is owned by Kathryn Proctor.

	Assets				=	Liab.	+	Owner's Equity			
	Cash +	Accts. Rec. +	Supp. +	Equip.	=	Accts. Pay. +		K. Proctor, Capital +	Rev.	−	Exp.
Balances, Aug. 1	7,200	1,800 +	5,400 +	10,000	=	1,200 +		23,200 +	0	−	0
Paid for utilities	−600										+600
New balances	6,600 +	1,800 +	5,400 +	10,000	=	1,200 +		23,200 +	0	−	600
Performed services for cash	+6,000								+6,000		
New balances	12,600 +	1,800 +	5,400 +	10,000	=	1,200 +		23,200 +	6,000	−	600
Paid a creditor	−600					−600					
New balances	12,000 +	1,800 +	5,400 +	10,000	=	600 +		23,200 +	6,000	−	600
Performed services on credit		+4,800							+4,800		
New balances	12,000 +	6,600 +	5,400 +	10,000	=	600 +		23,200 +	10,800	−	600
Paid salaries	−5,400										+5,400
New balances	6,600 +	6,600 +	5,400 +	10,000	=	600 +		23,200 +	10,800	−	6,000
Paid telephone bill	−480										+480
New balances	6,120 +	6,600 +	5,400 +	10,000	=	600 +		23,200 +	10,800	−	6,480
Withdrew cash for personal expenses	−1,200							−1,200			
New balances	4,920 +	6,600 +	5,400 +	10,000	=	600 +		22,000 +	10,800	−	6,480

INSTRUCTIONS

Analyze each transaction carefully. Prepare an income statement and a statement of owner's equity for the month. Prepare a balance sheet for August 31, 20X1. List the expenses in detail on the income statement.

Analyze: In order to complete the statement of owner's equity, which amount was transferred from the income statement?

Critical Thinking Problem 2.1

Financial Statements

The following account balances are for Ping Chung, Certified Public Accountant, as of April 30, 20X1.

Cash	$120,000
Accounts Receivable	48,000
Maintenance Expense	18,400
Advertising Expense	15,560
Fees Earned	107,200
Ping Chung, Capital, April 1	?
Salaries Expense	52,000
Machinery	84,000
Accounts Payable	52,800
Ping Chung, Withdrawals for April	27,200

INSTRUCTIONS

Using the accounting equation form, determine the balance for Ping Chung, Capital, April 1, 20X1. Prepare an income statement and a statement of owner's equity for the month ended April 30, 20X1, and a balance sheet for April 30, 20X1. List the expenses on the income statement in alphabetical order.

Analyze: What net change in owner's equity occurred during the month of April?

Critical Thinking Problem 2.2

Accounting for a New Company

Santiago Madrid opened a gym and fitness studio called Perfect Body Fitness and Spa Center at the beginning of November of the current year. It is now the end of December, and Madrid is trying to determine whether he made a profit during his first two months of operations. You offer to help him and ask to see his accounting records. He shows you a shoe box and tells you that every piece of paper pertaining to the business is in that box.

As you go through the material in the shoe box, you discover the following:

a. A receipt from Clark Properties for $18,000 rent on the exercise studio for November and December.

b. Bank deposit slips totaling $15,000 for money collected from customers who attended exercise classes.

c. An invoice for $80,000 for exercise equipment. The first payment is not due until December 31.

d. A bill for $4,200 from the maintenance service that cleans the studio. Madrid has not yet paid this bill.

e. A December 19 parking ticket for $150. Madrid says he was in a hurry that morning to get to the Fitness Center on time and forgot to put money in the parking meter.

f. A handwritten list of customers and fees for the classes they have taken. As the customers attend the classes, Madrid writes their names and the amount of each customer's fee on the list. As customers pay, Madrid crosses their names off the list. Fees not crossed off the list amount to $6,400.

g. A credit card receipt for $1,200 for printing flyers advertising the grand opening of the Center. For convenience, Madrid used his personal credit card.

h. A credit card receipt for $1,400 for four warm-up suits Madrid bought to wear at the studio. He also put this purchase on his personal credit card.

Use the concepts you have learned in this chapter to help Madrid.

1. Prepare an income statement for the first two months of operation of Perfect Body Fitness and Spa Center.
2. How would you evaluate the results of the first two months of operation?
3. What advice would you give Madrid concerning his system of accounting?

BUSINESS CONNECTIONS

Interpreting Results

Managerial FOCUS

1. After examining financial data for a monthly period, the owner of a small business expressed surprise that the firm's cash balance had decreased during the month even though there was substantial net income. Do you think this owner is right to expect cash to increase because of a substantial net income? Why or why not?
2. Is it reasonable to expect that all new businesses will have a net income from the first month's operations? From the first year's operations?
3. Why should managers be concerned with changes in the amount of creditors' claims against the business?
4. How does an accounting system help managers control operations and make sound decisions?

Internal Control for Accounts Receivable

Internal Control and FRAUD PREVENTION

A good system of internal control requires business entities to have well-documented (written) policies and procedures on accounts receivables. These policies and procedures should cover segregation of duties of staff, credit and collection policies, and the review and reconciliation of accounting records. Segregation of duties of staff should require different employees to perform invoicing, accounts receivable collection, and review and reconciliation of accounting records. Credit and collection policies should establish guidelines covering to whom credit will be granted, the terms of the credit, maximum credit limits, and collection guidelines for any past due accounts. The review and reconciliation of accounting records should establish policies for ensuring that the amount that appears on the balance sheet for accounts receivable agrees with the totals for individual credit customers. Additionally, individual customer accounts should be periodically classified based on the aging of accounts receivable (days from inception of receivable to the reconciliation date). Under each of these internal control policies (segregation of duties, credit and collection policies, and reconciliation of accounting records), describe five accounting controls that you believe would ensure a good system of internal control for accounts receivable.

Income Statement

Financial Statement ANALYSIS

Review the following excerpt from the 2018 consolidated statement of income for Southwest Airlines Co. Answer the questions that follow.

Southwest Airlines Co.
Consolidated Statement of Income
Years Ended December 31, 2018 and 2017

	2018	2017
Operating Revenues (in millions):		
Passenger	$20,455	$19,763
Freight	175	173
Other	1,335	1,210
Total operating revenues	21,965	21,146
Net Income	$2,465	$3,357

Analyze:

1. Although the format for the heading of an income statement can vary from company to company, the heading should contain the answers to who, what, and when. List the answers to each question for the statement presented above.

2. What three types of revenue are reflected on this statement?

3. The net income of $2.465 billion reflected on Southwest Airlines Co.'s consolidated statement of income for 2018 will be transferred to the next financial statement to be prepared. Net income is needed to complete which statement?

Analyze Online: Find the *Investor Relations* section of the Southwest Airlines Co. website (www.southwest.com) and answer the following questions.

4. What total operating revenues did Southwest Airlines Co. report for the most recent quarter?

5. Find the most recent press release posted on the website. Read the press release, and summarize the topic discussed. What effect, if any, do you think this will have on company earnings? Why?

Working to Provide Accurate Data

TEAMWORK

Gloria's Fabrics is a large fabric provider to the general public. The accounting office has three employees: accounts receivable clerk, accounts payable clerk, and full charge bookkeeper. The accounts receivable clerk creates the sales invoices and records the cash receipts, the accounts payable clerk creates and pays the purchase orders, and the full charge bookkeeper reconciles the checking account. Assign each group member one of the three jobs. Identify the accounts and describe the transactions that would be recorded by the person doing that assigned job. What effect would each transaction have on each account? How would each member of the accounting department work together to present accurate information for the decision makers?

Answers to Comprehensive Self Review

1. Buying for cash results in an immediate decrease in cash; buying on account results in a liability recorded as accounts payable.

2. The opposite side of the accounting equation will decrease because a decrease in assets results in a corresponding decrease in either a liability or the owner's equity.

3. The payment of $1,200 to a creditor on account.

4. Revenue increases owner's equity. Expenses decrease owner's equity.

5. The income statement is prepared first because the net income or loss is needed to complete the statement of owner's equity. The statement of owner's equity is prepared next to update the change in owner's equity. The balance sheet is prepared last.

Analyzing Business Transactions Using T Accounts

Chapter 3

Jonathan Weiss/Shutterstock

www.att.com

When Alexander Graham Bell invented the telephone in 1876, and gave birth to the company that would become AT&T, he had no idea that a century and a half later, millions of people worldwide would be relying on his "namesake" to call, text, and e-mail the people in their lives. Since being formed in 1877, AT&T has broadened its offerings through new-product development and diversification. In June 2018, AT&T completed its acquisition of Time Warner, Inc. The overarching objective of the acquisition was to combine Time Warner's content (Warner Bros., HBO, and Turner) with AT&T's distribution to elevate AT&T's long-term strategy of being the global leader in telecommunications, media and entertainment, and technology.

Keeping track of the multitude of transactions initiated by the variety of services provided by AT&T is the job of its accountants. However, because the accounting equation table is just too clumsy to be used in a company that has thousands upon thousands of transactions every month, accountants use a more streamlined recordkeeping approach. Accountants throughout the world rely instead on a double-entry system of debits and credits.

thinking critically

How might accountants in 1877 have recorded The Bell Telephone Company's first telephone service revenue transaction? How did this transaction affect the fundamental accounting equation?

LEARNING OBJECTIVES

- **3-1** Set up T accounts for assets, liabilities, and owner's equity.
- **3-2** Analyze business transactions and enter them in the accounts.
- **3-3** Determine the balance of an account.
- **3-4** Set up T accounts for revenue and expenses.
- **3-5** Prepare a trial balance from T accounts.
- **3-6** Prepare an income statement, a statement of owner's equity, and a balance sheet.
- **3-7** Develop a chart of accounts.
- **3-8** Define the accounting terms new to this chapter.

NEW TERMS

account balance
accounts
chart of accounts
classification
credit
debit
double-entry system
drawing account
footing
normal balance
permanent account
slide
T account
temporary account
transposition
trial balance

Section 1

SECTION OBJECTIVES

>> 3-1 Set up T accounts for assets, liabilities, and owner's equity.
WHY IT'S IMPORTANT
The T account is an important visual tool used as an alternative to the fundamental accounting equation.

>> 3-2 Analyze business transactions and enter them in the accounts.
WHY IT'S IMPORTANT
Accountants often use T accounts to help analyze and classify business transactions.

>> 3-3 Determine the balance of an account.
WHY IT'S IMPORTANT
Accurate account balances contribute to a reliable accounting system.

TERMS TO LEARN

account balance
accounts
classification
footing
normal balance
T account

Transactions That Affect Assets, Liabilities, and Owner's Equity

In this chapter, you will learn how to record the changes caused by business transactions. This recordkeeping is a basic part of accounting systems.

Asset, Liability, and Owner's Equity Accounts

The accounting equation is one tool for analyzing the effects of business transactions. However, businesses do not record transactions in equation form. Instead, businesses establish separate records, called **accounts,** for assets, liabilities, and owner's equity. Use of accounts helps owners and staff analyze, record, classify, summarize, and report financial information. Accounts are recognized by their **classification** as assets, liabilities, or owner's equity. Asset accounts show the property a business owns. Liability accounts show the debts of the business. Owner's equity accounts show the owner's financial interest in the business. Each account has a name that describes the type of property, the debt, or the financial interest.

Accountants use T accounts to analyze transactions. A **T account** consists of a vertical line and a horizontal line that resemble the letter **T**. The name of the account is written on the horizontal (top) line. Increases and decreases in the account are entered on either side of the vertical line.

The following are T accounts for assets, liabilities, and owner's equity:

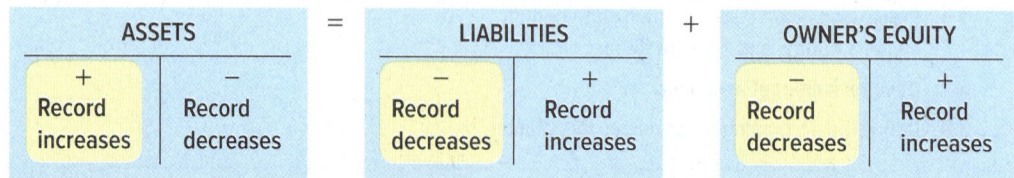

Recording a Cash Investment

Asset accounts show items of value owned by a business. Trayton Eli invested $100,000 in the business. Sergio Sanchez, the office manager for Eli's Consulting Services, set up a *Cash* account. Cash is an asset. Assets appear on the left side of the accounting equation. Cash increases appear on the left side of the *Cash* T account. Decreases are shown on the right side. Sanchez entered the cash investment of $100,000 **(a)** on the left side of the *Cash* account.

T accounts normally do not have plus and minus signs. We show them to help you identify increases (+) and decreases (−) in accounts.

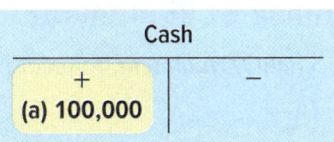

>> **3-1 OBJECTIVE**
Set up T accounts for assets, liabilities, and owner's equity.

recall

The Accounting Equation
Assets = Liabilities + Owner's Equity

>> **3-2 OBJECTIVE**
Analyze business transactions and enter them in the accounts.

Sergio Sanchez set up an account for owner's equity called *Trayton Eli, Capital*. Owner's equity appears on the right side of the accounting equation (Assets = Liabilities + Owner's Equity). Increases in owner's equity appear on the right side of the T account. Decreases in owner's equity appear on the left side. Sanchez entered the investment of $100,000 **(a)** on the right side of the *Trayton Eli, Capital* account.

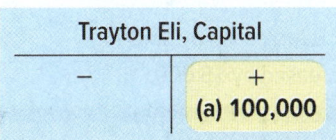

Use these steps to analyze the effects of the business transactions:

1. Analyze the financial event.
   - Identify the accounts affected.
   - Classify the accounts affected.
   - Determine the amount of increase or decrease for each account.
2. Apply the left-right rules for each account affected.
3. Make the entry in T-account form.

BUSINESS TRANSACTION

Trayton Eli withdrew $100,000 from personal savings and deposited it in the new business checking account for Eli's Consulting Services.

ANALYSIS
a. The asset account *Cash* is increased by $100,000.
a. The owner's equity account, *Trayton Eli, Capital,* is increased by $100,000.

LEFT-RIGHT RULES

LEFT   Increases to asset accounts are recorded on the left side of the T account. Record $100,000 on the left side of the *Cash* T account.

RIGHT   Increases to owner's equity accounts are recorded on the right side of the T account. Record $100,000 on the right side of the *Trayton Eli, Capital* T account.

T-ACCOUNT PRESENTATION

Cash		Trayton Eli, Capital	
+	−	−	+
(a) 100,000			(a) 100,000

Recording a Cash Purchase of Equipment

Sergio Sanchez set up an asset account, **Equipment,** to record the purchase of a computer and other equipment.

BUSINESS TRANSACTION

Eli's Consulting Services issued a $5,000 check to purchase a computer and other equipment.

ANALYSIS
b. The asset account **Equipment** is increased by $5,000.
b. The asset account **Cash** is decreased by $5,000.

LEFT-RIGHT RULES

LEFT Increases to asset accounts are recorded on the left side of the T account. Record $5,000 on the left side of the **Equipment** T account.

RIGHT Decreases to asset accounts are recorded on the right side of the T account. Record $5,000 on the right side of the **Cash** T account.

T-ACCOUNT PRESENTATION

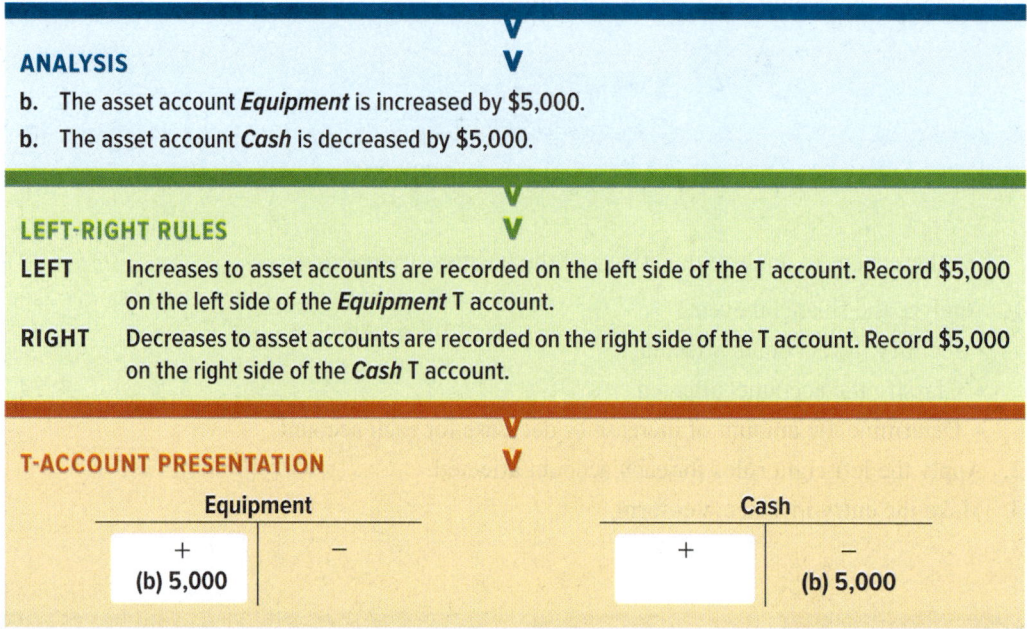

Let's look at the T accounts to review the effects of the transactions. Sanchez entered $5,000 **(b)** on the left (increase) side of the **Equipment** account. He entered $5,000 **(b)** on the right (decrease) side of the **Cash** account. Notice that the **Cash** account shows the effects of two transactions.

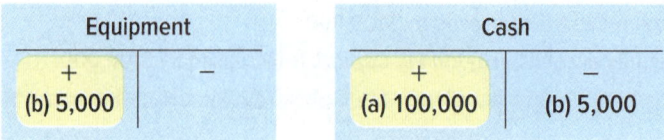

Recording a Credit Purchase of Equipment

Liabilities are amounts a business owes its creditors. Liabilities appear on the right side of the accounting equation (Assets = Liabilities + Owner's Equity). Increases in liabilities are on the right side of liability T accounts. Decreases in liabilities are on the left side of liability T accounts.

BUSINESS TRANSACTION

The firm bought office equipment for $6,000 on account from Office Plus.

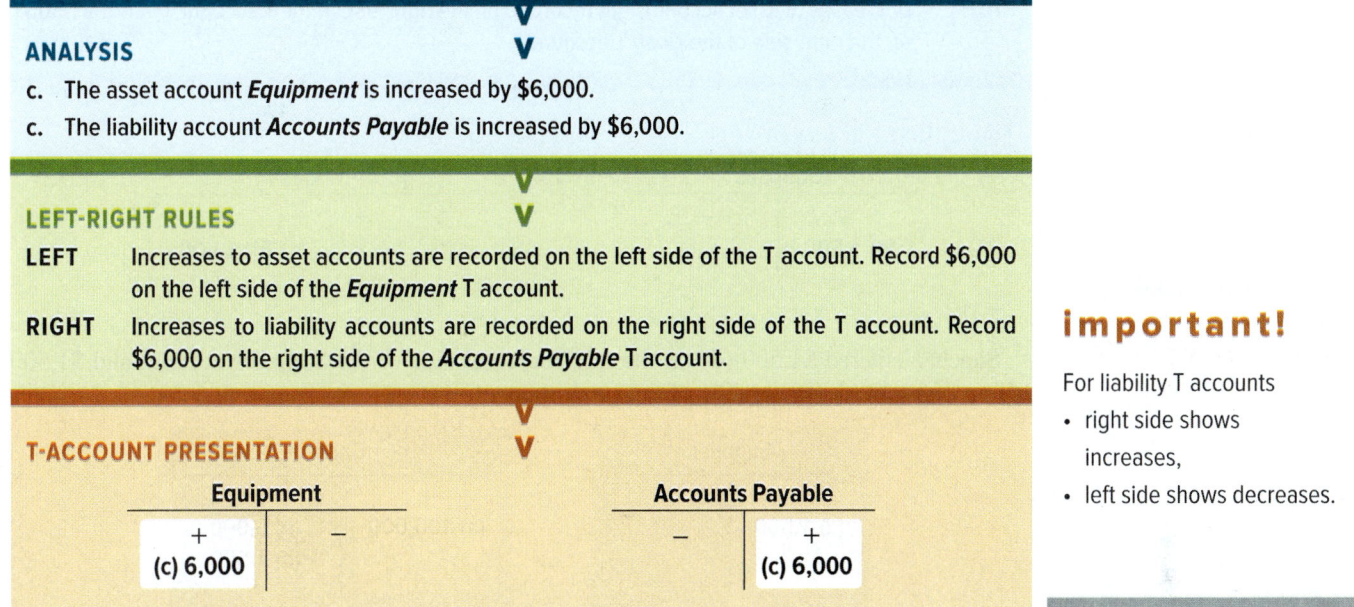

ANALYSIS
c. The asset account *Equipment* is increased by $6,000.
c. The liability account *Accounts Payable* is increased by $6,000.

LEFT-RIGHT RULES
LEFT Increases to asset accounts are recorded on the left side of the T account. Record $6,000 on the left side of the *Equipment* T account.
RIGHT Increases to liability accounts are recorded on the right side of the T account. Record $6,000 on the right side of the *Accounts Payable* T account.

important!
For liability T accounts
- right side shows increases,
- left side shows decreases.

T-ACCOUNT PRESENTATION

Equipment	Accounts Payable
+ | −	− | +
(c) 6,000	(c) 6,000

Let's look at the T accounts to review the effects of the transactions. Sanchez entered $6,000 **(c)** on the left (increase) side of the *Equipment* account. It now shows two transactions. He entered $6,000 **(c)** on the right (increase) side of the *Accounts Payable* account.

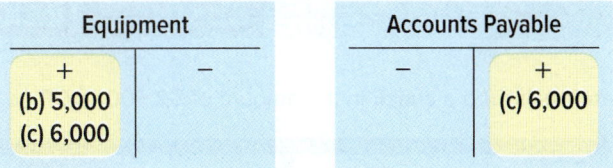

Recording a Cash Purchase of Supplies

Sergio Sanchez set up an asset account called *Supplies.*

BUSINESS TRANSACTION

Eli's Consulting Services issued a check for $1,500 to Office Delux Inc. to purchase office supplies.

ANALYSIS
d. The asset account *Supplies* is increased by $1,500.
d. The asset account *Cash* is decreased by $1,500.

LEFT-RIGHT RULES

LEFT Increases to asset accounts are recorded on the left side of the T account. Record $1,500 on the left side of the **Supplies** T account.

RIGHT Decreases to asset accounts are recorded on the right side of the T account. Record $1,500 on the right side of the **Cash** T account.

T-ACCOUNT PRESENTATION

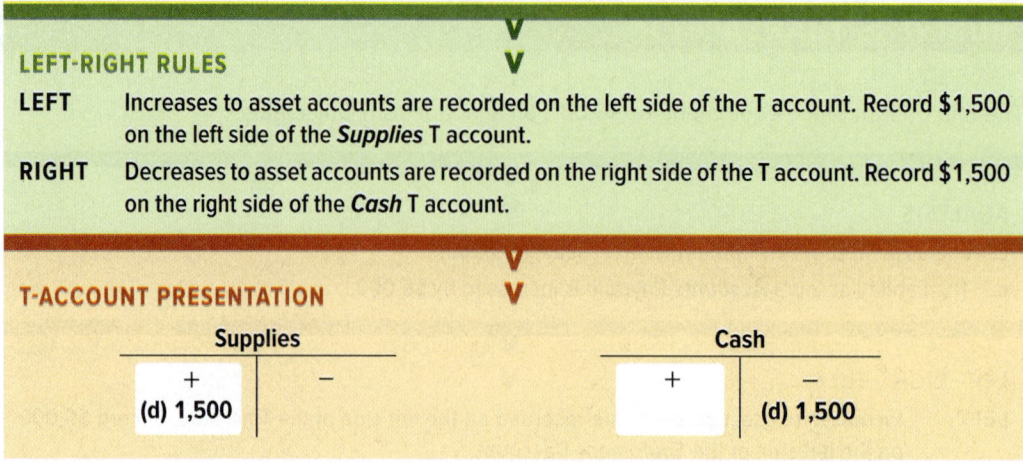

Sanchez entered $1,500 (**d**) on the left (increase) side of the **Supplies** account and $1,500 (**d**) on the right (decrease) side of the **Cash** account.

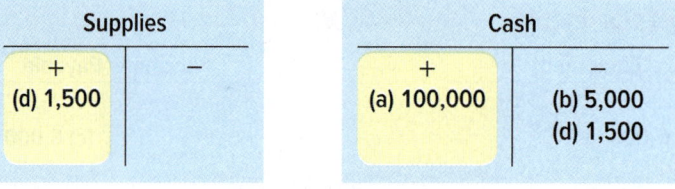

Notice that the **Cash** account now shows three transactions: the initial investment by the owner (**a**), the cash purchase of equipment (**b**), and the cash purchase of supplies (**d**).

Recording a Payment to a Creditor

On November 30, the business paid $2,500 to Office Plus to apply against the debt of $6,000 shown in **Accounts Payable**.

BUSINESS TRANSACTION

Eli's Consulting Services issued a check in the amount of $2,500 to Office Plus.

ANALYSIS

e. The asset account **Cash** is decreased by $2,500.
e. The liability account **Accounts Payable** is decreased by $2,500.

LEFT-RIGHT RULES

LEFT Decreases to liability accounts are recorded on the left side of the T account. Record $2,500 on the left side of the **Accounts Payable** T account.

RIGHT Decreases to asset accounts are recorded on the right side of the T account. Record $2,500 on the right side of the **Cash** T account.

T-ACCOUNT PRESENTATION

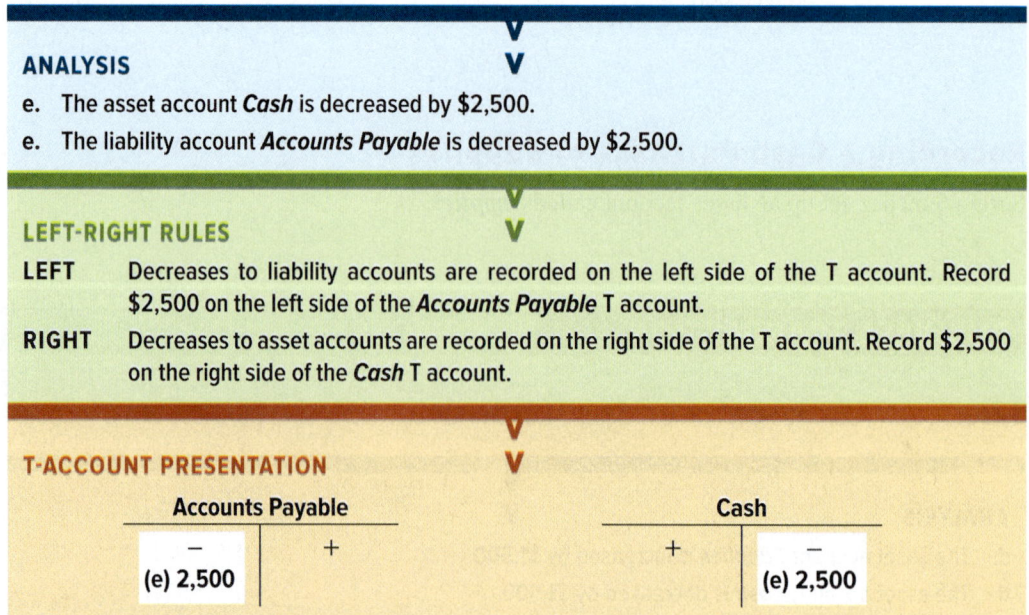

Let's look at the T accounts to review the effects of the transactions. Sanchez entered $2,500 **(e)** on the right (decrease) side of the *Cash* account. He entered $2,500 **(e)** on the left (decrease) side of the *Accounts Payable* account. Notice that both accounts show the effects of several transactions.

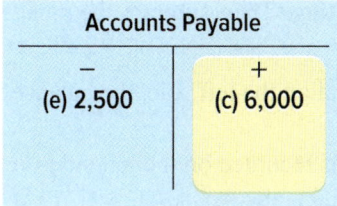
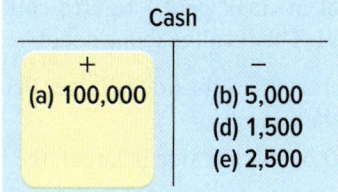

Recording Prepaid Rent

In November, Eli's Consulting Services was required to pay the December and January rent in advance. Sanchez set up an asset account called *Prepaid Rent.*

BUSINESS TRANSACTION

Eli's Consulting Services issued a check for $8,000 to pay rent for the months of December and January.

ANALYSIS
f. The asset account *Prepaid Rent* is increased by $8,000.
f. The asset account *Cash* is decreased by $8,000.

LEFT-RIGHT RULES
LEFT Increases to asset accounts are recorded on the left side of the T account. Record $8,000 on the left side of the *Prepaid Rent* T account.
RIGHT Decreases to asset accounts are recorded on the right side of the T account. Record $8,000 on the right side of the *Cash* T account.

T-ACCOUNT PRESENTATION

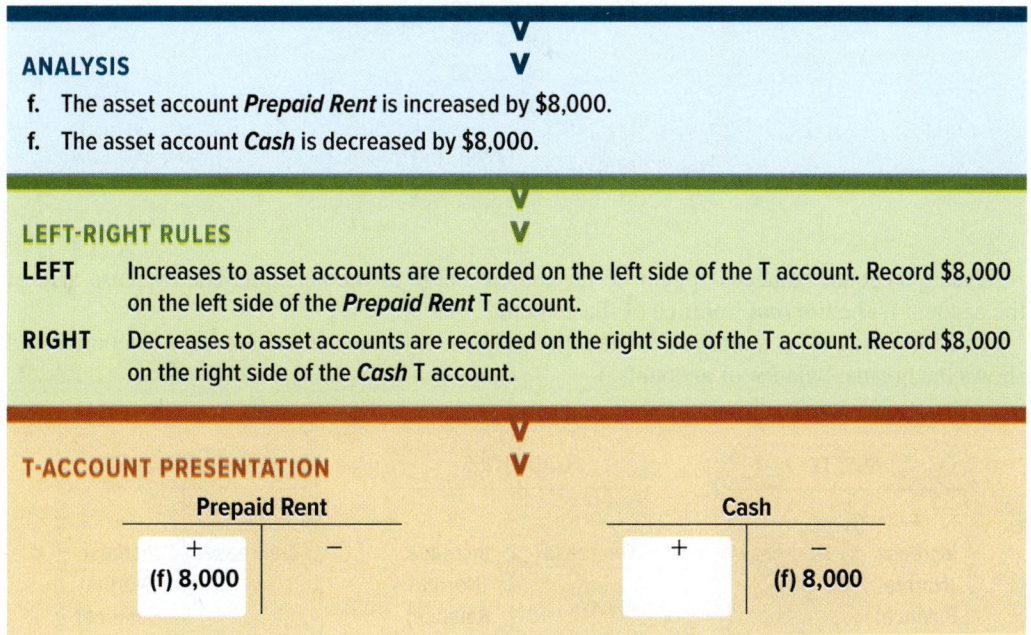

Let's review the T accounts to see the effects of the transactions. Sanchez entered $8,000 **(f)** on the left (increase) side of the *Prepaid Rent* account. He entered $8,000 **(f)** on the right (decrease) side of the *Cash* account.

Notice that the *Cash* account shows the effects of numerous transactions. It shows initial investment **(a)**, equipment purchase **(b)**, supplies purchase **(d)**, payment on account **(e)**, and advance rent payment **(f)**.

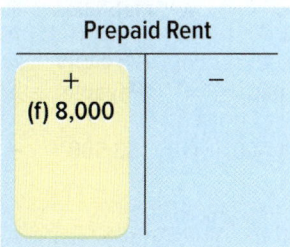

>> 3-3 OBJECTIVE

Determine the balance of an account.

Account Balances

An **account balance** is the difference between the amounts on the two sides of the account. First add the figures on each side of the account. If the column has more than one figure, enter the total in small pencil figures called a **footing.** Then subtract the smaller total from the larger total. The result is the account balance.

- If the total on the right side is larger than the total on the left side, the balance is recorded on the right side.
- If the total on the left side is larger, the balance is recorded on the left side.
- If an account shows only one amount, that amount is the balance.
- If an account contains entries on only one side, the total of those entries is the account balance.

Let's look at the **Cash** account for Eli's Consulting Services. The left side shows $100,000. The total of the right side is $17,000. Subtract the footing of $17,000 from $100,000. The result is the account balance of $83,000. The account balance is shown on the left side of the account.

```
              Cash
        +           −
   (a) 100,000   (b) 5,000
                 (d) 1,500
                 (e) 2,500
                 (f) 8,000
                 17,000 ← Footing
   Bal. 83,000
```

Usually account balances appear on the increase side of the account. The increase side of the account is the **normal balance** of the account.

The following is a summary of the procedures to increase or decrease accounts and shows the normal balance of accounts.

ABOUT ACCOUNTING

Law Enforcement

The FBI and other law enforcement agencies recruit accountants to investigate criminal conduct. Perhaps the most famous use of accounting by law enforcers is the conviction of Al Capone for tax evasion after he could not be jailed for his ties to organized crime.

```
   ASSETS          =    LIABILITIES        +    OWNER'S EQUITY
  +         −             −        +             −        +
Increase  Decrease      Decrease  Increase     Decrease  Increase
(Normal                           (Normal                (Normal
Balance)                          Balance)               Balance)
```

Figure 3.1 shows a summary of the account balances for Eli's Consulting Services. Figure 3.2 shows a balance sheet prepared for November 30, 20X1.

In equation form, the firm's position after these transactions is:

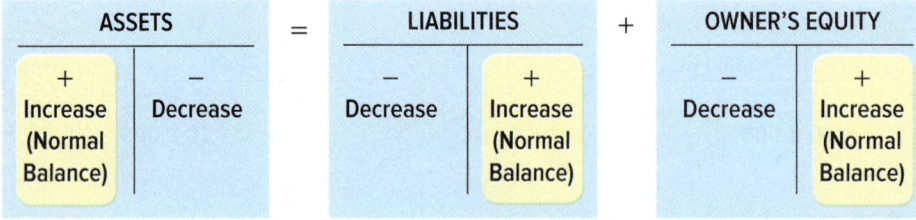

Assets						=	Liabilities	+	Owner's Equity
Cash	+	Supp.	+	Prepaid Rent	+	Equip.	=	Accounts Payable	+	Trayton Eli, Capital
$83,000	+	$1,500	+	$8,000	+	$11,000	=	$3,500	+	$100,000

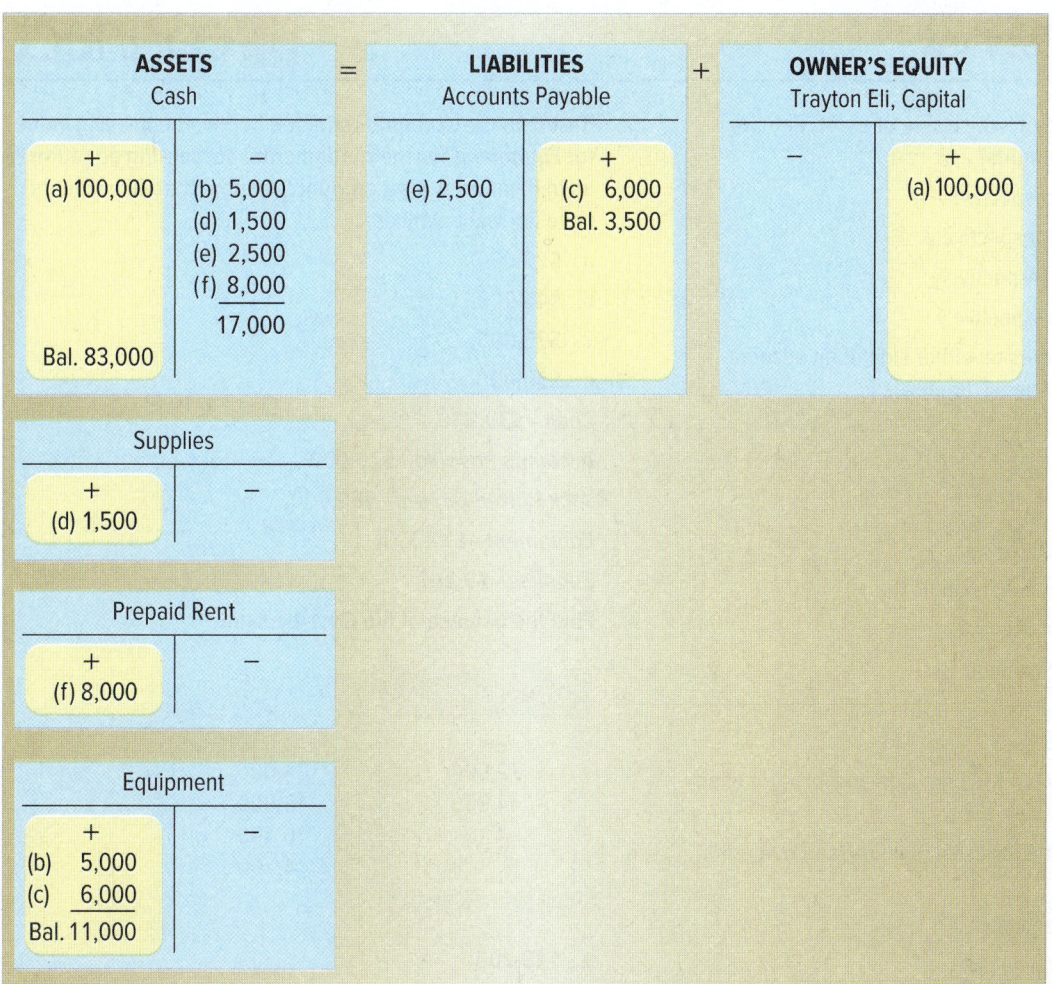

FIGURE 3.1

T-Account Balances for Eli's Consulting Services

FIGURE 3.2 Balance Sheet for Eli's Consulting Services

Assets		Liabilities	
		Eli's Consulting Services	
		Balance Sheet	
		November 30, 20X1	
Cash	83 000 00	Accounts Payable	3 500 00
Supplies	1 500 00		
Prepaid Rent	8 000 00	Owner's Equity	
Equipment	11 000 00	Trayton Eli, Capital	100 000 00
Total Assets	103 500 00	Total Liabilities and Owner's Equity	103 500 00

Notice how the balance sheet reflects the fundamental accounting equation.

Section 1 Review

1. Increases are recorded on which side of asset, liability, and owner's equity accounts?
   a. credit, debit, debit respectively
   b. credit, credit, credit respectively
   c. debit, credit, credit respectively
   d. debit, credit, debit respectively

2. The sum of several entries on either side of an account that is entered in small pencil figures is a:
   a. calculation.
   b. summation.
   c. footing.
   d. balance.

3. The normal balance of an account is the:
   a. decrease side of the account.
   b. increase side of the account.
   c. the difference between the left side and right side of an account.
   d. the difference between the right side and left side of an account.

4. The normal balance side for asset, liability, and owner's equity accounts is:
   a. left, left, right respectively.
   b. left, right, right respectively.
   c. right, right, left respectively.
   d. right, right, right respectively.

5. The Richey Company purchased new equipment for $40,400 from Office Supplies, Inc., to be paid in 30 days. Which of the following is correct?
   a. *Equipment* is increased by $40,400; *Accounts Payable* is decreased by $40,400.
   b. *Equipment* is increased by $40,400; *Accounts Payable* is increased by $40,400.
   c. *Equipment* is decreased by $40,400; *Accounts Payable* is increased by $40,400.
   d. *Equipment* is increased by $40,400; *Cash* is decreased by $40,400.

6. Based on the accounts reflected below, the missing value for *Equipment* for the fundamental accounting equation to be in balance is what amount? Assume that all accounts have normal balances.
   a. $20,000
   b. $40,000
   c. $25,000
   d. $30,000

   Cash—$30,800
   Accounts Payable—$20,000
   Jack Carter, Capital—$60,000
   Equipment—$XX,XXX
   Supplies—$9,200

7. Find the balance of the *Cash* account.

Cash	
+	−
72,000	24,000
44,000	10,000
	10,400
	4,700

   a. $48,200
   b. $66,900
   c. $64,000
   d. $116,000

Section 2

SECTION OBJECTIVES	TERMS TO LEARN
>> 3-4 Set up T accounts for revenue and expenses. **WHY IT'S IMPORTANT** T accounts help you understand the effects of all business transactions. **>> 3-5** Prepare a trial balance from T accounts. **WHY IT'S IMPORTANT** The trial balance is an important check of accuracy at the end of the accounting period. **>> 3-6** Prepare an income statement, a statement of owner's equity, and a balance sheet. **WHY IT'S IMPORTANT** Financial statements summarize the financial activities and condition of the business. **>> 3-7** Develop a chart of accounts. **WHY IT'S IMPORTANT** Businesses require a system that allows accounts to be easily identified and located.	chart of accounts credit debit double-entry system drawing account permanent account slide temporary account transposition trial balance

Transactions That Affect Revenue, Expenses, and Withdrawals

Let's examine the revenue and expense transactions of Eli's Consulting Services for December to see how they are recorded.

Revenue and Expense Accounts

Some owner's equity accounts are classified as revenue or expense accounts. Separate accounts are used to record revenue and expense transactions.

Recording Revenue from Services Sold for Cash

During December, the business earned $36,000 in revenue from clients who paid cash for bookkeeping, accounting, and consulting services. This involved several transactions. Sergio Sanchez entered $36,000 **(g)** on the left (increase) side of the asset account *Cash*.

>> **3-4 OBJECTIVE**
Set up T accounts for revenue and expenses.

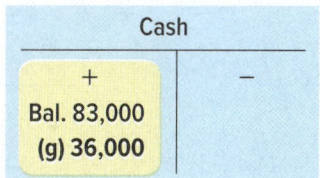

How is the increase in owner's equity recorded? One way would be to record the $36,000 on the right side of the **Trayton Eli, Capital** account. However, the preferred way is to keep revenue separate from the owner's investment until the end of the accounting period. Therefore, Sanchez opened a revenue account for **Fees Income.**

Sanchez entered $36,000 (**g**) on the right side of the **Fees Income** account. Revenues increase owner's equity. Increases in owner's equity appear on the right side of the T account. Therefore, increases in revenue appear on the right side of revenue T accounts.

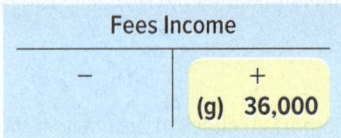

The right side of the revenue account shows increases and the left side shows decreases. Decreases in revenue accounts are rare but might occur because of corrections or transfers.

Let's review the effects of the transactions. Sanchez entered $36,000 (**g**) on the left (increase) side of the **Cash** account and $36,000 (**g**) on the right (increase) side of the **Fees Income** account.

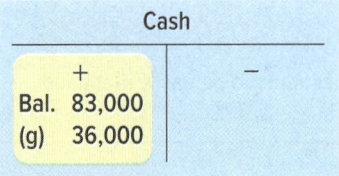 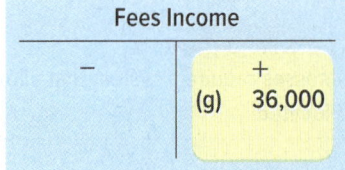

At this point, the firm needs just one revenue account. Most businesses have separate accounts for different types of revenue. For example, sales of goods such as clothes are recorded in the revenue account **Sales.**

Recording Revenue from Services Sold on Credit

In December, Eli's Consulting Services earned $11,000 from various charge account clients. Sanchez set up an asset account, **Accounts Receivable.**

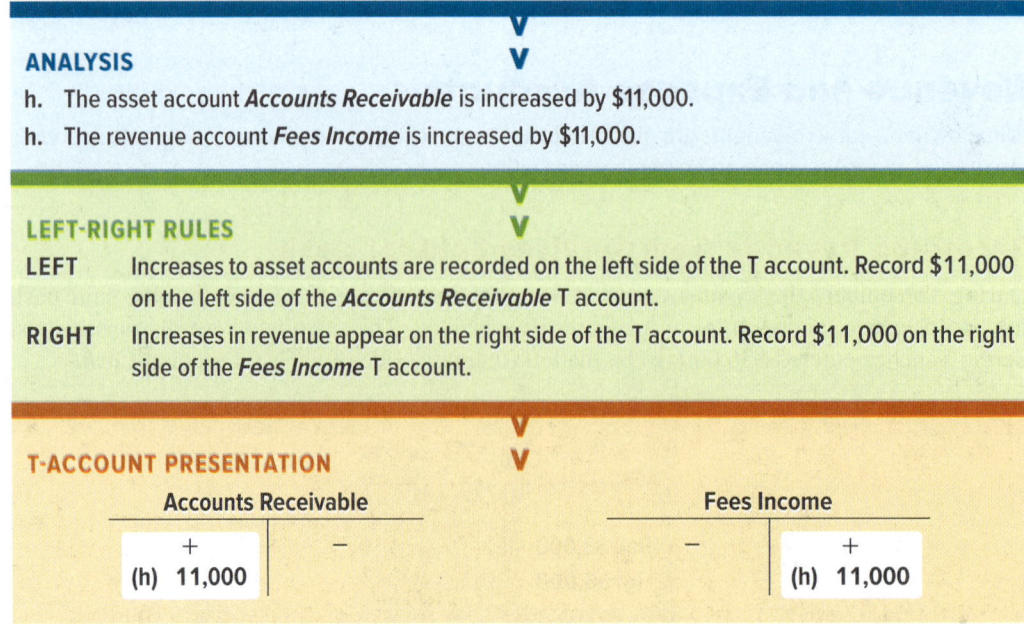

Let's review the effects of the transactions. Sanchez entered $11,000 **(h)** on the left (increase) side of the *Accounts Receivable* account and $11,000 **(h)** on the right (increase) side of the *Fees Income* account.

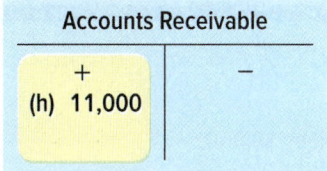

Recording Collections from Accounts Receivable

Charge account clients paid $6,000, reducing the amount owed to Eli's Consulting Services.

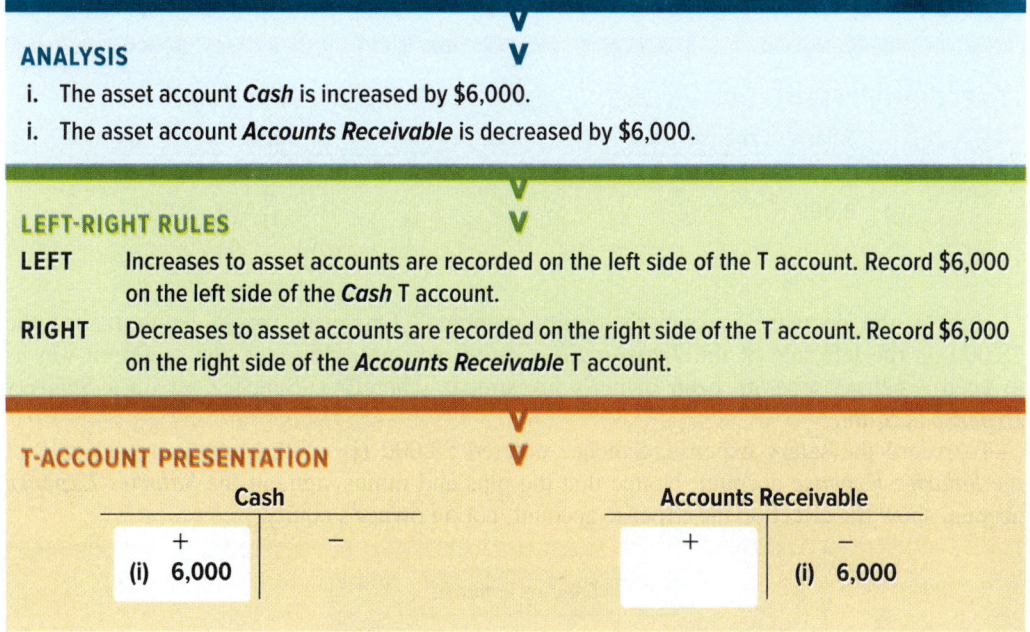

ANALYSIS
i. The asset account *Cash* is increased by $6,000.
i. The asset account *Accounts Receivable* is decreased by $6,000.

LEFT-RIGHT RULES
LEFT Increases to asset accounts are recorded on the left side of the T account. Record $6,000 on the left side of the *Cash* T account.
RIGHT Decreases to asset accounts are recorded on the right side of the T account. Record $6,000 on the right side of the *Accounts Receivable* T account.

T-ACCOUNT PRESENTATION

Let's review the effects of the transactions. Sanchez entered $6,000 **(i)** on the left (increase) side of the *Cash* account and $6,000 **(i)** on the right (decrease) side of the *Accounts Receivable* account. Notice that revenue is not recorded when cash is collected from charge account clients. The revenue was recorded when the sales on credit were recorded **(h)**.

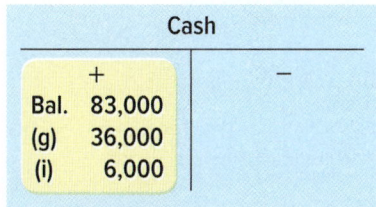

Recording an Expense for Salaries

Expenses decrease owner's equity. Decreases in owner's equity appear on the left side of the T account. Therefore, increases in expenses (which are decreases in owner's equity) are recorded on the left side of expense T accounts. Decreases in expenses are recorded on the right side of the T accounts. Decreases in expenses are rare but may result from corrections or transfers.

recall

Expense
An expense is an outflow of cash, the use of other assets, or the incurring of a liability.

BUSINESS TRANSACTION

In December, Eli's Consulting Services paid $8,000 in salaries.

ANALYSIS
j. The asset account *Cash* is decreased by $8,000.
j. The expense account *Salaries Expense* is increased by $8,000.

LEFT-RIGHT RULES
LEFT   Increases in expenses appear on the left side of the T account. Record $8,000 on the left side of the *Salaries Expense* T account.
RIGHT Decreases in asset accounts are recorded on the right side of the T account. Record $8,000 on the right side of the *Cash* T account.

T-ACCOUNT PRESENTATION

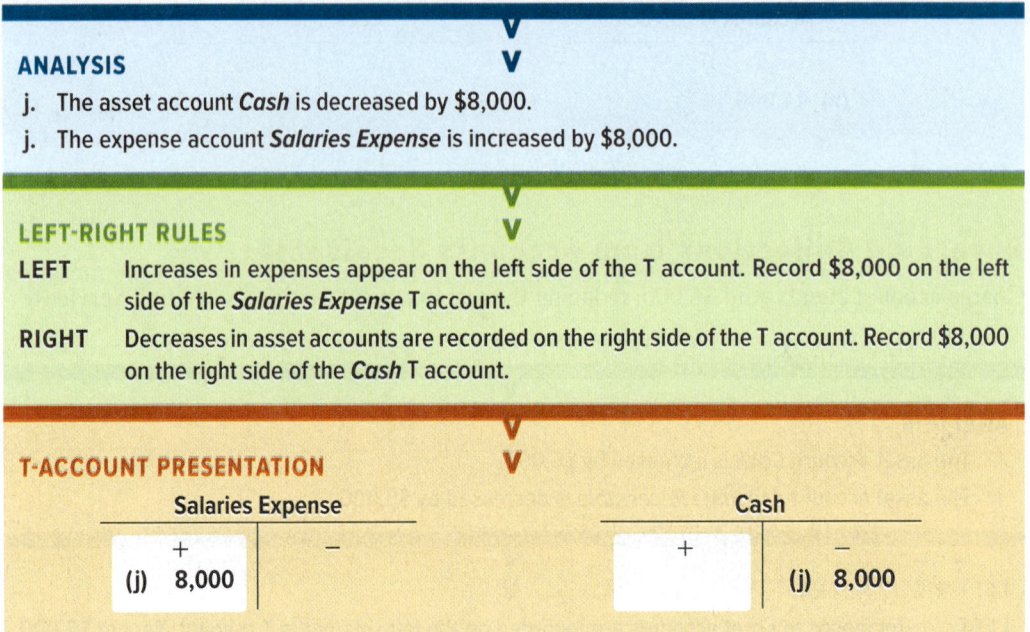

How is the decrease in owner's equity recorded? One way would be to record the $8,000 on the left side of the *Trayton Eli, Capital* account. However, the preferred way is to keep expenses separate from owner's investment. Therefore, Sanchez set up a *Salaries Expense* account.

To record the salary expense, Sanchez entered $8,000 **(j)** on the left (increase) side of the *Salaries Expense* account. Notice that the plus and minus signs in the *Salaries Expense* account show the effect on the expense account, not on owner's equity.

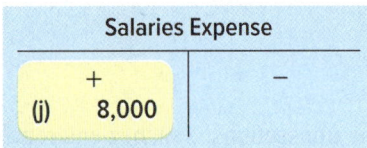

Sanchez entered $8,000 **(j)** on the right (decrease) side of the *Cash* T account.

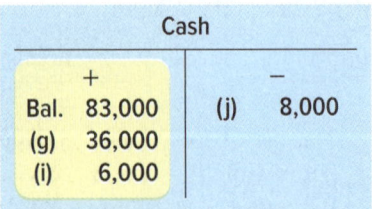

Most companies have numerous expense accounts. The various expense accounts appear in the Expenses section of the income statement.

Recording an Expense for Utilities

At the end of December, Eli's Consulting Services received a $650 bill for utilities. Sanchez set up an account for *Utilities Expense.*

BUSINESS TRANSACTION

Eli's Consulting Services issued a check for $650 to pay the utilities bill.

ANALYSIS
k. The asset account *Cash* is decreased by $650.
k. The expense account *Utilities Expense* is increased by $650.

LEFT-RIGHT RULES
LEFT   Increases in expenses appear on the left side of the T account. Record $650 on the left side of the *Utilities Expense* T account.
RIGHT Decreases to asset accounts are recorded on the right side of the T account. Record $650 on the right side of the *Cash* T account.

T-ACCOUNT PRESENTATION

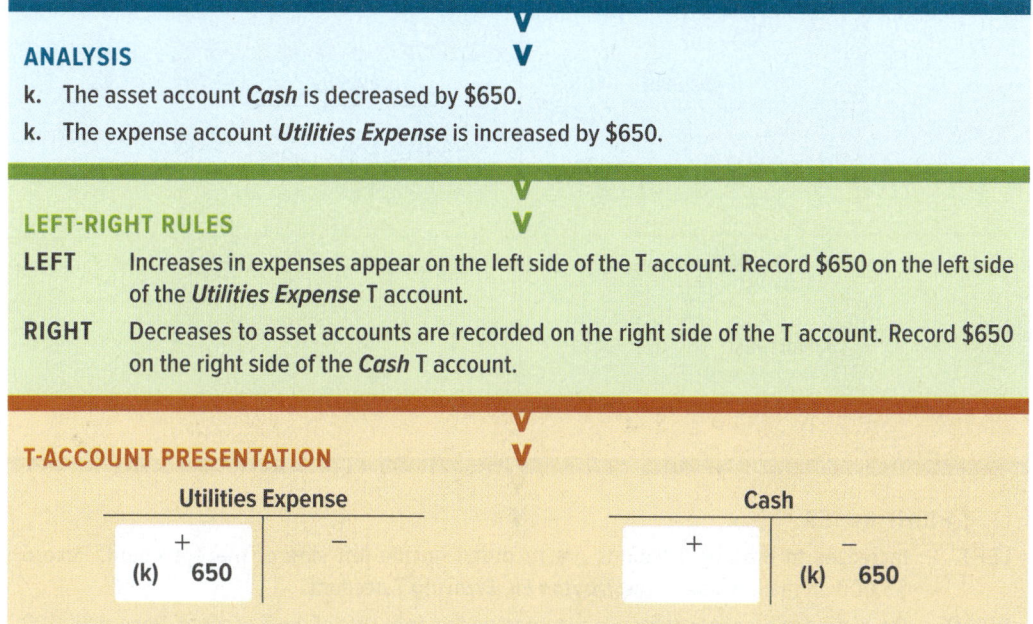

Let's review the effects of the transactions.

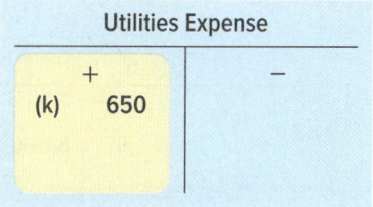

The Drawing Account

In sole proprietorships and partnerships, the owners generally do not pay themselves salaries. To obtain funds for personal living expenses, owners make withdrawals of cash. The withdrawals are against previously earned profits that have become part of capital or against profits that are expected in the future.

Since withdrawals decrease owner's equity, withdrawals could be recorded on the left side of the capital account. However, the preferred way is to keep withdrawals separate from the owner's capital account until the end of the accounting period. An owner's equity account called a **drawing account** is set up to record withdrawals. Increases in the drawing account (which are decreases in owner's equity) are recorded on the left side of the drawing T accounts.

BUSINESS TRANSACTION

Trayton Eli wrote a check to withdraw $5,000 cash for personal use.

ANALYSIS
l. The asset account *Cash* is decreased by $5,000.
l. The owner's equity account *Trayton Eli, Drawing* is increased by $5,000.

FIGURE 3.3

The Relationship Between Owner's Equity and Revenue, Expenses, and Withdrawals

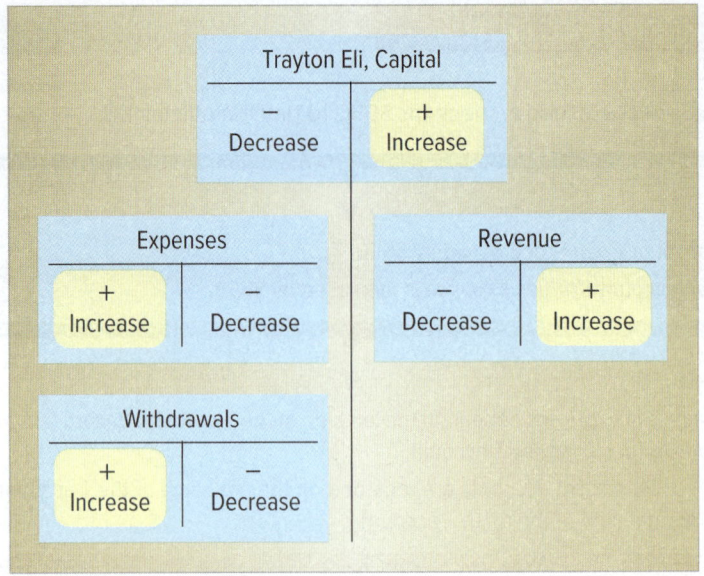

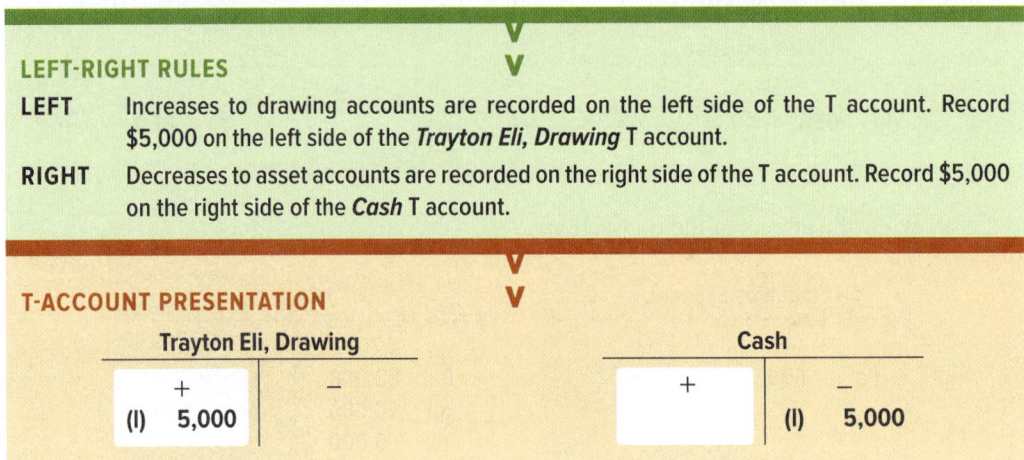

Let's review the transactions. Sanchez entered $5,000 **(l)** on the right (decrease) side of the asset account **Cash** and $5,000 **(l)** on the left (increase) side of *Trayton Eli, Drawing*. Note that the plus and minus signs show the effect on the drawing account, not on owner's equity.

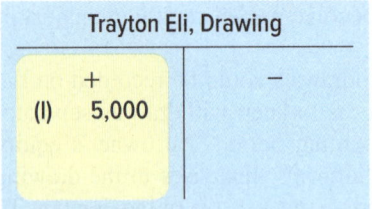

Figure 3.3 shows a summary of the relationship between the capital account and the revenue, expense, and drawing accounts.

important!

Normal Balances

Debit:	Credit:
Asset	Liability
Expense	Revenue
Drawing	Capital

The Rules of Debit and Credit

Accountants do not use the terms *left side* and *right side* when they talk about making entries in accounts. Instead, they use the term **debit** for an entry on the left side and **credit** for an entry on the right side. Figure 3.4 summarizes the rules for debits and credits. The accounting system is called the **double-entry system.** This is because each transaction has at least two entries—a debit and a credit.

FIGURE 3.4 Rules for Debits and Credits

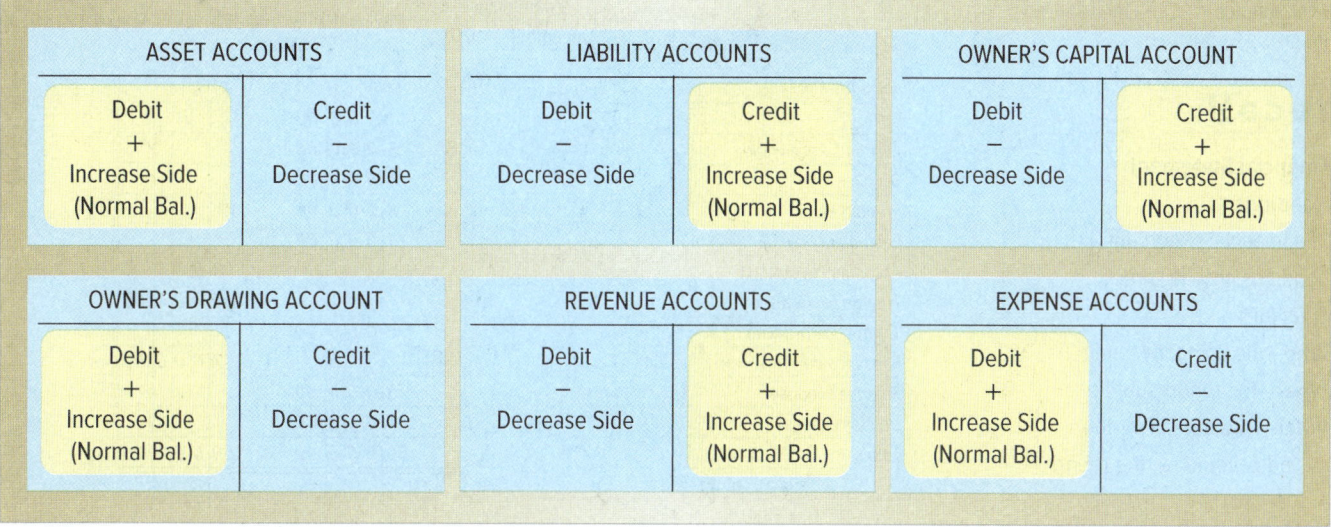

After the December transactions for Eli's Consulting Services are recorded, the account balances are calculated. Figure 3.5 shows the account balances at the end of December. Notice that the fundamental accounting equation remains in balance (Assets = Liabilities + Owner's Equity).

FIGURE 3.5 End-of-December 20X1 Account Balances

ASSETS = **LIABILITIES** + **OWNER'S EQUITY**

Cash

Bal.	83,000	(j)	8,000
(g)	36,000	(k)	650
(i)	6,000	(l)	5,000
	125,000		13,650
Bal.	111,350		

Accounts Payable

		Bal.	3,500

Trayton Eli, Capital

		Bal.	100,000

Accounts Receivable

(h)	11,000	(i)	6,000
Bal.	5,000		

Trayton Eli, Drawing

(l)	5,000		

Supplies

Bal.	1,500		

Fees Income

		(g)	36,000
		(h)	11,000
		Bal.	47,000

Prepaid Rent

Bal.	8,000		

Salaries Expense

(j)	8,000		

Equipment

Bal.	11,000		

Utilities Expense

(k)	650		

FIGURE 3.6

Trial Balance

recall

Financial Statement Headings

The financial statement headings answer three questions:

Who—the company name
What—the report subtitle
When—the date of, or the period covered by, the report

Eli's Consulting Services
Trial Balance
December 31, 20X1

ACCOUNT NAME	DEBIT	CREDIT
Cash	111 350 00	
Accounts Receivable	5 000 00	
Supplies	1 500 00	
Prepaid Rent	8 000 00	
Equipment	11 000 00	
Accounts Payable		3 500 00
Trayton Eli, Capital		100 000 00
Trayton Eli, Drawing	5 000 00	
Fees Income		47 000 00
Salaries Expense	8 000 00	
Utilities Expense	650 00	
Totals	150 500 00	150 500 00

>> 3-5 OBJECTIVE

Prepare a trial balance from T accounts.

The Trial Balance

Once the account balances are computed, a trial balance is prepared. The **trial balance** is a statement that tests the accuracy of total debits and credits after transactions have been recorded. If total debits do not equal total credits, there is an error. Figure 3.6 shows the trial balance for Eli's Consulting Services. To prepare a trial balance, perform the following steps:

1. Enter the trial balance heading showing the company name, report title, and closing date for the accounting period.
2. List the account names in the same order as they appear on the financial statements.
   - Assets
   - Liabilities
   - Owner's Equity
   - Revenue
   - Expenses
3. Enter the ending balance of each account in the appropriate Debit or Credit column.
4. Total the Debit column.
5. Total the Credit column.
6. Compare the total debits with the total credits.

MANAGERIAL IMPLICATIONS <<

FINANCIAL STATEMENTS

- Recording entries into accounts provides an efficient method of gathering data about the financial affairs of a business.
- A chart of accounts is usually similar from company to company; balance sheet accounts are first, followed by income statement accounts.
- A trial balance proves the financial records are in balance.
- The income statement reports the revenue and expenses for the period and shows the net income or loss.
- The statement of owner's equity shows the change in owner's equity during the period.
- The balance sheet summarizes the assets, liabilities, and owner's equity of the business on a given date.
- Owners, managers, creditors, banks, and many others use financial statements to make decisions about the business.

THINKING CRITICALLY

What are some possible consequences of not recording financial data correctly?

Understanding Trial Balance Errors

If the totals of the Debit and Credit columns are equal, the financial records are in balance. If the totals of the Debit and Credit columns are not equal, there is an error. The error may be in the trial balance, or it may be in the financial records. Some common errors are:

- adding trial balance columns incorrectly;
- recording only half a transaction—for example, recording a debit but not recording a credit, or vice versa;
- recording both halves of a transaction as debits or credits rather than recording one debit and one credit;
- recording an amount incorrectly from a transaction;
- recording a debit for one amount and a credit for a different amount;
- making an error when calculating the account balances.

Finding Trial Balance Errors

If the trial balance does not balance, try the following procedures:

1. Check the arithmetic. If the columns were originally added from top to bottom, verify the total by adding from bottom to top.
2. Check that the correct account balances were transferred to the correct trial balance columns.
3. Check the arithmetic used to compute the account balances.
4. Check that each transaction was recorded correctly in the accounts by tracing the amounts to the analysis of the transaction.

Sometimes you can determine the type of the error by the amount of the difference between the trial balance columns. Compute the difference between the debit total and the credit total. If the difference is evenly divisible by 2, a debit might be recorded as a credit, or a credit recorded as a debit.

If the difference is evenly divisible by 9, there might be a transposition. A **transposition** occurs when the digits of a number are switched (357 for 375). The test for a transposition is:

$$\begin{array}{r} 375 \\ -357 \\ \hline 18 \end{array} \qquad 18/9 = 2$$

Also check for slides. A **slide** occurs when the decimal point is misplaced (375 for 37.50). We can test for a slide in the following manner:

$$\begin{array}{r} 375.00 \\ -37.50 \\ \hline 337.50 \end{array} \qquad 337.50/9 = 37.50$$

Financial Statements

>> **3-6 OBJECTIVE**
Prepare an income statement, a statement of owner's equity, and a balance sheet.

After the trial balance is prepared, the financial statements are prepared. Figure 3.7 shows the financial statements for Eli's Consulting Services. The amounts are taken from the trial balance. As you study the financial statements, note that net income from the income statement is used on the statement of owner's equity. Also note that the ending balance of the *Trayton Eli, Capital* account, computed on the statement of owner's equity, is used on the balance sheet.

Chart of Accounts

>> **3-7 OBJECTIVE**
Develop a chart of accounts.

A **chart of accounts** is a list of all the accounts used by a business. Figure 3.8 shows the chart of accounts for Eli's Consulting Services. Each account has a number and a name. The balance sheet accounts are listed first, followed by the income statement accounts. The account number is assigned based on the type of account.

FIGURE 3.7

Financial Statements for Eli's Consulting Services

Eli's Consulting Services
Income Statement
Month Ended December 31, 20X1

Revenue			
Fees Income			47 000 00
Expenses			
Salaries Expense		8 000 00	
Utilities Expense		6 50 00	
Total Expenses			8 650 00
Net Income			38 350 00

Eli's Consulting Services
Statement of Owner's Equity
Month Ended December 31, 20X1

Trayton Eli, Capital, December 1, 20X1		100 000 00
Net Income for December	38 350 00	
Less Withdrawals for December	5 000 00	
Increase in Capital		33 350 00
Trayton Eli, Capital, December 31, 20X1		133 350 00

Eli's Consulting Services
Balance Sheet
December 31, 20X1

Assets		Liabilities	
Cash	111 350 00	Accounts Payable	3 500 00
Accounts Receivable	5 000 00		
Supplies	1 500 00		
Prepaid Rent	8 000 00	Owner's Equity	
Equipment	11 000 00	Trayton Eli, Capital	133 350 00
Total Assets	136 850 00	Total Liabilities and Owner's Equity	136 850 00

Asset Accounts	100–199	Revenue Accounts	400–499
Liability Accounts	200–299	Expense Accounts	500–599
Owner's Equity Accounts	300–399		

important!

Balance Sheet Accounts
The amounts on the balance sheet are carried forward to the next accounting period.

Notice that the accounts are not numbered consecutively. For example, asset account numbers jump from 101 to 111 and then to 121, 137, and 141. In each block of numbers, gaps are left so that additional accounts can be added when needed.

Permanent and Temporary Accounts

important!

Income Statement Accounts
The amounts on the income statement are transferred to the capital account at the end of the accounting period.

The asset, liability, and owner's equity accounts appear on the balance sheet at the end of an accounting period. The balances of these accounts are then carried forward to start the new period. Because they continue from one accounting period to the next, these accounts are called **permanent accounts** or *real accounts*.

Revenue and expense accounts appear on the income statement. The drawing account appears on the statement of owner's equity. These accounts classify and summarize changes in owner's equity during the period. They are called **temporary accounts** or *nominal accounts* because the balances in these accounts are transferred to the capital account at the end of the accounting period. In the next period, these accounts start with zero balances.

FIGURE 3.8
Chart of Accounts

Eli's Consulting Services
Chart of Accounts

Account Number	Account Name
Balance Sheet Accounts	
100–199	**ASSETS**
101	Cash
111	Accounts Receivable
121	Supplies
137	Prepaid Rent
141	Equipment
200–299	**LIABILITIES**
202	Accounts Payable
300–399	**OWNER'S EQUITY**
301	Trayton Eli, Capital
Statement of Owner's Equity Account	
302	Trayton Eli, Drawing
Income Statement Accounts	
400–499	**REVENUE**
401	Fees Income
500–599	**EXPENSES**
511	Salaries Expense
514	Utilities Expense

Section 2 Review

1. What is the increase side for *Cash; Accounts Payable;* and *Trayton Eli, Capital?*
   a. right, left, right respectively
   b. left, left, left respectively
   c. left, right, right respectively
   d. right, right, right respectively

2. An error in which the digits of a number are switched—for example, 571 is recorded as 517—is an example of a:
   a. switch.
   b. summation.
   c. slide.
   d. transposition.

3. An error in which the decimal point is misplaced—for example, when 317 is written as 3.17—is an example of a:
   a. slide.
   b. transposition.
   c. switch.
   d. summation.

4. The trial balance includes all of the following except:
   a. list of all accounts.
   b. balances of all accounts.
   c. equality of debits and credits.
   d. income or loss for the period.

5. Which account has a normal debit balance?
   a. *Accounts Payable*
   b. *Jeffery Wells, Drawing*
   c. *Jeffery Wells, Capital*
   d. *Fees Income*

6. The company owner took $5,000 cash for personal use. What is the entry for this transaction?
   a. debit *Cash* and credit *Caleb Parker, Capital*
   b. debit *Cash* and credit *Caleb Parker, Drawing*
   c. debit *Caleb Parker, Drawing* and credit *Cash*
   d. debit *Caleb Parker, Capital* and credit *Cash*

7. Errors in the Parker Interiors trial balance include all items below except:
   a. *C. Parker, Drawing* should be debited.
   b. *Fees Income* should be credited.
   c. total debits and total credits should equal $51,000.
   d. *Equipment* should be credited.

Parker Interiors
Trial Balance
December 31, 20X1

	DEBIT	CREDIT
Cash	15 000 00	
Accts. Rec.	10 000 00	
Equip.	7 000 00	
Accts. Pay.		15 000 00
C. Parker, Capital		22 000 00
C. Parker, Drawing		10 000 00
Fees Income	14 000 00	
Rent Exp.	2 000 00	
Supplies Exp.	2 000 00	
Telephone Exp.	5 000 00	
Totals	55 000 00	47 000 00

REVIEW Chapter Summary

In this chapter, you have learned how to use T accounts to help analyze and record business transactions. A chart of accounts can be developed to easily identify all the accounts used by a business. After determining the balance for all accounts, the trial balance is prepared to test the accuracy of total debits and credits after transactions have been recorded.

Learning Objectives

3-1 Set up T accounts for assets, liabilities, and owner's equity.

T accounts consist of two lines, one vertical and one horizontal, that resemble the letter T. The account name is written on the top line. Increases and decreases to the account are entered on either the left side or the right side of the vertical line.

3-2 Analyze business transactions and enter them in the accounts.

Each business transaction is analyzed for its effects on the fundamental accounting equation, Assets = Liabilities + Owner's Equity. Then these effects are recorded in the proper accounts. Accounts are classified as assets, liabilities, or owner's equity.

- Increases in an asset account appear on the debit, or left, side because assets are on the left side of the accounting equation. The credit, or right, side records decreases.
- An increase in a liability account is recorded on the credit, or right, side. The left, or debit, side of a liability account is used for recording decreases.
- Increases in owner's equity are shown on the credit (right) side of an account. Decreases appear on the debit (left) side.
- The drawing account is used to record the withdrawal of cash from the business by the owner. The drawing account decreases owner's equity.

3-3 Determine the balance of an account.

The difference between the amounts recorded on the two sides of an account is known as the balance of the account.

3-4 Set up T accounts for revenue and expenses.

- Revenue accounts increase owner's equity; therefore, increases are recorded on the credit side of revenue accounts.
- Expenses are recorded on the debit side of the expense accounts because expenses decrease owner's equity.

3-5 Prepare a trial balance from T accounts.

The trial balance is a statement to test the accuracy of the financial records. Total debits should equal total credits.

3-6 Prepare an income statement, a statement of owner's equity, and a balance sheet.

The income statement is prepared to report the revenue and expenses for the period. The statement of owner's equity is prepared to analyze the change in owner's equity during the period. Then the balance sheet is prepared to summarize the assets, liabilities, and owner's equity of the business at the end of the period.

3-7 Develop a chart of accounts.

A firm's list of accounts is called its chart of accounts. Accounts are arranged in a predetermined order and are numbered for handy reference and quick identification. Typically, accounts are numbered in the order in which they appear on the financial statements. Balance sheet accounts come first, followed by income statement accounts.

3-8 Define the accounting terms new to this chapter.

Glossary

Account balance (p. 62) The difference between the amounts recorded on the two sides of an account

Accounts (p. 56) Written records of the assets, liabilities, and owner's equity of a business

Chart of accounts (p. 73) A list of the accounts used by a business to record its financial transactions

Classification (p. 56) A means of identifying each account as an asset, liability, or owner's equity

Credit (p. 70) An entry on the right side of an account

Debit (p. 70) An entry on the left side of an account

Double-entry system (p. 70) An accounting system that involves recording the effects of each transaction as debits and credits

Drawing account (p. 69) A special type of owner's equity account set up to record the owner's withdrawal of cash from the business

Footing (p. 62) A small pencil figure written at the base of an amount column showing the sum of the entries in the column

Normal balance (p. 62) The increase side of an account

Permanent account (p. 74) An account that is kept open from one accounting period to the next

Slide (p. 73) An accounting error involving a misplaced decimal point

T account (p. 56) A type of account, resembling a T, used to analyze the effects of a business transaction

Temporary account (p. 74) An account whose balance is transferred to another account at the end of an accounting period

Transposition (p. 73) An accounting error involving misplaced digits in a number

Trial balance (p. 72) A statement to test the accuracy of total debits and credits after transactions have been recorded

Comprehensive Self Review

1. What is a chart of accounts?
2. What are withdrawals, and how are they recorded?
3. What type of accounts are found on the balance sheet?
4. On which side of asset, liability, and owner's equity accounts are decreases recorded?
5. Your friend has prepared financial statements for her business. She has asked you to review the statements for accuracy. The trial balance debit column totals $91,000 and the credit column totals $104,000. What steps would you take to find the error?

(Answers to Comprehensive Self Review are at the end of the chapter.)

Discussion Questions

1. What are accounts?
2. What is the purpose of a chart of accounts?
3. In what order do accounts appear in the chart of accounts?
4. When a chart of accounts is created, number gaps are left within groups of accounts. Why are these number gaps necessary?
5. Accounts are classified as permanent or temporary accounts. What do these classifications mean?
6. How is the balance of an account determined?
7. Indicate whether each of the following types of account would normally have a debit balance or a credit balance:
    a. An asset account
    b. A liability account
    c. The owner's capital account
    d. A revenue account
    e. An expense account
8. The terms *debit* and *credit* are often used in describing the effects of transactions on different accounts. What do these terms mean?

9. Why is *Prepaid Rent* considered an asset account?
10. Why is the modern system of accounting usually called the double-entry system?
11. Are the following accounts permanent or temporary accounts?
    a. *Fees Income*
    b. *Johnny Jones, Drawing*
    c. *Accounts Payable*
    d. *Accounts Receivable*
    e. *Johnny Jones, Capital*
    f. *Prepaid Rent*
    g. *Cash*
    h. *Advertising Expense*
    i. *Utilities Expense*
    j. *Equipment*
    k. *Salaries Expense*
    l. *Prepaid Insurance*

APPLICATIONS

Exercises

Setting up T accounts.

◀ **Exercise 3.1**
Objective 3-1

Johnson Cleaning Service has the following account balances on December 31, 20X1. Set up a T account for each account and enter the balance on the proper side of the account.

| Cash | $ 76,000 | Accounts Payable | 96,800 |
| Equipment | 184,000 | Elicia Johnson, Capital | 163,200 |

Using T accounts to analyze transactions.

◀ **Exercise 3.2**
Objective 3-2

Haden Fry decided to start a dental practice. The first five transactions for the business follow. For each transaction, (1) determine which two accounts are affected, (2) set up T accounts for the affected accounts, and (3) enter the debit and credit amounts in the T accounts.

1. Haden invested $90,000 cash in the business.
2. Paid $30,000 in cash for equipment.
3. Performed services for cash amounting to $9,000.
4. Paid $3,800 in cash for advertising expense.
5. Paid $3,000 in cash for supplies.

Determining debit and credit balances.

◀ **Exercise 3.3**
Objective 3-3

Indicate whether each of the following accounts normally has a debit balance or a credit balance:

1. Cash
2. Blaine Brownell, Capital
3. Fee Income
4. Accounts Payable
5. Supplies
6. Equipment
7. Accounts Receivable
8. Salaries Expense

Exercise 3.4
Objective 3-3

▶ **Identifying debits and credits.**

In each of the following sentences, fill in the blanks with the word *debit* or *credit*:

1. Revenue accounts normally have __?__ balances. These accounts increase on the __?__ side and decrease on the __?__ side.
2. Liability accounts normally have __?__ balances. These accounts increase on the __?__ side and decrease on the __?__ side.
3. Expense accounts normally have __?__ balances. These accounts increase on the __?__ side and decrease on the __?__ side.
4. Asset accounts normally have __?__ balances. These accounts increase on the __?__ side and decrease on the __?__ side.
5. The owner's capital account normally has a __?__ balance. This account increases on the __?__ side and decreases on the __?__ side.

Exercise 3.5
Objective 3-3

▶ **Determining account balances.**

The following T accounts show transactions that were recorded by Residential Relocators, a firm that specializes in local housing rentals. The entries for the first transaction are labeled with the letter (a), the entries for the second transaction with the letter (b), and so on. Determine the balance of each account.

Cash					Scott Hamilton, Capital		
(a)	95,000	(b)	23,000			(a)	95,000
(d)	15,000	(e)	350				
(g)	1,500	(h)	5,500				
		(i)	2,500				

Accounts Receivable					Scott Hamilton, Drawing	
(f)	5,000	(g)	1,500	(i)	2,500	

Supplies			Fees Income		
(b)	23,000			(d)	15,000
				(f)	5,000

Equipment			Salaries Expense	
(c)	40,000		(h)	5,500

Accounts Payable			Telephone Expense	
	(c)	40,000	(e)	350

Exercise 3.6
Objectives 3-5, 3-6

▶ **Preparing a trial balance and an income statement.**

Using the account balances from Exercise 3.5, prepare a trial balance and an income statement for Residential Relocators. The trial balance is for December 31, 20X1, and the income statement is for the month ended December 31, 20X1.

Exercise 3.7
Objective 3-6

▶ **Preparing a statement of owner's equity and a balance sheet.**

From the trial balance and the net income or net loss determined in Exercise 3.6, prepare a statement of owner's equity and a balance sheet for Residential Relocators as of December 31, 20X1.

Exercise 3.8
Objective 3-7

Preparing a chart of accounts.

The accounts that will be used by Metro Moving Company follow. Prepare a chart of accounts for the firm. Classify the accounts by type, arrange them in an appropriate order, and assign suitable account numbers.

Salaries Expense	Office Supplies
Prepaid Rent	Accounts Payable
Fees Income	Cash
Accounts Receivable	Utilities Expense
Telephone Expense	Office Equipment
Carmen Alexis, Capital	Carmen Alexis, Drawing

PROBLEMS

Problem Set A

Problem 3.1A
Objective 3-1

Using T accounts to record transactions involving assets, liabilities, and owner's equity.

The following transactions occurred at several different businesses and are not related.

INSTRUCTIONS

Analyze each of the transactions. For each, decide what accounts are affected and set up T accounts. Record the effects of the transaction in the T accounts.

TRANSACTIONS

1. Serena Hamilton, an owner, made an additional investment of $42,000 in cash.
2. A firm purchased equipment for $20,000 in cash.
3. A firm sold some surplus office furniture for $3,400 in cash.
4. A firm purchased a computer for $3,700, to be paid in 60 days.
5. A firm purchased office equipment for $22,400 on credit. The amount is due in 60 days.
6. James Taylor, owner of Taylor Travel Agency, withdrew $12,000 of his original cash investment.
7. A firm bought a delivery truck for $38,500 on credit; payment is due in 90 days.
8. A firm issued a check for $7,200 to a supplier in partial payment of an open account balance.

Analyze: List the transactions that directly affected an owner's equity account.

Problem 3.2A
Objectives 3-1, 3-2

Using T accounts to record transactions involving assets, liabilities, and owner's equity.

The following transactions took place at Willis Counseling Services, a business established by Raymond Willis.

INSTRUCTIONS

For each transaction, set up T accounts from this list: *Cash; Office Furniture; Office Equipment; Automobile; Accounts Payable; Raymond Willis, Capital;* and *Raymond Willis, Drawing.* Analyze each transaction. Record the amounts in the T accounts affected by that transaction.

TRANSACTIONS

1. Raymond Willis invested $50,000 cash in the business.
2. Purchased office furniture for $17,000 in cash.
3. Bought a fax machine for $675; payment is due in 30 days.
4. Purchased a used car for the firm for $17,800 in cash.
5. Willis invested an additional $15,500 cash in the business.
6. Bought a new computer for $1,250; payment is due in 60 days.
7. Paid $675 to settle the amount owed on the fax machine.
8. Willis withdrew $5,200 in cash for personal expenses.

Analyze: Which transactions affected asset accounts?

Problem 3.3A
Objectives 3-2, 3-4

▶ **Using T accounts to record transactions involving revenues and expenses.**

The following occurred during June at Brown Financial Planning.

INSTRUCTIONS

Analyze each transaction. Use T accounts to record these transactions and be sure to put the name of the account on the top of each account. Record the effects of the transaction in the T accounts.

TRANSACTIONS

1. Purchased office supplies for $12,000 in cash.
2. Delivered monthly statements; collected fee income of $65,700.
3. Paid the current month's office rent of $9,500.
4. Completed professional financial planning; billed client for $16,000.
5. Client paid fee of $4,000 for weekly counseling, previously billed.
6. Paid office salaries of $18,400.
7. Paid telephone bill of $1,080.
8. Billed client for $12,000 fee for preparing a comprehensive financial plan.
9. Purchased office supplies of $4,400 on account.
10. Paid office salaries of $18,400.
11. Collected $12,000 from client who was billed.
12. Clients paid a total of $36,400 cash for fees.

Analyze: How much cash did the business spend during the month?

Problem 3.4A
Objectives 3-1, 3-2, 3-4

▶ **Using T accounts to record all business transactions.**

The following accounts and transactions are for Vincent Sutton, Landscape Consultant.

INSTRUCTIONS

Analyze the transactions. Record each in the appropriate T accounts. Identify each entry in the T accounts by writing the letter of the transaction next to the entry.

ASSETS
Cash
Accounts Receivable
Office Furniture
Office Equipment

LIABILITIES
Accounts Payable
OWNER'S EQUITY
Vincent Sutton, Capital
Vincent Sutton, Drawing
REVENUE
Fees Income
EXPENSES
Rent Expense
Utilities Expense
Salaries Expense
Telephone Expense
Miscellaneous Expense

TRANSACTIONS

a. Sutton invested $90,000 in cash to start the business.
b. Paid $6,000 for the current month's rent.
c. Bought office furniture for $10,580 in cash.
d. Performed services for $8,200 in cash.
e. Paid $1,250 for the monthly telephone bill.
f. Performed services for $14,000 on credit.
g. Purchased a computer and copier for $18,000; paid $7,200 in cash immediately with the balance due in 30 days.
h. Received $7,000 from credit clients.
i. Paid $2,800 in cash for office cleaning services for the month.
j. Purchased office chairs for $5,800; received credit terms of 30 days.
k. Purchased office equipment for $22,000 and paid half of this amount in cash immediately; the balance is due in 30 days.
l. Issued a check for $9,400 to pay salaries.
m. Performed services for $14,500 in cash.
n. Performed services for $16,000 on credit.
o. Collected 8,000 on accounts receivable from charge customers.
p. Issued a check for $2,900 in partial payment of the amount owed for office chairs.
q. Paid $725 to a duplicating company for photocopy work performed during the month.
r. Paid $1,280 for the monthly electric bill.
s. Sutton withdrew $5,500 in cash for personal expenses.

Analyze: What liabilities does the business have after all transactions have been recorded?

Preparing financial statements from T accounts.

◀ **Problem 3.5A**
Objectives 3-3, 3-5, 3-6

The accountant for the firm owned by Vincent Sutton prepares financial statements at the end of each month.

INSTRUCTIONS

Use the figures in the T accounts for Problem 3.4A to prepare a trial balance, an income statement, a statement of owner's equity, and a balance sheet. (The first line of the statement headings should read "Vincent Sutton, Landscape Consultant.") Assume that the transactions took place during the month ended June 30, 20X1. Determine the account balances before you start work on the financial statements.

Analyze: What is the change in owner's equity for the month of June?

Problem Set B

Problem 3.1B
Objectives 3-1, 3-2

▶ **Using T accounts to record transactions involving assets, liabilities, and owner's equity.**

The following transactions occurred at several different businesses and are not related.

INSTRUCTIONS

Analyze each of the transactions. For each transaction, set up T accounts. Record the effects of the transaction in the T accounts.

TRANSACTIONS

1. A firm purchased equipment for $32,000 in cash.
2. The owner, Gwendolyn Kelly, withdrew $8,000 cash.
3. A firm sold a piece of surplus equipment for $6,000 in cash.
4. A firm purchased a used delivery truck for $24,000 in cash.
5. A firm paid $7,200 in cash to apply against an account owed.
6. A firm purchased office equipment for $10,000. The amount is to be paid in 60 days.
7. Kawonza Carter, owner of the company, made an additional investment of $40,000 in cash.
8. A firm paid $3,000 by check for office equipment that it had previously purchased on credit.

Analyze: Which transactions affect liability accounts?

Problem 3.2B
Objectives 3-1, 3-2

▶ **Using T accounts to record transactions involving assets, liabilities, and owner's equity.**

The following transactions took place at Aircraft Maintenance Company.

INSTRUCTIONS

For each transaction, set up T accounts from the following list: *Cash; Shop Equipment; Store Equipment; Truck; Accounts Payable; Shirley Cosby, Capital;* and *Shirley Cosby, Drawing.* Analyze each transaction. Record the effects of the transactions in the T accounts.

TRANSACTIONS

1. Shirley Cosby invested $40,000 cash in the business.
2. Purchased shop equipment for $3,600 in cash.
3. Bought store equipment for $2,400; payment is due in 30 days.
4. Purchased a used truck for $25,800 in cash.
5. Cosby gave the firm her personal tools that have a fair market value of $6,200.
6. Bought a used cash register for $2,850; payment is due in 30 days.
7. Paid $550 in cash to apply to the amount owed for store fixtures.
8. Cosby withdrew $3,250 in cash for personal expenses.

Analyze: Which transactions affect the *Cash* account?

Problem 3.3B
Objectives 3-1, 3-2, 3-4

▶ **Using T accounts to record transactions involving revenue and expenses.**

The following transactions took place at P and W Capital Investments.

INSTRUCTIONS

Analyze each of the transactions. For each transaction, decide what accounts are affected and set up T accounts. Record the effects of the transaction in the T accounts.

TRANSACTIONS

1. Paid $4,800 for the current month's rent.
2. Performed services for $9,000 in cash.
3. Paid salaries of $6,900.
4. Performed additional services for $12,500 on credit.
5. Paid $1,580 for the monthly telephone bill.
6. Collected $6,500 from accounts receivable.
7. Received a $297 refund for an overcharge on the telephone bill.
8. Performed services for $8,560 on credit.
9. Paid $950 in cash for the monthly electric bill.
10. Paid $875 in cash for gasoline purchased for the firm's van during the month.
11. Received $3,500 from charge account customers.
12. Performed services for $9,400 in cash.

Analyze: What total cash was collected for Accounts Receivable during the month?

Using T accounts to record all business transactions.

◀ **Problem 3.4B**
Objectives 3-1, 3-2, 3-4

The accounts and transactions of Brian Carter, Counselor and Attorney at Law, follow.

INSTRUCTIONS

Analyze the transactions. Record each in the appropriate T accounts. Use plus and minus signs in front of the amounts to show the increases and decreases. Identify each entry in the T accounts by writing the letter of the transaction next to the entry.

ASSETS
Cash
Accounts Receivable
Office Furniture
Office Equipment
Automobile

LIABILITIES
Accounts Payable

OWNER'S EQUITY
Brian Carter, Capital
Brian Carter, Drawing

REVENUE
Fees Income

EXPENSES
Automobile Expense
Rent Expense
Utilities Expense
Salaries Expense
Telephone Expense

TRANSACTIONS

a. Brian Carter invested $150,000 in cash to start the business.
b. Paid $8,500 for the current month's rent.
c. Bought a used automobile for the firm for $38,500 in cash.
d. Performed services for $21,500 in cash.

e. Paid $1,850 for automobile repairs.
f. Performed services for $12,800 on credit.
g. Purchased office chairs for $6,500 on credit.
h. Received $6,500 from credit clients.
i. Paid $4,200 to reduce the amount owed for the office chairs.
j. Issued a check for $1,610 to pay the monthly utility bill.
k. Purchased office equipment for $22,800 and paid half of this amount in cash immediately; the balance is due in 30 days.
l. Issued a check for $18,900 to pay salaries.
m. Performed services for $9,450 in cash.
n. Performed services for $6,500 on credit.
o. Paid $1,076 for the monthly telephone bill.
p. Collected $4,200 on accounts receivable from charge customers.
q. Purchased additional office equipment and received a bill for $6,880 due in 30 days.
r. Paid $900 in cash for gasoline purchased for the automobile during the month.
s. Brian Carter withdrew $8,000 in cash for personal expenses.

Analyze: What outstanding amount is owed to the company from its credit customers?

Problem 3.5B ▶ Preparing financial statements from T accounts.

Objectives 3-3, 3-5, 3-6

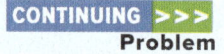

The accountant for the firm owned by Brian Carter prepares financial statements at the end of each month.

INSTRUCTIONS

Use the figures in the T accounts for Problem 3.4B to prepare a trial balance, an income statement, a statement of owner's equity, and a balance sheet. (The first line of the statement headings should read "Brian Carter, Counselor and Attorney at Law.") Assume that the transactions took place during the month ended April 30, 20X1. Determine the account balances before you start work on the financial statements.

Analyze: What net change in owner's equity occurred during the month of April?

Critical Thinking Problem 3.1

Financial Condition

At the beginning of the summer, Humphrey Nelson was looking for a way to earn money to pay for his college tuition in the fall. He decided to start a lawn service business in his neighborhood. To get the business started, Humphrey used $6,000 from his savings account to open a checking account for his new business, Elegant Lawn Care. He purchased two used power mowers and various lawn care tools for $2,000, and paid $3,600 for a used truck to transport the mowers.

Several of his neighbors hired him to cut their grass on a weekly basis. He sent these customers monthly bills. By the end of the summer, they had paid him $4,800 in cash and owed him another $2,400. Humphrey also cut grass on an as-needed basis for other neighbors, who paid him $4,000.

During the summer, Humphrey spent $800 for gasoline for the truck and mowers. He paid $4,000 to a friend who helped him on several occasions. An advertisement in the local paper cost $800. Now, at the end of the summer, Humphrey is concerned because he has only $3,600 left in his checking account. He says, "I worked hard all summer and have only $3,600 to show for it. It would have been better to leave the money in the bank."

Prepare an income statement, a statement of owner's equity (for the three month period ended August 31, 20X1), and a balance sheet (dated August 31, 20X1) for Elegant Lawn Care. Explain to Humphrey whether or not he is "better off" than he was at the beginning of the summer. (Hint: T accounts might be helpful in organizing the data.)

Critical Thinking Problem 3.2

Sole Proprietorship

Brenda Jo Smith is an architect who operates her own business. The accounts and transactions for the business follow.

INSTRUCTIONS

(1) Analyze the transactions for January 20X1. Record each in the appropriate T accounts. Identify each entry in the T account by writing the letter of the transaction next to the entry.

(2) Determine the account balances. Prepare a trial balance, an income statement, a statement of owner's equity, and a balance sheet for Brenda Jo Smith, Architect.

ASSETS
Cash
Accounts Receivable
Office Furniture
Office Equipment

LIABILITIES
Accounts Payable

OWNER'S EQUITY
Brenda Jo Smith, Capital
Brenda Jo Smith, Drawing

REVENUE
Fees Income

EXPENSES
Advertising Expense
Utilities Expense
Salaries Expense
Telephone Expense
Miscellaneous Expense

TRANSACTIONS

a. Brenda Jo Smith invested $20,000 in cash to start the business.
b. Paid $2,000 for advertisements in a design magazine.
c. Purchased office furniture for $2,300 in cash.
d. Performed services for $4,550 in cash.
e. Paid $210 for the monthly telephone bill.
f. Performed services for $2,130 on credit.
g. Purchased a fax machine for $325; paid $75 in cash, with the balance due in 30 days.
h. Paid a bill for $550 from the office cleaning service.
i. Received $1,560 from clients on account.
j. Purchased office chairs for $545; received credit terms of 30 days.
k. Paid $4,000 for salaries.
l. Issued a check for $225 in partial payment of the amount owed for office chairs.
m. Received $2,300 in cash for services performed.
n. Issued a check for $460 for utilities expense.
o. Performed services for $2,150 on credit.

p. Collected $900 from clients on account.

q. Brenda Jo Smith withdrew $2,500 in cash for personal expenses.

r. Paid $600 to Copy Quick for photocopy work performed during the month.

Analyze: Using the basic accounting equation, what is the financial condition of Brenda Jo Smith's business at month-end?

BUSINESS CONNECTIONS

Managerial FOCUS

Informed Decisions

1. In discussing a firm's latest financial statements, a manager says that it is the "results on the bottom line" that really count. What does the manager mean?
2. If a firm's expenses equal or exceed its revenue, what actions might management take?
3. How can management find out, at any time, whether a firm can pay its bills as they become due?
4. How do the income statement and the balance sheet help management make sound decisions?

Internal Control and FRAUD PREVENTION

Segregation of Duties for Effective Internal Control

Gloria's Fabrics is a large fabric provider to the general public. The accounting office has three employees: accounts receivable clerk, accounts payable clerk, and a bookkeeper who manages the accounting function in the company. The accounts receivable clerk creates the sales invoices and records the cash receipts. The accounts payable clerk creates and pays purchase orders. The bookkeeper manages the accounting function, supervises all accounting office employees, and reconciles the checking account. Review the separation of duties for each employee: the accounts receivable clerk, the accounts payable clerk, and the bookkeeper. Identify the accounts and describe the transactions that would be recorded by that assigned job. Evaluate the internal control and the potential for fraud at Gloria's Fabrics. How would you restructure the job responsibilities of each employee in order to strengthen the internal control of the firm?

Financial Statement ANALYSIS

Management Letter and Annual Report

Annual reports released by publicly held companies include a letter to the stockholders written by the chief executive officer, chairman of the board, or president.

Analyze Online: Locate the Adobe Systems, Inc., website (www.adobe.com). Within *Investor Relations* in the *About Adobe* link in the *Menu,* find the annual report for the current year. Read the letter to the stockholders within the annual report.

Analyze:

1. What types of information can a company's management deliver using the letter to stockholders?
2. What annual revenue did Adobe Systems, Inc., report for fiscal 2018?
3. What amount of cash, cash equivalents, and short-term investments did Adobe have on hand at the end of 2018?
4. Are the financial results presented in the current year more or less favorable than those presented for fiscal 2017?
5. How much in operating cash flows did Adobe generate during fiscal year 2017?

TEAMWORK

Specific Chart of Accounts

A chart of accounts varies with each type of business as well as each company. In a group, compare and contrast the accounts that would appear in Cole's Real Estate Office, Sarah's Clothing Emporium, Neal's Grocery Store, and Tanner Plumbing Service. What accounts would appear in all companies? What accounts would be specific to each business?

Answers to Comprehensive Self Review

1. A list of the numbers and names of the accounts of a business. It provides a system by which the accounts of the business can be easily identified and located.
2. Cash taken from the business by the owner to obtain funds for personal living expenses. Withdrawals are recorded in a special type of owner's equity account called a drawing account.
3. The asset, liability, and owner's ending capital balance.
4. Decreases in asset accounts are recorded on the credit side. Decreases in liability and owner's equity accounts are recorded on the debit side. A decrease in the owner's drawing account is recorded on the credit side.
5.
   - Check the math by adding the columns again.
   - Determine whether the account balances are in the correct columns.
   - Check the accounts to see whether the balances in the accounts were computed correctly.
   - Check the accuracy of transactions recorded during the period.

The General Journal and the General Ledger

Chapter 4

Mayskyphoto/Shutterstock

www.boeing.com

Boeing was founded by William Boeing in 1916 as Pacific Aero Products; the company's name was changed to Boeing a year later. In 1917, Boeing employed 28 people; today, Boeing employs more than 150,000 people in more than 65 countries. Boeing also utilizes the talents and skills of hundreds of thousands of individuals who work for Boeing suppliers worldwide including 1.3 million people at 13,600 U.S. companies.

With corporate headquarters in Chicago, Illinois, Boeing is among the world's largest aircraft manufacturers. Boeing is the fifth largest defense contractor in the world based of 2018 revenue and the largest aerospace exporter in the United States based on 2018 revenue. Boeing operates and is organized into four segments: Commercial Airplanes; Defense, Space, and Security; Global Services; and Boeing Capital. More than 10,000 Boeing-built commercial jetliners are in service worldwide, which is almost 50 percent of the world fleet. Furthermore, about 90 percent of the world's cargo is transported on Boeing planes.

Boeing derives its income from the sales of products and the sales of services. For the fiscal year ended December 31, 2018, Boeing reported total revenue of $101.1 billion on record commercial deliveries of airplanes. Boeing also reported net earnings of $10.5 billion for the year 2018. Operating cash flow increased to $15.3 billion with strong liquidity of $8.6 billion in cash and marketable securities. In fiscal year 2018, Boeing won 893 new orders, raising its total company backlog to $490 billion (equal to seven years of production at current rates). For the 2019 fiscal year, Boeing expects revenue to be between $101.5 and $111.5 billion, including commercial airplane deliveries between 810 and 815. Operating cash flow for 2019 is expected to be between $17.0 and $17.5 billion.

thinking critically
How do you think Boeing would record the purchase of new manufacturing equipment that will be used for several years?

LEARNING OBJECTIVES
4-1 Record transactions in the general journal.
4-2 Prepare compound journal entries.
4-3 Post journal entries to general ledger accounts.
4-4 Correct errors made in the journal or ledger.
4-5 Define the accounting terms new to this chapter.

NEW TERMS
accounting cycle
audit trail
balance ledger form
chronological order
compound entry
correcting entry
general journal
general ledger
journal
journalizing
ledger
posting

Section 1

SECTION OBJECTIVES	TERMS TO LEARN
>> 4-1 Record transactions in the general journal. **WHY IT'S IMPORTANT** Written records for all business transactions are necessary. The general journal acts as the "diary" of the business. >> 4-2 Prepare compound journal entries. **WHY IT'S IMPORTANT** Compound entries contain several debits or credits for a single business transaction, creating efficiencies in journalizing.	accounting cycle audit trail chronological order compound entry general journal journal journalizing

The General Journal

The **accounting cycle** is a series of steps performed during each accounting period to classify, record, and summarize data for a business and to produce needed financial information. The first step in the accounting cycle is to analyze business transactions. You learned this skill in Chapter 3. The second step in the accounting cycle is to prepare a record of business transactions.

Journals

Business transactions are recorded in a **journal,** which is a diary of business activities. The journal lists transactions in **chronological order,** that is, in the order in which they occur. The journal is sometimes called the *record of original entry* because it is where transactions are first entered in the accounting records. There are different types of journals. This chapter will examine the general journal. You will become familiar with other journals in later chapters.

> Most corporations use accounting software to record business transactions. Industry-specific software is available for accounting firms, oil and gas companies, construction firms, medical firms, and any other industry-specific business enterprise.

>> **4-1 OBJECTIVE**
Record transactions in the general journal.

important!

The Diary of a Business
The general journal is similar to a diary. The general journal details, in chronological order, the economic events of the business.

The General Journal

The **general journal** is a financial record for entering all types of business transactions. **Journalizing** is the process of recording transactions in the general journal.

Figure 4.1 shows the general journal for Eli's Consulting Services. Notice that the general journal has a page number. To record a transaction, enter the year at the top of the Date column. In the Date column, write the month and day on the first line of the first entry. After the first entry, enter the year and month only when a new page is started or when the year or the month changes. In the Date column, write the day of each transaction on the first line of each transaction.

In the Description column, enter the account to be debited. Write the account name close to the left margin of the Description column, and enter the amount on the same line in the Debit column.

Enter the account to be credited on the line beneath the debit. Indent the account name about one-half inch from the left margin. Enter the amount on the same line in the Credit column.

Then enter a complete but concise description of the transaction in the Description column. Begin the description on the line following the credit. The description is indented about one inch from the left margin.

Write account names exactly as they appear in the chart of accounts. This will minimize errors when amounts are transferred from the general journal to the accounts.

FIGURE 4.1

General Journal Entry

	GENERAL JOURNAL			PAGE 1	
DATE	DESCRIPTION	POST. REF.	DEBIT	CREDIT	
20X1					1
Nov. 6	Cash		100 000 00		2
	Trayton Eli, Capital			100 000 00	3
	Investment by owner				4
					5

- Record the year first, then the month and day.
- Record the debit first.
- Indent about one-half inch and record the credit.
- Indent again and write the description.

Leave a blank line between general journal entries. Some accountants use this blank line to number each general journal entry.

When possible, the journal entry description should refer to the source of the information. For example, the journal entry to record a payment should include the check number in the description. Document numbers are part of the audit trail. The **audit trail** is a chain of references that makes it possible to trace information, locate errors, and prevent fraud. The audit trail provides a means of checking the journal entry against the original data on the documents.

Recording November Transactions in the General Journal

In Chapters 2 and 3, you learned a step-by-step method for analyzing business transactions. In this chapter, you will learn how to complete the journal entry for a business transaction in the same manner. Review the following steps before you continue:

1. Analyze the financial event:
   - Identify the accounts affected.
   - Classify the accounts affected.
   - Determine the amount of increase or decrease for each account affected.
2. Apply the rules of debit and credit:
   a. Which account is debited? For what amount?
   b. Which account is credited? For what amount?
3. Make the entry in T-account form.
4. Record the complete entry in general journal form.

important!

Audit Trail
To maintain the audit trail, descriptions should refer to document numbers whenever possible.

BUSINESS TRANSACTION

On November 6, Trayton Eli withdrew $100,000 from personal savings and deposited it in a new business checking account for Eli's Consulting Services.

MEMORANDUM 01

TO: Sergio Sanchez
FROM: Trayton Eli
DATE: November 6, 20X1
SUBJECT: Contributed personal funds to the business

I contributed $100,000 from my personal savings to Eli's Consulting Services.

ANALYSIS

a. The asset account *Cash* is increased by $100,000.
a. The owner's equity account, *Trayton Eli, Capital,* is increased by $100,000.

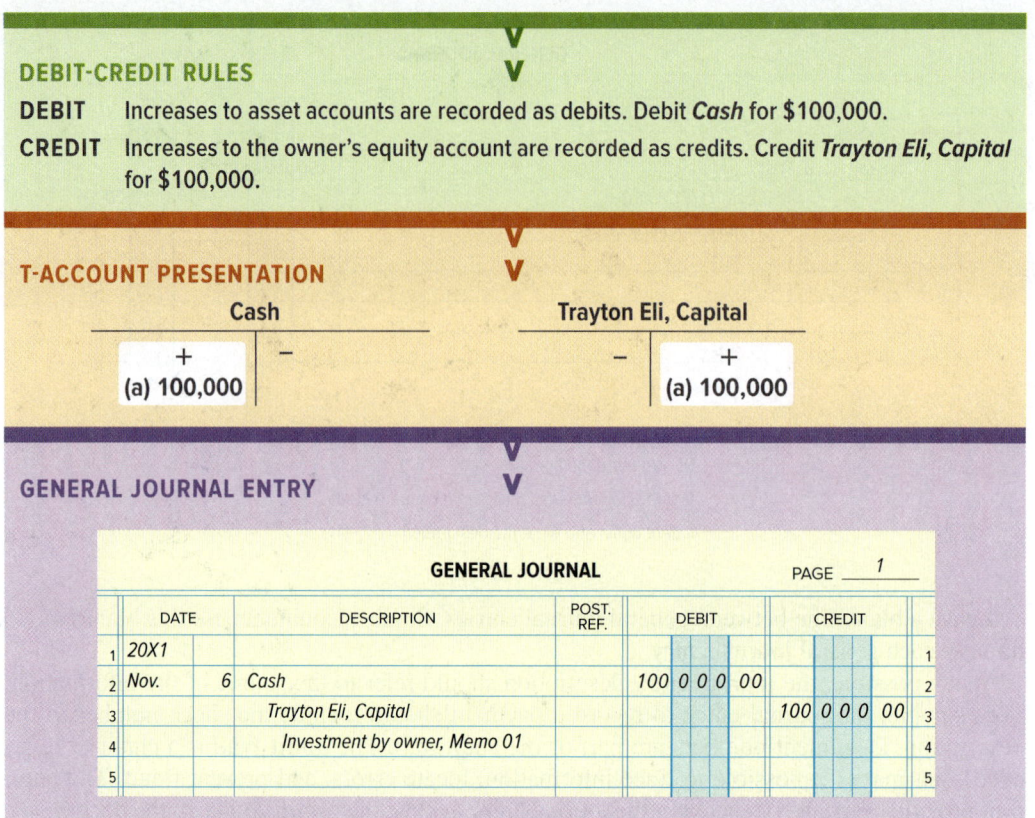

BUSINESS TRANSACTION

On November 7, Eli's Consulting Services issued Check 1001 for $5,000 to purchase a computer and other equipment.

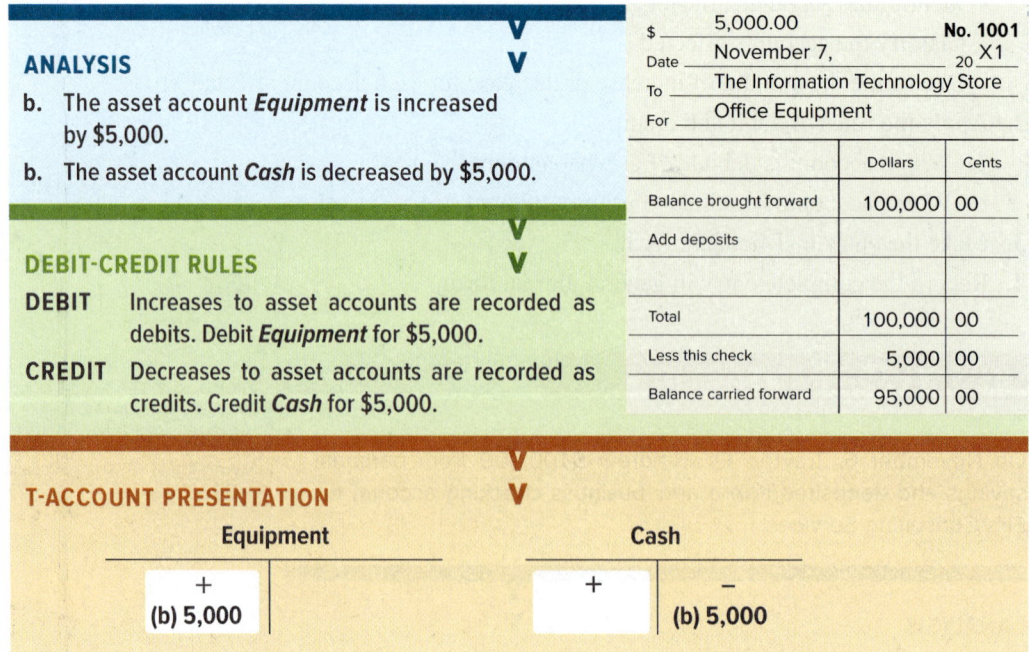

GENERAL JOURNAL ENTRY

	DATE	DESCRIPTION	POST. REF.	DEBIT	CREDIT	
6	Nov. 7	Equipment		5 0 0 0 00		6
7		Cash			5 0 0 0 00	7
8		Purchased equip., Check 1001				8

GENERAL JOURNAL — PAGE 1

The check number appears in the description and forms part of the audit trail for the transaction.

BUSINESS TRANSACTION

On November 10, Eli's Consulting Services purchased office equipment on account for $6,000.

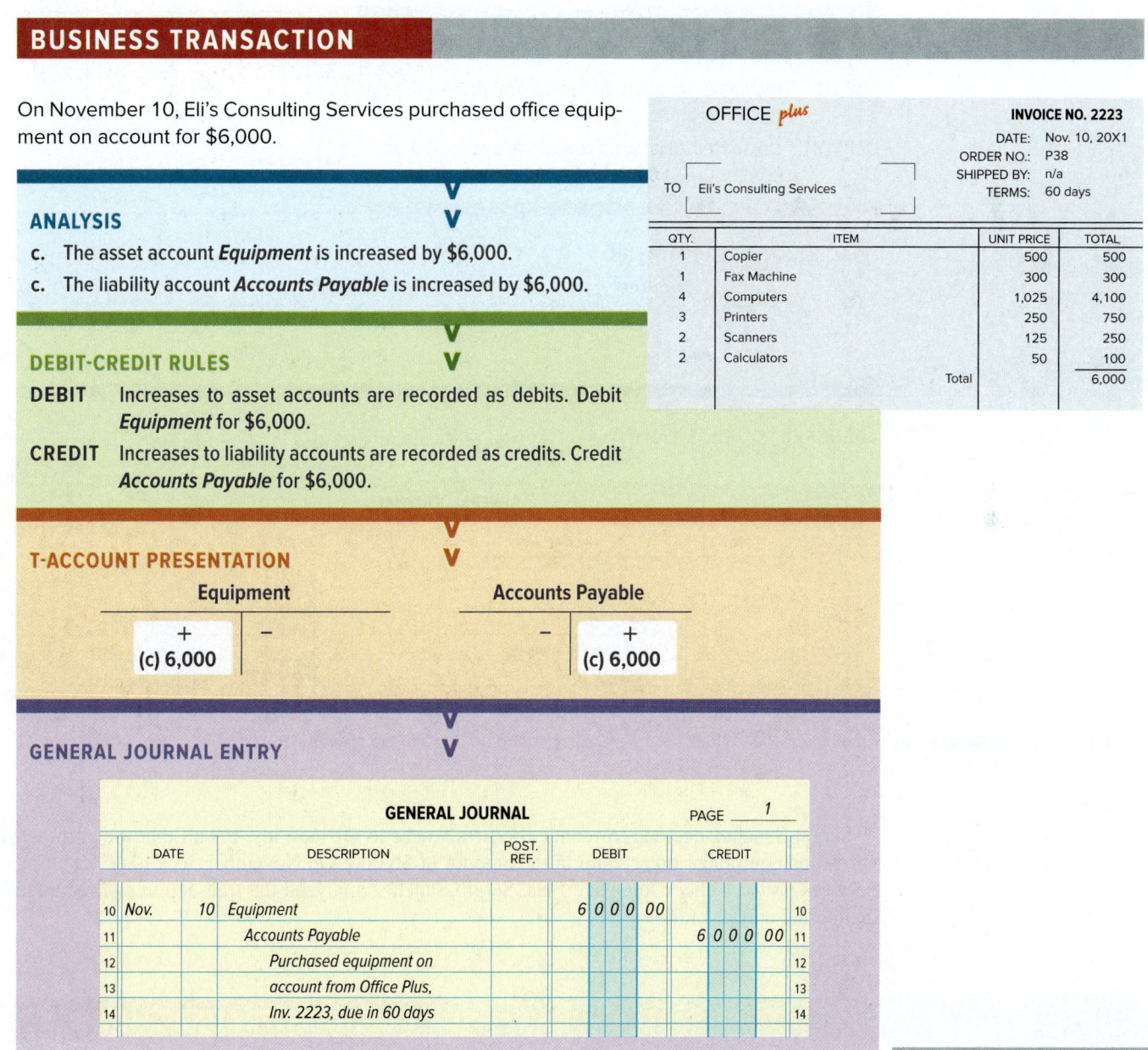

OFFICE *plus*

INVOICE NO. 2223
DATE: Nov. 10, 20X1
ORDER NO.: P38
SHIPPED BY: n/a
TERMS: 60 days

TO Eli's Consulting Services

QTY.	ITEM	UNIT PRICE	TOTAL
1	Copier	500	500
1	Fax Machine	300	300
4	Computers	1,025	4,100
3	Printers	250	750
2	Scanners	125	250
2	Calculators	50	100
		Total	6,000

ANALYSIS
c. The asset account **Equipment** is increased by $6,000.
c. The liability account **Accounts Payable** is increased by $6,000.

DEBIT-CREDIT RULES
DEBIT Increases to asset accounts are recorded as debits. Debit **Equipment** for $6,000.
CREDIT Increases to liability accounts are recorded as credits. Credit **Accounts Payable** for $6,000.

T-ACCOUNT PRESENTATION

Equipment		Accounts Payable	
+	−	−	+
(c) 6,000			(c) 6,000

GENERAL JOURNAL ENTRY

GENERAL JOURNAL — PAGE 1

	DATE	DESCRIPTION	POST. REF.	DEBIT	CREDIT	
10	Nov. 10	Equipment		6 0 0 0 00		10
11		Accounts Payable			6 0 0 0 00	11
12		Purchased equipment on				12
13		account from Office Plus,				13
14		Inv. 2223, due in 60 days				14

96 CHAPTER 4 The General Journal and the General Ledger

The supplier's name (Office Plus) and invoice number (2223) appear in the journal entry description and form part of the audit trail for the transaction. The journal entry can be checked against the data on the original document, Invoice 2223.

BUSINESS TRANSACTION

On November 28, Eli's Consulting Services purchased supplies for $1,500, Check 1002.

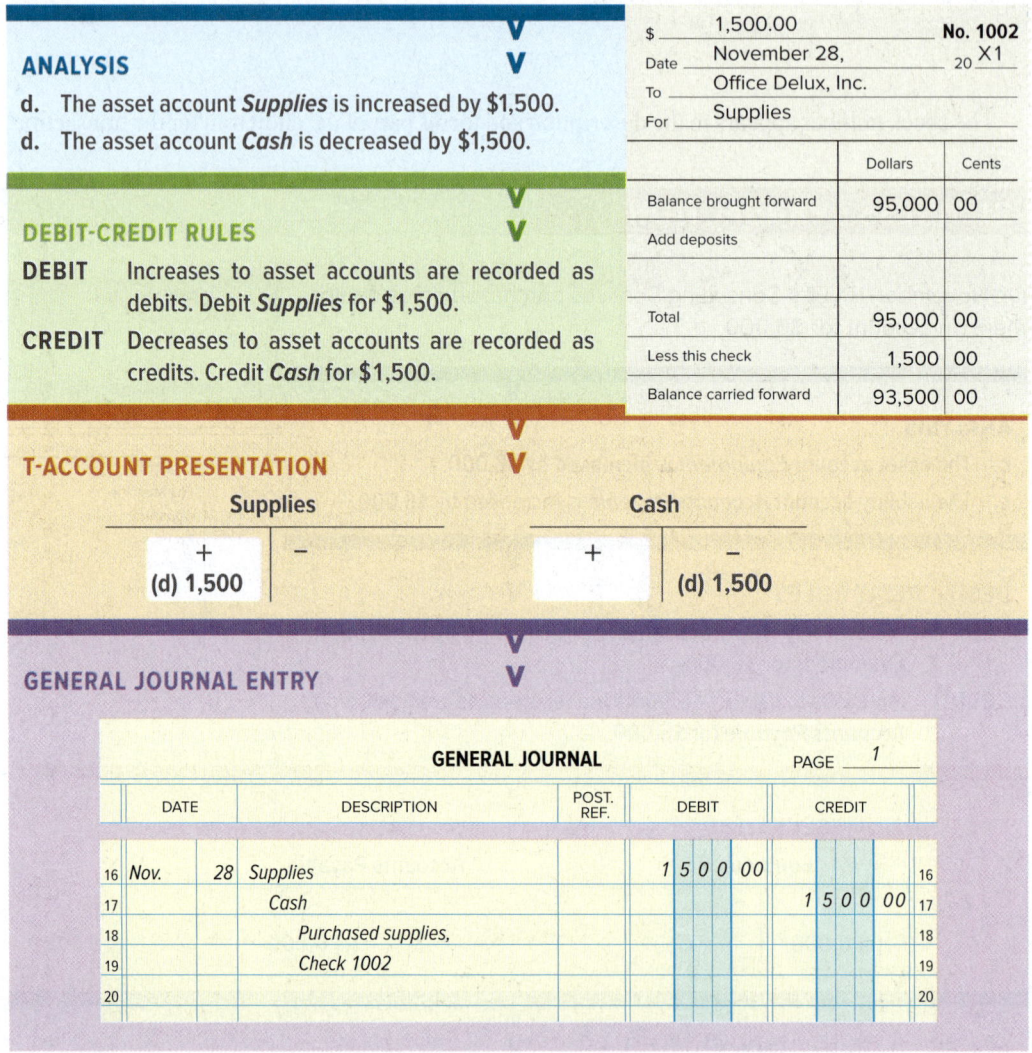

Sergio Sanchez decided to reduce the firm's debt to Office Plus. Recall that the firm had purchased equipment on account in the amount of $6,000. On November 30, Eli's Consulting Services issued a check to Office Plus. Sergio Sanchez analyzed the transaction and recorded the journal entry as follows.

BUSINESS TRANSACTION

On November 30, Eli's Consulting Services paid Office Plus $2,500 in partial payment of Invoice 2223, Check 1003.

ANALYSIS

e. The asset account **Cash** is decreased by $2,500.
e. The liability account **Accounts Payable** is decreased by $2,500.

DEBIT-CREDIT RULES

DEBIT Decreases to liability accounts are recorded as debits. Debit **Accounts Payable** for $2,500.

CREDIT Decreases to asset accounts are recorded as credits. Credit **Cash** for $2,500.

T-ACCOUNT PRESENTATION

Accounts Payable		Cash	
−	+	+	−
(e) 2,500			(e) 2,500

	2,500.00		No. 1003
$			
Date	November 30,		20 X1
To	Office Plus		
For	Payment on Account		

	Dollars	Cents
Balance brought forward	93,500	00
Add deposits		
Total	93,500	00
Less this check	2,500	00
Balance carried forward	91,000	00

GENERAL JOURNAL ENTRY

GENERAL JOURNAL PAGE 1

	DATE	DESCRIPTION	POST. REF.	DEBIT	CREDIT	
21	Nov. 30	Accounts Payable		2 5 0 0 00		21
22		Cash			2 5 0 0 00	22
23		Paid on account, Office Plus,				23
24		Invoice 2223, Check 1003				24

Notice that the general journal Description column includes three important items for the audit trail:

- the supplier name,
- the invoice number,
- the check number.

In the general journal, always enter debits before credits. This is the case even if the credit item is considered first when mentally analyzing the transaction.

Eli's Consulting Services issued a check in November to pay December and January rent in advance. Recall that the right to occupy facilities is considered a form of property. Sergio Sanchez analyzed the transaction and recorded the journal entry as follows.

BUSINESS TRANSACTION

On November 30, Eli's Consulting Services wrote Check 1004 for $8,000 to prepay rent for December and January.

	8,000.00		No. 1004
$			
Date	November 30,		20 X1
To	Davidson Properties		
For	Prepaid Rent		

	Dollars	Cents
Balance brought forward	91,000	00
Add deposits		
Total	91,000	00
Less this check	8,000	00
Balance carried forward	83,000	00

ANALYSIS

f. The asset account **Prepaid Rent** is increased by $8,000.
f. The asset account **Cash** is decreased by $8,000.

DEBIT-CREDIT RULES
DEBIT Increases to asset accounts are recorded as debits. Debit *Prepaid Rent* for $8,000.
CREDIT Decreases to asset accounts are recorded as credits. Credit *Cash* for $8,000.

T-ACCOUNT PRESENTATION

Prepaid Rent		Cash	
+	−	+	−
(f) 8,000			(f) 8,000

GENERAL JOURNAL ENTRY

GENERAL JOURNAL   PAGE 1

DATE	DESCRIPTION	POST. REF.	DEBIT	CREDIT
Nov. 30	Prepaid Rent		8 000 00	
	Cash			8 000 00
	Paid Dec. and Jan. rent			
	in advance; Check 1004			

Recording December Transactions in the General Journal

Eli's Consulting Services opened for business on December 1. Let's review the transactions that occurred in December. Refer to items **g** through **l** in Chapter 3 for the analysis of each transaction.

1. Performed services for $36,000 in cash.
2. Performed services for $11,000 on credit.
3. Received $6,000 in cash from credit clients on their accounts.
4. Paid $8,000 for salaries.
5. Paid $650 for a utility bill.
6. The owner withdrew $5,000 for personal expenses.

Figure 4.2 shows the entries in the general journal. In an actual business, transactions involving fees income and accounts receivable occur throughout the month and are recorded when they take place. For the sake of simplicity, these transactions are summarized and recorded as of December 31 for Eli's Consulting Services.

>> **4-2 OBJECTIVE**
Prepare compound journal entries

Preparing Compound Entries

So far, each journal entry consists of one debit and one credit. Some transactions require a **compound entry**—a journal entry that contains more than one debit or credit. In a compound entry, record all debits first, followed by the credits.

> When Allstate purchased an insurance division of CNA Financial Corporation, Allstate paid cash and issued a 10-year note payable (a promise to pay). Detailed accounting records are not available to the public, but a compound journal entry was probably used to record this transaction.

FIGURE 4.2

General Journal Entries for December

	GENERAL JOURNAL			PAGE 2
DATE	DESCRIPTION	POST. REF.	DEBIT	CREDIT
20X1				
Dec. 31	Cash		36 000 00	
	Fees Income			36 000 00
	Performed services for cash			
31	Accounts Receivable		11 000 00	
	Fees Income			11 000 00
	Performed services on credit			
31	Cash		6 000 00	
	Accounts Receivable			6 000 00
	Received cash from credit			
	clients on account			
31	Salaries Expense		8 000 00	
	Cash			8 000 00
	Paid monthly salaries to			
	employees, Checks			
	1005–1006			
31	Utilities Expense		650 00	
	Cash			650 00
	Paid monthly bill for utilities,			
	Check 1007			
31	Trayton Eli, Drawing		5 000 00	
	Cash			5 000 00
	Owner withdrew cash for			
	personal expenses,			
	Check 1008			

Suppose that on November 7, when Eli's Consulting Services purchased the equipment for $5,000, Trayton Eli paid $2,500 in cash and agreed to pay the balance in 30 days. This transaction is analyzed below.

BUSINESS TRANSACTION

On November 7, the firm purchased equipment for $5,000, issued Check 1001 for $2,500, and agreed to pay the balance in 30 days.

ANALYSIS

The asset account **Equipment** is increased by $5,000. The asset account **Cash** is decreased by $2,500. The liability account **Accounts Payable** is increased by $2,500.

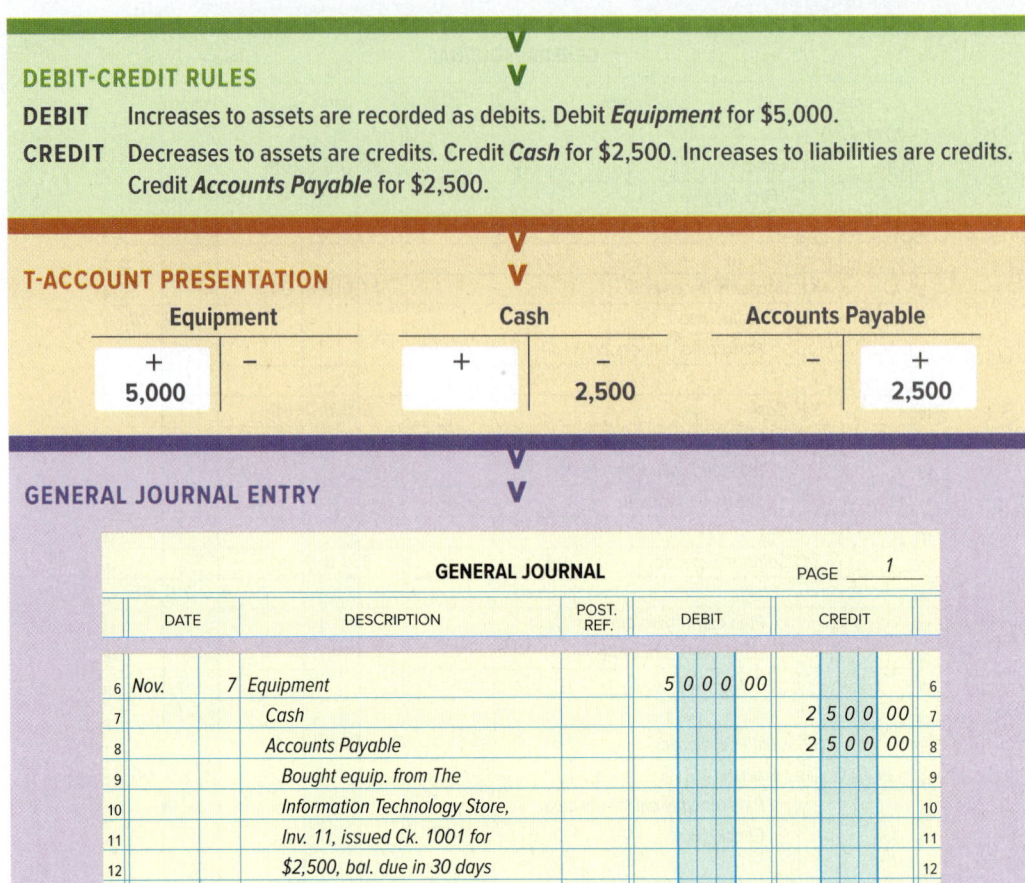

recall

Debits = Credits
No matter how many accounts are affected by a transaction, total debits must equal total credits.

Section 1 Review

1. The part of the journal entry to be recorded first is the:
   a. asset.
   b. credit.
   c. debit.
   d. liability.

2. A general journal is like a(n):
   a. address book.
   b. appointment calendar.
   c. diary.
   d. to-do list.

3. Checks and invoice numbers are included in the journal entry description to:
   a. validate the transaction.
   b. provide an audit trail.
   c. trace information through the accounting system.
   d. both b and c are correct.

4. The journal is referred to as the:
   a. record of final entry.
   b. record of original entry.
   c. record of permanent entry.
   d. record of temporary entry.

5. In a compound journal entry:
   a. if two accounts are debited, two accounts must be credited.
   b. if two accounts are debited, at least one account must be credited.
   c. total debits must equal total credits.
   d. Both b and c are correct.

6. Which of the reasons reflected below is the most accurate for including descriptions when making journal entries?
   a. The audit trail will be more difficult to follow.
   b. They eliminate the need for recording the transaction.
   c. They serve as a substitute for recording the transaction.
   d. The audit trail will be easier to follow.

Section 2

SECTION OBJECTIVES

>> **4-3** Post journal entries to general ledger accounts.
   WHY IT'S IMPORTANT
   The general ledger provides a permanent, classified record for a company's accounts.

>> **4-4** Correct errors made in the journal or ledger.
   WHY IT'S IMPORTANT
   Errors must be corrected to ensure a proper audit trail and to provide good information.

TERMS TO LEARN

balance ledger form
correcting entry
general ledger
ledger
posting

The General Ledger

You learned that a journal contains a chronological (day-by-day) record of a firm's transactions. Each journal entry shows the accounts and the amounts involved. Using the journal as a guide, you can enter transaction data in the accounts.

Ledgers

T accounts are used to analyze transactions quickly but are not used to maintain financial records. Instead, businesses keep account records on a special form that makes it possible to record all data efficiently. There is a separate form for each account. The account forms are kept in a book or binder called a **ledger.** The ledger is called the *record of final entry* because the ledger is the last place that accounting transactions are recorded.

The process of transferring data from the journal to the ledger is known as **posting.** Posting takes place after transactions are journalized. Posting is the third step of the accounting cycle.

The General Ledger

Every business has a general ledger. The **general ledger** is the master reference file for the accounting system. It provides a permanent, classified record of all accounts used in a firm's operations.

Ledger Account Forms

There are different types of general ledger account forms. Sergio Sanchez decided to use a balance ledger form. A **balance ledger form** shows the balance of the account after each entry is posted. Look at Figure 4.3. It shows the first general journal entry, the investment by the owner. It also shows the general ledger forms for **Cash** and **Trayton Eli, Capital.** On the ledger form, notice the:

- account name and number;
- columns for date, description, and posting reference (post. ref.);
- columns for debit, credit, balance debit, and balance credit.

important!

General Journal and General Ledger
The general journal is the record of *original* entry. The general ledger is the record of *final* entry.

FIGURE 4.3

Posting from the General Journal to the General Ledger

GENERAL JOURNAL   PAGE 1

DATE	DESCRIPTION	POST. REF.	DEBIT	CREDIT
20X1				
Nov. 6	Cash	101	100 000 00	
	Trayton Eli, Capital	301		100 000 00
	Investment by owner, Memo 01			

ACCOUNT Cash   **ACCOUNT NO.** 101

DATE	DESCRIPTION	POST. REF.	DEBIT	CREDIT	BALANCE DEBIT	BALANCE CREDIT
20X1						
Nov. 6		J1	100 000 00		100 000 00	

ACCOUNT Trayton Eli, Capital   **ACCOUNT NO.** 301

DATE	DESCRIPTION	POST. REF.	DEBIT	CREDIT	BALANCE DEBIT	BALANCE CREDIT
20X1						
Nov. 6		J1		100 000 00		100 000 00

ABOUT ACCOUNTING

Careers

How do you get to be the president of a large corporation in the United States? Probably by beginning your career as an accountant. More accountants have advanced to be presidents of large corporations than people with any other background.

>> 4-3 OBJECTIVE

Post journal entries to general ledger accounts.

recall

Normal Balance

The normal balance of an account is its increase side.

Posting to the General Ledger

Examine Figure 4.4. On November 7, Sergio Sanchez made a general journal entry to record the purchase of equipment. To post the data from the journal to the general ledger, Sanchez entered the debit amount in the Debit column in the *Equipment* account and the credit amount in the Credit column in the *Cash* account.

In the general journal, identify the first account listed. In Figure 4.4, *Equipment* is the first account. In the general ledger, find the ledger form for the first account listed. In Figure 4.4, this is the *Equipment* ledger form.

The steps to post from the general journal to the general ledger follow:

1. On the ledger form, enter the date of the transaction. Enter a description of the entry, if necessary. Usually routine entries do not require descriptions.
2. On the ledger form, enter the general journal page in the Posting Reference column. On the *Equipment* ledger form, the **J1** in the Posting Reference column indicates that the journal entry is recorded on page 1 of the general journal. The letter **J** refers to the general journal.
3. On the ledger form, enter the debit amount in the Debit column or the credit amount in the Credit column. In Figure 4.4 on the *Equipment* ledger form, $5,000 is entered in the Debit column.
4. On the ledger form, compute the balance and enter it in the Debit Balance column or the Credit Balance column. In Figure 4.4, the balance in the *Equipment* account is a $5,000 debit.
5. On the general journal, enter the ledger account number in the Posting Reference column. In Figure 4.4, the account number 141 is entered in the Posting Reference column next to "Equipment."

Repeat the process for the next account in the general journal. In Figure 4.4, Sanchez posted the credit amount from the general journal to the *Cash* ledger account. Notice on the *Cash* ledger form that he entered the credit of $5,000 and then computed the account balance. After the transaction is posted, the balance of the *Cash* account is $95,000.

Be sure to enter the numbers in the Posting Reference columns. This indicates that the entry was posted and ensures against posting the same entry twice. Posting references are part of the audit trail. They allow a transaction to be traced from the ledger to the journal entry, and then to the source document.

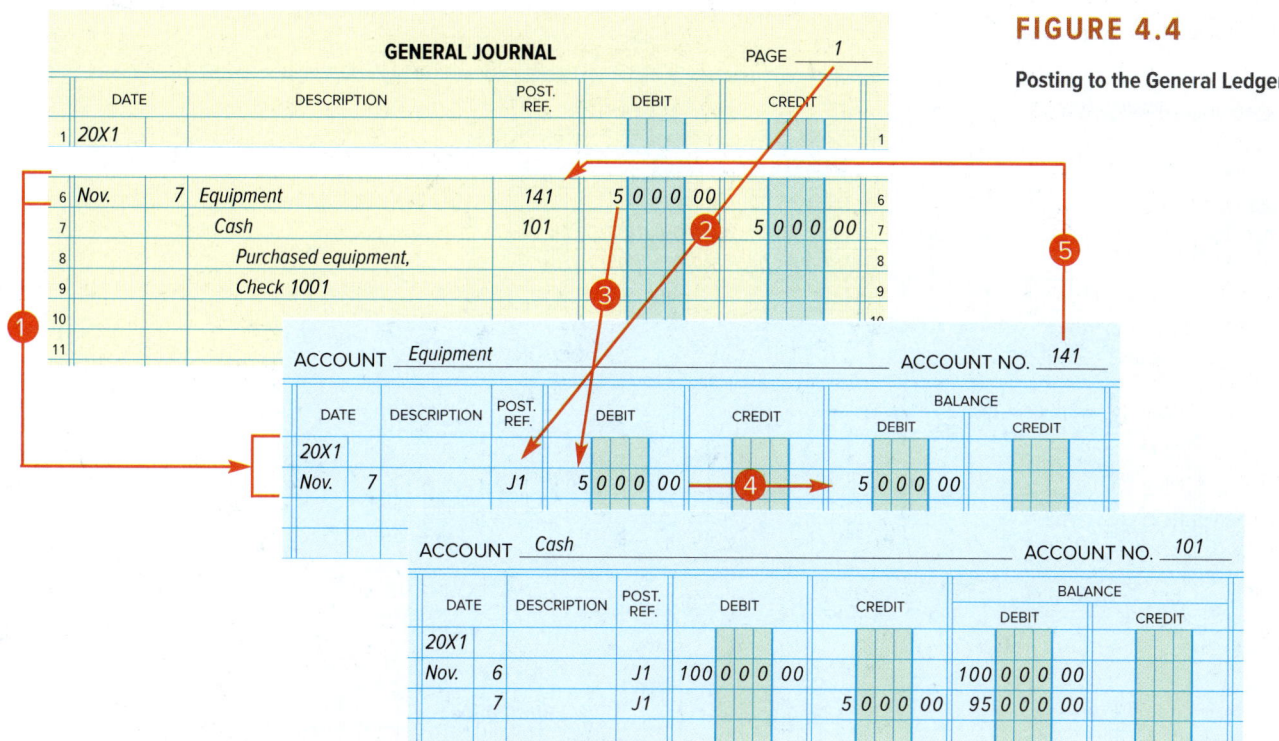

FIGURE 4.4

Posting to the General Ledger

Figure 4.5 shows the general ledger after all the entries for November and December are posted.

Each ledger account provides a complete record of the increases and decreases to that account. The balance ledger form also shows the current balance for the account.

In the general ledger accounts, the balance sheet accounts appear first and are followed by the income statement accounts. The order is:

- assets
- liabilities
- owner's equity
- revenue
- expenses

This arrangement speeds the preparation of the trial balance and the financial statements.

FIGURE 4.5

Posted General Ledger Accounts

ACCOUNT: Cash   ACCOUNT NO. 101

DATE		DESCRIPTION	POST. REF.	DEBIT	CREDIT	BALANCE DEBIT	BALANCE CREDIT
20X1							
Nov.	6		J1	100 000 00		100 000 00	
	7		J1		5 000 00	95 000 00	
	28		J1		1 500 00	93 500 00	
	30		J1		2 500 00	91 000 00	
	30		J1		8 000 00	83 000 00	
Dec.	31		J2	36 000 00		119 000 00	
	31		J2	6 000 00		125 000 00	
	31		J2		8 000 00	117 000 00	
	31		J2		650 00	116 350 00	
	31		J2		5 000 00	111 350 00	

(continued)

FIGURE 4.5 (continued)

ACCOUNT Accounts Receivable **ACCOUNT NO.** 111

DATE	DESCRIPTION	POST. REF.	DEBIT	CREDIT	BALANCE DEBIT	BALANCE CREDIT
20X1						
Dec. 31		J2	11 000 00		11 000 00	
31		J2		6 000 00	5 000 00	

ACCOUNT Supplies **ACCOUNT NO.** 121

DATE	DESCRIPTION	POST. REF.	DEBIT	CREDIT	BALANCE DEBIT	BALANCE CREDIT
20X1						
Nov. 28		J1	1 500 00		1 500 00	

ACCOUNT Prepaid Rent **ACCOUNT NO.** 137

DATE	DESCRIPTION	POST. REF.	DEBIT	CREDIT	BALANCE DEBIT	BALANCE CREDIT
20X1						
Nov. 30		J1	8 000 00		8 000 00	

ACCOUNT Equipment **ACCOUNT NO.** 141

DATE	DESCRIPTION	POST. REF.	DEBIT	CREDIT	BALANCE DEBIT	BALANCE CREDIT
20X1						
Nov. 7		J1	5 000 00		5 000 00	
10		J1	6 000 00		11 000 00	

ACCOUNT Accounts Payable **ACCOUNT NO.** 202

DATE	DESCRIPTION	POST. REF.	DEBIT	CREDIT	BALANCE DEBIT	BALANCE CREDIT
20X1						
Nov. 10		J1		6 000 00		6 000 00
30		J1	2 500 00			3 500 00

ACCOUNT Trayton Eli, Capital **ACCOUNT NO.** 301

DATE	DESCRIPTION	POST. REF.	DEBIT	CREDIT	BALANCE DEBIT	BALANCE CREDIT
20X1						
Nov. 6		J1		100 000 00		100 000 00

ACCOUNT Trayton Eli, Drawing **ACCOUNT NO.** 302

DATE	DESCRIPTION	POST. REF.	DEBIT	CREDIT	BALANCE DEBIT	BALANCE CREDIT
20X1						
Dec. 31		J2	5 000 00		5 000 00	

(continued)

FIGURE 4.5 (continued)

ACCOUNT	Fees Income				ACCOUNT NO.	401	
DATE	DESCRIPTION	POST. REF.	DEBIT	CREDIT	BALANCE DEBIT	BALANCE CREDIT	
20X1							
Dec. 31		J2		36 000 00		36 000 00	
31		J2		11 000 00		47 000 00	

ACCOUNT	Salaries Expense				ACCOUNT NO.	511	
DATE	DESCRIPTION	POST. REF.	DEBIT	CREDIT	BALANCE DEBIT	BALANCE CREDIT	
20X1							
Dec. 31		J2	8 000 00		8 000 00		

ACCOUNT	Utilities Expense				ACCOUNT NO.	514	
DATE	DESCRIPTION	POST. REF.	DEBIT	CREDIT	BALANCE DEBIT	BALANCE CREDIT	
20X1							
Dec. 31		J2	650 00		650 00		

Correcting Journal and Ledger Errors

Entries in the general journal and posting to the general ledger are made using accounting software that will not journalize or post entries that do not balance. However, this does not prevent entries to or posting of incorrect amounts or to incorrect accounts. For example, an entry may be made to credit cash when the items were purchased on account (accounts payable) or an entry may be journalized or posted to supplies when the correct account may be equipment. When errors are made in accounting records, they should be adjusted by making a **correcting entry,** a journal entry made to correct the erroneous entry. A correcting entry reflects the reality of the transaction that occurred.

>> **4-4 OBJECTIVE**
Correct errors made in the journal or ledger.

recall

Order of Accounts
The general ledger lists accounts in the same order as they appear on the trial balance: assets, liabilities, owner's equity, revenue, and expenses.

MANAGERIAL IMPLICATIONS <<

ACCOUNTING SYSTEMS

- Business managers should be sure that their firms have efficient procedures for recording transactions.
- A well-designed accounting system allows timely and accurate posting of data to the ledger accounts.
- The information that appears in the financial statements is taken from the general ledger.
- Since management uses financial information for decision making, it is essential that the financial statements be prepared quickly at the end of each period and that they contain the correct amounts.

- The promptness and accuracy of the statements depend on the efficiency of the recording process.
- A well-designed accounting system has a strong audit trail.
- Every business should be able to trace amounts through the accounting records and back to the documents where the transactions were first recorded.

THINKING CRITICALLY

What are the consequences of not having a good audit trail?

Let's look at an example. On September 1, an automobile repair shop purchased some shop equipment for $18,000 in cash. By mistake, the journal entry debited the *Office Equipment* account rather than the *Shop Equipment* account, as follows.

	GENERAL JOURNAL			PAGE 16
DATE	DESCRIPTION	POST. REF.	DEBIT	CREDIT
20X1				
Sept. 1	Office Equipment	141	18 000 00	
	Cash	101		18 000 00
	Purchased equipment,			
	Check 1104			

To correct the error, a correcting journal entry was prepared and posted. The correcting entry debits *Shop Equipment* and credits *Office Equipment* for $18,000. This entry transfers $18,000 out of the *Office Equipment* account and into the *Shop Equipment* account.

	GENERAL JOURNAL			PAGE 28
DATE	DESCRIPTION	POST. REF.	DEBIT	CREDIT
20X1				
Oct. 1	Shop Equipment	151	18 000 00	
	Office Equipment	141		18 000 00
	To correct error made on			
	Sept. 1 when a purchase			
	of shop equipment was			
	recorded as office			
	equipment			

Section 2 Review

1. Posting references are made in ledger accounts and in the journal to:
   a. indicate the entry has been posted.
   b. ensure against posting the same information twice.
   c. Both a and b are correct.
   d. Neither a nor b is correct.

2. If a journal entry that contains an error has been posted, erase the entry and change the posting in the ledger accounts.
   a. True
   b. False

3. Once an incorrect journal entry has been posted, the incorrect amounts remain in the general ledger accounts.
   a. True
   b. False

4. What is entered in the Posting Reference column of the general journal?
   a. the ledger account number
   b. the date of the transaction
   c. the amount of the transaction
   d. a description of the transaction

5. **The general journal organizes accounting information in:**
   a. account order.
   b. alphabetical order.
   c. date order.
   d. chronological order.
6. **The general ledger organizes accounting information in:**
   a. account order.
   b. alphabetical order.
   c. date order.
   d. chronological order.
7. **The second step in the accounting cycle is to:**
   a. provide a description of the transaction.
   b. analyze the transaction.
   c. journalize the transaction.
   d. post the transaction.

Chapter 4 REVIEW — Chapter Summary

In this chapter, you have studied the method for journalizing business transactions in the records of a company. The details of each transaction are then posted to the general ledger. A well-designed accounting system provides for prompt and accurate journalizing and posting of all transactions.

Learning Objectives

4-1 Record transactions in the general journal.

- Recording transactions in a journal is called journalizing, the second step in the accounting cycle.
    - A journal is a daily record of transactions.
    - A written analysis of each transaction is contained in a journal.
- The general journal is widely used in business. It can accommodate all kinds of business transactions. Use the following steps to record a transaction in the general journal:
    - Number each page in the general journal. The page number will be used as a posting reference.
    - Enter the year at the top of the Date column. After that, enter the year only when a new page is started or when the year changes.
    - Enter the month and day in the Date column of the first line of the first entry. After that, enter the month only when a new page is started or when the month changes. Always enter the day on the first line of a new entry.
    - Enter the name of the account to be debited in the Description column.
    - Enter the amount to be debited in the Debit column.
    - Enter the name of the account to be credited on the next line. Indent the account name about one-half inch.
    - Enter the amount to be credited in the Credit column.
    - Enter a complete but concise description on the next line. Indent the description about one inch.
- Note that the debit portion is always recorded first.
- If possible, include source document numbers in descriptions in order to create an audit trail.

4-2 Prepare compound journal entries.

A transaction might require a journal entry that contains several debits or credits. All debits are recorded first, followed by the credits.

4-3 Post journal entries to general ledger accounts.

- Posting to the general ledger is the third step in the accounting cycle. Posting is the transfer of data from journal entries to ledger accounts.
- The individual accounts together form a ledger. All the accounts needed to prepare financial statements are found in the general ledger.
- Use the following steps to post a transaction.
    - On the ledger form:
        1. Enter the date of the transaction. Enter the description, if necessary.
        2. Enter the posting reference in the Posting Reference column. When posting from the general journal, use the letter **J** followed by the general journal page number.
        3. Enter the amount in either the Debit column or the Credit column.
        4. Compute the new balance and enter it in either the Debit Balance column or the Credit Balance column.
    - On the general journal:
        5. Enter the ledger account number in the Posting Reference column.
- To summarize the steps of the accounting cycle discussed so far:
    1. Analyze transactions.
    2. Journalize transactions.
    3. Post transactions.

4-4 Correct errors made in the journal or ledger.

To ensure honesty and to provide a clear audit trail, erasures are not permitted in a journal. A correcting entry is journalized and posted to correct a previous mistake. Posting references in the journal and the ledger accounts cross reference the entries and form another part of the audit trail. They make it possible to trace or recheck any transaction.

4-5 Define the accounting terms new to this chapter.

Glossary

Accounting cycle (p. 92) A series of steps performed during each accounting period to classify, record, and summarize data for a business and to produce needed financial information

Audit trail (p. 93) A chain of references that makes it possible to trace information, locate errors, and prevent fraud

Balance ledger form (p. 101) A ledger account form that shows the balance of the account after each entry is posted

Chronological order (p. 92) Organized in the order in which the events occur

Compound entry (p. 98) A journal entry with more than one debit or credit

Correcting entry (p. 105) A journal entry made to correct an erroneous entry

General journal (p. 92) A financial record for entering all types of business transactions; a record of original entry

General ledger (p. 101) A permanent, classified record of all accounts used in a firm's operation; a record of final entry

Journal (p. 92) The record of original entry

Journalizing (p. 92) Recording transactions in a journal

Ledger (p. 101) The record of final entry

Posting (p. 101) Transferring data from a journal to a ledger

Comprehensive Self Review

1. What is recorded in the Posting Reference column of a general journal?
2. Why is the ledger called the "record of final entry"?
3. How do you correct an incorrect journal entry that has not been posted?
4. Give examples of items that might appear in an audit trail.
5. Which of the following shows both the debits and credits of the entire transaction?
    a. An entry in the general journal
    b. A posting to a general ledger account

(Answers to Comprehensive Self Review are at the end of the chapter.)

Discussion Questions

1. What is the purpose of a journal?
2. In what order are accounts arranged in the general ledger? Why?
3. What is a ledger?
4. What is posting?
5. What are posting references? Why are they used?
6. What is the accounting cycle?
7. What is a compound journal entry?
8. What is the value of having a description for each general journal entry?
9. What procedure is used to record an entry in the general journal?
10. How should corrections be made in the general journal?
11. What is an audit trail? Why is it desirable to have an audit trail?

APPLICATIONS

Exercises

Exercise 4.1
Objective 4-1

▶ **Analyzing transactions.**

Selected accounts from the general ledger of the Escobedo Shipping Service follow. Analyze the following transactions and indicate by number what accounts should be debited and credited for each transaction.

    101 Cash
    111 Accounts Receivable
    121 Supplies
    131 Equipment
    202 Accounts Payable
    301 Rosa Escobedo, Capital
    401 Fees Income
    511 Rent Expense
    514 Salaries Expense
    517 Utilities Expense

TRANSACTIONS

1. Gave a cash refund of $875 to a customer because of a lost package. (The customer had previously paid in cash.)
2. Sent a check for $1,250 to the utility company to pay the monthly bill.
3. Provided services for $8,700 on credit.
4. Purchased new equipment for $6,400 and paid for it immediately by check.
5. Issued a check for $5,300 to pay a creditor on account.
6. Performed services for $16,775 in cash.
7. Collected $6,250 from credit customers.
8. The owner made an additional investment of $25,000 in cash.
9. Purchased supplies for $2,350 on credit.
10. Issued a check for $3,750 to pay the monthly rent.

Exercise 4.2
Objective 4-1

▶ **Recording transactions in the general journal.**

Selected accounts from the general ledger of Martin Consulting Services follow. Record the general journal entries that would be made to record the following transactions. Be sure to include dates and descriptions in these entries.

    101 Cash
    111 Accounts Receivable
    121 Supplies
    137 Prepaid Rent
    139 Automobile
    141 Equipment
    202 Accounts Payable
    301 Marcus Martin, Capital
    302 Marcus Martin, Drawing
    401 Fees Income
    511 Rent Expense
    514 Salaries Expense
    517 Telephone Expense

DATE	TRANSACTIONS
20X1	
Sept. 1	Marcus Martin invested $40,000 in cash to start the firm.
4	Purchased office equipment for $4,350 on credit from Zappo, Inc.; received Invoice 8925, payable in 30 days.
16	Purchased an automobile that will be used to visit clients; issued Check 1001 for $28,000 in full payment.
20	Purchased supplies for $550; paid immediately with Check 1002.
23	Returned damaged supplies for a cash refund of $105.
30	Issued Check 1003 for $2,100 to Zappo, Inc., as payment on account for Invoice 8925.
30	Withdrew $3,000 in cash for personal expenses.
30	Issued Check 1004 for $4,500 to pay the rent for October.
30	Performed services for $11,325 in cash.
30	Paid $480 for monthly telephone bill, Check 1005.

Posting to the general ledger.

Post the journal entries that you prepared for Exercise 4.2 to the general ledger. Use the account names shown in Exercise 4.2.

◀ **Exercise 4.3**
Objectives 4-1, 4-3
CONTINUING >>>
Problem

Compound journal entries.

The following transactions took place at the Pimental Employment Agency during November 20X1. Record the general journal entries that would be made for these transactions. Use a compound entry for each transaction.

◀ **Exercise 4.4**
Objective 4-2

DATE	TRANSACTIONS
Nov. 5	Performed services for Executive Job Search, Inc., for $30,000; received $12,500 in cash and the client promised to pay the balance in 60 days.
18	Purchased equipment for $550 and some supplies for $750 from Office Supply; issued Check 1008 for the total.
23	Received Invoice 1890 for $4,350 from Automotive Technicians Repair for repairs to the firm's automobile; issued Check 1009 for half the amount and arranged to pay the other half in 30 days.

Recording a correcting entry.

On June 10, 20X1, an employee of Williams Corporation mistakenly debited *Telephone Expense* rather than *Utilities Expense* when recording a bill of $2,000 for the May utility service. The error was discovered on June 30. Prepare a general journal entry to correct the error.

◀ **Exercise 4.5**
Objective 4-4

Recording a correcting entry.

On August 22, 20X1, an employee of Bell Company mistakenly debited the *Truck Expense* account rather than the *Repair Expense* account when recording a bill of $1,025 for repairs. The error was discovered on October 1. Prepare a general journal entry to correct the error.

◀ **Exercise 4.6**
Objective 4-4

PROBLEMS

Problem Set A

Problem 4.1A
Objective 4-1

▶ **Recording transactions in the general journal.**

The transactions that follow took place at the Cedar Hill Recreation and Sports Arena during September 20X1. This firm has indoor courts where customers can play tennis for a fee. It also rents equipment and offers tennis lessons.

INSTRUCTIONS

Record each transaction in the general journal, using the following chart of accounts. Be sure to number the journal page 1 and to write the year at the top of the Date column. Include a description for each entry.

ASSETS
101 Cash
111 Accounts Receivable
121 Supplies
134 Prepaid Rent
141 Equipment

LIABILITIES
202 Accounts Payable

OWNER'S EQUITY
301 Terry Pohlen, Capital
302 Terry Pohlen, Drawing

REVENUE
401 Fees Income

EXPENSES
511 Equipment Repair Expense
512 Rent Expense
513 Salaries Expense
514 Telephone Expense
517 Utilities Expense

DATE		TRANSACTIONS
Sept.	1	Issued Check 1169 for $3,000 to pay the September rent.
	5	Performed services for $8,000 in cash.
	6	Performed services for $5,900 on credit.
	10	Paid $1,150 for monthly telephone bill; issued Check 1170.
	11	Paid for equipment repairs of $1,250 with Check 1171.
	12	Received $2,500 on account from credit clients.
	15	Issued Checks 1172–1177 for $6,200 for salaries.
	18	Issued Check 1178 for $2,965 to purchase supplies.
	19	Purchased new tennis rackets for $5,250 on credit from The Tennis Supply Shop; received Invoice 3108, payable in 30 days.
	20	Issued Check 1179 for $4,820 to purchase new nets. (Equip.)
	21	Received $1,500 on account from credit clients.
	21	Returned a damaged net and received a cash refund of $1,140.
	22	Performed services for $4,450 in cash.
	23	Performed services for $7,050 on credit.
	26	Issued Check 1180 for $975 to purchase supplies.
	28	Paid the monthly electric bill of $1,875 with Check 1181.
	30	Issued Checks 1182–1187 for $6,200 for salaries.
	30	Issued Check 1188 for $7,500 cash to Terry Pohlen for personal expenses.

Analyze: If the company paid a bill for supplies on October 1, what check number would be included in the journal entry description?

Journalizing and posting transactions.

On October 1, 20X1, Helen Kennedy opened an advertising agency. She plans to use the chart of accounts listed below.

Problem 4.2A

Objectives 4-1, 4-2, 4-3

INSTRUCTIONS

1. Journalize the transactions. Number the journal page 1, write the year at the top of the Date column, and include a description for each entry.
2. Post to the ledger accounts. Before you start the posting process, open accounts by entering account names and numbers in the headings. Follow the order of the accounts in the chart of accounts.

ASSETS
101 Cash
111 Accounts Receivable
121 Supplies
141 Office Equipment
151 Art Equipment

LIABILITIES
202 Accounts Payable

OWNER'S EQUITY
301 Helen Kennedy, Capital
302 Helen Kennedy, Drawing

REVENUE
401 Fees Income

EXPENSES
511 Office Cleaning Expense
514 Rent Expense
517 Salaries Expense
520 Telephone Expense
523 Utilities Expense

DATE		TRANSACTIONS
Oct.	1	Helen Kennedy invested $70,000 cash in the business.
	2	Paid October office rent of $4,000; issued Check 1001.
	5	Purchased desks and other office furniture for $18,000 from Office Furniture Mart, Inc.; received Invoice 6704 payable in 60 days.
	6	Issued Check 1002 for $4,100 to purchase art equipment.
	7	Purchased supplies for $1,670; paid with Check 1003.
	10	Issued Check 1004 for $800 for office cleaning service.
	12	Performed services for $4,200 in cash and $1,800 on credit. (Use a compound entry.)
	15	Returned damaged supplies for a cash refund of $300.
	18	Purchased a computer for $3,000 from Office Furniture Mart, Inc., Invoice 7108; issued Check 1005 for a $1,750 down payment, with the balance payable in 30 days. (Use one compound entry.)
	20	Issued Check 1006 for $9,500 to Office Furniture Mart, Inc., as payment on account for Invoice 6704.
	26	Performed services for $4,800 on credit.
	27	Paid $375 for monthly telephone bill; issued Check 1007.
	30	Received $4,200 in cash from credit customers.
	30	Issued Check 1008 to pay the monthly utility bill of $1,080.
	30	Issued Checks 1009–1011 for $9,000 for salaries.

Analyze: What is the balance of account 202 in the general ledger?

Problem 4.3A
Objective 4-4

Recording correcting entries.

The following journal entries were prepared by an employee of International Marketing Company who does not have an adequate knowledge of accounting.

INSTRUCTIONS

Examine the journal entries carefully to locate the errors. Prepare journal entries to correct the errors. Assume that **Office Equipment** and **Office Supplies** were recorded at the correct values. However, the items were paid for entirely in cash, not on credit. Assume the errors are found and corrected on the last day of the month.

GENERAL JOURNAL PAGE 3

DATE		DESCRIPTION	POST. REF.	DEBIT	CREDIT
20X1					
April	1	Accounts Payable		15 800 00	
		Fees Income			15 800 00
		Performed services on credit			
	2	Cash		600 00	
		Telephone Expense			600 00
		Paid for March telephone			
		service, Check 1917			
	3	Office Equipment		8 200 00	
		Office Supplies		900 00	
		Accounts Payable			9 100 00
		Purchased file cabinet and			
		office supplies, Check 1918			

Analyze: After the correcting journal entries have been posted, what effect do the correcting entries have on the company's reported assets?

Journalizing and posting transactions.

◀ **Problem 4.4A**
Objectives 4-1, 4-2, 4-3

Four transactions for Airline Maintenance and Repair Shop that took place in November 20X1 appear below, along with the general ledger accounts used by the company.

INSTRUCTIONS

Record the transactions in the general journal and post them to the appropriate ledger accounts. Be sure to number the journal page 1 and to write the year at the top of the Date column.

Cash	101	Equipment	151
Accounts Receivable	111	Accounts Payable	202
Office Supplies	121	Edith Porras, Capital	301
Tools	131	Fees Income	401
Machinery	141		

DATE		TRANSACTIONS
Nov.	1	Edith Porras invested $75,000 in cash plus tools with a fair market value of $15,000 to start the business.
	2	Purchased equipment for $13,500 and supplies for $1,700 from Airline Equipment Company, Invoice 551; issued Check 100 for $5,500 as a down payment with the balance due in 30 days.
	10	Performed services for Worldwide Airlines for $33,200, which paid $15,800 in cash with the balance due in 30 days.
	20	Purchased machinery for $8,000 from Craft Machinery, Inc., Invoice 779; issued Check 101 for $1,500 in cash as a down payment with the balance due in 30 days.

Analyze: What liabilities does the business owe as of November 30?

Problem Set B

Problem 4.1B
Objective 4-1

▶ **Recording transactions in the general journal.**

The transactions listed below took place at Prasad Building Cleaning Service during September 20X1. This firm cleans commercial buildings for a fee.

INSTRUCTIONS

Analyze and record each transaction in the general journal. Choose the account names from the chart of accounts shown below. Be sure to number the journal page 1 and to write the year at the top of the Date column. Include a description for each entry.

ASSETS
101 Cash
111 Accounts Receivable
121 Cleaning Supplies
131 Office Supplies
134 Prepaid Rent
141 Equipment

LIABILITIES
202 Accounts Payable

OWNER'S EQUITY
301 Victor Prasad, Capital
302 Victor Prasad, Drawing

REVENUE
401 Fees Income

EXPENSES
511 Equipment Repair Expense
514 Salaries Expense
521 Telephone Expense
524 Utilities Expense

DATE		TRANSACTIONS
Sept.	1	Victor Prasad invested $75,000 in cash to start the business.
	1	Issued Check 1000 for $4,000 to pay the September rent.
	2	Purchased used equipment for $22,000 from Pope Equipment Supplies, Invoice 2101; issued Check 1001 for $12,000 with the balance due in 30 days.
	3	Issued Check 1002 for $1,800 for cleaning supplies.
	4	Issued Check 1003 for $2,050 for office supplies.
	6	Performed services for $6,000 in cash.
	8	Performed services for $7,500 on credit.
	9	Paid $850 for monthly telephone bill; issued Check 1004.
	10	Issued Check 1005 for $975 for equipment repairs.
	12	Received $3,250 from credit clients.
	14	Issued Checks 1006–1007 for $1,500 to pay salaries.
	18	Performed services for $8,200 in cash.
	20	Issued Check 1008 for $2,275 for the monthly electric bill.
	26	Performed services for $8,950 in cash.
	30	Issued Checks 1009–1010 for $1,500 to pay salaries.
	30	Issued Check 1011 for $9,500 to Victor Prasad to pay for personal expenses.

Analyze: How many transactions affected expense accounts?

Journalizing and posting transactions.

In June 20X1, Chan Lee opened a photography studio that provides services to public and private schools. His firm's financial activities for the first month of operations and the chart of accounts appear below.

Problem 4.2B

Objectives 4-1, 4-2, 4-3

INSTRUCTIONS

1. Journalize the transactions. Number the journal page 1 and write the year at the top of the Date column. Describe each entry.
2. Post to the ledger accounts. Before you start the posting process, open the accounts by entering the names and numbers in the headings. Follow the order of the accounts in the chart of accounts.

ASSETS
101 Cash
111 Accounts Receivable
121 Supplies
141 Office Equipment
151 Photographic Equipment

LIABILITIES
202 Accounts Payable

OWNER'S EQUITY
301 Chan Lee, Capital
302 Chan Lee, Drawing

REVENUE
401 Fees Income

EXPENSES
511 Office Cleaning Expense
514 Rent Expense
517 Salaries Expense
520 Telephone Expense
523 Utilities Expense

DATE		TRANSACTIONS
June	1	Chan Lee invested $20,000 cash in the business.
	2	Issued Check 1001 for $2,000 to pay the June rent.
	5	Purchased desks and other office furniture for $9,500 from Office Supply, Inc.; received Invoice 5312, payable in 60 days.
	6	Issued Check 1002 for $2,100 to purchase photographic equipment.
	7	Purchased supplies for $550; paid with Check 1003.
	10	Issued Check 1004 for $800 for office cleaning service.
	12	Performed services for $2,600 in cash and $2,600 on credit. (Use one compound entry.)
	15	Returned damaged supplies; received a $180 cash refund.
	18	Purchased a computer for $2,250 from Dallas Office Supply, Invoice 304; issued Check 1005 for a $500 down payment. The balance is payable in 30 days. (Use one compound entry.)
	20	Issued Check 1006 for $2,500 to Office Supply, Inc., as payment on account for office furniture, Invoice 5312.
	26	Performed services for $2,500 on credit.
	27	Paid $632 for monthly telephone bill; issued Check 1007.
	30	Received $2,300 in cash from credit clients on account.
	30	Issued Check 1008 to pay the monthly utility bill of $750.
	30	Issued Checks 1009—1011 for $6,550 for salaries.

Analyze: What was the *Cash* account balance after the transaction of June 27 was recorded?

Problem 4.3B
Objective 4-4

▶ **Recording correcting entries.**

All the journal entries shown below contain errors. The entries were prepared by an employee of Helena Corporation who does not have an adequate knowledge of accounting.

INSTRUCTIONS

Examine the journal entries carefully to locate the errors. Prepare journal entries to correct the errors. Assume that *Office Supplies* and *Office Equipment* were recorded at the correct values. However, the items were purchased with cash. Check 1602 was properly processed in the accounting records and was not for the January 3, 20X1, items purchased. Assume the errors are found and corrected on the last day of the month.

GENERAL JOURNAL   PAGE __1__

DATE		DESCRIPTION	POST. REF.	DEBIT	CREDIT
20X1					
Jan.	1	Accounts Payable		1 100 00	
		Fees Income			1 100 00
		Performed services on credit			
	2	Cash		750 00	
		Telephone Expense			750 00
		Paid for January telephone			
		service, Check 1601			
	3	Office Equipment		1 250 00	
		Office Supplies		250 00	
		Accounts Payable			1 500 00
		Purchased file cabinet and			
		office supplies, Check 1602			

Analyze: After the correcting journal entries have been posted, what effect do the correcting entries have on the reported assets of the company?

Journalizing and posting transactions.

Problem 4.4B
Objectives 4-1, 4-2, 4-3

Several transactions that occurred during December 20X1, the first month of operation for Wells' Accounting Services, follow. The company uses the general ledger accounts listed below.

INSTRUCTIONS
Record the transactions in the general journal (page 1) and post to the appropriate accounts.

Cash	101	Furniture & Fixtures	151
Accounts Receivable	111	Accounts Payable	202
Office Supplies	121	Carolyn Wells, Capital	301
Computers	131	Fees Income	401
Office Equipment	141		

DATE		TRANSACTIONS
Dec.	3	Carolyn Wells began business by depositing $50,000 cash into a business checking account.
	4	Purchased a computer for $5,000 cash.
	5	Purchased furniture and fixtures on account for $15,000.
	6	Purchased office equipment for $5,600 cash.
	10	Rendered services to client and sent bill for $6,400.
	11	Purchased office supplies for $2,100 in cash.
	15	Received invoice for furniture purchased on December 5 and paid it.

Analyze: Describe the activity for account 202 during the month.

Critical Thinking Problem 4.1

Financial Statements

French Taylor is a new staff accountant for Fashion House Beauty Supply. He has asked you to review the financial statements prepared for April to find and correct any errors. Review the income statement and balance sheet that follow and identify the errors Taylor made (he did not prepare a statement of owner's equity). Prepare a corrected income statement and balance sheet, as well as a statement of owner's equity, for Fashion House Beauty Supply.

Fashion House Beauty Supply
Income Statement
April 30, 20X1

Revenue		
Fees Income		42 800 00
Expenses		
Salaries Expense	10 800 00	
Rent Expense	3 200 00	
Repair Expense	910 00	
Utilities Expense	1 820 00	
Drawing	5 200 00	
Total Expenses		21 030 00
Net Income		26 470 00

Fashion House Beauty Supply
Balance Sheet
Month Ended April 30, 20X1

Assets		Liabilities	
Land	25 000 00	Accounts Receivable	13 870 00
Building	42 000 00		
Cash	17 000 00	Owner's Equity	
Accounts Payable	6 100 00	French Taylor, Capital, April 1, 20X1	70 900 00
Total Assets	80 100 00	Total Liabilities and Owner's Equity	84 770 00

Critical Thinking Problem 4.2

Start-Up Business

On June 1, 20X1, Jenna Davis opened the Leadership Coaching Agency. She plans to use the chart of accounts given below.

INSTRUCTIONS

1. Journalize the transactions. Be sure to number the journal pages and write the year at the top of the Date column. Include a description for each entry.
2. Post to the ledger accounts. Before you start the posting process, open the accounts by entering the account names and numbers in the headings. Using the list of accounts below, assign appropriate account numbers and place them in the correct order in the ledger.
3. Prepare a trial balance.
4. Prepare the income statement.
5. Prepare a statement of owner's equity.
6. Prepare the balance sheet.

ACCOUNTS

Cash	Jenna Davis, Drawing
Accounts Receivable	Fees Income
Supplies	Advertising Expense
Office Furniture	Rent Expense
Recording Equipment	Salaries Expense
Accounts Payable	Telephone Expense
Jenna Davis, Capital	Utilities Expense

DATE		TRANSACTIONS
June	1	Jenna Davis invested $40,000 cash to start the business.
	2	Issued Check 201 for $2,000 to pay the June rent for the office.
	3	Purchased desk and other office furniture for $12,000 from Lowe's Office Supply, Invoice 5103; issued Check 202 for a $2,000 down payment with the balance due in 30 days.
	4	Issued Check 203 for $1,700 for supplies.
	6	Performed services for $7,000 in cash.
	7	Issued Check 204 for $3,000 to pay for advertising expense.
	8	Purchased recording equipment for $15,000 from Special Moves, Inc., Invoice 2122; issued Check 205 for a down payment of $5,000 with the balance due in 30 days.
	10	Performed services for $5,500 on account.
	11	Issued Check 206 for $3,000 to Lowe's Office Supply as payment on account.
	12	Performed services for $10,000 in cash.
	15	Issued Check 207 for $6,200 to pay an employee's salary.
	18	Received payments of $4,000 from credit clients on account.
	20	Issued Check 208 for $6,000 to Special Moves, Inc., as payment on account.
	25	Issued Check 209 in the amount of $375 for the monthly telephone bill.
	27	Issued Check 210 in the amount of $980 for the monthly electric bill.
	28	Issued Check 211 to Jenna Davis for $5,000 for personal living expenses.
	30	Issued Check 212 for $6,200 to pay the salary of an employee.

Analyze: How many postings were made to the *Cash* account?

BUSINESS CONNECTIONS

Business Records

1. How might a poor set of recording procedures affect the flow of information to management?
2. Why should management be concerned about the efficiency of a firm's procedures for journalizing and posting transactions?
3. Why should management insist that a firm's accounting system have a strong audit trail?
4. The owner of a new business recently questioned the accountant about the value of having both a journal and a ledger. The owner believes that it is a waste of effort to enter data about transactions in two different records. How would you explain the value of having both records?

Circumventing Internal Control

An essential element of a strong system on internal control and fraud prevention is the segregation of duties of employees. Segregation of duties increases the likelihood that a single employee does not have the ability to steal assets of the business and to cover up that illegal activity. For example, an employee who receives cash from customers for payment on account does not journalize and/or post the transaction in the general journal and the general ledger. However, the ability of a business to achieve optimal segregation of duties may be limited due to the small number of individuals employed.

Assume, however, that a business has achieved optimal segregation of duties. Then answer the two questions reflected below.

1. How might employees steal assets of a business in spite of optimal segregation of duties and an excellent system of internal control?
2. What additional measures can a company take to safeguard against employees circumventing an excellent system of internal control including optimal segregation of duties?

Balance Sheet

Review the following excerpt taken from the Walmart consolidated balance sheet as of January 31, 2018.

Analyze:

Walmart Stores, Inc. Consolidated Balance Sheet January 31, 2018	
(Amounts in millions)	
Property and Equipment:	
Property and Equipment (net)	$107.7
Property Under Capital Leases:	
Property Under Capital Leases (net)	$7.143

1. When the accountant for Walmart records a purchase of property and equipment, what type of account is debited? If Walmart purchases equipment on credit, what account might be credited?
2. What type of source document might be reflected in the journal entry to record the purchase of equipment?
3. If the accounting manager reviewed the *Equipment* account in the general ledger, what types of information might be listed there?

Analyze Online: Locate the website for Walmart (https://corporate.walmart.com/), which provides an online store for consumers as well as corporate information. Within the website, locate the consolidated balance sheet for the current year.

4. What is the balance reported for cash and cash equivalents at January 31 of the current year?
5. What is the balance reported for inventories at January 31 of the current year?

Audit Trail

An audit trail allows an individual to track a transaction from the journal entry to the general ledger through to the financial statements. The audit trail can also find all the transactions that comprise the dollar amount for each account listed on the income statement and balance sheet. Your team has been assigned the duty to diagram the audit trail for your company. In your diagram, show several transactions and how they would be tracked from the journal entry to the financial statements and back to the journal entry.

TEAMWORK

Answers to Comprehensive Self Review

1. The general ledger account number.
2. It is the last accounting record in which a transaction is recorded.
3. Errors made in journal entries whether posted or not must be made through correcting entries.
4. Check number.
   Invoice number for goods purchased on credit from a vendor.
   Invoice number for services billed to a charge account customer.
   Memorandum number.
5. a. An entry in the general journal.

Adjustments and the Worksheet Chapter 5

www.kpmg.com

Financial information prepared by accountants is used by others to make a variety of decisions. This financial information must be both accurate and complete by including all activity that took place during the reporting period. How do users of financial information, such as owners, managers, employees, creditors, investors, customers, and taxing and regulatory authorities, know if the amounts being reported are a true representation of a company's financial performance? Financial services firms, such as KPMG International Cooperative (KPMG), work to verify the accuracy and reliability of a company's financial information.

mimisim/Shutterstock

KPMG's roots can be traced back to 1891 when William Barclay Peat became the head of the accounting firm where he began his career and renamed it William Barclay Peat & Company. A subsequent series of mergers over nearly a century culminated in the forming of KPMG in 1987. KPMG and its member firms employ over 207,000 individuals working in 153 countries around the world. These dedicated professionals provide accounting, audit, tax, and other financial-related services to their clients. KPMG earns its revenue through the time spent performing these services. For the fiscal year ended September 30, 2018, KPMG reported $28.96 billion in revenue. Though all clients did not make immediate payments, KPMG must recognize the $28.96 billion in revenue at the time the services are performed. Through adjusting entries, introduced in this chapter, business entities are ensured of reflecting revenue within the financial statements for the appropriate accounting period. KPMG also incurs expenses, the costs necessary to earn revenue. Some examples of these expenses include employees' wages and benefits, office rent, travel, business insurance, office supplies, and utilities. To properly measure the company's financial performance, it is important to make certain that the expenses incurred in earning revenue are recorded in the same period as the revenue that generated the expenses. Matching expenses to revenues also is accomplished through adjusting entries and provides business entities with the most accurate financial results.

thinking critically

Careful recordkeeping is critical to all businesses, large and small. Why does matching these revenues and expenses within the same year matter so much?

LEARNING OBJECTIVES

5-1 Complete a trial balance on a worksheet.
5-2 Prepare adjustments for unrecorded business transactions.
5-3 Complete the worksheet.
5-4 Prepare an income statement, statement of owner's equity, and balance sheet from the completed worksheet.
5-5 Journalize and post the adjusting entries.
5-6 Define the accounting terms new to this chapter.

NEW TERMS

account form balance sheet
adjusting entries
adjustments
book value
contra account
contra asset account
depreciation
prepaid expenses
report form balance sheet
salvage value
straight-line depreciation
worksheet

Section 1

SECTION OBJECTIVES

>> **5-1** Complete a trial balance on a worksheet.

WHY IT'S IMPORTANT
Time and effort can be saved when the trial balance is prepared directly on the worksheet. Amounts can be easily transferred to other sections of the worksheet.

>> **5-2** Prepare adjustments for unrecorded business transactions.

WHY IT'S IMPORTANT
Not all business transactions occur between separate business entities. Some financial events occur within a business and need to be recorded.

TERMS TO LEARN

adjusting entries
adjustments
book value
contra account
contra asset account
depreciation
prepaid expenses
salvage value
straight-line depreciation
worksheet

The Worksheet

Financial statements are completed as soon as possible in order to be useful. One way to speed the preparation of financial statements is to use a worksheet. A **worksheet** is a form used to gather all data needed at the end of an accounting period to prepare the financial statements. Preparation of the worksheet is the fourth step in the accounting cycle.

Figure 5.1 shows a common type of worksheet. The heading shows the company name, report title, and period covered. In addition to the Account Name column, this worksheet contains five sections: Trial Balance, Adjustments, Adjusted Trial Balance, Income Statement, and Balance Sheet. Each section includes a Debit column and a Credit column. The worksheet has 10 columns in which to enter dollar amounts.

The Trial Balance Section

>> **5-1 OBJECTIVE**
Complete a trial balance on a worksheet.

recall

Trial Balance
If total debits do not equal total credits, there is an error in the financial records. The error must be found and corrected.

Refer to Figure 5.2 as you read about how to prepare the Trial Balance section of the worksheet.

1. Enter the general ledger account names.
2. Transfer the general ledger account balances to the Debit and Credit columns of the Trial Balance section.
3. Total the Debit and Credit columns to prove that the trial balance is in balance.
4. Place a double rule under each Trial Balance column to show that the work in that column is complete.

FIGURE 5.1
Ten-Column Worksheet

Eli's Consulting Services
Worksheet
Month Ended December 31, 20X1

ACCOUNT NAME	TRIAL BALANCE		ADJUSTMENTS	
	DEBIT	CREDIT	DEBIT	CREDIT
1				
2				
3				
4				
5				

FIGURE 5.2 A Partial Worksheet

Eli's Consulting Services
Worksheet
Month Ended December 31, 20X1

	ACCOUNT NAME	TRIAL BALANCE DEBIT	TRIAL BALANCE CREDIT	ADJUSTMENTS DEBIT	ADJUSTMENTS CREDIT
1	Cash	111 350 00			
2	Accounts Receivable	5 000 00			
3	Supplies	1 500 00			(a) 500 00
4	Prepaid Rent	8 000 00			(b) 4 000 00
5	Equipment	11 000 00			
6	Accumulated Depreciation—Equipment				(c) 183 00
7	Accounts Payable		3 500 00		
8	Trayton Eli, Capital		100 000 00		
9	Trayton Eli, Drawing	5 000 00			
10	Fees Income		47 000 00		
11	Salaries Expense	8 000 00			
12	Utilities Expense	650 00			
13	Supplies Expense			(a) 500 00	
14	Rent Expense			(b) 4 000 00	
15	Depreciation Expense—Equipment			(c) 183 00	
16	Totals	150 500 00	150 500 00	4 683 00	4 683 00

Notice that the trial balance has four new accounts: *Accumulated Depreciation—Equipment, Supplies Expense, Rent Expense,* and *Depreciation Expense—Equipment.* These accounts have zero balances now, but they will be needed later as the worksheet is completed.

The Adjustments Section

Usually, account balances change because of transactions with other businesses or individuals. For Eli's Consulting Services, the account changes recorded in Chapter 4 were caused by transactions with the firm's suppliers, customers, landlord, and employees. It is easy to recognize, journalize, and post these transactions as they occur.

Some changes are not caused by transactions with other businesses or individuals. They arise from the internal operations of the firm during the accounting period. Journal entries made to update accounts for previously unrecorded items are called **adjustments** or **adjusting entries.** These changes are first entered on the worksheet at the end of each accounting period. The worksheet provides a convenient form for gathering the information and determining the effects of the changes. Let's look at the adjustments made by Eli's Consulting Services on December 31, 20X1.

>> 5-2 OBJECTIVE
Prepare adjustments for unrecorded business transactions.

Trial Balance

On the trial balance, accounts are listed in this order: assets, liabilities, owner's equity, revenue, and expenses.

Adjusting for Supplies Used

On November 28, 20X1, Eli's Consulting Services purchased $1,500 of supplies. On December 31, the trial balance shows a $1,500 balance in the **Supplies** account. This amount is too high because some of the supplies were used during December.

An adjustment must be made for the supplies used. Otherwise, the asset account **Supplies** is overstated because fewer supplies are actually on hand. The expense account **Supplies Expense** is understated. The cost of the supplies used represents an operating expense that has not been recorded.

On December 31, Sergio Sanchez counted the supplies. Remaining supplies totaled $1,000. This meant that supplies amounting to $500 were used during December ($1,500 − $1,000 = $500). At the end of December, an adjustment must be made to reflect the supplies used. The adjustment reduces the **Supplies** account to $1,000, the amount of supplies remaining. It increases the **Supplies Expense** account by $500 for the amount of supplies used. Notice that the adjustment for supplies is based on actual usage.

Refer to Figure 5.2 to review the adjustment on the worksheet: a debit of $500 to **Supplies Expense** and a credit of $500 to **Supplies**. Both the debit and credit are labeled *(a)* to identify the two parts of the adjustment.

Supplies is a type of prepaid expense. **Prepaid expenses** are items that are acquired and paid for in advance of their use. Other common prepaid expenses are prepaid rent, prepaid insurance, and prepaid advertising. When cash is paid for these items, amounts are debited to **Prepaid Rent, Prepaid Insurance,** and **Prepaid Advertising;** all are asset accounts. As prepaid expenses are used, an adjustment is made to reduce the asset accounts and to increase the related expense accounts.

ABOUT ACCOUNTING

Accounting Software

The use of accounting software eliminates the need to prepare a worksheet. However, adjusting entries must always be made to properly reflect account balances at the end of a reporting period.

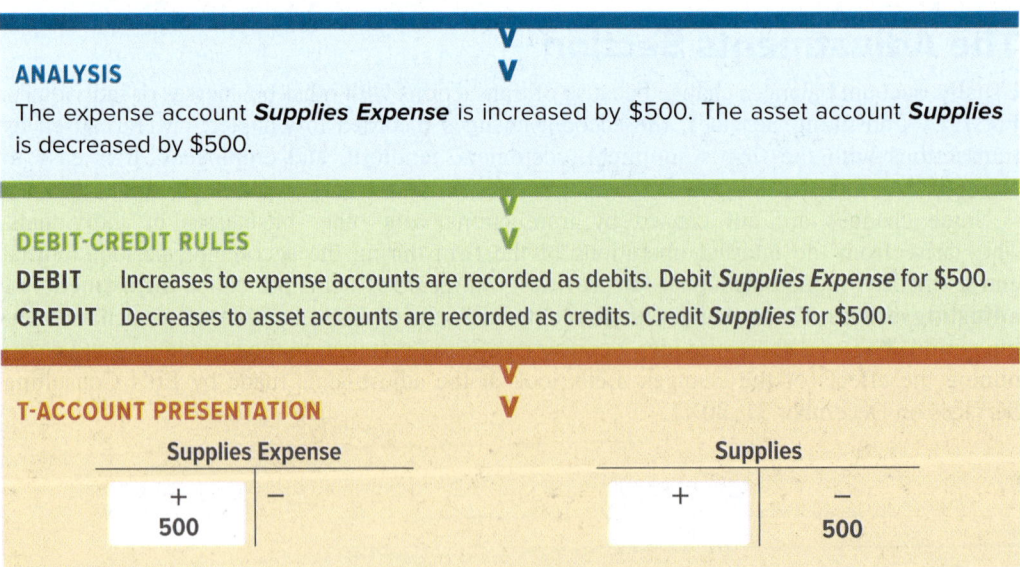

Let's review the effect of the adjustment on the asset account **Supplies**. Recall that the **Supplies** account already had a balance of $1,500. If no adjustment is made, the balance would remain at $1,500, even though only $1,000 of supplies are left.

```
                    Supplies
            +                       −
    Bal.    1,500       Adj.      500
    Bal.    1,000
```

Adjusting for Expired Rent

On November 30, 20X1, Eli's Consulting Services paid $8,000 rent for December and January. The right to occupy facilities for the specified period is an asset. The $8,000 was debited to **Prepaid Rent,** an asset account. On December 31, 20X1, the **Prepaid Rent** balance is $8,000. This is too high because one month of rent has been used. The expired rent is $4,000 ($8,000 ÷ 2 months). At the end of December, an adjustment is made to reflect the expired rent.

ADJUSTMENT

Record the adjustment for expired rent.

ANALYSIS
The expense account **Rent Expense** is increased by $4,000. The asset account **Prepaid Rent** is decreased by $4,000.

DEBIT-CREDIT RULES
DEBIT   Increases to expense accounts are recorded as debits. Debit *Rent Expense* for $4,000.
CREDIT Decreases to asset accounts are recorded as credits. Credit *Prepaid Rent* for $4,000.

T-ACCOUNT PRESENTATION

```
        Rent Expense                        Prepaid Rent
      +            −                       +           −
    4,000                                           4,000
```

Let's review the effect of the adjustment on the asset account **Prepaid Rent.** The beginning balance of $8,000 represents prepaid rent for the months of December and January. By December 31, the prepaid rent for the month of December is "used up." The adjustment reducing **Prepaid Rent** recognizes the expense of occupying the facilities in December. The $4,000 ending balance represents prepaid rent for the month of January.

important!

Prepaid Expense
Prepaid rent is recorded as an asset at the time it is paid. As time elapses, the asset is used up. An adjustment is made to reduce the asset and to recognize rent expense.

```
                  Prepaid Rent
            +                       −
    Bal.    8,000       Adj.     4,000
    Bal.    4,000
```

Refer again to Figure 5.2 to review the adjustment on the worksheet: a debit of $4,000 to **Rent Expense** and a credit of $4,000 to **Prepaid Rent**. Both parts of the adjustment are labeled *(b)*.

Adjusting for Depreciation

There is one more adjustment to make at the end of December. It involves the equipment purchased in November. The cost of long-term assets such as equipment is not recorded as an expense when purchased. Instead, the cost is recorded as an asset and spread over the time the assets are used for the business. **Depreciation** is the process of allocating the cost of long-term assets over their expected useful lives. There are many ways to calculate depreciation. Eli's Consulting Services uses the **straight-line depreciation** method. This method results in an equal amount of depreciation being charged to each accounting period during the asset's useful life. The formula for straight-line depreciation is

$$\text{Depreciation} = \frac{\text{Cost} - \text{Salvage value}}{\text{Estimated useful life}}$$

Salvage value is an estimate of the amount that may be received by selling or disposing of an asset at the end of its useful life.

Eli's Consulting Services purchased $11,000 worth of equipment. The equipment has an estimated useful life of five years and no salvage value. The depreciation for December, the first month of operations, is $183 (rounded).

$$\frac{\$11,000 - \$0}{60 \text{ months}} = \$183 \text{ (rounded)}$$

1. Convert the asset's useful life from years to months: 5 years × 12 months = 60 months.
2. Divide the total depreciation to be taken by the total number of months: $11,000 ÷ 60 = $183 (rounded).
3. Record depreciation expense of $183 each month for the next 60 months.

> Conoco Inc. depreciates property such as refinery equipment, pipelines, and deepwater drill ships on a straight-line basis over the estimated life of each asset, ranging from 15 to 25 years.

important!

Contra Accounts
The normal balance for a contra account is the opposite of the related account.

Accumulated Depreciation is a contra asset account. The normal balance of an asset account is a *debit*. The normal balance of a contra asset account is a *credit*.

As the cost of the equipment is gradually transferred to expense, its recorded value as an asset must be reduced. This procedure cannot be carried out by directly decreasing the balance in the asset account. Generally accepted accounting principles require that the original cost of a long-term asset continue to appear in the asset account until the firm has used up or disposed of the asset.

The adjustment for depreciation is recorded in a contra account entitled *Accumulated Depreciation—Equipment*. A **contra account** has a normal balance that is opposite that of a related account. For example, the *Equipment* account is an asset and has a normal debit balance. *Accumulated Depreciation—Equipment* is a **contra asset account** with a normal credit balance, which is opposite the normal balance of an asset account. The adjustment to reflect depreciation for December is a $183 debit to *Depreciation Expense—Equipment* and a $183 credit to *Accumulated Depreciation—Equipment*.

The *Accumulated Depreciation—Equipment* account is a record of all depreciation taken on the equipment. The financial records show the original cost of the equipment (*Equipment,* $11,000) and all depreciation taken (*Accumulated Depreciation—Equipment,* $183). The difference between the two accounts is called book value. **Book value** is that portion of an asset's original cost that has not yet been depreciated. Three amounts are reported on the financial statements for equipment:

Equipment	$11,000
Less accumulated depreciation	−183
Equipment at book value	$10,817

ADJUSTMENT

Record the adjustment for depreciation.

ANALYSIS

The expense account *Depreciation Expense—Equipment* is increased by $183. The contra asset account *Accumulated Depreciation—Equipment* is increased by $183.

DEBIT-CREDIT RULES

DEBIT Increases to expense accounts are recorded as debits. Debit *Depreciation Expense—Equipment* for $183.

CREDIT Increases to contra asset accounts are recorded as credits. Credit *Accumulated Depreciation—Equipment* for $183.

T-ACCOUNT PRESENTATION

Depreciation Expense—Equipment		Accumulated Depreciation—Equipment	
+	−	−	+
183			183

Refer to Figure 5.2 to review the depreciation adjustment on the worksheet. The two parts of the adjustment are labeled *(c)*.

If Eli's Consulting Services had other kinds of long-term tangible assets, an adjustment for depreciation would be made for each one. Long-term tangible assets include land, buildings, equipment, trucks, automobiles, furniture, and fixtures. Depreciation is calculated on all long-term tangible assets except land. Land is not depreciated.

Notice that each adjustment involved a balance sheet account (an asset or a contra asset) and an income statement account (an expense). When all adjustments have been entered, total and rule the Adjustments columns. Be sure that the totals of the Debit and Credit columns are equal. If they are not, locate and correct the error or errors before continuing. Figure 5.2 shows the completed Adjustments section.

Section 1 Review

1. Adjusting entries are:
   a. journal entries made to correct accounts for previous errors in recording transactions.
   b. journal entries made to update accounts for previously unrecorded items.
   c. journal entries made to record the original transaction.
   d. journal entries made to ledger accounts to record the original transaction.

2. Prepaid expenses are adjusted at the end of the accounting period in order to:
   a. properly reflect the remaining cost of the asset available for use by the business.
   b. properly reflect the portion of the cost the asset used by the business.
   c. Neither a nor b is correct.
   d. Both a and b are correct.

3. A worksheet:
   a. is a form used to gather all data needed at the end of the account period to prepare the financial statements.
   b. is a form to facilitate the efficient preparation of the financial statements.
   c. has five sections: trial balance, adjustments, adjusted trial balance, income statement, and balance sheet.
   d. All of the above are correct.

4. A firm paid $9,000 for supplies during the accounting period. At the end of the accounting period, the firm had $5,800 of supplies on hand. What adjustment is entered on the worksheet?
   a. *Supplies* is debited for $3,200 and *Supplies Expense* is credited for $3,200.
   b. *Supplies Expense* is debited for $3,200 and *Supplies* is credited for $3,200.
   c. *Supplies* is debited for $9,000 and *Supplies Expense* is credited for $9,000.
   d. *Supplies Expense* is debited for $5,800 and *Supplies* is credited for $5,800.

5. On January 1, a firm paid $42,000 for six months' rent, January through June. What is the adjustment for rent expense at the end of January?
   a. *Rent Expense* is debited for $42,000 and *Prepaid Rent* is credited for $42,000.
   b. *Prepaid Rent* is debited for $7,000 and *Rent Expense* is credited for $7,000.
   c. *Rent Expense* is debited for $7,000 and *Prepaid Rent* is credited for $7,000.
   d. No adjustment is made until the end of June.

6. Three years ago, Overnight Delivery bought a delivery truck for $80,000. The truck has no salvage value and a five-year useful life. What is the book value of the truck at the end of three years?
   a. $48,000
   b. $32,000
   c. $64,000
   d. $16,000

Section 2

SECTION OBJECTIVES	TERMS TO LEARN
>> 5-3 Complete the worksheet. **WHY IT'S IMPORTANT** The worksheet summarizes both internal and external financial events of a period. **>> 5-4 Prepare an income statement, statement of owner's equity, and balance sheet from the completed worksheet.** **WHY IT'S IMPORTANT** Using a worksheet saves time in preparing the financial statements. **>> 5-5 Journalize and post the adjusting entries.** **WHY IT'S IMPORTANT** Adjusting entries update the financial records of the business.	account form balance sheet report form balance sheet

Financial Statements

The worksheet is used to prepare the financial statements. Preparing financial statements is the fifth step in the accounting cycle.

The Adjusted Trial Balance Section

The next task is to prepare the Adjusted Trial Balance section.

1. Combine the figures from the Trial Balance section and the Adjustments section of the worksheet. Record the computed results in the Adjusted Trial Balance columns.
2. Total the Debit and Credit columns in the Adjusted Trial Balance section. Confirm that debits equal credits.

Figure 5.3 shows the completed Adjusted Trial Balance section of the worksheet. The accounts that do not have adjustments are simply extended from the Trial Balance section to the Adjusted Trial Balance section. For example, the **Cash** account balance of $111,350 is recorded in the Debit column of the Adjusted Trial Balance section without change.

The balances of accounts that are affected by adjustments are recomputed. Look at the **Supplies** account. It has a $1,500 debit balance in the Trial Balance section and shows a $500 credit in the Adjustments section. The new balance is $1,000 ($1,500 − $500). It is recorded in the Debit column of the Adjusted Trial Balance section.

Use the following guidelines to compute the amounts for the Adjusted Trial Balance section.

- If the account has a debit balance in the Trial Balance section and a debit entry in the Adjustments section, add the two amounts.

>> 5-3 OBJECTIVE
Complete the worksheet.

If the Trial Balance section has a:	AND if the entry in the Adjustments section is a:	Then:
Debit balance	Debit	Add the amounts.
Debit balance	Credit	Subtract the credit amount.
Credit balance	Credit	Add the amounts.
Credit balance	Debit	Subtract the debit amount.

FIGURE 5.3 A Partial Worksheet

Eli's Consulting Services
Worksheet
Month Ended December 31, 20X1

	ACCOUNT NAME	TRIAL BALANCE DEBIT	TRIAL BALANCE CREDIT	ADJUSTMENTS DEBIT	ADJUSTMENTS CREDIT
1	Cash	111 350 00			
2	Accounts Receivable	5 000 00			
3	Supplies	1 500 00			(a) 500 00
4	Prepaid Rent	8 000 00			(b) 4 000 00
5	Equipment	11 000 00			
6	Accumulated Depreciation—Equipment				(c) 183 00
7	Accounts Payable		3 500 00		
8	Trayton Eli, Capital		100 000 00		
9	Trayton Eli, Drawing	5 000 00			
10	Fees Income		47 000 00		
11	Salaries Expense	8 000 00			
12	Utilities Expense	650 00			
13	Supplies Expense			(a) 500 00	
14	Rent Expense			(b) 4 000 00	
15	Depreciation Expense—Equipment			(c) 183 00	
16	Totals	150 500 00	150 500 00	4 683 00	4 683 00
17	Net Income				

- If the account has a debit balance in the Trial Balance section and a credit entry in the Adjustments section, subtract the credit amount.
- If the account has a credit balance in the Trial Balance section and a credit entry in the Adjustments section, add the two amounts.
- If the account has a credit balance in the Trial Balance section and a debit entry in the Adjustments section, subtract the debit amount.

Prepaid Rent has a Trial Balance debit of $8,000 and an Adjustments credit of $4,000. Enter $4,000 ($8,000 − $4,000) in the Adjusted Trial Balance Debit column.

Four accounts that started with zero balances in the Trial Balance section are affected by adjustments. They are **Accumulated Depreciation—Equipment, Supplies Expense, Rent Expense,** and **Depreciation Expense—Equipment.** The figures in the Adjustments section are simply extended to the Adjusted Trial Balance section. For example, **Accumulated Depreciation—Equipment** has a zero balance in the Trial Balance section and a $183 credit in the Adjustments section. Extend the $183 to the Adjusted Trial Balance Credit column.

Once all account balances are recorded in the Adjusted Trial Balance section, total and rule the Debit and Credit columns. Be sure that total debits equal total credits. If they are not equal, find and correct the error or errors.

The Income Statement and Balance Sheet Sections

The Income Statement and Balance Sheet sections of the worksheet are used to separate the amounts needed for the balance sheet and the income statement. For example, to prepare an income statement, all revenue and expense account balances must be in one place.

Starting at the top of the Adjusted Trial Balance section, examine each general ledger account. For accounts that appear on the balance sheet, enter the amount in the appropriate column of the Balance Sheet section. For accounts that appear on the income statement, enter the amount in the appropriate column of the Income Statement section. Take care to enter debit amounts in the Debit column and credit amounts in the Credit column.

ADJUSTED TRIAL BALANCE		INCOME STATEMENT		BALANCE SHEET		
DEBIT	CREDIT	DEBIT	CREDIT	DEBIT	CREDIT	
111 350 00						1
5 000 00						2
1 000 00						3
4 000 00						4
11 000 00						5
	183 00					6
	3 500 00					7
	100 000 00					8
5 000 00						9
	47 000 00					10
8 000 00						11
650 00						12
500 00						13
4 000 00						14
183 00						15
150 683 00	150 683 00					16
						17

Preparing the Balance Sheet Section

Refer to Figure 5.4 as you learn how to complete the worksheet. Asset, liability, and owner's equity accounts appear on the balance sheet. The first five accounts that appear on the worksheet are assets. Extend the asset accounts to the Debit column of the Balance Sheet section. The next account, **Accumulated Depreciation—Equipment,** is a contra asset account. Extend it to the Credit column of the Balance Sheet section. Extend **Accounts Payable** and **Trayton Eli, Capital** to the Credit column of the Balance Sheet section. Extend **Trayton Eli, Drawing** to the Debit column of the Balance Sheet section.

Preparing the Income Statement Section

Revenue and expense accounts appear on the income statement. Extend the **Fees Income** account to the Credit column of the Income Statement section. The last five accounts on the worksheet are expense accounts. Extend these accounts to the Debit column of the Income Statement section.

After all account balances are transferred from the Adjusted Trial Balance section of the worksheet to the financial statement sections, total the Debit and Credit columns in the Income Statement section. For Eli's Consulting Services, the debits (expenses) total $13,333 and the credits (revenue) total $47,000.

Next, total the columns in the Balance Sheet section. For Eli's Consulting Services, the debits (assets and drawing account) total $137,350 and the credits (contra asset, liabilities, and owner's equity) total $103,683.

Return to the Income Statement section. The totals of these columns are used to determine the net income or net loss. Subtract the smaller column total from the larger one. Enter the difference on the line below the smaller total. In the Account Name column, enter "Net Income" or "Net Loss."

In this case, the total of the Credit column, $47,000, exceeds the total of the Debit column, $13,333. The Credit column total represents revenue. The Debit column total represents expenses. The difference between the two amounts is a net income of $33,667. Enter $33,667 in the Debit column of the Income Statement section.

> **recall**
>
> **Locating Errors**
> If total debits do not equal total credits, find the difference between total debits and total credits. If the difference is divisible by 9, there could be a transposition error. If the difference is divisible by 2, an amount could be entered in the wrong (Debit or Credit) column.

FIGURE 5.4 A Completed Worksheet

Eli's Consulting Services
Worksheet
Month Ended December 31, 20X1

	ACCOUNT NAME	TRIAL BALANCE DEBIT	TRIAL BALANCE CREDIT	ADJUSTMENTS DEBIT	ADJUSTMENTS CREDIT
1	Cash	111 350 00			
2	Accounts Receivable	5 000 00			
3	Supplies	1 500 00			(a) 500 00
4	Prepaid Rent	8 000 00			(b) 4 000 00
5	Equipment	11 000 00			
6	Accumulated Depreciation—Equipment				(c) 183 00
7	Accounts Payable		3 500 00		
8	Trayton Eli, Capital		100 000 00		
9	Trayton Eli, Drawing	5 000 00			
10	Fees Income		47 000 00		
11	Salaries Expense	8 000 00			
12	Utilities Expense	650 00			
13	Supplies Expense			(a) 500 00	
14	Rent Expense			(b) 4 000 00	
15	Depreciation Expense—Equipment			(c) 183 00	
16	Totals	150 500 00	150 500 00	4 683 00	4 683 00
17	Net Income				
18					

important!

Net Income
The difference between the Debit and Credit columns of the Income Statement section represents net income. The difference between the Debit and Credit columns of the Balance Sheet section should equal the net income amount.

Net income causes a net increase in owner's equity. As a check on accuracy, the amount in the Balance Sheet Debit column is subtracted from the amount in the Credit column and compared to net income. In the Balance Sheet section, subtract the smaller column total from the larger one. The difference should equal the net income or net loss computed in the Income Statement section. Enter the difference on the line below the smaller total. For Eli's Consulting Services, enter $33,667 in the Credit column of the Balance Sheet section.

Total the Income Statement and Balance Sheet columns. Make sure that total debits equal total credits for each section.

Eli's Consulting Services had a net income. If it had a loss, the loss would be entered in the Credit column of the Income Statement section and the Debit column of the Balance Sheet section. "Net Loss" would be entered in the Account Name column on the worksheet.

Preparing Financial Statements

When the worksheet is complete, the next step is to prepare the financial statements, starting with the income statement. Preparation of the financial statements is the fifth step in the accounting cycle.

>> **5-4 OBJECTIVE**
Prepare an income statement, statement of owner's equity, and balance sheet from the completed worksheet.

Preparing the Income Statement

Use the Income Statement section of the worksheet to prepare the income statement. Figure 5.5 shows the income statement for Eli's Consulting Services. Compare it to the worksheet in Figure 5.4.

If the firm had incurred a net loss, the final amount on the income statement would be labeled "Net Loss."

ADJUSTED TRIAL BALANCE		INCOME STATEMENT		BALANCE SHEET		
DEBIT	CREDIT	DEBIT	CREDIT	DEBIT	CREDIT	
111 350 00				111 350 00		1
5 000 00				5 000 00		2
1 000 00				1 000 00		3
4 000 00				4 000 00		4
11 000 00				11 000 00		5
	183 00				183 00	6
	3 500 00				3 500 00	7
	100 000 00				100 000 00	8
5 000 00				5 000 00		9
	47 000 00		47 000 00			10
8 000 00		8 000 00				11
650 00		650 00				12
500 00		500 00				13
4 000 00		4 000 00				14
183 00		183 00				15
150 683 00	150 683 00	13 333 00	47 000 00	137 350 00	103 683 00	16
		33 667 00			33 667 00	17
		47 000 00	47 000 00	137 350 00	137 350 00	18

Preparing the Statement of Owner's Equity

The statement of owner's equity reports the changes that have occurred in the owner's financial interest during the reporting period. Use the data in the Balance Sheet section of the worksheet, as well as the net income or net loss figure, to prepare the statement of owner's equity.

- From the Balance Sheet section of the worksheet, use the amounts for owner's capital; owner's withdrawals, if any; and owner's investments, if any.
- From the Income Statement section of the worksheet, use the amount calculated for net income or net loss.

The statement of owner's equity is prepared before the balance sheet because the ending capital balance is needed to prepare the balance sheet. The statement of owner's equity reports the change in owner's capital during the period ($28,667) as well as the ending capital ($128,667). Figure 5.6 shows the statement of owner's equity for Eli's Consulting Services.

Preparing the Balance Sheet

The accounts listed on the balance sheet are taken directly from the Balance Sheet section of the worksheet. Figure 5.7 shows the balance sheet for Eli's Consulting Services.

Note that the equipment's book value is reported on the balance sheet ($10,817). Do not confuse book value with market value. Book value is the portion of the original cost that has not been depreciated. *Market value* is what a willing buyer will pay a willing seller for the asset. Market value may be higher or lower than book value.

Notice that the amount for **Trayton Eli, Capital,** $128,667, comes from the statement of owner's equity.

FIGURE 5.5

Income Statement

Eli's Consulting Services
Income Statement
Month Ended December 31, 20X1

Revenue		
Fees Income		47 000 00
Expenses		
Salaries Expense	8 000 00	
Utilities Expense	650 00	
Supplies Expense	500 00	
Rent Expense	4 000 00	
Depreciation Expense—Equipment	183 00	
Total Expenses		13 333 00
Net Income		33 667 00

FIGURE 5.6

Statement of Owner's Equity

Eli's Consulting Services
Statement of Owner's Equity
Month Ended December 31, 20X1

Trayton Eli, Capital, December 1, 20X1		100 000 00
Net Income for December	33 667 00	
Less Withdrawals for December	5 000 00	
Increase in Capital		28 667 00
Trayton Eli, Capital, December 31, 20X1		128 667 00

FIGURE 5.7

Balance Sheet

Eli's Consulting Services
Balance Sheet
December 31, 20X1

Assets		
Cash		111 350 00
Accounts Receivable		5 000 00
Supplies		1 000 00
Prepaid Rent		4 000 00
Equipment	11 000 00	
Less Accumulated Depreciation	183 00	10 817 00
Total Assets		132 167 00
Liabilities and Owner's Equity		
Liabilities		
Accounts Payable		3 500 00
Owner's Equity		
Trayton Eli, Capital		128 667 00
Total Liabilities and Owner's Equity		132 167 00

The balance sheet in Figure 5.7 is prepared using the report form. The **report form balance sheet** lists the asset accounts first, followed by liabilities and owner's equity. Chapters 2 and 3 illustrated the **account form balance sheet,** with assets on the left and liabilities and owner's equity on the right. The report form is widely used because it provides more space for entering account names and its format is easier to prepare.

Some companies show long-term assets at a net amount. "Net" means that accumulated depreciation has been subtracted from the original cost. For example, The Boeing Company's consolidated statement of financial position as of December 31, 2018, reflects:

The net amounts for Property, plant, and equipment that appears on the balance sheet for 2018 and 2017 are $12,645 million and $12,672 million, respectively. These amounts are net of accumulated depreciation of $18,568 and $17,641 million for December 31, 2018, and December 31, 2017, respectively.

Figure 5.8A through Figure 5.8G provide a step-by-step demonstration of how to complete the worksheet and financial statements for Eli's Consulting Services.

FIGURE 5.8A Worksheet Summary

The worksheet is used to gather all the data needed at the end of an accounting period to prepare the financial statements. The worksheet heading contains the name of the company (**WHO**), the title of the statement being prepared (**WHAT**), and the period covered (**WHEN**). The worksheet contains 10 money columns that are arranged in five sections labeled Trial Balance, Adjustments, Adjusted Trial Balance, Income Statement, and Balance Sheet. Each section includes a Debit column and a Credit column.

The information reflected in the worksheet below is for Eli's Consulting Services for the period ending December 31, 2019. The illustrations that follow will highlight the preparation of each part of the worksheet.

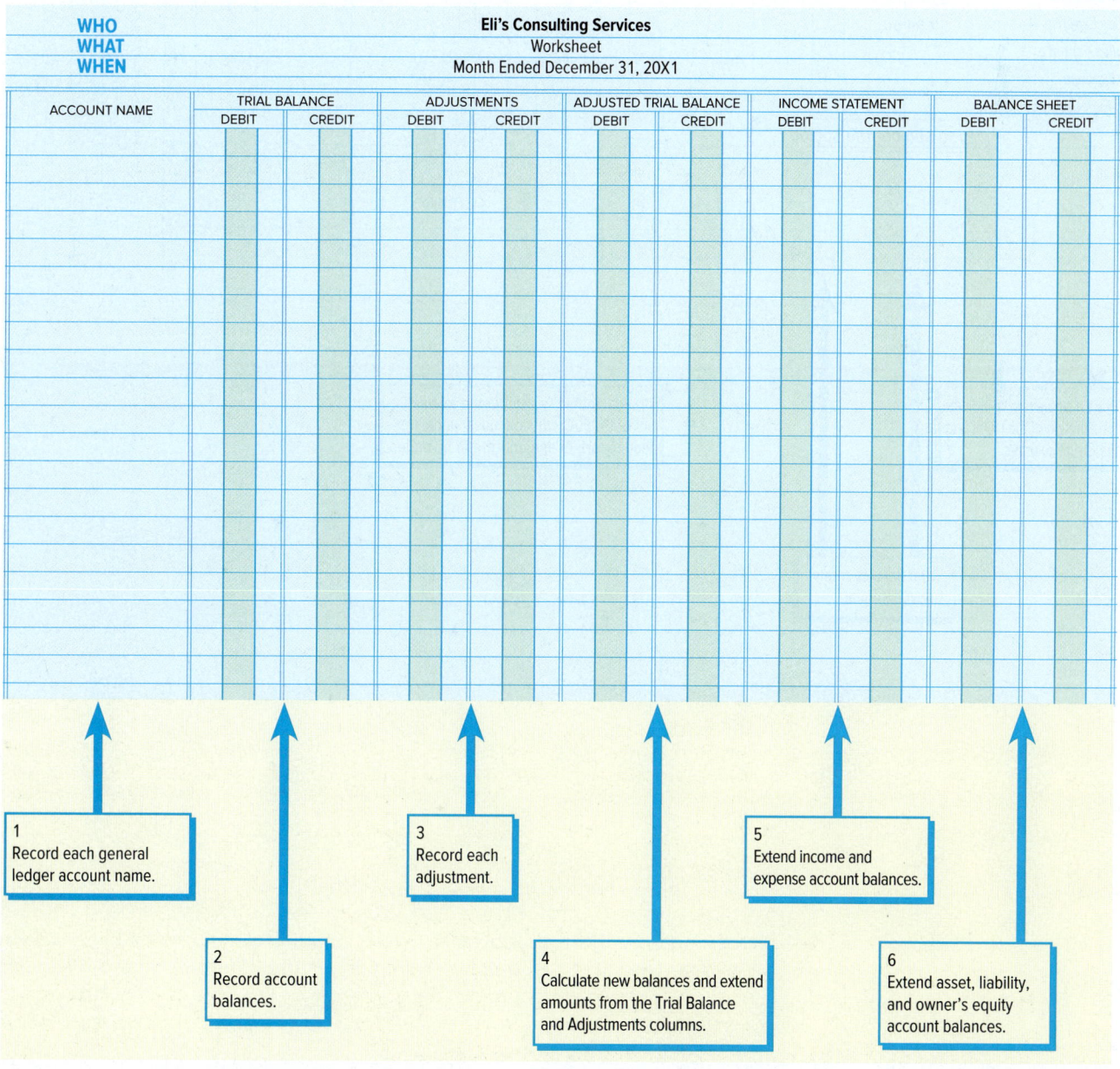

FIGURE 5.8B The Trial Balance Columns

The first step in preparing the worksheet for Eli's Consulting Services is to list the general ledger accounts and their balances in the Account Name and Trial Balance sections of the worksheet. The equality of total debits and credits is proved by totaling the Debit and Credit columns.

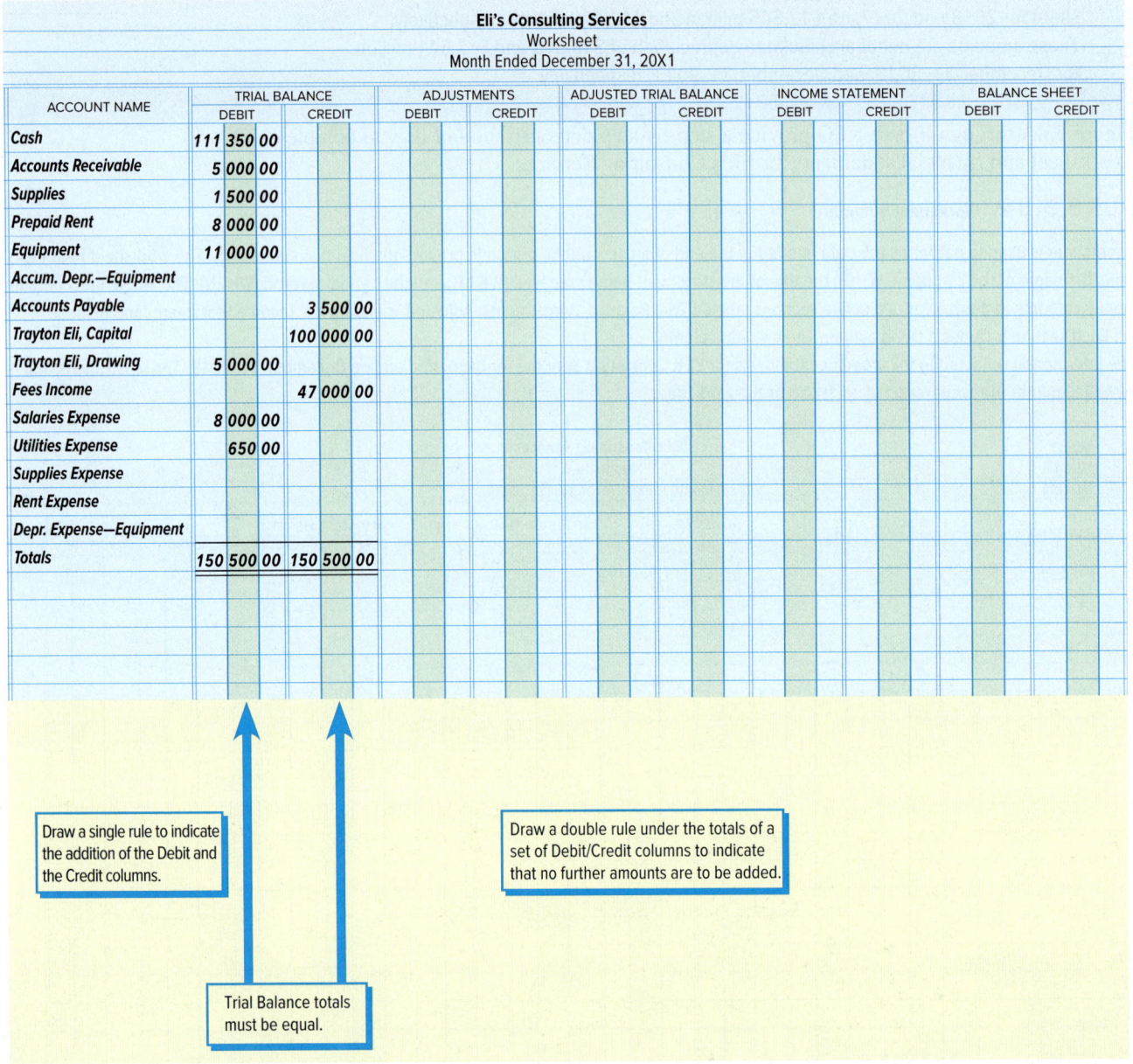

FIGURE 5.8C The Adjustments

The data in the general ledger accounts at the end of an accounting period do not present a complete picture of the firm's financial affairs even though transactions have been recorded accurately throughout the period. Certain financial changes have occurred with the business as a result of its operations that have not yet been entered in the accounting records. These changes must be recognized and recorded at the end of the accounting period. The Adjustments section of the worksheet is used to record these changes. The Adjustments section of the worksheet for Eli's Consulting Services reflects three adjustments. Notice that the debit and credit parts of each adjustment are identified by a letter. After all adjustments are entered, the Debit and Credit columns of the Adjustments section are totaled to test that total debits equal total credits.

Eli's Consulting Services
Worksheet
Month Ended December 31, 20X1

ACCOUNT NAME	TRIAL BALANCE		ADJUSTMENTS		ADJUSTED TRIAL BALANCE		INCOME STATEMENT		BALANCE SHEET	
	DEBIT	CREDIT	DEBIT	CREDIT	DEBIT	CREDIT	DEBIT	CREDIT	DEBIT	CREDIT
Cash	111 350 00									
Accounts Receivable	5 000 00									
Supplies	1 500 00			(a) 500 00						
Prepaid Rent	8 000 00			(b) 4 000 00						
Equipment	11 000 00									
Accum. Depr.—Equipment				(c) 183 00						
Accounts Payable		3 500 00								
Trayton Eli, Capital		100 000 00								
Trayton Eli, Drawing	5 000 00									
Fees Income		47 000 00								
Salaries Expense	8 000 00									
Utilities Expense	650 00									
Supplies Expense			(a) 500 00							
Rent Expense			(b) 4 000 00							
Depr. Expense—Equipment			(c) 183 00							
Totals	150 500 00	150 500 00	4 683 00	4 683 00						

Draw a single rule to indicate that the columns are to be added.

Total debits must equal total credits.

Draw a double rule under the Debit/Credit column total.

FIGURE 5.8D The Adjusted Trial Balance

The third set of columns is the Adjusted Trial Balance. The balance for the accounts in this set of columns is obtained by combining the amounts in the Trial Balance columns with the amounts in the Adjustments columns. If no adjustment is made to an account, the amount in the Trial Balance column is extended to the appropriate column in the Adjusted Trial Balance section. If an adjustment is made to an account, the adjustment amount is added to or subtracted from the Trial Balance amount and the new total is extended to the appropriate column in the Adjusted Trial Balance section.

Eli's Consulting Services
Worksheet
Month Ended December 31, 20X1

ACCOUNT NAME	TRIAL BALANCE DEBIT	TRIAL BALANCE CREDIT	ADJUSTMENTS DEBIT	ADJUSTMENTS CREDIT	ADJUSTED TRIAL BALANCE DEBIT	ADJUSTED TRIAL BALANCE CREDIT	INCOME STATEMENT DEBIT	INCOME STATEMENT CREDIT	BALANCE SHEET DEBIT	BALANCE SHEET CREDIT
Cash	111 350 00				111 350 00					
Accounts Receivable	5 000 00				5 000 00					
Supplies	1 500 00			(a) 500 00	1 000 00					
Prepaid Rent	8 000 00			(b) 4 000 00	4 000 00					
Equipment	11 000 00				11 000 00					
Accum. Depr.—Equipment				(c) 183 00		183 00				
Accounts Payable		3 500 00				3 500 00				
Trayton Eli, Capital		100 000 00				100 000 00				
Trayton Eli, Drawing	5 000 00				5 000 00					
Fees Income		47 000 00				47 000 00				
Salaries Expense	8 000 00				8 000 00					
Utilities Expense	650 00				650 00					
Supplies Expense			(a) 500 00		500 00					
Rent Expense			(b) 4 000 00		4 000 00					
Depr. Expense—Equipment			(c) 183 00		183 00					
Totals	150 500 00	150 500 00	4 683 00	4 683 00	150 683 00	150 683 00				

Draw a single rule to indicate that the columns are to be added.

Total debits must equal total credits.

Draw a double rule under the Debit/Credit column totals.

Adjustments and the Worksheet   CHAPTER 5   143

FIGURE 5.8E The Financial Statement Columns

The accounts from the Adjusted Trial Balance columns are next extended to the columns of the statements on which the accounts will appear. The account balances for the asset, liability, and owner's capital accounts are extended to the Balance Sheet columns. The owner's drawing account balance is extended to the Balance Sheet Debit column and will be used when the formal statement of owner's equity is prepared. The balances of the revenue and expense accounts are extended to the Income Statement columns.

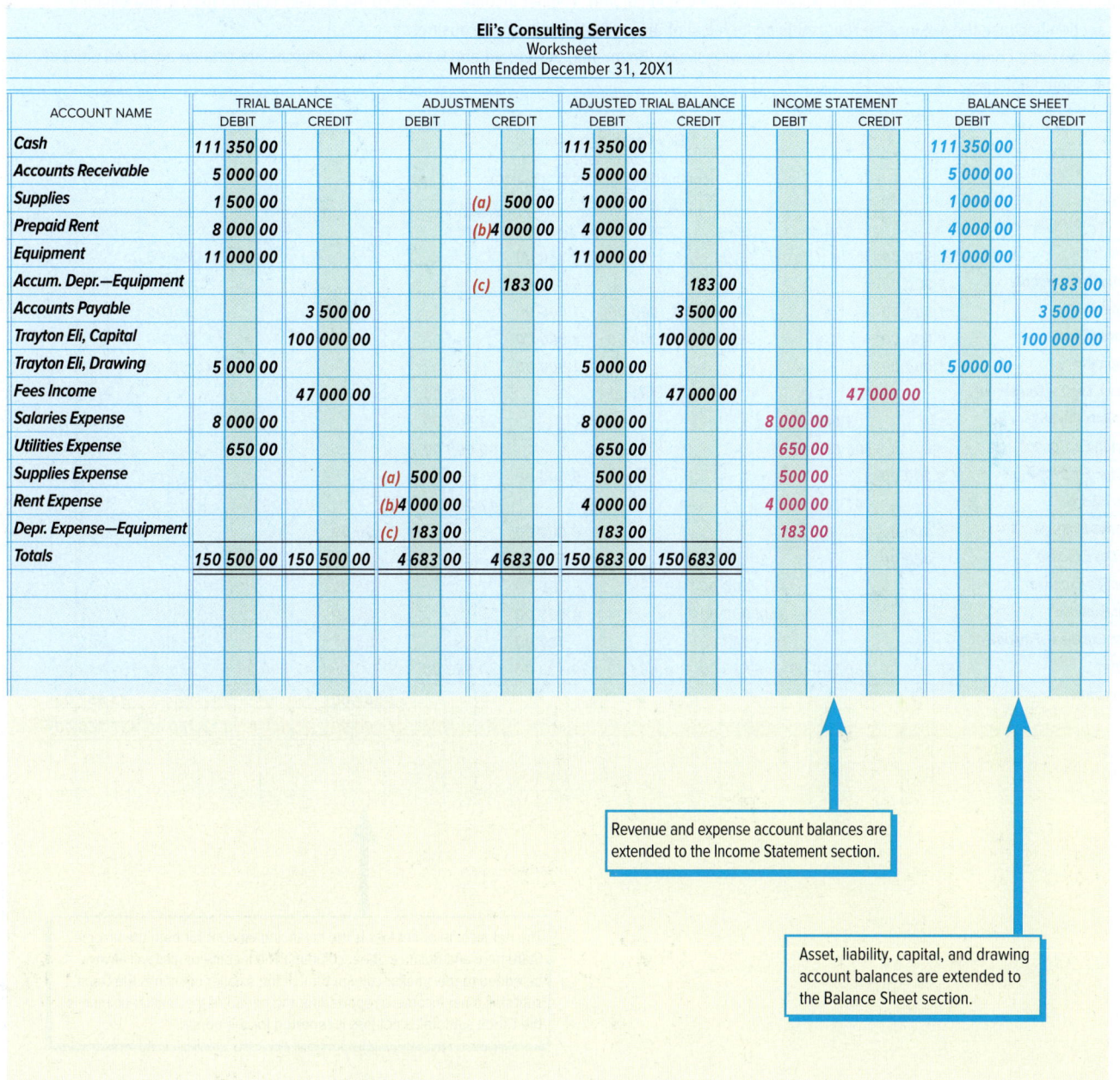

Revenue and expense account balances are extended to the Income Statement section.

Asset, liability, capital, and drawing account balances are extended to the Balance Sheet section.

FIGURE 5.8F Determining Net Income or Net Loss

After all account balances have been transferred to the financial statement sections, the columns in the Income Statement and Balance Sheet sections are totaled. The difference between the larger and smaller column totals represents the net income or net loss for the period. In the case of Eli's Consulting Services, the difference of $33,667.00 represents the net income for the period because the smaller column in the Income Statement section is the Debit column. This balance indicates that the firm had more revenue for the period than expenses. Notice that the smaller column in the Balance Sheet section of the worksheet is the Credit column. The net income is added to the smaller column total in the Balance Sheet section because the net income represents an increase of the owner's equity in the business.

After the net income or net loss is recorded on the worksheet, the Income Statement and Balance Sheet columns are totaled again. All pairs of columns should balance.

Eli's Consulting Services
Worksheet
Month Ended December 31, 20X1

ACCOUNT NAME	TRIAL BALANCE DEBIT	TRIAL BALANCE CREDIT	ADJUSTMENTS DEBIT	ADJUSTMENTS CREDIT	ADJUSTED TRIAL BALANCE DEBIT	ADJUSTED TRIAL BALANCE CREDIT	INCOME STATEMENT DEBIT	INCOME STATEMENT CREDIT	BALANCE SHEET DEBIT	BALANCE SHEET CREDIT
Cash	111 350 00				111 350 00				111 350 00	
Accounts Receivable	5 000 00				5 000 00				5 000 00	
Supplies	1 500 00			(a) 500 00	1 000 00				1 000 00	
Prepaid Rent	8 000 00			(b) 4 000 00	4 000 00				4 000 00	
Equipment	11 000 00				11 000 00				11 000 00	
Accum. Depr.—Equipment				(c) 183 00		183 00				183 00
Accounts Payable		3 500 00				3 500 00				3 500 00
Trayton Eli, Capital		100 000 00				100 000 00				100 000 00
Trayton Eli, Drawing	5 000 00				5 000 00				5 000 00	
Fees Income		47 000 00				47 000 00		47 000 00		
Salaries Expense	8 000 00				8 000 00		8 000 00			
Utilities Expense	650 00				650 00		650 00			
Supplies Expense			(a) 500 00		500 00		500 00			
Rent Expense			(b) 4 000 00		4 000 00		4 000 00			
Depr. Expense—Equipment			(c) 183 00		183 00		183 00			
Totals	150 500 00	150 500 00	4 683 00	4 683 00	150 683 00	150 683 00	13 333 00	47 000 00	137 350 00	103 683 00
Net Income							33 667 00			33 667 00
							47 000 00	47 000 00	137 350 00	137 350 00

The net income or net loss is the balancing amount for both the Income Statement and Balance Sheet columns. The income or loss will always be added to the smaller column total. If the smaller column is the Debit subtotal, a net income is reported for the period. If the smaller column is the Credit subtotal, a net loss is reported for the period.

FIGURE 5.8G Preparing the Financial Statements

The information needed to prepare the financial statements is obtained from the worksheet.

Eli's Consulting Services
Income Statement
Month Ended December 31, 20X1

Revenue		
Fees Income		47 000 00
Expenses		
Salaries Expense	8 000 00	
Utilities Expense	650 00	
Supplies Expense	500 00	
Rent Expense	4 000 00	
Depreciation Expense—Equipment	183 00	
Total Expenses		13 333 00
Net Income		33 667 00

When expenses for the period are less than revenue, a net income results. The net income is transferred to the statement of owner's equity.

Eli's Consulting Services
Statement of Owner's Equity
Month Ended December 31, 20X1

Trayton Eli, Capital, December 1, 20X1		100 000 00
Net Income for December	33 667 00	
Less Withdrawals for December	5 000 00	
Increase in Capital		28 667 00
Trayton Eli, Capital, December 31, 20X1		128 667 00

The withdrawals are subtracted from the net income for the period to determine the change in owner's equity.

Eli's Consulting Services
Balance Sheet
December 31, 20X1

Assets		
Cash		111 350 00
Accounts Receivable		5 000 00
Supplies		1 000 00
Prepaid Rent		4 000 00
Equipment	11 000 00	
Less Accumulated Depreciation	183 00	10 817 00
Total Assets		132 167 00
Liabilities and Owner's Equity		
Liabilities		
Accounts Payable		3 500 00
Owner's Equity		
Trayton Eli, Capital		128 667 00
Total Liabilities and Owner's Equity		132 167 00

The ending capital balance is transferred from the statement of owner's equity to the balance sheet.

Summary of Financial Statements

The Income Statement

The income statement is prepared directly from the data in the Income Statement section of the worksheet. The heading of the income statement contains the name of the firm (WHO), the name of the statement (WHAT), and the period covered by the statement (WHEN). The revenue section of the statement is prepared first. The revenue account name is obtained from the Account Name column of the worksheet. The balance of the revenue account is obtained from the Credit column of the Income Statement section of the worksheet. The expenses section of the income statement is prepared next. The expense account titles are obtained from the Account Name column of the worksheet. The balance of each expense account is obtained from the Debit column of the Income Statement section of the worksheet.

Determining the net income or net loss for the period is the last step in preparing the income statement. If the firm has more revenue than expenses, a net income is reported for the period. If the firm has more expenses than revenue, a net loss is reported. The net income or net loss reported must agree with the amount calculated on the worksheet.

The Statement of Owner's Equity

The statement of owner's equity is prepared from the data in the Balance Sheet section of the worksheet and the general ledger capital account. The statement of owner's equity is prepared before the balance sheet so that the amount of the ending capital balance is available for presentation on the balance sheet. The heading of the statement contains the name of the firm (WHO), the name of the statement (WHAT), and the date of the statement (WHEN).

The statement begins with the capital account balance at the beginning of the period. Next, the increase or decrease in the owner's capital account is determined. The increase or decrease is computed by adding the net income (or subtracting the net loss) for the period to any additional investments made by the owner during the period and subtracting withdrawals for the period. The increase or decrease is added to the beginning capital balance to obtain the ending capital balance.

The Balance Sheet

The balance sheet is prepared from the data in the Balance Sheet section of the worksheet and the statement of owner's equity. The balance sheet reflects the assets, liabilities, and owner's equity of the firm on the balance sheet date. The heading of the statement contains the name of the firm (WHO), the name of the statement (WHAT), and the date of the statement (WHEN).

The assets section of the statement is prepared first. The asset account titles are obtained from the Account Name column of the worksheet. The balance of each asset account is obtained from the Debit column of the Balance Sheet section of the worksheet. The balance of each contra asset account, such as accumulated depreciation, is obtained from the Credit column of the Balance Sheet section of the worksheet. The liability and owner's equity section is prepared next. The liability and owner's equity account titles are obtained from the Account Name column of the worksheet. The balance of each liability account is obtained from the Credit column of the Balance Sheet section of the worksheet. The ending balance for the owner's capital account is obtained from the statement of owner's equity. Total liabilities and owner's equity must equal total assets.

Journalizing and Posting Adjusting Entries

The worksheet is a tool. It is used to determine the effects of adjustments on account balances. It is also used to prepare the financial statements. However, the worksheet is not part of the permanent accounting record.

After the financial statements are prepared, the adjustments shown on the worksheet must become part of the permanent accounting record. Each adjustment is journalized and posted to the general ledger accounts. Journalizing and posting adjusting entries is the sixth step in the accounting cycle.

For Eli's Consulting Services, three adjustments are needed to provide a complete picture of the firm's operating results and its financial position. Adjustments are needed for supplies expense, rent expense, and depreciation expense.

Refer to Figure 5.4 for data needed to record the adjustments. Enter the words "Adjusting Entries" in the Description column of the general journal. Some accountants prefer to start a new page when they record the adjusting entries. Then journalize the adjustments in the order in which they appear on the worksheet.

After journalizing the adjusting entries, post them to the general ledger accounts. Figure 5.9 shows how the adjusting entries for Eli's Consulting Services on December 31, 20X1, were journalized and posted. Account numbers appear in the general journal Posting Reference column because all entries have been posted. In each general ledger account, the word "Adjusting" appears in the Description column.

Remember that the worksheet is not part of the accounting records. Adjustments that are on the worksheet must be recorded in the general journal and posted to the general ledger in order to become part of the permanent accounting records.

>> 5-5 OBJECTIVE
Journalize and post the adjusting entries.

FIGURE 5.9

Journalized and Posted Adjusting Entries

GENERAL JOURNAL PAGE 3

DATE	DESCRIPTION	POST. REF.	DEBIT	CREDIT
20X1	*Adjusting Entries*			
Dec. 31	Supplies Expense	517	500 00	
	Supplies	121		500 00
31	Rent Expense	520	4 000 00	
	Prepaid Rent	137		4 000 00
31	Depr. Expense—Equipment	523	183 00	
	Accum. Depr.—Equipment	142		183 00

ACCOUNT **Supplies** ACCOUNT NO. **121**

DATE	DESCRIPTION	POST. REF.	DEBIT	CREDIT	BALANCE DEBIT	BALANCE CREDIT
20X1						
Nov. 28		J1	1 500 00		1 500 00	
Dec. 31	Adjusting	J3		500 00	1 000 00	

ACCOUNT **Prepaid Rent** ACCOUNT NO. **137**

DATE	DESCRIPTION	POST. REF.	DEBIT	CREDIT	BALANCE DEBIT	BALANCE CREDIT
20X1						
Nov. 30		J2	8 000 00		8 000 00	
Dec. 31	Adjusting	J3		4 000 00	4 000 00	

ACCOUNT **Accumulated Depreciation—Equipment** ACCOUNT NO. **142**

DATE	DESCRIPTION	POST. REF.	DEBIT	CREDIT	BALANCE DEBIT	BALANCE CREDIT
20X1						
Dec. 31	Adjusting	J3		183 00		183 00

ACCOUNT **Supplies Expense** ACCOUNT NO. **517**

DATE	DESCRIPTION	POST. REF.	DEBIT	CREDIT	BALANCE DEBIT	BALANCE CREDIT
20X1						
Dec. 31	Adjusting	J3	500 00		500 00	

ACCOUNT **Rent Expense** ACCOUNT NO. **520**

DATE	DESCRIPTION	POST. REF.	DEBIT	CREDIT	BALANCE DEBIT	BALANCE CREDIT
20X1						
Dec. 31	Adjusting	J3	4 000 00		4 000 00	

ACCOUNT **Depreciation Expense—Equipment** ACCOUNT NO. **523**

DATE	DESCRIPTION	POST. REF.	DEBIT	CREDIT	BALANCE DEBIT	BALANCE CREDIT
20X1						
Dec. 31	Adjusting	J3	183 00		183 00	

MANAGERIAL IMPLICATIONS

WORKSHEETS

- The worksheet permits quick preparation of the financial statements. Quick preparation of financial statements allows management to obtain timely information.
- Timely information allows management to:
  - evaluate the results of operations,
  - evaluate the financial position of the business,
  - make decisions.
- The worksheet provides a convenient form for gathering information and determining the effects of internal changes, such as:
  - recording an expense for the use of a long-term asset like equipment,
  - recording the actual use of prepaid items.
- The more accounts that a firm has in its general ledger, the more useful the worksheet is in speeding the preparation of the financial statements.
- It is important to management that the appropriate adjustments are recorded in order to present a complete and accurate picture of the firm's financial affairs.

THINKING CRITICALLY
Why is it necessary to record an adjustment for depreciation?

Section 2 Review

1. The worksheet is a tool that aids in the preparation of the financial statements. Any changes in account balances recorded on the worksheet are not shown in the general journal and the general ledger until the adjusting entries have been journalized and posted.
   a. True
   b. False

2. All of the following amounts appear on the statement of owner's equity except:
   a. net income or net loss for the period.
   b. additional investments by the owner for the period.
   c. the fair market value of the net assets of the business.
   d. the beginning and ending balance of owner's equity.

3. On the report form balance sheet, the liabilities and owner's equity are listed to the right of the assets. On the account form, the liabilities and owner's equity are listed under the assets.
   a. True
   b. False

4. *Accumulated Depreciation—Equipment* is a(n):
   a. contra asset account.
   b. contra liability account.
   c. liability account.
   d. asset account.

5. On a worksheet, the adjusted balance of the *Supplies* account is extended to the:
   a. balance sheet debit column.
   b. balance sheet credit column.
   c. income statement credit column.
   d. income statement debit column.

6. Paxton Office Supply Company purchased equipment for $80,000. *Depreciation Expense* for the month is $1,600. What is the balance of the *Equipment* account after posting the depreciation entry?
   a. $78,400
   b. $81,600
   c. $80,000
   d. $1,600

5 Chapter REVIEW Chapter Summary

At the end of the operating period, adjustments for internal events are recorded to update the accounting records. In this chapter, you have learned how the accountant uses the worksheet and adjusting entries to accomplish this task.

Learning Objectives

5-1 Complete a trial balance on a worksheet.

A worksheet is normally used to save time in preparing the financial statements. Preparation of the worksheet is the fourth step in the accounting cycle. The trial balance is the first section of the worksheet to be prepared.

5-2 Prepare adjustments for unrecorded business transactions.

Some changes arise from the internal operations of the firm itself. Adjusting entries are made to record these changes. Any adjustments to account balances should be entered in the Adjustments section of the worksheet.

- Prepaid expenses are expense items that are acquired and paid for in advance of their use. At the time of their acquisition, these items represent assets and are recorded in asset accounts. As they are used, their cost is transferred to expense by means of adjusting entries at the end of each accounting period.

  Examples of general ledger asset accounts and the related expense accounts follow:

Asset Accounts	Expense Accounts
Supplies	Supplies Expense
Prepaid Rent	Rent Expense
Prepaid Insurance	Insurance Expense

- Depreciation is the process of allocating the cost of a long-term tangible asset to operations over its expected useful life. Part of the asset's cost is charged off as an expense at the end of each accounting period during the asset's useful life. The straight-line method of depreciation is widely used. The formula for straight-line depreciation is:

$$\text{Depreciation} = \frac{\text{Cost} - \text{Salvage value}}{\text{Estimated useful life}}$$

5-3 Complete the worksheet.

An adjusted trial balance is prepared to prove the equality of the debits and credits after adjustments have been entered on the worksheet. Once the Debit and Credit columns have been totaled and ruled, the Income Statement and Balance Sheet columns of the worksheet are completed. The net income or net loss for the period is determined, and the worksheet is completed.

5-4 Prepare an income statement, statement of owner's equity, and balance sheet from the completed worksheet.

All figures needed to prepare the financial statements are properly reflected on the completed worksheet. The accounts are arranged in the order in which they must appear on the income statement and balance sheet. Preparation of the financial statements is the fifth step of the accounting cycle.

5-5 Journalize and post the adjusting entries.

After the financial statements have been prepared, the accountant must make permanent entries in the accounting records for the adjustments shown on the worksheet. The adjusting entries are then posted to the general ledger. Journalizing and posting the adjusting entries is the sixth step in the accounting cycle.

To summarize the steps of the accounting cycle discussed so far:

1. Analyze transactions.
2. Journalize transactions.
3. Post the journal entries.
4. Prepare a worksheet.
5. Prepare financial statements.
6. Record adjusting entries.

5-6 Define the accounting terms new to this chapter.

Glossary

Account form balance sheet (p. 138) A balance sheet that lists assets on the left and liabilities and owner's equity on the right (see also Report form balance sheet)

Adjusting entries (p. 127) Journal entries made to update accounts for items that were not recorded during the accounting period

Adjustments (p. 127) See Adjusting entries

Book value (p. 131) That portion of an asset's original cost that has not yet been depreciated

Contra account (p. 130) An account with a normal balance that is opposite that of a related account

Contra asset account (p. 130) An asset account with a credit balance, which is contrary to the normal balance of an asset account

Depreciation (p. 130) Allocation of the cost of a long-term asset to operations during its expected useful life

Prepaid expenses (p. 128) Expense items acquired, recorded, and paid for in advance of their use

Report form balance sheet (p. 138) A balance sheet that lists the asset accounts first, followed by liabilities and owner's equity

Salvage value (p. 130) An estimate of the amount that could be received by selling or disposing of an asset at the end of its useful life

Straight-line depreciation (p. 130) Allocation of an asset's cost in equal amounts to each accounting period of the asset's useful life

Worksheet (p. 126) A form used to gather all data needed at the end of an accounting period to prepare financial statements

Comprehensive Self Review

1. The *Drawing* account is extended to which column of the worksheet?
2. Why is the net income for a period recorded in the Balance Sheet section of the worksheet as well as the Income Statement section?
3. Is the normal balance for *Accumulated Depreciation* a debit or credit balance?
4. Why are assets depreciated?
5. The *Supplies* account has a debit balance of $9,000 in the Trial Balance column. The Credit column in the Adjustments section is $3,600. What is the new balance? The new balance will be extended to which column of the worksheet?

(Answers to Comprehensive Self Review are at the end of the chapter.)

Discussion Questions

1. What effect does each of the following items have on net income?
   a. The owner withdrew cash from the business.
   b. Credit customers paid on outstanding balances that were past due.
   c. The business bought equipment on account.
   d. The business journalized and posted an adjustment for depreciation of equipment.
2. What effect does each item in Question 1 have on owner's equity?
3. Why is it necessary to journalize and post adjusting entries?
4. What three amounts are reported on the balance sheet for a long-term asset such as equipment?

5. What is book value?
6. How does a contra asset account differ from a regular asset account?
7. Why is an accumulated depreciation account used in making the adjustment for depreciation?
8. Are the following assets depreciated? Why or why not?
   a. Prepaid Insurance
   b. Delivery Truck
   c. Land
   d. Manufacturing Equipment
   e. Prepaid Rent
   f. Furniture
   g. Store Equipment
   h. Prepaid Advertising
   i. Computers
9. How does the straight-line method of depreciation work?
10. Give three examples of assets that are subject to depreciation.
11. Why is it necessary to make an adjustment for supplies used?
12. What are prepaid expenses? Give four examples.
13. What adjustment would be recorded for expired insurance?
14. A firm purchases machinery, which has an estimated useful life of 10 years and no salvage value, for $60,000 at the beginning of the accounting period. What is the adjusting entry for depreciation at the end of one month if the firm uses the straight-line method of depreciation?

APPLICATIONS

Exercises

Exercise 5.1

Objective 5-2

▶ **Calculating adjustments.**

Determine the necessary end-of-June adjustments for Conner Company.

1. On June 1, 20X1, Conner Company, a new firm, paid $16,800 rent in advance for a seven-month period. The $16,800 was debited to the **Prepaid Rent** account.
2. On June 1, 20X1, the firm bought supplies for $12,580. The $12,580 was debited to the **Supplies** account. An inventory of supplies at the end of June showed that items costing $9,275 were on hand.
3. On June 1, 20X1, the firm bought equipment costing $108,000. The equipment has an expected useful life of nine years and no salvage value. The firm will use the straight-line method of depreciation.

Exercise 5.2

Objective 5-2

▶ **Calculating adjustments.**

For each of the following situations, determine the necessary adjustments.

1. A firm purchased a three-year insurance policy for $27,000 on July 1, 20X1. The $27,000 was debited to the **Prepaid Insurance** account. What adjustment should be made to record expired insurance on the firm's July 31, 20X1, worksheet?
2. On December 1, 20X1, a firm signed a contract with a local radio station for advertising that will extend over a two-year period. The firm paid $72,000 in advance and debited the amount to **Prepaid Advertising.** What adjustment should be made to record expired advertising on the firm's December 31, 20X1, worksheet?

Worksheet through Adjusted Trial Balance.

On January 31, 20X1, the general ledger of Johnson Company showed the following account balances. Prepare the worksheet through the Adjusted Trial Balance section. Assume that every account has the normal debit or credit balance. The worksheet covers the month of January.

► **Exercise 5.3**
Objectives 5-1, 5-2

ACCOUNTS	
Cash	63,000
Accounts Receivable	22,500
Supplies	9,000
Prepaid Insurance	8,200
Equipment	91,500
Accum. Depr.—Equip.	0
Accounts Payable	16,700
Elicia Johnson, Capital	81,950
Fees Income	117,000
Rent Expense	10,600
Salaries Expense	10,850
Supplies Expense	0
Insurance Expense	0
Depreciation Expense—Equipment	0

ADDITIONAL INFORMATION:

a. Supplies used during January totaled $5,700.
b. Expired insurance totaled $2,050.
c. Depreciation expense for the month was $1,850.

Correcting net income.

Assume that a firm reports net income of $135,000 prior to making adjusting entries for the following items: expired rent, $10,500; depreciation expense, $12,300; and supplies used, $5,400.

Assume that the required adjusting entries have not been made. What effect do these errors have on the reported net income?

► **Exercise 5.4**
Objective 5-2

Journalizing and posting adjustments.

Lancaster Company must make three adjusting entries on December 31, 20X1.

a. Supplies used, $11,000 (supplies totaling $18,000 were purchased on December 1, 20X1, and debited to the *Supplies* account).
b. Expired insurance, $8,200; on December 1, 20X1, the firm paid $49,200 for six months' insurance coverage in advance and debited *Prepaid Insurance* for this amount.
c. Depreciation expense for equipment, $5,800.

Make the journal entries for these adjustments and post the entries to the general ledger accounts: Use page 3 of the general journal for the adjusting entries. Use the following accounts and numbers.

► **Exercise 5.5**
Objective 5-5

Supplies	121
Prepaid Insurance	131
Accum. Depr.—Equip.	142
Depreciation Exp.—Equip.	517
Insurance Expense	521
Supplies Expense	523

PROBLEMS

Problem Set A

Problem 5.1A
Objectives 5-2, 5-3

▶ **Completing the worksheet.**

The trial balance of Ortiz Company as of January 31, 20X1, after the company completed the first month of operations, is shown in the partial worksheet below.

INSTRUCTIONS

Complete the worksheet by making the following adjustments: supplies on hand at the end of the month, $4,200; expired insurance, $5,500; depreciation expense on equipment for the period, $1,600.

Analyze: How does the insurance adjustment affect *Prepaid Insurance*?

Ortiz Company
Worksheet (Partial)
Month Ended January 31, 20X1

	ACCOUNT NAME	TRIAL BALANCE DEBIT	TRIAL BALANCE CREDIT	ADJUSTMENTS DEBIT	ADJUSTMENTS CREDIT
1	Cash	105 000 00			
2	Accounts Receivable	21 800 00			
3	Supplies	39 400 00			
4	Prepaid Insurance	66 000 00			
5	Equipment	109 000 00			
6	Accumulated Depreciation—Equipment				
7	Accounts Payable		25 800 00		
8	Frank Ortiz, Capital		253 000 00		
9	Frank Ortiz, Drawing	15 400 00			
10	Fees Income		114 200 00		
11	Supplies Expense				
12	Insurance Expense				
13	Salaries Expense	32 200 00			
14	Depreciation Expense—Equipment				
15	Utilities Expense	4 200 00			
16	Totals	393 000 00	393 000 00		

Problem 5.2A
Objectives 5-1, 5-2, 5-3

▶ **Reconstructing a partial worksheet.**

The **adjusted** trial balance of Campus Book Store and Supply Company as of November 30, 20X1, after the firm's first month of operations, appears below.

Appropriate adjustments have been made for the following items:

a. Supplies used during the month, $5,800.
b. Expired rent for the month, $7,000.
c. Depreciation expense for the month, $1,900.

INSTRUCTIONS

1. Record the Adjusted Trial Balance in the Adjusted Trial Balance columns of the worksheet.
2. Prepare the adjusting entries in the Adjustments columns.
3. Complete the Trial Balance columns of the worksheet prior to making the adjusting entries.

Analyze: What was the balance of *Prepaid Rent* prior to the adjusting entry for expired rent?

Campus Book Store and Supply Company
Adjusted Trial Balance
November 30, 20X1

Account Name	Debit	Credit
Cash	$ 46,150	
Accounts Receivable	7,624	
Supplies	9,200	
Prepaid Rent	42,000	
Equipment	55,000	
Accumulated Depreciation—Equipment		$ 1,900
Accounts Payable		18,000
Stanley Ingram, Capital		83,674
Stanley Ingram, Drawing	8,000	
Fees Income		97,100
Depreciation Expense—Equipment	1,900	
Rent Expense	7,000	
Salaries Expense	17,000	
Supplies Expense	5,800	
Utilities Expense	1,000	
Totals	$200,674	$200,674

◀ **Problem 5.3A**
Objective 5-4

Preparing financial statements from the worksheet.

The completed worksheet for Chavarria Corporation as of December 31, 20X1, after the company had completed the first month of operation, appears below.

INSTRUCTIONS

1. Prepare an income statement.
2. Prepare a statement of owner's equity. The owner made no additional investments during the month.
3. Prepare a balance sheet (use the report form).

Analyze: If the adjustment to *Prepaid Advertising* had been $6,800 instead of $3,400, what net income would have resulted?

◀ **Problem 5.4A**
Objectives 5-2, 5-3, 5-4, 5-5

Preparing a worksheet and financial statements, journalizing adjusting entries, and posting to ledger accounts.

Shayla Green owns Creative Designs. The trial balance of the firm for January 31, 20X1, the first month of operations, is shown below.

INSTRUCTIONS

1. Complete the worksheet for the month.
2. Prepare an income statement, statement of owner's equity, and balance sheet. No additional investments were made by the owner during the month.
3. Journalize and post the adjusting entries. Use 3 for the journal page number. Use the following account numbers: **Supplies,** 121; **Prepaid Advertising,** 130; **Prepaid Rent,** 131; **Accumulated Depreciation—Equipment,** 142; **Supplies Expense,** 517; **Advertising Expense,** 519; **Rent Expense,** 520; **Depreciation Expense—Equipment,** 523.

End-of-the-month adjustments must account for the following items:

a. Supplies were purchased on January 1, 20X1; inventory of supplies on January 31, 20X1, is $3,200.
b. The prepaid advertising contract was signed on January 1, 20X1, and covers a four-month period.

Chavarria Corporation
Worksheet
Month Ended December 31, 20X1

ACCOUNT NAME	TRIAL BALANCE DEBIT	TRIAL BALANCE CREDIT	ADJUSTMENTS DEBIT	ADJUSTMENTS CREDIT
1 Cash	78 200 00			
2 Accounts Receivable	13 000 00			
3 Supplies	12 100 00			(a) 7 000 00
4 Prepaid Advertising	20 400 00			(b) 3 400 00
5 Equipment	85 000 00			
6 Accumulated Depreciation—Equipment				(c) 1 700 00
7 Accounts Payable		13 000 00		
8 Isabel Chavarria, Capital		109 000 00		
9 Isabel Chavarria, Drawing	8 200 00			
10 Fees Income		115 500 00		
11 Supplies Expense			(a) 7 000 00	
12 Advertising Expense			(b) 3 400 00	
13 Depreciation Expense—Equipment			(c) 1 700 00	
14 Salaries Expense	17 800 00			
15 Utilities Expense	2 800 00			
16 Totals	237 500 00	237 500 00	12 100 00	12 100 00
17 Net Income				

c. Rent of $4,200 expired during the month.

d. Depreciation is computed using the straight-line method. The equipment has an estimated useful life of 10 years with no salvage value.

Analyze: If the adjusting entries had not been made for the month, by what amount would net income be overstated or understated?

Creative Designs
Worksheet (Partial)
Month Ended January 31, 20X1

ACCOUNT NAME	TRIAL BALANCE DEBIT	TRIAL BALANCE CREDIT
1 Cash	73 000 00	
2 Accounts Receivable	27 200 00	
3 Supplies	19 500 00	
4 Prepaid Advertising	24 800 00	
5 Prepaid Rent	50 400 00	
6 Equipment	67 200 00	
7 Accumulated Depreciation—Equipment		
8 Accounts Payable		33 100 00
9 Shayla Green, Capital		122 000 00
10 Shayla Green, Drawing	16 000 00	
11 Fees Income		148 200 00
12 Advertising Expense		
13 Depreciation Expense—Equipment		
14 Rent Expense		
15 Salaries Expense	21 400 00	
16 Supplies Expense		
17 Utilities Expense	3 800 00	
18 Totals	303 300 00	303 300 00

	ADJUSTED TRIAL BALANCE		INCOME STATEMENT		BALANCE SHEET	
	DEBIT	CREDIT	DEBIT	CREDIT	DEBIT	CREDIT
1	78 200 00				78 200 00	
2	13 000 00				13 000 00	
3	5 100 00				5 100 00	
4	17 000 00				17 000 00	
5	85 000 00				85 000 00	
6		1 700 00				1 700 00
7		13 000 00				13 000 00
8		109 000 00				109 000 00
9	8 200 00				8 200 00	
10		115 500 00		115 500 00		
11	7 000 00		7 000 00			
12	3 400 00		3 400 00			
13	1 700 00		1 700 00			
14	17 800 00		17 800 00			
15	2 800 00		2 800 00			
16	239 200 00	239 200 00	32 700 00	115 500 00	206 500 00	123 700 00
17			82 800 00			82 800 00
18			115 500 00	115 500 00	206 500 00	206 500 00

Problem Set B

Completing the worksheet.

The trial balance of Lazo Company as of February 28, 20X1, appears below.

◀ **Problem 5.1B**
Objectives 5-2, 5-3

Lazo Company
Worksheet (Partial)
Month Ended February 28, 20X1

	ACCOUNT NAME	TRIAL BALANCE		ADJUSTMENTS	
		DEBIT	CREDIT	DEBIT	CREDIT
1	Cash	73 000 00			
2	Accounts Receivable	6 400 00			
3	Supplies	4 200 00			
4	Prepaid Rent	24 000 00			
5	Equipment	46 000 00			
6	Accumulated Depreciation—Equipment				
7	Accounts Payable		12 000 00		
8	Thomas Lazo, Capital		98 500 00		
9	Thomas Lazo, Drawing	3 000 00			
10	Fees Income		54 000 00		
11	Depreciation Expense—Equipment				
12	Rent Expense				
13	Salaries Expense	6 300 00			
14	Supplies Expense				
15	Utilities Expense	1 600 00			
16	Totals	164 500 00	164 500 00		

INSTRUCTIONS

1. Record the trial balance in the Trial Balance section of the worksheet.
2. Complete the worksheet by making the following adjustments: supplies on hand at the end of the month, $2,200; expired rent, $2,000; depreciation expense for the period, $1,000.

Analyze: Why do you think the account *Accumulated Depreciation—Equipment* has a zero balance on the trial balance shown?

Problem 5.2B

Objectives 5-1, 5-2, 5-3

▶ **Reconstructing a partial worksheet.**

The **adjusted** trial balance of Sergio Mendez, Attorney-at-Law, as of November 30, 20X1, after the company had completed the first month of operations, appears below.

Appropriate adjustments have been made for the following items:

a. Supplies used during the month, $14,400.
b. Expired rent for the month, $13,600.
c. Depreciation expense for the month, $2,200.

Sergio Mendez, Attorney-at-Law
Adjusted Trial Balance
Month Ended November 30, 20X1

Account Name	Debit	Credit
Cash	$140,200	
Accounts Receivable	34,000	
Supplies	27,200	
Prepaid Rent	163,200	
Equipment	264,000	
Accumulated Depreciation—Equipment		$ 2,200
Accounts Payable		68,000
Sergio Mendez, Capital		320,000
Sergio Mendez, Drawing	24,000	
Fees Income		342,800
Salaries Expense	43,200	
Utilities Expense	7,000	
Supplies Expense	14,400	
Rent Expense	13,600	
Depreciation Expense—Equipment	2,200	
Totals	$733,000	$733,000

INSTRUCTIONS

1. Record the adjusted trial balance in the Adjusted Trial Balance columns of the worksheet.
2. Prepare the adjusting entries in the Adjustments columns.
3. Complete the Trial Balance columns of the worksheet prior to making the adjusting entries.

Analyze: Which contra asset account is on the adjusted trial balance?

Preparing financial statements from the worksheet.

◀ **Problem 5.3B**
Objective 5-4

The completed worksheet for JP's Accounting Services for the month ended December 31, 20X1, appears on the next page.

INSTRUCTIONS
1. Prepare an income statement.
2. Prepare a statement of owner's equity. The owner made no additional investments during the month.
3. Prepare a balance sheet.

Analyze: By what total amount did the value of assets reported on the balance sheet decrease due to the adjusting entries?

Preparing a worksheet and financial statements, journalizing adjusting entries, and posting to ledger accounts.

◀ **Problem 5.4B**
Objectives 5-2, 5-3, 5-4, 5-5

Christopher Foster owns Estate Planning and Investments Company. The trial balance of the firm for June 30, 20X1, the first month of operations, is shown below.

Estate Planning and Investments Company
Worksheet (Partial)
Month Ended June 30, 20X1

	ACCOUNT NAME	TRIAL BALANCE DEBIT	TRIAL BALANCE CREDIT	ADJUSTMENTS DEBIT	ADJUSTMENTS CREDIT
1	Cash	78 800 00			
2	Accounts Receivable	24 400 00			
3	Supplies	30 400 00			
4	Prepaid Advertising	57 600 00			
5	Prepaid Rent	144 000 00			
6	Equipment	192 000 00			
7	Accumulated Depreciation—Equipment				
8	Accounts Payable		43 200 00		
9	Christopher Foster, Capital		240 400 00		
10	Christopher Foster, Drawing	16 000 00			
11	Fees Income		295 200 00		
12	Advertising Expense				
13	Depreciation Expense—Equipment				
14	Rent Expense				
15	Salaries Expense	30 400 00			
16	Supplies Expense				
17	Utilities Expense	5 200 00			
18	Totals	578 800 00	578 800 00		
19					

INSTRUCTIONS
1. Complete the worksheet for the month.
2. Prepare an income statement, statement of owner's equity, and balance sheet. No additional investments were made by the owner during the month.
3. Journalize and post the adjusting entries. Use 3 for the journal page number. Use the account numbers provided in Problem 5.4A.

JP's Accounting Services
Worksheet
Month Ended December 31, 20X1

#	ACCOUNT NAME	TRIAL BALANCE DEBIT	TRIAL BALANCE CREDIT	ADJUSTMENTS DEBIT	ADJUSTMENTS CREDIT
1	Cash	33 900 00			
2	Accounts Receivable	4 400 00			
3	Supplies	3 000 00			(a) 1 200 00
4	Prepaid Advertising	8 000 00			(b) 1 600 00
5	Fixtures	36 000 00			
6	Accumulated Depreciation—Fixtures				(c) 600 00
7	Accounts Payable		15 000 00		
8	Jackie Peaches, Capital		60 000 00		
9	Jackie Peaches, Drawing	6 000 00			
10	Fees Income		62 660 00		
11	Supplies Expense			(a) 1 200 00	
12	Advertising Expense			(b) 1 600 00	
13	Depreciation Expense—Fixtures			(c) 600 00	
14	Rent Expense	7 000 00			
15	Salaries Expense	37 200 00			
16	Utilities Expense	2 160 00			
17	Totals	137 660 00	137 660 00	3 400 00	3 400 00
18	Net Income				

End-of-month adjustments must account for the following:

a. The supplies were purchased on June 1, 20X1; inventory of supplies on June 30, 20X1, showed a value of $12,000.

b. The prepaid advertising contract was signed on June 1, 20X1, and covers a four-month period.

c. Rent of $12,000 expired during the month.

d. Depreciation is computed using the straight-line method. The equipment has an estimated useful life of five years with no salvage value.

Analyze: Why are the costs that reduce the value of equipment not directly posted to the asset account *Equipment*?

Critical Thinking Problem 5.1

The Effect of Adjustments

Assume you are the accountant for Catalina Industries. John Catalina, the owner of the company, is in a hurry to receive the financial statements for the year ended December 31, 20X1, and asks you how soon they will be ready. You tell him you have just completed the trial balance and are getting ready to prepare the adjusting entries. Mr. Catalina tells you not to waste time preparing adjusting entries but to complete the worksheet without them and prepare the financial statements based on the data in the trial balance. According to him, the adjusting entries will not make that much difference. The trial balance shows the following account balances:

Prepaid Rent	$ 84,000
Supplies	36,000
Building	470,000
Accumulated Depreciation—Building	28,000

ADJUSTED TRIAL BALANCE		INCOME STATEMENT		BALANCE SHEET	
DEBIT	CREDIT	DEBIT	CREDIT	DEBIT	CREDIT
33,900 00				33,900 00	
4,400 00				4,400 00	
1,800 00				1,800 00	
6,400 00				6,400 00	
36,000 00				36,000 00	
	600 00				600 00
	15,000 00				15,000 00
	60,000 00				60,000 00
6,000 00				6,000 00	
	62,660 00		62,660 00		
1,200 00		1,200 00			
1,600 00		1,600 00			
600 00		600 00			
7,000 00		7,000 00			
37,200 00		37,200 00			
2,160 00		2,160 00			
		49,760 00	62,660 00	88,500 00	75,600 00
		12,900 00			12,900 00
138,260 00	138,260 00	62,660 00	62,660 00	88,500 00	88,500 00

If the income statement were prepared using trial balance amounts, the net income would be $191,120. A review of the company's records reveals the following information:

1. Rent of $84,000 was paid on July 1, 20X1, for 12 months.
2. Purchases of supplies during the year totaled $36,000. An inventory of supplies taken at year-end showed supplies on hand of $5,440.
3. The building was purchased three years ago and has an estimated life of 30 years and a salvage value of $50,000.
4. No adjustments have been made to any of the accounts during the year.

Write a memo to Mr. Catalina explaining the effect on the financial statements of omitting the adjustments. Indicate the change to net income that results from the adjusting entries.

Critical Thinking Problem 5.2

Worksheet and Financial Statements

The account balances for the Pittman International Company on January 31, 20X1, follow. The balances shown are after the first month of operations.

101	Cash	$18,475	401	Fees Income	$30,925
111	Accounts Receivable	3,400	511	Advertising Expense	1,500
121	Supplies	2,150	514	Depr. Expense—Equip.	0
131	Prepaid Insurance	15,000	517	Insurance Expense	0
141	Equipment	24,000	518	Rent Expense	2,500
142	Accum. Depr.—Equip.	0	519	Salaries Expense	6,700
202	Accounts Payable	6,000	520	Supplies Expense	0
301	Reginald Pittman, Capital	40,000	523	Telephone Expense	350
302	Reginald Pittman, Drawing	2,000	524	Utilities Expense	850

INSTRUCTIONS

1. Prepare the Trial Balance section of the worksheet.
2. Record the following adjustments in the Adjustments section of the worksheet:
   a. Supplies used during the month amounted to $1,050.
   b. The amount in the **Prepaid Insurance** account represents a payment made on January 1, 20X1, for six months of insurance coverage.
   c. The equipment, purchased on January 1, 20X1, has an estimated useful life of 10 years with no salvage value. The firm uses the straight-line method of depreciation.
3. Complete the worksheet.
4. Prepare an income statement, statement of owner's equity, and balance sheet (use the report form).
5. Record the balances in the selected general ledger accounts, then journalize and post the adjusting entries. Use 3 for the journal page number.

Analyze: If the useful life of the equipment had been 12 years instead of 10 years, how would net income have been affected?

BUSINESS CONNECTIONS

Understanding Adjustments

Managerial FOCUS

1. A building owned by Hopewell Company was recently valued at $850,000 by a real estate expert. The president of the company is questioning the accuracy of the firm's latest balance sheet because it shows a book value of $550,000 for the building. How would you explain this situation to the president?
2. At the beginning of the year, Mandela Company purchased a new building and some expensive new machinery. An officer of the firm has asked you whether this purchase will affect the firm's year-end income statement. What answer would you give?
3. Suppose the president of a company where you work as an accountant questions whether it is worthwhile for you to spend time making adjustments at the end of each accounting period. How would you explain the value of the adjustments?
4. How does the worksheet help provide vital information to management?

Internal Controls for Journal Entries

Internal Control and FRAUD PREVENTION

Journal entries and adjusting journal entries can be used to conceal theft of company assets as well as to inflate a company's profits or deflate company losses. One of the biggest bankruptcies and biggest accounting scandals in the United States occurred at a company called WorldCom. To hide falling profitability, WorldCom recorded expenses as investments, which increased its profits by the amount of the expenses that were capitalized. To hide the theft of supplies, an employee might hide the theft by making an adjusting entry to cover up the supplies taken. Suppose a company purchases supplies during the period of $10,000 and actually has $5,000 of supplies on hand at the end of the period. If an employee steals $2,000 of supplies, to cover it up the employee makes an adjusting journal entry debiting Supplies Expense for $7,000 (instead of $5,000) and credits Supplies for $7,000 (instead of $5,000). The commission of fraudulent accounting crime by WorldCom and several other companies led to the passage of the Sarbanes-Oxley Act in 2002. The Sarbanes-Oxley Act (discussed in Chapter 1) strengthened accounting disclosure requirements and significantly increased penalties for fraudulent accounting.

To prevent journal entry fraud, what are some basic internal control procedures for recording journal entries (including adjusting journal entries) that should exist in every company?

Depreciation

Financial Statement ANALYSIS

DuPont reported depreciation expense of $1,308 million on its consolidated financial statements for the period ended December 31, 2018. The following excerpt is taken from the company's consolidated balance sheet for the same year:

(Dollars in millions, except per share) December 31, 2018

Property, Plant and Equipment	$13,906
Less: Accumulated depreciation	1,720
Net property, plant, and equipment	$12,186

Analyze:

1. What percentage of the original cost of property, plant, and equipment was depreciated *during* 2018?
2. What percentage of property, plant, and equipment cost was depreciated *as of* December 31, 2018?
3. If the company continued to record depreciation expense at this level each year, how many years remain until all assets would be fully depreciated? (Assume no salvage values.)

Analyze Online: Connect to the DuPont website (www.dupont.com). Click on the *Investors* link to find information on quarterly earnings.

4. What is the most recent quarterly earnings statement presented? What period does the statement cover?
5. For the most recent quarter, what depreciation expense was reported?

Matching Expenses and Revenue

TEAMWORK

Edward Foster is a building contractor. He and his customer have agreed that he will submit a bill to them when he is 25 percent complete, 50 percent complete, 75 percent complete, and 100 percent complete. For example, he has a $300,000 room addition. When he has completed 25 percent, he will bill his customer $25,000. The problem occurs when he is 40 percent complete and has incurred expenses but cannot bill his customer. How can his revenue and expenses match? Discuss in a group several ways that Edward's accountants could solve this problem. What accounts would be used?

Answers to Comprehensive Self Review

1. Debit column of the Balance Sheet section.
2. Net income causes a net increase in owner's equity.
3. Credit balance.
4. To allocate the cost of the assets to operations during their expected useful lives.
5. $5,400 ($9,000 − $3,600). Debit column of the Balance Sheet section.

Closing Entries and the Postclosing Trial Balance

Chapter 6

Royalty-Free/Corbis

www.carnival.com

The folks at Carnival Cruise Lines have made it their business to help people enjoy their leisure time. For nearly 40 years, Carnival has made luxurious ocean cruising a reasonable vacation option for many individuals. Often, for under $100 per person per day, passengers can enjoy a seven-day Caribbean cruise on a ship with soaring atriums, expansive spas, children's facilities, and double promenades offering a myriad of entertainment venues.

Since the TSS *Mardi Gras* made its first voyage in 1972, Carnival Corporation has grown to become the most popular cruise line in the world, attracting four million guests annually. Carnival Cruise Lines is the flagship company of Carnival Corporation & plc, the largest cruise vacation group in the world, with a portfolio of cruise brands in North America, Europe, Australia, and Asia. Headquartered in Miami, Florida, and London, England, Carnival Corporation & plc generated $18.9 billion in revenues in 2018 and realized a total net income of $3.2 billion.

When a company has been around as long as Carnival, much of its success is dependent on being able to compare its revenues and expenses from one year to the next. In order to do this, Carnival needs to separate revenues and expenses into separate accounting periods so that it can "start fresh" each year. This separation enables the company to evaluate how it is performing from one year to the next. It can help the company pinpoint problem areas—for example, higher ship-to-shore excursion costs—but it can also spotlight improvements—for example, increased revenues in the onboard casinos.

thinking critically

How do Carnival's managers use financial statements to evaluate performance? How might these evaluations affect business policies or strategies?

LEARNING OBJECTIVES	NEW TERMS
6-1 Journalize and post closing entries.	closing entries
6-2 Prepare a postclosing trial balance.	*Income Summary* account
6-3 Interpret financial statements.	interpret
6-4 Review the steps in the accounting cycle.	postclosing trial balance
6-5 Define the accounting terms new to this chapter.	

Section 1

> **SECTION OBJECTIVES**
>
> **>> 6-1** Journalize and post closing entries.
>
> **WHY IT'S IMPORTANT**
> A business ends its accounting cycle at a given point in time. The closing process prepares the accounting records for the beginning of a new accounting cycle.
>
> **TERMS TO LEARN**
>
> closing entries
> *Income Summary* account

Closing Entries

In Chapter 5, we discussed the worksheet and the adjusting entries. In this chapter, you will learn about closing entries.

The Closing Process

The seventh step in the accounting cycle is to journalize and post closing entries. **Closing entries** are journal entries that:

- transfer the results of operations (net income or net loss) to owner's equity,
- reduce revenue, expense, and drawing account balances to zero.

THE *INCOME SUMMARY* ACCOUNT

The *Income Summary* **account** is a special owner's equity account that is used only in the closing process to summarize results of operations. *Income Summary* has a zero balance after the closing process, and it remains with a zero balance until after the closing procedure for the next period.

FIGURE 6.1 Worksheet for Eli's Consulting Services

Eli's Consulting Services
Worksheet
Month Ended December 31, 20X1

	ACCOUNT NAME	TRIAL BALANCE DEBIT	TRIAL BALANCE CREDIT	ADJUSTMENTS DEBIT	ADJUSTMENTS CREDIT
1	Cash	111 350 00			
2	Accounts Receivable	5 000 00			
3	Supplies	1 500 00			(a) 500 00
4	Prepaid Rent	8 000 00			(b) 4 000 00
5	Equipment	11 000 00			
6	Accum. Dep.—Equipment				(c) 183 00
7	Accounts Payable		3 500 00		
8	Trayton Eli, Capital		100 000 00		
9	Trayton Eli, Drawing	5 000 00			
10	Fees Income		47 000 00		
11	Salaries Expense	8 000 00			
12	Utilities Expense	650 00			
13	Supplies Expense			(a) 500 00	
14	Rent Expense			(b) 4 000 00	
15	Dep. Expense—Equipment			(c) 183 00	
16					
17	Totals	150 500 00	150 500 00	4 683 00	4 683 00
18	Net Income				
19					

Income Summary is classified as a temporary owner's equity account. Other names for this account are *Revenue and Expense Summary* and *Income and Expense Summary.*

Steps in the Closing Process

There are four steps in the closing process:

1. Transfer the balance of the revenue account to the *Income Summary* account.
2. Transfer the expense account balances to the *Income Summary* account.
3. Transfer the balance of the *Income Summary* account to the owner's capital account.
4. Transfer the balance of the drawing account to the owner's capital account.

The worksheet contains the data necessary to make the closing entries. Refer to Figure 6.1 as you study each closing entry.

Step 1: Transfer Revenue Account Balances

On December 31, the worksheet for Eli's Consulting Services shows one revenue account, *Fees Income*. It has a credit balance of $47,000. To *close* an account means to reduce its balance to zero. In the general journal, enter a debit of $47,000 to close the *Fees Income* account. To balance the journal entry, enter a credit of $47,000 to the *Income Summary* account. This closing entry transfers the total revenue for the period to the *Income Summary* account and reduces the balance of the revenue account to zero.

The analysis of this closing entry is shown below. In this chapter, the visual analyses will show the beginning balances in all T accounts in order to illustrate closing entries.

>> 6-1 OBJECTIVE

Journalize and post closing entries.

ADJUSTED TRIAL BALANCE		INCOME STATEMENT		BALANCE SHEET		
DEBIT	CREDIT	DEBIT	CREDIT	DEBIT	CREDIT	
111 350 00				111 350 00		1
5 000 00				5 000 00		2
1 000 00				1 000 00		3
4 000 00				4 000 00		4
11 000 00				11 000 00		5
	183 00				183 00	6
	3 500 00				3 500 00	7
	100 000 00				100 000 00	8
5 000 00				5 000 00		9
	47 000 00		47 000 00			10
8 000 00		8 000 00				11
650 00		650 00				12
500 00		500 00				13
4 000 00		4 000 00				14
183 00		183 00				15
						16
150 683 00	150 683 00	13 333 00	47 000 00	137 350 00	103 683 00	17
		33 667 00			33 667 00	18
		47 000 00	47 000 00	137 350 00	137 350 00	19

important!

Income Summary Account
The *Income Summary* account does not have an increase or decrease side and no normal balance side.

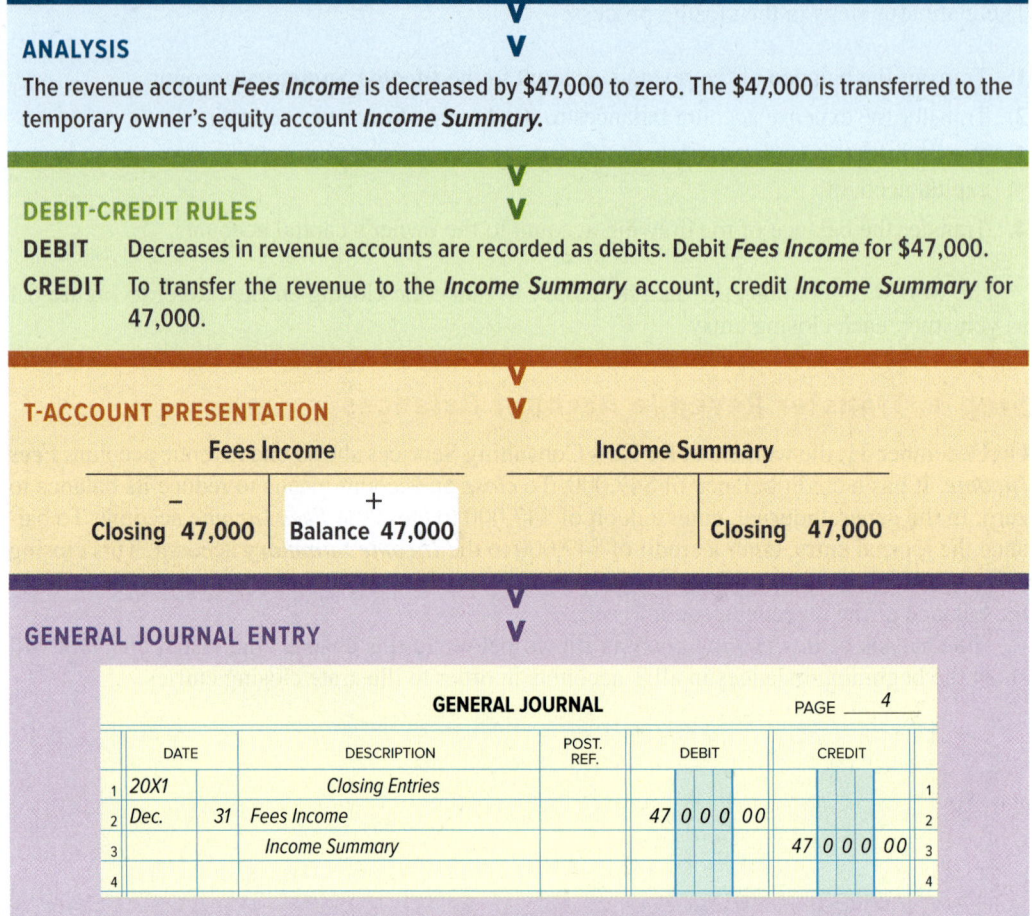

Write "Closing Entries" in the Description column of the general journal on the line above the first closing entry.

> The Home Depot, Inc., reported sales of $108.2 billion for the fiscal year ended February 3, 2019. To close the revenue, the company would debit the *Sales* account and credit the *Income Summary* account.

Step 2: Transfer Expense Account Balances

The Income Statement section of the worksheet for Eli's Consulting Services lists five expense accounts. Since expense accounts have debit balances, enter a credit in each account to reduce its balance to zero. Debit the total of the expenses, $13,333, to the *Income Summary* account. This closing entry transfers total expenses to the *Income Summary* account and reduces the balances of the expense accounts to zero. This is a compound journal entry; it has more than one credit.

CLOSING ENTRY

Second Closing Entry—Close Expenses to Income Summary

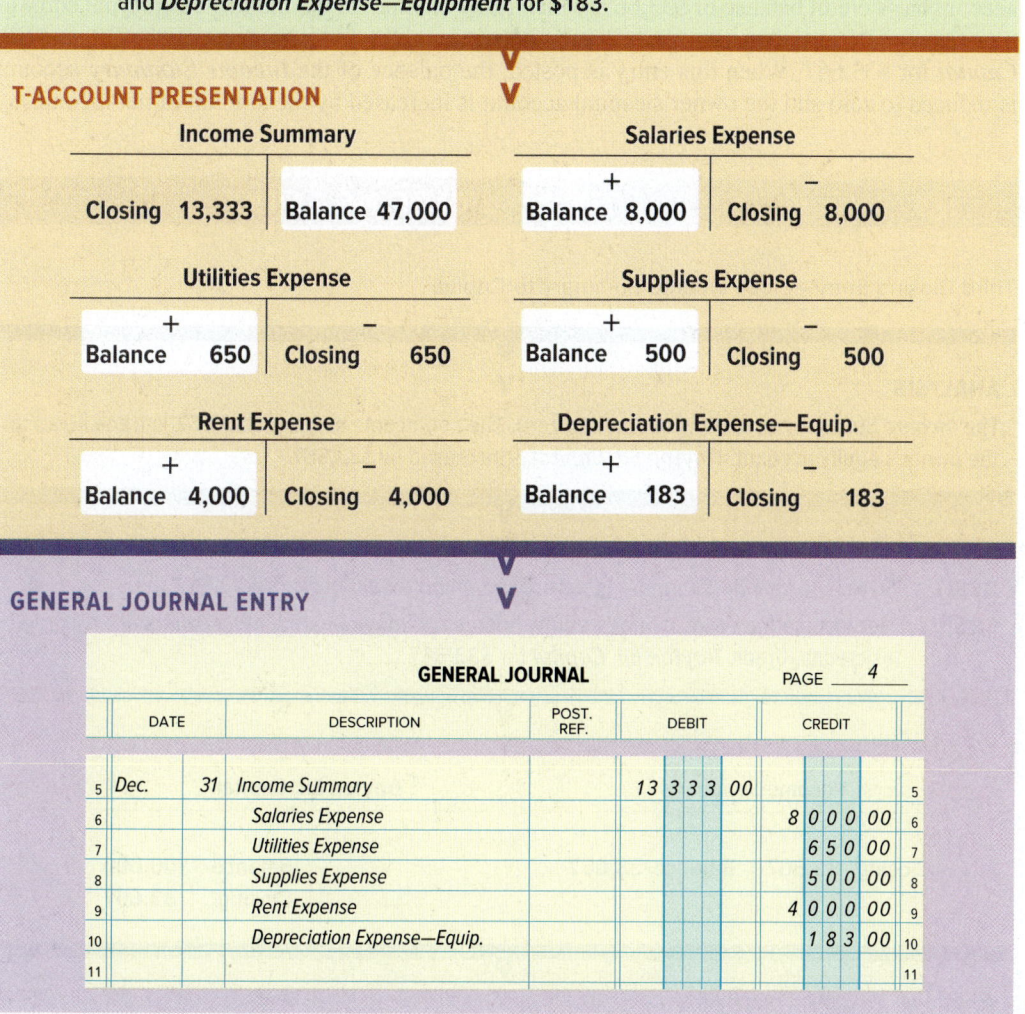

ANALYSIS
The five expense account balances are reduced to zero. The total, $13,333, is transferred to the temporary owner's equity account *Income Summary*.

DEBIT-CREDIT RULES
DEBIT To transfer the expenses to the *Income Summary* account, debit *Income Summary* for $13,333.
CREDIT Decreases to expense accounts are recorded as credits. Credit *Salaries Expense* for $8,000, *Utilities Expense* for $650, *Supplies Expense* for $500, *Rent Expense* for $4,000, and *Depreciation Expense—Equipment* for $183.

T-ACCOUNT PRESENTATION

Income Summary		Salaries Expense	
Closing 13,333	Balance 47,000	Balance 8,000	Closing 8,000

Utilities Expense		Supplies Expense	
Balance 650	Closing 650	Balance 500	Closing 500

Rent Expense		Depreciation Expense—Equip.	
Balance 4,000	Closing 4,000	Balance 183	Closing 183

GENERAL JOURNAL ENTRY

GENERAL JOURNAL PAGE 4

DATE	DESCRIPTION	POST. REF.	DEBIT	CREDIT
Dec. 31	Income Summary		13 333 00	
	Salaries Expense			8 000 00
	Utilities Expense			650 00
	Supplies Expense			500 00
	Rent Expense			4 000 00
	Depreciation Expense—Equip.			183 00

recall
Revenue
Revenue increases owner's equity.

recall
Expenses
Expenses decrease owner's equity.

After the second closing entry, the *Income Summary* account reflects all of the entries in the Income Statement columns of the worksheet.

Income Summary

Dr.		Cr.	
Closing	13,333	Closing	47,000
		Balance	33,667

> The Home Depot, Inc., reported total operating expenses of $21.63 billion for its fiscal year ended February 3, 2019. At the end of the fiscal year, accountants for Home Depot, Inc., transferred the balances of all expense accounts to the *Income Summary* account.

Step 3: Transfer Net Income or Net Loss to Owner's Equity

The next step in the closing process is to transfer the balance of *Income Summary* to the owner's capital account. After the revenue and expense accounts are closed, the *Income Summary* account has a credit balance of $33,667, which is net income for the month. The journal entry to transfer net income to owner's equity is a debit to *Income Summary* and a credit to *Trayton Eli, Capital* for $33,667. When this entry is posted, the balance of the *Income Summary* account is reduced to zero and the owner's capital account is increased by the amount of net income.

CLOSING ENTRY

Third Closing Entry—Close Income Summary to Capital

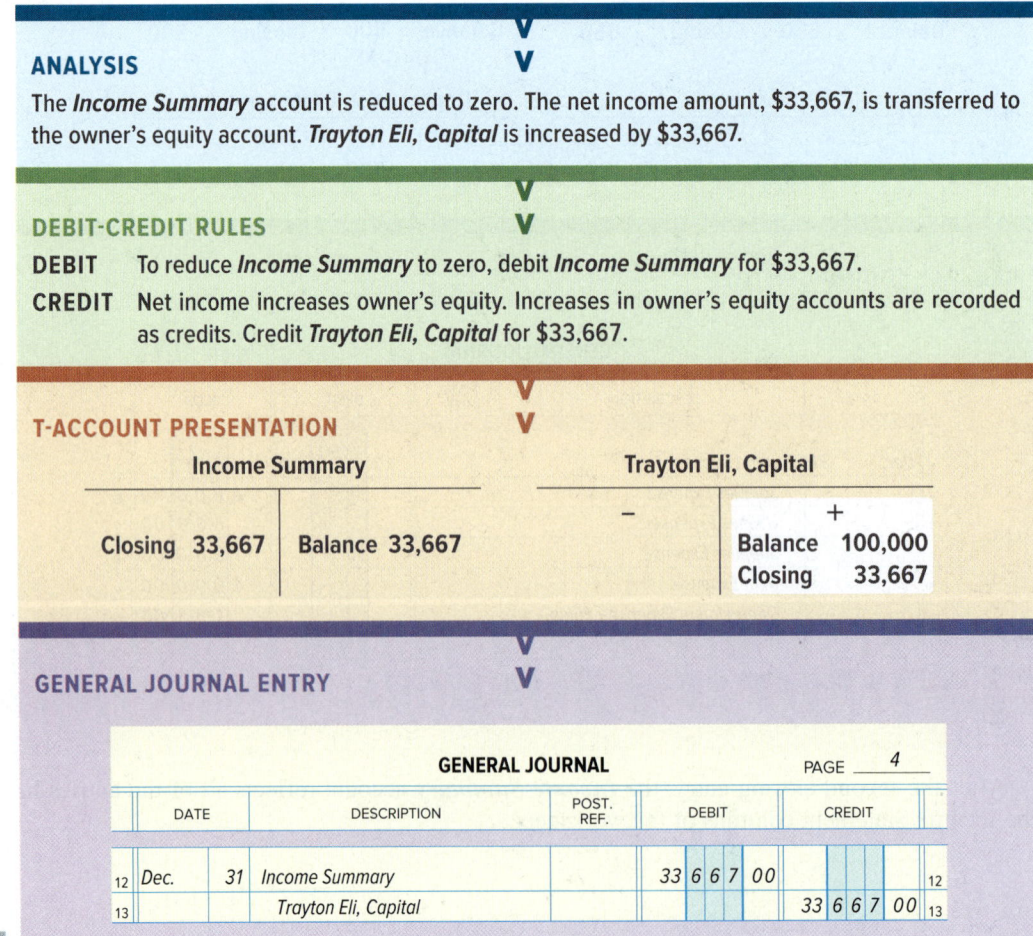

ANALYSIS
The *Income Summary* account is reduced to zero. The net income amount, $33,667, is transferred to the owner's equity account. *Trayton Eli, Capital* is increased by $33,667.

DEBIT-CREDIT RULES
DEBIT To reduce *Income Summary* to zero, debit *Income Summary* for $33,667.
CREDIT Net income increases owner's equity. Increases in owner's equity accounts are recorded as credits. Credit *Trayton Eli, Capital* for $33,667.

T-ACCOUNT PRESENTATION

Income Summary		Trayton Eli, Capital	
−		−	+
Closing 33,667	Balance 33,667		Balance 100,000
			Closing 33,667

GENERAL JOURNAL ENTRY

GENERAL JOURNAL   PAGE 4

DATE	DESCRIPTION	POST. REF.	DEBIT	CREDIT
Dec. 31	Income Summary		33 66 7 00	
	Trayton Eli, Capital			33 66 7 00

After the third closing entry, the *Income Summary* account has a zero balance. The summarized expenses ($13,333) and revenue ($47,000) have been transferred to the owner's equity account ($33,667 net income).

Income Summary			
Dr.		Cr.	
Expenses	13,333	Revenue	47,000
Net Inc.	33,667		
Balance	0		

Trayton Eli, Capital			
Dr.		Cr.	
−		+	
		Balance	100,000
		Net Inc.	33,667
		Balance	133,667

Step 4: Transfer the Drawing Account Balance to Capital

You will recall that withdrawals are funds taken from the business by the owner for personal use. Withdrawals are recorded in the drawing account. Withdrawals are not expenses of the business. They do not affect net income or net loss.

Withdrawals appear in the statement of owner's equity as a deduction from capital. Therefore, the drawing account is closed directly to the capital account.

When this entry is posted, the balance of the drawing account is reduced to zero and the owner's capital account is decreased by the amount of the withdrawals.

recall

Withdrawals
Withdrawals decrease owner's equity.

CLOSING ENTRY

Fourth Closing Entry—Close Withdrawals to Capital

ANALYSIS
The drawing account balance is reduced to zero. The balance of the drawing account, $5,000, is transferred to the owner's equity account.

DEBIT-CREDIT RULES

DEBIT Decreases in owner's equity accounts are recorded as debits. Debit *Trayton Eli, Capital* for $5,000.

CREDIT Decreases in the drawing account are recorded as credits. Credit *Trayton Eli, Drawing* for $5,000.

T-ACCOUNT PRESENTATION

Trayton Eli, Capital			
−		+	
Closing	5,000	Balance	133,667

Trayton Eli, Drawing			
+		−	
Balance	5,000	Closing	5,000

GENERAL JOURNAL ENTRY

GENERAL JOURNAL   PAGE 4

DATE		DESCRIPTION	POST. REF.	DEBIT	CREDIT
Dec.	31	Trayton Eli, Capital		5 000 00	
		Trayton Eli, Drawing			5 000 00

The new balance of the *Trayton Eli, Capital* account agrees with the amount listed in the Owner's Equity section of the balance sheet.

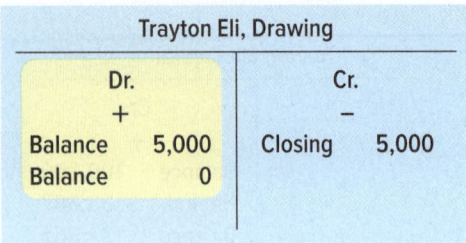

Figure 6.2 shows the general journal and general ledger for Eli's Consulting Services after the closing entries are recorded and posted. Note that:

- "Closing" is entered in the Description column of the ledger accounts;
- the balance of *Trayton Eli, Capital* agrees with the amount shown on the balance sheet for December 31;
- the ending balances of the drawing, revenue, and expense accounts are zero.

This example shows the closing process at the end of one month. Usually businesses make closing entries at the end of the fiscal year only.

FIGURE 6.2

Closing Process Completed: General Journal and General Ledger

Step 1 Close revenue.

Step 2 Close expense accounts.

Step 3 Close Income Summary.

Step 4 Close Drawing account.

GENERAL JOURNAL   PAGE 4

	DATE	DESCRIPTION	POST. REF.	DEBIT	CREDIT
1	20X1	Closing Entries			
2	Dec. 31	Fees Income	401	47 000 00	
3		Income Summary	309		47 000 00
4					
5	31	Income Summary	309	13 333 00	
6		Salaries Expense	511		8 000 00
7		Utilities Expense	514		650 00
8		Supplies Expense	517		500 00
9		Rent Expense	520		4 000 00
10		Depreciation Expense—Equip.	523		183 00
11					
12	31	Income Summary	309	33 667 00	
13		Trayton Eli, Capital	301		33 667 00
14					
15	31	Trayton Eli, Capital	301	5 000 00	
16		Trayton Eli, Drawing	302		5 000 00
17					

ACCOUNT Trayton Eli, Capital   ACCOUNT NO. 301

DATE	DESCRIPTION	POST. REF.	DEBIT	CREDIT	BALANCE DEBIT	BALANCE CREDIT
20X1						
Nov. 6		J1		100 000 00		100 000 00
Dec. 31	Closing	J4		33 667 00		133 667 00
31	Closing	J4	5 000 00			128 667 00

Closing Entries and the Postclosing Trial Balance

ACCOUNT Trayton Eli, Drawing   ACCOUNT NO. 302

DATE	DESCRIPTION	POST. REF.	DEBIT	CREDIT	BALANCE DEBIT	BALANCE CREDIT
20X1						
Dec. 31		J2	5 000 00		5 000 00	
31	Closing	J4		5 000 00	– 0 –	

ACCOUNT Income Summary   ACCOUNT NO. 309

DATE	DESCRIPTION	POST. REF.	DEBIT	CREDIT	BALANCE DEBIT	BALANCE CREDIT
20X1						
Dec. 31	Closing	J4		47 000 00		47 000 00
31	Closing	J4	13 333 00			33 667 00
31	Closing	J4	33 667 00			– 0 –

ACCOUNT Fees Income   ACCOUNT NO. 401

DATE	DESCRIPTION	POST. REF.	DEBIT	CREDIT	BALANCE DEBIT	BALANCE CREDIT
20X1						
Dec. 31		J2		36 000 00		36 000 00
31		J2		11 000 00		47 000 00
31	Closing	J4	47 000 00			– 0 –

ACCOUNT Salaries Expense   ACCOUNT NO. 511

DATE	DESCRIPTION	POST. REF.	DEBIT	CREDIT	BALANCE DEBIT	BALANCE CREDIT
20X1						
Dec. 31		J2	8 000 00		8 000 00	
31	Closing	J4		8 000 00	– 0 –	

ACCOUNT Utilities Expense   ACCOUNT NO. 514

DATE	DESCRIPTION	POST. REF.	DEBIT	CREDIT	BALANCE DEBIT	BALANCE CREDIT
20X1						
Dec. 31		J2	650 00		650 00	
31	Closing	J4		650 00	– 0 –	

ACCOUNT Supplies Expense   ACCOUNT NO. 517

DATE	DESCRIPTION	POST. REF.	DEBIT	CREDIT	BALANCE DEBIT	BALANCE CREDIT
20X1						
Dec. 31	Adjusting	J3	500 00		500 00	
31	Closing	J4		500 00	– 0 –	

(continued)

FIGURE 6.2 (continued)

ACCOUNT Rent Expense **ACCOUNT NO.** 520

DATE	DESCRIPTION	POST. REF.	DEBIT	CREDIT	BALANCE DEBIT	BALANCE CREDIT
20X1						
Dec. 31	Adjusting	J3	4 000 00		4 000 00	
31	Closing	J4		4 000 00	–0–	

ACCOUNT Depreciation Expense—Equipment **ACCOUNT NO.** 523

DATE	DESCRIPTION	POST. REF.	DEBIT	CREDIT	BALANCE DEBIT	BALANCE CREDIT
20X1						
Dec. 31	Adjusting	J3	183 00		183 00	
31	Closing	J4		183 00	–0–	

You have now seen seven steps of the accounting cycle. The steps we have discussed are (1) analyze transactions, (2) journalize the transactions, (3) post the transactions, (4) prepare a worksheet, (5) prepare financial statements, (6) record adjusting entries, and (7) record closing entries. Two steps remain. They are (8) prepare a postclosing trial balance and (9) interpret the financial information.

Section 1 Review

1. **What is the journal entry to close the drawing account?**
   a. debit the *Capital* account and credit the *Drawing* account
   b. debit the *Drawing* account and credit the *Capital* account
   c. debit the *Revenue* account and credit the *Drawing* account
   d. debit *Drawing Expense* and credit the *Drawing* account

2. **The *Income Summary* account is a temporary:**
   a. liability account.
   b. expense account.
   c. drawing account.
   d. owner's equity account.

3. **The fourth step in the closing process is to**
   a. interpret the financial information.
   b. prepare a worksheet.
   c. analyze transactions.
   d. journalize the transactions.

4. **After the closing entries are posted, which account normally has a balance other than zero?**
   a. *Capital*
   b. *Rent Expense*
   c. *Income Summary*
   d. *Fees Income*

5. **After closing, which accounts have zero balances?**
   a. liability and capital accounts
   b. asset and liability accounts
   c. revenue, drawing, and expense accounts
   d. liability, drawing, and expense accounts

6. **The business owner removes supplies that are worth $1,200 from the company stockroom. She intends to take them home for personal use. What effect will this have on the company's net income?**
   a. Net income will decrease by $1,200.
   b. Net income will increase by $1,200.
   c. No effect on net income.
   d. Net income will decrease by $2,400.

Section 2

SECTION OBJECTIVES	TERMS TO LEARN
>> 6-2 Prepare a postclosing trial balance. **WHY IT'S IMPORTANT** The postclosing trial balance helps the accountant identify any errors in the closing process. >> 6-3 Interpret financial statements. **WHY IT'S IMPORTANT** Financial statements contain information that can impact and drive operating decisions and plans for the future of the company. >> 6-4 Review the steps in the accounting cycle. **WHY IT'S IMPORTANT** Proper treatment of data as it flows through the accounting system ensures reliable financial reports.	interpret postclosing trial balance

Using Accounting Information

In this section, we will complete the accounting cycle for Eli's Consulting Services.

Preparing the Postclosing Trial Balance

The eighth step in the accounting cycle is to prepare the postclosing trial balance, or *after-closing trial balance*. The **postclosing trial balance** is a statement that is prepared to prove the equality of total debits and credits. It is the last step in the end-of-period routine. The postclosing trial balance verifies that:

- total debits equal total credits;
- revenue, expense, and drawing accounts have zero balances.

On the postclosing trial balance, the only accounts with balances are the permanent accounts:

- assets
- liabilities
- owner's equity

Figure 6.3 shows the postclosing trial balance for Eli's Consulting Services.

>> 6-2 OBJECTIVE

Prepare a postclosing trial balance.

FIGURE 6.3

Postclosing Trial Balance

Eli's Consulting Services
Postclosing Trial Balance
December 31, 20X1

ACCOUNT NAME	DEBIT	CREDIT
Cash	111 350 00	
Accounts Receivable	5 000 00	
Supplies	1 000 00	
Prepaid Rent	4 000 00	
Equipment	11 000 00	
Accumulated Depreciation—Equipment		183 00
Accounts Payable		3 500 00
Trayton Eli, Capital		128 667 00
Totals	132 350 00	132 350 00

Finding and Correcting Errors

If the postclosing trial balance does not balance, there are errors in the accounting records. Find and correct the errors before continuing. Refer to Chapter 3 for tips on how to find common errors. Also use the audit trail to trace data through the accounting records to find errors.

>> **6-3 OBJECTIVE**

Interpret financial statements.

Interpreting the Financial Statements

The ninth and last step in the accounting cycle is interpreting the financial statements. Management needs timely and accurate financial information to operate the business successfully. To **interpret** the financial statements means to understand and explain the meaning and importance of information in accounting reports. Information in the financial statements provides answers to many questions:

- What is the cash balance?
- How much do customers owe the business?
- How much does the business owe suppliers?
- What is the profit or loss?

> Managers of The Home Depot, Inc., use the corporation's financial statements to answer questions about the business. How much cash does our business have? What net earnings did our company report this year? For the fiscal year ended February 3, 2019, The Home Depot, Inc., reported an ending cash balance of $1.8 billion and net earnings of $11.1 billion.

Figure 6.4 shows the financial statements for Eli's Consulting Services at the end of its first accounting period. By interpreting these statements, management learns that:

- the cash balance is $111,350,
- customers owe $5,000 to the business,
- the business owes $3,500 to its suppliers,
- the profit was $33,667.

FIGURE 6.4

End-of-Month Financial Statements

Eli's Consulting Services
Income Statement
Month Ended December 31, 20X1

Revenue		
Fees Income		47 000 00
Expenses		
Salaries Expense	8 000 00	
Utilities Expense	650 00	
Supplies Expense	500 00	
Rent Expense	4 000 00	
Depreciation Expense—Equipment	183 00	
Total Expenses		13 333 00
Net Income for the Month		33 667 00

Eli's Consulting Services
Statement of Owner's Equity
Month Ended December 31, 20X1

Trayton Eli, Capital, December 1, 20X1		100 000 00
Net Income for December	33 667 00	
Less Withdrawals for December	5 000 00	
Increase in Capital		28 667 00
Trayton Eli, Capital, December 31, 20X1		128 667 00

Eli's Consulting Services
Balance Sheet
December 31, 20X1

Assets		
Cash		111 350 00
Accounts Receivable		5 000 00
Supplies		1 000 00
Prepaid Rent		4 000 00
Equipment	11 000 00	
Less Accumulated Depreciation	183 00	10 817 00
Total Assets		132 167 00
Liabilities and Owner's Equity		
Liabilities		
Accounts Payable		3 500 00
Owner's Equity		
Trayton Eli, Capital		128 667 00
Total Liabilities and Owner's Equity		132 167 00

ABOUT ACCOUNTING

Professional Consultants Professionals in the consulting field, such as accountants and lawyers, need to understand accounting so they can bill for services performed. Because clients have different billing rates depending on the service performed, specialized software is used to manage the paperwork and keep track of the billings and payments.

> **6-4 OBJECTIVE**
>
> Review the steps in the accounting cycle.

The Accounting Cycle

You have learned about the entire accounting cycle as you studied the financial affairs of Eli's Consulting Services during its first month of operations. Figure 6.5 summarizes the steps in the accounting cycle.

Step 1. **Analyze transactions.** Analyze source documents to determine their effects on the basic accounting equation. The data about transactions appears on a variety of source documents such as:
- sales slips,
- purchase invoices,
- credit memorandums,
- check stubs.

Step 2. **Journalize the transactions.** Record the effects of the transactions in a journal.

Step 3. **Post the journal entries.** Transfer data from the journal to the general ledger accounts.

Step 4. **Prepare a worksheet.** At the end of each period, prepare a worksheet.
- Use the Trial Balance section to prove the equality of debits and credits in the general ledger.
- Use the Adjustments section to enter changes in account balances that are needed to present an accurate and complete picture of the financial affairs of the business.
- Use the Adjusted Trial Balance section to verify the equality of debits and credits after the adjustments. Extend the amounts from the Adjusted Trial Balance section to the Income Statement and Balance Sheet sections.
- Use the Income Statement and Balance Sheet sections to prepare the financial statements.

Step 5. **Prepare financial statements.** Prepare financial statements to report information to owners, managers, and other interested parties.
- The income statement shows the results of operations for the period.
- The statement of owner's equity reports the changes in the owner's financial interest during the period.
- The balance sheet shows the financial position of the business at the end of the period.

> **recall**
>
> **The Accounting Cycle**
>
> The accounting cycle is a series of steps performed during each period to classify, record, and summarize data to produce needed financial information.

FIGURE 6.5

The Accounting Cycle

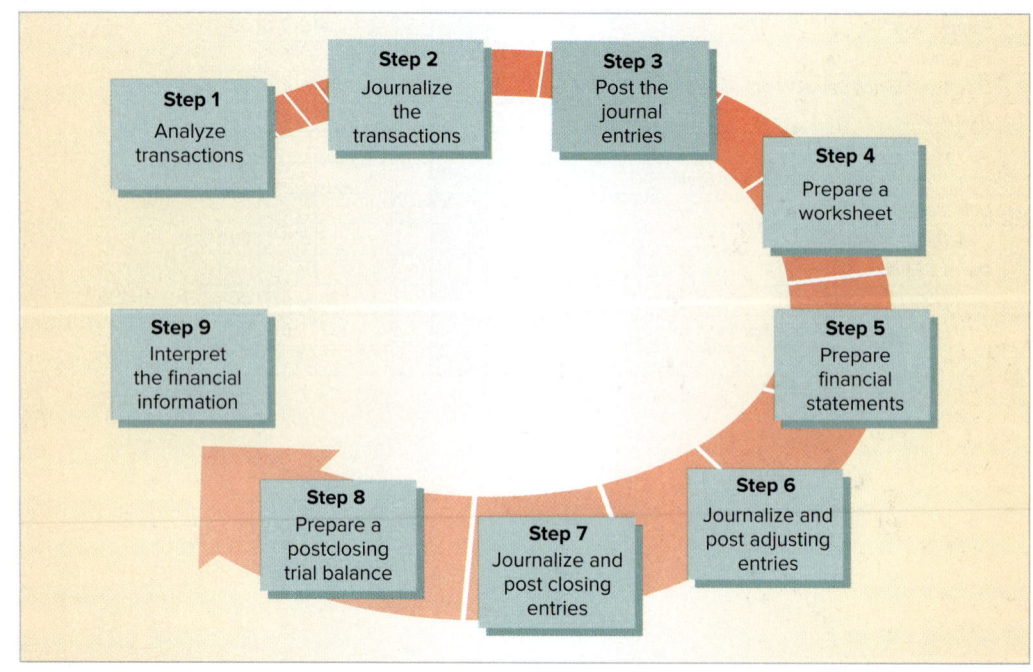

Step 6. Journalize and post the adjusting entries. Use the worksheet to journalize and post adjusting entries. The adjusting entries are a permanent record of the changes in account balances shown on the worksheet.

Step 7. Journalize and post the closing entries. Journalize and post the closing entries to:
- transfer net income or net loss to owner's equity;
- reduce the balances of the revenue, expense, and drawing accounts to zero.

Step 8. Prepare a postclosing trial balance. The postclosing trial balance shows that the general ledger is in balance after the closing entries are posted. It is also used to verify that there are zero balances in revenue, expense, and drawing accounts.

Step 9. Interpret the financial information. Use financial statements to understand and communicate financial information and to make decisions. Accountants, owners, managers, and other interested parties interpret financial statements by comparing such things as profit, revenue, and expenses from one accounting period to the next.

> In addition to financial statements, Adobe Systems, Inc., prepares a Financial Highlights report. This report lists total assets, revenue, net income, and the number of worldwide employees for the past five years.

After studying the accounting cycle of Eli's Consulting Services, you have an understanding of how data flow through a simple accounting system for a small business:

- Source documents are analyzed.
- Transactions are recorded in the general journal.
- Transactions are posted from the general journal to the general ledger.
- Financial information is proved, adjusted, and summarized on the worksheet.
- Financial information is reported on financial statements.

Figure 6.6 illustrates this data flow.

As you will learn in later chapters, some accounting systems have more complex records, procedures, and financial statements. However, the steps of the accounting cycle and the underlying accounting principles remain the same.

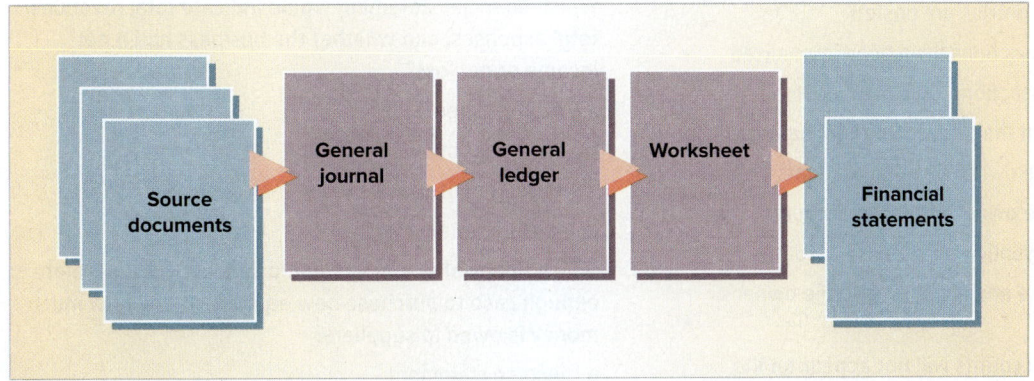

FIGURE 6.6

Flow of Data Through a Simple Accounting System

MANAGERIAL IMPLICATIONS

FINANCIAL STATEMENTS

- Management needs timely and accurate financial information to control operations and make decisions.
- A well-designed and well-run accounting system provides reliable financial statements to management.
- Although management is not involved in day-to-day accounting procedures and end-of-period processes, the efficiency of the procedures affects the quality and promptness of the financial information that management receives.

THINKING CRITICALLY

If you owned or managed a business, how often would you want financial statements prepared? Why?

Section 2 Review

1. What are the last three steps (7th, 8th, and 9th) in the accounting cycle?
    a. post the journal entries, journalize transactions, analyze transactions
    b. prepare financial statements, prepare a worksheet, prepare postclosing trial balance
    c. journalize and post closing entries, prepare a postclosing trial balance, interpret the financial statements
    d. intrepret the financial information, analyze transactions, journalize transactions

2. Why is a postclosing trial balance prepared?
    a. to ensure the general journal is in balance after the adjusting and closing entries are journalized
    b. to ensure the general ledger is in balance after the adjusting and closing entries are posted
    c. to ensure that all transactions have been journalized
    d. to ensure that all transactions have been posted

3. What accounts appear on the postclosing trial balance?
    a. asset, liability, and the owner's capital accounts
    b. asset, liability, and the owner's drawing accounts
    c. asset, liability, and revenue and expense accounts
    d. asset, liability, revenue and expense, and the owner's drawing accounts

4. Which of the following accounts will not appear on the postclosing trial balance?
    a. *B. J. Hall, Capital*
    b. *B. J. Hall, Drawing*
    c. *Accounts Payable*
    d. *Cash*

5. After the revenue and expense accounts are closed, *Income Summary* has a credit balance of $80,000. What does this figure represent?
    a. Net loss of $80,000
    b. Net profit of $80,000
    c. Owner's withdrawal of $80,000
    d. Net increase in owner's equity of $80,000

6. Which financial statement would indicate how much customers owe to the business?
    a. income statement
    b. balance sheet
    c. statement of owner's equity
    d. statement of cash flows

7. Which financial statement would indicate total revenues, total expenses, and whether the business had a net income or net loss?
    a. balance sheet
    b. statement of owner's equity
    c. statement of cash flows
    d. income statement

8. Which financial statement would indicate whether there is enough cash to purchase new equipment and how much money is owed to suppliers?
    a. income statement
    b. balance sheet
    c. statement of owner's equity
    d. statement of cash flows

REVIEW Chapter Summary

After the worksheet and financial statements have been completed and adjusting entries have been journalized and posted, the closing entries are recorded and a postclosing trial balance is prepared.

Learning Objectives

6-1 Journalize and post closing entries.

Journalizing and posting the closing entries is the seventh step in the accounting cycle. Closing entries transfer the results of operations to owner's equity and reduce the balances of the revenue and expense accounts to zero. The worksheet provides the data necessary for the closing entries. A temporary owner's equity account, *Income Summary,* is used. There are four steps in the closing process:

1. The balance of the revenue account is transferred to the *Income Summary* account.

    Debit *Revenue*

    Credit *Income Summary*

2. The balances of the expense accounts are transferred to the *Income Summary* account.

    Debit *Income Summary*

    Credit *Expenses*

3. The balance of the *Income Summary* account—net income or net loss—is transferred to the owner's capital account.

    If *Income Summary* has a credit balance:

    Debit *Income Summary*

    Credit *Owner's Capital*

    If *Income Summary* has a debit balance:

    Debit *Owner's Capital*

    Credit *Income Summary*

4. The drawing account is closed to the owner's capital account.

    Debit *Owner's Capital*

    Credit *Drawing*

After the closing entries have been posted, the capital account reflects the results of operations for the period. The revenue and expense accounts, with zero balances, are ready to accumulate data for the next period.

6-2 Prepare a postclosing trial balance.

Preparing the postclosing trial balance is the eighth step in the accounting cycle. A postclosing trial balance is prepared to test the equality of total debit and credit balances in the general ledger after the adjusting and closing entries have been recorded. This report lists only permanent accounts open at the end of the period—asset, liability, and the owner's capital accounts. The temporary accounts—revenue, expenses, drawing, and *Income Summary*—apply only to one accounting period and do not appear on the postclosing trial balance.

6-3 Interpret financial statements.

The ninth step in the accounting cycle is interpreting the financial statements. Business decisions must be based on accurate and timely financial information.

6-4 Review the steps in the accounting cycle.

The accounting cycle consists of a series of steps that are repeated in each fiscal period. These steps are designed to classify, record, and summarize the data needed to produce financial information.

The steps of the accounting cycle are:

1. Analyze transactions.
2. Journalize the transactions.
3. Post the journal entries.
4. Prepare a worksheet.
5. Prepare financial statements.
6. Journalize and post adjusting entries.
7. Journalize and post closing entries.
8. Prepare a postclosing trial balance.
9. Interpret the financial information.

6-5 Define the accounting terms new to this chapter.

Glossary

Closing entries (p. 166) Journal entries that transfer the results of operations (net income or net loss) to owner's equity and reduce the revenue, expense, and drawing account balances to zero

Income Summary account (p. 166) A special owner's equity account that is used only in the closing process to summarize the results of operations

Interpret (p. 176) To understand and explain the meaning and importance of something (such as financial statements)

Postclosing trial balance (p. 175) A statement that is prepared to prove the equality of total debits and credits after the closing process is completed

Comprehensive Self Review

1. What three financial statements are prepared during the accounting cycle?
2. A firm has the following expenses: **Rent Expense,** $3,600; **Salaries Expense,** $7,000; **Supplies Expense,** $1,500. Give the entry to close the expense accounts.
3. A firm has $90,000 in revenue for the period. Give the entry to close the **Fees Income** account.
4. What is the last step in the accounting cycle?
5. Is the following statement true or false? Why? "All owner's equity accounts appear on the postclosing trial balance."

(Answers to Comprehensive Self Review are at the end of the chapter.)

Discussion Questions

1. Name the steps of the accounting cycle.
2. Where does the accountant obtain the data needed for the closing entries?
3. Why is a postclosing trial balance prepared?
4. Where does the accountant obtain the data needed for the adjusting entries?
5. Briefly describe the flow of data through a simple accounting system.
6. Why does the accountant record closing entries at the end of a period?
7. What is the accounting cycle?
8. How is the *Income Summary* account used in the closing procedure?
9. What accounts appear on a postclosing trial balance?
10. What three procedures are performed at the end of each accounting period before the financial information is interpreted?

APPLICATIONS

Exercises

Exercise 6.1
Objective 6-1

▶ **Journalize closing entries.**

On December 31, 20X1, the ledger of Hunter Company contained the following account balances:

Cash	$33,000	Jessica Hunter, Drawing	$26,000
Accounts Receivable	2,900	Fees Income	53,750
Supplies	2,100	Depreciation Expense	2,750

Equipment	26,000	Salaries Expense	17,000
Accumulated Depreciation	2,500	Supplies Expense	3,000
Accounts Payable	3,000	Telephone Expense	2,600
Jessica Hunter, Capital	60,750	Utilities Expense	4,650

All the accounts have normal balances. Journalize the closing entries. Use 4 as the general journal page number.

Accounting cycle. ◀ **Exercise 6.2**
Objective 6-4

Following are the steps in the accounting cycle. Arrange the steps in the proper sequence.

1. Prepare a worksheet.
2. Journalize and post adjusting entries.
3. Analyze transactions.
4. Journalize the transactions.
5. Post the journal entries.
6. Journalize and post closing entries.
7. Interpret the financial information.
8. Prepare a postclosing trial balance.
9. Prepare financial statements.

Postclosing trial balance. ◀ **Exercise 6.3**
Objective 6-2

From the following list, identify the accounts that will appear on the postclosing trial balance.

ACCOUNTS

1. Cash
2. Accounts Receivable
3. Supplies
4. Equipment
5. Accumulated Depreciation
6. Accounts Payable
7. Brianna Celina, Capital
8. Brianna Celina, Drawing
9. Fees Income
10. Depreciation Expense
11. Salaries Expense
12. Supplies Expense
13. Utilities Expense

Financial statements. ◀ **Exercise 6.4**
Objective 6-3

Managers often consult financial statements for specific types of information. Indicate whether each of the following items would appear on the income statement, the statement of owner's equity, or the balance sheet. Use *I* for the income statement, *E* for the statement of owner's equity, and *B* for the balance sheet. If an item appears on more than one statement, use all letters that apply to that item.

1. Cash on hand
2. Owner's withdrawals for the period
3. Accounts Payable of the business
4. Total expenses for the period
5. Book value of the firm's equipment
6. Original cost of the firm's equipment
7. Depreciation expensed on the firm's equipment for the period
8. Accumulated depreciation on the firm's equipment

9. Accounts receivable of the business
10. Cost of supplies used during the period
11. Supplies on hand
12. Owner's capital at the end of the period
13. Net income for the period
14. Total assets of the business
15. Revenue earned during the period

Exercise 6.5
Objective 6-1

▶ **Closing entries.**

The *Income Summary* and *Violante Autro, Capital* accounts for Autro Production Company at the end of its accounting period follow.

ACCOUNT: Income Summary — ACCOUNT NO. 399

DATE	DESCRIPTION	POST. REF.	DEBIT	CREDIT	BALANCE DEBIT	BALANCE CREDIT
20X1						
Dec. 31	Closing	J4		67 000 00		67 000 00
31	Closing	J4	35 900 00			31 100 00
31	Closing	J4	31 100 00			– 0 –

ACCOUNT: Violante Autro, Capital — ACCOUNT NO. 301

DATE	DESCRIPTION	POST. REF.	DEBIT	CREDIT	BALANCE DEBIT	BALANCE CREDIT
20X1						
Dec. 1		J1		120 000 00		120 000 00
31	Closing	J4		31 100 00		151 100 00
31	Closing	J4	11 000 00			140 100 00

Complete the following statements:

1. Total revenue for the period is _____.
2. Total expenses for the period are _____.
3. Net income for the period is _____.
4. Owner's withdrawals for the period are _____.

Exercise 6.6
Objective 6-1

▶ **Closing entries.**

The ledger accounts of Aveeno Company appear as follows on March 31, 20X1:

ACCOUNT NO.	ACCOUNT	BALANCE
101	Cash	$ 80,000
111	Accounts Receivable	59,820
121	Supplies	10,600
131	Prepaid Insurance	25,000
141	Equipment	118,000
142	Accumulated Depreciation—Equipment	41,320
202	Accounts Payable	14,000
301	Mesia Aveeno, Capital	130,000
302	Mesia Aveeno, Drawing	13,000
401	Fees Income	374,460
510	Depreciation Expense—Equipment	21,160

511	Insurance Expense	11,400
514	Rent Expense	33,000
517	Salaries Expense	166,000
518	Supplies Expense	5,600
519	Telephone Expense	6,800
523	Utilities Expense	9,400

All accounts have normal balances. Journalize and post the closing entries. Use 4 as the page number for the general journal in journalizing the closing entries. Use account number 399 for the *Income Summary* account.

Closing entries.

◀ Exercise 6.7
Objective 6-1

On December 31, the *Income Summary* account of Ballon Company has a debit balance of $222,000 after revenue of $234,000 and expenses of $456,000 were closed to the account. **Kenneth Ballon, Drawing** has a debit balance of $24,000 and **Kenneth Ballon, Capital** has a credit balance of $348,000. Record the journal entries necessary to complete closing the accounts. What is the new balance of **Kenneth Ballon, Capital**?

Accounting cycle.

◀ Exercise 6.8
Objective 6-4

Complete a chart of the accounting cycle by writing the steps of the cycle in their proper sequence.

PROBLEMS

Problem Set A

Adjusting and closing entries.

◀ Problem 6.1A
Objective 6-1

Research Associates, owned by Alex Raman, is retained by large companies to test consumer reaction to new products. On January 31, 20X1, the firm's worksheet showed the following adjustments data: (a) supplies used, $2,340; (b) expired rent, $13,000; and (c) depreciation on office equipment, $4,580. The balances of the revenue and expense accounts listed in the Income Statement section of the worksheet and the drawing account listed in the Balance Sheet section of the worksheet are given below:

REVENUE AND EXPENSE ACCOUNTS		
401	Fees Income	$109,800 Cr.
511	Depr. Expense—Office Equipment	4,580 Dr.
514	Rent Expense	13,000 Dr.
517	Salaries Expense	49,500 Dr.
520	Supplies Expense	2,340 Dr.
523	Telephone Expense	1,350 Dr.
526	Travel Expense	10,390 Dr.
529	Utilities Expense	1,250 Dr.
DRAWING ACCOUNT		
302	Alex Raman, Drawing	11,000 Dr.

INSTRUCTIONS

1. Record the adjusting entries in the general journal, page 3.
2. Record the closing entries in the general journal, page 4.

Analyze: What closing entry is required to close a drawing account?

Problem 6.2A
Objective 6-1, 6-2

▶ **Journalizing and posting adjusting and closing entries and preparing a postclosing trial balance.**

A completed worksheet for The Best Group is shown below.

INSTRUCTIONS

1. Record balances as of December 31, 20X1, in the ledger accounts.
2. Journalize (use 3 as the page number) and post the adjusting entries. Use account number 131 for Prepaid Advertising and the same account numbers for all other accounts shown in Mini-Practice Set 1 for Eli's Consulting Services' chart of accounts.
3. Journalize (use 4 as the page number) and post the closing entries.
4. Prepare a postclosing trial balance.

Analyze: How many accounts are listed in the Adjusted Trial Balance section? How many accounts are listed on the postclosing trial balance?

Problem 6.3A
Objective 6-1

▶ **Journalizing and posting closing entries.**

On December 31, after adjustments, Ponthieu Company's ledger contains the following account balances:

101	Cash	$ 47,200 Dr.
111	Accounts Receivable	17,800 Dr.
121	Supplies	4,000 Dr.
131	Prepaid Rent	40,600 Dr.
141	Equipment	64,000 Dr.
142	Accumulated Depreciation—Equip.	2,000 Cr.
202	Accounts Payable	8,500 Cr.
301	Louis Ponthieu, Capital (12/1/20X1)	85,620 Cr.
302	Louis Ponthieu, Drawing	8,200 Dr.

The Best Group
Worksheet
Month Ended December 31, 20X1

	ACCOUNT NAME	TRIAL BALANCE		ADJUSTMENTS		
		DEBIT	CREDIT		DEBIT	CREDIT
1	Cash	93 400 00				
2	Accounts Receivable	13 000 00				
3	Supplies	8 000 00		(a)		3 400 00
4	Prepaid Advertising	32 000 00		(b)		4 000 00
5	Equipment	85 000 00				
6	Accumulated Depreciation—Equipment			(c)		3 400 00
7	Accounts Payable		13 000 00			
8	Randy Best, Capital		142 000 00			
9	Randy Best, Drawing	9 400 00				
10	Fees Income		103 500 00			
11	Supplies Expense			(a)	3 400 00	
12	Advertising Expense			(b)	4 000 00	
13	Depreciation Expense—Equipment			(c)	3 400 00	
14	Salaries Expense	15 400 00				
15	Utilities Expense	2 300 00				
16	Totals	258 500 00	258 500 00		10 800 00	10 800 00
17	Net Income					
18						
19						

401	Fees Income	163,600 Cr.
511	Advertising Expense	5,800 Dr.
514	Depreciation Expense—Equip.	1,000 Dr.
517	Rent Expense	4,600 Dr.
519	Salaries Expense	38,800 Dr.
523	Utilities Expense	7,720 Dr.

INSTRUCTIONS

1. Record the balances in the ledger accounts as of December 31.
2. Journalize the closing entries in the general journal, page 4. Use account number 399 for the *Income Summary* account.
3. Post the closing entries to the general ledger accounts.

Analyze: What is the balance of the *Salaries Expense* account after closing entries are posted?

Worksheet, journalizing and posting adjusting and closing entries, and the postclosing trial balance.

◄ **Problem 6.4A**
Objectives 6-1, 6-2

A partially completed worksheet for At Home Pet Care Service, a firm that grooms pets at the owner's home, follows.

INSTRUCTIONS

1. Record balances as of December 31 in the ledger accounts.
2. Prepare the worksheet.
3. Journalize (use 3 as the journal page number) and post the adjusting entries. Use account number 131 for *Prepaid Advertising* and the same account numbers for all other accounts shown in Mini-Practice Set 1 for Eli's Consulting Services' chart of accounts.
4. Journalize (use 4 as the journal page number) and post the closing entries.
5. Prepare a postclosing trial balance.

ADJUSTED TRIAL BALANCE		INCOME STATEMENT		BALANCE SHEET	
DEBIT	CREDIT	DEBIT	CREDIT	DEBIT	CREDIT
93,400.00				93,400.00	
13,000.00				13,000.00	
4,600.00				4,600.00	
28,000.00				28,000.00	
85,000.00				85,000.00	
	3,400.00				3,400.00
	13,000.00				13,000.00
	142,000.00				142,000.00
9,400.00				9,400.00	
	103,500.00		103,500.00		
3,400.00		3,400.00			
4,000.00		4,000.00			
3,400.00		3,400.00			
15,400.00		15,400.00			
2,300.00		2,300.00			
261,900.00	261,900.00	28,500.00	103,500.00	233,400.00	158,400.00
		75,000.00			75,000.00
		103,500.00	103,500.00	233,400.00	233,400.00

At Home Pet Care Service
Worksheet
Month Ended December 31, 20X1

	ACCOUNT NAME	TRIAL BALANCE DEBIT	TRIAL BALANCE CREDIT	ADJUSTMENTS DEBIT	ADJUSTMENTS CREDIT
1	Cash	64 1 0 0 00			
2	Accounts Receivable	10 9 0 0 00			
3	Supplies	12 0 0 0 00			(a) 4 2 0 0 00
4	Prepaid Advertising	8 0 0 0 00			(b) 3 8 0 0 00
5	Equipment	42 0 0 0 00			
6	Accumulated Depreciation—Equipment				(c) 1 1 6 0 00
7	Accounts Payable		12 0 0 0 00		
8	Larry Sims, Capital		91 0 0 0 00		
9	Larry Sims, Drawing	6 0 0 0 00			
10	Fees Income		53 2 0 0 00		
11	Salaries Expense	11 6 0 0 00			
12	Utilities Expense	1 6 0 0 00			
13	Supplies Expense			(a) 4 2 0 0 00	
14	Advertising Expense			(b) 3 8 0 0 00	
15	Depreciation Expense—Equipment			(c) 1 1 6 0 00	
16	Totals	156 2 0 0 00	156 2 0 0 00	9 1 6 0 00	9 1 6 0 00

Analyze: What total debits were posted to the general ledger to complete all closing entries for the month of December?

Problem Set B

Problem 6.1B

Objective 6-1

▶ **Adjusting and closing entries.**

Tobias Cleaning and Maintenance, owned by Triana Tobias, provides cleaning services to hotels, motels, and hospitals. On January 31, 20X1, the firm's worksheet showed the following adjustment data. The balances of the revenue and expense accounts listed in the Income Statement section of the worksheet and the drawing account listed in the Balance Sheet section of the worksheet are also given.

ADJUSTMENTS

a. Supplies used, $4,290
b. Expired insurance, $2,220
c. Depreciation on machinery, $1,680

REVENUE AND EXPENSE ACCOUNTS

401	Fees Income	$49,200 Cr.
511	Depreciation Expense—Machinery	1,680 Dr.
514	Insurance Expense	2,220 Dr.
517	Rent Expense	4,500 Dr.
520	Salaries Expense	24,000 Dr.
523	Supplies Expense	4,290 Dr.
526	Telephone Expense	315 Dr.

529	Utilities Expense	960 Dr.
DRAWING ACCOUNT		
302	Triana Tobias, Drawing	3,600 Dr.

INSTRUCTIONS

1. Record the adjusting entries in the general journal, page 3.
2. Record the closing entries in the general journal, page 4. Use account numbers provided in Mini-Practice Set 1 for any account number not given.

Analyze: What effect did the adjusting entry for expired insurance have on the *Insurance Expense* account?

Journalizing and posting adjusting and closing entries and preparing a postclosing trial balance.

◄ **Problem 6.2B**
Objectives 6-1, 6-2

A completed worksheet for Elegant Lawn Nursery and Landscape is shown below.

INSTRUCTIONS

1. Record the balances as of December 31 in the ledger accounts.
2. Journalize (use 3 as the page number) and post the adjusting entries. Use account number 131 for *Prepaid Advertising* and the same account numbers for all other accounts as shown in Mini-Practice Set 1 for Eli's Consulting Services' chart of accounts.
3. Journalize (use 4 as the page number) and post the closing entries.
4. Prepare a postclosing trial balance.

Analyze: What total credits were posted to the general ledger to complete the closing entries?

Journalizing and posting closing entries.

◄ **Problem 6.3B**
Objective 6-1

On December 31, after adjustments, The Pollock Family Farm's ledger contains the following account balances.

101	Cash	$21,374 Dr.
111	Accounts Receivable	5,400 Dr.
121	Supplies	2,750 Dr.
131	Prepaid Rent	17,325 Dr.
141	Equipment	27,000 Dr.
142	Accumulated Depreciation—Equip.	675 Cr.
202	Accounts Payable	7,313 Cr.
301	Bruce Pollock, Capital (12/1/20X1)	43,088 Cr.
302	Bruce Pollock, Drawing	2,700 Dr.
401	Fees Income	40,998 Cr.
511	Advertising Expense	2,475 Dr.
514	Depreciation Expense—Equip.	675 Dr.
517	Rent Expense	1,575 Dr.
519	Salaries Expense	8,100 Dr.
523	Utilities Expense	2,700 Dr.

INSTRUCTIONS

1. Record the balances in the ledger accounts as of December 31.
2. Journalize the closing entries in the general journal, page 4. Use account number 399 for the *Income Summary* account
3. Post the closing entries to the general ledger accounts.

Analyze: List the accounts affected by closing entries for the month of December.

Elegant Lawn Nursery and Landscape
Worksheet
Month Ended December 31, 20X1

	ACCOUNT NAME	TRIAL BALANCE DEBIT	TRIAL BALANCE CREDIT	ADJUSTMENTS DEBIT	ADJUSTMENTS CREDIT
1	Cash	32 400 00			
2	Accounts Receivable	6 000 00			
3	Supplies	6 000 00			(a) 3 000 00
4	Prepaid Advertising	9 000 00			(b) 1 200 00
5	Equipment	60 000 00			
6	Accumulated Depreciation—Equipment				(c) 1 500 00
7	Accounts Payable		9 000 00		
8	Karen Preston, Capital		82 200 00		
9	Karen Preston, Drawing	8 400 00			
10	Fees Income		46 800 00		
11	Supplies Expense			(a) 3 000 00	
12	Advertising Expense			(b) 1 200 00	
13	Depreciation Expense—Equipment			(c) 1 500 00	
14	Salaries Expense	14 400 00			
15	Utilities Expense	1 800 00			
16	Totals	138 000 00	138 000 00	5 700 00	5 700 00
17	Net Income				

Problem 6.4B
Objectives 6-1, 6-2, 6-4

▶ **Worksheet, journalizing and posting adjusting and closing entries, and the postclosing trial balance.**

A partially completed worksheet for Rissa Potter, CPA, for the month ending June 30, 20X1, is shown below.

Rissa Potter, CPA
Worksheet
Month Ended June 30, 20X1

	ACCOUNT NAME	TRIAL BALANCE DEBIT	TRIAL BALANCE CREDIT	ADJUSTMENTS DEBIT	ADJUSTMENTS CREDIT
1	Cash	31 950 00			
2	Accounts Receivable	11 340 00			
3	Supplies	15 750 00			(a) 2 700 00
4	Computers	28 800 00			
5	Accumulated Depreciation—Computers		2 880 00		(b) 240 00
6	Accounts Payable		12 600 00		
7	Rissa Potter, Capital		62 235 00		
8	Rissa Potter, Drawing	12 000 00			
9	Fees Income		67 950 00		
10	Salaries Expense	37 725 00			
11	Supplies Expense			(a) 2 700 00	
12	Depreciation Expense—Computers			(b) 240 00	
13	Travel Expense	5 400 00			
14	Utilities Expense	2 700 00			
15	Totals	145 665 00	145 665 00	2 940 00	2 940 00

ADJUSTED TRIAL BALANCE		INCOME STATEMENT		BALANCE SHEET		
DEBIT	CREDIT	DEBIT	CREDIT	DEBIT	CREDIT	
32 400 00				32 400 00		1
6 000 00				6 000 00		2
3 000 00				3 000 00		3
7 800 00				7 800 00		4
60 000 00				60 000 00		5
	1 500 00				1 500 00	6
	9 000 00				9 000 00	7
	82 200 00				82 200 00	8
8 400 00				8 400 00		9
	46 800 00		46 800 00			10
3 000 00		3 000 00				11
1 200 00		1 200 00				12
1 500 00		1 500 00				13
14 400 00		14 400 00				14
1 800 00		1 800 00				15
139 500 00	139 500 00	21 900 00	46 800 00	117 600 00	92 700 00	16
		24 900 00			24 900 00	17
		46 800 00	46 800 00	117 600 00	117 600 00	18

INSTRUCTIONS

1. Record the balances as of June 30 in the ledger accounts.
2. Prepare the worksheet.
3. Journalize (use 3 as the journal page number) and post the adjusting entries. Use account number 121 for **Supplies;** 131 for **Computers;** 142 for the *Accumulated Depreciation* account; 309 for *Income Summary;* 517 for **Supplies Expense;** 519 for *Travel Expense;* and 523 for **Depreciation Expense**.
4. Journalize (use 4 as the journal page number) and post the closing entries.
5. Prepare a postclosing trial balance.

Analyze: What is the reported net income for the month of June for Rissa Potter, CPA?

Critical Thinking Problem 6.1

The Closing Process

The Trial Balance section of the worksheet for Fashion World for the period ended December 31, 20X1, appears below. Adjustments data are also given.

ADJUSTMENTS

a. Supplies used, $7,200
b. Expired insurance, $4,800
c. Depreciation expense for machinery, $2,400

INSTRUCTIONS

1. Complete the worksheet.
2. Prepare an income statement.
3. Prepare a statement of owner's equity.

Fashion World
Worksheet
Month Ended December 31, 20X1

ACCOUNT NAME	TRIAL BALANCE		ADJUSTMENTS	
	DEBIT	CREDIT	DEBIT	CREDIT
1 Cash	81 600 00			
2 Accounts Receivable	18 000 00			
3 Supplies	14 400 00			(a) 7 200 00
4 Prepaid Insurance	21 600 00			(b) 4 800 00
5 Machinery	168 000 00			
6 Accumulated Depreciation—Machinery				(c) 2 400 00
7 Accounts Payable		27 000 00		
8 Angela Cruz, Capital		149 160 00		
9 Angela Cruz, Drawing	12 000 00			
10 Fees Income		165 000 00		
11 Supplies Expense			(a) 7 200 00	
12 Insurance Expense			(b) 4 800 00	
13 Salaries Expense	22 200 00			
14 Depreciation Expense—Machinery			(c) 2 400 00	
15 Utilities Expense	3 360 00			
16 Totals	341 160 00	341 160 00	14 400 00	14 400 00

4. Prepare a balance sheet.
5. Journalize the adjusting entries in the general journal, page 3.
6. Journalize the closing entries in the general journal, page 4.
7. Prepare a postclosing trial balance.

Analyze: If the adjusting entry for expired insurance had been recorded in error as a credit to *Insurance Expense* and a debit to *Prepaid Insurance* for $2,400, what reported net income would have resulted?

Critical Thinking Problem 6.2

Owner's Equity

Kimberly Ashley, the bookkeeper for Interiors Designs, has just finished posting the closing entries for the year to the ledger. She is concerned about the following balances:

Capital account balance in the general ledger:	$194,200
Ending capital balance on the statement of owner's equity:	111,200

Ashley knows that these amounts should agree and asks for your assistance in reviewing her work.
  Your review of the general ledger of Interiors Designs reveals a beginning capital balance of $100,000. You also review the general journal for the accounting period and find the closing entries shown below.

1. What errors did Kimberly Ashley make in preparing the closing entries for the period?
2. Prepare a general journal entry to correct the errors made.
3. Explain why the balance of the capital account in the ledger after closing entries have been posted will be the same as the ending capital balance on the statement of owner's equity.

GENERAL JOURNAL				PAGE 15	
DATE	DESCRIPTION	POST. REF.	DEBIT	CREDIT	
20X1	Closing Entries				1
Dec. 31	Fees Income		196 000 00		2
	Accumulated Depreciation		17 000 00		3
	Accounts Payable		66 000 00		4
	Income Summary			279 000 00	5
					6
31	Income Summary		184 800 00		7
	Salaries Expense			156 000 00	8
	Supplies Expense			10 000 00	9
	Depreciation Expense			4 800 00	10
	Wade Wilson, Drawing			14 000 00	11

BUSINESS CONNECTIONS

Interpreting Financial Statements

1. An officer of Westway Corporation recently commented that when he receives the firm's financial statements, he looks at just the bottom line of the income statement—the line that shows the net income or net loss for the period. He said that he does not bother with the rest of the income statement because "it's only the bottom line that counts." He also does not read the balance sheet. Do you think this manager is correct in the way he uses the financial statements? Why or why not?

2. The president of Brown Corporation is concerned about the firm's ability to pay its debts on time. What items on the balance sheet would help her to assess the firm's debt-paying ability?

3. Why is it important that a firm's financial records be kept up-to-date and that management receive the financial statements promptly after the end of each accounting period?

4. What kinds of operating and general policy decisions might be influenced by data on the financial statements?

Internal Control and Fraud Prevention and Certified Bookkeeper

Internal control and fraud prevention is an area tested on the Certified Bookkeeper's exam. Certification in your field indicates you have a certain level of education and training. Go to the American Institute of Professional Bookkeepers' website at www.aipb.org. From the certification program icon, determine the three requirements to become a certified bookkeeper and the four areas tested on the exam.

Income Statement

In 2018, CSX Corporation, which operates under the name Surface Transportation, reported operating expenses of $7,381 million. A partial list of the company's operating expenses follows. CSX Corporation reported revenues of $12,250 million for the year.

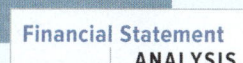

Consolidated Income Statement
(Dollars in millions)

Revenue	$12,250
Operating Expenses	
(Dollars in millions)	
Labor and Fringe Benefits	$2,738
Materials, Supplies, and Other	1,967
Fuel	1,046
Depreciation	1,331
Equipment and Other Rents	395

Analyze:

1. If the given categories represent the related general ledger accounts, what journal entry would be made to close the expense accounts at year-end?
2. What journal entry would be made to close the revenue accounts?

Analyze Online: Locate the website for CSX Corporation (www.csx.com). Click on *Investors*. Within the *Annual Report* link, find the most recent annual report.

3. On the consolidated statement of earnings, what was the amount reported for operating expenses?
4. What percentage increase or decrease does this figure represent from the operating expenses reported in the prior fiscal year?

TEAMWORK

Accounting Cycle

Understanding the steps in the accounting cycle is important to get accurate information about the financial condition of your company. In teams, make strips of paper with the nine steps of the accounting cycle. Give two or three strips to each member of the group. Each team member needs to put his or her strips in the proper order of the nine steps.

Answers to Comprehensive Self Review

1. Income statement, statement of owner's equity, and balance sheet.
2. Income Summary   12,100
        Rent Expense   3,600
        Salaries Expense   7,000
        Supplies Expense   1,500
3. Fees Income   90,000
        Income Summary   90,000
4. Interpret the financial statements.
5. False. The *temporary* owner's equity accounts do not appear on the postclosing trial balance. The temporary owner's equity accounts are the drawing account and ***Income Summary.***

Mini-Practice Set 1

Service Business Accounting Cycle

Eli's Consulting Services

This project will give you an opportunity to apply your knowledge of accounting principles and procedures by handling all the accounting work of Eli's Consulting Services for the month of January 2020.

Assume that you are the chief accountant for Eli's Consulting Services. During January, the business will use the same types of records and procedures that you learned about in Chapters 1 through 6. The chart of accounts for Eli's Consulting Services has been expanded to include a few new accounts. Follow the instructions to complete the accounting records for the month of January.

INTRODUCTION

Eli's Consulting Services
Chart of Accounts

Assets	Revenue
101 Cash	401 Fees Income
111 Accounts Receivable	**Expenses**
121 Supplies	511 Salaries Expense
134 Prepaid Insurance	514 Utilities Expense
137 Prepaid Rent	517 Supplies Expense
141 Equipment	520 Rent Expense
142 Accumulated Depreciation—Equipment	523 Depreciation Expense—Equipment
Liabilities	526 Advertising Expense
202 Accounts Payable	529 Maintenance Expense
Owner's Equity	532 Telephone Expense
301 Trayton Eli, Capital	535 Insurance Expense
302 Trayton Eli, Drawing	
309 Income Summary	

INSTRUCTIONS

1. Open the general ledger accounts and enter the balances for January 1, 20X2. Obtain the necessary figures from the postclosing trial balance prepared on December 31, 20X1, which appears in Figure 6.3.
2. Analyze each transaction and record it in the general journal. Use page 3 to begin January's transactions.
3. Post the transactions to the general ledger accounts.
4. Prepare the Trial Balance section of the worksheet.
5. Prepare the Adjustments section of the worksheet.
   a. Compute and record the adjustment for supplies used during the month. An inventory taken on January 31 showed supplies of $9,400 on hand.
   b. Compute and record the adjustment for expired insurance for the month.
   c. Record the adjustment for one month of expired rent of $4,000.
   d. Record the adjustment for depreciation of $183 on the old equipment for the month. The first adjustment for depreciation for the new equipment will be recorded in February.
6. Complete the worksheet.
7. Prepare an income statement for the month.
8. Prepare a statement of owner's equity.

9. Prepare a balance sheet using the report form.
10. Journalize and post the adjusting entries.
11. Journalize and post the closing entries.
12. Prepare a postclosing trial balance.

Analyze: Compare the January 31 balance sheet you prepared with the December 31 balance sheet shown in Figure 6.4.

a. What changes occurred in total assets, liabilities, and the owner's ending capital?
b. What changes occurred in the *Cash* and *Accounts Receivable* accounts?
c. Has there been an improvement in the firm's financial position? Why or why not?

DATE		TRANSACTIONS
Jan.	2	Purchased supplies for $14,000; issued Check 1015.
	2	Purchased a one-year insurance policy for $16,800; issued Check 1016.
	7	Sold services for $30,000 in cash and $20,000 on credit during the first week of January.
	12	Collected a total of $8,000 on account from credit customers during the first week of January.
	12	Issued Check 1017 for $7,200 to pay for special promotional advertising to new businesses on the local radio station during the month.
	13	Collected a total of $9,000 on account from credit customers during the second week of January.
	14	Returned supplies that were damaged for a cash refund of $1,500.
	15	Sold services for $41,400 in cash and $4,600 on credit during the second week of January.
	20	Purchased supplies for 10,000 from White's, Inc.; received Invoice 2384 payable in 30 days.
	20	Sold services for $25,000 in cash and $7,000 on credit during the third week of January.
	20	Collected a total of $11,200 on account from credit customers during the third week of January.
	21	Issued Check 1018 for $14,130 to pay for maintenance work on the office equipment.
	22	Issued Check 1019 for $7,200 to pay for special promotional advertising to new businesses in the local newspaper.
	23	Received the monthly telephone bill for $2,050 and paid it with Check 1020.
	26	Collected a total of $3,200 on account from credit customers during the fourth week of January.
	27	Issued Check 1021 for $6,000 to Office Plus as payment on account for Invoice 2223.
	28	Sent Check 1022 for $5,350 in payment of the monthly bill for utilities.
	29	Sold services for $38,000 in cash and $5,500 on credit during the fourth week of January.
	31	Issued Checks 1023–1027 for $65,600 to pay the monthly salaries of the regular employees and three part-time workers.
	31	Issued Check 1028 for $24,000 for personal use.
	31	Issued Check 1029 for $8,300 to pay for maintenance services for the month.
	31	Purchased additional equipment for $30,000 from Contemporary Equipment Company; issued Check 1030 for $20,000 and bought the rest on credit. The equipment has a five-year life and no salvage value.
	31	Sold services for $15,200 in cash and $3,240 on credit on January 31.

Accounting for Sales and Accounts Receivable

Chapter 7

Kristoffer Tripplaar/Alamy

www.mccormickcorporation.com

Variety is the spice of life, and McCormick & Company, Inc., provides a wide variety of spices to consumer and industrial customers in more than 110 countries. In 1889, Willoughby M. McCormick started the company in a basement and sold his flavors and extracts door to door. The company grew quickly but faced a major setback in 1904 when a fire destroyed all of the company's assets and records. The devastation of losing everything pushed Willoughby McCormick to nearly give up on his company, but his dedication to his employees compelled him to rebuild the company, and it has continued to grow since.

However, the contributions of the company are not limited to the sales of spices and extracts. In addition to the continued development and production of innovative new products, McCormick has built a legacy of establishing industry quality standards, improving employee relations and working conditions, and developing a legacy of charitable donations and organizations. McCormick is committed to taking responsibility for its products—and the world around them.

McCormick sells to a rapidly growing base of consumer and industrial customers, earning sales of $4.8 billion during 2017 and having a reported $555.1 million of accounts receivable at the end of 2017. The accuracy and reliability of recording sales and collecting accounts receivable are crucial to the continued success of McCormick and its continued commitment to its employees and the communities it serves.

thinking critically
Do you think that McCormick & Company varies the discounts that it offers to its various industrial customers?

LEARNING OBJECTIVES

- **7-1** Record credit sales in a sales journal.
- **7-2** Post from the sales journal to the general ledger accounts.
- **7-3** Post from the sales journal to the customers' accounts in the accounts receivable subsidiary ledger.
- **7-4** Record sales returns and allowances in the general journal.
- **7-5** Post sales returns and allowances.
- **7-6** Prepare a schedule of accounts receivable.
- **7-7** Compute trade discounts.
- **7-8** Record credit card sales in appropriate journals.
- **7-9** Calculate sales tax due.
- **7-10** Define the accounting terms new to this chapter.

NEW TERMS

accounts receivable ledger
charge-account sales
contra revenue account
control account
credit memorandum
discount on credit card sales
invoice
list price
manufacturing business
merchandise inventory
merchandising business
net price
net sales
open-account credit
periodic inventory system
perpetual inventory system
retail business
sales allowance
sales journal
sales return
Sales Returns and Allowances
schedule of accounts receivable
service business
special journal
subsidiary ledger
trade discount
wholesale business

Section 1

SECTION OBJECTIVES	TERMS TO LEARN
>> 7-1 Record credit sales in a sales journal. **WHY IT'S IMPORTANT** Credit sales are a major source of revenue for many businesses. The sales journal is an efficient option for recording large volumes of credit sales transactions. >> 7-2 Post from the sales journal to the general ledger accounts. **WHY IT'S IMPORTANT** A well-designed accounting system prevents repetitive tasks.	manufacturing business merchandise inventory merchandising business periodic inventory system perpetual inventory system retail business sales journal service business special journal subsidiary ledger

Merchandise Sales

When an accounting system is developed for a firm, one important consideration is the nature of the firm's operations. The three basic types of businesses are a **service business,** which sells services; a **merchandising business,** which sells goods that it purchases for resale; and a **manufacturing business,** which sells goods that it produces.

Trayton Eli's Consulting Services, the firm that was described in Chapters 2 through 6, is a service business. The firm that we will examine next, Maxx-Out Sporting Goods, is a merchandising business that sells the latest sporting goods and sportswear for men, women, and children. It is a **retail business,** which sells goods and services directly to individual consumers. Maxx-Out Sporting Goods is a sole proprietorship owned and operated by Max Ferraro, who was formerly a sales manager for a major retail clothing store.

Maxx-Out Sporting Goods must account for purchases and sales of goods, and for **merchandise inventory**—the stock of goods that is kept on hand. Refer to the chart of accounts for Maxx-Out Sporting Goods below. You will learn about the accounts in this and following chapters.

Due to the relatively small size of its operations, Maxx-Out Sporting Goods does not keep track of its inventory daily. Maxx-Out Sporting Goods uses a **periodic inventory system.** In a periodic inventory system, the cost of inventory on hand must be determined by counting merchandise inventory in stock.

Larger businesses need to know the number of units and the unit cost for inventory on hand at all times. These businesses use a perpetual inventory system. In a **perpetual inventory system,** the amount of inventory on hand is adjusted for each sale, purchase, or return. Electronic equipment, such as point-of-sale cash registers and scanners, helps track inventory balances. The accounting for a perpetual system is discussed in the appendix to Chapter 9.

To allow for efficient recording of financial data, the accounting systems of most merchandising businesses include special journals and subsidiary ledgers.

Special Journals and Subsidiary Ledgers

A **special journal** is a journal that is used to record only one type of transaction. A **subsidiary ledger** is a ledger that contains accounts of a single type. Table 7.1 lists the journals and ledgers that merchandising businesses generally use in their accounting systems. In this chapter, we will discuss the sales journal and the accounts receivable subsidiary ledger.

important!

Business Classifications
The term *merchandising* refers to the type of business operation, not the type of legal entity. Maxx-Out Sporting Goods could have been a partnership or a corporation instead of a sole proprietorship.

TABLE 7.1

Journals and Ledgers Used by Merchandising Businesses

JOURNALS	
Type of Journal	**Purpose**
Sales	To record sales of merchandise on credit
Purchases	To record purchases of merchandise on credit
Cash receipts	To record cash received from all sources
Cash payments	To record all disbursements of cash
General	To record all transactions that are not recorded in another special journal and all adjusting and closing entries

LEDGERS	
Type of Ledger	**Content**
General	Assets, liabilities, owner's equity, revenue, and expense accounts
Accounts receivable	Accounts for credit customers
Accounts payable	Accounts for creditors

Maxx-Out Sporting Goods Chart of Accounts

Assets
- 101 Cash
- 105 Petty Cash Fund
- 109 Notes Receivable
- 111 Accounts Receivable
- 112 Allowance for Doubtful Accounts
- 116 Interest Receivable
- 121 Merchandise Inventory
- 126 Prepaid Insurance
- 127 Prepaid Interest
- 129 Supplies
- 131 Store Equipment
- 132 Accumulated Depreciation—Store Equipment
- 141 Office Equipment
- 142 Accumulated Depreciation—Office Equipment

Liabilities
- 201 Notes Payable—Trade
- 202 Notes Payable—Bank
- 205 Accounts Payable
- 216 Interest Payable
- 221 Social Security Tax Payable
- 222 Medicare Tax Payable
- 223 Employee Income Tax Payable
- 225 Federal Unemployment Tax Payable
- 227 State Unemployment Tax Payable
- 229 Salaries Payable
- 231 Sales Tax Payable

Owner's Equity
- 301 Max Ferraro, Capital
- 302 Max Ferraro, Drawing
- 399 Income Summary

Revenue
- 401 Sales
- 451 Sales Returns and Allowances
- 491 Interest Income
- 493 Miscellaneous Income

Cost of Goods Sold
- 501 Purchases
- 502 Freight In
- 503 Purchases Returns and Allowances
- 504 Purchases Discounts

Expenses
- 611 Salaries Expense—Sales
- 612 Supplies Expense
- 614 Advertising Expense
- 617 Cash Short or Over
- 626 Depreciation Expense—Store Equipment
- 634 Rent Expense
- 637 Salaries Expense—Office
- 639 Insurance Expense
- 641 Payroll Taxes Expense
- 643 Utilities Expense
- 649 Telephone Expense
- 651 Uncollectible Accounts Expense
- 657 Bank Fees Expense
- 658 Delivery Expense
- 659 Depreciation Expense—Office Equipment
- 691 Interest Expense
- 693 Miscellaneous Expense

The Sales Journal

The **sales journal** is used to record only sales of merchandise on credit. To understand the need for a sales journal, consider how credit sales made at Maxx-Out Sporting Goods would be entered and posted using a general journal and general ledger. Refer to Figure 7.1.

FIGURE 7.1

Journalizing and Posting Credit Sales

GENERAL JOURNAL PAGE 2

DATE	DESCRIPTION	POST. REF.	DEBIT	CREDIT
20X1				
Jan. 3	Accounts Receivable	111	702 00	
	Sales Tax Payable	231		52 00
	Sales	401		650 00
	Sold merchandise on			
	credit to Ann Anh,			
	Sales Slip 1101			
8	Accounts Receivable	111	648 00	
	Sales Tax Payable	231		48 00
	Sales	401		600 00
	Sold merchandise on			
	credit to Cathy Ball,			
	Sales Slip 1102			
11	Accounts Receivable	111	756 00	
	Sales Tax Payable	231		56 00
	Sales	401		700 00
	Sold merchandise on			
	credit to Barbara Coe, Sales			
	Slip 1103			
15	Accounts Receivable	111	324 00	
	Sales Tax Payable	231		24 00
	Sales	401		300 00
	Sold merchandise on			
	credit to Amalia Rodriguez,			
	Sales Slip 1104			

ACCOUNT Accounts Receivable   ACCOUNT NO. 111

DATE	DESCRIPTION	POST. REF.	DEBIT	CREDIT	BALANCE DEBIT	BALANCE CREDIT
20X1						
Jan. 1	Balance	✓			3240 00	
3		J2	702 00		3942 00	
8		J2	648 00		4590 00	
11		J2	756 00		5346 00	
15		J2	324 00		5670 00	

(continued)

Note the word "Balance" in the ledger accounts. To record beginning balances, enter the date in the Date column, the word "Balance" in the Description column, a check mark in the Posting Reference column, and the amount in the Debit or Credit Balance column.

Most state and many local governments impose a sales tax on retail sales of certain goods and services. Businesses are required to collect this tax from their customers and send it to the proper tax agency at regular intervals. When goods or services are sold on credit, the sales tax is usually recorded at the time of the sale even though it will not be collected immediately. A liability account called **Sales Tax Payable** is credited for the sales tax charged.

FIGURE 7.1 (continued)

ACCOUNT **Sales Tax Payable**   ACCOUNT NO. **231**

DATE	DESCRIPTION	POST. REF.	DEBIT	CREDIT	BALANCE DEBIT	BALANCE CREDIT
20X1						
Jan. 1	Balance	✓				756 00
3		J2		52 00		808 00
8		J2		48 00		856 00
11		J2		56 00		912 00
15		J2		24 00		936 00

ACCOUNT **Sales**   ACCOUNT NO. **401**

DATE	DESCRIPTION	POST. REF.	DEBIT	CREDIT	BALANCE DEBIT	BALANCE CREDIT
20X1						
Jan. 3		J2		650 00		650 00
8		J2		600 00		1,250 00
11		J2		700 00		1,950 00
15		J2		300 00		2,250 00

As you can see, a great amount of repetition is involved in both journalizing and posting these sales. The four credit sales made on January 3, 8, 11, and 15 required four separate entries in the general journal and involved four debits to **Accounts Receivable,** four credits to **Sales Tax Payable,** four credits to **Sales** (the firm's revenue account), and four descriptions. The posting of 12 items to the three general ledger accounts represents still further duplication of effort. This recording procedure is not efficient for a business that has a substantial number of credit sales each month.

Recording Transactions in a Sales Journal

A special journal intended only for credit sales provides a more efficient method of recording these transactions. Figure 7.2 shows the January credit sales of Maxx-Out Sporting Goods recorded in a sales journal. Since Maxx-Out Sporting Goods is located in a state that has an

>> **7-1 OBJECTIVE**
Record credit sales in a sales journal.

FIGURE 7.2
A Sales Journal

SALES JOURNAL   PAGE **1**

	DATE	SALES SLIP NO.	CUSTOMER'S ACCOUNT DEBITED	POST. REF.	ACCOUNTS RECEIVABLE DEBIT	SALES TAX PAYABLE CREDIT	SALES CREDIT	
1	20X1							1
2	Jan. 3	1101	Ann Anh		702 00	52 00	650 00	2
3	8	1102	Cathy Ball		648 00	48 00	600 00	3
4	11	1103	Barbara Coe		756 00	56 00	700 00	4
5	15	1104	Amalia Rodriguez		324 00	24 00	300 00	5
6	18	1105	Fred Wu		810 00	60 00	750 00	6
7	21	1106	Linda Carter		486 00	36 00	450 00	7
8	28	1107	Kim Ramirez		108 00	8 00	100 00	8
9	29	1108	Mesia Davis		1,080 00	80 00	1,000 00	9
10	31	1109	Alma Sanchez		972 00	72 00	900 00	10
11	31	1110	Ann Anh		270 00	20 00	250 00	11
12								12

FIGURE 7.3

Customer's Sales Slip

Maxx-Out Sporting Goods
2007 Trendsetter Lane
Dallas, Texas 75268-0967

DATE: 1/3/X1 SALESPERSON: S. Harris AUTH.

Goods Taken [X]   To Be Delivered [ ]

Send to:

Special Instructions:

I authorize this purchase to be charged on my account.

Signature: Ann Anh

SALES SLIP 1101

Qty.	Description	Unit Price	Amount
1	Olympic weight set	350.00	350.00
1	Mountain Bike	300.00	300.00
		Sales Tax	52.00
		Amount	702.00

NAME: Ann Anh
ADDRESS: 8913 South Hampton Road
Dallas, TX 75232-6002

---

8 percent sales tax on retail transactions, its sales journal includes a Sales Tax Payable Credit column. For the sake of simplicity, the sales journal shown here includes a limited number of transactions. The firm actually has many more credit sales each month.

Notice that the headings and columns in the sales journal speed up the recording process. No general ledger account names are entered. Only one line is needed to record all information for each transaction—date, sales slip number, customer's name, debit to **Accounts Receivable,** credit to **Sales Tax Payable,** and credit to **Sales.** Since the sales journal is used for a single purpose, there is no need to enter any descriptions. Thus, a great deal of repetition is avoided.

Entries in the sales journal are usually made daily. In a retail business such as Maxx-Out Sporting Goods, the data needed for each entry is taken from a copy of the customer's sales slip, as shown in Figure 7.3.

Many small retail firms use a sales journal similar to the one shown in Figure 7.2. However, keep in mind that special journals vary in format according to the needs of individual businesses.

> **recall**
>
> **Journals**
> A journal is a day-to-day record of a firm's transactions.

>> **7-2 OBJECTIVE**
> Post from the sales journal to the general ledger accounts.

Posting from a Sales Journal

A sales journal not only simplifies the initial recording of credit sales, it also eliminates a great deal of repetition in posting these transactions. With a sales journal, it is not necessary to post each credit sale individually to general ledger accounts. Instead, summary postings are made at the end of the month after the amount columns of the sales journal are totaled. See Figure 7.4 for an illustration of posting from the sales journal to the general ledger.

In actual practice, before any posting takes place, the equality of the debits and credits recorded in the sales journal is proved by comparing the column totals. The proof for the sales journal in Figure 7.4 is given below. All multicolumn special journals should be proved in a similar manner before their totals are posted.

Proof of Sales Journal	
	Debits
Accounts Receivable Debit column	$6,156.00
	Credits
Sales Tax Payable Credit column	$ 456.00
Sales Credit column	5,700.00
	$6,156.00

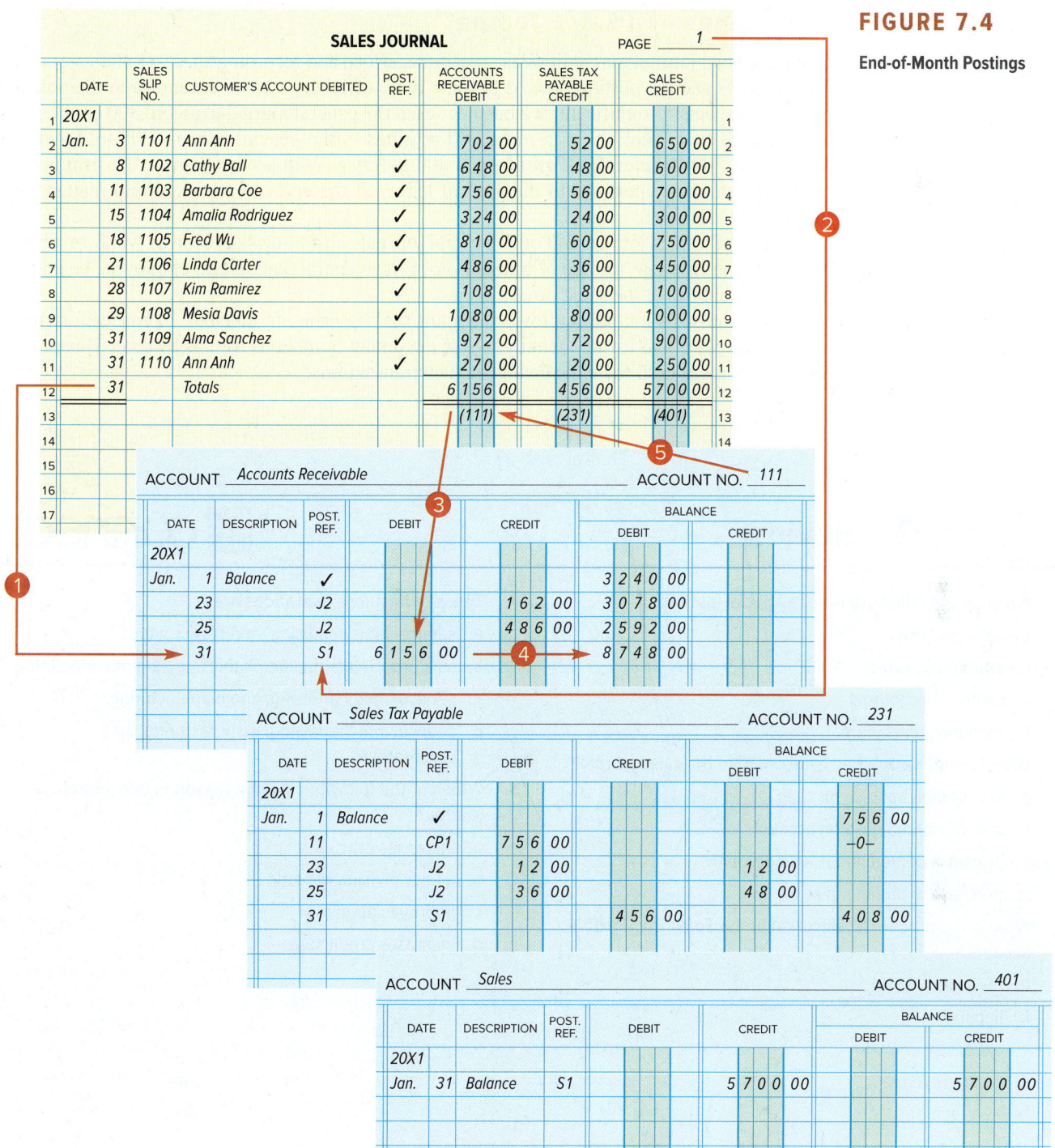

FIGURE 7.4

End-of-Month Postings

After the equality of the debits and credits has been verified, the sales journal is ruled and the column totals are posted to the general ledger accounts involved. To indicate that the postings have been made, the general ledger account numbers are entered in parentheses under the column totals in the sales journal. The abbreviation S1 is written in the Posting Reference column of the accounts, showing that the data was posted from page 1 of the sales journal.

The check marks in the sales journal in Figure 7.4 indicate that the amounts have been posted to the individual customer accounts. Posting from the sales journal to the customer accounts in the subsidiary ledger is illustrated later in this chapter.

Advantages of a Sales Journal

Using a special journal for credit sales saves time, effort, and recording space. Both the journalizing process and the posting process become more efficient, but the advantage in the posting process is especially significant. If a business used the general journal to record 300 credit sales a month, the firm would have to make 900 postings to the general ledger—300 to **Accounts Receivable,** 300 to **Sales Tax Payable,** and 300 to **Sales.** With a sales journal, the firm makes only three summary postings to the general ledger at the end of each month no matter how many credit sales were entered.

The use of a sales journal and other special journals also allows division of work. In a business with a fairly large volume of transactions, it is essential that several employees be able to record transactions at the same time.

Finally, the sales journal improves the audit trail by bringing together all entries for credit sales in one place and listing them by source document number as well as by date. This procedure makes it easier to trace the details of such transactions.

> **important!**
>
> **Posting**
> When posting from the sales journal, post information moving from left to right across the ledger form.

Section 1 Review

1. Which of the following is not a special journal?
   a. sales journal
   b. purchases journal
   c. contra sales journal
   d. cash payments journal

2. What type of transaction is recorded in the sales journal?
   a. sale of merchandise for cash
   b. sale of merchandise on account
   c. purchase of merchandise on account
   d. purchase of merchandise for cash

3. What is the proper classification of the *Sales Tax Payable* account?
   a. revenue
   b. liability
   c. expense
   d. contra revenue

4. Types of business operations are
   a. service, merchandising, and corporation.
   b. sole proprietorship, merchandising, and manufacturing.
   c. service, merchandising, and manufacturing.
   d. service, merchandising, manufacturing, and corporation.

5. Which of the following is not a reason to use a sales journal?
   a. increases efficiency
   b. allows division of work
   c. improves audit trail
   d. increases credit sales

Section 2

SECTION OBJECTIVES	TERMS TO LEARN
>> 7-3 Post from the sales journal to the customers' accounts in the accounts receivable subsidiary ledger. **WHY IT'S IMPORTANT** This ledger contains individual records that reflect all transactions of each customer. >> 7-4 Record sales returns and allowances in the general journal. **WHY IT'S IMPORTANT** Companies can see how much revenue is lost due to merchandise problems. >> 7-5 Post sales returns and allowances. **WHY IT'S IMPORTANT** Accurate, up-to-date customer records contribute to overall customer satisfaction. >> 7-6 Prepare a schedule of accounts receivable. **WHY IT'S IMPORTANT** This schedule provides a snapshot of amounts due from customers.	accounts receivable ledger contra revenue account control account credit memorandum net sales sales allowance sales return *Sales Returns and Allowances* schedule of accounts receivable

Accounts Receivable

A business that extends credit to customers must manage its accounts receivable carefully. Accounts receivable represent a substantial asset for many businesses, and this asset must be converted into cash in a timely manner. Otherwise, a firm may not be able to pay its bills even though it has a large volume of sales and earns a satisfactory profit.

The Accounts Receivable Ledger

The accountant needs detailed information about the transactions with credit customers and the balances owed by such customers at all times. This information is provided by an **accounts receivable ledger** with individual accounts for all credit customers. The accounts receivable ledger is referred to as a subsidiary ledger because it is separate from and subordinate to the general ledger.

Using an accounts receivable ledger makes it possible to verify that customers are paying their balances on time and that they are within their credit limits. The accounts receivable ledger also provides a convenient way to answer questions from credit customers. Customers may ask about their current balances or about a possible billing error.

The accounts for credit customers are maintained in a balance ledger form with three money columns, as shown in Figure 7.5 nearby. Notice that this form does not contain a column for indicating the type of account balance. The balances in the customer accounts are presumed to be debit balances since asset accounts normally have debit balances. However, occasionally there is a credit balance because a customer has overpaid an amount owed or has returned goods that were already paid for. One common procedure for dealing with this situation is to circle the balance in order to show that it is a credit amount.

For a small business such as Maxx-Out Sporting Goods, customer accounts are alphabetized in the accounts receivable ledger. Larger firms and firms that use accounting software programs assign an account number to each credit customer and arrange the customer accounts in numeric order. Postings to the accounts receivable ledger are usually made daily so that the customer accounts can be kept up to date at all times.

Posting a Credit Sale

>> **7-3 OBJECTIVE**

Post from the sales journal to the customers' accounts in the accounts receivable subsidiary ledger.

Each credit sale recorded in the sales journal is posted to the appropriate customer's account in the accounts receivable ledger, as shown in Figure 7.5. The date, the sales slip number, and the amount that the customer owes as a result of the sale are transferred from the sales journal to the customer's account. The amount is taken from the Accounts Receivable Debit column of the journal and is entered in the Debit column of the account. Next, the new balance is determined and recorded.

To show that the posting has been completed, a check mark (✓) is entered in the sales journal and the abbreviation S1 is entered in the Posting Reference column of the customer's account. As noted before, this abbreviation identifies page 1 of the sales journal.

Posting Cash Received on Account

When the transaction involves cash received on account from a credit customer, the cash collected is first recorded in a cash receipts journal. (The necessary entry in the cash receipts journal is discussed in Chapter 9.) The cash is then posted to the individual customer account in the accounts receivable ledger. Figure 7.6 shows a posting for cash received on January 7 from Ann Anh, a credit customer of Maxx-Out Sporting Goods.

>> **7-4 OBJECTIVE**

Record sales returns and allowances in the general journal.

Sales Returns and Allowances

A sale is entered in the accounting records when the goods are sold or the service is provided. If something is wrong with the goods or service, the firm may take back the goods, resulting in a **sales return,** or give the customer a reduction in price, resulting in a **sales allowance.**

When a return or allowance is related to a credit sale, the normal practice is to issue a document called a **credit memorandum** to the customer rather than giving a cash refund. The

FIGURE 7.5

Posting from the Sales Journal to the Accounts Receivable Ledger

FIGURE 7.6

Posting for Cash Received on Account

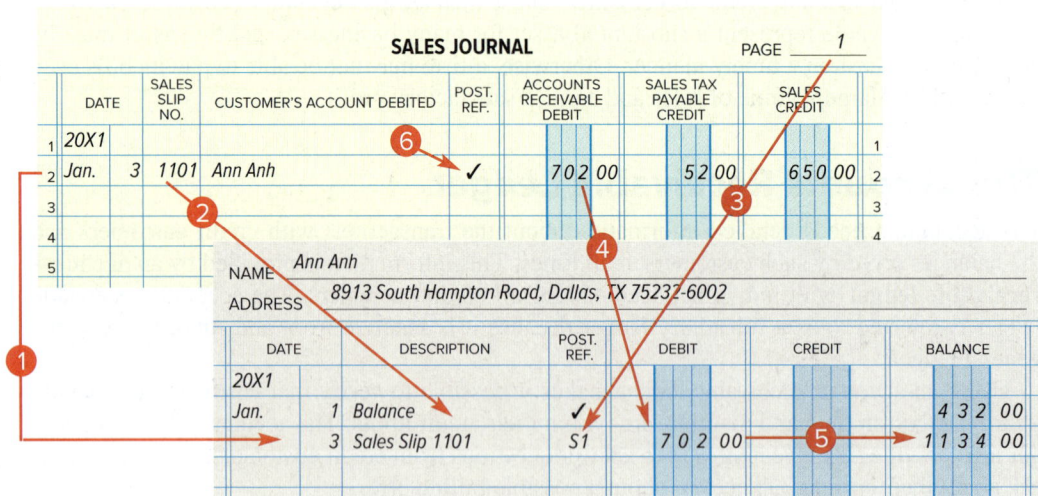

credit memorandum states that the customer's account is being reduced by the amount of the return or allowance plus any sales tax. A copy of the credit memorandum provides the data needed to enter the transaction in the firm's accounting records.

A debit to the **Sales Returns and Allowances** account is preferred to making a direct debit to **Sales.** This procedure gives a complete record of sales returns and allowances for each accounting period. Business managers use this record as a measure of operating efficiency. The **Sales Returns and Allowances** account is a **contra revenue account** because it has a debit balance, which is contrary, or opposite, to the normal credit balance for a revenue account.

BUSINESS TRANSACTION

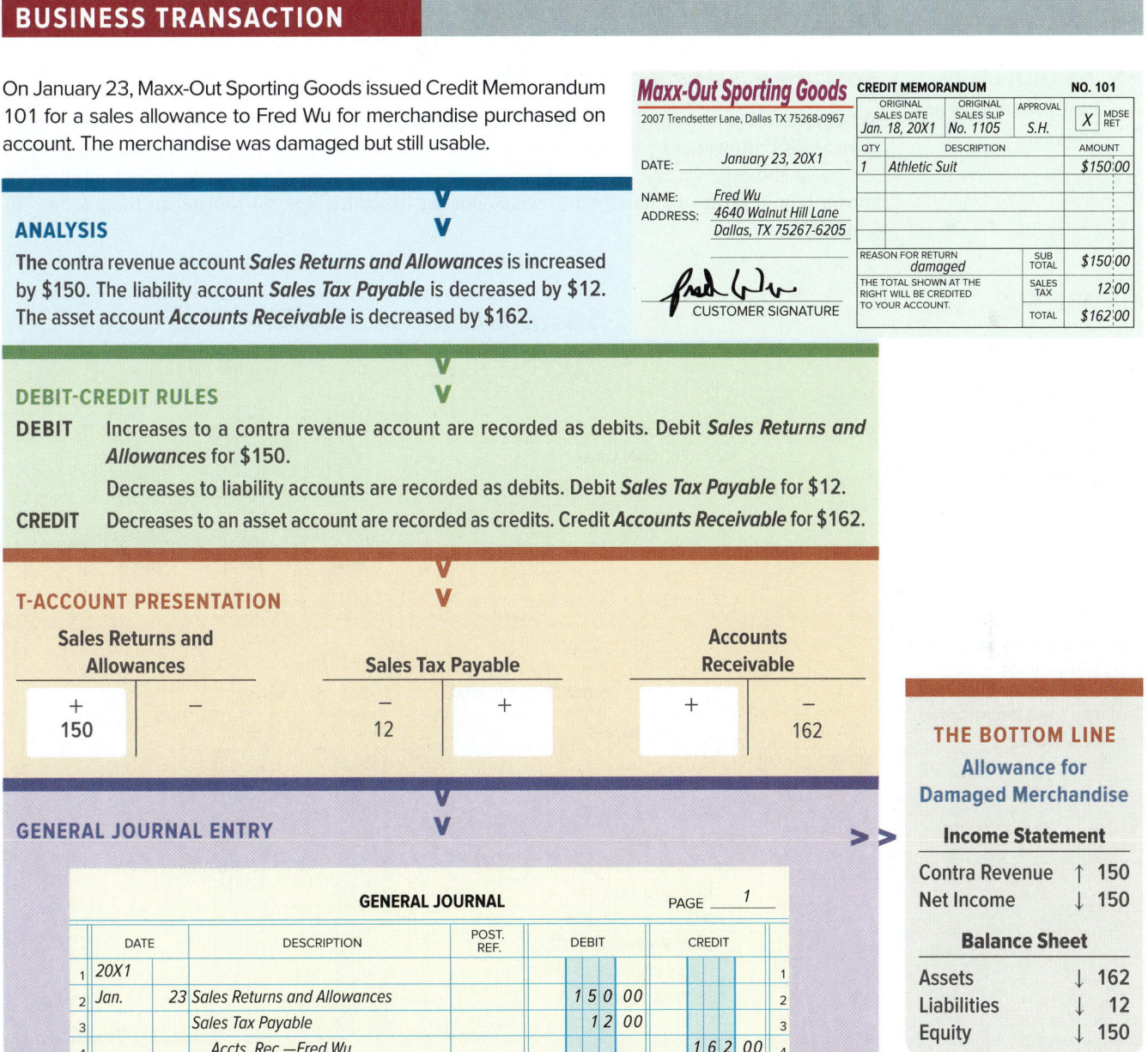

What is the ultimate effect of this transaction on the financial statements? An increase in contra revenue causes a decrease in net income. Note that the $150 decrease in net income causes a $150 decrease in owner's equity. The asset **Accounts Receivable** is decreased, and the liability **Sales Tax Payable** is also decreased. The eventual effect of this transaction on the income statement and the balance sheet is summarized in the box titled *The Bottom Line*.

Recording Sales Returns and Allowances

Depending on the volume of sales returns and allowances, a business may use a general journal to record these transactions, or it may use a special sales returns and allowances journal.

Using the General Journal for Sales Returns and Allowances A small firm that has a limited number of sales returns and allowances each month has no need to establish a special journal for such transactions. Instead, the required entries are made in the general journal.

Using a Sales Returns and Allowances Journal In a business having many sales returns and allowances, it is efficient to use a special journal for these transactions. An example of a *sales returns and allowances journal* is shown in Figure 7.7.

>> 7-5 OBJECTIVE

Post sales returns and allowances.

Posting a Sales Return or Allowance

Whether sales returns and allowances are recorded in the general journal or in a special sales returns and allowances journal, each of these transactions must be posted from the general ledger to the appropriate customer's account in the accounts receivable ledger. Figure 7.8 shows how a return of merchandise was posted from the general journal to the account of Linda Carter.

FIGURE 7.7

Sales Returns and Allowances Journal

SALES RETURNS AND ALLOWANCES JOURNAL PAGE 8

	DATE	SALES SLIP NO.	CUSTOMER'S ACCOUNT CREDITED	POST. REF.	ACCOUNTS RECEIVABLE CREDIT	SALES TAX PAYABLE DEBIT	SALES RET. & ALLOW. DEBIT	
1	20X1							1
2	Jan. 23	1105	Fred Wu	✓	162 00	12 00	150 00	2
3	25	1106	Linda Carter	✓	486 00	36 00	450 00	3
4								4
17	31		Totals		3 240 00	240 00	3 000 00	17
18					(111)	(231)	(451)	18
19								19

FIGURE 7.8

Posting a Sales Return to the Customer's Account

GENERAL JOURNAL PAGE 1

	DATE	DESCRIPTION	POST. REF.	DEBIT	CREDIT	
1	20X1					1
6	Jan. 25	Sales Returns and Allowances	451	450 00		6
7		Sales Tax Payable	231	36 00		7
8		Accounts Rec./Linda Carter	111 ✓		486 00	8
9		Accepted a return of				9
10		defective merchandise,				10
11		Credit Memorandum 102;				11
12		original sale made on Sales				12
13		Slip 1106 of January 21.				13
14						14

NAME Linda Carter
ADDRESS 1819 Belt Line Road, Dallas, Texas 75267-6318

DATE	DESCRIPTION	POST. REF.	DEBIT	CREDIT	BALANCE
20X1					
Jan. 1	Balance	✓			54 00
21	Sales Slip 1106	S1	486 00		540 00
25	CM 102	J1		486 00	54 00

Because the credit amount in the general journal entry for this transaction requires two postings, the account number 111 and a check mark are entered in the Posting Reference column of the journal. The 111 indicates that the amount was posted to the *Accounts Receivable* account in the general ledger, and the check mark indicates that the amount was posted to the customer's account in the accounts receivable ledger. Notice that a diagonal line was used to separate the two posting references.

Refer to Figure 7.7, which shows a special sales returns and allowances journal instead of a general journal. The account numbers at the bottom of each column are the posting references for the three general ledger accounts: *Accounts Receivable, Sales Tax Payable,* and *Sales Returns and Allowances.* The check marks in the Posting Reference column show that the credits were posted to individual customer accounts in the accounts receivable subsidiary ledger.

Remember that a business can use the general journal or special journals for transactions related to credit sales. A special journal is an efficient option for recording and posting large numbers of transactions.

Figure 7.9 shows the accounts receivable ledger after posting is completed.

Reporting Net Sales

At the end of each accounting period, the balance of the *Sales Returns and Allowances* account is subtracted from the balance of the *Sales* account in the Revenue section of the income statement. The resulting figure is the **net sales** for the period.

For example, assume the *Sales Returns and Allowances* account contains a balance of $600 at the end of January. Also assume the *Sales* account has a balance of $25,700 at the end of January. The Revenue section of the firm's income statement will appear as follows.

Maxx-Out Sporting Goods	
Income Statement (Partial)	
Month Ended January 31, 20X1	
Revenue	
Sales	$25,700
Less Sales Returns and Allowances	600
Net Sales	$25,100

ABOUT ACCOUNTING

Investing in Ethics

Are ethical companies—those with a strong internal enforcement policy—really more profitable? Yes, according to a study by Dr. Curtis Verschoor of DePaul University. Verschoor reports, "of the 87 companies where an ethics code was clearly stated, the average Market Value Added (MVA) was 2.5 times larger than for those not mentioning a code of ethics or conduct."

FIGURE 7.9

Accounts Receivable Ledger

NAME Ann Anh
ADDRESS 8913 South Hampton Road, Dallas, Texas 75232-6002

DATE		DESCRIPTION	POST. REF.	DEBIT	CREDIT	BALANCE
20X1						
Jan.	1	Balance	✓			432 00
	3	Sales Slip 1101	S1	702 00		1134 00
	7		CR1		432 00	702 00
	31	Sales Slip 1110	S1	270 00		972 00

NAME Cathy Ball
ADDRESS 7517 Woodrow Wilson Lane, Dallas, Texas 75267-6205

DATE		DESCRIPTION	POST. REF.	DEBIT	CREDIT	BALANCE
20X1						
Jan.	8	Sales Slip 1102	S1	648 00		648 00

(continued)

FIGURE 7.9
(continued)

NAME Vickie Bowman
ADDRESS 1712 Red Bird Lane, Dallas, Texas 75267-6502

DATE	DESCRIPTION	POST. REF.	DEBIT	CREDIT	BALANCE
20X1					
Jan. 1	Balance	✓			270 00
11		CR1		270 00	– 0 –

NAME Linda Carter
ADDRESS 1819 Belt Line Road, Dallas, Texas 75267-6318

DATE	DESCRIPTION	POST. REF.	DEBIT	CREDIT	BALANCE
20X1					
Jan. 1	Balance	✓			54 00
21	Sales Slip 1106	S1	486 00		540 00
25	CM 102	J1		486 00	54 00

NAME Barbara Coe
ADDRESS 1864 Elm Street, Dallas, Texas 75267-6205

DATE	DESCRIPTION	POST. REF.	DEBIT	CREDIT	BALANCE
20X1					
Jan. 1	Balance	✓			1 080 00
11	Sales Slip 1103	S1	756 00		1 836 00
13		CR1		540 00	1 296 00

NAME Mesia Davis
ADDRESS 1008 University Boulevard, Dallas, Texas 75267-6318

DATE	DESCRIPTION	POST. REF.	DEBIT	CREDIT	BALANCE
20X1					
Jan. 1	Balance	✓			216 00
29	Sales Slip 1108	S1	1 080 00		1 296 00
31		CR1		275 00	1 021 00

NAME Kim Ramirez
ADDRESS 5787 Valley View Lane, Dallas, Texas 75267-6318

DATE	DESCRIPTION	POST. REF.	DEBIT	CREDIT	BALANCE
20X1					
Jan. 1	Balance	✓			216 00
28	Sales Slip 1107	S1	108 00		324 00
31		CR1		108 00	216 00

FIGURE 7.9

(continued)

NAME Amalia Rodriguez
ADDRESS 8108 Sherman Drive, Dallas, Texas 75267-6205

DATE		DESCRIPTION	POST. REF.	DEBIT	CREDIT	BALANCE
20X1						
Jan.	1	Balance	✓			648 00
	15	Sales Slip 1104	S1	324 00		972 00

NAME Alma Sanchez
ADDRESS 1382 Clark Road, Dallas, Texas 75267-6205

DATE		DESCRIPTION	POST. REF.	DEBIT	CREDIT	BALANCE
20X1						
Jan.	1	Balance	✓			108 00
	16		CR1		108 00	– 0 –
	31	Sales Slip 1109	S1	972 00		972 00

NAME Fred Wu
ADDRESS 4640 Walnut Hill Lane, Dallas, Texas 75267-6205

DATE		DESCRIPTION	POST. REF.	DEBIT	CREDIT	BALANCE
20X1						
Jan.	1	Balance	✓			216 00
	18	Sales Slip 1105	S1	810 00		1026 00
	22		CR1		400 00	626 00
	23	CM 101	J1		162 00	464 00

Schedule of Accounts Receivable

>> **7-6 OBJECTIVE**
Prepare a schedule of accounts receivable.

The use of an accounts receivable ledger does not eliminate the need for the *Accounts Receivable* account in the general ledger. This account remains in the general ledger and continues to appear on the balance sheet at the end of each fiscal period. However, the *Accounts Receivable* account is now considered a control account. A **control account** serves as a link between a subsidiary ledger and the general ledger. Its balance summarizes the balances of its related accounts in the subsidiary ledger.

At the end of each month, after all the postings have been made from the sales journal, the cash receipts journal, and the general journal to the accounts receivable ledger, the balances in the accounts receivable ledger must be proved against the balance of the *Accounts Receivable* general ledger account. First, a **schedule of accounts receivable,** which lists the subsidiary ledger account balances, is prepared. The total of the schedule is compared with the balance of the *Accounts Receivable* account. If the two figures are not equal, errors must be located and corrected.

On January 31, the accounts receivable ledger at Maxx-Out Sporting Goods contains the accounts shown in Figure 7.9. To prepare a schedule of accounts receivable, the names of all customers with account balances are listed with the amount of their unpaid balances. Next, the figures are added to find the total owed to the business by its credit customers.

> Best Buy Co., Inc., reported accounts receivable of approximately $1.0 billion at February 3, 2018.

FIGURE 7.10

Schedule of Accounts Receivable and the Accounts Receivable Account

Maxx-Out Sporting Goods
Schedule of Accounts Receivable
January 31, 20X1

Ann Anh	972 00
Cathy Ball	648 00
Linda Carter	54 00
Barbara Coe	1 296 00
Mesia Davis	1 021 00
Kim Ramirez	216 00
Amalia Rodriguez	972 00
Alma Sanchez	972 00
Fred Wu	464 00
Total	6 615 00

ACCOUNT Accounts Receivable   **ACCOUNT NO.** 111

DATE	DESCRIPTION	POST. REF.	DEBIT	CREDIT	BALANCE DEBIT	BALANCE CREDIT
20X1						
Jan. 1	Balance	✓			3 240 00	
23		J1		162 00	3 078 00	
25		J1		486 00	2 592 00	
31		S1	6 156 00		8 748 00	
31		CR1		2 133 00	6 615 00	

A comparison of the total of the schedule of accounts receivable prepared at Maxx-Out Sporting Goods on January 31 and the balance of the **Accounts Receivable** account in the general ledger shows that the two figures are the same, as shown in Figure 7.10. The posting reference CR1 refers to the cash receipts journal, which is discussed in Chapter 9.

In addition to providing a proof of the subsidiary ledger, the schedule of accounts receivable serves another function. It reports information about the firm's accounts receivable at the end of the month. Management can review the schedule to see exactly how much each customer owes.

Section 2 Review

1. If a business has sales of $252,000 and $3,000 of sales returns and allowances, what is the amount of net sales?
    a. $255,000
    b. $252,000
    c. $249,000
    d. None of these is correct.

2. Which of the following is *not* true concerning a sales allowance?
    a. The customer's accounts receivable balance is reduced.
    b. The customer must return the damaged merchandise.
    c. A credit memorandum is issued to the customer.
    d. None of these is correct.

3. Which of the following is true concerning the accounts receivable ledger?
    a. Postings to the accounts receivable ledger from the sales journal are made once monthly.
    b. The accounts receivable ledger contains individual balances of amounts owed to vendors.
    c. The accounts receivable ledger contains individual balances of amounts owed by credit customers.
    d. Postings to the accounts receivable ledger from the purchases journal are made daily.

4. Where is net sales reported?
   a. sales general ledger account
   b. general journal
   c. income statement
   d. sales journal
5. Which of the following general ledger accounts would appear in a sales returns and allowances journal?
   a. *Sales Returns and Allowances, Sales Tax Payable, Accounts Receivable*
   b. *Sales Returns and Allowances, Sales, Accounts Receivable*
   c. *Sales Returns, Sales Allowances, Sales*
   d. *Sales Returns and Allowances, Sales, Accounts Payable*
6. A company issues a credit memorandum to a customer for returned merchandise. The merchandise was originally sold for $200 plus a sales tax of 5%. What is the amount of the credit memorandum?
   a. $205
   b. $210
   c. $200
   d. $190

Section 3

SECTION OBJECTIVES	TERMS TO LEARN
>> 7-7 Compute trade discounts. **WHY IT'S IMPORTANT** Trade discounts allow for flexible pricing structures. >> 7-8 Record credit card sales in appropriate journals. **WHY IT'S IMPORTANT** Credit cards are widely used in merchandising transactions. >> 7-9 Calculate sales tax due. **WHY IT'S IMPORTANT** Businesses are legally responsible for accurately reporting and remitting sales taxes.	charge-account sales discount on credit card sales invoice list price net price open-account credit trade discount wholesale business

Special Topics in Merchandising

Merchandisers have many accounting concerns. These include pricing, credit, and sales taxes.

Credit Sales for a Wholesale Business

The operations of Maxx-Out Sporting Goods are typical of those of many retail businesses—businesses that sell goods and services directly to individual consumers. In contrast, a **wholesale business** is a manufacturer or distributor of goods that sells to retailers or large consumers such as hotels and hospitals. The basic procedures used by wholesalers to handle sales and accounts receivable are the same as those used by retailers. However, many wholesalers offer cash discounts and trade discounts, which are not commonly found in retail operations. If the business does not offer a cash discount, the payment terms would be net 30, abbreviated as n/30, meaning payment is due by 30 days after the invoice date.

The procedures used in connection with cash discounts are examined in Chapter 9. The handling of trade discounts is described here.

>> **7-7 OBJECTIVE**
Compute trade discounts.

Computing Trade Discounts

A wholesale business offers goods to trade customers at less than retail prices. This price adjustment is based on the volume purchased by trade customers and takes the form of a **trade discount,** which is a reduction from the **list price**—the established retail price. There may be a single trade discount or a series of discounts for each type of goods. The **net price** (list price less all trade discounts) is the amount the wholesaler records in its sales journal. Publishing separate trade discounts can simplify the pricing structure appearing in product catalogs and brochures, while providing the company the flexibility to change the discounts offered through separate updates. Additionally, companies can raise the discount offered as the volume of product purchased increases, promoting customer loyalty.

The same goods may be offered to different customers at different trade discounts, depending on the size of the order and the costs of selling to the various types of customers.

Single Trade Discount Suppose the list price of goods is $1,500 and the trade discount is 40 percent. The amount of the discount is $600, and the net price to be shown on the invoice and recorded in the sales journal is $900.

List price	$1,500
Less 40% discount ($1,500 × 0.40)	600
Invoice price	$ 900

important!

Trade Discounts
The amount of sales revenue recorded is the list price minus the trade discount.

Series of Trade Discounts If the list price of goods is $1,500 and the trade discount is quoted in a series such as 25 and 15 percent, a different net price will result.

List price	$1,500.00
Less first discount ($1,500 × 0.25)	375.00
Difference	$1,125.00
Less second discount ($1,125 × 0.15)	168.75
Invoice price	$ 956.25

Using a Sales Journal for a Wholesale Business

Since sales taxes apply only to retail transactions, a wholesale business does not need to account for such taxes. Its sales journal may therefore be as simple as the one illustrated in Figure 7.11. This sales journal has a single amount column. The total of this column is posted to the general ledger at the end of the month as a debit to the **Accounts Receivable** account and a credit to the **Sales** account (Figure 7.12). During the month, the individual entries in the sales journal are posted to the customer accounts in the accounts receivable ledger.

Wholesale businesses issue invoices. An **invoice** is a customer billing for merchandise bought on credit. Copies of the invoices are used to enter the transactions in the sales journal.

The next merchandising topic, credit policies, applies to both wholesalers and retailers. The discussion in this textbook focuses on credit policies and accounting for retail firms.

> **important!**
>
> **Special Journal Format**
> Special journals such as the sales journal can vary in format from company to company.

FIGURE 7.11

Wholesaler's Sales Journal

SALES JOURNAL — PAGE 1

	DATE	INVOICE NO.	CUSTOMER'S ACCOUNT DEBITED	POST. REF.	ACCOUNTS RECEIVABLE DR. SALES CR.
1	20X1				
2	Jan. 3	7099	Gabbert's Hardware Company		18 600 00
25	31	7151	Neal's Department Store		4 200 00
26	31		Total		40 875 00
27					(111/401)

FIGURE 7.12

General Ledger Accounts

ACCOUNT **Accounts Receivable**   ACCOUNT NO. **111**

DATE	DESCRIPTION	POST. REF.	DEBIT	CREDIT	BALANCE DEBIT	BALANCE CREDIT
20X1						
Jan. 1	Balance	✓			46 700 00	
31		S1	40 875 00		87 575 00	

ACCOUNT **Sales**   ACCOUNT NO. **401**

DATE	DESCRIPTION	POST. REF.	DEBIT	CREDIT	BALANCE DEBIT	BALANCE CREDIT
20X1						
Jan. 31		S1		40 875 00		40 875 00

Credit Policies

The use of credit is considered to be one of the most important factors in the rapid growth of modern economic systems. Sales on credit are made by large numbers of wholesalers and retailers of goods and by many professional people and service businesses. The assumption is that the volume of both sales and profits will increase if buyers are given a period of a month or more to pay for the goods or services they purchase.

However, the increase in profits a business expects when it grants credit will be realized only if each customer completes the transaction by paying for the goods or services purchased. If payment is not received, the expected profits become actual losses and the purpose for granting the credit is defeated. Business firms try to protect against the possibility of such losses by investigating a customer's credit record and ability to pay for purchases before allowing any credit to the customer.

Professional people such as doctors, lawyers, architects, and owners of small businesses like Maxx-Out Sporting Goods usually make their own decisions about granting credit. Such decisions may be based on personal judgment or on reports available from credit bureaus, information supplied by other creditors, and credit ratings supplied by national firms such as Dun & Bradstreet.

> Dun & Bradstreet is a leader in providing credit information. The company's common stock trades on the New York Stock Exchange. Its ticker symbol is DNB. For the year ended December 31, 2017, the company reported revenues of $1.74 billion.

Larger businesses maintain a credit department to determine the amounts and types of credit that should be granted to customers. In addition to using credit data supplied by institutions, the credit department may obtain financial statements and related reports from customers who have applied for credit. This information is analyzed to help determine the maximum amount of credit that may be granted and suitable credit terms for the customer. Financial statements that have been audited by certified public accountants are used extensively by credit departments.

Even though the credit investigation is thorough, some accounts receivable become uncollectible. Unexpected business developments, errors of judgment, incorrect financial data, and many other causes may lead to defaults in payments by customers. Experienced managers know that some uncollectible accounts are to be expected in normal business operations and that limited losses indicate that a firm's credit policies are sound. Provisions for such limited losses from uncollectible accounts are usually made in budgets and other financial projections.

Each business must develop credit policies that achieve maximum sales with minimum losses from uncollectible accounts:

- A credit policy that is too tight results in a low level of losses at the expense of increases in sales volume.
- A credit policy that is too lenient may result in increased sales volume accompanied by a high level of losses.

Good judgment based on knowledge and experience must be used to achieve a well-balanced credit policy.

Different types of credit have evolved with the growing economy and changing technology. The different types of credit require different accounting treatments.

Accounting for Different Types of Credit Sales

The most common types of credit sales are:

- open-account credit,
- business credit cards,
- bank credit cards,
- cards issued by credit card companies.

Open-Account Credit The form of credit most commonly offered by professional people and small businesses permits the sale of services or goods to the customer with the understanding that the amount is to be paid at a later date. This type of arrangement is called **open-account credit.** It is usually granted on the basis of personal acquaintance or knowledge of the customer. However, formal credit checks may also be used. The amount involved in each transaction is usually small, and payment is expected within 30 days or on receipt of a monthly statement. Open-account sales are also referred to as **charge-account sales.**

Maxx-Out Sporting Goods uses the open-account credit arrangement. Sales transactions are recorded as debits to the *Accounts Receivable* account and credits to the *Sales* account. Collections on account are recorded as debits to the *Cash* account and credits to the *Accounts Receivable* account.

Business Credit Cards Many retail businesses, especially large ones such as department store chains and gasoline companies, provide their own credit cards (sometimes called charge cards) to customers who have established credit. Whenever a sale is completed using a business credit card, a sales slip is prepared in the usual manner. Then the sales slip and the credit card are placed in a mechanical device that prints the customer's name, account number, and other data on all copies of the sales slip. Many companies use computerized card readers and sales registers that print out a sales slip with the customer information and a line for the customer's signature. Some businesses require that the salesclerk contact the credit department by telephone or computer terminal to verify the customer's credit status before completing the transaction.

Business credit card sales are similar to open-account credit sales. A business credit card sale is recorded as:

- a debit to *Accounts Receivable,*
- a credit to a revenue account such as *Sales.*

A customer payment is recorded as:

- a debit to *Cash,*
- a credit to *Accounts Receivable.*

Bank Credit Cards Retailers can provide credit while minimizing or avoiding the risk of losses from uncollectible accounts by accepting bank credit cards. The most widely accepted bank credit cards are MasterCard and Visa. Many banks participate in one or both of these credit card programs, and other banks have their own credit cards. Bank credit cards are issued to consumers directly by banks.

A business may participate in these credit card programs by meeting conditions set by the bank. Banks review such factors as:

- The business's financial history.
- The industry in which the business operates.
- The type of business: online, physical store, or both.
- Any past merchant account history.

A credit card sale is processed when the customer inserts the chip end of the credit card into an electronic terminal (see Figure 7.13). The terminal transmits information to the bank or credit card company using an Internet connection.

When a business makes a sale to a customer using a bank credit card, it acquires an asset that can be converted into cash immediately without responsibility for later collection from the customer. In most cases, the bank deposits the cash from the sale into the business's bank account the same day.

Banks charge the business a fee, called a **discount on credit card sales,** for processing the sale. The discount is usually between 1.5 and 4 percent of the amount charged. Depending on the arrangements that have been made, the bank will deduct the discount and immediately credit the depositor's checking account with the net amount of the sale, or it will credit the depositor's checking account for the full amount of the sale and deduct the discount at the end of the month. If the second procedure is used, the total discount for the month's sales will appear on the bank statement.

The bank is responsible for collecting from the cardholder. If any amounts are uncollectible, the bank sustains the loss. For the retailer, bank credit card sales are like cash sales. The

FIGURE 7.13

Credit Card Reader

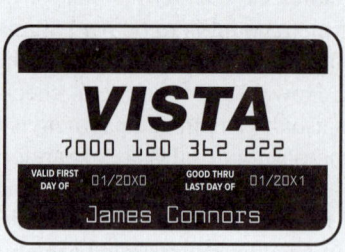

Photo: ©Africa Studio/Shutterstock; Image: McGraw-Hill Education

FIGURE 7.14

Credit Card Receipt

```
                MAXX-OUT SPORTING GOODS
                       DALLAS, TX
                *******************************
     SWEATSUIT                         $125.00
     SALES TAX                          $10.00
     TOTAL                             $135.00
     NAME :
     CONNORS/JAMES
     TYPE :
     PURCHASED                          SWIPED
     VISTA
     ***********222
     INVOICE #                       08789798234
     AUTH CODE :                          12345
     DATE :                            01/28/X1
     TIME                                 17:02

                  James Connors
                  _____
                  Signature :
```

accounting procedures for such sales are therefore quite similar to the accounting procedures for cash sales, which will be discussed in Chapter 9. If the business is billed once each month for the bank's discount, the total amount involved in the daily deposit of the credit card sales slips is debited to **Cash** and credited to **Sales.**

Credit Card Companies Credit cards such as American Express and Diners Club are issued by business firms or subsidiaries of business firms that are operated for the special purpose of handling credit card transactions. The potential cardholder must submit an application and pay an annual fee to the credit card company. If the credit references are satisfactory, the credit card is issued. It is normally reissued at one-year intervals so long as the company's credit experience with the cardholder remains satisfactory.

Hotels, restaurants, airline companies, many types of retail stores, and a wide variety of other businesses accept these credit cards. When making sales to cardholders, sellers usually prepare their own sales slip or bill and then complete a special sales slip required by the credit card company (see Figure 7.14). As with the sales slips for bank credit cards, the forms must be imprinted with the identifying data on the customer's card and signed by the customer. Such sales slips are sometimes referred to as *sales invoices, sales drafts,* or *sales vouchers.* The term used varies from one credit card company to another.

The seller acquires an account receivable from the credit card company rather than from the customer. At approximately one-month intervals, the credit card company bills the cardholders

Accounting for Credit Card Sales

The procedure used to account for credit card sales is similar to the procedure for recording open-account credit sales. However, the account receivable is with the credit card company, not with the cardholders who buy the goods or services.

There are two basic methods of recording these sales. Businesses that have few transactions with credit card companies normally debit the amounts of such sales to the usual **Accounts Receivable** account in the general ledger and credit them to the same **Sales** account that is used for cash sales and other types of credit sales. An individual account for each credit card company is set up in the accounts receivable subsidiary ledger. This method of recording sales is shown in Figure 7.15.

Payment from a credit card company is recorded in the cash receipts journal, a procedure discussed in Chapter 9. Fees charged by the credit card companies for processing these sales are debited to an account called **Discount Expense on Credit Card Sales.** For example, assume that American Express charges a 7 percent discount fee on the sale charged by Wilson Davis on January 3 and remits the balance to the firm. This transaction would be recorded in the cash receipts journal by debiting **Cash** for $502.20, debiting **Discount Expense on Credit Card Sales** for $37.80, and crediting **Accounts Receivable** for $540.00.

Firms that do a large volume of business with credit card companies may debit all such sales to a special **Accounts Receivable from Credit Card Companies** account in the general ledger, thus separating this type of receivable from the accounts receivable resulting from open-account credit sales. A special account called **Sales—Credit Card Companies** is credited for the revenue from these transactions. Figure 7.16 shows how the necessary entries are made in the sales journal.

>> **7-8 OBJECTIVE**

Record credit card sales in appropriate journals.

FIGURE 7.15

Recording Credit Card Company Sales

SALES JOURNAL PAGE 17

	DATE	SALES SLIP NO.	CUSTOMER'S ACCOUNT DEBITED	POST. REF.	ACCOUNTS RECEIVABLE DEBIT	SALES TAX PAYABLE CREDIT	SALES CREDIT	
1	20X1							1
2	Jan. 3	533	American Express		540 00	40 00	500 00	2
3			(Wilson Davis)					3
26	11	651	MasterCard		216 00	16 00	200 00	26
27			(Teresa Logan)					27
28								28

FIGURE 7.16 Recording Sales for Accounts Receivable from Credit Card Companies

SALES JOURNAL PAGE 7

	DATE	SALES SLIP NO.	CUSTOMER'S ACCOUNT DEBITED	POST. REF.	ACCOUNTS RECEIVABLE DEBIT	ACCT. REC.— CREDIT CARD COMPANIES DEBIT	SALES TAX PAYABLE CREDIT	SALES CREDIT	SALES— CREDIT CARD COMPANIES CREDIT	
1	20X1									1
2	Jan. 3		Summary of credit card sales/			972 00	72 00		900 00	2
3			American Express							3
5										5
16	11		Summary of credit card sales/			540 00	40 00		500 00	16
17			MasterCard							17
29	31		Totals			4860 00	360 00		4500 00	29
30						(114)	(231)		(404)	30
31										31

Sales Taxes

Many cities and states impose a tax on retail sales. Sales taxes imposed by city and state governments vary. However, the procedures used to account for these taxes are similar.

A sales tax may be levied on all retail sales, but often certain items are exempt. In most cases, the amount of the sales tax is stated separately and then added to the retail price of the merchandise.

> According to the Tax Foundation, Lake Providence, Louisiana, at 12%, had the highest combined state and local sales tax rate in the country during 2017.

The retailer is required to collect sales tax from customers, make periodic (usually monthly) reports to the taxing authority, and pay the taxes due when the reports are filed. The government may allow the retailer to retain part of the tax as compensation for collecting it.

>> 7-9 OBJECTIVE
Calculate sales tax due.

Preparing the State Sales Tax Return

At the end of each month, after the accounts have all been posted, Maxx-Out Sporting Goods prepares the sales tax return. The information required for the monthly return comes from the accounting data of the current month. Three accounts are involved: **Sales Tax Payable, Sales,** and **Sales Returns and Allowances.** In some states, the sales tax return is filed quarterly rather than monthly.

The procedures to file a sales tax return are similar to those used by Maxx-Out Sporting Goods on February 7 when it filed the monthly sales tax return for January with the state tax commissioner. The firm's sales are subject to an 8 percent state sales tax. To highlight the data needed, the January postings are shown in the ledger accounts in Figure 7.17.

FIGURE 7.17

Ledger Account Postings for Sales Tax

ACCOUNT: Sales Tax Payable — ACCOUNT NO. 231

DATE	DESCRIPTION	POST. REF.	DEBIT	CREDIT	BALANCE DEBIT	BALANCE CREDIT
20X1						
Jan. 1	Balance	✓				756 00
11		CP1	756 00			-0-
23		J1	12 00		12 00	
25		J1	36 00		48 00	
31		S1		456 00		408 00
31		CR1		1800 00		2208 00

ACCOUNT: Sales — ACCOUNT NO. 401

DATE	DESCRIPTION	POST. REF.	DEBIT	CREDIT	BALANCE DEBIT	BALANCE CREDIT
20X1						
Jan. 31		S1		5700 00		5700 00
31		CR1		22500 00		28200 00

ACCOUNT: Sales Returns and Allowances — ACCOUNT NO. 451

DATE	DESCRIPTION	POST. REF.	DEBIT	CREDIT	BALANCE DEBIT	BALANCE CREDIT
20X1						
Jan. 23		J1	150 00		150 00	
25		J1	450 00		600 00	

Using these figures as a basis, the amount of the firm's taxable gross sales for January is determined as follows:

Cash Sales	$22,500
Credit Sales	5,700
Total Sales	$28,200
Less Sales Returns and Allowances	600
Taxable Gross Sales for January	$27,600

> **THE BOTTOM LINE**
> **Retail Sales**
>
> **Income Statement**
> Revenue ↑ 27,600
> Net Income ↑ 27,600
>
> **Balance Sheet**
> Assets ↑ 29,808
> Liabilities ↑ 2,208
> Equity ↑ 27,600

The 8 percent sales tax on the gross sales of $27,600 amounts to $2,208.00. Note that the firm's increase in assets (**Cash** and **Accounts Receivable**) is equal to sales revenue plus the sales tax liability on that revenue.

In the state where Maxx-Out Sporting Goods is located, a retailer who files the sales tax return (see Figure 7.19) on time and who pays the tax when it is due is entitled to a discount. The discount is intended to compensate the retailer, at least in part, for acting as a collection agent for the government. The discount rate depends on the amount of tax to be paid. For amounts over $1,000, the rate is 1 percent of the total tax due. For Maxx-Out Sporting Goods, the discount for January is determined as follows:

Taxable Gross Sales for January	$27,600.00
8% Sales Tax Rate	× 0.08
Sales Tax Due	$ 2,208.00
1% Discount Rate	× 0.01
Discount	$ 22.08
Sales Tax Due	$ 2,208.00
Discount	(22.08)
Net Sales Tax Due	$ 2,185.92

The firm sends a check for the net sales tax due with the sales tax return. The accounting entry made to record this payment includes a debit to **Sales Tax Payable** and a credit to **Cash** (for $2,185.92 in this case). After the amount of the payment is posted, the balance in the **Sales Tax Payable** account should be equal to the discount, as shown in Figure 7.18. Slight differences can arise because the tax collected at the time of the sale is determined by a tax bracket method that can give results slightly more or less than the final computations on the tax return.

FIGURE 7.18

Effect of Paying Sales Tax

ACCOUNT _Sales Tax Payable_ ACCOUNT NO. _231_

DATE	DESCRIPTION	POST. REF.	DEBIT	CREDIT	BALANCE DEBIT	BALANCE CREDIT
20X1						
Jan. 1	Balance	✓				756 00
11		CP1	756 00			–0–
23		J1	12 00		12 00	
25		J1	36 00		48 00	
31		S1		456 00		408 00
31		CR1		1800 00		2208 00
Feb. 6		CP1	2185 92			22 08

Tax payment ← (2185 92) Amount of discount ← (22 08)

FIGURE 7.19

State Sales Tax Return

SALES TAX RETURN

	LICENSE NUMBER	**STATE TAX COMMISSION**
ALWAYS REFER TO THIS NUMBER WHEN WRITING THE DIVISION →	217539	SALES AND USE TAX DIVISION DRAWER 20 CAPITAL CITY, STATE 78711 RETURN REQUESTED
—IMPORTANT— ANY CHANGE IN OWNERSHIP REQUIRES A NEW LICENSE: NOTIFY THIS DIVISION IMMEDIATELY.		
This return DUE on the 1st day of month following period covered by the return, and becomes DELINQUENT on the 21st day.	37-9462315 FED. E.I. NO. OR S.S NO.	*January 31, 20X1* —Sales for period ending—

MAKE ALL REMITTANCES PAYABLE TO STATE TAX COMMISSIOIN DO NOT SEND CASH STAMPS NOT ACCEPTED

OWNER'S NAME AND LOCATION

Maxx-Out Sporting Goods
2007 Trendsetter Lane
Dallas, Texas 75268-0967

	COMPUTATION OF SALES TAX	For Taxpayer's Use	Do Not Use This Column
1.	TOTAL Gross proceeds of sales or Gross Receipts (to include rentals)	27,600.00	
2.	Add cost of personal property purchased on a RETAIL LICENSE FOR RESALE but USED BY YOU or YOUR EMPLOYEES, including GIFTS and PREMIUMS	–0–	
3.	USE TAX—Add cost of personal property purchased outside of STATE for your use, storage, or consumption	–0–	
4.	Total (Lines 1, 2, and 3)	27,600.00	
5.	LESS ALLOWABLE DEDUCTIONS (Must be itemized on reverse side)	–0–	
6.	Net taxable total (Line 4 minus Line 5)	27,600.00	
7.	Sales and Use Tax Due (8% of Line 6)	2,208.00	
8.	LESS TAXPAYER'S DISCOUNT—(Deductible only when amount of TAX due is not delinquent at time of payment) →	22.08	
	IF LINE 7 IS LESS THAN $100.00 —DEDUCT 3% IF LINE 7 IS $100 BUT LESS THAN $1,000.00 —DEDUCT 2% IF LINE 7 IS $1,000.00 OR MORE —DEDUCT 1%		
9.	NET AMOUNT OF TAX PAYABLE (Line 7 minus Line 8)	2,185.92	
	Add the following penalty and interest if return or remittance is late.		
10.	Specific Penalty: 25% of tax _____ $ _____		
11.	Interest: 1/2 of 1% per month from due date until paid. $ _____ TOTAL PENALTY AND INTEREST →		
12.	TOTAL TAX, PENALTY AND INTEREST	2,185.92	
13.	Subtract credit memo No.		
14.	TOTAL AMOUNT DUE (IF NO SALES MADE SO STATE)	2,185.92	

I certify that this return, including the accompanying schedules or statements, has been examined by me and to the best of my knowledge and belief, a true and complete return, made in good faith, for the period stated, pursuant to the provisions of the Code of Laws, 20–, and Acts Amendatory Thereto.

URGENT—SEE THAT LICENSE NUMBER IS ON RETURN

Max Ferraro
SIGNATURE

Owner   February 7, 20X1
Owner, partner or title   Date

Return must be signed by owner or if corporation, authorized person.

Division Use Only

If there is a balance in the *Sales Tax Payable* account after the sales tax liability is satisfied, the balance is transferred to an account called *Miscellaneous Income* by a general journal entry. This entry consists of a debit to *Sales Tax Payable* and a credit to *Miscellaneous Income*.

Recording Sales Tax in the Sales Account

In some states, retailers can credit the entire sales price plus tax to the *Sales* account. At the end of each month or quarter, they must remove from the *Sales* account the amount of tax included and transfer that amount to the *Sales Tax Payable* account. Assume that during January a retailer whose sales are all taxable sells merchandise for a total price of $20,250, which includes an 8 percent tax. The entry to record these sales is summarized in general journal form shown here.

>> **THE BOTTOM LINE**
>
> **Discount on Sales Tax**
>
> **Income Statement**
> Misc. Income ↑ 22.08
> Net Income ↑ 22.08
>
> **Balance Sheet**
> Assets   No Effect
> Liabilities   ↓ 22.08
> Equity   ↑ 22.08

GENERAL JOURNAL PAGE 4

DATE		DESCRIPTION	POST. REF.	DEBIT	CREDIT
20X1					
Jan.	31	Accounts Receivable	111	20,250.00	
		Sales	401		20,250.00
		To record total sales and			
		sales tax collected during			
		the month			

At the end of the month, the retailer must transfer the sales tax from the *Sales* account to the *Sales Tax Payable* account. The first step in the transfer process is to determine the amount of tax involved. The sales tax payable is computed as follows.

MANAGERIAL IMPLICATIONS <<

CREDIT SALES

- Credit sales are a major source of revenue in many businesses, and accounts receivable represent a major asset.
- Management needs up-to-date and correct information about both sales and accounts receivable in order to monitor the financial health of the firm.
- Special journals save time and effort and reduce the cost of accounting work.
- In a retail firm that must handle sales tax, the sales journal and the cash receipts journal provide a convenient method of recording the amounts owed for sales tax.
  - When the data is posted to the Sales Tax Payable account in the general ledger, the firm has a complete and systematic record that speeds the completion of the periodic sales tax return.
  - The firm has detailed proof of its sales tax figures in the case of a tax audit.

- An accounts receivable subsidiary ledger provides management and the credit department with up-to-date information about the balances owed by all customers.
  - This information is useful in controlling credit and collections.
  - Detailed information helps in evaluating the effectiveness of credit policies.
  - Management must keep a close watch on the promptness of customer payments because much of the cash needed for day-to-day operations usually comes from payments on accounts receivable.
- A well-balanced credit policy helps increase sales volume but also keeps losses from uncollectible accounts at an acceptable level.
- Retailers are liable for any sales taxes not collected. This situation can be avoided with an efficient control system.

THINKING CRITICALLY

What are some possible consequences of out-of-date accounts receivable records?

Sales + tax	= $20,250
100% of sales + 8% of sales	= $20,250
108% of sales	= $20,250
Sales	= $20,250/1.08
Sales	= $18,750
Tax	= $18,750 × 0.08 = $1,500

The firm then makes the following entry to transfer the liability from the *Sales* account.

GENERAL JOURNAL PAGE 4

	DATE	DESCRIPTION	POST. REF.	DEBIT	CREDIT	
1	20X1					1
8	Jan. 31	Sales	401	1500 00		8
9		Sales Tax Payable	231		1500 00	9
10		To transfer sales tax				10
11		payable from the Sales				11
12		account to the liability				12
13		account				13
14						14
15						15

The retailer in this example originally recorded the entire sales price plus tax in the *Sales* account. The sales tax was transferred to the *Sales Tax Payable* account at the end of the month.

Section 3 Review

1. Which of the following are common types of credit sales?
   a. bank credit cards
   b. business credit cards
   c. open-account credit
   d. All answers are correct.

2. What account is used to record sales tax owed by a business to a city or state?
   a. *Sales Tax Expense*
   b. *Sales Tax Payable*
   c. *Sales Tax Receivable*
   d. *Sales*

3. A company that buys $4,000 of goods from a wholesaler offering trade discounts of 20 and 10 percent will pay what amount for the goods?
   a. $1,760
   b. $2,800
   c. $2,880
   d. $2,780

4. If a wholesale business offers a trade discount of 35 percent on a sale of $7,200, what is the amount of the discount?
   a. $240
   b. $252
   c. $2,400
   d. $2,520

5. A customer uses a credit card to purchase merchandise of $1,000, plus a 5% sales tax, from Royal Menswear. The credit card company charges a 2% discount fee on the transaction. How much will the credit card company pay Royal Menswear for this transaction?
   a. $1,030
   b. $1,070
   c. $1,050
   d. $1,029

REVIEW Chapter Summary

The nature of the operations of a business, the volume of its transactions, and other factors influence the design of an accounting system. In this chapter, you have learned about the use of special journals and subsidiary ledgers suitable for a merchandising business. These additional journals and ledgers increase the efficiency of recording credit transactions and permit the division of labor.

Learning Objectives

7-1 Record credit sales in a sales journal.

The sales journal is used to record credit sales transactions, usually on a daily basis. For sales transactions that include sales tax, the sales tax liability is recorded at the time of the sale to ensure that company records reflect the appropriate amount of sales tax liability.

7-2 Post from the sales journal to the general ledger accounts.

At the end of each month, the sales journal is totaled, proved, and ruled. Column totals are then posted to the general ledger. Using a sales journal rather than a general journal to record sales saves the time and effort of posting individual entries to the general ledger during the month.

7-3 Post from the sales journal to the customers' accounts in the accounts receivable subsidiary ledger.

The accounts of individual credit customers are kept in a subsidiary ledger called the accounts receivable ledger. Daily postings are made to this ledger from the sales journal, the cash receipts journal, and the general journal or the sales returns and allowances journal. The current balance of a customer's account is computed after each posting so that the amount owed is known at all times.

7-4 Record sales returns and allowances in the general journal.

Sales returns and allowances are usually debited to a contra revenue account. A firm with relatively few sales returns and allowances could use the general journal to record these transactions.

7-5 Post sales returns and allowances.

Sales returns and allowances transactions must be posted to the general ledger and to the appropriate accounts receivable subsidiary ledgers. The balance of the *Sales Returns and Allowances* account is subtracted from the balance of the *Sales* account to show net sales on the income statement.

7-6 Prepare a schedule of accounts receivable.

Each month a schedule of accounts receivable is prepared. It is used to prove the subsidiary ledger against the *Accounts Receivable* account. It also reports the amounts due from credit customers.

7-7 Compute trade discounts.

Wholesale businesses often offer goods to trade customers at less than retail prices. Trade discounts are expressed as a percentage off the list price. Multiply the list price by the percentage trade discount offered to compute the dollar amount. Sales are recorded net of the trade discounts.

7-8 Record credit card sales in appropriate journals.

Credit sales are common, and different credit arrangements are used. Businesses that have few transactions with credit card companies normally record these transactions in the sales journal by debiting the usual *Accounts Receivable* account in the general ledger and crediting the same *Sales* account that is used for cash sales.

7-9 Prepare the state sales tax return.

In states and cities that have a sales tax, the retailer must prepare a sales tax return and send the total tax collected to the taxing authority.

7-10 Define the accounting terms new to this chapter.

Glossary

Accounts receivable ledger (p. 205) A subsidiary ledger that contains credit customer accounts

Charge-account sales (p. 217) Sales made through the use of open-account credit or one of various types of credit cards

Contra revenue account (p. 207) An account with a debit balance, which is contrary to the normal balance for a revenue account

Control account (p. 211) An account that links a subsidiary ledger and the general ledger since its balance summarizes the balances of the accounts in the subsidiary ledger

Credit memorandum (p. 206) A note verifying that a customer's account is being reduced by the amount of a sales return or sales allowance plus any sales tax that may have been involved

Discount on credit card sales (p. 217) A fee charged by the credit card companies for processing sales made with credit cards

Invoice (p. 215) A customer billing for merchandise bought on credit

List price (p. 214) An established retail price

Manufacturing business (p. 198) A business that sells goods that it has produced

Merchandise inventory (p. 198) The stock of goods a merchandising business keeps on hand

Merchandising business (p. 198) A business that sells goods purchased for resale

Net price (p. 214) The list price less all trade discounts

Net sales (p. 209) The difference between the balance in the *Sales* account and the balance in the *Sales Returns and Allowances* account

Open-account credit (p. 217) A system that allows the sale of services or goods with the understanding that payment will be made at a later date

Periodic inventory system (p. 198) An inventory system in which the merchandise inventory balance is only updated when a physical inventory is taken

Perpetual inventory system (p. 198) An inventory system that tracks the inventories on hand at all times

Retail business (p. 198) A business that sells directly to individual consumers

Sales allowance (p. 206) A reduction in the price originally charged to customers for goods or services

Sales journal (p. 199) A special journal used to record sales of merchandise on credit

Sales return (p. 206) A firm's acceptance of a return of goods from a customer

Sales Returns and Allowances (p. 207) A contra revenue account where sales returns and sales allowances are recorded; sales returns and allowances are subtracted from sales to determine net sales

Schedule of accounts receivable (p. 211) A listing of all balances of the accounts in the accounts receivable subsidiary ledger

Service business (p. 198) A business that sells services

Special journal (p. 198) A journal used to record only one type of transaction

Subsidiary ledger (p. 198) A ledger dedicated to accounts of a single type and showing details to support a general ledger account

Trade discount (p. 214) A reduction from list price

Wholesale business (p. 214) A business that manufactures goods for or distributes goods to retail businesses or large consumers such as hotels and hospitals

Comprehensive Self Review

1. Name the two different time periods usually covered in sales tax returns.
2. What is a control account?
3. Why does a small merchandising business usually need a more complex set of financial records and statements than a small service business?
4. Why is it useful for a firm to have an accounts receivable ledger?
5. Explain how service, merchandising, and manufacturing businesses differ from each other.

(Answers to Comprehensive Self Review are at the end of the chapter.)

Discussion Questions

1. How are the net sales for an accounting period determined?
2. What purposes does the schedule of accounts receivable serve?
3. How do retail and wholesale businesses differ?
4. Why is a sales return or allowance usually recorded in a special *Sales Returns and Allowances* account rather than being debited to the *Sales* account?
5. How is a multicolumn special journal proved at the end of each month?
6. What kind of account is *Sales Returns and Allowances*?
7. The sales tax on a credit sale is not collected from the customer immediately. When is this tax usually entered in a firm's accounting records? What account is used to record this tax?
8. In a particular state, the sales tax rate is 5 percent of sales. The retailer is allowed to record both the selling price and the tax in the same account. Explain how to compute the sales tax due when this method is used.
9. What two methods are commonly used to record sales involving credit cards issued by credit card companies?
10. What procedure does a business use to collect amounts owed to it for sales on credit cards issued by credit card companies?
11. When a firm makes a sale involving a credit card issued by a credit card company, does the firm have an account receivable with the cardholder or with the credit card company?
12. What is the discount on credit card sales? What type of account is used to record this item?
13. Why are bank credit card sales similar to cash sales for a business?
14. What is open-account credit?
15. What is a trade discount? Why do some firms offer trade discounts to their customers?

APPLICATIONS

Exercises

Identifying the journal to record transactions.

Exercise 7.1
Objective 7-1

The accounting system of Great Harvest Healthy Foods includes the journals listed below. Indicate the specific journal in which each of the transactions listed below would be recorded.

JOURNALS

Cash receipts journal   Sales journal   Purchases journal
Cash payments journal   General journal

DATE		TRANSACTIONS
May	1	Purchased merchandise on credit.
	2	Sold merchandise on credit.
	3	Accepted a return of merchandise from a credit customer.
	4	Sold merchandise for cash.
	5	Gave an allowance for damaged merchandise.
	6	Received a payment on account from a credit customer.
	7	Issued a check to pay a creditor on account.
	8	Received an additional cash investment from the owner.

Exercise 7.2

Objectives 7-1, 7-2, 7-3, 7-4

▶ **Identifying the accounts used to record sales and related transactions.**

The transactions below took place at Washington Outdoor Adventures, a retail business that sells outdoor clothing and camping equipment. Indicate the numbers of the general ledger accounts that would be debited and credited to record each transaction.

GENERAL LEDGER ACCOUNTS

101	Cash	401	Sales
111	Accounts Receivable	451	Sales Returns and Allowances
231	Sales Tax Payable		

DATE		TRANSACTIONS
May	1	Sold merchandise on credit; the transaction involved sales tax.
	2	Received checks from credit customers on account.
	3	Accepted a return of merchandise from a credit customer; the original sale involved sales tax.
	4	Sold merchandise for cash; the transaction involved sales tax.
	5	Gave an allowance to a credit customer for damaged merchandise; the original sale involved sales tax.
	6	Provided a cash refund to a customer who returned merchandise; the original sale was made for cash and involved sales tax.

Exercise 7.3

Objective 7-1

▶ **Recording credit sales.**

The following transactions took place at Washington Outdoor Adventures during June. Enter these transactions in a sales journal like the one shown in Figure 7.2. Use 18 as the page number for the sales journal.

DATE		TRANSACTIONS
June	1	Sold a tent and other items on credit to Justin McGowan; issued Sales Slip 1101 for $700 plus sales tax of $70.
	2	Sold a backpack, an air mattress, and other items to Ann Teng; issued Sales Slip 1102 for $550 plus sales tax of $55.
	3	Sold a lantern, cooking utensils, and other items to Tony Morales; issued Sales Slip 1103 for $280 plus sales tax of $28.

Exercise 7.4

Objective 7-1

▶ **Recording sales returns and allowances.**

Record the general journal entries for the following transactions of The Linen Barn that occurred in July. Use 15 as the page number for the general journal.

DATE		TRANSACTIONS
July	5	Accepted a return of damaged merchandise from Ann Dickinson, a credit customer; issued Credit Memorandum 301 for $882, which includes sales tax of $42; the original sale was made on Sales Slip 1610 of June 30.
	21	Gave an allowance to Roberta Bishop, a credit customer, for merchandise that was slightly damaged but usable; issued Credit Memorandum 302 for $546, which includes sales tax of $26; the original sale was made on Sales Slip 1663 of July 17.

Exercise 7.5
Objective 7-2

Posting from the sales journal.
The sales journal for Carolina Company is shown below. Describe how the amounts would be posted to the general ledger accounts.

SALES JOURNAL PAGE 1

	DATE	SALES SLIP NO.	CUSTOMER'S ACCOUNT DEBITED	POST. REF.	ACCOUNTS RECEIVABLE DEBIT	SALES TAX PAYABLE CREDIT	SALES CREDIT	
1	20X1							1
2	July 2	1101	Scott Cohen		540 00	40 00	500 00	2
3	7	1102	Julia Hoang		864 00	64 00	800 00	3
11	31	1110	Barbara Baxter		324 00	24 00	300 00	11
12	31		Totals		6 480 00	480 00	6 000 00	12
13					(111)	(231)	(401)	13
14								14

Exercise 7.6
Objective 7-7

Computing a trade discount.
Rossi Wholesalers made sales using the following list prices and trade discounts. What amount will be recorded for each sale in the sales journal?

1. List price of $950 and trade discount of 10 percent
2. List price of $3,080 and trade discount of 20 percent
3. List price of $1,800 and trade discount of 25 percent

Exercise 7.7
Objective 7-7

Computing a series of trade discounts.
Oliver's English Gardens, a wholesale firm, made sales using the following list prices and trade discounts. What amount will be recorded for each sale in the sales journal?

1. List price of $7,000 and trade discounts of 30 and 10 percent
2. List price of $4,200 and trade discounts of 20 and 5 percent
3. List price of $10,800 and trade discounts of 25 and 15 percent

Exercise 7.8
Objective 7-9

Computing the sales tax due and recording its payment.
The balances of certain accounts of Camille Corporation on April 30, 20X1, were as follows:

Sales	$330,000
Sales Returns and Allowances	4,500

The firm's net sales are subject to an 8 percent sales tax. Prepare the general journal entry to record payment of the sales tax payable on April 30, 20X1.

Exercise 7.9
Objective 7-6

Preparing a schedule of accounts receivable.
The accounts receivable ledger for Modern Vintage Antiques follows below.

1. Prepare a schedule of accounts receivable as of January 31, 20X1.
2. What should be the balance in the *Accounts Receivable* (control) account?

Exercise 7.10
Objective 7-5

▶ Posting sales returns and allowances.
Post the following journal entries to the appropriate ledger accounts. Assume the following account balances as of March 1, 20X1:

Accounts Receivable (control account)	$1,788
Accounts Receivable—Carol Fountain	940
Accounts Receivable—Rich Jones	848

NAME Stella Bianco
ADDRESS 917 Broadway, New York, NY 10018

DATE	DESCRIPTION	POST. REF.	DEBIT	CREDIT	BALANCE
20X1					
Jan. 1	Balance	✓			1 4 7 5 00
2	Sales Slip 1801	S1	6 4 0 00		2 1 1 5 00

NAME Edward Charleston
ADDRESS 2022 5th Avenue, New York, NY 10018

DATE	DESCRIPTION	POST. REF.	DEBIT	CREDIT	BALANCE
20X1					
Jan. 1	Balance	✓			3 7 8 00
27	Sales Slip 1824	S1	1 8 9 00		5 6 7 00
31		CR1		1 8 4 00	3 8 3 00

NAME Neal Feingold
ADDRESS 98 Houston Street, New York, NY 10018

DATE	DESCRIPTION	POST. REF.	DEBIT	CREDIT	BALANCE
20X1					
Jan. 1	Balance	✓			3 2 4 00
15	Sales Slip 1812	CR1		3 2 4 00	– 0 –
31		S1	7 5 6 00		7 5 6 00

NAME Don Peterson
ADDRESS 5063 Park Avenue, New York, NY 10019

DATE	DESCRIPTION	POST. REF.	DEBIT	CREDIT	BALANCE
20X1					
Jan. 1	Balance	✓			6 4 8 00
20	Sales Slip 1819	S1	2 1 6 00		8 6 4 00
21		CR1		4 5 0 00	4 1 4 00
22	Sales Slip 1822	S1	8 1 0 00		1 2 2 4 00

NAME Maria Sanchez
ADDRESS 2111 West 32nd Street, New York, NY 10019

DATE	DESCRIPTION	POST. REF.	DEBIT	CREDIT	BALANCE
20X1					
Jan. 1	Balance	✓			4 8 6 00
31	Sales Slip 1840	S1	2 2 1 4 00		2 7 0 0 00

NAME Ann Yang
ADDRESS 721 Lexington Avenue, New York, NY 10027

DATE	DESCRIPTION	POST. REF.	DEBIT	CREDIT	BALANCE
20X1					
Jan. 1	Balance	✓			2 3 7 6 00
12		CR1		1 1 8 8 00	1 1 8 8 00
17	Sales Slip 1817	S1	9 8 4 00		2 1 7 2 00

GENERAL JOURNAL
PAGE 42

DATE		DESCRIPTION	POST. REF.	DEBIT	CREDIT
20X1					
Mar.	14	Sales Returns and Allowances		300 00	
		Sales Tax Payable		24 00	
		Accounts Rec.—Carol Fountain			324 00
		Accepted return on defective			
		merchandise, Credit Memo			
		101; original sale of Feb. 23,			
		Sales Slip 1101			
	22	Sales Returns and Allowances		50 00	
		Sales Tax Payable		4 00	
		Accounts Rec.—Rich Jones			54 00
		Gave allowance for damaged			
		merchandise, Credit Memo			
		102; original sale Mar. 15,			
		Sales Slip 1150			

PROBLEMS

Problem Set A

Recording credit sales and posting from the sales journal.

Great Lakes Appliances is a retail store that sells household appliances. Merchandise sales are subject to an 8 percent sales tax. The firm's credit sales for July are listed below, along with the general ledger accounts used to record these sales. The balance shown for *Accounts Receivable* is for the beginning of the month.

◀ Problem 7.1A

Objectives 7-1, 7-2

DATE		TRANSACTIONS
July	1	Sold a dishwasher to Jim Hernandez; issued Sales Slip 501 for $1,025 plus sales tax of $82.
	6	Sold a washer to Helen Thai; issued Sales Slip 502 for $2,300 plus sales tax of $184.
	11	Sold a high-definition television set to Rich James; issued Sales Slip 503 for $2,475 plus sales tax of $198.
	17	Sold an electric dryer to Mary Schneider; issued Sales Slip 504 for $1,150 plus sales tax of $92.
	23	Sold a trash compactor to Vickie Colombo; issued Sales Slip 505 for $775 plus sales tax of $62.
	27	Sold a home entertainment system to Jeff Budd; issued Sales Slip 506 for $1,600 plus sales tax of $128.
	29	Sold an electric range to Michelle Ly; issued Sales Slip 507 for $1,325 plus sales tax of $106.
	31	Sold a microwave oven to Pete Moloney; issued Sales Slip 508 for $500 plus sales tax of $40.

INSTRUCTIONS

1. Open the general ledger accounts and enter the balance of *Accounts Receivable* for July 1.
2. Record the transactions in a sales journal like the one shown in Figure 7.4. Use 8 as the journal page number.
3. Total, prove, and rule the sales journal as of July 31.
4. Post the column totals from the sales journal to the proper general ledger accounts.

GENERAL LEDGER ACCOUNTS

- 111 Accounts Receivable, $32,000 Dr.
- 231 Sales Tax Payable
- 401 Sales

Analyze: What percentage of credit sales was for entertainment items?

Problem 7.2A ▶ Journalizing, posting, and reporting sales transactions.

Objectives 7-1, 7-2, 7-4

Towncenter Furniture specializes in modern living room and dining room furniture. Merchandise sales are subject to an 8 percent sales tax. The firm's credit sales and sales returns and allowances for February 20X1 are reflected below, along with the general ledger accounts used to record these transactions. The balances shown are for the beginning of the month.

DATE	TRANSACTIONS
Feb. 1	Sold a living room sofa to Sun Yoo; issued Sales Slip 1615 for $4,790 plus sales tax of $383.20.
5	Sold three recliners to Jacqueline Moore; issued Sales Slip 1616 for $2,350 plus sales tax of $188.
9	Sold a dining room set to Hazel Tran; issued Sales Slip 1617 for $6,550 plus sales tax of $524.
11	Accepted a return of one damaged recliner from Jacqueline Moore that was originally sold on Sales Slip 1616 of February 5; issued Credit Memorandum 702 for $1,026, which includes sales tax of $76.00.
17	Sold living room tables and bookcases to Ann Brown; issued Sales Slip 1618 for $9,550 plus sales tax of $764.
23	Sold eight dining room chairs to Domingo Salas; issued Sales Slip 1619 for $3,650 plus sales tax of $292.
25	Gave Ann Brown an allowance for scratches on her bookcases; issued Credit Memorandum 703 for $702, which includes sales tax of $52; the bookcases were originally sold on Sales Slip 1618 of February 17.
27	Sold a living room sofa and four chairs to Jose Saucedo; issued Sales Slip 1620 for $4,225 plus sales tax of $338.
28	Sold a dining room table to Mimi Yuki; issued Sales Slip 1621 for $2,050 plus sales tax of $164.
28	Sold a living room modular wall unit to Alan Baker; issued Sales Slip 1622 for $3,900 plus sales tax of $312.

INSTRUCTIONS

1. Open the general ledger accounts and enter the balances for February 1.
2. Record the transactions in a sales journal and in a general journal. Use 8 as the page number for the sales journal and 24 as the page number for the general journal.
3. Post the entries from the general journal to the general ledger.
4. Total, prove, and rule the sales journal as of February 28.

5. Post the column totals from the sales journal.
6. Prepare the heading and the Revenue section of the firm's income statement for the month ended February 28, 20X1.

GENERAL LEDGER ACCOUNTS

- 111 Accounts Receivable, $16,636 Dr.
- 231 Sales Tax Payable, $7,270 Cr.
- 401 Sales
- 451 Sales Returns and Allowances

Analyze: Based on the beginning balance of the *Sales Tax Payable* account, what was the amount of net sales for January? (Hint: Sales tax returns are filed and paid to the state quarterly.)

Recording sales transactions, posting to the accounts receivable ledger, and preparing a schedule of accounts receivable.

◄ Problem 7.3A
Objectives 7-1, 7-2, 7-3, 7-4, 7-5, 7-6

Elegant Dining sells china, glassware, and other gift items that are subject to an 8 percent sales tax. The shop uses a general journal and a sales journal similar to those illustrated in this chapter. All customers have payment terms of n/30.

DATE		TRANSACTIONS
Nov.	1	Sold china to Paola Jimenez; issued Sales Slip 1001 for $1,250 plus $100 sales tax.
	5	Sold a brass serving tray to Janet Hutchison; issued Sales Slip 1002 for $1,850 plus $148 sales tax.
	6	Sold a vase to Charles Brown; issued Sales Slip 1003 for $450 plus $36 sales tax.
	10	Sold a punch bowl and glasses to Terri Namala; issued Sales Slip 1004 for $1,450 plus $116 sales tax.
	14	Sold a set of serving bowls to Dorothy Watts; issued Sales Slip 1005 for $300 plus $24 sales tax.
	17	Gave Terri Namala an allowance because of a broken glass discovered when unpacking the punch bowl and glasses sold on November 10, Sales Slip 1004; issued Credit Memorandum 102 for $176.00, which includes sales tax of $13.
	21	Sold a coffee table to Teresa Yu; issued Sales Slip 1006 for $2,950 plus $236 sales tax.
	24	Sold sterling silver teaspoons to Hank O'Connor; issued Sales Slip 1007 for $350 plus $28 sales tax.
	25	Gave Teresa Yu an allowance for scratches on her coffee table sold on November 21, Sales Slip 1006; issued Credit Memorandum 103 for $396, which includes $29 in sales tax.
	30	Sold a clock to Elena Bratianu; issued Sales Slip 1008 for $3,550 plus $284 sales tax.

INSTRUCTIONS

1. Record the transactions for November in the proper journal. Use 6 as the page number for the sales journal and 16 as the page number for the general journal.
2. Immediately after recording each transaction, post to the accounts receivable ledger.
3. Post the amounts from the general journal daily. Post the sales journal amount as a total at the end of the month.
4. Prepare a schedule of accounts receivable. Compare the balance of the *Accounts Receivable* control account with the total of the schedule.

Analyze: Which customer has the highest balance owed at November 30?

Problem 7.4A
Objectives 7-1, 7-2, 7-3, 7-4, 7-5, 7-6

Recording sales transactions, posting to the accounts receivable ledger, and preparing a schedule of accounts receivable.

Bella Floral Designs is a wholesale shop that sells flowers, plants, and plant supplies. The transactions shown below took place during January. All customers have credit terms of n/30.

DATE	TRANSACTIONS
Jan. 3	Sold a floral arrangement to Thomas Florist; issued Invoice 1081 for $600.
8	Sold potted plants to Carter Garden Supply; issued Invoice 1082 for $825.
9	Sold floral arrangements to Thomasville Flower Shop; issued Invoice 1083 for $482.
10	Sold corsages to Moore's Flower Shop; issued Invoice 1084 for $630.
15	Gave Thomasville Flower Shop an allowance because of withered blossoms discovered in one of the floral arrangements sold on Invoice 1083 on January 9; issued Credit Memorandum 101 for $60.
20	Sold table arrangements to Cedar Hill Floral Shop; issued Invoice 1085 for $580.
22	Sold plants to Applegate Nursery; issued Invoice 1086 for $780.
25	Sold roses to Moore's Flower Shop; issued Invoice 1087 for $437.
27	Sold several floral arrangements to Thomas Florist; issued Invoice 1088 for $975.
31	Gave Thomas Florist an allowance because of withered blossoms discovered in one of the floral arrangements sold on Invoice 1088 on January 27; issued Credit Memorandum 102 for $200.

INSTRUCTIONS

1. Record the transactions in the proper journal. Use 7 as the page number for the sales journal and 11 as the page number for the general journal.
2. Immediately after recording each transaction, post to the accounts receivable ledger.
3. Post the amounts from the general journal daily. Post the sales journal amount as a total at the end of the month.
4. Prepare a schedule of accounts receivable. Compare the balance of the *Accounts Receivable* control account with the total of the schedule.

Analyze: Damaged goods decreased sales by what dollar amount? By what percentage amount?

Problem Set B

Problem 7.1B
Objectives 7-1, 7-2

Recording credit sales and posting from the sales journal.

Awesome Appliances is a retail store that sells household appliances. Merchandise sales are subject to an 8 percent sales tax. The firm's credit sales for June are listed below Instruction 4, along with the general ledger accounts used to record these sales. The balance shown for Accounts Receivable is for the beginning of the month.

INSTRUCTIONS

1. Open the general ledger accounts and enter the balance of *Accounts Receivable* for June 1.
2. Record the transactions in a sales journal like the one shown in Figure 7.4. Use 8 as the journal page number.

3. Total, prove, and rule the sales journal as of June 30.
4. Post the column totals from the sales journal to the proper general ledger accounts.

DATE		TRANSACTIONS
June	1	Sold a dishwasher to Emir Bahar; issued Sales Slip 201 for $600 plus sales tax of $48.
	6	Sold a washer to Gilbert Gomez; issued Sales Slip 202 for $925 plus sales tax of $74.
	11	Sold a high-definition television set to Terrell Johnson; issued Sales Slip 203 for $1,950 plus sales tax of $156.
	17	Sold an electric dryer to Barbara Odom; issued Sales Slip 204 for $750 plus sales tax of $60.
	23	Sold a trash compactor to Nish Patel; issued Sales Slip 205 for $475 plus sales tax of $38.
	27	Sold a portable television set to June Kim; issued Sales Slip 206 for $300 plus sales tax of $24.
	29	Sold an electric range to Jim Park; issued Sales Slip 207 for $525 plus sales tax of $42.
	30	Sold a microwave oven to Patty Bustos; issued Sales Slip 208 for $300 plus sales tax of $24.

GENERAL LEDGER ACCOUNTS

111	Accounts Receivable, $81,500 Dr.
231	Sales Tax Payable
401	Sales

Analyze: What percentage of sales was for entertainment items?

Journalizing, posting, and reporting sales transactions.

◀ **Problem 7.2B**
Objectives 7-1, 7-2, 7-4, 7-5

The Furniture Lot is a retail store that specializes in modern living room and dining room furniture. Merchandise sales are subject to an 8 percent sales tax. The firm's credit sales and sales returns and allowances for June are reflected below, along with the general ledger accounts used to record these transactions. The balances shown are for the beginning of the month.

INSTRUCTIONS
1. Open the general ledger accounts and enter the balances for June 1.
2. Record the transactions in a sales journal and a general journal. Use 9 as the page number for the sales journal and 26 as the page number for the general journal.
3. Post the entries from the general journal to the general ledger.
4. Total, prove, and rule the sales journal as of June 30.
5. Post the column totals from the sales journal.
6. Prepare the heading and the Revenue section of the firm's income statement for the month ended June 30, 20X1.

GENERAL LEDGER ACCOUNTS

111	Accounts Receivable, $24,150 Dr.
231	Sales Tax Payable, $4,515 Cr.
401	Sales
451	Sales Returns and Allowances

DATE	TRANSACTIONS
June 1	Sold a living room sofa to Kenya Jackson; issued Sales Slip 1601 for $2,525 plus sales tax of $202.
5	Sold three recliners to Carmen Cruz; issued Sales Slip 1602 for $1,500 plus sales tax of $120.
9	Sold a dining room set to Lu Chang; issued Sales Slip 1603 for $6,025 plus sales tax of $482.
11	Accepted a return of a damaged chair from Carmen Cruz; the chair was originally sold on Sales Slip 1602 of June 5; issued Credit Memorandum 215 for $540, which includes sales tax of $40.
17	Sold living room tables and bookcases to Rick Jones; issued Sales Slip 1604 for $4,000 plus sales tax of $320.
23	Sold eight dining room chairs to Demitri Brown; issued Sales Slip 1605 for $2,400 plus sales tax of $192.
25	Gave Rick Jones an allowance for scratches on his bookcases; issued Credit Memorandum 216 for $270, which includes sales tax of $20; the bookcases were originally sold on Sales Slip 1604 of June 17.
27	Sold a living room sofa and four chairs to Paul Rivera; issued Sales Slip 1606 for $2,575 plus sales tax of $206.
29	Sold a dining room table to Rosie Seltz; issued Sales Slip 1607 for $1,150 plus sales tax of $92.
30	Sold a living room modular wall unit to Jim Mayor; issued Sales Slip 1608 for $3,100 plus sales tax of $248.

Analyze: Based on the beginning balance of the *Sales Tax Payable* account, what was the amount of total net sales for April and May? (Hint: Sales tax returns are filed and paid to the state quarterly.)

Problem 7.3B
Objectives 7-1, 7-2, 7-3, 7-4, 7-5, 7-6

Recording sales transactions, posting to the accounts receivable ledger, and preparing a schedule of accounts receivable.

Wine Country Gift Shop sells cards, supplies, and various holiday gift items. All sales are subject to a sales tax of 8 percent. The shop uses a sales journal and general journal. All customers have credit terms of n/30.

DATE	TRANSACTIONS
Feb. 3	Sold Michelle Benoit a box of holiday greeting cards for $50 plus sales tax of $4 on Sales Slip 201.
4	Sold Ken Hamlett a Valentine's Day party pack for $200 plus sales tax of $16 on Sales Slip 202.
5	Desiree Navarro bought 10 boxes of Valentine's Day gift packs for her office. Sales Slip 203 was issued for $200 plus sales tax of $16.
8	Sold Amy Peloza a set of crystal glasses for $400 plus sales tax of $32 on Sales Slip 204.
9	Larry Edwards purchased two statues for $300 plus $24 sales tax on Sales Slip 205.
9	Gave Desiree Navarro an allowance because of incomplete items in some gift packs; issued Credit Memorandum 101 for $81, which includes sales tax of $6.
10	Sold Gordon Dunn a Valentine Birthday package for $150 plus $12 sales tax on Sales Slip 206.

DATE	(cont.) TRANSACTIONS
13	Gave Amy Peloza an allowance of $50 because of two broken glasses in the set she purchased on February 8. Credit Memorandum 102 was issued for the allowance plus sales tax of $4.
14	Sold Michelle Benoit 10 boxes of gift candy for $175 plus sales tax of $14 on Sales Slip 207.
15	Sold a punch serving set with glasses for $150 to Ken Gilly. Sales tax of $12 was included on Sales Slip 208.
20	Sold Ned Jones a box of holiday greeting cards for $100 plus sales tax of $8 on Sales Slip 209.
22	Sold Adriana Almeida a set of crystal glasses for $425 plus sales tax of $34 on Sales Slip 210.
28	Melissa Thomas purchased three statues for $600 plus $48 sales tax on Sales Slip 211.

INSTRUCTIONS

1. Record the credit sale transactions for February in the proper journal. Use 6 as the page number for the sales journal and 16 as the page number for the general journal.
2. Immediately after recording each transaction, post to the accounts receivable ledger.
3. Post the entries to the appropriate accounts.
4. Prepare a schedule of accounts receivable and compare the balance due with the amount shown in the *Accounts Receivable* control account.

Analyze: How many postings were made to the general ledger?

Recording sales transactions, posting to the accounts receivable ledger, and preparing a schedule of accounts receivable.

◀ **Problem 7.4B**
Objectives 7-1, 7-2, 7-3, 7-4, 7-5, 7-6

The Vintage Nursery is a wholesale shop that sells flowers, plants, and plant supplies. The transactions shown below took place during February. All customers have credit terms of n/30.

DATE		TRANSACTIONS
Feb.	3	Sold a floral arrangement to Thompson Funerals; issued Invoice 2201 for $400.
	8	Sold potted plants to Meadows Nursery; issued Invoice 2202 for $800.
	9	Sold floral arrangements to DeSoto Flower Shop; issued Invoice 2203 for $1,050.
	10	Sold corsages to Lovelace Nursery; issued Invoice 2204 for $700.
	15	Gave DeSoto Flower Shop an allowance because of withered blossoms discovered in one of the floral arrangements sold on Invoice 2203 on February 9; issued Credit Memorandum 105 for $100.
	20	Sold table arrangements to Lovelace Nursery; issued Invoice 2205 for $650.
	22	Sold plants to Southwest Nursery; issued Invoice 2206 for $850.
	25	Sold roses to Denton Flower Shop; issued Invoice 2207 for $450.
	27	Sold several floral arrangements to Thompson Funerals; issued Invoice 2208 for $750.
	28	Gave Thompson Funerals an allowance because of withered blossoms discovered in one of the floral arrangements sold on Invoice 2208 on February 27; issued Credit Memorandum 106 for $75.

INSTRUCTIONS

1. Record the transactions in the proper journal. Use 5 as the page number for the sales journal and 10 as the page number for the general journal.
2. Immediately after recording each transaction, post to the accounts receivable ledger.
3. Post the amounts from the general journal daily. Post the sales journal amount as a total at the end of the month.
4. Prepare a schedule of accounts receivable. Compare the balance of the *Accounts Receivable* control account with the total of the schedule.

Analyze: Damaged goods decreased sales by what dollar amount? By what percentage amount?

Critical Thinking Problem 7.1

Wholesaler Transactions

Matrix Toy Company sells toys and games to retail stores. The firm offers a trade discount of 40 percent on toys and 30 percent on games. Its credit sales and sales returns and allowances transactions for August are shown below. The general ledger accounts used to record these transactions are listed below. The balance shown for *Accounts Receivable* is as of the beginning of August.

INSTRUCTIONS

1. Open the general ledger accounts and enter the balance of *Accounts Receivable* for August 1.
2. Set up an accounts receivable subsidiary ledger. Open an account for each of the credit customers listed below and enter the balances as of August 1. Enter n/45 in the blank space after "Terms." This means each customer has 45 days to pay for the merchandise it purchased.

Bombay's Department Store	$28,900
The Game Store	
Little Annie's Toy Store	30,500
Pinkerton Toy Center	
Reader's Bookstores	
Super Game Center	19,010

3. Record the transactions in a sales journal and in a general journal. Use 9 as the page number for the sales journal and 25 as the page number for the general journal. Be sure to enter each sale at its net price.
4. Post the individual entries from the sales journal and the general journal.
5. Total and rule the sales journal as of August 31.
6. Post the column total from the sales journal to the proper general ledger accounts.
7. Prepare the heading and the Revenue section of the firm's income statement for the month ended August 31.
8. Prepare a schedule of accounts receivable for August 31.
9. Check the total of the schedule of accounts receivable against the balance of the *Accounts Receivable* account in the general ledger. The two amounts should be equal.

GENERAL LEDGER ACCOUNTS

- 111 Accounts Receivable, $78,410 Dr.
- 401 Sales
- 451 Sales Returns and Allowances

DATE	TRANSACTIONS
August 1	Sold toys to Bombay's Department Store; issued Invoice 1001, which shows a list price of $19,500 and a trade discount of 40 percent.
5	Sold games to Reader's Bookstores; issued Invoice 1002, which shows a list price of $21,250 and a trade discount of 30 percent.
9	Sold games to Super Game Center; issued Invoice 1003, which shows a list price of $7,500 and a trade discount of 30 percent.
14	Sold toys to Little Annie's Toy Store; issued Invoice 1004, which shows a list price of $26,400 and a trade discount of 40 percent.
18	Accepted a return of all the games shipped to Super Game Center because they were damaged in transit; issued Credit Memo 151 for the original sale made on Invoice 1003 on August 9.
22	Sold toys to The Game Store; issued Invoice 1005, which shows a list price of $16,200 and a trade discount of 40 percent.
26	Sold games to Bombay's Department Store; issued Invoice 1006, which shows a list price of $20,600 and a trade discount of 30 percent.
30	Sold toys to Pinkerton Toy Center; issued Invoice 1007, which shows a list price of $22,800 and a trade discount of 40 percent.

Analyze: What is the effect on net sales if the company offers a series of trade discounts on toys (25 percent, 15 percent) instead of a single 40 percent discount?

Critical Thinking Problem 7.2

Retail Store

Tony Zendejas is the owner of Housewares Galore, a housewares store that sells a wide variety of items for the kitchen, bathroom, and home. Housewares Galore offers a company credit card to customers.

The company has experienced an increase in sales since the company credit card was introduced. Tony is considering replacing his manual system of recording sales with electronic point-of-sale cash registers that are linked to a computer.

Cash sales are now rung up by the salesclerks on a cash register that generates a tape listing total cash sales at the end of the day. For credit sales, salesclerks prepare handwritten sales slips that are forwarded to the accountant for manual entry into the sales journal and accounts receivable ledger.

The electronic register system Tony is considering would use an optical scanner to read coded labels attached to the merchandise. As the merchandise is passed over the scanner, the code is sent to the computer. The computer is programmed to read the code and identify the item being sold, record the amount of the sale, maintain a record of total sales, update the inventory record, and keep a record of cash received.

If the sale is a credit transaction, the customer's company credit card number is swiped through a card reader connected with the register. The computer updates the customer's account in the accounts receivable ledger stored in computer memory.

If this system is used, many of the accounting functions are done automatically as sales are entered into the register. At the end of the day, the computer prints a complete sales journal, along with up-to-date balances for the general ledger and the accounts receivable ledger accounts related to sales transactions.

Listed below are four situations that Tony is eager to eliminate. Would use of an electronic point-of-sale system as described above reduce or prevent these problems? Why or why not?

1. The accountant did not post a sale to the customer's subsidiary ledger account.
2. The salesclerk did not charge a customer for an item.
3. The customer purchased merchandise using a stolen credit card.
4. The salesclerk was not aware that the item purchased was on sale and did not give the customer the sale price.

BUSINESS CONNECTIONS

Retail Sales

Managerial FOCUS

1. How does the *Sales Returns and Allowances* account provide management with a measure of operating efficiency? What problems might be indicated by a high level of returns and allowances?

2. Suppose you are the accountant for a small chain of clothing stores. Up to now, the firm has offered open-account credit to qualified customers but has not allowed the use of bank credit cards. The president of the chain has asked your advice about changing the firm's credit policy. What advantages might there be in eliminating the open-account credit and accepting bank credit cards instead? Do you see any disadvantages?

3. Suppose a manager in your company has suggested that the firm not hire an accountant to advise it on tax matters and to file tax returns. He states that tax matters are merely procedural in nature and that anyone who can read the tax form instructions can do the necessary work. Comment on this idea.

4. During the past year, Cravens Company has had a substantial increase in its losses from uncollectible accounts. Assume that you are the newly hired controller of this firm and that you have been asked to find the reason for the increase. What policies and procedures would you investigate?

5. Why is it usually worthwhile for a business to sell on credit even though it will have some losses from uncollectible accounts?

6. How can a firm's credit policy affect its profitability?

7. How can efficient accounting records help management maintain sound credit and collection policies?

8. Why should management insist that all sales on credit and other transactions affecting the firm's accounts receivable be journalized and posted promptly?

Internal Control and FRAUD PREVENTION

Sales Returns and Allowances

Credit memos are created when a product is returned. A debit to *Sales Returns and Allowances* and a credit to *Accounts Receivable* is recorded when a credit memo is created. A credit memo will reduce *Accounts Receivable* and write off the invoice. You have noticed that the Accounts Receivable clerk, Wes, has created an abnormally high number of credit memos. You notice the inventory does not reflect the additional inventory resulting from the *Sales Returns and Allowances.* What would you do? How can the company safeguard against such possible fraud?

Financial Statement ANALYSIS

Home Depot

Income Statement

An excerpt from the Consolidated Statements of Earnings for The Home Depot, Inc., is presented below. Review the financial data and answer the following analysis questions:

(Amounts in millions except per share data) Fiscal Year	2018	2017	2016
Revenues:			
Net Sales	$108,203	$100,904	$94,595

Analyze:

1. The Home Depot, Inc.'s statement reports one figure for net sales. Name one account whose balance may have been deducted from the *Sales* account balance to determine a net sales amount.

2. The data presented demonstrate a steady increase in net sales over the three-year period. By what amount and by what percentage have net sales of 2018 increased from sales of 2016?

Analyze Online: Find the most recent consolidated statements of comprehensive income on The Home Depot, Inc., website (www.homedepot.com). Click on *Investor Relations,* then *Financial Reports,* then *Annual Reports,* then select the link for the most recent annual report.

3. What dollar amount is reported for net sales for the most recent year?
4. What is the trend in net sales over the last three years?
5. What are some possible reasons for this trend?

Customer to Vendor

Divide into groups of four individuals. Your company is named Cole's Cooking Supplies. Assign one person as Cole's sales associate; one as the company's Accounts Receivable clerk; one as the customer, Louisa's Cooking School; and one as Louisa's Accounts Payable clerk. Record the transaction each individual would record from a sale of $50,000 for cooking supplies.

TEAMWORK

Answers to Comprehensive Self Review

1. The month and the quarter.
2. A control account is an account that serves as a link between a subsidiary ledger and the general ledger because its balance summarizes the balances of the accounts in the subsidiary ledger.
3. A merchandising business must account for the purchase and sale of goods and for its merchandise inventory.
4. It contains detailed information about the transactions with credit customers and shows the balances owed by credit customers at all times.
5. A service business sells services; a merchandising business sells goods that it has purchased for resale; and a manufacturing business sells goods that it has produced.

Accounting for Purchases and Accounts Payable

Chapter 8

QualityHD/Shutterstock

www.bedbathandbeyond.com

Bed Bath & Beyond is a retailer with inventory of a wide selection of domestic merchandise and home furnishings. Starting out, it sold a limited selection of merchandise at its store in Springfield, New Jersey, then called Bed 'n Bath. In response to growing competition in the domestics market, the number of products offered was increased in 1985 and the name was changed to Bed Bath & Beyond. It has since grown to operate several subsidiaries and has further expanded its product selection to include specially commissioned, limited-edition items from emerging fashion and home designers and has expanded its customer base to include institutional customers in the hospitality, cruise line, health care, and other industries.

Bed Bath & Beyond is committed to serving its customers and is dedicated to continually increasing the convenience of its shopping experience and selection of merchandise. It offers extensive breadth, depth, and differentiation of its merchandise to better engage its customers, whatever their interests. Its products can be viewed and purchased in-store, online, and through a mobile device, and it offers in-store pickup or direct shipping.

For its twelve-month fiscal year ended March 3, 2018, Bed Bath & Beyond reported sales of nearly $12.35 billion, amounting to an increase of 1.09 percent from the twelve months ended February 25, 2017. The company purchased merchandise from approximately 11,100 suppliers in its fiscal year ended March 3, 2018, making meticulous recordkeeping of purchases and accounts payable imperative. Knowing amounts due to vendors and payment due dates enables the company to effectively manage its cash flow.

thinking critically
Do you think that companies such as Bed Bath & Beyond pay their bills at the last possible minute? Why or why not?

LEARNING OBJECTIVES

8-1 Record purchases of merchandise on credit in a three-column purchases journal.

8-2 Post from the three-column purchases journal to the general ledger accounts.

8-3 Post credit purchases from the purchases journal to the accounts payable subsidiary ledger.

8-4 Record purchases returns and allowances in the general journal and post them to the **Accounts Payable** account in the general ledger and to the accounts payable subsidiary ledger.

8-5 Prepare a schedule of accounts payable.

8-6 Compute the net delivered cost of purchases.

8-7 Demonstrate a knowledge of the procedures for effective internal control of purchases.

8-8 Define the accounting terms new to this chapter.

NEW TERMS

accounts payable ledger
cash discount
cost of goods sold
Freight In account
purchase allowance
purchase invoice
purchase order
purchase requisition
purchase return
Purchases account
purchases discount
purchases journal
receiving report
sales discount
sales invoice
schedule of accounts payable
Transportation In account

Section 1

SECTION OBJECTIVES

>> **8-1** Record purchases of merchandise on credit in a three-column purchases journal.

WHY IT'S IMPORTANT
Most merchandisers purchase goods on credit, and the use of a special journal improves efficiency when recording these transactions.

>> **8-2** Post from the three-column purchases journal to the general ledger accounts.

WHY IT'S IMPORTANT
Summary postings from the purchases journal minimize repetitive tasks.

TERMS TO LEARN

cash discount
cost of goods sold
Freight In account
purchase invoice
purchase order
purchase requisition
Purchases account
purchases discount
purchases journal
receiving report
sales discount
sales invoice
Transportation In account

Merchandise Purchases

In this chapter, you will learn how Maxx-Out Sporting Goods manages its purchases of goods for resale and its accounts payable.

Accounting for Purchases

Most merchandising businesses purchase goods on credit under open-account arrangements. A large firm usually has a centralized purchasing department that is responsible for locating suppliers, obtaining price quotations, negotiating credit terms, and placing orders. In small firms, purchasing activities are handled by a single individual, usually the owner or manager.

Purchasing Procedures

When a sales department needs goods, it sends the purchasing department a purchase requisition (Figure 8.1). A **purchase requisition** lists the items to be ordered. It is signed by someone with the authority to approve requests for merchandise, usually the manager of the sales department. The purchasing department selects a supplier that can furnish the goods at a competitive price and then issues a purchase order (Figure 8.2). The **purchase order** specifies the exact items, quantity, price, and credit terms. It is signed by someone with authority to approve purchases, usually the purchasing agent.

When the goods arrive at the business, they are inspected. A **receiving report** is prepared to show the quantity and condition of the goods received. The purchasing department receives a copy of the receiving report and compares it to the purchase order. If defective goods or the wrong quantity of goods is received, the purchasing department contacts the supplier and settles the problem.

Figure 8.3 shows the invoice, or *bill,* for items ordered and shipped. The customer, Maxx-Out Sporting Goods, calls it a **purchase invoice.** The supplier, International Sportsman, calls it a **sales invoice.** The customer's accounting department compares the invoice to copies of the purchase order and receiving report. The accounting department checks the quantities, prices, and math on the invoice and then records the purchase. It is important to record purchases in the accounting records as soon as the invoice is verified. Shortly before the due date of the invoice, the accounting department issues a check to the supplier and records the payment.

> A typical Home Depot store stocks between 30,000 and 40,000 different products during the year, including both national brand name and Home Depot brand name items.

FIGURE 8.1

Purchase Requisition

Maxx-Out Sporting Goods
2007 Trendsetter Lane
Dallas, TX 75268-0967

PURCHASE REQUISITION

No. __325__

DEPARTMENT __Men's__   DATE OF REQUEST __January 2, 20X1__
ADVISE ON DELIVERY __Max Ferraro__   DATE REQUIRED __January 25, 20X1__

QUANTITY	DESCRIPTION
10	Assorted colors men's sweatsuits

APPROVED BY _____   REQUESTED BY _____

FOR PURCHASING DEPARTMENT USE ONLY

PURCHASE ORDER __9001__   ISSUED TO: __International Sportsman__
DATE __January 5, 20X1__   __1718 Sherry Lane__
   __Denton, TX 75267-6205__

FIGURE 8.2

Purchase Order

Maxx-Out Sporting Goods
2007 Trendsetter Lane
Dallas, TX 75268-0967

PURCHASE ORDER

To: __International Sportsman__
__1718 Sherry Lane__
__Denton, TX 75267-6205__

Date: __January 5, 20X1__
Order No: __9001__
Terms: __n/30__
FOB: __Denton__

QUANTITY	ITEM	UNIT PRICE	TOTAL
10	Assorted colors men's sweatsuits	55.00	550.00

APPROVED BY __Max Ferraro__

FIGURE 8.3

Invoice

International Sportsman
1718 Sherry Lane
Denton, TX 75267-6205

INVOICE NO. 7985

SOLD TO: Maxx-Out Sporting Goods
2007 Trendsetter Lane
Dallas, TX 75268-0967

DATE: January 23, 20X1
ORDER NO.: 9001
SHIPPED BY: Metroplex Express
TERMS: n/30

YOUR ORDER NO.	SALESPERSON	TERMS
9001		n/30
DATE SHIPPED	SHIPPED BY	FOB
January 23, 20X1	Metroplex Express	Denton

QUANTITY	DESCRIPTION	UNIT PRICE	TOTAL
10	Assorted colors men's sweatsuits	55 00	550 00
	Freight		50 00
	Total		600 00

The *Purchases* Account

The purchase of merchandise for resale is a cost of doing business. The purchase of merchandise is debited to the ***Purchases*** **account.** *Purchases* is a temporary account classified as a cost of goods sold account. The **cost of goods sold** is the actual cost to the business of the merchandise sold to customers.

Cost of goods sold accounts follow the debit and credit rules of expense accounts. The *Purchases* account is increased by debits and decreased by credits. Its normal balance is a debit. In the chart of accounts, the cost of goods sold accounts appear just before the expense accounts.

> Walmart purchases private-label products from suppliers and markets these as Walmart brands. Products such as Ol'Roy™ dog food, Equate health and beauty items, and Special Kitty cat food and cat care products are purchased at lower costs than nationally known brands, enabling Walmart to sell these items at a lower price to its customers.

important!

Purchases on credit and Freight Charges

The purchases journal is used to record *only credit purchases of merchandise for resale.* Credit purchases of other items used in the business are recorded in the general journal. *Freight In* is debited for transportation charges on merchandise inventory that are paid by the buyer. Transportation charges for other asset purchases are not debited to *Freight In* but to the asset account charged when the asset was purchased. For example, if freight is paid for purchase of equipment, the *Equipment* account would be debited for the freight charges.

Freight Charges for Purchases

Sometimes the buyer pays the freight charge—the cost of shipping the goods from the seller's warehouse to the buyer's location. There are two ways to handle the freight charges paid by the buyer:

- The buyer is billed directly by the transportation company for the freight charge. The buyer issues a check directly to the freight company.
- The seller pays the freight charge and includes it on the invoice. The invoice includes the price of the goods and the freight charge.

The freight charge is debited to the ***Freight In*** or ***Transportation In* account.** This is a cost of goods sold account showing transportation charges for merchandise purchased. The buyer enters three elements in the accounting records:

Price of goods (debit ***Purchases***)	$550.00
Freight charge (debit ***Freight In***)	50.00
Total invoice (credit ***Accounts Payable***)	$600.00

Purchases		Freight In		Accounts Payable	
Dr.	Cr.	Dr.	Cr.	Dr.	Cr.
+	+	+	−	−	+
550		50			600

The Purchases Journal

For most merchandising businesses, it is not efficient to enter purchases of goods in the general journal. Instead, credit purchases of merchandise are recorded in a special journal called the **purchases journal.**

The following illustrates how the first four credit purchases shown in the Purchases Journal below appear in a general journal. Each entry involves a debit to *Purchases* and *Freight In* and a credit to *Accounts Payable* plus a detailed explanation.

These four general journal entries require 12 separate postings to general ledger accounts: 4 to *Purchases,* 4 to *Freight In,* and 4 to *Accounts Payable.* As you can see from the ledger accounts that follow, it takes a great deal of time and effort to post these entries.

>> **8-1 OBJECTIVE**
Record purchases of merchandise on credit in a three-column purchases journal.

	GENERAL JOURNAL			PAGE 1	
DATE	DESCRIPTION	POST. REF.	DEBIT	CREDIT	
20X1					1
Jan. 3	Purchases	501	2 675 00		2
	Freight In	502	190 00		3
	Accounts Payable	205		2 865 00	4
	Purchased merchandise from				5
	Active Designs, Invoice 5879,				6
	dated January 2, 20X1,				7
	terms 2/10, n/30				8
					9
5	Purchases	501	3 880 00		10
	Freight In	502	175 00		11
	Accounts Payable	205		4 055 00	12
	Purchased merchandise from				13
	The Sports Warehouse, Invoice 633,				14
	dated January 3, 20X1,				15
	terms n/30				16
					17
6	Purchases	501	2 900 00		18
	Freight In	502	240 00		19
	Accounts Payable	205		3 140 00	20
	Purchased merchandise from				21
	The Modern Sportsman,				22
	Invoice 8011, dated				23
	January 4, 20X1, terms n/30				24
					25
7	Purchases	501	3 675 00		26
	Freight In	502	260 00		27
	Accounts Payable	205		3 935 00	28
	Purchased merchandise from				29
	World of Sports, Invoice 4321,				30
	dated January 4, 20X1,				31
	terms 2/10, n/30				

ACCOUNT Accounts Payable   ACCOUNT NO. 205

DATE	DESCRIPTION	POST. REF.	DEBIT	CREDIT	BALANCE DEBIT	BALANCE CREDIT
20X1						
Jan. 1	Balance	✓				10 800 00
3		J1		2 865 00		13 665 00
5		J1		4 055 00		17 720 00
6		J1		3 140 00		20 860 00
7		J1		3 935 00		24 795 00

ACCOUNT Purchases   ACCOUNT NO. 501

DATE	DESCRIPTION	POST. REF.	DEBIT	CREDIT	BALANCE DEBIT	BALANCE CREDIT
20X1						
Jan. 3		J1	2 675 00		2 675 00	
5		J1	3 880 00		6 555 00	
6		J1	2 900 00		9 455 00	
7		J1	3 675 00		13 130 00	

ACCOUNT Freight In   **ACCOUNT NO.** 502

DATE		DESCRIPTION	POST. REF.	DEBIT	CREDIT	BALANCE DEBIT	BALANCE CREDIT
20X1							
Jan.	3		J1	190 00		190 00	
	5		J1	175 00		365 00	
	6		J1	240 00		605 00	
	7		J1	260 00		865 00	

Figure 8.4 shows the purchases journal for Maxx-Out Sporting Goods. Remember that the purchases journal is only for credit purchases of merchandise for resale to customers. Notice how the columns efficiently organize the data about the credit purchases. The purchases journal makes it possible to record each purchase on a single line. In addition, there is no need to enter account names and descriptions.

Recording Transactions in a Purchases Journal

Use the information on the purchase invoice to make the entry in the purchases journal:

1. Enter the date, supplier name, invoice number, invoice date, and credit terms.
2. In the Accounts Payable Credit column, enter the total owed to the supplier.
3. In the Purchases Debit column, enter the price of the goods purchased.
4. In the Freight In Debit column, enter the freight amount.

The total of the Purchases Debit and Freight In Debit columns must equal the amount entered in the Accounts Payable Credit column.

The invoice date and credit terms determine when payment is due. The following credit terms often appear on invoices:

- *Net 30 days*, or *n/30*, means that payment in full is due 30 days after the date of the invoice.
- *Net 10 days EOM*, or *n/10 EOM*, means that payment in full is due 10 days after the end of the month in which the invoice was issued.
- *2% 10 days, net 30 days*, or *2/10, n/30*, means that if payment is made within 10 days of the invoice date, the customer can take a 2 percent discount. Otherwise, payment in full is due in 30 days.

The 2 percent discount is a **cash discount;** it is a discount offered by suppliers to encourage quick payment by customers. To the customer it is known as a **purchases discount.** To the supplier it is known as a **sales discount.**

FIGURE 8.4 Purchases Journal

PURCHASES JOURNAL   PAGE 1

DATE		PURCHASED FROM	INVOICE NUMBER	INVOICE DATE	TERMS	POST. REF.	ACCOUNTS PAYABLE CREDIT	PURCHASES DEBIT	FREIGHT IN DEBIT
20X1									
Jan.	3	Active Designs	5879	01/02/X1	2/10, n/30		2865 00	2675 00	190 00
	5	The Sports Warehouse	633	01/03/X1	n/30		4055 00	3880 00	175 00
	6	The Modern Sportsman	8011	01/04/X1	n/30		3140 00	2900 00	240 00
	7	World of Sports	4321	01/04/X1	2/10, n/30		3935 00	3675 00	260 00
	19	Athletic Equipment, Inc.	8997	01/15/X1	2/10, n/30		4200 00	3860 00	340 00
	23	International Sportsman	7985	01/22/X1	n/30		600 00	550 00	50 00
	31						18795 00	17540 00	1255 00

FIGURE 8.5 Posting to the General Ledger

PURCHASES JOURNAL PAGE 1

DATE		PURCHASED FROM	INVOICE NUMBER	INVOICE DATE	TERMS	POST. REF.	ACCOUNTS PAYABLE CREDIT	PURCHASES DEBIT	FREIGHT IN DEBIT
20X1									
Jan.	3	Active Designs	5879	01/02/X1	2/10, n/30	✓	2 865 00	2 675 00	190 00
	5	The Sports Warehouse	633	01/03/X1	n/30	✓	4 055 00	3 880 00	175 00
	6	The Modern Sportsman	8011	01/04/X1	n/30	✓	3 140 00	2 900 00	240 00
	7	World of Sports	4321	01/04/X1	2/10, n/30	✓	3 935 00	3 675 00	260 00
	19	Athletic Equipment, Inc.	8997	01/15/X1	2/10, n/30	✓	4 200 00	3 860 00	340 00
	23	International Sportsman	7985	01/22/X1	n/30	✓	600 00	550 00	50 00
	31						18 795 00	17 540 00	1 255 00
							(205)	(501)	(502)

ACCOUNT Accounts Payable **ACCOUNT NO.** 205

DATE	DESCRIPTION	POST. REF.	DEBIT	CREDIT	BALANCE DEBIT	BALANCE CREDIT
20X1						
Jan. 1	Balance	✓				10 800 00
31		P1		18 795 00		29 595 00

ACCOUNT Purchases **ACCOUNT NO.** 501

DATE	DESCRIPTION	POST. REF.	DEBIT	CREDIT	BALANCE DEBIT	BALANCE CREDIT
20X1						
Jan. 31		P1	17 540 00		17 540 00	

ACCOUNT Freight In **ACCOUNT NO.** 502

DATE	DESCRIPTION	POST. REF.	DEBIT	CREDIT	BALANCE DEBIT	BALANCE CREDIT
20X1						
Jan. 31		P1	1 255 00		1 255 00	

Posting to the General Ledger

The purchases journal simplifies the posting process. Summary amounts are posted at the end of the month. Refer to Figure 8.5 as you learn how to post from the purchases journal to the general ledger accounts.

Total the Accounts Payable Credit, the Purchases Debit, and the Freight In Debit columns. Before posting, prove the equality of the debits and credits recorded in the purchases journal.

>> **8-2 OBJECTIVE**
Post from the three-column purchases journal to the general ledger accounts.

Proof of Purchases Journal

	Debits
Purchases Debit column	$17,540.00
Freight In Debit column	1,255.00
	$18,795.00
	Credits
Accounts Payable Credit column	$18,795.00

important!

Cash Discounts
In the purchases journal, record the amount shown on the invoice. The cash discount is recorded when the payment is made.

After the equality of debits and credits is verified, rule the purchases journal. The steps to post the column totals to the general ledger follow:

1. Locate the *Accounts Payable* ledger account.
2. Enter the date.
3. Enter the posting reference, P1. The **P** is for purchases journal. The **1** is the purchases journal page number.
4. Enter the amount from the Accounts Payable Credit column in the purchases journal in the Credit column of the *Accounts Payable* ledger account.
5. Compute the new balance and enter it in the Balance Credit column.
6. In the purchases journal, enter the *Accounts Payable* ledger account number (205) under the column total.
7. Repeat the steps for the Purchases Debit and Freight In Debit columns.

During the month, the individual entries in the purchases journal are posted to the creditor accounts in the accounts payable ledger. The check marks in the purchases journal in Figure 8.5 indicate that these postings have been completed. This procedure is discussed later in this chapter.

Advantages of a Purchases Journal

Every business has certain types of transactions that occur over and over again. A well-designed accounting system includes journals that permit efficient recording of such transactions. In most merchandising firms, purchases of goods on credit take place often enough to make it worthwhile to use a purchases journal.

A special journal for credit purchases of merchandise saves time and effort when recording and posting purchases. The use of a purchases journal and other special journals allows for the division of accounting work among different employees. The purchases journal strengthens the audit trail. All credit purchases are recorded in one place, and each entry refers to the number and date of the invoice.

Section 1 Review

1. What type of transaction is recorded in the purchases journal?
   a. purchases of equipment on credit
   b. purchases of equipment for cash
   c. purchases of merchandise inventory for cash
   d. purchases of merchandise inventory on credit

2. Freight charges paid by the buyer of merchandise are debited to
   a. *Merchandise Inventory.*
   b. *Freight In.*
   c. *Purchasing Expense.*
   d. *Sales Expense.*

3. Which of the following best describes the *Purchases* account?
   a. a contra revenue account with a normal debit balance
   b. a contra cost of goods sold account with a normal credit balance
   c. a cost of goods sold account with a normal debit balance
   d. a cost of goods sold account with a normal credit balance

4. A purchase invoice for $5,000 has credit terms of 1/10, n/30. Assuming the invoice is paid within 10 days, the amount paid is
   a. $4,995.
   b. $5,050.
   c. $5,000.
   d. $4,950.

5. When the sales department needs goods, what document is sent to the purchasing department?
   a. purchase order
   b. sales order
   c. purchase requisition
   d. sales requisition

6. What form is sent to the supplier to order goods?
   a. purchase invoice
   b. purchase order
   c. sales order
   d. sales invoice

7. Which of the following columns are included in a purchases journal?
   a. Accounts Payable Credit, Purchases Debit, Freight In Debit
   b. Accounts Payable Debit, Purchases Debit, Freight In Debit
   c. Accounts Receivable Debit, Purchases Debit, Freight In Debit
   d. Accounts Receivable Credit, Purchases Debit, Freight In Debit

8. If freight is paid for the purchase of equipment to be used by the business, the freight charges are debited to
   a. *Freight In.*
   b. *Merchandise Inventory.*
   c. *Purchasing Expense.*
   d. *Equipment.*

Section 2

SECTION OBJECTIVES	TERMS TO LEARN
>> 8-3 Post credit purchases from the purchases journal to the accounts payable subsidiary ledger. **WHY IT'S IMPORTANT** Up-to-date records allow prompt payment of invoices.	accounts payable ledger purchase allowance purchase return schedule of accounts payable
>> 8-4 Record purchases returns and allowances in the general journal and post them to the *Accounts Payable* account in the general ledger and to the accounts payable subsidiary ledger. **WHY IT'S IMPORTANT** For unsatisfactory goods received, an allowance or return is reflected in the accounting records.	
>> 8-5 Prepare a schedule of accounts payable. **WHY IT'S IMPORTANT** This schedule provides a snapshot of amounts owed to suppliers.	
>> 8-6 Compute the net delivered cost of purchases. **WHY IT'S IMPORTANT** This is an important component in measuring operational results.	
>> 8-7 Demonstrate a knowledge of the procedures for effective internal control of purchases. **WHY IT'S IMPORTANT** Businesses try to prevent fraud, errors, and holding excess inventory.	

Accounts Payable

Businesses that buy merchandise on credit can conduct more extensive operations and use financial resources more effectively than if they paid cash for all purchases. It is important to pay invoices on time so that the business maintains a good credit reputation with its suppliers.

The Accounts Payable Ledger

Businesses need detailed records in order to pay invoices promptly. The **accounts payable ledger** provides information about the individual accounts for all creditors. The accounts payable ledger is a subsidiary ledger; it is separate from and subordinate to the general ledger. The accounts payable ledger contains a separate account for each creditor. Each account shows purchases, payments, and returns and allowances. The balance of the account shows the amount owed to the creditor.

Figure 8.6 shows the accounts payable ledger account for International Sportsman. Notice that the Balance column does not indicate whether the balance is a debit or a credit. The form assumes that the balance will be a credit because the normal balance of liability accounts is a credit. A debit balance may exist if more than the amount owed was paid to the creditor or if returned goods were already paid for. If the balance is a debit, circle the amount to show that the account does not have the normal balance.

Small businesses like Maxx-Out Sporting Goods arrange the accounts payable ledger in alphabetical order. Large businesses and businesses that use computerized accounting systems assign an account number to each creditor and arrange the accounts payable ledger in numeric order.

FIGURE 8.6

Accounts Payable Ledger Account

NAME	International Sportsman			TERMS	n/30		
ADDRESS	1718 Sherry Lane, Dallas, Texas 75267-6205						
DATE	DESCRIPTION	POST. REF.	DEBIT		CREDIT		BALANCE
20X1							
Jan. 1	Balance	✓					1 600 00
23	Invoice 7985, 01/23/X1	P1			600 00		2 200 00

Posting a Credit Purchase

To keep the accounting records up to date, invoices are posted to the accounts payable subsidiary ledger every day. Refer to Figure 8.6 as you learn how to post to the accounts payable ledger.

1. Locate the accounts payable ledger account for the creditor International Sportsman.
2. Enter the date.
3. In the Description column, enter the invoice number and date.
4. In the Posting Reference column, enter the purchases journal page number.
5. Enter the amount from the Accounts Payable Credit column in the purchases journal in the Credit column of the accounts payable subsidiary ledger.
6. Compute and enter the new balance in the Balance column.
7. In the purchases journal (Figure 8.5), enter a check mark (✓) in the Posting Reference column. This indicates that the transaction is posted in the accounts payable subsidiary ledger.

>> **8-3 OBJECTIVE**
Post credit purchases from the purchases journal to the accounts payable subsidiary ledger.

Posting Cash Paid on Account

When the transaction involves cash paid on account to a supplier, the payment is first recorded in a cash payments journal. (The cash payments journal is discussed in Chapter 9.) The cash payment is then posted to the individual creditor's account in the accounts payable ledger. Figure 8.7 shows a posting for cash paid to a creditor on January 27.

Purchases Returns and Allowances

When merchandise arrives, it is examined to confirm that it is satisfactory. Occasionally, the wrong goods are shipped, or items are damaged or defective. A **purchase return** is when the business returns the goods. A **purchase allowance** is when the purchaser keeps the goods but receives a reduction in the price of the goods. The supplier issues a credit memorandum for the return or allowance. The credit memorandum reduces the amount that the purchaser owes.

Purchases returns and allowances are entered in the ***Purchases Returns and Allowances*** account, not in the ***Purchases*** account. The ***Purchases Returns and Allowances*** account is a complete record of returns and allowances. Business managers analyze this account to identify problem suppliers.

Purchases Returns and Allowances is a contra cost of goods sold account. The normal balance of cost of goods sold accounts is a debit. The normal balance of ***Purchases Returns and Allowances,*** a contra cost of goods sold account, is a credit.

>> **8-4 OBJECTIVE**
Record purchases returns and allowances in the general journal and post them to the *Accounts Payable* account in the general ledger and to the accounts payable subsidiary ledger.

recall

Subsidiary Ledger
The total of the accounts in the subsidiary ledger must equal the control account balance.

Recording Purchases Returns and Allowances

Maxx-Out Sporting Goods received merchandise from International Sportsman on January 23. Some goods were damaged, and the supplier granted a $100 purchase allowance. Maxx-Out Sporting Goods recorded the full amount of the invoice, $600, in the purchases journal. The purchase allowance was recorded separately in the general journal.

254 CHAPTER 8 Accounting for Purchases and Accounts Payable

FIGURE 8.7

Posting a Payment Made on Account

NAME	International Sportsman			TERMS	n/30	
ADDRESS	1718 Sherry Lane, Dallas, Texas 75267-6205					
DATE	DESCRIPTION	POST. REF.	DEBIT		CREDIT	BALANCE
20X1						
Jan. 1	Balance	✓				1 600 00
23	Invoice 7985, 01/23/X1	P1			600 00	2 200 00
27		CP1	1 000 00			1 200 00

BUSINESS TRANSACTION

On January 30, Maxx-Out Sporting Goods received a credit memorandum for $100 from International Sportsman as an allowance for damaged merchandise.

International Sportsman
1718 Sherry Lane
Dallas, TX 75267-6205

TO: Maxx-Out Sporting Goods
2007 Trendsetter Lane
Dallas, TX 75268-0967

CREDIT MEMORANDUM
NUMBER: 103
DATE: January 30, 20X1

ORIGINAL INVOICE: 7985
INVOICE DATE: January 23, 20X1
DESCRIPTION: Credit for damaged merchandise: $100.00

ANALYSIS
The liability account **Accounts Payable** is decreased by $100. The contra cost of goods sold account **Purchases Returns and Allowances** is increased by $100.

DEBIT-CREDIT RULES
DEBIT Decreases to liabilities are debits. Debit **Accounts Payable** for $100.
CREDIT Increases to contra cost of goods sold accounts are recorded as credits. Credit **Purchases Returns and Allowances** for $100.

T-ACCOUNT PRESENTATION

Accounts Payable		Purchases Returns and Allowances	
−	+	−	+
100			100

GENERAL JOURNAL ENTRY

		GENERAL JOURNAL		PAGE 1		
	DATE	DESCRIPTION	POST. REF.	DEBIT	CREDIT	
15	Jan. 30	Accounts Payable/International Sportsman		100 00		15
16		Purchases Returns and Allowances			100 00	16
17		Received Credit Memo 103 for				17
18		damaged merchandise returned;				18
19		original Invoice 7985,				19
20		January 23, 20X1				20

THE BOTTOM LINE

Purchase Allowance

Income Statement
Contra Cost of
 Goods Sold ↑ 100
Net Income ↑ 100

Balance Sheet
Liabilities ↓ 100
Equity ↑ 100

FIGURE 8.8

Posting to a Creditor's Account

	GENERAL JOURNAL			PAGE __1__	
DATE	DESCRIPTION	POST. REF.	DEBIT	CREDIT	
20X1					1
Jan. 30	Accounts Payable/International Sportsman	205 ✓	100 00		16
	Purchases Returns and Allowances	503		100 00	17
	Received Credit Memo 103 for				18
	damaged merchandise				19
	returned; original				20
	Invoice 7985, January 23, 20X1				21

NAME International Sportsman TERMS n/30
ADDRESS 1718 Sherry Lane, Dallas, Texas 75267-6205

DATE	DESCRIPTION	POST. REF.	DEBIT	CREDIT	BALANCE
20X1					
Jan. 1	Balance	✓			1600 00
23	Invoice 7985, 01/23/X1	P1		600 00	2200 00
27		CP1	1000 00		1200 00
30	CM 103	J1	100 00		1100 00

recall

Contra Accounts
The *Purchases Returns and Allowances* account is a contra account. Contra accounts have normal balances that are the opposite of related accounts. For example, the normal balance of *Purchases Returns and Allowances* is credit, where the normal balance of *Purchases* is debit.

Notice that this entry includes a debit to **Accounts Payable** and a credit to **Purchases Returns and Allowances.** In addition, there is a debit to the creditor's account in the accounts payable subsidiary ledger. Businesses that have few returns and allowances use the general journal to record these transactions. Businesses with many returns and allowances use a special journal for purchases returns and allowances.

Posting a Purchases Return or Allowance

Whether recorded in the general journal or in a special journal, it is important to promptly post returns and allowances to the creditor's account in the accounts payable ledger. Refer to Figure 8.8 to learn how to post purchases returns and allowances to the supplier's account.

1. Enter the date.
2. In the Description column, enter the credit memorandum number.
3. In the Posting Reference column, enter the general journal page number.
4. Enter the amount of the return or allowance in the Debit column.
5. Compute the new balance and enter it in the Balance column.
6. In the general journal, enter a check mark (✓) to show that the transaction was posted to the creditor's account in the accounts payable subsidiary ledger.

After the transaction is posted to the general ledger, enter the **Purchases Returns and Allowances** ledger account number in the Posting Reference column.

Schedule of Accounts Payable

The total of the individual creditor accounts in the subsidiary ledger must equal the balance of the *Accounts Payable* control account. To prove that the control account and the subsidiary ledger are equal, businesses prepare a **schedule of accounts payable**—a list of all balances owed to creditors. Figure 8.9 shows the accounts payable subsidiary ledger for Maxx-Out Sporting Goods on January 31.

Figure 8.10 shows the schedule of accounts payable for Maxx-Out Sporting Goods. Notice that the accounts payable control account balance is $20,245. This equals the total on the schedule of accounts payable. If the amounts are not equal, it is essential to locate and correct the errors.

>> 8-5 OBJECTIVE
Prepare a schedule of accounts payable.

FIGURE 8.9

The Accounts Payable Ledger

NAME: Active Designs   TERMS: 2/10, n/30
ADDRESS: 2313 Belt Line Road, Dallas, Texas 75267-6205

DATE		DESCRIPTION	POST. REF.	DEBIT	CREDIT	BALANCE
20X1						
Jan.	1	Balance	✓			2 200 00
	3	Invoice 5879, 01/02/X1	P1		2 865 00	5 065 00
	13		CP1	3 200 00		1 865 00
	30		CP1	800 00		1 065 00

NAME: Athletic Equipment, Inc.   TERMS: 2/10, n/30
ADDRESS: 1027 St James Avenue, Dallas, Texas 75267-6205

DATE		DESCRIPTION	POST. REF.	DEBIT	CREDIT	BALANCE
20X1						
Jan.	19	Invoice 8997, 01/15/X1	P1		4 200 00	4 200 00

NAME: International Sportsman   TERMS: n/30
ADDRESS: 1718 Sherry Lane, Dallas, Texas 75267-6205

DATE		DESCRIPTION	POST. REF.	DEBIT	CREDIT	BALANCE
20X1						
Jan.	1	Balance	✓			1 600 00
	23	Invoice 7985, 01/23/X1	P1		600 00	2 200 00
	27		CP1	1 000 00		1 200 00
	30	CM 103	J1	100 00		1 100 00

NAME: The Modern Sportsman   TERMS: n/30
ADDRESS: 2860 Jackson Drive, Dallas, Texas 75267-6205

DATE		DESCRIPTION	POST. REF.	DEBIT	CREDIT	BALANCE
20X1						
Jan.	1	Balance	✓			1 600 00
	6	Invoice 8011, 01/04/X1	P1		3 140 00	4 740 00

NAME: The Sports Warehouse   TERMS: n/30
ADDRESS: 1313 Sunset Drive, Dallas, Texas 75267-6205

DATE		DESCRIPTION	POST. REF.	DEBIT	CREDIT	BALANCE
20X1						
Jan.	1	Balance	✓			2 400 00
	5	Invoice 633, 01/03/X1	P1		4 055 00	6 455 00
	17		CP1	4 250 00		2 205 00

NAME: World of Sports   TERMS: 2/10, n/30
ADDRESS: 1729 Parker Road, Dallas, Texas 75267-6205

DATE		DESCRIPTION	POST. REF.	DEBIT	CREDIT	BALANCE
20X1						
Jan.	1	Balance	✓			3 000 00
	7	Invoice 4321, 01/04/X1	P1		3 935 00	6 935 00

FIGURE 8.10

Schedule of Accounts Payable and the Accounts Payable Account

Maxx-Out Sporting Goods
Schedule of Accounts Payable
January 31, 20X1

Active Designs	1,065.00
Athletic Equipment, Inc.	4,200.00
International Sportsman	1,100.00
The Modern Sportsman	4,740.00
The Sports Warehouse	2,205.00
World of Sports	6,935.00
Total	20,245.00

ACCOUNT: Accounts Payable   ACCOUNT NO. 205

DATE	DESCRIPTION	POST. REF.	DEBIT	CREDIT	BALANCE DEBIT	BALANCE CREDIT
20X1						
Jan. 1	Balance					10,800.00
30		J1	100.00			10,700.00
31		P1		18,795.00		29,495.00
31		CP1	9,250.00			20,245.00

Determining the Cost of Purchases

The **Purchases** account accumulates the cost of merchandise bought for resale. The income statement of a merchandising business contains a section showing the total cost of purchases. This section combines information about the cost of the purchases, freight in, and purchases returns and allowances for the period. Maxx-Out Sporting Goods has the following general ledger account balances at January 31:

Purchases	$17,540
Freight In	1,255
Purchases Returns and Allowances	100

The net delivered cost of purchases for Maxx-Out Sporting Goods for January is calculated as follows:

Purchases	$17,540
Freight In	1,255
Delivered Cost of Purchases	$18,795
Less Purchases Returns and Allowances	100
Net Delivered Cost of Purchases	$18,695

For firms that do not have freight charges, the amount of net purchases is calculated as follows:

Purchases	$17,540
Less Purchases Returns and Allowances	100
Net Purchases	$17,440

>> 8-6 OBJECTIVE
Compute the net delivered cost of purchases.

In Chapter 13, you will see how the complete income statement for a merchandising business is prepared. You will learn about the Cost of Goods Sold section and how the net delivered cost of purchases is used in calculating the results of operations.

>> **8-7 OBJECTIVE**

Demonstrate a knowledge of the procedures for effective internal control of purchases.

Internal Control of Purchases

Internal controls are the company's policies and procedures in place to safeguard assets, ensure reliability of accounting data, and promote compliance with management policies and applicable laws. Because of the large amount of money spent to purchase goods, businesses should develop careful procedures to control purchases and payments. A business should ensure its control process includes sufficient safeguards to:

- create written proof that purchases and payments are authorized;
- ensure that different people are involved in the process of buying goods, receiving goods, and making payments.

Separating duties among employees provides a system of checks and balances. In a small business with just a few employees, it might be very difficult to separate duties. This means the owner must be involved in daily operations. Even a small business, however, should design a set of control procedures as effective as resources allow. Effective systems for small businesses should have the following controls in place:

ABOUT ACCOUNTING

Employee Fraud

In its 2018 Global Study on Occupational Fraud and Abuse, the Association of Certified Fraud Examiners reported that small businesses lose nearly twice as much per fraud scheme than do larger organizations.

1. All purchases should be made only after proper authorization has been given in writing.
2. Goods should be carefully checked when received. They should then be compared with the purchase order and with the invoice received from the supplier.
3. The purchase order, receiving report, and invoice should be checked to confirm that the information on the documents is in agreement.
4. The computations on the invoice should be checked for accuracy.
5. Authorization for payment should be made by someone other than the person who ordered the goods.
6. Another person should write the check for payment.
7. Prenumbered forms should be used for purchase requisitions, purchase orders, and checks. The numbers on the documents issued should be verified periodically to make sure all forms can be accounted for.

Medium- and large-sized businesses often use the voucher system. As a business grows, the owner finds it increasingly difficult to be involved in all the firm's transactions. The owner cannot personally approve or sign all checks. That's when the internal controls provided by the voucher system become increasingly important.

Controls built into a voucher system include the following:

- All liabilities are authorized. For example, a properly approved purchase order is required for each purchase of merchandise on account.
- All payments are made by check.
- All checks are issued based on a properly approved voucher.
- Vouchers are used to cover bills and invoices received from outside parties.
- All bills and invoices are verified before they are approved for payment.
- Only experienced and responsible employees are allowed to approve bills and invoices for payment.
- Invoices are attached to the vouchers to provide supporting documentation.
- Different employees approve the vouchers, record the vouchers and payments, and sign and mail the checks.
- All paid vouchers, including supporting documentation, are kept on file for a specified period of time.

MANAGERIAL IMPLICATIONS

ACCOUNTING FOR PURCHASES

- Management and the accounting staff need to work together to make sure that there are good internal controls over purchasing.
- A carefully designed system of checks and balances protects the business against fraud, errors, and excessive investment in merchandise.
- The accounting staff needs to record transactions efficiently so that up-to-date information about creditors is available.
- Using the purchases journal and the accounts payable subsidiary ledger improves efficiency.
- To maintain a good credit reputation with suppliers, it is important to have an accounting system that ensures prompt payment of invoices.

- A well-run accounting system provides management with information about cash: cash required to pay suppliers, short-term loans needed to cover temporary cash shortages, and cash available for short-term investments.
- Separate accounts for recording purchases, freight charges, and purchases returns and allowances make it easy to analyze the elements in the cost of purchases.

THINKING CRITICALLY
As a manager, what internal controls would you put in your accounting system?

Section 2 Review

1. Which of the following would report the balance owed to an individual supplier?
   a. the accounts receivable ledger
   b. the accounts payable ledger
   c. the *Accounts Receivable* account in the general ledger
   d. the *Accounts Payable* balance in the general ledger

2. Which of the following best describes the *Purchases Returns and Allowances* account?
   a. a contra cost of goods sold account with a normal credit balance
   b. a contra cost of goods sold account with a normal debit balance
   c. a contra revenue account with a normal credit balance
   d. a contra revenue account with a normal debit balance

3. Purchases returns and purchases allowances are normally recorded in the
   a. purchases journal.
   b. sales journal.
   c. cash receipts journal.
   d. general journal.

4. A firm has a debit balance of $62,450 in its *Purchases* account and a credit balance of $2,875 in its *Purchases Returns and Allowances* account. What are net purchases for the period?
   a. $62,450
   b. $65,325
   c. $59,575
   d. None of these is correct.

5. A firm has the following account balances: *Purchases,* $40,000; *Freight In,* $2,000; and *Purchases Returns and Allowances,* $1,600. What is the amount of the net delivered cost of purchases?
   a. $40,400
   b. $43,600
   c. $36,400
   d. $39,600

6. A firm receives an invoice that reflects the price of goods as $1,375 and the freight charge as $92. Which of the following accounts are debited when this transaction is recorded?
   a. Debit *Purchases,* $1,375, and *Freight In,* $92.
   b. Debit *Purchases,* $1,467.
   c. Debit *Merchandise Inventory,* $1,375, and *Freight In,* $92.
   d. Debit *Merchandise Inventory,* $1,467.

7. The net delivered cost of purchases for the period appears on the
   a. balance sheet.
   b. income statement.
   c. schedule of accounts payable.
   d. statement of owner's equity.

8. Which of the following is not a good internal control over purchases?
    a. Computations on the vendor's invoice should be checked for accuracy.
    b. Authorization for payment should be made by someone other than the person who ordered the goods.
    c. The person authorizing the purchase should be the same person who writes the check for payment.
    d. Prenumbered forms should be used for purchase requisitions, purchase orders, and checks.

9. In the accounts payable ledger, a supplier's account has a beginning balance of $4,800. A transaction of $1,600 is posted from the purchases journal. What is the balance of the supplier's account?
    a. $3,200 debit
    b. $3,200 credit
    c. $6,400 debit
    d. $6,400 credit

REVIEW Chapter Summary

In this chapter, you have learned about the accounting journals and ledgers required for the efficient processing of purchases for a business. Businesses with strong internal controls establish and follow procedures for approving requests for new merchandise, choosing suppliers, placing orders with suppliers, checking goods after they arrive, identifying invoices, and approving payments.

Learning Objectives

8-1 Record purchases of merchandise on credit in a three-column purchases journal.

Purchases and payments on account must be entered in the firm's accounting records promptly and accurately. Most merchandising businesses normally purchase goods on credit. The most efficient system for recording purchases on credit is the use of a special purchases journal. With this type of journal, only one line is needed to enter all the data.

The purchases journal is used only to record the credit purchase of goods for resale. General business expenses are not recorded in the purchases journal.

8-2 Post from the three-column purchases journal to the general ledger accounts.

The use of the three-column purchases journal simplifies the posting process because nothing is posted to the general ledger until the month's end. Then, summary postings are made to the *Purchases, Freight In,* and *Accounts Payable* accounts.

8-3 Post credit purchases from the purchases journal to the accounts payable subsidiary ledger.

An accounts payable subsidiary ledger helps a firm keep track of the amounts it owes to creditors. Postings are made to this ledger on a daily basis.

- Each credit purchase is posted from the purchases journal to the accounts payable subsidiary ledger.
- Each payment on account is posted from the cash payments journal to the accounts payable subsidiary ledger.

8-4 Record purchases returns and allowances in the general journal and post them to the *Accounts Payable* account in the general ledger and to the accounts payable subsidiary ledger.

Returns and allowances on purchases of goods are credited to an account called *Purchases Returns and Allowances.* These transactions may be recorded in the general journal or in a special purchases returns and allowances journal. Each return or allowance on a credit purchase is posted to the accounts payable subsidiary ledger.

8-5 Prepare a schedule of accounts payable.

At the month's end, a schedule of accounts payable is prepared. The schedule lists the balances owed to the firm's creditors and proves the accuracy of the subsidiary ledger. The total of the schedule of accounts payable is compared with the balance of the *Accounts Payable* account in the general ledger, which acts as a control account. The two amounts should be equal.

8-6 Compute the net delivered cost of purchases.

The net delivered cost of purchases is computed by adding the cost of purchases and freight in, then subtracting any purchases returns and allowances. Net delivered cost of purchases is reported in the Cost of Goods Sold section of the income statement.

8-7 Demonstrate a knowledge of the procedures for effective internal control of purchases.

Purchases and payments should be properly authorized and processed with appropriate documentation to provide a system of checks and balances. A division of responsibilities within the purchases process ensures strong internal controls.

8-8 Define the accounting terms new to this chapter.

Glossary

Accounts payable ledger (p. 252) A subsidiary ledger that contains a separate account for each creditor

Cash discount (p. 248) A discount offered by suppliers for payment received within a specified period of time

Cost of goods sold (p. 244) The actual cost to the business of the merchandise sold to customers

Freight In **account** (p. 246) An account showing transportation charges for items purchased

Purchase allowance (p. 253) A price reduction from the amount originally billed

Purchase invoice (p. 244) A bill received for goods purchased

Purchase order (p. 244) An order to the supplier of goods specifying items needed, quantity, price, and credit terms

Purchase requisition (p. 244) A list sent to the purchasing department showing the items to be ordered

Purchase return (p. 253) Return of unsatisfactory goods

Purchases **account** (p. 246) An account used to record cost of goods bought for resale during a period

Purchases discount (p. 248) A cash discount offered to the customers for payment within a specified period

Purchases journal (p. 246) A special journal used to record the purchase of goods on credit

Receiving report (p. 244) A form showing quantity and condition of goods received

Sales discount (p. 248) A cash discount offered by the supplier for payment within a specified period

Sales invoice (p. 244) A supplier's billing document

Schedule of accounts payable (p. 255) A list of all balances owed to creditors

Transportation In **account** (p. 246) See *Freight In* account

Comprehensive Self Review

1. What type of account is *Purchases Returns and Allowances*?
2. What is a cash discount and why is it offered?
3. What is the purpose of the *Freight In* account?
4. What is the purpose of a purchase requisition? A purchase order?
5. What is the difference between a receiving report and an invoice?

(Answers to Comprehensive Self Review are at the end of the chapter.)

Discussion Questions

1. Why are the invoice date and terms recorded in the purchases journal?
2. What major safeguards should be built into a system of internal control for purchases of goods?
3. What is the purpose of a credit memorandum?
4. What is a purchase allowance?
5. What is a purchase return?
6. What is a schedule of accounts payable? Why is it prepared?
7. What is the relationship of the *Accounts Payable* account in the general ledger to the accounts payable subsidiary ledger?
8. What type of accounts are kept in the accounts payable ledger?
9. Why is it useful for a business to have an accounts payable ledger?
10. How is the net delivered cost of purchases computed?

11. What journals can be used to enter various merchandise purchase transactions?
12. What is the difference between a purchase invoice and a sales invoice?
13. What is the normal balance of the *Purchases* account?
14. On what financial statement do the accounts related to purchases of merchandise appear? In which section of this statement are they reported?
15. Why is the use of a *Purchases Returns and Allowances* account preferred to crediting these transactions to *Purchases*?
16. What do the following credit terms mean?
    a. n/30
    b. 2/10, n/30
    c. n/10 EOM
    d. n/20
    e. 1/10, n/20
    f. 3/5, n/30
    g. n/15 EOM
17. A business has purchased some new equipment for use in its operations, not for resale to customers. The terms of the invoice are n/30. Should this transaction be entered in the purchases journal? If not, where should it be recorded?

APPLICATIONS

Exercises

Identifying the journals used to record purchases and related transactions.

◀ **Exercise 8.1**
Objective 8-1

The accounting system of Rose and Tea Fine Kitchenware includes the following journals. Indicate which journal is used to record each transaction.

JOURNALS

Cash receipts journal
Cash payments journal
Purchases journal
Sales journal
General journal

TRANSACTIONS

1. Purchased merchandise for $4,000; the terms are 2/10, n/30.
2. Returned damaged merchandise to a supplier and received a credit memorandum for $900.
3. Issued a check for $4,600 to a supplier as a payment on account.
4. Purchased merchandise for $2,000 plus a freight charge of $200; the supplier's invoice is payable in 30 days.
5. Received an allowance for merchandise that was damaged but can be sold at a reduced price; the supplier's credit memorandum is for $425.
6. Purchased merchandise for $3,725 in cash.

Exercise 8.2
Objective 8-1

▶ **Identifying journals used to record purchases and related transactions.**

The following transactions took place at Extreme Bikers. Indicate the general ledger account numbers that would be debited and credited to record each transaction.

GENERAL LEDGER ACCOUNTS

101   Cash
205   Accounts Payable
501   Purchases
502   Freight In
503   Purchases Returns and Allowances

TRANSACTIONS

1. Purchased merchandise for $1,500; the terms are 2/10, n/30.
2. Returned damaged merchandise to a supplier and received a credit memorandum for $300.
3. Issued a check for $800 to a supplier as a payment on account.
4. Purchased merchandise for $2,400 plus a freight charge of $260; the supplier's invoice is payable in 30 days.
5. Received an allowance for merchandise that was damaged but can be sold at a reduced price; the supplier's credit memorandum is for $400.
6. Purchased merchandise for $4,200 in cash.

Exercise 8.3
Objective 8-1

▶ **Recording credit purchases.**

The following transactions took place at AutoQuest Car Parts during the first week of July. Indicate how these transactions would be entered in a purchases journal like the one shown in this chapter.

DATE		TRANSACTIONS
July	1	Purchased batteries for $1,980 plus a freight charge of $105 from Everlife Batteries Corporation; received Invoice 6812, dated June 27, which has terms of n/30.
	3	Purchased mufflers for $4,250 plus a freight charge of $99 from Performance Mufflers; received Invoice 441, dated June 30, which has terms of 1/10, n/60.
	5	Purchased car radios for $2,740 plus freight of $137 from Xtreme Sounds Shop, Inc.; received Invoice 5601, dated July 1, which has terms of 2/10, n/30.
	10	Purchased truck tires for $6,270 from Specialty Tire Company; received invoice 1102, dated July 8, which has terms of 2/10, n/30. The seller paid the freight charges.

Exercise 8.4
Objective 8-4

▶ **Recording a purchase return.**

On March 19, Beautiful Kitchens, a retail store, received Credit Memorandum 244 for $4,125 from M & J Appliance Corporation. The credit memorandum covered a return of damaged trash compactors originally purchased on Invoice 4101 dated February 3. Prepare the general journal entry that Beautiful Kitchens would make for this transaction.

Exercise 8.5
Objective 8-4

▶ **Recording a purchase allowance.**

On April 7, Fisher & Sons Appliances was given an allowance of $1,210 by Modern Kitchens, which issued Credit Memorandum 112. The allowance was for scratches on stoves that were originally purchased on Invoice 911 dated March 20. Prepare the general journal entry that Fisher & Sons Appliances would make for this transaction.

Determining the cost of purchases.

Exercise 8.6
Objective 8-4

On June 30 the general ledger of Newport Clothiers, a clothing store, showed a balance of $65,895 in the *Purchases* account, a balance of $2,125 in the *Freight In* account, and a balance of $1,280 in the *Purchases Returns and Allowances* account. What was the delivered cost of the purchases made during June? What was the net delivered cost of these purchases?

Errors in recording purchase transactions.

Exercise 8.7
Objectives 8-1, 8-4

The following errors were made in recording transactions in posting from the purchases journal. How will these errors be detected?

a. A credit of $2,000 to the Thomastown Furniture Company account in the accounts payable ledger was posted as $200.

b. The Accounts Payable column total of the purchases journal was understated by $300.

c. An invoice of $1,680 for merchandise from Johnson Company was recorded as having been received from Baxton Company, another supplier.

d. A $500 payment to Baxton Company was debited to Johnson Company.

Determining the cost of purchases.

Exercise 8.8
Objective 8-4

Complete the following schedule by supplying the missing information.

Net Delivered Cost of Purchases	Case A	Case B
Purchases	(a)	95,420
Freight In	4,200	(c)
Delivered Cost of Purchases	97,600	(d)
Less Purchases Returns and Allowances	(b)	3,855
Net Delivered Cost of Purchases	93,750	97,770

PROBLEMS

Problem Set A

Journalizing credit purchases and purchases returns and allowances and posting to the general ledger.

Problem 8.1A
Objectives 8-1, 8-2, 8-3

Lens Queen is a retail store that sells cameras and photography supplies. The firm's credit purchases and purchases returns and allowances transactions for June 20X1 appear below, along with the general ledger accounts used to record these transactions. The balance shown in *Accounts Payable* is for the beginning of June.

INSTRUCTIONS

1. Open the general ledger accounts and enter the balance of *Accounts Payable* for June 1, 20X1.
2. Record the transactions in a three-column purchases journal and in a general journal. Use 14 as the page number for the purchases journal and 38 as the page number for the general journal.
3. Post entries from the general journal to the general ledger accounts.
4. Total and rule the purchases journal as of June 30.
5. Post the column totals from the purchases journal to the proper general ledger accounts.
6. Compute the net delivered cost of purchases for the firm for the month of June.

GENERAL LEDGER ACCOUNTS

205 Accounts Payable, $14,154 Cr.
501 Purchases
502 Freight In
503 Purchases Returns and Allowances

DATE		TRANSACTIONS
June	1	Purchased digital cameras for $2,000 plus a freight charge of $205 from American Photo Equipment, Invoice 4241, dated May 27; the terms are 60 days net.
	8	Purchased film for $1,389 from Foto Suppliers, Invoice 1102, dated June 3, net payable in 45 days.
	12	Purchased lenses for $911 from Gem Lenses, Invoice 7282, dated June 9; the terms are 1/10, n/60.
	18	Received Credit Memorandum 110 for $375 from American Photo Equipment for defective cameras that were returned; they were originally purchased on Invoice 4241, dated May 27.
	20	Purchased film for $1,150 plus freight of $70 from Foto Suppliers, Invoice 1148, dated June 15, net payable in 45 days.
	23	Purchased camera cases for $1,951 from Quality Cases, Invoice 3108, dated June 18, net due and payable in 45 days.
	28	Purchased lens filters for $2,420 plus freight of $115 from Sublime Stills, Invoice 5027, dated June 24; the terms are 2/10, n/30.
	30	Received Credit Memorandum 1108 for $285 from Quality Cases; the amount is an allowance for damaged but usable goods purchased on Invoice 3108, dated June 18.

(**Note:** Save your working papers for use in Problem 8.2A.)

Analyze: What total purchases were posted to the *Purchases* general ledger account for June?

Problem 8.2A
Objectives 8-4, 8-6

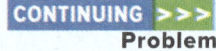

Posting to the accounts payable ledger and preparing a schedule of accounts payable.

This problem is a continuation of Problem 8.1A.

INSTRUCTIONS

1. Set up an accounts payable subsidiary ledger for Lens Queen. Open an account for each of the creditors listed below and enter the balances as of June 1, 20X1. Arrange the accounts payable ledger in alphabetical order.
2. Post the individual entries from the purchases journal and the general journal prepared in Problem 8.1A.
3. Prepare a schedule of accounts payable for June 30.
4. Check the total of the schedule of accounts payable against the balance of the *Accounts Payable* account in the general ledger. The two amounts should be equal.

Creditors		
Name	Terms	Balance
Foto Suppliers	n/45	$10,430
Quality Cases	n/45	1,150
American Photo Equipment	n/60	
Gem Lenses	1/10, n/60	2,574
Sublime Stills	2/10, n/30	

Analyze: What amount is owed to Gem Lenses on June 30?

Problem 8.3A
Objectives 8-1, 8-2, 8-3, 8-4, 8-5, 8-6

Journalizing credit purchases and purchases returns and allowances, computing the net delivered cost of goods, posting to the general ledger, posting to the accounts payable ledger, and preparing a schedule of accounts payable.

The Old English Garden Shop is a retail store that sells garden equipment, furniture, and supplies. Its credit purchases and purchases returns and allowances for July are listed below. The general ledger accounts used to record these transactions are also provided. The balance shown is for the beginning of July 20X1.

INSTRUCTIONS
PART I
1. Open the general ledger accounts and enter the balance of *Accounts Payable* for July 1.
2. Record the transactions in a three-column purchases journal and in a general journal. Use 8 as the page number for the purchases journal and 20 as the page number for the general journal.
3. Post the entries from the general journal to the proper general ledger accounts.
4. Total, prove, and rule the purchases journal as of July 31.
5. Post the column totals from the purchases journal to the proper general ledger accounts.
6. Compute the net delivered cost of the firm's purchases for the month of July.

GENERAL LEDGER ACCOUNTS
205 Accounts Payable, $35,980 Cr.

501 Purchases

502 Freight In

503 Purchases Returns and Allowances

DATE		TRANSACTIONS
July	1	Purchased lawn mowers for $9,410 plus a freight charge of $269 from Charleston Corporation, Invoice 1011, dated June 26, net due and payable in 60 days.
	5	Purchased outdoor chairs and tables for $4,470 plus a freight charge of $562 from Cedarbrook Garden Center, Invoice 639, dated July 2, net due and payable in 45 days.
	9	Purchased grass seed for $1,525 from Lawn and Gardens Supply, Invoice 8164, dated July 5; the terms are 30 days net.
	16	Received Credit Memorandum 110 for $500 from Cedarbrook Garden Center; the amount is an allowance for scratches on some of the chairs and tables originally purchased on Invoice 639, dated July 2.
	19	Purchased fertilizer for $1,300 plus a freight charge of $266 from Lawn and Gardens Supply, Invoice 9050, dated July 15; the terms are 30 days net.
	21	Purchased hoses from Dunn Rubber Company for $3,790 plus a freight charge of $264, Invoice 1785, dated July 17; terms are 1/15, n/60.
	28	Received Credit Memorandum 223 for $530 from Dunn Rubber Company for damaged hoses that were returned; the goods were purchased on Invoice 1785, dated July 17.
	31	Purchased lawn sprinkler systems for $10,610 plus a freight charge of $298 from Warren Industrial Products, Invoice 8985, dated July 26; the terms are 2/10, n/30.

INSTRUCTIONS
PART II

1. Set up an accounts payable subsidiary ledger for The Old English Garden Shop. Open an account for each of the creditors listed below and enter the balances as of July 1.
2. Post the individual entries from the purchases journal and the general journal prepared in Part I.
3. Prepare a schedule of accounts payable for July 31, 20X1.
4. Check the total of the schedule of accounts payable against the balance of the *Accounts Payable* account in the general ledger. The two amounts should be equal.

Creditors		
Name	Terms	Balance
Cedarbrook Garden Center	n/45	$11,220
Charleston Corporation	n/60	18,220
Dunn Rubber Company	1/15, n/60	
Lawn and Gardens Supply	n/30	6,540
Warren Industrial Products	2/10, n/30	

Analyze: What total freight charges were posted to the general ledger for the month of July?

Problem 8.4A
Objectives 8-1, 8-2, 8-3, 8-4, 8-5, 8-6

▶ **Journalizing credit purchases and purchases returns and allowances, posting to the general ledger, posting to the accounts payable ledger, and preparing a schedule of accounts payable.**

Office Plus is a retail business that sells office equipment, furniture, and supplies. Its credit purchases and purchases returns and allowances for September are shown below. The general ledger accounts and the creditors' accounts in the accounts payable subsidiary ledger used to record these transactions are also provided. All balances shown are for the beginning of September.

INSTRUCTIONS

1. Open the general ledger accounts and enter the balance of *Accounts Payable* for September 1, 20X1.
2. Open the creditors' accounts in the accounts payable subsidiary ledger and enter the balances for September 1.
3. Record the transactions in a three-column purchases journal and in a general journal. Use 5 as the page number for the purchases journal and 14 as the page number for the general journal.
4. Post to the accounts payable subsidiary ledger daily.
5. Post the entries from the general journal to the proper general ledger accounts at the end of the month.
6. Total and rule the purchases journal as of September 30.
7. Post the column totals from the purchases journal to the proper general ledger accounts.
8. Prepare a schedule of accounts payable and compare the balance of the *Accounts Payable* control account with the schedule of accounts payable.

GENERAL LEDGER ACCOUNTS

205 Accounts Payable, $28,356 Cr.
501 Purchases
502 Freight In
503 Purchases Returns and Allowances

Creditors		
Name	Terms	Balance
Apex Office Machines, Inc.	n/60	$11,060
Brown Paper Company	1/10, n/30	2,220
Dalton Office Furniture Company	n/30	9,676
Davis Corporation	n/30	
Zenn Furniture, Inc.	2/10, n/30	5,400

DATE		TRANSACTIONS
Sept.	3	Purchased desks for $8,020 plus a freight charge of $222 from Dalton Office Furniture Company, Invoice 4213, dated August 29; the terms are 30 days net.
	7	Purchased computers for $12,300 from Apex Office Machines, Inc., Invoice 9217, dated September 2, net due and payable in 60 days.
	10	Received Credit Memorandum 511 for $700 from Dalton Office Furniture Company; the amount is an allowance for damaged but usable desks purchased on Invoice 4213, dated August 29.
	16	Purchased file cabinets for $2,656 plus a freight charge of $134 from Davis Corporation, Invoice 8066, dated September 11; the terms are 30 days net.
	20	Purchased electronic desk calculators for $1,100 from Apex Office Machines, Inc., Invoice 11011, dated September 15, net due and payable in 60 days.
	23	Purchased bond paper and copy machine paper for $8,500 plus a freight charge of $100 from Brown Paper Company, Invoice 6498, dated September 18; the terms are 1/10, n/30.
	28	Received Credit Memorandum 312 for $980 from Apex Office Machines, Inc., for defective calculators that were returned; the calculators were originally purchased on Invoice 11011, dated September 15.
	30	Purchased office chairs for $3,940 plus a freight charge of $170 from Zenn Furniture, Inc., Invoice 696, dated September 25; the terms are 2/10, n/30.

Analyze: What total amount was recorded for purchases returns and allowances in the month of September? What percentage of total purchases does this represent?

Problem Set B

Journalizing credit purchases and purchases returns and allowances and posting to the general ledger.

◀ **Problem 8.1B**
Objectives 8-1, 8-2, 8-3

Mountain Ski Shop is a retail store that sells ski equipment and clothing. The firm's credit purchases and purchases returns and allowances during May 20X1 follow, along with the general ledger accounts used to record these transactions. The balance shown in *Accounts Payable* is for the beginning of May.

INSTRUCTIONS

1. Open the general ledger accounts and enter the balance of *Accounts Payable* for May 1, 20X1.
2. Record the transactions in a three-column purchases journal and in a general journal.
   Use 15 as the page number for the purchases journal and 38 as the page number for the general journal.

3. Post the entries from the general journal to the proper general ledger accounts.
4. Total and rule the purchases journal as of May 31.
5. Post the column totals from the purchases journal to the proper general ledger accounts.
6. Compute the net delivered cost of purchases of the firm for the month of May.

GENERAL LEDGER ACCOUNTS

205   Accounts Payable, $21,608 Cr.
501   Purchases
502   Freight In
503   Purchases Returns and Allowances

DATE	TRANSACTIONS
May 1	Purchased ski boots for $6,600 plus a freight charge of $120 from East Coast Snow Shop, Invoice 6572, dated April 28; the terms are 45 days net.
8	Purchased skis for $12,500 from May-Day Ski Shop, Invoice 4916, dated May 2; the terms are net payable in 30 days.
9	Received Credit Memorandum 155 for $1,050 from East Coast Snow Shop for damaged ski boots that were returned; the boots were originally purchased on Invoice 6572, dated April 28.
12	Purchased ski jackets for $5,200 from Fashion Ski Wear, Invoice 986, dated May 11, net due and payable in 60 days.
16	Purchased ski poles for $2,650 from May-Day Ski Shop, Invoice 5011, dated May 15; the terms are n/30.
22	Purchased ski pants for $3,160 from Winter Sports Clothing, Invoice 4019, dated May 16; the terms are 1/10, n/60.
28	Received Credit Memorandum 38 for $480 from May-Day Ski Shop for defective ski poles that were returned; the items were originally purchased on Invoice 5011, dated May 15.
31	Purchased sweaters for $3,630 plus a freight charge of $220 from Golden Skis & Clothing, Invoice 8354, dated May 27; the terms are 2/10, n/30.

(**Note:** Save your working papers for use in Problem 8.2B.)

Analyze: What total accounts payable were posted from the purchases journal to the general ledger for the month?

Problem 8.2B
Objectives 8-4, 8-6

▶ **Posting to the accounts payable ledger and preparing a schedule of accounts payable.**

This problem is a continuation of Problem 8.1B.

INSTRUCTIONS

1. Set up an accounts payable subsidiary ledger for Mountain Ski Shop. Open an account for each of the creditors listed below and enter the balances as of May 1, 20X1. Arrange the accounts payable ledger in alphabetical order.
2. Post the individual entries from the purchases journal and the general journal prepared in Problem 8.1B.
3. Prepare a schedule of accounts payable for May 31.

4. Check the total of the schedule of accounts payable against the balance of the *Accounts Payable* account in the general ledger. The two amounts should be equal.

Creditors		
Name	Terms	Balance
May-Day Ski Shop	n/30	$1,700
Fashion Ski Wear	n/60	8,720
Winter Sports Clothing	1/10, n/60	5,000
East Coast Snow Shop	n/45	6,188
Golden Skis & Clothing	2/10, n/30	

Analyze: What amount did Mountain Ski Shop owe to its supplier East Coast Snow Shop on May 31?

◀ **Problem 8.3B**
Objectives 8-1, 8-2, 8-3, 8-4, 8-5, 8-6

Journalizing credit purchases and purchases returns and allowances, computing the net delivered cost of goods, posting to the general ledger, posting to the accounts payable ledger, and preparing a schedule of accounts payable.

The Green Thumb is a retail store that sells garden equipment, furniture, and supplies. Its credit purchases and purchases returns and allowances for December are shown below. The general ledger accounts used to record these transactions are also provided. The balance shown is for the beginning of December 20X1.

INSTRUCTIONS
PART I
1. Open the general ledger accounts and enter the balance of *Accounts Payable* for December 1.
2. Record the transactions in a three-column purchases journal and in a general journal. Use 8 as the page number for the purchases journal and 20 as the page number for the general journal.
3. Post the entries from the general journal to the proper general ledger accounts.
4. Total, prove, and rule the purchases journal as of December 31.
5. Post the column totals from the purchases journal to the proper general ledger accounts.
6. Compute the net delivered cost of the firm's purchases for the month of December.

GENERAL LEDGER ACCOUNTS
205 Accounts Payable, $14,490 Cr.
501 Purchases
502 Freight In
503 Purchases Returns and Allowances

DATE		TRANSACTIONS
Dec.	1	Purchased lawn mowers for $7,780 plus a freight charge of $376 from PowerTools Inc., Invoice 2110, dated November 26, net due and payable in 45 days.
	5	Purchased outdoor chairs and tables for $6,200 plus a freight charge of $150 from Patio Dudes, Invoice 633, dated December 2; the terms are 1/15, n/60.
	9	Purchased grass seed for $1,148 from Summer Lawn Center, Invoice 1127, dated December 4; the terms are 30 days net.

(continued)

DATE	(cont.) TRANSACTIONS
16	Received Credit Memorandum 101 for $300 from Patio Dudes; the amount is an allowance for scratches on some of the chairs and tables originally purchased on Invoice 633, dated December 2.
19	Purchased fertilizer for $1,850 plus a freight charge of $126 from Summer Lawn Center, Invoice 1131, dated December 15; the terms are 30 days net.
21	Purchased garden hoses for $960 plus a freight charge of $96 from EXH Rubber Company, Invoice 8517, dated December 17; the terms are n/60.
28	Received Credit Memorandum 210 for $90 from EXH Rubber Company for damaged hoses that were returned; the goods were purchased on Invoice 8517, dated December 17.
31	Purchased lawn sprinkler systems for $4,200 plus a freight charge of $225 from Chatham Industries, Invoice 8819, dated December 26; the terms are 2/10, n/30.

INSTRUCTIONS
PART II

1. Set up an accounts payable subsidiary ledger for The Green Thumb. Open an account for each of the following creditors and enter the balances as of December 1.
2. Post the individual entries from the purchases journal and the general journal prepared in Part I.
3. Prepare a schedule of accounts payable for December 31.
4. Check the total of the schedule of accounts payable against the balance of the *Accounts Payable* account in the general ledger. The two amounts should be equal.

Creditors		
Name	Terms	Balance
Chatham Industries	2/10, n/30	$3,150
EXH Rubber Company	n/60	3,850
Patio Dudes	1/15, n/60	
PowerTools, Inc.	n/45	4,842
Summer Lawn Center	n/30	2,648

Analyze: By what amount did *Accounts Payable* increase during the month of December?

Problem 8.4B
Objectives 8-1, 8-2, 8-3, 8-4, 8-5, 8-6

▶ **Journalizing credit purchases and purchases returns and allowances, posting to the general ledger, posting to the accounts payable ledger, and preparing a schedule of accounts payable.**

Cards 'n More is a retail card, novelty, and business supply store. Its credit purchases and purchases returns and allowances for February 20X1 appear below. The general ledger accounts and the creditors' accounts in the accounts payable subsidiary ledger used to record these transactions are also provided. The balance shown is for the beginning of February.

INSTRUCTIONS

1. Open the general ledger accounts and enter the balance of *Accounts Payable* for February.
2. Open the creditors' accounts in the accounts payable subsidiary ledger and enter the balances for February 1, 20X1.

3. Record each transaction in the appropriate journal, purchases or general. Use page 4 in the purchases journal and page 12 in the general journal.
4. Post entries to the accounts payable subsidiary ledger daily.
5. Post entries in the general journal to the proper general ledger accounts at the end of the month.
6. Total and rule the purchases journal as of February 28.
7. Post the totals to the appropriate general ledger accounts.
8. Calculate the net delivered cost of purchases.
9. Prepare a schedule of accounts payable and compare the balance of the *Accounts Payable* control account with the schedule of accounts payable.

GENERAL LEDGER ACCOUNTS

203	Accounts Payable, $15,700 credit balance
501	Purchases
502	Freight In
503	Purchases Returns and Allowances

Creditors		
Name	**Terms**	**Balance**
Business Supplies, Inc.	n/30	$8,000
Holiday and Gift Cards	2/10, n/30	4,000
Packing and Shipping Center	2/10, n/30	3,700
Snazzy Business Cards	1/10, n/45	

DATE		TRANSACTIONS
Feb.	5	Purchased copy paper from Packing and Shipping Center for $2,100 plus $100 shipping charges on Invoice 502, dated February 2.
	8	Purchased assorted holiday cards from Holiday and Gift Cards on Invoice 2808, $1,950, dated February 5.
	12	Purchased five boxes of novelty items from Holiday and Gift Cards for a total cost of $900, Invoice 2904, dated February 8.
	13	Purchased a tray of cards from Snazzy Business Cards on Invoice 2013 for $620, dated February 9.
	19	Purchased forms from Business Supplies, Inc., for $1,975 plus shipping charges of $75 on Invoice 2019, dated February 16.
	20	One box of cards purchased on February 8 from Holiday and Gift Cards was water damaged. Received Credit Memorandum 102 for $180.
	21	Toner supplies are purchased from Business Supplies, Inc., for $3,600 plus shipping charges of $110, Invoice 1376, dated February 19.
	27	Received Credit Memorandum 118 for $130 from Holiday and Gift Cards as an allowance for damaged novelty items purchased on February 12.

Analyze: What total amount did Cards 'n More pay in freight charges during the month of February? What percentage of delivered cost of purchases does this represent?

Critical Thinking Problem 8.1

Merchandising: Sales and Purchases

Fashion Standards is a retail clothing store. Sales of merchandise and purchases of goods on account for January 20X1, the first month of operations, appear below.

INSTRUCTIONS

1. Record the purchases of goods on account on page 1 of a three-column purchases journal.
2. Record the sales of merchandise on account on page 1 of a sales journal.
3. Post the entries from the purchases journal and the sales journal to the individual accounts in the accounts payable and accounts receivable subsidiary ledgers. Use the following account numbers:

    Accounts Receivable 111

    Accounts Payable 205

    Sales Tax Payable 231

    Sales 401

    Purchases 501

    Freight In 502

    All customers have n/30 credit terms.

4. Total, prove, and rule the journals as of January 31.
5. Post the column totals from the special journals to the proper general ledger accounts.
6. Prepare a schedule of accounts payable for January 31.
7. Prepare a schedule of accounts receivable for January 31.

		PURCHASES OF GOODS ON ACCOUNT
Jan.	3	Purchased dresses for $4,500 plus a freight charge of $120 from Fashion Expo, Invoice 101, dated December 26; the terms are net 30 days.
	5	Purchased handbags for $3,480 plus a freight charge of $89 from Tru Totes & Co., Invoice 223, dated December 28; the terms are 2/10, n/30.
	7	Purchased blouses for $3,000 plus a freight charge of $75 from Extreme Fashions, Invoice 556, dated January 3; the terms are 2/10, n/30.
	9	Purchased casual pants for $2,360 from Comfy Casuals, Invoice 110, dated January 5; terms are n/30.
	12	Purchased business suits for $6,400 plus a freight charge of $150 from Professional Wears, Invoice 104, dated January 9; the terms are 2/10, n/30.
	18	Purchased shoes for $3,120 plus freight of $80 from City Walks, Invoice 118, dated January 14; the terms are n/60.
	25	Purchased hosiery for $1,025 from Silky Legs Express, Invoice 1012, dated January 20; the terms are 2/10, n/30.
	29	Purchased scarves and gloves for $1,600 from Comfy Casuals, Invoice 315, dated January 26; the terms are n/30.
	31	Purchased party dresses for $7,500 plus a freight charge of $250 from Special Occasions Dress Shop, Invoice 1044, dated January 27; the terms are 2/10, n/30.

		SALES OF MERCHANDISE ON ACCOUNT
Jan.	4	Sold two dresses to Vivian Cho; issued Sales Slip 101 for $600 plus $48 sales tax.
	5	Sold a handbag to Dina Bates; issued Sales Slip 102 for $525 plus $42 sales tax.
	6	Sold four blouses to Julia Adams; issued Sales Slip 103 for $400 plus $32 sales tax.
	10	Sold casual pants and a blouse to Cheryl Scott; issued Sales Slip 104 for $350 plus $28 sales tax.
	14	Sold a business suit to Alleen De Revere; issued Sales Slip 105 for $500 plus $40 sales tax.
	17	Sold hosiery, shoes, and gloves to Sasha Ramirez; issued Sales Slip 106 for $625 plus $50 sales tax.
	21	Sold dresses and scarves to Elaine Patterson; issued Sales Slip 107 for $1,500 plus $120 sales tax.
	24	Sold a business suit to Andrea Aguilar; issued Sales Slip 108 for $500 plus $40 sales tax.
	25	Sold shoes to Tracy Mai; issued Sales Slip 109 for $300 plus $24 sales tax.
	29	Sold a casual pants set to Toni Garcia; issued Sales Slip 110 for $600 plus $48 sales tax.
	31	Sold a dress and handbag to Linda Martin; issued Sales Slip 111 for $950 plus $76 sales tax.

Analyze: What is the net delivered cost of purchases for the month of January?

Critical Thinking Problem 8.2

Internal Control

Celeste Renard, owner of Sensual Linens Shop, was preparing checks for payment of the current month's purchase invoices when she realized that there were two invoices from Passionate Linens Company, each for the purchase of 100 red, heart-imprinted king-size linen sets. Renard thinks that Passionate Linens Company must have billed Sensual Linens Shop twice for the same shipment because she knows the shop would not have needed two orders for 100 red linen sets within a month.

1. How can Renard determine whether Passionate Linens Company billed Sensual Linens Shop in error or whether Sensual Linens Shop placed two identical orders for red, heart-imprinted linen sets?

2. If two orders were placed, how can Renard prevent duplicate purchases from happening in the future?

BUSINESS CONNECTIONS

Cash Management

1. Why should management be concerned about paying its invoices on a timely basis?
2. Why is it important for a firm to maintain a satisfactory credit rating?

Managerial | FOCUS

3. Suppose you are the new controller of a small but growing company and you find that the firm has a policy of paying cash for all purchases of goods even though it could obtain credit. The president of the company does not like the idea of having debts, but the vice president thinks this is a poor business policy that will hurt the firm in the future. The president has asked your opinion. Would you agree with the president or the vice president? Why?

4. How would excessive investment in merchandise harm a business?

5. How can good internal controls over purchases protect a firm from fraud and errors and from excessive investment in merchandise?

6. Why should management be concerned about internal controls over purchases?

Internal Control and FRAUD PREVENTION

Adding New Vendors

Anna Abraham is the accounts payable clerk for Jiffy Delivery Service. This company runs 10 branches in the San Diego area. The company pays for a variety of expenses. Anna writes the checks for each of the vendors and the controller signs the checks. Anna has decided she needs a raise and the controller has told her to wait for six months. Anna has devised a plan to get a raise on her own. She creates a new vendor for her friend's business with the name John's Car Detailing. She also creates two purchase orders for car detailing service from John's for $75 and $70. She writes checks to John's Car Detailing to pay these invoices. She knows the controller will sign all checks only looking at the checks over $100. She delivers the checks to John, who will deposit the checks in his bank account. John then writes a check to her for $145. Is this a good way for Anna to obtain a raise? Is it an ethical practice? Eventually what will be the effect of her actions? What can the company do to prevent this type of behavior?

Financial Statement ANALYSIS

Home Depot

Income Statement

The following financial statement excerpt is taken from the *2018 Annual Report (for the fiscal year ended February 3, 2019)* for The Home Depot, Inc.

Consolidated Statements of Earnings

(In millions)	For the fiscal year ended	
	February 3, 2019	January 28, 2018
Net Sales	$108,203	$100,904
Cost of Sales	71,043	66,548
Gross Profit	$37,160	$34,356

1. The Cost of Sales amount on The Home Depot, Inc., consolidated statements of earnings represents the net cost of the goods that were sold for the period. For the year ended February 3, 2019, what percentage of net sales was the cost of sales? For the year ended January 28, 2018?

2. What factors might affect a merchandising company's cost of sales from one period to another?

TEAMWORK

Payment Terms

A company needs to develop an objective for paying bills. Does it want to stretch its cash flow as far as it can? Does it want to have a good reputation of always paying bills on time? Does it want to be sure to get paid by its customers before they pay their vendors? In a group, discuss what would be the best payment terms to use for each objective and its impact on the company.

Answers to Comprehensive Self Review

1. A contra cost of goods sold account.
2. A price reduction offered to encourage quick payment of invoices by customers.
3. To accumulate freight charges paid for purchases.
4. The purchase requisition is used by a sales department to notify the purchasing department of the items wanted. The purchase order is prepared by the purchasing department to order the necessary goods at an appropriate price from the selected supplier.
5. The receiving report shows the quantity of goods received and the condition of the goods. The invoice shows quantities and prices; it is the document from which checks are prepared in payment of purchases.

Cash Receipts, Cash Payments, and Banking Procedures

Chapter 9

www.chase.com

JPMorgan Chase & Co. (Chase) is a leading global financial services firm and one of the largest banking institutions in the United States, with operations worldwide. Chase had approximately $2.5 trillion in assets and $255.7 billion in equity as of December 31, 2017. Under the J.P. Morgan and Chase brands, the company serves millions of customers in the United States and many of the world's largest corporate and institutional clients.

A major strategy for the Consumer and Community Banking Division has been to build lifetime, engaged relationships with customers. According to Gordon Smith, co-president and chief operating officer, JPMorgan Chase & Co., and CEO, Consumer & Community Banking, Chase made several improvements around the customer experience in 2017, including facial recognition in its app, a fully mobile bank pilot (Finn), real-time payments using Chase QuickPay^{SM} with Zelle, and a simpler online application for business banking customers.

East pop/Shutterstock

Chase online banking allows businesses to view account activity, pay bills, transfer funds, receive electronic payments from customers, and view monthly statements from a personal computer.

In addition to online banking via personal computer, the Chase mobile app allows customers to view account balances and history, scan and deposit checks electronically, and pay bills with a mobile device. Chase also offers its customers various account alerts, including e-mail or text alerts when certain transactions exceed a customer-set limit. The number of Chase customers using mobile devices has more than doubled in recent years.

thinking critically
What types of payments could be processed by a small business using electronic banking?

LEARNING OBJECTIVES

- **9-1** Record cash receipts in a cash receipts journal.
- **9-2** Account for cash short or over.
- **9-3** Post from the cash receipts journal to subsidiary and general ledgers.
- **9-4** Record cash payments in a cash payments journal.
- **9-5** Post from the cash payments journal to subsidiary and general ledgers.
- **9-6** Demonstrate a knowledge of procedures for a petty cash fund.
- **9-7** Demonstrate a knowledge of internal control procedures for cash.
- **9-8** Demonstrate knowledge of how to write a check, endorse checks, prepare a bank deposit slip, and maintain a checkbook balance.
- **9-9** Reconcile the monthly bank statement.
- **9-10** Record any adjusting entries required from the bank reconciliation.
- **9-11** Understand how businesses use online banking to manage cash activities.
- **9-12** *Appendix:* Record transactions for a retailer using the perpetual inventory system.
- **9-13** Define the accounting terms new to this chapter.

NEW TERMS

bank reconciliation statement
blank endorsement
bonding
canceled check
cash
cash payments journal
cash receipts journal
cash register proof
Cash Short or Over account
check
credit memorandum
debit memorandum
deposit in transit
deposit slip
dishonored (NSF) check
drawee

drawer
electronic funds transfer (EFT)
endorsement
full endorsement
negotiable
outstanding checks
payee
petty cash analysis sheet
petty cash fund
petty cash voucher
postdated check
promissory note
restrictive endorsement
service charge
statement of account

Section 1

SECTION OBJECTIVES	TERMS TO LEARN
9-1 Record cash receipts in a cash receipts journal. **WHY IT'S IMPORTANT** The cash receipts journal is an efficient option for recording incoming cash. **9-2** *Account for cash short or over.* **WHY IT'S IMPORTANT** Discrepancies in cash are a possible indication that cash is mismanaged. **9-3** Post from the cash receipts journal to subsidiary and general ledgers. **WHY IT'S IMPORTANT** The subsidiary and general ledgers must hold accurate, up-to-date information about cash transactions.	cash cash receipts journal cash register proof *Cash Short or Over* account petty cash fund promissory note statement of account

Cash Receipts

Cash is the business asset that is most easily lost, mishandled, or even stolen. A well-managed business has careful procedures for controlling cash and recording cash transactions.

Cash Transactions

In accounting, the term **cash** is used for currency, coins, checks, money orders, and funds on deposit in a bank. Most cash transactions involve checks and electronic transfers of funds.

Cash Receipts

The type of cash receipts depends on the nature of the business. Supermarkets receive checks as well as currency and coins. Department stores receive checks in the mail, or by electronic payment, from charge account customers. Cash received by wholesalers is usually in the form of checks.

Cash Payments

For safety and convenience, most businesses make payments by check. Sometimes a limited number of transactions are paid with currency and coins. The **petty cash fund** is used to handle payments involving small amounts of money, such as postage stamps, delivery charges, and minor purchases of office supplies. Some businesses maintain a fund to provide cash for business-related travel and entertainment expenses.

The Cash Receipts Journal

To improve the accounting for cash receipts, many businesses use a special **cash receipts journal.** The cash receipts journal simplifies the recording of transactions and eliminates repetition in posting.

FIGURE 9.1 Cash Receipts Journal

CASH RECEIPTS JOURNAL   PAGE __1__

DATE	DESCRIPTION	POST. REF.	ACCOUNTS RECEIVABLE CREDIT	SALES TAX PAYABLE CREDIT	SALES CREDIT	OTHER ACCOUNTS CREDIT			CASH DEBIT
						ACCOUNT NAME	POST. REF.	AMOUNT	
20X1									
Jan. 7	Ann Anh		702 00						702 00
8	Cash Sales			360 00	4 500 00				4 860 00
11	Vickie Bowman		270 00						270 00
12	Investment					M. Ferraro, Capital		15 000 00	15 000 00
13	Barbara Coe		540 00						540 00
15	Cash Sales			384 00	4 800 00	Cash Short/Over		(18 00)	5 166 00
16	Alma Sanchez		108 00						108 00
17	Cash Refund					Supplies		75 00	75 00
22	Fred Wu		400 00						400 00
22	Cash Sales			400 00	5 000 00				5 400 00
29	Cash Sales			216 00	2 700 00	Cash Short/Over		16 00	2 932 00
31	Kim Ramirez		108 00						108 00
31	Mesia Davis		275 00						275 00
31	Cash Sales			440 00	5 500 00				5 940 00
31	Note Collection/					Notes Receivable		800 00	
	Stacee Fairley					Interest Income		36 00	836 00

Recording Transactions in the Cash Receipts Journal

The format of the cash receipts journal varies according to the needs of each business. Figure 9.1 shows the cash receipts journal for Maxx-Out Sporting Goods, which has two major sources of cash receipts: checks from credit customers who are making payments on account and currency and coins from cash sales.

The cash receipts journal has separate columns for the accounts frequently used when recording cash receipts. There are columns for:

- debits to *Cash,*
- credits to *Accounts Receivable* for payments received on account,
- credits to *Sales* and *Sales Tax Payable* for cash sales.

At the end of the month, the totals of these columns are posted to the general ledger.

Notice the Other Accounts Credit section, which is for entries that do not fit into one of the special columns. Entries in the Other Accounts Credit section are individually posted to the general ledger.

Cash Sales and Sales Taxes Maxx-Out Sporting Goods uses a cash register to record cash sales and to store currency and coins. As each transaction is entered, the cash register prints a receipt for the customer. It also records the sale and the sales tax on an audit tape locked inside the machine. At the end of the day, when the machine is cleared, the cash register prints the transaction totals on the audit tape. The manager of the store removes the audit tape, and a cash register proof is prepared. The **cash register proof** is a verification that the amount in the cash register agrees with the amount shown on the audit tape. The cash register proof is used to record cash sales and sales tax in the cash receipts journal. The currency and coins are deposited in the firm's bank.

Refer to Figure 9.1, the cash receipts journal for Maxx-Out Sporting Goods. To keep it simple, it shows weekly, rather than daily, cash sales entries. Look at the January 8 entry. The steps to record the January 8 sales follow:

1. Enter the sales tax collected, $360.00, in the Sales Tax Payable Credit column.
2. Enter the sales, $4,500.00, in the Sales Credit column.

>> **9-1 OBJECTIVE**
Record cash receipts in a cash receipts journal.

ABOUT ACCOUNTING

Automated Teller Machines

The first ATM in the United States was installed by Chemical Bank on September 2, 1969. According to PaymentsSource, there are now more than 100,000 bank-owned ATMs in the U.S. alone.

3. Enter the cash received, $4,860.00, in the Cash Debit column.
4. Confirm that total credits equal total debits ($360.00 + $4,500.00 = $4,860.00).

>> **9-2 OBJECTIVE**
Account for cash short or over.

Cash Short or Over Occasionally, errors occur when making change. When errors happen, the cash in the cash register is either more than or less than the cash listed on the audit tape. When cash in the register is more than the audit tape, cash is over. When cash in the register is less than the audit tape, cash is short. Cash tends to be short more often than over because customers are more likely to notice and complain if they receive too little change.

Record short or over amounts in the **Cash Short or Over account.** If the account has a credit balance, there is an overage, which is treated as revenue. If the account has a debit balance, there is a shortage, which is treated as an expense.

Figure 9.1 shows how cash overages and shortages appear in the cash receipts journal. Look at the January 29 entry. Cash sales were $2,700. Sales tax collected was $216. The cash drawer was over $16. Overages are recorded as credits. Notice that the account name and the overage are entered in the Other Accounts Credit section.

Now look at the January 15 entry. This time the cash register was short. Shortages are recorded as debits. Debits are not the normal balance of the Other Accounts Credit column, so the debit entry is circled. The debit entry may also be enclosed in parentheses.

Businesses that have frequent entries for cash shortages and overages add a Cash Short or Over column to the cash receipts journal.

important!

Cash Short or Over

Expect errors when employees make change, but investigate large and frequent errors. They may indicate dishonesty or incompetence, neither of which is a good attribute in employees.

Cash Received on Account Maxx-Out Sporting Goods makes sales on account and bills customers once a month. It sends a **statement of account** that shows the transactions during the month and the balance owed. Customers are asked to pay within 30 days of receiving the statement. Checks from credit customers are entered in the cash receipts journal, and then the checks are deposited in the bank.

Figure 9.1 shows how cash received on account is recorded. Look at the January 7 entry for Ann Anh. The check amount is entered in the Accounts Receivable Credit and the Cash Debit columns.

Cash Discounts on Sales Maxx-Out Sporting Goods, like most retail businesses, does not offer cash discounts. However, many wholesale businesses offer cash discounts to customers who pay within a certain time period. For example, a wholesaler may offer a 1 percent discount if the customer pays within 10 days. To the wholesaler this is a *sales discount.* Sales discounts are recorded when the payment is received. Sales discounts are recorded in a contra revenue account, **Sales Discounts.** Businesses with many sales discounts add a Sales Discounts Debit column to the cash receipts journal.

Additional Investment by the Owner Figure 9.1 shows that on January 12, owner Max Ferraro invested an additional $15,000 in Maxx-Out Sporting Goods. He intends to use the money to expand the product line. The account name and amount are entered in the Other Accounts Credit section. The debit is entered in the Cash Debit column.

Receipt of a Cash Refund Sometimes a business receives a cash refund for supplies, equipment, or other assets that are returned to the supplier. Figure 9.1 shows that on January 17, Maxx-Out Sporting Goods received a $75 cash refund for supplies that were returned to the seller. The account name and amount are entered in the Other Accounts Credit section. The debit is entered in the Cash Debit column.

Collection of a Promissory Note and Interest A **promissory note** is a written promise to pay a specified amount of money on a certain date. Most notes require that interest is paid at a specified rate. Businesses use promissory notes to extend credit for some sales transactions.

Sometimes promissory notes are used to replace an accounts receivable balance when the account is overdue. For example, on July 31 Maxx-Out Sporting Goods accepted a six-month promissory note from Stacee Fairley, who owed $800 on account (see Figure 9.2). Fairley had asked for more time to pay his balance. Maxx-Out Sporting Goods agreed to grant more time if Fairley signed a promissory note with 9 percent annual interest. The note provides more legal protection than an account receivable. The interest is compensation for the delay in receiving payment.

Cash Receipts, Cash Payments, and Banking Procedures CHAPTER 9 283

FIGURE 9.2

A Promissory Note

```
$ 800.00                                          July 31, 20X0

  Six Months       AFTER DATE  I   PROMISE TO PAY

TO THE ORDER OF  Maxx-Out Sporting Goods

  Eight Hundred and no/100                              DOLLARS

PAYABLE AT  First Texas Bank

VALUE RECEIVED with interest at 9%

NO. 30    DUE  January 31, 20X1              Stacee Fairley
```

On the date of the transaction, July 31, Maxx-Out Sporting Goods recorded a general journal entry to increase notes receivable and to decrease accounts receivable for $800. The asset account **Notes Receivable** was debited and **Accounts Receivable** was credited.

	GENERAL JOURNAL			PAGE 16	
DATE	DESCRIPTION	POST. REF.	DEBIT	CREDIT	
20X0					1
July 31	Notes Receivable	109	800 00		2
	Accounts Receivable/Stacee Fairley	111 ✓		800 00	3
	Received a 6-month, 9% note from				4
	Stacee Fairley to replace open account				5

On January 31, the due date of the note, Maxx-Out Sporting Goods received a check for $836 from Fairley. This sum covered the amount of the note ($800) and the interest owed for the six-month period ($36). Figure 9.1 shows the entry in the cash receipts journal. The account names, **Notes Receivable** and **Interest Income,** and the amounts are entered on two lines in the Other Accounts Credit section. The debit is in the Cash Debit column.

Posting from the Cash Receipts Journal

During the month, the amounts recorded in the Accounts Receivable Credit column are posted to individual accounts in the accounts receivable subsidiary ledger. Similarly, the amounts that appear in the Other Accounts Credit column are posted individually to the general ledger accounts during the month. The "CR1" posting references in the *Cash Short or Over* general ledger account below show that the entries appear on the first page of the cash receipts journal.

>> **9-3 OBJECTIVE**

Post from the cash receipts journal to subsidiary and general ledgers.

ACCOUNT Cash Short or Over					ACCOUNT NO. 617	
					BALANCE	
DATE	DESCRIPTION	POST. REF.	DEBIT	CREDIT	DEBIT	CREDIT
20X1						
Jan. 15		CR1	18 00		18 00	
29		CR1		16 00	2 00	

Posting the Column Totals At the end of the month, the cash receipts journal is totaled and the equality of debits and credits is proved.

Proof of Cash Receipts Journal

	Debits
Cash Debit column	$42,612.00
	Credits
Accounts Receivable Credit column	$ 2,403.00
Sales Tax Payable Credit column	1,800.00
Sales Credit column	22,500.00
Other Accounts Credit column	15,909.00
Total Credits	$42,612.00

Figure 9.3 shows the cash receipts journal after all posting is completed.

When the cash receipts journal has been proved, rule the columns and post the totals to the general ledger. Figure 9.4 shows how to post from the cash receipts journal to the general ledger accounts.

To post a column total to a general ledger account, enter "CR1" in the Posting Reference column to show that the entry is from the first page of the cash receipts journal. Enter the column total in the general ledger account Debit or Credit column. Figure 9.4 shows the entries to **Accounts Receivable** (1), **Sales Tax Payable** (2), **Sales** (3), and **Cash** (4). Compute the new balance for each account and enter it in the Balance Debit or Balance Credit column.

Enter the general ledger account numbers under the column totals on the cash receipts journal. The (X) in the Other Accounts Credit Amount column indicates that the individual amounts were posted to the general ledger, so the total of the column is not posted.

Posting to the Accounts Receivable Ledger

To keep customer balances current, accountants post entries from the Accounts Receivable Credit column to the customers'

FIGURE 9.3 Posted Cash Receipts Journal

CASH RECEIPTS JOURNAL   PAGE 1

DATE		DESCRIPTION	POST. REF.	ACCOUNTS RECEIVABLE CREDIT	SALES TAX PAYABLE CREDIT	SALES CREDIT	OTHER ACCOUNTS CREDIT			CASH DEBIT
							ACCOUNT NAME	POST. REF.	AMOUNT	
20X1										
Jan.	7	Ann Anh	✓	702 00						702 00
	8	Cash Sales			360 00	4 500 00				4 860 00
	11	Vickie Bowman	✓	270 00						270 00
	12	Investment					M. Ferraro, Capital	301	15 000 00	15 000 00
	13	Barbara Coe	✓	540 00						540 00
	15	Cash Sales			384 00	4 800 00	Cash Short/Over	617	18 00	5 166 00
	16	Alma Sanchez	✓	108 00						108 00
	17	Cash Refund					Supplies	129	75 00	75 00
	22	Fred Wu	✓	400 00						400 00
	22	Cash Sales			400 00	5 000 00				5 400 00
	29	Cash Sales			216 00	2 700 00	Cash Short/Over	617	16 00	2 932 00
	31	Kim Ramirez	✓	108 00						108 00
	31	Mesia Davis	✓	275 00						275 00
	31	Cash Sales			440 00	5 500 00				5 940 00
	31	Note Collection/					Notes Receivable	109	800 00	
		Stacee Fairley					Interest Income	491	36 00	836 00
		Totals		2 403 00	1 800 00	22 500 00			15 909 00	42 612 00
				(111)	(231)	(401)			(X)	(101)

FIGURE 9.4 Posting from the Cash Receipts Journal

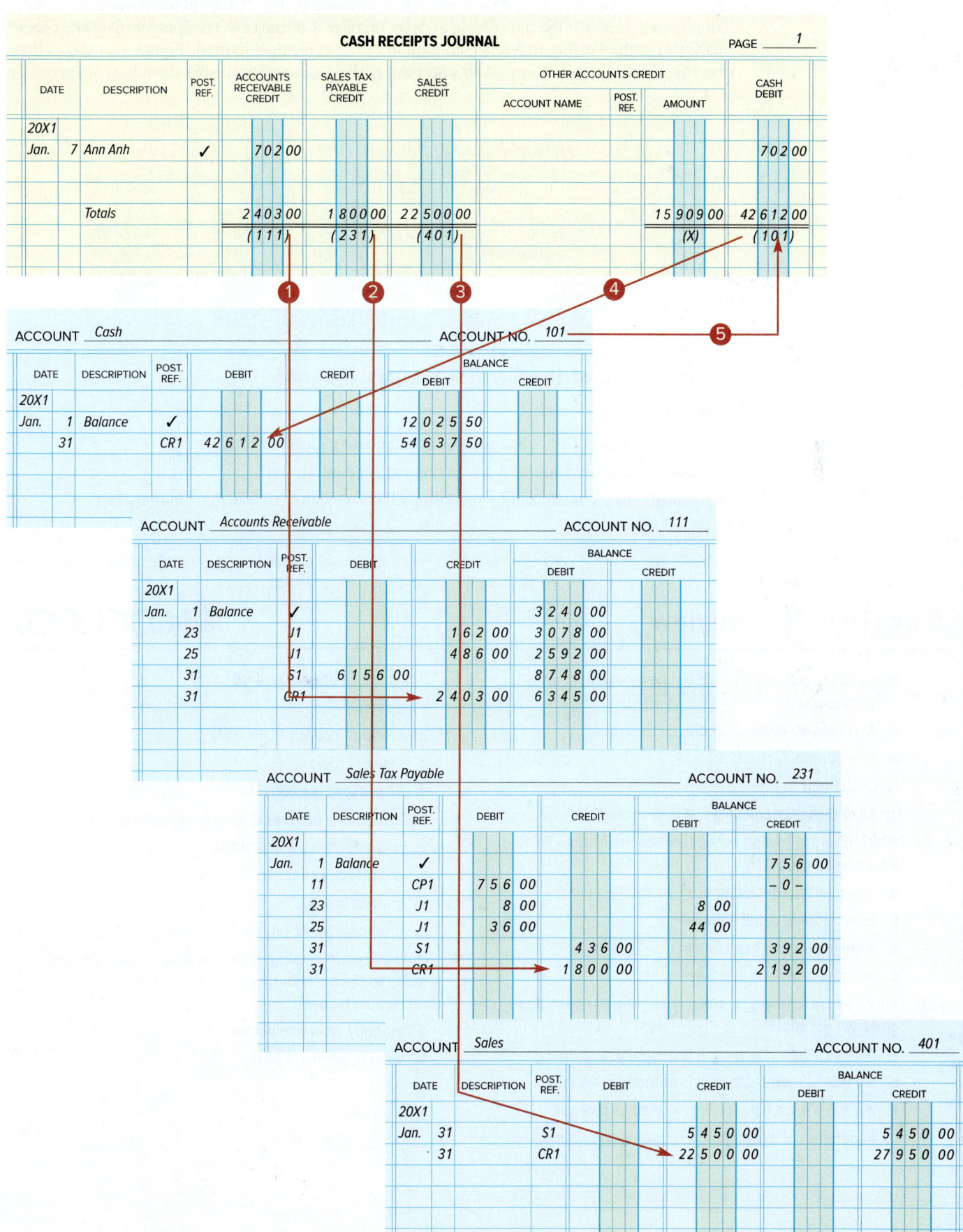

accounts in the accounts receivable subsidiary ledger daily. For example, on January 7, $702 was posted to Ann Anh's account in the subsidiary ledger. The "CR1" in the Posting Reference column indicates that the transaction appears on page 1 of the cash receipts journal. The check mark (✓) in the Posting Reference column in the cash receipts journal (Figure 9.4) shows that the amount was posted to Ann Anh's account in the accounts receivable subsidiary ledger.

NAME Ann Anh
ADDRESS 8913 South Hampton Road, Dallas, Texas 75232-6002

DATE		DESCRIPTION	POST. REF.	DEBIT	CREDIT	BALANCE
20X1						
Jan.	1	Balance	✓			432 00
	3	Sales Slip 1101	S1	702 00		1134 00
	7		CR1		702 00	432 00
	31	Sales Slip 1110	S1	267 50		699 50

Advantages of the Cash Receipts Journal

The cash receipts journal:

- saves time and effort when recording and posting cash receipts,
- allows for the division of work among the accounting staff,
- strengthens the audit trail by recording all cash receipts transactions in one place.

Section 1 Review

1. Which of the following would not be a column in a cash receipts journal?
   a. Accounts Receivable Credit
   b. Sales Credit
   c. Cash Debit
   d. All of these are columns in a cash receipts journal.

2. Which of the following best describes the *Notes Receivable* account?
   a. asset, normal debit balance
   b. asset, normal credit balance
   c. revenue, normal debit balance
   d. revenue, normal credit balance

3. Which of the following is true concerning the *Cash Short and Over* account?
   a. If it has a credit balance, it is treated as expense.
   b. If it has a credit balance, it is treated as revenue.
   c. If it has a debit balance, it is treated as revenue.
   d. Regardless of its balance, it is treated as expense.

4. Which items are considered cash?
   a. currency
   b. funds on deposit in the bank
   c. money orders
   d. All of these are correct.

5. Collection of a note receivable is recorded in the
   a. accounts receivable journal.
   b. cash receipts journal.
   c. general journal.
   d. promissory note journal.

6. How often are postings from the cash receipts journal made to the customers' accounts in the accounts receivable ledger?
   a. monthly, at end of month
   b. weekly, at end of week
   c. daily
   d. annually

Section 2

SECTION OBJECTIVES	TERMS TO LEARN
>> 9-4 Record cash payments in a cash payments journal. **WHY IT'S IMPORTANT** The cash payments journal is an efficient option for recording payments by check. >> 9-5 Post from the cash payments journal to subsidiary and general ledgers. **WHY IT'S IMPORTANT** The subsidiary and general ledgers must hold accurate, up-to-date information about cash transactions. >> 9-6 Demonstrate a knowledge of procedures for a petty cash fund. **WHY IT'S IMPORTANT** Businesses use the petty cash fund to pay for small operating expenditures. >> 9-7 Demonstrate a knowledge of internal control procedures for cash. **WHY IT'S IMPORTANT** Internal controls safeguard business assets.	bonding cash payments journal petty cash analysis sheet petty cash voucher

Cash Payments

A good system of internal control requires that payments be made by check. In a good internal control system, duties concerning custody of cash and checks are separated from recording cash or checks. For example, one employee approves payments, another employee prepares the checks, and another employee records the transactions.

The Cash Payments Journal

Unless a business has just a few cash payments each month, the process of recording these transactions in the general journal is time-consuming. The **cash payments journal** is a special journal used to record transactions involving the payment of cash.

Recording Transactions in the Cash Payments Journal

Refer to Figure 9.5 for Maxx-Out Sporting Goods' cash payments journal. Notice that there are separate columns for the accounts frequently used when recording cash payments— *Cash, Accounts Payable,* and *Purchases Discounts.* At the end of the month, the totals of these columns are posted to the general ledger.

The Other Accounts Debit section is for entries that do not fit into one of the special columns. Entries in the Other Accounts Debit section are individually posted to the general ledger.

Payments for Expenses Businesses write checks for a variety of expenses each month. In January, Maxx-Out Sporting Goods issued checks for rent, electricity, telephone service,

>> **9-4 OBJECTIVE**
Record cash payments in a cash payments journal.

FIGURE 9.5 Cash Payments Journal

CASH PAYMENTS JOURNAL PAGE 1

DATE	CK. NO.	DESCRIPTION	POST. REF.	ACCOUNTS PAYABLE DEBIT	OTHER ACCOUNTS DEBIT — ACCOUNT TITLE	POST. REF.	AMOUNT	PURCHASES DISCOUNTS CREDIT	CASH CREDIT
20X1									
Jan. 3	111	January rent			Rent Expense		1500 00		1500 00
10	112	Store fixtures			Store Equipment		2400 00		2400 00
11	113	Tax remittance			Sales Tax Payable		756 00		756 00
11	114	World of Sports		3935 00				78 70	3856 30
13	115	Active Designs		2865 00				57 30	2807 70
14	116	Store Supplies			Supplies		900 00		900 00
15	117	Withdrawal			M. Ferraro, Drawing		3000 00		3000 00
17	118	Electric bill			Utilities Expense		318 00		318 00
17	119	The Sports Warehouse		4250 00					4250 00
21	120	Telephone bill			Telephone Expense		276 00		276 00
25	121	Newspaper ad			Advertising Expense		840 00		840 00
27	122	International Sportsman		1000 00					1000 00
30	123	Active Designs		1135 00					1135 00
31	124	World of Sports		565 00					565 00
31	125	January payroll			Salaries Expense		4950 00		4950 00
31	126	Purchase of goods			Purchases		3200 00		3200 00
31	127	Freight charge			Freight In		175 00		175 00
31	128	Cash refund			Sales Returns & Allow.		160 00		
					Sales Tax Payable		12 80		172 80
31	129	Note Paid to			Notes Payable		6000 00		
		Metroplex Equip. Co.			Interest Expense		300 00		6300 00
31	130	Establish Petty Cash fund			Petty Cash Fund		175 00		175 00
		TOTALS		13750 00			24962 80	136 00	38576 80

advertising, and salaries. Refer to the January 3 entry for rent expense in Figure 9.5. Notice that the account name and amount are entered in the Other Accounts Debit section. The credit is in the Cash Credit column.

Payments on Account Merchandising businesses usually make numerous payments on account for goods that were purchased on credit. If there is no cash discount, the entry in the cash payments journal is a debit to **Accounts Payable** and a credit to **Cash**. For an example of a payment without a discount, refer to the January 27 entry for International Sportsman in Figure 9.5.

Purchases Discounts is a contra cost of goods sold account that appears in the Cost of Goods Sold section of the income statement. Purchases discounts are subtracted from purchases to obtain net purchases.

For an example of a payment with a discount, refer to the January 13 entry for Active Designs in Figure 9.5. Maxx-Out Sporting Goods takes a 2 percent discount for paying within the discount period ($2,865 × 0.02 = $57.30). When there is a cash discount, three elements must be recorded:

- Debit **Accounts Payable** for the invoice amount, $2,865.
- Credit **Purchases Discounts** for the amount of the discount, $57.30.
- Credit **Cash** for the amount of cash paid, $2,807.70.

---

recall

Discount Terms

The terms 2/10, n/30 mean that if payment is made within 10 days, the customer can take a 2 percent discount. Otherwise, payment in full is due in 30 days.

> Debit cards (also called check cards) look like credit cards or ATM (automated teller machine) cards but operate like cash or a personal check. In this context, debit means "subtract" so when you use your debit card, you are subtracting your money from your bank account. Funds on deposit with a bank represent a liability from the bank's perspective. By debiting accounts when depositors use their debit cards, the bank reduces the depositors' account balances and also reduces the bank's liabilities to depositors. Debit cards are accepted almost everywhere including grocery stores, retail stores, gasoline stations, and restaurants. Debit cards are popular because they offer an alternative to carrying checks or cash. Transactions completed using a debit card will appear on your bank statement.

Cash Purchases of Equipment and Supplies Businesses use cash to purchase equipment, supplies, and other assets. These transactions are recorded in the cash payments journal. In January, Maxx-Out Sporting Goods issued checks for store fixtures and store supplies. Refer to the entries on January 10 and 14 in Figure 9.5. Notice that the account names and amounts appear in the Other Accounts Debit section. The credits are recorded in the Cash Credit column.

Payment of Taxes Retail businesses collect sales tax from their customers. Periodically, the sales tax is remitted to the taxing authority. Refer to the entry on January 11 in Figure 9.5. Maxx-Out Sporting Goods issued a check for $756 to pay the December sales tax. Notice that the account name and amount appear in the Other Accounts Debit section. The credit is in the Cash Credit column.

Cash Purchases of Merchandise Most merchandising businesses buy their goods on credit. Occasionally, purchases are made for cash. These purchases are recorded in the cash payments journal. Refer to the January 31 entry for the purchase of goods in Figure 9.5.

Payment of Freight Charges Freight charges on purchases of goods are handled in two ways. In some cases, the seller pays the freight charge and then includes it on the invoice. This method was covered in Chapter 8. The other method is for the buyer to pay the transportation company when the goods arrive. The buyer issues a check for the freight charge and records it in the cash payments journal. Refer to the entry on January 31 in Figure 9.5. The account name and amount appear in the Other Accounts Debit section. The credit is in the Cash Credit column.

Payment of a Cash Refund When a customer purchases goods for cash and later returns them or receives an allowance, the customer is usually given a cash refund. Refer to the January 31 entry in Figure 9.5. Maxx-Out Sporting Goods issued a check for $172.80 to a customer who returned a defective item. When there is a cash refund, three elements are recorded:

- Debit *Sales Returns and Allowances* for the amount of the purchase, $160.00.
- Debit *Sales Tax Payable* for the sales tax, $12.80.
- Credit *Cash* for the amount of cash paid, $172.80.

Notice that the debits in the Other Accounts Debit section appear on two lines because two general ledger accounts are debited.

Payment of a Promissory Note and Interest A promissory note can be issued to settle an overdue account or to obtain goods, equipment, or other property. For example, on August 4 Maxx-Out Sporting Goods issued a 180-day promissory note for $6,000 to purchase store fixtures from Metroplex Equipment Company. The note had an interest rate of 10 percent. Maxx-Out Sporting Goods recorded this transaction in the general journal by debiting *Store Equipment* and crediting *Notes Payable,* a liability account.

	GENERAL JOURNAL			PAGE 16
DATE	DESCRIPTION	POST. REF.	DEBIT	CREDIT
20X0				
Aug. 4	Store Equipment	131	6 000 00	
	Notes Payable	201		6 000 00
	Issued a 6-month, 10% note to			
	Metroplex Equipment Company for			
	purchase of new store fixtures			

On January 31, Maxx-Out Sporting Goods issued a check for $6,300 in payment of the note, $6,000, and the interest, $300. This transaction was recorded in the cash payments journal in Figure 9.5.

- Debit *Notes Payable,* $6,000.
- Debit *Interest Expense,* $300.
- Credit *Cash,* $6,300.

Notice that the debits in the Other Accounts Debit section appear on two lines.

>> **9-5 OBJECTIVE**

Post from the cash payments journal to subsidiary and general ledgers.

Posting from the Cash Payments Journal

During the month, the amounts recorded in the Accounts Payable Debit column are posted to individual accounts in the accounts payable subsidiary ledger. The amounts in the Other Accounts Debit column are also posted individually to the general ledger accounts during the month. For example, the January 3 entry in the cash payments journal was posted to the **Rent Expense** account. The "CP1" indicates that the entry is recorded on page 1 of the cash payments journal.

ACCOUNT Rent Expense					ACCOUNT NO. 634	
DATE	DESCRIPTION	POST. REF.	DEBIT	CREDIT	BALANCE DEBIT	CREDIT
20X1						
Jan. 3		CP1	1 500 00		1 500 00	

Posting the Column Totals At the end of the month, the cash payments journal is totaled and proved. The total debits must equal the total credits.

Proof of Cash Payments Journal	
	Debits
Accounts Payable Debit column	$13,750.00
Other Accounts Debit column	24,962.80
Total Debits	$38,712.80
	Credits
Purchases Discount Credit column	$ 136.00
Cash Credit column	38,576.80
Total Credits	$38,712.80

FIGURE 9.6 Posted Cash Payments Journal

CASH PAYMENTS JOURNAL   PAGE 1

DATE	CK. NO.	DESCRIPTION	POST. REF.	ACCOUNTS PAYABLE DEBIT	OTHER ACCOUNTS DEBIT			PURCHASES DISCOUNTS CREDIT	CASH CREDIT
					ACCOUNT TITLE	POST. REF.	AMOUNT		
20X1									
Jan. 3	111	January rent			Rent Expense	634	1 500 00		1 500 00
10	112	Store fixtures			Store Equipment	131	2 400 00		2 400 00
11	113	Tax remittance			Sales Tax Payable	231	756 00		756 00
11	114	World of Sports	✓	3 935 00				78 70	3 856 30
13	115	Active Designs	✓	2 865 00				57 30	2 807 70
14	116	Store Supplies			Supplies	129	900 00		900 00
15	117	Withdrawal			M. Ferraro, Drawing	302	3 000 00		3 000 00
17	118	Electric bill			Utilities Expense	643	318 00		318 00
17	119	The Sports Warehouse	✓	4 250 00					4 250 00
21	120	Telephone bill			Telephone Expense	649	276 00		276 00
25	121	Newspaper ad			Advertising Expense	614	840 00		840 00
27	122	International Sportsman	✓	1 000 00					1 000 00
30	123	Active Designs	✓	1 135 00					1 135 00
31	124	World of Sports	✓	565 00					565 00
31	125	January payroll			Salaries Expense	637	4 950 00		4 950 00
31	126	Purchase of goods			Purchases	501	3 200 00		3 200 00
31	127	Freight charge			Freight In	502	175 00		175 00
31	128	Cash refund			Sales Returns & Allow.	451	160 00		
					Sales Tax Payable	231	12 80		172 80
31	129	Note Paid to Metroplex			Notes Payable	201	6 000 00		
		Equipment Company			Interest Expense	691	300 00		6 300 00
31	130	Establish Petty Cash fund			Petty Cash Fund	105	175 00		175 00
31		Totals		13 750 00			24 962 80	136 00	38 576 80
				(205)			(X)	(504)	(101)

Figure 9.6 shows the January cash payments journal after posting for Maxx-Out Sporting Goods. Notice that the account numbers appear in the Posting Reference column of the Other Accounts Debit section to show that the amounts were posted.

When the cash payments journal has been proved, rule the columns and post the totals to the general ledger. Figure 9.7 shows how to post from the cash payments journal to the general ledger accounts.

To post a column total to a general ledger account, enter "CP1" in the Posting Reference column to show that the entry is from page 1 of the cash payments journal.

Enter the column total in the general ledger account Debit or Credit column. Figure 9.7 shows the entries to **Accounts Payable** (1), **Purchases Discounts** (2), and **Cash** (3). Compute the new balance and enter it in the Balance Debit or Balance Credit column.

Enter the general ledger account numbers under the column totals on the cash payments journal. The (X) in the Other Accounts Debit column indicates that the individual accounts were posted to the general ledger, so the column total was not posted.

Posting to the Accounts Payable Ledger To keep balances current, accountants post entries from the Accounts Payable Debit column of the cash payments journal to the vendor accounts in the accounts payable subsidiary ledger daily. For example, on January 13, $2,865 was posted to Active Designs's account in the subsidiary ledger. The "CP1" in the Posting Reference column indicates that the entry is recorded on page 1 of the cash payments journal. The check mark (✓) in the Posting Reference column of the cash payments journal (Figure 9.7) shows that the amount was posted to the supplier's account in the accounts payable subsidiary ledger.

Advantages of the Cash Payments Journal

The cash payments journal:

- saves time and effort when recording and posting cash payments,
- allows for a division of labor among the accounting staff,
- improves the audit trail because all cash payments are recorded in one place and listed by check number.

FIGURE 9.7 Posted General Ledger Accounts

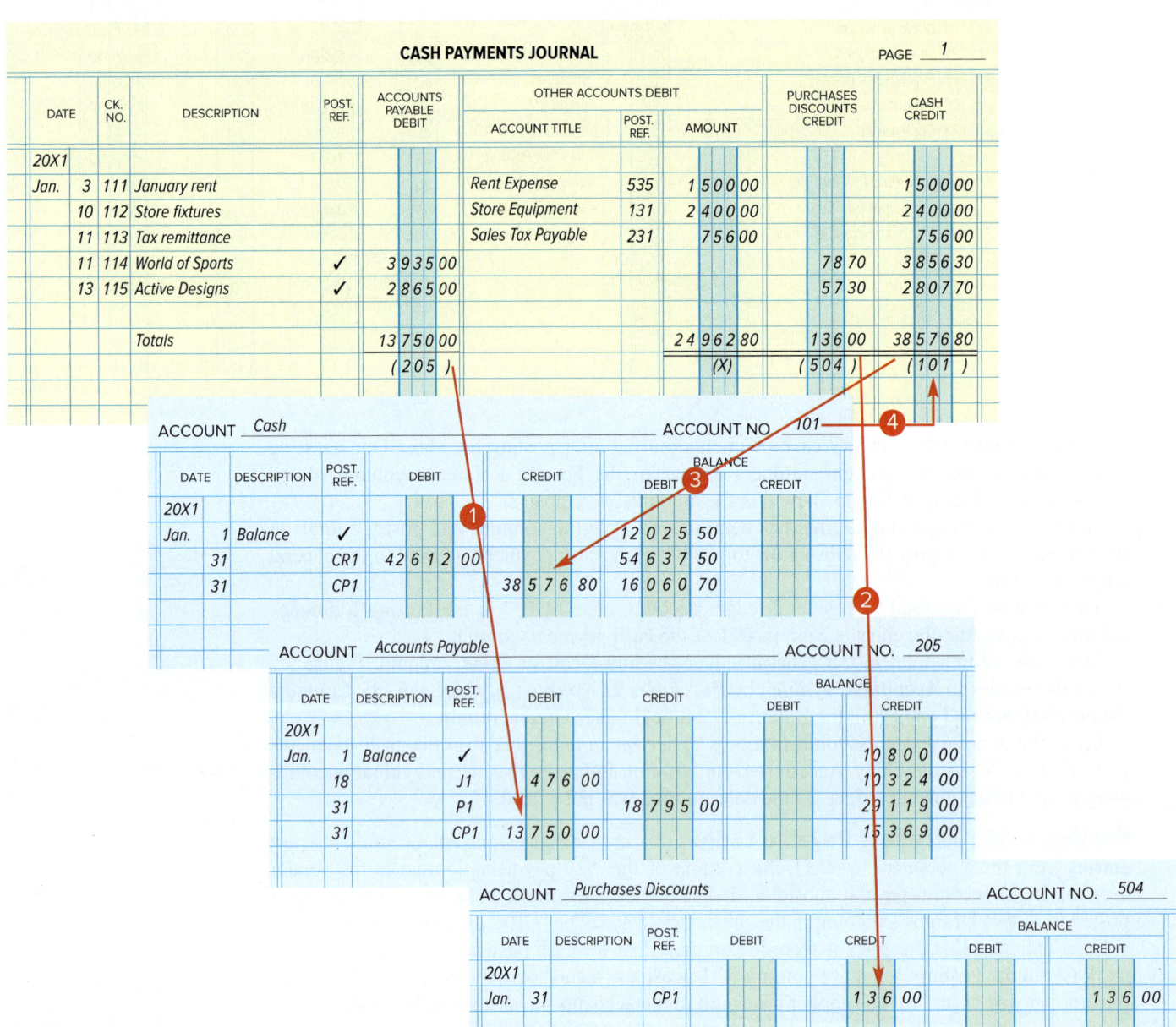

The Petty Cash Fund

In a well-managed business, most bills are paid by check. However, there are times when small expenditures are made with currency and coins. Most businesses use a petty cash fund to pay for small expenditures. Suppose that in the next two hours the office manager needs a $4 folder for a customer. It is not practical to obtain an approval and write a check for $4 in the time available. Instead, the office manager takes $4 from the petty cash fund to purchase the folder.

Establishing the Fund

The amount of the petty cash fund depends on the needs of the business. Usually the office manager, cashier, or assistant is in charge of the petty cash fund. The cashier is responsible for petty cash. To set up the petty cash fund, Maxx-Out Sporting Goods wrote a $175 check to the cashier. She cashed the check and put the currency in a locked cash box.

The establishment of the petty cash fund should be recorded in the cash payments journal. Debit **Petty Cash Fund** in the Other Accounts Debit section of the journal and enter the credit in the Cash Credit column.

Making Payments from the Fund

Petty cash fund payments are limited to small amounts. A **petty cash voucher** is used to record the payments made from the petty cash fund. The petty cash voucher shows the voucher number, amount, purpose of the expenditure, and account to debit. The person receiving the funds signs the voucher, and the person who controls the petty cash fund initials the voucher. Figure 9.8 shows a petty cash voucher for $16.25 for office supplies.

The Petty Cash Analysis Sheet

Most businesses use a **petty cash analysis sheet** to record transactions involving petty cash. The Receipts column shows cash put in the fund, and the Payments column shows the cash paid out. There are special columns for accounts that are used frequently, such as **Supplies, Freight In,** and **Miscellaneous Expense.** There is an Other Accounts Debit column for entries that do not fit in a special column. Figure 9.9 shows the petty cash analysis sheet for Maxx-Out Sporting Goods for February.

Replenishing the Fund The total vouchers plus the cash on hand should always equal the amount of the fund—$175 for Maxx-Out Sporting Goods. Replenish the petty cash fund at the end of each month or sooner if the fund is low. Refer to Figures 9.9 and 9.10 as you learn how to replenish the petty cash fund.

1. Total the columns on the petty cash analysis sheet.
2. Prove the petty cash fund by adding cash on hand and total payments. This should equal the petty cash fund balance ($15.25 + $159.75 = $175.00).

>> **9-6 OBJECTIVE**
Demonstrate a knowledge of procedures for a petty cash fund.

important!

Petty Cash
Only one person controls the petty cash fund. That person should keep receipts for all expenditures.

FIGURE 9.8

Petty Cash Voucher

PETTY CASH VOUCHER 1			
NOTE: This form must be computer processed or filled out in black ink.			
DESCRIPTION OF EXPENDITURE	**ACCOUNTS TO BE CHARGED**	**AMOUNT**	
Office supplies	Supplies 129	16	25
	Total	16	25

RECEIVED THE SUM OF _Sixteen_ DOLLARS AND _25/100_ CENTS
SIGNED _L.T. Green_ DATE _2/3/X1_ APPROVED BY _M.F._ DATE _2/3/X1_
Metroplex Office Supply Co.

FIGURE 9.9 Petty Cash Analysis Sheet

						DELIVERY	MISC.	OTHER ACCOUNTS DEBIT	
DATE	VOU. NO.	DESCRIPTION	RECEIPTS	PAYMENTS	SUPPLIES DEBIT	EXPENSE DEBIT	EXPENSE DEBIT	ACCOUNT TITLE	AMOUNT
20X1									
Feb. 1		Establish fund	175 00						
3	1	Office supplies		16 25	16 25				
6	2	Delivery service		24 00		24 00			
11	3	Withdrawal		25 00				M. Ferraro, Drawing	25 00
15	4	Postage stamps		37 00			37 00		
20	5	Delivery service		17 50		17 50			
26	6	Window washing		26 00			26 00		
28	7	Store supplies		14 00	14 00				
28		Totals	175 00	159 75	30 25	41 50	63 00		25 00
28		Balance on hand		15 25					
			175 00	175 00					
28		Balance on hand	15 25						
28		Replenish fund	159 75						
28		Carried forward	175 00						

FIGURE 9.10 Reimbursing the Petty Cash Fund

					OTHER ACCOUNTS DEBIT			PURCHASES	CASH
DATE	CK. NO.	DESCRIPTION	POST. REF.	ACCOUNTS PAYABLE DEBIT	ACCOUNT TITLE	POST. REF.	AMOUNT	DISCOUNTS CREDIT	CREDIT
20X1									
Feb. 28	191	Replenish Petty Cash fund			Supplies	129	30 25		
					M. Ferraro, Drawing	302	25 00		
					Delivery Expense	523	41 50		
					Miscellaneous Expense	593	63 00		159 75

3. Write a check to restore the petty cash fund to its original balance.
4. Record the check in the cash payments journal. Refer to the petty cash analysis sheet for the accounts and amounts to debit. Notice that the debits appear on four lines of the Other Accounts Debit section. The credit appears in the Cash Credit column.

Any shortages or overages in the petty cash fund are handled similarly to the change fund as discussed in Section 1.

Internal Control of the Petty Cash Fund

Whenever there is valuable property or cash to protect, appropriate safeguards must be established. Petty cash is no exception. The following internal control procedures apply to petty cash:

1. Use the petty cash fund only for small payments that cannot conveniently be made by check.
2. Limit the amount set aside for petty cash to the approximate amount needed to cover one month's payments from the fund.
3. Write petty cash fund checks to the person in charge of the fund, not to the order of "Cash."

4. Assign one person to control the petty cash fund. This person has sole control of the money and is the only one authorized to make payments from the fund.
5. Keep petty cash in a safe, a locked cash box, or a locked drawer.
6. Prepare a petty cash voucher for each payment. The voucher should be signed by the person who receives the money and should show the payment details. This provides an audit trail for the fund. Additionally, obtain a vendor's invoice or other receipt as documentation for each petty cash voucher.

Internal Control over Cash

>> 9-7 OBJECTIVE

Demonstrate a knowledge of internal control procedures for cash.

In a well-managed business, there are internal control procedures for handling and recording cash receipts and cash payments. The internal control over cash should be tailored to the needs of the business. Accountants play a vital role in designing, establishing, and monitoring the cash control system. In developing internal control procedures for cash, certain basic principles must be followed.

Control of Cash Receipts

As noted already, cash is the asset that is most easily stolen, lost, or mishandled. Yet cash is essential to carrying on business operations. It is important to protect all cash receipts to make sure that funds are available to pay expenses and take care of other business obligations. The following are essential cash receipt controls:

1. Have only designated employees receive and handle cash whether it consists of checks and money orders or currency and coins. These employees should be carefully chosen for reliability and accuracy and should be carefully trained. In some businesses, employees who handle cash are bonded. **Bonding** is the process by which employees are investigated by an insurance company. Employees who pass the background check can be bonded; that is, the employer can purchase insurance on the employees. If the bonded employees steal or mishandle cash, the business is insured against the loss.
2. Keep cash receipts in a cash register, a locked cash drawer, or a safe while they are on the premises.
3. Make a record of all cash receipts as the funds come into the business. For checks, endorse each check when received. For currency and coins, this record is the audit tape in a cash register or duplicate copies of numbered sales slips. The use of a cash register provides an especially effective means of control because the machine automatically produces a tape showing the amounts entered. This tape is locked inside the cash register until it is removed by a supervisor.
4. Before a bank deposit is made, check the funds to be deposited against the record made when the cash was received. The employee who checks the deposit should be someone other than the one who receives or records the cash.
5. Deposit cash receipts in the bank promptly—every day or several times a day. Deposit the funds intact—do not make payments directly from the cash receipts. The person who makes the bank deposit should be someone other than the one who receives and records the funds.
6. Enter cash receipts transactions in the accounting records promptly. The person who records cash receipts should not be the one who receives or deposits the funds.
7. Have the monthly bank statement sent to and reconciled by someone other than the employees who handle, record, and deposit the funds.

One of the advantages of efficient procedures for handling and recording cash receipts is that the funds reach the bank sooner. Cash receipts are not kept on the premises for more than a short time, which means that the funds are safer and are readily available for paying bills owed by the firm.

Control of Cash Payments

It is important to control cash payments so that the payments are made only for authorized business purposes. The following are essential cash payment controls:

1. Make all payments by check except for payments from special-purpose cash funds such as a petty cash fund.
2. Issue checks only with an approved bill, invoice, or other document that describes the reason for the payment.
3. Have only designated personnel, who are experienced and reliable, approve bills and invoices.
4. Have checks prepared and recorded in the checkbook or check register by someone other than the person who approves the payments.
5. Have still another person sign and mail the checks to creditors. Consider requiring two people to sign all checks greater than a predesignated amount.
6. Use prenumbered check forms. Periodically the numbers of the checks that were issued and the numbers of the blank check forms remaining should be verified to make sure that all check numbers are accounted for.
7. During the bank reconciliation process, compare the canceled checks, or an image of the canceled check on the bank website, to the checkbook or check register. The person who does the bank reconciliation should be someone other than the person who prepares or records the checks.
8. Enter promptly in the accounting records all cash payment transactions. The person who records cash payments should not be the one who approves payments or the one who writes the checks.

Small businesses usually cannot achieve the division of responsibility recommended for cash receipts and cash payments. However, no matter what size the firm, efforts should be made to set up effective control procedures for cash.

Section 2 Review

1. A cash refund given to a customer for returned goods would be recorded in the
   a. cash receipts journal.
   b. general journal.
   c. cash payments journal.
   d. purchases journal.
2. Which of the following is the entry to record payment of a note payable with interest?
   a. debit *Cash*, credit *Notes Payable*, credit *Interest Expense*
   b. debit *Notes Payable*, debit *Interest Expense*, credit *Cash*
   c. debit *Cash*, credit *Notes Receivable*, credit *Interest Expense*
   d. debit *Notes Receivable*, debit *Interest Expense*, credit *Cash*
3. The entry to record replenishing the petty cash fund will usually
   a. have several debits, with a credit to *Petty Cash*.
   b. have several credits, with a debit to *Petty Cash*.
   c. have several credits, with a debit to *Cash*.
   d. have several debits, with a credit to *Cash*.
4. To take the discount, what is the payment date for an invoice dated January 21 with terms 3/15, n/30?
   a. February 5
   b. February 4
   c. February 3
   d. February 7
5. Cash purchases of merchandise are recorded in the
   a. cash receipts journal.
   b. general journal.
   c. cash payments journal.
   d. purchases journal.

6. **Which of the following is not a good control over cash receipts?**
   a. Enter cash receipts in the accounting records promptly.
   b. Keep cash receipts in a cash register, locked cash drawer, or a safe while they are on the premises.
   c. Bond employees who receive and handle cash receipts.
   d. The same person should receive all cash receipts, enter them in the accounting records, and make the bank deposit.

7. **Which of the following is not a good control over cash payments?**
   a. Someone other than the person approving payments should record them in the accounting records.
   b. The person doing the bank reconciliation should not prepare or record checks.
   c. Use petty cash to make most payments to be more efficient.
   d. Enter all cash payments in the accounting records promptly.

Section 3

SECTION OBJECTIVES	TERMS TO LEARN
>> 9-8 Write a check, endorse checks, prepare a bank deposit slip, and maintain a checkbook balance. **WHY IT'S IMPORTANT** Banking tasks are basic practices in every business. >> 9-9 Reconcile the monthly bank statement. **WHY IT'S IMPORTANT** Reconciliation of the bank statement provides a good control of cash. >> 9-10 Record any adjusting entries required from the bank reconciliation. **WHY IT'S IMPORTANT** Certain items are not recorded in the accounting records during the month. >> 9-11 Understand how businesses use online banking to manage cash activities. **WHY IT'S IMPORTANT** Many businesses use online banking to manage a significant portion of cash activities.	bank reconciliation statement blank endorsement canceled check check credit memorandum debit memorandum deposit in transit deposit slip dishonored (NSF) check drawee drawer electronic funds transfer (EFT) endorsement full endorsement negotiable outstanding checks payee postdated check restrictive endorsement service charge

Banking Procedures

Businesses with good internal control systems safeguard cash. Many businesses make a daily bank deposit, and some make two or three deposits a day. Keeping excess cash is a dangerous practice. Also, frequent bank deposits provide a steady flow of funds for the payment of expenses.

Writing Checks

A **check** is a written order signed by an authorized person, the **drawer,** instructing a bank, the **drawee,** to pay a specific sum of money to a designated person or business, the **payee.** The checks in Figure 9.11 are **negotiable,** which means that ownership of the checks can be transferred to another person or business.

Before writing the check, complete the check stub. In Figure 9.11, the check stub for Check 111 shows:

- Date: January 3, 20X1
- Payee: Carter Real Estate Group
- Purpose: January rent
- Balance brought forward: $12,025.50
- Check amount: $1,500.00
- Balance: $10,525.50

Once the stub has been completed, fill in the check. Carefully enter the date, the payee, and the amount in figures and words. Draw a line to fill any empty space after the payee's name and after the amount in words. To be valid, checks need an authorized signature. For Maxx-Out Sporting Goods, only Max Ferraro, the owner, is authorized to sign checks.

FIGURE 9.11 Checks and Check Stubs

No. 111 BAL BRO'T FOR'D **12,025 50**	**Maxx-Out Sporting Goods** 2007 Trendsetter Lane Dallas, TX 75268-0967	**No. 111** 11-8640 / 1210
January 3, 20 X1	DATE January 3, 20 X1	
Carter Real Estate Group	PAY TO THE ORDER OF Carter Real Estate Group	$ 1,500.00
TO ORDER OF January rent FOR	One thousand five hundred 00/100 DOLLARS	
TOTAL 12,025 50	FIRST TEXAS NATIONAL BANK Dallas, TX 75267-6205	
AMOUNT THIS CHECK 1,500 00	MEMO Rent for January Max Ferraro	
BALANCE 10,525 50	⑆1210D8640⑆ ‖⁎38C1498867‖⁎	
No. 112 BAL BRO'T FOR'D **10,525 50**	**Maxx-Out Sporting Goods** 2007 Trendsetter Lane Dallas, TX 75268-0967	**No. 112** 11-8640 / 1210
January 10, 20 X1	DATE January 10, 20 X1	
The Retail Equip. Ctr.	PAY TO THE ORDER OF The Retail Equipment Center	$ 2,400.00
TO ORDER OF store fixtures FOR	Two thousand four hundred 00/100 DOLLARS	
TOTAL 10,525 50	FIRST TEXAS NATIONAL BANK Dallas, TX 75267-6205	
AMOUNT THIS CHECK 2,400 00	MEMO store fixtures Max Ferraro	
BALANCE 8,125 50	⑆1210D8640⑆ ‖⁎38C1498867‖⁎	

Figure 9.11 shows the check stub for Check 112, a cash purchase from The Retail Equipment Center for $2,400. After Check 112, the account balance is $8,125.50 ($10,525.50 − $2,400.00).

Endorsing Checks

Each check needs an endorsement to be deposited. The **endorsement** is a written authorization that transfers ownership of a check. After the payee transfers ownership to the bank by an endorsement, the bank has a legal right to collect payment from the drawer, the person or business that issued the check. If the check cannot be collected, the payee guarantees payment to all subsequent holders.

Several forms of endorsement are shown in Figure 9.12. Endorsements are placed on the back of the check, on the left, near the perforated edge where the check was separated from the stub.

A **blank endorsement** is the signature of the payee that transfers ownership of the check without specifying to whom or for what purpose. Checks with a blank endorsement can be further endorsed by anyone who has the check, even if the check is lost or stolen.

A **full endorsement** is a signature transferring a check to a specific person, business, or bank. Only the person, business, or bank named in the full endorsement can transfer it to someone else.

The safest endorsement is the **restrictive endorsement.** A restrictive endorsement is a signature that transfers the check to a specific party for a specific purpose, usually for deposit to a bank account. Most businesses restrictively endorse the checks they receive using a rubber stamp or a check processing machine.

Preparing the Deposit Slip

>> 9-8 OBJECTIVE
Demonstrate knowledge of how to write a check, endorse checks, prepare a bank deposit slip, and maintain a checkbook balance.

Businesses prepare a **deposit slip** to record each deposit of cash or checks to a bank account. Usually the bank provides deposit slips preprinted with the account name and number. Figure 9.13 shows the deposit slip for the January 8 deposit for Maxx-Out Sporting Goods.

Notice the printed numbers on the lower edge of the deposit slip. These are the same numbers on the bottom of the checks, Figure 9.11. The numbers are printed using a special magnetic

FIGURE 9.12

Types of Check Endorsement

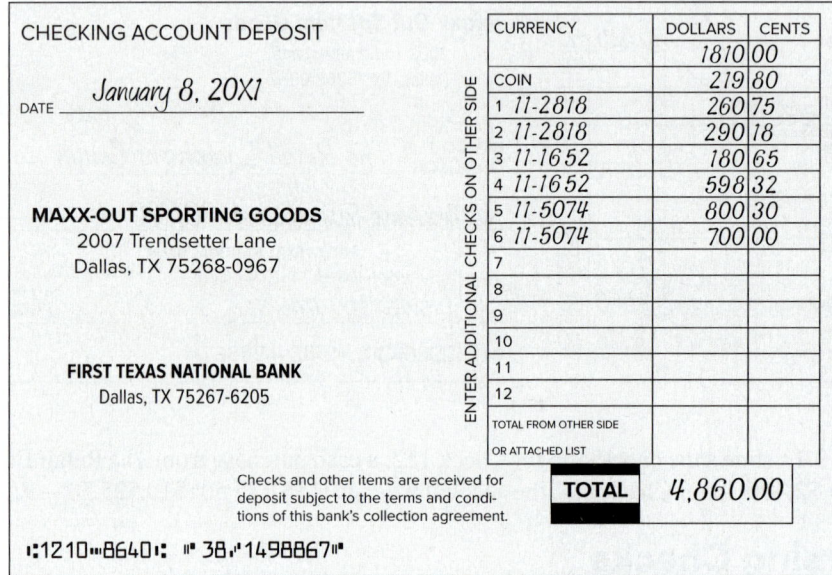

FIGURE 9.13

Deposit Slip

ink character recognition (MICR) type that can be "read" by machine. Deposit slips and checks encoded with MICR are rapidly and efficiently processed by machine.

- The 12 indicates that the bank is in the 12th Federal Reserve District.
- The 10 is the routing number used in processing the document.
- The 8640 identifies First Texas National Bank.
- The 38 14 98867 is the account number.

The deposit slip for Maxx-Out Sporting Goods shows the date, January 8. Currency is the paper money, $1,810.00. Coin is the amount in coins, $219.80. The checks and money orders are individually listed. Some banks ask that the *American Bankers Association (ABA) transit number* for each check be entered on the deposit slip. The transit number appears on the top part of the fraction that appears in the upper right corner of the check. In Figure 9.11, the transit number is 11-8640.

Many banks now allow businesses to deposit checks to an automated teller machine (ATM) without using deposit slips. The ATM receipt provides the depositor with images of the checks deposited as well as the total amount of the deposit.

Handling Postdated Checks

Occasionally, a business will receive a postdated check. A **postdated check** is dated some time in the future. If the business receives a postdated check, it should not deposit it before the date on the check. Otherwise, the check could be refused by the drawer's bank. Postdated checks are written by drawers who do not have sufficient funds to cover the check. The drawer expects to have adequate funds in the bank by the date on the check. Issuing or accepting postdated checks is not a proper business practice.

Reconciling the Bank Statement

Once a month, the bank sends a statement of the deposits received and the checks paid for each account. Figure 9.14 shows the bank statement for Maxx-Out Sporting Goods. It shows a day-to-day listing of all transactions during the month. A code, explained at the bottom,

>> 9-9 OBJECTIVE
Reconcile the monthly bank statement.

FIGURE 9.14

Bank Statement

FIRST TEXAS NATIONAL BANK

MAXX-OUT SPORTING GOODS 1-877-TEXBANK
2007 Trendsetter Lane
Dallas, TX 75268-0967

Account Number: 38-14-98867   January 1–January 31, 20X1
Activity Summary:

Balance, January 1	$ 12,025.50
Deposits and credits	36,672.00
Withdrawals and debits	(25,189.00)
Balance, January 31	$ 23,508.50

DATE	DESCRIPTION	DEPOSITS/ CREDITS	WITHDRAWALS/ DEBITS	BALANCE
1/1/X1	Opening balance			$ 12,025.50
1/7/X1	Deposit	702.00		12,727.50
1/7/X1	Check No. 111		1,500.00	11,227.50
1/8/X1	Check No. 112		2,400.00	8,827.50
1/8/X1	Deposit	4,860.00		13,687.50
1/11/X1	Deposit	270.00		13,957.50
1/11/X1	Check No. 113		756.00	13,201.50
1/12/X1	Check No. 114		3,856.30	9,345.20
1/12/X1	Deposit	15,000.00		24,345.20
1/13/X1	Check No. 115		2,807.70	21,537.50
1/13/X1	Deposit	540.00		22,077.50
1/15/X1	Deposit	5,166.00		27,243.50
1/15/X1	Check No. 116		900.00	26,343.50
1/17/X1	Deposit	108.00		26,451.50
1/17/X1	Check No. 117		3,000.00	23,451.50
1/17/X1	Check No. 118		318.00	23,133.50
1/18/X1	Deposit	75.00		23,208.50
1/18/X1	Check No. 119		4,250.00	18,958.50
1/18/X1	Check No. 120		276.00	18,682.50
1/22/X1	Deposit	400.00		19,082.50
1/22/X1	Deposit	5,400.00		24,482.50
1/22/X1	Check No. 121		840.00	23,642.50
1/22/X1	Check No. 122		1,000.00	22,642.50
1/22/X1	Check No. 10087		1,600.00	21,042.50
1/29/X1	Deposit	2,932.00		23,974.50
1/29/X1	Debit for NSF Check		525.00	23,449.50
1/31/X1	Deposit	108.00		23,557.50
1/31/X1	Deposit	275.00		23,832.50
1/31/X1	Credit for funds collected	836.00		24,668.50
1/31/X1	Service fee for NSF check		25.00	24,643.50
1/31/X1	Check No. 123		1,135.00	24,508.50
	Totals	36,672.00	25,189.00	

identifies transactions that do not involve checks or deposits. For example, SC indicates a service charge. The last column of the bank statement shows the account balance at the beginning of the period, after each day's transactions, and at the end of the period.

Canceled checks are checks paid by the bank during the month. Canceled checks are proof of payment. They are filed after the bank reconciliation is complete. Most banks store a digital picture of the check available to the account holder on the bank's website. Some banks enclose canceled checks with the bank statement.

Usually there is a difference between the ending balance shown on the bank statement and the balance shown in the checkbook. A bank reconciliation determines why the difference exists and brings the records into agreement.

Changes in the Checking Account Balance

A **credit memorandum** explains any addition, other than a deposit, to the checking account. For example, when a note receivable is due, the bank may collect the note from the maker and place the proceeds in the checking account. The amount collected appears on the bank statement, and the credit memorandum showing the details of the transaction is enclosed with the bank statement.

A **debit memorandum** explains any deduction, other than a check, from the checking account. Service charges and dishonored checks appear as debit memorandums.

Bank **service charges** are fees charged by banks to cover the costs of maintaining accounts and providing services, such as the use of the night deposit box and the collection of promissory notes. The debit memorandum shows the type and amount of each service charge.

Figure 9.15 shows a debit memorandum for a $525.00 dishonored check. A **dishonored check** is one that is returned to the depositor unpaid. Normally, checks are dishonored because there are insufficient funds in the drawer's account to cover the check. The bank usually stamps the letters *NSF,* for *Not Sufficient Funds,* on the check. The business records a journal entry to debit *Accounts Receivable* and credit *Cash* for the amount of the dishonored check.

When a check is dishonored, the business contacts the drawer to arrange for collection. The drawer can ask the business to redeposit the check because the funds are now in the account. If so, the business records the check deposit again. Sometimes, the business requests a cash payment.

The Bank Reconciliation Process: An Illustration

When the bank statement is received, it is reconciled with the financial records of the business. On February 5, Maxx-Out Sporting Goods received the bank statement shown in Figure 9.14. The ending cash balance according to the bank is $23,508.50. On January 31, the *Cash* account, called the *book balance of cash,* is $16,060.70. The same amount appears on the check stub at the end of January.

Sometimes the difference between the bank balance and the book balance is due to errors. The bank might make an arithmetic error, give credit to the wrong depositor, or charge a check

FIGURE 9.15

Debit Memorandum

DEBIT: MAXX-OUT SPORTING GOODS	FIRST TEXAS NATIONAL BANK
2007 Trendsetter Lane	
Dallas, TX 75268-0967	
38-14-98867	DATE: January 31, 20X1

NSF Check - David Newhouse	525 00

APPROVED: *Max Ferraro*

FIGURE 9.16

Bank Reconciliation Statement

Maxx-Out Sporting Goods			
Bank Reconciliation Statement			
January 31, 20X1			
Balance on Bank Statement			23 508 50
Additions:			
Deposit of January 31 in transit	5 940 00		
Check incorrectly charged to account	1 600 00	7 540 00	
			31 048 50
Deductions for outstanding checks:			
Check 124 of January 31		565 00	
Check 125 of January 31	4 950 00		
Check 126 of January 31	3 200 00		
Check 127 of January 31		175 00	
Check 128 of January 31		172 80	
Check 129 of January 31	6 300 00		
Check 130 of January 31		175 00	
Total Checks Outstanding		15 537 80	
Adjusted Bank Balance		15 510 70	
Balance in Books		16 060 70	
Deductions:			
NSF Check from David Newhouse	525 00		
Bank Service Charge	25 00	550 00	
Adjusted Book Balance		15 510 70	

against the wrong account. Some banks require that errors in the bank statement be reported within a short period of time. The errors made by businesses include not recording a check or deposit, or recording a check or deposit for the wrong amount.

Other than errors, there are four reasons why the book balance of cash may not agree with the balance on the bank statement.

1. **Outstanding checks** are checks that are recorded in the cash payments journal but have not been paid by the bank.
2. **Deposit in transit** is a deposit that is recorded in the cash receipts journal but that reaches the bank too late to be shown on the monthly bank statement.
3. Service charges and other deductions are not recorded in the business records.
4. Deposits, such as the collection of promissory notes, are not recorded in the business records.

Figure 9.16 shows a **bank reconciliation statement** that accounts for the differences between the balance on the bank statement and the book balance of cash. The bank reconciliation statement format is:

	First Section		Second Section
	Bank statement balance		Book balance
+	deposits in transit	+	deposits not recorded
−	outstanding checks	−	deductions
+ or −	bank errors	+ or −	errors in the books
	Adjusted bank balance		Adjusted book balance

When the bank reconciliation statement is complete, the adjusted bank balance must equal the adjusted book balance.

The bank reconciliation process involves comparing items in the company's records to those on the bank statement. Use the following steps to prepare the bank reconciliation statement:

First Section

1. Enter the balance on the bank statement, $23,508.50.
2. Compare the deposits in the checkbook with the deposits on the bank statement. Maxx-Out Sporting Goods had one deposit in transit. On January 31, receipts of $5,940.00 were placed in the bank's night deposit box. The bank recorded the deposit on February 1. The deposit will appear on the February bank statement. Additionally, if any deposits in transit are on the previous month's bank reconciliation, ensure they are listed on the current month's bank statement.
3. List the outstanding checks.
   - Put the canceled checks in numeric order. For businesses that do not receive canceled checks, obtain a listing of checks cleared during the period from the bank's website.
   - Compare the canceled checks to the check stubs, verifying the check numbers and amounts.
   - Examine the endorsements to make sure that they agree with the names of the payees.
   - List the checks that have not cleared the bank.
   - Maxx-Out Sporting Goods has seven outstanding checks totaling $15,537.80.
   - Additionally, if any outstanding checks are listed on the previous month's bank reconciliation, ensure they are included in the current month's bank statement. If they are not, they are still outstanding and should be included in the current month's bank reconciliation.
4. While reviewing the canceled checks for Maxx-Out Sporting Goods, Max Ferraro found a $1,600 check issued by The Dress Barn. The $1,600 was deducted from Maxx-Out Sporting Goods' account; it should have been deducted from the account for The Dress Barn. This is a bank error. Max Ferraro contacted the bank about the error. The correction will appear on the next bank statement. The bank error amount is added to the bank statement balance on the bank reconciliation statement.
5. The adjusted bank balance is $15,510.70.

important!

Adjusted Book Balance

Journal entries are required to record additions and deductions that appear on the bank statement but have not been recorded in the general ledger. These items are located under the "Balance in Books" section of the bank reconciliation.

Second Section

1. Enter the balance in books from the *Cash* account, $16,060.70.
2. Record any deposits made by the bank that have not been recorded in the accounting records. Maxx-Out Sporting Goods did not have any.
3. Record deductions made by the bank. There are two items:
   - the NSF check for $525,
   - the bank service charge for $25.
4. Record any errors in the accounting records that were discovered during the reconciliation process. Maxx-Out Sporting Goods did not have any errors in January.
5. The adjusted book balance is $15,510.70.

Notice that the adjusted bank balance and the adjusted book balance agree.

>> **9-10 OBJECTIVE**

Record any adjusting entries required from the bank reconciliation.

Adjusting the Financial Records

Items in the second section of the bank reconciliation statement include additions and deductions made by the bank that do not appear in the accounting records. Businesses prepare journal entries to record these items in the books.

For Maxx-Out Sporting Goods, two entries must be made. The first entry is for the NSF check from David Newhouse, a credit customer. The second entry is for the bank service charge. The effect of the two items is a decrease in the *Cash* account balance.

MANAGERIAL IMPLICATIONS

CASH

- It is important to safeguard cash against loss and theft.
- Management and the accountant need to work together:
  - to make sure that there are effective controls for cash receipts and cash payments,
  - to monitor the internal control system to make sure that it functions properly,
  - to develop procedures that ensure the quick and efficient recording of cash transactions.
- To make decisions, management needs up-to-date information about the cash position so that it can anticipate cash shortages and arrange loans or arrange for the temporary investment of excess funds.
- Management and the accountant need to establish controls over the banking activities—depositing funds, issuing checks, recording checking account transactions, and reconciling the monthly bank statement.

THINKING CRITICALLY

How would you determine how much cash to keep in the business checking account, as opposed to in a short-term investment?

BUSINESS TRANSACTION

The January bank reconciliation statement (Figure 9.16) shows an NSF check of $525 and a bank service charge of $25.

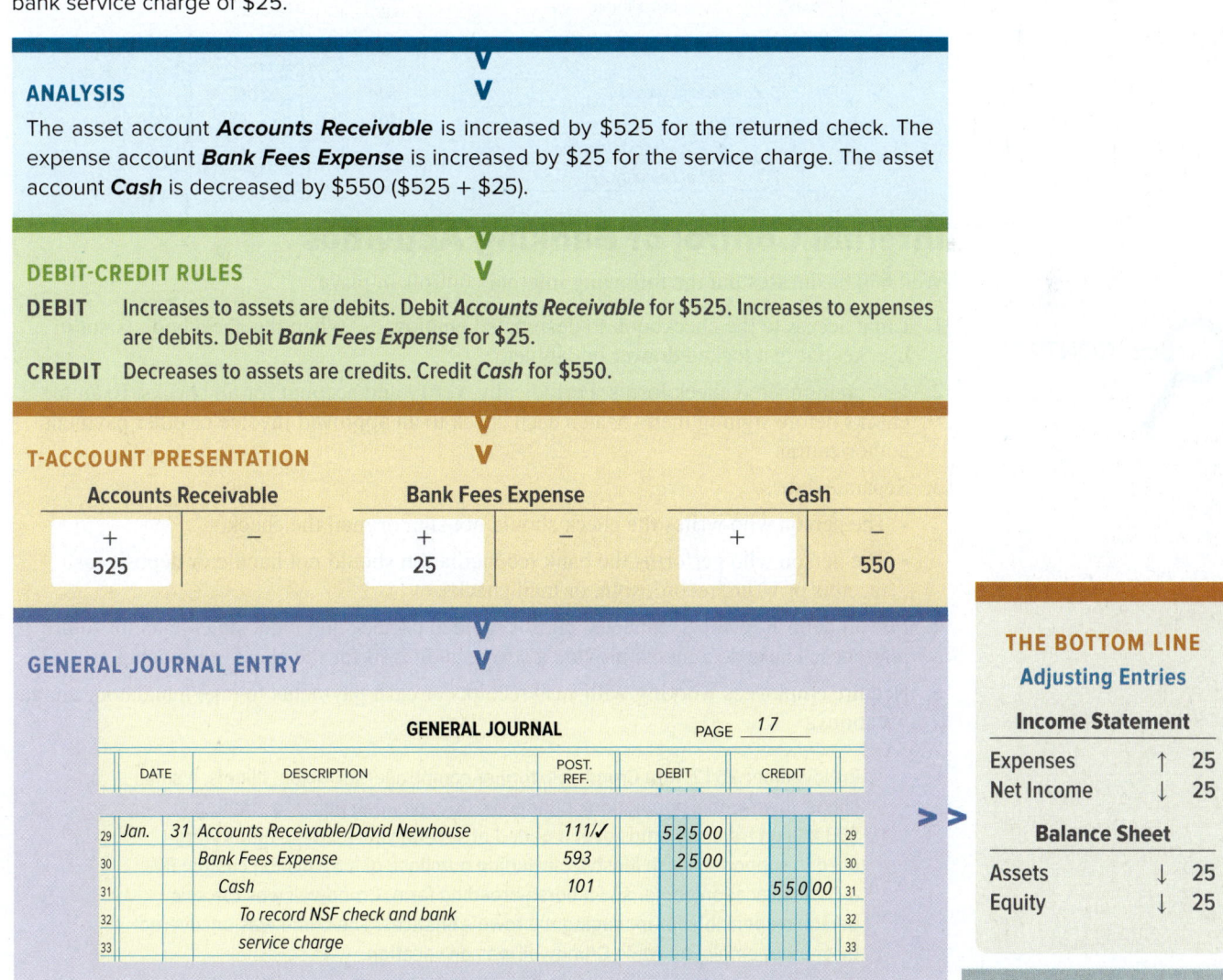

After posting, the *Cash* account appears as follows.

ACCOUNT Cash						ACCOUNT NO. 101	
DATE	DESCRIPTION	POST. REF.	DEBIT	CREDIT		BALANCE	
						DEBIT	CREDIT
20X1							
Jan. 1	Balance	✓				12 025 50	
31		CR1	42 612 00			54 637 50	
31		CP1		38 576 80		16 060 70	
31		J17		550 00		15 510 70	

Notice that $15,510.70 is the adjusted bank balance, the adjusted book balance, and the general ledger *Cash* balance. A notation is made on the latest check stub to deduct the amounts ($525 and $25). The notation includes the reasons for the deductions.

Sometimes the bank reconciliation reveals an error in the firm's financial records. For example, the February bank reconciliation for Maxx-Out Sporting Goods found that Check 151 was written for $465. The amount on the bank statement is $465. However, the check was recorded in the accounting records as $445. The business made a $20 error when recording the check. Maxx-Out Sporting Goods prepared the following journal entry to correct the error. The $20 is also deducted on the check stub.

		GENERAL JOURNAL			PAGE 18	
	DATE	DESCRIPTION	POST. REF.	DEBIT	CREDIT	
1	20X1					1
2						2
29	Feb. 28	Advertising Expense	514	20 00		29
30		Cash	101		20 00	30
31		To correct error for check				31
32		151 of February 22				32

Internal Control of Banking Activities

Well-run businesses put the following internal controls in place:

1. Limit access to the checkbook to designated employees. When the checkbook is not in use, keep it in a locked drawer or cabinet.
2. Use prenumbered check forms. Periodically, verify and account for all checks. Examine checks before signing them. Match each check to an approved invoice or other payment authorization.
3. Separate duties.
   - The person who writes the check should not sign or mail the check.
   - The person who performs the bank reconciliation should not handle or deposit cash receipts or write, record, sign, or mail checks.
4. File all deposit receipts, canceled checks, voided checks, and bank statements for future reference. These documents provide a strong audit trail for the checking account.
5. Require employees working with cash receipts or cash payments to take mandatory annual vacations.

> In November 2012, Rita Crundwell, former comptroller for Dixon, Illinois, a small Illinois town with a population of under 16,000, pleaded guilty to stealing $53 million from city funds over a period of several years. These funds were used to support a lavish lifestyle, including purchase of a $2 million custom RV, a Florida vacation home, and a horse-breeding farm. Crundwell was the sole person responsible for managing the town's finances. The crime was uncovered by another employee while Crundwell was on vacation.

Using Online Banking

Many businesses now manage a significant portion of their cash activities using online banking. Online banking offers many features to make businesses more efficient. These features include:

- Businesses can initiate **electronic funds transfers (EFT)** to vendors from a computer instead of writing checks.
- Payments to government agencies for taxes can be submitted online, using the government agency website, to avoid late payment penalties.
- Businesses can receive EFT from customers, rather than receiving checks in the mail. This is especially important in transacting cash receipts from foreign customers. Routine payments, such as those for utilities expenses and loan payments, can be automatically deducted from the company's bank account.
- Businesses can deposit checks from customers using a dedicated scanning device.
- Many banks offer security alerts for such instances as changes in mailing addresses and ATM and automatic payment withdrawals that exceed specified limits. Such alerts are often sent to the responsible company official via e-mail or phone text messages. When an alert is received, the company should view account activity online to ensure cash transactions are legitimate.

>> 9-11 OBJECTIVE
Understand how businesses use online banking to manage cash activities.

There are usually no source documents for the transactions listed above. The accountant should check bank activity online frequently to ensure all EFT and other transactions initiated electronically are recorded in the accounting records.

For example, the online account activity of Western Imports and Exports for July 29, 30, and 31, 20X1, is shown in Figure 9.17. The company's accountant was out of town during that period.

In matching these transactions to the company's **Cash** account in the general ledger, the accountant identified the following unrecorded transactions:

1. The loan payment on 7/30/20X1 was an automatic debit by Western Equipment for the company's monthly payment on an equipment loan. The loan does not bear interest.
2. The ACH credit on 7/30/20X1 was an EFT payment sent by Baden Holding, a German customer, on account.
3. The bill payment of 7/30/20X1 was an automatic debit by West Communications (telephone).
4. The ATM withdrawal of 7/31/20X1 was for personal use by the owner, Susan De Angelis.

FIGURE 9.17 Online Account Activity

Business Checking			Account #987-654321		
Date	Type	Description	Additions	Payments	Balance
7/31/20X1	ATM	ATM withdrawal		$200.00	$27,819.91
7/31/20X1	Check	Check #1421 (view)		$1,225.95	$28,019.91
7/30/20X1	Bill payment	Online payment		$248.52	$29,245.86
7/30/20X1	Check	Check #1420 (view)		$428.20	$29,494.38
7/30/20X1	ACH credit	Baden Holding	$10,200.00		$29,922.58
7/30/20X1	Deposit	Deposit ID #8989	$5,400.00		$19,722.58
7/30/20X1	Loan payment	Online transfer to WC XXX		$3,900.00	$14,322.58
7/29/20X1	Check	Check #1422 (view)		$850.00	$18,222.58

The accountant recorded these transactions in the general journal, as follows:

	GENERAL JOURNAL			PAGE 10
DATE	DESCRIPTION	POST. REF.	DEBIT	CREDIT
20X1				
July 30	Notes Payable		3 900 00	
	Cash			3 900 00
	To record loan payment to Western			
	Equipment			
30	Cash		10 200 00	
	Accounts Receivable/Baden Holding			10 200 00
	To record EFT received on account			
	from Baden Holding			
30	Telephone Expense		248 52	
	Cash			248 52
	To record online payment to			
	West Communications			
31	Susan De Angelis, Drawing		200 00	
	Cash			200 00
	To record ATM withdrawal by			
	Susan De Angelis for personal use			

In addition to the internal controls over banking activities discussed earlier, companies using online banking should allow only authorized check signors access to the company's online account. Those authorized should review bank activity online daily to ensure no suspicious activity has occurred. Additionally, log-in information, such as user identification and passwords, should be changed frequently.

> According to Javelin Strategy, the number of identity theft victims in the United States rose to 16.7 million in 2017.

Section 3 Review

1. What is the term for the person or firm issuing a check?
   a. drawee
   b. drawer
   c. payee
   d. bank

2. Why does a payee endorse a check before depositing it?
   a. It is the legal process by which the payee transfers ownership of the check to the bank.
   b. It is a form of identification verification.
   c. The check will be paid faster by the bank if it is endorsed.
   d. All of these are correct.

3. Which of these bank reconciliation items requires journal entries?
   a. outstanding checks
   b. deposits in transit
   c. a check properly written by the company but paid at the wrong amount by the bank
   d. an NSF check from a customer

4. On the bank reconciliation, outstanding checks should be
   a. added to the balance on bank statement.
   b. deducted from the balance on bank statement.
   c. added to the balance in books.
   d. deducted from the balance in books.

5. Which of the following does not require an adjustment to the financial records?
   a. deposits in transit
   b. bank service charge
   c. a check that was incorrectly recorded by the firm at $115 but was paid by the bank at its correct amount of $1,115
   d. an NSF check from a customer
6. On the bank reconciliation statement, you would not find a list of
   a. deposits in transit.
   b. canceled checks.
   c. outstanding checks.
   d. NSF checks.
7. The following data was taken from a firm's bank reconciliation statement: book balance, $7,910; deposit in transit, $150; NSF check from a customer, $200; outstanding checks, $5,000; bank service charge, $10. Its adjusted book balance is
   a. $7,720.
   b. $8,120.
   c. $7,700.
   d. $8,100.

>> **9-12 OBJECTIVE**

Appendix: Record transactions for a retailer using the perpetual inventory system.

APPENDIX TO CHAPTER 9:
The Perpetual Inventory System

Merchandising companies sell products, not services. Their accounting practices are different from those of service companies. We will focus on these differences and explain the general ledger accounts used by merchandising companies.

The distribution channel is the means that manufacturers of products use to sell their products to consumers. A common example of the distribution channel is:

Manufacturer sells to *Wholesaler* who sells to *Retailer* who sells to *Consumer.*

In this appendix, we learn to record transactions for a retailer. We will use a general journal to record transactions.

The accounting for sales and purchases discussed in Chapters 7, 8, and 9 assumed use of the periodic inventory system. When the periodic system is used, the inventory records are only updated when a physical inventory is taken. A physical inventory is an actual count of units on hand. This system is adequate for smaller businesses such as Maxx-Out Sporting Goods.

Larger businesses require up-to-date information of inventories on hand and use the perpetual inventory system. The perpetual inventory system updates both the general ledger merchandise inventory account and inventory items in the inventory ledger with each purchase, sale, and return. Using a perpetual inventory system requires a substantial investment in point-of-sale cash registers, scanning devices, back office hardware, and computer software.

Perpetual inventory management systems give management more control over the company's inventory. Management can use computers to access inventory records to know exactly how much of each item in inventory is on hand. This assists management in inventory control and purchasing activities. The perpetual inventory system also allows for cycle counts of inventory. A cycle count is an inventory management procedure in which only certain inventory items are counted and compared with the perpetual inventory records. Shortages of inventory on hand can be investigated and corrective actions taken.

In this appendix, we will introduce Big 10 Sporting Goods, a multistate retailer selling sporting goods and sporting apparel. Big 10 Sporting Goods must account for purchases, sales, returns of goods, and *merchandise inventory*—the stock of goods on hand.

Big 10 Sporting Goods uses the perpetual inventory method. We will first examine purchasing transactions entered into by Big 10 Sporting Goods, then sales transactions by Big 10 Sporting Goods.

Purchasing Transactions

When the perpetual inventory system is used, the **Merchandise Inventory** account is used to record purchases and purchase returns of merchandise inventory. It is also used to record freight costs of merchandise inventory purchased. **Merchandise Inventory** is an asset account with a normal debit balance.

The **Merchandise Inventory** account replaces the **Purchases, Purchases Returns,** and **Freight In** accounts used in the periodic inventory system.

Big 10 Sporting Goods engaged in the following purchases transactions during the month of September 20X1. The accounting for these transactions is illustrated below. Descriptions have been omitted.

Purchases and Cash Payments with Freight Charges

If the freight terms are free on board (FOB) shipping point, the buyer pays the freight charge—the cost of shipping the goods from the seller's warehouse to the buyer's location. If the freight terms are FOB destination, the seller pays the freight charges. There are two ways to handle the freight charges paid by the buyer:

- The buyer is billed directly by the transportation company for the freight charge. The buyer issues a check directly to the freight company.

- The seller pays the freight charge and includes it on the invoice. The invoice includes the price of the goods and the freight charge.

On September 1 and September 2, Big 10 Sporting Goods engaged in purchases of merchandise. The transaction on September 1 involved the purchase of merchandise for cash, with no freight charges. The September 2 transaction was for the purchase of merchandise on account, with freight charges. The accounting for these transactions follows.

BUSINESS TRANSACTION

On September 1, Big 10 Sporting Goods purchased merchandise for cash, $12,000.

GENERAL JOURNAL ENTRY

GENERAL JOURNAL

DATE	DESCRIPTION	POST. REF.	DEBIT	CREDIT
20X1				
Sept. 1	Merchandise Inventory		12 000 00	
	Cash			12 000 00

BUSINESS TRANSACTION

On September 2, Big 10 Sporting Goods recorded a purchase of weight-lifting equipment for $9,500 plus freight of $250 from Sledge Hammer Strength; the terms are 1/10, n/30.

GENERAL JOURNAL ENTRY

GENERAL JOURNAL

DATE	DESCRIPTION	POST. REF.	DEBIT	CREDIT
20X1				
Sept. 2	Merchandise Inventory ($9,500 + $250)		9 750 00	
	Accounts Payable/Sledge Hammer Strength			9 750 00

Purchase Returns and Allowances

When merchandise arrives, it is examined to confirm that it is satisfactory. Occasionally, the wrong goods are shipped, or items are damaged or defective. A *purchase return* is when the business returns the goods. A *purchase allowance* is when the purchaser keeps the goods but receives a reduction in the price of the goods. The supplier issues a credit memorandum for the return or allowance. The credit memorandum reduces the amount that the purchaser owes.

A purchase return by Big 10 Sporting Goods to Sledge Hammer Strength follows.

BUSINESS TRANSACTION

On September 5, Big 10 Sporting Goods returned damaged merchandise purchased on September 2 from Sledge Hammer Strength; it received Credit Memorandum 302 for $400.

GENERAL JOURNAL ENTRY

	DATE	DESCRIPTION	POST. REF.	DEBIT	CREDIT	
1	20X1					1
8	Sept. 5	Accounts Payable/Sledge Hammer Strength		400 00		8
9		Merchandise Inventory			400 00	9

Recording Purchases Discounts

The accounting for purchases discounts received is illustrated below.

BUSINESS TRANSACTION

On September 11, Big 10 Sporting Goods paid the amount due to Sledge Hammer Strength for the purchase of September 2, less the return on September 5, taking the 1 percent discount.

GENERAL JOURNAL ENTRY

	DATE	DESCRIPTION	POST. REF.	DEBIT	CREDIT	
1	20X1					1
11	Sept. 11	Accounts Payable/Sledge Hammer Strength ($9,750 − $400)		9 350 00		11
12		Merchandise Inventory [1% × ($9,500 − $400)]			91 00	12
13		Cash ($9,750 − $400 − $91)			9 259 00	13

The 1 percent discount reduces the cost of the merchandise purchased. As **Merchandise Inventory** is an asset account, we credit **Merchandise Inventory** to reflect the decrease in its cost.

Purchases discounts are calculated only on the cost of the merchandise purchased, less any returns. Purchases discounts are not allowed on freight charges.

Recording Merchandise Purchased with Trade Discounts

Many wholesale businesses offer goods to trade customers with the price computed using trade discounts. This is often done to simplify pricing. Publishing separate trade discounts can simplify the pricing structure appearing in product catalogs and brochures, while providing the company the flexibility to change the discounts offered through separate updates. Additionally, companies can raise the discount offered as the volume of the product purchased increases, promoting customer loyalty.

There may be a single trade discount or a series of discounts for each type of goods. The same goods may be offered to different customers at different trade discounts, depending on the size of the order and the costs of selling to the various types of customers.

A vendor of Big 10 Sporting Goods, Modern Sportsman, offers merchandise for sale with a list price of $10,000, with trade discounts of 20 percent and 10 percent, terms 2/10, n/30.

On September 15, Big 10 Sporting Goods purchases merchandise with a list price of $10,000 from Modern Sportsman. The amount owed for the purchase is computed as follows:

List price	$10,000.00
Less first discount ($10,000 × 20%)	2,000.00
Difference	$ 8,000.00
Less second discount ($8,000 × 10%)	800.00
Invoice price	$ 7,200.00

The journal entry to record the purchase on September 15 follows:

GENERAL JOURNAL

DATE	DESCRIPTION	POST. REF.	DEBIT	CREDIT
20X1				
Sept. 15	Merchandise Inventory		7,200 00	
	Accounts Payable/Modern Sportsman			7,200 00

On September 24, Big 10 Sporting Goods pays the amount owed to Modern Sportsman, less the 2 percent discount. The entry to record the payment is below.

GENERAL JOURNAL

DATE	DESCRIPTION	POST. REF.	DEBIT	CREDIT
20X1				
Sept. 24	Accounts Payable/Modern Sportsman		7,200 00	
	Merchandise Inventory (2% × $7,200)			144 00
	Cash ($7,200 − $144)			7,056 00

Sales Transactions

There are several new accounts used in accounting for sales transactions when the perpetual inventory method is employed. These new accounts are summarized below.

Name of Account	Type of Account	Normal Balance	Used to Record
Sales	Revenue	CR	Sales of merchandise inventory
Sales Tax Payable	Liability	CR	Sales tax charged to customers
Sales Discounts	Contra revenue	DR	Early payment discounts given to buyer by seller
Sales Returns and Allowance	Contra revenue	DR	Products returned by buyer on the seller's books
Credit Card Expense	Expense	DR	Fees charged by credit card companies to seller
Cost of Goods Sold	Expense	DR	The cost of merchandise sold to companies

Big 10 Sporting Goods engaged in the following sales transactions during the month of September 20X1. Big 10 Sporting Goods sells merchandise for cash, on account, and to customers using bank credit cards. The accounting for these transactions is illustrated below. Big 10 Sporting Goods must charge 5 percent sales tax on all purchases. Descriptions have been omitted.

Recording Sales with Sales Tax Payable for Cash and on Account

For merchandising companies, the revenue account is called *Sales*. Revenue is recorded when the product is sold to the customer. Additionally, perpetual inventory accounting requires a second entry when sales are made. This entry debits the *Cost of Goods Sold* account and credits the *Merchandise Inventory* account. The *Cost of Goods Sold* account shows the actual cost of the merchandise sold to customers and is classified as an expense in a perpetual inventory system. *Merchandise Inventory* is an asset account whose balance represents the cost of merchandise inventory on hand.

Most state and many local governments impose a sales tax on the sale of certain goods and services. Businesses are required to collect this tax from their customers and pay it to the proper tax agency at regular intervals. When taxable goods and services are sold on account, the sales tax is usually recorded at the time of sale, even though it will be collected from the customer later. A liability account called *Sales Tax Payable* is credited for the sales tax charged.

Below are two sales transactions of Big 10 Sporting Goods involving sales tax.

BUSINESS TRANSACTION

On September 1, Big 10 Sporting Goods recorded cash sales, $28,000, plus sales tax of $1,400. The cost of the merchandise sold was $14,000.

GENERAL JOURNAL ENTRY

GENERAL JOURNAL

	DATE		DESCRIPTION	POST. REF.	DEBIT	CREDIT	
1	20X1						1
2	Sept.	1	Cash ($28,000 + $1,400)		29 400 00		2
3			Sales			28 000 00	3
4			Sales Tax Payable ($28,000 × 5%)			1 400 00	4
5							5
6		1	Cost of Goods Sold		14 000 00		6
7			Merchandise Inventory			14 000 00	7

BUSINESS TRANSACTION

On September 2, Big 10 Sporting Goods recorded a sale of sporting apparel to Richard Santo on account, terms 1/10, net 30, $1,000, plus $50 tax. The cost of the merchandise sold was $550.

GENERAL JOURNAL ENTRY

GENERAL JOURNAL

	DATE		DESCRIPTION	POST. REF.	DEBIT	CREDIT	
1	20X1						1
9	Sept.	2	Accounts Receivable/Richard Santo ($1,000 + $50)		1 050 00		9
10			Sales			1 000 00	10
11			Sales Tax Payable ($1,000 × 5%)			50 00	11
13		2	Cost of Goods Sold		550 00		13
14			Merchandise Inventory			550 00	14

Recording Sales Returns and Sales Allowances

If the customer is dissatisfied with the goods received, the firm may take back the goods, resulting in a *sales return.* Or it may negotiate a reduction in the sales price, resulting in a *sales allowance.*

If the goods returned were initially paid for with cash, the customer will receive a cash refund. When a return or allowance is related to a credit sale, the normal practice is to issue a document called a *credit memorandum* to the customer instead of giving the customer a cash refund. The credit memorandum documents the reduction in the customer's account balance, crediting the customer's account receivable for the amount of the return or allowance. If the sale was made with sales tax added, the sales tax paid on the goods returned will also be credited to the customer's account. Both sales returns and sales allowances are recorded in a contra revenue account, **Sales Returns and Allowances.**

The perpetual inventory method requires two entries to record a return of product by the customer. The first entry records the credit memorandum given to the customer. The second entry records the return of merchandise to stock.

In the case of a sales allowance, only the first entry to record the credit memorandum is recorded, as the customer is keeping the merchandise.

The transaction below describes how Big 10 Sporting Goods would record the issuance of a credit memorandum to a customer for return of damaged goods.

BUSINESS TRANSACTION

On September 5, Big 10 Sporting Goods accepted a return of goods from Richard Santo. The items were originally sold on September 2. Big 10 Sporting Goods issued Credit Memorandum 202 to Richard Santo for $200. The cost of the returned items was $110.

GENERAL JOURNAL ENTRY

GENERAL JOURNAL

	DATE		DESCRIPTION	POST. REF.	DEBIT	CREDIT	
1	20X1						1
16	Sept.	5	Sales Tax Payable ($200 × 5%)		10 00		16
17			Sales Returns and Allowances		200 00		17
18			Accounts Receivable ($200 + $10)			210 00	18
20		5	Merchandise Inventory		110 00		20
21			Cost of Goods Sold			110 00	21

Cash Discounts on Sales

Many companies selling products offer payment terms to certain customers. Additionally, they may offer discounts on the price of the merchandise if the invoice is paid within a specified time period to encourage quicker payment. This is done to improve a firm's cash flow. The invoice date and credit terms determine when payment is due. The following credit terms often appear on invoices:

- *Net 30 days,* or *n/30,* means that payment in full is due 30 days after the date of the invoice.
- *Net 10 days EOM,* or *n/10 EOM,* means that payment in full is due 10 days after the end of the month in which the invoice was issued.
- *2 percent 10 days, net 30 days,* or *2/10, n/30,* means that if payment is made within 10 days of the invoice date, the customer can take a 2 percent discount. Otherwise, payment in full is due in 30 days. Note that discounts are not allowed on any freight portion of the invoice.

Big 10 Sporting Goods offers a 1 percent discount if the customer pays within 10 days of the invoice; otherwise, the amount is due in whole in 30 days. This credit term is expressed on the invoice as 1/10, n/30. To the seller, this is a *sales discount.* Sales discounts are recorded when the payment is received. Sales discounts are recorded in a contra revenue account, **Sales Discounts.**

The accounting for sales discounts is illustrated in the transaction below.

BUSINESS TRANSACTION

On September 11, Big 10 Sporting Goods received payment from Richard Santo for the sale of September 2, less the return on September 5 and less the cash discount.

GENERAL JOURNAL ENTRY

GENERAL JOURNAL

	DATE	DESCRIPTION	POST. REF.	DEBIT	CREDIT
1	20X1				
22	Sept. 11	Sales Discounts [(1% × ($1,000 − $200)]		8 00	
23		Cash ($1,050 − $210 − $8)		8 32 00	
24		Accounts Receivable ($1,050 − $210)			8 40 00

Bank Credit Cards

Retailers can provide credit while minimizing or avoiding the risk of losses from uncollectible accounts by accepting bank credit cards. The most widely accepted bank credit cards are MasterCard and Visa. Many banks participate in one or both of these credit card programs and other banks have their own credit cards. Bank credit cards are issued to consumers directly by banks. A business may participate in these credit card programs by meeting conditions set by the bank. Banks review such factors as:

- The business's financial history.
- The industry in which the business operates.
- The type of business: online, physical store, or both.
- Any past merchant account history.

When a sale is made to a cardholder, the sale is processed electronically. The customer inserts his or her credit card into a card reading device. The card reading device transmits information to the bank using an Internet connection.

Sales made to customers paying with bank credit cards are treated as cash sales. In most cases, the amount processed on the card is transferred to the seller's bank account the same day. Fees charged by the credit card company for processing these sales are debited to an account called **Credit Card Expense.** It is important to note these fees are charged on the total amount of the sale plus any sales tax.

For example, assume Big 10 Sporting Goods sells merchandise on September 15 totaling $20,000 to customers using bank credit cards, plus 5 percent sales tax. The bank credit card company charges a 2 percent fee to process the transactions. The cost of the merchandise sold was $13,500.

Cash would be debited for $20,580, computed as follows:

Merchandise sales	$20,000.00
Plus sales tax ($20,000 × 5%)	1,000.00
Subtotal	21,000.00
Less bank fee ($21,000 × 2%)	420.00
Debit to **Cash**	$20,580.00

The following journal entry records the sales made to customers using bank credit cards on September 15.

GENERAL JOURNAL

DATE	DESCRIPTION	POST. REF.	DEBIT	CREDIT
20X1				
Sept. 15	Credit Card Expense		420 00	
	Cash		20 580 00	
	Sales			20 000 00
	Sales Tax Payable			1 000 00
15	Cost of Goods Sold		13 500 00	
	Merchandise Inventory			13 500 00

Posting Transactions to Subsidiary Ledgers

The posting of transactions from the general journal to the accounts receivable ledger is discussed in Chapter 7. The posting of transactions from the general journal to the accounts payable ledger is discussed in Chapter 8. When the perpetual inventory method is used, such postings are done in the same manner demonstrated in Chapters 7 and 8.

Chapter 9 REVIEW — Chapter Summary

In this chapter, you have learned the basic principles of accounting for cash payments and cash receipts.

Learning Objectives

9-1 Record cash receipts in a cash receipts journal.

Use of special journals leads to an efficient recording process for cash transactions. The cash receipts journal has separate columns for the accounts used most often for cash receipt transactions.

9-2 Account for cash short or over.

Errors can occur when making change. Cash register discrepancies should be recorded using the expense account *Cash Short or Over.*

9-3 Post from the cash receipts journal to subsidiary and general ledgers.

Individual accounts receivable amounts are posted to the subsidiary ledger daily. Figures in the Other Accounts Credit column are posted individually to the general ledger during the month. All other postings are done on a summary basis at month-end.

9-4 Record cash payments in a cash payments journal.

The cash payments journal has separate columns for the accounts used most often, eliminating the need to record the same account names repeatedly.

9-5 Post from the cash payments journal to subsidiary and general ledgers.

Individual accounts payable amounts are posted daily to the accounts payable subsidiary ledger. Amounts listed in the Other Accounts Debit column are posted individually to the general ledger during the month. All other postings are completed on a summary basis at the end of the month.

9-6 Demonstrate a knowledge of procedures for a petty cash fund.

Although most payments are made electronically or by check, small payments are often made through a petty cash fund. A petty cash voucher is prepared for each payment and signed by the person receiving the money. The person in charge of the fund records expenditures on a petty cash analysis sheet. The fund is replenished with a check for the sum spent. An entry is made in the cash payments journal to debit the accounts involved.

9-7 Demonstrate a knowledge of internal control procedures for cash.

All businesses need a system of internal controls to protect cash from theft and mishandling and to ensure accurate records of cash transactions. A checking account is essential to store cash safely and to make cash payments efficiently. For maximum control over outgoing cash, all payments should be made by check except those from carefully controlled special-purpose cash funds such as a petty cash fund.

9-8 Write a check, endorse checks, prepare a bank deposit slip, and maintain a checkbook balance.

Check writing requires careful attention to details. If a standard checkbook is used, the stub should be completed before the check so that it will not be forgotten. The stub gives the data needed to journalize the payment.

9-9 Reconcile the monthly bank statement.

A bank statement should be immediately reconciled with the cash balance in the firm's financial records. Usually, differences are due to deposits in transit, outstanding checks, and bank service charges, but many factors can cause lack of agreement between the bank balance and the book balance.

9-10 Record any adjusting entries required from the bank reconciliation.

Some differences between the bank balance and the book balance may require that the firm's records be adjusted after the bank statement is reconciled. Journal entries are recorded and then posted to correct the *Cash* account balance and the checkbook balance.

9-11 Understand how businesses use online banking to manage cash activities.

Many businesses now use online banking to receive cash payments from customers and to initiate cash payments.

9-12 *Appendix:* Record transactions for a retailer using the perpetual inventory system.

Perpetual inventory systems give management more control over the company's inventory, and assist management in inventory control and purchasing activities.

9-13 Define the accounting terms new to this chapter.

Glossary

Bank reconciliation statement (p. 303) A statement that accounts for all differences between the balance on the bank statement and the book balance of cash

Blank endorsement (p. 299) A signature of the payee written on the back of the check that transfers ownership of the check without specifying to whom or for what purpose

Bonding (p. 295) The process by which employees are investigated by an insurance company that will insure the business against losses through employee theft or mishandling of funds

Canceled check (p. 302) A check paid by the bank on which it was drawn

Cash (p. 280) In accounting, currency, coins, checks, money orders, and funds on deposit in a bank

Cash payments journal (p. 287) A special journal used to record transactions involving the payment of cash

Cash receipts journal (p. 280) A special journal used to record and post transactions involving the receipt of cash

Cash register proof (p. 281) A verification that the amount of currency and coins in a cash register agrees with the amount shown on the cash register audit tape

Cash Short or Over **account** (p. 282) An account used to record any discrepancies between the amount of currency and coins in the cash register and the amount shown on the audit tape

Check (p. 298) A written order signed by an authorized person instructing a bank to pay a specific sum of money to a designated person or business

Credit memorandum (p. 302) A form that explains any addition, other than a deposit, to a checking account

Debit memorandum (p. 302) A form that explains any deduction, other than a check or other electronic payment transaction, from a checking account

Deposit in transit (p. 303) A deposit that is recorded in the cash receipts journal but that reaches the bank too late to be shown on the monthly bank statement

Deposit slip (p. 299) A form prepared to record the deposit of cash or checks to a bank account

Dishonored (NSF) check (p. 302) A check returned to the depositor unpaid because of insufficient funds in the drawer's account; also called an NSF check

Drawee (p. 298) The bank on which a check is written

Drawer (p. 298) The person or firm issuing a check

Electronic funds transfer (EFT) (p. 307) An electronic transfer of money from one account to another

Endorsement (p. 299) A written authorization that transfers ownership of a check

Full endorsement (p. 299) A signature transferring a check to a specific person, firm, or bank

Negotiable (p. 298) A financial instrument whose ownership can be transferred to another person or business

Outstanding checks (p. 303) Checks that have been recorded in the cash payments journal but have not yet been paid by the bank

Payee (p. 298) The person or firm to whom a check is payable

Petty cash analysis sheet (p. 293) A form used to record transactions involving petty cash

Petty cash fund (p. 280) A special-purpose fund used to handle payments involving small amounts of money

Petty cash voucher (p. 293) A form used to record the payments made from a petty cash fund

Postdated check (p. 300) A check dated some time in the future

Promissory note (p. 282) A written promise to pay a specified amount of money on a specific date

Restrictive endorsement (p. 299) A signature that transfers a check to a specific party for a stated purpose

Service charge (p. 302) A fee charged by a bank to cover the costs of maintaining accounts and providing services

Statement of account (p. 282) A form sent to a firm's customers showing transactions during the month and the balance owed

Comprehensive Self Review

1. Describe a full endorsement.
2. What is a petty cash voucher?
3. When is the petty cash fund replenished?
4. What are the advantages of using special journals for cash receipts and cash payments?
5. What does the term *cash* mean in business?

(Answers to Comprehensive Self Review are at the end of the chapter.)

Discussion Questions

1. Why is a bank reconciliation prepared?
2. Why are journal entries sometimes needed after the bank reconciliation is prepared?
3. Give some reasons why the bank balance and the book balance of cash might differ.
4. What is the book balance of cash?
5. What procedures are used to achieve internal control over banking activities?
6. What information is shown on the bank statement?
7. What is a check?
8. What type of information is entered on a check stub? Why should a check stub be prepared before the check is written?
9. Why are MICR numbers printed on deposit slips and checks?
10. Which type of endorsement is most appropriate for a business to use?
11. How are cash shortages and overages recorded?
12. When are petty cash expenditures entered in a firm's accounting records?
13. Describe the major controls for petty cash.
14. What type of account is **Purchases Discounts**? How is this account presented on the income statement?
15. How does a firm record a payment on account to a creditor when a cash discount is involved? Which journal is used?
16. How does a wholesale business record a check received on account from a customer when a cash discount is involved? Which journal is used?
17. Why do some wholesale businesses offer cash discounts to their customers?
18. What is a promissory note? What entry is made to record the collection of a promissory note and interest? Which journal is used?
19. Describe the major controls for cash payments.
20. Explain what *bonding* means. How does bonding relate to safeguarding cash?
21. Describe the major controls for cash receipts.
22. Explain the meaning of the following terms:

a. Canceled check
b. Outstanding check
c. Deposit in transit
d. Debit memorandum
e. Credit memorandum
f. Dishonored check
g. Blank endorsement
h. Deposit slip
i. Drawee
j. Restrictive endorsement
k. Payee
l. Drawer
m. Service charge

Discussion Questions 23, 24, 25, and 26 refer to the Appendix to this chapter.

23. The following statements concern the use of online banking. Identify whether each is true or false.
    a. Businesses can use online banking to send tax payments to government agencies.
    b. Businesses can use online banking to send, but not receive, electronic fund transfers.
    c. Bank security alerts are usually sent via registered mail.
    d. Only authorized check signers should have access to the company's online bank account.
    e. Bank log-in information should be changed frequently.

24. What account is debited for the purchase of merchandise inventory when (a) the periodic system is used and (b) the perpetual inventory system is used?

25. What account is credited for the return of merchandise inventory when (a) the periodic system is used and (b) the perpetual inventory system is used?

26. What account is debited for freight charges on merchandise inventory purchases when (a) the periodic system is used and (b) the perpetual inventory system is used?

27. What account is credited for a cash discount taken by the purchaser when (a) the periodic system is used and (b) the perpetual system is used?

APPLICATIONS

Exercises

Recording cash receipts.

◀ **Exercise 9.1**
Objectives 9-1, 9-2

The following transactions took place at Nickie's Sports Gear during the first week of October 20X1. Record these transactions in a cash receipts journal. Use 12 as the page number for the cash receipts journal.

DATE		TRANSACTIONS
Oct.	1	Had cash sales of $7,600 plus sales tax of $608; there was a cash overage of $12.
	2	Collected $980 on account from James Lynn, a credit customer.
	3	Had cash sales of $5,400 plus sales tax of $432.
	4	Nickie Martin, the owner, made an additional cash investment of $27,000.
	6	Had cash sales of $7,400 plus sales tax of $592; there was a cash shortage of $20.

Exercise 9.2
Objective 9-4

▶ **Recording cash payments.**

The following transactions took place at Nickie's Sports Gear during the first week of October 20X1. Record these transactions in a cash payments journal. Use 15 as the page number of the cash payments journal.

DATE		TRANSACTIONS
Oct.	1	Issued Check 3850 for $3,900 to pay the monthly rent.
	1	Issued Check 3851 for $3,400 to Hunter Company, a creditor, on account.
	2	Issued Check 3852 for $13,750 to purchase new equipment.
	2	Issued Check 3853 for $8,160 to remit sales tax to the state sales tax authority.
	3	Issued Check 3854 for $1,960 to Sports Emporium, a creditor, on account for invoice of $2,000 less cash discount of $40.
	4	Issued Check 3855 for $3,725 to purchase merchandise.
	6	Issued Check 3856 for $5,000 as a cash withdrawal for personal use by Nickie Martin, the owner.

Exercise 9.3
Objective 9-6

▶ **Recording the establishment of a petty cash fund.**

On January 2, The Orange Legal Clinic issued Check 2108 for $400 to establish a petty cash fund. Indicate how this transaction would be recorded in a cash payments journal. Use 1 as the page number for the cash payments journal.

Exercise 9.4
Objective 9-6

▶ **Recording the replenishment of a petty cash fund.**

On January 2, Vanessa's Floral Supplies Inc. issued Check 3100 for $400 to establish a petty cash fund. On January 31, Check 3159 was issued to replenish the petty cash fund. An analysis of payments from the fund showed these totals: **Supplies,** $78; **Delivery Expense,** $209; and **Miscellaneous Expense,** $16. Indicate how this transaction would be recorded in a cash payments journal. Use 1 as the page number for the cash payments journal.

Exercise 9.5
Objectives 9-9, 9-10

▶ **Preparing a bank reconciliation statement.**

Johnson Corporation received a bank statement showing a balance of $15,900 as of October 31, 20X1. The firm's records showed a book balance of $15,572 on October 31. The difference between the two balances was caused by the following items. Prepare a bank reconciliation statement and necessary journal entries for the firm as of October 31. Use 14 as the page number for the general journal.

1. A debit memorandum for an NSF check from Mike Hart for $342.
2. Three outstanding checks: Check 7017 for $134, Check 7098 for $45, and Check 7107 for $1,560.
3. A bank service charge of $12.
4. A deposit in transit of $1,057. The deposit was made on October 31 using the bank's ATM machine after the bank had closed.

Exercise 9.6
Objectives 9-9, 9-10

▶ **Analyzing bank reconciliation items.**

At Livermore Delivery and Courier Service, the following items were found to cause a difference between the bank statement and the firm's records. Indicate whether each item will affect the bank balance or the book balance when the bank reconciliation statement is prepared. Also indicate which items will require an accounting entry after the bank reconciliation is completed.

1. A deposit in transit.
2. A debit memorandum for a dishonored check.
3. A credit memorandum for a promissory note that the bank collected for Livermore.
4. An error found in Livermore's records, which involves the amount of a check. The firm's checkbook and cash payments journal indicate $808 as the amount, but the canceled check itself and the listing on the bank statement show that $880 was the actual sum.

5. An outstanding check.
6. A bank service charge.
7. A check issued by another firm that was charged to Livermore's account by mistake.

Preparing a bank reconciliation statement. ◀ Exercise 9.7

Venturi Office Supplies received a bank statement showing a balance of $73,027 as of March 31, 20X1. The firm's records showed a book balance of $72,987 on March 31. The difference between the two balances was caused by the following items. Prepare a bank reconciliation statement for the firm as of March 31 and the necessary journal entries. Use 8 as the page number for the general journal.

Objectives 9-9, 9-10

1. A debit memorandum for $40, which covers the bank's collection fee for the note.
2. A deposit in transit of $3,700.
3. A check for $378 issued by another firm that was mistakenly charged to Venturi's account.
4. A debit memorandum for an NSF check of $4,643 issued by Wilson Construction Company, a credit customer.
5. Outstanding checks: Check 3782 for $1,250; Check 3840 for $151.
6. A credit memorandum for a $7,400 noninterest-bearing note receivable that the bank collected for the firm.

Determining the adjusted bank balance. ◀ Exercise 9.8

Flores Company received a bank statement showing a balance of $13,000 on November 30, 20X1. During the bank reconciliation process, Flores Company's accountant noted the following bank errors:

Objective 9-9

1. A check for $153 issued by Flora, Inc., was mistakenly charged to Flores Company's account.
2. Check 2782 was written for $100 but was paid by the bank as $1,100.
3. Check 2920 for $87 was paid by the bank twice.
4. A deposit for $570 on November 22 was credited by the bank for $750.

Assuming outstanding checks total $2,170, prepare the adjusted bank balance section of the November 30, 20X1, bank reconciliation.

Journalizing electronic transactions. ◀ Exercise 9.9

After returning from a three-day business trip, the accountant for Southeast Sales, Johanna Estrada, checked bank activity in the company's checking account online. The activity for the last three days follows.

Objective 9-11

Business Checking		Account #123456-987			
Date	Type	Description	Additions	Payments	Balance
09/24/20X1	Loan Payment	Online Transfer to HMG XXXX		$3,500.00	$15,675.06
09/24/20X1	Deposit	DEPOSIT ID NUMBER 8888	$2,269.60		$19,175.06
09/23/20X1	Check	CHECK #1554 (view)		$3,500.00	$16,905.46
09/23/20X1	Bill Payment	Online Payment		$36.05	$20,405.46
09/22/20X1	Check	CHECK #1553 (view)		$240.00	$20,441.51
09/22/20X1	Check	CHECK #1551 (view)		$1,750.00	$20,681.51
09/22/20X1	ACH Credit	Edwards UK AP PAYMENT	$8,900.00		$22,431.51
09/22/20X1	ATM	ATM WITHDRAWAL		$240.00	$13,531.51

After matching these transactions to the company's *Cash* account in the general ledger, Johanna noted the following unrecorded transactions:

1. The ATM withdrawal on 9/22/20X1 was for personal use by the owner, Robert Savage.
2. The ACH credit on 9/22/20X1 was an electronic funds payment received on account from Edwards UK, a credit customer located in Great Britain.

3. The bill payment made 9/23/20X1 was to Waste Control Trash Services (utilities).
4. The loan payment on 9/24/20X1 was an automatic debit by Central Motors for the company's monthly payment on a loan for its automobiles. The loan does not bear interest.

Prepare the journal entries in a general journal to record the four transactions above. Use 21 as the page number.

Exercise 9.10
Appendix
Objective 9-12

▶ **Normal balances.**

Identify the normal balance of the following accounts. Use "Dr." for debit or "Cr." for credit.

1. _____ Merchandise Inventory
2. _____ Sales Tax Payable
3. _____ Sales
4. _____ Sales Discounts
5. _____ Sales Returns and Allowances
6. _____ Cost of Goods Sold
7. _____ Credit Card Expense

Exercise 9.11
Appendix
Objective 9-12

▶ **Recording purchases made for cash and on account.**

Rubino Corporation engaged in the following transactions during June. The company uses the perpetual inventory system. Record these transactions in a general journal.

DATE		TRANSACTIONS
20X1		
June	4	Purchased merchandise on account from Katz Company; Invoice 100 for $2,050; terms n/30.
	15	Recorded purchases for cash, $2,540.
	30	Paid amount due to Katz Company for the purchase on June 4.

Exercise 9.12
Appendix
Objective 9-12

▶ **Recording purchases with purchases returns and purchases discounts.**

Record the following transactions of Evelyn's Designs in a general journal. The company uses the perpetual inventory system.

DATE		TRANSACTIONS
20X1		
April	1	Purchased merchandise on credit from American Fabricators, Invoice 885, $2,000; terms 1/10, n/30; freight of $100 was paid by American Fabricators and added to the invoice (total invoice amount, $2,100).
	9	Paid amount due to American Fabricators for the purchase of April 1, less the 1 percent discount, Check 457.
	15	Purchased merchandise on credit from Kalyagin Company, Invoice 145, $600; terms 1/10, n/30; freight of $50 prepaid by Kalyagin and added to the invoice.
	17	Returned damaged merchandise purchased on April 15 from Kalyagin Company; received Credit Memorandum 332 for $200.
	24	Paid the amount due to Kalyagin Company for the purchase of April 15, less the return on April 17, taking the 1 percent discount, Check 470.

Exercise 9.13
Appendix
Objective 9-12

Recording sales made for cash and on account.

Wang Corporation operates in a state with no sales tax. The company uses the perpetual inventory system. Record the following transactions in a general journal. Use 1 as the page number for the general journal.

DATE	TRANSACTIONS
20X1	
June 5	Sold merchandise on account to Brown Company; issued Sales Slip 1200 for $1,025, terms n/30. The cost of the merchandise sold was $733.
15	Recorded cash sales, $1,990. The cost of merchandise sold was $1,388.
30	Received payment on account due from Brown Company for the sale on June 5.

Exercise 9.14
Appendix
Objective 9-12

Recording sales made for cash and on account, with 8 percent sales tax, and sales returns.

Record the following transactions of Fashion Park in a general journal. Use 1 as the page number for the general journal. Fashion Park must charge 8 percent sales tax on all sales. The company uses the perpetual inventory system.

DATE	TRANSACTIONS
20X1	
April 2	Sold merchandise for cash, $2,500 plus sales tax. The cost of merchandise sold was $1,500.
3	The customer purchasing merchandise for cash on April 2 returned $250 of the merchandise; provided a cash refund to the customer. The cost of returned merchandise was $150.
4	Sold merchandise on credit to Jordan Clark; issued Sales Slip 908 for $1,050 plus tax, terms n/30. The cost of the merchandise sold was $630.
6	Accepted return of merchandise from Jordan Clark; issued Credit Memorandum 302 for $150 plus tax. The original sale was made on Sales Slip 908 of April 4. The cost of returned merchandise was $90.
30	Received payment on account from Jordan Clark in payment of her purchase of April 4, less the return on April 6.

Exercise 9.15
Appendix
Objective 9-12

Recording a sale made on account, with a sales discount.

On April 1, Manning Meat Distributors sold merchandise on account to Fichman's Franks for $3,700 on Invoice 1001, terms 2/10, n/30. The cost of merchandise sold was $2,200. Payment was received in full from Fichman's Franks, less discount, on April 10.

Record the transactions for Manning Meat Distributors on April 1 and April 10. The company uses the perpetual inventory system. Use 1 as the journal page number.

Exercise 9.16
Appendix
Objective 9-12

Journalizing merchandising transactions for buyer and seller.

Bushell Company (buyer) and Schiff, Inc. (seller), engaged in the following transactions during February 20X1. Schiff, Inc. operates in a state with no sales tax.

BUSHELL COMPANY

DATE		TRANSACTIONS
20X1		
Feb.	10	Purchased merchandise for $5,500 from Schiff, Inc., Invoice 1980, terms 1/10, n/30.
	13	Received Credit Memorandum 230 from Schiff, Inc., for damaged merchandise totaling $600 that was returned; the goods were purchased on Invoice 1980, dated February 10.
	19	Paid amount due to Schiff, Inc., for Invoice 1980 of February 10, less the return of February 13 and less the cash discount, Check 2010.

SCHIFF, INC.

DATE		TRANSACTIONS
20X1		
Feb.	10	Sold merchandise for $5,500 on account to Bushell Company, Invoice 1980, terms 1/10, n/30. The cost of merchandise sold was $4,400.
	13	Issued Credit Memorandum 230 to Bushell Company for damaged merchandise totaling $600 that was returned; the goods were purchased on Invoice 1980, dated February 10. The cost of the returned goods was $480.
	19	Received payment from Bushell Company for Invoice 1980 of February 10, less the return of February 13 and less the cash discount, Check 2010.

Both companies use the perpetual inventory system. Journalize the transactions above in a general journal for both Bushell Company and Schiff, Inc. Use 20 as the journal page for both companies.

PROBLEMS

Problem Set A

Problem 9.1A

Objectives 9-1, 9-2, 9-3

▶ **Journalizing cash receipts and posting to the general ledger.**

Car Geek is a retail store that sells car care products over the Internet. The firm's cash receipts for February and the general ledger accounts used to record these transactions are shown below.

INSTRUCTIONS

1. Open the general ledger accounts and enter the balances as of February 1, 20X1.
2. Record the transactions in a cash receipts journal. Use 4 as the page number.
3. Post the individual entries from the Other Accounts Credit section of the cash receipts journal to the proper general ledger accounts.
4. Total and rule the cash receipts journal as of February 28, 20X1.
5. Post the column totals from the cash receipts journal to the proper general ledger accounts.

SELECTED GENERAL LEDGER ACCOUNTS

101 Cash	$ 4,860 Dr.
109 Notes Receivable	700 Dr.
111 Accounts Receivable	4,025 Dr.
129 Supplies	510 Dr.
231 Sales Tax Payable	245 Cr.
301 Ken Sato, Capital	33,000 Cr.
401 Sales	
491 Interest Income	
620 Cash Short or Over	

DATE		TRANSACTIONS
Feb.	3	Received $400 from Kelly Stott, a credit customer, on account.
	5	Received a cash refund of $110 for damaged supplies.
	7	Had cash sales of $3,800 plus sales tax of $304 during the first week of February; there was a cash shortage of $50.
	9	Ken Sato, the owner, invested an additional $14,000 cash in the business.
	12	Received $280 from Jamie Garrison, a credit customer, in payment of her account.
	14	Had cash sales of $3,550 plus sales tax of $284 during the second week of February; there was an overage of $18.
	16	Received $350 from Michael Hunt, a credit customer, to apply toward his account.
	19	Received a check from Kay Pitts to pay her $700 promissory note plus interest of $28.
	21	Had cash sales of $4,050 plus sales tax of $324 during the third week of February.
	25	Al Harris, a credit customer, sent a check for $480 to pay the balance he owes.
	28	Had cash sales of $3,100 plus sales tax of $248 during the fourth week of February; there was a cash shortage of $26.

Analyze: What total accounts receivable were collected in February?

Journalizing cash payments, recording petty cash, and posting to the general ledger.

◀ **Problem 9.2A**
Objectives 9-4, 9-5, 9-6

The cash payments of The Aristocrats Jewels, a retail business, for June and the general ledger accounts used to record these transactions appear below.

INSTRUCTIONS

1. Open the general ledger accounts and enter the balances as of June 1.
2. Record all payments by check in a cash payments journal; use 8 as the page number.
3. Record all payments from the petty cash fund on a petty cash analysis sheet; use 8 as the sheet number.
4. Post the individual entries from the Other Accounts Debit section of the cash payments journal to the proper general ledger accounts.

5. Total, prove, and rule the petty cash analysis sheet as of June 30. Record the replenishment of the fund and the final balance on the sheet.
6. Total, prove, and rule the cash payments journal as of June 30.
7. Post the column totals from the cash payments journal to the proper general ledger accounts.

SELECTED GENERAL LEDGER ACCOUNTS

101 Cash	$46,740 Dr.
105 Petty Cash Fund	
129 Supplies	1,160 Dr.
201 Notes Payable	4,200 Cr.
205 Accounts Payable	19,880 Cr.
231 Sales Tax Payable	5,200 Cr.
302 Larry Jennings, Drawing	
451 Sales Returns and Allowances	
504 Purchases Discounts	
611 Delivery Expense	
620 Rent Expense	
623 Salaries Expense	
626 Telephone Expense	
634 Interest Expense	
635 Miscellaneous Expense	

DATE		TRANSACTIONS
June	1	Issued Check 4121 for $3,500 to pay the monthly rent.
	2	Issued Check 4122 for $5,200 to remit the state sales tax.
	3	Issued Check 4123 for $2,880 to Perfect Timing Watch Company, a creditor, in payment of Invoice 6808, dated May 5.
	4	Issued Check 4124 for $250 to establish a petty cash fund. (After journalizing this transaction, be sure to enter it on the first line of the petty cash analysis sheet.)
	5	Paid $40 from the petty cash fund for office supplies, Petty Cash Voucher 1.
	7	Issued Check 4125 for $4,368 to Perry Corporation in payment of a $4,200 promissory note and interest of $168.
	8	Paid $30 from the petty cash fund for postage stamps, Petty Cash Voucher 2.
	10	Issued Check 4126 for $604 to a customer as a cash refund for a defective watch that was returned; the original sale was made for cash.
	12	Issued Check 4127 for $286 to pay the telephone bill.
	14	Issued Check 4128 for $5,831 to International Jewelry Company, a creditor, in payment of Invoice 8629, dated May 6 ($5,950), less a cash discount ($119).
	15	Paid $19 from the petty cash fund for delivery service, Petty Cash Voucher 3.
	17	Issued Check 4129 for $960 to purchase store supplies.
	20	Issued Check 4130 for $3,920 to Nelsons Jewelry and Accessories, a creditor, in payment of Invoice 1513, dated June 12 ($4,000), less a cash discount ($80).
	22	Paid $34 from the petty cash fund for a personal withdrawal by Larry Jennings, the owner, Petty Cash Voucher 4.

DATE	9.2A (cont.) TRANSACTIONS
25	Paid $40 from the petty cash fund to have the store windows washed and repaired, Petty Cash Voucher 5.
27	Issued Check 4131 for $3,750 to Classy Creations, a creditor, in payment of Invoice 667, dated May 30.
30	Paid $34 from the petty cash fund for delivery service, Petty Cash Voucher 6.
30	Issued Check 4132 for $7,925 to pay the monthly salaries.
30	Issued Check 4133 for $6,000 to Larry Jennings, the owner, as a withdrawal for personal use.
30	Issued Check 4134 for $197 to replenish the petty cash fund. (Foot the columns of the petty cash analysis sheet in order to determine the accounts that should be debited and the amounts involved.)

Analyze: What total payments were made from the petty cash fund for the month?

Journalizing sales and cash receipts and posting to the general ledger.

◀ **Problem 9.3A**
Objectives 9-1, 9-2, 9-3

Awesome Sounds is a wholesale business that sells musical instruments. Transactions involving sales and cash receipts for the firm during April 20X1 follow, along with the general ledger accounts used to record these transactions.

INSTRUCTIONS

1. Open the general ledger accounts and enter the balances as of April 1, 20X1.
2. Record the transactions in a sales journal, a cash receipts journal, and a general journal. Use 7 as the page number for each of the special journals and 17 as the page number for the general journal.
3. Post the entries from the general journal to the general ledger.
4. Total, prove, and rule the special journals as of April 30, 20X1.
5. Post the column totals from the special journals to the proper general ledger accounts.
6. Prepare the heading and the Revenue section of the firm's income statement for the month ended April 30.

GENERAL LEDGER ACCOUNTS

101 Cash	$17,400 Dr.
109 Notes Receivable	
111 Accounts Receivable	22,000 Dr.
401 Sales	
451 Sales Returns and Allowances	
452 Sales Discounts	

DATE	TRANSACTIONS
April 1	Sold merchandise for $4,900 to Soprano Music Center; issued Invoice 9312 with terms of 2/10, n/30.
3	Received a check for $1,960 from Music Supply Store in payment of Invoice 6718 of March 25 ($2,000), less a cash discount ($40).
5	Sold merchandise for $1,825 in cash to a new customer who has not yet established credit.
8	Sold merchandise for $5,500 to Music Warehouse; issued Invoice 9313 with terms of 2/10, n/30.

(continued)

DATE	9.3A (cont.) TRANSACTIONS
10	Soprano Music Center sent a check for $4,802 in payment of Invoice 9312 of April 1 ($4,900), less a cash discount ($98).
15	Accepted a return of damaged merchandise from Music Warehouse; issued Credit Memorandum 105 for $900; the original sale was made on Invoice 9313 of April 8.
19	Sold merchandise for $11,500 to Eagleton Music Center; issued Invoice 9314 with terms of 2/10, n/30.
23	Collected $3,225 from Sounds From Yesterday for Invoice 6725 of March 25.
26	Accepted a two-month promissory note for $6,500 from Country Music Store in settlement of its overdue account; the note has an interest rate of 12 percent.
28	Received a check for $11,270 from Eagleton Music Center in payment of Invoice 9314, dated April 19 ($11,500), less a cash discount ($230).
30	Sold merchandise for $10,800 to Contemporary Sounds, Inc.; issued Invoice 9315 with terms of 2/10, n/30.

Analyze: What total sales on account were made in the month of April, prior to any returns or allowances?

Problem 9.4A
Objectives 9-4, 9-5

▶ **Journalizing purchases, cash payments, and purchases discounts; posting to the general ledger.**

The Hike and Bike Outlet is a retail store. Transactions involving purchases and cash payments for the firm during June 20X1 are listed below, as are the general ledger accounts used to record these transactions.

INSTRUCTIONS

1. Open the general ledger accounts and enter the balances as of June 1, 20X1.
2. Record the transactions in a purchases journal, a cash payments journal, and a general journal. Use 8 as the page number for each of the special journals and 20 as the page number for the general journal.
3. Post the entries from the general journal and from the Other Accounts Debit section of the cash payments journal to the proper general ledger accounts.
4. Total, prove, and rule the special journals as of June 30.
5. Post the column totals from the special journals to the general ledger.
6. Show how the firm's net cost of purchases would be reported on its income statement for the month ended June 30.

GENERAL LEDGER ACCOUNTS

101 Cash	$25,900 Dr.
131 Equipment	68,000 Dr.
201 Notes Payable	
205 Accounts Payable	4,980 Cr.
501 Purchases	
503 Purchases Ret. and Allow.	
504 Purchases Discounts	
611 Rent Expense	
614 Salaries Expense	
617 Telephone Expense	

DATE		TRANSACTIONS
June	1	Issued Check 1101 for $3,700 to pay the monthly rent.
	3	Purchased merchandise for $4,100 from Perfect Fit Shoe Shop, Invoice 746, dated June 1; the terms are 2/10, n/30.
	5	Purchased new store equipment for $5,700 from Bigtown Company, Invoice 9067 dated June 4, net payable in 30 days.
	7	Issued Check 1102 for $1,570 to Take a Break Clothing Company, a creditor, in payment of Invoice 3342 of May 9.
	8	Issued Check 1103 for $4,018 to Perfect Fit Shoe Shop, a creditor, in payment of Invoice 746 dated June 1 ($4,100), less a cash discount ($82).
	12	Purchased merchandise for $2,500 from Jim's Sweat Shop, Invoice 9922, dated June 9, net due and payable in 30 days.
	15	Issued Check 1104 for $438 to pay the monthly telephone bill.
	18	Received Credit Memorandum 203 for $700 from Jim's Sweat Shop for defective goods that were returned; the original purchase was made on Invoice 9922 dated June 9.
	21	Purchased new store equipment for $10,750 from LA Sports Equipment Company; issued a three-month promissory note with interest at 12 percent.
	23	Purchased merchandise for $6,200 from Beautiful Trails, Invoice 1927, dated June 20; terms of 2/10, n/30.
	25	Issued Check 1105 for $1,600 to Jim's Sweat Shop, a creditor, as payment on account, Invoice 7416 dated May 28.
	28	Issued Check 1106 for $6,076 to Beautiful Trails, a creditor, in payment of Invoice 1927 of June 20 ($6,200), less a cash discount ($124).
	30	Purchased merchandise for $2,180 from The Jogging Shoe LLC, Invoice 4713, dated June 26; the terms are 1/10, n/30.
	30	Issued Check 1107 for $6,800 to pay the monthly salaries of the employees.

Analyze: Assuming that all relevant information is included in this problem, what total liabilities does the company have at month-end?

Preparing a bank reconciliation statement and journalizing entries to adjust the cash balance.

◀ **Problem 9.5A**
Objectives 9-9, 9-10

On May 2, 20X1, PHF Vacations received its April bank statement from First City Bank and Trust. Enclosed with the bank statement, which appears below, was a debit memorandum for $210 that covered an NSF check issued by Doris Fisher, a credit customer. The firm's checkbook contained the following information about deposits made and checks issued during April. The balance of the *Cash* account and the checkbook on April 30, 20X1, was $3,012.

DATE		TRANSACTIONS	
April	1	Balance	$6,099
	1	Check 1207	110
	3	Check 1208	400
	5	Deposit	450
	5	Check 1209	325
	10	Check 1210	3,000
			(continued)

DATE	9.5A (cont.) TRANSACTIONS	
17	Check 1211	60
19	Deposit	200
22	Check 1212	8
23	Deposit	200
26	Check 1213	250
28	Check 1214	18
30	Check 1215	16
30	Deposit	250

FIRST CITY BANK AND TRUST

PHF Vacations 1-877-123-9876
1718 Jade Lane
San Diego, CA 92111-4998

Account Number: 23-11070-08 April 1–30, 20X1
Activity Summary:

Balance, April 1	$ 6,099.00
Deposits and credits	850.00
Withdrawals and debits	(4,370.00)
Balance, April 30	$ 2,579.00

DATE	DESCRIPTION	DEPOSITS/CREDITS	WITHDRAWALS/DEBITS	BALANCE
4/1/X1	Opening balance			$6,099.00
4/6/X1	Deposit	450.00		6,549.00
4/6/X1	Check No. 1207		110.00	6,439.00
4/10/X1	Check No. 1208		400.00	6,039.00
4/10/X1	Check No. 1209		325.00	5,714.00
4/13/X1	Check No. 1210		3,000.00	2,714.00
4/14/X1	Service fee		7.00	2,707.00
4/20/X1	Deposit	200.00		2,907.00
4/22/X1	Check No. 1211		60.00	2,847.00
4/25/X1	Deposit	200.00		3,047.00
4/26/X1	Check No. 1212		8.00	3,039.00
4/29/X1	Debit for NSF Check		210.00	2,829.00
4/29/X1	Check No. 1213		250.00	2,579.00
	Totals	850.00	4,370.00	

INSTRUCTIONS

1. Prepare a bank reconciliation statement for the firm as of April 30, 20X1.
2. Record general journal entries for any items on the bank reconciliation statement that must be journalized. Date the entries April 30, 20X1.

Analyze: What checks remain outstanding after the bank statement has been reconciled?

Preparing a bank reconciliation statement and journalizing entries to adjust the cash balance.

◀ **Problem 9.6A**
Objectives 9-9, 9-10

On August 31, 20X1, the balance in the checkbook and the *Cash* account of the Sonoma Creek Bed and Breakfast was $13,031. The balance shown on the bank statement on the same date was $13,997.

NOTES

a. The firm's records indicate that a $1,600 deposit dated August 30 and a $601 deposit dated August 31 do not appear on the bank statement.

b. A service charge of $28 and a debit memorandum of $230 covering an NSF check have not yet been entered in the firm's records. (The check was issued by Andy Stein, a credit customer.)

c. The following checks were issued but have not yet been paid by the bank:

   Check 712, $120
   Check 713, $130
   Check 716, $250
   Check 736, $577
   Check 739, $78
   Check 741, $120

d. A credit memorandum shows that the bank collected a $2,095 note receivable and interest of $55 for the firm. These amounts have not yet been entered in the firm's records.

INSTRUCTIONS

1. Prepare a bank reconciliation statement for the firm as of August 31.
2. Record general journal entries for items on the bank reconciliation statement that must be journalized. Date the entries August 31, 20X1.

Analyze: What effect did the journal entries recorded as a result of the bank reconciliation have on the fundamental accounting equation?

Correcting errors revealed by a bank reconciliation.

◀ **Problem 9.7A**
Objectives 9-9, 9-10

During the bank reconciliation process at Fontes & Barone Consultancy on May 2, 20X1, the following two errors were discovered in the firm's records.

1. The checkbook and the cash payments journal indicated that Check 2206 dated April 17 was issued for $696 to make a cash purchase of supplies. However, examination of the canceled check and the listing on the bank statement showed that the actual amount of the check was $96.

2. The checkbook and the cash payments journal indicated that Check 2247 dated April 20 was issued for $140 to pay a utility bill. However, examination of the canceled check and the listing on the bank statement showed that the actual amount of the check was $410.

INSTRUCTIONS

1. Prepare the adjusted book balance section of the firm's bank reconciliation statement. The book balance as of April 30 was $25,275. The errors listed above are the only two items that affect the book balance.
2. Prepare general journal entries to correct the errors. Use page 11 and date the entries April 30, 20X1. Check 2206 was correctly debited to *Supplies* on April 17, and Check 2247 was debited to *Utilities Expense* on April 20.

Analyze: If the errors described had not been corrected, would net income for the period be overstated or understated? By what amount?

Problem 9.8A
Objectives 9-9, 9-10, 9-11

▶ **Preparing a bank reconciliation statement and journalizing entries to adjust the cash balance.**

On August 1, 20X1, the accountant for Western Exports downloaded the company's July 31, 20X1, bank statement from the bank's website. The balance shown on the bank statement was $28,810. The July 31, 20X1, balance in the *Cash* account in the general ledger was $13,687.

Jenny Iglesias, the accountant for Western Exports, noted the following differences between the bank's records and the company's *Cash* account in the general ledger.

a. An electronic funds transfer for $14,900 from Defontaine Equipement, a customer located in France, was received by the bank on July 31.

b. Check 1422 was correctly written and recorded for $1,200. The bank mistakenly paid the check for $1,230.

c. The accounting records indicate that Check 1425 was issued for $69 to make a purchase of supplies. However, examination of the check online showed that the actual amount of the check was for $99.

d. A deposit of $850 made after banking hours on July 31 did not appear on the July 31 bank statement.

e. The following checks were outstanding: Check 1429 for $1,254 and Check 1430 for $146.

f. An automatic debit of $267 on July 31 from CentralComm for telephone service appeared on the bank statement but had not been recorded in the company's accounting records.

INSTRUCTIONS

1. Prepare a bank reconciliation for the firm as of July 31.
2. Record general journal entries for the items on the bank reconciliation that must be journalized. Date the entries July 31, 20X1. Use 19 as the page number.

Analyze: What effect on total expenses occurred as a result of the general journal entries recorded?

Problem 9.9A
Appendix
Objective 9-12

▶ **Recording transactions using the perpetual inventory system.**

The following transactions took place at Fabulous Fashions Outlet during July 20X1. Fabulous Fashions Outlet uses a perpetual inventory system. The firm operates in a state with no sales tax. Record the transactions in a general journal. Use 8 as the page number for the general journal.

DATE		TRANSACTIONS
20X1		
July	1	Purchased dresses for $4,200 plus a freight charge of $200 from Funky Fashions, Invoice 101, dated July 1; the terms are 2/10, n/30.
	5	Sold two dresses on account to Alice Rivera, terms 1/10, n/30; issued Sales Slip 788 for $700. The cost of the dresses sold was $560.
	7	Received Credit Memorandum 210 for $650 from Funky Fashions for damaged dresses returned; the goods were purchased on Invoice 101 dated July 1.
	9	Accepted a return of a dress from Alice Rivera; the dress was originally sold on Sales Slip 788 of July 5; issued Credit Memorandum 89 for $300. The cost of the returned dress was $240.
	10	Issued Check 1255 to pay the amount due to Funky Fashions for Invoice 101, dated July 1, less the return of July 7 and less the cash discount.
	15	Received payment from Alice Rivera for the sale of July 5, less the return of July 9 and less the cash discount.
	15	Recorded sales on credit cards for the two-week period ended July 15, $13,900; the bank charges a 3 percent fee on all credit card sales. The cost of merchandise sold was $11,100.

DATE	9.9A (cont.) TRANSACTIONS
17	Purchased merchandise on account from American Rags for $3,000, subject to trade discounts of 40 percent and 10 percent, terms 1/10, n/30, Invoice 2078.
26	Paid amount owed to American Rags for the purchase of July 17, less discount, Check 1285.

Analyze: What percentage of the total amount due to Funky Fashions for the purchase on July 1 is due to the freight charge?

Problem Set B

Journalizing cash receipts and posting to the general ledger.

◀ **Problem 9.1B**
Objectives 9-1, 9-2, 9-3

Ez Suppliers is a retail store that sells cards, business supplies, and novelties. The firm's cash receipts during June 20X1 and the general ledger accounts used to record these transactions appear below.

INSTRUCTIONS

1. Open the general ledger accounts and enter the balances as of June 1.
2. Record the transactions in a cash receipts journal. (Use page 14.)
3. Post the individual entries from the Other Accounts Credit section of the cash receipts journal to the proper general ledger accounts.
4. Total and rule the cash receipts journal as of June 30.
5. From the cash receipts journal, post the totals to the general ledger.

SELECTED GENERAL LEDGER ACCOUNTS

102 Cash	$2,200
111 Accounts Receivable	7,400
115 Notes Receivable	1,700
129 Office Supplies	800
231 Sales Tax Payable	400
302 Roma Horvat, Capital	8,600
401 Sales	
791 Interest Income	

DATE		TRANSACTIONS
June	3	Received $300 from The Copy Center, a credit customer.
	4	Received a check for $1,802 from Amy Whitesides to pay her note receivable; the total included $102 of interest.
	5	Received a $198 refund for damaged supplies purchased from Forms-R-Us.
	7	Recorded cash sales of $1,700 plus sales tax payable of $136.
	10	Received $900 from Gi Hahn, a credit customer.
	13	Roma Horvat, the owner, contributed additional capital of $12,000 to the business.

(continued)

DATE	9.1B (cont.) TRANSACTIONS
14	Recorded cash sales of $1,450 plus sales tax of $116.
18	Received $1,760 from Kathy Harris, a credit customer.
19	Received $1,000 from Nancy Matthews, a credit customer.
21	Recorded cash sales of $1,150 plus sales tax of $92.
27	Received $750 from Al Rizzo, a credit customer.

Analyze: Assuming that all relevant information is included in this problem, what are total assets for Ez Suppliers at June 30, 20X1?

Problem 9.2B
Objectives 9-4, 9-5, 9-6

▶ **Journalizing cash payments and recording petty cash; posting to the general ledger.**

The cash payments of European Gift Shop, a retail business, for September and the general ledger accounts used to record these transactions appear below.

INSTRUCTIONS

1. Open the general ledger accounts and enter the balances as of September 1, 20X1.
2. Record all payments by check in a cash payments journal. Use 12 as the page number.
3. Record all payments from the petty cash fund on a petty cash analysis sheet with special columns for *Delivery Expense* and *Miscellaneous Expense.* Use 12 as the sheet number.
4. Post the individual entries from the Other Accounts Debit section of the cash payments journal to the proper general ledger accounts.
5. Total and rule the petty cash analysis sheet as of September 30, then record the replenishment of the fund and the final balance on the sheet.
6. Total and rule the cash payments journal as of September 30.
7. Post the column totals from the cash payments journal to the proper general ledger accounts.

SELECTED GENERAL LEDGER ACCOUNTS

101 Cash	$21,530 Dr.	504 Purchases Discounts
105 Petty Cash Fund		511 Delivery Expense
141 Equipment	43,000 Dr.	611 Interest Expense
201 Notes Payable	1,000 Cr.	614 Miscellaneous Expense
205 Accounts Payable	9,800 Cr.	620 Rent Expense
231 Sales Tax Payable	1,344 Cr.	623 Salaries Expense
302 Fred Lynn, Drawing		626 Telephone Expense
451 Sales Ret. and Allow.		

DATE		TRANSACTIONS
Sept.	1	Issued Check 401 for $1,344 to remit sales tax to the state tax commission.
	2	Issued Check 402 for $1,700 to pay the monthly rent.
	4	Issued Check 403 for $100 to establish a petty cash fund. (After journalizing this transaction, be sure to enter it on the first line of the petty cash analysis sheet.)
	5	Issued Check 404 for $1,470 to Elegant Glassware, a creditor, in payment of Invoice 6793, dated August 28 ($1,500), less a cash discount ($30).

DATE	9.2B (cont.) TRANSACTIONS
6	Paid $12.00 from the petty cash fund for delivery service, Petty Cash Voucher 1.
9	Purchased store equipment for $1,000; issued Check 405.
11	Paid $16 from the petty cash fund for office supplies, Petty Cash Voucher 2 (charge to **Miscellaneous Expense**).
13	Issued Check 406 for $970 to Taylor Company, a creditor, in payment of Invoice 7925, dated August 15.
14	Issued Check 407 for $425 to a customer as a cash refund for a defective watch that was returned; the original sale was made for cash.
16	Paid $10 from the petty cash fund for a personal withdrawal by Fred Lynn, the owner, Petty Cash Voucher 3.
18	Issued Check 408 for $187 to pay the monthly telephone bill.
21	Issued Check 409 for $833 to African Imports, a creditor, in payment of Invoice 1822, dated September 13 ($850), less a cash discount ($17).
23	Paid $13 from the petty cash fund for postage stamps, Petty Cash Voucher 4 (charge to Miscellaneous Expense).
24	Issued Check 410 for $1,040 to Zachary Corporation in payment of a $1,000 promissory note and interest of $40.
26	Issued Check 411 for $1,240 to Atlantic Ceramics, a creditor, in payment of Invoice 3510, dated August 29.
27	Paid $10 from the petty cash fund for delivery service, Petty Cash Voucher 5.
28	Issued Check 412 for $1,500 to Fred Lynn, the owner, as a withdrawal for personal use.
30	Issued Check 413 for $2,500 to pay the monthly salaries of the employees.
30	Issued Check 414 for $61 to replenish the petty cash fund. (Foot the columns of the petty cash analysis sheet in order to determine the accounts that should be debited and the amounts involved.)

Analyze: What was the amount of total debits to general ledger liability accounts during the month of September?

Journalizing sales and cash receipts and posting to the general ledger.

◀ **Problem 9.3B**
Objectives 9-1, 9-2, 9-3

Royal Kitchen Supplies is a wholesale business. The transactions involving sales and cash receipts for the firm during August 20X1 and the general ledger accounts used to record these transactions are listed below.

INSTRUCTIONS

1. Open the general ledger accounts and enter the balances as of August 1, 20X1.
2. Record the transactions in a sales journal, a cash receipts journal, and a general journal. Use 10 as the page number for each of the special journals and 24 as the page number for the general journal.
3. Post the entries from the general journal to the proper general ledger accounts.
4. Total and rule the special journals as of August 31, 20X1.
5. Post the column totals from the special journals to the proper general ledger accounts.
6. Prepare the heading and the Revenue section of the firm's income statement for the month ended August 31, 20X1.

GENERAL LEDGER ACCOUNTS

101 Cash	$15,070 Dr.	401 Sales
109 Notes Receivable		451 Sales Returns and Allowances
111 Accounts Receivable	22,507 Dr.	452 Sales Discounts

DATE		TRANSACTIONS
Aug.	1	Received a check for $6,468 from Construction Supply Company in payment of Invoice 8277 dated July 21 ($6,600), less a cash discount ($132).
	2	Sold merchandise for $19,450 to Jamison Builders; issued Invoice 2978 with terms of 2/10, n/30.
	4	Accepted a three-month promissory note for $12,000 from Davis Custom Homes to settle its overdue account; the note has an interest rate of 12 percent.
	7	Sold merchandise for $18,550 to Branch Construction Company; issued Invoice 2979 with terms of 2/10, n/30.
	11	Collected $19,061 from Jamison Builders for Invoice 2978 dated August 2 ($19,450), less a cash discount ($389.00).
	14	Sold merchandise for $7,050 in cash to a new customer who has not yet established credit.
	16	Branch Construction Company sent a check for $18,179 in payment of Invoice 2979 dated August 7 ($18,550), less a cash discount ($371.00).
	22	Sold merchandise for $6,850 to Contemporary Homes; issued Invoice 2980 with terms of 2/10, n/30.
	24	Received a check for $6,000 from Garcia Homes Center to pay Invoice 2877, dated July 23.
	26	Accepted a return of damaged merchandise from Contemporary Homes; issued Credit Memorandum 101 for $550; the original sale was made on Invoice 2980, dated August 22.
	31	Sold merchandise for $17,440 to Denton County Builders; issued Invoice 2981 with terms of 2/10, n/30.

Analyze: What total sales on account were made in August? Include sales returns and allowances in your computation.

Problem 9.4B
Objectives 9-4, 9-5

▶ **Journalizing purchases, cash payments, and purchases discounts; posting to the general ledger.**

Contemporary Appliance Center is a retail store that sells a variety of household appliances. The firm operates in a state with no sales tax. Transactions involving purchases and cash payments for the firm during December 20X1 and the general ledger accounts used to record these transactions appear below.

INSTRUCTIONS

1. Open the general ledger accounts and enter the balances in these accounts as of December 1, 20X1.
2. Record the transactions in a purchases journal, a cash payments journal, and a general journal. Use 12 as the page number for each of the special journals and 30 as the page number for the general journal.
3. Post the entries from the general journal and from the Other Accounts Debit section of the cash payments journal to the proper accounts in the general ledger.
4. Total and rule the special journals as of December 31, 20X1.
5. Post the column totals from the special journals to the general ledger accounts.
6. Show how the firm's cost of purchases would be reported on its income statement for the month ended December 31, 20X1.

GENERAL LEDGER ACCOUNTS

101 Cash	$60,700 Dr.
131 Equipment	68,000 Dr.
201 Notes Payable	
205 Accounts Payable	7,600 Cr.
501 Purchases	
503 Purchases Returns and Allowances	
504 Purchases Discounts	
611 Rent Expense	
614 Salaries Expense	
617 Telephone Expense	

DATE		TRANSACTIONS
Dec.	1	Purchased merchandise for $6,600 from Alexis Products for Homes, Invoice 6559, dated November 28; the terms are 2/10, n/30.
	2	Issued Check 1801 for $3,000 to pay the monthly rent.
	4	Purchased new store equipment for $14,000 from Kesterson Company; issued a two-month promissory note with interest at 10 percent.
	6	Issued Check 1802 for $6,468 to Alexis Products for Homes, a creditor, in payment of Invoice 6559, dated November 28 ($6,600), less a cash discount ($132).
	10	Purchased merchandise for $9,200 from the Baxter Corporation, Invoice 5119, dated December 7; terms of 2/10, n/30.
	13	Issued Check 1803 for $265 to pay the monthly telephone bill.
	15	Issued Check 1804 for $9,016 to Baxter Corporation, a creditor, in payment of Invoice 5119, dated December 7 ($9,200), less a cash discount ($184).
	18	Purchased merchandise for $12,400 from Household Appliance Center, Invoice 7238, dated December 16; terms of 3/10, n/30.
	20	Purchased new store equipment for $6,000 from Safety Security Systems Inc., Invoice 536, dated December 17, net payable in 45 days.
	21	Issued Check 1805 for $4,200 to Chain Lighting and Appliances, a creditor, in payment of Invoice 7813, dated November 23.
	22	Purchased merchandise for $5,800 from Zale Corporation, Invoice 3161, dated December 19, net due in 30 days.
	24	Issued Check 1806 for $12,028 to Household Appliance Center, a creditor, in payment of Invoice 7238, dated December 16 ($12,400), less a cash discount ($372).
	28	Received Credit Memorandum 201 for $1,050 from Zale Corporation for damaged goods that were returned; the original purchase was made on Invoice 3161, dated December 19.
	31	Issued Check 1807 for $6,500 to pay the monthly salaries of the employees.

Analyze: List the dates for transactions in December that would be categorized as expenses of the business.

Preparing a bank reconciliation statement and journalizing entries to adjust the cash balance.

◀ **Problem 9.5B**
Objectives 9-9, 9-10

On October 7, 20X1, Peter Chen, Attorney-at-Law, received his September bank statement from First Texas National Bank. Enclosed with the bank statement was a debit memorandum for $118 that covered an NSF check issued by Annette Cole, a credit customer. The firm's checkbook contained the following information about deposits made and checks issued during September. The balance of the *Cash* account and the checkbook on September 30 was $8,134.

INSTRUCTIONS

1. Prepare a bank reconciliation statement for the firm as of September 30, 20X1.
2. Record general journal entries for any items on the bank reconciliation statement that must be journalized. Date the entries September 30, 20X1.

DATE		TRANSACTIONS	
Sept.	1	Balance	$6,500
	1	Check 104	100
	3	Check 105	10
	3	Deposit	500
	6	Check 106	225
	10	Deposit	410
	11	Check 107	200
	15	Check 108	75
	21	Check 109	60
	22	Deposit	730
	25	Check 110	16
	25	Check 111	80
	27	Check 112	140
	28	Deposit	900

FIRST TEXAS NATIONAL BANK

Peter Chen, Attorney-at-Law 1-877-987-6543
3510 North Central Expressway
Dallas, TX 75232-2709

Account Number: 22-5654-30   September 1–30, 20X1
Activity Summary:

Balance, September 1	$ 6,500.00
Deposits and credits	1,640.00
Withdrawals and debits	(816.50)
Balance, September 30	$ 7,323.50

DATE	DESCRIPTION	DEPOSITS/CREDITS	WITHDRAWALS/DEBITS	BALANCE
9/1/X1	Opening balance			$6,500.00
9/3/X1	Deposit	500.00		7,000.00
9/6/X1	Check No. 104		100.00	6,900.00
9/11/X1	Deposit	410.00		7,310.00
9/11/X1	Check No. 105		10.00	7,300.00
9/11/X1	Check No. 107		200.00	7,100.00
9/15/X1	Check No. 106		225.00	6,875.00
9/19/X1	Check No. 109		60.00	6,815.00
9/23/X1	Deposit	730.00		7,545.00
9/25/X1	Check No. 110		16.00	7,529.00
9/25/X1	Check No. 111		80.00	7,449.00
9/28/X1	Debit for NSF Check		118.00	7,331.00
9/28/X1	Service charge		7.50	7,323.50
	Totals	1,640.00	816.50	

Analyze: How many checks were paid (cleared the bank) according to the September 30 bank statement?

Preparing a bank reconciliation statement and journalizing entries to adjust the cash balance.

◀ **Problem 9.6B**
Objectives 9-9, 9-10

On July 31, 20X1, the balance in Northwest Appliances's checkbook and *Cash* account was $9,318.59. The balance shown on the bank statement on the same date was $10,442.03.

NOTES

a. The following checks were issued but have not yet been paid by the bank: Check 533 for $251.95, Check 535 for $222.50, and Check 537 for $642.40.

b. A credit memorandum shows that the bank has collected a $1,437 note receivable and interest of $30 for the firm. These amounts have not yet been entered in the firm's records.

c. The firm's records indicate that a deposit of $991.07 made on July 31 does not appear on the bank statement.

d. A service charge of $24.34 and a debit memorandum of $445 covering an NSF check have not yet been entered in the firm's records. (The check was issued by Bob Walker, a credit customer.)

INSTRUCTIONS

1. Prepare a bank reconciliation statement for the firm as of July 31, 20X1.
2. Record general journal entries for any items on the bank reconciliation statement that must be journalized. Date the entries July 31, 20X1.

Analyze: After all journal entries have been recorded and posted, what is the balance in the *Cash* account at July 31, 20X1?

Correcting errors revealed by a bank reconciliation.

◀ **Problem 9.7B**
Objectives 9-9, 9-10

During the bank reconciliation process at Awesome Dudes Moving Corporation on March 2, 20X1, the following errors were discovered in the firm's records.

a. The checkbook and the cash payments journal indicated that Check 1301 dated February 18 was issued for $382 to pay for hauling expenses. However, examination of the canceled check and the listing on the bank statement showed that the actual amount of the check was $238.

b. The checkbook and the cash payments journal indicated that Check 1322 dated February 24 was issued for $604 to pay a telephone bill. However, examination of the canceled check and the listing on the bank statement showed that the actual amount of the check was $640.

INSTRUCTIONS

1. Prepare the adjusted book balance section of the firm's bank reconciliation statement. The book balance as of February 28, 20X1, was $19,661. The errors listed are the only two items that affect the book balance.
2. Prepare general journal entries to correct the errors. Date the entries February 28, 20X1. Check 1301 was debited to *Hauling Expense* on February 18 and Check 1322 was debited to *Telephone Expense* on February 24.

Analyze: What net change to the *Cash* account occurred as a result of the correcting journal entries?

Preparing a bank reconciliation statement and journalizing entries to adjust the cash balance.

◀ **Problem 9.8B**
Objectives 9-9, 9-10, 9-11

On December 1, 20X1, Sofia Sartori, the accountant for Classic Appliances, downloaded the company's November 30, 20X1, bank statement from the bank's website. The balance shown on the bank statement was $30,734. The November 30, 20X1, balance in the *Cash* account in the general ledger was $17,630.

Sofia noted the following differences between the bank's records and the company's *Cash* account in the general ledger.

a. The following checks were outstanding: Check 4129 for $1,592 and Check 4130 for $229.

b. A deposit of $1,234 made after banking hours on November 30 did not appear on the November 30 bank statement.

c. An automatic debit of $923 on November 30 from ClearComm for telephone service appeared on the bank statement but had not been recorded in the company's accounting records.

d. An electronic funds transfer for $13,150 from Bella Cucina, a customer located in Italy, was received by the bank on November 30.

e. Check 4122 was correctly written and recorded for $1,300. The bank mistakenly paid the check for $1,100.

f. The accounting records indicate that Check 4125 was issued for $980 to make a purchase of equipment. However, examination of the check online showed that the actual amount of the check was for $890.

INSTRUCTIONS

1. Prepare a bank reconciliation for the firm as of November 30.
2. Record general journal entries for the items on the bank reconciliation that must be journalized. Date the entries November 30, 20X1. Use 44 as the page number.

Analyze: What effect did the journal entries recorded as a result of the bank reconciliation have on total assets?

Problem 9.9B Appendix
Objective 9-12

▶ **Recording transactions using the perpetual inventory system.**

The following transactions took place at Grow-Right Garden Center during June 20X1. Grow-Right Garden Center uses a perpetual inventory system. Grow-Right Garden Center operates in a state with no sales tax. Record the transactions in a general journal. Use 10 as the page number for the general journal.

DATE		TRANSACTIONS
20X1		
June	1	Purchased lawn mowers for $6,080 plus a freight charge of $320 from Mow Down Corporation, Invoice 201, dated June 1; the terms are 2/10, n/30.
	5	Sold garden tools and supplies on account to Art Garcia, terms 1/10, n/30; issued Sales Slip 888 for $1,500. The cost of the merchandise sold was $750.
	7	Received Credit Memorandum 310 for $550 from Mow Down Corporation for defective lawn mowers returned; the goods were purchased on Invoice 201 dated June 1.
	9	Accepted a return of various garden tools and supplies from Art Garcia; the items were originally sold on Sales Slip 888 of June 5. Issued Credit Memorandum 89 for $200. The cost of the returned items was $100.
	10	Issued Check 1555 to pay the amount due to Mow Down Corporation for Invoice 201, dated June 1, less the return of June 7 and less the cash discount.
	15	Received payment from Art Garcia for the sale of June 5, less the return of June 9 and less the cash discount.
	15	Recorded sales on credit cards for the two-week period ended June 15, $16,000; the bank charges a 2 percent fee on all credit card sales. The cost of merchandise sold was $7,950.
	17	Purchased merchandise on account from Patio Dudes for $8,000, subject to trade discounts of 30 percent and 5 percent, terms 1/10, n/30, Invoice 2178.
	26	Paid amount owed to Patio Dudes for the purchase of June 17, Check 1598.

Analyze: Assume 20 lawn mowers were purchased from Mow Down Corporation on June 1. What was the average cost per lawn mower purchased on June 1? (Hint: Include the freight charges as part of the cost of the lawn mowers.)

Critical Thinking Problem 9.1

Special Journals

During September 20X1, Interior Designs Specialty Shop, a retail store, had the transactions listed below. The general ledger accounts used to record these transactions are also provided below.

INSTRUCTIONS

1. Open the general ledger accounts and enter the balances as of September 1, 20X1.
2. Record the transactions in a sales journal, a cash receipts journal, a purchases journal, a cash payments journal, and a general journal. Use page 12 as the page number for each of the special journals and page 32 as the page number for the general journal.
3. Post the entries from the general journal to the proper general ledger accounts.
4. Post the entries from the Other Accounts Credit section of the cash receipts journal to the proper general ledger accounts.
5. Post the entries from the Other Accounts Debit section of the cash payments journal to the proper general ledger accounts.
6. Total and rule the special journals as of September 30.
7. Post the column totals from the special journals to the proper general ledger accounts.
8. Set up an accounts receivable ledger for Interior Designs Specialty Shop. Open an account for each of the customers listed below and enter the balances as of September 1. All of these customers have terms of n/30.

Credit Customers	
Name	Balance 9/01/X1
Rachel Carter	
Mesia Davis	$1,260.00
Robert Kent	1,730.00
Pam Lawrence	
David Prater	1,050.00
Henry Tolliver	
Jason Williams	2,100.00

9. Post the individual entries from the sales journal, the cash receipts journal, and the general journal to the accounts receivable subsidiary ledger.
10. Prepare a schedule of accounts receivable for September 30, 20X1.
11. Check the total of the schedule of accounts receivable against the balance of the *Accounts Receivable* account in the general ledger. The two amounts should be the same.

Creditors		
Name	Balance 9/01/X1	Terms
Booker, Inc.		n/45
McKnight Corporation	$5,500	1/10, n/30
Nelson Craft Products		2/10, n/30
Rocker Company		n/30
Reed Millings Company		2/10, n/30
Sadler Floor Coverings	1,940	n/30
Wells Products	2,120	n/30

12. Set up an accounts payable subsidiary ledger for Interior Designs Specialty Shop. Open an account for each of the creditors listed above and enter the balances as of September 1, 20X1.
13. Post the individual entries from the purchases journal, the cash payments journal, and the general journal to the accounts payable subsidiary ledger.
14. Prepare a schedule of accounts payable for September 30, 20X1.
15. Check the total of the schedule of accounts payable against the balance of the *Accounts Payable* account in the general ledger. The two amounts should be the same.

GENERAL LEDGER ACCOUNTS

101 Cash	$18,945 Dr.	451 Sales Returns and Allowances
109 Notes Receivable		501 Purchases
111 Accounts Receivable	6,140 Dr.	502 Freight In
121 Supplies	710 Dr.	503 Purchases Returns and Allowances
131 Inventory	29,365 Dr.	504 Purchases Discounts
201 Notes Payable		611 Cash Short or Over
205 Accounts Payable	9,560 Cr.	614 Rent Expense
231 Sales Tax Payable		617 Salaries Expense
301 Sergio Cortez, Capital	45,600 Cr.	619 Utilities Expense
401 Sales		

DATE		TRANSACTIONS
Sept.	1	Received a check for $1,050 from David Prater to pay his account.
	1	Issued Check 1401 for $1,940 to Sadler Floor Coverings, a creditor, in payment of Invoice 6325 dated August 3.
	2	Issued Check 1402 for $2,500 to pay the monthly rent.
	3	Sold a table on credit for $650 plus sales tax of $52.00 to Pam Lawrence, Sales Slip 1850.
	5	Sergio Cortez, the owner, invested an additional $15,000 cash in the business in order to expand operations.
	6	Had cash sales of $3,900 plus sales tax of $312 during the period September 1–6; there was a cash shortage of $20.
	6	Purchased carpeting for $4,450 from Reed Millings Company, Invoice 827, dated September 3; terms of 2/10, n/30.
	6	Issued Check 1403 for $158 to Tri-City Trucking Company to pay the freight charge on goods received from Reed Millings Company.
	8	Purchased store supplies for $370 from Rocker Company, Invoice 4204, dated September 6, net amount due in 30 days.
	8	Sold chairs on credit for $950 plus sales tax of $76.00 to Henry Tolliver, Sales Slip 1851.
	11	Accepted a two-month promissory note for $2,100 from Jason Williams to settle his overdue account; the note has an interest rate of 10 percent.
	11	Issued Check 1404 for $4,361 to Reed Millings Company, a creditor, in payment of Invoice 827 dated September 3 ($4,450) less a cash discount ($89).
	13	Had cash sales of $3,850 plus sales tax of $308 during the period September 8–13.
	14	Purchased carpeting for $3,700 plus a freight charge of $84 from Wells Products, Invoice 9453, dated September 11, net due and payable in 30 days.
	15	Collected $1,260 on account from Mesia Davis.

DATE	(cont.) TRANSACTIONS
17	Gave a two-month promissory note for $5,500 to McKnight Corporation, a creditor, to settle an overdue balance; the note bears interest at 12 percent.
19	Sold a lamp on credit to Rachel Carter for $250 plus sales tax of $20, Sales Slip 1852.
20	Had cash sales of $4,100 plus sales tax of $328 during the period September 15–20; there was a cash shortage of $9.00.
21	Purchased area rugs for $2,800 from Nelson Craft Products, Invoice 677, dated September 18; the terms are 2/10, n/30.
22	Issued Check 1405 for $306 to pay the monthly utility bill.
23	Granted an allowance to Rachel Carter for scratches on the lamp that she bought on Sales Slip 1852 of September 19; issued Credit Memorandum 151 for $54, which includes a price reduction of $50 and sales tax of $4.
24	Received Credit Memorandum 110 for $300 from Nelson Craft Products for a damaged rug that was returned; the original purchase was made on Invoice 677 dated September 18.
24	Robert Kent sent a check for $1,730 to pay the balance he owes.
25	Issued Check 1406 for $3,600 to make a cash purchase of merchandise.
26	Issued Check 1407 for $2,450 to Nelson Craft Products, a creditor, in payment of Invoice 677 of September 18 ($2,800), less a return ($300) and a cash discount ($50).
27	Purchased hooked rugs for $4,200 plus a freight charge of $128 from Booker, Inc., Invoice 1368, dated September 23, net payable in 45 days.
27	Had cash sales of $4,800 plus sales tax of $384 during the period September 22–27.
28	Issued Check 1408 for $2,120 to Wells Products, a creditor, in payment of Invoice 8984 dated August 30.
29	Sold a cabinet on credit to Mesia Davis for $1,200 plus sales tax of $96, Sales Slip 1853.
30	Had cash sales of $1,500 plus sales tax of $120 for September 29–30; there was a cash overage of $10.
30	Issued Check 1409 for $6,800 to pay the monthly salaries of the employees.

Analyze: What were the total cash payments for September?

Critical Thinking Problem 9.2

Cash Controls

Mike Ryan is the owner of Ryan Contractors, a successful small construction company. He spends most of his time out of the office supervising work at various construction sites, leaving the operation of the office to the company's cashier/bookkeeper, Gloria Anderson. Gloria makes bank deposits, pays the company's bills, maintains the accounting records, and prepares monthly bank reconciliations.

Recently a friend told Mike that while he was at a party he overheard Gloria bragging that she paid for her new clothes with money from the company's cash receipts. She said her boss would never know because he never checks the cash records.

Mike admits that he does not check on Gloria's work. He now wants to know if Gloria is stealing from him. He asks you to examine the company's cash records to determine whether Gloria has stolen cash from the business and, if so, how much.

Your examination of the company's cash records reveals the following information:

1. Gloria prepared the following August 31, 20X1, bank reconciliation.

Balance in books, August 31, 20X1		$18,786
Additions:		
Outstanding checks		
Check 1780	$ 792	
Check 1784	1,819	
Check 1806	384	2,695
		$21,481
Deductions:		
Deposit in transit, August 28, 20X1	$4,882	
Bank service charge	10	4,892
Balance on bank statement, August 31, 20X1		$16,589

2. An examination of the general ledger shows the **Cash** account with a balance of $18,786 on August 31, 20X1.
3. The August 31 bank statement shows a balance of $16,589.
4. The August 28 deposit of $4,882 does not appear on the August 31 bank statement.
5. A comparison of canceled checks returned with the August 31 bank statement with the cash payments journal reveals the following checks as outstanding:

Check 1590	$ 363
Check 1680	1,318
Check 1724	586
Check 1780	792
Check 1784	1,819
Check 1806	384

Prepare a bank reconciliation using the format presented in this chapter for the month of August. Assume there were no bank or bookkeeping errors in August. Did Gloria take cash from the company? If so, how much and how did she try to conceal the theft? How can Mike improve his company's internal controls over cash?

BUSINESS CONNECTIONS

Cash Management

Managerial FOCUS

1. The new accountant for Asheville Hardware Center, a large retail store, found the following weaknesses in the firm's cash-handling procedures. How would you explain to management why each of these procedures should be changed?

   a. No cash register proof is prepared at the end of each day. The amount of money in the register is considered the amount of cash sales for the day.

   b. Small payments are sometimes made from the currency and coins in the cash register. (The store has no petty cash fund.)

   c. During busy periods for the firm, cash receipts are sometimes kept on the premises for several days before a bank deposit is made.

   d. When funds are removed from the cash register at the end of each day, they are placed in an unlocked office cabinet until they are deposited.

   e. The person who makes the bank deposits also records them in the checkbook, journalizes cash receipts, and reconciles the bank statement.

2. Why should management be concerned about having accurate information about the firm's cash position available at all times?
3. Many banks now offer a variety of computer services to clients. Why is it not advisable for a firm to pay its bank to complete the reconciliation procedure at the end of each month?
4. Assume that you are the newly hired controller at Norton Company and that you have observed the following banking procedures in use at the firm. Would you change any of these procedures? Why or why not?
   a. A blank endorsement is made on all checks to be deposited.
   b. The checkbook is kept on the top of a desk so that it will be handy.
   c. The same person prepares bank deposits, issues checks, and reconciles the bank statement.
   d. The reconciliation process usually takes place two or three weeks after the bank statement is received.
   e. The bank statement and the canceled checks are thrown away after the reconciliation process is completed.
   f. As a shortcut in the reconciliation process, there is no attempt to compare the endorsements on the back of the canceled checks with the names of the payees shown on the face of these checks.
5. Why should management be concerned about achieving effective internal control over cash receipts and cash payments?
6. How does management benefit when cash transactions are recorded quickly and efficiently?
7. Why do some companies require that all employees who handle cash be bonded?
8. Why is it a good practice for a business to make all payments by check or electronic funds transfer except for minor payments from a petty cash fund?

Cash Controls

Jim Sullivan owns Auto Spa, an automated car wash and car detailer. Auto Spa also sells snacks and gift items in its waiting area. Auto Spa has one cash register, where all payments from customers are received. There is a $400 change fund in the cash register. There are two cash register clerks, George and Alice, who work two different shifts during the day. Jim prints out a cash register tape at the end of the day, but doesn't compare it to the deposit.

Jim noticed an increase in business during the first week of August, but the bank deposits were less than Jim thought they would be. He contacted you for advice. By comparing the sales per the cash register tapes to the bank deposits, you find approximately $840 missing from the bank deposits for the first week of August.

What controls should Jim implement to prevent this fraud from occurring in the future?

Balance Sheet

The following excerpt is taken from The Home Depot, Inc., *2018 Annual Report (for the fiscal year ended February 3, 2019)*:

The Home Depot, Inc. Consolidated Balance Sheets		
	As of	
amounts in millions	February 3, 2019	January 28, 2018
ASSETS		
Current Assets:		
Cash and cash equivalents*	$ 1,778	$ 3,595
Total assets	$44,003	$44,529
*Cash and Cash Equivalents: Short-term investments that have maturities of three months or less when purchased are considered to be cash equivalents.		

Home Depot

Analyze:

1. What percentage of total assets is made up of cash and cash equivalents at February 3, 2019?
2. Cash receipt and cash payment transactions affect the total value of a company's assets. By what amount did the category "Cash and cash equivalents" change from January 28, 2018, to February 3, 2019?
3. If accountants at The Home Depot, Inc., failed to record cash receipts of $150,000 on February 3, 2019, what impact would this error have on the balance sheet category "Cash and cash equivalents"?

TEAMWORK

Internal Controls of Cash

You and four friends have decided to create a new service company called Unpacking for You. Your company unpacks for families once they have moved into a new house. Your business is primarily a cash business. Each family will pay you $100 for each room that is unpacked on the same day you finish the service. How will your business make sure that the payment from the customer is valid? How will you ensure that you will receive the cash when the customer pays the employee in cash?

Answers to Comprehensive Self Review

1. A full endorsement contains the name of the payee plus the name of the firm or bank to whom the check is payable. The endorsement is written or printed on the back of the check.
2. A record of when a payment is made from petty cash, the amount and purpose of the expenditure, and the account to be charged.
3. Petty cash can be replenished at any time if the fund runs low, but it should be replenished at the end of each month so that all expenses for the month are recorded.
4. Special journals eliminate repetition in postings; the initial recording of transactions is faster.
5. Checks, money orders, and funds on deposit in a bank as well as currency and coins.

Payroll Computations, Records, and Payment

Chapter **10**

www.hrblock.com

Following World War II, Henry Bloch and his brother, Leon, founded United Business Company, an accounting services firm, by borrowing $5,000. Leon decided to go to law school, so Henry brought his other brother, Richard, into the company. The business focus was not on taxes, but in 1955, they ran an ad for their tax preparation services, and the small office in Kansas City was flooded with calls. It seems just as the IRS was phasing out its free tax preparation services and turning taxpayers away, the Bloch brothers were advertising their services.

The 1955 tax season was so successful, United Business Company decided to change its name to H&R Block and shifted its focus from general accounting services to tax preparation. Today, H&R Block employs quite a few more employees than it did in 1950 (more than 70,000 in a recent report), and with those added employees, the company's payroll responsibilities have also grown. Not only does it file tax returns for its clients, it also, as an employer, must deduct appropriate taxes from employees' paychecks.

H&R Block is currently the largest consumer tax services company in the United States. It operates through approximately 12,000 retail operations.

Joe Raedle/Getty Images

thinking critically

What kinds of taxes and other deductions come out of an H&R Block employee's paycheck? What deductions come out of yours?

LEARNING OBJECTIVES

- **10-1** Explain the major federal laws relating to employee earnings and withholding.
- **10-2** Compute gross earnings of employees.
- **10-3** Determine employee deductions for social security tax.
- **10-4** Determine employee deductions for Medicare tax.
- **10-5** Determine employee deductions for income tax.
- **10-6** Enter gross earnings, deductions, and net pay in the payroll register.
- **10-7** Journalize payroll transactions in the general journal.
- **10-8** Maintain an earnings record for each employee.
- **10-9** Define the accounting terms new to this chapter.

NEW TERMS

commission basis
compensation record
employee
Employee's Withholding Allowance Certificate (Form W-4)
exempt employees
federal unemployment taxes (FUTA)
hourly rate basis
independent contractor
individual earnings record
Medicare tax
payroll register
piece-rate basis
salary basis
social security (FICA or OASDI) tax
Social Security Act
state unemployment taxes (SUTA)
tax-exempt wages
time and a half
wage-bracket table method
workers' compensation insurance

Section 1

SECTION OBJECTIVES	TERMS TO LEARN
10-1 Explain the major federal laws relating to employee earnings and withholding. **WHY IT'S IMPORTANT** Tax and labor laws protect the rights of both the employee and the employer. Income tax withholding laws ensure continued funding of certain federal and state programs.	employee federal unemployment taxes (FUTA) independent contractor Medicare tax social security (FICA or OASDI) tax Social Security Act state unemployment taxes (SUTA) time and a half workers' compensation insurance

Payroll Laws and Taxes

A large component of the activity of any business is concerned with payroll work. Payroll accounting is so important that it requires special consideration.

Who Is an Employee?

Payroll accounting relates only to earnings of those individuals classified as employees. An **employee** is hired by and works under the control and direction of the employer. Usually the employer provides the tools or equipment used by the employee, sets the employee's working hours, and determines how the employee completes the job. Examples of employees are the company president, the bookkeeper, the sales clerk, and the warehouse worker. All employee earnings are subject to payroll taxes, and those taxes are reported on a calendar-year basis.

In contrast to an employee, an **independent contractor** is paid by the company to carry out a specific task or job but is not under the direct supervision or control of the company. The independent contractor is told what needs to be done, but the means of doing the job are left to the independent contractor. The Internal Revenue Service (IRS) has a list of guidelines to determine if a vendor meets the definition of independent contractor. Typical examples of independent contractors are the accountant who performs the independent audit, the outside attorney who renders legal advice, and the consultant who installs a new accounting system.

This text addresses issues related to employees but not to independent contractors. When dealing with independent contractors, businesses do not have to follow federal labor laws regulating minimum rates of pay and maximum hours of employment. The business is not required to withhold or match payroll taxes on amounts paid to independent contractors. The independent contractor is responsible for paying all payroll taxes related to income.

>> **10-1 OBJECTIVE**
Explain the major federal laws relating to employee earnings and withholding.

Federal Employee Earnings and Withholding Laws

Since the 1930s, many federal and state laws have affected the relationship between employers and employees. Some of these laws deal with working conditions, including hours and earnings. Others relate to income tax withholding. Some concern taxes that are levied against the employer to provide specific employee benefits.

The Fair Labor Standards Act

The *Fair Labor Standards Act* of 1938, often referred to as the Wage and Hour Law or FLSA, applies only to firms engaged directly or indirectly in interstate commerce. It sets a minimum hourly rate of pay and maximum hours of work per week to be performed at the regular rate of pay. When this book was printed, the minimum federal hourly rate of pay was $7.25, and the maximum number of hours at the regular pay rate was 40 hours per week. When an employee works more than 40 hours in a week, the employee earns at least one and one-half times the regular hourly rate of pay for the extra hours. This overtime rate is called **time and a half.** Even if the federal law does not apply to them, many employers pay time and a half for overtime because of union contracts or simply as good business practice. It should be noted that some states have a minimum hourly pay rate that exceeds the federal minimum hourly rate of pay, and employers, when this occurs, must recognize the difference and account for it accordingly.

Social Security Tax

The *Federal Insurance Contributions Act (FICA)* is commonly referred to as the **Social Security Act.** The act, first passed in the 1930s, has been amended frequently. Social Security's Old-Age, Survivors, and Disability Insurance (OASDI) program provides the following benefits:

- Retirement benefits when a worker reaches the eligible retirement age.
- Benefits for the dependents of the retired worker.
- Benefits for the worker and the worker's dependents when the worker is disabled.

These retirement and disability benefits are paid by the **social security tax,** sometimes called the **FICA or OASDI tax.** Both the employer and the employee pay an equal amount of social security tax. The employer is required to withhold social security tax from the employee's pay. On the schedule provided by the IRS, the employer sends the social security tax withheld to the federal government.

The rate of the social security tax has remained constant for many years at 6.2 percent. The earning amount subject to this tax is indexed and so increases each year, according to congressional action. In 2019, the social security tax rate was 6.2 percent of the first $132,900 of salary or wages paid to each employee. In examples and problems, this text uses a social security tax rate of 6.2 percent of the first $132,900 of salary or wages.

Medicare Tax

The Medicare tax is closely related to the social security tax. Prior to 1992, it was a part of the social security tax. The **Medicare tax** is a tax levied equally on employees and employers to provide medical care for the employee and the employee's spouse after each has reached 65.

In recent years, the Medicare tax rate has remained constant at 1.45 percent. The Medicare tax applies to all salaries and wages paid during the year. The employer is required to withhold the Medicare tax from the employee's pay and send it to the federal government on the schedule established by the IRS.

Note that the social security tax is paid on a maximum amount of earnings with no additional tax paid on earnings that cross the ceiling limit (in this text we will use $132,900 as the ceiling wage subject to social security). An individual who earns more than $132,900 in a calendar year will not pay any social security tax on earnings above the $132,900 amount. The Medicare tax does not have an earnings base limit. Therefore, the Medicare tax applies to *all* earnings paid during the year.

Federal Income Tax

Employers are required to withhold from employees' earnings an estimated amount of income tax that will be payable by the employee on the earnings. The amount depends on several factors like single/married, how frequently employee is paid, and number of dependents. Later in this chapter you will learn how to determine the amount to withhold from an employee's paycheck.

---

important!

Wage Base Limit

The social security tax has a wage base maximum ceiling on which taxes are paid and withheld. There is no maximum wage base limit for the Medicare tax. All salaries and wages are subject to the Medicare tax. The Affordable Care Act created an additional Medicare tax of 0.9 percent on single taxpayers with earnings in excess of $200,000 (that means single high-income earners will pay 1.45 percent in Medicare taxes on all earnings and an additional 0.9 percent of Medicare taxes on earnings in excess of $200,000). Employers will not be taxed on this additional Medicare tax.

State and Local Taxes

Many states, and some local governments, have a state/local income tax. In those localities, employers are required to withhold state/local income taxes from employees' earnings. The state/local income tax withholding rules are generally almost identical to those governing federal income tax withholding, but they require separate general ledger accounts in the firm's accounting system because those taxes are submitted to the state and/or local government.

Employer's Payroll Taxes and Insurance Costs

Remember that employers withhold social security and Medicare taxes from employees' earnings. In addition to those withholdings, employers pay social security and Medicare taxes on their employees' earnings. Employers are also required to pay federal and state taxes for unemployment benefits to assist employees who are laid off while they search for a new job. In addition to taxes, employers are required in most situations to purchase workers' compensation insurance in the event a worker is injured on the job. This insurance is not a tax but an operating expense—more on this later in the chapter.

Social Security Tax

The employer's share of the social security tax is 6.2 percent up to the earnings maximum subject to this tax. (In this text, the social security tax is 6.2 percent of the first $132,900 of earnings.) Periodically the employer pays (typically through electronic deposits) to the federal government the social security tax withheld from gross wages/earnings plus the employer's share of the social security tax.

	Social Security
Employee (pays through withholding)	6.2%
Employer (pays equal amount)	6.2
Total	12.4%

Medicare Tax

The employer's share of Medicare tax is 1.45 percent of earnings. Like the social security tax, Medicare taxes must be deposited with the federal government. The Medicare tax withheld from gross earnings plus the employer's share of the Medicare tax is the amount to be deposited.

The Medicare tax rates the employer remits to the federal government are shown below:

	Medicare
Employee (pays through withholding)	1.45%
Employer (pays equal amount)	1.45%
Total	2.90%

Federal Unemployment Tax

The *Federal Unemployment Tax Act (FUTA)* provides benefits for employees who become unemployed. Taxes levied by the federal government against employers to benefit unemployed workers are called **federal unemployment taxes (FUTA).** Employers pay the entire amount of these taxes. In this text, we assume that the taxable earnings base is $7,000. That is, the tax applies to the first $7,000 of each employee's earnings for the year. As this text is written, the FUTA tax rate was 6.0 percent, but it can be reduced by the state unemployment tax rate. In examples and problems, this text uses a FUTA tax rate of 6.0 percent. These rates will be used in all payroll examples. Table 10.1 summarizes payroll tax liabilities. Note that the column for Unemployment Tax would apply to state and federal unemployment.

TABLE 10.1

Summary of Payroll Tax Liabilities (Who Pays)

Federal Income Tax	Social Security Tax	Medicare Tax	Unemployment Tax
Employee	Employee Employer	Employee Employer	Employer

The employee pays these taxes by the withholding of the tax from the periodic wage payment.

The employer pays these taxes through the deposits/filing and reporting on the appropriate forms.

State Unemployment Tax

The federal and state unemployment programs work together to provide benefits for employees who become unemployed. Employers pay all of the **state unemployment taxes (SUTA)**. Often, the earnings base for the federal and state unemployment taxes are the same: the first $7,000 of each employee's earnings for the year. For many states the SUTA tax rate is 5.4 percent. States may periodically adjust the state unemployment tax rate and amount of earnings subject to the unemployment tax based on the state's history of employment in specific industries.

The federal unemployment tax rate (6.0 percent) can be reduced by the rate charged by the state (5.4 percent in this example), so the effective FUTA rate can be as low as 0.6 percent (6.0 percent − 5.4 percent).

SUTA tax	5.4%
FUTA tax rate	6.0%
Less SUTA tax	(5.4)
Net FUTA tax	0.6
Total federal and state unemployment tax	6.0%

Workers' Compensation Insurance

Workers' compensation insurance is not a tax, but insurance that protects employees against losses from job-related injuries or illnesses, or compensates their families if death occurs in the course of the employment. Workers' compensation requirements are defined by each state, not the federal government. Most states mandate workers' compensation insurance.

Typically, a company will pay the workers' compensation insurance premium at the beginning of the year, and later in the year the rate may be adjusted by the insurance company based on claims against the company. Rates may also be separated by job roles and responsibilities within the business. So, if you are a warehousing company, the company will likely be charged a higher premium rate for workers on the floor of the warehouse moving freight around than the rate charged for the office personnel. As stated earlier in the text, the cost of this insurance is an operating expense charged against current earnings.

Employee Records Required by Law

> Many companies outsource payroll duties to professional payroll companies. ADP, Inc., is the world's largest provider of payroll services and employee information systems.

Federal laws require that certain payroll records be maintained. For each employee the employer must keep a record of:

- the employee's name, address, social security number, and date of birth;
- hours worked each day and week, and wages paid at the regular and overtime rates (certain exceptions exist for employees who earn salaries);

- cumulative wages paid throughout the year;
- amount of income tax, social security tax, and Medicare tax withheld for each pay period;
- proof that the employee is a U.S. citizen or has a valid work permit;
- cost of employer-sponsored health insurance coverage if provided by the employer.

Section 1 Review

1. What is "time and a half"?
   a. 11:30 am
   b. 150% times employee base rate of pay
   c. the FUTA rate of tax on quarterly earnings
   d. means you owe federal income tax plus another 50%

2. How are unemployment insurance benefits financed?
   a. They are financed by taxing the employee and withholding from gross earnings.
   b. Employers pay the entire tax based on an amount determined by state and federal governments.
   c. The total cost of unemployment (FUTA and SUTA) is shared equally by employees and employers.
   d. Congress allocates funds to pay all costs related to unemployment benefits.

3. How are social security benefits financed?
   a. All social security benefits are from dollars withheld from employee pay.
   b. Employers totally fund social security.
   c. State governments fund social security.
   d. Employees and employers both fund social security.

4. The purpose of FUTA is to provide benefits for
   a. employees who become unemployed.
   b. employees who become injured while on the job.
   c. retired workers.
   d. disabled employees.

5. Who pays the social security tax?
   a. employee only
   b. employer only
   c. both employee and employer
   d. none of the above

Section 2

SECTION OBJECTIVES	TERMS TO LEARN
>> 10-2 Compute gross earnings of employees. **WHY IT'S IMPORTANT** Payroll is a large part of business activity.	commission basis
>> 10-3 Determine employee deductions for social security tax. **WHY IT'S IMPORTANT** Employers are legally responsible for collecting and remitting this tax.	Employee's Withholding Allowance Certificate (Form W-4) exempt employees hourly rate basis payroll register
>> 10-4 Determine employee deductions for Medicare tax. **WHY IT'S IMPORTANT** Employers have legal responsibility.	piece-rate basis salary basis tax-exempt wages wage-bracket table method
>> 10-5 Determine employee deductions for income tax. **WHY IT'S IMPORTANT** Employers are legally responsible.	
>> 10-6 Enter gross earnings, deductions, and net pay in the payroll register. **WHY IT'S IMPORTANT** The payroll register provides information needed to prepare paychecks.	

Calculating Earnings and Taxes

Brandon Express Company is a sole proprietorship owned and managed by Sarah Brandon. The company imports furniture and novelty items to sell over the Internet. It has five employees. The three shipping clerks and the shipping supervisor are paid on an hourly basis. The office clerk is paid a weekly salary. Payday is each Monday; it covers the wages and salaries earned the previous week. The employees are subject to withholding of social security, Medicare, and federal income taxes. The business pays social security and Medicare taxes, and federal and state unemployment insurance taxes. The business is required by state law to carry workers' compensation insurance. Because it is involved in interstate commerce, Brandon Express Company is subject to the Fair Labor Standards Act.

From time to time, Sarah Brandon, the owner, makes cash withdrawals to cover her personal expenses. The withdrawals by the owner of a sole proprietorship are not treated as salaries or wages but as reductions in owner's equity.

Computing Total Earnings of Employees

The first step in preparing payroll is to compute the gross wages or salary for each employee. There are several ways to compute earnings:

Hourly rate basis workers earn a stated rate per hour. Gross pay depends on the number of hours worked.

Salary basis workers earn an agreed-upon amount for each week, month, or other period.
Commission basis workers, usually salespeople, earn a percentage of net sales.
Piece-rate basis manufacturing workers are paid based on the number of units produced.

> Walmart has approximately 2.3 million employees in its worldwide operations (1.5 million in the U.S.), which include Walmart discount stores, Sam's Clubs, the distribution centers, and the home office. It has operations in North America, Central and South America, Asia, and the UK.

>> **10-2 OBJECTIVE**
Compute gross earnings of employees.

Determining Pay for Hourly Employees

Two pieces of data are needed to compute gross pay for hourly rate basis employees: the number of hours worked during the payroll period and the rate of pay.

Hours Worked

At Brandon Express Company, the shipping supervisor keeps a weekly time sheet. Each day she enters the hours worked by each shipping clerk. At the end of the week, the office clerk uses the time sheet to compute the total hours worked and to prepare the payroll.

Many businesses use time and attendance systems for hourly employees. Businesses utilizing time clocks may have a physical time clock near the employee entrance, or time may be captured by the computer work location for each person. Those with physical time clocks ask each employee to insert a time card in the time clock to record the times of arrival and departure. The payroll clerk collects this data at the end of the week, determines the hours worked by each employee, and multiplies the number of hours by the pay rate to compute the gross pay and withholdings. Most businesses utilize a payroll software program to calculate earnings, withholdings, and net pay.

Gross Pay

Alicia Martinez, Jorge Rodriguez, and George Dunlap are shipping clerks at Brandon Express Company. They are hourly employees. Their gross pay for the week that ended January 6 is determined as follows:

- Martinez worked 40 hours. She earns $10 an hour. Her gross pay is $400 (40 hours × $10).
- Rodriguez worked 40 hours. He earns $9.50 an hour. His gross pay is $380 (40 × $9.50).
- Dunlap earns $9 per hour. He worked 45 hours. He is paid 40 hours at regular pay and 5 hours at time and a half. There are two ways to compute Dunlap's gross pay:

  1. The Wage and Hour Law method identifies the *overtime premium,* the amount the firm could have saved if all the hours were paid at the regular rate. The overtime premium rate is $4.50, one-half of the regular rate ($9 × ½ = $4.50).

Total hours × regular rate:	
45 hours × $9	$405.00
Overtime premium:	
5 hours × $4.50	22.50
Gross pay	$427.50

recall

Owner Withdrawals
Withdrawals by the owner of a sole proprietorship are debited to a temporary owner's equity account (in this case, *Sarah Brandon, Drawing*). Withdrawals are not treated as salary or wages but serve to reduce the owner's equity or capital. The sole proprietor will pay income and earnings taxes on the net taxable income of the sole proprietor business entity, not the withdrawals.

2. The second method identifies how much the employee earned by working overtime.

Regular earnings:	
40 hours × $9	$360.00
Overtime earnings:	
5 hours × $13.50 ($9 × 1½)	67.50
Gross pay	$427.50

Cecilia Wu is the shipping supervisor at Brandon Express Company. She is an hourly employee. She earns $14 an hour, and she worked 40 hours. Her gross pay is $560 (40 × $14).

Withholdings for Hourly Employees Required by Law

Recall that three deductions from employees' gross pay are required by federal law: social security tax, Medicare tax, and federal income tax withholding.

Social Security Tax The social security tax is levied on both the employer and the employee. This text calculates social security tax using a 6.2 percent tax rate on the first $132,900 of wages paid during the calendar year. **Tax-exempt wages** are earnings in excess of the base amount set by the Social Security Act ($132,900). Tax-exempt wages are not subject to social security withholding.

If an employee works for more than one employer during the year, the social security tax is deducted and matched by each employer. When the employee files a federal income tax return, any excess social security tax withheld from the employee's earnings is refunded by the government or applied to payment of the employee's federal income taxes.

To determine the amount of social security tax to withhold from an employee's pay, multiply the taxable wages by the social security tax rate. Round the result to the nearest cent.

The following shows the social security tax deductions for Brandon Express Company's hourly employees.

>> **10-3 OBJECTIVE**
Determine employee deductions for social security tax.

Employee	Gross Pay	Tax Rate	Tax
Alicia Martinez	$400.00	6.2%	$ 24.80
Jorge Rodriguez	380.00	6.2	23.56
George Dunlap	427.50	6.2	26.51
Cecilia Wu	560.00	6.2	34.72
Total social security tax withheld			$109.59

Medicare Tax The Medicare tax is paid by both the employee and the employer. To compute the Medicare tax to withhold from the employee's paycheck, multiply the wages by the Medicare tax rate, 1.45 percent. The following shows the Medicare tax deduction for the hourly employees.

>> **10-4 OBJECTIVE**
Determine employee deductions for Medicare tax.

Employee	Gross Pay	Tax Rate	Tax
Alicia Martinez	$400.00	1.45%	$ 5.80
Jorge Rodriguez	380.00	1.45	5.51
George Dunlap	427.50	1.45	6.20
Cecilia Wu	560.00	1.45	8.12
Total Medicare tax			$25.63

>> 10-5 OBJECTIVE

Determine employee deductions for income tax.

Federal Income Tax A substantial portion of the federal government's revenue comes from the income tax on individuals, most of which is withheld by employers and deposited to the government within specified, regular periods. Employers are required by law to withhold federal income tax from employees' pay. Periodically the employer pays the federal income tax withheld to the federal government. After the end of the year, the employee files an income tax return. If the amount of federal income tax withheld does not cover the amount of income tax due, the employee pays the balance. If too much federal income tax has been withheld, the employee receives a refund.

> The federal income tax is a pay-as-you-go tax. There are two ways to pay. If you are an employee, your employer will withhold income tax from your pay based on your instructions in Form W-4. If you do not pay tax through withholdings, or do not pay enough taxes through withholdings because of income from other sources, you might have to pay estimated taxes. Individuals who are in business for themselves generally have to pay taxes through the estimated tax system. The Electronic Federal Tax Payment System (EFTPS) is a free service from the IRS through which taxpayers can use the Internet to pay their federal taxes, especially **1040** estimated taxes.

important!

Pay-As-You-Go

Employee income tax withholding is designed to place employees on a pay-as-you-go basis in paying their federal income tax.

Withholding Allowances The amount of federal income tax to withhold from an employee's earnings depends on the:

- earnings during the pay period,
- length of the pay period,
- marital status,
- number of withholding allowances.

Determining the number of withholding allowances for some taxpayers is complex. In the simplest circumstances, a taxpayer claims a withholding allowance for:

- the taxpayer,
- a spouse who does not also claim an allowance,
- each dependent for whom the taxpayer provides more than half the support during the year.

As the number of withholding allowances increases, the amount of federal income tax withheld decreases. The goal is to claim the number of withholding allowances so that the federal income tax withheld is about the same as the employee's tax liability for those earnings reported on the individual income tax return.

To claim withholding allowances, employees complete **Employee's Withholding Allowance Certificate, Form W-4.** The employee gives the completed Form W-4 to the employer. If the number of exemption allowances decreases, the employee must file a new Form W-4 within 10 days. If the number of exemption allowances increases, the employee may, but is not required to, file another Form W-4. If an employee does not file a Form W-4, the employer withholds federal income tax based on zero withholding allowances.

Figure 10.1 shows Form W-4 for Alicia Martinez. Notice that on Line 5, Martinez claims one withholding allowance.

important!

Get It in Writing

Employers need a signed Form W-4 in order to change the employee's federal income tax withholding.

Computing Federal Income Tax Withholding Although there are several ways to compute the federal income tax to withhold from an employee's earnings, the **wage-bracket table method** is almost universally used. The wage-bracket tables are in *Publication 15, Circular E.* This publication contains withholding tables for weekly, biweekly, semimonthly, monthly, and daily or miscellaneous payroll periods for single and married persons. Figure 10.2 shows partial tables for single and married persons who are paid weekly.

Use the following steps to determine the amount to withhold:

1. Choose the table for the pay period and the employee's marital status.
2. Find the row in the table that matches the wages earned. Find the column that matches the number of withholding allowances claimed on Form W-4. The income tax to withhold is the intersection of the row and the column.

As an example, let's determine the amount to withhold from Cecilia Wu's gross pay. Wu is married, claims two withholding allowances, and earned $560 for the week:

1. Go to the table for married persons paid weekly, Figure 10.2B.
2. Find the line covering wages between $560 and $570. Find the column for two withholding allowances. The tax to withhold is $30; this is where the row and the column intersect.

Using the wage-bracket tables, can you find the federal income tax amounts to withhold for Martinez, Rodriguez, and Dunlap?

Employee	Gross Pay	Marital Status	Withholding Allowances	Income Tax Withholding
Alicia Martinez	$400.00	Married	1	$ 19.00
Jorge Rodriguez	380.00	Single	1	34.00
George Dunlap	427.50	Single	3	23.00
Cecilia Wu	560.00	Married	2	30.00
				$106.00

Other Deductions Required by Law Most states and some local governments require employers to withhold state and local income taxes from earnings. A couple of additional withholdings from employees include court orders for child support or other type of court-ordered garnishments. Employers, when ordered by a court, are required to withhold amounts designated in the court order—known as a garnishment—and remit those amounts to the proper authorities.

In some states, employers are also required to withhold disability or other taxes. The procedures are similar to those for federal income tax withholding. Apply the tax rate to the earnings, or use withholding tables.

FIGURE 10.1 Form W-4 (Partial)

FIGURE 10.2A

Sample Federal Withholding Tax Tables (Partial) for Single Persons—Weekly Payroll Period

SINGLE Persons—WEEKLY Payroll Period (For Wages Paid Through December 20X1)

If the wages are —		And the number of withholding allowances claimed is —										
At least	But less than	0	1	2	3	4	5	6	7	8	9	10
		The amount of income tax to be withheld is —										
$0	$55	$0	$0	$0	$0	$0	$0	$0	$0	$0	$0	$0
55	60	1	0	0	0	0	0	0	0	0	0	0
60	65	1	0	0	0	0	0	0	0	0	0	0
65	70	2	0	0	0	0	0	0	0	0	0	0
70	75	2	0	0	0	0	0	0	0	0	0	0
75	80	3	0	0	0	0	0	0	0	0	0	0
80	85	3	0	0	0	0	0	0	0	0	0	0
85	90	4	0	0	0	0	0	0	0	0	0	0
90	95	4	0	0	0	0	0	0	0	0	0	0
95	100	5	0	0	0	0	0	0	0	0	0	0
100	105	5	0	0	0	0	0	0	0	0	0	0
105	110	6	0	0	0	0	0	0	0	0	0	0
110	115	6	0	0	0	0	0	0	0	0	0	0
115	120	7	1	0	0	0	0	0	0	0	0	0
120	125	7	1	0	0	0	0	0	0	0	0	0
125	130	8	2	0	0	0	0	0	0	0	0	0
130	135	8	2	0	0	0	0	0	0	0	0	0
135	140	9	3	0	0	0	0	0	0	0	0	0
140	145	9	3	0	0	0	0	0	0	0	0	0
145	150	10	4	0	0	0	0	0	0	0	0	0
150	155	10	4	0	0	0	0	0	0	0	0	0
155	160	11	5	0	0	0	0	0	0	0	0	0
160	165	11	5	0	0	0	0	0	0	0	0	0
165	170	12	6	0	0	0	0	0	0	0	0	0
170	175	12	6	0	0	0	0	0	0	0	0	0
175	180	13	7	1	0	0	0	0	0	0	0	0
180	185	13	7	1	0	0	0	0	0	0	0	0
185	190	14	8	2	0	0	0	0	0	0	0	0
190	195	14	8	2	0	0	0	0	0	0	0	0
195	200	15	9	3	0	0	0	0	0	0	0	0
200	210	16	9	3	0	0	0	0	0	0	0	0
210	220	18	10	4	0	0	0	0	0	0	0	0
220	230	19	11	5	0	0	0	0	0	0	0	0
230	240	21	12	6	1	0	0	0	0	0	0	0
240	250	22	13	7	2	0	0	0	0	0	0	0
250	260	24	15	8	3	0	0	0	0	0	0	0
260	270	25	16	9	4	0	0	0	0	0	0	0
270	280	27	18	10	5	0	0	0	0	0	0	0
280	290	28	19	11	6	0	0	0	0	0	0	0
290	300	30	21	12	7	1	0	0	0	0	0	0
300	310	31	22	13	8	2	0	0	0	0	0	0
310	320	33	24	15	9	3	0	0	0	0	0	0
320	330	34	25	16	10	4	0	0	0	0	0	0
330	340	36	27	18	11	5	0	0	0	0	0	0
340	350	37	28	19	12	6	0	0	0	0	0	0
350	360	39	30	21	13	7	1	0	0	0	0	0
360	370	40	31	22	14	8	2	0	0	0	0	0
370	380	42	33	24	15	9	3	0	0	0	0	0
380	390	43	34	25	17	10	4	0	0	0	0	0
390	400	45	36	27	18	11	5	0	0	0	0	0
400	410	46	37	28	20	12	6	0	0	0	0	0
410	420	48	39	30	21	13	7	1	0	0	0	0
420	430	49	40	31	23	14	8	2	0	0	0	0
430	440	51	42	33	24	15	9	3	0	0	0	0
440	450	52	43	34	26	17	10	4	0	0	0	0
450	460	54	45	36	27	18	11	5	0	0	0	0
460	470	55	46	37	29	20	12	6	0	0	0	0
470	480	57	48	39	30	21	13	7	1	0	0	0
480	490	58	49	40	32	23	14	8	2	0	0	0
490	500	60	51	42	33	24	15	9	3	0	0	0
500	510	61	52	43	35	26	17	10	4	0	0	0
510	520	63	54	45	36	27	18	11	5	0	0	0
520	530	64	55	46	38	29	20	12	6	0	0	0
530	540	66	57	48	39	30	21	13	7	1	0	0
540	550	67	58	49	41	32	23	14	8	2	0	0
550	560	69	60	51	42	33	24	15	9	3	0	0
560	570	70	61	52	44	35	26	17	10	4	0	0
570	580	72	63	54	45	36	27	18	11	5	0	0
580	590	73	64	55	47	38	29	20	12	6	0	0
590	600	75	66	57	48	39	30	21	13	7	1	0

This table does not contain actual withholding amounts for the year 20X1 and should not be used to determine payroll withholdings for 20X1.

Withholdings Not Required by Law

There are many payroll deductions not required by law but made by agreement between the employee and the employer. Some examples are:

- group life insurance,
- group medical insurance

FIGURE 10.2B

Sample Federal Withholding Tax Tables (Partial) for Married Persons—Weekly Payroll Period

MARRIED Persons—WEEKLY Payroll Period (For Wages Paid Through December 20X1)

If the wages are —		And the number of withholding allowances claimed is —										
At least	But less than	0	1	2	3	4	5	6	7	8	9	10
		The amount of income tax to be withheld is —										
$0	$125	$0	$0	$0	$0	$0	$0	$0	$0	$0	$0	$0
125	130	0	0	0	0	0	0	0	0	0	0	0
130	135	0	0	0	0	0	0	0	0	0	0	0
135	140	0	0	0	0	0	0	0	0	0	0	0
140	145	0	0	0	0	0	0	0	0	0	0	0
145	150	0	0	0	0	0	0	0	0	0	0	0
150	155	0	0	0	0	0	0	0	0	0	0	0
155	160	0	0	0	0	0	0	0	0	0	0	0
160	165	1	0	0	0	0	0	0	0	0	0	0
165	170	1	0	0	0	0	0	0	0	0	0	0
170	175	2	0	0	0	0	0	0	0	0	0	0
175	180	2	0	0	0	0	0	0	0	0	0	0
180	185	3	0	0	0	0	0	0	0	0	0	0
185	190	3	0	0	0	0	0	0	0	0	0	0
190	195	4	0	0	0	0	0	0	0	0	0	0
195	200	4	0	0	0	0	0	0	0	0	0	0
200	210	5	0	0	0	0	0	0	0	0	0	0
210	220	6	0	0	0	0	0	0	0	0	0	0
220	230	7	1	0	0	0	0	0	0	0	0	0
230	240	8	2	0	0	0	0	0	0	0	0	0
240	250	9	3	0	0	0	0	0	0	0	0	0
250	260	10	4	0	0	0	0	0	0	0	0	0
260	270	11	5	0	0	0	0	0	0	0	0	0
270	280	12	6	0	0	0	0	0	0	0	0	0
280	290	13	7	1	0	0	0	0	0	0	0	0
290	300	14	8	2	0	0	0	0	0	0	0	0
300	310	15	9	3	0	0	0	0	0	0	0	0
310	320	16	10	4	0	0	0	0	0	0	0	0
320	330	17	11	5	0	0	0	0	0	0	0	0
330	340	18	12	6	0	0	0	0	0	0	0	0
340	350	19	13	7	1	0	0	0	0	0	0	0
350	360	20	14	8	2	0	0	0	0	0	0	0
360	370	21	15	9	3	0	0	0	0	0	0	0
370	380	22	16	10	4	0	0	0	0	0	0	0
380	390	23	17	11	5	0	0	0	0	0	0	0
390	400	24	18	12	6	0	0	0	0	0	0	0
400	410	25	19	13	7	1	0	0	0	0	0	0
410	420	26	20	14	8	2	0	0	0	0	0	0
420	430	27	21	15	9	3	0	0	0	0	0	0
430	440	28	22	16	10	4	0	0	0	0	0	0
440	450	30	23	17	11	5	0	0	0	0	0	0
450	460	31	24	18	12	6	0	0	0	0	0	0
460	470	33	25	19	13	7	1	0	0	0	0	0
470	480	34	26	20	14	8	2	0	0	0	0	0
480	490	36	27	21	15	9	3	0	0	0	0	0
490	500	37	28	22	16	10	4	0	0	0	0	0
500	510	39	30	23	17	11	5	0	0	0	0	0
510	520	40	31	24	18	12	6	0	0	0	0	0
520	530	42	33	25	19	13	7	1	0	0	0	0
530	540	43	34	26	20	14	8	2	0	0	0	0
540	550	45	36	27	21	15	9	3	0	0	0	0
550	560	46	37	29	22	16	10	4	0	0	0	0
560	570	48	39	30	23	17	11	5	0	0	0	0
570	580	49	40	32	24	18	12	6	0	0	0	0
580	590	51	42	33	25	19	13	7	1	0	0	0
590	600	52	43	35	26	20	14	8	2	0	0	0
600	610	54	45	36	27	21	15	9	3	0	0	0
610	620	55	46	38	29	22	16	10	4	0	0	0
620	630	57	48	39	30	23	17	11	5	0	0	0
630	640	58	49	41	32	24	18	12	6	0	0	0
640	650	60	51	42	33	25	19	13	7	1	0	0
650	660	61	52	44	35	26	20	14	8	2	0	0
660	670	63	54	45	36	27	21	15	9	3	0	0
670	680	64	55	47	38	29	22	16	10	4	0	0
680	690	66	57	48	39	30	23	17	11	5	0	0
690	700	67	58	50	41	32	24	18	12	6	0	0
700	710	69	60	51	42	33	25	19	13	7	1	0
710	720	70	61	53	44	35	26	20	14	8	2	0
720	730	72	63	54	45	36	27	21	15	9	3	0
730	740	73	64	56	47	38	29	22	16	10	4	0

This table does not contain actual withholding amounts for the year 20X1 and should not be used to determine payroll withholdings for 20X1.

- company retirement plans,
- bank or credit union savings plans or loan repayments,
- U.S. saving bonds purchase plans,
- stocks and other investment purchase plans,
- employer loan repayments,
- union dues.

These and other payroll deductions increase the payroll recordkeeping work but do not involve any new principles or procedures. They are handled in the same way as the deductions for social security, Medicare, and federal income taxes. The amounts withheld from the employee's pay are recorded as liabilities on payday; the liabilities are debited (to remove) when paid.

Brandon Express Company pays all medical insurance premiums for each employee. If the employee chooses to have medical coverage for a spouse or dependent, the company deducts $40 per week for coverage of the spouse/child. Dunlap and Wu each has $40 per week deducted to obtain the medical coverage.

Determining Pay for Salaried Employees

A salaried employee earns a specific sum of money for each payroll period. The office clerk at Brandon Express Company earns a weekly salary.

Hours Worked

Salaried workers who do not hold supervisory jobs are covered by the provisions of the Wage and Hour Law that deal with maximum hours and overtime premium pay. Employers keep time records for all nonsupervisory salaried workers to make sure that their hourly earnings meet the legal requirements.

Salaried employees who hold supervisory or managerial positions are called **exempt employees.** They are not subject to the maximum hour and overtime premium pay provisions of the Wage and Hour Law. As such, these employee do not receive any additional pay for time worked in excess of 40 hours per week.

Gross Earnings

Cynthia Booker is the office clerk at Brandon Express Company. During the first week of January, she worked 40 hours, her regular schedule. There are no overtime earnings because she did not work more than 40 hours during the week. Her salary of $480 is her gross pay for the week.

Withholdings for Salaried Employees Required by Law

The procedures for withholding taxes for salaried employees are the same as for withholding for hourly rate employees. Apply the tax rate to the earnings, or use withholding tables.

Recording Payroll Information for Employees

A payroll register is prepared for each pay period. The **payroll register** shows all the payroll information for the pay period.

>> **10-6 OBJECTIVE**
Enter gross earnings, deductions, and net pay in the payroll register.

The Payroll Register

Figure 10.3 shows the payroll register for Brandon Express Company for the week ended January 6. Note that all employees were paid for eight hours on January 1,

FIGURE 10.3 Payroll Register

PAYROLL REGISTER   **WEEK BEGINNING**   *January 1, 20X1*

NAME	NO. OF ALLOW.	MARITAL STATUS	CUMULATIVE EARNINGS	NO. OF HRS.	RATE/ SALARY	EARNINGS REGULAR	EARNINGS OVERTIME	GROSS AMOUNT	CUMULATIVE EARNINGS
Martinez, Alicia	1	M		40	10.00	400 00		400 00	400 00
Rodriguez, Jorge	1	S		40	9.50	380 00		380 00	380 00
Dunlap, George	3	S		45	9.00	360 00	67 50	427 50	427 50
Wu, Cecilia	2	M		40	14.00	560 00		560 00	560 00
Booker, Cynthia	1	S		40	480.00	480 00		480 00	480 00
			0 00			2 180 00	67 50	2 247 50	2 247 50
(A)	(B)		(C)	(D)	(E)	(F)	(G)	(H)	(I)

a holiday. To learn how to complete the payroll register, refer to Figure 10.3 and follow these steps:

1. *Columns A, B, and E.* Enter the employee's name (Column A), number of withholding allowances and marital status (Column B), and rate of pay (Column E). In a computerized payroll system, this information is entered once and is automatically retrieved each time payroll is prepared.

2. *Column C.* The Cumulative Earnings column (Column C) shows the total earnings for the calendar year before the current pay period. This figure is needed to determine whether the employee has exceeded the earnings limit for the social security and FUTA taxes. Since this is the first payroll period of the year, there are no cumulative earnings prior to the current pay period.

3. *Column D.* In Column D, enter the total number of hours worked in the current period. This data comes from the weekly time sheet.

4. *Columns F, G, and H.* Using the hours worked and the pay rate, calculate regular pay (Column F), the overtime earnings (Column G), and gross pay (Column H).

5. *Column I.* Calculate the cumulative earnings after this pay period (Column I) by adding the beginning cumulative earnings (Column C) and the current period's gross pay (Column H).

6. *Columns J, K, and L.* The Taxable Wages columns show the earnings subject to taxes for social security (Column J), Medicare (Column K), and FUTA (Column L). Only the earnings at or under the earnings limit are included in these columns.

7. *Columns M, N, O, and P.* The Deductions columns show the withholding for social security tax (Column M), Medicare tax (Column N), federal income tax (Column O), and medical insurance (Column P).

8. *Column Q.* Subtract the deductions (Columns M, N, O, and P) from the gross earnings (Column H). Enter the results in the Net Amount column (Column Q). This is the amount paid to each employee.

9. *Column R.* Enter the check number in Column R.

10. *Columns S and T.* The payroll register's last two columns classify employee earnings as office salaries (Column S) or shipping wages (Column T).

When the payroll data for all employees has been entered in the payroll register, total the columns. Check the balances of the following columns:

■ Total regular earnings plus total overtime earnings must equal the gross amount (Columns F + G = Column H).

AND ENDING January 6, 20X1   **PAID** January 8, 20X1

TAXABLE WAGES			DEDUCTIONS				DISTRIBUTION			
SOCIAL SECURITY	MEDICARE	FUTA	SOCIAL SECURITY	MEDICARE	INCOME TAX	HEALTH INSURANCE	NET AMOUNT	CHECK NO.	OFFICE SALARIES	SHIPPING WAGES
400 00	400 00	400 00	24 80	5 80	19 00		350 40	1601		400 00
380 00	380 00	380 00	23 56	5 51	34 00		316 93	1602		380 00
427 50	427 50	427 50	26 51	6 20	23 00	40 00	331 79	1603		427 50
560 00	560 00	560 00	34 72	8 12	30 00	40 00	447 16	1604		560 00
480 00	480 00	480 00	29 76	6 96	49 00		394 28	1605	480 00	
2 247 50	2 247 50	2 247 50	139 35	32 59	155 00	80 00	1 840 56		480 00	1 767 50
(J)	(K)	(L)	(M)	(N)	(O)	(P)	(Q)	(R)	(S)	(T)

- The total gross amount less total deductions must equal the total net amount.

Gross amount		$2,247.50
Less deductions:		
Social security tax	$139.35	
Medicare tax	32.59	
Income tax	155.00	
Health insurance	80.00	
Total deductions		406.94
Net amount		$1,840.56

- The office salaries and the shipping wages must equal gross earnings (Columns S + T = Column H).

The payroll register supplies all the information to make the journal entry to record the payroll. Journalizing the payroll is discussed in Section 3.

Section 2 Review

1. Which one of the following is not a required deduction from payroll required by federal law?
   a. FUTA tax
   b. social security tax
   c. federal income tax
   d. Medicare tax

2. Which factor(s) does not determine the amount of federal income tax to be withheld from an employee's earnings?
   a. state where employee lives
   b. number of dependents the employee claims
   c. marital status
   d. the frequency of payroll payments

3. What does being classified an "exempt" employee mean?
   a. level of dangerous work being performed by employees
   b. can take off work any time desired
   c. employee does not have to pay medicare tax
   d. generally speaking, not eligible for any overtime pay

4. Which of the following affects the amount of Medicare tax to be withheld from an hourly rate employee's pay?
   a. medical insurance premium
   b. marital status
   c. withholding allowances claimed on Form W-4
   d. hours worked resulting in higher gross pay

5. Stacy Carter worked 48 hours during the week ending November 17. Her regular rate is $9 per hour. Calculate her gross earnings for the week.
   a. $432
   b. $492
   c. $468
   d. $444

Section 3

SECTION OBJECTIVES	TERMS TO LEARN
>> 10-7 Journalize payroll transactions in the general journal. **WHY IT'S IMPORTANT** Payroll cost is an operating expense. >> 10-8 Maintain an earnings record for each employee. **WHY IT'S IMPORTANT** Federal law requires that employers maintain records.	compensation record individual earnings record

Recording Payroll Information

In this section you will learn how to prepare paychecks and journalize and post payroll transactions by following the January payroll activity for Brandon Express Company.

Recording Payroll

Recording payroll involves two separate entries: one to record the payroll expense and another to pay the employees. The general journal entry to record the payroll expense is based on the payroll register. The gross pay is debited to *Shipping Wages Expense* for the shipping clerks and supervisor and to *Office Salaries Expense* for the office clerk. Each type of deduction is credited to a separate liability account *(Social Security Tax Payable, Medicare Tax Payable, Employee Income Tax Payable, Health Insurance Premiums Payable)*. Net pay is credited to the liability account *Salaries and Wages Payable.*

Refer to Figure 10.3 to see how the data on the payroll register is used to prepare the January 8 payroll journal entry for Brandon Express Company. Following is an analysis of the entry.

>> **10-7 OBJECTIVE**
Journalize payroll transactions in the general journal.

BUSINESS TRANSACTION

The information in the payroll register (Figure 10.3) is used to record the payroll expense.

ANALYSIS

The expense account **Office Salaries Expense** is increased by $480.00. The expense account **Shipping Wages Expense** is increased by $1,767.50. The liability account for each deduction is increased: **Social Security Tax Payable,** $139.35; **Medicare Tax Payable,** $32.59; **Employee Income Tax Payable,** $155.00; **Health Insurance Premiums Payable,** $80.00. The liability account **Salaries and Wages Payable** is increased by the net amount of the payroll, $1,840.56.

366 CHAPTER 10 Payroll Computations, Records, and Payment

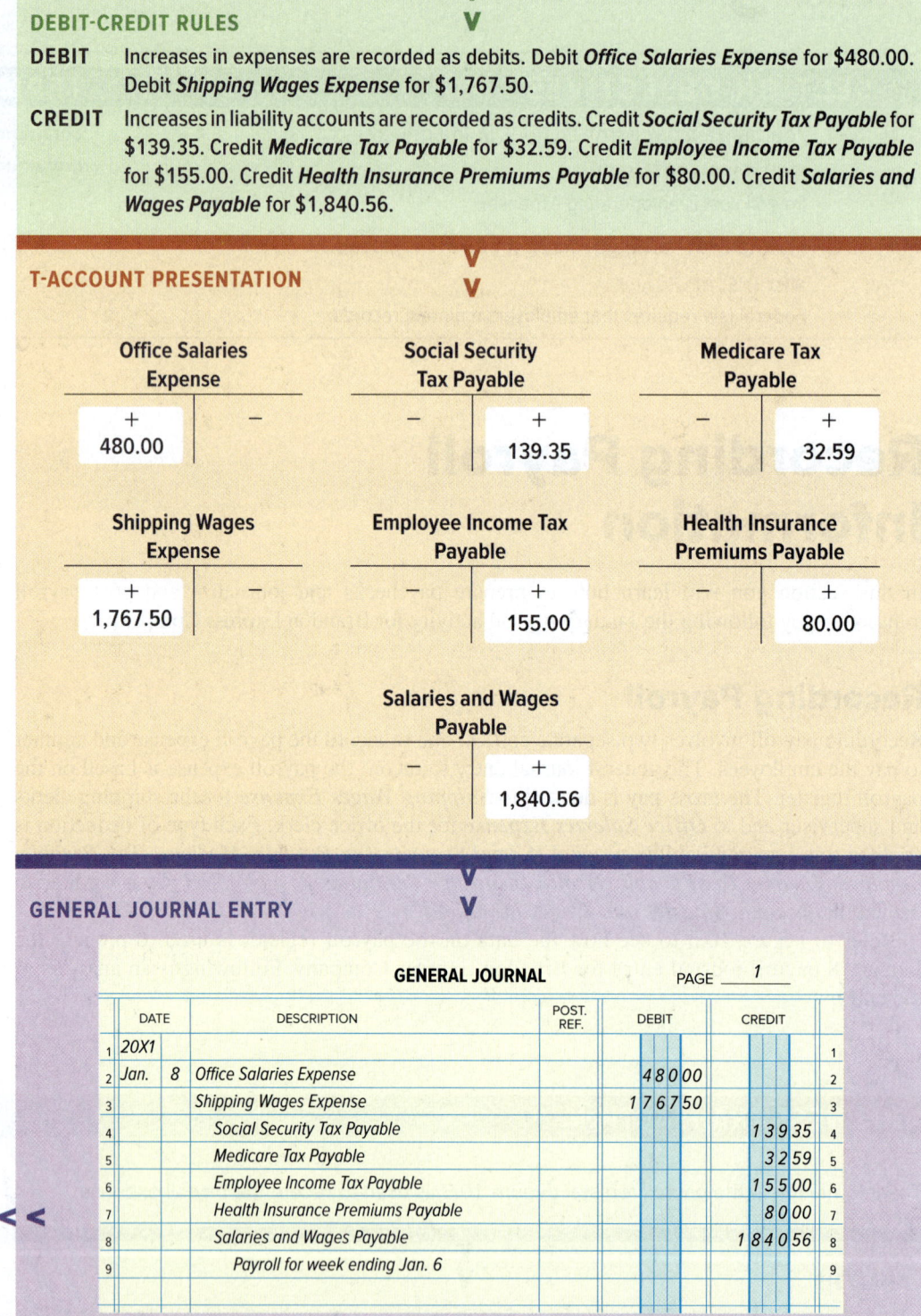

DEBIT-CREDIT RULES

DEBIT Increases in expenses are recorded as debits. Debit *Office Salaries Expense* for $480.00. Debit *Shipping Wages Expense* for $1,767.50.

CREDIT Increases in liability accounts are recorded as credits. Credit *Social Security Tax Payable* for $139.35. Credit *Medicare Tax Payable* for $32.59. Credit *Employee Income Tax Payable* for $155.00. Credit *Health Insurance Premiums Payable* for $80.00. Credit *Salaries and Wages Payable* for $1,840.56.

T-ACCOUNT PRESENTATION

Office Salaries Expense: + 480.00
Social Security Tax Payable: + 139.35
Medicare Tax Payable: + 32.59
Shipping Wages Expense: + 1,767.50
Employee Income Tax Payable: + 155.00
Health Insurance Premiums Payable: + 80.00
Salaries and Wages Payable: + 1,840.56

GENERAL JOURNAL ENTRY

GENERAL JOURNAL   PAGE 1

DATE	DESCRIPTION	POST. REF.	DEBIT	CREDIT
20X1				
Jan. 8	Office Salaries Expense		480 00	
	Shipping Wages Expense		1767 50	
	Social Security Tax Payable			139 35
	Medicare Tax Payable			32 59
	Employee Income Tax Payable			155 00
	Health Insurance Premiums Payable			80 00
	Salaries and Wages Payable			1840 56
	Payroll for week ending Jan. 6			

THE BOTTOM LINE
Record Payroll

Income Statement
Expenses ↑ $2,247.50
Net Income ↓ $2,247.50

Balance Sheet
Liabilities ↑ $2,247.50
Equity ↓ $2,247.50

Southwest Airlines Co. recorded salaries, wages, and benefits of more than $7.32 billion for the year ended December 31, 2017.

Paying Employees

Most businesses pay their employees by check or by direct deposit. By using these methods, the business avoids the inconvenience and risk involved in dealing with currency.

Paying by Check

Paychecks may be deducted on the firm's regular checking account or on a payroll bank account. The check stub, an e-check stub, or deposit information e-mail shows information about the employee's gross earnings, deductions, and net pay. Employees should keep this item as a record of their payroll data. The check number is entered in the Check Number column of the payroll register (Figure 10.3, Column R). The canceled check (or e-record) provides a record of the payment, and the employee's endorsement serves as a receipt. Following is an analysis of the transaction to pay Brandon Express Company's employees.

important!

Payroll Liabilities
All deductions from employee gross pay are liabilities for the employer.

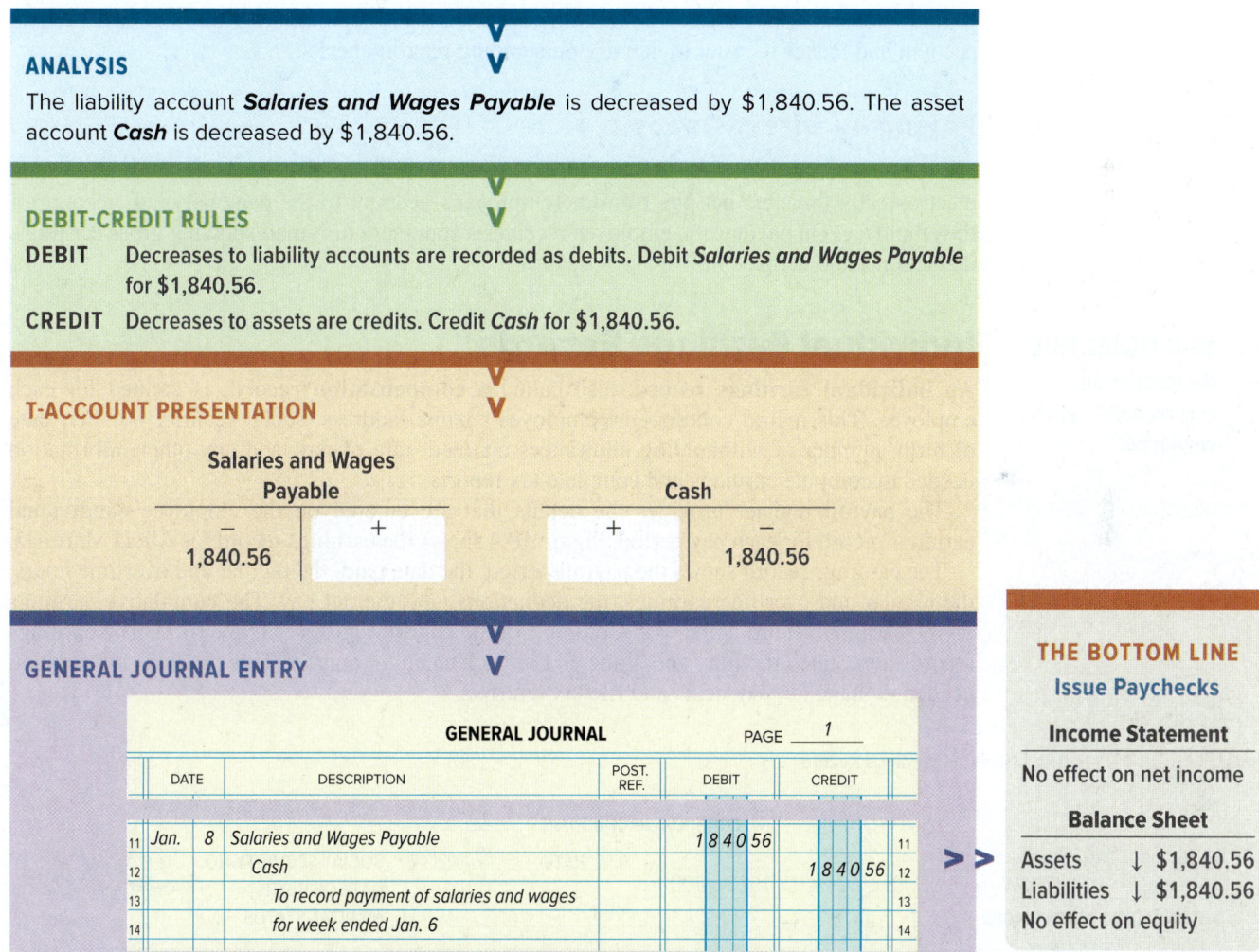

BUSINESS TRANSACTION

On January 8, Brandon Express Company wrote five checks for payroll, check numbers 1601–1605.

ANALYSIS
The liability account **Salaries and Wages Payable** is decreased by $1,840.56. The asset account **Cash** is decreased by $1,840.56.

DEBIT-CREDIT RULES
DEBIT Decreases to liability accounts are recorded as debits. Debit *Salaries and Wages Payable* for $1,840.56.
CREDIT Decreases to assets are credits. Credit *Cash* for $1,840.56.

T-ACCOUNT PRESENTATION

Salaries and Wages Payable		Cash	
−	+	+	−
1,840.56			1,840.56

GENERAL JOURNAL ENTRY

DATE	DESCRIPTION	POST. REF.	DEBIT	CREDIT
Jan. 8	Salaries and Wages Payable		1,840.56	
	Cash			1,840.56
	To record payment of salaries and wages			
	for week ended Jan. 6			

THE BOTTOM LINE

Issue Paychecks

Income Statement
No effect on net income

Balance Sheet
Assets   ↓ $1,840.56
Liabilities ↓ $1,840.56
No effect on equity

Checks Written on a Separate Payroll Account Many businesses write payroll checks (either physically or electronically) from a separate payroll bank account. This is a two-step process:

1. A check is drawn on the regular bank account for the total amount of net pay and deposited in the payroll bank account.
2. Individual payroll checks are issued from the payroll bank account.

important!

Separate Payroll Account
Using a separate payroll account facilitates the bank reconciliation and provides better internal control.

MANAGERIAL IMPLICATIONS >>

LAWS AND CONTROLS

- It is management's responsibility to ensure that the payroll procedures and records comply with federal, state, and local laws.
- For most businesses, wages and salaries are a large part of operating expenses. Payroll records help management to keep track of and control expenses.
- Management should investigate large or frequent overtime expenditures.
- To prevent errors and fraud, management periodically should have the payroll records audited and payroll procedures evaluated.
- Two common payroll frauds are the overstatement of hours worked and the issuance of checks to nonexistent employees.

THINKING CRITICALLY
What controls would you put in place to prevent payroll fraud?

Using a separate payroll account simplifies the bank reconciliation of the regular checking account and makes it easier to identify outstanding payroll checks.

Paying by Direct Deposit

The most popular method of paying employees is the direct deposit method. The bank electronically transfers net pay from the employer's account to the personal bank account of the employee. On payday, the employee receives a statement or e-mail showing gross earnings, deductions, and net pay.

>> 10-8 OBJECTIVE

Maintain an earnings record for each employee.

Individual Earnings Records

An **individual earnings record,** also called a **compensation record,** is created for each employee. This record contains the employee's name, address, social security number, date of birth, number of withholding allowances claimed, rate of pay, and any other information needed to compute earnings and complete tax reports.

The payroll register provides the details that are entered on the employee's individual earnings record for each pay period. Figure 10.4 shows the earnings record for Alicia Martinez.

The earnings record shows the payroll period, the date paid, the regular and overtime hours, the regular and overtime earnings, the deductions, and the net pay. The cumulative earnings on the earnings record agree with Column I of the payroll register (Figure 10.3). The earnings records are totaled monthly and at the end of each calendar quarter. This provides information needed to make tax payments and file tax returns.

FIGURE 10.4 An Individual Earnings Record

EARNINGS RECORD FOR 20X1

NAME: Alicia Martinez
ADDRESS: 1712 Windmill Hill Lane, Dallas, TX 75232-6002
WITHHOLDING ALLOWANCES: 1
RATE: $10 per hour
SOCIAL SECURITY NO.: 123-45-6789
DATE OF BIRTH: November 23, 1979
MARITAL STATUS: M

PAYROLL NO.	DATE WK. END.	DATE PAID	HOURS RG	HOURS OT	EARNINGS REGULAR	EARNINGS OVERTIME	EARNINGS TOTAL	EARNINGS CUMULATIVE	DEDUCTIONS SOCIAL SECURITY	DEDUCTIONS MEDICARE	DEDUCTIONS INCOME TAX	DEDUCTIONS OTHER	NET PAY
1	1/06	1/08	40		400 00		400 00	400 00	24 80	5 80	19 00		350 40
2	1/13	1/15	40		400 00		400 00	800 00	24 80	5 80	19 00		350 40
3	1/20	1/22	40		400 00		400 00	1200 00	24 80	5 80	19 00		350 40
4	1/27	1/29	40		400 00		400 00	1600 00	24 80	5 80	19 00		350 40
	January				1600 00		1600 00		99 20	23 20	76 00		1401 60

Completing January Payrolls

Figure 10.5 shows the entire cycle of computing, paying, journalizing, and posting payroll data. In order to complete the January payroll for Brandon Express Company, assume that all employees worked the same number of hours each week of the month as they did the first week. Thus, they had the same earnings, deductions, and net pay each week.

Entry to Record Payroll

As illustrated earlier in this section, one general journal entry is made to record the weekly payroll for all employees of Brandon Express Company. This general journal entry records the payroll expense and liability, but not the payments to employees. Since we are assuming an identical payroll for each week of the month, each of the four weekly payrolls requires general journal entries identical to the one shown in Figure 10.5. Notice how the payroll register column totals are recorded in the general journal.

Entry to Record Payment of Payroll

The weekly entries in the general journal to record payments to employees debit **Salaries and Wages Payable** and credit **Cash.**

Postings to Ledger Accounts

The entries to record the weekly payroll expense and liability amounts are posted from the general journal to the accounts in the general ledger. The total of the Salaries and Wages Payable Debit column in the cash payments journal is posted to the **Salaries and Wages Payable** general ledger account.

> **ABOUT ACCOUNTING**
>
> **Tax Returns**
>
> The top 20 percent of U.S. wage earners (those making more than $150,000) will pay about 87 percent of all federal income for the U.S. (*Online Wall Street Journal,* November 9, 2018.)

FIGURE 10.5 Journalizing and Posting Payroll Data

AND ENDING January 6, 20X1   PAID January 8, 20X1

TAXABLE WAGES			DEHUCTIONS				DISTRIBUTION			
SOCIAL SECURITY	MEDICARE	FUTA	SOCIAL SECURITY	MEDICARE	INCOME TAX	HEALTH INSURANCE	NET AMOUNT	CHECK NO.	OFFICE SALARIES	SHIPPING WAGES
400 00	400 00	400 00	24 80	5 80	19 00		350 40	1601		400 00
380 00	380 00	380 00	23 56	5 51	34 00		316 93	1602		380 00
427 50	427 50	427 50	26 51	6 20	23 00	40 00	331 79	1603		427 50
560 00	560 00	560 00	34 72	8 12	30 00	40 00	447 16	1604		560 00
480 00	480 00	480 00	29 76	6 96	49 00		394 28	1605	480 00	
2 247 50	2 247 50	2 247 50	139 35	32 59	155 00	80 00	1 840 56		480 00	1 767 50
(J)	(K)	(L)	(M)	(N)	(O)	(P)	(Q)	(R)	(S)	(T)

1	20X1					1
2	Jan.	8	Office Salaries Expense	541	480 00	2
3			Shipping Wages Expense	542	1 767 50	3
4			Social Security Tax Payable	221		139 35	4
5			Medicare Tax Payable	222		32 59	5
6			Employee Income Tax Payable	223		155 00	6
7			Health Insurance Premiums Payable	224		80 00	7
8			Salaries and Wages Payable	229		1 840 56	8
9			Payroll for week ending Jan. 6				9

(continued)

370 CHAPTER 10 Payroll Computations, Records, and Payment

FIGURE 10.5 (continued)

1	20X1								1
2	Jan.	8	Office Salaries Expense	541	480 00				2
3			Shipping Wages Expense	542	1 767 50				3
4			Social Security Tax Payable	221			139 35		4
5			Medicare Tax Payable	222			32 59		5
6			Employee Income Tax Payable	223			155 00		6
7			Health Insurance Premiums Payable	224			80 00		7
8			Salaries and Wages Payable	229			1 840 56		8
9			Payroll for week ending Jan. 6						9

Office Salaries Expense
1/08	480.00
1/15	480.00
1/22	480.00
1/29	480.00

Medicare Tax Payable
1/08	32.59
1/15	32.59
1/22	32.59
1/29	32.59

Shipping Wages Expense
1/08	1,767.50
1/15	1,767.50
1/22	1,767.50
1/29	1,767.50

Employee Income Tax Payable
1/08	155.00
1/15	155.00
1/22	155.00
1/29	155.00

Health Ins. Premiums Payable
1/08	80.00
1/15	80.00
1/22	80.00
1/29	80.00

Social Security Tax Payable
1/08	139.35
1/15	139.35
1/22	139.35
1/29	139.35

Salaries and Wages Payable
1/08	1,840.56	1/08	1,840.56
1/15	1,840.56	1/15	1,840.56
1/22	1,840.56	1/22	1,840.56
1/29	1,840.56	1/29	1,840.56

GENERAL JOURNAL PAGE 1

	DATE		DESCRIPTION	POST. REF.	DEBIT	CREDIT	
1	20X1						1
2	Jan.	8	Salaries and Wages Payable		1 840 56		2
3			Cash			1 840 56	3
4			To record payment of				4
5			salaries and wages				5
6			for week				6
7			ended Jan. 6				7

Section 3 Review

1. What is (are) a good reason(s) for using a payroll bank account for payroll that is separated from your operating bank account?
   a. easier to audit payroll transactions
   b. easier to find an individual's payroll transaction if check is lost
   c. quicker bank reconciliation of payroll checking account
   d. all of the above

2. What accounts are affected when payroll checks are written?
   a. *Cash* is debited for gross earnings.
   b. *Cash* is credited for net earnings.
   c. *Federal Income Tax* is debited.
   d. *Accounts Payable* is credited.

3. Which of the following is recorded on an individual earnings record?
   a. gross earnings each pay period
   b. federal income tax withheld each pay period
   c. social security tax withheld each pay period
   d. all of the above

4. Details related to all employees' gross earnings, deductions, and net pay for a period are found in the
   a. payroll register.
   b. individual earnings record.
   c. general journal.
   d. cash payments journal.

5. Payroll deductions are recorded in a separate
   a. asset account.
   b. expense account.
   c. liability account.
   d. revenue account.

10 Chapter REVIEW Chapter Summary

The main goal of payroll work is to compute the gross wages or salaries earned by each employee, the amounts to be deducted for various taxes and other purposes, and the net amount payable.

Learning Objectives

10-1 Explain the major federal laws relating to employee earnings and withholding.

Several federal laws affect payroll.

- The federal Wage and Hour Law limits to 40 the number of hours per week an employee can work at the regular rate of pay. For more than 40 hours of work a week, an employer involved in interstate commerce must pay one and one-half times the regular rate.

- Federal laws require that the employer withhold at least three taxes from the employee's pay: the employee's share of social security tax, the employee's share of Medicare tax, and federal income tax. Instructions for computing these taxes are provided by the government.

- If required, state disability and other income taxes can also be deducted. Other deductions may include court orders for various items.

- Voluntary deductions can also be made.

10-2 Compute gross earnings of employees.

To compute gross earnings for an employee, it is necessary to know whether the employee is paid using an hourly rate basis, a salary basis, a commission basis, or a piece-rate basis.

10-3 Determine employee deductions for social security tax.

The social security tax is levied in an equal amount on both the employer and the employee. The tax is a percentage of the employee's gross wages during a calendar year up to a maximum wage base limit.

10-4 Determine employee deductions for Medicare tax.

The Medicare tax is levied in an equal amount on both the employer and the employee. There is no wage base limit for Medicare taxes. Under the Affordable Care Act, higher-income wage earners are now subject to an additional Medicare tax of 0.9 percent in addition to the regular Medicare tax of 1.45 percent. Unlike the regular Medicare tax, this additional tax on high-income wage earners is paid only by the individuals; the business does not match the amount.

10-5 Determine employee deductions for income tax.

Income taxes are deducted from an employee's paycheck by the employer and then are paid to the government periodically. Although several methods can be used to compute the amount of federal income tax to be withheld from employee earnings, the wage-bracket table method is most often used. The wage-bracket tables are in *Publication 15, Circular E, Employer's Tax Guide*. Withholding tables for various pay periods for single and married persons are contained in *Circular E*.

10-6 Enter gross earnings, deductions, and net pay in the payroll register.

Daily records of the hours worked by each non-supervisory employee are kept. Using these hourly time sheets, the payroll clerk computes the employees' earnings, deductions, and net pay for each payroll period and records the data in a payroll register.

10-7 Journalize payroll transactions in the general journal.

The payroll register is used to prepare a general journal entry to record payroll expense and liability amounts. A separate journal entry is made to record payments to employees.

10-8 Maintain an earnings record for each employee.

At the beginning of each year, the employer sets up an individual earnings record for each employee. The amounts in the payroll register are posted to the individual earnings records throughout the year so that the firm has detailed payroll information for each employee. At the end of the year, employers provide reports that show gross earnings and total deductions to each employee.

10-9 Define the accounting terms new to this chapter.

Glossary

Commission basis (p. 356) A method of paying employees according to a percentage of net sales

Compensation record (p. 368) *See* Individual earnings record

Employee (p. 350) A person who is hired by and works under the control and direction of the employer

Employee's Withholding Allowance Certificate, Form W-4 (p. 358) A form used to claim exemption (withholding) allowances

Exempt employees (p. 362) Salaried employees who hold supervisory or managerial positions who are not subject to the maximum hour and overtime pay provisions of the Wage and Hour Law

Federal unemployment taxes (FUTA) (p. 352) Taxes levied by the federal government against employers to benefit unemployed workers

Hourly rate basis (p. 355) A method of paying employees according to a stated rate per hour

Independent contractor (p. 350) One who is paid by a company to carry out a specific task or job but is not under the direct supervision or control of the company

Individual earnings record (p. 368) An employee record that contains information needed to compute earnings and complete tax reports

Medicare tax (p. 351) A tax levied on employees and employers to provide medical care for the employee and the employee's spouse after each has reached age 65

Payroll register (p. 362) A record of payroll information for each employee for the pay period

Piece-rate basis (p. 356) A method of paying employees according to the number of units produced

Salary basis (p. 356) A method of paying employees according to an agreed-upon amount for each week or month

Social Security Act (p. 351) A federal act providing certain benefits for employees and their families; officially the Federal Insurance Contributions Act

Social security (FICA or OASDI) tax (p. 351) A tax imposed by the Federal Insurance Contributions Act and collected on employee earnings to provide retirement and disability benefits

State unemployment taxes (SUTA) (p. 353) Taxes levied by a state government against employers to benefit unemployed workers

Tax-exempt wages (p. 357) Earnings in excess of the base amount set by the Social Security Act

Time and a half (p. 351) Rate of pay for an employee's work in excess of 40 hours a week

Wage-bracket table method (p. 358) A simple method to determine the amount of federal income tax to be withheld using a table provided by the government

Workers' compensation insurance (p. 353) Insurance that protects employees against losses from job-related injuries or illnesses, or compensates their families if death occurs in the course of the employment

Comprehensive Self Review

1. What is the purpose of the payroll register?
2. How does an independent contractor differ from an employee?
3. From an accounting and internal control viewpoint, would it be preferable to pay employees by check or cash? Explain.
4. How is the amount of social security tax to be withheld from an employee's earnings determined?
5. What is the purpose of workers' compensation insurance?

(Answers to Comprehensive Self Review are at the end of the chapter.)

Discussion Questions

1. How does the Fair Labor Standards Act affect the wages paid by many firms? What types of firms are regulated by the act?
2. What factors affect how much federal income tax must be withheld from an employee's earnings?

3. What aspects of employment are regulated by the Fair Labor Standards Act? What is another commonly used name for this act?
4. What is an exempt employee?
5. How are the federal and state unemployment taxes related?
6. Does the employee bear any part of the SUTA tax? Explain.
7. Give two examples of common payroll fraud.
8. How are earnings determined when employees are paid on the hourly rate basis?
9. What is the purpose of the Medicare tax?
10. What is the purpose of the social security tax?
11. How does the direct deposit method of paying employees operate?
12. What are the four bases for determining employee gross earnings?
13. What is the simplest method for finding the amount of federal income tax to be deducted from an employee's gross pay?
14. What publication of the Internal Revenue Service provides information about the current federal income tax rates and the procedures that employers should use to withhold federal income tax from an employee's earnings?
15. How does the salary basis differ from the hourly rate basis of paying employees?

APPLICATIONS

Exercises

Exercise 10.1
Objective 10-2

▶ **Computing gross earnings.**

The hourly rates of four employees of European Enterprises follow, along with the hours that these employees worked during one week. Determine the gross earnings of each employee.

Employee No.	Hourly Rate	Hours Worked
1	$10.25	38
2	9.75	35
3	11.00	40
4	12.00	35

Exercise 10.2
Objective 10-2

▶ **Computing regular earnings, overtime earnings, and gross pay.**

During one week, four production employees of Morgan Manufacturing Company worked the hours shown below. All these employees receive overtime pay at one and one-half times their regular hourly rate for any hours worked beyond 40 in a week. Determine the regular earnings, overtime earnings, and gross earnings for each employee.

Employee No.	Hourly Rate	Hours Worked
1	$11.00	46
2	10.62	47
3	10.46	38
4	10.80	48

Exercise 10.3
Objective 10-3

Determining social security withholding.

The monthly salaries for December and the year-to-date earnings of the employees of Cross Consulting Company as of November 30 follow.

Employee No.	December Salary	Year-to-Date Earnings Through November 30
1	$ 8,500	$ 76,500
2	10,000	70,000
3	10,500	115,500
4	12,000	120,000

Determine the amount of social security tax to be withheld from each employee's gross pay for December. Assume a 6.2 percent social security tax rate and an earnings base of $132,900 for the calendar year.

Exercise 10.4
Objective 10-4
CONTINUING >>> Problem

Determining deduction for Medicare tax.

Using the earnings data given in Exercise 10.3, determine the amount of Medicare tax to be withheld from each employee's gross pay for December. Assume a 1.45 percent Medicare tax rate and that all salaries and wages are subject to the tax.

Exercise 10.5
Objective 10-5

Determining federal income tax withholding.

Data about the marital status, withholding allowances, and weekly salaries of the four office workers at Ollie's Office Supply Company follow. Use the tax tables in Figure 10.2 to find the amount of federal income tax to be deducted from each employee's gross pay.

Employee No.	Marital Status	Withholding Allowances	Weekly Salary
1	M	2	$675
2	S	1	565
3	M	2	665
4	S	1	495

Exercise 10.6
Objective 10-7

Recording payroll transactions in the general journal.

Private Investigations has two office employees. A summary of their earnings and the related taxes withheld from their pay for the week ending June 7, 20X1, follows.

	Ann Queen	Donald Tender
Gross earnings	$730.00	$1,290.00
Social security deduction	(45.26)	(79.98)
Medicare deduction	(10.59)	(18.71)
Income tax withholding	(73.00)	(230.00)
Net pay for week	$601.15	$ 961.31

1. Prepare the general journal entry to record the company's payroll for the week. Use the account names given in this chapter. Use 16 as the page number for the general journal.
2. Prepare the general journal entry to summarize the checks to pay the weekly payroll.

Exercise 10.7

Objective 10-7

▶ **Journalizing payroll transactions.**

On July 31, the payroll register for Red Company showed the following totals for the month: gross earnings, $38,950; social security tax, $2,414.90; Medicare tax, $564.78; income tax, $5,842.00; and net amount due, $30,128.32. Of the total earnings, $30,500.00 was for sales salaries and $8,450.00 was for office salaries. Prepare a general journal entry to record the monthly payroll of the firm on July 31. Use 20 as the page number for the general journal.

PROBLEMS

Problem Set A

Problem 10.1A

Objectives 10-2, 10-3, 10-4, 10-5, 10-7

▶ **Computing gross earnings, determining deductions, journalizing payroll transactions.**

Robin Market works for Cycle Industries. Her pay rate is $14.50 per hour and she receives overtime pay at one and one-half times her regular hourly rate for any hours worked beyond 40 in a week. During the pay period that ended December 31, 20X1, Robin worked 42 hours. She is married and claims three withholding allowances on her W-4 form. Robin's cumulative earnings prior to this pay period total $32,000. This week's wages are subject to the following deductions:

1. Social Security tax at 6.2 percent
2. Medicare tax at 1.45 percent
3. Federal income tax (use the withholding table shown in Figure 10.2B)
4. Health and disability insurance premiums, $180
5. Charitable contribution, $25

INSTRUCTIONS

1. Compute Robin's regular, overtime, gross, and net pay.
2. Assuming the weekly payroll has been recorded, journalize the payment of her wages for the week ended December 31. Use 54 as the page number for the general journal.

Analyze: Based on Robin's cumulative earnings through December 31, how much overtime pay did she earn this year?

Problem 10.2A

Objectives 10-2, 10-3, 10-4, 10-5

▶ **Computing gross earnings, determining deductions, preparing payroll register, journalizing payroll transactions.**

Country Covers has four employees and pays them on an hourly basis. During the week beginning June 24 and ending June 30, these employees worked the hours shown below. Information about hourly rates, marital status, withholding allowances, and cumulative earnings prior to the current pay period also appears below.

Employee	Regular Hours Worked	Hourly Rate	Marital Status	Withholding Allowances	Cumulative Earnings
Roma Brandon	48	$11.50	M	4	$16,975
Carlos Cortez	40	11.20	M	1	16,080
Jane Jorgus	48	12.70	M	1	17,640
Winter Wise	50	10.70	S	2	14,660

INSTRUCTIONS

1. Enter the basic payroll information for each employee in a payroll register. Record the employee's name, number of withholding allowances, marital status, total and overtime hours, and regular hourly rate. Consider any hours worked beyond 40 in the week as overtime hours.
2. Compute the regular, overtime, and gross earnings for each employee. Enter the figures in the payroll register.
3. Compute the amount of social security tax to be withheld from each employee's earnings. Assume a 6.2 percent social security rate on the first $132,900 earned by the employee during the year. Enter the figures in the payroll register.
4. Compute the amount of Medicare tax to be withheld from each employee's earnings. Assume a 1.45 percent Medicare tax rate on all salaries and wages earned by the employee during the year. Enter the figures in the payroll register.
5. Determine the amount of federal income tax to be withheld from each employee's total earnings. Use the tax tables in Figure 10.2. Enter the figures in the payroll register.
6. Compute the net pay of each employee and enter the figures in the payroll register.
7. Total and prove the payroll register.
8. Prepare a general journal entry to record the payroll for the week ended June 30. Use 15 as the page number for the general journal.
9. Record the general journal entry to summarize payment of the payroll on July 3.

Analyze: What are Jane Jorgus's cumulative earnings on June 30?

Computing gross earnings, determining deductions, preparing payroll register, journalizing payroll transactions.

◀ **Problem 10.3A**
Objectives 10-2, 10-3, 10-4, 10-5

Alex Wilson operates On-Time Courier Service. The company has four employees who are paid on an hourly basis. During the workweek beginning December 15 and ending December 21, 20X1, employees worked the number of hours shown below. Information about their hourly rates, marital status, and withholding allowances also appears below, along with their cumulative earnings for the year prior to the December 15–21 payroll period.

Employee	Hours Worked	Regular Hourly Rate	Marital Status	Withholding Allowances	Cumulative Earnings
Grace Dodger	47	$16.70	M	4	$32,860
Ron Dollar	49	26.90	M	3	53,972
Alex Garcia	43	28.50	S	1	57,300
Red Russell	40	13.70	S	0	26,620

INSTRUCTIONS

1. Enter the basic payroll information for each employee in a payroll register. Record the employee's name, number of withholding allowances, marital status, total and overtime hours, and regular hourly rate. Consider any hours worked beyond 40 in the week as overtime hours.
2. Compute the regular, overtime, and gross earnings for each employee. Enter the figures in the payroll register.
3. Compute the amount of social security tax to be withheld from each employee's gross earnings. Assume a 6.2 percent social security rate on the first $132,900 earned by the employee during the year. Enter the figures in the payroll register.
4. Compute the amount of Medicare tax to be withheld from each employee's gross earnings. Assume a 1.45 percent Medicare tax rate on all salaries and wages earned by the employee during the year. Enter the figures in the payroll register.

5. Determine the amount of federal income tax to be withheld from each employee's total earnings. Use the tax tables in Figure 10.2 to determine the withholding for Russell. Withholdings are $112.00 for Dodger, $323.00 for Garcia, and $258 for Dollar. Enter the figures in the payroll register.

6. Compute the net amount due each employee and enter the figures in the payroll register.

7. Total and prove the payroll register. Dodger and Russell are office workers. Garcia and Dollar are delivery workers.

8. Prepare a general journal entry to record the payroll for the week ended December 21, 20X1. Use 32 as the page number for the general journal.

9. Prepare a general journal entry on December 23 to summarize payment of wages for the week.

Analyze: What percentage of total taxable wages was delivery wages?

Problem 10.4A
Objectives 10-2, 10-3, 10-4, 10-5, 10-6, 10-7

Computing gross earnings, determining deductions and net amount due, journalizing payroll transactions.

Metro Media Company pays its employees monthly. Payments made by the company on October 31 follow. Cumulative amounts for the year paid to the persons prior to the October 31 payroll are also given.

1. Tori Parker, president, gross monthly salary of $20,000; gross earnings prior to October 31, $160,000.

2. Carolyn Catz, vice president, gross monthly salary of $14,000; gross earnings paid prior to October 31, $126,000.

3. Michelle Clark, independent accountant who audits the company's accounts and performs consulting services, $16,500; gross amounts paid prior to October 31, $42,500.

4. Will Wu, treasurer, gross monthly salary of $6,000; gross earnings prior to October 31, $54,000.

5. Payment to Review Services for monthly services of Tom Bradley, an editorial expert, $6,000; amount paid to Review Services prior to October 31, $30,000.

INSTRUCTIONS

1. Use an earnings ceiling of $132,900 for social security taxes and a tax rate of 6.2 percent and a tax rate of 1.45 percent on all earnings for Medicare taxes. Prepare a schedule showing the following information:

    a. Each employee's cumulative earnings prior to October 31.

    b. Each employee's gross earnings for October.

    c. The amounts to be withheld for each payroll tax from each employee's earnings; the employee's income tax withholdings are Parker, $5,600; Catz, $4,200; Wu, $1,320.

    d. The net amount due each employee.

    e. The total gross earnings, the total of each payroll tax deduction, and the total net amount payable to employees.

2. Prepare the general journal entry to record the company's payroll on October 31. Use journal page 22. Omit explanations.

3. Prepare the general journal entry to record payments to employees on October 31.

Analyze: What distinguishes an employee from an independent contractor?

Problem Set B

Problem 10.1B
Objectives 10-2, 10-3, 10-4, 10-5, 10-7

Computing gross earnings, determining deductions, journalizing payroll transactions.

Alan Johnson works for CAT Commercial Builders, Inc. His pay rate is $14.00 per hour and he receives overtime pay at one and one-half times his regular hourly rate for any hours worked beyond 40 in a week. During the pay period ended December 31, 20X1, Alan worked 48 hours.

Alan is married and claims three withholding allowances on his W-4 form. His cumulative earnings prior to this pay period total $29,260. Allan's wages are subject to the following deductions:

1. Social security tax at 6.2 percent
2. Medicare tax at 1.45 percent
3. Federal income tax (use the withholding table shown in Figure 10.2B)
4. Health insurance premiums, $150
5. Credit Union savings, $25

INSTRUCTIONS

1. Compute Alan's regular, overtime premium earnings, gross, and net pay.
2. Assuming the weekly payroll has been recorded, journalize the payment of his wages for the week ended December 31, 20X1. Use journal page 18.

Analyze: Based on Alan's cumulative earnings through December 31, how much overtime pay did he earn this year?

Computing earnings, determining deductions and net amount due, preparing payroll register, journalizing payroll transactions.

◀ **Problem 10.2B**
Objectives 10-2, 10-3, 10-4, 10-5

The four employees for ACWorks are paid on an hourly basis. During the week of December 25–31, 20X1, these employees worked the hours indicated. Information about their hourly rates, marital status, withholding allowances, and cumulative earnings prior to the current pay period also appears below.

Employee	Hours Worked	Regular Hourly Rate	Marital Status	Withholding Allowances	Cumulative Earnings
Betty Brooks	45	$12.80	M	3	$ 44,179.00
Cynthia Carter	48	13.40	M	2	53,015.00
Mary Easley	44	29.50	M	4	82,748.00
James Periot	30	37.00	S	2	104,486.00

INSTRUCTIONS

1. Enter the basic payroll information for each employee in a payroll register. Record the employee's name, number of withholding allowances, marital status, total hours, overtime hours, and regular hourly rate. Consider any hours worked beyond 40 in the week as overtime hours.
2. Compute the regular earnings, overtime premium, and gross earnings for each employee. Enter the figures in the payroll register.
3. Compute the amount of social security tax to be withheld from each employee's gross earnings. Assume a 6.2 percent social security tax rate on the first $132,900 earned by each employee during the year. Enter the figures in the payroll register.
4. Compute the amount of Medicare tax to be withheld from each employee's gross earnings. Assume a 1.45 percent Medicare tax rate on all earnings for each employee during the year. Enter the figure on the payroll register.
5. Determine the amount of federal income tax to be withheld from each employee's gross earnings. Income tax withholdings are $235 for Easley and $238 for Periot. Enter these figures in the payroll register.
6. Compute the net amount due each employee and enter the figures in the payroll register.
7. Complete the payroll register for the store employees.

8. Prepare a general journal entry to record the payroll for the week ended December 31, 20X1. Use page 18 for the journal.

9. Record the general journal entry to summarize the payment on December 31, 20X1, of the net amount due employees.

Analyze: What is the difference between the amount credited to the **Cash** account on December 31, 20X1, for the payroll week ended December 31 and the amount debited to **Wages Expense** for the same payroll period? What causes the difference between the two figures?

Problem 10.3B ▶ Computing earnings, determining deductions and net amount due, preparing payroll register, journalizing payroll transactions.

Objectives 10-2, 10-3, 10-4, 10-5

Barbara Merino operates Merino Consulting Services. She has four employees and pays them on an hourly basis. During the week ended November 12, 20X1, her employees worked the number of hours shown below. Information about their hourly rates, marital status, withholding allowances, and cumulative earnings for the year prior to the current pay period also appears below.

Employee	Hours Worked	Regular Hourly Rate	Marital Status	Withholding Allowances	Cumulative Earnings
Kathryn Allen	43	$10.50	M	3	$26,565
Calvin Cooke	36	10.25	S	2	25,933
Maria Vasquez	45	29.75	M	4	75,268
Hollie Visage	41	32.75	S	2	82,858

INSTRUCTIONS

1. Enter the basic payroll information for each employee in a payroll register. Record the employee's name, number of withholding allowances, marital status, total hours, overtime hours, and regular hourly rate. Consider any hours worked beyond 40 in the week as overtime hours.
2. Compute the regular earnings, overtime premium, and gross earnings for each employee. Enter the figures in the payroll register.
3. Compute the amount of social security tax to be withheld from each employee's gross earnings. Assume a 6.2 percent social security rate on the first $132,900 earned by the employee during the year. Enter the figures in the payroll register.
4. Compute the amount of Medicare tax to be withheld from each employee's gross earnings. Assume a 1.45 percent Medicare tax rate on all earnings paid during the year. Enter the figures in the payroll register.
5. Use the tax tables in Figure 10.2 to determine the federal income tax to be withheld. Federal income tax to be withheld from Vasquez's pay is $192 and from Visage's pay is $267. Enter the figures in the payroll register.
6. Compute the net amount due each employee and enter the figures in the payroll register.
7. Complete the payroll register. Allen and Cooke are office workers. Earnings for Vasquez and Visage are charged to consulting wages.
8. Prepare a general journal entry to record the payroll for the week ended November 12, 20X1. Use the account titles given in this chapter. Use journal page 32.
9. Prepare the general journal entry to summarize payment of amounts due employees on November 15, 20X1.

Analyze: What total deductions were taken from employee paychecks for the pay period ended November 12?

Problem 10.4B ▶ Computing gross earnings, determining deductions and net amount due, journalizing payroll transactions.

Objectives 10-2, 10-3, 10-4, 10-5, 10-7

Daily Operations pays its employees monthly. Payments made by the company on November 30, 20X1, follow. Cumulative amounts paid to the persons named prior to the November 30 payroll are also given.

1. Dave Orlando, president, gross monthly salary of $18,000; gross earnings prior to November 30, $180,000.
2. Sue Stamos, vice president, gross monthly salary of $12,000; gross earnings paid prior to November 30, $120,000.
3. Caley Marie, independent media buyer who purchases media contracts for companies and performs other public relations consulting services, $15,650; gross amounts paid prior to November 30, $45,000.
4. Claire Hayakawa, treasurer, gross monthly salary of $6,500; gross earnings prior to November 30, $65,000.
5. Payment to the Canal Marketing Group for monthly services of Anna Canal, a marketing and public relations expert, $10,000; amount paid to the Canal Marketing Group prior to November 30, $46,500.

INSTRUCTIONS

1. Use an earnings ceiling of $132,900 and a tax rate of 6.2 percent for social security taxes and a tax rate of 1.45 percent on all earnings for Medicare taxes. Prepare a schedule showing the following information:
   a. Each employee's cumulative earnings prior to November 30.
   b. Each employee's gross earnings for November.
   c. The amounts to be withheld for each payroll tax from each employee's earnings; the employee's income tax withholdings are Orlando, $4,760; Stamos, $3,000; Hayakawa, $1,200.
   d. The net amount due each employee.
   e. The total gross earnings, the total of each payroll tax deduction, and the total net amount payable to employees.
2. Give the general journal entry to record the company's payroll on November 30. Use journal page 24. Omit explanations.
3. Give the general journal entry to record payments to employees on November 30.

Analyze: In what month in 20X1 did Stamos reach the withholding limit for social security?

Critical Thinking Problem 10.1

Payroll Accounting

Delta Company pays salaries and wages on the last day of each month. Payments made on December 31, 20X1, for amounts incurred during December are shown below. Cumulative amounts paid prior to the December 31 payroll for the persons named are also shown.

a. Francis Fisher, president, gross monthly salary, $12,000; gross earnings paid prior to December 31, $132,000.
b. Sandy Swartz, vice president, gross monthly salary, $10,000; gross earnings paid prior to December 31, $100,000.
c. Juan Rios, independent accountant who audits the company's accounts and performs certain consulting services, $10,000; gross amount paid prior to December 31, $25,000.
d. Harry House, treasurer, gross monthly salary, $5,500; gross earnings paid prior to December 31, $60,500.
e. Payment to Daily Security Services for Eddie Martin, a security guard who is on duty on Saturdays and Sundays, $1,000; amount paid to Daily Security Services prior to December 31, $10,000.

INSTRUCTIONS

1. Using the tax rates and earnings ceilings given in this chapter, prepare a schedule showing the following information:
   a. Each employee's cumulative earnings prior to December 31.

b. Each employee's gross earnings for December.

c. The amounts to be withheld for each payroll tax from each employee's earnings (employee income tax withholdings for Fisher are $3,080; for Swartz, $2,500; and for House, $800).

d. The net amount due each employee.

e. The total gross earnings, the total of each payroll tax deduction, and the total net amount payable to employees.

2. Record the general journal entry for the company's payroll on December 31. Use journal page 32.

3. Record the general journal entry for payments to employees on December 31.

Analyze: What is the balance of the *Salaries Payable* account after all payroll entries have been posted for the month?

Critical Thinking Problem 10.2

Payroll Internal Controls

Several years ago, Kat Cortz opened Ocho Tacos, a restaurant specializing in homemade tacos. The restaurant was so successful that the company expanded, and now operates eight restaurants in the local area.

Cortez tells you that when she first started, she handled all aspects of the business herself. Now that there are eight Ocho Tacos, she depends on the managers of each restaurant to make decisions and oversee day-to-day operations. Cortez oversees operations at the company's headquarters, which is located at the first Ocho Tacos.

Each manager interviews and hires new employees for a restaurant. The new employee is required to complete a W-4, which is sent by the manager to the headquarters office. Each restaurant has a time clock and employees are required to clock in/out as they arrive/depart. Blank time cards are kept in a box under the time clock. At the beginning of each week, employees complete the top of the card they will use during the week. The manager collects the cards at the end of the week and sends them to headquarters.

Cortez hired a cousin, Anna, to prepare the payroll instead of assigning this task to the accounting staff. Because she is a relative, Cortez trusts her and has confidence that confidential payroll information will not be divulged to other employees.

When Anna receives a W-4 for a new employee, she sets up an individual earnings record for the employee. Each week, using the time cards sent by each restaurant's manager, she computes the gross pay, deductions, and net pay for all the employees. She then posts details to the employees' earnings records and prepares and signs the payroll checks. The checks are sent to the managers, who distribute them to the employees.

As long as Anna receives a time card for an employee, she prepares a paycheck. If she fails to get a time card for an employee, she checks with the manager to see if the employee was terminated or has quit. At the end of the month, Anna reconciles the payroll bank account and prepares quarterly and annual payroll tax returns.

1. Identify any weaknesses in Ocho Tacos's payroll system.
2. Identify one way a manager could defraud Ocho Tacos under the present payroll system.
3. What internal control procedures would you recommend to Cortez to protect against the fraud you identified above?

BUSINESS CONNECTIONS

Managerial FOCUS

Cash Management

1. Why should managers check the amount spent for overtime?
2. The new controller for CAR Company, a manufacturing firm, has suggested to management that the business change from paying the factory employees in cash to paying them by check. What reasons would you offer to support this suggestion?

3. Why should management make sure that a firm has an adequate set of payroll records?
4. How can detailed payroll records help managers control expenses?

Salary vs. Hourly

Susie's Sweater Factory employs two managers for the factory. These managers work 12 hours per day at $16 per hour. After eight hours, they receive overtime pay. Management is trying to cut costs. They have decided to promote the managers to a salary position. The managers will be offered a daily salary of $200. Since they would be promoted to a salary position, they will not receive overtime. The company has required they accept the promotion or find employment elsewhere. Is it ethical for the company to offer the managers a salary position? Is it ethical to require the employee to accept the promotion? Should the managers accept the promotion?

Internal Control and FRAUD PREVENTION

Balance Sheet

The Home Depot, Inc., reported the following data in its FY 2018 10-K *(for the fiscal year ended February 3, 2019)*:

Financial Statement ANALYSIS

Home Depot

The Home Depot, Inc. and Subsidiaries		
Consolidated Balance Sheets		
(in millions except per share amounts)	February 3, 2019	January 28, 2018
Current liabilities:		
Accrued salaries and related expenses	1,506	1,640
Total current liabilities	16,716	16,194

Analyze:

1. What percentage of total current liabilities is made up of accrued salaries and related expenses at February 3, 2019?
2. By what amount did accrued salaries and related expenses change from fiscal 2017 to fiscal 2018?

Cycle to Pay Employee

There are many approvals needed to create a paycheck for an employee. Divide into groups of five to identify the jobs necessary to create a paycheck for an employee. Describe the function and, if necessary, the journal entry for each job.

TEAMWORK

Answers to Comprehensive Self Review

1. To record in one place all information about an employee's earnings and withholdings for the period.
2. An employee is one who is hired by the employer and who is under the control and direction of the employer. An independent contractor is paid by the company to carry out a specific task or job and is not under the direct supervision and control of the employer.
3. By check because there is far less possibility of mistake, lost money, or fraud. The check serves as a receipt and permanent record of the transaction.
4. Social security taxes are determined by multiplying the amount of taxable earnings by the social security tax rate.
5. To compensate workers for losses suffered from job-related injuries or to compensate their families if the employee's death occurs in the course of employment.

Payroll Taxes, Deposits, and Reports

Chapter 11

Friedrich Stark/Alamy

www.ford.com

The U.S.-based auto manufacturer Ford Motor Company was incorporated by Henry Ford on June 16, 1903. Henry Ford is credited with producing the Model T, one of the best-selling vehicles of all time, selling more than 15 million vehicles! More recently, the company has made history with the F-150 truck, becoming the best-selling vehicle in the United States for the past 30+ years. But its most important credit goes to introducing the assembly-line manufacturing process in the U.S.

Another remarkable act by Ford was to increase the factory workers' pay to $5 per day, which was about double the existing pay rate for factory workers at the time. Along with paying more, it also reduced the normal manufacturing work shift from nine hours to eight. These two changes benefited both the workers and the company; the combination of higher pay and fewer working hours significantly decreased employee turnover and increased vehicle production. With eight-hour shifts, the Ford factory could operate 24 hours per day with three eight-hour shifts. By increasing employee wages, Ford enabled many employees to purchase Ford vehicles.

Sales for the third quarter of 2018 totaled $36.5 billion. On the employee front, the company reported in the 2017 Annual Report employing approximately 202,000 people in all operations. Imagine the tax reporting required for this company with operations around the world!

thinking critically

What types of benefits do you think are important to people working in industries such as manufacturing? What would be important to you?

LEARNING OBJECTIVES

- **11-1** Explain how and when payroll taxes are paid to the government.
- **11-2** Compute and record the employer's social security and Medicare taxes.
- **11-3** Record deposit of social security, Medicare, and employee income taxes.
- **11-4** Prepare an Employer's Quarterly Federal Tax Return, Form 941.
- **11-5** Prepare Wage and Tax Statement (Form W-2) and Annual Transmittal of Wage and Tax Statements (Form W-3).
- **11-6** Compute and record liability for federal and state unemployment taxes and record payment of the taxes.
- **11-7** Prepare an Employer's Federal Unemployment Tax Return, Form 940.
- **11-8** Compute and record workers' compensation insurance premiums.
- **11-9** Define the accounting terms new to this chapter.

NEW TERMS

Employer's Annual Federal Unemployment Tax Return, Form 940
Employer's Quarterly Federal Tax Return, Form 941
experience rating system
merit rating system
Transmittal of Wage and Tax Statements, Form W-3
unemployment insurance program
Wage and Tax Statement, Form W-2
withholding statement

Section 1

SECTION OBJECTIVES

>> **11-1** Explain how and when payroll taxes are paid to the government.
   WHY IT'S IMPORTANT
   Employers are required by law to deposit payroll taxes.

>> **11-2** Compute and record the employer's social security and Medicare taxes.
   WHY IT'S IMPORTANT
   Accounting records should reflect all liabilities.

>> **11-3** Record deposit of social security, Medicare, and employee income taxes.
   WHY IT'S IMPORTANT
   Payments decrease the payroll tax liability.

>> **11-4** Prepare an Employer's Quarterly Federal Tax Return, Form 941.
   WHY IT'S IMPORTANT
   Completing a federal tax return is part of the employer's legal obligation.

>> **11-5** Prepare Wage and Tax Statement (Form W-2) and Annual Transmittal of Wage and Tax Statements (Form W-3).
   WHY IT'S IMPORTANT
   Employers are legally required to provide end-of-year payroll information.

TERMS TO LEARN

Employer's Quarterly Federal Tax Return, Form 941
Transmittal of Wage and Tax Statements, Form W-3
Wage and Tax Statement, Form W-2
withholding statement

Social Security, Medicare, and Employee Income Tax

In Chapter 10, you learned that the law requires employers to act as collection agents for certain taxes due from employees. In this chapter, you will learn how to compute the employer's taxes, make tax payments, and file the required tax returns and reports.

>> **11-1 OBJECTIVE**
Explain how and when payroll taxes are paid to the government.

Payment of Payroll Taxes

The payroll register provides information about wages subject to payroll taxes. Figure 11.1 shows a portion of the payroll register for Brandon Express Company for the week ending January 6.

Employers make tax deposits for the following taxes that are withheld from employee gross wages: federal income tax, social security tax, and Medicare tax. In addition, the employer must also deposit an amount equal to the social security and Medicare taxes withheld from employees' wages. If a check is written to cover these taxes, the deposits are made in a Federal Reserve Bank or other authorized financial institution. Businesses usually make these payroll tax deposits at their own bank or more typically through online deposits.

If the business makes the deposit electronically (the preferred method), the *Electronic Federal Tax Payment System (EFTPS)* is used. This is a system for electronically depositing employment taxes using a telephone or a computer. Electronic filing of taxes due is now required in most instances. An employer *must* use EFTPS if the annual federal tax deposits are more than $200,000. Employers who are required to make electronic deposits and do not do so can be subject to a 10 percent penalty.

FIGURE 11.1 Portion of a Payroll Register

AND ENDING January 6, 20X1   PAID January 8, 20X1

TAXABLE WAGES			DEDUCTIONS				DISTRIBUTION			
SOCIAL SECURITY	MEDICARE	FUTA	SOCIAL SECURITY	MEDICARE	INCOME TAX	HEALTH INSURANCE	NET AMOUNT	CHECK NO.	OFFICE SALARIES	SHIPPING WAGES
400 00	400 00	400 00	24 80	5 80	19 00		350 40	1601		400 00
380 00	380 00	380 00	23 56	5 51	34 00		316 93	1602		380 00
427 50	427 50	427 50	26 51	6 20	23 00	40 00	331 79	1603		427 50
560 00	560 00	560 00	34 72	8 12	30 00	40 00	447 16	1604		560 00
480 00	480 00	480 00	29 76	6 96	49 00		394 28	1605	480 00	
2 247 50	2 247 50	2 247 50	139 35	32 59	155 00	80 00	1 840 56		480 00	1 767 50

The frequency of deposits depends on the amount of tax liability. The amount currently owed is compared to the tax liability threshold. For simplicity, this textbook uses $2,500 as the tax liability threshold.

The deposit schedules are not related to how often employees are paid. The deposit schedules are based on the amount currently owed and the amount reported in the lookback period. The *lookback period* is a four-quarter period ending on June 30 of the preceding year.

1. If the amount owed is less than $2,500, payment is due quarterly with the payroll tax return (Form 941).

    Example. An employer's tax liability is as follows:

January	$ 580
February	640
March	620
	$1,840

    Since the accumulated tax liability did not reach $2,500 or more, at any time during the quarter, no deposit is required during the quarter. The employer may pay the total amount due with the payroll tax returns.

2. If the amount owed is $2,500 or more, the schedule is determined from the total taxes reported on Form 941 during the lookback period.

    a. If the amount reported in the lookback period was $50,000 or less, the employer is subject to the *Monthly Deposit Schedule Rule*. Monthly payments are due on the 15th day of the following month. For example, the January payment is due by February 15.

    b. If the amount reported in the lookback period was more than $50,000, the employer is subject to the *Semiweekly Deposit Schedule Rule*. "Semiweekly" refers to the fact that deposits are due on either Wednesdays or Fridays, depending on the employer's payday.

    - If payday is a Wednesday, Thursday, or Friday, the deposit is due on the following Wednesday.
    - If payday is a Saturday, Sunday, Monday, or Tuesday, the deposit is due on the following Friday.

    c. For new employers with no lookback period, if the amount owed is $2,500 or more, payments are due under the Monthly Deposit Schedule Rule.

3. If the total accumulated tax liability reaches $100,000 or more on any day, a deposit is due on the next banking day. This applies even if the employer is on a monthly or a semiweekly deposit schedule.

Employer's Social Security and Medicare Tax Expenses

Remember that both employers and employees pay social security and Medicare taxes. Figure 11.1 shows the *employee's* share of these payroll taxes. The *employer* pays the same amount of payroll taxes. At the assumed rate of 6.2 percent for social security and 1.45 percent for Medicare tax, the employer's tax liability is $343.88.

>> 11-2 OBJECTIVE
Compute and record the employer's social security and Medicare taxes.

important!

In addition to keeping good records on taxes withheld from employees, the Affordable Care Act provisions are requiring businesses with a designated number of minimum employees to report on health insurance benefits. Many of these reporting requirements (and taxes) will be tracked and reported through the summary earnings report and other federal filings. When writing this revision, there were legal actions over the Affordable Care Act as to its legality.

CHAPTER 11 — Payroll Taxes, Deposits, and Reports

important!

Tax Liability

The employer's tax liability is the amount owed for:

- employee withholdings (income tax, social security tax, Medicare tax);
- employer's matching amounts of social security and Medicare taxes withheld from employees.

	Employee (Withheld)	Employer (Matched)
Social security	$139.35	$139.35
Medicare	32.59	32.59
	$171.94	$171.94
Total	$343.88	

In Chapter 10, you learned how to record employee payroll deductions. The entry to record the employer's share (commonly called "matching") of social security and Medicare taxes is made at the end of each payroll period. The debit is to the **Payroll Taxes Expense** account. The credits are to the same liability accounts used to record the employee's share of payroll taxes.

BUSINESS TRANSACTION

On January 8, Brandon Express Company recorded the employer's share of social security and Medicare taxes. The information on the payroll register (Figure 11.1) is used to record the payroll taxes expense.

ANALYSIS
The expense account *Payroll Taxes Expense* is increased by the employer's share of social security and Medicare taxes, $171.94. The liability account *Social Security Tax Payable* is increased by $139.35. The liability account *Medicare Tax Payable* is increased by $32.59.

DEBIT-CREDIT RULES
DEBIT Increases to expense accounts are recorded as debits. Debit *Payroll Taxes Expense* for $171.94.

CREDIT Increases to liability accounts are recorded as credits. Credit *Social Security Tax Payable* for $139.35. Credit *Medicare Tax Payable* for $32.59.

T-ACCOUNT PRESENTATION

Payroll Taxes Expense	Social Security Tax Payable	Medicare Tax Payable
+ −	− +	− +
171.94	139.35	32.59

GENERAL JOURNAL ENTRY

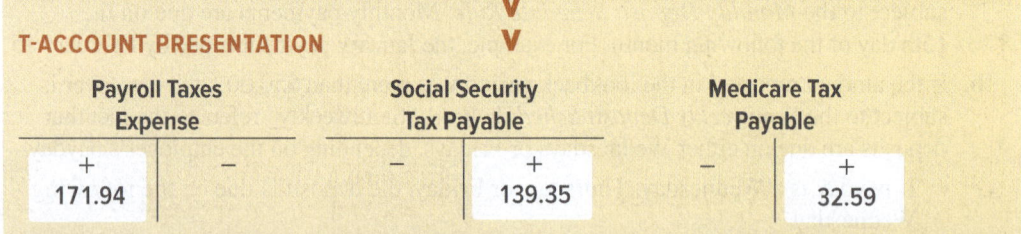

GENERAL JOURNAL PAGE 1

DATE	DESCRIPTION	POST. REF.	DEBIT	CREDIT
20X1				
Jan. 8	Payroll Taxes Expense		171 94	
	Social Security Tax Payable			139 35
	Medicare Tax Payable			32 59
	To record social security and			
	Medicare taxes for Jan. 8 payroll			

THE BOTTOM LINE
Employer's Payroll Taxes

Income Statement
- Expenses ↑ 171.94
- Net Income ↓ 171.94

Balance Sheet
- Liabilities ↑ 171.94
- Equity ↓ 171.94

> According to the Social Security Administration, benefits were being paid to approximately 67 million men, women, and children in 2018. It is essential that earnings are correctly reported so that future benefits can be calculated accurately.

Recording the Payment of Taxes Withheld

At the end of January, the accounting records for Brandon Express Company contained the following information:

	Employee (Withheld)	Employer (Matched)	Total
Social security	$ 557.40	$557.40	$1,114.80
Medicare	130.36	130.36	260.72
Federal income tax	620.00	—	620.00
Total	$1,307.76	$687.76	$1,995.52

>> **11-3 OBJECTIVE**
> Record deposit of social security, Medicare, and employee income taxes.

Brandon Express Company is on a monthly payment schedule. The amount reported in the lookback period is less than $50,000. The payroll tax liability for the quarter ending March 31, 2019, is more than $2,500. (Recall that this textbook uses $2,500 as the tax liability threshold.) A tax payment is due on the 15th day of the following month, February 15.

The tax liability for the first quarter is deposited electronically.

The entry to record the tax deposit is shown below. The entry is shown in general journal form for illustration purposes only. (Brandon Express Company actually uses a cash payments journal.)

GENERAL JOURNAL PAGE 2

DATE	DESCRIPTION	POST. REF.	DEBIT	CREDIT
20X1				
Feb. 15	Social Security Tax Payable		1,114.80	
	Medicare Tax Payable		260.72	
	Employee Income Tax Payable		620.00	
	Cash			1,995.52
	Deposit of payroll taxes withholding			
	at First State Bank			

February Payroll Records

There were four weekly payroll periods in February. Each hourly employee worked the same number of hours each week and had the same gross pay and deductions as in January. The office clerk earned her regular salary and had the same deductions as in January. At the end of the month:

- the individual earnings records were updated;
- the taxes were deposited before March 15;
- the tax deposit was recorded in the cash payments journal.

March Payroll Records

There were five weekly payroll periods in March. Assume that the payroll period ended on March 31, and the payday was on March 31. Also assume that the earnings and deductions of the employees were the same for each week as in January and February. At the end of the month, the individual earnings records were updated, the taxes were deposited, and the tax deposit was recorded in the cash payments journal.

Quarterly Summary of Earnings Records

At the end of each quarter, the individual earnings records are totaled. This involves adding the columns in the Earnings, Deductions, and Net Pay sections. Figure 11.2 shows the earnings record, posted and summarized, for Alicia Martinez for the first quarter.

Table 11.1 shows the quarterly totals for each employee of Brandon Express Company. This information is taken from the individual earnings records. Through the end of the first quarter, no employee has exceeded the social security earnings limit ($132,900), and the FUTA/SUTA limit ($7,000) has only been exceeded by Cecilia Wu.

>> 11-4 OBJECTIVE
Prepare an Employer's Quarterly Federal Tax Return, Form 941.

Employer's Quarterly Federal Tax Return

Each quarter an employer files an **Employer's Quarterly Federal Tax Return, Form 941** with the Internal Revenue Service. Form 941 must be filed by all employers subject to federal income tax withholding, social security tax, or Medicare tax, with certain exceptions as specified in *Publication 15, Circular E*. This tax return provides information about employee earnings, the tax liability for each month in the quarter, and the deposits made.

FIGURE 11.2 Individual Earnings Record

EARNINGS RECORD FOR 20X1

NAME: Alicia Martinez
ADDRESS: 1712 Windmill Hill Lane, Dallas TX 75232-6002
WITHHOLDING ALLOWANCES: 1
RATE: $10 per hour
SOCIAL SECURITY NO.: 123-45-6789
DATE OF BIRTH: October 31, 1979
MARITAL STATUS: M

PAYROLL NO.	DATE WK. END.	DATE PAID	HOURS RG	HOURS OT	REGULAR	OVERTIME	TOTAL	CUMULATIVE	SOCIAL SECURITY	MEDICARE	INCOME TAX	OTHER	NET PAY
1	1/06	1/08	40		400 00		400 00	400 00	24 80	5 80	19 00		350 40
2	1/13	1/15	40		400 00		400 00	400 00	24 80	5 80	19 00		350 40
3	1/20	1/22	40		400 00		400 00	400 00	24 80	5 80	19 00		350 40
4	1/27	1/29	40		400 00		400 00	400 00	24 80	5 80	19 00		350 40
	January				1600 00		1600 00	1600 00	99 20	23 20	76 00		1401 60
1	2/03	2/05	40		400 00		400 00	400 00	24 80	5 80	19 00		350 40
2	2/10	2/12	40		400 00		400 00	400 00	24 80	5 80	19 00		350 40
3	2/17	2/19	40		400 00		400 00	400 00	24 80	5 80	19 00		350 40
4	2/24	2/25	40		400 00		400 00	400 00	24 80	5 80	19 00		350 40
	February				1600 00		1600 00	1600 00	99 20	23 20	76 00		1401 60
1	3/03	3/05	40		400 00		400 00	400 00	24 80	5 80	19 00		350 40
2	3/10	3/12	40		400 00		400 00	400 00	24 80	5 80	19 00		350 40
3	3/17	3/19	40		400 00		400 00	400 00	24 80	5 80	19 00		350 40
4	3/24	3/26	40		400 00		400 00	400 00	24 80	5 80	19 00		350 40
5	3/31	3/31	40		400 00		400 00	400 00	24 80	5 80	19 00		350 40
	March				2000 00		2000 00	2000 00	124 00	29 00	95 00		1752 00
	First Quarter				5200 00		5200 00	5200 00	322 40	75 40	247 00		4555 20

| Employee | Taxable Earnings |||| Deductions |||
	Total Earnings	Social Security	Medicare	SUTA & FUTA	Social Security	Medicare Tax	Income Tax
Alicia Martinez	5,200.00	5,200.00	5,200.00	5,200.00	322.40	75.40	247.00
Jorge Rodriguez	4,940.00	4,940.00	4,940.00	4,940.00	306.28	71.63	442.00
George Dunlap	5,557.50	5,557.50	5,557.50	5,557.50	344.57	80.58	299.00
Cecilia Wu	7,280.00	7,280.00	7,280.00	7,000.00	451.36	105.56	390.00
Cynthia Booker	6,240.00	6,240.00	6,240.00	6,240.00	386.88	90.48	637.00
Totals	29,217.50	29,217.50	29,217.50	28,937.50	1,811.49	423.65	2,015.00

TABLE 11.1

Summary of Earnings, Quarter Ended March 31, 20X1

> The Social Security Administration administers the Old Age and Survivors, Disability Insurance, and Supplemental Security Income programs. These programs are funded by the social security taxes collected from employees and matched by employers. The system currently takes in more in revenue from the 12.4 percent payroll taxes than it pays out in benefits. The trust fund is expected to begin paying out more in benefits than it collects in the mid-2030s.

When to File Form 941 The due date for Form 941 is the last day of the month following the end of each calendar quarter. If the taxes for the quarter were deposited when due, the due date is extended by 10 days.

Completing Form 941 Figure 11.3 shows Form 941 for Brandon Express Company. Form 941 is prepared using the data on the quarterly summary of earnings records shown in Table 11.1. Let's examine Form 941.

- Use the preprinted form if it is available. Otherwise, enter the employer's name, address, and identification number at the top of Form 941. Check the applicable quarter.
- *Line 1* is completed for each quarter. Enter the number of employees for the pay periods indicated.
- *Line 2* shows total wages and tips subject to withholding. For Brandon Express Company the total subject to withholding is $29,217.50.
- *Line 3* shows the total employee income tax withheld during the quarter, $2,015.00.
- *Line 4* is checked if no wages or tips are subject to social security or Medicare tax.
- *Line 5a* shows the total amount of wages that are subject to social security taxes, $29,217.50. The amount is multiplied by the combined social security rate, 12.4 percent.

Social Security Tax:	
Employee's share	6.2%
Employer's share	6.2
Total	12.4%

The amount of taxes is $3,622.97 ($29,217.50 × 12.4%).

- *Line 5b* is left blank since no employees at Tomlin Furniture Company had taxable social security tips.

important!

Quarters

A quarter is a three-month period. There are four quarters in a year:

- 1st quarter: January, February, March
- 2nd quarter: April, May, June
- 3rd quarter: July, August, September
- 4th quarter: October, November, December

FIGURE 11.3 Employer's Quarterly Federal Tax Return, Form 941

Form **941 for 20X1:** Employer's **QUARTERLY** Federal Tax Return
Department of the Treasury — Internal Revenue Service

950114
OMB No. 1545-0029

Employer identification number (EIN): 75-1234567

Name (not your trade name): Sarah Brandon

Trade name (if any): Brandon Express Company

Address: 5910 Lake June Road
City: Dallas State: TX ZIP code: 75232-6017

Report for this Quarter . . . (Check one.)

- [X] 1: January, February, March
- [ ] 2: April, May, June
- [ ] 3: July, August, September
- [ ] 4: October, November, December

Instructions and prior year forms are available at www.irs.gov/form941.

Read the separate instructions before you complete Form 941. Type or print within the boxes.

Part 1: Answer these questions for this quarter.

1. Number of employees who received wages, tips, or other compensation for the pay period including: *Mar. 12* (Quarter 1), *June 12* (Quarter 2), *Sept. 12* (Quarter 3), or *Dec. 12* (Quarter 4) — **1** | 5

2. Wages, tips, and other compensation — **2** | 29,217.50

3. Federal income tax withheld from wages, tips, and other compensation — **3** | 2,015.00

4. If no wages, tips, and other compensation are subject to social security or Medicare tax — [ ] Check and go to line 6.

		Column 1		Column 2
5a	Taxable social security wages	29,217.50	× .124 =	3,622.97
5b	Taxable social security tips	.	× .124 =	.
5c	Taxable Medicare wages & tips	29,217.50	× .029 =	847.31
5d	Taxable wages & tips subject to Additional Medicare Tax withholding	.	× .009 =	.

5e. Add Column 2 from lines 5a, 5b, 5c, and 5d — **5e** | 4,470.28

5f. Section 3121(q) Notice and Demand—Tax due on unreported tips (see instructions) — **5f** | .

6. Total taxes before adjustments. Add lines 3, 5e, and 5f — **6** | 6,485.28

7. Current quarter's adjustment for fractions of cents — **7** | .

8. Current quarter's adjustment for sick pay — **8** | .

9. Current quarter's adjustments for tips and group-term life insurance — **9** | .

10. Total taxes after adjustments. Combine lines 6 through 9 — **10** | 6,485.28

11. Total deposits for this quarter, including overpayment applied from a prior quarter and overpayments applied from Form 941-X, 941-X (PR), 944-X, 944-X (PR), or 944-X (SP) filed in the current quarter — **11** | 6,485.28

12. **Balance due.** If line 10 is more than line 11, enter the difference and see instructions — **12** |

13. **Overpayment.** If line 11 is more than line 10, enter the difference | . | Check one: [ ] Apply to next return. [ ] Send a refund.

▶ You MUST complete both pages of Form 941 and SIGN it.

For Privacy Act and Paperwork Reduction Act Notice, see the back of the Payment Voucher. Cat. No. 17001Z

Next ▶
Form **941**

FIGURE 11.3 (continued)

950214

Name *(not your trade name)*: Sarah Brandon

Employer identification number (EIN): 75-1234567

Part 2: Tell us about your deposit schedule and tax liability for this quarter.

If you are unsure about whether you are a monthly schedule depositor or a semiweekly schedule depositor, see Pub. 15 (Circular E), section 11.

14 Check one:

☐ Line 10 on this return is less than $2,500 or line 10 on the return for the prior quarter was less than $2,500, and you did not incur a $100,000 next-day deposit obligation during the current quarter. If line 10 for the prior quarter was less than $2,500 but line 10 on this return is $100,000 or more, you must provide a record of your federal tax liability. If you are a monthly schedule depositor, complete the deposit schedule below; if you are a semiweekly schedule depositor, attach Schedule B (Form 941). Go to Part 3.

☒ **You were a monthly schedule depositor for the entire quarter.** Enter your tax liability for each month and total liability for the quarter, then go to Part 3.

Tax liability:		
Month 1	1995	52
Month 2	1995	52
Month 3	2494	24
Total liability for quarter	6485	28	Total must equal line 10.

☐ **You were a semiweekly schedule depositor for any part of this quarter.** Complete Schedule B (Form 941), Report of Tax Liability for Semiweekly Schedule Depositors, and attach it to Form 941.

Part 3: Tell us about your business. If a question does NOT apply to your business, leave it blank.

15 If your business has closed or you stopped paying wages . . . . ☐ Check here, and
    enter the final date you paid wages   /   /

16 If you are a seasonal employer and you do not have to file a return for every quarter of the year . . ☐ Check here.

Part 4: May we speak with your third-party designee?

Do you want to allow an employee, a paid tax preparer, or another person to discuss this return with the IRS? See the instructions for details.

☐ Yes. Designee's name and phone number _____

Select a 5-digit Personal Identification Number (PIN) to use when talking to the IRS. ☐ ☐ ☐ ☐ ☐

☒ No.

Part 5: Sign here. You MUST complete both pages of Form 941 and SIGN it.

Under penalties of perjury, I declare that I have examined this return, including accompanying schedules and statements, and to the best of my knowledge and belief, it is true, correct, and complete. Declaration of preparer (other than taxpayer) is based on all information of which preparer has any knowledge.

X Sign your name here: *Sarah Brandon*

Print your name here: Sarah Brandon
Print your title here: Owner

Date: 04 / 30 / 20X1

Best daytime phone: 972-709-4567

Paid Preparer Use Only

Check if you are self-employed . . . ☐

Preparer's name	
Preparer's signature	
Firm's name (or yours if self-employed)	
Address	
City	State	

PTIN:
Date: /   /
EIN:
Phone:
ZIP code:

Form **941**

- *Line 5c* shows the total amount of wages that are subject to Medicare taxes, $29,217.50. The amount is multiplied by the combined Medicare tax rate, 2.9 percent.

Medicare Tax:	
Employee's share	1.45%
Employer's share	1.45
Total	2.90%

  The amount of taxes is $847.31 ($29,217.50 × 2.90%).

- *Line 5d* is left blank since no employees were subject to the additional Medicare tax withholding.
- *Line 5e* shows the total social security and Medicare taxes, $4,470.28.
- *Line 5f* is left blank since no employees had taxable social security tips.
- *Line 6* shows the total tax liability for withheld income taxes, social security, and Medicare Taxes, $6,485.28.
- *Line 7* is for adjustments due to rounding. No rounding adjustments this quarter.
- *Line 8* is for adjustments due to sick pay. No sick pay adjustments this quarter.
- *Line 9* is for adjustments for tips and group-term life insurance. No such adjustments this quarter.
- *Line 10* shows total taxes after adjustments, $6,485.28.
- *Line 11* shows total deposits made during the quarter including overpayments applied from a prior quarter, $6,485.28.
- Any balance due is entered on *Line 12* or an overpayment is entered on *Line 13*.
- *Line 14* shows the monthly deposits made by Brandon Express Company.

Notice that on Line 14 if the amount of taxes is less than $2,500, the amount may be paid with the return or with a financial depositor. There is no need to complete the record of monthly deposits. Since the amount of taxes due for Brandon Express Company is greater than $2,500, and Brandon is a monthly depositor, the record of monthly tax deposits must be completed on Line 14. The total deposits shown on Line 14 must equal the taxes shown on Line 10.

If the employer did not deduct enough taxes from an employee's earnings, the business pays the difference. The deficiency is debited to **Payroll Taxes Expense.**

>> **11-5 OBJECTIVE**

Prepare Wage and Tax Statement (Form W-2) and Annual Transmittal of Wage and Tax Statements (Form W-3).

Wage and Tax Statement, Form W-2

Employers provide a **Wage and Tax Statement, Form W-2** to each employee by January 31 for the previous calendar year's earnings. Form W-2 is sometimes called a **withholding statement.** Form W-2 contains information about the employee's earnings and tax withholdings for the year. The information for Form W-2 comes from the employee's earnings record. Many employers now furnish this form in electronic form.

Employees who stop working for the business during the year may ask that a Form W-2 be issued early. The Form W-2 must be issued within 30 days after the request or after the final wage payment, whichever is later.

Figure 11.4 shows Form W-2 for Alicia Martinez. This is the standard form provided by the Internal Revenue Service (IRS). Some employers use a "substitute" Form W-2 that is approved by the IRS. The substitute form permits the employer to list total deductions and to reconcile the gross earnings, the deductions, and the net pay. If the firm issues 250 or more Forms W-2, the returns must be filed electronically.

At least four copies of each of Form W-2 are prepared:

1. One copy for the employer to send to the Social Security Administration, which shares the information with the IRS.
2. One copy for the employee to attach to the federal income tax return.

---

recall

Tax Calculations
Social security and Medicare taxes are calculated by multiplying the taxable wages by the tax rate.

important!

Form W-2
The employer must provide each employee with a Wage and Tax Statement, Form W-2, by January 31 of the following year. All payroll forms are revised each year. Those used in the text are illustrative of current forms at the time of publication.

FIGURE 11.4 Wage and Tax Statement, Form W-2

22222 Void ☐	**a** Employee's social security number 123-45-6789	For Official Use Only ▶ OMB No. 1545-0008

b Employer identification number (EIN) 75-1234567	**1** Wages, tips, other compensation — 20,800.00 **2** Federal income tax withheld — 988.00
c Employer's name, address, and ZIP code Brandon Express Company 5910 Lake June Road Dallas, TX 75232-6017	**3** Social security wages — 20,800.00 **4** Social security tax withheld — 1,289.60 **5** Medicare wages and tips — 20,800.00 **6** Medicare tax withheld — 301.60 **7** Social security tips **8** Allocated tips
d Control number	**9** **10** Dependent care benefits
e Employee's first name and initial: Alicia Last name: Martinez Suff.	**11** Nonqualified plans **12a** See instructions for box 12
1712 Windmill Hill Lane Dallas, Texas 75232-6002	**13** Statutory employee ☐ Retirement plan ☐ Third-party sick pay ☐ **12b** **14** Other **12c** **12d**
f Employee's address and ZIP code	
15 State: TX Employer's state ID number: 12-9876500	**16** State wages, tips, etc. 20800.00 **17** State income tax **18** Local wages, tips, etc. **19** Local income tax **20** Locality name

Form **W-2** Wage and Tax Statement   **20X1**   Department of the Treasury—Internal Revenue Service
For Privacy Act and Paperwork Reduction Act Notice, see the separate instructions.
Copy A For Social Security Administration — Send this entire page with Form W-3 to the Social Security Administration; photocopies are **not** acceptable.   Cat. No. 10134D

Do Not Cut, Fold, or Staple Forms on This Page

3. One copy for the employee's records.
4. One copy for the employer's records.

If there is a state income tax, two more copies of Form W-2 are prepared:

5. One copy for the employer to send to the state tax department.
6. One copy for the employee to attach to the state income tax return.

Additional copies are prepared if there is a city or county income tax.

Annual Transmittal of Wage and Tax Statements, Form W-3

The **Transmittal of Wage and Tax Statements, Form W-3,** is submitted with Forms W-2 to the Social Security Administration. Form W-3 reports the total social security wages; total Medicare wages; total social security tax withheld; total Medicare tax withheld; total wages, tips, and other compensation; total federal income tax withheld; and other information.

A copy of Form W-2 for each employee is attached to Form W-3. Form W-3 is due by the last day of February following the end of the calendar year. The Social Security Administration shares the tax information on Forms W-2 with the Internal Revenue Service. Figure 11.5 shows the completed Form W-3 for Brandon Express Company.

The amounts on Form W-3 must equal the sums of the amounts on the attached Forms W-2. For example, the amount entered in Box 1 of Form W-3 must equal the sum of the amounts entered in Box 1 of all the Forms W-2.

The amounts on Form W-3 also must equal the sums of the amounts reported on the Forms 941 during the year. For example, the social security wages reported on the Form W-3 must equal the sum of the social security wages reported on the four Forms 941.

The filing of Form W-3 marks the end of the routine procedures needed to account for payrolls and for payroll tax withholdings.

ABOUT ACCOUNTING

IRS Electronic Filing

While filing of individual and business income tax returns is steadily increasing (approximately 86.3% for individuals in 2015), the IRS reported in late 2015 that the e-filing of all Form 94x series was only 33.3%. The stated goal is 80% of employment tax returns to be filed electronically.

FIGURE 11.5 Transmittal of Wage and Tax Statements, Form W-3

Control number: 33333	OMB No. 1545-0008
Kind of Payer: 941 (X)	
Kind of Employer: None apply (X)	
c Total number of Forms W-2: 5	
e Employer identification number (EIN): 75-1234567	
f Employer's name: Brandon Express Company	
g Employer's address and ZIP code: 5910 Lake June Road, Dallas, TX 75232-6017	
1 Wages, tips, other compensation: 116,870.00	**2** Federal income tax withheld: 8,060.00
3 Social security wages: 116,870.00	**4** Social security tax withheld: 7,245.96
5 Medicare wages and tips: 116,870.00	**6** Medicare tax withheld: 1,697.60
15 State: TX	Employer's state ID number: 12-9876500
Employer's contact person: Sarah Brandon	Employer's telephone number: 972-709-4567
Signature: Sarah Brandon	Title: Owner	Date: 2/10/20X2

Form **W-3** Transmittal of Wage and Tax Statements — 20X1
Department of the Treasury, Internal Revenue Service

Section 1 Review

1. The Form W-2 is used to report all but the following:
   a. gross earnings for the year.
   b. total federal income tax withheld from employee earnings for the year.
   c. total payroll taxes the company paid this year.
   d. total Medicare tax withheld from employee earnings for the year.

2. How does a business deposit federal payroll taxes?
   a. Employees deposit their own taxes due at a bank.
   b. The company makes the deposit at any bank.
   c. The company makes the deposit using bitcoin.
   d. The deposit is made at a national bank by the company.

3. What is the purpose of Form 941?
   a. accounts for all employee gross wages and federal tax–required withholdings during a quarter
   b. used to calculate the federal unemployment tax due for a quarter
   c. reports the yearly amounts of gross wages and required federal tax withholdings
   d. used to calculate the state unemployment tax due for a quarter

4. Which tax is paid equally by the employee and employer?
   a. federal income tax
   b. state income tax
   c. social security tax
   d. federal unemployment tax

5. Employers usually record social security taxes in the accounting records at the end of:
   a. each payroll period.
   b. each month.
   c. each quarter.
   d. the year.

Section 2

SECTION OBJECTIVES	TERMS TO LEARN
>> 11-6 Compute and record liability for federal and state unemployment taxes and record payment of the taxes. **WHY IT'S IMPORTANT** Businesses need to record all payroll tax liabilities. **>> 11-7** Prepare an Employer's Federal Unemployment Tax Return, Form 940. **WHY IT'S IMPORTANT** The unemployment insurance programs provide support to individuals during temporary periods of unemployment. **>> 11-8** Compute and record workers' compensation insurance premiums. **WHY IT'S IMPORTANT** Businesses need insurance to cover workplace injury claims.	Employer's Annual Federal Unemployment Tax Return, Form 940 experience rating system merit rating system unemployment insurance program

Unemployment Tax and Workers' Compensation

In Section 1, we discussed taxes that are withheld from employees' earnings and, in some cases, matched by the employer. In this section, we will discuss payroll-related expenses that are paid solely by the employer.

Unemployment Compensation Insurance Taxes

The unemployment compensation tax program, often called the **unemployment insurance program,** provides unemployment compensation through a tax levied on employers.

Coordination of Federal and State Unemployment Rates

The unemployment insurance program is a federal program that encourages states to provide unemployment insurance for employees working in the state. The federal government allows a credit—or reduction—in the federal unemployment tax for amounts charged by the state for unemployment taxes.

This text assumes that the federal unemployment tax rate is 6.0 percent less a state unemployment tax credit of 5.4 percent; thus, the federal tax rate is reduced to 0.6 percent (6.0 percent − 5.4 percent). The earnings limits for the federal and the state unemployment taxes are usually the same, $7,000.

A few states levy an unemployment tax on the employee. The tax is withheld from employee pay and remitted by the employer to the state.

For businesses that provide steady employment, the state unemployment tax rate may be lowered based on an **experience rating system,** or a **merit rating system.** Under the experience rating system, the state tax rate may be reduced to less than 1 percent for businesses that provide steady employment. In contrast, some states levy penalty rates as high as 10 percent for employers with poor records of providing steady employment.

The reduction of state unemployment taxes because of favorable experience ratings does not affect the credit allowable against the federal tax. An employer may take a credit against the federal unemployment tax as though it were paid at the normal state rate even though the employer actually pays the state a lower rate.

Because of its experience rating, Brandon Express Company pays a state unemployment tax of 4.0 percent, which is less than the standard rate of 5.4 percent. Note that the business may take the credit for the full amount of the state rate (5.4 percent) against the federal rate, even though the business actually pays a state rate of 4.0 percent.

>> 11-6 OBJECTIVE

Compute and record liability for federal and state unemployment taxes and record payment of the taxes.

Computing and Recording Unemployment Taxes

Brandon Express Company records its state and federal unemployment tax expense at the end of each payroll period. The unemployment taxes for the payroll period ending January 6 are as follows:

Federal unemployment tax	($2,247.50 × 0.006)	=	$ 13.49
State unemployment tax	($2,247.50 × 0.040)	=	89.90
Total unemployment taxes		=	$103.39

The entry to record the employer's unemployment payroll taxes follows.

	GENERAL JOURNAL			PAGE 1
DATE	DESCRIPTION	POST. REF.	DEBIT	CREDIT
20X1				
Jan. 8	Payroll Taxes Expense		103 39	
	Federal Unemployment Tax Payable			13 49
	State Unemployment Tax Payable			89 90
	Unemployment taxes on			
	weekly payroll			

Reporting and Paying State Unemployment Taxes

In most states, the due date for the state unemployment tax return is the last day of the month following the end of the quarter. Generally, the tax is paid, electronically, with the return.

Employer's Quarterly Report Each state requires reporting of wages for unemployment tax purposes. Since Brandon Express Company is located in Texas, it will complete the Texas state unemployment tax form and submit the tax due. Generally, each state requires quarterly reporting of wages and depositing of state unemployment taxes due. Amounts of wages subject to tax and the state tax rate are determined by each state.

Brandon Express Company submits the report and issues a check payable to the state tax authority for the amount due. The entry is recorded in the cash payments journal. The transaction is shown here in general journal form for purposes of illustration:

	GENERAL JOURNAL			PAGE
DATE	DESCRIPTION	POST. REF.	DEBIT	CREDIT
20X1				
Apr. 29	State Unemployment Tax Payable		1 157 50	
	Cash			1 157 50
	Paid SUTA taxes for quarter			
	ending March 31			

Earnings in Excess of Base Amount State unemployment tax is paid on the first $7,000 of annual earnings for each employee. Earnings over $7,000 are not subject to state unemployment tax.

For example, Cecilia Wu earns $560 every week of the year. Table 11.1 shows that she earned $7,280 at the end of the first quarter. In the four weeks of January, February, and March, she earned $2,240 ($560 × 4).

	Earnings	Cumulative Earnings
January	$2,240	$2,240
February	2,240	4,480
March	2,240	6,720
March, week 5	560	7,280

In the fifth week of March, Wu earned $560, but only $280 of it is subject to state unemployment tax ($7,000 earnings limit − $6,720 cumulative earnings = $280). For the rest of the calendar year, Wu's earnings are not subject to state unemployment tax.

Reporting and Paying Federal Unemployment Taxes

The rules for reporting and depositing federal unemployment taxes differ from those used for social security and Medicare taxes.

Depositing Federal Unemployment Taxes Generally, federal unemployment tax payments are electronically deposited through EFTPS. Deposits are made quarterly and are due on the last day of the month following the end of the quarter.

The federal unemployment tax is calculated at the end of each quarter. It is computed by multiplying the first $7,000 of each employee's wages by 0.006. A deposit is required when more than $500 of federal unemployment tax is owed. If $500 or less is owed, no deposit is due. Any deposit due of $500 or more should be electronically deposited.

For example, suppose that a business calculates its federal unemployment tax to be $325 at the end of the first quarter. Since it is not more than $500, no deposit is due. At the end of the second quarter, it calculates its federal unemployment taxes on second quarter wages to be $200. The total undeposited unemployment tax now is more than $500, so a deposit is required.

First quarter undeposited tax	$325
Second quarter undeposited tax	200
Total deposit due	$525

In the case of Brandon Express Company, the company owed $173.63 in federal unemployment tax at the end of March. Since this is less than $500, no deposit is due.

Month	Taxable Earnings Paid	Rate	Tax Due	Deposit Due Date
January	$ 8,990.00	0.006	$ 53.94	April 30
February	8,990.00	0.006	53.94	April 30
March	10,957.50	0.006	65.75	April 30
Total	$28,937.50		$173.63	

The payment of federal unemployment tax is recorded by debiting the *Federal Unemployment Tax Payable* account and crediting the *Cash* account.

Reporting Federal Unemployment Tax, Form 940 Tax returns are not due quarterly for the federal unemployment tax. The employer submits an annual return. The **Employer's Annual Federal Unemployment Tax Return, Form 940,** is a preprinted government form

>> 11-7 OBJECTIVE
Prepare an Employer's Federal Unemployment Tax Return, Form 940.

used to report unemployment taxes for the calendar year. It is due by January 31 of the following year. The due date is extended to February 10 if all tax deposits were made on time.

The information needed to complete Form 940 comes from the annual summary of individual earnings records and from the state unemployment tax returns filed during the year.

Figure 11.6 shows Form 940 prepared for Brandon Express Company. Refer to it as you learn how to complete Form 940.

PART 1: Asks the filer if he or she was required to pay SUTA tax in more than one state.

PART 2: Determine your FUTA tax before adjustments.

- *Line 3* shows the total compensation paid to employees, $116,870.00.
- *Line 4* is blank because there were no exempt payments.
- *Line 5* shows the compensation that exceeds the $7,000 earnings limit, $81,870 ($116,870 − $35,000).
- *Line 6* shows the wages not subject to federal unemployment tax, $81,870.
- *Line 7* shows the taxable wages for the year, $35,000. This amount must agree with the total taxable FUTA wages shown on the individual employee earnings records for the year.
- *Line 8* shows the FUTA tax, $210 ($35,000 × 0.006).

PART 3: Determine your adjustments.

- *Lines 9, 10, and 11* are blank because the company had no adjustments.

PART 4: Determine your FUTA tax and balance due or overpayment.

- *Line 12* shows the total FUTA tax, after adjustments, $210.
- *Line 13* shows the FUTA tax deposited during the year, $0.
- *Line 14* shows the balance due, $210.
- *Line 15* is blank because there is no overpayment.

PART 5: Report your FUTA tax liability by quarter. This section is not applicable to Brandon Express Company because its total FUTA liability is less than $500.

>> 11-8 OBJECTIVE

Compute and record workers' compensation insurance premiums.

Workers' Compensation Insurance

Workers' compensation provides benefits for employees who are injured on the job. The insurance premium, which is paid by the employer, depends on the risk involved with the work performed. It is important to classify earnings according to the type of work the employees perform and to summarize labor costs according to the insurance premium classifications.

For instance, workers' compensation insurance will cost much more for workers in a coal mine or on an oil rig than it will for workers in an office setting. Insurance companies will have different rates for each category of risk of a company's workers.

There are two ways to handle workers' compensation insurance. The method a business uses depends on the number of its employees.

Estimated Annual Premium in Advance Employers who have few employees pay an estimated premium in advance. At the end of the year, the employer calculates the actual premium. If the actual premium is more than the estimated premium paid, the employer pays the balance due. If the actual premium is less than the estimated premium paid, the employer receives a refund.

Brandon Express Company has two work classifications: office work and shipping work. The workers' compensation premium rates are:

Office workers	$0.45 per $100 of labor costs
Shipping workers	1.25 per $100 of labor costs

The insurance premium rates recognize that injuries are more likely to occur to shipping workers than to office workers. Based on employee earnings for the previous year, Brandon Express Company paid an estimated premium of $1,000 for the new year. The payment was made on January 15.

Payroll Taxes, Deposits, and Reports CHAPTER 11 401

FIGURE 11.6 Employer's Annual Federal Unemployment Tax Return, Form 940

Form **940 for 20X1:** Employer's Annual Federal Unemployment (FUTA) Tax Return
Department of the Treasury — Internal Revenue Service

850113
OMB No. 1545-0028

Employer identification number (EIN): 75-1234567

Name (not your trade name): Sarah Brandon

Trade name (if any): Brandon Express Company

Address: 5910 June Lake Road

City: Dallas **State:** TX **ZIP code:** 75322-6017

Type of Return (Check all that apply.)
- a. Amended
- b. Successor employer
- c. No payments to employees in 2019
- d. Final: Business closed or stopped paying wages

Instructions and prior-year forms are available at www.irs.gov/form940.

Read the separate instructions before you complete this form. Please type or print within the boxes.

Part 1: Tell us about your return. If any line does NOT apply, leave it blank. See instructions before completing Part 1.

1a If you had to pay state unemployment tax in one state only, enter the state abbreviation . **1a** TX

1b If you had to pay state unemployment tax in more than one state, you are a multi-state employer . . . **1b** ☐ Check here. Complete Schedule A (Form 940).

2 If you paid wages in a state that is subject to CREDIT REDUCTION . . . **2** ☐ Check here. Complete Schedule A (Form 940).

Part 2: Determine your FUTA tax before adjustments. If any line does NOT apply, leave it blank.

3 Total payments to all employees . . . **3** 116870.00

4 Payments exempt from FUTA tax . . . **4**

Check all that apply:
- 4a ☐ Fringe benefits
- 4b ☐ Group-term life insurance
- 4c ☐ Retirement/Pension
- 4d ☐ Dependent care
- 4e ☐ Other

5 Total of payments made to each employee in excess of $7,000 . . . **5** 81870.00

6 Subtotal (line 4 + line 5 = line 6) . . . **6** 81870.00

7 Total taxable FUTA wages (line 3 – line 6 = line 7) (see instructions) . . . **7** 35000.00

8 FUTA tax before adjustments (line 7 × .006 = line 8) . . . **8** 210.00

Part 3: Determine your adjustments. If any line does NOT apply, leave it blank.

9 If ALL of the taxable FUTA wages you paid were excluded from state unemployment tax, multiply line 7 by .054 (line 7 × .054 = line 9). Go to line 12 . . . **9**

10 If SOME of the taxable FUTA wages you paid were excluded from state unemployment tax, OR you paid ANY state unemployment tax late (after the due date for filing Form 940), complete the worksheet in the instructions. Enter the amount from line 7 of the worksheet . . . **10**

11 If credit reduction applies, enter the total from Schedule A (Form 940) . . . **11**

Part 4: Determine your FUTA tax and balance due or overpayment. If any line does NOT apply, leave it blank.

12 Total FUTA tax after adjustments (lines 8 + 9 + 10 + 11 = line 12) . . . **12** 210.00

13 FUTA tax deposited for the year, including any overpayment applied from a prior year . . . **13** 0.00

14 Balance due (If line 12 is more than line 13, enter the excess on line 14.)
- If line 14 is more than $500, you must deposit your tax.
- If line 14 is $500 or less, you may pay with this return. (see instructions) . . . **14** 210.00

15 Overpayment (If line 13 is more than line 12, enter the excess on line 15 and check a box below.) . . . **15**

▶ You **MUST** complete both pages of this form and **SIGN** it.   Check one: ☐ Apply to next return. ☐ Send a refund.

Next ▶

For Privacy Act and Paperwork Reduction Act Notice, see the back of Form 940-V, Payment Voucher.   Cat. No. 112340   Form **940**

FIGURE 11.6 (continued)

850212

Name *(not your trade name)*
Sarah Brandon

Employer identification number (EIN)
75-123456

Part 5: Report your FUTA tax liability by quarter only if line 12 is more than $500. If not, go to Part 6.

16 Report the amount of your FUTA tax liability for each quarter; do NOT enter the amount you deposited. If you had no liability for a quarter, leave the line blank.

16a 1st quarter (January 1 – March 31) . . . . 16a [   ] •

16b 2nd quarter (April 1 – June 30) . . . . 16b [   ] •

16c 3rd quarter (July 1 – September 30) . . . . 16c [   ] •

16d 4th quarter (October 1 – December 31) . . . . . . 16d [   ] •

17 Total tax liability for the year (lines 16a + 16b + 16c + 16d = line 17) 17 [   ] • Total must equal line 12.

Part 6: May we speak with your third-party designee?

Do you want to allow an employee, a paid tax preparer, or another person to discuss this return with the IRS? See the instructions for details.

☐ Yes. Designee's name and phone number

Select a 5-digit Personal Identification Number (PIN) to use when talking to IRS

☒ No.

Part 7: Sign here. You MUST complete both pages of this form and SIGN it.

Under penalties of perjury, I declare that I have examined this return, including accompanying schedules and statements, and to the best of my knowledge and belief, it is true, correct, and complete, and that no part of any payment made to a state unemployment fund claimed as a credit was, or is to be, deducted from the payments made to employees. Declaration of preparer (other than taxpayer) is based on all information of which preparer has any knowledge.

✗ Sign your name here *Sarah Brandon*

Print your name here **Sarah Brandon**

Print your title here **Owner**

Date **01 / 31 / 20X2**

Best daytime phone **972-123-8766**

Paid Preparer Use Only Check if you are self-employed . ☐

Preparer's name

Preparer's signature

Firm's name (or yours if self-employed)

Address

City   State

PTIN

Date / /

EIN

Phone

ZIP code

Page **2**

Form **940**

GENERAL JOURNAL PAGE _____

DATE	DESCRIPTION	POST. REF.	DEBIT	CREDIT
20X1				
Jan. 15	Prepaid Workers' Compensation Insurance		1 000 00	
	Cash			1 000 00
	Estimated workers' compensation			
	insurance for 20X1			

At the end of the year, the actual premium was computed to be $1,261.20. The actual premium was computed by applying the proper rates to the payroll data for the year:

- The office wages were $24,960.

  ($24,960 ÷ $100) × $0.45 =

  249.60 × $0.45 = $112.32

- The shipping wages were $91,910.

  ($91,910 ÷ $100) × $1.25 =

  919.1 × $1.25 = $1,148.88

- Total premium for year = $1,261.20

Classification	Payroll	Rate	Premium
Office work	$24,960	$0.45 per $100	$ 112.32
Shipping work	91,910	1.25 per $100	1,148.88
Total premium for year			$1,261.20
Less estimated premium paid			1,000.00
Balance of premium due			$ 261.20

On December 31, the balance due to the insurance company is recorded as a liability by an adjusting entry. Brandon Express Company owes $261.20 ($1,261.20 − $1,000.00) for the workers' compensation insurance.

MANAGERIAL IMPLICATIONS <<

PAYROLL TAXES

- Management must ensure that payroll taxes are computed properly and paid on time.
- In order to avoid penalties, it is essential that a business prepares its payroll tax returns accurately and files the returns and required forms promptly.
- The payroll system should ensure that payroll reports are prepared in an efficient manner.
- Managers need to be familiar with all payroll taxes and how they impact operating expenses.
- Managers must be knowledgeable about unemployment tax regulations in their state because favorable experience ratings can reduce unemployment tax expense.
- Management is responsible for developing effective internal control procedures over payroll operations and ensuring that they are followed.

THINKING CRITICALLY

What accounting records are used to prepare Form 941?

	GENERAL JOURNAL			PAGE	
DATE	DESCRIPTION	POST. REF.	DEBIT	CREDIT	
20X1					1
Dec. 31	Workers' Compensation Insurance Expense		261 20		2
	Workers' Compensation Insurance Payable			261 20	3
					4

Additionally, an adjusting journal would be recorded on December 31, 20X1, for prepaid workers' compensation insurance expired.

Suppose that at the beginning of the year on January 15, 20X1, Brandon Express Company had paid an estimated premium of $1,400 instead of $1,000. The actual premium at the end of the year was $1,261.20. The company would be due a refund from the insurance company for the amount overpaid, $138.80 ($1,400.00 − $1,261.20).

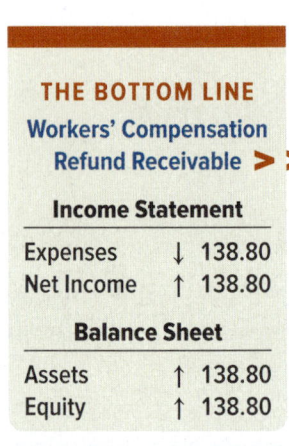

Deposit and Monthly Premium Payments Employers with many employees may use a different method to handle workers' compensation insurance. At the beginning of the year, they make large deposits, often 25 percent of the estimated annual premium. From January through November, they pay the actual premium due based on an audit of the month's wages. The premium for the last month is deducted from the deposit. Any balance is refunded or applied toward the following year's deposit.

Internal Control over Payroll Operations

Now that we have examined the basic accounting procedures used for payrolls and payroll taxes, let's look at some internal control procedures that are recommended to protect payroll operations.

1. Assign only highly responsible, well-trained employees to work in payroll operations.
2. Keep payroll records in a secured location. Train payroll employees to maintain confidentiality about pay rates and other information in the payroll records.
3. Add new employees to the payroll system and make all changes in employee pay rates only with proper written authorization from management.
4. Make changes to an employee's withholding allowances based only on a Form W-4 properly completed and signed by the employee.
5. Make voluntary deductions from employee earnings based only on a signed authorization from the employee.
6. Have the payroll authorizations examined by someone other than the person who prepares them. Compare each check/deposit to the entry for the employee in the payroll register.
7. If still issuing actual payroll checks, have them distributed to the employees by someone other than the person who prepares them.
8. Have the monthly payroll bank account statement received and reconciled by someone other than the person who prepares the payroll checks.
9. Prompt bank reconciliation of the payroll checking account should be completed each month. It is important to track any returned checks or deposits so employees receive payment for work performed.
10. Maintain files of all authorization forms for adding new employees, changing pay rates, and making voluntary deductions. Also retain all Forms W-4.

Section 2 Review

1. Why is it important for workers' compensation wages to be classified according to the type of work performed?
   a. The company will likely pay a different rate on each classification.
   b. Some classifications are exempt from workers' compensation rates.
   c. Federal law requires classification.
   d. The wages must be reported by classifications on Form 941.

2. Who pays the federal unemployment tax and the state unemployment tax?
   a. Congress appropriates money to pay these taxes.
   b. State governments appropriate money to pay these taxes.
   c. Employees pay both taxes.
   d. Employers pay both taxes for employees.

3. How does a favorable experience rating affect the state unemployment tax rate?
   a. It will likely reduce the SUTA amount due.
   b. It makes the FUTA tax less.
   c. It will make the FUTA tax more.
   d. It will make state Medicare tax withheld more on employees.

4. State unemployment taxes are filed:
   a. monthly.
   b. quarterly.
   c. yearly.
   d. at the end of each pay period.

5. The federal unemployment taxes are reported on:
   a. Form 941.
   b. Form 8109.
   c. Form W-3.
   d. Form 940.

Chapter 11 Review

Chapter Summary

Employers must pay social security, SUTA, FUTA, and Medicare taxes. They must also collect federal and state income taxes from their employees and then remit those taxes to the appropriate taxing authorities. In this chapter, you have learned how to compute the employer's taxes and how to file the required tax returns and reports.

Learning Objectives

11-1 Explain how and when payroll taxes are paid to the government.

Employers act as collection agents for social security, Medicare, and federal income taxes withheld from employee earnings. Employers must remit these sums that are withheld from employee earnings but also must make a deposit for the business matching the amounts withheld from employees for social security and Medicare taxes to the government. These taxes must be deposited in an authorized depository, usually a commercial bank. The methods and schedules for deposits vary according to the sums involved.

11-2 Compute and record the employer's social security and Medicare taxes.

Employers should multiply the social security and Medicare tax rates by taxable wages to compute the employer's portion of taxes due.

11-3 Record deposit of social security, Medicare, and employee income taxes.

As taxes are paid to the government, the accounting records should be updated to reflect the payment, thereby reducing tax liability accounts.

11-4 Prepare an Employer's Quarterly Federal Tax Return, Form 941.

The Form 941 reports wages paid, federal employee income tax withheld, and applicable social security and Medicare taxes.

11-5 Prepare Wage and Tax Statement (Form W-2) and Annual Transmittal of Wage and Tax Statements (Form W-3).

By the end of January, each employee must be given a Wage and Tax Statement, Form W-2, showing the previous year's earnings and withholdings for social security, Medicare, and employee income tax. The employer files a Transmittal of Wage and Tax Statements, Form W-3, with copies of employees' Forms W-2. Form W-3 is due by the last day of February following the end of the calendar year.

11-6 Compute and record liability for federal and state unemployment taxes and record payment of the taxes.

Unemployment insurance taxes are paid by the employer to both state and federal governments. State unemployment tax returns differ from state to state but usually require a list of employees, their social security numbers, and taxable wages paid. The rate of state unemployment tax depends on the employer's experience rating. The net federal unemployment tax rate can be as low as 0.6 percent based on assumptions in this chapter.

11-7 Prepare an Employer's Federal Unemployment Tax Return, Form 940.

An Employer's Annual Federal Unemployment Tax Return, Form 940, must be filed in January for the preceding calendar year. The form shows the total wages paid, the amount of wages subject to unemployment tax, and the federal unemployment tax owed for the year. A credit is allowed against gross federal tax for unemployment tax charged under state plans, up to 5.4 percent of wages subject to the federal tax.

11-8 Compute and record workers' compensation insurance premiums.

By state law, employers might be required to carry workers' compensation insurance. For companies with a few employees, an estimated premium is paid at the start of the year. A final settlement is made with the insurance company on the basis of an audit of the payroll after the end of the year. Premiums vary according to the type of work performed by each employee. Other premium payment plans can be used for larger employers.

11-9 Define the accounting terms new to this chapter.

Glossary

Employer's Annual Federal Unemployment Tax Return, Form 940 (p. 399) Preprinted government form used by the employer to report unemployment taxes for the calendar year

Employer's Quarterly Federal Tax Return, Form 941 (p. 390) Preprinted government form used by the employer to report payroll tax information relating to social security, Medicare, and employee income tax withholding to the Internal Revenue Service

Experience rating system (p. 397) A system that rewards an employer for maintaining steady employment conditions by reducing the firm's state unemployment tax rate

Merit rating system (p. 397) *See* Experience rating system

Transmittal of Wage and Tax Statements, Form W-3 (p. 395) Preprinted government form submitted with Forms W-2 to the Social Security Administration

Unemployment insurance program (p. 397) A program that provides unemployment compensation through a tax levied on employers

Wage and Tax Statement, Form W-2 (p. 394) Preprinted government form that contains information about an employee's earnings and tax withholdings for the year

Withholding statement (p. 394) *See* Wage and Tax Statement, Form W-2

Comprehensive Self Review

1. What is Form W-3?
2. Is the ceiling on earnings subject to unemployment taxes larger than or smaller than the ceiling on earnings subject to the social security tax?
3. How do the FUTA and SUTA taxes relate to each other?
4. Under the monthly deposit schedule rule, when must deposits for employee income tax and other withheld taxes be made?
5. Which of the following factors determine the frequency of deposits of social security, Medicare, and income tax withholdings?
    a. Experience rating.
    b. Amount of taxes reported in the lookback period.
    c. Company's net income.
    d. Amount of taxes currently owed.
    e. How often employees are paid.

(Answers to Comprehensive Self Review are at the end of the chapter.)

Discussion Questions

1. Which of the following are withheld from employees' earnings?
    a. FUTA
    b. income tax
    c. Medicare
    d. social security
    e. SUTA
    f. workers' compensation
2. What does "monthly" refer to in the Monthly Deposit Schedule Rule?
3. What does "semiweekly" refer to in the Semiweekly Deposit Schedule Rule?

4. What is EFTPS? When is EFTPS required?
5. What is a business tax identification number?
6. What are the four taxes levied on employers?
7. What is the lookback period?
8. What is the purpose of Form W-3? When must it be issued? To whom is it sent?
9. When must Form W-2 be issued? To whom is it sent?
10. What happens if the employer fails to deduct enough employee income tax or FICA tax from employee earnings?
11. How can an employer keep informed about changes in the rates and bases for the social security, Medicare, and FUTA taxes?
12. When is the premium for workers' compensation insurance usually paid?
13. Who pays for workers' compensation insurance?
14. What is Form 941? How often is the form filed?
15. Is the employer required to deposit the federal unemployment tax during the year? Explain.
16. A state charges a basic SUTA tax rate of 5.4 percent. Because of an excellent experience rating, an employer in the state has to pay only 1.0 percent of the taxable payroll as state tax. What is the percentage to be used in computing the credit against the federal unemployment tax?
17. What is the purpose of Form 940? How often is it filed?
18. What is the purpose of allowing a credit against the FUTA for state unemployment taxes?
19. Why was the unemployment insurance system established?

APPLICATIONS

Exercises

Exercise 11.1
Objective 11-1

▶ **Depositing payroll taxes.**

Given the following scenario, choose the best answer. At the end of the quarter, the business owed $2,000 in total payroll taxes. The amount due must be deposited:

a. on the last business day of the quarter.

b. on the last day of the quarter.

c. on the day Form 941 for the quarter is due.

d. on the first day of the next quarter.

Exercise 11.2
Objective 11-3

▶ **Recording deposit of social security, Medicare, and income taxes.**

After Copper Corporation paid its employees on July 15 and recorded the corporation's share of payroll taxes for the payroll paid that date, the firm's general ledger showed a balance of $20,584 in the **Social Security Tax Payable** account, a balance of $4,814 in the **Medicare Tax Payable** account, and a balance of $19,920 in the **Employee Income Tax Payable** account. On July 16, the business issued a check to deposit the taxes owed in the First City Bank. Record this transaction in general journal form. Use 24 as the page number for the general journal.

Exercise 11.3
Objectives 11-2, 11-6

▶ **Computing employer's payroll taxes.**

At the end of the weekly payroll period on June 30, the payroll register of Known Consultants showed employee earnings of $50,000. Determine the firm's payroll taxes for the period. Use a social security rate of 6.2 percent, Medicare rate of 1.45 percent, FUTA rate of 0.6 percent, and SUTA rate of 5.4 percent. Consider all earnings subject to social security tax and Medicare tax and $40,000 subject to FUTA and SUTA taxes.

Depositing federal unemployment tax.

On March 31, the *Federal Unemployment Tax Payable* account in the general ledger of The Argosy Company showed a balance of $1,507. This represents the FUTA tax owed for the first quarter of the year. On April 30, the firm deposited the amount owed in the First National Bank. Record this transaction in general journal form. Use 14 as the page number for the general journal.

◀ **Exercise 11.4**
Objective 11-6

Computing SUTA tax.

On April 30, Quality Furniture Company prepared its state unemployment tax return for the first quarter of the year. The firm had taxable wages of $85,000. Because of a favorable experience rating, Quality pays SUTA tax at a rate of 1.4 percent. How much SUTA tax did the firm owe for the quarter?

◀ **Exercise 11.5**
Objective 11-6

Paying SUTA tax.

On June 30, the *State Unemployment Tax Payable* account in the general ledger of Your Office Supplies showed a balance of $2,148. This represents the SUTA tax owed for the second quarter of the year. On July 31, the business issued a check to the state unemployment insurance fund for the amount due. Record this payment in general journal form. Use 30 as the page number for the general journal.

◀ **Exercise 11.6**
Objective 11-6

Computing FUTA tax.

On January 31, AC Gourmet Shop prepared its Employer's Annual Federal Unemployment Tax Return, Form 940. During the previous year, the business paid total wages of $462,150 to its 14 employees. Of this amount, $98,000 was subject to FUTA tax. Using a rate of 0.6 percent, determine the FUTA tax owed and the balance due on January 31, when Form 940 was filed. A deposit of $300 was made during the past year that applied to total tax due.

◀ **Exercise 11.7**
Objective 11-6

Computing workers' compensation insurance premiums.

Meri Medical Supplies estimates that its office employees will earn $175,000 next year and its factory employees will earn $600,000. The firm pays the following rates for workers' compensation insurance: $0.60 per $100 of wages for the office employees and $7.50 per $100 of wages for the factory employees. Determine the estimated premium for each group of employees and the total estimated premium for next year.

◀ **Exercise 11.8**
Objective 11-8

PROBLEMS

Problem Set A

Computing and recording employer's payroll tax expense.

The payroll register of Exterior Cleaning Company showed total employee earnings of $5,000 for the payroll period ended July 14.

◀ **Problem 11.1A**
Objectives 11-2, 11-6

INSTRUCTIONS

1. Compute the employer's payroll taxes for the period. Use rates of 6.2 percent for the employer's share of the social security tax, 1.45 percent for Medicare tax, 0.6 percent for FUTA tax, and 5.4 percent for SUTA tax. All earnings are taxable.
2. Prepare a general journal entry to record the employer's payroll taxes for the period. Use journal page 30.

Analyze: Which of the above taxes are paid by the employee and matched by the employer?

Problem 11.2A
Objectives 11-2, 11-3

Computing employer's social security tax, Medicare tax, and unemployment taxes.

A payroll summary for Mark Consulting Company, owned by Mark Fronke, for the quarter ending June 30, 20X1, appears below. The firm made the required tax deposits as follows:

a. For April taxes, paid on May 15.
b. For May taxes, paid on June 17.

Date Wages Paid		Total Earnings	Social Security Tax Deducted	Medicare Tax Deducted	Income Tax Withheld
April	8	$ 3,400.00	$ 210.80	$ 49.30	$ 338.00
	15	3,700.00	229.40	53.65	365.00
	22	4,100.00	254.20	59.45	338.00
	29	4,400.00	272.80	63.80	436.00
		$15,600.00	$ 967.20	$226.20	$1,477.00
May	5	$ 3,200.00	$ 198.40	$ 46.40	$ 318.00
	12	3,400.00	210.80	49.30	338.00
	19	3,400.00	210.80	49.30	338.00
	26	4,400.00	272.80	63.80	436.00
		$14,400.00	$ 892.80	$208.80	$1,430.00
June	2	$ 3,700.00	$ 229.40	$ 53.65	$ 365.00
	9	3,400.00	210.80	49.30	338.00
	16	4,400.00	272.80	63.80	436.00
	23	3,400.00	210.80	49.30	338.00
	30	3,200.00	198.40	46.40	318.00
		$18,100.00	$1,122.20	$262.45	$1,795.00
Total		$48,100.00	$2,982.20	$697.45	$4,702.00

INSTRUCTIONS

1. Using the tax rates given below, and assuming that all earnings are taxable, make the general journal entry on April 8, 20X1, to record the employer's payroll tax expense on the payroll ending that date. Use journal page 12.

Social security	6.2 percent
Medicare	1.45
FUTA	0.6
SUTA	5.4

2. Prepare the entries in general journal form to record deposit of the employee income tax withheld and the social security and Medicare taxes (employee and employer shares) on May 15 for April taxes and on June 17 for May taxes.

Analyze: How were the amounts for *Income Tax Withheld* determined?

Problem 11.3A
Objectives 11-4, 11-6
CONTINUING >>> Problem

This is a continuation of Problem 11.2A for Mark Consulting Company; recording payment of taxes and preparing employer's quarterly federal tax return.

1. On July 15, the firm issued a check to deposit the federal income tax withheld and the FICA tax (both employee and employer shares for the third month [June]). Based on your computations in Problem 11.2A, record the issuance of the check in general journal form. Use journal page 24.

2. Complete Form 941 in accordance with the discussions in this chapter. Use a 12.4 percent social security rate and a 2.9 percent Medicare rate in computations. Use the following address for the company: 2300 East Ocean Blvd., Long Beach, CA 90802. Use 75-4444444 as the employer identification number. Date the return July 31, 20X1. Mr. Fronke's phone number is 562-709-3654.

Analyze: Based on the entries that you have recorded, what is the balance of the *Employee Income Tax Payable* account at July 15?

Problem 11.4A
Objectives 11-6, 11-7

Computing and recording unemployment taxes; completing Form 940.

Certain transactions and procedures relating to federal and state unemployment taxes follow for Robin's Nest LLC, a retail store owned by Robin Roberts. The firm's address is 2007 Lovely Lane, Dallas, TX 75268-0967. The firm's phone number is 972-456-1200. The employer's federal and state identification numbers are 75-9462315 and 37-9462315, respectively. Carry out the procedures as instructed in each of the following steps.

INSTRUCTIONS

1. Compute the state unemployment insurance tax owed on the employees' wages for the quarter ended March 31, 20X1. This information will be shown on the employer's quarterly report to the state agency that collects SUTA tax. The employer has recorded the tax on each payroll date. Although the state charges a 5.4 percent unemployment tax rate, Robin's Nest LLC's rate is only 1.7 percent because of its experience rating. The employee earnings for the first quarter are shown below. All earnings are subject to SUTA tax.

Name of Employee	Total Earnings
Suzi Roma	$ 4,500
Jo Guyton	3,800
Gloria Bermudez	4,800
Anna Scott	5,600
Anita Thomas	3,500
Terri Wong	3,000
Total	$25,200

2. On April 30, 20X1, the firm issued a check to the state employment commission for the amount computed above. In general journal form, record the issuance of the check. Use journal page 82.

Analyze: Why is the business experience rating important with regard to the state unemployment tax rate?

Problem 11.5A
Objectives 11-6, 11-7

CONTINUING >>> Problem

This is a continuation of Problem 11.4A for Robin's Nest LLC; computing and recording unemployment taxes; completing Form 940.

1. Complete Form 940, the Employer's Annual Federal Unemployment Tax Return. Assume that all wages have been paid and that all quarterly payments have been submitted to the state as required. The payroll information for 20X1 appears below. The federal tax deposits were submitted as follows: a deposit of $151.20 on April 21, a deposit of $124.80 on July 22, and a deposit of $72.00 on October 21. Date the unemployment tax return January 28, 20X2. A check for the balance due as per line 14, Part 4, will be sent with Form 940.

Quarter Ended	Total Wages Paid	Wages Paid in Excess of $7,000	State Unemployment Tax Paid
Mar. 31	$ 25,200.00	–0–	$ 428.40
June 30	30,800.00	$ 10,000.00	353.60
Sept. 30	37,000.00	25,000.00	204.00
Dec. 31	49,000.00	42,000.00	119.00
Totals	$142,000.00	$77,000.00	$1,105.00

2. In general journal form, record issuance of a check on January 28, 20X2, for the balance of FUTA tax due for 20X1. Use journal page 15.

Analyze: What total debits were made to liability accounts for entries you recorded in Problem 11.4A and Problem 11.5A?

Problem 11.6A
Objective 11-8

Computing and recording workers' compensation insurance premiums.

The following information relates to Ponte Manufacturing Company's workers' compensation insurance premiums for 20X1. On January 15, 20X1, the company estimated its premium for workers' compensation insurance for the year on the basis of that data.

Work Classification	Amount of Estimated Wages	Insurance Rates
Office work	$ 64,000	$0.30/$100
Shop work	308,000	$6.00/$100

INSTRUCTIONS

1. Compute the estimated premiums.
2. Record in general journal form payment of the estimated premium on January 15, 20X1. Use 8 as the page number.
3. On January 4, 20X2, an audit of the firm's payroll records showed that it had actually paid wages of $69,960 to its office employees and wages of $315,320 to its shop employees. Compute the actual premium for the year and the balance due the insurance company or the credit due the firm.
4. Prepare the general journal entry on December 31, 20X1, to adjust the *Workers' Compensation Insurance Expense* account. Use 98 as the page number.

Analyze: If all wages were attributable to shop employees, what premium estimate would have been calculated and recorded on January 15, 20X1?

Problem Set B

Computing and recording employer's payroll tax expense.

The payroll register of Auto Detailers showed total employee earnings of $6,000 for the week ended April 8.

◀ **Problem 11.1B**
Objectives 11-2, 11-6

INSTRUCTIONS

1. Compute the employer's payroll taxes for the period. The tax rates are as follows:

Social security	6.2 percent
Medicare	1.45
FUTA	0.6
SUTA	5.4

2. Prepare a general journal entry to record the employer's payroll taxes for the period. Use journal page 62.

Analyze: If the SUTA tax rate had been 3.0 percent, what total employer payroll taxes would have been recorded?

Computing employer's social security tax, Medicare tax, and unemployment taxes.

◀ **Problem 11.2B**
Objectives 11-2, 11-3

A payroll summary for Today's Teen owned by Nikki Davis, for the quarter ending September 30, 20X1, appears below. The business made the following electronic deposits of payroll taxes:

a. August 15 for July taxes.
b. September 15 for August taxes.

Date Wages Paid		Total Earnings	Social Security Tax Withheld	Medicare Tax Withheld	Federal Income Tax Withheld
July	7	$ 2,000.00	$ 124.00	$ 29.00	$ 175.00
	14	2,000.00	124.00	29.00	175.00
	21	2,100.00	130.20	30.45	190.00
	28	1,980.00	122.76	28.71	160.00
		$ 8,080.00	$ 500.96	$117.16	$ 700.00
Aug.	4	$ 2,100.00	$ 130.20	$ 30.45	190.00
	11	2,400.00	148.80	34.80	210.00
	18	2,400.00	148.80	34.80	210.00
	25	2,600.00	161.20	37.70	230.00
		$ 9,500.00	$ 589.00	$137.75	$ 840.00
Sept.	1	$ 2,000.00	$ 124.00	$ 29.00	$ 175.00
	8	2,100.00	130.20	30.45	190.00
	15	2,100.00	130.20	30.45	190.00
	22	2,200.00	136.40	31.90	200.00
	29	1,900.00	117.80	27.55	160.00
		$10,300.00	$ 638.60	$149.35	$ 915.00
Totals		$27,880.00	$1,728.56	$404.26	$2,455.00

INSTRUCTIONS

1. Prepare the general journal entry on July 7, 20X1, to record the employer's payroll tax expense on the payroll ending that date. Use journal page 31. All earnings are subject to the following taxes:

Social security	6.2 percent
Medicare	1.45
FUTA	0.6
SUTA	2.2

2. Make the entries in general journal form to record deposit of the employee income tax withheld and the social security and Medicare taxes (both employees' withholding and employer's matching portion) on August 15 for July taxes and on September 15 for the August taxes.

Analyze: How much would a SUTA rate of 1.5 percent reduce the tax for the payroll of July 7?

Problem 11.3B
Objectives 11-4, 11-6

This is a continuation of Problem 11.2B for Today's Teen; recording payment of taxes and preparing employer's quarterly federal tax return.

1. On October 15, the firm made a deposit through EFTPS for the federal income tax withheld and the FICA tax (both employees' withholding and employer's matching portion). Based on your computations in Problem 11.2B, record the issuance of the check in general journal form. Use journal page 31.

2. Complete Form 941 in accordance with the discussions in this chapter and the instructions on the form. Use a 12.4 percent social security rate and a 2.9 percent Medicare rate in computations. Use the following address for the company: 12001 Pioneer Blvd., Artesia, CA 90650. The firm's phone number is 562-860-5451. Use 75-5555555 as the employer identification number. Date the return October 31, 20X1.

Analyze: What total taxes were deposited with the IRS for the quarter ended September 30, 20X1?

Problem 11.4B
Objectives 11-6, 11-7

Computing and recording unemployment taxes; completing Form 940.

Certain transactions and procedures relating to federal and state unemployment taxes are given below for Latest Greatest, a retail store owned by John Marion. The firm's address is 4560 LBJ Freeway, Dallas, TX 75232-6002. The firm's phone number is 972-456-1201. The employer's federal and state identification numbers are 75-9999999 and 37-6789015, respectively. Carry out the procedures as instructed in each step.

INSTRUCTIONS

1. Compute the state unemployment insurance tax owed for the quarter ended March 31, 20X1. This information will be shown on the employer's quarterly report to the state agency that collects SUTA tax. The employer has recorded the tax expense and liability on each payroll date. Although the state charges a 5.4 percent unemployment tax rate, Latest Greatest has received a favorable experience rating and therefore pays only a 2.3 percent state tax rate. The employee earnings for the first quarter are given below. All earnings are subject to SUTA tax.

Name of Employee	Total Earnings
Marty Morris	$ 4,500
Chris Cantori	3,600
Cailey Marie	3,600
Yvonne Martinez	4,200
Cney Caz	2,000
John Phan	2,400
Total	$20,300

2. On April 30, 20X1, the firm issued a check for the amount computed above. Record the transaction in general journal form. Use journal page 21.

Analyze: If Marty Morris made the same amount for the quarter ended June 30, 20X1, how much of his earnings would be subject to the federal unemployment tax?

This is a continuation of Problem 11.4B for Latest Greatest; computing and recording unemployment taxes; completing Form 940.

◀ **Problem 11.5B**
Objectives 11-6, 11-7

CONTINUING >>>
Problem

1. Complete Form 940, the Employer's Annual Federal Unemployment Tax Return. Assume that all wages have been paid and that all quarterly payments have been submitted to the state as required. The payroll information for 20X1 appears below. The firm's FUTA tax liability by quarter follows: first quarter, $121.80; second quarter, $106.50; third quarter, $87.00; and fourth quarter, $24.00. The firm made the correct 1st and 2nd quarter FUTA deposits. Date the unemployment tax return January 27, 20X2. A check for the balance due will be sent with Form 940.

Quarter Ended	Total Wages Paid	Wages Paid in Excess of $7,000	State Unemployment Tax Paid
Mar. 31	$ 20,300.00	–0–	$ 466.90
June 30	21,250.00	$ 3,500.00	408.25
Sept. 30	24,500.00	10,000.00	333.50
Dec. 31	28,000.00	24,000.00	92.00
Totals	$ 94,050.00	$ 37,500.00	$1,300.65

2. On January 27, 20X2, the firm paid the amount shown on line 14, Part 4 of Form 940. In general journal form, record the payment. Use journal page 48.

Analyze: What is the balance of the *Federal Unemployment Tax Payable* account after paying the FUTA amount due on January 27, 20X2?

Computing and recording premiums on workers' compensation insurance.

◀ **Problem 11.6B**
Objective 11-8

The following information is for Union Express Delivery Service's workers' compensation insurance premiums. On January 15, 20X1, the company estimated its premium for workers' compensation insurance for the year on the basis of the following data:

Work Classification	Amount of Estimated Wages	Insurance Rates
Office work	$ 50,000	$0.50/$100
Delivery work	308,000	$6.00/$100

INSTRUCTIONS

1. Use the information to compute the estimated premium for the year.
2. A check was issued to pay the estimated premium on January 17, 20X1. Record the transaction in general journal form. Use 7 as the page number.
3. On January 19, 20X2, an audit of the firm's payroll records showed that it had actually paid wages of $52,970 to its office employees and wages of $316,240 to its delivery employees. Compute the actual premium for the year and the balance due the insurance company or the credit due the firm.
4. Give the general journal entry to adjust the *Workers' Compensation Insurance Expense* account. Date the entry December 31, 20X1. Use 88 as the page number.

Analyze: What is the balance of the *Workers' Compensation Insurance Expense* account at December 31, 20X1, after all journal entries have been posted?

Critical Thinking Problem 11.1

Determining Employee Status

In each of the following independent situations, decide whether the business organization should treat the person being paid as an employee and should withhold social security, Medicare, and employee income taxes from the payment made.

1. George Jacobs owns and operates a cigar shop as a sole proprietor. Jacobs withdraws $2,000 a week from the cigar shop.

2. Alicia Ankar is a court reporter. She has an office at the Metro Court Reporting Center but pays no rent. The manager of the center receives requests from attorneys for court reporters to take depositions at legal hearings. The manager then chooses a court reporter who best meets the needs of the client and contacts the court reporter chosen. The court reporter has the right to refuse to take on the job, and the court reporter controls his or her working hours and days. Clients make payments to the center, which deducts a 25 percent fee for providing facilities and rendering services to support the court reporter. The balance is paid to the court reporter. During the current month, the center collected fees of $40,000 for Ankar, deducted $10,000 for the center's fee, and remitted the remainder to Ankar.

3. Ken, a registered nurse, has retired from full-time work. However, because of his experience and special skills, on each Monday, Wednesday, and Thursday he assists Dr. Grace Ann, a dermatologist. Ken is paid an hourly fee by Dr. Ann. During the current week, his hourly fees totaled $600.

4. After working several years as an editor for a trade magazine, Kate quit her job to stay at home with her two small children. Later, the magazine asked her to work in her home performing editorial work as needed. Kate is paid an hourly fee for the work she performs. In some cases, she goes to the company's offices to pick up or return a manuscript. In other cases, the firm sends a manuscript to her, or she returns one by e-mail. During the current month, Kate's hourly earnings totaled $1,200.

5. ILC carries on very little business activity. It merely holds land and certain assets. The board of directors has concluded that it needs no employees. It has decided instead to pay David John, one of the shareholders, a consulting fee of $24,000 per year to serve as president, secretary, and treasurer and to manage all the affairs of the company. John spends an average of one hour per week on the corporation's business affairs. However, his fee is fixed regardless of how few or how many hours he works.

Analyze: What characteristics do the persons you identified as "employees" have in common?

Critical Thinking Problem 11.2

Comparing Employees and Independent Contractors

The *Valley Voice* is a local newspaper that is published Monday through Friday. It sells 90,000 copies daily. The paper is currently in a profit squeeze, and the publisher, Tom Turkey, is looking for ways to reduce expenses.

A review of current distribution procedures reveals that the *Valley Voice* employs 100 truck drivers to drop off bundles of newspapers to 1,300 teenagers who deliver papers to individual homes. The drivers are paid an hourly wage while the teenagers receive 4 cents for each paper they deliver.

Turkey is considering an alternative method of distributing the papers, which he says has worked in other cities the size of Flower Mound (where the *Valley Voice* is published). Under the new system, the newspaper would retain 20 truck drivers to transport papers to five distribution centers around the city. The distribution centers are operated by independent contractors who would be responsible for making their own arrangements to deliver papers to subscribers' homes. The 20 drivers retained by the *Valley Voice* would receive the same hourly rate as they currently earn, and the independent contractors would receive 20 cents for each paper delivered.

1. What payroll information does Turkey need in order to make a decision about adopting the alternative distribution method?

2. Assume the following information:
   a. The average driver earns $42,000 per year.
   b. Average employee income tax withholding is 15 percent.
   c. The social security tax is 6.2 percent of the first $132,900 of earnings.
   d. The Medicare tax is 1.45 percent of all earnings.
   e. The state unemployment tax is 5 percent, and the federal unemployment tax is 0.6 percent, of the first $7,000 of earnings.
   f. Workers' compensation insurance is 70 cents per $100 of wages.
   g. The paper pays $300 per month for health insurance for each driver and contributes $250 per month to each driver's pension plan.
   h. The paper has liability insurance coverage for all teenage carriers that costs $100,000 per year.

   Prepare a schedule showing the costs of distributing the newspapers under the current system and the proposed new system. Based on your analysis, which system would you recommend to Turkey?

3. What other factors, monetary and nonmonetary, might influence your decision?

BUSINESS CONNECTIONS

Payroll

Managerial FOCUS

1. Carolina Customs recently discovered that a payroll clerk had issued checks to nonexistent employees for several years and cashed the checks himself. The company does not have any internal control procedures for its payroll operations. What specific controls might have led to the discovery of this fraud more quickly or discouraged the payroll clerk from even attempting the fraud?

2. Johnson Company has 24 employees. Some employees work in the office, others in the warehouse, and still others in the retail store. In the company's records, all employees are simply referred to as "general employees." Explain to management why this is not an acceptable practice.

3. Why should management be concerned about the accuracy and promptness of payroll tax deposits and payroll tax returns?

4. What is the significance to management of the experience rating system used to determine the employer's tax under the state unemployment insurance laws?

Ghost Employee

Internal Control and FRAUD PREVENTION

Nicky Norton owns a boutique dress shop that has been very successful. He employs 3 sales associates who get paid $10 per hour for a 40-hour week. He decides to open up another dress shop on the other side of town. He hires three more sales associates with the same pay arrangements. After three months, Norton notices the new store is not making the same profit as the other stores. His sales have doubled and his expenses are the same proportion except for wages. He knows that each sales associate should receive $1,720 each month, yet his total wages expense for the month is $12,040. He worries that he is not paying close enough attention to the old store. What is his problem? Should he discuss this problem with all the sales associates?

Employee Data

Financial Statement ANALYSIS

Home Depot

The Home Depot, Inc., reported the following data in its Form 10-K filing *(for the fiscal year ended February 3, 2019):*

Number of employees at February 3, 2019	413,000
Contributions to employees' retirement plans during the year ended February 3, 2019	$211 million

Analyze: Assume all employees receive contributions to their retirement plan. What was the average retirement plan contribution made by The Home Depot for full-time employees?

TEAMWORK

Determining Information

Wages and payroll tax expense are the largest costs that a company incurs. At times, a company has a problem paying wages and cash deposits for payroll taxes. Your company has a cash flow problem. In a group of four employees, brainstorm ways to cut the costs of wages and payroll taxes.

Answers to Comprehensive Self Review

1. Form W-3 is sent to the Social Security Administration. It reports the total social security wages; total Medicare wages; total social security and Medicare taxes withheld; total wages, tips, and other compensation; total employee income tax withheld; and other information.
2. Smaller
3. A credit, with limits, is allowed against the federal tax for unemployment tax charged by the state.
4. By the 15th day of the following month.
5. **b.** Amount of taxes reported in the lookback period
   d. Amount of taxes currently owed

Accruals, Deferrals, and the Worksheet

Chapter 12

McGraw-Hill Education/Jill Braaten, photographer

www.starbucks.com

The mission of Starbucks is to inspire and nurture the human spirit—one person, one cup, and one neighborhood at a time. Starting out as a single storefront opened in 1971 in Seattle, Washington, it has expanded to 27,339 stores across 75 countries since its founding. In its fiscal year ended October 1, 2017, the number of Starbucks stores increased by 2,254. At October 1, 2017, Starbucks employed approximately 277,000 people worldwide.

From its start as a roaster and retailer of coffee, tea, and spices, Starbucks' product offerings have expanded to include several different blends of coffee, handcrafted beverages, coffee- and tea-brewing equipment, mugs, packaged edibles, books, and more. Starbucks' beverages and merchandise are also sold at other retail establishments, such as grocery stores.

Starbucks offers a staple menu of coffee and tea beverages year round, as well as a seasonal menu that it continually updates, in addition to developing new flavors and products to offer variety to existing customers and to appeal to new customers. For fiscal year 2017, Starbucks reported net revenues of $22.4 billion, an increase of 5 percent over the previous fiscal year.

With increasing sales and ever-expanding distribution channels, managing inventory levels and purchasing requirements is crucial. Starbucks must order merchandise with enough lead time to have it in stores ahead of demand. At the same time, it must closely monitor in-store inventory levels so as to not have excess inventory and still have the ability to stock new incoming products.

thinking critically
What types of inventory issues do you think Starbucks must address at the end of each year?

LEARNING OBJECTIVES

12-1 Determine the adjustment for merchandise inventory, and enter the adjustment on the worksheet.

12-2 Compute adjustments for accrued and prepaid expense items, and enter the adjustments on the worksheet.

12-3 Compute adjustments for accrued and deferred income items, and enter the adjustments on the worksheet.

12-4 Complete a 10-column worksheet.

12-5 Define the accounting terms new to this chapter.

NEW TERMS

accrual basis
accrued expenses
accrued income
deferred expenses
deferred income
inventory sheet
net income line
property, plant, and equipment
unearned income
updated account balances

Section 1

SECTION OBJECTIVES	TERMS TO LEARN
>> 12-1 Determine the adjustment for merchandise inventory, and enter the adjustment on the worksheet. **WHY IT'S IMPORTANT** The change in merchandise inventory affects the financial statements. **>> 12-2** Compute adjustments for accrued and prepaid expense items, and enter the adjustments on the worksheet. **WHY IT'S IMPORTANT** Each expense item needs to be assigned to the accounting period in which it helped to earn revenue. **>> 12-3** Compute adjustments for accrued and deferred income items, and enter the adjustments on the worksheet. **WHY IT'S IMPORTANT** The accrual basis of accounting states that income is recognized in the period it is earned.	accrual basis accrued expenses accrued income deferred expenses deferred income inventory sheet property, plant, and equipment unearned income

Calculating and Recording Adjustments

In Chapter 5, you learned how to make adjustments so that all revenue and expenses that apply to a fiscal period appear on the income statement for that period. In this chapter, you will learn more about adjustments and how they affect Whiteside Antiques, a retail merchandising business owned by Bill Whiteside.

The Accrual Basis of Accounting

Financial statements usually are prepared using the **accrual basis** of accounting because it most nearly attains the goal of matching expenses and revenue in an accounting period.

- *Revenue is recognized when earned, not necessarily when the cash is received.* Revenue is recognized when the sale is complete. A sale is complete when title to the goods passes to the customer or when the service is provided. For sales on account, revenue is recognized when the sale occurs even though the cash is not collected immediately.

- *Expenses are recognized when incurred or used, not necessarily when cash is paid.* Each expense is assigned to the accounting period in which it helped to earn revenue for the business, even if cash is not paid at that time. This is often referred to as *matching revenues and expenses*.

Sometimes cash changes hands before the revenue or expense is recognized. For example, insurance premiums are normally paid in advance, and the coverage extends over several accounting periods. When this occurs, the accountant debits the Prepaid Insurance account. The Prepaid Insurance account is referred to as a prepaid, or deferred, expense.

In other cases, cash changes hands after the revenue or expense has been recognized. For example, employees might work during December but be paid in January of the following year. As you will see below, the accountant credits Salaries Payable to record the amount of salaries earned but net yet paid at the end of the accounting period. Salary Payable is referred to as an accrued liability.

Because of these timing differences, adjustments are made to ensure that revenue and expenses are recognized in the appropriate period.

Using the Worksheet to Record Adjustments

The worksheet is used to assemble data about adjustments and to organize the information for the financial statements. The worksheet for Whiteside Antiques will be prepared in the same manner as covered in Chapter 5. Figure 12.1 shows the first two sections of the worksheet for Whiteside Antiques. Let's review how to prepare the worksheet:

- Enter the trial balance in the Trial Balance section. Total the columns. Be sure that total debits equal total credits.
- Enter the adjustments in the Adjustments section. Use the same letter to identify the debit part and the credit part of each adjustment. Total the columns. Be sure that total debits equal total credits.
- For each account, combine the amounts in the Trial Balance section and the Adjustments section. Enter the results in the Adjusted Trial Balance section, total the columns, and make sure that total debits equal total credits.
- Extend account balances to the Income Statement and Balance Sheet sections and complete the worksheet.

Adjustment for Merchandise Inventory

Merchandise inventory consists of the goods that a business has on hand for sale to customers. An asset account called merchandise inventory is maintained in the general ledger. During the accounting period, all purchases of merchandise are debited to the **Purchases** account. All sales of merchandise are credited to the revenue account **Sales.**

Notice that no entries are made directly to the **Merchandise Inventory** account during the accounting period. Consequently, when the trial balance is prepared at the end of the period, the **Merchandise Inventory** account still shows the *beginning* inventory for the period.

At the end of each period, a business determines the *ending* balance of the **Merchandise Inventory** account. The first step in determining the ending inventory is to count the number of units of each type of item on hand. As the merchandise is counted, the quantity on hand is entered on an inventory sheet. The **inventory sheet** lists the quantity of each type of goods a firm has in stock. This process is called a physical inventory. For each item, the quantity is multiplied by the unit cost to find the totals per item. The totals for all items are added to compute the total cost of merchandise inventory.

The trial balance for Whiteside Antiques shows **Merchandise Inventory** of $52,000. Based on a count taken on December 31, merchandise inventory at the end of the year actually totaled $47,000. Whiteside Antiques needs to adjust the **Merchandise Inventory** account to reflect the balance at the end of the year.

The adjustment is made in two steps, using the accounts **Merchandise Inventory** and **Income Summary.**

1. The beginning inventory ($52,000) is taken off the books by transferring the account balance to the **Income Summary** account. This entry is labeled **(a)** on the worksheet in Figure 12.1 and is illustrated in T-account form below.

Merchandise Inventory		Income Summary	
Bal. 52,000	Adj. 52,000	Adj. 52,000	

   ————(a)————

2. The ending inventory ($47,000) is placed on the books by debiting **Merchandise Inventory** and crediting **Income Summary.** This entry is labeled **(b)** on the worksheet in Figure 12.1.

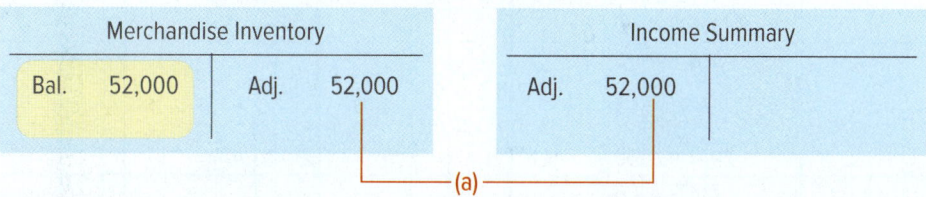

> **important!**
>
> **Recognize**
> The word "recognize" means to record in the accounting records.

>> **12-1 OBJECTIVE**
> Determine the adjustment for merchandise inventory, and enter the adjustment on the worksheet.

> **recall**
>
> **Income Summary**
> The *Income Summary* account is a temporary owner's equity account used in the closing process.

FIGURE 12.1 10-Column Worksheet—Partial

Whiteside Antiques
Worksheet
Year Ended December 31, 20X1

ACCOUNT NAME	TRIAL BALANCE DEBIT	TRIAL BALANCE CREDIT	ADJUSTMENTS DEBIT		ADJUSTMENTS CREDIT	
1. Cash	13 136 00					
2. Petty Cash Fund	100 00					
3. Notes Receivable	1 200 00					
4. Accounts Receivable	32 000 00					
5. Allowance for Doubtful Accounts		250 00			(c)	800 00
6. Interest Receivable			(m)	30 00		
7. Merchandise Inventory	52 000 00		(b)	47 000 00	(a)	52 000 00
8. Prepaid Insurance	7 350 00				(k)	2 450 00
9. Prepaid Interest	225 00				(l)	150 00
10. Supplies	6 300 00				(j)	4 975 00
11. Store Equipment	30 000 00					
12. Accumulated Depreciation—Store Equipment					(d)	2 400 00
13. Office Equipment	5 000 00					
14. Accumulated Depreciation—Office Equipment					(e)	700 00
15. Notes Payable—Trade		2 000 00				
16. Notes Payable—Bank		9 000 00				
17. Accounts Payable		24 129 00				
18. Interest Payable					(i)	20 00
19. Social Security Tax Payable		1 084 00			(g)	74 40
20. Medicare Tax Payable		250 00			(g)	17 40
21. Employee Income Taxes Payable		990 00				
22. Federal Unemployment Tax Payable					(h)	7 20
23. State Unemployment Tax Payable					(h)	64 80
24. Salaries Payable					(f)	1 200 00
25. Sales Tax Payable		7 200 00				
26. Bill Whiteside, Capital		61 221 00				
27. Bill Whiteside, Drawing	27 600 00					
28. Income Summary			(a)	52 000 00	(b)	47 000 00
29. Sales		561 650 00				
30. Sales Returns and Allowances	12 500 00					
31. Interest Income		136 00			(m)	30 00
32. Miscellaneous Income		366 00				
33. Purchases	321 500 00					
34. Freight In	9 800 00					
35. Purchases Returns and Allowances		3 050 00				
36. Purchases Discounts		3 130 00				
37. Salaries Expense—Sales	78 490 00		(f)	1 200 00		
38. Advertising Expense	7 425 00					
39. Cash Short or Over	125 00					
40. Supplies Expense			(j)	4 975 00		

FIGURE 12.1 (continued)

	ACCOUNT NAME	TRIAL BALANCE		ADJUSTMENTS	
		DEBIT	CREDIT	DEBIT	CREDIT
41	Depreciation Expense—Store Equipment			(d) 2 400 00	
42	Rent Expense	27 600 00			
43	Salaries Expense—Office	26 500 00			
44	Insurance Expense			(k) 2 450 00	
45	Payroll Taxes Expense	7 205 00		(g) 91 80	
46				(h) 72 00	
47	Telephone Expense	1 875 00			
48	Uncollectible Accounts Expense			(c) 800 00	
49	Utilities Expense	5 925 00			
50	Depreciation Expense—Office Equipment			(e) 700 00	
51	Interest Expense	600 00		(i) 20 00	
52				(l) 150 00	
53	Totals	674 456 00	674 456 00	111 888 80	111 888 80

The effect of this adjustment is to remove the beginning merchandise inventory balance and replace it with the ending merchandise inventory balance. Merchandise inventory is adjusted in two steps on the worksheet because both the beginning and the ending inventory figures appear on the income statement, which is prepared directly from the worksheet.

The merchandise inventory adjustment is not necessary if the perpetual inventory system is used.

> Amazon.com, Inc. reported inventories of $16 billion in its December 31, 2017, balance sheet.

Adjustment for Loss from Uncollectible Accounts

Credit sales are made with the expectation that the customers will pay the amount due later. Sometimes the account receivable is never collected. Losses from uncollectible accounts are classified as operating expenses.

Under accrual accounting, the expense for uncollectible accounts is recorded in the same period as the related sale. The expense is estimated because the actual amount of uncollectible accounts is not known until later periods. To match the expense for uncollectible accounts with the sales revenue for the same period, the estimated expense is debited to an account named **Uncollectible Accounts Expense.**

Several methods exist for estimating the expense for uncollectible accounts. Whiteside Antiques uses the *percentage of net credit sales* method. The rate used is based on the company's past experience with uncollectible accounts and management's assessment of current business conditions. Whiteside Antiques estimates that four-fifths of 1 percent (0.80 percent) of net credit sales will be uncollectible. Net credit sales for the year were $100,000. The estimated expense for uncollectible accounts is $800 ($100,000 × 0.0080).

The entry to record the expense for uncollectible accounts includes a credit to a contra asset account, **Allowance for Doubtful Accounts.** This account appears on the balance sheet as follows:

Accounts Receivable	$32,000
Allowance for Doubtful Accounts ($800 + $250)	1,050
Net Accounts Receivable	$30,950

>> **12-2 OBJECTIVE**
Compute adjustments for accrued and prepaid expense items, and enter the adjustments on the worksheet.

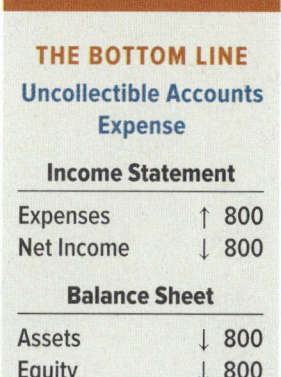

Adjustment (c) appears on the worksheet in Figure 12.1 for the expense for uncollectible accounts.

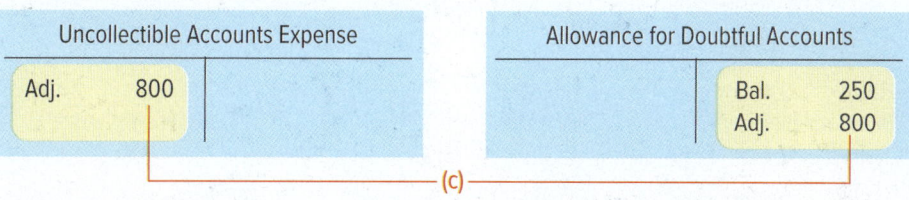

When a specific account becomes uncollectible, it is written off:

- The entry is a debit to **Allowance for Doubtful Accounts** and a credit to **Accounts Receivable.**
- The customer's account in the accounts receivable subsidiary ledger is also reduced.

Uncollectible Accounts Expense is not affected by the write-off of individual accounts identified as uncollectible. It is used only when the end-of-period adjustment is recorded.

Notice that net income is decreased at the end of the period when the adjustment for *estimated* expense for uncollectible accounts is made. When a specific customer account is written off, net income is *not* affected. The write-off of a specific account affects only the balance sheet accounts *Accounts Receivable* (asset) and *Allowance for Doubtful Accounts* (contra asset).

The balance of *Allowance for Doubtful Accounts* is reduced throughout the year as customer accounts are written off. Notice that *Allowance for Doubtful Accounts* already has a credit balance of $250 in the Trial Balance section of the worksheet. When the estimate of uncollectible accounts expense is based on sales, any remaining balance from previous periods is not considered when recording the adjustment.

> Microsoft Corporation reported an allowance for doubtful accounts of $377 million on total accounts receivable of approximately $26.9 billion in its June 30, 2018, balance sheet.

Adjustments for Depreciation

Most businesses have long-term assets that are used in the operation of the business. These are often referred to as **property, plant, and equipment.** Property, plant, and equipment includes buildings, trucks, automobiles, machinery, furniture, fixtures, office equipment, and land.

Property, plant, and equipment costs are not charged to expense accounts when purchased. Instead, the cost of a long-term asset is allocated over the asset's expected useful life by depreciation. This process involves the gradual transfer of acquisition cost to expense. This concept was first introduced in Chapter 5. There is one exception. Land is not depreciated.

There are many ways to calculate depreciation. Whiteside Antiques uses the straight-line method, so an equal amount of depreciation is taken in each year of the asset's useful life. The formula for straight-line depreciation is:

$$\frac{\text{Cost} - \text{Salvage value}}{\text{Estimated useful life}} = \text{Depreciation}$$

Salvage value is an estimate of the amount that could be obtained from the sale or disposition of an asset at the end of its useful life. Cost minus salvage value is called the *depreciable base*.

Depreciation of Store Equipment The trial balance shows that Whiteside Antiques has $30,000 of store equipment with a 10-year useful life. The estimated salvage value is $6,000. The amount of annual depreciation expense using the straight-line method is $2,400, calculated as follows:

Cost of store equipment	$30,000
Salvage value	(6,000)
Depreciable base	$24,000
Estimated useful life	10 years

$$\frac{\$30{,}000 - \$6{,}000}{10 \text{ years}} = \$2{,}400 \text{ per year}$$

The annual depreciation expense is $2,400. Adjustment **(d)** appears on the worksheet in Figure 12.1 for the depreciation expense for store equipment.

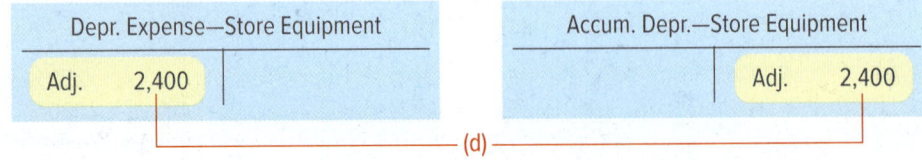

Depreciation of Office Equipment Whiteside Antiques reports $5,000 of office equipment on the trial balance. What is the amount of annual depreciation expense using the straight-line method if estimated salvage value is $800 and estimated life is six years?

Cost of office equipment	$5,000
Salvage value	(800)
Depreciable base	$4,200
Estimated useful life	6 years

$$\frac{\$5{,}000 - \$800}{6 \text{ years}} = \$700 \text{ per year}$$

Annual depreciation expense is $700. Adjustment **(e)** appears on the worksheet in Figure 12.1 for depreciation expense for office equipment.

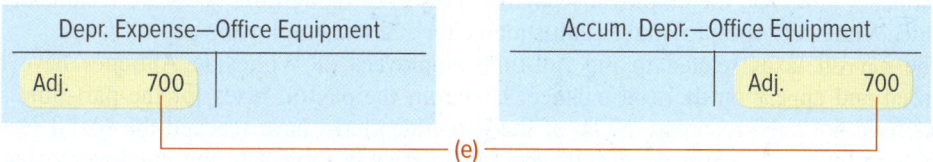

As discussed in Chapter 5, **Accumulated Depreciation** is a contra asset account. It has a normal credit balance, which is opposite the normal balance of an asset account.

Most companies do not purchase items of property, plant, or equipment at the beginning of the year, but as needed. In this case, a partial year of depreciation must be calculated and recorded.

For example, assume a company purchased store equipment for $30,000 on October 1, 20X1. The store equipment has a useful life of 10 years and an estimated salvage value of $6,000. The depreciation expense for the year ended December 31, 20X1, for the store equipment is $600, calculated as follows.

Cost of store equipment	$30,000
Salvage value	(6,000)
Depreciable base	$24,000
Divided by useful life, in months (10 years × 12)	120
Depreciation per month	$ 200
Multiplied by months used in 20X1 (Oct., Nov., Dec.)	3
Depreciation for 20X1	$ 600

> **important!**
>
> **Depreciation**
> To calculate monthly straight-line depreciation, divide the depreciable base (cost less salvage value) by the number of months in the useful life.

Adjustments for Accrued Expenses

Many expense items are paid for, recorded, and used in the same accounting period. However, some expense items are paid for and recorded in one period but used in a later period. Other expense items are used in one period and paid for in a later period. In these situations, adjustments are made so that the financial statements show all expenses in the appropriate period.

Accrued expenses are expenses that relate to (are used in) the current period but have not yet been paid and do not yet appear in the accounting records. Whiteside Antiques makes adjustments for three types of accrued expenses:

- accrued salaries
- accrued payroll taxes
- accrued interest on notes payable

Because accrued expenses involve amounts that must be paid in the future, the adjustment for each item is a debit to an expense account and a credit to a liability account.

Accrued Salaries At Whiteside Antiques, all full-time sales and office employees are paid semimonthly—on the 15th and the last day of the month. The trial balance in Figure 12.1 shows the correct salaries expense for the full-time employees for the year. From December 28 to January 3, the firm hired several part-time sales clerks for the year-end sale. Through December 31, 20X1, these employees earned $1,200. The part-time salaries expense has not yet been recorded because the employees will not be paid until January 3, 20X2. An adjustment is made to record the amount owed, but not yet paid, as of the end of December.

Adjustment **(f)** appears on the worksheet in Figure 12.1 for accrued salaries.

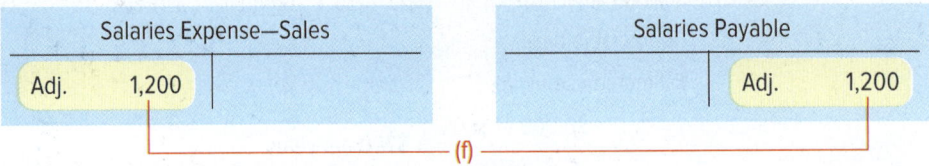

> **important!**
>
> **The Matching Principle**
> Adjustments for accrued expenses match the expense to the period in which the expense took place.

Accrued Payroll Taxes Payroll taxes are not legally owed until the salaries are paid. Businesses that want to match revenue and expenses in the appropriate period make adjustments to accrue the employer's payroll taxes even though the taxes are technically not yet due. Whiteside Antiques makes adjustments for accrued employer's payroll taxes.

The payroll taxes related to the full-time employees of Whiteside Antiques have been recorded and appear on the trial balance. However, the payroll taxes for the part-time sales clerks have not been recorded. None of the part-time clerks have reached the social security wage base limit. The entire $1,200 of accrued salaries is subject to the employer's share of social security and Medicare taxes. The accrued employer's payroll taxes are:

Social security tax	$1,200 × 0.0620 =	$74.40
Medicare tax	$1,200 × 0.0145 =	17.40
Total accrued payroll taxes		$91.80

Adjustment **(g)** appears on the worksheet in Figure 12.1 for accrued payroll taxes.

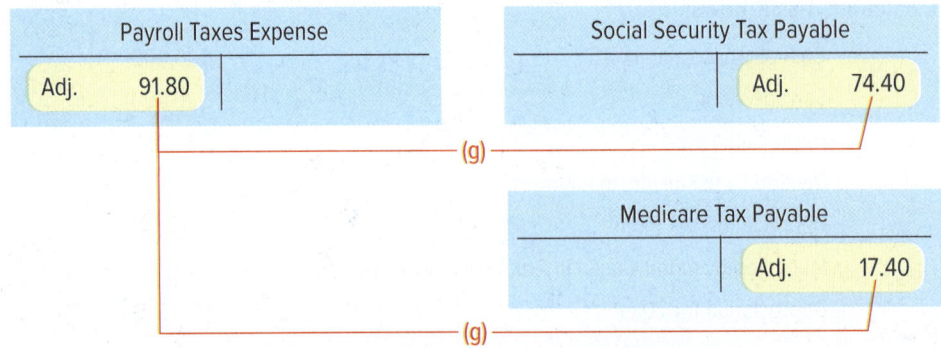

The entire $1,200 of accrued salaries is also subject to unemployment taxes. The unemployment tax rates for Whiteside Antiques are 0.6 percent for federal and 5.4 percent for state.

Federal unemployment tax	$1,200 × 0.006 =	$ 7.20
State unemployment tax	$1,200 × 0.054 =	64.80
Total accrued taxes		$72.00

Adjustment **(h)** appears on the worksheet in Figure 12.1 for accrued unemployment taxes.

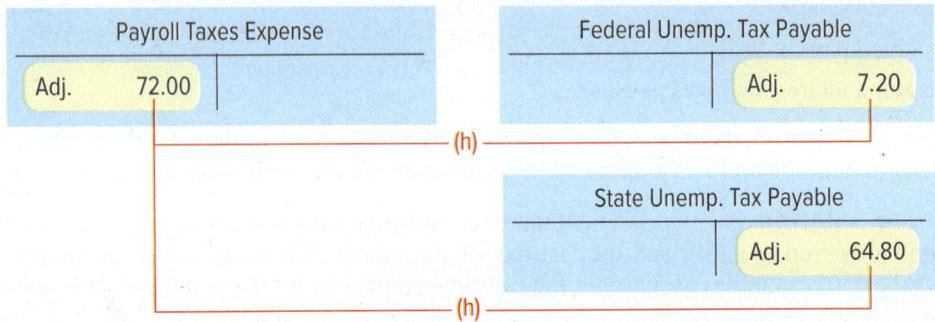

Accrued Interest on Notes Payable On December 1, 20X1, Whiteside Antiques issued a two-month note for $2,000, with annual interest of 12 percent. The note was recorded in the *Notes Payable—Trade* account. Whiteside Antiques will pay the interest when the note matures on February 1, 20X2. However, the interest expense is incurred day by day and should be allocated to each fiscal period involved in order to obtain a complete and accurate picture of expenses. The accrued interest amount is determined by using the interest formula Principal × Rate × Time.

$$\text{Principal} \times \text{Rate} \times \text{Time}$$
$$\$2{,}000 \times 0.12 \times 1/12 = \$20$$

The fraction 1/12 represents one month, which is 1/12 of a year.

Adjustment **(i)** appears on the worksheet in Figure 12.1 for the accrued interest expense.

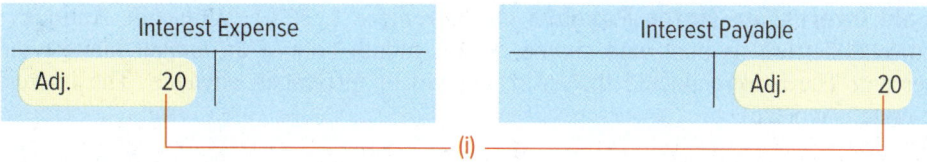

Other Accrued Expenses Most businesses pay property taxes to state and local governments. They accrue these taxes at the end of the accounting period. Adjustments might also be necessary for commissions, professional services, and many other accrued expenses.

> In its December 31, 2017, balance sheet, JetBlue Airways Corporation reported the following current liabilities (all in millions of dollars): Accounts payable, $378; Air traffic liability, $1,215; Accrued salaries, wages, and benefits, $313; Other accrued liabilities, $293; and Current maturities of long-term debt and capital leases, $196.

Adjustments for Prepaid Expenses

Prepaid expenses, or **deferred expenses,** are expenses that are paid for and recorded before they are used. Often a portion of a prepaid item remains unused at the end of the period; it is applicable to future periods. When paid for, these items are recorded as assets. At the end of the period, an adjustment is made to recognize as an expense the portion used during the period. Whiteside Antiques makes adjustments for three types of prepaid expenses:

- prepaid supplies
- prepaid insurance
- prepaid interest on notes payable

The adjusting entries for supplies used and insurance expired were introduced in Chapter 5. The adjusting entry for prepaid interest on notes payable is new to this chapter.

Supplies Used When supplies are purchased, they are debited to the asset account *Supplies.* On the trial balance in Figure 12.1, *Supplies* has a balance of $6,300. A physical count on December 31 showed $1,325 of supplies on hand. This means that $4,975 ($6,300 − $1,325) of supplies were used during the year. An adjustment is made to charge the cost of supplies used to the current year's operations and to reflect the value of the supplies on hand.

Adjustment **(j)** appears on the worksheet in Figure 12.1 for supplies expense.

Supplies Expense		Supplies	
Adj. 4,975		Bal. 6,300	Adj. 4,975

(j)

Expired Insurance On January 2, 20X1, Whiteside Antiques wrote a check for $7,350 for a three-year insurance policy. The asset account **Prepaid Insurance** was debited for $7,350. On December 31, 20X1, one year of insurance had expired. An adjustment for $2,450 ($7,350 × 1/3) was made to charge the cost of the expired insurance to operations and to decrease **Prepaid Insurance** to reflect the prepaid insurance premium that remains.

Adjustment **(k)** appears on the worksheet in Figure 12.1 for the insurance.

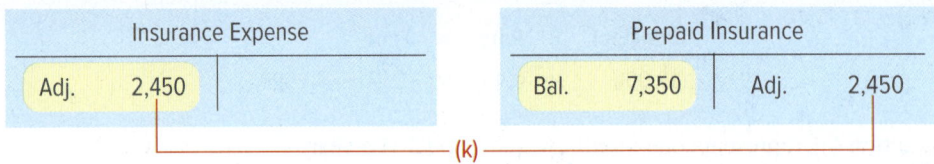

Prepaid Interest on Notes Payable On November 1, 20X1, Whiteside Antiques borrowed $9,000 from its bank and signed a three-month note at an annual interest rate of 10 percent. The bank deducted the entire amount of interest in advance. The interest for three months is $225.

$$\text{Principal} \times \text{Rate} \times \text{Time}$$
$$\$9,000 \times 0.10 \times 3/12 = \$225$$

important!

Some assets and liabilities always require adjustments Although prepaid expenses are usually charged to an asset account when they are paid, some businesses charge most prepayments to expense. In either case, at the time financial statements are prepared, the accounts must be adjusted to show the correct expense and prepayment.

Whiteside Antiques received $8,775 ($9,000 − $225). The transaction was recorded as a debit to **Cash** for $8,775, a debit to **Prepaid Interest** for $225, and a credit to **Notes Payable—Bank** for $9,000.

On December 31, two months of prepaid interest ($225 × 2/3 = $150) had been incurred and needed to be recorded as an expense. The adjustment consists of a debit to **Interest Expense** and a credit to **Prepaid Interest**.

Adjustment **(l)** appears on the worksheet in Figure 12.1 for the interest expense.

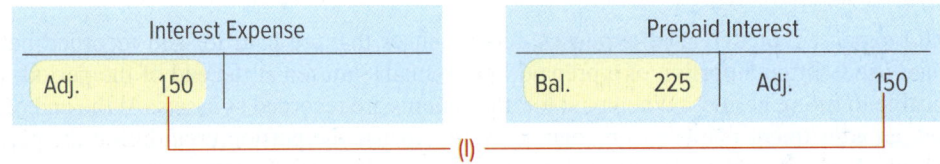

Other Prepaid Expenses Other common prepaid expenses are prepaid rent, prepaid advertising, and prepaid taxes. When paid, the amounts are debited to the asset accounts **Prepaid Rent, Prepaid Advertising,** and **Prepaid Taxes.** At the end of each period, an adjustment is made to transfer the portion used from the asset account to an expense account. For example, the adjustment for expired rent would be a debit to **Rent Expense** and a credit to **Prepaid Rent.**

Alternative Method Some businesses use a different method for prepaid expenses. At the time cash is paid, they debit an expense account (not an asset account). At the end of each period, they make an adjustment to transfer the portion that is not used from the expense account to an asset account.

Suppose that Whiteside used this alternative method when purchasing the three-year insurance policy. On January 1, 20X1, the transaction would have been recorded as a debit to **Insurance Expense** for $7,350 and a credit to **Cash** for $7,350. On December 31, 20X1, after the insurance coverage for one year had expired, coverage for two years remained. The adjustment would be recorded as a debit to **Prepaid Insurance** for $4,900 ($7,350 × 2/3) and a credit to **Insurance Expense** for $4,900.

Identical amounts appear on the financial statements at the end of each fiscal period, no matter which method is used to handle prepaid expenses.

Adjustments for Accrued Income

Accrued income is income that has been earned but not yet received and recorded. On December 31, 20X1, Whiteside Antiques had accrued interest on notes receivable.

Accrued Interest on Notes Receivable Interest-bearing notes receivable are recorded at face value and are carried in the accounting records at this value until they are collected. The interest income is recorded when it is received, which is normally when the note matures. However, interest income is earned day by day. At the end of the period, an adjustment is made to recognize interest income earned but not yet received or recorded.

On November 1, 20X1, Whiteside Antiques accepted a four-month, 15 percent note for $1,200 from a customer. The note and interest are due on March 1, 20X2. As of December 31, 20X1, interest income for two months (November and December) was earned but not received. The amount of earned interest income is $30.

$$\text{Principal} \times \text{Rate} \times \text{Time}$$
$$\$1{,}200 \times 0.15 \times 2/12 = \$30$$

Adjustment **(m)** appears on the worksheet in Figure 12.1 for the interest income. To record the interest income of $30 earned, but not yet received, an adjustment debiting the asset account *Interest Receivable* and crediting a revenue account called *Interest Income* is made.

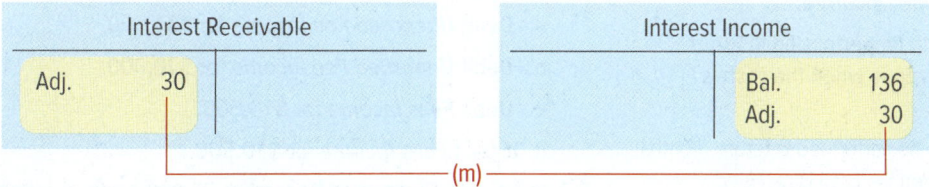

Adjustments for Unearned Income

Unearned income, or **deferred income,** exists when cash is received before income is earned. Under the accrual basis of accounting, only income that has been earned appears on the income statement. Whiteside Antiques has no unearned income. The following is an example of unearned income for another business.

Unearned Subscription Income for a Publisher Magazine publishers receive cash in advance for subscriptions. When the publisher receives the cash, it is unearned income and is a liability. It is a liability because the publisher has an obligation to provide magazines during the subscription period. As the magazines are sent to the subscribers, income is earned and the liability decreases.

Tech Publishing Corporation publishes *Consumer Technology Today.* When subscriptions are received, **Cash** is debited and **Unearned Subscription Income,** a liability account, is credited. At the end of the year, *Unearned Subscription Income* had a balance of $450,000. During the year, $184,000 of magazines were delivered; income was earned in the amount of $184,000. The adjustment to recognize income is a debit to **Unearned Subscription Income** for $184,000 and a credit to **Subscription Income** for $184,000.

After the adjustment, the *Unearned Subscription Income* account has a balance of $266,000, which represents subscriptions for future periods.

Unearned Subscription Income			
12/31 Adj.	184,000	12/31 Bal.	450,000
		12/31 Bal.	266,000

Other Unearned Income Items Other types of unearned income include management fees, rental income, legal fees, architectural fees, construction fees, and advertising income. The cash received in advance is recorded as unearned income. As the income is earned, the amount is transferred from the liability account to a revenue account.

>> **12-3 OBJECTIVE**
Compute adjustments for accrued and deferred income items, and enter the adjustments on the worksheet.

recall

Two Ways to Record Transactions
Earlier in this chapter you learned that prepaid expenses are usually charged to an asset account when paid, but may be charged to an expense account at that time. Likewise, unearned income is usually credited to a liability account when received, but may be credited to an income account. Be sure to understand how the transaction was originally entered before you begin making the adjusting entry.

Alternative Method Some businesses use a different method to handle unearned income. At the time the cash is received, a credit is made to a revenue account (not a liability account). At the end of each period, the adjustment transfers the portion that is not earned to a liability account. For example, suppose Tech Publishing Corporation uses this method. When cash for subscriptions is received, it is credited to *Subscription Income*. At the end of the period, an adjustment is made to transfer the unearned income to a liability account. The entry is a debit to *Subscription Income* and a credit to *Unearned Subscription Income*.

Identical amounts appear on the financial statements at the end of each fiscal period no matter which method is used to handle unearned income.

Section 1 Review

1. Which of the following is not true concerning the accrual basis of accounting?
   a. Revenues are recognized when earned.
   b. Expenses are recognized when incurred.
   c. Cash received for services to be performed in future months is recognized as revenue when the cash is received.
   d. Cash received for services to be performed in future months is recognized as a liability when the cash is received.

2. A company has merchandise inventory at the beginning of the year of $14,000 and merchandise inventory at the end of the year of $18,000. Which of the following would be included in the adjusting entry to place the ending inventory on the books?
   a. Debit *Income Summary* for $14,000.
   b. Credit *Income Summary* for $18,000.
   c. Debit *Merchandise Inventory* for $14,000.
   d. Credit *Merchandise Inventory* for $18,000.

3. MJF Company has net credit sales of $2,500,000 and estimates bad debts at 0.5 percent of net credit sales. Which of the following journal entries would be used to record estimated uncollectible accounts receivable?
   a. Debit *Uncollectible Accounts Expense* for $12,500, and credit *Allowance for Doubtful Accounts* for $12,500.
   b. Debit *Uncollectible Accounts Expense* for $12,500, and credit *Accounts Receivable* for $12,500.
   c. Debit *Uncollectible Accounts Expense* for $125,000, and credit *Allowance for Doubtful Accounts* for $125,000.
   d. Debit *Uncollectible Accounts Expense* for $125,000, and credit *Accounts Receivable* for $125,000.

4. In Caymus Company's December 31 trial balance, a credit balance of $31,500 appears in *Unearned Fee Income*. This amount represents cash received from a customer on November 1 covering work to be performed by Caymus in November through January. At December 31, Caymus had earned $10,500 of the amount received on November 1. Which of the following would be used to adjust the *Unearned Fees Income* account on December 31?
   a. Debit *Unearned Fee Income* for $31,500.
   b. Debit *Unearned Fee Income* for $20,000.
   c. Debit *Fees Income* for $10,500.
   d. Credit *Fees Income* for $10,500.

5. In Naranjo Company's December 31 trial balance, a debit balance of $18,000 is found in the *Prepaid Rent* account. A payment of $18,000 for prepayment of six months' rent was made on September 1. Which of the following would be used to adjust the *Prepaid Rent* account on December 31?
   a. Debit *Rent Expense* for $18,000.
   b. Debit *Prepaid Rent* for $18,000.
   c. Debit *Rent Expense* for $12,000.
   d. Debit *Prepaid Rent* for $12,000.

6. Calderone Company purchased office equipment for $9,000 on October 1 of the current year. The office equipment has a useful life of six years and salvage value of $360. What is the amount of depreciation expense for the current year ending December 31?
   a. $120
   b. $360
   c. $1,440
   d. $1,080

7. Debtor Company borrowed $10,000 on a six-month note payable on November 1 of the current year. The note bears interest at an annual interest rate of 9 percent. What is the amount of accrued interest payable at December 31 of the current year?
   a. $900
   b. $75
   c. $750
   d. $150

Section 2

SECTION OBJECTIVES	TERMS TO LEARN
>> 12-4 Complete a 10-column worksheet. **WHY IT'S IMPORTANT** Using the worksheet is a convenient way to gather the information needed for the financial statements.	net income line updated account balances

Completing the Worksheet

After all adjustments have been entered on the worksheet, total the Adjustments Debit and Credit columns and verify that debits and credits are equal. The next step in the process is to prepare the Adjusted Trial Balance section.

Preparing the Adjusted Trial Balance Section

>> **12-4 OBJECTIVE**
Complete a 10-column worksheet.

Figure 12.2 shows the completed worksheet for Whiteside Antiques. The Adjusted Trial Balance section of the worksheet is completed as follows:

1. Combine the amount in the Trial Balance section and the Adjustments section for each account.
2. Enter the results in the Adjusted Trial Balance section. The accounts that do not have adjustments are simply extended from the Trial Balance section to the Adjusted Trial Balance section. For example, the balance of the **Cash** account is recorded in the Debit column of the Adjusted Trial Balance section without change.
3. The accounts that are affected by adjustments are recomputed. Follow these rules to combine amounts on the worksheet:

Trial Balance Section	Adjustments Section	Action
Debit	Debit	Add
Debit	Credit	Subtract
Credit	Credit	Add
Credit	Debit	Subtract

- If the account has a debit balance in the Trial Balance section and a debit entry in the Adjustments section, add the two amounts. Look at the **Salaries Expense—Sales** account. It has a $78,490 debit balance in the Trial Balance section and a $1,200 debit entry in the Adjustments section. The new balance is $79,690 ($78,490 + $1,200). It is entered in the Debit column of the Adjusted Trial Balance section.

- If the account has a debit balance in the Trial Balance section and a credit entry in the Adjustments section, subtract the credit amount. Look at the **Supplies** account. It has a $6,300 debit balance in the Trial Balance section and a $4,975 credit entry in the Adjustments section. The new balance is $1,325 ($6,300 − $4,975). It is entered in the Debit column of the Adjusted Trial Balance section.

- If the account has a credit balance in the Trial Balance section and a credit entry in the Adjustments section, add the two amounts. Look at **Allowance for Doubtful Accounts**. It has a $250 credit balance in the Trial Balance section and an $800 credit entry in the Adjustments section. The new balance is $1,050 ($250 + $800). It is entered in the Credit column of the Adjusted Trial Balance section.

FIGURE 12.2 10-Column Worksheet—Complete

Whiteside Antiques
Worksheet
Year Ended December 31, 20X1

	ACCOUNT NAME	TRIAL BALANCE DEBIT	TRIAL BALANCE CREDIT	ADJUSTMENTS DEBIT		ADJUSTMENTS CREDIT	
1	Cash	13,136.00					
2	Petty Cash Fund	100.00					
3	Notes Receivable	1,200.00					
4	Accounts Receivable	32,000.00					
5	Allowance for Doubtful Accounts		250.00			(c)	800.00
6	Interest Receivable			(m)	30.00		
7	Merchandise Inventory	52,000.00		(b)	47,000.00	(a)	52,000.00
8	Prepaid Insurance	7,350.00				(k)	2,450.00
9	Prepaid Interest	225.00				(l)	150.00
10	Supplies	6,300.00				(j)	4,975.00
11	Store Equipment	30,000.00					
12	Accumulated Depreciation—Store Equipment					(d)	2,400.00
13	Office Equipment	5,000.00					
14	Accumulated Depreciation—Office Equipment					(e)	700.00
15	Notes Payable—Trade		2,000.00				
16	Notes Payable—Bank		9,000.00				
17	Accounts Payable		24,129.00				
18	Interest Payable					(i)	20.00
19	Social Security Tax Payable		1,084.00			(g)	74.40
20	Medicare Tax Payable		250.00			(g)	17.40
21	Employee Income Taxes Payable		990.00				
22	Federal Unemployment Tax Payable					(h)	7.20
23	State Unemployment Tax Payable					(h)	64.80
24	Salaries Payable					(f)	1,200.00
25	Sales Tax Payable		7,200.00				
26	Bill Whiteside, Capital		61,221.00				
27	Bill Whiteside, Drawing	27,600.00					
28	Income Summary			(a)	52,000.00	(b)	47,000.00
29	Sales		561,650.00				
30	Sales Returns and Allowances	12,500.00					
31	Interest Income		136.00			(m)	30.00
32	Miscellaneous Income		366.00				
33	Purchases	321,500.00					
34	Freight In	9,800.00					
35	Purchases Returns and Allowances		3,050.00				
36	Purchases Discounts		3,130.00				
37	Salaries Expense—Sales	78,490.00		(f)	1,200.00		
38	Advertising Expense	7,425.00					
39	Cash Short or Over	125.00					
40	Supplies Expense			(j)	4,975.00		

ADJUSTED TRIAL BALANCE		INCOME STATEMENT		BALANCE SHEET		
DEBIT	CREDIT	DEBIT	CREDIT	DEBIT	CREDIT	
13 136 00				13 136 00		1
100 00				100 00		2
1 200 00				1 200 00		3
32 000 00				32 000 00		4
	1 050 00				1 050 00	5
	30 00				30 00	6
47 000 00				47 000 00		7
4 900 00				4 900 00		8
	75 00				75 00	9
1 325 00				1 325 00		10
30 000 00				30 000 00		11
	2 400 00				2 400 00	12
5 000 00				5 000 00		13
	700 00				700 00	14
	200 00				200 00	15
	900 00				900 00	16
	24 129 00				24 129 00	17
	20 00				20 00	18
	1 158 40				1 158 40	19
	267 40				267 40	20
	990 00				990 00	21
	7 20				7 20	22
	64 80				64 80	23
	1 200 00				1 200 00	24
	7 200 00				7 200 00	25
	61 221 00				61 221 00	26
27 600 00				27 600 00		27
52 000 00	47 000 00	52 000 00	47 000 00			28
	561 650 00		561 650 00			29
12 500 00		12 500 00				30
	166 00		166 00			31
	366 00		366 00			32
321 500 00		321 500 00				33
9 800 00		9 800 00				34
	3 050 00		3 050 00			35
	3 130 00		3 130 00			36
79 690 00		79 690 00				37
7 425 00		7 425 00				38
125 00		125 00				39
4 975 00		4 975 00				40

FIGURE 12.2 (continued)

	ACCOUNT NAME	TRIAL BALANCE		ADJUSTMENTS	
		DEBIT	CREDIT	DEBIT	CREDIT
41	Depreciation Expense—Store Equipment			(d) 2 400 00	
42	Rent Expense	27 600 00			
43	Salaries Expense—Office	26 500 00			
44	Insurance Expense			(k) 2 450 00	
45	Payroll Taxes Expense	7 205 00		(g) 91 80	
46				(h) 72 00	
47	Telephone Expense	1 875 00			
48	Uncollectible Accounts Expense			(c) 800 00	
49	Utilities Expense	5 925 00			
50	Depreciation Expense—Office Equipment			(e) 700 00	
51	Interest Expense	600 00		(i) 20 00	
52				(l) 150 00	
53	Totals	674 456 00	674 456 00	111 888 80	111 888 80
54	Net Income				
55					
56					

- If the account has a credit balance in the Trial Balance section and a debit entry in the Adjustments section, subtract the debit amount. Whiteside Antiques had no such adjustments.

The Adjusted Trial Balance section now contains the **updated account balances** that will be used in preparing the financial statements.

Look at the *Income Summary* account. Recall that the debit entry in this account removed the *beginning* balance from **Merchandise Inventory** and the credit entry added the *ending* balance to **Merchandise Inventory**. Notice that the debit and credit amounts in *Income Summary* are not combined in the Adjusted Trial Balance section.

The **Merchandise Inventory** adjustments were required as Whiteside Antiques uses the periodic inventory method. If Whiteside Antiques used the perpetual inventory method, these inventory adjustments would not have been entered in the worksheet.

Once all the updated account balances have been entered in the Adjusted Trial Balance section, total and rule the columns. Confirm that total debits equal total credits.

Preparing Income Statement and Balance Sheet Sections

To complete the Income Statement and Balance Sheet sections of the worksheet, identify the accounts that appear on the balance sheet. On Figure 12.2, the accounts from **Cash** through **Bill Whiteside, Drawing** appear on the balance sheet. For each account, enter the amount in the appropriate Debit or Credit column of the Balance Sheet section of the worksheet.

For accounts that appear on the income statement, **Sales** through **Interest Expense**, enter the amounts in the appropriate Debit or Credit column of the Income Statement section. The *Income Summary* debit and credit amounts are also entered in the Income Statement section of the worksheet. Notice that the debit and credit amounts in *Income Summary* are not combined in the Income Statement section.

Calculating Net Income or Net Loss

Once all account balances have been entered in the financial statement sections of the worksheet, the net income or net loss for the period is determined.

1. Total the Debit and Credit columns in the Income Statement section. For Whiteside Antiques, the debits total $564,403.80 and the credits total $615,362.00. Since the credits exceed the debits, the difference represents net income of $50,958.20.

ADJUSTED TRIAL BALANCE		INCOME STATEMENT		BALANCE SHEET		
DEBIT	CREDIT	DEBIT	CREDIT	DEBIT	CREDIT	
2 400 00		2 400 00				41
27 600 00		27 600 00				42
26 500 00		26 500 00				43
2 450 00		2 450 00				44
7 368 80		7 368 80				45
						46
1 875 00		1 875 00				47
800 00		800 00				48
5 925 00		5 925 00				49
700 00		700 00				50
770 00		770 00				51
						52
726 769 80	726 769 80	564 403 80	615 362 00	162 366 00	111 407 80	53
		50 958 20			50 958 20	54
		615 362 00	615 362 00	162 366 00	162 366 00	55
						56

2. To balance the Debit and Credit columns in the Income Statement section, enter $50,958.20 in the Debit column of the Income Statement section. Total each column again and record the final total of each column ($615,362.00) on the worksheet.
3. Total the columns in the Balance Sheet section. Total debits are $162,366.00 and total credits are $111,407.80. The difference must equal the net income for the year, $50,958.20.
4. Enter $50,958.20 in the Credit column of the Balance Sheet section. Total each column again and record the final total in each column ($162,366.00).
5. Rule the Debit and Credit columns in all sections to show that the worksheet is complete.

MANAGERIAL IMPLICATIONS

EFFECT OF ADJUSTMENTS ON FINANCIAL STATEMENTS

- If managers are to know the true revenue, expenses, and net income or net loss for a period, the matching process is necessary.
- If accounts are not adjusted, the financial statements will be incomplete, misleading, and of little help in evaluating operations.
- Managers need to be familiar with the procedures and underlying assumptions used by the accountant to make adjustments because adjustments increase or decrease net income.
- Managers need information about uncollectible accounts expense in order to review the firm's credit policy. If losses are too high, management might tighten the requirements for obtaining credit. If losses are very low, management might investigate whether easing credit requirements would increase net income.
- The worksheet is a useful device for gathering data about adjustments and for preparing the financial statements.
- Managers are keenly interested in receiving timely financial statements, especially the income statement, which shows the results of operations.
- Managers are also interested in the prompt preparation of the balance sheet because it shows the financial position of the business at the end of the period.

THINKING CRITICALLY

What are some possible consequences of not making adjusting entries?

Notice that the net income is recorded in two places on the **net income line** of the worksheet. It is recorded in the Credit column of the Balance Sheet section because net income *increases* owner's equity. It is recorded in the Debit column of the Income Statement section to balance the two columns in that section.

Section 2 Review

1. Which of the following best describes the *Accumulated Depreciation* account?
   a. a contra-asset account with a normal debit balance
   b. a contra-asset account with a normal credit balance
   c. an expense account with a normal debit balance
   d. an expense account with a normal credit balance

2. A company failed to record depreciation expense. Which of the following is not true?
   a. The company's net income will be overstated.
   b. The company's total assets will be overstated.
   c. The owner's equity will be overstated.
   d. The company's total liabilities will be overstated.

3. The *Sales* account will appear in which of the following in the worksheet?
   a. Income Statement Debit column
   b. Balance Sheet Debit column
   c. Income Statement Credit column
   d. Balance Sheet Credit column

4. The amount of net income appears on the worksheet in the:
   a. Credit column of the Adjusted Trial Balance section.
   b. Debit column of the Balance Sheet section.
   c. Credit column of the Income Statement section.
   d. Debit column of the Income Statement section.

5. The *Notes Payable* account appears on the worksheet in the:
   a. Credit column of the Balance Sheet section.
   b. Debit column of the Balance Sheet section.
   c. Credit column of the Income Statement section.
   d. Debit column of the Income Statement section.

6. The *Merchandise Inventory* account appears on the worksheet in the:
   a. Credit column of the Balance Sheet section.
   b. Debit column of the Balance Sheet section.
   c. Credit column of the Income Statement section.
   d. Debit column of the Income Statement section.

7. The *Unearned Fees* account appears on the worksheet in the:
   a. Credit column of the Balance Sheet section.
   b. Debit column of the Balance Sheet section.
   c. Credit column of the Income Statement section.
   d. Debit column of the Income Statement section.

REVIEW Chapter Summary

Accrual basis accounting requires that all revenue and expenses for a fiscal period be matched and reported on the income statement to determine net income or net loss for the period. In this chapter, you have learned the techniques used to adjust accounts so that they accurately reflect the operations of the period.

Learning Objectives

12-1 Determine the adjustment for merchandise inventory, and enter the adjustment on the worksheet.

Merchandise inventory consists of goods that a business has on hand for sale to customers. When the trial balance is prepared at the end of the period, the *Merchandise Inventory* account still reflects the beginning inventory. Before the financial statements can be prepared, *Merchandise Inventory* must be updated to reflect the ending inventory for the period. The actual quantity of the goods on hand at the end of the period must be counted. Then the adjustment is completed in two steps:

1. Remove the beginning inventory balance from the *Merchandise Inventory* account. Debit *Income Summary*; credit *Merchandise Inventory*.
2. Add the ending inventory to the *Merchandise Inventory* account. Debit *Merchandise Inventory*; credit *Income Summary*.

12-2 Compute adjustments for accrued and prepaid expense items, and enter the adjustments on the worksheet.

Expense accounts are adjusted at the end of the period so that they correctly reflect the current period. Examples of adjustments include provision for uncollectible accounts and depreciation. Other typical adjustments of expense accounts involve accrued expenses and prepaid expenses.

- Accrued expenses are expense items that have been incurred or used but not yet paid or recorded. They include salaries, payroll taxes, interest on notes payable, and property taxes.
- Prepaid expenses are expense items that a business pays for and records before it actually uses the items. Rent, insurance, and advertising paid in advance are examples.

12-3 Compute adjustments for accrued and deferred income items, and enter the adjustments on the worksheet.

Revenue accounts are adjusted at the end of the period so that they correctly reflect the current period.

- Adjustments can affect either accrued income or deferred income.
- Accrued income is income that has been earned but not yet received and recorded.
- Deferred, or unearned, income is income that has not yet been earned but has been received.

12-4 Complete a 10-column worksheet.

When all adjustments have been entered on the worksheet, the worksheet is completed so that the financial statements can be prepared easily.

1. Figures in the Trial Balance section are combined with the adjustments to obtain an adjusted trial balance.
2. Each item in the Adjusted Trial Balance section is extended to the Income Statement or the Balance Sheet section of the worksheet.
3. The Income Statement columns are totaled and the net income or net loss is determined and entered in the net income line.
4. The amount of net income or net loss is entered in the net income line in the Balance Sheet section. After net income or net loss is added, the total debits must equal the total credits in the Balance Sheet section columns.

12-5 Define the accounting terms new to this chapter.

Glossary

Accrual basis (p. 420) A system of accounting by which all revenues and expenses are matched and reported on financial statements for the applicable period, regardless of when the cash related to the transaction is received or paid

Accrued expenses (p. 425) Expense items that relate to the current period but have not yet been paid and do not yet appear in the accounting records

Accrued income (p. 429) Income that has been earned but not yet received and recorded

Deferred expenses (p. 427) *See* Prepaid expenses

Deferred income (p. 429) *See* Unearned income

Inventory sheet (p. 421) A form used to list the quantity and type of goods a firm has in stock

Net income line (p. 436) The worksheet line immediately following the column totals on which net income (or net loss) is recorded in two places: the Income Statement section and the Balance Sheet section

Property, plant, and equipment (p. 424) Long-term assets that are used in the operation of a business and that are subject to depreciation (except for land, which is not depreciated)

Unearned income (p. 429) Income received before it is earned

Updated account balances (p. 434) The amounts entered in the Adjusted Trial Balance section of the worksheet

Comprehensive Self Review

1. Why is the accrual basis of accounting usually preferred?
2. What is meant by the term "accrued income"?
3. How, if at all, does "accrued income" differ from "unearned income"?
4. A completed worksheet for Holiday Company on December 31, 20X1, showed a total of $930,000 in the Debit column of the Income Statement section and a total credit of $902,000 in the Credit column. Does this represent a profit or a loss for the year? How much?
5. On July 1, 20X1, a landlord received $36,000 cash from a tenant, covering rent from July 1, 20X1, through June 30, 20X2. The payment received was credited to *Unearned Rent Income*. Assuming no entry has been made in the *Unearned Rent Income* account since the payment was received, what would be the adjusting entry on December 31, 20X1?
6. On July 1, 20X1, a landlord received $36,000 cash from a tenant, covering rent from that date through June 30, 20X2. The payment was credited to *Rent Income*. Assuming no entry has been made in the income account since receipt of the payment, what would be the adjusting entry on December 31, 20X1?

(Answers to Comprehensive Self Review are at the end of the chapter.)

Discussion Questions

1. What adjustment is made to record the estimated expense for uncollectible accounts?
2. When a specific account receivable is deemed uncollectible, it is written off by debiting _____ and crediting _____.
3. *Income Summary* amounts are extended to which statement columns on the worksheet?
4. Why is depreciation recorded?
5. What types of assets are subject to depreciation? Give three examples of such assets.
6. Explain the meaning of the following terms that relate to depreciation:
    a. Salvage value
    b. Depreciable base
    c. Useful life
    d. Straight-line method
7. What adjustment is made for depreciation on office equipment?
8. What is an accrued expense? Give three examples of items that often become accrued expenses.
9. What adjustment is made to record accrued salaries?

10. What is a prepaid expense? Give three examples of prepaid expense items.
11. How is the cost of an insurance policy recorded when the policy is purchased?
12. What adjustment is made to record expired insurance?
13. What is the alternative method of handling prepaid expenses?
14. What is accrued income? Give an example of an item that might produce accrued income.
15. What adjustment is made for accrued interest on a note receivable?
16. What is unearned income? Give two examples of items that would be classified as unearned income.
17. How is unearned income recorded when it is received?
18. What adjustment is made to record income earned during a period?
19. What is the alternative method of handling unearned income?
20. *Unearned Fees Income* is classified as which type of account?
21. How does the worksheet help the accountant to prepare financial statements more efficiently?

APPLICATIONS

Exercises

Determining the adjustments for inventory.

◀ Exercise 12.1
Objective 12-1

The beginning inventory of SoCal Wholesalers was $121,000, and the ending inventory is $116,500. What entries are needed at the end of the fiscal period to adjust *Merchandise Inventory*?

Determining the adjustments for inventory.

◀ Exercise 12.2
Objective 12-1

The Income Statement section of the Johnson Company worksheet for the year ended December 31, 20X1, has $201,000 recorded in the Debit column and $216,250 in the Credit column on the line for the *Income Summary* account. What were the beginning and ending balances for *Merchandise Inventory*?

Preparing adjustments for uncollectible accounts, depreciation, and payroll items.

◀ Exercise 12.3
Objective 12-2

For each of the following independent situations, prepare the adjusting entry that must be made at December 31, 20X1. Omit descriptions.

   a. During the year 20X1, Alenikov Company had net credit sales of $2,020,000. Past experience shows that 1.5 percent of the firm's net credit sales result in uncollectible accounts.

   b. Equipment purchased by Fronke Consultancy for $42,500 on January 2, 20X1, has an estimated useful life of eight years and an estimated salvage value of $3,500. Prepare the adjusting entry to record depreciation for the year ended December 31, 20X1.

   c. On December 31, 20X1, Moloney Plumbing Supply owed wages of $12,200 to its factory employees, who are paid weekly.

   d. On December 31, 20X1, Moloney Plumbing Supply owed the employer's social security (6.2 percent) and Medicare (1.45 percent) taxes on the entire $12,200 of accrued wages for its factory employees.

   e. On December 31, 20X1, Moloney Plumbing Supply owed federal (0.6 percent) and state (5.4 percent) unemployment taxes on the entire $12,200 of accrued wages for its factory employees.

Preparing adjustments for accrued and prepaid expense items.

◀ Exercise 12.4
Objective 12-2

For each of the following independent situations, prepare the adjusting entry that must be made on December 31, 20X1. Omit descriptions.

   a. On December 31, 20X1, the *Notes Payable* account at Tsang Manufacturing Company had a balance of $18,000. This balance represented a three-month, 8.5 percent note issued on November 1.

b. On January 2, 20X1, Hitech Computer Consultants purchased flash drives, paper, and other supplies for $6,230 in cash. On December 31, 20X1, an inventory of supplies showed that items costing $1,620 were on hand. The **Supplies** account has a balance of $6,230.

c. On October 1, 20X1, South Dakota Manufacturing paid a premium of $14,640 in cash for a one-year insurance policy. On December 31, 20X1, the **Prepaid Insurance** account has a balance of $14,640.

d. On June 1, 20X1, Headcase Beauty Salon signed a one-year advertising contract with a local radio station and issued a check for $13,200 to pay the total amount owed. On December 31, 20X1, the **Prepaid Advertising** account has a balance of $13,200.

Exercise 12.5
Objective 12-2

▶ **Recording adjustments for prepaid interest.**

On December 1, 20X1, Jenny's Java Joint borrowed $50,000 from its bank in order to expand its operations. The firm issued a four-month, 9 percent note for $50,000 to the bank and received $48,500 in cash because the bank deducted the interest for the entire period in advance. Prepare the journal entry that would be made to record this transaction and the adjustment for prepaid interest that should be recorded for the year ended December 31, 20X1. Omit descriptions. Round your answers to the nearest dollar.

Exercise 12.6
Objective 12-2

▶ **Recording adjustments for accrued interest.**

On December 31, 20X1, the **Notes Payable** account at Cherie's Boutique Shop had a balance of $72,000. This amount represented funds borrowed on a six-month, 6 percent note from the firm's bank on December 1. Prepare the adjusting journal entry for interest expense on this note that should be recorded for the year ended December 31, 20X1. Omit descriptions.

Exercise 12.7
Objective 12-3

▶ **Recording adjustments for accrued and deferred income items.**

For each of the following independent situations, prepare the adjusting entry that must be made at December 31, 20X1. Omit descriptions.

a. On December 31, 20X1, the **Notes Receivable** account at Sufen Materials Corporation had a balance of $25,000, which represented a six-month, 6 percent note received from a customer on September 1.

b. During the week ended June 7, 20X1, McCormick Media received $90,000 from customers for subscriptions to its magazine *Modern Business*. On December 31, 20X1, an analysis of the **Unearned Subscription Revenue** account showed that 60 percent of the subscriptions were earned in 20X1.

c. On November 1, 20X1, Perez Realty Company rented a commercial building to a new tenant and received $37,200 in advance to cover the rent for six months. Upon receipt, the $37,200 was recorded in the **Unearned Rent** account.

d. On November 1, 20X1, the Mighty Bucks Hockey Club sold season tickets for 60 home games, receiving $9,200,000. Upon receipt, the $9,200,000 was recorded in the **Unearned Season Tickets Income** account. At December 31, 20X1, the Mighty Bucks Hockey Club had played 6 home games.

PROBLEMS

Problem Set A

Problem 12.1A
Objectives 12-2, 12-3

▶ **Recording adjustments for accrued and prepaid items and unearned income.**

Based on the information below, record the adjusting journal entries that must be made for Kisling Distributors on June 30, 20X1. The company has a June 30 fiscal year-end. Use 18 as the page number for the general journal.

a.–b. *Merchandise Inventory,* before adjustment, has a balance of $7,800. The newly counted inventory balance is $8,300.

c. **Unearned Seminar Fees** has a balance of $6,300, representing prepayment by customers for five seminars to be conducted in June, July, and August 20X1. Two seminars had been conducted by June 30, 20X1.

d. **Prepaid Insurance** has a balance of $13,800 for six months' insurance paid in advance on May 1, 20X1.

e. Store equipment costing $6,530 was purchased on March 31, 20X1. It has a salvage value of $530 and a useful life of five years.

f. Employees have earned $280 that has not been paid at June 30, 20X1.

g. The employer owes the following taxes on wages not paid at June 30, 20X1: SUTA, $8.40; FUTA, $1.68; Medicare, $4.06; and social security, $17.36.

h. Management estimates uncollectible accounts expense at 1 percent of sales. This year's sales were $2,300,000.

i. **Prepaid Rent** has a balance of $7,050 for six months' rent paid in advance on March 1, 20X1.

j. The **Supplies** account in the general ledger has a balance of $430. A count of supplies on hand at June 30, 20X1, indicated $165 of supplies remain.

k. The company borrowed $4,800 from Second Bancorp on June 1, 20X1, and issued a four-month note. The note bears interest at 9 percent.

Analyze: After all adjusting entries have been journalized and posted, what is the balance of the *Prepaid Rent* account?

Recording adjustments for accrued and prepaid expense items and unearned income.

◀ **Problem 12.2A**
Objectives 12-2, 12-3

On July 1, 20X1, Cherie Wang established Cherie Wang Financial Services. Selected transactions for the first few days of July follow.

INSTRUCTIONS

1. Record the transactions on page 1 of the general journal. Omit descriptions. Assume that the firm initially records prepaid expenses as assets and unearned income as a liability. Omit explanations.

2. Record the adjusting journal entries that must be made on July 31, 20X1, on page 2 of the general journal. Omit descriptions.

DATE		TRANSACTIONS
20X1		
July	1	Signed a lease for an office and issued Check 101 for $14,700 to pay the rent in advance for six months.
	1	Borrowed money from Bancorp West by issuing a four-month, 9 percent note for $40,000; received $38,800 because the bank deducted the interest in advance.
	1	Signed an agreement with Kroll Corp. to provide financial services for one year at $7,000 per month; received the entire fee of $84,000 in advance. The $84,000 was credited to Unearned Financial Service Fees.
	1	Purchased office equipment for $15,900 from Office Outfitters; issued a two-month, 12 percent note in payment. The equipment is estimated to have a useful life of five years and a $1,500 salvage value. The equipment will be depreciated using the straight-line method.
	1	Purchased a one-year insurance policy and issued Check 102 for $1,740 to pay the entire premium.
	3	Purchased office furniture for $16,080 from Furniture Warehouse; issued Check 103 for $8,480 and agreed to pay the balance in 60 days. The equipment has an estimated useful life of four years and a $1,200 salvage value. The office furniture will be depreciated using the straight-line method.
	5	Purchased office supplies for $2,010 with Check 104. Assume $900 of supplies are on hand July 31, 20X1.

Analyze: What balance should be reflected in *Unearned* **Financial Service Fees** at July 31, 20X1?

Problem 12.3A ▶ Recording adjustments for accrued and prepaid expense items and earned income.

Objectives 12-2, 12-3

On July 31, 20X1, after one month of operation, the general ledger of Michael Mendoza, CPA, contained the accounts and balances given below.

INSTRUCTIONS

1. Prepare a partial worksheet with the following sections: Trial Balance, Adjustments, and Adjusted Trial Balance. Use the data about the firm's accounts and balances to complete the Trial Balance section.
2. Enter the adjustments described below in the Adjustments section. Identify each adjustment with the appropriate letter.
3. Complete the Adjusted Trial Balance section.

ACCOUNTS AND BALANCES

Cash	$26,710	Dr.
Accounts Receivable	2,440	Dr.
Supplies	960	Dr.
Prepaid Rent	10,500	Dr.
Prepaid Insurance	2,820	Dr.
Prepaid Advertising	400	Dr.
Furniture	14,760	Dr.
Accumulated Depreciation—Furniture		
Equipment	7,250	Dr.
Accumulated Depreciation—Equipment		
Notes Payable	17,700	Cr.
Accounts Payable	5,500	Cr.
Interest Payable		
Unearned Accounting Fees	6,600	Cr.
Michael Mendoza, Capital	34,720	Cr.
Michael Mendoza, Drawing	3,600	Dr.
Accounting Fees	9,600	Cr.
Salaries Expense	4,200	Dr.
Utilities Expense	270	Dr.
Telephone Expense	210	Dr.
Supplies Expense		
Rent Expense		
Insurance Expense		
Advertising Expense		
Depreciation Expense—Furniture		
Depreciation Expense—Equipment		
Interest Expense		

ADJUSTMENTS

a. On July 31, an inventory of the supplies showed that items costing $530 were on hand.
b. On July 1, the firm paid $10,500 in advance for three months of rent.
c. On July 1, the firm purchased a one-year insurance policy for $2,820.
d. On July 1, the firm paid $400 for four months of advertising. The ads began running in July.
e. On July 1, the firm purchased office furniture for $14,760. The furniture is expected to have a useful life of six years and a salvage value of $1,800.

f. On July 1, the firm purchased office equipment for $7,250. The equipment is expected to have a useful life of five years and a salvage value of $1,850.

g. On July 1, the firm issued a three-month, 6 percent note for $17,700.

h. On July 1, the firm received a consulting fee of $6,600 in advance for a one-year period.

Analyze: By what total amount were the expense accounts of the business adjusted?

Recording adjustments and completing the worksheet.

◄ **Problem 12.4A**

Objectives 12-1, 12-2, 12-3, 12-4

The Green Thumb Gardener is a retail store that sells plants, soil, and decorative pots. On December 31, 20X1, the firm's general ledger contained the accounts and balances that appear below.

INSTRUCTIONS

1. Prepare the Trial Balance section of a 10-column worksheet. The worksheet covers the year ended December 31, 20X1.
2. Enter the adjustments below in the Adjustments section of the worksheet. Identify each adjustment with the appropriate letter.
3. Complete the worksheet.

ACCOUNTS AND BALANCES

Account	Balance	
Cash	$ 6,700	Dr.
Accounts Receivable	3,600	Dr.
Allowance for Doubtful Accounts	62	Cr.
Merchandise Inventory	12,300	Dr.
Supplies	1,300	Dr.
Prepaid Advertising	1,080	Dr.
Store Equipment	8,700	Dr.
Accumulated Depreciation—Store Equipment	1,600	Cr.
Office Equipment	2,200	Dr.
Accumulated Depreciation—Office Equipment	380	Cr.
Accounts Payable	2,725	Cr.
Social Security Tax Payable	530	Cr.
Medicare Tax Payable	88	Cr.
Federal Unemployment Tax Payable		
State Unemployment Tax Payable		
Salaries Payable		
Beth Argo, Capital	30,677	Cr.
Beth Argo, Drawing	21,000	Dr.
Sales	95,048	Cr.
Sales Returns and Allowances	1,200	Dr.
Purchases	49,400	Dr.
Purchases Returns and Allowances	530	Cr.
Rent Expense	7,000	Dr.
Telephone Expense	690	Dr.
Salaries Expense	15,100	Dr.
Payroll Taxes Expense	1,370	Dr.
Income Summary		
Supplies Expense		
Advertising Expense		
Depreciation Expense—Store Equipment		
Depreciation Expense—Office Equipment		
Uncollectible Accounts Expense		

ADJUSTMENTS

a.–b. Merchandise inventory on December 31, 20X1, is $13,321.

c. During 20X1, the firm had net credit sales of $45,000; the firm estimates that 0.5 percent of these sales will result in uncollectible accounts.

d. On December 31, 20X1, an inventory of the supplies showed that items costing $325 were on hand.

e. On October 1, 20X1, the firm signed a six-month advertising contract for $1,080 with a local newspaper and paid the full amount in advance.

f. On January 2, 20X0, the firm purchased store equipment for $8,700. At that time, the equipment was estimated to have a useful life of five years and a salvage value of $700.

g. On January 2, 20X0, the firm purchased office equipment for $2,200. At that time, the equipment was estimated to have a useful life of five years and a salvage value of $300.

h. On December 31, 20X1, the firm owed salaries of $1,930 that will not be paid until 20X2.

i. On December 31, 20X1, the firm owed the employer's social security tax (assume 6.2 percent) and Medicare tax (assume 1.45 percent) on the entire $1,930 of accrued wages.

j. On December 31, 20X1, the firm owed federal unemployment tax (assume 0.6 percent) and state unemployment tax (assume 5.4 percent) on the entire $1,930 of accrued wages.

Analyze: By what amount were the assets of the business affected by adjustments?

Problem 12.5A ▶ Recording adjustments and completing the worksheet.

Objectives 12-1, 12-2, 12-3, 12-4

CONTINUING >>> Problem

Healthy Eating Foods Company is a distributor of nutritious snack foods such as granola bars. On December 31, 20X1, the firm's general ledger contained the accounts and balances that follow.

INSTRUCTIONS

1. Prepare the Trial Balance section of a 10-column worksheet. The worksheet covers the year ended December 31, 20X1.

2. Enter the adjustments in the Adjustments section of the worksheet. Identify each adjustment with the appropriate letter.

3. Complete the worksheet.

Note: This problem will be required to complete Problem 13.4A in Chapter 13.

ACCOUNTS AND BALANCES

Account	Balance	
Cash	$ 30,100	Dr.
Accounts Receivable	35,200	Dr.
Allowance for Doubtful Accounts	420	Cr.
Merchandise Inventory	86,000	Dr.
Supplies	10,400	Dr.
Prepaid Insurance	5,400	Dr.
Office Equipment	8,300	Dr.
Accum. Depreciation—Office Equipment	2,650	Cr.
Warehouse Equipment	28,000	Dr.
Accum. Depreciation—Warehouse Equipment	9,600	Cr.
Notes Payable—Bank	32,000	Cr.
Accounts Payable	12,200	Cr.
Interest Payable		
Social Security Tax Payable	1,680	Cr.
Medicare Tax Payable	388	Cr.
Federal Unemployment Tax Payable		
State Unemployment Tax Payable		

ACCOUNTS AND BALANCES (CONT.)

Salaries Payable		
Phillip Tucker, Capital	108,684	Cr.
Phillip Tucker, Drawing	56,000	Dr.
Sales	653,778	Cr.
Sales Returns and Allowances	10,000	Dr.
Purchases	350,000	Dr.
Purchases Returns and Allowances	9,200	Cr.
Income Summary		
Rent Expense	36,000	Dr.
Telephone Expense	2,200	Dr.
Salaries Expense	160,000	Dr.
Payroll Taxes Expense	13,000	Dr.
Supplies Expense		
Insurance Expense		
Depreciation Expense—Office Equip.		
Depreciation Expense—Warehouse Equip.		
Uncollectible Accounts Expense		
Interest Expense		

ADJUSTMENTS

a.–b. Merchandise inventory on December 31, 20X1, is $78,000.

c. During 20X1, the firm had net credit sales of $560,000; past experience indicates that 0.5 percent of these sales should result in uncollectible accounts.

d. On December 31, 20X1, an inventory of supplies showed that items costing $1,180 were on hand.

e. On May 1, 20X1, the firm purchased a one-year insurance policy for $5,400.

f. Three years ago the firm purchased office equipment for $8,300. At that time, the equipment was estimated to have a useful life of six years and a salvage value of $350.

g. Three years ago the firm purchased warehouse equipment for $28,000. At that time, the equipment was estimated to have a useful life of five years and a salvage value of $4,000.

h. On November 1, 20X1, the firm issued a four-month, 12 percent note for $32,000.

i. On December 31, 20X1, the firm owed salaries of $5,000 that will not be paid until 20X2.

j. On December 31, 20X1, the firm owed the employer's social security tax (assume 6.2 percent) and Medicare tax (assume 1.45 percent) on the entire $5,000 of accrued wages.

k. On December 31, 20X1, the firm owed the federal unemployment tax (assume 0.6 percent) and the state unemployment tax (assume 5.4 percent) on the entire $5,000 of accrued wages.

Analyze: When the financial statements for Healthy Eating Foods Company are prepared, what net income will be reported for the period ended December 31, 20X1?

◄ Problem 12.6A
Objectives 12-1, 12-2, 12-3, 12-4

Recording adjustments and completing the worksheet.

Enoteca Fine Wines is a retail store selling vintage wines. On December 31, 20X1, the firm's general ledger contained the accounts and balances below. All account balances are normal.

Cash	$ 29,886
Accounts Receivable	1,500
Prepaid Advertising	480

Supplies	300
Merchandise Inventory	15,000
Store Equipment	27,000
Accumulated Depreciation—Store Equipment	3,000
Office Equipment	6,000
Accumulated Depreciation—Office Equipment	1,500
Notes Payable, due 20X2	20,000
Accounts Payable	4,705
Wages Payable	
Social Security Tax Payable	
Medicare Tax Payable	
Unearned Seminar Fees	8,000
Interest Payable	
Vincent Carbone, Capital	32,700
Vincent Carbone, Drawing	14,110
Income Summary	
Sales	154,970
Sales Discounts	200
Seminar Fee Income	
Purchases	91,000
Purchases Returns and Allowances	1,500
Freight In	225
Rent Expense	13,200
Wages Expense	24,000
Payroll Taxes Expense	3,324
Depreciation Expense—Store Equipment	
Depreciation Expense—Office Equipment	
Advertising Expense	
Supplies Expense	
Interest Expense	150

INSTRUCTIONS:

1. Prepare the Trial Balance section of a 10-column worksheet. The worksheet covers the year ended December 31, 20X1.
2. Enter the adjustments below in the Adjustments section of the worksheet. Identify each adjustment with the appropriate letter.
3. Complete the worksheet.

ADJUSTMENTS:

a.–b. Merchandise inventory at December 31, 20X1, was counted and determined to be $14,000.

c. The amount recorded as prepaid advertising represents $480 paid on September 1, 20X1, for 12 months of advertising.

d. The amount of supplies on hand at December 31 was $130.

e. Depreciation on store equipment was $3,800 for 20X1.

f. Depreciation on office equipment was $1,250 for 20X1.

g. Unearned seminar fees represent $8,000 received on November 1, 20X1, for four seminars. At December 31, three of these seminars had been conducted.

h. Wages owed but not paid at December 31 were $500.

i. On December 31, 20X1, the firm owed the employer's social security tax ($31.00) and Medicare tax ($7.25).

j. The note payable bears interest at 6 percent per annum. Two months of interest is owed at December 31, 20X1.

Analyze: What was the amount of revenue earned by conducting seminars during the year ended December 31, 20X1?

Problem Set B

Recording adjustments for accrued and prepaid items and unearned income.

◀ **Problem 12.1B**
Objectives 12-2, 12-3

Based on the information below, record the adjusting journal entries that must be made for D. Johnson Products, LLC, on December 31, 20X1. The company has a December 31 fiscal year-end. Use 18 as the page number for the general journal.

a.–b. *Merchandise Inventory,* before adjustment, has a balance of $9,600. The newly counted inventory balance is $10,500.

c. *Unearned Seminar Fees* has a balance of $18,800, representing prepayment by customers for four seminars to be conducted in December 20X1 and January 20X2. Three seminars had been conducted by December 31, 20X1.

d. *Prepaid Insurance* has a balance of $13,200 for six months' insurance paid in advance on November 1, 20X1.

e. Store equipment costing $12,000 was purchased on September 1, 20X1. It has a salvage value of $600 and a useful life of five years.

f. Employees have earned $2,000 of wages not paid at December 31, 20X1.

g. The employer owes the following taxes on wages not paid at December 31, 20X1: SUTA, $60.00; FUTA, $12.00; Medicare, $29.00; and social security, $124.00.

h. Management estimates uncollectible accounts expense at 1.5 percent (0.015) of sales. This year's sales were $3,250,000.

i. *Prepaid Rent* has a balance of $20,250 for nine months' rent paid in advance on August 1, 20X1.

j. The *Supplies* account in the general ledger has a balance of $780. A count of supplies on hand at December 31, 20X1, indicated $150 of supplies remain.

k. The company borrowed $22,500 on a two-month note payable dated December 1, 20X1. The note bears interest at 8 percent.

Analyze: After all adjusting entries have been journalized and posted, what is the balance of the *Unearned Seminar Fees* account?

Recording adjustments for accrued and prepaid expense items and unearned income.

◀ **Problem 12.2B**
Objectives 12-2, 12-3

On June 1, 20X1, William Tsang established his own consulting firm. Selected transactions for the first few days of June follow.

1. Record the transactions on page 1 of the general journal. Omit descriptions. Assume that the firm initially records prepaid expenses as assets and unearned income as a liability.

2. Record the adjusting journal entries that must be made on June 30, 20X1, on page 2 of the general journal. Omit descriptions.

DATE	TRANSACTIONS
20X1	
June 1	Signed a lease for an office and issued Check 101 for $30,000 to pay the rent in advance for one year.
1	Borrowed money from Southwestern Trust Bank by issuing a three-month, 10 percent note for $18,000; received $17,550 because the bank deducted interest in advance.
1	Signed an agreement with Michelle's Party Supplies to provide consulting services for one year at $3,250 per month; received the entire fee of $39,000 in advance.
1	Purchased office equipment for $34,200 from Equipment Warehouse; issued a three-month, 6 percent note in payment. The equipment is estimated to have a useful life of six years and an $1,800 salvage value, and will be depreciated using the straight-line method.
1	Purchased a one-year insurance policy and issued Check 102 for $3,360 to pay the entire premium.
3	Purchased office furniture for $10,400 from Furniture Gallery; issued Check 103 for $5,400 and agreed to pay the balance in 60 days. The furniture is estimated to have a useful life of 10 years and an $800 salvage value, and will be depreciated using the straight-line method.
5	Purchased office supplies for $955 with Check 104; assume $525 of supplies are on hand June 30, 20X1.

Analyze: At the end of calendar year 20X1, how much of the rent paid on June 1 will have been charged to expense?

Problem 12.3B ▶
Objectives 12-2, 12-3

Recording adjustments for accrued and prepaid expense items and unearned income.

On September 30, 20X1, after one month of operation, the general ledger of Cross Country Travels contained the accounts and balances shown below.

INSTRUCTIONS

1. Prepare a partial worksheet with the following sections: Trial Balance, Adjustments, and Adjusted Trial Balance. Use the data about the firm's accounts and balances to complete the Trial Balance section.
2. Enter the adjustments described below in the Adjustments section. Identify each adjustment with the appropriate letter. (Some items may not require adjustments.)
3. Complete the Adjusted Trial Balance section.

ACCOUNTS AND BALANCES

Cash	$27,560	Dr.
Supplies	740	Dr.
Prepaid Rent	4,200	Dr.
Prepaid Advertising	3,900	Dr.
Prepaid Interest	450	Dr.
Furniture	4,840	Dr.
Accumulated Depreciation—Furniture		
Equipment	9,000	Dr.
Accumulated Depreciation—Equipment		

ACCOUNTS AND BALANCES (CONT.)

Notes Payable	20,250	Cr.
Accounts Payable	5,650	Cr.
Interest Payable		
Unearned Travel Fees	22,000	Cr.
Sandy Yung, Capital	6,980	Cr.
Sandy Yung, Drawing	2,000	Dr.
Travel Fees		
Salaries Expense	1,600	Dr.
Telephone Expense	120	Dr.
Entertainment Expense	220	Dr.
Supplies Expense		
Rent Expense		
Insurance Expense		
Advertising Expense		
Depreciation Expense—Furniture		
Depreciation Expense—Equipment		
Interest Expense		

ADJUSTMENTS

a. On September 30, an inventory of the supplies showed that items costing $605 were on hand.
b. On September 1, the firm paid $4,200 in advance for three months of rent.
c. On September 1, paid $3,900 in advance for six months of insurance.
d. On September 1, the firm paid $450 in advance for three months of advertising. The ads started running in September.
e. On September 1, the firm purchased office furniture for $4,840. The furniture is expected to have a useful life of 10 years and a salvage value of $280.
f. On September 3, the firm purchased equipment for $9,000. The equipment is expected to have a useful life of six years and a salvage value of $1,080.
g. On September 1, the firm issued a two-month, 6 percent note for $20,000.
h. During September, the firm received $22,000 of fees in advance. An analysis of the firm's records shows that $5,000 applies to services provided in September and the rest pertains to future months.

Analyze: What was the net dollar effect on net income of the adjustments to the accounting records of the business?

Recording adjustments and completing the worksheet.

◀ **Problem 12.4B**

Objectives 12-1, 12-2, 12-3, 12-4

Fun Depot is a retail store that sells toys, games, and bicycles. On December 31, 20X1, the firm's general ledger contained the following accounts and balances.

INSTRUCTIONS

1. Prepare the Trial Balance section of a 10-column worksheet. The worksheet covers the year ended December 31, 20X1.
2. Enter the adjustments below in the Adjustments section of the worksheet. Identify each adjustment with the appropriate letter.
3. Complete the worksheet.

ACCOUNTS AND BALANCES

Cash	$ 26,400	Dr.
Accounts Receivable	22,700	Dr.
Allowance for Doubtful Accounts	320	Cr.
Merchandise Inventory	138,000	Dr.
Supplies	11,600	Dr.
Prepaid Advertising	5,280	Dr.
Store Equipment	32,500	Dr.
Accumulated Depreciation—Store Equipment	5,760	Cr.
Office Equipment	8,400	Dr.
Accumulated Depreciation—Office Equipment	1,440	Cr.
Accounts Payable	8,600	Cr.
Social Security Tax Payable	5,920	Cr.
Medicare Tax Payable	1,368	Cr.
Federal Unemployment Tax Payable		
State Unemployment Tax Payable		
Salaries Payable		
Janie Fielder, Capital	112,250	Cr.
Janie Fielder, Drawing	100,000	Dr.
Sales	1,043,662	Cr.
Sales Returns and Allowances	17,200	Dr.
Purchases	507,600	Dr.
Purchases Returns and Allowances	5,040	Cr.
Rent Expense	125,000	Dr.
Telephone Expense	4,280	Dr.
Salaries Expense	164,200	Dr.
Payroll Taxes Expense	15,200	Dr.
Income Summary		
Supplies Expense		
Advertising Expense	6,000	Dr.
Depreciation Expense—Store Equipment		
Depreciation Expense—Office Equipment		
Uncollectible Accounts Expense		

ADJUSTMENTS

a.–b. Merchandise inventory on December 31 is $148,000.

c. During 20X1, the firm had net credit sales of $440,000. The firm estimates that 0.7 percent of these sales will result in uncollectible accounts.

d. On December 31, an inventory of the supplies showed that items costing $2,960 were on hand.

e. On September 1, 20X1, the firm signed a six-month advertising contract for $5,280 with a local newspaper and paid the full amount in advance.

f. On January 2, 20X0, the firm purchased store equipment for $32,500. At that time, the equipment was estimated to have a useful life of five years and a salvage value of $3,700.

g. On January 2, 20X0, the firm purchased office equipment for $8,400. At that time, the equipment was estimated to have a useful life of five years and a salvage value of $1,200.

h. On December 31, the firm owed salaries of $8,000 that will not be paid until 20X2.

i. On December 31, the firm owed the employer's social security tax (assume 6.2 percent) and Medicare tax (assume 1.45 percent) on the entire $8,000 of accrued wages.

j. On December 31, the firm owed federal unemployment tax (assume 0.6 percent) and state unemployment tax (assume 5.4 percent) on the entire $8,000 of accrued wages.

Analyze: If the adjustment for advertising had not been recorded, what would the reported net income have been?

Recording adjustments and completing the worksheet.

◀ **Problem 12.5B**

Whatnots is a retail seller of cards, novelty items, and business products. On December 31, 20X1, the firm's general ledger contained the following accounts and balances.

Objectives 12-1, 12-2, 12-3, 12-4

INSTRUCTIONS

1. Prepare the Trial Balance section of a 10-column worksheet. The worksheet covers the year ended December 31, 20X1.

2. Enter the adjustments in the Adjustments section of the worksheet. Identify each adjustment with the appropriate letter.

3. Complete the worksheet.

Note: This problem will be required to complete Problem 13.4B in Chapter 13.

ACCOUNTS AND BALANCES

Cash	$ 3,235	Dr.
Accounts Receivable	6,910	Dr.
Allowance for Doubtful Accounts	600	Cr.
Merchandise Inventory	16,985	Dr.
Supplies	750	Dr.
Prepaid Insurance	2,400	Dr.
Store Equipment	6,000	Dr.
Accumulated Depreciation—Store Equip.	2,000	Cr.
Store Fixtures	15,760	Dr.
Accumulated Depreciation—Store Fixtures	4,100	Cr.
Notes Payable	4,000	Cr.
Accounts Payable	600	Cr.
Interest Payable		
Social Security Tax Payable		
Medicare Tax Payable		
Federal Unemployment Tax Payable		
State Unemployment Tax Payable		
Salaries Payable		
Preston Allen, Capital	39,780	Cr.
Preston Allen, Drawing	8,000	Dr.
Sales	236,560	Cr.
Sales Returns and Allowances	6,000	Dr.
Purchases	160,000	Dr.
Purchases Returns and Allowances	2,000	Cr.
Income Summary		
Rent Expense	18,000	Dr.

ACCOUNTS AND BALANCES (CONT.)

Telephone Expense	2,400	Dr.
Salaries Expense	40,000	Dr.
Payroll Tax Expense	3,200	Dr.
Income Summary		
Supplies Expense		
Insurance Expense		
Depreciation Expense—Store Equipment		
Depreciation Expense—Store Fixtures		
Interest Expense		
Uncollectible Accounts Expense		

ADJUSTMENTS

a.–b. Merchandise inventory on hand on December 31 is $15,840.

c. During 20X1, the firm had net credit sales of $160,000. Past experience indicates that 0.8 percent of these sales should result in uncollectible accounts.

d. On December 31, an inventory of supplies showed that items costing $245 were on hand.

e. On July 1, 20X1, the firm purchased a one-year insurance policy for $2,400.

f. Three years ago the firm purchased store equipment for $6,000. The equipment was estimated to have a five-year useful life and a salvage value of $1,000.

g. Three years ago the firm purchased store fixtures for $15,760. At the time of the purchase, the fixtures were assumed to have a useful life of seven years and a salvage value of $1,410.

h. On October 1, 20X1, the firm issued a six-month, $4,000 note payable at 9 percent interest with a local bank.

i. At year-end (December 31, 20X1), the firm owed salaries of $1,450 that will not be paid until January 20X2.

j. On December 31, 20X1, the firm owed the employer's social security tax (assume 6.2 percent) and Medicare tax (assume 1.45 percent) on the entire $1,450 of accrued wages.

k. On December 31, 20X1, the firm owed federal unemployment tax (assume 0.6 percent) and state unemployment tax (assume 5.0 percent) on the entire $1,450 of accrued wages.

Analyze: After all adjustments have been recorded, what is the net book value of the company's assets?

Problem 12.6B ▶ Recording adjustments and completing the worksheet.

Objectives 12-1, 12-2, 12-3, 12-4

Gamer's Paradise is a retail store that sells computer games, owned by Matt Huffman. On December 31, 20X1, the firm's general ledger contained the accounts and balances below. All account balances are normal.

Cash	$36,465
Accounts Receivable	2,669
Prepaid Advertising	2,880
Supplies	425
Merchandise Inventory	18,500
Store Equipment	30,000
Accumulated Depreciation—Store Equipment	3,000
Office Equipment	6,000
Accumulated Depreciation—Office Equipment	1,500
Notes Payable, due 20X2	22,500

Accounts Payable	7,725
Wages Payable	
Social Security Tax Payable	
Medicare Tax Payable	
Unearned Seminar Fees	8,500
Interest Payable	
Matt Huffman, Capital	46,200
Matt Huffman, Drawing	20,000
Income Summary	
Sales	166,060
Sales Discounts	180
Seminar Fee Income	
Purchases	92,500
Purchases Returns and Allowances	770
Freight In	275
Rent Expense	26,400
Wages Expense	18,000
Payroll Taxes Expense	1,811
Depreciation Expense—Store Equipment	
Depreciation Expense—Office Equipment	
Advertising Expense	
Supplies Expense	
Interest Expense	150

INSTRUCTIONS

1. Prepare the Trial Balance section of a 10-column worksheet. The worksheet covers the year ended December 31, 20X1.
2. Enter the adjustments below in the Adjustments section of the worksheet. Identify each adjustment with the appropriate letter.
3. Complete the worksheet.

ADJUSTMENTS

a.–b. Merchandise inventory at December 31, 20X1, was counted and determined to be $21,200.

c. The amount recorded as prepaid advertising represents $2,880 paid on September 1, 20X1, for six months of advertising.

d. The amount of supplies on hand at December 31 was $105.

e. Depreciation on store equipment was $4,500 for 20X1.

f. Depreciation on office equipment was $1,000 for 20X1.

g. Unearned seminar fees represent $8,500 received on November 1, 20X1, for five seminars. At December 31, three of these seminars had been conducted.

h. Wages owed but not paid at December 31 were $800.

i. On December 31, the firm owed the employer's social security tax ($49.60) and Medicare tax ($11.60).

j. The note payable bears interest at 8 percent per annum. Two months of interest is owed at December 31, 20X1.

Analyze: How did the balance of merchandise inventory change during the year ended December 31, 20X1?

Critical Thinking Problem 12.1

Completing the Worksheet

The unadjusted trial balance of Ben's Jewelers on December 31, 20X1, the end of its fiscal year, appears below.

INSTRUCTIONS

1. Copy the unadjusted trial balance onto a worksheet and complete the worksheet using the following information:

    a.–b. Ending merchandise inventory, $98,700.

    c. Uncollectible accounts expense, $1,000.

    d. Store supplies on hand December 31, 20X1, $625.

    e. Office supplies on hand December 31, 20X1, $305.

    f. Depreciation on store equipment, $11,360.

    g. Depreciation on office equipment, $3,300.

    h. Accrued sales salaries, $4,000, and accrued office salaries, $1,000.

    i. Social security tax on accrued salaries, $326; Medicare tax on accrued salaries, $76. (Assumes that tax rates have increased.)

    j. Federal unemployment tax on accrued salaries, $56; state unemployment tax on accrued salaries, $270.

2. Journalize the adjusting entries on page 30 of the general journal. Omit descriptions.
3. Journalize the closing entries on page 32 of the general journal. Omit descriptions.
4. Compute the following:

    a. net sales

    b. net delivered cost of purchases

    c. cost of goods sold

    d. net income or net loss

    e. balance of **Ben Waites, Capital** on December 31, 20X1.

Analyze: What change(s) to **Ben Waites, Capital** will be reported on the statement of owner's equity?

BEN'S JEWELERS Trial Balance December 31, 20X1		
Cash	$ 13,050	Dr
Accounts Receivable	49,900	Dr.
Allowance for Doubtful Accounts	2,000	Cr.
Merchandise Inventory	105,900	Dr.
Store Supplies	4,230	Dr.
Office Supplies	2,950	Dr.
Store Equipment	113,590	Dr.
Accumulated Depreciation—Store Equipment	13,010	Cr.
Office Equipment	27,640	Dr.
Accumulated Depreciation—Office Equipment	4,930	Cr.
Accounts Payable	4,390	Cr.

BEN'S JEWELERS
Trial Balance
December 31, 20X1

Salaries Payable		
Social Security Tax Payable		
Medicare Tax Payable		
Federal Unemployment Tax Payable		
State Unemployment Tax Payable		
Ben Waites, Capital	166,310	Cr.
Ben Waites, Drawing	30,000	Dr.
Income Summary		
Sales	862,230	Cr.
Sales Returns and Allowances	7,580	Dr.
Purchases	504,810	Dr.
Purchases Returns and Allowances	4,240	Cr.
Purchases Discounts	10,770	Cr.
Freight In	7,000	Dr.
Salaries Expense—Sales	75,950	Dr.
Rent Expense	35,500	Dr.
Advertising Expense	12,300	Dr.
Store Supplies Expense		
Depreciation Expense—Store Equipment		
Salaries Expense—Office	77,480	Dr.
Uncollectible Accounts Expense		
Payroll Taxes Expense		
Office Supplies Expense		
Depreciation Expense—Office Equipment		

Critical Thinking Problem 12.2

Net Profit

When Sandra Michaels's father took seriously ill suddenly, Sandra had just completed the semester in college, so she stepped in to run the family business, ASAP Couriers, until it could be sold. Under her father's direction, the company was a successful operation and provided ample money to meet the family's needs.

Sandra was majoring in biology in college and knew little about business or accounting, but she was eager to do a good job of running the business so it would command a good selling price. Since all of the services performed were paid in cash, Sandra figured that she would do all right as long as the *Cash* account increased. Thus, she was delighted to watch the cash balance increase from $24,800 at the beginning of the first month to $64,528 at the end of the second month—an increase of $39,728 during the two months she had been in charge. When she was presented an income statement for the two months by the company's bookkeeper, she could not understand why it did not show that amount as income but instead reported only $19,700 as net income.

Knowing that you are taking an accounting class, Sandra brings the income statement, shown below, to you and asks if you can help her understand the difference.

ASAP COURIERS
Income Statement
Months of June and July, 20X1

Operating Revenues		
Delivery Fees		$205,018
Operating Expenses		
Salaries and Related Taxes	$128,224	
Gasoline and Oil	32,500	
Repairs Expense	6,470	
Supplies Expense	2,268	
Insurance Expense	2,856	
Depreciation Expense	13,000	
Total Operating Expense		185,318
Net Income		$ 19,700

In addition, Sandra permits you to examine the accounting records, which show that the balance of **Salaries Payable** was $2,680 at the beginning of the first month but had increased to $7,140 at the end of the second month. Most of the balance in the **Insurance Expense** account reflects monthly insurance payments covering only one month each. However, the **Prepaid Insurance** account had decreased $300 during the two months, and all supplies had been purchased before Sandra took over. The balances of the company's other asset and liability accounts showed no changes.

1. Explain the cause of the difference between the increase in the **Cash** account balance and the net income for the two months.
2. Prepare a schedule that accounts for this difference.

BUSINESS CONNECTIONS

Out of Balance
The president of Tower Copper Company has told you to go out to the factory and count merchandise inventory. He said the stockholders were coming for a meeting next week and he wanted to put on a good show. He asked you to make the inventory a bit heavier by counting the first and last rows twice. The higher ending inventory will result in higher net income. What should you do?

Balance Sheet
McCormick and Company, Inc., reported the following in its *2018 Annual Report:*

Consolidated Balance Sheet

at November 30 (millions)	2018	2017
Assets		
Cash and cash equivalents	$ 96.6	$ 186.8
Trade accounts receivable, less allowances	518.1	555.1
Inventories	786.3	793.3
Prepaid expenses and other current assets	78.9	81.8
Total current assets	1,479.9	1,617.0
Property, plant, and equipment, net	985.1	809.1

Analyze:

1. Based on the information presented above, which categories might require adjusting entries at the end of an operating period?
2. List the potential adjusting entries. Disregard dollar amounts.
3. By what percentage did McCormick's cash and cash equivalents decrease from 2017 to 2018?

Both Sellers and Servers Adjust

Accruals and deferrals can vary for each company. The adjusting entries for a service company will differ from those of a merchandising company. Brainstorm the adjusting entries' similarities and differences for a service company and a merchandising company.

TEAMWORK

Answers to Comprehensive Self Review

1. The accrual method properly matches expenses with revenues in each accounting period so that statement users can rely on the financial statements prepared for each period.
2. Accrued income is income that has been earned but that has not yet been received in cash or other assets.
3. Accrued income is income earned but not yet received. Unearned income is the reverse of accrued income: It is an amount that has been received but has not yet been earned.
4. This represents a loss because expenses are greater than income. The loss is $28,000.
5. *Unearned Rent Income* will be debited for $18,000 and *Rent Income* will be credited for $18,000.
6. *Rent Income* will be debited for $18,000 and *Unearned Rent Income* will be credited for that amount.

Financial Statements and Closing Procedure

Chapter 13

Susan Montgomery/Shutterstock

www.vitaminshoppe.com

Vitamin Shoppe, Inc., is an omnichannel merchandising business that operates 785 locations throughout the United States and Puerto Rico. The company carries 900 brands, which encompass 26,000 unique products. These products include a wide variety of vitamins, minerals, and sports nutrition supplements. As a result of the complex nature of the business, Vitamin Shoppe has multiple elements that contribute to its calculation of net income. This complexity also results in the existence of different classes of assets and liabilities. Therefore, Vitamin Shoppe uses classified financial statements to report its financial results, which are more extensive versions of the financial statements to which you were previously introduced.

For the fiscal year ended December 30, 2017, Vitamin Shoppe reported net sales of $1.18 billion and a net loss of $252 million. However, within the classified income statements, there are a number of subtotals between these amounts. To arrive at these subtotals, Vitamin Shoppe reports cost of goods sold of $821 million; selling, general, and administrative expenses of $345 million; and net interest expense of $9.7 million, among other items. The company's classified balance sheets similarly display multiple asset categories (current assets, net property and equipment, goodwill) and multiple liability categories (current liabilities, net convertible notes, deferred rent).

Vitamin Shoppe defines success as "providing a fulfilling customer experience to each person who shops in our store." In pursuit of this goal, the company will continue to focus on both customer needs and retail fundamentals, while embracing the current digital transformation. Presenting information within classified financial statements ensures that current and potential investors and creditors can more fully appreciate the myriad activities that lead to the company's bottom line.

thinking critically

Given that it operates retail nutrition stores, what types of expenses do you think Vitamin Shoppe includes within the selling, general, and administrative expenses category on its classified income statement?

LEARNING OBJECTIVES

- **13-1** Prepare a classified income statement from the worksheet.
- **13-2** Prepare a statement of owner's equity from the worksheet.
- **13-3** Prepare a classified balance sheet from the worksheet.
- **13-4** Journalize and post the adjusting entries.
- **13-5** Journalize and post the closing entries.
- **13-6** Prepare a postclosing trial balance and calculate various financial ratios.
- **13-7** Journalize and post reversing entries.
- **13-8** Define the accounting terms new to this chapter.

NEW TERMS

accounts receivable turnover
average collection period
average number of days in inventory
classified financial statement
condensed income statement
current assets
current liabilities
current ratio
gross profit
gross profit percentage
inventory turnover
liquidity
long-term liabilities
multiple-step income statement
plant and equipment
reversing entries
single-step income statement
working capital

Section 1

SECTION OBJECTIVES	TERMS TO LEARN
>> 13-1 Prepare a classified income statement from the worksheet. **WHY IT'S IMPORTANT** To help decision makers, financial information needs to be presented in a meaningful and easy-to-use way. **>> 13-2** Prepare a statement of owner's equity from the worksheet. **WHY IT'S IMPORTANT** The statement of owner's equity reports changes to and balances in the owner's equity account. **>> 13-3** Prepare a classified balance sheet from the worksheet. **WHY IT'S IMPORTANT** Grouping accounts helps financial statement users to identify total assets, equity, and financial obligations of the business.	classified financial statement condensed income statement current assets current liabilities gross profit liquidity long-term liabilities multiple-step income statement plant and equipment single-step income statement

Preparing the Financial Statements

The information needed to prepare the financial statements is on the worksheet in the Income Statement and Balance Sheet sections. At the end of the period, Whiteside Antiques prepares three financial statements: income statement, statement of owner's equity, and balance sheet, based on the worksheet you studied in Chapter 12. The income statement and the balance sheet are arranged in a classified format. On **classified financial statements,** revenues, expenses, assets, and liabilities are divided into groups of similar accounts and a subtotal is given for each group. This makes the financial statements more useful to the readers.

> The annual report of the Coca-Cola Company includes Consolidated Balance Sheets, Consolidated Statements of Income, and Consolidated Statements of Shareowners' Equity. The annual report also contains a table of Selected Financial Data that reports five consecutive years of summarized financial information.

>> **13-1 OBJECTIVE**
Prepare a classified income statement from the worksheet.

The Classified Income Statement

A classified income statement is sometimes called a **multiple-step income statement** because several subtotals are computed before net income is calculated. The simpler income statement you learned about in previous chapters is called a **single-step income statement.** It lists all revenues in one section and all expenses in another section. Only one computation is necessary to determine the net income (Total Revenue − Total Expenses = Net Income).

Figure 13.1 shows the classified income statement for Whiteside Antiques. Refer to it as you learn how to prepare a multiple-step income statement.

Operating Revenue

The first section of the classified income statement contains the revenue from operations. This is the revenue earned from normal business activities. Other income is presented separately near the bottom of the statement. For Whiteside Antiques, all operating revenue comes from sales of merchandise.

FIGURE 13.1 Classified Income Statement

Whiteside Antiques
Income Statement
Year Ended December 31, 20X1

Operating Revenue				
Sales				561,650.00
Less Sales Returns and Allowances				12,500.00
Net Sales				549,150.00
Cost of Goods Sold				
Merchandise Inventory, Jan. 1, 20X1			52,000.00	
Purchases		321,500.00		
Freight In		9,800.00		
Delivered Cost of Purchases		331,300.00		
Less Purchases Returns and Allowances	3,050.00			
Purchases Discounts	3,130.00	6,180.00		
Net Delivered Cost of Purchases			325,120.00	
Total Merchandise Available for Sale			377,120.00	
Less Merchandise Inventory, Dec. 31, 20X1			47,000.00	
Cost of Goods Sold				330,120.00
Gross Profit on Sales				219,030.00
Operating Expenses				
Selling Expenses				
Salaries Expense—Sales		79,690.00		
Advertising Expense		7,425.00		
Cash Short or Over		125.00		
Supplies Expense		4,975.00		
Depreciation Expense—Store Equipment		2,400.00		
Total Selling Expenses			94,615.00	
General and Administrative Expenses				
Rent Expense		27,600.00		
Salaries Expense—Office		26,500.00		
Insurance Expense		2,450.00		
Payroll Taxes Expense		7,368.80		
Telephone Expense		1,875.00		
Uncollectible Accounts Expense		800.00		
Utilities Expense		5,925.00		
Depreciation Expense—Office Equipment		700.00		
Total General and Administrative Expenses			73,218.80	
Total Operating Expenses				167,833.80
Net Income from Operations				51,196.20
Other Income				
Interest Income		166.00		
Miscellaneous Income		366.00		
Total Other Income			532.00	
Other Expenses				
Interest Expense			770.00	
Net Nonoperating Expense				238.00
Net Income for Year				50,958.20

Because Whiteside Antiques is a retail firm, it does not offer sales discounts to its customers. If it did, the sales discounts would be deducted from total sales in order to compute net sales. The net sales amount is computed as follows:

>Sales
>(Sales Returns and Allowances)
>(Sales Discounts)
>―――――――――
>Net Sales

The parentheses indicate that the amount is subtracted. Net sales for Whiteside Antiques are $549,150 for 20X1.

Cost of Goods Sold

The Cost of Goods Sold section contains information about the cost of the merchandise that was sold during the period. Three elements are needed to compute the cost of goods sold: beginning inventory, net delivered cost of purchases, and ending inventory. The format is:

For Whiteside Antiques, the net delivered cost of purchases is $325,120 and the cost of goods sold is $330,120. **Merchandise Inventory** is the one account that appears on both the income statement and the balance sheet. Beginning and ending merchandise inventory balances appear on the income statement. Ending merchandise inventory also appears on the balance sheet in the Assets section.

Gross Profit on Sales

The **gross profit** on sales is the difference between the net sales and the cost of goods sold. For Whiteside, net sales is the revenue earned from selling antique items. Cost of goods sold is what Whiteside paid for the antiques that were sold during the fiscal period. Gross profit is what is left to cover operating and other expenses and provide a profit. The format is:

>Net Sales
>(Cost of Goods Sold)
>―――――――――
>Gross Profit on Sales

The gross profit on sales is $219,030.

Operating Expenses

Operating expenses are expenses that arise from normal business activities. Whiteside Antiques separates operating expenses into two categories: *Selling Expenses* and *General and Administrative Expenses*. The selling expenses relate directly to the marketing, sale, and delivery of goods. The general and administrative expenses are necessary for business operations but are not directly connected with the sales function. Rent, utilities, and salaries for office employees are examples of general and administrative expenses.

Merchandising firms often use warehouses to store inventory. These firms would have an additional operating expense category: *Warehouse Expenses*.

Net Income or Net Loss from Operations

Keeping operating and nonoperating income separate helps financial statement users learn about the operating efficiency of the firm. The format for determining net income (or net loss) from operations is:

> Gross Profit on Sales
> (Total Operating Expenses)
> ―――――――――――――――
> Net Income (or Net Loss) from Operations

For Whiteside Antiques, net income from operations is $51,196.20.

Other Income and other Expenses

Income that is earned from sources other than normal business activities appears in the Other Income section. For Whiteside Antiques, other income includes interest on notes receivable and one miscellaneous income item.

Expenses that are not directly connected with business operations appear in the Other Expenses section. The only other expense for Whiteside Antiques is interest expense.

Net Income or Net Loss

Net income is all the revenue minus all the expenses. For Whiteside Antiques, net income is $50,958.20. If there is a net loss, it appears in parentheses. Net income or net loss is used to prepare the statement of owner's equity.

Condensed Income Statement

Many companies provide condensed financial statements to vendors and creditors. A **condensed income statement** summarizes much of the detail into a few lines of information. A condensed income statement for Whiteside Antiques is prepared below, in whole dollars.

Whiteside Antiques
Income Statement
Year Ended December 31, 20X1

Net Sales		549,150
Cost of Goods Sold		330,120
Gross Profit		219,030
Operating Expenses:		
Selling Expenses	94,615	
General and Administrative Expenses	73,219	
Total Operating Expenses		167,834
Net Income from Operations		51,196
Other Expense, Net		238
Net Income for Year		50,958

The Statement of Owner's Equity

>> **13-2 OBJECTIVE**
Prepare a statement of owner's equity from the worksheet.

The statement of owner's equity reports the changes that occurred in the owner's financial interest during the period. Figure 13.2 shows the statement of owner's equity for Whiteside Antiques. The ending capital balance for Bill Whiteside, $84,579.20, is used to prepare the balance sheet.

The Classified Balance Sheet

>> **13-3 OBJECTIVE**
Prepare a classified balance sheet from the worksheet.

The classified balance sheet divides the various assets and liabilities into groups. Figure 13.3 shows the balance sheet for Whiteside Antiques. Refer to it as you learn how to prepare a classified balance sheet.

FIGURE 13.2
Statement of Owner's Equity

Whiteside Antiques
Statement of Owner's Equity
Year Ended December 31, 20X1

Bill Whiteside, Capital, January 1, 20X1			61 221 00
Net Income for Year	50 958 20		
Less Withdrawals for the Year	27 600 00		
Increase in Capital			23 358 20
Bill Whiteside, Capital, December 31, 20X1			84 579 20

FIGURE 13.3
Classified Balance Sheet

ABOUT ACCOUNTING
Financial Reports
Most large companies present comparative condensed income statements and balance sheets. The Securities and Exchange Commission requires most publicly traded corporations to present three years of income statements and two years of balance sheets. This provides users information that helps assess the progress in profit and financial strength of the company.

Whiteside Antiques
Balance Sheet
December 31, 20X1

Assets			
Current Assets			
Cash			13 136 00
Petty Cash Fund			100 00
Notes Receivable			1 200 00
Accounts Receivable		32 000 00	
Less Allowance for Doubtful Accounts		1 050 00	30 950 00
Interest Receivable			30 00
Merchandise Inventory			47 000 00
Prepaid Expenses			
Supplies		1 325 00	
Prepaid Insurance		4 900 00	
Prepaid Interest		75 00	6 300 00
Total Current Assets			98 716 00
Plant and Equipment			
Store Equipment	30 000 00		
Less Accumulated Depreciation	2 400 00	27 600 00	
Office Equipment	5 000 00		
Less Accumulated Depreciation	700 00	4 300 00	
Total Plant and Equipment			31 900 00
Total Assets			130 616 00
Liabilities and Owner's Equity			
Current Liabilities			
Notes Payable—Trade		2 000 00	
Notes Payable—Bank		9 000 00	
Accounts Payable		24 129 00	
Interest Payable		20 00	
Social Security Tax Payable		1 158 40	
Medicare Tax Payable		267 40	
Employee Income Tax Payable		990 00	
Federal Unemployment Tax Payable		7 20	
State Unemployment Tax Payable		64 80	
Salaries Payable		1 200 00	
Sales Tax Payable		7 200 00	
Total Current Liabilities			46 036 80
Owner's Equity			
Bill Whiteside, Capital			84 579 20
Total Liabilities and Owner's Equity			130 616 00

Current Assets

Current assets consist of cash, items that will normally be converted into cash within one year, and items that will be used up within one year. Current assets are usually listed in order of liquidity. **Liquidity** is the ease with which an item can be converted into cash. Current assets are vital to the survival of a business because they provide the funds needed to pay bills and meet expenses. The current assets for Whiteside Antiques total $98,716.

Plant and Equipment

Noncurrent assets are called *long-term assets.* An important category of long-term assets is plant and equipment. **Plant and equipment** consists of property that will be used in the business for longer than one year. For many businesses, plant and equipment represents a sizable investment. The balance sheet shows three amounts for each category of plant and equipment:

> Asset
> (Accumulated depreciation)
> Book value

For Whiteside Antiques, total plant and equipment is $31,900.

Current Liabilities

Current liabilities are the debts that must be paid within one year. They are usually listed in order of priority of payment. Management must ensure that funds are available to pay current liabilities when they become due in order to maintain the firm's good credit reputation. For Whiteside Antiques, total current liabilities are $46,036.80.

Long-Term Liabilities

Long-term liabilities are debts of the business that are due more than one year in the future. Although repayment of long-term liabilities might not be due for several years, management must make sure that periodic interest is paid promptly. Long-term liabilities include mortgages, notes payable, and loans payable. Whiteside Antiques had no long-term liabilities on December 31, 20X1.

Owner's Equity

Whiteside Antiques prepares a separate statement of owner's equity that reports all information about changes that occurred in Bill Whiteside's financial interest during the period. The ending balance of the owner's capital account is transferred from that statement to the Owner's Equity section of the balance sheet.

recall

Book Value
Book value is the portion of the original cost that has not been depreciated. Usually, book value bears no relation to the market value of the asset.

Section 1 Review

1. Roberto Company has sales of $1,000,000, sales returns and allowances of $10,000, sales discounts of $2,000, and salary expense—sales of $120,000. What is the amount of net sales?
   a. $1,012,000
   b. $988,000
   c. $1,132,000
   d. $868,000

2. Kelley Company has beginning inventory of $125,000, purchases of $950,000, purchases returns and allowances of $25,000, freight-in of $10,000, and ending inventory of $118,000. What is the amount of the cost of goods sold?
   a. $922,000
   b. $928,000
   c. $992,000
   d. $942,000

3. Chen Company has net sales of $500,000, cost of goods sold of $300,000, and interest expense of $10,000. What is the amount of gross profit on sales?
   a. $200,000
   b. $198,000
   c. $202,000
   d. none of these

4. Which of the following is not a current asset?
   a. merchandise inventory
   b. a note receivable due in 11 months
   c. prepaid insurance covering the next eight months
   d. a note receivable due in 13 months

5. How should purchases returns and allowances be shown on the income statement?
   a. as Other Income
   b. as an addition to the delivered cost of purchases
   c. as a deduction from the delivered cost of purchases
   d. as Other Expenses

6. Which of these is not a general and administrative expense?
   a. rent expense
   b. salaries expense—office
   c. advertising expense
   d. uncollectible accounts expense

7. The balance of *James Wilson, Capital* at the beginning of the period was $50,000. During the period, his company had net income of $40,000, and he withdrew $35,000 from the business for personal use. What is the amount of the *James Wilson, Capital* account at the end of the accounting period?
   a. $125,000
   b. $5,000
   c. $45,000
   d. $55,000

8. Which of the following would not be classified as Plant and Equipment on a balance sheet?
   a. prepaid insurance
   b. autos
   c. store equipment
   d. office equipment

Section 2

SECTION OBJECTIVES	TERMS TO LEARN
>> 13-4 Journalize and post the adjusting entries. **WHY IT'S IMPORTANT** Adjusting entries match revenue and expenses to the proper periods. **>> 13-5** Journalize and post the closing entries. **WHY IT'S IMPORTANT** The temporary accounts are closed in order to prepare for the next accounting period. **>> 13-6** Prepare a postclosing trial balance. **WHY IT'S IMPORTANT** The general ledger must remain in balance. **>> 13-7** Journalize and post reversing entries. **WHY IT'S IMPORTANT** Reversing entries are made so that transactions can be recorded in the usual way in the next accounting period.	accounts receivable turnover average collection period average number of days in inventory current ratio gross profit percentage inventory turnover reversing entries working capital

Completing the Accounting Cycle

The complete accounting cycle was presented in Chapter 6. In this section, we will complete the accounting cycle for Whiteside Antiques.

Journalizing and Posting the Adjusting Entries

All adjustments are shown on the worksheet. After the financial statements have been prepared, the adjustments are made a permanent part of the accounting records. They are recorded in the general journal as adjusting journal entries and are posted to the general ledger.

>> **13-4 OBJECTIVE**
Journalize and post the adjusting entries.

Journalizing the Adjusting Entries

Figure 13.4 shows the adjusting journal entries for Whiteside Antiques. Each adjusting entry shows how the adjustment was calculated. Supervisors and auditors need to understand, without additional explanation, why the adjustment was made.

Let's review the types of adjusting entries made by Whiteside Antiques:

Type of Adjustment	Worksheet Reference	Purpose
Inventory	(a–b)	Removes beginning inventory and adds ending inventory to the accounting records.
Expense	(c–e)	Matches expense to revenue for the period; the credit is to a contra asset account. Required for bad debts and depreciation.
Accrued Expense	(f–i)	Matches expense to revenue for the period; the credit is to a liability account.
Prepaid Expense	(j–l)	Matches expense to revenue for the period; the credit is to an asset account.
Accrued Income	(m)	Recognizes income earned in the period. The debit is to an asset account.

FIGURE 13.4

Adjusting Entries in the General Journal

GENERAL JOURNAL

PAGE 25

DATE		DESCRIPTION	POST. REF.	DEBIT	CREDIT
		Adjusting Entries			
20X1		(Adjustment a)			
Dec.	31	Income Summary	399	52 000 00	
		Merchandise Inventory	121		52 000 00
		To transfer beginning inventory			
		to Income Summary			
		(Adjustment b)			
	31	Merchandise Inventory	121	47 000 00	
		Income Summary	399		47 000 00
		To record ending inventory			
		(Adjustment c)			
	31	Uncollectible Accounts Expense	685	800 00	
		Allowance For Doubtful Accounts	112		800 00
		To record estimated loss			
		from uncollectible accounts			
		based on 0.80% of net			
		credit sales of $100,000			
		(Adjustment d)			
	31	Depreciation Expense—Store Equip.	620	2 400 00	
		Accum. Depreciation—Store Equip.	132		2 400 00
		To record depreciation			
		for 20X1 as shown by			
		schedule on file			
		(Adjustment e)			
	31	Depreciation Expense—Office Equip.	689	700 00	
		Accum. Depreciation—Office Equip.	142		700 00
		To record depreciation			
		for 20X1 as shown by			
		schedule on file			
		(Adjustment f)			
	31	Salaries Expense—Sales	602	1 200 00	
		Salaries Payable	229		1 200 00
		To record accrued salaries			
		of part-time sales clerks			
		for Dec. 28–31			

(continued)

FIGURE 13.4

Adjusting Entries in the General Journal (continued)

GENERAL JOURNAL PAGE 26

DATE		DESCRIPTION	POST. REF.	DEBIT	CREDIT
		Adjusting Entries			
20X1		(Adjustment g)			
Dec.	31	Payroll Taxes Expense	665	91 80	
		Social Security Tax Payable	221		74 40
		Medicare Tax Payable	223		17 40
		To record accrued payroll			
		taxes on accrued salaries			
		for Dec. 28–31			
		(Adjustment h)			
	31	Payroll Taxes Expense	665	72 00	
		Fed. Unemployment Tax Payable	225		7 20
		State Unemployment Tax Payable	227		64 80
		To record accrued payroll			
		taxes on accrued salaries			
		for Dec. 28–31			
		(Adjustment i)			
	31	Interest Expense	695	20 00	
		Interest Payable	216		20 00
		To record interest on a			
		2-month, $2,000, 12%			
		note payable dated			
		Dec. 1, 20X1			
		($2,000 x .12 x 1/12)			
		(Adjustment j)			
	31	Supplies Expense	615	4 975 00	
		Supplies	129		4 975 00
		To record supplies used			
		(Adjustment k)			
	31	Insurance Expense	660	2 450 00	
		Prepaid Insurance	126		2 450 00
		To record expired			
		insurance on 3-year			
		policy purchased for			
		$7,350 on Jan. 2, 20X1			

(continued)

FIGURE 13.4

Adjusting Entries in the General Journal (continued)

		GENERAL JOURNAL			PAGE 27
	DATE	DESCRIPTION	POST. REF.	DEBIT	CREDIT
1	20X1	(Adjustment l)			
2	Dec. 31	Interest Expense	695	150 00	
3		Prepaid Interest	127		150 00
4		To record transfer of 2/3			
5		of prepaid interest of			
6		$225 for a 3-month,			
7		10% note payable issued			
8		to bank on Nov. 1, 20X1			
9					
10		(Adjustment m)			
11		31 Interest Receivable	116	30 00	
12		Interest Income	491		30 00
13		To record accrued interest			
14		earned on a 4-month,			
15		15% note receivable			
16		dated Nov. 1, 20X1			
17		($1,200 x 0.15 x 2/12)			

Posting the Adjusting Entries

After the adjustments have been recorded in the general journal, they are promptly posted to the general ledger. The word *Adjusting* is entered in the Description column of the general ledger account. This distinguishes it from entries for transactions that occurred during that period. After the adjusting entries have been posted, the general ledger account balances match the amounts shown in the Adjusted Trial Balance section of the worksheet in Figure 12.2.

>> **13-5 OBJECTIVE**

Journalize and post the closing entries.

Journalizing and Posting the Closing Entries

At the end of the period, the temporary accounts are closed. The temporary accounts are the revenue, cost of goods sold, expense, income summary, and drawing accounts.

Journalizing the Closing Entries

We were first introduced to closing journal entries in Chapter 6. Due to the additional accounts required for merchandising companies, the closing journal entries are more complex for a merchandising firm.

The Income Statement section of the worksheet in Figure 12.2 provides the data needed to prepare closing entries. There are four steps in the closing process:

1. Close revenue accounts and cost of goods sold accounts with credit balances to *Income Summary.*
2. Close expense accounts and cost of goods sold accounts with debit balances to *Income Summary.*
3. Close *Income Summary,* which now reflects the net income or loss for the period, to owner's capital.
4. Close the drawing account to owner's capital.

Step 1: **Closing the Revenue Accounts and the Cost of Goods Sold Accounts with Credit Balances.** The first entry closes the revenue accounts and other temporary income statement accounts with credit balances. Look at the Income Statement section of the worksheet in Figure 12.2. There are five items listed in the Credit column, not including *Income Summary*. Debit each account, except *Income Summary*, for its balance. Credit *Income Summary* for the total, $568,362.

	GENERAL JOURNAL			PAGE 28
DATE	DESCRIPTION	POST. REF.	DEBIT	CREDIT
20X1	Closing Entries			
Dec. 31	Sales	401	561 650 00	
	Interest Income	491	166 00	
	Miscellaneous Income	493	366 00	
	Purchases Returns and Allowances	503	3 050 00	
	Purchases Discounts	504	3 130 00	
	Income Summary			568 362 00

Step 2: **Closing the Expense Accounts and the Cost of Goods Sold Accounts with Debit Balances.** The Debit column of the Income Statement section of the worksheet in Figure 12.2 shows the expense accounts and the cost of goods sold accounts with debit balances. Credit each account, *except Income Summary,* for its balance. Debit *Income Summary* for the total, $512,403.80.

	GENERAL JOURNAL			PAGE 28
DATE	DESCRIPTION	POST. REF.	DEBIT	CREDIT
20X1				
Dec. 31	Income Summary	399	512 403 80	
	Sales Returns and Allowances	451		12 500 00
	Purchases	501		321 500 00
	Freight In	502		9 800 00
	Salaries Expense—Sales	602		79 690 00
	Advertising Expense	605		7 425 00
	Cash Short or Over	610		125 00
	Supplies Expense	615		4 975 00
	Depreciation Expense—Store Equip.	620		2 400 00
	Rent Expense	640		27 600 00
	Salaries Expense—Office	645		26 500 00
	Insurance Expense	660		2 450 00
	Payroll Taxes Expense	665		7 368 80
	Telephone Expense	680		1 875 00
	Uncollectible Accounts Expense	685		800 00
	Utilities Expense	687		5 925 00
	Depreciation Expense—Office Equip.	689		700 00
	Interest Expense	695		770 00

Step 3: **Closing the *Income Summary* Account.** After the first two closing entries have been posted, the balance of the *Income Summary* account is equal to the net income or net loss for the period. The third closing entry transfers the *Income*

Summary balance to the owner's capital account. *Income Summary* after the second closing entry has a balance of $50,958.20.

Income Summary			
12/31	52,000.00	12/31	47,000.00
12/31	512,403.80	12/31	568,362.00
	564,403.80		615,362.00
		Bal.	50,958.20

Adjusting Entries (a–b)
Closing Entries

Keep in mind the first debit and the first credit in the *Income Summary* account above resulted from the adjusting journal entries for *Merchandise Inventory* discussed in Chapter 12. For Whiteside Antiques, the third closing entry is as follows. This closes the *Income Summary* account, which remains closed until it is used in the end-of-period process for the next year.

	GENERAL JOURNAL		PAGE 28	
DATE	DESCRIPTION	POST. REF.	DEBIT	CREDIT
Dec. 31	Income Summary	399	50 958 20	
	Bill Whiteside, Capital	301		50 958 20

Step 4: Closing the Drawing Account. This entry closes the drawing account and updates the capital account so that its balance agrees with the ending capital reported on the statement of owner's equity and on the balance sheet.

	GENERAL JOURNAL		PAGE 28	
DATE	DESCRIPTION	POST. REF.	DEBIT	CREDIT
Dec. 31	Bill Whiteside, Capital	301	27 600 00	
	Bill Whiteside, Drawing	302		27 600 00

Posting the Closing Entries

The closing entries are posted from the general journal to the general ledger. The word *Closing* is entered in the Description column of each account that is closed. After the closing entry is posted, each temporary account balance is zero.

>> **13-6 OBJECTIVE**

Prepare a postclosing trial balance and calculate various financial ratios.

Preparing a Postclosing Trial Balance

After the closing entries have been posted, prepare a postclosing trial balance to confirm that the general ledger is in balance. Only the accounts that have balances—the asset, liability, and owner's capital accounts—appear on the postclosing trial balance. The postclosing trial balance matches the amounts reported on the balance sheet. To verify this, compare the postclosing trial balance, Figure 13.5, with the balance sheet, Figure 13.3.

If the postclosing trial balance shows that the general ledger is out of balance, find and correct the error or errors immediately. Any necessary correcting entries must be journalized and posted so that the general ledger is in balance before any transactions can be recorded for the new period.

FIGURE 13.5

Postclosing Trial Balance

Whiteside Antiques
Postclosing Trial Balance
December 31, 20X1

ACCOUNT NAME	DEBIT	CREDIT
Cash	13 136 00	
Petty Cash Fund	100 00	
Notes Receivable	1 200 00	
Accounts Receivable	32 000 00	
Allowance for Doubtful Accounts		1 050 00
Interest Receivable	30 00	
Merchandise Inventory	47 000 00	
Supplies	1 325 00	
Prepaid Insurance	4 900 00	
Prepaid Interest	75 00	
Store Equipment	30 000 00	
Accumulated Depreciation—Store Equipment		2 400 00
Office Equipment	5 000 00	
Accumulated Depreciation—Office Equipment		700 00
Notes Payable—Trade		2 000 00
Notes Payable—Bank		9 000 00
Accounts Payable		24 129 00
Interest Payable		20 00
Social Security Tax Payable		1 158 40
Medicare Tax Payable		267 40
Employee Income Taxes Payable		990 00
Federal Unemployment Tax Payable		7 20
State Unemployment Tax Payable		64 80
Salaries Payable		1 200 00
Sales Tax Payable		7 200 00
Bill Whiteside, Capital		84 579 20
Totals	134 766 00	134 766 00

Interpreting the Financial Statements

Interested parties analyze the financial statements to evaluate the results of operations and to make decisions. Interpreting financial statements requires an understanding of the business and the environment in which it operates as well as the nature and limitations of accounting information. Ratios and other measurements are used to analyze and interpret financial statements. Seven such measurements are used by Whiteside Antiques.

The **gross profit percentage** reveals the amount of gross profit from each sales dollar. The gross profit percentage is calculated by dividing gross profit by net sales. For Whiteside Antiques, gross profit was almost 40 cents for every dollar of net sales.

$$\frac{\text{Gross profit}}{\text{Net sales}} = \frac{\$219{,}030}{\$549{,}150} = 0.3988 = 39.9\%$$

> In its income statement for the fiscal year ended February 3, 2018, The Gap, Inc., reported gross profit of $6,066 million on net sales of $15,855 million, resulting in a gross profit percentage of 38.3 percent.

Working capital is the difference between total current assets and total current liabilities. It is a measure of the firm's ability to pay its current obligations. Whiteside Antiques' working capital is $52,679.20, calculated as follows:

$$\text{Current assets} - \text{Current liabilities} = \$98{,}716.00 - \$46{,}036.80 = \$52{,}679.20$$

important!

Current Ratio
Banks and other lenders look closely at the current ratio of each loan applicant.

The **current ratio** is a relationship between current assets and current liabilities that provides a measure of a firm's ability to pay its current debts. Whiteside has $2.14 in current assets for every dollar of current liabilities. The current ratio may also be compared to that of other firms in the same business. The current ratio is calculated in the following manner:

$$\frac{\text{Current assets}}{\text{Current liabilities}} = \frac{\$98,716.00}{\$46,036.80} = 2.14 \text{ to } 1$$

> Microsoft reported current assets of **$169.7 billion** and current liabilities of **$58.5 billion** on June 30, 2018. The current ratio shows that the business has **$2.90** of current assets for each dollar of current liabilities.

Inventory turnover shows the number of times inventory is replaced during the accounting period. Inventory turnover is calculated in the following manner:

$$\text{Inventory turnover} = \frac{\text{Cost of goods sold}}{\text{Average inventory}}$$

$$\text{Average inventory} = \frac{\text{Beginning inventory} + \text{Ending inventory}}{2}$$

$$\text{Average inventory} = \frac{\$52,000 + \$47,000}{2} = \$49,500$$

$$\text{Inventory turnover} = \frac{\$330,120}{\$49,500} = 6.67 \text{ times}$$

For Whiteside Antiques, the average inventory for the year was $49,500. The inventory turnover was 6.67; that is, inventory was replaced about seven times during the year.

We can use the inventory turnover to estimate the average number of days it takes to sell inventory once purchased. The **average collection period** is computed by dividing 365 days by the inventory turnover. For Whiteside Antiques, its **average number of days in inventory** for 20X1 was approximately 54.7 days, calculated as:

$$\text{Average number of days in inventory} = \frac{365}{6.67} = 54.7 \text{ days}$$

A company needs to collect accounts receivable promptly. This minimizes the amount of working capital tied up in receivables and improves cash flow. The **accounts receivable turnover** measures the reasonableness of accounts receivable outstanding and can be used to estimate the average collection period of accounts receivable.

> In 2017, Amazon.com reported cost of goods sold of approximately **$111.9 billion** and average inventory balances of approximately **$13.8 billion**. The inventory turnover was **8.11 times**, meaning it takes Amazon.com on average **45 days** to sell its inventory.

The accounts receivable turnover is computed as follows:

$$\text{Accounts receivable turnover} = \frac{\text{Net credit sales}}{\text{Average accounts receivable}}$$

Assume the net credit sales for Whiteside Antiques were $326,975 in 20X1 and that the balance of accounts receivable at December 31, 20X0, was $28,500. The average accounts receivable are $29,725, calculated as:

$$\text{Average accounts receivable} = \frac{\$28,500 + \$30,950}{2} = \$29,725$$

The accounts receivable balances used above are after deducting the allowance for doubtful accounts. The accounts receivable turnover is 11. The calculation follows.

$$\text{Accounts receivable turnover} = \frac{\$326,975}{\$29,725} = 11.0 \text{ times}$$

We can use the accounts receivable turnover to estimate the average collection period. The average collection period is computed by dividing 365 days by the accounts receivable turnover. For Whiteside Antiques, its average collection period in 20X1 was 33.2 days, calculated as:

$$\text{Average collection period} = \frac{365 \text{ days}}{11.0} = 33.2 \text{ days}$$

If Whiteside Antiques grants credit terms of n/30 days, its average collection period would be considered satisfactory.

The following table summarizes the ratios discussed in this chapter.

Name of Ratio	Ratio Formula	Purpose of Ratio
Working capital (expressed in dollars)	Current assets − Current liabilities	To measure a firm's ability to pay its current obligations.
Current ratio	Current assets ÷ Current liabilities	This is another measure of a firm's ability to pay its current obligations. The current ratio may be compared to other firms in the same business.
Gross profit percentage	Gross profit ÷ Net sales	To calculate the amount of gross profit earned from each dollar of sales.
Inventory turnover	Cost of goods sold ÷ Average inventory* *Average inventory = [(Beginning inventory + Ending inventory) ÷ 2]	To calculate and evaluate the company's efficiency in purchasing and selling merchandise inventory.
Average number of days in inventory	365 days ÷ inventory turnover	To calculate the average number of days it takes to sell merchandise inventory after it is purchased.
Accounts receivable turnover	Net credit sales ÷ Average accounts receivable* *Average accounts receivable (A/R) = [(Beginning A/R + Ending A/R) ÷ 2]	To calculate and evaluate the company's efficiency in granting credit and collecting cash from credit customers.
Average collection period	365 days ÷ accounts receivable turnover	To calculate the average number of days it takes for a business to receive cash from credit customers.

Journalizing and Posting Reversing Entries

>> 13-7 OBJECTIVE
Journalize and post reversing entries.

Some adjustments made at the end of one period can cause problems in the next period. **Reversing entries** are made to reverse the effect of certain adjustments. This helps prevent errors in recording payments or cash receipts in the new accounting period.

Let's use adjustment (**f**) as an illustration of how reversing entries are helpful. On December 31, Whiteside Antiques owed $1,200 of salaries to its part-time sales clerks. The salaries will be paid in January. To recognize the salaries expense in December, adjustment (**f**) was made to debit *Salaries Expense—Sales* for $1,200 and credit *Salaries Payable* for $1,200. The adjustment was recorded and posted in the accounting records.

476 CHAPTER 13 Financial Statements and Closing Procedure

recall

Accrual Basis
Revenues are recognized when earned, and expenses are recognized when incurred or used, regardless of when cash is received or paid.

By payday on January 3, the part-time sales clerks have earned $1,700:

$1,200 earned in December
$ 500 earned in January

The entry to record the January 3 payment of the salaries is a debit to **Salaries Expense—Sales** for $500, a debit to **Salaries Payable** for $1,200, and a credit to **Cash** for $1,700. This entry recognizes the salary expense for January and reduces the **Salaries Payable** account to zero.

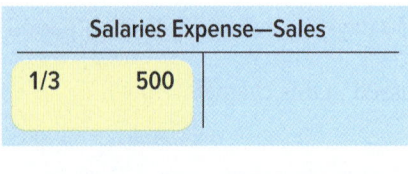

To record this transaction, the accountant had to review the adjustment in the end-of-period records and allocate the amount paid between the expense and liability accounts. This review is time-consuming, can cause errors, and is sometimes forgotten.

Reversing entries provide a way to guard against oversights, eliminate the review of accounting records, and simplify the entry made in the new period. As an example of a reversing entry, we will analyze the same transaction (January 3 payroll of $1,700) if reversing entries are made.

First, record the adjustment on December 31. Then record the reversing entry on January 1. Note that the reversing entry is the exact opposite (the reverse) of the adjustment. After the reversing entry is posted, the **Salaries Payable** account shows a zero balance and the **Salaries Expense—Sales** account has a credit balance. This is unusual because the normal balance of an expense account is a debit.

GENERAL JOURNAL PAGE 25

DATE	DESCRIPTION	POST. REF.	DEBIT	CREDIT
20X1	Adjusting Entries			
	(Adjustment f)			
Dec. 31	Salaries Expense—Sales	602	1 200 00	
	Salaries Payable	229		1 200 00

GENERAL JOURNAL PAGE 29

DATE	DESCRIPTION	POST. REF.	DEBIT	CREDIT
20X2	Reversing Entries			
Jan. 1	Salaries Payable	229	1 200 00	
	Salaries Expense—Sales	602		1 200 00

ACCOUNT	Salaries Payable				ACCOUNT NO. 229	
DATE	DESCRIPTION	POST. REF.	DEBIT	CREDIT	BALANCE DEBIT	BALANCE CREDIT
20X1						
Dec. 31	Adjusting	J25		1 200 00		1 200 00
20X2						
Jan. 1	Reversing	J29	1 200 00			—0—

ACCOUNT	Salaries Expense—Sales				ACCOUNT NO. 602	
DATE	DESCRIPTION	POST. REF.	DEBIT	CREDIT	BALANCE DEBIT	BALANCE CREDIT
20X1						
Dec. 31	Balance				78 490 00	
31	Adjusting	J25	1 200 00		79 690 00	
31	Closing	J28		79 690 00	—0—	
20X2						
Jan. 1	Reversing	J29		1 200 00		1 200 00

On January 3, the payment of $1,700 of salaries is recorded in the normal manner. Notice that this entry reduces cash and increases the expense account for the entire $1,700. It does not allocate the $1,700 between the expense and liability accounts.

	GENERAL JOURNAL			PAGE 30	
DATE	DESCRIPTION	POST. REF.	DEBIT	CREDIT	
20X1					1
Jan. 3	Salaries Expense—Sales	602	1 700 00		2
	Cash	101		1 700 00	3

After this entry is posted, the expenses are properly allocated between the two periods: $1,200 in December and $500 in January. The **Salaries Payable** account has a zero balance. The accountant did not have to review the previous records or allocate the payment between two accounts when the salaries were paid.

ACCOUNT	Salaries Expense—Sales				ACCOUNT NO. 602	
DATE	DESCRIPTION	POST. REF.	DEBIT	CREDIT	BALANCE DEBIT	BALANCE CREDIT
20X1						
Dec. 31	Balance				78 490 00	
31	Adjusting	J25	1 200 00		79 690 00	
31	Closing	J28		79 690 00	—0—	
20X2						
Jan. 1	Reversing	J29		1 200 00		1 200 00
3		J30	1 700 00		500 00	

Identifying Items for Reversal

Not all adjustments need to be reversed. Normally, reversing entries are made for accrued items that involve future payments or receipts of cash. Reversing entries are not made for uncollectible accounts, depreciation, and prepaid expenses—if they are initially recorded as assets. However, when prepaid expenses are initially recorded as expenses (the alternative method), the end-of-period adjustment needs to be reversed.

Whiteside Antiques makes reversing entries for:

- accrued salaries—adjustment **(f)**,
- accrued payroll taxes—adjustments **(g)** and **(h)**,
- interest payable—adjustment **(i)**,
- interest receivable—adjustment **(m)**.

Journalizing Reversing Entries

We just analyzed the reversing entry for accrued salaries, adjustment **(f)**. The next two reversing entries are for accrued payroll taxes. Making these reversing entries means that the accountant does not have to review the year-end adjustments before recording the payment of payroll taxes in the next year.

GENERAL JOURNAL PAGE 29

	DATE	DESCRIPTION	POST. REF.	DEBIT	CREDIT	
1	20X2					1
6	Jan. 1	Social Security Tax Payable	221	74 40		6
7		Medicare Tax Payable	223	17 40		7
8		Payroll Taxes Expense	665		91 80	8
9		To reverse adjusting entry				9
10		(g) made Dec. 31, 20X1				10
11						11
12	1	Federal Unemployment Tax Payable	225	7 20		12
13		State Unemployment Tax Payable	227	64 80		13
14		Payroll Taxes Expense	665		72 00	14
15		To reverse adjusting entry				15
16		(h) made Dec. 31, 20X1				16

The next reversing entry is for accrued interest expense. The reversing entry that follows prevents recording difficulties when the note is paid on February 1.

GENERAL JOURNAL PAGE 29

	DATE	DESCRIPTION	POST. REF.	DEBIT	CREDIT	
17						17
18	1	Interest Payable	216	20 00		18
19		Interest Expense	695		20 00	19
20		To reverse adjusting entry				20
21		(i) made Dec. 31, 20X1				21

In addition to adjustments for accrued expenses, Whiteside Antiques made two adjustments for accrued income items. The next reversing entry is for accrued interest income on the note receivable. Whiteside will receive cash for the note and the interest on March 1. The reversing entry eliminates any difficulties in recording the interest income when the note is paid on March 1.

GENERAL JOURNAL PAGE 29

	DATE	DESCRIPTION	POST. REF.	DEBIT	CREDIT	
22						22
23	1	Interest Income	491	30 00		23
24		Interest Receivable	116		30 00	24
25		To reverse adjusting entry				25
26		(m) made Dec. 31, 20X1				26

After the reversing entry has been posted, the *Interest Receivable* account has a zero balance and the *Interest Income* account has a debit balance of $30. This is unusual because the normal balance of *Interest Income* is a credit.

On March 1, Whiteside Antiques received a check for $1,260 in payment of the note ($1,200) and the interest ($60). The transaction is recorded in the normal manner as a debit to *Cash* for $1,260, a credit to *Notes Receivable* for $1,200, and a credit to *Interest Income* for $60.

Refer to the *Interest Income* general ledger account below. After this entry has been posted, interest income is properly allocated between the two periods, $30 in the previous year and $30 in the current year. The balance of *Interest Receivable* is zero. The accountant does not have to review the year-end adjustments before recording the receipt of the principal and interest relating to the note receivable on March 1.

ACCOUNT: Interest Receivable   ACCOUNT NO. 116

DATE		DESCRIPTION	POST. REF.	DEBIT	CREDIT	BALANCE DEBIT	BALANCE CREDIT
20X1							
Dec.	31	Adjusting	J27	30 00		30 00	
20X2							
Jan.	1	Reversing	J29		30 00	—0—	

ACCOUNT: Interest Income   ACCOUNT NO. 491

DATE		DESCRIPTION	POST. REF.	DEBIT	CREDIT	BALANCE DEBIT	BALANCE CREDIT
20X1							
Dec.	31	Balance					136 00
	31	Adjusting	J27		30 00		166 00
	31	Closing	J28	166 00			—0—
20X2							
Jan.	1	Reversing	J29	30 00		30 00	
Mar.	1		CR3		60 00		30 00

Review of the Accounting Cycle

In Chapters 7, 8, and 9, Maxx-Out Sporting Goods was used to introduce accounting procedures, records, and statements for merchandising businesses. In Chapters 12 and 13, Whiteside Antiques was used to illustrate the end-of-period activities for merchandising businesses. Underlying the various procedures described were the steps in the accounting cycle. Let's review the accounting cycle.

1. *Analyze transactions.* Transaction data comes into an accounting system from a variety of source documents—sales slips, purchase invoices, credit memorandums, check stubs, and so on. Each document is analyzed to determine the accounts and amounts affected.
2. *Journalize the data about transactions.* Each transaction is recorded in either a special journal or the general journal.
3. *Post the data about transactions.* Each transaction is transferred from the journal to the ledger accounts. Merchandising businesses typically maintain several subsidiary ledgers in addition to the general ledger.
4. *Prepare a worksheet.* At the end of each period, a worksheet is prepared. The Trial Balance section of the worksheet is used to prove the equality of the debits and credits in the general ledger. Adjustments are entered in the Adjustments section so that the financial statements will be prepared using the accrual basis of accounting. The Adjusted Trial Balance section is used to prove the equality of the debits and credits of the updated account balances. The Income Statement and Balance Sheet sections are used to arrange data in an orderly manner.

ABOUT ACCOUNTING

Professional Conduct

In September 1998, the Securities and Exchange Commission (SEC) defined improper professional conduct by accountants. The new rule allowed the SEC to censure, suspend, or bar accountants who violate it. The American Institute of Certified Public Accountants (AICPA) supported the rule. The rule led to the dissolution of Arthur Andersen, one of the nation's "big five" firms of certified public accountants, in 2003 following the imposition of severe sanctions on the firm in the "Enron Affair," in which Arthur Andersen was the auditor for Enron. The Sarbanes-Oxley Act has further strengthened the SEC's power over professional conduct by accountants that audit publicly traded companies.

5. *Prepare financial statements.* A formal set of financial statements is prepared to report information to interested parties.
6. *Journalize and post adjusting entries.* Adjusting entries are journalized and posted in the accounting records. This creates a permanent record of the changes shown on the worksheet.
7. *Journalize and post closing entries.* Closing entries are journalized and posted in order to transfer the results of operations to owner's equity and to prepare the temporary accounts for the next period. The closing entries reduce the temporary account balances to zero.
8. *Prepare a postclosing trial balance.* The postclosing trial balance confirms that the general ledger is still in balance and that the temporary accounts have zero balances.
9. *Interpret the financial information.* The accountant, owners, managers, and other interested parties interpret the information shown in the financial statements and other less-formal financial reports that might be prepared. This information is used to evaluate the results of operations and the financial position of the business and to make decisions.

In addition to the nine steps listed here, some firms record reversing entries. Reversing entries simplify the recording of cash payments for accrued expenses and cash receipts for accrued income.

Figure 13.6 shows the flow of data through an accounting system that uses special journals and subsidiary ledgers. The system is composed of subsystems that perform specialized functions.

The accounts receivable area records transactions involving sales and cash receipts and maintains the individual accounts for credit customers. This area also handles billing for credit customers.

The accounts payable area records transactions involving purchases and cash payments and maintains the individual accounts for creditors.

The general ledger and financial reporting area records transactions in the general journal, maintains the general ledger accounts, performs the end-of-period procedures, and prepares financial statements. This area is the focal point for the accounting system because all transactions eventually flow into the general ledger. In turn, the general ledger provides the data that appear in the financial statements.

MANAGERIAL IMPLICATIONS

FINANCIAL STATEMENTS

- Managers carefully study the financial statements to evaluate the operating efficiency and financial strength of the business.
- A common analysis technique is to compare the data on current statements with the data from previous statements. This can reveal developing trends.
- In large businesses, financial statements are compared with the published financial reports of other companies in the same industry.
- In order to evaluate information on classified financial statements, managers need to understand the nature and significance of the groupings.
- Management ensures that closing entries are promptly made so that transactions for the new period can be recorded. Any significant delay means that valuable information, such as the firm's cash position, may not be available or up to date.
- The efficiency and effectiveness of the adjusting and closing procedures can have a positive effect on the annual independent audit. For example, detailed descriptions in the general journal make it easy for the auditor to understand the adjusting entries.

THINKING CRITICALLY

How can managers use the financial statements to learn about a company's operating efficiency?

FIGURE 13.6 Flow of Financial Data through an Accounting System

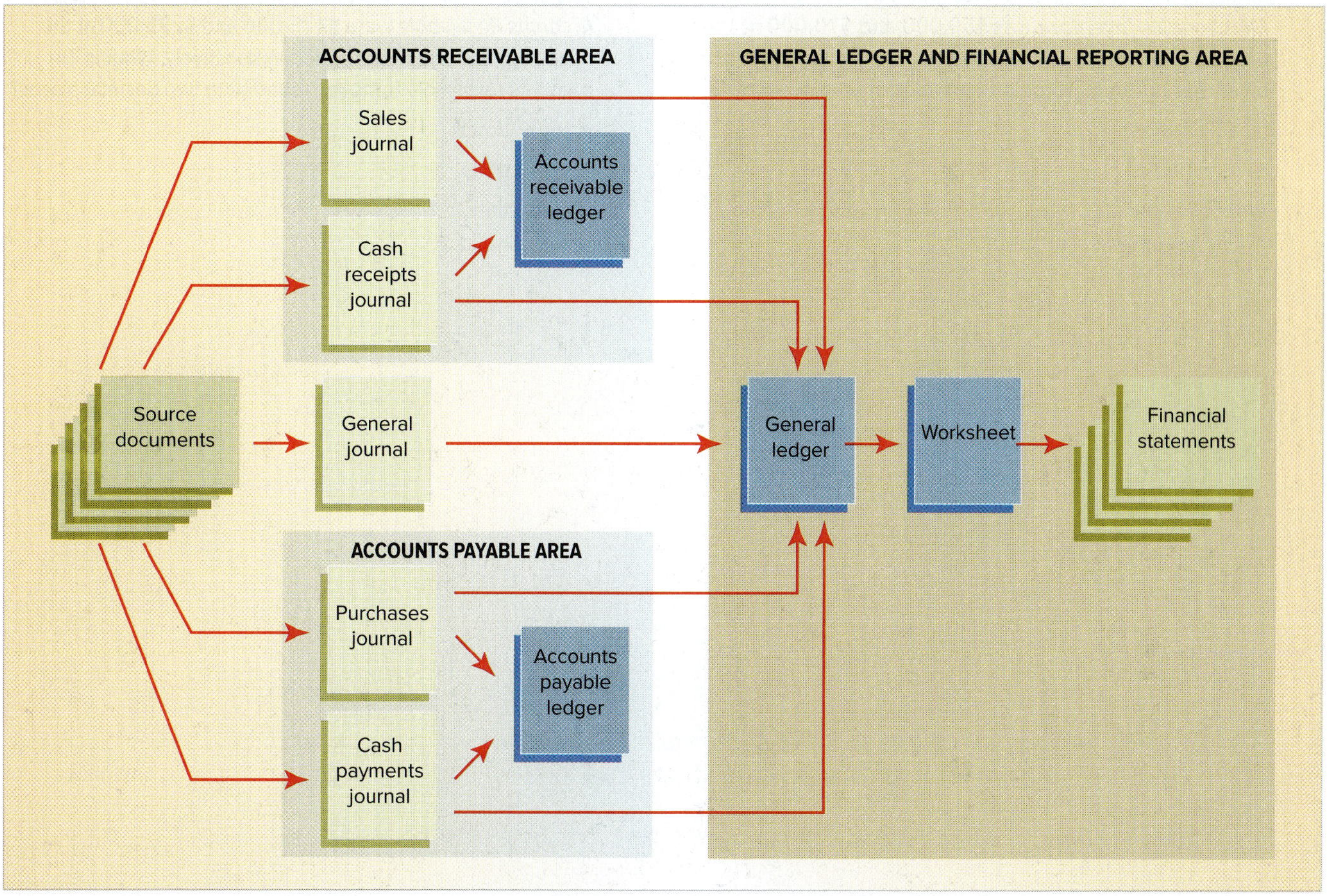

Section 2 Review

1. Which of the following accounts would not appear on the postclosing trial balance?
   a. *Cash*
   b. *Accumulated Depreciation—Office Equipment*
   c. *Supplies*
   d. *Supplies Expense*

2. The purpose of the second closing entry is to:
   a. close expense accounts and cost of goods sold accounts with debit balances.
   b. close expense accounts and cost of goods sold accounts with credit balances.
   c. close revenue accounts and cost of goods sold accounts with debit balances.
   d. close revenue accounts and cost of goods sold accounts with credit balances.

3. The Office Warehouse had the following account balances: *Cash,* $25,000; *Accounts Receivable,* $75,000; *Merchandise Inventory,* $85,000; *Equipment,* $225,000; *Accumulated Depreciation—Equipment,* $45,000; *Accounts Payable,* $50,000; *Salaries Payable,* $15,000; and *Notes Payable—Long-Term,* $70,000. What is the current ratio, rounded to two decimal places?
   a. 2.70 to 1
   b. 2.85 to 1
   c. 3.04 to 1
   d. 1.37 to 1

4. A reversing entry is made for an end-of-period adjustment that recorded:
   a. estimated bad debts for the period.
   b. an accrued expense that involves future cash payments.
   c. a transfer of an amount from a prepaid expense account to an expense account.
   d. the change in merchandise inventory.

5. Vanessa Company reported net sales of $1,000,000, cost of goods sold of $600,000, and gross profit of $400,000. *Merchandise Inventory* was $50,000 and $70,000 at the beginning and end of the period, respectively. What is the inventory turnover, rounded to two decimal places?

   a. 6.67 times
   b. 8.57 times
   c. 10.00 times
   d. 12.00 times

6. Marco Company reported net credit sales of $1,500,000, cost of goods sold of $800,000, and gross profit of $700,000. *Accounts Receivable* were $175,000 and $225,000 at the beginning and end of the period, respectively. What is the accounts receivable turnover, rounded to two decimal places?

   a. 6.67 times
   b. 3.50 times
   c. 4.00 times
   d. 7.50 times

REVIEW Chapter Summary

In this chapter, you have learned how to prepare classified financial statements from the worksheet and how to close the accounting records for the period.

Learning Objectives

13-1 Prepare a classified income statement from the worksheet.

- A classified income statement for a merchandising business usually includes these sections: Operating Revenue, Cost of Goods Sold, Gross Profit on Sales, Operating Expenses, and Net Income.
- To make the income statement even more useful, operating expenses may be broken down into categories, such as selling expenses and general and administrative expenses.
- Income earned from sources other than normal business activities appears in the Other Income section. Expenses not directly connected with business operations appear in the Other Expenses section.

13-2 Prepare a statement of owner's equity from the worksheet.

A statement of owner's equity is prepared to provide detailed information about the changes in the owner's financial interest during the period. The ending owner's capital balance is used to prepare the balance sheet.

13-3 Prepare a classified balance sheet from the worksheet.

- Assets are usually presented in two groups: current assets, and plant and equipment. Current assets consist of cash, items to be converted into cash within one year, and items to be used up within one year. Plant and equipment consists of property that will be used for a long time in the operations of the business.
- Liabilities are also reported in two categories: current liabilities and long-term liabilities. Current liabilities will normally be paid within one year. Long-term liabilities are due in more than one year.

13-4 Journalize and post the adjusting entries.

When the year-end worksheet and financial statements have been completed, adjusting entries are recorded in the general journal and posted to the general ledger. The data comes from the worksheet Adjustments section.

13-5 Journalize and post the closing entries.

After the adjusting entries have been journalized and posted, the closing entries should be recorded in the records of the business. The data in the Income Statement section of the worksheet can be used to journalize the closing entries.

13-6 Prepare a postclosing trial balance.

To confirm that the general ledger is still in balance after the adjusting and closing entries have been posted, a postclosing trial balance is prepared.

13-7 Journalize and post reversing entries.

At the start of each new period, most firms follow the practice of reversing certain adjustments that were made in the previous period.

- This is done to avoid recording problems with transactions that will occur in the new period.
- Usually, only adjusting entries for accrued expenses and accrued income need to be reversed. Of these, usually only accrued expense and income items involving future payments and receipts of cash can cause difficulties later and should be reversed.
- The use of reversing entries is optional. Reversing entries save time, promote efficiency, and help to achieve a proper matching of revenue and expenses in each period.
- With reversing entries, there is no need to examine each transaction to see whether a portion applies to the past period and then divide the amount of the transaction between the two periods.

13-8 Define the accounting terms new to this chapter.

Glossary

Accounts receivable turnover (p. 474) A measure of the speed with which sales on account are collected; the ratio of net credit sales to average receivables

Average collection period (p. 474) The ratio of 365 days to the accounts receivable turnover; also called the *number of days' sales in receivables*

Average number of days in inventory (p. 474) The average number of days for merchandise inventory to be sold after it is purchased

Classified financial statement (p. 460) A format by which revenues and expenses on the income statement, and assets and liabilities on the balance sheet, are divided into groups of similar accounts and a subtotal is given for each group

Condensed income statement (p. 463) An income statement summarizing detailed income statement accounts into a few lines of information

Current assets (p. 465) Assets consisting of cash, items that normally will be converted into cash within one year, and items that will be used up within one year

Current liabilities (p. 465) Debts that must be paid or otherwise satisfied within one year

Current ratio (p. 474) A relationship between current assets and current liabilities that provides a measure of a firm's ability to pay its current debts (current ratio = current assets ÷ current liabilities)

Gross profit (p. 462) The difference between net sales and the cost of goods sold (gross profit = net sales − cost of goods sold)

Gross profit percentage (p. 473) The amount of gross profit from each dollar of sales (gross profit percentage = gross profit ÷ net sales)

Inventory turnover (p. 474) The number of times inventory is purchased and sold during the accounting period (inventory turnover = cost of goods sold ÷ average inventory)

Liquidity (p. 465) The ease with which an item can be converted into cash; the ability of a business to pay its debts when due

Long-term liabilities (p. 465) Debts of a business that are due more than one year in the future

Multiple-step income statement (p. 460) A type of income statement on which several subtotals are computed before the net income is calculated

Plant and equipment (p. 465) Property that will be used in the business for longer than one year

Reversing entries (p. 475) Journal entries made to reverse the effect of certain adjusting entries involving accrued income or accrued expenses to avoid problems in recording future payments or receipts of cash in a new accounting period

Single-step income statement (p. 460) A type of income statement where only one computation is needed to determine the net income (total revenue − total expenses = net income)

Working capital (p. 473) The measure of the ability of a company to meet its current obligations; the excess of current assets over current liabilities

Comprehensive Self Review

1. Explain the difference between a single-step income statement and a multiple-step income statement. Which is normally favored?
2. What journal entry(ies) is (are) made in the adjustment column for beginning and ending inventories?
3. Why would a photocopy machine used in the office not be considered a current asset?
4. Immediately after closing entries are posted, which of the following types of accounts will have zero balances? Select all that apply.
    a. asset accounts
    b. expense accounts
    c. liability accounts
    d. owner's drawing account
    e. *Income Summary* account
    f. owner's capital account
    g. revenue accounts
5. Which of the following should have a debit balance in the adjusted trial balance?
    a. *Sales Returns and Allowances*
    b. *Purchases Discounts*
    c. *Salaries Payable*
    d. *Unearned Rental Income*

6. Describe the entry that would be made to close the *Income Summary* account in each of the following cases. The owner of the firm is Jan Hanson.

   a. There is net income of $58,000.

   b. There is a net loss of $8,000.

7. Give the sequence in which the following journal entries are posted to the accounts.

   a. adjusting entries

   b. entries to close expense accounts

   c. entries to close revenue accounts

   d. reversing entries

(Answers to Comprehensive Self Review are at the end of the chapter.)

Discussion Questions

1. Give an example of an expense that is classified as Other Expense in the income statement.
2. Which section of the income statement contains information about the purchases made during the period and the beginning and ending inventories?
3. What are operating expenses? Are financing expenses included in operating expenses?
4. What is the purpose of the balance sheet?
5. Give examples of some current assets that usually are classified as Current Assets on the balance sheet.
6. How do current liabilities and long-term liabilities differ?
7. What information is provided by the statement of owner's equity?
8. What account balances or other amounts are included on two different financial statements for the period? Which statements are involved?
9. What is the purpose of the postclosing trial balance?
10. What types of accounts, permanent or temporary, appear on the postclosing trial balance?
11. If the totals of the adjusted trial balance Debit and Credit columns are equal, but the postclosing trial balance does not balance, what is the likely cause of the problem?
12. What types of adjustments are reversed?
13. On December 31, Klein Company made an adjusting entry debiting *Interest Receivable* and crediting *Interest Income* for $300 of accrued interest. What reversing entry, if any, should be recorded for this item on January 1?
14. Various adjustments made at Adams Company are listed below. Which of the adjustments would normally be reversed?

    a. Adjustment for accrued payroll taxes expense

    b. Adjustment for supplies used

    c. Adjustment for depreciation on the building

    d. Adjustment for estimated uncollectible accounts

    e. Adjustment for accrued interest income

    f. Adjustment for beginning inventory

    g. Adjustment for ending inventory

    h. Adjustment to record portion of insurance premiums that have expired

15. If the owner invests additional capital in the business during the month, how would that new investment be shown in the financial statements?
16. What are the steps in the accounting cycle?

17. Jarrett Company's inventory turnover ratio was nine times in 20X1 and eight times in 20X2. Did Jarrett Company sell its inventory more quickly, or more slowly, in 20X2 compared to 20X1?

18. Fuji Company had a current ratio of 2.0 in 20X1 and 2.2 in 20X2. Does this signify an improvement or decline in Fuji Company's liquidity from 20X1 to 20X2?

APPLICATIONS

Exercises

Exercise 13.1
Objective 13-1

▶ **Classifying income statement items.**

The accounts listed below appear on the worksheet of Commonwealth Crafts. Indicate the section of the classified income statement in which each account will be reported.

SECTIONS OF CLASSIFIED INCOME STATEMENT
a. Operating Revenue
b. Cost of Goods Sold
c. Operating Expenses
d. Other Income
e. Other Expenses

ACCOUNTS
1. Purchases Returns and Allowances
2. Telephone Expense
3. Sales Returns and Allowances
4. Purchases
5. Interest Income
6. Merchandise Inventory
7. Interest Expense
8. Sales
9. Depreciation Expense—Store Equipment
10. Rent Expense
11. Sales Discounts
12. Supplies Expense
13. Freight In
14. Purchases Discounts
15. Uncollectible Accounts Expense

Exercise 13.2
Objective 13-3

▶ **Classifying balance sheet items.**

The following accounts appear on the worksheet of Commonwealth Crafts at December 31, 20X1. Indicate the section of the classified balance sheet in which each account will be reported.

SECTIONS OF CLASSIFIED BALANCE SHEET
a. Current Assets
b. Plant and Equipment
c. Current Liabilities

d. Long-Term Liabilities

e. Owner's Equity

ACCOUNTS

1. Accounts Receivable
2. Truck
3. Prepaid Rent
4. Notes Payable, due 20X5
5. Office Supplies
6. Accounts Payable
7. Merchandise Inventory
8. John O'Hare, Capital
9. Cash
10. Unearned Revenue
11. Notes Receivable, due 20X2
12. Accumulated Depreciation—Truck
13. Notes Payable, due 20X2
14. John O'Hare, Drawing
15. Interest Payable

Preparing a classified income statement.

◄ **Exercise 13.3**
Objective 13-1

The worksheet of Lantz's Office Supplies contains the following revenue, cost, and expense accounts. Prepare a classified income statement for this firm for the year ended December 31, 20X1. The merchandise inventory amounted to $59,775 on January 1, 20X1, and $52,725 on December 31, 20X1. The expense accounts numbered 611 through 617 represent selling expenses, and those numbered 631 through 646 represent general and administrative expenses.

ACCOUNTS

401	Sales	$265,950	Cr.
451	Sales Returns and Allowances	4,350	Dr.
491	Miscellaneous Income	400	Cr.
501	Purchases	108,600	Dr.
502	Freight In	1,975	Dr.
503	Purchases Returns and Allowances	3,600	Cr.
504	Purchases Discounts	1,800	Cr.
611	Salaries Expense—Sales	45,300	Dr.
614	Store Supplies Expense	2,310	Dr.
617	Depreciation Expense—Store Equipment	1,510	Dr.
631	Rent Expense	13,500	Dr.
634	Utilities Expense	6,200	Dr.
637	Salaries Expense—Office	21,100	Dr.
640	Payroll Taxes Expense	5,800	Dr.
643	Depreciation Expense—Office Equipment	570	Dr.
646	Uncollectible Accounts Expense	720	Dr.
691	Interest Expense	740	Dr.

Exercise 13.4
Objective 13-2

▶ **Preparing a statement of owner's equity.**

The worksheet of Lantz's Office Supplies contains the following owner's equity accounts. Use this data and the net income determined in Exercise 13.3 to prepare a statement of owner's equity for the year ended December 31, 20X1. No additional investments were made during the period.

ACCOUNTS

| 301 | Terri Lantz, Capital | $68,760 | Cr. |
| 302 | Terri Lantz, Drawing | 40,700 | Dr. |

Exercise 13.5
Objective 13-3

▶ **Preparing a classified balance sheet.**

The worksheet of Lantz's Office Supplies contains the following asset and liability accounts. The balance of the **Notes Payable** account consists of notes that are due within a year. Prepare a balance sheet dated December 31, 20X1. Obtain the ending capital for the period from the statement of owner's equity completed in Exercise 13.4.

ACCOUNTS

101	Cash	$12,655	Dr.
107	Change Fund	500	Dr.
111	Accounts Receivable	15,140	Dr.
112	Allowance for Doubtful Accounts	860	Cr.
121	Merchandise Inventory	52,725	Dr.
131	Store Supplies	1,100	Dr.
133	Prepaid Interest	130	Dr.
141	Store Equipment	11,200	Dr.
142	Accum. Depreciation—Store Equipment	1,180	Cr.
151	Office Equipment	3,400	Dr.
152	Accum. Depreciation—Office Equipment	500	Cr.
201	Notes Payable	5,500	Cr.
203	Accounts Payable	6,725	Cr.
216	Interest Payable	110	Cr.
231	Sales Tax Payable	1,890	Cr.

Exercise 13.6
Objective 13-5

▶ **Recording closing entries.**

On December 31, 20X1, the Income Statement columns of the worksheet for The Sax Shop contained the following information. Give the entries that should be made in the general journal to close the revenue, cost of goods sold, expense, and other temporary accounts. Use journal page 16.

INCOME STATEMENT COLUMNS

	Debit	Credit
Income Summary	$ 40,000	$ 43,000
Sales		291,500
Sales Returns and Allowances	4,400	
Sales Discounts	3,600	
Interest Income		230
Purchases	135,200	

	Debit	Credit
Freight In	2,700	
Purchases Returns and Allowances		1,500
Purchases Discounts		2,630
Rent Expense	24,000	
Utilities Expense	3,630	
Telephone Expense	1,940	
Salaries Expense	67,100	
Payroll Taxes Expense	5,370	
Supplies Expense	1,580	
Depreciation Expense	3,000	
Interest Expense	420	
Totals	$292,940	$338,860

Assume further that the owner of the firm is Mark Fronke and that the *Mark Fronke, Drawing* account had a balance of $39,700 on December 31, 20X1.

Journalizing reversing entries.

◀ **Exercise 13.7**
Objective 13-7

Examine the following adjusting entries and determine which ones should be reversed. Show the reversing entries that should be recorded in the general journal as of January 1, 20X2. Include appropriate descriptions.

20X1	(Adjustment a)		
Dec. 31	Uncollectible Accounts Expense	4,175.00	
	Allowance for Doubtful Accounts		4,175.00
	To record estimated loss from uncollectible accounts based on 0.5% of net credit sales, $835,000		
	(Adjustment b)		
31	Supplies Expense	4,700.00	
	Supplies		4,700.00
	To record supplies used during the year		
	(Adjustment c)		
31	Insurance Expense	3,300.00	
	Prepaid Insurance		3,300.00
	To record expired insurance on 1-year $13,200 policy purchased on Oct. 1		
	(Adjustment d)		
31	Depreciation. Exp.—Store Equipment	14,300.00	
	Accum. Depreciation—Store Equip.		14,300.00
	To record depreciation		
	(Adjustment e)		
31	Salaries Expense—Office	5,800.00	
	Salaries Payable		5,800.00
	To record accrued salaries for Dec. 29–31		
	(Adjustment f)		

		Debit	Credit
31	Payroll Taxes Expense	443.70	
	Social Security Tax Payable		359.60
	Medicare Tax Payable		84.10
	To record accrued payroll taxes on accrued salaries: social security, 6.2% × $5,800 = $359.60; Medicare, 1.45% × $5,800 = $84.10		
	(Adjustment g)		
31	Interest Expense	600.00	
	Interest Payable		600.00
	To record accrued interest on a 4-month, 6% trade note payable dated Oct. 1: $40,000 × 0.06 × 3/12 = $600		
	(Adjustment h)		
31	Interest Receivable	400.00	
	Interest Income		400.00
	To record interest earned on 9-month, 8% note receivable dated July 1: $10,000 × 0.08 × 6/12 = $400		

Exercise 13.8

Objective 13-6

▶ **Preparing a postclosing trial balance.**

The Adjusted Trial Balance section of the worksheet for Hendricks Janitorial Supplies follows. The owner made no additional investments during the year. Prepare a postclosing trial balance for the firm on December 31, 20X1.

ACCOUNTS

	Debit	Credit
Cash	$ 21,600	
Accounts Receivable	62,800	
Allowance for Doubtful Accounts		$ 220
Merchandise Inventory	187,200	
Supplies	6,240	
Prepaid Insurance	3,160	
Equipment	52,000	
Accumulated Depreciation—Equipment		22,800
Accounts Payable		8,700
Social Security Tax Payable		1,490
Medicare Tax Payable		410
James Hendricks, Capital		281,640
James Hendricks, Drawing	75,000	
Income Summary	181,000	187,200
Sales		778,000
Sales Returns and Allowances	15,400	
Purchases	487,900	
Freight In	6,400	
Purchases Returns and Allowances		9,500

	Debit	Credit
Purchases Discounts		6,300
Rent Expense	34,800	
Telephone Expense	6,340	
Salaries Expense	124,140	
Payroll Taxes Expense	12,700	
Supplies Expense	7,600	
Insurance Expense	1,660	
Depreciation Expense—Equipment	9,100	
Uncollectible Accounts Expense	1,220	
Totals	$1,296,260	$1,296,260

Calculating ratios.   ◀ Exercise 13.9
Objective 13-6

The following selected accounts were taken from the financial records of Sonoma Valley Distributors at December 31, 20X1. All accounts have normal balances.

Cash	$31,340
Accounts Receivable	67,900
Note Receivable, due 20X2	10,250
Merchandise Inventory	36,000
Prepaid Insurance	4,350
Supplies	1,410
Equipment	63,500
Accumulated Depreciation, Equipment	23,500
Note Payable to Bank, due 20X2	34,000
Accounts Payable	27,000
Interest Payable	350
Sales	545,500
Sales Discounts	3,400
Cost of Goods Sold	348,540

Accounts Receivable at December 31, 20X0, was $52,550. **Merchandise Inventory** at December 31, 20X0, was $58,200. Based on the account balances above, calculate the following:

a. The gross profit percentage
b. Working capital
c. The current ratio
d. The inventory turnover
e. The accounts receivable turnover. All sales were on credit.

Calculating the accounts receivable turnover and the inventory turnover.   ◀ Exercise 13.10
Objective 13-6

Tsang Company reports the following in its most recent year of operations:

- Net sales, $2,000,000 (all on account)
- Cost of goods sold, $977,500
- Gross profit, $1,022,500
- Accounts receivable, beginning of year, $220,000

- Accounts receivable, end of year, $280,000
- Merchandise inventory, beginning of year, $110,000
- Merchandise inventory, end of year, $120,000

Based on these balances, compute:

a. The accounts receivable turnover
b. The average collection period
c. The inventory turnover
d. The average number of days in inventory

Exercise 13.11 ▶ **Preparing a summarized income statement; computing ratios.**

Objectives 13-1, 13-6, 13-7, 13-8, 13-9, 13-10, 13-11

Selected accounts and other information from the records of Calderone Company for the year ended December 31 follow:

Merchandise Inventory, January 1	$ 20,000
Merchandise Inventory, December 31	22,000
Sales Returns and Allowances	1,000
Store Supplies Expense	3,000
Sales Salaries Expense	30,000
Sales	218,000
Purchases	50,000
Rent Expense	37,000
Sales Commissions Expense	4,200
Freight In	1,500
Purchases Discounts	400
Depreciation Expense—Office Equipment	3,000
Depreciation Expense—Store Equipment	6,000
Utilities Expense	8,000
Office Salaries Expense	25,000
Interest Expense	400
Interest Income	1,200

1. Compute the following items that would appear on a classified income statement. The company combines both selling and general and administrative expenses into a single line, Operating Expenses.

   a. Net sales
   b. Cost of goods sold
   c. Gross profit
   d. Operating expenses
   e. Net income from operations
   f. Other income, net
   g. Net income for year

2. Prepare a summarized income statement for Calderone Company for the current year. Use the condensed income statement following Objective 13-1 as an example.

3. Compute the following ratios:

   a. Gross profit percentage
   b. Inventory turnover

PROBLEMS

Problem Set A

Preparing classified financial statements.

Superior Hardwood Company distributes hardwood products to small furniture manufacturers. The adjusted trial balance data given below is from the firm's worksheet for the year ended December 31, 20X1.

◀ **Problem 13.1A**
Objectives 13-1, 13-2, 13-3

INSTRUCTIONS

1. Prepare a classified income statement for the year ended December 31, 20X1. The expense accounts represent warehouse expenses, selling expenses, and general and administrative expenses.
2. Prepare a statement of owner's equity for the year ended December 31, 20X1. No additional investments were made during the year.
3. Prepare a classified balance sheet as of December 31, 20X1. The mortgage payable extends for more than a year.

ACCOUNTS

	Debit	Credit
Cash	$ 34,100	
Petty Cash Fund	500	
Notes Receivable, due 20X2	11,800	
Accounts Receivable	86,000	
Allowance for Doubtful Accounts		$ 6,000
Merchandise Inventory	234,000	
Warehouse Supplies	2,860	
Office Supplies	1,420	
Prepaid Insurance	10,200	
Land	46,000	
Building	178,000	
Accumulated Depreciation—Building		54,000
Warehouse Equipment	37,000	
Accumulated Depreciation—Warehouse Equipment		17,400
Delivery Equipment	51,000	
Accumulated Depreciation—Delivery Equipment		19,600
Office Equipment	25,000	
Accumulated Depreciation—Office Equipment		12,000
Notes Payable, due 20X2		20,200
Accounts Payable		49,000
Interest Payable		580
Mortgage Payable		61,000
Loans Payable, Long-term		17,000
Charles Ronie, Capital (Jan. 1)		452,460
Charles Ronie, Drawing	127,000	

ACCOUNTS (CONT.)

	Debit	Credit
Income Summary	244,000	234,000
Sales		1,685,000
Sales Returns and Allowances	18,200	
Interest Income		1,580
Purchases	767,000	
Freight In	13,800	
Purchases Returns and Allowances		8,440
Purchases Discounts		11,160
Warehouse Wages Expense	199,600	
Warehouse Supplies Expense	7,100	
Depreciation Expense—Warehouse Equipment	5,800	
Salaries Expense—Sales	269,200	
Travel and Entertainment Expense	21,500	
Delivery Wages Expense	60,330	
Depreciation Expense—Delivery Equipment	9,800	
Salaries Expense—Office	70,600	
Office Supplies Expense	4,000	
Insurance Expense	6,200	
Utilities Expense	9,290	
Telephone Expense	6,520	
Payroll Taxes Expense	59,000	
Property Taxes Expense	5,600	
Uncollectible Accounts Expense	5,800	
Depreciation Expense—Building	9,000	
Depreciation Expense—Office Equipment	4,000	
Interest Expense	8,200	
Totals	$2,649,420	$2,649,420

Analyze: What is the current ratio for this business?

Problem 13.2A

Objectives 13-1, 13-2, 13-3

GL

▶ **Preparing classified financial statements.**

Good to Go Auto Products distributes automobile parts to service stations and repair shops. The adjusted trial balance data that follows is from the firm's worksheet for the year ended December 31, 20X1.

INSTRUCTIONS

1. Prepare a classified income statement for the year ended December 31, 20X1. The expense accounts represent warehouse expenses, selling expenses, and general and administrative expenses.
2. Prepare a statement of owner's equity for the year ended December 31, 20X1. No additional investments were made during the year.
3. Prepare a classified balance sheet as of December 31, 20X1. The mortgage payable extends for more than one year.

ACCOUNTS

	Debit	Credit
Cash	$ 99,000	
Petty Cash Fund	600	
Notes Receivable, due 20X2	15,000	
Accounts Receivable	140,200	
Allowance for Doubtful Accounts		$ 3,800
Interest Receivable	150	
Merchandise Inventory	128,500	
Warehouse Supplies	3,300	
Office Supplies	700	
Prepaid Insurance	4,640	
Land	16,000	
Building	107,000	
Accumulated Depreciation—Building		16,700
Warehouse Equipment	19,800	
Accumulated Depreciation—Warehouse Equipment		9,500
Office Equipment	9,400	
Accumulated Depreciation—Office Equipment		3,900
Notes Payable, due 20X2		15,000
Accounts Payable		56,900
Interest Payable		400
Notes Payable, Long-term		17,000
Mortgage Payable		20,000
Colin O'Brien, Capital (Jan. 1)		326,870
Colin O'Brien, Drawing	70,650	
Income Summary	131,400	128,500
Sales		1,110,300
Sales Returns and Allowances	8,400	
Interest Income		580
Purchases	463,000	
Freight In	9,800	
Purchases Returns and Allowances		13,650
Purchases Discounts		9,240
Warehouse Wages Expense	108,600	
Warehouse Supplies Expense	5,800	
Depreciation Expense—Warehouse Equipment	3,400	
Salaries Expense—Sales	151,700	
Travel Expense	24,000	
Delivery Expense	37,425	
Salaries Expense—Office	85,000	
Office Supplies Expense	1,220	
Insurance Expense	9,875	

ACCOUNTS (CONT.)

	Debit	Credit
Utilities Expense	8,000	
Telephone Expense	3,280	
Payroll Taxes Expense	31,600	
Building Repairs Expense	3,700	
Property Taxes Expense	16,400	
Uncollectible Accounts Expense	3,580	
Depreciation Expense—Building	5,600	
Depreciation Expense—Office Equipment	1,620	
Interest Expense	4,000	
Totals	$1,732,340	$1,732,340

Analyze: What percentage of total operating expenses is attributable to warehouse expenses?

Problem 13.3A ▶ Preparing classified financial statements.

Objectives 13-1, 13-2, 13-3

Obtain all data necessary from the worksheet prepared for Enoteca Fine Wines in Problem 12.6A at the end of Chapter 12. Then follow the instructions to complete this problem.

INSTRUCTIONS

1. Prepare a classified income statement for the year ended December 31, 20X1. The company does not classify its operating expenses as selling expenses and general and administrative expenses.

2. Prepare a statement of owner's equity for the year ended December 31, 20X1. No additional investments were made during the year.

3. Prepare a classified balance sheet as of December 31, 20X1.

Analyze: What is the inventory turnover for Enoteca Fine Wines?

Problem 13.4A ▶ Journalizing adjusting, closing, and reversing entries.

Objectives 13-4, 13-5, 13-7

Obtain all data that is necessary from the worksheet prepared for Healthy Eating Foods Company in Problem 12.5A at the end of Chapter 12. Then follow the instructions to complete this problem.

INSTRUCTIONS

1. Record adjusting entries in the general journal as of December 31, 20X1. Use 25 as the first journal page number. Include descriptions for the entries.

2. Record closing entries in the general journal as of December 31, 20X1. Include descriptions.

3. Record reversing entries in the general journal as of January 1, 20X2. Include descriptions.

Analyze: Assuming that the firm did not record a reversing entry for salaries payable, what entry is required when salaries of $6,000 are paid on January 3?

Problem 13.5A ▶ Journalizing adjusting and reversing entries.

Objectives 13-4, 13-7

The data below concerns adjustments to be made at Tea Leaf Importers.

INSTRUCTIONS

1. Record the adjusting entries in the general journal as of December 31, 20X1. Use 25 as the first journal page number. Include descriptions.

2. Record reversing entries in the general journal as of January 1, 20X2. Include descriptions.

ADJUSTMENTS

a. On November 1, 20X1, the firm signed a lease for a warehouse and paid rent of $42,000 in advance for a six-month period.

b. On December 31, 20X1, an inventory of supplies showed that items costing $1,920 were on hand. The balance of the *Supplies* account was $9,885.

c. A depreciation schedule for the firm's equipment shows that a total of $9,750 should be charged off as depreciation in 20X1.

d. On December 31, 20X1, the firm owed salaries of $12,200 that will not be paid until January 20X2.

e. On December 31, 20X1, the firm owed the employer's social security (6.2 percent) and Medicare (1.45 percent) taxes on all accrued salaries.

f. On September 1, 20X1, the firm received a six-month, 9 percent note for $6,500 from a customer with an overdue balance.

Analyze: After the adjusting entries have been posted, what is the balance of the *Prepaid Rent* account on January 1, 20X2?

Problem Set B

Preparing classified financial statements.

◀ **Problem 13.1B**
Objectives 13-1, 13-2, 13-3

ComputerGeeks.com is a retail store that sells computers, laptops, supplies, and other electronic devices. The adjusted trial balance data given below is from the firm's worksheet for the year ended December 31, 20X1.

INSTRUCTIONS

1. Prepare a classified income statement for the year ended December 31, 20X1. The expense accounts represent warehouse expenses, selling expenses, and general and administrative expenses.

2. Prepare a statement of owner's equity for the year ended December 31, 20X1. No additional investments were made during the year.

3. Prepare a classified balance sheet as of December 31, 20X1. The mortgage payable extends for more than one year.

ACCOUNTS

	Debit	Credit
Cash	$ 12,200	
Petty Cash Fund	100	
Notes Receivable, due 20X2	3,200	
Accounts Receivable	19,250	
Allowance for Doubtful Accounts		$ 2,250
Merchandise Inventory	35,400	
Warehouse Supplies	775	
Office Supplies	780	
Prepaid Insurance	2,200	
Land	7,642	
Building	48,500	
Accumulated Depreciation—Building		13,000
Warehouse Equipment	8,000	
Accumulated Depreciation—Warehouse Equipment		2,300

ACCOUNTS (CONT.)

	Debit	Credit
Delivery Equipment	16,400	
Accumulated Depreciation—Delivery Equipment		3,600
Office Equipment	6,000	
Accumulated Depreciation—Office Equipment		2,500
Notes Payable, due 20X2		4,000
Accounts Payable		14,140
Interest Payable		240
Mortgage Payable		15,950
Loans Payable, Long-term		4,000
Bruce Zaro, Capital (Jan. 1)		60,940
Bruce Zaro, Drawing	24,000	
Income Summary	33,125	35,400
Sales		429,800
Sales Returns and Allowances	3,150	
Interest Income		462
Purchases	179,600	
Freight In	2,200	
Purchases Returns and Allowances		2,520
Purchases Discounts		2,350
Warehouse Wages Expense	38,900	
Warehouse Supplies Expense	1,790	
Depreciation Expense—Warehouse Equipment	1,400	
Salaries Expense—Sales	67,200	
Travel and Entertainment Expense	6,300	
Delivery Wages Expense	26,900	
Depreciation Expense—Delivery Equipment	2,440	
Salaries Expense—Office	15,900	
Office Supplies Expense	1,150	
Insurance Expense	1,500	
Utilities Expense	2,400	
Telephone Expense	1,380	
Payroll Taxes Expense	15,250	
Property Taxes Expense	1,750	
Uncollectible Accounts Expense	1,050	
Depreciation Expense—Building	3,000	
Depreciation Expense—Office Equipment	1,020	
Interest Expense	1,600	
Totals	$593,452	$593,452

Analyze: What is the gross profit percentage for the year ended December 31, 20X1?

Preparing classified financial statements.

Problem 13.2B
Objectives 13-1, 13-2, 13-3

Hog Wild is a retail firm that sells motorcycles, parts, and accessories. The adjusted trial balance data given below is from the firm's worksheet for the year ended December 31, 20X1.

INSTRUCTIONS

1. Prepare a classified income statement for the year ended December 31, 20X1. The expense accounts represent warehouse expenses, selling expenses, and general and administrative expenses.
2. Prepare a statement of owner's equity for the year ended December 31, 20X1. No additional investments were made during the year.
3. Prepare a classified balance sheet as of December 31, 20X1. The mortgage payable extends for more than one year.

ACCOUNTS

	Debit	Credit
Cash	$ 14,350	
Petty Cash Fund	200	
Notes Receivable, due 20X2	6,000	
Accounts Receivable	54,600	
Allowance for Doubtful Accounts		$ 5,000
Interest Receivable	200	
Merchandise Inventory	87,915	
Warehouse Supplies	3,700	
Office Supplies	1,800	
Prepaid Insurance	6,900	
Land	20,400	
Building	53,100	
Accumulated Depreciation—Building		8,400
Warehouse Equipment	24,000	
Accumulated Depreciation—Warehouse Equipment		4,000
Office Equipment	12,800	
Accumulated Depreciation—Office Equipment		1,800
Notes Payable, due 20X2		8,000
Accounts Payable		32,500
Interest Payable		1,800
Notes Payable, Long-term		6,000
Mortgage Payable		35,875
Nick Henry, Capital (Jan. 1)		198,710
Nick Henry, Drawing	56,000	
Income Summary	88,980	87,915
Sales		608,417
Sales Returns and Allowances	9,400	
Interest Income		720
Purchases	230,050	
Freight In	9,600	

ACCOUNTS (CONT.)

	Debit	Credit
Purchases Returns and Allowances		6,420
Purchases Discounts		5,760
Warehouse Wages Expense	64,300	
Warehouse Supplies Expense	4,300	
Depreciation Expense—Warehouse Equipment	2,400	
Salaries Expense—Sales	78,900	
Travel Expense—Sales	21,000	
Delivery Expense	35,400	
Salaries Expense—Office	57,500	
Office Supplies Expense	1,360	
Insurance Expense	9,500	
Utilities Expense	6,912	
Telephone Expense	4,370	
Payroll Taxes Expense	19,200	
Building Repairs Expense	3,100	
Property Taxes Expense	11,700	
Uncollectible Accounts Expense	2,900	
Depreciation Expense—Building	3,200	
Depreciation Expense—Office Equipment	1,680	
Interest Expense	3,600	
Totals	$1,011,317	$1,011,317

Analyze: What is the inventory turnover for Hog Wild?

Problem 13.3B

Objectives 13-1, 13-2, 13-3

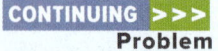

Preparing classified financial statements.

Obtain all data necessary from the worksheet prepared for Gamer's Paradise in Problem 12.6B at the end of Chapter 12. Then follow the instructions to complete this problem.

INSTRUCTIONS

1. Prepare a classified income statement for the year ended December 31, 20X1. The company does not classify its operating expenses as selling expenses and general and administrative expenses.
2. Prepare a statement of owner's equity for the year ended December 31, 20X1. No additional investments were made during the year.
3. Prepare a classified balance sheet as of December 31, 20X1.

Analyze: What is the amount of working capital for Gamer's Paradise?

Problem 13.4B

Objectives 13-4, 13-5, 13-7

Journalizing adjusting, closing, and reversing entries.

Obtain all data that is necessary from the worksheet prepared for Whatnots in Problem 12.5B at the end of Chapter 12. Then follow the instructions to complete this problem.

INSTRUCTIONS

1. Record adjusting entries in the general journal as of December 31, 20X1. Use 29 as the first journal page number. Include descriptions for the entries.

2. Record closing entries in the general journal as of December 31, 20X1. Include descriptions.
3. Record reversing entries in the general journal as of January 1, 20X2. Include descriptions.

Analyze: Assuming that the company did not record a reversing entry for salaries payable, what entry is required when salaries of $2,600 are paid on January 4? (Ignore payroll taxes withheld.)

Journalizing adjusting and reversing entries.

◀ **Problem 13.5B**
Objectives 13-4, 13-7

The data below concerns adjustments to be made at Mendocino Creek Wine Company.

INSTRUCTIONS

1. Record the adjusting entries in the general journal as of December 31, 20X1. Use 25 as the first journal page number. Include descriptions.
2. Record reversing entries in the general journal as of January 1, 20X2. Include descriptions.

ADJUSTMENTS

a. On August 1, 20X1, the firm signed a six-month advertising contract with a trade magazine and paid the entire amount, $27,900, in advance. *Prepaid Advertising* had a balance of $27,900 on December 31, 20X1.

b. On December 31, 20X1, an inventory of supplies showed that items costing $940 were on hand. The balance of the *Supplies* account was $7,680.

c. A depreciation schedule for the firm's store equipment shows that a total of $13,100 should be charged off as depreciation for 20X1.

d. On December 31, 20X1, the firm owed salaries of $13,200 that will not be paid until January 20X2.

e. On December 31, 20X1, the firm owed the employer's social security (6.2 percent) and Medicare (1.45 percent) taxes on all accrued salaries.

f. On November 1, 20X1, the firm received a three-month, 6 percent note for $7,000 from a customer with an overdue balance.

Analyze: After the adjusting entries have been posted, what is the balance of the *Prepaid Advertising* account on December 31?

Critical Thinking Problem 13.1

Year-End Processing

Programs Plus is a retail firm that sells computer programs for home and business use. Programs Plus operates in a state with no sales tax. On December 31, 20X1, its general ledger contained the accounts and balances shown below:

ACCOUNTS	BALANCES	
Cash	$15,280	Dr.
Accounts Receivable	26,600	Dr.
Allowance for Doubtful Accounts	95	Cr.
Merchandise Inventory	62,375	Dr.
Supplies	6,740	Dr.
Prepaid Insurance	2,380	Dr.
Equipment	34,000	Dr.
Accumulated Depreciation—Equipment	10,100	Cr.
Notes Payable	7,264	Cr.
Accounts Payable	6,500	Cr.
Social Security Tax Payable	560	Cr.

ACCOUNTS (CONT.)

ACCOUNTS	BALANCES	
Medicare Tax Payable	130	Cr.
Yasser Tousson, Capital	93,620	Cr.
Yasser Tousson, Drawing	50,000	Dr.
Sales	514,980	Cr.
Sales Returns and Allowances	9,600	Dr.
Purchases	319,430	Dr.
Freight In	3,600	Dr.
Purchases Returns and Allowances	7,145	Cr.
Purchases Discounts	5,760	Cr.
Rent Expense	14,500	Dr.
Telephone Expense	2,164	Dr.
Salaries Expense	92,000	Dr.
Payroll Taxes Expense	7,300	Dr.
Interest Expense	185	Dr.

The following accounts had zero balances:

- Salaries Payable
- Interest Payable
- Income Summary
- Supplies Expense
- Insurance Expense
- Depreciation Expense—Equipment
- Uncollectible Accounts Expense

The data needed for the adjustments on December 31 are as follows:

a.–b. Ending merchandise inventory, $67,850.

c. Uncollectible accounts, 0.5 percent of net credit sales of $245,000.

d. Supplies on hand December 31, $1,020.

e. Expired insurance, $1,190.

f. *Depreciation Expense—Equipment,* $5,600.

g. Accrued interest expense on notes payable, $325.

h. Accrued salaries, $2,100.

i. *Social Security Tax Payable* (6.2 percent) and *Medicare Tax Payable* (1.45 percent) of accrued salaries.

INSTRUCTIONS

1. Prepare a worksheet for the year ended December 31, 20X1.
2. Prepare a classified income statement. The firm does not divide its operating expenses into selling and administrative expenses.
3. Prepare a statement of owner's equity. No additional investments were made during the period.
4. Prepare a classified balance sheet. All notes payable are due within one year.
5. Journalize the adjusting entries. Use 25 as the first journal page number.

6. Journalize the closing entries.
7. Journalize the reversing entries.

Analyze: By what percentage did the owner's capital account change in the period from January 1, 20X1, to December 31, 20X1?

Critical Thinking Problem 13.2

Classified Balance Sheet

Brandon Marchand is the owner of Divine Jewels, a store specializing in gold, platinum, and special stones. During the past year, in response to increased demand, Brandon doubled his selling space by expanding into the vacant building space next door to his store. This expansion has been expensive because of the need to increase inventory and to purchase new store fixtures and equipment, including carpeting and state-of-the-art built-in fixtures. Brandon notes that the company's cash position has decreased and he is worried about future demands on cash to finance the growth.

Brandon presents you with a statement showing the assets, liabilities, and his equity for year-end 20X0 and 20X1, and asks your opinion on the company's ability to pay for the recent expansion. He did not have income and expense data available at the time. He commented that he had not made any new investment in the business in the past two years and was not financially able to do so presently. The information presented is shown below:

	December 31, 20X0	December 31, 20X1
Assets		
Cash	$ 150,000	$ 40,000
Accounts Receivable	45,000	91,500
Inventory	105,000	234,000
Prepaid Expenses	6,000	9,000
Store Fixtures and Equipment	180,000	395,000
Total Assets	$486,000	$769,500
Liabilities and Owner's Equity		
Liabilities		
Notes Payable (due in 4 years)	$ 90,000	$ 250,000
Accounts Payable	132,000	176,000
Salaries Payable	18,000	19,500
Total Liabilities	$240,000	$445,500
Owner's Equity		
Brandon Marchand, Capital	246,000	324,000
Total Liabilities and Owner's Equity	$486,000	$769,500

INSTRUCTIONS

1. Prepare classified balance sheets for Divine Jewels for December 31, 20X0, and December 31, 20X1. (Ignore depreciation.)
2. Based on the information presented in the classified balance sheets, what is your opinion of Divine Jewels' ability to pay its current bills in a timely manner?
3. What is the advantage of a classified balance sheet over a balance sheet that is not classified?

BUSINESS CONNECTIONS

Managerial FOCUS

Understanding Financial Statements

1. Why should management be concerned about the efficiency of the end-of-period procedures?
2. Spectrum Company had an increase in sales and net income during its last fiscal year, but cash decreased and the firm was having difficulty paying its bills by the end of the year. What factors might cause a shortage of cash even though a firm is profitable?
3. For the last three years, the balance sheet of Smith Hardware Center, a large retail store, has shown a substantial increase in merchandise inventory. Why might management be concerned about this development?
4. Why is it important to compare the financial statements of the current year with those of prior years?
5. Should a manager be concerned if the balance sheet shows a large increase in current liabilities and a large decrease in current assets? Explain your answer.
6. The latest income statement prepared at Patel Company shows that net sales increased by 10 percent over the previous year and selling expenses increased by 25 percent. Do you think that management should investigate the reasons for the increase in selling expenses? Why or why not?
7. Why is it useful for management to compare a firm's financial statements with financial information from other companies in the same industry?

Helping Your Boss May Be Wrong

Generally accepted accounting principles require that the principal amount due in the upcoming year on long-term debt be presented as a current liability on the balance sheet. This requires the accountant to make a journal entry to remove the current year's principal from the long-term liabilities and record it as a current liability. This entry reduces the long-term liabilities and increases the current liabilities. You are the bookkeeper for Southern Tools. Southern Tools has a bank loan that requires a current ratio of 1.5 to 1. The owner has asked that you not make the adjusting entry to take the current portion from the long-term liabilities. You know if you make the adjusting entry the bank will probably require the entire amount of Southern Tools' loan to be repaid immediately. What should you do?

Balance Sheet

McCormick & Company, Inc., is a global leader in the manufacture, marketing, and distribution of spices, seasoning mixes, condiments, and other products to the food industry. McCormick & Company, Inc., reported the following in its *2018 Annual Report*:

Consolidated Balance Sheet		
(in millions)	November 30	
	2018	**2017**
Total Current Assets	$1,479.9	$1,617.0
Total Assets	$10,256.4	$10,385.8
Total Current Liabilities	$2,001.7	$1,947.3
Total Liabilities	$7,074.2	$7,814.9

Analyze:

1. What is the current ratio for both 2018 and 2017?
2. Did the current ratio improve or decline from 2017 to 2018?
3. The company reported net sales of $5,408.9 million and gross profit of $2,371.6 million for its fiscal year ended November 30, 2018. What is the gross profit percentage for this period?

Analyzing Home Depot

Ratios are an important part of financial analysis. Divide into groups of two or three. Each person should choose one year from the The Home Depot *Annual Report* in Appendix A. Calculate the current ratio, gross profit percentage, and inventory turnover. Is The Home Depot doing better or worse than the previous year? What account is causing this change?

> **TEAMWORK**
>
> **Home Depot**

Answers to Comprehensive Self Review

1. Single-step: all revenues listed in one section and all related costs and expenses in another section. Multiple-step: various sections in which subtotals and totals are computed in arriving at net income. Multistep statements are generally preferred.

2. An entry in the debit column on the *Income Summary* line and a credit to *Merchandise Inventory* for the amount of beginning inventory closes the beginning inventory. A debit on the *Merchandise Inventory* line and a credit to *Income Summary* for the amount of ending inventory sets up the ending inventory.

3. It generally has a life of more than one year and is used in business operations.

4. **b.** expense accounts **e.** *Income Summary* account
   d. owner's drawing account **g.** revenue accounts

5. **a.** *Sales Returns and Allowances*

6. **a.** Debit *Income Summary* and credit *Jan Hanson, Capital* for $58,000.
   b. Debit *Jan Hanson, Capital* and credit *Income Summary* for $8,000.

7. **a.** adjusting entries; **c.** entries to close revenue accounts; **b.** entries to close expense accounts; **d.** reversing entries

Mini-Practice Set 2

Merchandising Business Accounting Cycle

The Fashion Rack

INTRODUCTION

The Fashion Rack is a retail merchandising business that sells brand-name clothing at discount prices. The firm is owned and managed by Teresa Lojay, who started the business on April 1, 20X1. This project will give you an opportunity to put your knowledge of accounting into practice as you handle the accounting work of The Fashion Rack during the month of October 20X1.

The Fashion Rack has a monthly accounting period. The firm's chart of accounts is shown below. The journals used to record transactions are the sales journal, purchases journal, cash receipts journal, cash payments journal, and general journal. Postings are made from the journals to the accounts receivable ledger, accounts payable ledger, and general ledger. The employees are paid at the end of the month. A computerized payroll service prepares all payroll records and checks.

INSTRUCTIONS

1. Open the general ledger accounts and enter the balances for October 1, 20X1. Obtain the necessary figures from the postclosing trial balance prepared on September 30, 20X1, which is shown below. (If you are using the *Study Guide & Working Papers,* you will find that the general ledger accounts are already open.)

2. Open the subsidiary ledger accounts and enter the balances for October 1, 20X1. Obtain the necessary figures from the schedule of accounts payable and schedule of accounts receivable prepared on September 30, 20X1, which appears below. (If you are using the *Study Guide & Working Papers,* you will find that the subsidiary ledger accounts are already open.)

3. Analyze the transactions for October and record each transaction in the proper journal. (Use 10 as the number for the first page of each special journal and 16 as the number for the first page of the general journal.)

4. Post the individual entries that involve customer and creditor accounts from the journals to the subsidiary ledgers on a daily basis. Post the individual entries that appear in the general journal and in the Other Accounts sections of the cash receipts and cash payments journals to the general ledger on a daily basis.

5. Total, prove, and rule the special journals as of October 31, 20X1.

6. Post the column totals from the special journals to the general ledger accounts.

The Fashion Rack
Chart of Accounts

Assets			Liabilities		
101	Cash		203	Accounts Payable	
111	Accounts Receivable		221	Social Security Tax Payable	
112	Allowance for Doubtful Accounts		222	Medicare Tax Payable	
121	Merchandise Inventory		223	Employee Income Tax Payable	
131	Supplies		225	Federal Unemployment Tax Payable	
133	Prepaid Insurance		227	State Unemployment Tax Payable	
135	Prepaid Advertising		229	Salaries Payable	
141	Equipment		231	Sales Tax Payable	
142	Accumulated Depreciation—Equipment				

The Fashion Rack			
Chart of Accounts (continued)			
Owner's Equity		**Expenses**	
301	Teresa Lojay, Capital	611	Advertising Expense
302	Teresa Lojay, Drawing	614	Depreciation Expense—Equipment
399	Income Summary	617	Insurance Expense
Revenues		620	Uncollectible Accounts Expense
401	Sales	623	Janitorial Services Expense
402	Sales Returns and Allowances	626	Payroll Taxes Expense
Cost of Goods Sold		629	Rent Expense
501	Purchases	632	Salaries Expense
502	Freight In	635	Supplies Expense
503	Purchases Returns and Allowances	638	Telephone Expense
504	Purchases Discounts	644	Utilities Expense

7. Check the accuracy of the subsidiary ledgers by preparing a schedule of accounts receivable and a schedule of accounts payable as of October 31, 20X1. Compare the totals with the balances of the **Accounts Receivable** account and the **Accounts Payable** account in the general ledger.

8. Check the accuracy of the general ledger by preparing a trial balance in the first two columns of a 10-column worksheet. Make sure that the total debits and the total credits are equal.

9. Complete the Adjustments section of the worksheet. Use the following data. Identify each adjustment with the appropriate letter.

    a. During October, the firm had net credit sales of $10,140. From experience with similar businesses, the previous accountant had estimated that 1.0 percent of the firm's net credit sales would result in uncollectible accounts. Record an adjustment for the expected loss from uncollectible accounts for the month of October.

    b. On October 31, an inventory of the supplies showed that items costing $2,740 were on hand. Record an adjustment for the supplies used in October.

    c. On September 30, 20X1, the firm purchased a six-month insurance policy for $8,400. Record an adjustment for the expired insurance for October.

    d. On October 1, 20X1, the firm signed a three-month advertising contract for $5,100 with a local cable television station and paid the full amount in advance. Record an adjustment for the expired advertising for October.

    e. On April 1, 20X1, the firm purchased equipment for $83,000. The equipment was estimated to have a useful life of five years and a salvage value of $12,500. Record an adjustment for depreciation on the equipment for October.

    f.–g. Based on a physical count, ending merchandise inventory was determined to be $82,260.

10. Complete the Adjusted Trial Balance section of the worksheet.
11. Determine the net income or net loss for October and complete the worksheet.
12. Prepare a classified income statement for the month ended October 31, 20X1. (The firm does not divide its operating expenses into selling and administrative expenses.)
13. Prepare a statement of owner's equity for the month ended October 31, 20X1.
14. Prepare a classified balance sheet as of October 31, 20X1.
15. Journalize and post the adjusting entries using general journal page 17.
16. Prepare and post the closing entries using general journal page 18.
17. Prepare a postclosing trial balance.

DATE		TRANSACTIONS
Oct.	1	Issued Check 601 for $4,400 to pay Properties Management, Inc., the monthly rent.
	1	Signed a three-month radio advertising contract with Cable Station KTLE for $5,100; issued Check 602 to pay the full amount in advance.
	2	Received $520 from Megan Greening, a credit customer, in payment of her account.
	2	Issued Check 603 for $17,820 to remit the sales tax owed for July through September to the State Tax Commission.
	2	Issued Check 604 for $7,673.40 to A Fashion Statement, a creditor, in payment of Invoice 9387 ($7,830), less a cash discount ($156.60).
	3	Sold merchandise on credit for $2,480 plus sales tax of $124 to Mariam Salib, Sales Slip 241.
	4	Issued Check 605 for $1,050 to BMX Supply Co. for supplies.
	4	Issued Check 606 for $8,594.60 to Unique Styles, a creditor, in payment of Invoice 5671 ($8,770), less a cash discount ($175.40).
	5	Collected $1,700.00 on account from Amy Trinh, a credit customer.
	5	Accepted a return of merchandise from Mariam Salib. The merchandise was originally sold on Sales Slip 241, dated October 3; issued Credit Memorandum 18 for $630, which includes sales tax of $30.
	5	Issued Check 607 for $1,666 to Classy Threads, a creditor, in payment of Invoice 3292 ($1,700), less a cash discount ($34).
	6	Had cash sales of $18,600 plus sales tax of $930 during October 1–6.
	8	Received a check from James Helmer, a credit customer, for $832 to pay the balance he owes.
	8	Issued Check 608 for $1,884 to deposit social security tax ($702), Medicare tax ($162), and federal income tax withholding ($1,020) from the September payroll. Record this check in the cash payments journal.
	9	Sold merchandise on credit for $2,050 plus sales tax of $102.50 to Emma Maldonado, Sales Slip 242.
	10	Issued Check 609 for $1,525 to pay *The Daily News* for a newspaper advertisement that appeared in October.
	11	Purchased merchandise for $4,820 from A Fashion Statement, Invoice 9422, dated October 8; the terms are 2/10, n/30.
	12	Issued Check 610 for $395 to pay freight charges to Ace Freight Company, the trucking company that delivered merchandise from A Fashion Statement on September 27 and October 11.
	13	Had cash sales of $13,200 plus sales tax of $660 during October 8–13.
	15	Sold merchandise on credit for $1,940 plus sales tax of $97 to James Helmer, Sales Slip 243.
	16	Purchased discontinued merchandise from Acme Jobbers; paid for it immediately with Check 611 for $5,120.
	16	Received $510 on account from Mariam Salib, a credit customer.
	16	Issued Check 612 for $4,723.60 to A Fashion Statement, a creditor, in payment of Invoice 9422 ($4,820.00), less cash discount ($96.40).
	18	Issued Check 613 for $7,400 to Teresa Lojay as a withdrawal for personal use.
	20	Had cash sales of $13,500 plus sales tax of $675 during October 15–20.
	22	Issued Check 614 to City Utilities for $1,492 to pay the monthly electric bill.

DATE	(cont.) TRANSACTIONS
24	Sold merchandise on credit for $820 plus sales tax of $41 to Megan Greening, Sales Slip 244.
25	Purchased merchandise for $3,580 from Classy Threads, Invoice 3418, dated October 23; the terms are 2/10, n/30.
26	Issued Check 615 to Regional Telephone for $940 to pay the monthly telephone bill.
27	Had cash sales of $14,240 plus sales tax of $712 during October 22–27.
29	Received Credit Memorandum 175 for $430 from Classy Threads for defective goods that were returned. The original purchase was recorded on October 25.
29	Sold merchandise on credit for $3,450 plus sales tax of $172.50 to Amy Trinh, Sales Slip 245.
29	Recorded the October payroll. The records prepared by the payroll service show the following totals: earnings, $10,800; social security, $702.00; Medicare, $162.00; income tax, $1,020; and net pay, $8,916. The excess withholdings corrected an error made in withholdings in September.
29	Recorded the employer's payroll taxes, which were calculated by the payroll service: social security, $702; Medicare, $162; federal unemployment tax, $118; and state unemployment tax, $584. This, too, reflects an understatement of taxes recorded in September and corrected in this month.
30	Purchased merchandise for $4,080 from Unique Styles, Invoice 5821, dated October 26; the terms are 1/10, n/30.
31	Issued Checks 616 through 619, totaling $8,916.00, to employees to pay October payroll. For the sake of simplicity, enter the total of the checks on a single line in the cash payments journal.
31	Issued Check 620 for $525 to A+ Janitors for October janitorial services.
31	Had cash sales of $1,800 plus sales tax of $90 for October 29–31.

The Fashion Rack
Postclosing Trial Balance
September 30, 20X1

ACCOUNT NAME	DEBIT	CREDIT
Cash	59 800 00	
Accounts Receivable	6 210 00	
Allowance for Doubtful Accounts		420 00
Merchandise Inventory	88 996 00	
Supplies	4 100 00	
Prepaid Insurance	8 400 00	
Equipment	83 000 00	
Accumulated Depreciation—Equipment		7 050 00
Accounts Payable		18 300 00
Social Security Tax Payable		702 00
Medicare Tax Payable		162 00
Employee Income Tax Payable		1 020 00
Federal Unemployment Tax Payable		512 00
State Unemployment Tax Payable		1 268 00
Sales Tax Payable		17 820 00
Teresa Lojay, Capital		203 252 00
Totals	250 506 00	250 506 00

The Fashion Rack
Schedule of Accounts Payable
September 30, 20X1

A Fashion Statement	7 830 00
Classy Threads	1 700 00
Unique Styles	8 770 00
Total	18 300 00

The Fashion Rack
Schedule of Accounts Receivable
September 30, 20X1

Ashley Butler	795 00
Megan Greening	520 00
James Helmer	832 00
Emma Maldonado	232 00
Jim Price	1 621 00
Mariam Salib	510 00
Amy Trinh	1 700 00
Total	6 210 00

Accounting Principles and Reporting Standards

Chapter 14

James Leynse/Getty Images

www.fasb.org

A company's financial information is used by many individuals and entities, both internal and external to the company, to make financial decisions. Therefore, the company's financial information needs to be an accurate and credible representation of the company's financial performance. Since 1973, the Financial Accounting Standards Board (FASB) has been establishing standards of financial accounting that govern the preparation of financial reports by nongovernmental entities. These standards of financial reporting serve as the rules for properly recording and reporting the company's financial activities. The FASB standards are officially recognized as authoritative by the Securities and Exchange Commission (SEC) and the American Institute of Certified Public Accountants (AICPA).

The FASB is comprised of seven full-time members with diverse backgrounds in accounting, finance, and business. Each member must be completely independent of any and all firms or institutions that may be affected or governed by the FASB principles.

The FASB's mission is to establish and improve the standards of financial accounting and reporting used by nongovernmental companies to assist them in providing information that is useful in decision making. They utilize a comprehensive process incorporating input from a broad spectrum of participants. Once a financial reporting issue has been identified, the issue is analyzed and, if deemed necessary, added to the FASB's technical agenda. The FASB further analyzes and discusses the issue at public meetings and solicits input from a broad spectrum of stakeholders. The FASB then issues an exposure draft of the issue, solicits additional input, and may hold public discussions on the proposed issue. All input is further analyzed by the board to carefully consider the issue at hand and all stakeholder input received. Only after considerable analysis of the benefits to be provided by a new standard does the board decide to approve or deny any additions or changes to the financial reporting standards.

The FASB has adopted a collective process of establishing a consistent set of rules for the recording and reporting of financial performance and results. If the FASB's standards are followed, the result should be a set of financial reports that are informative and useful in decision making.

thinking critically

If a company was to change its revenue recognition policy, why would it be important to report this change in the financial notes of the company's annual report?

LEARNING OBJECTIVES

14-1 Understand the process used to develop generally accepted accounting principles.

14-2 Identify the major accounting standards-setting bodies and their roles in the standards-setting process.

14-3 Describe the users and uses of financial reports.

14-4 Identify and explain the qualitative characteristics of accounting information.

14-5 Describe and explain the basic assumptions about accounting reports.

14-6 Explain and apply the basic principles of accounting.

14-7 Describe and apply the modifying constraints on accounting principles.

14-8 Define the accounting terms new to this chapter.

NEW TERMS

conceptual framework
conservatism
cost-benefit test
full disclosure principle
going concern assumption
historical cost basis principle
industry practice constraint
matching principle
materiality constraint
monetary unit assumption
neutrality concept
periodicity of income assumption
private sector
public sector
qualitative characteristics
realization
revenue recognition principle
transparency

Section 1

SECTION OBJECTIVES

>> **14-1** Understand the process used to develop generally accepted accounting principles.

WHY IT'S IMPORTANT
Knowing how accounting principles are developed helps in understanding the logic underlying accounting and therefore helps learn rules.

>> **14-2** Identify the major accounting standards-setting bodies and their roles in the standards-setting process.

WHY IT'S IMPORTANT
Documents relating to accounting principles and standards are filled with references to organizations involved in standards setting. To understand standards, it is necessary to understand the roles of these organizations.

>> **14-3** Describe the users and uses of financial reports.

WHY IT'S IMPORTANT
Principles and standards of accounting can be developed in a logical way only if it is known who the users of the statements are and what uses they make of the statements.

TERMS TO LEARN

conceptual framework
private sector
public sector

Generally Accepted Accounting Principles

In previous chapters, you learned how to record business transactions and summarize them in financial statements. Financial statements are prepared using generally accepted accounting principles and rules. In the first section of this chapter, you will learn how these principles and rules are developed. In the second section, you will learn about the conceptual framework of accounting underlying all financial reporting for business enterprises.

The Need for Generally Accepted Accounting Principles

In order to ensure that they are meaningful and useful, financial statements are prepared using generally accepted accounting principles (GAAP). GAAP is used whether the business is a sole proprietorship managed by the owner or is a large company such as Macy's. GAAP allows the financial statements of different companies to be compared and meaningful conclusions drawn from the comparison. It also allows a company to compare its own statements from period to period.

>> **14-1 OBJECTIVE**
Understand the process used to develop generally accepted accounting principles.

The Development of Generally Accepted Accounting Principles

Accepted accounting principles are developed in several ways in the United States. In the past, unique accounting procedures and practices became widely used over time by specific industries or in accounting for specific transactions. These industry practices have sometimes become accepted as GAAP even though they may not be entirely consistent with the general requirements. In some cases, accounting rules result from a decision by the authoritative rule-making organization to permit more than one method because of industry practice. This is true, for example, in the oil and gas industries, in which two methods of accounting for certain activities are allowed by the Securities and Exchange Commission (SEC). The use of two methods may yield widely differing results.

For the past half-century, however, accounting principles in the United States have been developed through a cooperative effort between the **private sector** (business) and the **public sector** (government). The Securities and Exchange Commission is the legal rule-making body from the public sector, and the Financial Accounting Standards Board (FASB) is the primary representative of the private sector. Most official pronouncements of accounting principles and rules today represent a joint effort of these two organizations.

>> **14-2 OBJECTIVE**
Identify the major accounting standards-setting bodies and their roles in the standards-setting process.

The Securities and Exchange Commission

In 1934, the Congress of the United States established the Securities and Exchange Commission (SEC) to administer the Securities Act of 1933 and the Securities Exchange Act of 1934. Among its powers, the SEC has authority to define accounting terms and to prescribe accounting principles for companies under its jurisdiction. The SEC also determines the form and content of accounting reports that are required to be filed with the SEC. The SEC regulates the financial reporting of publicly held corporations (basically, companies whose stocks are traded in the securities exchanges and over-the-counter markets). The SEC is a dominant force in accounting because its rules must be followed by publicly held companies. Historically, however, the SEC has used its powers sparingly, preferring to let the accounting profession develop accounting principles and financial reporting standards, which are then usually adopted by the SEC as official rules. The Sarbanes-Oxley Act, passed by the U.S. Congress in 2002 in reaction to the "accounting scandals" of public companies in the early 2000s, reaffirms the SEC's role as the authoritative accounting rule-making body. The Act goes further to permit the SEC to accept the accounting and reporting rules developed by "a private-sector organization," provided certain requirements are met. Section 108 of the Act states: ". . . the Commission may recognize as 'generally accepted' for purposes of the securities laws, any accounting principles established by a standard setting body"* (meeting certain tests). In April 2003, the SEC officially recognized the FASB as the accounting standard setter under Sarbanes-Oxley.

ABOUT
ACCOUNTING
Authority of the SEC
The SEC is given statutory power to establish accounting and reporting rules for publicly held companies. Thus, it has the "final voice" in accounting principles for those companies.

Public Company Accounting Oversight Board

The Sarbanes-Oxley Act also created the Public Company Accounting Oversight Board (PCAOB). The PCAOB is a private-sector, nonprofit corporation whose purpose is to oversee the CPA firms auditing publicly held companies. The PCAOB has five members who are appointed by the SEC. Two members of the PCAOB (and only two) must be CPAs.

The PCAOB has the power to, among other things, set auditing, quality control, ethics, independence, and other standards for CPA firms engaged in auditing publicly held companies. This includes regulating the nonaudit services CPA firms provide to their audit clients, such as tax and consulting services. This authority was given to the PCAOB as a reaction to audit failures at several publicly held companies including WorldCom and Enron. Many people felt the auditors' independence from their clients had been impaired because of the large amount of fees they earned from consulting and tax services.

The Financial Accounting Standards Board

Since 1973, the Financial Accounting Standards Board (FASB) has been the designated organization in the private sector for establishing standards of financial accounting that govern the preparation of financial reports by nongovernmental entities. Those standards are officially recognized as authoritative by the Securities and Exchange Commission and the American Institute of Certified Public Accountants. The mission of the FASB is to establish and improve standards of financial accounting and reporting that foster financial reporting by nongovernmental entities that provide decision-useful information to investors and other users of financial reports.

* U.S. Securities and Exchange Commission

> **ABOUT ACCOUNTING**
>
> **Sources of Accounting Rules**
>
> The FASB is the authoritative rule-making body in the private sector. Because the SEC is empowered to accept the FASB's rules, it is regarded as the primary source of accounting principles. In addition, the AICPA requires its members to certify that audited statements conform to GAAP.

> **important!**
>
> **The Conceptual Framework**
>
> The conceptual framework is the foundation underlying all generally accepted accounting principles and reporting practices. It is very important in your study of accounting.

From its inception in 1973 until 2013, the authoritative pronouncements of the FASB were known as *Statements of Financial Accounting Standards,* or simply Standards. More than 160 such standards were issued. In mid-2010, the FASB introduced the *Financial Accounting Standards Board Accounting Standards Codification.* The Codification organized GAAP into a structure that is much easier for a professional to study and define the generally accepted accounting principle relating to a particular account or accounting issue. The Codification is now the source of all authoritative nongovernmental GAAP. All GAAP related to assets are now found in the section of the Codification for Assets (ASC300 Assets)—likewise for all other areas of accounting. Subject areas are referred to as a topic. All previous level U.S. GAAP are superseded by the Codification.

The FASB's work is based on a fundamental framework of accounting, developed under its **conceptual framework** project. The goal of the project is to provide a cohesive set of closely related objectives and concepts to be used in developing accounting and reporting standards. The FASB has issued eight *Statements of Financial Accounting Concepts* that provide the guidelines on which the official *Statements of Financial Accounting Standards* are to be based. The process used by the FASB in developing the conceptual framework statements reflects deductive reasoning and involves essentially the following steps:

1. Define the goals and objectives of accounting.
2. Identify users of financial reports and the uses made of the reports.
3. Examine the qualitative characteristics that make accounting information useful.
4. Identify and define the financial elements such as assets, liabilities, revenues, and expenses, whose inclusion and classification make financial statements meaningful and useful.
5. Establish the form and content of financial statements.
6. Set forth fundamental recognition criteria.
7. Develop measurement standards for financial elements that appear in the financial statements.

Section 108 of the 2002 Sarbanes-Oxley Act requires the SEC to "conduct a study on the adoption by the United States financial reporting system of a principles-based accounting system." The FASB itself conducted a study and issued a report in October 2002. In July 2003, the SEC completed its study and made its report to Congress. The result is an intention for the FASB to issue "objectives-oriented standards" and to "address deficiencies in the conceptual framework." The goal is to arrive at an "internally consistent" and "complete" framework. The Codification helps achieve this desired result.

For the most recent activities and pronouncements of the FASB and projects (including the conceptual framework project), visit www.FASB.org.

The American Institute of Certified Public Accountants

The American Institute of Certified Public Accountants (AICPA) is the national organization of certified public accountants. Prior to formation of the FASB, the AICPA's Accounting Principles Board was recognized by the SEC as the preeminent private-sector group in developing accounting rules. Although the AICPA has much less authority and a less-active role in the development of accounting standards than it held before its APB was superseded by the FASB in 1973, it continues to play an important role through its Accounting Standards Executive Committee (AcSEC). AcSEC issues three important types of documents:

> **ABOUT ACCOUNTING**
>
> **The AICPA's Role**
>
> Although the AICPA is no longer the authoritative accounting rule maker, it continues to play an important role in developing accounting principles.

1. **Accounting and auditing guides.** These releases provide guidance on accounting matters not addressed directly by the FASB and summarize the accounting and auditing practices in specific industries—for example, casinos, airlines, insurance companies, and oil- and gas-producing companies.
2. **Statements of position (SOPs).** SOPs provide guidance on a financial accounting question that has been raised until the FASB issues an official pronouncement on the topic.
3. **Practice bulletins.** Practice bulletins express the AICPA's position on narrow accounting issues that have not been considered by the FASB or SEC.

In addition to its work through AcSEC, the AICPA regulates auditing practices and takes the lead role in developing and enforcing ethical standards for auditors. In this role, the AICPA gives the statements of the FASB additional support by requiring that AICPA members make sure the companies being audited follow the accounting and reporting standards specified in the FASB Statements.

For the most recent activities and pronouncements of the AICPA, visit www.AICPA.org.

Federal and State Agencies Other Than the SEC

Historically, many other federal and state agencies have strongly influenced accounting and reporting standards. Regulatory agencies have had the power to prescribe detailed systems of accounting for public utilities, including the railroad and electric power industries. These agencies are concerned with regulation of price and competition more than with the development of accounting principles. As a result, the accounting and reporting requirements imposed on regulated industries frequently have not reflected GAAP.

Similarly, federal income tax requirements have had an impact on financial accounting. Businesses are not required to use the same financial accounting and tax accounting practices. However, some taxpayers adopt tax accounting rules where possible to avoid keeping two sets of records. This is possible if the tax requirements do not conflict with authoritative financial accounting principles. There almost inevitably are differences between required tax treatment and required GAAP. These differences often give rise to a unique accounting problem: the requirement that the current financial income statement should reflect the tax expense applicable to the income reported in the financial statements even though the actual tax paid is different because it is not levied on the income reported in the financial statement.

Other Organizations in the United States

Other organizations and groups have over several decades been instrumental in the development and evolution of accounting principles and rules. The American Accounting Association (AAA) is one such organization. About half its members teach accounting. Many of them have written textbooks and articles dealing with accounting principles and concepts and often are involved in other accounting organizations, including the FASB. In a variety of ways, the AAA has been able to stimulate acceptance of the principles it has helped develop and perfect over the years.

As early as 1930, the New York Stock Exchange (NYSE) required corporations whose securities were traded on a public stock exchange to publish annual reports. Later, quarterly reports were required. Since 1933, the NYSE has insisted upon independent audits for all corporations that applied to have their securities (stocks and bonds) listed on the exchange.

ABOUT
ACCOUNTING
The AICPA has many resources on its website to help you learn about IFRS. www.aicpa.org

The International Accounting Standards Board

Accounting principles vary from country to country. The International Accounting Standards Board (IASB) was formed to develop accounting standards that can be adopted throughout the world for publicly traded companies. The mission of the IASB is to develop International Financial Reporting Standards (IFRS) that bring transparency, accountability, and efficiency to financial markets around the world. The organization has issued about 40 "International Accounting Standards." The International Financial Reporting Standards Foundation is an independent, nonprofit foundation that was created in 2000 to oversee the IASB. Accounting professionals have begun using the terminology of IFRS in reference to all internationally accepted accounting principles. In an important move, in 2002 the European Union voted to require companies whose securities are traded on exchanges in member countries to prepare financial reports on the basis of IASB Standards.

Accounting rule-making bodies in the United States historically have been reluctant to recognize as "authoritative" the standards issued by the IASB or its predecessor, the International Accounting Standards Committee (IASC). Presently, however, the SEC, the FASB, the International Accounting Standards Board, and accounting rule-making bodies from many countries are working toward the convergence of the standards issued by each organization. Because of this, new rules developed by the FASB and by the IASB have become more consistent with one another. The two organizations and accounting rule-setting bodies from other countries have worked closely in developing almost identical standards on new issues.

Section 108 of the Sarbanes-Oxley Act, in describing the attributes of a private-sector organization that might be accepted as the accounting standards setter, included the following text: ". . . considers, in adopting accounting principles, . . . the extent to which international convergence on high quality accounting standards is necessary or appropriate in the public interest and for the protection of investors."*

It can be reasonably expected that the gap between accounting statements in countries around the world will decrease dramatically in the next decade as more countries adopt IFRS for financial statements.

For the most recent activities and pronouncements of the IASB and projects (including the Conceptual Framework Project), visit www.IFRS.org.

The FASB and IASB Conceptual Framework Project

At their joint meeting in October 2004, the FASB and the IASB decided to add to their respective agendas a joint project to develop a common conceptual framework that both boards would use as a basis for their accounting standards. In late 2010, the boards effectively deferred work on the joint project until other more urgent convergence projects were finalized. Subsequently, in December 2012, the IASB decided to reactivate the conceptual framework project as an IASB-only comprehensive project.

Before being suspended, the joint IASB/FASB project was being conducted in a number of phases. Phase A, Objectives and Qualitative Characteristics, of the conceptual framework project was completed in September 2010. Phase B, Elements and Recognition; Phase C, Measurement; Phase D, Reporting Entity; and Phase E, Presentation and Disclosure, will be further considered as part of the IASB-only comprehensive project.

Users and Uses of Financial Reports

>> **14-3 OBJECTIVE**
Describe the users and uses of financial reports.

In its conceptual framework, the FASB concluded that financial reporting rules should concentrate on providing information that is helpful to current and potential investors and creditors in making investment and credit decisions. The focus is not on providing information to management, tax authorities, or regulatory agencies because they have access to specific information from the firm's records not available to the public and often the information they need is not the same as that needed by investors and creditors.

In its conceptual framework project, the FASB also concluded that the information needed by investors and creditors should help them assess the likelihood of receiving a future cash flow, the amount of such a cash flow, and the time when the cash flow may be received. This conclusion is based on the idea that investors and creditors expect to receive a cash flow directly or indirectly from the business entity:

- *directly* from the distribution of the company's earnings or
- *indirectly* through the disposition of their interests for cash.

Thus, financial report users need information about:

- profits
- economic resources (assets)
- claims against the assets (liabilities and owner's equity)
- changes in assets and in the claims against the assets

Information about profits appears in the income statement. Information about assets, liabilities, and owner's equity is provided primarily in the balance sheet.

The statement of cash flows provides information about the cash received from major sources during the period and the uses made of that cash. The statement of cash flows is discussed in Chapter 24.

>ABOUT
>**ACCOUNTING**
>
>**Accounting Is Designed for Users**
>
>In order to develop accounting principles and reporting standards, it is necessary to know for whom reports are being prepared and to what uses they are put.

---

* Library of Congress

Certain analyses of the financial statements also supply meaningful information about the results of operations and the financial condition of a business. The analysis of financial statements is discussed in Chapter 23.

It is clear from the actions of the SEC and the FASB that they interpret the Sarbanes-Oxley Act to require a stronger conceptual framework of accounting. It is equally clear that the two organizations also agree that accounting standards must be based on the conceptual framework. The SEC's 2006 report to the Congress on "principles-based" accounting observed that the first characteristic of objectives-based standards, dictated by the Sarbanes-Oxley Act, is that any standard must "be based on an improved and consistently applied framework." It is essential that accounting students understand the framework.

Section 1 Review

1. Select the governmental entity that has final oversight of the development of accounting principles:
   a. American Institute of Certified Public Accountants (AICPA).
   b. Internal Revenue Service (IRS).
   c. Securities and Exchange Commission (SEC).
   d. Financial Accounting Standards Board (FASB).

2. The Financial Accounting Standards Board (FASB) project designed to develop basic concepts, assumptions, and principles is called:
   a. Accounting Framework Project.
   b. Conceptual Framework Project.
   c. Generally Accepted Accounting Framework Project.
   d. Concept Vision Framework Project.

3. Two major reasons the pronouncements of the Financial Accounting Standards Board have had a major influence on accounting in this country are:
   a. the SEC traditionally relies on FASB as the provider of accounting standards.
   b. entities that do not follow pronouncements of the FASB are heavily fined.
   c. the AICPA requires members to follow the FASB rules.
   d. a and b are correct.
   e. a and c are correct.

4. Saber Corporation is a corporation with only two shareholders (owners). Saber Corporation is a publicly held corporation required to file financial statements with the SEC.
   a. True
   b. False

5. Which organization has the power to limit nonaudit services by CPA firms to their clients?
   a. Financial Accounting Standards Board
   b. Public Company Accounting Oversight Board
   c. International Accounting Standards Board
   d. Securities and Exchange Commission

6. Which organization is an independent, private-sector body that develops and approves International Financial Reporting Standards (IFRS)?
   a. Financial Accounting Standards Board
   b. Public Accounting Oversight Board
   c. International Accounting Standards Board
   d. Securities and Exchange Commission

7. Which organization develops and issues most of the accounting standards?
   a. Financial Accounting Standards Board
   b. Public Accounting Oversight Board
   c. International Accounting Standards Board
   d. Securities and Exchange Commission

8. Which organization has legal responsibility for setting accounting requirements for publicly held corporations?
   a. Financial Accounting Standards Board
   b. Public Accounting Oversight Board
   c. International Accounting Standards Board
   d. Securities and Exchange Commission

9. To an investor, an auditor's notation that financial statements are "not prepared in conformity with GAAP" means:
   a. the statements are unreliable.
   b. the statements are not presented in accordance with established accounting principles.
   c. the statements may be unreliable.
   d. a, b, and c are correct.
   e. b and c are correct.

Section 2

SECTION OBJECTIVES	TERMS TO LEARN
14-4 Identify and explain the qualitative characteristics of accounting information. **WHY IT'S IMPORTANT** The qualitative characteristics provide the users a basis for relying on the statements. **14-5** Describe and explain the basic assumptions about accounting reports. **WHY IT'S IMPORTANT** The accountant bases financial reports on standard assumptions, so an understanding of these assumptions is essential to understanding reports. **14-6** Explain and apply the basic principles of accounting. **WHY IT'S IMPORTANT** All accounting reports rest on the basic principles. Knowledge of the principles is essential to prepare statements and to understand statements. **14-7** Describe and apply the modifying constraints on accounting principles. **WHY IT'S IMPORTANT** Modifying conventions may justify or require the modification of basic accounting principles.	conservatism cost-benefit test full disclosure principle going concern assumption historical cost basis principle industry practice constraint matching principle materiality constraint monetary unit assumption neutrality concept periodicity of income assumption qualitative characteristics realization revenue recognition principle transparency

The IASB's Conceptual Framework of Accounting

The rules of accounting that you are learning in this textbook are all based on the existing conceptual framework developed as a separate project with the IASB. The objective of the project is to improve financial reporting by providing a more complete, clear, and updated set of concepts. In May 2015, the IASB issued Exposure Draft 2015-3, *Conceptual Framework for Financial Reporting*. The exposure draft was more complete than the previously existing conceptual framework because it addressed areas that were either not covered or not covered in enough detail, clarified some aspects of the previously existing conceptual framework, and updated parts of the existing conceptual framework that were out of date.

In March 2018 the IASB published its revised *Conceptual Framework for Financial Reporting*. The 2018 *Conceptual Framework* is structured into an introductory explanation on the status and purpose of the Conceptual Framework, eight chapters, and a glossary. Reflected below is a summary of the chapters and topics covered in the final *Framework*.

A detailed discussion of the *Framework* is beyond the scope of this text. However, four levels of concepts in the conceptual framework—(1) qualitative characteristics of financial

Summary of Main Aspects of the *Conceptual Framework*	
Chapter	Topic
1	Status and Purpose of the *Conceptual Framework*
	The objective of general purpose financial reporting
2	Qualitative characteristics of useful financial information
3	Financial statements and the reporting entity
4	The elements of financial statements
5	Recognition and derecognition
6	Measurement
7	Presentation and disclosure
8	Concepts of capital and capital maintenance
Appendix A	Glossary

reports, (2) basic assumptions underlying financial reports, (3) basic accounting principles, and (4) modifying constraints—are discussed below. An understanding of these elements will be of great benefit in this course as you learn how to account for and report various transactions affecting the financial statements.

Qualitative Characteristics of Financial Reports

The **qualitative characteristics** are the qualities that make accounting information useful for decision making by investors, creditors, and other users. The meanings of most of these characteristics are self-evident from their names.

Qualitative Characteristics	
Decision Usefulness	
Relevance	Faithful Representation
Confirmatory Value*	Completeness
Predictive Value*	Neutrality
*(Value must be Material)	Freedom from Error

Fundamental Qualitative Characteristics

Relevance and faithful representation are the two qualitative characteristics of financial reports. These two characteristics are closely related and interdependent. First, the information should be relevant to decision makers. Further, the information should be a faithful representation of business activities. However, the framework assumes that financial statement users will have a basic knowledge of business and economics and they will devote an appropriate amount of time to studying and analyzing the statements. Published financial reports are not designed for individuals who do not possess such knowledge.

Relevance

Relevance means that accounting information is capable of making a difference in a decision by the report user. Conversely, if information is not capable of being useful to the user in

>> **14-4 OBJECTIVE**
Identify and explain the qualitative characteristics of accounting information.

making a decision, it is not relevant. In order for accounting information to be relevant in making a difference in decision making, it must have confirmatory value, predictive value, or both. Generally, relevant information will possess both of these components. Both of these components must be material in order to be relevant.

Confirmatory Value Information that helps the statement user verify fulfillment or nonfulfillment of prior expectations or decisions is said to have confirmatory value. For example, a quarterly income statement may provide evidence that prior expectations have been met. In this context, confirmatory value deals with verifying past expectations. However, information providing confirmatory value may also be useful in predicting future results.

Predictive Value If information is relevant, it will help statement users in making predictions or forecasts about the meaning and ultimate outcome of events giving rise to the information.

If information is relevant, it must be material in amount or nature that is sufficient to affect a decision. If information is not material, it need not be reported in accordance with GAAP. Materiality is an entity-specific aspect of relevance based on the nature or magnitude of items to which the information relates. A complete discussion of materiality is discussed under modifying constraints later in the chapter.

Faithful Representation

To be a faithful representation of business activities, accounting information must be complete, neutral, and free from error. Faithful representation is the concept that data shown in the financial reports reflect what really happened. If an entity reports sales of $544,000, that figure should reflect the true sales for the period. In order for financial information to be a faithful representation of business activities, the information must be complete, neutral, and free from error.

Completeness Information is complete when it includes everything necessary to reflect what happened for all of the business activities for which the firm is reporting.

Neutrality Information is neutral if the financial statements are objectively prepared and are free from bias (that is, they do not favor one group of users over the other). The information should be prepared in such a way that it is helpful and seen in the same manner by all groups.

Freedom from Error Information is free from error if the information is the best available. The conceptual framework acknowledges limitations in achieving a faithful representation due to inherent uncertainties, estimates, and assumptions. Accordingly, financial information may not always be entirely free from errors, but it is expected to reflect unbiased judgments and due diligence in applying appropriate accounting principles.

Enhancing Qualitative Characteristics

Comparability, timeliness, verifiability, and understandability are attributes that enhance the relevance and faithful representation of financial information. These attributes should be maximized individually and together.

Comparability Comparability means that the financial data is presented in such a manner that it can be meaningfully compared with the same data for other companies. Comparability enables users to identify similarities and differences among items, both between different accounting periods within a set of financial statements and across different reporting entities. Uniform and consistent accounting principles provide support for achieving this goal.

Timeliness Firms must disclose accounting information in a timely manner. Timeliness refers to information being made available to users early enough to use it in the decision process.

Verifiability Verifiability is indicated when independent measures obtain similar results. If persons outside the entity arrive at different conclusions about measurements, then the financial information cannot be said to be verifiable.

Understandability Understandability means that users of the accounting information must be able to comprehend the information within the context of the decisions that they are making. This is a user-specific quality because users will differ in their ability to comprehend any set of information.

Underlying Assumptions

The FASB's conceptual framework lists four assumptions financial statement users should be able to assume that preparers of the statements have made in preparing the statements.

>> **14-5 OBJECTIVE**
Describe and explain the basic assumptions about accounting reports.

Underlying Assumptions
Separate Economic Entity
Going Concern
Monetary Unit
Periodicity of Income

Separate Economic Entity Assumption

Accounting records are kept for a specific business or activity. The separate economic entity assumption assumes that the business is separate from its owners. Transactions in the records of a business and the resulting financial statements reflect the affairs of the business—not the affairs of the owners.

It is easy to understand the separate assumption for a corporation such as Microsoft because Microsoft is legally separate from its owners. However, the separate entity concept applies equally to sole proprietorships and partnerships, even though the owners may be legally liable for all debts of the business and for actions carried out on behalf of the business.

Going Concern Assumption

When transactions are recorded and financial statements are prepared, it is assumed that the business is a **going concern**—that is, it will continue to operate indefinitely. This assumption permits businesses to record property and equipment as assets at their cost without having to be concerned about what they are worth in case of liquidation in the near future.

Monetary Unit Assumption

There are two aspects to the **monetary unit assumption.** First is the idea that expressing financial facts and events is meaningful only when they can be expressed in monetary terms. The entity may possess many assets, usually intangible—such as goodwill it has created among customers—that cannot be specifically identified and their values determined. If these assets cannot be expressed in meaningful monetary amounts, an attempt to include them in the financial statements would result in the violation of one or more of the qualitative characteristics or basic assumptions. Similarly, there may be potential liabilities, such as a lawsuit that has been filed against the entity but appears to have little validity. However, it may be appropriate or even necessary to discuss such potential assets or liabilities in disclosures accompanying the statements in order to give a full presentation, even though they do not possess the characteristics necessary to assign a monetary value to them.

The second aspect of the monetary unit assumption is that the value of money is stable. The assumption that the value of the monetary unit is stable allows the cost of assets purchased many years ago to be added to the costs of recently purchased assets of the same kind and the total dollar amount reported on the financial statements. This means that it is deemed to be unnecessary for accountants to convert dollars spent in different years, when the purchasing

ABOUT
ACCOUNTING
The Business and Its Owners as Separate Entities
If the business entity is a sole proprietorship, it may be difficult to think in terms of the owner and the business as separate entities.

power might be quite different, to a common unit of purchasing power. This assumption has been criticized because the value of money does not, in fact, remain stable. Its purchasing power changes substantially over the years. Proposals have been made for abandoning the stable monetary concept, but the practical problems involved and the objectivity and reliability of historical cost figures have prevailed to this time.

Periodicity of Income Assumption

The income statement covers a certain time period and the balance sheet is prepared as of the end of that time period. It is assumed that the activities of the business can be separated into time periods with revenues and expenses being assigned on a logical basis to those periods. This assumption is called the **periodicity of income assumption.** In reality, the final results of a business are known only when the business ceases to exist. When all assets are sold and all liabilities paid, the owners can determine the amount of the overall profit or loss. However, owners, creditors, and other interested parties cannot wait until a business is dissolved to make decisions. Operating and financing decisions must be made constantly throughout the life of the business. Many of these decisions are based on profit or loss for a specified period of time. Others are based on assets and liabilities as of the end of the period. Accountants have developed techniques, including the accrual basis of accounting, to prepare financial statements at regular intervals to meet the goals implied by this assumption. Many, if not most, of the concepts you learn in accounting result from the periodicity assumption.

Although the fiscal year is generally perceived as the standard accounting period, the SEC and FASB require that the same accounting rules be applied in measuring income for each quarter. Many businesses assume that the periodicity assumption can be extended even further to monthly financial statements. Obviously the assumption of periodicity has more validity for some types of business. For example, a merchandising business can measure assets, liabilities, revenues, and expenses easily each quarter, or even each month. However, an enterprise growing timber may find it much more difficult to get an accurate measure of financial results each quarter.

>> **14-6 OBJECTIVE**
Explain and apply the basic principles of accounting.

recall

Recording Assets and Depreciation
Property, plant, and equipment assets are recorded at historical, or original, cost. Depreciation is recorded in a separate accumulated depreciation account.

General Principles

Four basic principles to serve as guides to preparing financial statements are presented in the FASB's basic concepts:

Basic Principles
Historical Cost Basis
Revenue Recognition
Matching
Full Disclosure

Historical Cost Basis Principle

Business transactions are, with few exceptions, recorded on a **historical cost basis,** which is the amount of consideration, expressed in monetary terms, involved in a transaction through dealings in the market between the business and outsiders. Assets are generally carried at historical cost, adjusted for depreciation, until they are removed from use and disposed of. Historical cost is the cost when an asset is acquired. Historical cost is preferred to some possible alternatives to cost because cost, when determined in an "arm's length" transaction with independent outsiders, is an objective, verifiable measure of initial economic value. The alternatives to using cost involve some measure or estimate of value, which is generally neither an objective nor verifiable quantity. As a result of this principle, generally an asset is recorded and remains in the account at its original cost even though its value may increase to an amount materially in excess of cost.

There are, however, important exceptions to the general rule that historical cost remains the basic carrying amount in the financial reports. For example, certain current assets—those that will be converted into cash within the next year—are carried at "the lower of cost or market" because market value is a reasonable measure of the amount that can be expected to be received for the asset within the next 12 months. Investments in securities that are expected to be sold within the next year would be shown at their market value rather than cost. *Accounts Receivable* is usually shown at the amount expected to be collected from customers, through the use of an *Allowance for Doubtful Accounts.* In addition, an asset included in plant and equipment is shown at its "impaired value" (a complex calculation) if it is apparent that future net cash flows from its future use will be less than its present book value. Nevertheless, the cost principle remains a fundamental concept in financial reporting.

Revenue Recognition Principle

One of the greatest challenges an accountant faces is determining the period in which to record revenue and report it on the income statement. Revenue represents the inflow of new assets resulting from the sale of goods or services to an outsider. Under the **revenue recognition principle,** revenue is recognized when it is both earned and realized. The earning process is completed when the product or service has been delivered and related costs have been incurred. Usually **realization** is deemed to occur at the point at which a sale is made or a service is rendered to an outsider and delivery has been made. This is the point at which new assets are created in the form of money or in claims against others (usually taking the form of accounts receivable). The realization principle requires objective, verifiable evidence of both the earning and realization of revenue in order for income to be recorded.

However, the realization principle is the subject of much criticism. For example, if a company owns stock in another publicly traded corporation, some accountants believe that an increase in the market value of the stock should be recognized as income. This practice would, in most cases, violate the realization principle, which suggests that gain should not be recognized until the stock is sold. Accountants who support the realization principle are concerned that the "gain" might be eliminated by a decrease in stock price before the stock is sold.

There are some exceptions to the realization principle for reporting revenue. For example, contractors who build long-term projects often report income on a "percentage-of-completion" basis. If a bridge takes three years to complete, a portion of the estimated profit can be recognized by the contractor each year under the percentage-of-completion method.

In contrast, some businesses, especially service providers such as physicians, architects, and accountants, frequently recognize income only when cash is received, not when it is earned, because the rate of losses from uncollectible accounts is very high in these businesses.

Revenue from Contracts with Customers

In recognition of the challenges with the revenue recognition principle discussed above, in May 2014 the FASB issued *Accounting Standard Update (ASU) 2014-09, Revenue from Contracts with Customers (Topic 606),* and the IASB issued *International Financial Reporting Standards (IFRS) 15, Revenue from Contracts with Customers.* The new revenue recognition standards are not intended to change either the timing of receivable recognition or the subsequent accounting for receivables for merchandise or services unless there is a contract with separate performance obligations.

Topic 606 defines a new core principle for recognizing revenue for contracts within the scope of the standard. An entity shall recognize revenue to depict the transfer of promised goods or services to customers in an amount that reflects the consideration to which the entity expects to be entitled in exchange for those goods or services.

This core principle differs significantly from the current core principle of revenue recognition under U.S. GAAP. Specifically, the concept of an earning process has been eliminated and the concepts of realization and realizability have been eliminated. Instead, the core principle is based

---

important!

Criteria for Revenue Recognition

Two tests must be met before revenue can be recognized: (1) the revenue must have been earned and (2) the revenue must have been realized.

important!

When Is Revenue Earned?

Revenue is earned when the entity has done all that it has to do to be entitled to all benefits to be received from the sale or service.

important!

When Is Revenue Realized?

Revenue is realized when cash, financial claims, or other assets have been received as a result of the income-earning activity.

important!

A detailed discussion of *ASU 2014-09, Revenue from Contracts with Customers (Topic 606),* is covered in intermediate accounting and is beyond the scope of this text. However, *Topic 606* does not change the accounting for receivables for merchandise or services unless there is a contract with separate performance obligations. Consequently, *Topic 606* has no impact on the discussion of accounting for sales and accounts receivable discussed in Chapter 7 of this text.

recall

Why Adjustments Are Made
End-of-period adjustments are made to record income and expenses in the appropriate accounting period. The goal of adjustments is to match revenues and expenses.

important!

Importance of Notes in Statements
The notes to the financial statements explain or give details of items shown in the financial statements. These notes are considered an integral part of the statements and are audited by the independent auditor.

on concepts that do not have much significance in current revenue accounting standards. Going forward, the concept of transferring promised goods or services to customers would be essential to the timing (when) of revenue recognition. The concept of consideration to which the entity expects to be entitled would be essential to the measurement (how much) of revenue recognition.

An entity recognizes revenue in accordance with the core principles by applying the following five steps to the revenue recognition process:

1. Identify the contracts.
2. Identify the performance obligations in the contract.
3. Determine the transaction price.
4. Allocate the transaction price to the contract's performance obligations.
5. Recognize revenue when (or as) the entity satisfies a performance obligation. If an entity receives revenue (cash, deposits, etc.) in advance of performance, that revenue is unearned and should be reported as a short-term (recognition period is one year or less) or long-term (recognition period longer than one year) liability.

The effective dates of the above changes are for annual reporting periods beginning after December 15, 2017, for public entities and for annual reporting periods beginning after December 15, 2018, for nonpublic entities.

Matching Principle

To properly measure income, revenue must be matched against expired costs incurred in earning the revenue. This concept is called the **matching principle.** Many of the controversial questions in accounting involve determining when a cost should be charged as an expense. Accountants seek systematic, rational approaches for determining when to recognize revenue and when costs should be charged against revenue.

There are numerous ways to match revenue and expenses. Here are some examples:

- Manufacturing costs are identified with specific products and are charged to cost of goods sold when the products are sold.
- The cost of a building is recorded as an asset. Depreciation expense is recognized over the periods in which the asset is expected to help earn revenues for the business.
- Insurance premiums cover specific periods and are charged to expense over those periods.
- General office salaries do not clearly benefit future periods and are charged to expense when they are incurred.

The matching principle has given rise to a process referred to as the accrual basis of accounting, which you learned about in Chapter 12. The accrual basis calls for recognizing revenues or expenses in the period to which they apply, rather than in some later period when the cash is received or paid. The adjustments for prepaid rent, expired insurance, unearned income, and salaries payable that you learned in Chapter 12 were made under the accrual method of accounting to conform to the matching principle.

Full Disclosure Principle

The **full disclosure principle** requires that all information that might affect the user's interpretation of the profitability and financial position of a business must be disclosed in the financial statements or in notes to the statements.

The accountant and company management are constantly faced with the question: "How much information is enough and how much is too much?" In recent years, there have been numerous lawsuits charging that the financial statements did not disclose facts that would have influenced investor or creditor decisions. As a result, accountants must be careful to include sufficient information so that an informed reader can obtain a complete understanding of the financial position of the business.

A primary emphasis of the SEC in financial reporting is "full disclosure." The SEC's full-disclosure policy is essentially that any information that would be likely, if disclosed, to change the user's interpretation of the statement should be disclosed. As a result, the basic financial statements may occupy only two or three pages in a corporation's annual report, but the "notes to the financial statements" explaining the items in the statements may occupy 10 or 12 pages. Because of federal regulatory legislation enacted in recent years, there is even more pressure to increase disclosures in order to help statement users better understand and evaluate the company's financial affairs.

In recent years, much attention has been given in the news media to the idea of **transparency** in financial reporting. Both the SEC and FASB have focused recently on the topic of transparency in their public comments and in their authoritative pronouncements. Essentially, this notion is that the financial statements and the related disclosures taken together should permit interested users to receive a clear and concise understanding of the activities of the enterprise and its financial affairs.

Modifying Constraints

The accounting principles and their underlying assumptions provide a framework for analyzing business transactions in determining the accounting treatment they should be given in the financial reports. However, a number of practical considerations are recognized as constraining or modifying the application of the general principles. Here are the most important of these constraints:

Constraints
Materiality
Cost-Benefit Test
Conservatism
Industry Practice

Materiality

Materiality refers to the significance of an item of financial data in relation to other financial data. The rigid application of the recommended accounting treatment of an item may depend on whether or not the item is considered material in light of other items in the financial reports. Suppose that during the year a small business purchases small items of equipment, each costing $200, but with a total cost of $1,800. If the company's usual net income is only $15,000, the $1,800 cost would likely be considered material. As a result, the concept of matching would require that the assets be capitalized and depreciated. However, if Walmart purchased items of equipment costing only $1,800, the amount would be insignificant and the company likely would simply charge the costs to expense when purchased. The difference in either net income or total assets as a result of deciding to charge the cost to expense instead of capitalizing it would be insignificant. This example suggests that the materiality constraint goes hand-in-hand with the cost-benefit test.

Cost-Benefit Test

Sometimes it is difficult and expensive to gather information to fully comply with an accounting principle or rule that should theoretically be applied in preparing financial statements. As a result, the conceptual framework suggests that it may be necessary to use the **cost-benefit test** to determine whether the increased cost of complying with an accounting principle or standard is justified by the benefit (increased usefulness of the statements) that would result if the preferred treatment is followed.

For example, a large business may purchase thousands of inexpensive small tools with useful lives ranging from six months to two years. In theory, those tools lasting more than one year should be capitalized and their costs depreciated. However, the entity might have to incur large costs to simply keep records and identify the individual tools. The difference that might result in annual income from using the theoretically correct accounting treatment, compared to

important!

When Supplemental Information Should Be Provided
Supplemental information is information that is helpful to understanding the statements. However, it may be low in reliability or not essential to an understanding of the statements. It may be required by the FASB or SEC, or it may be voluntarily provided.

>> **14-7 OBJECTIVE**
Describe and apply the modifying constraints on accounting principles.

important!

What Is a Material Item?
The IASB updated the definition of materiality through an amendment to *IAS 1, Presentation of Financial Statements,* and *IAS 8, Accounting Policies, Changes in Accounting Estimates and Errors.* Under the new definition, information is material if omitting or obscuring it could reasonably be expected to influence the decisions that the primary users of general-purpose financial statements make on the basis of those financial statements, which provide financial information about a specific entity. It is difficult to develop firm rules or guides to be followed in determining whether an item is material or is immaterial. A rule of thumb sometimes followed is that if an individual item, or the total of all items, being considered is less than 5 percent of net income, the items are not material. However, other factors must be considered, and this rule of thumb is by no means a standard.

that resulting from simply charging the tools to expense when they are purchased, may be very small. As a result the tools would likely be charged to expense when purchased.

As suggested earlier, the cost-benefit constraint goes hand in hand with the materiality constraint. In some instances, an improvement in financial reporting resulting from applying a theoretically superior treatment to a transaction may be so small when compared to income that almost any cost of implementing the theoretically correct approach might warrant ignoring the conceptual rule. Conversely, even though an item might appear to be immaterial, that is no justification for applying the materiality constraint and arbitrarily applying a treatment that does not correspond with GAAP without applying the cost-benefit test.

Conservatism

Accountants have long followed a doctrine of conservatism. **Conservatism** in accounting is the idea that "when in doubt, take the conservative action." Thus, if there is no clear evidence of how a transaction or situation should be accounted for or if there are two or more equally acceptable treatments of the transaction, the accountant should choose the conservative approach. The conservative approach is the one that would result in the least possible reported income or largest reported loss. In accounting, the conservatism notion comes into play when there is little evidence, or there is conflicting evidence, about the facts or their interpretation.

For example, Carpet Company purchased a new machine designed specifically to produce a single product and with a useful physical life of 10 years. However, there is a strong likelihood that the product will be replaced in about five years by newer products and that the machine will be of no further use to the company when that occurs. In this circumstance, conservatism dictates that the machine be depreciated over five years.

On the other hand, if there is no reason to think that the machine will not be used to manufacture the product for 10 years, but the owner feels that "you just can't ever be sure how long it might last, so we should be conservative and depreciate it over five years," it would be inappropriate to use the five-year life for depreciation. The conservatism constraint does not override other accounting concepts and principles that are clearly appropriate in the circumstances. Conservatism is not a constraint to be applied without considering other factors.

Industry Practice

Historically, existing accounting practices in certain industries have sometimes become acceptable as GAAP. Typically this situation exists in an industry where there are unusual tax laws or regulatory requirements, an industry that has unusually high risks, or one that has activities or transactions to which it is difficult to apply GAAP. One example where GAAP has evolved to conform to **industry practice** is the public utility industry. For many decades, public utilities treated interest incurred on money borrowed to build a power plant as a cost of the plant, just like the cost of cement or steel. Public utility regulatory agencies required or permitted interest to be included in the cost of the plant, rather than charged to an interest expense account. This accounting practice has come to be required under GAAP for all construction projects, regardless of the industry.

The Impact of Generally Accepted Accounting Principles

This book contains many references to accounting principles, assumptions, and modifying constraints. Being familiar with these concepts will help you understand how individual transactions are accounted for and why they are handled in a specific way. Often businesses encounter new or unusual transactions that give rise to accounting questions that do not appear to have simple solutions. Almost invariably, the solutions to these questions will fall back on the concepts discussed in this chapter. Thus, an understanding of these concepts is essential to your understanding of complex accounting issues.

ABOUT ACCOUNTING

The Cost-Benefit Test

In many cases, the cost-benefit relationship is very difficult to determine. Both costs and, especially, benefits are hard to measure. Benefits are often difficult to quantify and verify.

ABOUT ACCOUNTING

What "Conservatism" Does Not Mean in Accounting

In the past, accountants have been accused of being overly conservative, to the point that they were encouraged to understate assets. This is not a proper understanding of the constraint of conservatism.

ABOUT ACCOUNTING

Special Accounting Rules for Specific Industries

Most of the accounting practices related to specific industries have been adjusted to fit into the conceptual framework. In cases where they have not (e.g., the oil industry), it is because of unusual operating activities or high risks involved.

MANAGERIAL IMPLICATIONS

FINANCIAL STATEMENTS

- Management relies on the information in financial statements to make decisions.
- Management needs to understand the underlying principles used to prepare financial statements.
- Managers of large businesses compare their financial statements with those of their competitors. The universal application of accounting assumptions, principles, and modifying conventions allows financial statements to be compared.
- Proper accounting using generally accepted accounting principles can help prevent lawsuits by financial statement users.
- Full disclosure of pertinent information in financial statements and accompanying notes can reduce the possibility of lawsuits.

THINKING CRITICALLY

What are some income statement and balance sheet items that could mislead investors?

Section 2 Review

1. Historical cost is used to initially record transactions because it is:
   a. subjective and verifiable.
   b. objective and verifiable.
   c. material and subjective.
   d. subject to change.

2. The two qualitative characteristics of financial reports are:
   a. relevance and faithful representation.
   b. comparability and timeliness.
   c. verifiability and understandability.
   d. relevance and materiality.

3. Going concern is the assumption that an entity will operate indefinitely.
   a. True
   b. False

4. Comparability refers to the ability to compare and contrast one company's statements with another company's statements.
   a. True
   b. False

5. The four basic assumptions underlying financial accounting are:
   a. materiality, cost-benefit, conservatism, and industry practice.
   b. separate entity, materiality, cost-benefit, and industry practice.
   c. separate entity, going concern, monetary unit of measurement, and periodicity of income.
   d. going concern, conservatism, industry practice, and materiality.

6. Materiality is whether the omission of an item or not following GAAP for an item is likely to change the user's interpretation of statements. Factors that might be considered in determining materiality are total assets, net income, total liabilities, and owner's equity.
   a. True
   b. False

In Questions 7–10, indicate which underlying assumption or modifying convention is most important in each situation.

7. Samuels Company prepares financial statements for each quarter of the year.
   a. materiality
   b. stable monetary unit
   c. separate entity
   d. periodicity of income

8. Bowman Corporation immediately charges to expense any asset costing less than $400.
   a. materiality
   b. stable monetary unit
   c. separate entity
   d. periodicity of income

9. Karen Germany purchased a building for her business in 20X1 for $500,000. In 20X9, the building is still being used and has a remaining expected life of 25 years. Germany points out that cumulative inflation has been about 50 percent since 20X1, so she proposes changing the asset account from $500,000 to $750,000.
   a. materiality
   b. stable monetary unit
   c. separate entity
   d. periodicity of income

10. Walker Company issues each month a check to James Walker, the sole proprietor, for $10,000 because he deems this a reasonable payment for the time he spends in the business. The amount paid is not charged to *Salary Expense* but to his *Drawing* account.
    a. materiality
    b. stable monetary unit
    c. separate entity
    d. periodicity of income

Questions 11 and 12 are based on the facts below:

One week ago, Jason Williams was appointed manager of the company for which you work. He has looked at the draft of the annual report for last year, scheduled to be issued in a few days. He states that the company needs to "take no chances" and should be conservative in its reporting. He has asked for your opinion on the appropriate treatment of each of the situations below.

11. The company is engaged in several lawsuits, some of which are very material. The company's lawyer and its former manager think the suits are almost certain to be decided in favor of your employer and, therefore, they plan to ignore them in the financial reports. The new manager wants to either show a potential loss as an expense or disclose the lawsuits in notes to the statements.
    a. disclose the existence of the lawsuits
    b. record a loss of the lawsuit

12. Because losses from bad debts have been running at a fairly high rate (5 percent of net sales), he proposes that revenue should not be recognized from credit sales until the money is actually collected from customers.
    a. record the sale less an allowance for uncollectible accounts
    b. do not record the sale until the credit sale is collected

REVIEW   Chapter Summary

The increasing interest of a large and diverse group—government, owners, analysts, creditors, and economists—in financial reports ensures continuing progress in the search for accounting principles that will make the reports more meaningful, useful, and reliable. In this chapter, you have learned how accounting principles are developed and the roles of various organizations and groups in that development. In addition, you have learned fundamental facts about the International Accounting Standards Board's conceptual framework underlying modern-day financial reports. The importance of underlying qualitative characteristics, underlying assumptions, and basic principles in this framework has been stressed.

Learning Objectives

14-1 Understand the process used to develop generally accepted accounting principles.

In the United States, GAAP are developed cooperatively by the public and private sectors. Although the SEC has power to establish accounting rules for publicly held companies, it usually delegates the job to the private sector through the FASB.

14-2 Identify the major accounting standards-setting bodies and explain their roles in the standards-setting process.

The SEC has legislative responsibility for developing accounting and reporting rules for publicly held companies but has authority to accept standards set by the FASB. The AICPA, the AAA, and governmental regulatory bodies also have played a role in developing GAAP. The PCAOB regulates CPA firms that audit publicly traded companies.

14-3 Describe the users and uses of financial reports.

The users of statements are the present and potential investors and creditors who use the statements in making credit and investment decisions. The focus is on information to help users assess future cash flows.

14-4 Identify and explain the qualitative characteristics of accounting information.

The Fundamental Qualitative Characteristics are:
- Relevance
  - Confirmatory value
  - Predictive value
- Faithful Representation
  - Completeness
  - Neutrality
  - Freedom from error

The Enhancing Qualitative Characteristics are:
- Comparability
- Timeliness
- Verifiability
- Understandability

14-5 Describe and explain the basic assumptions about accounting reports.

Major assumptions that preparers of financial reports should generally make:
- The business is an economic entity separate and apart from its owner(s).
- The entity will remain a going concern.
- Monetary terms are the significant feature of economic data.
- Income is periodic, so that income can be meaningfully measured for each period and compared with other periods.

14-6 Explain and apply the basic principles of accounting.

- Transactions are recorded on a cost basis.
- Revenues are recognized when earned and realized.
- Revenues and costs should be matched in the financial reports for appropriate periods.
- Full disclosure means that all information that might affect the reader's interpretation of the statements should be disclosed.

14-7 Describe and apply the modifying constraints on accounting principles.

The modifying constraints are factors that may in some cases overrule the necessity to apply GAAP.

These constraints are:
- Materiality
- Cost-benefits test
- Conservatism
- Industry practice

14-8 Define the accounting terms new to this chapter.

Glossary

Conceptual framework (p. 514) A basic framework developed by the FASB to provide conceptual guidelines for financial statements. The most important features are statements of qualitative features of statements, basic assumptions underlying statements, basic accounting principles, and modifying constraints

Conservatism (p. 526) The concept that revenue and assets should be understated rather than overstated if GAAP allows alternatives. Similarly, expenses and liabilities should be overstated rather than understated

Cost-benefit test (p. 525) If accounting concepts suggest a particular accounting treatment for an item, but it appears that the theoretically correct treatment would require an unreasonable amount of work, the accountant may analyze the benefits and costs of the preferred treatment to see if the benefit gained from its adoption is justified by the cost

Full disclosure principle (p. 524) The requirement that all information that might affect the user's interpretation of the profitability and financial condition of a business be disclosed in the financial statements or in notes to the statements

Going concern assumption (p. 521) The assumption that a firm will continue to operate indefinitely

Historical cost basis principle (p. 522) The principle that requires assets and services to be recorded at their cost at the time they are acquired and that, generally, long-term assets remain at historical costs in the asset accounts

Industry practice constraint (p. 526) In a few limited cases, unusual operating characteristics of an industry, usually based on risk, for which special accounting principles and procedures have been developed. These may not conform completely with GAAP for other industries

Matching principle (p. 524) The concept that revenue and the costs incurred in earning the revenue should be matched in the appropriate accounting periods

Materiality constraint (p. 525) The significance of an item in relation to a particular situation or set of facts

Monetary unit assumption (p. 521) It is assumed that only those items and events that can be measured in monetary terms are included in the financial statements. An inherent part of this assumption is that the monetary unit is stable. Thus, assets purchased one year may be combined in the accounts with those purchased in other years even though the dollars used in each year actually may have different purchasing power

Neutrality concept (p. 520) The concept that information in financial statements cannot be selected or presented in a way to favor one set of interested parties over another

Periodicity of income assumption (p. 522) The concept that economic activities of an entity can be divided logically and identified with specific time periods, such as the year or quarter

Private sector (p. 513) This is the nongovernmental sector of society; in an accounting context, it is the business sector, which is represented in developing accounting principles by the Financial Accounting Standards Board (FASB)

Public sector (p. 513) The government sector, which is represented in developing accounting principles by the Securities and Exchange Commission (SEC)

Qualitative characteristics (p. 519) Traits necessary for credible financial statements: relevance (confirmatory and predictive value), faithful representation (completeness, neutrality, and freedom from error), comparability, timeliness, verifiability, and understandability

Realization (p. 523) The concept that revenue occurs when goods or services, merchandise, or other assets are exchanged for cash or claims to cash

Revenue recognition principle (p. 523) Revenue is recognized when it has been earned and realized

Transparency (p. 525) Information provided in the financial statements and notes accompanying them should provide a clear and accurate picture of the financial affairs of the company. The key to this idea is that of disclosure

Comprehensive Self Review

1. What is the full disclosure principle? How are disclosures made in financial reports?
2. How does the AICPA still have an influence on the development of accounting principles and standards?
3. In what circumstances is industry practice likely to be a factor in "generally accepted accounting principles"?
4. Why should one become familiar with IFRS?
5. If the "stable monetary assumption" were not made, what impact would this likely have on recordkeeping and financial statements?
6. Explain the matching principle. What impact does this principle have on end-of-period adjustments?

(Answers to Comprehensive Self Review are at the end of the chapter.)

Discussion Questions

1. Why is a conceptual framework necessary in developing accounting standards and rules?
2. What is meant by full disclosure?
3. What are the two most important bodies or organizations involved in developing generally accepted accounting principles in the United States?
4. Why is it desirable to have a set of fundamental concepts to be used in developing accounting standards and rules?
5. How will U.S. companies be affected by IFRS?
6. What is meant by the concept of neutrality in accounting?
7. Explain the qualitative characteristic of comparability.
8. How is the matching concept related to the accrual basis of accounting?
9. It can be argued that the cost principle is dependent on the going concern assumption. Why?
10. How does the materiality convention affect day-to-day accounting?
11. How are the concepts of materiality and cost-benefit related?
12. What is the periodicity of income concept?
13. In recent years, there have been many charges, some of them substantiated, that large companies have manipulated business transactions and accounting records to move income from one year to another in order to change the income reported in different years. Suggest three concepts, assumptions, principles, or conventions that such manipulation would violate.
14. Many current assets are not shown at historic cost in the financial statements. For example, inventories are usually shown at the "lower of cost or market." What concepts or conventions warrant this practice?
15. What two tests must be met in order for revenues to be recognized by public entities for reporting periods beginning before December 15, 2017?
16. What criteria must exist in order for revenues to be recognized by public entities for reporting periods beginning after December 15, 2017?

APPLICATIONS

Exercises

Exercise 14.1

Objectives 14-5, 14-6

▶ **Applying accounting principles and concepts.**

For each of the following cases, respond to the question and indicate the accounting principle or concept that applies.

1. Princeton, LLC, paid insurance premiums of $9,600 on December 1, 20X1. These premiums covered a two-year period beginning on that date. What amount, from this payment, should the corporation show as insurance expense for the year 20X1? What accounting principles, conventions, or assumptions support your answer?

2. Alexa Watson buys and sells real estate. On December 31, 20X1, her inventory of property included a tract of undeveloped land for which she had paid $450,000. The fair market value of the land was $900,000 at that date. How much income should Watson report for 20X1 in connection with this land? Why?

3. Washington Building Company signed a contract with a customer on November 1, 20X1. The contract called for construction of a building to begin by December 31, 20X1, and to be completed by December 31, 20X2. The contract price was $18.0 million. Washington estimated that the building would cost $12.0 million. On November 15, 20X1, the customer was required to make an advance payment of $2,000,000. No work was done on the project until January 20X2. How much income from the project should Washington report in 20X1? Why?

Exercise 14.2

Objectives 14-5, 14-6, 14-7

▶ **Applying accounting principles and concepts.**

For each of the following cases, respond to the question asked and indicate the accounting principle or concept that applies.

1. Patterson Company purchased many small tools during 20X1 at a total cost of $3,000. Some tools were expected to last for a few weeks, some for several months, and some for several years. Patterson's income for 20X1 will be about $1.75 million. How should Patterson account for the small tools in order to be theoretically correct? As a practical matter, how should Patterson account for these tools? Why?

2. Selena Cantu is the sole proprietor of The In and Out Mini Market. Cantu's accountant insists that she keep a detailed record of money and merchandise that she takes out of the business for personal use. Why?

3. At the end of each fiscal period, the accountant for New Zealand Company requires that a careful inventory be made of the office supplies and that the amount on hand be reported as an asset and the amount used during the period be reported as an expense. Why?

Exercise 14.3

Objectives 14-5, 14-6

▶ **Applying accounting principles and concepts.**

For each of the following cases, respond to the question asked and indicate the accounting principle or concept that applies.

1. Sanchez Company has decided to charge off as a loss the portion of its accounts receivable that it estimates will be uncollectible. The accounts involved resulted from the current year's sales. Is this correct or incorrect accounting? Why?

2. On March 15 of last year, Zane Inc. purchased land for $420,000, on which it planned to construct an office building. At the end of the year, the land had increased in value to $520,000. Nevertheless, Zane recognized no income as a result of the increase in value. Is this correct or incorrect accounting? Why?

3. Three years ago, Williamson Company purchased a machine for $600,000. The machine is expected to have no salvage value. Nevertheless, Williamson continues to keep the asset's cost in its accounting records and to depreciate the asset over its 10-year useful life. Is this correct or incorrect accounting? Why?

Applying accounting principles and concepts.

For each of the following cases, respond to the question asked and indicate the accounting principle or concept that applies.

1. Lane Company charges off the cost of all magazine advertising in the year it is incurred even though the advertising probably results in some sales in later years. Why?
2. Clark Company's net income is about $3.2 million a year. Clark charges to expense all property insurance premiums when paid. Last year approximately $9,600 of these premiums represented amounts applicable to future years. Is this proper? Why or why not?
3. Castillo Products Corporation charges all of its marketing costs to expense when incurred. Why?

◀ **Exercise 14.4**
Objectives 14-6, 14-7

Applying accounting principles and concepts.

Ryan & Sabo sells copy equipment. It grants all customers a 12-month warranty, agreeing to make necessary repairs within the following 12-month after-sale period free of charge. At the end of each year, the company estimates the total cost to be incurred during the next period under the warranties for equipment sold during the current period and charges that amount to expense, crediting a liability account. Is this appropriate accounting? Why or why not?

◀ **Exercise 14.5**
Objective 14-6

Applying accounting principles and concepts.

Diamond Jewelers has never borrowed money. Because of rapid growth, on June 25, 20X1, John Peoples, the owner, applied for a loan of $300,000 from his bank. The banker asked Peoples for copies of financial reports of Diamond Jewelers for 20X0 and quarterly statements for 20X1. Peoples had never prepared formal financial statements for the business. He and the company's bookkeeper obtained some information from his 20X0 income tax return and estimated other items for which information was not readily available. He took the statements to the banker on July 2. The banker expressed his concern over the statements. What are the most important fundamental financial reporting concepts that seem to have been violated?

◀ **Exercise 14.6**
Objective 14-6

PROBLEMS

Problem Set A

Understanding how and why accounting and auditing principles and standards are developed.

Read each of the following statements carefully and indicate whether each is true or false.

1. Accounting principles and standards are based on the assumption that statements will be read by individuals who have little understanding of accounting and reporting.
2. The PCAOB regulates CPA firms that audit nonpublic companies.
3. The FASB is a division of the Internal Revenue Service.
4. The American Institute of CPAs has, in the past, had a strong influence on the development of auditing principles.
5. Many nonpublic companies are not required to follow GAAP.

◀ **Problem 14.1A**
Objectives 14-1, 14-2, 14-3

6. The Sarbanes-Oxley Act places great emphasis on internal controls and fraud prevention.
7. The FASB and the IASB are working toward convergence of U.S. financial reporting standards and those of the International Accounting Standards Board
8. Because of the Sarbanes-Oxley Act, it is probable that the FASB/IASB conceptual framework will become less important in developing accounting principles and standards.
9. The FASB Standards are designed primarily for the use of the IRS.
10. The IASB has authority to accept or reject financial accounting principles and standards developed by the FASB.

Problem 14.2A

Objectives 14-4, 14-5, 14-6

Applying accounting principles and concepts.

The accounting treatment or statement presentation of various items is discussed below. The items pertain to unrelated businesses.

INSTRUCTIONS

Indicate in each case whether the item has been handled in accordance with generally accepted accounting principles. If so, indicate the key basic concept that has been followed. If not, indicate which concept has been violated and tell how the item should have been recorded or presented.

1. At the beginning of 20X1, Dawson Company bought a building for $4,000,000. At the end of 20X1, the building's value was appraised at $4,500,000. Because there was an increase in value, the company did not record depreciation on the building and also did not increase the $4,000,000 recorded in the building account at time of purchase.
2. On December 31, 20X1, the balance sheet of Haskel Transport Company reported prepaid insurance at $12,000. The prepaid insurance reflects the refund value of a three-year fire insurance policy that originally cost $18,000 on January 1, 20X0.
3. Paxley Company manufactured machinery for its own use at a cost of $800,000. The lowest bid from an outsider was $900,000. Nevertheless, the company recorded the machinery at $800,000.
4. The equipment of Thorntree Country Club has a book value (cost less accumulated depreciation) of $760,000. However, the equipment could not be sold for more than $500,000 today. The company's owner thinks that the machinery should nevertheless be reported on the balance sheet at $760,000 and depreciated over its useful life because the equipment is being used regularly in the business and it is expected to be used profitably for the next five years—the remaining useful life that is being used for depreciation purposes.
5. On December 31, 20X1, an account receivable of $6,400 due from Robert Adams, who is in the county jail on charges of passing bad checks, is not included in the balance sheet. The owner of the business has written off the amount because he feels certain that the debt will not be paid, even though Adams insists that he will pay after he gets out of jail and finds a job.
6. The assets listed in the accounting records of Johnson Pharmacy include a money market account of Samuel Johnson, owner of the business. Johnson has established the savings account so that if he needs to invest more cash in the pharmacy, it will be readily available.

Analyze: If Dawson Company uses the accounting treatment described in item 1, is net income overstated or understated for 20X1?

Problem 14.3A

Objectives 14-5, 14-6

Reconstructing an income statement to reflect proper accounting principles.

Samuel Cox, owner of Cox Video Center, sent the income statement shown below to several of his creditors who had asked for financial statements. The business is a sole proprietorship that sells audio and other electronic equipment. One of the creditors looked over the income statement and reported that it did not conform to generally accepted accounting principles.

INSTRUCTIONS

Prepare an income statement in accordance with generally accepted accounting principles.

Cox Video Center Income Statement December 31, 20X1		
Cash Collected from Customers		$699,000
Cost of Goods Sold		
Merchandise Inventory, Jan. 1	$ 77,000	
Payments to Suppliers	440,000	
	517,000	
Less Merchandise Inventory, Dec. 31	87,000	
Cost of Goods Sold		430,000
Gross Profit on Sales		269,000
Operating Expenses		
Salaries of Employees	$ 81,500	
Salary of Owner	31,200	
Office Expense	32,000	
Depreciation Expense	21,520	
Income Tax of Owner	9,000	
Payroll Taxes Expense	10,000	
Advertising and Other Selling Expenses	23,900	
Repairs Expense	13,000	
Insurance Expense	5,400	
Interest Expense	13,000	
Utility and Telephone Expense	19,500	
Legal and Audit Expense	4,500	
Miscellaneous Expense	29,500	
Total Expenses		294,020
Net Loss from Operations		(25,020)
Increase in Appraised Value of Land During Year		28,000
Net Income		$ 2,980

The following additional information was made available by Cox:

a. On January 1, 20X1, accounts receivable from customers totaled $27,700. On December 31, 20X1, the receivables totaled $34,000.

b. No effort has been made to charge off worthless accounts. An analysis shows that $1,800 of the accounts receivable on December 31, 20X1, will never be collected.

c. The beginning and ending merchandise inventories were valued at their estimated selling price. The cost of the ending inventory is determined to be $49,500, and the cost of the beginning inventory is determined at $45,800.

d. On January 1, 20X1, suppliers of merchandise were owed $40,200, while on December 31, 20X1, these debts were $46,425.

e. The owner paid himself a salary of $2,600 per month from the funds of the business and charged this amount to an account called **Salary of Owner**.

f. The owner also withdrew cash from the firm's bank account to pay himself $4,900 interest on his capital investment. This amount was charged to **Interest Expense**.

g. A check for $9,000 to cover the owner's personal income tax for the previous year was issued from the firm's bank account. This was charged to **Income Tax of Owner**.

h. Depreciation on assets was computed at 8 percent of the gross profit. An analysis of assets showed that the original cost of the equipment and fixtures was $67,500. Their estimated useful life is 12 years with no salvage value. The building cost $152,750. Its useful life is expected to be 25 years with no salvage value.

i. Included in **Repairs Expense** was $6,600 paid on December 22 for a new parking lot completed that day.

j. The increase in land value was based on an appraisal by a qualified real estate appraiser.

Analyze: What is the gross profit percentage based on the income statement you prepared?

Problem 14.4A ▶ Reconstructing a balance sheet to reflect proper accounting principles.

Objectives 14-5, 14-6

Sadie Hawkins owns The Education Supply Center, a small store that sells educational supplies. Hawkins recently approached the local bank for a loan to finance a planned expansion of her store. Hawkins prepared the balance sheet shown below and submitted it to one of the bank's loan officers in support of her loan application.

INSTRUCTIONS

1. Identify any errors in the balance sheet, and explain why they should be considered errors.
2. Prepare a corrected balance sheet in accordance with generally accepted accounting principles.

The following additional information was made available by Hawkins:

The Education Supply Center
Balance Sheet
December 31, 20X1

Assets

Cash	$ 28,800
Accounts Receivable	34,000
Inventory	82,000
Equipment (cost)	70,000
Personal Residence	416,000
Supplies	4,320
Family Auto	80,000
Total Assets	$715,120

Liabilities and Owner's Equity

Accounts Payable	$ 34,900
Note Payable on Family Car	26,000
Mortgage on House	224,000
Sadie Hawkins, Capital	430,220
Total Liabilities and Owner's Equity	$715,120

a. The inventory has an original cost of $65,800. It is listed on the balance sheet at the estimated selling price.

b. The cash listed on the balance sheet includes $7,400 in Sadie Hawkins' personal account. The remainder of the cash is in the store's account.

c. The store recently purchased a delivery truck for $78,000, financed through a bank loan. The bank has legal title to the truck. To date, the store has paid $22,000 on the loan. Of the remaining $56,000 liability, $21,200 is current and the remainder long-term. Hawkins did not include the truck or the liability on the balance sheet because neither she nor the business owns it.

d. Depreciation allowable to date is $14,000 on the equipment and $10,000 on the truck.

Analyze: If Hawkins knew that $1,800 of accounts receivable was not collectible, what should be done to reflect this fact on the records of the business? On the balance sheet?

Applying accounting principles and concepts.

◀ **Problem 14.15A**
Objectives 14-5, 14-6, 14-7

For each of the unrelated situations below, identify the accounting principle or concept violated (if a violation exists) and explain the nature of the violation. If you believe that the treatment is in accordance with GAAP, state the major principle or concept in support.

1. Van Road Equipment Company manufactures paving equipment. It pays its salespeople a commission of 15 percent of the sales price as their remuneration. During 20X1, its sales were $10,000,000 and commissions were $1,500,000. In the income statement, sales are shown as $8,500,000.

2. Website Sales and Exchanges Company sells such items as discontinued products and merchandise purchased from bankrupt companies. Freight costs on goods purchased are quite high. The company adds the freight costs to the purchase price and treats the total as cost of inventory.

3. Each year the Information Technology Support Center has a large number of uncollectible accounts. The company charges uncollectible accounts to expense when they are written off. On the average, this is about 18 months after the due date of the account.

4. Zang Builders uses a large quantity of small tools. The annual purchases of the tools, which have a life of about two years, are approximately 2 percent of the company's net income for the year. Zang has followed the practice of capitalizing the cost of the tools and depreciating the cost over two years. The owner asks why the accountant spends so much time on "bookkeeping" and tells her to simply charge the tools to expense when they are purchased.

5. Joseph Wong owns a travel tour service. Customers must make a deposit of one-half the tour price at the time they book reservations. The balance is due 60 days prior to departure. Partial refunds are provided, depending on the date of cancellation. At the time deposits are received, Wong records them as revenue. Refunds are treated as expenses at the time they are made.

Analyze: What is the effect on sales of the procedure used by Van Road Equipment Company in question 1, above?

Problem Set B

Understanding how and why accounting and auditing principles and standards are developed.

◀ **Problem 14.1B**
Objectives 14-1, 14-2, 14-3

Read each of the following statements carefully and indicate whether each is true or false.

1. The FASB and IASB have placed little emphasis on cash flows in their conceptual framework.
2. Providing useful information to investors is one of the major considerations of the FASB in developing financial reporting standards.
3. The Sarbanes-Oxley Act suggests a principles approach to establishing accounting standards.
4. The PCAOB has the power to set independence standards for CPA firms that audit publicly traded companies.
5. Because tax rules and financial accounting are the same, federal income tax requirements have had little impact on financial accounting in the United States.
6. The SEC is the private sector's voice in the accounting rule-making process.

7. The FASB Accounting Standards Codification is now the single source of authoritative U.S. GAAP for nongovernmental entities.

8. Although accounting rule-making organizations in the United States have been reluctant to embrace international accounting standards, there is now a move toward developing congruence between U.S. and international standards.

9. The requirements of state and federal regulatory bodies, such as commissions regulating public utilities, have had little impact on accounting standards in this country.

10. The balance sheet is the statement user's primary source of information about cash flows in a business.

Problem 14.2B ▶ **Applying accounting principles and concepts.**

Objectives 14-5, 14-6

Objectives 14-5, 14-6

The accounting treatment or statement presentation of various items is discussed below. The items pertain to unrelated businesses.

INSTRUCTIONS

Indicate in each case whether the item has been handled in accordance with generally accepted accounting principles. If so, indicate which of the basic concepts has been followed. If not, indicate which concept has been violated and tell how the item should have been recorded or presented.

1. On December 31, 20X0, Mixon Corporation valued its inventory according to an acceptable accounting method. On December 31, 20X1, the inventory was valued by a different but also acceptable method, and on December 31, 20X2, the inventory was valued by the method that was used in 20X0.

2. Republic Manufacturing Company makes air cleaning units. The cost of manufacturing a particular unit is $1,500. However, when the inventory amounts are computed for the balance sheet, the amount used for this unit is $1,800, the normal selling price.

3. In 20X1, Wilson Bakeries had sales of $66 million, all on credit. Statistics of the company for prior years show that losses from uncollectible accounts are equal to about 3.0 percent of sales each year. However, Wilson Bakeries charges off a loss from uncollectible accounts only when a specific account is found to be uncollectible.

4. On October 1, 20X1, Hatten Manufacturing Company purchased some highly specialized, custom-made equipment for $360,000. Because the equipment is of no use to anyone else and has no salvage value, it was recorded in the asset account at $1. The equipment is projected to be used regularly in the business until the equipment wears out, approximately six years from the date of its purchase.

5. Each year Richland Development Company values its investments in land at the current market price.

6. Included on the balance sheet of Special Touch Massage Center is the personal automobile of Brecha Hogan, the owner.

Analyze: If the equipment described in item 4 is depreciated using the straight-line method and has no salvage value, what amount should be charged to expense for the year ended December 31, 20X1?

Problem 14.3B ▶ **Reconstructing an income statement to reflect proper accounting principles.**

Objectives 14-4, 14-5, 14-6

The income statement shown below was prepared by Karen Carter, owner of Karen's Beauty Supplies. The business is a sole proprietorship that sells skin and hair care products. An accountant who looked at the income statement told Carter that the statement does not conform to generally accepted accounting principles.

INSTRUCTIONS

Prepare an income statement for Karen's Beauty Supplies in accordance with generally accepted accounting principles.

Karen's Beauty Supplies
Income Statement
Year Ended December 31, 20X1

Cash Receipts from Customers		$255,000
Cost of Goods Sold		
Merchandise Inventory, Jan. 1	$ 19,000	
Payments to Creditors	176,000	
	195,000	
Less Merchandise Inventory, Dec. 31	25,000	
Cost of Goods Sold		170,000
Gross Profit on Sales		85,000
Expenses		
Salaries Expense	$ 32,500	
Insurance Expense	1,600	
Payroll Taxes Expense	2,800	
Repairs Expense	1,850	
Supplies and Other Office Expenses	3,750	
Advertising and Other Selling Expenses	6,400	
Utilities Expense	3,200	
Interest Expense	3,350	
Total Expenses		55,950
Net Income from Operations		29,550
Increase in Market Value of Store Equipment		3,750
Net Income for Year		$ 33,300

The following additional information was made available by Carter:

a. On January 1, 20X1, accounts receivable from customers totaled $17,500. On December 31, 20X1, receivables totaled $15,125.

b. On December 31, 20X1, accounts receivable amounting to $1,100 were expected to be uncollectible.

c. On January 1, 20X1, accounts payable owed to merchandise suppliers were $11,000. On December 31, 20X1, the outstanding accounts payable were $17,855.

d. Included in **Salaries Expense** is $9,000 that Carter was "paid" for her personal work in the business.

e. Included in **Interest Expense** is $1,700 that Carter withdrew as interest on her capital investment.

f. Miscellaneous repairs of $750 were charged to **Store Equipment** during the year. No new equipment was purchased.

g. Carter explains that because the estimated value of her store equipment has increased by $3,750 during the year, no depreciation expense was recorded. The store equipment cost $28,000 and had an estimated useful life of 10 years with estimated salvage value of $2,000.

Analyze: The entries required to correct situations a.–g. would affect several permanent accounts for Karen's Beauty Supplies. List the permanent accounts affected.

Problem 14.4B

Objectives 14-4, 14-5, 14-6

Reconstructing a balance sheet to reflect proper accounting principles.

Country Cooking Prepared Meals is a retail shop owned by Beatrice Wilson. She wants to expand her business and has submitted the following balance sheet to her bank as part of the business loan application.

INSTRUCTIONS

1. Identify any errors in the balance sheet and explain why they should be considered errors.
2. Prepare a corrected balance sheet in accordance with generally accepted accounting principles.

Country Cooking Prepared Meals
Balance Sheet
December 31, 20X1

Assets

Cash	$ 18,000
Accounts Receivable	4,250
Inventory	19,275
Store Fixtures	14,000
Store Equipment	8,000
Personal Residence	170,000
Personal Automobile	16,625
Total Assets	$250,150

Liabilities and Owner's Equity

Accounts Payable	$ 14,000
Note Payable on Personal Automobile	8,275
Mortgage Payable on Personal Residence	55,250
Beatrice Wilson, Capital	172,625
Total Liabilities and Owner's Equity	$250,150

The following additional information is provided by Wilson:

a. The inventory has an original cost of $17,500. Wilson has valued it on the balance sheet at what it would cost today.

b. Wilson has counted $4,000 in her personal savings account in the business cash account.

c. The store fixtures, shown at original cost, were purchased two years ago. No depreciation has been taken on them. Depreciation for the two years, based on their estimated life of 10 years, would be $2,800.

d. The store equipment cost $9,600. No depreciation has been computed on the equipment, but it has been written down to its estimated replacement cost by a charge to expense. Depreciation on the equipment's original cost for the 24 months since its purchase would be $1,900.

e. Both the personal residence and personal automobile are only occasionally used for business purposes.

Analyze: Based on the new balance sheet that you have prepared, what are the total current assets for Country Cooking Prepared Meals?

Applying accounting principles and concepts.

For each of the unrelated situations below, identify the accounting principle or concept violated (if a violation exists) and explain the nature of the violation. If you believe that the treatment is in accordance with GAAP, state this as your position and defend it.

◀ **Problem 14.5B**

Objectives 14-5, 14-6, 14-7

1. A building repair company opened for business in late 20X1. On December 31 the *Services Revenue* account contained a balance of $504,000. Of that amount, $126,000 represents deposits received on contracts for services to be performed in January and February 20X2.

2. In recent years, Ultimate Home Designs has enjoyed rapid growth in profits because of customer loyalty and its reputation of putting the needs of customers first. The company recently debited an account called *Goodwill* in the amount of $300,000. The owner says this reflects the company's success in the business and the true worth of the business. The offsetting credit was to the *Owner's Equity* account.

3. Forest Hills Company manufactures a product requiring several parts. The company manufactures the parts, even though almost all competitors purchase the parts from outside sources, because Forest Hills can manufacture the parts for about 15 percent less than it would have to pay for the parts. Forest Hills thinks that comparability is very important in financial reporting, so when the parts are manufactured, they are recorded at what the purchase price would have been. At the same time, income is recorded equal to the difference between actual cost and the hypothetical purchase price. The *Inventory of Parts* account reflects this outside purchase price, and the *Finished Products Inventory* also reflects the hypothetical purchase price of the part used in manufacturing the products.

4. Lopez Company sold for $550,000 land that was purchased 10 years ago for $440,000. Even though the general price level had doubled during this period, Martinez reported a profit of $110,000 on the sale.

5. L. T. Allen owns Allen Computer Services. His annual net income is $750,000 and his owner's equity is $1,350,000. In December 20X1 an irate customer sued Allen for $2,000,000, alleging that an error made by Allen had resulted in damages of that amount. Allen's attorney thinks there may be substantial liability. Allen does not disclose the suit in the financial statements sent to the firm's banker and to providers of equipment and services.

Analyze: Refer to situation 2, above. Assume that in item 2, Wilson Company bought all of the assets of Ultimate Home Designs, paying an amount equal to book value for all assets, including $300,000 for goodwill. Also assume that the actual values of all the other assets purchased were equal to the purchase price. Do you think that it would be appropriate for Wilson Company to record the purchase price of the goodwill at the $300,000 paid for it?

Critical Thinking Problem 14.1

Judgment Call

Logistics Distribution Center receives a number of different products in its warehouse. Logistics distributes these products by truck to customers within a radius of 150 miles. The company is located near the Jackson Regional Airport, which is owned and operated by the city of Jackson. Most of the products are received by rail or truck, but some are received by air.

The city and the local Chamber of Commerce have announced a joint undertaking to build a new divided highway to connect the airport with the interstate highway approximately three miles away. The Chamber of Commerce is attempting to raise $4,000,000 as its contribution to the new highway's cost. The Chamber has asked the 10 largest enterprises in the city to make substantial contributions. Logistics has been asked to contribute $1,000,000 of the total amount.

At a meeting of Logistics's board of directors, the request was considered. It was pointed out that although Logistics is not located on the route of the proposed new road, the road's construction would speed up access of trucks to the warehouse and should substantially increase the value of Logistics's property. It is difficult to measure the benefits of either of these factors. The company's president suggested that a major reason for making the contribution was to get good publicity and to improve the company's image in the community. "It is good advertising," he said.

The company's controller is asked how the contribution would be accounted for in the company's accounts. A major question is whether the $1,000,000 should be:

- charged to expense when the contribution is made (thus reducing income of that period),
- capitalized as part of the cost of the land owned by the company in the area (increasing assets and not affecting income), or
- recorded as an asset and charged to expense over a period of 10 years (thus increasing assets in the short run and spreading out the effects of the contribution on income).

What answer would you give if you were the controller? In your answer, consider the principles, assumptions, and concepts that you have studied in this chapter.

Critical Thinking Problem 14.2
Applying GAAP

Assume that you are an independent CPA performing audits of financial statements. In the course of your work, you encounter the following independent situations. Review each of the situations. If you consider the treatment to be in conformity with generally accepted accounting principles and concepts, explain why. If you do not, explain which principle or concept has been violated and how the situation should have been reported.

1. South Pacific Oil and Gas Company produces oil and gas from the ground. It drills wells to attempt to find the oil and gas and to produce any minerals found. On average, about one out of four wells that the company drills produces oil and gas. Drilling costs range from $350,000 to $1,500,000 for each well. The company has adopted a rule that if the well results in finding oil and gas that can be produced profitably, the drilling costs will be recorded as an asset. If a dry hole results, the drilling costs are charged to expense.

2. R & R Vacation Resort recognizes room rental revenue on the date that a reservation is made. For the summer season, many guests make reservations as far as a year in advance of their intended visit.

3. The Traders Village Store spends a large sum on advertising for various sales promotions during the year. The advertising includes "institutional" ads designed to bring in customers in future years. The owner is sure that the advertising will generate revenue in future periods, but she has no idea of how much revenue will be produced or over what period of time it will be earned. In the current year, $500,000 was paid for advertising, and all of this amount was charged as an expense in the current period.

4. Machinery and Equipment Supply Company has constructed special-purpose equipment designed to manufacture other equipment that will be sold to computer chip manufacturers. Due to the special nature of this equipment, it has virtually no resale value to any other company. Therefore, the company has charged the entire cost to construct the equipment, $90 million, to expense in the current period.

5. Carson Company prepares financial statements four times each year. For convenience, these statements are prepared when business is slow and the accounting staff is less busy with other matters. Last year "quarterly" financial statements were prepared for the five-month period ended May 31, the two-month period ended July 31, the three-month period ended October 31, and the two-month period ended December 31.

6. In its regional office, Northwestern Stores purchases at least 150 storage bins each year. These baskets cost approximately $30 each and have useful lives ranging from two to six years. They are depreciated over a period of four years, the estimated average life. One of the company's accountants has suggested that the costs of the baskets should be charged to expense at the time they are purchased.

Analyze: If item 2 were recorded as described, what possible implications would this have for stockholders in the company?

BUSINESS CONNECTIONS

Judgment and Objectivity

Managerial FOCUS

1. A new manager of a retail company suggests that the company should prepare its income statement on the basis of cash receipts and cash expenditures (except for the acquisition of fixed assets, such as plant and equipment). He argues that managers, investors, creditors, and others are more interested in cash receipts and disbursements than in accrual-based accounting. Do you think he is correct? Explain.
2. In what situations would the going concern assumption *not* be useful to management?
3. What arguments can be given that the historical cost framework should be abandoned?
4. How can the element of personal judgment, which is involved in such matters as estimates of salvage value and useful life, be minimized to preserve the objectivity of an accounting system?

The Sarbanes-Oxley Act

Internal Control and FRAUD PREVENTION

The Sarbanes-Oxley Act of 2002 (Public Law 107-204) was enacted on July 30, 2002. The Act is also known as the Public Accounting Reform and Investor Protection Act and the Corporate and Auditing Accountability, Responsibility, and Transparency Act. The Act contains 11 titles, which were enacted as a reaction to a number of major corporate and accounting scandals, including Enron and WorldCom. Research this Act by finding it on the Internet. What is the subject of each of the 11 titles of the Act?

Notes to Financial Statements

Refer to The Home Depot, Inc., financial statements *(for the fiscal year ended February 3, 2019)* in Appendix A.

Financial Statement ANALYSIS

Home Depot

1. Discuss the qualitative characteristics of comparability and understandability in relation to the financial statements presented. In your opinion, do the statements satisfy these two criteria required by the FASB for financial reporting?
2. "Notes to Consolidated Financial Statements" are published along with the financial statements of a fiscal period, offering detailed information on significant accounting policies and financial data. Review the consolidated balance sheets and excerpts from "Notes to Consolidated Financial Statements." Are the company's merchandise inventories represented on the balance sheet? Describe the discussion found in Note 1 and the principle addressed by it.

Accounting Conventions

TEAMWORK

Every business manager should know and implement the four basic general accounting principles. Divide into four groups. Each group should choose one of the four basic accounting principles and pass out 3×5 cards to each student in the group. Ask each student to write on the card an example of a violation of and compliance with the accounting principle represented by the group. When completed, each student group should present their work to the class for discussion.

Answers to Comprehensive Self Review

1. The full disclosure principle is that all events and factors that are likely to impact the interpretation of the statements should be disclosed. Disclosures can be made in parenthetical notes to the statements or by "notes to the statements" (deemed to be an integral part of the statements). In addition, "supplemental notes" that may not be directly related to amounts shown in the statements may be included.
2. The AICPA influence is primarily through its committees that examine current issues arising in practice for which there is no clear guidance from the FASB. The Sarbanes-Oxley Act gives express power to the SEC to accept rules developed by (one) private-sector organization, so it is possible that the direct impact of AICPA pronouncements will be limited in the future.

3. Industry practice is likely to be an important consideration where there are unique operating circumstances or unique contracts involved in that industry and there is no clearly preferable application of the conceptual framework.

4. The FASB and the SEC have made commitments to work with the International Accounting Standards Board on having U.S. GAAP align or converge more closely with international accounting standards.

5. The result would be that record keeping would be much more complicated, probably involving separate accounts for transactions (such as machinery purchases) made in each year. Another approach might be to attempt to keep all records in terms of "value" at the statement date.

6. Applicable costs should be matched with revenues in the income statement the same year—generally in the year of sale. This requires adjustments for prepaid and accrued expenses and for unearned and accrued income items, as well as such items as depreciation and uncollectible accounts.

Accounts Receivable and Uncollectible Accounts

Chapter 15

Sundry Photography/Shutterstock

www.amazon.com

Amazon is the most valuable public company in the world. Founded in 1994 by Jeffrey Bezos, Amazon.com, Inc., doing business as Amazon, is also the largest Internet company as measured by revenue in the world. With approximately 566,000 employees, it is the second largest employer in the United States. Amazon serves worldwide consumers through both retail websites and physical stores. In its press release on earnings for 2018, Amazon reported a net sales increase of 31% based on sales of $232.9 billion, compared with $177.9 billion in 2017. Income was earned through a variety of segments, including Prime (a subscription-based shipping and video service with over 100 million global members); Amazon's web services; Amazon's Marketplace (through which hundreds of millions of unique products are offered for sale by Amazon and third-party sellers); Amazon Devices (smart technology devices, many of which utilize Amazon's Alexa service); and Whole Foods (acquired on August 28, 2017).

While Amazon continues to report strong sales year after year, these sales figures do not always result in the collection of cash. Extending credit to customers is necessary to remain competitive and facilitates customer utilization more efficiently. However, there are also risks in selling services on credit. Not only must Amazon wait 15, 30, 60, or more days to receive payment from customers, there is the risk that some customers may not pay at all. Companies must accept the realization that some customers will be unable to pay the amount owed. Therefore, an estimate of the dollar amount that may not be collected must be established and reported on its financial statements.

At the end of each accounting year, Amazon must make its best estimate of the probable losses inherent in its customer receivables. The year-end estimate is based on actual historical losses experienced, trends in customer payment frequency, judgments of the possible effects of the economic conditions, and the financial health of specific customers and market sectors. At December 31, 2018, Amazon customers owed a total of $9.5 billion, of which $118 million, approximately 1.24 percent of the amount owed, was estimated to be uncollectible. This may seem like a huge amount of its services for which it will not receive payment; however, for companies that extend credit to their customers, it is considered a normal cost of doing business.

thinking critically

What do you think Amazon could do to minimize its uncollectible accounts?

LEARNING OBJECTIVES

15-1 Record the estimated expense from uncollectible accounts receivable using the allowance method.
15-2 Write off uncollectible accounts using the allowance method.
15-3 Record the collection of accounts previously written off using the allowance method.
15-4 Record losses from uncollectible accounts using the direct charge-off method.
15-5 Record the collection of accounts previously written off using the direct charge-off method.
15-6 Recognize common internal controls for accounts receivable.
15-7 Define the accounting terms new to this chapter.

NEW TERMS

aging the accounts receivable
allowance method
direct charge-off method
valuation account

Section 1

SECTION OBJECTIVES

>> 15-1 Record the estimated expense from uncollectible accounts receivable using the allowance method.

WHY IT'S IMPORTANT
Assets should not be overstated. In accordance with the matching principle, bad debt losses are matched with the related sales revenue.

>> 15-2 Charge off uncollectible accounts using the allowance method.

WHY IT'S IMPORTANT
When an account is uncollectible, it should be charged off. The accounts receivable ledger should contain complete and accurate information so that future credit decisions are sound.

>> 15-3 Record the collection of accounts previously written off using the allowance method.

WHY IT'S IMPORTANT
Customers' accounts should reflect actual payment histories.

TERMS TO LEARN

aging the accounts receivable
allowance method
direct charge-off method
valuation account

The Allowance Method of Accounting for Uncollectible Accounts

important!

The Credit Manager
The credit manager plays a very important role in improving profitability of the business.

Most businesses extend credit to their customers because it increases sales revenues. Manufacturing enterprises, wholesale distributors, and organizations providing services to other businesses typically sell an overwhelming portion of their goods and services on credit. Service businesses such as medical providers, attorneys, accountants, auto repair garages, and others offering services to individuals also frequently extend credit. Almost invariably, when a business extends credit, some customers will not pay their bills. A firm's credit department and its management try to reduce the losses from uncollectible accounts. Typically, a customer seeking credit privileges must complete a credit application form. The applicant must provide financial information requested. In most cases, the applicant's credit record is checked through a credit report obtained from a credit agency. A credit report shows the payment record of a customer and some reports include historical or other information concerning the business or person about whom inquiry is being made.

However, no matter what tools are used, it is almost impossible to forecast with certainty whether a specific customer will prove to be a good risk. If a company has no credit losses, the business may be losing substantial sales by having a credit policy that is too restrictive. Management must constantly balance the risk of higher credit losses resulting from giving credit to more applicants or from setting higher limits on the amount of credit extended individual customers (both of which may lead to increased losses) against the possibility of losing sales volume as a result of giving credit to fewer customers or setting lower limits on each customer. Losses resulting from failure of customers to pay the amounts owed, called "uncollectible accounts expense" or "losses from uncollectible accounts," or sometimes referred to as "bad debts expense," are a normal cost of doing business.

A basic question faced in accounting for uncollectible accounts is determining when they should be charged to expense. A corollary question is how to determine the amount to be charged to expense during each accounting period. Related issues for the accountant are how to make the resulting accounting entries and how to show the information in the financial statements.

Methods of Accounting for Uncollectible Accounts

Two methods are used to account for uncollectible accounts. These are the "allowance method" and the "direct charge-off method." The latter is sometimes called the "specific charge-off method."

The Allowance Method

Under the **allowance method,** an estimate is made and recorded each year of the bad debt losses applicable to sales of that year, even though it may be a year or more before it is known which specific accounts are uncollectible. At the end of the accounting period, the estimated loss for the period is debited to *Uncollectible Accounts Expense* and credited to *Allowance for Doubtful Accounts.* This approach matches the estimated expense from uncollectible accounts to the revenue in the period the revenue is recognized. *Allowance for Doubtful Accounts* is subtracted from *Accounts Receivable* on the balance sheet. The net accounts receivable reflects the amount that the business thinks will be collected. For this reason, the allowance account is called a **valuation account.** The allowance method meets two of the basic concepts in the FASB's conceptual framework. The principle of matching revenues and related costs is applied. In addition, current assets that will be converted into cash should not be shown at more than the amount expected to be realized when they are converted. Because of these characteristics, the allowance method is required under generally accepted accounting principles.

The Direct Charge-Off Method

Under the **direct charge-off method,** losses from uncollectible accounts are recorded only when specific customers' accounts become uncollectible. When that occurs, the balance due is removed from *Accounts Receivable* and the customer's account in the subsidiary ledger and is charged to *Uncollectible Accounts Expense.* The direct charge-off method is used primarily by small businesses, many of whom do not have external audits. Consistent with the concept of materiality, the direct charge-off method is also used by large businesses that have relatively insignificant accounts receivable. The direct charge-off method does not reflect generally accepted accounting principles because a loss from sales on account in one year frequently will not be charged to expense until a subsequent year (a violation of the matching principle) if the direct charge-off method is followed. In addition, the accounts receivable are shown at an amount greater than will ultimately be realized in cash from them. Federal income tax laws now require that the direct charge-off method be used in preparing the federal tax return. The allowance method is not acceptable for tax purposes. Using the direct charge-off method for financial reporting as well as income tax purposes reduces the amount of time spent in accounting for uncollectible accounts. As a result, the tax requirement leads some businesses to also use the direct charge-off method for financial reporting purposes.

Because the allowance method is the generally accepted procedure and is therefore much more widely used, details of that method are discussed before the direct charge-off method is examined in detail.

Applying the Allowance Method

You will learn how to use the allowance method to account for losses from uncollectible accounts by studying Kathy's Kitchens, a retail store selling kitchen appliances, gadgets, and kitchen remodeling services. Kathy's Kitchens is owned by Kathy Kaymark and has been in business several years. The store offers charge accounts to customers who meet its credit standards. Kathy sends customers statements of their accounts on the last day of each month,

important!

When Uncollectible Accounts Expense Is Recorded Under the Allowance Method
Under the allowance method, uncollectible accounts expense is recorded at the end of the period as an adjusting entry.

important!

Matching Uncollectible Accounts with Sales
The allowance method matches the uncollectible accounts expense with sales in the period the sales are recorded.

important!

Recording Uncollectible Accounts Expense Under the Direct Charge-Off Method
Under the direct charge-off method, bad debt expense is recorded when a customer's account becomes uncollectible.

important!

Uncollectible Accounts
Only the direct charge-off method is allowed for federal income tax purposes. The use of the allowance method is required under generally accepted accounting principles.

and the balance owed is due by the 20th day of the following month. Kathy understands that the allowance method is preferred to the direct charge-off method, so she has adopted the allowance method.

>> **15-1 OBJECTIVE**
Record the estimated expense from uncollectible accounts receivable using the allowance method.

Recording the Estimated Expense from Uncollectible Accounts When the Allowance Method Is Used

At the end of 20X0, Kathy analyzed the bad debts record in prior years and also the amounts owed currently by each customer. On the basis of this analysis, along with information from her trade association about typical bad debt losses in that type of business and from talks with other merchants in similar businesses in the community, Kathy estimated the provision for uncollectible accounts necessary at year-end 20X0 to be $1,900. Do not be concerned with the details of how this amount was determined. Three methods, to be examined later in this chapter, are commonly used as a basis for the estimate. At this point, we are interested only in the basic concepts of the recording procedure.

When adjusting entries were made at the end of the year 20X0, the estimated loss ($1,900) was recorded as a debit to the expense account *Uncollectible Accounts Expense,* sometimes called *Bad Debts Expense* or *Losses from Uncollectible Accounts.* This account is shown in the income statement as a general expense or as a selling expense, depending on which department in the business has responsibility for making credit decisions. Good internal controls generally suggest that the credit function should not be in the sales department, a department very interested in increasing sales. As a result, *Uncollectible Accounts Expense* is usually shown under General Expenses.

The credit part of the adjusting entry was to *Allowance for Doubtful Accounts.* Sometimes the allowance account is called *Allowance for Bad Debts* or *Allowance for Uncollectible Accounts.* Here is the journal entry made at the end of 20X0 in the records of Kathy's Kitchens:

important!

Uncollectible Accounts Expense on the Income Statement

Usually, *Uncollectible Accounts Expense* is shown as a general expense.

GENERAL JOURNAL PAGE 1

DATE	DESCRIPTION	POST. REF.	DEBIT	CREDIT
	Adjusting Entries			
20X0				
Dec. 31	Uncollectible Accounts Expense		1 900 00	
	Allowance for Doubtful Accounts			1 900 00

Remember that *Allowance for Doubtful Accounts,* which reflects the estimate of losses to be incurred on sales already made, is shown on the balance sheet as a deduction from *Accounts Receivable.* Assuming that there was a zero balance in *Allowance for Doubtful Accounts* prior to the adjusting entry, that account will have a credit balance of $1,900 on December 31, 20X0, after the above adjusting entry. The allowance account is a *contra* account because it is subtracted from an asset account (*Accounts Receivable*) in the balance sheet. It reduces the carrying value of the asset and is referred to as a valuation account. Here is how the accounts receivable information appeared on the balance sheet for Kathy's Kitchens on December 31, 20X0:

THE BOTTOM LINE
Uncollectible Accounts Adjustment

Income Statement
Expenses	↑ 1,900
Net Income	↓ 1,900

Balance Sheet >>
Assets	↓ 1,900
Equity	↓ 1,900

recall

Contra Asset Account
Allowance for Doubtful Accounts is a contra asset account. Its normal balance is a credit. It is reported in the balance sheet as a deduction from *Accounts Receivable* to provide an estimate of collectible receivables. For this reason, it is called a valuation account.

Kathy's Kitchens
Balance Sheet (partial)
December 31, 20X0

Current Assets		
Cash		$ 9,320
Accounts Receivable	$46,400	
Less Allowance for Doubtful Accounts	1,900	44,500

The $44,500 balance is often called the net realizable value of accounts receivable.

Alternatively, the balance sheet may show only the net amount of **Accounts Receivable,** after subtracting out the allowance, with the amount of the allowance shown in a parenthetical note.

> At December 31, 2018, The Coca-Cola Company reported *trade accounts receivable, less allowances,* of approximately $3.4 billion. This amount was net of allowances totaling $489 million.

Note again that under the allowance method, the financial statements reflect the matching principle. The estimated expense for losses on sales made in 20X0 is deducted in the 20X0 income statement—the same year that the related revenues from sales were reported. Also, the net **Accounts Receivable** on the balance sheet reflects the amount expected to be received in cash from the debtors.

Factors Used to Compute the Year-End Provision for Uncollectible Accounts

In the discussion of Kathy's Kitchens' provision for uncollectible accounts at the end of 20X0, you were not told how the $1,900 provision was determined. The end-of-year estimate of the amount to be charged to **Uncollectible Accounts Expense** and credited to the **Allowance for Doubtful Accounts** is usually based on one of three factors:

- net credit sales for the year,
- total accounts receivable on December 31,
- aging of accounts receivable on December 31.

When the amount of net credit sales for the year is the basis for the provision, it is often said that the preparer is using the "income statement approach." Using sales as the estimation base emphasizes the importance of matching uncollectible accounts expense with the net credit sales generated in the same year. In this approach, the key factor is the matching principle. When the provision is based on total accounts receivable or the aging of accounts receivable, the emphasis is on the balance sheet, so it is often called the "balance sheet approach." It emphasizes the appropriate valuation of receivables—not showing the net receivables at an amount greater than the cash expected to be received from their collection.

The calculations of the uncollectible accounts adjustment for Kathy's Kitchens on December 31, 20X1, under each of these three approaches illustrate how they are determined. During 20X1, Kathy's Kitchens had net credit sales of $600,000. Accounts receivable at the end of the year totaled $49,000. There was a credit balance of $1,900 in the allowance account on January 1, 20X1. Assume that accounts totaling $1,792 were charged off in 20X1, so that there is a credit balance of $108 in **Allowance for Doubtful Accounts** prior to adjusting entries on December 31. Here is how the three approaches would be applied by Kathy's Kitchens.

Percentage of Net Credit Sales

One way to estimate uncollectible accounts expense is to multiply the net credit sales by a percentage. The percentage is based on the company's previous experience with losses from uncollectible accounts. New businesses often base the percentage on the experience of other businesses in the same industry. The percentage is calculated as follows:

$$\frac{\text{Losses from uncollectible accounts}}{\text{Net credit sales}}$$

Net credit sales is calculated as total credit sales minus the sales returns and allowances on credit sales.

Kathy's Kitchens estimates that three-quarters of 1 percent (0.0075) of the net credit sales will be uncollectible. If net credit sales in 20X1 are $600,000, the estimated loss from uncollectible accounts is $4,500 (0.0075 × $600,000). This is the amount to be charged to **Uncollectible**

important!

Reporting Uncollectible Accounts Under GAAP
The allowance method meets the conservatism constraint.

important!

Effects of Different Estimation Bases on Entries
The accounts used to record the provision are the same for all three estimation bases. The difference is in how the amount of adjustment is computed.

important!

Matching Costs and Revenues
Although basing the uncollectible account estimate on receivables is not tied directly to sales for the year, generally the accounts receivable balance will reflect sales made in the current year. For this reason, accountants say that this approach is "matching revenues and costs."

important!

Using Total Sales as the Base
Some companies do not have separate data for sales on account and cash sales. In that case, the percentage may be applied to total sales. If the ratio between cash sales and credit sales changes from year to year, this is not a satisfactory approach.

recall

Basing Bad Debts on Sales Provides Matching

If the estimate of uncollectible accounts is based on sales, emphasis is being placed on the matching of revenues and expenses in the income statement.

Accounts Expense and credited to *Allowance for Doubtful Accounts* in the adjusting entry. It is entered on the worksheet and is later recorded in the general journal, along with other adjusting entries.

	GENERAL JOURNAL			PAGE 1
DATE	DESCRIPTION	POST. REF.	DEBIT	CREDIT
20X1	Adjusting Entries			
Dec. 31	Uncollectible Accounts Expense	561	4 500 00	
	Allowance for Doubtful Accounts	112		4 500 00
	To record estimated bad debt losses			
	for the year, based on 0.75 percent of			
	net credit sales of $600,000			

important!

Ignore the Balance in the Valuation Account in Making the Adjustment

If the uncollectible account provision is based on sales, the existing debit or credit balance in the allowance account is ignored in making the provision.

Note again that the expense charge is the focal point when sales are used as the basis for the estimate. The balance in the allowance account before the adjustment is ignored in determining how much will be charged to expense and credited to the allowance account. This is why the method is referred to as an "income statement approach."

Percentage of Total Accounts Receivable

Some accountants think that it is more important to focus on the balance in the allowance account than on the amount charged to expense. Under their approach, it is necessary to first determine the amount in the accounts estimated to be uncollectible and to adjust the *Allowance for Doubtful Accounts* to that amount. The offsetting debit to expense is the result of focusing on the balance sheet accounts.

A simple approach to determining the appropriate balance for *Allowance for Doubtful Accounts* is to apply a single percentage to the balance of the *Accounts Receivable* account. This percentage is typically based on the experience of the company during the last three or four years. The average of accounts that became uncollectible during each year of the base period is calculated. Similarly, the average of accounts receivable at the end of each base period year is determined. Then the ratio of the average uncollectible accounts to the average ending balance of accounts receivable is computed. The ratio is applied to the *Accounts Receivable* balance at the date of the computation to arrive at the estimated worthless accounts. Kathy's Kitchens decides to use the ratio of average uncollectible accounts for the last three years to the ending balance in *Accounts Receivable* for the three years. The records of Kathy's Kitchens show the following:

important!

Focus on Uncollectible Amount

Many accountants think that basing the allowance on accounts receivable focuses more sharply on the critical question of the amount in the accounts that is uncollectible than does a charge-off based on sales.

Year	Accounts Receivable	Uncollectible Accounts
1	$ 39,600	$2,083
2	44,360	2,145
3	46,400	2,240
Total	$130,360	$6,468
Average	$ 43,453	$2,156

The average loss over the three-year period is 4.962 percent of accounts receivable.

$$\frac{\text{Average Uncollectible Accounts}}{\text{Average Accounts Receivable}} = \frac{\$2,156}{\$43,453} = 0.04962$$

recall

Emphasis on the Balance Sheet

If the adjusting entry for uncollectible account expense is based on receivables, the emphasis is being placed on the balance sheet.

It is customary to round the percentage of loss to the nearest one-tenth of one percent. Under this convention, Kathy's rate would be rounded to 5.0 percent.

If the balance of *Accounts Receivable* on December 31, 20X1, is $49,000, estimated uncollectible accounts will be $2,450 (0.05 × $49,000). Under the balance sheet approach, *Allowance for Doubtful Accounts* is adjusted to the amount estimated to be *uncollectible*. Assuming that the *Allowance for Doubtful Accounts* has a credit balance of $108 on December 31, before the adjusting entry has been made, it will be necessary to add $2,342 to the account to bring it to the desired balance ($2,450 − $108 = $2,342). Here is the necessary entry:

	GENERAL JOURNAL			PAGE 12
DATE	DESCRIPTION	POST. REF.	DEBIT	CREDIT
20X1				
Dec. 31	Uncollectible Accounts Expense		2,342.00	
	Allowance for Doubtful Accounts			2,342.00

After the entry has been posted, the *Allowance for Doubtful Accounts* has a credit balance of $2,450. If *Allowance for Doubtful Accounts* had a *debit* balance of $240 prior to the adjusting entry, it would be necessary to credit the allowance account for $2,690 ($2,450 + $240 = $2,690) to arrive at the required balance of $2,450.

Aging the Accounts Receivable

Another way to estimate uncollectible accounts is a procedure called **aging the accounts receivable.** This procedure involves classifying receivables according to how long they have been outstanding. The first step is to prepare an aging schedule. Figure 15.1 shows the aging schedule for Kathy's Kitchens. Each account is listed by name and balance. Each invoice is classified as current (within the credit period), 1–30 days past due, 31–60 days past due, or over 60 days past due. Notice that Robert Brown owes $400. Of this amount, $80 is over 60 days past due and $320 is between 31 and 60 days past due.

The longer an account is past due, the less likely it is to be collected. Following are estimated uncollectible percentages for each age group shown in the analysis of Kathy's receivables:

Category	Percentage Uncollectible
Current Accounts	0.5%
1–30 days past due	6.0%
31–60 days past due	20.0%
Over 60 days past due	60.0%

important!

Collect Accounts as Quickly as Possible

Experience has shown that the older an account receivable becomes, the less likely it is to be collected. Every effort should be made to collect accounts as quickly as possible to avoid collection issues in the future.

FIGURE 15.1

Kathy's Kitchens Aged Accounts Receivable Schedule

Kathy's Kitchens
Schedule of Accounts Receivable by Age
December 31, 20X1

Customer	Balance	Current	Past Due—Days		
			1–30	31–60	Over 60
Anderson, Nick	$ 820		$ 820		
Anh, Susie	1,200	$ 1,200			
Benson, Samuel	257	37		$ 200	$ 20
Brown, Robert	400			320	80
All other accounts	46,323	36,763	6,180	1,080	2,300
Totals	$49,000	$38,000	$7,000	$1,600	$2,400

important!

Aging the Accounts Receivable

The aged accounts receivable schedule serves several purposes.

- It proves that the accounts receivable subsidiary ledger balances with the accounts receivable control account.
- It identifies slow-paying customers so that focused collection efforts can be taken.
- It is used to estimate the amount of accounts that will become uncollectible.

Based on these percentages, the estimated uncollectible accounts on December 31 total $2,370:

Current	0.005	×	$38,000	=	$ 190
1–30 days past due	0.06	×	7,000	=	420
31–60 days past due	0.20	×	1,600	=	320
Over 60 days past due	0.60	×	2,400	=	1,440
Totals			$49,000		$2,370

Allowance for Doubtful Accounts should then be adjusted so that its ending balance is a $2,370 credit. On December 31, before adjustments have been made, *Allowance for Doubtful Accounts* has a credit balance of $108. A credit adjustment of $2,262 ($2,370 − $108) will bring the account balance to the desired amount.

```
         Allowance for Doubtful Accounts
         ───────────────┬───────────────
                −       │       +
                        │ Bal.    108.00
                        │ Adj.  2,262.00
                        │ Bal.  2,370.00
```

The adjustment is recorded in the general journal as follows:

GENERAL JOURNAL PAGE 1

	20X1		Adjusting Entries			
22	Dec.	31	Uncollectible Accounts Expense	561	2 262 00	
23			Allowance for Doubtful Accounts	112		2 262 00
24			To adjust allowance account to $2,370,			
25			based on aging of accounts receivable			

>> 15-2 OBJECTIVE

Write off uncollectible accounts using the allowance method.

important!

Removing a Charged-Off Account

When the allowance method is used, *Accounts Receivable* (and the customer's account) is always credited when an account is determined to be uncollectible.

Writing Off a Customer's Account Determined to Be Uncollectible When the Allowance Method Is Used

A basic rule is that the longer past due an account becomes, the less likely it is to be collectible. When it is concluded that a specific account is not collectible, it should be "charged off" or "written off." For example, on January 24, 20X1, Kathy's Kitchens concluded that the account of James McDonald should be charged off. Kathy's had sent him numerous letters, made several telephone calls, and sent a number of e-mails. The account had a balance of $224, resulting from a sale on August 22, 20X0.

The general journal entry required to charge off a customer's account when the allowance method is used is a simple one. *Accounts Receivable* and McDonald's account in the subsidiary ledger are credited to remove the amount due. The debit is to *Allowance for Doubtful Accounts*. When the allowance was credited previously by an adjusting entry, it was not known which specific accounts would be uncollectible. It is now assumed that the provision included McDonald's account, so there is no longer a need to include in *Allowance for Doubtful*

Accounts an amount to cover a future loss from McDonald's failure to pay this debt. Here is the journal entry to write off McDonald's account:

	GENERAL JOURNAL			PAGE 12
DATE	DESCRIPTION	POST. REF.	DEBIT	CREDIT
20X1				
Jan. 24	Allowance for Doubtful Accounts		224 00	
	Accounts Receivable/James McDonald			224 00

The debit to *Allowance for Doubtful Accounts* reduces the credit balance in that account. The total amount of accounts receivable charged off in 20X1 may be more than, or less than, the balance in *Allowance for Doubtful Accounts* at the start of the year. What happens if the amount debited to *Allowance for Doubtful Accounts* exceeds the beginning amount in the account? For example, what happens if during 20X1 Kathy's Kitchens removes from *Accounts Receivable* and charges to *Allowance for Doubtful Accounts* a total of $2,018? Remember that the balance in the allowance account was only $1,900 at the start of the year. Thus, at the end of 20X1 *Allowance for Doubtful Accounts* would contain a debit balance of $118 ($2,018 debit − $1,900 credit = $118 debit). On the other hand, if the amount of uncollectible accounts charged off in 20X1 is only $1,700, there would have been a credit balance of $200 ($1,900 credit − $1,700 debit = $200 credit) in the allowance account before adjustments at the end of 20X1. The existence of a debit balance or a credit balance in the allowance account before adjustments at the end of the year is not generally a cause for concern. When the adjusting entries have been made, that situation will be corrected. We will see later how this situation is handled in the adjustments at the end of 20X1. Obviously, management will need to keep close watch every year to make sure that the estimation process being used is reasonable and the allowance balance is adequate, but not excessive.

It is important to remember that the charge-off of a specific account receivable has no impact on total assets if the allowance method is used. The credit to the asset account *Accounts Receivable* is exactly the same amount as the debit to the contra account *Allowance for Doubtful Accounts,* so there is no change in the net amount of *Accounts Receivable.*

important!
Balance in the Allowance Account
Allowance for Doubtful Accounts may have either a debit or credit balance before adjusting entries are posted.

important!
Is the Provision Reasonable?
It is very important for management to analyze the estimation process each year to assure that the provision for uncollectible accounts is reasonable.

> At its fiscal year ending June 30, 2018, Microsoft Corporation's balance sheet showed "Accounts Receivable, Net" of approximately $26.5 billion. A note to the financial statements described activity in the allowance account for the year as follows:
>
> > The allowance for doubtful accounts reflects our best estimate of probable losses inherent in the accounts receivable balance. We determine the allowance based on known troubled accounts, historical experience, and other currently available evidence.
>
> The note goes further to analyze the allowance for doubtful accounts for 2018, which includes the following information in $millions.
>
> | | |
> |---|---|
> | Beginning balance (July 1, 2017) | $361 |
> | Charges to costs and expenses | +134 |
> | Write-offs and other | − 98 |
> | Balance at end of period (June 30, 2018) | $397 |

>> 15-3 OBJECTIVE
Record the collection of accounts previously written off using the allowance method.

Collecting an Account That Has Been Previously Written Off

Occasionally, an account that was written off is later collected, in whole or in part. When a firm uses the allowance method to provide for losses, the recovery of an account previously charged off as uncollectible requires two entries to record the transaction. The first entry reinstates the account receivable, and the second entry records the receipt of cash. For example, the recovery on February 9, 20X2, of the $160 account of Richard Strong, charged off on July 13, 20X1, is recorded in the general journal as follows:

THE BOTTOM LINE

Reinstating an Account Using the Allowance Method

Income Statement
No effect on net income

Balance Sheet
No effect on assets
No effect on equity

GENERAL JOURNAL   PAGE ___

DATE	DESCRIPTION	POST. REF.	DEBIT	CREDIT
20X2				
Feb. 09	Accounts Receivable/Richard Strong	111/✓	160 00	
	Allowance for Doubtful Accounts	112		160 00
	To reverse entry dated July 13, 20X1,			
	writing off this account, collected in			
	full today.			

An entry in the cash receipts journal is then made in the usual way to record the collection—by a debit to **Cash** and a credit to **Accounts Receivable.**

If the amount recovered is only part of the balance written off, an entry is made to restore *only the amount actually collected* unless the firm is almost certain that the remainder will be paid. For example, if Richard Strong pays only $60, that is the amount that will be reinstated unless Kathy's is reasonably sure the additional $100 Strong owes will be paid. After the proper reinstatement is made, an entry in the cash receipts journal is then made in the usual way to record the collection of the account receivable.

Section 1 Review

1. What accounting principle supports the allowance method for reporting uncollectible accounts?
   a. historical cost
   b. periodicity of income
   c. matching
   d. conservatism

2. Thompson Industries determines its provision for uncollectible accounts by applying an estimated loss percentage of 1 percent to net credit sales. In 20X1, net credit sales were $5,800,000. Prior to the adjusting entry, *Allowance for Doubtful Accounts* contained a credit balance of $5,000. How much will be charged to *Uncollectible Accounts Expense* in 20X1?
   a. $53,000
   b. $5,800
   c. $5,300
   d. $58,000

3. Palmer Company determines its allowance for doubtful accounts by applying an expected loss percentage of 1.8 percent to the total of accounts receivable, $1,500,000. Prior to the adjusting entry, the allowance account has a debit balance of $1,180. How much will be charged to expense in the adjusting entry?
   a. $27,000
   b. $28,180
   c. $25,820
   d. $2,818

4. Zion Company uses the allowance method to record uncollectible accounts. In January 20X1, it charged off the $450 account balance of Lexington as uncollectible. In June 20X1, Lexington paid the entire amount charged off. What journal entries are made at the time of receipt of payment?
   a. Debit *Allowance for Doubtful Accounts* $450; credit *Accounts Receivable/Lexington* $450.

b. Debit *Accounts Receivable/Lexington* $450; credit *Allowance for Doubtful Accounts* $450.

c. Debit *Cash* $450; credit *Accounts Receivable/Lexington* $450.

d. b and c are correct.

e. a and c are correct.

5. Assume the same facts as in question 4, above, except that Lexington made the repayment in 20X2. What journal entries would be made on receipt of payment?

   a. Debit *Accounts Receivable/Lexington* $450; credit *Allowance for Doubtful Accounts* $450.

   b. Debit *Cash* $450; credit *Accounts Receivable/Lexington* $450.

   c. a and b are correct.

   d. Debit *Cash* $450; credit *Sales Revenue* $450.

6. Haden Company bases its provision for uncollectible accounts on sales. At the end of each of the past four years, the ratio of *Allowance for Doubtful Accounts* to *Accounts Receivable* at the end of the year has been greater than it was for the prior year. What does this suggest?

   a. The ratio is greater than needed and should be reduced.

   b. The ratio is smaller than needed and should be increased.

   c. The ratio does not need to be adjusted.

   d. Neither a, b, nor c is correct.

7. The credit manager at Deluxe Office Supply has learned that a former customer who did not pay his debt, and whose account Deluxe had charged off as uncollectible, has just won the state lottery and the customer may now pay the debt. Should the customer's account be reinstated?

   a. Yes, the account should be reinstated because the former customer has the wherewithal to pay.

   b. No, nothing has happened to validate that the former customer intends to pay.

   c. Every effort should be made to collect the debt.

   d. a and c are correct.

   e. b and c are correct.

Section 2

SECTION OBJECTIVES

>> **15-4** Record losses from uncollectible accounts using the direct charge-off method.

WHY IT'S IMPORTANT
Some small businesses and larger businesses with immaterial amounts of accounts receivable use this method, even though it does not comply with GAAP. Also, the direct charge-off method is required for federal income tax reporting.

>> **15-5** Record the collection of accounts previously written off using the direct charge-off method.

WHY IT'S IMPORTANT
Customers' accounts should reflect actual payment histories.

>> **15-6** Recognize common internal controls for accounts receivable.

WHY IT'S IMPORTANT
There are many activities involving accounts receivable and uncollectible accounts that provide opportunities for mishandling of funds. The accountant should be aware of steps to be taken to provide protection.

Applying the Direct Charge-Off Method; Internal Control of Accounts Receivable

The direct charge-off method for recording uncollectible account expense is simple to apply, but it does not comply with generally accepted accounting principles. As discussed earlier in this chapter, however, the method is often used by small businesses and by some larger enterprises when the impact on financial statements would be immaterial. In addition, because it is required for federal income tax purposes, an understanding of the system is essential.

>> **15-4 OBJECTIVE**
Record losses from uncollectible accounts using the direct charge-off method.

Recording Uncollectible Accounts When the Direct Charge-Off Method Is Used

Earlier in this chapter it was pointed out that the direct charge-off method records uncollectible accounts expense at the time a specific customer's account is deemed to be uncollectible. Certain transactions of Romano's Auto Repair Shop will be used to demonstrate the accounting entries made when the direct charge-off method is used.

On December 22, 20X0, Romano made repairs to Mike Miller's RV, charging $520 to **Accounts Receivable** and to Miller's account in the accounts receivable subsidiary ledger. On July 10, 20X1, after several weeks of trying to collect the account, Romano discovered that Miller had left his job and moved to another state. Romano concludes that the account must be written off. The loss is debited to **Uncollectible Accounts Expense.** The credit is to **Accounts Receivable** and to Miller's account in the accounts receivable subsidiary ledger.

		GENERAL JOURNAL			PAGE ___	
DATE		DESCRIPTION	POST. REF.	DEBIT	CREDIT	
20X1						
July	10	Uncollectible Account Expense		520 00		
		Accounts Receivable/Mike Miller			520 00	
		To write off uncollectible account				

There are several important points to remember about the direct charge-off method:

- It does not always match revenue and expenses violating the matching principle. Revenue for the work done on Miller's vehicle was recognized in 20X0. The bad debt expense, however, is recorded in 20X1.
- It can overstate accounts receivable. Under this method, the *Accounts Receivable* balance reflects all outstanding unpaid accounts that have not been written off. No estimate is made for the accounts that might be uncollectible in the future.
- It is the only method acceptable for federal income tax purposes.

Collecting an Account Previously Written Off When the Direct Charge-Off Method Is Used

>> **15-5 OBJECTIVE**
Record the collection of accounts previously written off using the direct charge-off method.

Under the direct charge-off method, the appropriate entries to record the collection of an account after it has been charged off depend on whether the collection is made in the same accounting period that the account was written off or occurs in a subsequent period.

Payment Received in Period in Which Account Is Charged Off

In the above example, Miller's account of $520 was written off on July 10, 20X1, under the direct charge-off method. The entry was a debit to *Uncollectible Accounts Expense* and a credit to *Accounts Receivable.* Suppose that on October 29, 20X1, Romano's Auto Repair Shop received $520 from Miller in full payment of his account. It takes two entries to record the transaction. The first entry is to reinstate in *Accounts Receivable* the amount being paid. This entry, which simply reverses the entry made to charge off the account as uncollectible, is made so that the customer's account will show the full history of the customer's payment record. The credit is made to *Uncollectible Accounts Expense* so that the expense account for the period will not be overstated. To the extent that there is payment in the same year, there was no net expense for the year.

THE BOTTOM LINE
Reinstating an Account Using the Direct Charge-Off Method

Income Statement
Expenses ↓ 520
Net Income ↑ 520

Balance Sheet
Assets ↑ 520
Equity ↑ 520

		GENERAL JOURNAL			PAGE ___	
DATE		DESCRIPTION	POST. REF.	DEBIT	CREDIT	
20X1						
Oct.	29	Accounts Receivable/Mike Miller		520 00		
		Uncollectible Account Expense			520 00	
		To reinstate Miller's account receivable				
		that was written off on July 10 and				
		collected in full today.				

The second entry records the customer's payment in the cash receipts journal in the usual way, as a debit to *Cash* and a credit to *Accounts Receivable* (and to Miller's account).

> **recall**
>
> **Amount to Reinstate**
> The entry to reinstate a previously written-off account reinstates *only the amount actually collected* unless the firm is almost certain that the remainder will be received.

Payment Received in Period Subsequent to That in Which Account Was Charged Off

Suppose that the collection of Miller's account is made in January 20X2, a period subsequent to that of the charge-off. In that event, the entry to reinstate the account is a debit to **Accounts Receivable** and a credit to **Uncollectible Accounts Recovered.**

GENERAL JOURNAL				PAGE
DATE	DESCRIPTION	POST. REF.	DEBIT	CREDIT
20X2 Jan. 09	Accounts Receivable/Mike Miller		520 00	
	Uncollectible Accounts Recovered			520 00
	To reinstate Miller's account receivable			
	that was written off on July 10, 20X1,			
	and collected in full today.			

> **ABOUT ACCOUNTING**
>
> **Delinquent Invoices**
> Credit agency statistics suggest that between 70 and 80 percent of invoices that remain delinquent beyond one year are never paid.

If the amount recovered in a period subsequent to the write-off is credited to **Uncollectible Accounts Expense,** the expense for the period of recovery will be understated.

The balance in **Uncollectible Accounts Recovered** is shown on the income statement as Other Income.

Accounting for Other Receivables and Bad Debt Losses

As with accounts receivable, notes receivable and other receivables can prove uncollectible. Losses from uncollectible notes receivable and other receivables can be handled by the direct charge-off method or the allowance method. **Uncollectible Accounts Expense** and **Allowance for Doubtful Accounts** can be used for losses from all types of receivables.

MANAGERIAL IMPLICATIONS <<

MANAGING CREDIT

- It is essential that managers establish formal procedures for granting credit to customers, for tracking accounts receivable, for ensuring that customers are paying promptly, supervision of write-offs, and for collecting past-due accounts.
- Management needs to be informed about the losses from uncollectible accounts so they can:
  - establish effective credit policies,
  - weigh the cost of uncollectible account losses against the reduced sales volume caused by tight credit policies.
- Managers should use the allowance method for uncollectible accounts in order to match revenue and expenses.
- Managers are responsible for developing procedures to handle payments from customers whose accounts have been written off.

THINKING CRITICALLY

What reports would provide information to managers about how well the accounts receivable function is being managed?

Internal Control of Accounts Receivable

Internal control of the accounts receivable process is very important because accounts receivable represent one of the largest assets on the balance sheet for many companies. Common internal controls for accounts receivable include the following:

- Authorizing all credit sales.
- Developing procedures that ensure that all credit sales are recorded and customers' accounts are debited.
- Separating the following duties:
    - authorizing credit sales,
    - recording the accounts receivable transactions,
    - preparing bills or statements for customers,
    - mailing the bills or statements,
    - processing payments received from customers.
- Sending invoices and monthly statements.
- Authorizing charge-offs or write-offs of accounts.
- Aging the accounts receivable to allow management to identify and monitor slow-paying accounts.
- Investigating and taking appropriate action on past due accounts.
- Approving the write-off of accounts by authorized individuals only, and making the approvals in writing.
- Trying to collect past due accounts even if they have been written off.

>> **15-6 OBJECTIVE**
Recognize common internal controls for accounts receivable.

Section 2 Review

1. What basic accounting principle is the basis for criticizing the direct charge-off method for recording uncollectible accounts?
    a. historical cost
    b. revenue recognition
    c. periodicity of income
    d. matching

2. Under the direct charge-off method, when a specific account receivable is written off, what account is debited and what is the effect of the write-off on net income and on assets?
    a. Debit *Accounts Receivable;* the write-off decreases net income and total assets.
    b. Debit *Allowance for Uncollectible Accounts;* the write-off increases net income and total assets.
    c. Debit *Uncollectible Accounts Expense;* the write-off decreases net income and total assets.
    d. Debit *Uncollectible Accounts Expense;* the write-off increases net income and total assets.

3. If an account receivable of $900 charged off in 20X1 under the direct charge-off method is recovered in 20X2, in what way does accounting for the recovery differ from that used if the recovery had been made in 20X1?
    a. Recovery in the same year as the write-off is credited to *Uncollectible Accounts Expense.*
    b. Recovery in a subsequent year to the write-off is credited to *Uncollectible Accounts Recovered.*
    c. Both a and b are correct.
    d. Neither a nor b is correct.

4. On March 31, 20X1, Carter Company wrote off the $500 account of James Walker as uncollectible. The company uses the direct charge-off method. What account is debited and what account is credited to record the write-off?
    a. Debit *Uncollectible Accounts Expense;* credit *Accounts Receivable/James Walker.*
    b. Debit *Allowance for Uncollectible Accounts;* credit *Accounts Receivable/James Walker.*
    c. Debit *Uncollectible Accounts Recovered;* credit *Accounts Receivable/James Walker.*
    d. Debit *Accounts Receivable/James Walker;* credit *Uncollectible Accounts Expense.*

5. Assume the same facts as in question 4, except that Carter Company uses the allowance method. What account is debited and what account is credited to record the write-off?

a. Debit *Allowance for Doubtful Accounts;* credit *Accounts Receivable/James Walker.*

b. Debit *Accounts Receivable/James Walker;* credit *Allowance for Doubtful Accounts.*

c. Debit *Uncollectible Accounts Expense;* credit *Accounts Receivable/James Walker.*

d. Debit *Uncollectible Accounts Recovered;* credit *Accounts Receivable/James Walker.*

6. The following statements are true concerning the allowance method except:

   a. the allowance method is not exact and does not always match revenue and expenses.

   b. the allowance method can overstate accounts receivable.

   c. the allowance method is the only method acceptable for federal income tax purposes.

   d. the allowance method is the only method considered as generally accepted accounting.

7. If an account is written off under the direct charge-off method and is subsequently collected in a different accounting period, what account is debited and what account is credited to record the reinstatement and collection of the account?

   a. Debit *Uncollectible Accounts Recovered;* credit *Accounts Receivable/Customer.*

   b. Debit *Allowance for Doubtful Accounts;* credit *Accounts Receivable/Customer.*

   c. Debit *Accounts Receivable/Customer;* credit *Uncollectible Accounts Recovered.*

   d. Debit *Accounts Receivable/Customer;* credit *Allowance for Doubtful Accounts.*

   e. c and d are correct.

REVIEW Chapter Summary

When credit is extended, uncollectible accounts inevitably occur. Before receivables can be accurately presented in the balance sheet and net income can be properly measured, the accounts must be studied for possible adjustment to reflect such losses. In this chapter, you have learned how to adjust the value of receivables to account for uncollectible accounts.

Learning Objectives

15-1 Record the estimated expense from uncollectible accounts receivable using the allowance method.

The allowance method matches bad debt losses against revenue received in the same period. It is consistent with generally accepted accounting principles and is the preferred method for recognizing uncollectible accounts.

- The estimate of losses from uncollectible accounts can be based on a percentage (determined by experience) of credit sales. The estimated amount is debited to *Uncollectible Accounts Expense* and credited to *Allowance for Doubtful Accounts.*

- The estimate can be based on a single rate of expected noncollectibility of all accounts receivable. On the basis of past experience, the rate is applied to the balance of *Accounts Receivable* to determine the anticipated losses from the accounts. The balance in *Allowance for Doubtful Accounts* is adjusted to this estimated loss amount.

- The estimate of uncollectible accounts can also be based on the age of accounts receivable. A different percentage for credit losses is applied to each age group, and the resulting amounts are added together. The *Allowance for Doubtful Accounts* is adjusted to the balance computed in the aging total. The amount need to bring the *Allowance* up to date is debited to *Uncollectible Accounts Expense* and credited to the *Allowance for Doubtful Accounts.*

15-2 Charge off uncollectible accounts using the allowance method.

Under the allowance method, an account that proves uncollectible is written off by a debit to *Allowance for Doubtful Accounts* and a credit to both *Accounts Receivable* and the customer's account in the subsidiary ledger.

15-3 Record the collection of accounts previously written off using the allowance method.

Under the allowance method, if all or part of an account previously written off as uncollectible is subsequently paid, the amount being recovered is reinstated by a debit to *Accounts Receivable* and a credit to *Allowance for Doubtful Accounts* and the customer's account in the subsidiary ledger. Any cash paid at that time is recorded by debiting *Cash* and crediting *Accounts Receivable* and the customer's account in the subsidiary ledger.

15-4 Record losses from uncollectible accounts using the direct charge-off method.

Under the direct charge-off method of recording uncollectible accounts, *Uncollectible Accounts Expense* is debited at the time specific accounts receivable are deemed to be uncollectible. Because the expense resulting from uncollectible accounts may not be matched in the same accounting period with the revenue that gave rise to the receivable, this method is not generally acceptable. It does not conform to the matching principle. However, many small businesses, and even some larger ones with relatively small amounts of receivables, use the method. It is required to be used for federal income tax purposes.

15-5 Record the collection of accounts previously written off using the direct charge-off method.

Under the direct charge-off method, if an account previously charged off as uncollectible is subsequently collected in the same accounting period, the original entry to charge off the account (to the extent it is collected) is reversed. The reversing entry is a debit to *Accounts Receivable* and the customer's account in the subsidiary ledger and a credit to *Uncollectible Accounts Expense.* At the same time, an entry is made in the cash receipts journal debiting *Cash* and crediting *Accounts Receivable* and the customer's subsidiary ledger account. If the collection is made in a year subsequent to the year in which the write-off was recorded, the entry to record the reinstatement is a debit to *Accounts Receivable* and the customer's subsidiary account and a credit to *Uncollectible Accounts Recovered.* This is followed by a journal entry debiting *Cash* and crediting *Accounts Receivable* and the customer's subsidiary ledger account.

15-6 Recognize common internal controls for accounts receivable.

It is very important that management establish formal procedures for approving and granting credit, for keeping close watch on customers' accounts to assure they are paid promptly, and for properly assigning duties related to accounts receivable. A key element in internal control is to avoid giving any one person responsibility for a large number of the functions related to receivables. These functions include granting credit, recording accounts receivable transactions, preparing bills for customers, mailing the bills and statements, processing payments from customers, approving write-offs, and trying to collect past-due accounts.

15-7 Define the accounting terms new to this chapter.

Glossary

Aging the accounts receivable (p. 551) Classifying accounts receivable balances according to how long they have been outstanding

Allowance method (p. 547) A method of recording uncollectible accounts that estimates losses from uncollectible accounts and charges them to expense in the period when the sales are recorded

Direct charge-off method (p. 547) A method of recording uncollectible account losses as they occur

Valuation account (p. 547) An account, such as *Allowance for Doubtful Accounts,* whose balance is revalued or reappraised in light of reasonable expectations

Comprehensive Self Review

1. If the allowance method is used, what account is debited when an account is determined to be uncollectible?
2. Which method of accounting for uncollectible accounts, the direct charge-off method or the allowance method, is considered generally acceptable?
3. Which method of accounting for uncollectible accounts, the direct charge-off method or the allowance method, must be used for tax purposes?
4. A business using the direct charge-off method charged off the account of Samuel Adams in 20X1. Adams made full payment in 20X2. What account is credited when the account is reinstated?
5. In Blevins Company, the accounts receivable clerk prepares and mails statements to customers, opens mail, and makes a list of receipts, then deposits the cash and approves the write-off of delinquent accounts. Comment on this arrangement of duties.
6. When a specific account is written off under the allowance method, does the net accounts receivable balance increase or decrease? Why?

(Answers to Comprehensive Self Review are at the end of the chapter.)

Discussion Questions

1. Explain the purpose of the allowance method of accounting for losses from uncollectible accounts.
2. Name three approaches to estimating losses from uncollectible accounts when the allowance method is used.
3. Suppose that the estimate of uncollectible accounts is based on credit sales and that *Allowance for Doubtful Accounts* has a debit balance before the adjustment is made. Explain how this situation is handled.

4. If a company is interested primarily in matching expenses and revenues each period, would it base its estimate of uncollectible accounts on sales (or net credit sales) or on accounts receivable? Explain.

5. What is meant by aging the accounts receivable?

6. Under the allowance method, what account is credited in the adjusting entry to record estimated uncollectible accounts?

7. Under the allowance method, what entry is made when a specific customer's account is deemed to be uncollectible?

8. What basic accounting concepts, assumptions, principles, or constraints support the allowance method?

9. Explain how to record the collection of an account receivable in the same year in which it was previously written off if the allowance method of recording estimated doubtful accounts is used.

10. Suppose that the estimate of uncollectible accounts is based on the aging of accounts receivable and that the *Allowance for Uncollectible Accounts* has a credit balance before the adjustment is made. Explain how this situation is handled.

11. How is *Uncollectible Accounts Expense* shown on the income statement?

12. How is *Allowance for Doubtful Accounts* shown in the balance sheet?

13. Explain the direct charge-off method for recording uncollectible accounts expense.

14. What are the major weaknesses of the direct charge-off method?

15. Under what conditions would the direct charge-off method be appropriate?

16. What entry is made to record an uncollectible account under the direct charge-off method?

17. Under the direct charge-off method, what entry is made when a firm collects an account that was charged off in a prior year?

18. List some duties that should routinely be separated as part of the internal control procedures for accounts receivable.

19. List some common internal controls for accounts receivable.

20. At December 31, 20X1, Gerald Company had accounts receivable of $1,500,000 and an allowance for doubtful accounts of $8,250. On January 1, 20X2, Gerald Company wrote off a $1,500 bad debt against the allowance for doubtful accounts. There were no other accounts receivable transactions on January 1. What is the net realizable value of accounts receivable (a) before the bad debt write-off and (b) after the bad debt write-off?

APPLICATIONS

Exercises

Estimating and recording uncollectible accounts on the basis of net credit sales. ◄ Exercise 15.1

On December 31, 20X1, certain account balances at Galaxy Company were as follows before year-end adjustments:

Objective 15-1

Accounts Receivable	$ 941,500
Allowance for Uncollectible Accounts (credit)	1,860
Sales	9,205,500
Sales Returns and Allowances	38,650

A further examination of the records showed that the "Sales" included $956,200 of cash sales during the year. Of the sales returns and allowances, $33,300 came from credit sales. Assume that Galaxy Company estimates its losses from uncollectible accounts to be 0.2 percent of net credit sales. Compute the estimated amount of *Uncollectible Accounts Expense* for 20X1 and prepare the journal entry to record the provision for uncollectible accounts.

Exercise 15.2
Objective 15-1

▶ **Estimating and recording uncollectible accounts on the basis of accounts receivable when there is a credit balance in *Allowance for Doubtful Accounts*.**

Assume that Galaxy Company (Exercise 15.1) makes its estimate of uncollectible accounts on December 31 as 3.2 percent of total accounts receivable. Compute the estimated amount of uncollectible accounts and give the general journal entry to record the provision for uncollectible accounts. (Obtain any information you need from Exercise 15.1.)

Exercise 15.3
Objective 15-1

▶ **Estimating and recording uncollectible accounts on the basis of accounts receivable when there is a debit balance in *Allowance for Doubtful Accounts*.**

On December 31, 20X1, before adjusting entries, the balances of selected accounts of the Xavier Equipment Company were as follows:

Accounts Receivable	$930,000
Allowance for Uncollectible Accounts (debit balance)	3,000 dr.

The company has determined that historically about 3.4 percent of accounts receivable are never collected and uses this basis to determine its bad debts provision. Give the journal entry to record the company's estimated loss from uncollectible accounts on December 31.

Exercise 15.4
Objective 15-2

▶ **Recording actual uncollectible amounts under the allowance method.**

On April 30, 20X1, Richey Plumbing, which uses the allowance method, decided that the $14,800 account of Alexis Watson was worthless and should be written off. Give the general journal entry to record the write-off.

Exercise 15.5
Objective 15-3

▶ **Recording the collection of an account written off in the same year under the allowance method.**

On December 8, 20X1, after a threatened lawsuit by Richey Plumbing, Alexis Watson paid the $14,800 account charged off on April 30, 20X1 (Exercise 15.4). Give the entries in general journal form to reinstate Watson's account and to record the receipt of her check.

Exercise 15.6
Objective 15-3

▶ **Recording the collection of an account written off in a prior year under the allowance method.**

Assume the same facts as in Exercise 15.5, except that the recovery of the $14,800 from Alexis Watson was received on February 28, 20X2. Give the entry in general journal form to record the reinstatement of Watson's account and to record the receipt of her check.

Exercise 15.7
Objective 15-4

▶ **Recording uncollectible accounts using the direct charge-off method.**

Conrod Utilities Services Company uses the direct charge-off method to record uncollectible accounts. On September 10, 20X1, the company learned that Shirley Cosby, a customer who owed $3,360, had moved and left no forwarding address. Conrod Utilities concluded that no part of the debt was collectible. Prepare the general journal entry to write off the account.

Exercise 15.8
Objective 15-5

▶ **Recording collection of an account previously written off using the direct charge-off method.**

On December 8, 20X1, Conrod Utilities Services Company received a check for $1,680 from Shirley Cosby, whose $3,360 account was written off on September 10 (Exercise 15.7). In the accompanying letter, Cosby apologized and said she probably would be unable to pay any of the remaining balance. Give the general journal entry necessary (the entry in the cash receipts journal has been made).

Exercise 15.9
Objective 15-5

Recording collection of an account written off in a prior period under the direct charge-off method.

Use the information given in Exercise 15.8, except assume that Conrod Utilities received the check for $1,680 on January 28, 20X2 (instead of on December 8, 20X1). Give the general journal entry necessary. The cash receipt has already been entered in the cash receipts journal.

PROBLEMS

Problem Set A

Problem 15.1A
Objectives 15-1, 15-2, 15-3

Estimating and recording uncollectible accounts transactions on the basis of sales.

Euro Leather Products sells leather clothing at both wholesale and retail. The company has found that there is a higher rate of uncollectible accounts from retail credit sales than from wholesale credit sales. Euro computes its estimated loss from uncollectible accounts at the end of each year. The amount is based on the rates of loss that the firm has developed from experience for each division. A separate computation is made for each of the two types of sales. The firm uses the percentage of net credit sales method.

As of December 31, 20X1, **Accounts Receivable** has a balance of $402,000, and **Allowance for Doubtful Accounts** has a debit balance of $426. The following table provides a breakdown of the net credit sales for the year 20X1 and the estimated rates of loss:

Category	Amount	Estimated Rate of Loss
Wholesale	$2,140,000	0.6%
Retail	600,000	1.1

INSTRUCTIONS

1. Compute the estimated amount of uncollectible accounts expense for each of the two categories of net credit sales for the year.
2. Prepare an adjusting entry in general journal form to provide for the estimated uncollectible accounts on December 31, 20X1. Use **Uncollectible Accounts Expense**.
3. Show how **Accounts Receivable** and **Allowance for Doubtful Accounts** should appear on the balance sheet of Euro Leather Products as of December 31, 20X1.
4. On January 20, 20X2, the account receivable of Chris Cobb Clothiers, amounting to $930, is determined to be uncollectible and is to be written off. Record this transaction in the general journal.
5. On November 26, 20X2, the attorneys for Euro turned over a check for $930 that they obtained from Chris Cobb Clothiers in settlement of its account, which had been written off on January 20. The money has already been recorded in the cash receipts journal. Give the general journal entry to reverse the original write-off.

Analyze: When the financial statements are prepared for the year ended December 31, 20X1, what net accounts receivable should be reported?

Problem 15.2A

Objectives 15-1, 15-2, 15-3

Estimating and recording uncollectible account transactions on the basis of accounts receivable.

The schedule of accounts receivable by age, shown below, was prepared for the Lucero Company at the end of the firm's fiscal year on December 31, 20X1:

	LUCERO COMPANY Schedule of Accounts Receivable by Age December 31, 20X1				
				Past Due—Days	
Account	Balance	Current	1–30	31–60	Over 60
Adson, Paul	$ 850.00	$ 850.00			
Allen, Alfred	1,000.00		$ 700.00	$ 300.00	
Ash, John	516.00				$ 516.00
Bae, John	260.00	260.00			
Barker, Kelsie	144.00	94.00	50.00		
Bentley, Maggie	560.00	220.00	250.00	90.00	
Blair, Herman	116.00			74.00	42.00
(All other accts.)	47,054.00	39,576.00	5,000.00	1,536.00	942.00
Totals	$50,500.00	$41,000.00	$6,000.00	$2,000.00	$1,500.00

INSTRUCTIONS

1. Compute the estimated uncollectible accounts at the end of the year using the following rates:

Current	2%
1–30 days past due	4%
31–60 days past due	10%
Over 60 days past due	30%

2. As of December 31, 20X1, there is a credit balance of $308 in *Allowance for Doubtful Accounts.* Compute the amount of the adjustment for uncollectible accounts expense that must be made as part of the adjusting entries.

3. In general journal form, record the adjustment for the estimated losses. Use *Uncollectible Accounts Expense* and *Allowance for Doubtful Accounts.*

4. On May 10, 20X2, the $516 account receivable of John Ash was recognized as uncollectible. Record this entry.

5. On June 12, 20X2, a check for $300 was received from Zeke Martin to apply to his account, which had been written off on November 8, 20X1, as uncollectible. Record the reversal of the previous write-off in the general journal. The cash obtained has already been entered in the cash receipts journal.

6. Suppose that instead of aging the accounts receivable, the company estimated the uncollectible accounts to be 2 percent of the total accounts receivable on December 31, 20X1. Give the general journal entry to record the adjustment for estimated losses from uncollectible accounts. Assume that *Allowance for Doubtful Accounts* has a credit balance of $308 before the adjusting entry.

Analyze: What impact would the change in estimation method described in item 6 have on the net income for fiscal 20X1?

Using different methods to estimate uncollectible accounts.

◀ **Problem 15.3A**
Objective 15-1

The balances of selected accounts of the Davidson Company on December 31, 20X1, are given below:

Accounts Receivable	$ 850,000
Allowance for Doubtful Accounts (credit)	4,000
Total Sales	10,050,000
Sales Returns and Allowances (total)	250,000

(Credit sales were $8,600,000. Returns and allowances on these sales were $210,000.)

INSTRUCTIONS

1. Compute the amount to be charged to *Uncollectible Accounts Expense* under each of the following different assumptions:
   a. Uncollectible accounts are estimated to be 0.2 percent of net credit sales.
   b. Experience has shown that about 3.2 percent of the accounts receivable will prove worthless.
2. Suppose *Allowance for Doubtful Accounts* has a debit balance of $3,500 instead of a credit balance of $4,000, but all other account balances remain the same. Compute the amount to be charged to *Uncollectible Accounts Expense* under each assumption in item 1.

Analyze: If you were the owner of Davidson Company and wished to maximize profits reported for 20X1, which method would you prefer to use?

Recording uncollectible account transactions under the direct charge-off method.

◀ **Problem 15.4A**
Objectives 15-4, 15-5

Pittman Company records uncollectible accounts expense as they occur. Selected transactions for 20X1 and 20X2 are described below. The accounts involved in these transactions are *Notes Receivable, Accounts Receivable,* and *Uncollectible Accounts Expense.* Record each transaction in general journal form.

DATE		TRANSACTIONS
20X1		
Feb.	7	The $1,400 account receivable of Marie Cousins is determined to be uncollectible and is to be written off.
May	16	Because of the death of Heidi Martin, her account receivable of $2,200 is considered uncollectible and is to be written off.
July	2	Received $700 from Marie Cousins in partial payment of her account, which had been written off on February 7. The cash obtained has already been recorded in the cash receipts journal. There is doubt that the balance of Cousins's account will be collected.
July	29	Received $700 from Marie Cousins to complete payment of her account, which had been written off on February 7. The cash obtained has already been recorded in the cash receipts journal.
Aug.	18	The $850 account receivable of Neal Wilder is determined to be uncollectible and is to be written off.
20X2		
Sept.	28	Received $1,100 from the estate of Heidi Martin as part of the settlement of affairs. This amount is applicable to the account receivable written off on May 16, 20X1. The cash obtained has already been recorded in the cash receipts journal.

Analyze: Based on these transactions, what net uncollectible accounts expense was recorded for the year 20X1?

Problem Set B

Problem 15.1B
Objectives 15-1, 15-2, 15-3

▶ **Estimating and recording uncollectible account transactions on the basis of sales.**

Lord Taylor Plumbing Company provides plumbing installations for both business and individual customers. The company records sales for the two types of customers in separate *Sales* accounts. The company's experience has been that each type of sales has a different rate of losses from uncollectible accounts. Thus, the total that the company charges off for these losses at the end of each accounting period is based on two computations (one computation for each sales account). The firm uses the percentage of net credit sales method.

As of December 31, 20X1, *Accounts Receivable* has a balance of $281,500 and *Allowance for Doubtful Accounts* has a credit balance of $600. The following table provides a breakdown of the credit sales by division for the year 20X1 and the estimated rates of loss:

Division	Amount	Rate of Loss
Business	$1,800,000	0.4%
Individual	1,200,000	0.9%

INSTRUCTIONS

1. Compute the estimated amount of losses in uncollectible accounts expense for each of the two types of sales for the year.
2. Prepare an adjusting entry in general journal form to provide for the estimated losses from uncollectible accounts. Use *Uncollectible Accounts Expense* and *Allowance for Doubtful Accounts*.
3. Show how *Accounts Receivable* and *Allowance for Doubtful Accounts* should appear on the balance sheet of Lord Taylor Plumbing Company as of December 31, 20X1.
4. On January 28, 20X2, the account receivable of Brown Enterprises, amounting to $824, is determined to be uncollectible and is to be written off. Record the transaction in general journal form.
5. On June 15, 20X2, the attorneys for Lord Taylor Plumbing Company turned over a check for $400 that they obtained from Brown Enterprises in settlement of its account, which had been written off on January 28, 20X2. The money has already been entered in the cash receipts journal. Record the general journal entry to reinstate the proper amount of Brown's account.

Analyze: Assume that Lord Taylor Plumbing Company uses a predetermined 7.0 percent rate on total accounts receivable to compute the estimated amount of uncollectible accounts receivable. What would be the amount charged to *Uncollectible Accounts Expense* on December 31, 20X1?

Problem 15.2B
Objectives 15-1, 15-2, 15-3

▶ **Estimating and recording uncollectible account transactions on the basis of accounts receivable.**

The schedule of accounts receivable by age shown below was prepared for the Custom Windows Shop at the end of the firm's fiscal year on July 31, 20X1:

CUSTOM WINDOWS SHOP Schedule of Accounts Receivable by Age July 31, 20X1					
			Past Due—Days		
Account	Balance	Current	1–30	31–60	Over 60
Alvarado, Steve	$ 300.00	$ 175.00	$ 125.00		
Brass, Dennis	608.00	120.00	400.00	$ 88.00	
Chang, Charles	196.00	196.00			
Cook, Elaine	38.00	38.00			
Edwards, Brad	632.00			416.00	$ 216.00
Kieffer, Carl	264.00		264.00		
(All other accts.)	14,610.00	8,286.00	3,600.00	1,894.00	830.00
Totals	$16,648.00	$8,815.00	$4,389.00	$2,398.00	$1,046.00

INSTRUCTIONS

1. Compute the estimated uncollectible accounts at the end of the year using these rates:

Current	1%
1–30 days past due	4%
31–60 days past due	14%
Over 60 days past due	40%

2. As of July 31, 20X1, there is a debit balance of $310.00 in *Allowance for Doubtful Accounts*. Compute the amount of the adjustment for uncollectible accounts expense that must be made as part of the adjusting entries.

3. In general journal form, record the adjustment for the estimated losses. Use *Uncollectible Accounts Expense* and *Allowance for Doubtful Accounts*.

4. On August 28, 20X1, the account receivable of Jorge Urbina, amounting to $182, was recognized as uncollectible. Record this write-off in the general journal.

5. On September 21, 20X1, a check for $250 was received from Barry King to apply on his $250 account, which had been written off as uncollectible on December 19, 20X0. Record the reversal of the previous write-off in the general journal. The cash obtained has already been entered in the cash receipts journal.

6. Suppose that instead of aging the accounts receivable, the company estimated the uncollectible accounts to be 8 percent of the total accounts receivable on July 31, 20X1. Assume also that *Allowance for Doubtful Accounts* has a credit balance of $125.00 before the adjusting entry. Give the general journal entry to record the adjustment for estimated losses from uncollectible accounts.

Analyze: Based on the percentages presented in item 1, what is the average uncollectible rate for all accounts receivable for 20X1?

Problem 15.3B

Objectives 15-1, 15-2, 15-3

▶ **Using different methods to estimate uncollectible accounts.**

The balances of selected accounts of Greece Sportswear Company on December 31, 20X1, are given below. Credit sales totaled $9,620,000. The returns and allowances on these sales were $55,000.

Accounts Receivable	$905,0000
Allowance for Doubtful Accounts	1,530 (credit)
Total Sales	10,350,000
Total Sales Returns and Allowances	705,000

INSTRUCTIONS

1. Compute the amount to be charged to *Uncollectible Accounts Expense* under each of the following different sets of assumptions. Round computations to the nearest dollar.

   a. Bad debt losses are estimated to be 0.32 percent of net credit sales.

   b. Experience has shown that about 3.2 percent of the accounts receivable are uncollectible.

2. Suppose that *Allowance for Doubtful Accounts* has a *debit* balance of $1,530 instead of a credit balance of that amount before adjustments, but all other account balances remain the same. Compute the amount to be charged to *Uncollectible Accounts Expense* under each of the assumptions listed in the first instruction.

Analyze: Which method results in the highest uncollectible expense for the period?

Problem 15.4B

Objectives 15-4, 15-5

▶ **Recording transactions related to uncollectible accounts using the direct charge-off method.**

Interactive Planning Software uses the direct charge-off method to account for uncollectible accounts expenses as they occur. Selected transactions for 20X1 and 20X2 follow. The accounts involved are *Accounts Receivable, Notes Receivable,* and *Uncollectible Accounts Expense.* Record each transaction in general journal form.

DATE		TRANSACTIONS
20X1		
March	15	Antonio Castillo, a credit customer, dies owing the firm $6,000. The account is written off.
April	22	Barry Lewis, a credit customer who owes the firm $4,000, declares bankruptcy. The amount is considered uncollectible and written off.
June	16	The executor of the estate of Antonio Castillo sends the firm $1,600 in partial settlement of the account written off on March 15. The cash obtained has already been recorded.
July	13	The bankruptcy court sends the firm $2,400 in settlement of the account receivable of Barry Lewis that was written off on April 22. The cash obtained has already been recorded in the cash receipts journal.
Oct.	8	The account owed by a customer, Helen Demaris, in the amount of $2,700 is determined worthless and is written off.
20X2		
Feb.	12	Barry Lewis pays the remainder of the account that had previously been written off. (See transactions of April 22 and July 13). The cash obtained has already been recorded in the cash receipts journal.

Analyze: When the worksheet is prepared at the end of 20X1, what balance should be listed for *Uncollectible Accounts Expense*? Assume that the transactions given are the only transactions that affected the account.

Critical Thinking Problem 15.1

Managing Uncollectible Accounts

The Family Place Kitchen is a small chain of kitchen remodeling stores. The company's year-end trial balance on December 31, 20X1, included the information shown below:

Accounts Receivable	$495,220
Allowance for Doubtful Accounts (credit)	14,100

Net credit sales for 20X1 were $4,450,000. *Allowance for Doubtful Accounts* has not yet been adjusted.

INSTRUCTIONS

1. At the end of 20X1, the following additional accounts receivable are deemed uncollectible:

Hayward Anderson	$ 5,400
Richard Bennett	1,090
Donald O'Brian	2,100
Sergio Tirado	2,615
Columbus Wilkerson	1,550
Total	$12,755

    Prepare the December 31, 20X1, journal entry to write off the above accounts. Of the accounts to be charged off, $8,600 are more than 60 days past due and $4,155 are from 31 to 60 days past due. Post this transaction to the T-accounts for *Accounts Receivable* and *Allowance for Doubtful Accounts.*

2. Assume that the company uses the percentage of sales method to estimate uncollectible accounts expense. After analyzing the prior year's activities, management determined that losses from uncollectible accounts for 20X1 should be 0.32 percent of net credit sales. Prepare the necessary adjusting journal entry. Round calculations to the nearest dollar.

3. Assume that the company uses the aging of accounts receivable method. The following information was furnished by the credit manager for use in calculating the estimated loss from uncollectible accounts. The balances of accounts were computed prior to the charge-offs in item 1.

Receivable Category	Estimated Loss Rate	Balances of Accounts (before charge-offs)
Current	1%	$405,000
1–30 days past due	5%	45,000
31–60 days past due	10%	24,700
Over 60 days past due	40%	20,520
Total		$495,220

    Compute the estimated uncollectible accounts as of December 31, 20X1, rounded to the nearest dollar.

4. Prepare the necessary adjusting journal entry to record the estimated uncollectible accounts expense on December 31 using the aging method. Post this entry to the T-accounts for *Accounts Receivable* and *Allowance for Doubtful Accounts.*

Analyze: If a company has used three different methods for estimating uncollectible accounts for the past three years, which basic accounting principle may have been violated? Why?

Critical Thinking Problem 15.2

Credit Decisions and Consequences

Brecha Hogan is president of Hogan Company, a manufacturer of toys for children. For the past 10 years, the company has sold its product to both wholesale and retail dealers of toys in the northeastern United States. Over the years, the company has come to know its customers well. While all sales are made on credit, few credit losses have occurred. The company's experience has shown that an annual provision for uncollectible accounts of 0.3 of 1 percent of sales is adequate in the old territory.

Early in 20X1, Hogan Company decided to expand and develop a new sales base in the southeastern United States. Hogan was pleased when credit sales of $800,000 were achieved in the new territory during the year. To achieve this level of sales and get a foothold in the new territory, though, credit was allowed to some customers with lower credit ratings than had been granted in the past. Given its liberal credit policies in the new territory Hogan estimates that the provision in the new territory should be 4 percent above actual first year's losses in the initial period of development.

The credit losses connected with sales in the southeast became apparent by the end of 20X1. The following losses from new territory customers had been identified before year-end:

1. On September 30, it was determined that nothing could be collected from Bedford Toy Outlets, which owed Hogan $88,000. The account was written off.

2. On December 10, another new customer, Forever Young Fun Shops, which owed Hogan $220,000, entered receivership. On that date Hogan was offered, and accepted, a check for $110,000 in final settlement of the debt. The balance was charged off.

3. On December 18, Technology Toys went out of business, and no collection of the $26,800 owed Hogan is anticipated. The account was charged off.

The following additional information about the old territory became available on December 31:

- Sales in the old territory totaled $25,120,000 in 20X1. Sales in the new territory totaled $800,000 in 20X1.
- Accounts receivable of $90,400 attributed to customers in the old sales territory were determined to be uncollectible and were written off.

INSTRUCTIONS

1. Give the journal entry to record total sales for the old and new territory for Hogan Company for 20X1. All sales are on account. Use December 31, 20X1, as the date to record the entry.
2. Give the journal entries to record the write-off of accounts in the new territory.
3. Give the journal entry to record the write-off of accounts in the old territory.
4. Give the entry on December 31 to record uncollectible accounts expense for 20X1 for both territories. Make the calculation using the percentages developed by Hogan.
5. Assume that the *Allowance for Doubtful Accounts* had a credit balance of $24,800 on September 30 before any of the above entries were made. Calculate the balance in the allowance account after all of the above entries have been posted.

Analyze: Based on actual losses experienced by Hogan in the new territory, are the credit granting policies for the new territory too liberal? Explain.

BUSINESS CONNECTIONS

Uncollectible Accounts

Managerial FOCUS

1. Why would managers use the allowance method for recording uncollectible accounts instead of the direct charge-off method?
2. Should the sales department be given final authority for approving credit applications? Why?
3. Why is an account receivable that was written off as uncollectible reinstated if it is later collected?
4. Why does management separate the authority to charge off uncollectible accounts from the authority to receive customers' cash?

Internal Control for Accounts Receivable

Internal control of the accounts receivable process is very important because accounts receivable represent one of the largest assets on the balance sheet for many companies. Discuss at least nine common internal controls for accounts receivable.

Balance Sheet

McCormick & Company, Inc., reported the following in its *2018 Annual Report:*

Consolidated Balance Sheets at November 30, 2018 (millions)		
	2018	2017
Trade accounts receivable, less allowances of $6.4 for 2018 and $6.6 for 2017	$518.1	$555.1
Total current assets	$1,479.9	$1,617.0

Analyze:

1. What were total trade accounts receivable at November 30, 2018, before the allowance was deducted?
2. Compute the percentage increase or decrease in net trade accounts receivable from 2017 to 2018 reported on the consolidated balance sheet.
3. What percentage of total current assets on November 30, 2018, are made up of net trade accounts receivable?

Life of an Invoice

In small groups, create a scenario for the life of an invoice. How does a sale become uncollectible? Start at the sale of a product, when it became uncollectible, and finally when it was paid. Present each account receivable scenario to the class. Be sure to include all the journal entries.

Answers to Comprehensive Self Review

1. *Allowance for Doubtful Accounts*
2. Allowance method is generally accepted.
3. The direct charge-off method
4. *Uncollectible Accounts Recovered*
5. This is an unsatisfactory arrangement because there is no separation of duties and the current arrangement places in the hands of one person the opportunity to misappropriate funds and cover it up in the accounting records without detection by others.
6. Remains the same. The debit to *Allowance for Doubtful Accounts* offsets the credit to *Accounts Receivable.*

Notes Payable and Notes Receivable

Chapter 16

Tero Vesalainen/Shutterstock

www.bankofamerica.com

When a business wants to buy something, but doesn't have the immediate cash necessary to make the purchase, it may need to borrow money in order to accomplish its goals. That is where companies like Bank of America get involved.

Bank of America is an American multinational investment bank and financial services company based in Charlotte, North Carolina, with central hubs in New York City, London, Hong Kong, Minneapolis, and Toronto. It is the second largest banking institution in the United States after JP Morgan Chase. Its primary financial services revolve around commercial banking, wealth management, and investment banking. Founded in San Francisco, California, as the Bank of Italy in 1904, the bank was acquired in a Charlotte-based NationsBank acquisition for $62 billion. Following what then was the largest bank acquisition in history, Bank of America was founded. Through a series of mergers and acquisitions, the bank built upon its commerce banking business by establishing Merrill Lynch for wealth management in 2008 and Bank of America Merrill Lynch for investment banking in 2009.

As of August 2018, Bank of America has a $313.5 billion market capitalization, making it the 13th largest company in the world. As the sixth largest American public company, it reported sales of $102.98 billion as of June 2018. Bank of America was ranked number 24 on the 2018 Fortune 500 rankings of the largest U.S. corporations. As the largest lender in the United States in 2008 during the worst recession in 70 years, Bank of America has faced numerous challenges. But with a laser-focused strategy for survival, the bank not only has survived but is striving.

Looking across every customer group it serves—whether a retail customer, a small business, or a large corporate client—the company works to maintain and build strong relationships, and this strategy is driving results, and its prospects for the future are outstanding.

thinking critically

If a small business needs to borrow money, what considerations does it need to think about before it borrows the money?

LEARNING OBJECTIVES

- **16-1** Determine whether an instrument meets all the requirements of negotiability.
- **16-2** Calculate the interest on a note.
- **16-3** Determine the maturity date of a note.
- **16-4** Record routine notes payable transactions.
- **16-5** Record discounted notes payable transactions.
- **16-6** Record routine notes receivable transactions.
- **16-7** Compute the proceeds from a discounted note receivable, and record transactions related to discounting of notes receivable.
- **16-8** Understand how to use bank drafts and trade acceptances and how to record transactions related to those instruments.
- **16-9** Define the accounting terms new to this chapter.

NEW TERMS

- bank draft
- banker's year
- bill of lading
- cashier's check
- commercial draft
- contingent liability
- discounting
- draft
- face value
- interest
- maturity value
- negotiable instrument
- note payable
- note receivable
- principal
- sight draft
- time draft
- trade acceptance

Section 1

SECTION OBJECTIVES

>> 16-1 Determine whether an instrument meets all the requirements of negotiability.

WHY IT'S IMPORTANT
Companies use financial documents prepared according to legal standards.

>> 16-2 Calculate the interest on a note.

WHY IT'S IMPORTANT
Interest represents revenue or expense.

>> 16-3 Determine the maturity date of a note.

WHY IT'S IMPORTANT
Funds must be available to pay the note when due.

>> 16-4 Record routine notes payable transactions.

WHY IT'S IMPORTANT
The accounting records must reflect all the firm's financial obligations.

>> 16-5 Record discounted notes payable transactions.

WHY IT'S IMPORTANT
Interest on notes is sometimes deducted in advance.

TERMS TO LEARN

banker's year
discounting
face value
interest
maturity value
negotiable instrument
note payable
principal

Accounting for Notes Payable

In this chapter, you will learn about negotiable instruments, in particular, promissory notes.

>> 16-1 OBJECTIVE
Determine whether an instrument meets all the requirements of negotiability.

Negotiable Instruments

The law covering negotiable instruments is a part of the Uniform Commercial Code (UCC). The UCC has been adopted by all of the states. A **negotiable instrument** is a financial document, containing a promise or order to pay, that meets all the requirements of the UCC in order to be transferable to another party. The UCC requirements specify that to be negotiable, an instrument must:

- be in writing and must be signed by the maker or drawer,
- contain an unconditional promise or order to pay a definite amount of money,
- be payable either on demand or at a future time that is fixed or that can be determined,
- be payable to the order of a specific person or to the bearer,
- clearly name or identify the drawee if addressed to a drawee.

Checks are negotiable instruments. Another important negotiable instrument is the promissory note. Promissory notes may be either notes payable or notes receivable.

FIGURE 16.1 Promissory Note

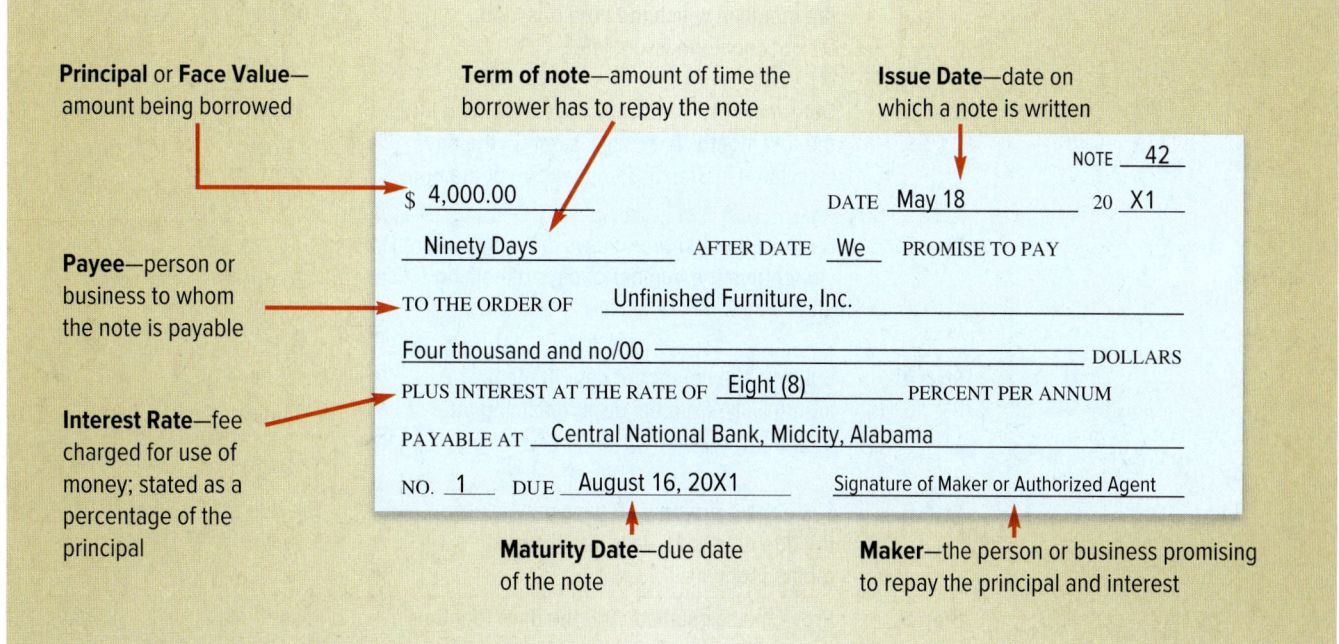

Notes Payable

On May 18, 20X1, Kathy's Kitchens purchased store equipment for $4,000 from Unfinished Furniture, Inc. The supplier agreed to accept payment in 90 days if Kathy Kaymark, the owner, signed the promissory note shown in Figure 16.1. A promissory note is a written promise to pay a certain amount of money at a specific future time. For Unfinished Furniture, Inc., the promissory note provides more legal protection than an account payable.

The promissory note is a negotiable instrument. It is in writing and signed by Kathy Kaymark, owner of Kathy's Kitchens. It is an unconditional promise to pay a definite sum, $4,000. It is payable on a date that can be determined exactly, 90 days after May 18. It is payable to a specific party, Unfinished Furniture, Inc. Although not necessary for negotiability, the note specifies a rate of interest, 8 percent. The maturity value of this note is $4,080.

Calculating the Interest on a Note

>> 16-2 OBJECTIVE
Calculate the interest on a note.

Interest is the fee charged for the use of money. Interest is calculated using the following formula:

$$\text{Interest} = \text{Principal} \times \text{Rate} \times \text{Time}$$

The time period is indicated in fractions of a year. A 360-day period, called a **banker's year,** is used for simplicity to calculate interest on a note. Interest on the note in Figure 16.1 is $80 ($4,000 × 0.08 × 90/360).

The note in Figure 16.1 shows a $4,000 amount, called the **principal, face value,** or *face amount.* The **maturity value** is the total amount (principal plus interest) that must be paid when a note comes due. For the note in Figure 16.1, the maturity value is $4,080 ($4,000 + $80).

Calculating the Maturity Date of a Note

>> 16-3 OBJECTIVE
Determine the maturity date of a note.

A note's maturity date is the number of days from the date of issue until it is due. The issue date itself is not counted. For example, a 30-day note issued on January 1 matures on January 31, 30 days after January 1. Let's find the maturity date for the note in Figure 16.1.

Step 1.	Determine the number of days remaining in the month in which the note is issued. Do not count the issue date.	31 days −18 days 13 days	in May issue date
Step 2.	Determine the number of days remaining after the first month. To do this, subtract the days calculated in Step 1 from the term of the note.	90 days −13 days 77 days	term of note May days remaining
Step 3.	Subtract the number of days in the next month (June) from the number of days remaining after Step 2.	77 days −30 days 47 days	in June remaining
Step 4.	Subtract the number of days in the next month (July) from the days remaining after Step 3.	47 days −31 days 16 days	in July remaining
Step 5.	Since there are only 16 days remaining, the due date is 16 days into the next month (August).	The due date is August 16.	
Step 6.	Prove the calculation. Add the days together to see if they equal the period of the note.	Proof: May June July August Total	13 days 30 days 31 days 16 days 90 days

Sometimes the term of a note is described in months instead of days. In this case, the maturity date is determined by counting ahead to the same date of the following month or months. For example, a three-month note issued on May 18 is due on August 18, regardless of the number of days in the period. If a note is issued at the end of a month, and there is no corresponding date in the month due, then the note is due on the first day of the following month. For example, a six-month note issued on August 30 should mature on February 30. Because there is no February 30, the note matures on March 1.

>> **16-4 OBJECTIVE**

Record routine notes payable transactions.

Recording the Issuance of a Note Payable

A **note payable** is a liability that represents a written promise by the maker of the note (the debtor) to pay another party (the creditor) a specified amount at a specified future date. The following shows how Kathy's Kitchens records the May 18 transaction to issue a 90-day, $4,000 note payable at 8 percent annual interest to purchase store equipment:

THE BOTTOM LINE

Issuance of Note Payable

Income Statement
No effect

Balance Sheet
Assets ↑ 4,000
Liabilities ↑ 4,000
No effect on equity

GENERAL JOURNAL PAGE 3

	DATE	DESCRIPTION	POST. REF.	DEBIT	CREDIT	
1	20X1					1
6	May 18	Store Equipment		4 000 00		6
7		Notes Payable—Trade			4 000 00	7
8		Issued note payable to Unfinished				8
9		Furniture, Inc., for purchase of store				9
10		equipment				10

Recording Payment of a Note and Interest

On the maturity date, August 16, Kathy's Kitchens pays the $4,000 principal plus the $80 in interest. This transaction is recorded as follows:

	GENERAL JOURNAL			PAGE 6	
DATE	DESCRIPTION	POST. REF.	DEBIT	CREDIT	
20X1					1
Aug 16	Notes Payable—Trade		4 000 00		11
	Interest Expense		80 00		12
	Cash			4 080 00	13
	Payment of May 18 note to				14
	Unfinished Furniture, Inc.				15

THE BOTTOM LINE
Payment of Note Payable

Income Statement
Expenses ↑ 80
Net Income ↓ 80

Balance Sheet
Assets ↓ 4,080
Liabilities ↓ 4,000
Equity ↓ 80

Renewing or Making a Partial Payment on a Note

If the issuer of a note asks and receives an extension to the maturity date, no additional accounting entries are required. On the extended maturity date, an entry is made to record payment of the note and interest for the entire period of the debt.

Sometimes at the maturity date only part of the note is paid. The partial payment is shown on the existing note, or the existing note is canceled and a new note is issued for the balance.

Recording the Issuance of a Discounted Note Payable

>> **16-5 OBJECTIVE**
Record discounted notes payable transactions.

Businesses often borrow money from banks and sign notes payable as evidence of the debts. Banks always charge interest on loans. For some promissory notes, such as the one to Unfinished Furniture, Inc., in Figure 16.1, interest is paid on the maturity date. The interest on a bank loan is usually paid at maturity. Often, however, the bank deducts the interest in advance, and the borrower receives only the difference between the face amount of the note and the interest on it to maturity. This practice of deducting the interest in advance from the principal on a note payable is called **discounting**.

On June 1, Kathy's Kitchens signed a $10,000, 6 percent, 60-day note payable with the bank. The note was issued at a discount. The interest is $100.

$$\text{Interest} = \text{Principal} \times \text{Rate} \times \text{Time}$$
$$\$100 = \$10,000 \times 0.06 \times (60/360)$$

The bank deducted the $100 interest from the face amount of the note, and Kathy's Kitchens received $9,900 ($10,000 − $100).

Kathy's Kitchens uses two note payable accounts—one for notes to vendors and the other for notes to the bank. The transaction is recorded as follows:

	GENERAL JOURNAL			PAGE 5	
DATE	DESCRIPTION	POST. REF.	DEBIT	CREDIT	
20X1					1
June 1	Cash		9 900 00		2
	Interest Expense		100 00		3
	Notes Payable—Bank			10 000 00	4
	To record note payable issued at				5
	a discount				6

THE BOTTOM LINE
Issuance of Discounted Note Payable

Income Statement
Expenses ↑ 100
Net Income ↓ 100

Balance Sheet
Assets ↑ 9,900
Liabilities ↑ 10,000
Equity ↓ 100

> **THE BOTTOM LINE**
>
> **Payment of Discounted Note Payable**
>
> **Income Statement**
> No effect on net income
>
> **Balance Sheet**
> Assets ↓ 10,000
> Liabilities ↓ 10,000
> No effect on equity

Recording the Payment of a Discounted Note Payable

At maturity, July 31, Kathy's Kitchens prepares a check for $10,000 to pay the note. There is no entry for interest expense because interest was paid and recorded when the note was issued. The entry is recorded as follows:

	GENERAL JOURNAL			PAGE 6
DATE	DESCRIPTION	POST. REF.	DEBIT	CREDIT
20X1				
July 31	Notes Payable—Bank		10 000 00	
	Cash			10 000 00
	Record payment of note			

Using a Notes Payable Register

If a business issues many notes payable, it is convenient to maintain a notes payable register. The notes payable register shows the important information about each note payable on a single line.

At the end of each accounting period, a schedule of notes payable is prepared from the information in the notes payable register. The schedule of notes payable must agree with the *Notes Payable* account in the general ledger.

For each note payable, the notes payable register shows the following information:

- the issue date;
- the payee;
- where the note is payable;
- the term of the note;
- the maturity date;
- the face amount;
- the interest rate, if any;
- the interest amount, if any.

Reporting Notes Payable and Interest Expense

Notes payable represent financial obligations of the business. They appear on the balance sheet as liabilities.

- Notes due within one year are classified as current liabilities.
- Notes due in more than one year are classified as long-term liabilities.

The notes presented in this chapter are current liabilities. Long-term liabilities are discussed in Chapter 22.

Interest expense appears on the income statement as a nonoperating expense. It is listed in the Other Income and Expenses section and is deducted from Income from Operations as follows:

Sales	$550,000
Cost of Goods Sold	(320,000)
Gross Profit on Sales	230,000
Operating Expenses	(164,000)
Income from Operations	66,000
Other Income and Expenses	
Interest Expense	(1,800)
Net Income	$ 64,200

Section 1 Review

1. How much cash will the borrower receive for a $12,000, 75-day, noninterest-bearing note discounted at 8 percent?
   a. $11,600
   b. $11,900
   c. $11,800
   d. $12,000

2. What is the maturity date of a 120-day note issued on April 10?
   a. July 8
   b. August 8
   c. September 8
   d. August 9

3. What is the interest due on a note for $15,000 at 8 percent for 75 days?
   a. $200
   b. $225
   c. $250
   d. $300

4. The total to be received when a note receivable is due is known as the:
   a. principal.
   b. maturity value.
   c. interest.
   d. face value.

5. Which of the following is not required for an instrument to be negotiable?
   a. It must be payable on demand or at a fixed or determinable date.
   b. It must contain an unconditional promise or order to pay a definite amount.
   c. It must be in writing.
   d. All of the above are required.

6. Notes due within one year are classified as current liabilities. Notes due in more than one year are classified as long-term liabilities.
   a. True
   b. False

7. Interest expense appears on the income statement as an operating expense and is listed in the Other Income and Expenses section and is deducted from Income from operations.
   a. True
   b. False

Section 2

SECTION OBJECTIVES	TERMS TO LEARN
>> 16-6 Record routine notes receivable transactions. **WHY IT'S IMPORTANT** Many businesses accept notes receivable from customers to purchase goods or to replace existing accounts receivable. **>> 16-7** Compute the proceeds from a discounted note receivable, and record transactions related to discounting of notes receivable. **WHY IT'S IMPORTANT** Businesses can raise cash by discounting notes receivable at the bank. **>> 16-8** Understand how to use bank drafts and trade acceptances and how to record transactions related to those instruments. **WHY IT'S IMPORTANT** Various financial instruments are used because they provide flexibility in cash management.	bank draft bill of lading cashier's check commercial draft contingent liability draft note receivable sight draft time draft trade acceptance

Accounting for Notes Receivable

Section 1 discussed promissory notes from the debtor's perspective. This section considers the creditor's perspective.

Notes Receivable

Some businesses allow customers to issue a promissory note to finance the purchase of goods. Sometimes a business requires a customer with an overdue account to sign a promissory note for the account balance. In these cases, the promissory note is classified as a **note receivable,** which is an asset that represents a creditor's written promise to pay a specified amount at a specified future date. There are many similarities between notes payable and notes receivable. Of course, the journal entries are different.

Noninterest-Bearing Notes Receivable

Customer Isabel Huang owes $1,500 to Kathy's Kitchens. The account is overdue, and Huang needs more time to pay. On September 18, Huang signs a 30-day, noninterest-bearing note for $1,500. In the event legal action becomes necessary, the note provides additional protection to Kathy's Kitchens.

1	20X1				1
2	Sept.	18	Notes Receivable	1 500 00	2
3			Accounts Receivable/Isabel Huang	1 500 00	3
4			To record 30-day note receivable to		4
5			replace an overdue account receivable		5

The maturity date of the note is October 18.

Days note is issued in September (30 − 18)	12 days
Days in October	18 days
Duration of note (proof)	30 days

At maturity when Huang pays the note, the entry in the cash receipts journal is a debit to *Cash* and a credit to *Notes Receivable.* Huang's note is marked "Paid" and returned to her.

Interest-Bearing Notes Receivable

Customers who do not pay their bills when due are expected to pay interest. Normally, promissory notes issued to replace overdue accounts are interest-bearing. Interest on notes is generally paid at the maturity date. On June 12, Kathy's Kitchens accepted a 60-day, 10 percent note for $1,200 from John Woods to replace his past-due account. The transaction is recorded as follows:

>> **16-6 OBJECTIVE**
Record routine notes receivable transactions.

	20X1				
	June	12	Notes Receivable	1 200 00	
			Accounts Receivable/John Woods		1 200 00
			To record 60-day note receivable to		
			replace an overdue account receivable		

The maturity date of the note is August 11.

Days note is issued in June (30 − 12)	18 days
Days in July	31 days
Total days to the end of July	49 days
Days in August to maturity (60 − 49 = 11)	11 days
Duration of note (proof)	60 days

The interest on $1,200 for 60 days at 10 percent is $20 ($1,200 × 0.10 × 60/360). Woods's payment of the note on the maturity date will include the $1,200 face amount of the note plus $20 interest. The payment would be recorded as follows:

	20X1				
	Aug.	11	Cash	1 220 00	
			Notes Receivable		1 200 00
			Interest Income		20 00
			Collection of John Woods's note		
			receivable		

Notes Receivable—Special Situations

Accountants must know how to record notes receivable for special situations.

Accounting for Partial Collection of a Note
On August 11, Kathy's Kitchens learned that John Woods could pay only half the $1,200 note receivable. Kathy's Kitchens agreed to extend the due date for another 30 days for half the principal, $600. Kathy's Kitchens accepted payment of $20 interest and $600 principal. Partial payments are applied first to interest and then to principal. The journal entry to record the transaction is as follows:

	20X1				
	Aug.	11	Cash	620 00	
			Notes Receivable		600 00
			Interest Income		20 00
			Collection of interest and one-half		
			of John Woods's note; balance renewed		
			for 30 days		

ABOUT ACCOUNTING

Annual Percentage Rate (APR)
Some lenders charge lower interest rates but add high fees; others do the reverse. The APR allows you to compare them on equal terms. It combines the fees and interest charges to give you the true annual interest rate.

The original note can be endorsed to reflect the partial payment and the new maturity date, or Kathy's Kitchens can cancel the original note and ask John Woods to sign a new interest-bearing note for $600.

Note Receivable Not Collected at Maturity If a note is not paid at maturity and there are no arrangements for renewal, the note is said to be "dishonored." Dishonored notes do not belong in the *Notes Receivable* account. If John Woods dishonored the original $1,200 note, the entry to transfer the balance out of *Notes Receivable* and back to *Accounts Receivable* would be as follows:

20X1				
Aug.	11	Accounts Receivable/John Woods	1,220.00	
		Notes Receivable		1,200.00
		Interest Income		20.00
		To charge back Woods's dishonored		
		note plus interest to maturity		

Note that Woods now owes the original balance of $1,200 plus $20 interest on the note. After a note is dishonored, interest continues to accrue on the note. The interest rate is usually specified by law. In most cases, it is higher than the rate shown on the note, although the parties may agree on a rate different from the statutory rate. Promissory notes usually require the maker to pay attorney's fees and all other costs incurred by the holder for efforts to collect the note.

Notes Received at the Time of a Sale Sometimes Kathy's Kitchens asks a customer to sign a promissory note at the time of sale. The transaction is recorded in the general journal as follows:

20X1				
Aug.	15	Notes Receivable	3,000.00	
		Sales		3,000.00
		Received 60-day, 9% note from		
		Sylvia Montes on sale of goods		

If a business routinely receives notes from customers at the time of sale, the transactions are recorded in a special Notes Receivable column of the sales journal.

Discounting a Note Receivable

A note receivable is an asset. At maturity date, the holder will receive cash for the note receivable. If the holder wants cash before the maturity date, the note can be discounted (sold) at the bank. The bank pays the holder the maturity value (principal plus any interest) minus the discount charge.

Noninterest-Bearing Note Receivable Discounted On September 18, Kathy's Kitchens needed cash to pay some bills. Kathy Kaymark decided to discount a 90-day, noninterest-bearing note receivable for $3,000 that the business received from John Nguyen on July 20. The maturity date of the note is October 18.

Days note is issued in July (31 − 20)	11 days
Days in August	31 days
Days in September	30 days
Total days to the end of September	72 days
Days in October to maturity (90 − 72)	18 days
Duration of note (proof)	90 days

On September 18, Kathy's Kitchens discounts the note at Central National Bank. The bank's discount rate is 10 percent.

Calculating the Discount and the Proceeds The steps to determine the discount and the proceeds on notes receivable follow:

Step 1. *Determine the maturity value of the note.* Because the note from Nguyen is noninterest-bearing, its maturity value and face amount are the same, $3,000.

Step 2. *Calculate the number of days in the discount period.* The discount period is the number of days from the discount date to the maturity date. The discount period is 30 days.

Days note is discounted in September (30 – 18)	12 days
Days in October until maturity	18 days
Total days in discount period	30 days

Step 3. *Compute the discount charged by the bank.* The discount formula is similar to the interest formula. The time is the number of days in the discount period. The discount is $25.

Discount = Maturity Value × Discount Rate × Discount Period
$25 = $3,000 × 0.10 × (30/360)

Step 4. *Calculate the proceeds,* the amount received from the bank. This is the maturity value of the note less the discount, $2,975 ($3,000 – $25).

Kathy's Kitchens received cash for the note 30 days before the note matured in exchange for a discount fee of $25.

The discount is debited to *Interest Expense.* The credit is to *Notes Receivable—Discounted,* a contra asset account. The following is the journal entry to record the discounting of the note receivable:

1	20X1					1
2	Sept.	18	Cash	2 975 00		2
3			Interest Expense	25 00		3
4			Notes Receivable—Discounted		3 000 00	4
5			To record discounting of			5
6			John Nguyen note			6

Contingent Liability for a Discounted Note When a note receivable is discounted, the party discounting the note endorses it. If the maker (Nguyen) does not pay the note at maturity, the bank can obtain payment from the endorser (Kathy's Kitchens). Hence, Kathy's Kitchens has a contingent liability of $3,000. A **contingent liability** can become a liability if certain things happen. Contingent liabilities are shown on the financial statements so that the users are aware that the business might have a liability in the future. The contingent liability for discounted notes receivable appears on the balance sheet as follows:

Notes Receivable	$7,400
Notes Receivable—Discounted	(3,000)
Net Notes Receivable	$4,400

Another common way to show contingent liabilities is to present the net notes receivable on the balance sheet and to include a note with the information about the discounted notes receivable.

Discounted Noninterest-Bearing Note Receivable at Maturity If on October 18, the maturity date, Nguyen pays the note, Kathy's Kitchens is no longer contingently liable for the note. The following journal entry removes the asset and the contingent liability:

1	20X1					1
2	Oct.	18	Notes Receivable—Discounted	3 000 00		2
3			Notes Receivable		3 000 00	3
4			Record payment of discounted note			4
5			of John Nguyen			5

>> **16-7 OBJECTIVE**
Compute the proceeds from a discounted note receivable, and record transactions related to discounting of notes receivable.

Suppose on October 18 Nguyen dishonored the note by not paying it. The bank filed a formal protest. Kathy's Kitchens became liable to the bank for the maturity value of the note plus a protest fee. Central National Bank deducted the note ($3,000) and the protest fee ($30) from the checking account for Kathy's Kitchens. The bank sent a debit memorandum with the dishonored note and the protest form to Kathy's Kitchens. The journal entries to record this transaction are as follows:

- Record the amount owed by Nguyen including the protest fee. Debit **Accounts Receivable/ John Nguyen** for $3,030 and credit **Cash** for $3,030.
- Debit **Notes Receivable—Discounted** for $3,000 and credit **Notes Receivable** for $3,000.

Kathy's Kitchens contacted Nguyen and asked for payment of the note. Payment was not received, so Kathy's Kitchens turned the note over to an attorney for collection.

Interest-Bearing Note Receivable Discounted Kathy Kaymark discounted another note receivable in order to meet cash needs. The $1,800, 90-day, 6 percent note was received from Kim Myers on September 29. The maturity date of the note is December 28.

Calculating the Discount and the Proceeds On November 28, Kathy's Kitchens discounted Myers's note at the bank at 10 percent. The steps to compute the discount and the proceeds on the note receivable follow:

Step 1. *Determine the maturity value of the note.* The interest is $27 ($1,800 × 0.06 × 90/360). The maturity value is the principal and interest, $1,827 ($1,800 + $27).

Step 2. *Calculate the number of days in the discount period.* The discount period is 30 days.

Days note is discounted in November (30 − 28)	2 days
Days in December until maturity	28 days
Total days in discount period	30 days

Step 3. *Compute the discount charged by the bank.* The bank charges $15.23, 10 percent of the maturity value for the discount period ($1,827 × 0.10 × 30/360).

Step 4. *Calculate the proceeds.* The proceeds are $1,811.77, the maturity value minus the discount ($1,827.00 − $15.23).

Interest income of $11.77 will be recorded. This represents the total interest used to compute the maturity value, minus the discount charged by the bank ($27.00 − $15.23 = $11.77). It also reflects the amount by which the proceeds from discounting the note exceed the principal of the note ($1,811.77 − $1,800.00 = $11.77).

GENERAL JOURNAL PAGE 10

DATE	DESCRIPTION	POST. REF.	DEBIT	CREDIT
20X1				
Nov. 28	Cash		1,811.77	
	Notes Receivable—Discounted			1,800.00
	Interest Income			11.77
	To record discounting of Kim Myers's note			

The amount received from discounting an interest-bearing note may be less than the face value of the note. In that event, **Interest Expense** would be debited for the difference. For example, if the discount rate charged by the bank when the Myers note, above, was discounted on November 28 is 20 percent, the discount would be $30.45 ($1,827 × .20 × 30/360), and the proceeds would have been $1,796.55 ($1,827.00 − $30.45). Here is the necessary entry:

	20X1				
	Nov.	28	Cash	1,796 55	
			Interest Expense	3 45	
			Notes Receivable—Discounted		1,800 00
			To record discounting of Myers's note		

Maturity of Discounted Interest-Bearing Note Receivable If the maker of a note receivable that has been discounted pays the holder of the note at maturity, the contingent liability of the endorser is ended. The endorser completely removes the note from the accounts. For example, if on the maturity date, December 28, Myers pays the Central National Bank, the entry below would be made:

	20X1				
	Dec.	28	Notes Receivable—Discounted	1,800 00	
			Notes Receivable		1,800 00
			To record payment by Myers of discounted note receivable		

If Myers dishonors the discounted note on December 28, the bank will deduct from Kathy's account the maturity value of the note, plus a small service fee—$25 in this example. Kathy's Kitchens would again remove the note from the accounts by debiting **Notes Receivable—Discounted** and crediting **Notes Receivable.** In addition, the entire amount that the bank deducted from Kathy's account would be charged back to **Accounts Receivable** and to Myers's account ($1,827 maturity value + $25 fee).

	20X1				
	Dec.	28	Notes Receivable—Discounted	1,800 00	
			Accounts Receivable/Kim Myers	1,852 00	
			Notes Receivable		1,800 00
			Cash		1,852 00
			To record dishonor of note by Myers		

The Notes Receivable Register

If a firm has many notes receivable, it is convenient to maintain a notes receivable register. For each note, the notes receivable register shows the date of the note, the maker, where the note is payable, the duration, the maturity date, the face amount, the rate of interest, and the amount of interest. For each discounted note, the register also shows the discount date and the bank holding the note.

Reporting Notes Receivable and Interest Income

Notes receivable appear on the balance sheet as assets.

- Notes that mature within one year are classified as current assets.
- Notes that mature in more than one year are classified as long-term assets.

The contra asset account **Notes Receivable—Discounted** appears as a deduction from **Notes Receivable.**

> Presentation of information in the balance sheet about notes payable and other liabilities varies widely from company to company. For example, a balance sheet prepared for SEC filing by Caterpillar, Inc., for December 31, 2018, showed total current liabilities of $28.2 billion. This number included $5.7 million of "Short-Term Borrowings." Presumably this number includes notes payable and other forms of short-term obligations.

Interest income is classified as nonoperating income. It is listed in the Other Income and Expenses section of the income statement and is added to income from operations. The discount charged for discounting notes is shown as interest expense in the Other Income and Expenses section and is deducted from income from operations. The income statement for a business that received and paid interest follows:

Sales		$550,000
Cost of Goods Sold		(320,000)
Gross Profit on Sales		230,000
Operating Expenses		(164,000)
Income from Operations		66,000
Other Income and Expenses		
Interest Income	$1,800	
Interest Expense	(2,350)	(550)
Net Income		$ 65,450

>> **16-8 OBJECTIVE**

Understand how to use bank drafts and trade acceptances and how to record transactions related to those instruments.

Drafts and Acceptances

Negotiable instruments include drafts and acceptances.

Drafts

A **draft** is a written order that requires one party (a person or business) to pay a stated sum of money to another party. A check is one type of draft. Other types are bank drafts and commercial drafts.

Bank Drafts A **bank draft** is a check written by a bank that orders another bank to pay the stated amount to a specific party. A bank draft is more readily accepted than a personal or business check. Bank drafts are used to pay debts to suppliers with whom credit has not been established.

A **cashier's check** is a draft on the issuing bank's own funds. Cashier's checks are sometimes used to pay bills. For the creditor, a cashier's check offers more protection than a business or personal check.

The business pays for the bank draft or cashier's check by issuing a business check to cover the amount of the draft or cashier's check plus the service charge.

On May 18, Kathy's Kitchens purchased a $1,412 bank draft and sent it to Home Supplies, Inc., to pay an overdue account payable to that company. The service charge for the bank draft was $12. The journal entry to record the transaction is as follows:

1	20X1				1
2	May	18	Accounts Payable/Home Supplies, Inc.	1400 00	2
3			Miscellaneous Bank Expense	12 00	3
4			Cash		1412 00	4
5			To record payment of past-due		5
6			account and bank charge with draft		6

Commercial Drafts A **commercial draft** is a note issued by one party that orders another party to pay a specified amount on a specified date. Commercial drafts are used for special shipment and collection situations. Commercial drafts may be either sight drafts or time drafts.

A **sight draft** is a commercial draft that is payable on presentation. When a sight draft is issued, no journal entry is made. When a sight draft is honored, the transaction is recorded as a cash receipt.

MANAGERIAL IMPLICATIONS

NEGOTIABLE INSTRUMENTS

- Because notes payable and notes receivable are negotiable instruments, they fall under the rules and regulations of the Uniform Commercial Code. Management needs to understand the rights, responsibilities, and obligations of the business for negotiable instruments.
- Management should carefully control and limit borrowing to minimize the interest charged for the use of funds.
- In a well-run business, managers ensure the prompt payment of debts to minimize interest expense and to maintain the company's credit rating.
- Management authorizes specific individuals to approve the use of debt.
- When cash is needed for current operations, managers need to know that notes receivable can be discounted.
- Good managers ensure that past due accounts receivable are converted into notes receivable because notes provide more legal protection and are more likely to be collected.
- Because notes and drafts are negotiable, management ensures that internal control procedures are in place.

THINKING CRITICALLY
Why might managers use outside sources of funds for their business operations? How do they acquire these funds?

Sight drafts are used to collect past-due accounts receivable. Customers are more likely to honor a sight draft than a collection letter. The sight draft is sent to the customer's bank. If the customer does not honor the draft, the customer's credit reputation at the bank can be damaged.

Sight drafts are also used to obtain cash on delivery when shipments are made to customers with poor credit or to new customers with no credit established. The sight draft is attached to a **bill of lading,** which is a business document that lists the goods accepted for transportation by a carrier. The bill of lading is sent to a bank near the customer. The customer pays the draft in order to get the bill of lading. The customer needs the bill of lading in order to obtain the goods. The collecting bank sends the money, less a collection fee, to the business issuing the draft. When the funds arrive, the business records the transaction as a cash sale and debits an expense account for the collection fee.

A **time draft** is a commercial draft that is payable during a specified period of time. The time period may be a specific date, or a specific number of days either after the date of the draft or after acceptance of the draft.

No journal entry is made when a time draft is issued. If the business honors (pays) the draft, the word "Accepted" is written on the draft and it is signed and dated. The business records the acceptance of a draft as a note payable. It is returned to the drawer, who records it as a note receivable.

Trade Acceptances

A **trade acceptance** is a form of commercial time draft used in transactions involving the sale of goods. The original transaction is recorded as a sale on credit. When the draft is accepted, it is accounted for as a promissory note. Merchants have fewer credit losses on trade acceptances than on accounts receivable. Trade acceptances can be discounted.

Internal Control of Notes Payable, Notes Receivable, and Drafts

The following are internal controls for notes payable, notes receivable, and drafts:

- Limit the number of people who can sign notes for the firm.
- Record all notes payable immediately.
- Identify a specific person or department to be responsible for prompt payment of interest and principal for notes payable.

- When paid, mark the note payable "Canceled" or "Paid" and file the note.
- Handle drafts as carefully as checks.
- Authorize only certain persons to accept notes.
- Record all notes receivable in the accounting records.
- Store notes receivable securely in a safe or fireproof vault to which access is limited.
- Verify and compare the actual notes receivable to the notes receivable register.
- Near the maturity date, inform the issuer of the approaching due date and the amount owed.
- If payment is not received on the due date, contact the issuer immediately.
- Review all past-due notes promptly and take necessary steps, including legal action, to ensure payment.

Section 2 Review

1. A note receivable with a maturity value of $6,200 is discounted at 10 percent with 90 days remaining until the maturity date. What are the proceeds from discounting the note?
   a. $6,100
   b. $6,045
   c. $6,090
   d. $6,200

2. Why do businesses sometimes accept notes receivable from customers?
   a. The note receivable provides greater legal protection than an account receivable.
   b. The customer is unable to pay the accounts receivable but is willing to provide a note with greater protection and an interest payment.
   c. Accepting the note is a viable alternative to writing the account off as uncollectible.
   d. All of the above are correct.

3. What does it mean to dishonor a note?
   a. The maker of the note pays the note when it is due.
   b. The maker of the note does not pay the note when it is due.
   c. The maker of the note requests an extension on the note.
   d. None of the above are correct.

4. The *Notes Receivable—Discounted* account:
   a. contains a debit balance.
   b. reflects the amounts due on dishonored notes receivable.
   c. is shown as a liability on the balance sheet.
   d. is deducted from *Notes Receivable* on the balance sheet.

5. A company that discounts an interest-bearing note receivable:
   a. always recognizes interest income when the note is discounted.
   b. never recognizes interest income when the note is discounted.
   c. recognizes interest income only if the proceeds from discounting exceed the maturity value of the note discounted.
   d. recognizes interest income if the proceeds exceed the face value of the note discounted.

6. When an interest-bearing note receivable is accepted instead of cash at the time of sale, the interest on the note increases the amount reported as sales.
   a. True
   b. False

7. Notes receivable appear on the balance sheet as assets. Notes that mature within one year are classified as current assets. Notes that mature in more than one year are classified as long-term assets.
   a. True
   b. False

REVIEW Chapter Summary

Chapter 16

In this chapter, you have learned how businesses use promissory notes, drafts, or trade acceptances to pay large amounts over a period of time. You have learned about negotiable instruments and how to record common notes payable and notes receivable transactions.

Learning Objectives

16-1 Determine whether an instrument meets all the requirements of negotiability.

A negotiable instrument is a financial document that:
- contains an order or promise to pay.
- meets all the requirements of the Uniform Commercial Code (UCC) to be transferable to another party.

The UCC requirements are as follows:
- It must be in writing.
- It must be signed by the maker.
- It must define the amount due and payment terms.
- It must list the payee.
- If addressed to a drawee, it must clearly name the person.

16-2 Calculate the interest on a note.

The borrower who signs a note payable usually pays interest on the amount borrowed. To determine the interest amount for any time period, use the formula Interest = Principal × Interest Rate × Time.

16-3 Determine the maturity date of a note.

The note's maturity date is determined at the time the note is issued, excluding the issue date itself.

16-4 Record routine notes payable transactions.

When purchasing an asset with a note, debit the asset account and credit *Notes Payable*. When paying the note payable, debit *Notes Payable* for the face of the note, debit *Interest Expense* for the interest, and credit *Cash* for the total paid (principal plus interest). *Interest Expense* appears on the income statement below Net Income from Operations in Other Income/Other Expense.

16-5 Record discounted notes payable transactions.

When money is borrowed on a note payable, the bank can deduct its interest charge immediately, called *discounting*. The borrower discounting a note payable receives the difference between the discount and the principal.

16-6 Record routine notes receivable transactions.

Notes receivable can be noninterest- or interest-bearing. Most firms charge interest.
- If the note receivable is issued at the time of a sale, record the transaction by debiting *Notes Receivable* and crediting *Sales*.
- If the note receivable results from a customer's failure to pay an account receivable, debit *Notes Receivable* and credit *Accounts Receivable*.
- The recipient credits *Interest Income* for interest received when the note is paid.

16-7 Compute the proceeds from a discounted note receivable, and record transactions related to discounting of notes receivable.

A firm with an immediate need for cash can discount a note receivable. Debit *Cash* for the proceeds, credit *Notes Receivable—Discounted* for the face value, and either debit *Interest Expense* (if the proceeds are less than the principal) or credit *Interest Income* (if the proceeds exceed the principal). *Notes Receivable—Discounted* represents a contingent liability. If the note's maker fails to pay at maturity, the business must pay the bank.

16-8 Understand how to use bank drafts and trade acceptances and how to record transactions related to those instruments.

Bank drafts, commercial drafts, and trade acceptances are negotiable instruments used in business.
- Bank drafts are checks written by a bank ordering another bank in which it has funds to pay the indicated amount to a specific person or business.
- Businesses issue commercial drafts to order a person or firm to pay a sum of money at a specific time.
- Trade acceptances arise from the sale of goods. The original transaction is recorded in the same way as a sale on credit. When the draft has been accepted, it is accounted for as a promissory note.

16-9 Define the accounting terms new to this chapter.

Glossary

Bank draft (p. 588) A check written by a bank that orders another bank to pay the stated amount to a specific party

Banker's year (p. 577) A 360-day period used to calculate interest on a note

Bill of lading (p. 589) A business document that lists goods accepted for transportation

Cashier's check (p. 588) A draft on the issuing bank's own funds

Commercial draft (p. 588) A note issued by one party that orders another party to pay a specified sum on a specified date

Contingent liability (p. 585) An item that can become a liability if certain things happen

Discounting (p. 579) Deducting the interest from the principal on a note payable or receivable in advance

Draft (p. 588) A written order that requires one party (a person or business) to pay a stated sum of money to another party

Face value (p. 577) An amount of money indicated to be paid, exclusive of interest or discounts

Interest (p. 577) The fee charged for the use of money

Maturity value (p. 577) The total amount (principal plus interest) payable when a note comes due

Negotiable instrument (p. 576) A financial document containing a promise or order to pay that meets all requirements of the Uniform Commercial Code in order to be transferable to another party

Note payable (p. 578) A liability representing a written promise by the maker of the note (the debtor) to pay another party (the creditor) a specified amount at a specified future date

Note receivable (p. 582) An asset representing a written promise by another party (the debtor) to pay the note holder (the creditor) a specified amount at a specified future date

Principal (p. 577) The amount shown on the face of a note

Sight draft (p. 588) A commercial draft that is payable on presentation

Time draft (p. 589) A commercial draft that is payable during a specified period of time

Trade acceptance (p. 589) A form of commercial time draft used in transactions involving the sale of goods

Comprehensive Self Review

1. What type of account is Notes Receivable—Discounted? How should the Notes Receivable—Discounted account be shown on the balance sheet?
2. Which account(s) will be debited and which will be credited when an interest-bearing note receivable that has been discounted is dishonored at the time of maturity?
3. How is maturity value of a note computed?
4. When is Interest Expense debited if an interest-bearing note payable is issued? If a note payable is discounted?
5. List the elements of a negotiable instrument.

(Answers to Comprehensive Self Review are at the end of the chapter.)

Discussion Questions

1. If a note dated February 28 has a three-month term, on what date must the note be paid?
2. What is the maturity value of a $9,000 note, bearing interest at 9 percent, and due 105 days after date of issue of the note?
3. What is meant by "discounting a note payable"?

4. How are notes payable maturing less than one year from the balance sheet date shown on the balance sheet?
5. Are notes payable likely to be given in borrowing money? The purchase of merchandise? The purchase of equipment? Why?
6. Explain why records must be kept of the due dates of all notes payable.
7. How, if at all, does computation of the maturity value of an interest-bearing note receivable differ from that for an interest-bearing note payable?
8. What is a dishonored note receivable?
9. What is meant by "discounting a note receivable"?
10. Explain how to compute the proceeds from discounting a note receivable.
11. When is a discounted note receivable considered a contingent liability?
12. Explain a cashier's check.
13. Explain a sight draft.
14. What are the requirements that must be met in order for a document to be negotiable?
15. What is the face amount of a note? The maturity value?
16. How does a note receivable differ from an account receivable?

APPLICATIONS

Exercises

Determining the due dates of notes.

◀ **Exercise 16.1**
Objective 16-3

Find the due date of each of the following notes:

1. A note dated May 19, 20X1, due in 120 days.
2. A note dated November 1, 20X1, due two years from that date.
3. A note dated April 10, 20X1, due six months from that date.

Determining the maturity value of notes.

◀ **Exercise 16.2**
Objectives 16-2, 16-3

Compute the maturity value for each of the following notes:

1. A note payable with a face amount of $50,000, dated June 15, 20X1, due in three months, bearing interest at 7 percent.
2. A note payable with a face amount of $44,000, dated May 5, 20X1, due in 45 days, bearing interest at 8 percent.

Computing the maturity value of notes payable.

◀ **Exercise 16.3**
Objective 16-3

Find the maturity value of each of the following notes payable:

1. A 60-day note, dated February 15, 20X1, with a face value of $52,000, bearing interest at 8 percent.
2. A six-month note, dated March 10, 20X1, with a face value of $21,600, bearing interest at 11 percent.

Recording the issuance of notes payable to borrow money.

◀ **Exercise 16.4**
Objectives 16-4, 16-5

During 20X1, Tolliver Company borrowed money at Natchez State Bank and Trust on two occasions. On June 8, the company borrowed $60,000, giving a 120-day, 5 percent note, and on September 8, the company discounted at 7 percent a $80,000, 90-day note payable.

1. Give entries in general journal form to record issuance of each of these notes.
2. Record in general journal form issuance of a check to pay each note.

Exercise 16.5
Objective 16-4

▶ **Recording a note given for a purchase of equipment.**

On August 1, 20X1, Martinez Company purchased a truck (delivery equipment) for $55,600, signing a 90-day, 8 percent note for the entire purchase price. Give the entry in general journal form to record the purchase of the equipment with the note and the payment of the note on the due date.

Exercise 16.6
Objective 16-7

▶ **Recording receipt of a note receivable and subsequent discounting of the note.**

On June 3, 20X1, Georgia State Company received a $10,400, 45-day, 10 percent note from Sampson Byrd, a customer whose account was past due.

1. Record in the general journal receipt of the note.
2. Give the entry in general journal form to record the discounting of this note receivable on June 18 at the Georgia State Bank and Trust. The bank charged a discount rate of 12 percent.

Exercise 16.7
Objective 16-7

▶ **Recording payment of a discounted note receivable.**

In general journal form, give the entry required by Georgia State Company when Sampson Byrd paid the note discounted in Exercise 16.6 on the maturity date.

Exercise 16.8
Objective 16-7

▶ **Recording a dishonored note receivable.**

Give the entries in general journal form that Georgia State Company would make if Sampson Byrd dishonored the note receivable discounted by Georgia State in Exercise 16.6, assuming the bank deducted the maturity value of the dishonored note plus a $55 service charge from Georgia State's bank account on the due date of the note.

PROBLEMS

Problem Set A

Problem 16.1A
Objective 16-2

▶ **Computing interest on notes payable.**

Keller Company issued the following notes during 20X1. Find the interest due on each of the notes, using the interest formula method. Show all calculations.

1. A $30,000 note at 9 percent for 180 days, issued February 15.
2. A $28,000 note at 12 percent for four months, issued October 3.
3. A $40,000 note at 10 percent for 180 days, issued October 18.

Analyze: What is the balance in *Notes Payable* on December 31, 20X1, assuming that all notes were paid when due?

Problem 16.2A
Objectives 16-2, 16-3, 16-4, 16-5

▶ **Recording transactions involving notes payable.**

Give the general journal entry to record each of the following transactions for Wilkinson Company:

1. Issued a 6-month, 9 percent note for $110,000 to purchase two forklifts on May 14, 20X1 (debit *Warehouse Equipment*).
2. Discounted its own 180-day, noninterest-bearing note with a principal amount of $80,000 at the California State Bank and Trust on May 28, 20X1. The bank charged a discount rate of 10 percent.
3. Paid the May 14 note on its due date.
4. Paid the note discounted on May 28 on its due date.

Analyze: What is the total interest expense for the year as a result of these transactions?

Computing interest and maturity value.

◀ **Problem 16.3A**
Objectives 16-2, 16-3

The following notes were received by Keller Company during 20X1:

Note No.	Date	Face Amount	Period	Interest Rate
21	Jan. 5	$30,000	3 months	8%
22	June 3	15,000	90 days	10%
23	Sept. 28	20,000	3 months	9%

Compute the maturity value of each note.

Analyze: What is the total interest expense on these notes for the year?

Computing the proceeds from discounted notes receivable.

◀ **Problem 16.4A**
Objectives 16-3, 16-7

The notes receivable held by the Tuttle Company on August 3, 20X1, are summarized below. On August 4, 20X1, Tuttle discounted all of these notes at Community Bank and Trust at a discount rate of 10 percent. Compute the net proceeds received from discounting each note.

Note No.	Date	Face Amount	Period	Interest Rate
31	Apr. 4, 20X1	$60,000	6 months	8%
32	June 11, 20X1	30,000	120 days	6%
33	July 31, 20X1	20,000	60 days	10%

Analyze: What is the net interest income or expense to be reported from these transactions assuming all notes are paid when due?

Recording the receipt, discounting, and payment of notes receivable.

◀ **Problem 16.5A**
Objectives 16-3, 16-4, 16-6, 16-7

On May 16, 20X1, Safeway Company received a 90-day, 8 percent, $10,500 interest-bearing note from Black Company in settlement of Black's past-due account. On June 30, Safeway discounted this note at Fargo Bank and Trust. The bank charged a discount rate of 13 percent. On August 14, Safeway received a notice that Black had paid the note and the interest on the due date. Give entries in general journal form to record these transactions.

Analyze: If the company prepared a balance sheet on July 31, 20X1, how should *Notes Receivable—Discounted* be presented on the statement?

Problem Set B

Computing interest on notes payable.

◀ **Problem 16.1B**
Objective 16-2

The notes listed below were issued by Louisiana Company during 20X1:

1. A $30,000 note at 10 percent for 90 days, issued on June 15.
2. A $60,000 note at 6 percent for 30 days, issued on August 21.
3. An $80,000 note at 7.5 percent for 6 months, issued on September 28.

Compute the interest due on each of the notes at maturity, using the interest formula method. Show all calculations.

Analyze: What would be the accrued interest payable on December 31 as a result of these transactions?

Recording transactions involving notes payable.

◀ **Problem 16.2B**
Objectives 16-2, 16-3, 16-4, 16-5

Give the general journal entry to record each of the following transactions:

1. On June 3, 20X1, Huddleston Company issued a 120-day, 9 percent note for $36,000 to purchase new office equipment.
2. Huddleston Company paid the June 3 note when it became due.

3. On September 18, 20X1, Huddleston Company borrowed money from the Hot Springs National Bank by discounting its own 90-day noninterest-bearing $60,000 note payable at a discount rate of 10 percent.

4. Huddleston Company paid the September 18 note when it became due.

Analyze: If Huddleston had borrowed $60,000 from the bank on September 18, signing a 90-day note, bearing interest of 10 percent, would these be more favorable or less favorable terms for Huddleston than discounting the $60,000 note at 10 percent? Why?

Problem 16.3B ▶ **Computing interest and maturity value.**

Objectives 16-2, 16-3

Ferrier Company received the notes listed below in 20X1. Compute the interest to be paid and the maturity value of each note. Show all computations.

Note No.	Date	Face Amount	Period	Interest Rate
30	May 4	$50,000	60 days	10.5%
31	July 8	40,000	90 days	8.5%
32	Aug. 20	60,000	4 months	9.0%

Analyze: Assuming all notes are paid when due, what would be the balance in *Notes Receivable* on July 31?

Problem 16.4B ▶ **Computing the proceeds from discounted notes receivable.**

Objective 16-7

The following notes receivable are held by the Rodriguez Company on January 1, 20X1. On January 2, 20X1, Rodriguez discounted all of these notes at First National Bank at a discount rate of 10 percent. Compute the net proceeds the firm received from discounting each note.

Note No.	Date	Face Amount	Period	Interest Rate
20	Sept. 20, 20X0	$15,000	120 days	8%
21	Sept. 10, 20X0	20,000	6 months	9%
22	Dec. 1, 20X0	25,000	120 days	12%

Analyze: How would *Notes Receivable* be shown on a balance sheet prepared on January 2, 20X1, after the transactions above have been entered?

Problem 16.5B ▶ **Recording the receipt, discounting, and payment of notes receivable.**

Objectives 16-2, 16-3, 16-4, 16-6, 16-7

On April 2, 20X1, Wu Company received a 6-month, 8 percent interest-bearing note from Jenna Blackmon in settlement of a past-due account receivable of $15,000. On May 3, Wu discounted this note at Mercantile State Bank. The bank charged a discount rate of 10 percent. On October 2, Wu received word that the note and interest had been paid in full.

1. Give all entries, in general journal form, to record these events.

2. Assume that Blackmon had failed to pay the note and that the bank charged Wu's account with the note and a $50 protest fee. Give the journal entry(ies) necessary to record these facts.

Analyze: What amount of interest income or interest expense will Wu report in 20X1 as a result of these transactions assuming Blackmon paid the note when due?

Critical Thinking Problem 16.1

Notes Receivable Discounted

Contemporary Furniture, a wholesale distributor of modern casual furniture, frequently accepts promissory notes from its customers at the time of sale. Because Contemporary Furniture regularly needs cash to meet its own obligations, it frequently discounts these notes at the bank.

Contemporary Furniture's accountant tells you that she does not bother to credit discounted notes to a *Notes Receivable—Discounted* account. Instead, she makes an entry debiting *Cash* and *Interest Expense* and crediting *Notes Receivable* (and *Interest Income* when appropriate). She says that using a *Notes Receivable—Discounted* account "just makes extra work, and, anyway, once the note is discounted, it becomes the bank's problem."

What is your reaction to the bookkeeper's comments?

Critical Thinking Problem 16.2

Notes Payable and Notes Receivable

James Howard owns Howard Auto Sales. He periodically borrows money from Bay City State Bank and Trust. He permits some customers to sign short-term notes for their purchases. He usually discounts these notes at the bank. Following are selected transactions that occurred in March 20X1.

INSTRUCTIONS

1. Record each of the March transactions in the general journal. (Omit explanations.)
2. Record the additional data related to these notes for months other than March in the general journal using the appropriate dates.

DATE		TRANSACTIONS
20X1		
Mar.	4	Mr. Howard borrows $20,000 from the bank on a note payable for the business. Terms of the note are 8 percent interest for 45 days.
	11	A 90-day $18,000 note payable to the bank is discounted at a rate of 10 percent.
	22	Sold a car to Darnell Jones for $30,000 on a 75-day note receivable, bearing interest at 10 percent.
	23	Discounted the Jones note with the bank. The bank charges a discount rate of 12 percent.
	25	Sold a car for $30,000 to Henry Thomas. Thomas paid $4,000 cash and signed a 30-day note, bearing interest at 10 percent, for the balance.
	28	Alfred Herron's account receivable is overdue. Howard requires him to sign a 12 percent, 30-day note for the balance of $11,000.

Additional Data

a. Howard pays all the company's notes payable on time.
b. Darnell Jones defaults on his $30,000 note and the bank charges the company's checking account for the maturity value of the note and a service fee of $60.
c. Henry Thomas pays his note on time.
d. Alfred Herron pays his note on time.

Analyze: What is the *Notes Payable* account balance on March 25?

BUSINESS CONNECTIONS

Cash Management

1. You are a member of Arrow Company's internal audit staff. A review of office practices indicates that an accounting assistant routinely makes arrangements with the bank for short-term notes payable and signs the notes. Evaluate this practice. Would you recommend any changes?
2. How can management use notes receivable as a way to acquire cash?
3. Under what circumstances would management insist on having a notes receivable register and/or a notes payable register?
4. As a manager, why would you insist that dishonored notes receivable be charged back to the *Accounts Receivable* control account and the maker's subsidiary ledger account?

Managerial FOCUS

Internal Control and FRAUD PREVENTION

Financial Statement ANALYSIS

Home Depot

Internal Control of Notes Receivable and Notes Payable

Internal control of notes receivable and notes payable is very important to a business because notes receivable and notes payable can represent significant assets and liabilities for a business. These assets and liabilities can have a material impact the liquidity of the firm. Discuss at least 12 common internal control procedures for notes receivable and notes payable.

Balance Sheet

The following excerpt was taken from The Home Depot, Inc., *Annual Report for the fiscal year ended February 3, 2019*. The Balance Sheet to the Consolidated Financial Statements contained the following details on the company's current and long-term debt.

(in millions)	2019	2018
Total current liabilities	$16,716	$16,194
Long-term debt, excluding current installments	26,807	24,267
Deferred income taxes	491	440
Other long-term liabilities	1,867	2,174
Total liabilities	45,881	43,075

Analyze:
1. What percentage of total debt is represented by the current portion in 2019? In 2018?
2. What percentage of total debt is represented by the long-term portion in 2019? In 2018?
3. If interest payments totaled $1,051 billion 2019, what average rate was paid on total debt? Use the end-of-year balance of liabilities for this computation.

Analyze Online: Find The Home Depot, Inc., website (www.homedepot.com). Recent financial reports are found within the *Investor Relations* link.

4. What is the fiscal period for the most recent annual report presented?
5. What long-term debt amount is reported on the balance sheet?
6. What amount of long-term debt matured in this fiscal period?

TEAMWORK

Negotiating Terms

A business manager should know how one company's transaction will affect another company. In teams of two students, assign one student to be the notes receivable clerk of the Heavenly Baths and another to be the notes payable clerk for Relax Haven, the borrowing company. Relax Haven cannot make the payment on a $20,000 invoice. Negotiate the necessary arrangements between the two parties.

Answers to Comprehensive Self Review

1. *Notes Receivable—Discounted* is a contra asset account. This means that it is deducted from *Notes Receivable* on the balance sheet.
2. Accounts debited and credited: ***Notes Receivable—Discounted*** will be debited and ***Notes Receivable*** will be credited. Also, ***Accounts Receivable*** and the customer's account in the subsidiary ledger will be debited and ***Cash*** will be credited.
3. Maturity value of the note is the sum of (a) the principal amount of the note and (b) interest on the principal amount at the rate specified, computed from the date the note is dated until the maturity date.
4. For an interest-bearing note issued, ***Interest Expense*** is debited when the note matures. The interest on a note payable discounted is recorded at the date of the discounting.
5. (a) must be in writing and signed by the maker; (b) contains an unconditional promise or order to pay a definite amount of money; (c) is payable on demand or at a time that can be determined; (d) is payable to the order of the bearer; and (e) if addressed to a drawee, the drawee must be clearly identified.

Merchandise Inventory

Chapter 17

www.samsclub.com

Sam's Club sells products through both membership warehouse clubs and eCommerce. The Club is one of three segments that comprise Walmart Inc. The first Sam's Club opened in Midwest City, Oklahoma, in 1983 and based on Walmart Inc.'s 2018 annual report, the number of stores has grown to 597 retail locations throughout the United States. Sam's Club sells products within six categories: grocery and consumables, fuel and other categories, home and apparel, technology, office and entertainment, and health and wellness. Sam's Club also sells a wide variety of products in each of its six product categories through its own Member's Mark brand. Net sales for the company grew to $59.2 billion in fiscal year 2018. This growth in net sales comprised approximately 12% of total net sales for Walmart Inc. Sam's Club reported $982 million in operating income for fiscal year 2018.

Ken Wolter/Shutterstock

The corporation's 2018 annual report indicates that Walmart Inc. "helps people around the world save money and live better." This is done at Sam's Club through both offering a variety of quality products in its retail locations and a wide variety of quality products in its retail locations and selling these products and more at the segment's website, where over 59,000 individual products are available for purchase. Given this staggering variety of products, inventory valuation is of utmost importance as it affects both the income statement and the balance sheet as the merchandise is sold and the inventory is reported on the balance sheet.

Sam's Club constantly restocks its inventory; however, the cost of this inventory constantly fluctuates. How does Sam's Club track the cost of each of its varied products? To address these price changes, Sam's Club uses a modified version of the last-in, first-out (LIFO) method of inventory valuation. This inventory valuation method provides Sam's Club with a consistent determination of inventory cost and cost of sales for financial reporting.

thinking critically

If at different times Sam's Club purchased two identical products at different prices, how would the sale of the lower-cost unit affect the company's financial statements compared to the sale of the higher-cost unit?

LEARNING OBJECTIVES

17-1 Compute inventory cost by applying four commonly used costing methods.

17-2 Compare the effects of different methods of inventory costing.

17-3 Compute inventory value under the lower of cost or net realizable value rule.

17-4 Estimate inventory cost using the gross profit method.

17-5 Estimate inventory cost using the retail method.

17-6 Define the accounting terms new to this chapter.

NEW TERMS

average cost method
first-in, first-out (FIFO) method
gross profit method
last-in, first-out (LIFO) method
lower of cost or net realizable value rule
markdown
markon
markup
net realizable value
periodic inventory
perpetual inventory
physical inventory
retail method
specific identification method
weighted average method

Section 1

SECTION OBJECTIVES	TERMS TO LEARN
17-1 Compute inventory cost by applying four commonly used costing methods. **WHY IT'S IMPORTANT** Factors such as industry practices, merchandise types, and business operations affect how a business assigns costs to inventories. **17-2** Compare the effects of different methods of inventory costing. **WHY IT'S IMPORTANT** Inventory valuation affects the net income or net loss of a business.	average cost method first-in, first-out (FIFO) method last-in, first-out (LIFO) method periodic inventory perpetual inventory physical inventory specific identification method weighted average method

Inventory Costing Methods

Businesses report information about merchandise inventory on the financial statements. This section covers four methods used to compute the value of merchandise inventory based on original cost.

Importance of Inventory Valuation

Assigning an appropriate value to merchandise inventory is important because the *Merchandise Inventory* account appears on both the balance sheet and the income statement. Often inventory represents the largest current asset on the balance sheet. Inventory valuation also affects the net income or net loss reported on the income statement.

A higher ending inventory value results in a lower cost of goods sold, which results in higher income from operations. On the other hand, a lower ending inventory value results in a higher cost of goods sold, which results in a lower income from operations.

> On its consolidated balance sheet for the fiscal year ended February 3, 2019, The Home Depot reported inventories of $13.9 billion. Inventory represents 31.6 percent of the company's total assets of $44.0 billion.

We learned in Chapter 12 that many firms value merchandise inventory at the original cost of the items on hand. Merchandise inventory is counted at the end of the accounting period. The inventory value is calculated by multiplying the number of units on hand by the cost per item. Taking an actual count of the number of units of each type of good on hand is known as taking a **physical inventory.** An inventory system in which the amount of goods on hand is determined by periodic counts is called a **periodic inventory** system. It is the method that we use in this chapter.

Some businesses need to know the number of units and the unit cost for the inventory on hand at all times. These businesses use a **perpetual inventory** system, in which inventory is based on a running total number of units. Electronic equipment, such as point-of-sale cash registers and scanners, helps track all of the items as they are purchased and sold. For a complete discussion of the perpetual inventory method, see the appendix to Chapter 9.

Assigning Costs to Inventory

The cost of sold merchandise is transferred from the balance sheet (current assets) to the income statement (cost of goods sold). The amount of cost that is transferred depends on the method used to value inventory. Four methods are commonly used to value inventory. Accountants choose the method that works best for the industry and the company.

Specific Identification Method

The **specific identification method** of inventory valuation is based on the actual cost of each item of merchandise. Cost of goods sold is the exact cost of the specific merchandise sold, and the ending inventory balance is the exact cost of the specific inventory items on hand. Businesses that sell high-priced or one-of-a-kind items, such as art and automobile dealers, use the specific identification method. However, this method is not practical for a business where hundreds of similar items of relatively small unit value are carried in inventory.

Average Cost Method

The **average cost method** uses the average cost of units of an item available for sale during the period to arrive at the value of ending inventory. It is advantageous to use the average cost method when a company's inventory is composed of many similar items that are not subject to significant price and style changes. Table 17.1, which provides an example of the average cost method, contains the following information:

- There were 200 units in beginning inventory valued at $18 each.
- There were three purchases during the year, at different costs.
- The beginning inventory and purchases are added together to determine that during the year 1,000 units were available for sale at a total cost of $20,600.
- The average cost per unit is $20.60 ($20,600 ÷ 1,000).
- A physical inventory count showed 206 units on hand on December 31.
- During the year, 794 units were sold (1,000 − 206).
- Under the average cost method, the total cost of units available for sale ($20,600) is divided between the financial statements as follows:
    - Balance sheet—ending inventory is $4,243.60 (206 units × $20.60).
    - Income statement—cost of goods sold is $16,356.40 (794 units × $20.60).

This method is sometimes referred to as the **weighted average method** because it considers the number of units in each purchase and the unit purchase price to compute a "weighted average" cost per unit.

>> **17-1 OBJECTIVE**
Compute inventory cost by applying four commonly used costing methods.

important!

Physical Inventory
Whether a perpetual or periodic inventory system is used, a physical inventory should be taken at least once a year.

recall

Cost of Goods Sold
The formula for cost of goods sold is

   Beginning inventory
+ Purchases
− Ending inventory
= Cost of goods sold

TABLE 17.1

Average Cost Method of Inventory Valuation

Explanation	Number of Units	Unit Cost	Total Cost
Beginning inventory, January 1, 20X1	200	$18.00	$ 3,600.00
Purchases:			
February 19	400	20.00	8,000.00
May 12	300	22.00	6,600.00
October 3	100	24.00	2,400.00
Total merchandise available for sale	1,000		$20,600.00
Average cost ($20,600 ÷ 1,000 = $20.60)			
Ending inventory, December 31, 20X1	206	20.60	$ 4,243.60
Cost of goods sold ($20,600 − $4,243.60)	794	20.60	$16,356.40

The average cost method of inventory valuation is relatively simple to use, but it reflects the limitations of any procedure that involves average figures. The average unit cost is not related to any specific unit, and it does not clearly reveal price changes. In highly competitive businesses that are subject to considerable model or style upgrades and price fluctuations, it is desirable to have a more specific and revealing method of cost determination.

> The Coca-Cola Company's inventories are shown in the company's *2018 Annual Report* as $2.766 billion, which is approximately 9.0 percent of its total current assets. A note to the financial statements comments: "Inventories are valued at the lower of cost or net realizable value. We determine cost on the basis of average cost or first-in, first-out methods."

First-In, First-Out Method

recall

Disclosure

The method of inventory valuation must be disclosed in the financial reports.

For most businesses, the physical flow of inventory is "the first item purchased is the first item sold." This certainly makes sense for perishable items. Some businesses assign inventory costs using this flow. The **first-in, first-out method** of inventory valuation, usually referred to as **FIFO,** assumes that the oldest merchandise is sold first.

Let's calculate ending inventory under FIFO using the information in Table 17.1. During the period, 794 units were sold. Under FIFO the "first cost in is the first cost transferred out" to cost of goods sold. This matches the earliest costs with the revenue from the units sold. So the cost of the ending inventory is computed by using the cost of the most recent purchases.

Table 17.2 shows that the cost assigned to the 206 units in ending inventory is $4,732.00: 100 units purchased in October at $24 and 106 units purchased in May at $22, for a total of 206 units. During the period, there was $20,600.00 of inventory available for sale. Under the FIFO method, the cost is divided between the financial statements as follows:

- Balance sheet—ending inventory is $4,732.00.
- Income statement—cost of goods sold is $15,868 ($20,600 − $4,732).

TABLE 17.2

FIFO Method of Inventory Costing

Explanation	Number of Units	Unit Cost	Total Cost
From purchase of October 3, 20X1	100	$24.00	$2,400.00
From purchase of May 12, 20X1	106	22.00	2,332.00
Ending inventory	206		$4,732.00

> A company can use several inventory valuation methods. Most inventory costs for Dole Food Company, Inc., are determined principally on a first-in, first-out basis. However, specific identification and average cost methods are used for certain packing material and operating inventories.

Last-In, First-Out Method

important!

Inventory Costing and Net Income

Gross profit on sales and net income are affected by the inventory costing method.

The **last-in, first-out (LIFO) method** assumes that the most recently purchased merchandise is sold first, and thus assigns the most recent costs to cost of goods sold. The "last cost in is the first cost transferred out" to cost of goods sold. Thus, the cost of ending inventory is computed using the cost of the oldest merchandise on hand during the period.

Using the figures from Table 17.1 but applying the LIFO method, Table 17.3 shows that the cost assigned to the 206 units in ending inventory is 200 at $18 from the beginning inventory and 6 at $20 from the February 19 purchase. During the period, there was $20,600 of inventory available for sale. Under the LIFO method, the cost is divided between the financial statements as follows:

- Balance sheet—ending inventory is $3,720.00.
- Income statement—cost of goods sold is $16,880 ($20,600 − $3,720).

Under the LIFO method, the balance sheet reflects the earliest costs. The cost of goods sold reflects the costs applicable to the most recent purchases.

TABLE 17.3 LIFO Method of Inventory Valuation

Explanation	Number of Units	Unit Cost	Total Cost
Beginning inventory, Jan. 1, 20X1	200	$18.00	$3,600.00
From purchase of February 19	6	20.00	120.00
Ending inventory, Dec. 31, 20X1	206		$3,720.00

Comparing Results of Inventory Costing Methods

Table 17.4 shows the results obtained for the average cost, FIFO, and LIFO inventory methods. The ending inventory is highest under FIFO and lowest under LIFO. The cost of goods sold is highest under LIFO and lowest under FIFO. This is true because costs have risen during the year.

Remember the following important points about inventory valuation methods:

- Except for specific identification, the physical flow of inventory and the costs assigned to inventory are not specifically matched. Average, FIFO, and LIFO cost methods *assign* costs to inventory but do not track the cost to the specific inventory item.
- Businesses can use separate inventory valuation methods for different classes of inventory.
- Following the consistency principle, once a business adopts an inventory valuation method, it uses that method consistently from one period to the next. A business cannot change its inventory valuation method at will, although a one-time change is acceptable.
- A business can use one inventory costing method for financial accounting purposes and another for federal income tax, with the exception of LIFO costing. A taxpayer who adopts LIFO for federal tax purposes must also adopt it for financial accounting purposes.

>> **17-2 OBJECTIVE**
Compare the effects of different methods of inventory costing.

TABLE 17.4 Comparison of Results of Inventory Costing Methods

Explanation	Units	Unit Cost	Total Cost	Ending Inventory Valuation	Cost of Goods Sold
Beginning inventory, January 1, 20X1	200	$18.00	$ 3,600.00		
Purchases:					
February 19	400	20.00	8,000.00		
May 12	300	22.00	6,600.00		
October 3	100	24.00	2,400.00		
Total merchandise available for sale	1,000		$20,600.00		
1. Average cost method	206	$20.60		$4,243.60	$16,356.40
2. FIFO	100	24.00	$ 2,400.00		
	106	22.00	2,332.00		
	206		$ 4,732.00	$4,732.00	$15,868.00
3. LIFO	200	18.00	$ 3,600.00		
	6	20.00	120.00		
	206		$ 3,720.00	$3,720.00	$16,880.00

- FIFO focuses on the balance sheet. The most current costs are in ending inventory.
- LIFO focuses on the income statement and the matching principle. The most recent costs are matched with revenue. LIFO is considered the most conservative costing method in a period of rising prices.

A major argument supporting the LIFO method is that when sales are made, the goods sold must be replaced at current costs. It is logical that current costs incurred for replaced goods should be charged against the revenue leading to the replacement.

Because price trends represent a vital element in any inventory valuation, remember these basic rules:

- When prices are rising, cost of goods sold is highest and net income is lowest under LIFO. Therefore, in periods of inflation, LIFO results in the lowest income tax expense.
- When prices are falling, cost of goods sold is lower and net income is higher under LIFO.
- Whatever direction prices take, the average cost method almost always results in net income between the amounts obtained with FIFO and LIFO.

LIFO Use Internationally

Most of the major industrialized countries use the methods of accounting for inventories discussed in this chapter. In some countries, however, LIFO is not generally accepted.

Section 1 Review

1. Which generally accepted accounting principle requires firms to use the same method of inventory from year to year?
   a. matching
   b. conservatism
   c. consistency
   d. full disclosure

2. In a period of rising prices, which inventory method results in the lowest reported net income?
   a. average cost
   b. weighted average
   c. first-in, first-out (FIFO)
   d. last-in, first-out (LIFO)

3. Under FIFO costing, which costs are assigned to the goods sold during the period?
   a. most recent costs
   b. average costs
   c. specific costs
   d. oldest costs

4. Under which method is the cost of goods sold the same as the costs of the merchandise sold?
   a. average cost
   b. retail cost
   c. specific identification
   d. weighted average

5. Which method of inventory valuation is based on the total number of units available for sale during the period?
   a. periodic
   b. perpetual
   c. retail method
   d. weighted average

6. Beginning inventory plus purchases minus ending inventory equals:
   a. cost of goods sold.
   b. cost of purchases.
   c. ending inventory.
   d. average cost of inventory.

7. Which inventory valuation method focuses on the balance sheet?
   a. lifo (LIFO)
   b. fifo (FIFO)
   c. average cost
   d. specific identification

8. Which inventory valuation method focuses on the income statement?
   a. lifo (LIFO)
   b. fifo (FIFO)
   c. average cost
   d. specific identification

Section 2

SECTION OBJECTIVES	TERMS TO LEARN
>> 17-3 Compute inventory value under the lower of cost or net realizable value rule. **WHY IT'S IMPORTANT** The conservatism convention is important when determining the cost of inventory. **>> 17-4** Estimate inventory cost using the gross profit method. **WHY IT'S IMPORTANT** Often businesses need to determine the cost of inventory without taking a physical count. **>> 17-5** Estimate inventory cost using the retail method. **WHY IT'S IMPORTANT** The retail method provides an easy and quick estimation of the cost of the inventory.	gross profit method lower of cost or net realizable value rule markdown markon markup net realizable value retail method

Inventory Valuation and Control

According to the historical cost principle, assets are reported on the balance sheet at their historical cost. The conservatism convention, however, states that assets should not be overstated. This section discusses how to report the value of inventory when the cost is above the net realizable value.

Lower of Cost or Net Realizable Value Rule

>> **17-3 OBJECTIVE**
Compute inventory value under the lower of cost or net realizable value rule.

FASB ASU 2015-11 requires entities to measure most inventory at the lower of cost or net realizable value (NRV). The ASU defines **net realizable value** as the estimated selling price of an inventory item in the ordinary course of business, less reasonably predictable costs of completion, disposal, and transportation. If the net realizable value is lower than the original cost, the business uses the **lower of cost or net realizable value rule.** That is, inventory is reported at its original cost or its net realizable value, whichever is lower. There are three ways to apply the lower of cost or net realizable value rule: by item, in total, or by group.

Lower of Cost or Net Realizable Value by Item

Table 17.5 illustrates the lower of cost or net realizable value rule by item. Inventory consists of two groups of two stock items each. The report shows the quantity, cost, and NRV price of each item. Cost is determined using one of the acceptable methods—specific identification, average cost, FIFO, or LIFO. Each item's valuation basis (cost or net realizable value, whichever is lower) is determined; for item 2810, it is cost, $1.80, and for item 2870 it is NRV, $2.05. The quantity is multiplied by the valuation basis and the amounts are totaled. The inventory balance reported on the balance sheet is $1,461.25.

TABLE 17.5

Establishing Lower of Cost or Net Realizable Value by Item

Description	Quantity	Unit Price Cost	Unit Price NRV	Lower of Cost or NRV Valuation Basis	Lower of Cost or NRV Amount
Group 1					
Stock 2810	150	$1.80	$1.95	Cost	$ 270.00
Stock 2870	225	2.10	2.05	NRV	461.25
Total, Group 1					$ 731.25
Group 2					
Stock 4625	100	$3.10	$3.05	NRV	$ 305.00
Stock 4633	250	1.70	1.80	Cost	425.00
Total, Group 2					$ 730.00
Inventory valuation (lower of cost or NRV by item)					$1,461.25

Lower of Total Cost or Total Net Realizable Value

Table 17.6 illustrates the lower of cost or NRV rule applied to total inventory, not to individual items. The cost of inventory is computed using both cost and NRV and then the results are compared. Inventory is valued in the balance sheet at the lower amount, $1,477.50.

> ASU 2015-11 is effective for public business entities prospectively for annual periods beginning after December 15, 2016, and interim periods therein. For all other entities, the ASU is effective prospectively for annual periods beginning after December 15, 2016, and interim periods thereafter. Early application of the ASU was permitted. Upon transition, entities must disclose the nature and reason for the accounting change.

Lower of Cost or Net Realizable Value Rule by Groups

Another way to apply the lower of cost or NRV rule is by groups. The lower figure (cost or NRV) for each group is added to the lower figures for the other groups to obtain the total

TABLE 17.6

Establishing Lower of Total Cost or Total NRV Valuation

Description	Quantity	Unit Price Unit Cost	Unit Price Unit NRV	Total Cost	Total NRV
Group 1					
Stock 2810	150	$1.80	$1.95	$ 270.00	$ 292.50
Stock 2870	225	2.10	2.05	472.50	461.25
Total, Group 1				$ 742.50	$ 753.75
Group 2					
Stock 4625	100	$3.10	$3.05	$ 310.00	$ 305.00
Stock 4633	250	1.70	1.80	425.00	450.00
Total, Group 2				$ 735.00	$ 755.00
Total Inventory				$1,477.50	$1,508.75
Inventory valuation (lower of total cost or total NRV)					$1,477.50

TABLE 17.7

Establishing the Lower of Total Cost or Total NRV by Groups

Lower of cost or NRV valuation by group (as shown in Table 17.6)	
Group 1 cost	$ 742.50
Group 2 cost	735.00
Total inventory valuation	$1,477.50

inventory valuation. As shown in Table 17.7, the valuation basis of both Group 1 and Group 2 is cost. Inventory is valued on the balance sheet at $1,477.50.

Depending on the method used, inventory could appear on the balance sheet as one of the following amounts:

Lower of Cost or Net Realizable Value	
By Item	$1,461.25
By Total	1,477.50
By Group	1,477.50

Accountants select the method based on the size and variety of inventory, the margin of profit, industry practices, and plans for expansion.

- Some accountants believe that the total method should be used. They think that the lower of cost or net realizable value rule should apply to the total inventory, not item by item. If net realizable value of the inventory as a whole has not declined below cost, they believe inventory should be presented at historical cost.
- Other accountants prefer the group method because it does not reflect individual fluctuations as does the item method, and it does not lump together all types of items as does the total method.
- Some accountants choose the item method because it is the most conservative method. Almost without exception the item method results in the lowest inventory amount.

recall

Conservatism
According to the modifying convention of conservatism, if GAAP allows alternatives, assets in the balance sheet should be understated rather than overstated.

important!

Lower of Cost or Net Realizable Value Rule
If the net realizable value is less than the historical cost, the inventory is reported at net realizable value.

Inventory Estimation Procedures

Occasionally, managers need to know the inventory cost and cannot or do not want to take a physical count. For example, after a fire the business cannot count the items destroyed. However, for insurance and income tax purposes, the business must determine the cost of the goods destroyed. Two common techniques to estimate the cost of inventory are the gross profit method and the retail method.

Gross Profit Method of Inventory Valuation

The **gross profit method** assumes that the rate of gross profit on sales and the ratio of cost of goods sold to net sales are relatively constant from period to period. Applying these ratios to information that may be gleaned from the records on any date of the year permits an estimate to be made of the cost of inventory at the end of a period ending on that date. This process is illustrated for the Posey Corporation, whose inventory was destroyed by fire on June 30, 20X1. However, accounting records were not destroyed.

The averages of sales and data related to cost of goods sold in the two prior years for Posey Corporation, along with the computation of the gross profit and the cost of goods sold ratios, are determined:

Net sales	$850,000
Cost of goods sold	493,000
Gross profit on sales	$357,000
Gross profit rate	$357,000/$850,000 = 42%
Cost of goods sold to net sales ratio	$493,000/$850,000 = 58%

>> **17-4 OBJECTIVE**
Estimate inventory cost using the gross profit method.

These rates have been typical of those in prior years for the business. The accounting records for the period January 1 through June 30, date of the fire, show:

Inventory (at cost), January 1	$210,000
Net purchases, January 1 through June 30	315,000
Net sales, January 1 through June 30	450,000

The following steps are used to estimate the cost of inventory on hand at the time of the fire:

Step 1. *Estimate the cost of goods sold.* Sales were $450,000 for January 1 through June 30. Using the 58 percent ratio for cost of goods sold to net sales, based on averages for the prior two years, the estimated cost of goods sold is $261,000 ($450,000 × 0.58).

Step 2. *Determine the cost of goods available for sale.* Include in the computation freight-in charges and purchases returns.

Beginning inventory	$210,000
Net purchases	315,000
Cost of goods available for sale	$525,000

Step 3. *Compute the ending (destroyed) inventory.* Subtract the estimated cost of goods sold from the cost of goods available for sale.

Cost of goods available for sale (Step 2)	$525,000
Estimated cost of goods sold (Step 1)	(261,000)
Estimated cost of ending inventory	$264,000

The cost of inventory destroyed in the fire is estimated to be $264,000.

>> 17-5 OBJECTIVE

Estimate inventory cost using the retail method.

Retail Method of Inventory Valuation

The **retail method** estimates inventory cost by applying the ratio of cost to selling price in the current accounting period to the retail price of the inventory. This widely used method permits businesses to determine the approximate cost of ending inventory from the financial records. It makes it possible for the business to prepare financial statements easily and often without taking a physical inventory count.

Using the retail method, inventory is classified into groups of items that have about the same rate of markon. **Markon** is the difference between the cost and the initial retail price of merchandise.

MANAGERIAL IMPLICATIONS <<

INVENTORY

- Good managers carefully control inventory because it may represent a large part of the assets of the business.
- Management should help select an inventory costing method that is practical, reliable, and as simple as possible to apply.
- Management needs to understand how the inventory valuation method affects net income and income taxes.
- Based on the gross profit method of estimating inventory, managers can prepare budgets and financial statements when a physical inventory count is not practical or possible.

- Retail managers use the retail method of inventory valuation to estimate the cost of goods on hand. Department managers, who are not permitted to exceed their inventory budgets, use this method as often as every week.

THINKING CRITICALLY

Should the gross profit method or the retail method of calculating inventory replace the physical count of inventory?

The following steps use assumed figures to estimate the cost of inventory using the retail method:

Step 1. List the beginning inventory at both cost ($95,400) and retail ($138,700).

Step 2. When merchandise is purchased, record it at cost ($526,800 including $2,400 freight) and determine its retail value ($819,500).

Step 3. Compute merchandise available for sale at cost ($622,200) and at retail ($958,200).

Step 4. Determine net sales at retail ($815,300).

Step 5. Subtract retail sales from the retail merchandise available for sale. The difference is the ending inventory at retail ($958,200 − $815,300 = $142,900).

Step 6. Compute the cost ratio.

$$\frac{\text{Merchandise Available for Sale at Cost}}{\text{Merchandise Available for Sale at Retail}} = \frac{\$622,200}{\$958,200} = 65 \text{ percent}$$

Step 7. Multiply the ending inventory at retail by the cost ratio. The result is an estimate of the ending inventory cost, $92,885 ($142,900 × 0.65).

Step 8. Estimate the cost of goods sold by subtracting the ending inventory at cost from the merchandise available for sale at cost, $529,315 ($622,200 − $92,885).

The calculations for each step are shown below:

	Cost	Retail
Step 1: Beginning inventory	$ 95,400	$138,700
Step 2: Purchases	526,800	819,500
Step 3: Total merchandise available for sale	$622,200	$958,200
Step 4: Less sales		815,300
Step 5: Ending inventory priced at retail		$142,900
Step 6: Cost ratio = ($622,200 ÷ $958,200) = 65%		
Step 7: Conversion to approximate cost: Ending inventory at retail × Cost ratio = $142,900 × 0.65 Ending inventory at cost = $92,885		
Step 8: Cost of goods sold = $622,200 − $92,885 = $529,315		

The benefit of the retail method is that without counting inventory the business is able to estimate the ending inventory balance at cost.

The retail method is not as simple as this example suggests. Adjustments must be made for **markups,** price increases above the original markons, and markup cancellations. Adjustments are also made for **markdowns,** price reductions below the original markon, and for markdown cancellations. These details are not covered in this text.

A more accurate application of the retail method involves taking a physical inventory, which is facilitated by using scanning devices to capture the sales price marked on the merchandise. The physical inventory at retail is converted to cost by applying the cost ratio. For example, if the physical inventory count shows retail cost of $60,000 and the cost ratio is 66.67 percent, the cost of the inventory is estimated to be $40,000 ($60,000 × 0.667).

The retail method for determining cost is used by many large retailers. For example, in notes to its financial statements for the fiscal year ending February 3, 2019, The Home Depot, Inc., states:

> The majority of the Company's Merchandise Inventories are stated at the lower of cost (first-in first-out) or market, as determined by the retail inventory method. Certain subsidiaries, including retail operations in Canada and Mexico, and distribution centers, record merchandise inventories at the lower of cost or net realizable value as determined by the cost method. These merchandise inventories represent approximately 29% of the total merchandise inventory balance.

Internal Control of Inventories

The internal controls over inventory depend on the nature of the inventory. For example, controls for expensive jewelry are more elaborate than controls over lumber. Typical inventory controls are as follows:

- Limit access to inventory of small valuable items.
- Require documents, such as approved shipping orders, before allowing items to leave the warehouse.
- Take a physical inventory count at least annually to verify that the goods on hand match the amounts in the accounting records.
- Have an independent auditor observe the physical inventory count.
- Use spot checks to verify the counting techniques and the items' costs.
- Verify all sales and shipping invoices to ensure sales have been properly recorded and are being shipped to a valid shipping address.
- Establish and follow strict inventory policies and procedures, especially in the area of sales returns and allowances.

The notes to the financial statements of The Home Depot for the fiscal year ending February 3, 2019, stress the importance of periodic inventories when a perpetual inventory system is used.

ABOUT ACCOUNTING

Inventory Financing
Many businesses obtain credit based on their merchandise inventory. Inventory financing uses the inventory on hand as collateral for the credit line.

> Independent physical inventory counts or cycle counts are taken on a regular basis in each store and distribution center to ensure that amounts reflected in merchandise inventories are properly stated. Shrink (or in the case of excess inventory, "swell") is the difference between the recorded amount of inventory and the physical inventory. We calculate shrink based on actual inventory losses occurring as a result of physical inventory counts during each fiscal period and estimated inventory losses occurring between physical inventory counts. The estimate of shrink occurring in the interim period between physical inventory counts is calculated on a store-specific basis based on recent shrink results and current trends in the business.

New Technology in Inventory Control

One of the problems with the use of "bar scanners" in checking inventories is that the methodology requires "line of sight" contact between the scanner and the bar code on the merchandise. This often requires physical movement of goods in the warehouse in order to obtain the line of sight. This is true not only at time of inventory taking, but in searching for goods that have been "recalled" by the manufacturer and in finding goods to move from the warehouse to the salesroom. This may be labor intensive and slow.

In the summer of 2003, Walmart launched an RFID (radio frequency identification) initiative. It asked its largest 100 suppliers to apply a "passive" electronic tag to all pallets and cases of merchandise shipped to three of its distribution centers. The system enables the company to determine quickly whether merchandise is on hand in the warehouse or has been moved to the floor of the store. It is obvious that the technique could be very valuable, especially in the control of warehouse stocks.

The U.S. Department of Defense has announced a similar program using RFID, which means that two of the world's largest purchasers of goods plan to install the program. Other major retailers, such as Best Buy, Target, and The Home Depot, Inc., are also considering installing the technology. The system also promises to aid suppliers of merchandise in planning and controlling inventory sales to buyers using the program.

Up-to-date information about RFID can be obtained by accessing the website of the American Production and Inventory Control Society (www.apics.org).

Section 2 Review

1. Which accounting principles, concepts, or modifying conventions underlie the valuation of inventories at the lower of cost or net realizable value?
   a. consistency
   b. conservatism
   c. historical cost
   d. matching

2. The estimated selling price of an inventory item less reasonably predictable costs of completion, disposal, and transportation is called:
   a. net realizable value.
   b. net lower of cost or market.
   c. market.
   d. net selling price.

3. Three ways by which the lower of cost or net realizable value rule might be applied include all but:
   a. group by group.
   b. item by item.
   c. group of items.
   d. total cost and total net realizable value.

4. Of the three ways by which the lower of cost or net realizable value might be applied, which will give the lowest ending inventory valuation?
   a. group by group
   b. item by item
   c. group of items
   d. total cost and total net realizable value

5. A business would use the gross profit method instead of the retail method to estimate ending inventory when:
   a. the selling prices of items on hand are known.
   b. the selling prices of items on hand are not known.
   c. the costs of items on hand are known.
   d. the costs of items on hand are not known.

6. Under what circumstances would the gross profit method of estimating inventory be used?
   a. when inventory has been destroyed
   b. when an inventory estimate is quickly needed
   c. both a and b are correct
   d. neither a nor b is correct

7. Which of these inventory costing procedures does not require a physical count of the inventory items?
   a. retail method
   b. specific identification method
   c. lower of cost or net realizable value method
   d. average cost method

8. Which inventory method almost always gives a result between LIFO and FIFO?
   a. retail method
   b. specific identification method
   c. lower of cost or net realizable value method
   d. average cost method

17 Chapter REVIEW   Chapter Summary

It is important to account for merchandise inventory because the information appears on both the balance sheet and the income statement. Industry practices, merchandise unit costs, and merchandise price fluctuations affect how costs are assigned to inventory.

Learning Objectives

17-1 Compute inventory cost by applying four commonly used costing methods.

There are four common inventory cost flow assumptions.
- The specific identification method uses the actual purchase price of the specific items in inventory.
- The average cost method averages the cost of all like items for sale during the period to value the ending inventory unit cost.
- The FIFO method develops the cost of the ending inventory from the cost of the latest purchases.
- The LIFO method develops the cost of the ending inventory from the cost of beginning inventory and earlier purchases.

17-2 Compare the effects of different methods of inventory costing.

The method used affects the net income reported.
- With rising prices, LIFO gives a lower reported net income than FIFO, as well as lower income taxes payable.
- With falling prices, LIFO gives a higher reported net income than FIFO.
- The average cost method almost always gives a result between these.

17-3 Compute inventory value under the lower of cost or net realizable value rule.

- Assets are reported on financial statements at their historical cost. However, assets should not be overstated.
- If the net realizable value of an inventory item is below its original purchase cost, it is necessary to value the inventory at the net realizable value in the firm's financial records.
- Consequently, inventory is valued at either its original cost or its net realizable value, whichever is lower. This is called the lower of cost or net realizable value.
- Cost refers to the historical cost.
- Net realizable value refers to estimated net selling price of an an item.
- The lower of cost or net realizable value can be applied to individual items in the inventory, to groups of items, or to the inventory as a whole.

17-4 Estimate inventory cost using the gross profit method.

The gross profit method of estimating inventory assumes that the rate of gross profit on sales and the ratio of cost of goods sold to net sales are relatively constant from period to period. Ending inventory can be estimated using three steps:

1. Estimate the cost of goods sold by multiplying net sales by the normal ratio of cost of goods sold to net sales.
2. Determine goods available for sale by adding beginning inventory and net purchases.
3. Compute ending inventory by subtracting the estimated cost of goods sold (in step 1) from goods available for sale (in step 2).

17-5 Estimate inventory cost using the retail method.

The retail method uses the retail selling price of items remaining. The retail value is multiplied by the cost ratio of the current period to determine the approximate cost. This method entails a full consideration of markups, markup cancellations, markdowns, and markdown cancellations.

17-6 Define the accounting terms new to this chapter.

Glossary

Average cost method (p. 601) A method of inventory costing using the average cost of units of an item available for sale during the period to arrive at cost of the ending inventory

First-in, first-out (FIFO) method (p. 602) A method of inventory costing that assumes the oldest merchandise is sold first

Gross profit method (p. 607) A method of estimating inventory cost based on the assumption that the rate of gross profit on sales and the ratio of cost of goods sold to net sales are relatively constant from period to period

Last-in, first-out (LIFO) method (p. 602) A method of inventory costing that assumes that the most recently purchased merchandise is sold first

Lower of cost or net realizable value rule (p. 605) The principle by which inventory is reported at either its original cost or its net realizable value, whichever is lower

Markdown (p. 609) Price reduction below the original markon

Markon (p. 608) The difference between the cost and the initial retail price of merchandise

Markup (p. 609) A price increase above the original markon

Net realizable value (p. 605) The estimated selling price of an inventory item in the ordinary course of business, less reasonably predictable costs of completion, disposal, and transportation

Periodic inventory (p. 600) Inventory based on a periodic count of goods on hand

Perpetual inventory (p. 600) Inventory based on a running total of number of units

Physical inventory (p. 600) An actual count of the number of units of each type of good on hand

Retail method (p. 608) A method of estimating inventory cost by applying the ratio of cost to selling price in the current accounting period to the retail price of the inventory

Specific identification method (p. 601) A method of inventory costing based on the actual cost of each item of merchandise

Weighted average method (p. 601) *See* Average cost method

Comprehensive Self Review

1. Name four commonly used methods or assumptions for determining the cost of an inventory.
2. Under what circumstances would it be logical to use specific identification in determining the ending inventory?
3. How often should a physical inventory be taken?
4. What is the formula for the cost ratio used in the retail method of estimating inventory?
5. How do the gross profit method and the retail method used to estimate inventory differ, if at all?
6. Suggest two situations in which it might be desirable (or necessary) to estimate inventories without a physical count.

(Answers to Comprehensive Self Review are at the end of the chapter.)

Discussion Questions

1. Suggest some specific controls that management must provide over inventory in a business that sells diamonds.
2. Suggest two situations where it may be necessary or desirable to estimate the inventory without a physical count.
3. Explain the retail method of inventory estimation.
4. A company uses the *LIFO* inventory method to determine cost. One of the managers complains that this is improper. He states: "We always sell our oldest products first. So we should be using *first-in, first-out* inventory costing." What would you say in response to his comment?
5. In a period of rising prices, is the *LIFO* method or the *FIFO* method likely to yield the larger inventory cost?
6. Is the value of inventory likely to be lower if the cost or net realizable value rule is applied on an item-by-item basis, on a group basis, or to the inventory as a whole?

7. Explain how the lower of cost or net realizable value method is applied on a group basis.
8. What is meant by the term *net realizable value* as it is used in the lower of cost or net realizable value rule?
9. What is meant by the *first-in, first-out* assumption?
10. Explain briefly the average cost method.
11. Under what circumstances is the specific identification method for determining cost of inventory items logical?
12. Why is a perpetual inventory easier to maintain today than it would have been 50 years ago?
13. Does the maintenance of a perpetual inventory eliminate the need for taking physical inventory? Explain.
14. What impact does the ending inventory have on net income for the period covered by the financial statements?
15. What accounting principle or constraint underlies the lower of cost or net realizable value rule for inventory valuation.

APPLICATIONS

Exercises

Exercise 17.1
Objective 17-1

▶ **Using the various costing methods of inventory valuation.**

Information about Spiceland Company's inventory of one item follows. Compute the cost of the ending inventory under (1) the average cost method (round unit cost to the nearest cent), (2) the FIFO method, and (3) the LIFO method.

Explanation	Number of Units	Unit Cost
Beginning inventory, January 1	230	$365
Purchases:		
April	270	370
August	190	375
October	240	377
Ending inventory, December 31	230	

Exercise 17.2
Objective 17-3

▶ **Using the lower of cost or net realizable value method.**

The following information concerns four items that Katy Mayfield Clothiers for Women has in its ending inventory on December 31. Two of these items are in the accessories department, and two are in the women leisure wear department.

	Quantity	Unit Cost	Net Realizable Value
Accessories			
Item 620	250	$30	$ 33
Item 621	160	56	53
Women leisure wear			
Item 726	110	96	103
Item 727	140	92	90

1. What is the valuation of ending inventory if the firm uses the lower of cost or net realizable value method and applies it on an item-by-item basis?
2. If the company applies the lower of cost or net realizable value method on the basis of total cost or total net realizable value, what is the value of ending inventory?
3. If the company elects to apply the lower of cost or net realizable value method to inventory groups, what is the value of the ending inventory?

Determining the effect on income of different costing assumptions. ◀ Exercise 17.3
Given the choice between average cost, FIFO, and LIFO, which method will give the lowest net income and which will give the highest net income in a period of rising prices?

Objective 17-2

Estimating inventory cost under the gross profit method. ◀ Exercise 17.4
Use the following data to compute the estimated inventory cost for Peterson Company under the gross profit method:

Objective 17-4

Average gross profit rate: 30% of sales

Inventory on January 1 (at cost): $230,000

Purchases from January 1 to date of inventory estimate: $1,040,000

Net sales for period: $1,300,000

Estimating inventory cost under the retail method. ◀ Exercise 17.5
Based on the following data, compute the estimated cost of the ending inventory at Kenamond Company. Use the retail method.

Objective 17-5

	Cost	Retail
Beginning inventory	$225,000	$ 339,000
Purchases	325,000	490,000
Freight in	4,200	
Sales		507,000

PROBLEMS

Problem Set A

Computing inventory costs under different valuation methods. ◀ Problem 17.1A
The following data concerns inventory and purchases at Hinojosa Company:

Objectives 17-1, 17-2

Inventory, January 1	100 units at $113
Purchases:	
January 6	70 units at $112
January 15	54 units at $113
January 22	44 units at $106
Inventory, January 31	100 units

INSTRUCTIONS

Determine the cost of the ending inventory on January 31 under each of the following methods: (a) average cost method; (b) first-in, first-out (FIFO) method; and (c) last-in, first-out (LIFO) method. When using the average cost method, compute the unit cost to two decimal places.

Analyze: Which inventory valuation method resulted in the highest dollar amount for ending inventory?

Problem 17.2A ▶ **Computing inventory costs under different valuation methods and applying the lower of cost or net realizable value rule.**

Objectives 17-1, 17-3

The following data pertains to software packages in the inventory of the Investment Software division of Foreign Market Investment Outlets:

Inventory, January 1	110 units at $234
Purchases:	
May 10	80 units at $230
August 18	115 units at $228
October 1	110 units at $230
Inventory, December 31	115 units

INSTRUCTIONS

1. Determine the cost of the inventory on December 31 and the cost of goods sold for the year ending on that date under each of the following valuation methods: (a) FIFO, (b) LIFO, and (c) average cost. When using the average cost method, compute the unit cost to the nearest cent.

2. Assume that the net realizable value of each unit on December 31 is $231. Using the lower of cost or net realizable value rule, find the inventory amount under each of the methods given in instruction 1.

Analyze: What is the difference between the cost and net realizable value of the inventory using the LIFO method?

Problem 17.3A ▶ **Applying the lower of cost or net realizable value rule by different methods.**

Objective 17-3

This data is for selected inventory items at Kimble Supply Company:

	Quantity	Unit Cost	Net Realizable Value
Printer Cartridges			
Item 119	70	$ 37.00	37.50
Item 120	80	30.75	27.50
Item 121	110	34.00	29.50
Fax Machines			
Item 210	25	97.00	100.00
Item 211	20	203.00	197.00
Item 212	19	236.00	$221.00

INSTRUCTIONS

Determine the amount to be reported as the inventory valuation at cost or net realizable value, whichever is lower, under each of these methods:

1. Lower of cost or net realizable value for each item separately.
2. Lower of total cost or total net realizable value.
3. Lower of total cost or total net realizable value by group.

Analyze: Which valuation method will yield the highest net income?

Estimating inventory by the gross profit method.

Over the past several years, Buzman Electronics has had an average gross profit of 30 percent. At the end of 20X1, the income statement of the company included the following information:

Sales		$ 3,518,000
Cost of Goods		
Inventory, January 1, 20X1	$ 244,000	
Purchases	2,440,000	
Total Merchandise Available for Sale	2,684,000	
Less Inventory, December 31, 20X1	293,750	
Cost of Goods Sold		2,390,250
Gross Profit on Sales		$ 1,127,750

Investigation revealed that employees of the company had not taken an actual physical count of the inventory on December 31. Instead, they had merely estimated the inventory.

INSTRUCTIONS

Using the gross profit method of inventory estimation, verify the reasonableness (or lack of reasonableness) of the ending inventory shown on the income statement.

Analyze: If a physical inventory count on December 31, 20X1, revealed an ending inventory of $291,126, calculate the gross profit percentage to the nearest one-tenth of 1 percent.

◀ **Problem 17.4A**
Objective 17-4

Estimating inventory by the retail method.

The August 1 inventory of Thompson Company had a cost of $180,000 and a retail value of $250,000. During August, merchandise was purchased for $202,260 and marked to sell for $304,000. August sales totaled $272,000.

INSTRUCTIONS

1. Compute the retail value of the ending inventory as of August 31.
2. Compute the approximate cost of the ending inventory.
3. Compute the cost of goods sold during August.

Analyze: What is the amount of estimated gross profit on sales for the month ending August 31?

◀ **Problem 17.5A**
Objective 17-5

Applying the correct method of evaluating inventory.

Jamison Sailing Company sells boats as a supplement to its boat storage operations. Data for its boat sales for August 20X1 are given below. The beginning inventory on August 1 was composed of the following items:

	Cost	Retail
28' Starfish	$ 90,000	$114,000
30' Perch	130,000	170,000
24' Sea King	52,000	60,000
30' Holiday	92,000	120,000
20' Lake King	56,000	69,000

◀ **Problem 17.6A**
Objectives 17-1, 17-2

INSTRUCTIONS

Sales during the month were the 30' Holiday and the 20' Lake King, sold at the retail values shown on August 1.

1. What is the best method of valuing the ending inventory?
2. Determine the value of Jamison Sailing Company's ending inventory of items that were brought over from the beginning inventory using this method. Assume that the company's retail values had not changed.
3. Determine the cost of goods sold during August.

Analyze: What is the estimated gross profit on sales for August?

Problem Set B

Problem 17.1B
Objectives 17-1, 17-2

▶ **Computing inventory costs under different valuation methods.**

The following data relates to the inventory and purchases of item 125 for McCray Company during May:

Inventory, May 1	260 units at $21.00
Purchases:	
May 10	190 units at $20.75
May 19	140 units at $20.35
May 25	160 units at $20.40
Inventory, May 31	230 units

INSTRUCTIONS

Determine the cost of the ending inventory on May 31 under each of the following methods: (a) average cost method; (b) first-in, first-out (FIFO) method; and (c) last-in, first-out (LIFO) method. When using the average cost method, compute the unit cost to two decimal places.

Analyze: Which inventory amount will result in the highest income for the period?

Problem 17.2B
Objectives 17-1, 17-3

▶ **Computing inventory costs under different valuation methods and applying the lower of cost or net realizable value rule.**

The following data pertains to Model Q two-wheeled trailers in the inventory of Moss Travel Trailers Equipment Company during the year 20X1:

Inventory, January 1	50 units at $10,480
Purchases:	
February 27	38 units at $9,320
August 16	46 units at $9,300
November 19	34 units at $9,740
Inventory, December 31	36 units

INSTRUCTIONS

1. Determine the cost of the inventory on December 31 and the cost of goods sold for the year ending on that date under each of the following valuation methods: (a) FIFO, (b) LIFO, and (c) average cost. When using the average cost method, compute the unit cost to the nearest cent.
2. Assume that the net realizable value of each unit on December 31 is $9,700. Using the lower of cost or net realizable value rule, find the inventory amount under each of the methods given in instruction 1.

Analyze: Using the lower of cost or net realizable value rule, which inventory amount will result in the highest net income for the period?

Applying the lower of cost or net realizable value rule by different methods.

Problem 17.3B
Objective 17-3

The following data concerns inventory at Eddy's Boat & Bike Shop:

	Quantity	Unit Cost	Net Realizable Value
Motor Bike Department			
Model 705	64	$ 9,850	$ 9,675
Model 766	104	10,325	11,350
Model 815	52	12,600	12,750
Boat Department			
Model BX12	36	5,400	5,500
Model BX14	32	7,250	6,990
Model BX16	28	5,220	5,325

INSTRUCTIONS

Determine the amount that the company should report as the inventory valuation at cost or net realizable value, whichever is lower. Use each of the following three valuation methods:

1. Lower of cost or net realizable value for each item separately.
2. Lower of total cost or total net realizable value.
3. Lower of total cost or total net realizable value by group.

Analyze: Which valuation method will yield the highest net income?

Estimating inventory by the gross profit method.

Problem 17.4B
Objective 17-4

Over the last two years, Allison Company has averaged 35 percent gross profit. At the end of 20X1, the auditor found the following data in the records of the company:

Sales		$1,540,000
Cost of goods sold:		
Inventory, January 1, 20X1	$ 105,000	
Purchases	1,045,000	
Total merchandise available for sale	1,150,000	
Less inventory, December 31, 20X1	151,000	
Cost of goods sold		999,000
Gross profit on sales		$ 541,000

Inquiry by the auditor revealed that employees of Allison Company had estimated the inventory on December 31, 20X1, instead of taking a complete physical count.

INSTRUCTIONS

Using the gross profit method of inventory estimation, verify the reasonableness (or lack of reasonableness) of the inventory estimate made by the company's employees.

Analyze: If a physical inventory count on December 31, 20X1, revealed an ending inventory of $130,000, calculate the gross profit percentage.

Estimating inventory by the retail method.

Problem 17.5B
Objective 17-5

The April 1 inventory of Henderson Stores had a cost of $231,000 and a retail value of $335,000. During April, merchandise was purchased for $267,250 and marked to sell for $419,000. Freight in was $9,000. April sales totaled $537,500.

INSTRUCTIONS

1. Compute the retail value of the ending inventory as of April 30.
2. Compute the approximate cost of the ending inventory.
3. Compute the cost of goods sold during April.

Analyze: What is the gross profit on sales for the period ending April 30?

Problem 17.6B
Objectives 17-1, 17-2

Using the correct inventory valuation method.

Beasley Realty Group had two completed unsold buildings on hand on January 1, 20X1.

Unit 06-92: Cost, $395,000; retail price, $482,000

Unit 06-94: Cost, $436,500; retail price, $504,000

During the period January 1 through March 31, the company completed the following construction jobs:

	Cost	Sales Price
Unit 06-95	$950,000	$1,145,000
Unit 07-01	459,500	589,000
Unit 07-03	418,000	557,500
Unit 07-05	560,000	725,250

All the units except 06-92 and 07-05 were sold in the quarter ending March 31.

INSTRUCTIONS

1. Determine the appropriate costing method for inventory in this construction business.
2. What value should be reported in the balance sheet for the company for the unsold units on March 31? Assume that it is firmly believed that the two buildings will be sold for the retail price shown.
3. Determine the cost of goods sold in the first quarter, assuming that all buildings sold were sold for the retail prices listed.

Analyze: What is gross profit on sales for the quarter ending March 31?

Critical Thinking Problem 17.1

Inventory Estimation

Sadler Computer Supply Company has just been destroyed by fire. Fortunately, however, the computerized accounting records had been "backed up" and were in a remote computer location so that the records were not destroyed. The company does not use the retail method of accounting, so although beginning inventory at cost, purchases at cost, purchases returns and allowances, freight in, sales, sales returns and allowances, and other accounting information are available, the retail method of estimating inventory destroyed cannot be used.

What suggestion can you give for determining the estimated cost of the inventory destroyed? What information is needed, and where would this information be found?

Critical Thinking Problem 17.2

Inventory Estimation

One of Wells Company's retail outlets was destroyed by fire on March 18. All merchandise was burned. The company has fire insurance on its merchandise inventory. It will therefore file a claim for recovery of the cost of the lost inventory. Clearly, a physical inventory cannot be taken because the inventory has been destroyed. The branch's records were kept by the home office, and you have been asked to examine the records to determine an estimate of the cost of the lost merchandise. As of March 18, the firm's records disclosed the following data about the beginning inventory for the year, the merchandise purchases made during the period, and total sales during the period:

	Actual Cost	Retail Sales Price
Beginning inventory, January 1	$90,000	$117,600
Merchandise purchases, January 1–March 18	62,500	82,600
Freight on purchases	2,325	
Total sales, January 1–March 18		110,000

INSTRUCTIONS

Determine the approximate cost of the inventory destroyed on March 18.

Analyze: Based on the cost you have computed for merchandise inventory, calculate the cost of goods sold for the period.

BUSINESS CONNECTIONS

Inventory Methods

1. In what special situations are inventory estimation procedures extremely useful?
2. The manager of a retail store has become concerned about the time taken to count the merchandise on hand each quarter. She argues that too much time is spent on this activity, with a resulting high cost of labor. She suggests that the company need not take a physical inventory at all but could rely on the retail inventory estimation procedure to arrive at the cost of the inventory. Respond to this argument.
3. What are two specific managerial reasons for using the LIFO method of inventory valuation during a period of rising prices?
4. In order to achieve better control over its investment in inventory, the management of a retail store wishes to get an estimate of the cost of inventory at the close of business each week. Outline a procedure to obtain this estimate without actually taking a physical count.
5. Explain briefly how computers and other electronic devices, such as scanners, have made perpetual inventories more practical.
6. The purchasing manager of a retail store has suggested that the company should maintain a perpetual inventory. The controller opposes this suggestion. In your opinion, on what basis does the controller probably oppose the idea?

Internal Controls for Inventory

Inventory control measures vary depending on the type of product to be sold. Why are good internal control procedures so important? List at least four inventory control measures to prevent fraud.

Balance Sheet

The following excerpt was taken from The Home Depot, Inc., for the fiscal year ended February 3, 2019:

Consolidated Balance Sheets		
(Dollars in millions)	February 3, 2019	January 28, 2018
Assets		
Current Assets:		
Cash and cash equivalents	$ 1,776	$ 3,595
Receivables, net	1,936	1,952
Merchandise inventories	13,925	12,748
Other current assets	890	638
Total Current Assets	$18,529	$18,933

Analyze:

1. By what amount has merchandise inventory increased or decreased from January 28, 2018, to February 3, 2019?

2. What percentage of current assets is attributable to inventories at February 3, 2018?

Analyze Online: Locate The Home Depot, Inc., website (www.homedepot.com) and click on the *Corporate Information* link under *About Us,* then click on *Investor Relations.*

3. Find the most recent annual report. What method is used to assign cost to the merchandise inventory? (Hint: See the Notes to Consolidated Financial Statements).

4. What is the stated value of the most recent year's merchandise inventory?

TEAMWORK

Missing Inventory

Erica has a baby clothing shop called The Baby Store. Erica has worked in her shop for several months. Her sales have doubled each month. Erica has decided to hire Wendy, a sales associate, because she needs to be away from the shop on a regular basis. After several months, Erica noticed that her purchases increased but sales did not go up in the same proportion and inventory is low. She is finding her net income is lower than in previous months. Divide the class into two teams. Have Team One list and discuss the possible reasons for her decreased income. Have Team Two determine the actions that should be taken to correct the problem.

Answers to Comprehensive Self Review

1. Specific identification, average costing, FIFO, and LIFO.
2. When there are relatively few items and each has a high cost.
3. Generally, inventory is taken once a year. If there is a history of thefts, breakage, overstocking or understocking, or other operational problems, it may be necessary to make physical counts more often.
4. Cost ratio = Cost of merchandise available for sale/Retail sales price of merchandise available for sale.
5. The retail method assumes that records have been kept of all inventory transactions at sales price (including price adjustments of merchandise), as well as cost, so that the inventory value at sales price of the merchandise is always known and readily convertible to a cost basis. The gross profit method is used when the retail price of inventory is unknown and has to be computed. The gross profit method uses a historical percentage rate, whereas the retail method calculates the percentage using current amounts. Therefore, the retail method results in a more current gross profit percentage.
6. The most obvious cases are when a fire or theft has occurred. Any other situation where the inventory has been physically removed or when a quick estimate is needed may call for an estimate.

Property, Plant, and Equipment

Chapter 18

Pavel Kapysh/Shutterstock

www.keurigdrpepper.com

Keurig Dr Pepper (KDP) completed their merger in July 2018 and became one of the leading coffee and beverage companies in North America. The merger created the seventh largest company in the U.S. food and beverage sector and the third largest beverage company in North America with annual revenues of approximately $1.1 billion. KDP holds leadership positions in soft drinks, specialty coffee and tea, water, juice and juice drinks, and mixers, and markets the number one single-serve coffee brewing system in the U.S. The company maintains an unrivaled distribution system that enables its portfolio of more than 125 owned, licensed, and partner brands to be available nearly everywhere people shop and consume beverages. With a wide range of hot and cold beverages that meet virtually every consumer need, KDP key brands include Keurig, Dr Pepper, Green Mountain Coffee Roasters, Canada Dry, Snapple, Bai, Motts, and The Original Donut Shop. The company employs more than 25,000 employees and operates more than 120 offices, manufacturing plants, warehouses, and distribution centers across North America. KDP maintains headquarters in Burlington, MA, and Frisco, TX.

Prior to the merger, Dr Pepper Snapple Group, Inc. (DPS) and Keurig Green Mountain, Inc., operated as two separate companies. DPS was built over time through a series of mergers and acquisitions that brought together iconic beverage brands in North America within Cadbury Schweppes, building on the Schweppes business by adding brands such as Dr Pepper, Snapple, 7UP, Canada Dry, Motts, and A&W.

Keurig Green Mountain, Inc. (Keurig), operated as a leading producer of innovative single-serve brewing systems and specialty coffee in the United States and Canada. Green Mountain Coffee Roasters, Inc., was incorporated in July 1993 and acquired Keurig Incorporated in June 2006 to form Keurig. For more information on the merger, visit the link above for the new consolidated group.

The manufacture, bottling, and distribution of its beverages require a substantial investment in buildings, warehouses, machinery, and trucks. On December 31, 2018, KDP reported $2.310 billion in property, plant, and equipment, net of accumulated depreciation. The machinery and equipment will be used for several years, but as it becomes less reliable and efficient, it will be replaced with new, more cost-effective equipment. Regular assessments are made of the equipment's contributions to the company's vision to be the best beverage business in the Americas.

thinking critically

When Keurig Dr Pepper contemplates replacing older equipment with newer equipment, what factors would go into making the final decision?

LEARNING OBJECTIVES

- **18-1** Determine the amount to record as an asset's cost.
- **18-2** Compute and record depreciation of property, plant, and equipment by commonly used methods.
- **18-3** Apply the Modified Accelerated Cost Recovery System (MACRS) for federal income tax purposes.
- **18-4** Record sales of plant and equipment.
- **18-5** Record asset trade-ins using financial accounting rules and income tax requirements.
- **18-6** Compute and record depletion of natural resources.
- **18-7** Recognize asset impairment and understand the general concepts of accounting for impairment.
- **18-8** Compute and record amortization and impairment of intangible assets.
- **18-9** Define the accounting terms new to this chapter.

NEW TERMS

accelerated method of depreciation	intangible assets
amortization	loss
brand name	net book value
capitalized costs	net salvage value
computer software	patent
copyright	real property
declining-balance method	recoverability test
depletion	residual value
double-declining-balance (DDB) method	scrap value
franchise	sum-of-the-years'-digits method
gain	tangible personal property
goodwill	trade name
impairment	trademark
income tax method	units-of-output method
	units-of-production method

Section 1

SECTION OBJECTIVES	TERMS TO LEARN
>> 18-1 Determine the amount to record as an asset's cost. **WHY IT'S IMPORTANT** An asset's cost is used to compute depreciation and gain or loss on disposition. >> 18-2 Compute and record depreciation of property, plant, and equipment by commonly used methods. **WHY IT'S IMPORTANT** Business expenses include allocations of the costs of long-term assets. >> 18-3 Apply the Modified Accelerated Cost Recovery System (MACRS) for federal income tax purposes. **WHY IT'S IMPORTANT** The IRS has special rules for cost recovery of long-term assets.	accelerated method of depreciation capitalized costs declining-balance method double-declining-balance (DDB) method net book value net salvage value real property residual value scrap value sum-of-the-years'-digits method tangible personal property units-of-output method units-of-production method

Acquisition and Depreciation

Setting up and maintaining a business often requires a large investment in property, plant, and equipment—assets often referred to as *fixed assets* or *capital assets*. In this section, two aspects of accounting for property, plant, and equipment are discussed:

- The costs of acquiring the assets.
- The transfer of the costs of these assets to expense through depreciation.

>> **18-1 OBJECTIVE**
Determine the amount to record as an asset's cost.

Property, Plant, and Equipment Classifications

As discussed in Chapter 12, *property, plant, and equipment* includes real property and tangible personal property purchased for use in the business and having a life of more than one year. **Real property** consists of land, land improvements (such as sidewalks and parking lots), buildings, and other structures attached to the land. **Tangible personal property** includes machinery, equipment, furniture, and fixtures that can be removed and used elsewhere.

The property, plant, and equipment classification does not include assets purchased for investment reasons. For example, land purchased for investment purposes is classified as other assets or investments.

Acquisition of Property, Plant, and Equipment

An important issue in accounting for property, plant, and equipment is determining which costs should be capitalized. **Capitalized costs** are all costs recorded as part of the asset's cost.

Costs of Equipment and Other Tangible Personal Property

The total cost of an asset can consist of several elements. Each element is debited to the account for that asset. The acquisition cost of an asset includes:

- gross purchase price less discounts, including cash discounts for prompt payment;
- transportation costs;

- installation costs;
- costs of adjustments or modifications needed to prepare the asset for use.

On January 2, 20X1, Hazlenut Company purchased store equipment for $18,000 and paid state and local sales taxes of $1,400. Transportation costs were $680. When the equipment arrived, extra features needed to prepare the asset for use were installed at a cost of $800. The **Store Equipment** account is debited for $20,880, as summarized below:

Purchase price	$18,000
Sales taxes	1,400
Transportation costs	680
Modification and installation costs	800
Total acquisition cost of machine	$20,880

Cost of Land and Building

The cost of land includes its purchase price, legal costs in connection with the acquisition, abstracts, title insurance, recording fees, and any other costs paid by the purchaser that are related to the acquisition.

The acquisition cost of land purchased for a building site should include the net costs (less salvage) of removing unwanted buildings and grading and draining the land. Remember that land is not depreciated.

Land improvements include the cost of installing permanent walks or roadways, curbing, gutters, and drainage facilities. These costs are debited to the asset account **Land Improvements.** Land improvements are depreciated.

If land and a building are purchased together for a single price, the purchase price is allocated between the **Land** and **Building** accounts. The amount allocated to the building is depreciated. The amount allocated to land is not depreciated.

Assets Constructed by or for the Business

When a building or other property, plant, and equipment is constructed and used by the business, the capitalized costs include all costs of labor, materials, permits and fees, insurance, measurable direct overhead, and other reasonable and necessary costs of construction. Interest costs incurred on borrowed funds during the construction period are capitalized as part of the asset.

Depreciation of Property, Plant, and Equipment

Buildings, machinery, equipment, furniture, and fixtures are depreciated because they have a limited life and will get used up or deteriorate over time. Depreciation is the allocation of the cost of the asset over the asset's useful life. Depreciation does not refer to a decrease in the market value of the asset.

Recording Depreciation

Assets that are used for more than one year are capitalized. Asset account names are descriptive, for example, **Office Equipment, Store Equipment, Vehicles,** or **Buildings.** At the end of each accounting period, depreciation for the period is debited to **Depreciation Expense** and credited to a contra asset account, **Accumulated Depreciation. Accumulated Depreciation** shows all depreciation that has been taken during the asset's life.

For example, a business purchased a building for $500,000 on January 2, 20X1. At the end of the first year, annual depreciation expense of $12,500 was entered on the

---

important!

Tangible Personal Property
The term "personal" means that the property has a physical substance and is something other than real estate. Personal property is owned by the business, not by the individual owners.

ABOUT ACCOUNTING

Fixed Assets
According to Asset Advisors, a Florida consulting firm, fixed assets represent 35 to 50 percent of the typical Fortune 500 company's assets.

recall

Land
Land is not depreciated.
Land has an indefinite life.
Land does not deteriorate or get used up.

>> 18-2 OBJECTIVE
Compute and record depreciation of property, plant, and equipment by commonly used methods.

worksheet as an adjustment. It was recorded as an adjusting entry in the general journal as follows:

	Dec.	31	Depreciation Expense—Buildings	12 500 00	
			Accumulated Depreciation—Buildings		12 500 00
			To record depreciation for the year		

The balance sheet shows a long-term asset's cost minus its accumulated depreciation. The difference is its book value, also known as its **net book value.** Book value is rarely the same as fair market value, which is the asset's price on the open market. After two years of depreciation, the balance sheet presentation for the building is as follows:

Property, Plant, and Equipment	
Building	$500,000.00
Less Accumulated Depreciation	25,000.00
Net Book Value	$475,000.00

> In fiscal 2018. Keurig Dr Pepper recorded *Depreciation and Amortization Expense* of $468 million. On December 31, 2018, the cost of its property, plant, and equipment was shown in the balance sheet at a net book value of $2.310 billion.

Depreciation information shown on the financial statements or in notes accompanying the financial statements includes:

- depreciation expense for the period;
- balances in the depreciable asset accounts, classified according to their nature or their function;
- accumulated depreciation;
- description of the method(s) used to compute depreciation.

Depreciation Methods

recall

Determining Annual Depreciation

The asset cost, the estimated salvage value, and the estimated useful life are needed in order to determine the annual depreciation.

Several methods are used to compute depreciation. Some of them use salvage value in the calculation. Under these methods, assets are not depreciated below salvage value. *Salvage value,* **residual value,** or **scrap value** is an estimate of the amount that could be obtained from an asset's sale or disposition at the end of its useful life. The **net salvage value** is the salvage value of the asset less any costs to remove or sell it.

Straight-Line Method The straight-line method introduced in Chapter 5 is the most widely used method of computing depreciation expense for financial statement purposes. Under the straight-line method, an equal amount of depreciation is recorded for each period over the useful life of the asset. Figure 18.1 shows straight-line depreciation of $432 per year.

FIGURE 18.1

Straight-Line Depreciation

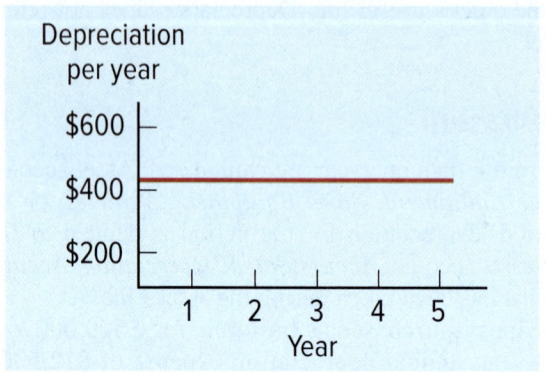

The formula for straight-line depreciation is as follows:

$$\text{Depreciation} = \frac{\text{Cost} - \text{Salvage value}}{\text{Estimated useful life}}$$

On January 2, 20X1, Hazlenut Company purchased office equipment for $2,400. The equipment has an estimated useful life of five years, with a net salvage value of $240. Using the straight-line method, the annual depreciation is $432 [($2,400 − $240)/5]. *Depreciation Expense—Office Equipment* will be debited for $432 and *Accumulated Depreciation—Office Equipment* will be credited for $432 each year.

When an asset is acquired during the year, depreciation is typically calculated to the nearest month. If the asset is acquired during the first 15 days of the month, depreciation is taken for the full month. If the asset is acquired after the 15th, depreciation starts in the following month. Suppose that Hazlenut Company purchased the office equipment on September 5. The monthly depreciation is $36 ($432 ÷ 12). Depreciation for the first year is $144 (4 months × $36). The journal entry is as follows:

	Dec.	31	Depreciation Expense—Office Equip.		144 00	
			Accumulated Depreciation—Office Equip.			144 00
			To record depreciation for four			
			months on equipment acquired			
			September 5			

Declining-Balance Method Under the **declining-balance method** of depreciation, the book value of an asset at the beginning of the year is multiplied by a percentage to determine depreciation for the year. The declining-balance method is an **accelerated method of depreciation,** which allocates greater amounts of depreciation to an asset's early years of useful life. The declining-balance computation ignores salvage value until the year in which the book value is reduced to estimated salvage value. Figure 18.2 illustrates the declining-balance method in graphical form.

One of the most common rates used is the **double-declining-balance (DDB).** DDB uses a rate equal to twice the straight-line rate and applies that rate to the book value of the asset at the beginning of the year. Follow these steps to calculate double-declining-balance depreciation on the office equipment for which straight-line depreciation was illustrated above:

Step 1: *Calculate the straight-line rate.*

$$\frac{100 \text{ percent}}{\text{Useful life}} = \frac{100 \text{ percent}}{5 \text{ years}} = 20 \text{ percent}$$

Step 2: *Calculate the double-declining rate.* The double-declining rate is the straight-line rate multiplied by 2, or 40 percent (20 percent × 2).

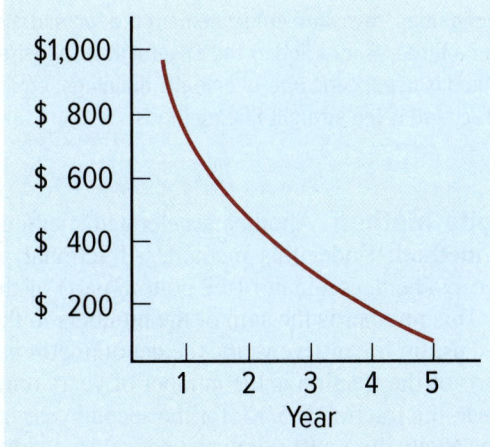

FIGURE 18.2

Declining-Balance Depreciation

TABLE 18.1

Depreciation under Double-Declining-Balance Method

Year	Beginning Book Value	Rate, %	Depreciation for Year	Depreciation to Date
1	$2,400.00	40	$960.00	$ 960.00
2	1,440.00	40	576.00	1,536.00
3	864.00	40	345.60	1,881.60
4	518.40	40	207.36	2,088.96
5	311.04	Limited	71.04	2,160.00

Book value at the end of five years = $240.00 ($2,400.00 − $2,160.00)

Step 3: *Compute depreciation for the period by multiplying the book value by the double-declining rate.* Repeat this step each year during the asset's useful life until the year in which the net book value would be less than salvage value.

Step 4: In the final year of depreciation, take only the amount of depreciation that will reduce the asset's net book value to its salvage value.

Here is how the double-declining-balance method would be applied to the asset purchased by Hazlenut Company:

- In the first year, the depreciation is $960 ($2,400 × 40%). *Note that salvage value is ignored in this computation.*

- At the start of the second year, the book value is $1,440 ($2,400 − $960). Depreciation for the second year is $576 ($1,440 × 40%). Note that the salvage value is again ignored in the computation.

- Similar computations are made in the third and fourth years and result in depreciation of $345.60 and $207.36 for the two years, respectively, as shown in Table 18.1. That table shows that the cumulative depreciation at the end of four years is $2,088.96. As a result, at the start of the fifth year, the asset's net book value is $311.04 ($2,400 cost − $2,088.96 depreciation taken = $311.04). This is only $71.04 greater than the estimated salvage ($311.04 − $240.00 = $71.04).

- *Remember that an asset should not be depreciated to a point that the net book value is less than the salvage value.* As a result, the depreciation for the fifth year is limited to $71.04 (unless there has been a change in the salvage value). Table 18.1 therefore shows depreciation for the fifth year is only $71.04. As a result, at the end of the fifth year, the accumulated depreciation will be $2,160 and the net book value at the end of the fifth year will be $240 ($2,400 cost − $2,160 accumulated depreciation), an amount equal to estimated salvage value.

> Hasbro, the maker of games, toys, and entertainment products, depreciates tools, dies, and molds over a three-year period or their useful lives, whichever is less. An accelerated method is used. Land improvements, buildings, equipment, and machinery are depreciated using straight-line methods.

Sum-of-the-Years'-Digits Method Another accelerated method of depreciation is the **sum-of-the-years'-digits method.** Under this method, a fractional part of the asset cost is charged to expense each year. The denominator (the bottom part) of the fraction is always the "sum of the years' digits." This number is the sum of the numbers in the asset's useful life. For a machine with an expected useful life of five years, the denominator is 15 (1 + 2 + 3 + 4 + 5). The numerator (the top part) of the fraction is the number of years remaining in the useful life of the asset. For the first year, the fraction is 5/15; for the second year it is 4/15; and so on. This fraction is multiplied by the acquisition cost minus the net salvage value of the asset.

TABLE 18.2

Comparison of Depreciation Methods

	Sum-of-the-Years'-Digits Method			Other Methods	
Year	Fraction	Cost Minus Salvage	Depreciation for Year	Declining Balance	Straight Line
1	5/15	$2,160.00	$ 720.00	$ 960.00	$ 432.00
2	4/15	2,160.00	576.00	576.00	432.00
3	3/15	2,160.00	432.00	345.60	432.00
4	2/15	2,160.00	288.00	207.36	432.00
5	1/15	2,160.00	144.00	71.04	432.00
Total depreciation, 5 years			$2,160.00	$2,160.00	$2,160.00

The first four columns of Table 18.2 show the sum-of-the-years'-digits method for the office equipment purchased by Hazlenut Company. Depreciation for the first year of the asset's life is $720 ($2,160 × 5/15) and for the second year of life, depreciation is $576 ($2,160 × 4/15). Table 18.2 compares this method with the other two commonly used methods.

Suppose that the equipment was purchased on September 5, 2019. Depreciation for the four months in 2019 would be a proportionate part of the depreciation for the first year of the asset's life, or $240 ($2,160 × 5/15 × 4/12).

For 2020, depreciation consists of the total of two parts: the depreciation for the remaining eight months of the first year (12 months) of life and depreciation for four months of the second year of life.

$2,160 × 5/15 (1st year fraction) × 8/12 (8 months)	$480
$2,160 × 4/15 (2nd year fraction) × 4/12 (4 months)	192
Depreciation for 2020	$672

Comparison of Depreciation Methods When choosing a depreciation method, much consideration is given to the matching principle. The goal is to match the cost of the asset to the periods when the asset provides benefits to the business. Review Table 18.2, which compares the three widely used methods. Notice that during the early years, the sum-of-the-years'-digits and declining-balance methods result in a larger depreciation expense than the straight-line method.

Accountants who favor the straight-line method believe that the asset provides equal benefits over its useful life. Many, however, suggest that accelerated depreciation is more logical than straight-line depreciation. They argue that typically assets are more productive in the early years of their lives, so greater benefit is gained from their use in those years. Additionally, repair costs and other maintenance costs are almost invariably higher when an asset gets older. The facts may suggest that straight-line depreciation results in a lower total cost per unit in the early years than in later years. Under the double-declining-balance and the sum-of-the-years'-digits methods, the higher depreciation costs in early years are partially offset by lower operating costs, so that there is a more nearly uniform total cost per unit of use.

Units-of-Output Method Under the straight-line and accelerated methods, depreciation is computed as a function of time. For some assets, depreciation is more directly related to the units of work produced. The **units-of-output method,** also known as the **units-of-production method,** calculates depreciation at the same rate for each unit produced. The unit of production may be measured in terms of the:

- physical quantities of production,
- number of hours the asset is used,
- other measures.

This method is often used to depreciate the cost of cars, trucks, and other motor vehicles, using miles as a measure of production.

Suppose that a business purchased a delivery truck for $64,000 in February 20X1. It is expected to be driven for 112,000 miles before being traded in and its expected salvage value at that time is $8,000. During 20X1, the truck was driven 17,400 miles.

Follow these steps to calculate depreciation under the units-of-production method:

Step 1: *Determine the depreciation per unit (per mile).* Divide the depreciable cost (the cost, minus estimated net salvage value) by the total miles expected to be driven during the truck's life.

$$\frac{\$64,000 - \$8,000}{112,000 \text{ miles}} = \$0.50 \text{ per mile driven}$$

Step 2: *Compute depreciation.* Multiply the number of units produced (miles driven) by the rate for each unit.

$$17,400 \text{ miles} \times \$0.50 \text{ per mile} = \$8,700$$

In its first year of operation, the truck would have depreciation expense of $8,700.

>> **18-3 OBJECTIVE**
Apply the Modified Accelerated Cost Recovery System (MACRS) for federal income tax purposes.

Federal Income Tax Requirements for "Cost Recovery" (Depreciation) of Property, Plant, and Equipment

The beginning accounting course focuses on financial accounting and reporting, so generally accepted accounting principles (GAAP) are of paramount importance. However, accountants commonly are involved in maintaining tax records and in preparing federal and state income tax returns. The treatments of many items of revenue and expense for income tax purposes differ greatly from those required under generally accepted accounting principles. It is therefore important that the accountant have a basic understanding of some of the major income tax rules that differ from financial accounting.

In addition, some small businesses that do not have audits by certified public accountants may adopt some tax requirements as part of their financial accounting in order to avoid confusion and duplication of work. One of those important differences is in the area of depreciation.

Federal income tax rules basically replace the depreciation rules of generally accepted accounting principles with the Modified Accelerated Cost Recovery System (MACRS), which applies to all assets purchased after December 31, 1986. (If appropriate, however, the taxpayer can use the units-of-production depreciation method instead of MACRS.)

MACRS was designed to encourage taxpayers to invest in business property and to simplify depreciation computations. Under MACRS, the portion of asset costs charged to expense is higher in the early years of an asset's life and lower in the later years. In that sense, it is akin to accelerated depreciation methods. This results in lower taxable income and tax savings in the early years with higher taxable income and taxes in later years.

Under MACRS, property is separated into defined classes. For tangible personal property, there are six classes of property. However, almost all personal property falls in three of those classes. Those three are:

- 5-year class—automobiles, lightweight trucks, computers, and certain special-purpose property.
- 7-year class—office furniture and fixtures and most manufacturing equipment.
- 10-year class—special purpose property, such as equipment used in the manufacture of food and tobacco products.

Under MACRS, the recovery periods for real property are:

- residential rental buildings—27.5 years.
- nonresidential buildings (office buildings) placed in service after May 12, 1993—39 years.
- nonresidential buildings placed in service on or before May 12, 1993—31.5 years.

Each MACRS class has a table of percentages. To determine the cost recovery (depreciation) under MACRS, multiply the asset's cost by the MACRS percentage. Salvage value is ignored. The following table shows the MACRS cost recovery for a $20,000 five-year asset, using the percentages required each year. Almost all businesses have assets in this rate class.

Year	Percent	Original Cost	Cost Recovery
1	20.00%	$20,000	$ 4,000
2	32.00	20,000	6,400
3	19.20	20,000	3,840
4	11.52	20,000	2,304
5	11.52	20,000	2,304
6	5.76	20,000	1,152
Totals	100.00%		$20,000

important!

Different Depreciation Methods Used

Most businesses use straight-line depreciation when preparing financial statements and MACRS when preparing tax returns.

Note that it takes six years to recover the entire cost of five-year properties. That is because MACRS uses the *half-year convention*. Regardless of purchase date, MACRS calculates depreciation for six months in the first year of the asset's life. The remaining six months of cost recovery are taken in the year after the end of the class life (in the sixth year for five-year property). (There are complex exceptions to the half-year convention.)

It is important that you know the basic concept of MACRS as demonstrated in the above example. It is also important to keep in mind that MACRS is not acceptable under GAAP.

Section 1 Review

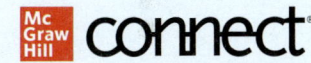

1. Tangible personal property includes all of the following except:
   a. machinery.
   b. equipment.
   c. furniture and fixtures.
   d. land.

2. The total cost of an asset includes all the following except:
   a. gross purchase price less discounts.
   b. transportation and freight to deliver the asset to the business.
   c. installation cost.
   d. utility cost related to the operation and use of the asset.

3. When an asset is constructed and used by the business, the capitalized cost includes all the following except:
   a. cost of labor to construct the asset.
   b. materials.
   c. permits and fees.
   d. measurable indirect cost.

4. Assuming a five-year life, a cost of $40,000, and an estimated net salvage value of $8,000, what would be the depreciation for the second year of the life of an asset if the double-declining-balance method is used?
   a. $6,400
   b. $8,000
   c. $9,600
   d. $16,000

5. An asset acquired on May 22, 20X1, cost $70,000, has an estimated useful life of five years, and has a net salvage value of $10,000. What is the amount of depreciation expense for 20X1 if the straight-line method is used?
   a. $7,000
   b. $8,000
   c. $8,200
   d. $14,000

6. What is the numerator and what is the denominator to be used in computing depreciation for the third year of use of an asset with a life of seven years if the sum-of-the-years'-digits method is used?
   a. numerator = 5; denominator = 28
   b. numerator = 6; denominator = 28
   c. numerator = 7; denominator = 20
   d. numerator = 8; denominator = 21

7. Which method of depreciation will result in a higher net income during the first year the asset is in use?
   a. straight-line
   b. sum-of-the-years'-digits
   c. declining-balance
   d. double-declining-balance

8. Land is not depreciated for all of the reasons below except:
   a. useful life is indefinite.
   b. land does not get used up.
   c. a and b are correct.
   d. Neither a nor b is correct.

Section 2

SECTION OBJECTIVES	TERMS TO LEARN
>> 18-4 Record sales of plant and equipment. **WHY IT'S IMPORTANT** Businesses routinely sell or dispose of plant assets that are no longer useful to the business. **>> 18-5** Record asset trade-ins using financial accounting rules and income tax requirements. **WHY IT'S IMPORTANT** Both methods are important to businesses.	gain income tax method loss

Disposition of Assets

The disposition of assets involves removing the asset's cost and its accumulated depreciation from the firm's accounting records. This section discusses the accounting treatment for three asset disposal methods: scrapping, sale, and trade-in.

Method of Disposition

Most business assets are eventually disposed of. They are either scrapped because they are worn out and have no value, sold because they are no longer needed by the business, or traded in on the purchase of new assets.

When assets are disposed of, the business often incurs a gain or a loss. A **gain** is the disposition of an asset for more than its book value. A **loss** is the disposition of an asset for less than its book value. The formula is:

$$\text{Proceeds} - \text{Book value} = \text{Gain or loss}$$

There is a gain when proceeds are higher than book value. There is a loss when proceeds are lower than book value.

A gain results from a peripheral activity of the business. In contrast, revenue involves the routine activities of the business such as selling goods and rendering services. A loss also results from a peripheral activity of the business. In contrast, expenses involve the day-to-day activities of the business.

The rules of debit and credit for gain accounts are the same as for revenue accounts. Similarly, expense accounts and loss accounts follow the same rules of debit and credit.

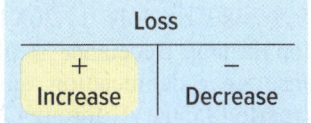
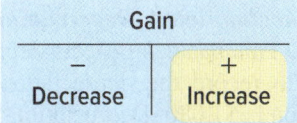

Disposal by Scrapping or Discarding

When an asset is worn out, often it is simply discarded. For example, the computer used by Sam's Discount Stores cost $5,250 and is fully depreciated. On June 30, the computer crashed and could not be repaired for a reasonable fee. It was worthless and was discarded. There were no proceeds from the disposal and no costs were incurred in the disposal. There is no gain or loss from the disposition:

Proceeds	$0
(Book value)	(0)
Gain or loss	$0

The following journal entry records the asset's disposal:

	June	30	Accum. Depreciation—Office Equipment		5 2 5 0 00		
			Office Equipment			5 2 5 0 00	
			Discarded computer				

If the discarded asset is not fully depreciated, depreciation is recorded up to the date of disposal. Suppose that the computer used by Sam's Discount Stores cost $5,250. Accumulated depreciation through December 31, 20X0, was $4,200. On June 30, 20X1, the computer crashed. The depreciation for the period January 1 through June 30 is $525. The depreciation is recorded through June 30 as follows: debit **Depreciation Expense** for $525 and credit **Accumulated Depreciation** for $525. After this entry, the **Accumulated Depreciation** account balance is $4,725 ($4,200 + 525). The book value of the computer is $525 ($5,250 − 4,725). There are no proceeds and no costs incurred for the disposal. There is a loss of $525 on the disposition.

Proceeds	$ 0
(Book value)	(525)
Gain or (loss)	$(525)

The entry to record the disposal of the computer removes the cost of the asset and its accumulated depreciation from the accounting records. The difference, book value, is recorded as a loss.

June	30	Accum. Depreciation—Office Equipment		4 7 2 5 00	
		Loss on Disposal of Fixed Assets		5 2 5 00	
		Office Equipment			5 2 5 0 00
		Discarded computer			

>> 18-4 OBJECTIVE

Record sales of plant and equipment.

Disposal by Sale

Sometimes useful assets are sold so the company can purchase better assets or because the assets are no longer needed. When an asset is sold, follow these steps to record the transaction:

Step 1. Record depreciation to the date of disposition.
Step 2. Remove the cost of the asset.
Step 3. Remove the accumulated depreciation.
Step 4. Record the proceeds.
Step 5. Determine and record the gain or loss, if any.

Several years ago, Hunter Laboratories purchased laboratory equipment for $12,000. The balance in **Accumulated Depreciation** was $6,480 on July 1, 20X1, the date the equipment is sold. This balance reflects depreciation through December 31 of the prior year. The first step is to record the depreciation expense since depreciation was last recorded. Annual depreciation is $1,080. Depreciation for the period January 1 through June 30 is therefore $540 ($1,080 ÷ 2). The entry is a debit to **Depreciation Expense—Laboratory Equipment** and a credit to **Accumulated Depreciation—Laboratory Equipment** for $540. After this entry, the **Accumulated Depreciation** account has a balance of $7,020 ($6,480 + 540) and the book value of the laboratory equipment is $4,980 ($12,000 − 7,020).

Sale for an Amount Equal to Book Value Suppose that the equipment was sold on account for book value, $4,980. Step 1, record depreciation to the date of disposition, has been illustrated. Steps 2–5 are as follows:

Step 2. *Remove the cost of the asset.* Credit **Laboratory Equipment** for $12,000.
Step 3. *Remove the accumulated depreciation.* Debit **Accumulated Depreciation— Laboratory Equipment** for $7,020.

Step 4. *Record the proceeds.* Debit **Accounts Receivable** for $4,980.
Step 5. *Determine and record the gain or loss, if any.*

Proceeds	$4,980
(Book value)	(4,980)
Gain or loss	$ 0

	GENERAL JOURNAL			PAGE 7	
DATE	DESCRIPTION	POST. REF.	DEBIT	CREDIT	
20X1					1
July 1	Accounts Receivable		4 980 00		22
	Accum. Depreciation—Laboratory Equipment		7 020 00		23
	Laboratory Equipment			12 000 00	24
	Sold laboratory equipment at				25
	book value				26

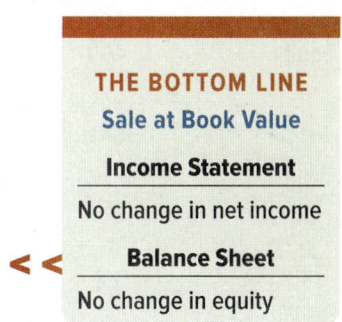

THE BOTTOM LINE
Sale at Book Value

Income Statement
No change in net income

Balance Sheet
No change in equity

Sale for More Than Book Value Suppose the equipment was sold on account for $5,520. The equipment was sold at a gain of $540.

Proceeds	$5,520
(Book value)	(4,980)
Gain	$ 540

The gain is recorded in the ***Gain on Sale of Equipment*** account. The gain is shown on the income statement in the Other Income section.

	GENERAL JOURNAL			PAGE 7	
DATE	DESCRIPTION	POST. REF.	DEBIT	CREDIT	
20X1					1
July 1	Accounts Receivable		5 520 00		22
	Accum. Depreciation—Laboratory Equipment		7 020 00		23
	Laboratory Equipment			12 000 00	24
	Gain on Sale of Equipment			540 00	25
	Sale of laboratory equipment				26
	at a gain				27

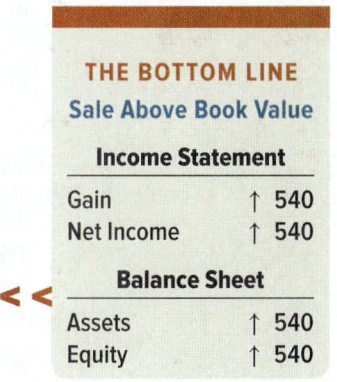

THE BOTTOM LINE
Sale Above Book Value

Income Statement
Gain ↑ 540
Net Income ↑ 540

Balance Sheet
Assets ↑ 540
Equity ↑ 540

Sale for Less Than Book Value Suppose the equipment was sold on account for $4,520. The equipment was sold at a loss of $460.

Proceeds	$4,520
(Book value)	(4,980)
Loss	($ 460)

The loss is recorded in the ***Loss on Sale of Equipment*** account. The loss appears on the income statement in the Other Expenses section.

> **THE BOTTOM LINE**
>
> **Sale Below Book Value**
>
> **Income Statement**
>
> Loss ↑ 460
> Net Income ↓ 460
>
> **Balance Sheet**
>
> Assets ↓ 460
> Equity ↓ 460

	GENERAL JOURNAL			PAGE 7
DATE	DESCRIPTION	POST. REF.	DEBIT	CREDIT
20X1				
July 1	Accounts Receivable		4 520 00	
	Accum. Depreciation—Laboratory Equipment		7 020 00	
	Loss on Sale of Equipment		460 00	
	Laboratory Equipment			12 000 00
	Sale of laboratory equipment			
	at a loss			

Some companies use a single account to record both gains and losses on sales of assets. The account is called *Gains and Losses on Sales of Assets.* It appears on the income statement in the Other Income section (if net gain) or Other Expenses section (if net loss).

>> **18-5 OBJECTIVE**
Record asset trade-ins using financial accounting rules and income tax requirements.

Disposal by Trade-In

Businesses often trade in old equipment when they purchase new equipment. Trade-in transactions are recorded in two steps:

Step 1. *Record the depreciation up to the date of trade-in.*

Step 2. *Record the trade-in of the old asset and the purchase of the new asset.*

Step 1 presents no new problem. Bringing the depreciation up to date involves precisely the same calculations that would be made if an asset were sold. Depreciation is recorded for the period beginning when the date of depreciation was last recorded and ending at the end of the month nearest the date of the trade-in.

Step 2 is somewhat more complicated.

a. *Under financial accounting rules, gains and losses on trade-ins are recorded as though the asset were sold.*

b. *For federal income tax purposes, neither gains nor losses are recognized on trade-ins.*

To illustrate the financial accounting rules and the income tax rules, we will examine a typical situation. Assume that on October 1, 20X1, Howard Company traded in an old truck acquired several years ago for $40,000, on a new truck. After bringing depreciation up to date, the total accumulated depreciation was $33,000, so that the book value was $7,000. The difference between the trade-in allowed and the agreed-on price of the truck is to be paid in cash.

Applying the Financial Accounting Rules for Trade-Ins

Actual gain or loss is the difference between the amount of allowance received on the trade-in and the book value of the old asset. The allowance is the difference between the fair value of the new asset and the amount of cash paid. For example, if Howard received a trade-in allowance of $7,800 on the old asset with a book value of $7,000, there is an implicit gain of $800. On the other hand, if the trade-in allowance is only $6,700 on an asset with a book value of $7,000, there is an implicit loss of $300.

Financial Accounting for Trade-in if Gain Is Realized on the Transaction Suppose that the new truck Howard acquired has an agreed-on price of $42,000, which is also its fair value. The dealer granted Howard a trade-in allowance of $7,800 and Howard paid cash of $34,200. As a result, Howard is deemed to have received $7,800 for the old truck. The implicit gain on the trade-in is $800 ($7,800 trade-in allowance minus $7,000 book value of the old truck.)

In this situation, the cost of the new asset is recorded at its fair market value and the difference between the trade-in allowance and book value of $800 is recorded as a gain.

Here are the steps to record the trade-in if there is a gain on the transaction:

Step 1. Remove the cost of the old asset ($40,000).
Step 2. Remove the accumulated depreciation for the old asset ($33,000).
Step 3. Record the payment ($34,200).
Step 4. Record the new asset at its fair market value ($42,000).
Step 5. Determine and record the gain ($800).

The journal entry to record the transaction would be:

	GENERAL JOURNAL			PAGE 7	
DATE	DESCRIPTION	POST. REF.	DEBIT	CREDIT	
20X1					1
Oct. 1	Truck (new)		42 000 00		2
	Accum. Depreciation (old truck)		33 000 00		3
	Truck (old)			40 000 00	4
	Gain on Trade-in of Truck			800 00	5
	Cash			34 200 00	6
	Trade-in of truck				7

Financial Accounting for Trade-in if Loss Is Realized on Transaction The above journal entry illustrates the financial accounting treatment for gains. For financial accounting purposes, losses are also recognized on trade-ins.

Suppose the amount allowed Howard as a trade-in value of the old asset had been $6,700, instead of $7,800, and Howard paid cash of $35,300 ($42,000 − $6,700). As a result, there would be a realized loss of $300 on the trade-in ($7,000 book value minus $6,700 received as trade-in allowance). Remember that for financial accounting purposes, losses *are* recognized. To record a trade-in under the financial accounting rules when there is a loss on the transaction, follow these steps:

Step 1. Remove the cost of the old asset ($40,000).
Step 2. Remove the accumulated depreciation for the old asset ($33,000).
Step 3. Record the payment ($35,300).
Step 4. Record the new asset at its fair market value ($42,000).
Step 5. Determine and record the loss ($300).

Here is the entry required to record the trade-in of the truck by Howard:

	GENERAL JOURNAL			PAGE 7	
DATE	DESCRIPTION	POST. REF.	DEBIT	CREDIT	
20X1					1
Oct. 1	Truck (new)		42 000 00		2
	Accum. Depreciation (old truck)		33 000 00		3
	Loss on Trade-in of Truck		300 00		4
	Truck (old)			40 000 00	5
	Cash			35 300 00	6
	Trade-in of truck at a loss				7

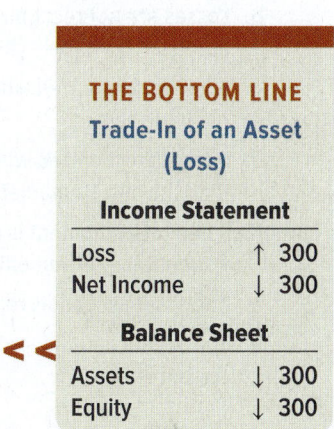

THE BOTTOM LINE

Trade-In of an Asset (Loss)

Income Statement

Loss	↑ 300
Net Income	↓ 300

Balance Sheet

Assets	↓ 300
Equity	↓ 300

Some smaller businesses follow the income tax rules discussed below in recording trade-in transactions because it may eliminate keeping two sets of records for the same transaction. It should be noted, however, that this is not always feasible because the cost and depreciation amounts may differ for financial accounting and tax purposes.

Applying the Income Tax Rules for Trade-Ins

The federal **income tax method** for trade-in transactions is easier than that for financial accounting because neither gain nor loss is recognized for tax purposes. The steps in applying the tax rules are:

Step 1. *Remove the cost of the old asset.*
Step 2. *Remove the accumulated depreciation for the old asset.*
Step 3. *Record the cash payment.*
Step 4. *Record the new asset at the sum of the book value of the old asset and the cash paid.*

Applying this basic rule to the two situations discussed above: (1) cash of $34,200 was paid on the trade-in and (2) cash of $35,300 was paid on the trade-in; no gain or loss would be recorded in either case for tax purposes. Assuming the same book value for both tax and financial reporting purposes (which is not the normal case because of the differences between depreciation calculations and MACRS cost recovery), in the first situation, the new truck would be recorded at $41,200 ($34,200 cash plus $7,000 book value of the old truck). In the second situation, the new truck would be recorded at $42,300 ($35,300 cash plus $7,000 book value of the old truck).

Section 2 Review

1. Under federal income tax rules, how are gains and losses on the trade-in of a like-kind asset treated?
    a. Gains and losses are recognized.
    b. Gains are recognized, but losses are not recognized.
    c. Neither gains nor losses are recognized.
    d. Losses are recognized, but gains are not recognized.

2. For financial reporting purposes, in what circumstances is a loss on the sale of a long-term asset recognized?
    a. A loss is recognized when the net book value exceeds the sales price.
    b. Losses are not recognized on the sale of long-term assets.
    c. A loss is recognized when the sales price exceeds the net book value.
    d. A loss is recognized when the net book value is less than the asset's market value.

3. If an item of equipment is retired and scrapped or sold, how should the retirement be accounted for?
    a. The asset account is removed from the books.
    b. The accumulated depreciation account is removed from the books.
    c. The difference between the proceeds or sales price and net book value is recorded as a gain or loss.
    d. All of the above, a, b, and c, are correct.

4. An asset that cost $20,000 and on which depreciation of $15,000 has been recorded is traded in on a new replacement asset. The sales price, also the fair value, of the new asset is $27,000. The owner of the old asset was given an allowance of $7,000 for the old asset and paid $20,000 in cash. For financial accounting purposes, what is the amount of gain or loss recorded?
    a. a gain of $2,000
    b. no gain or loss
    c. a loss of $2,000
    d. a gain of $7,000

5. An asset that cost $25,000 was retired and sold for $16,000 cash. Accumulated depreciation on the asset was $14,000. The entry to record this retirement and sale calls for recognizing:
    a. no gain or loss.
    b. a gain of $4,000.
    c. a loss of $9,000.
    d. a gain of $5,000.

6. If a company's fully depreciated asset that had no salvage value was scrapped but not removed from the accounting records, what would be the effect on the company's financial statements?
   a. The asset account and the accumulated depreciation account would be overstated by the same amount.
   b. There would be no effect on the net asset book value.
   c. Neither a nor b is correct.
   d. Both a and b are correct.

7. All of the following are steps in recording a trade-in of like-kind assets under the federal income tax method except:
   a. remove the cost of the old asset.
   b. remove the accumulated depreciation for the old asset.
   c. record the cash payment.
   d. record the gain or loss on the transaction.

8. Under the federal income tax method in recording a trade-in of a like-kind asset, at what amount is the new asset recorded?
   a. fair value
   b. the sum of the book value of the old plus the cash paid
   c. the cash paid in the transaction
   d. the sum of the fair value of the old plus the cash paid

Section 3

SECTION OBJECTIVES	TERMS TO LEARN
>> 18-6 Compute and record depletion of natural resources. **WHY IT'S IMPORTANT** Depletion matches an asset's costs with the benefits derived from its use. **>> 18-7** Recognize asset impairment and understand the general concepts of accounting for impairment. **WHY IT'S IMPORTANT** Sometimes assets do not retain their ability to generate expected revenues. In these cases, the asset cost is adjusted in the accounting records. **>> 18-8** Compute and record amortization and impairment of intangible assets. **WHY IT'S IMPORTANT** An intangible asset's cost is charged to expense over its assumed life.	amortization brand name computer software copyright depletion franchise goodwill impairment intangible assets patent recoverability test trade name trademark

Special Topics in Long-Term Assets

In the first two sections of this chapter, you have learned how to account for costs incurred in connection with the acquisition, operation, and disposition of property, plant, and equipment. These are very common transactions arising in almost every business. In the final section of the chapter, you will learn how to handle three less commonly encountered transactions related to assets of this type:

1. Depletion of costs of natural resources.
2. Impairment of property, plant, and equipment.
3. Costs incurred to acquire intangible assets.

In addition, you will learn some of the basic internal controls used to safeguard property, plant, and equipment—the asset category representing the largest investment of funds for most types of business.

Depletion

Natural resources such as iron ore, oil, gold, and coal are physically removed from the land in the production process. Businesses must know how to allocate the cost of natural resources as they are taken from their source. As the resources are extracted, part of their cost is charged to expense. **Depletion** is the term used to describe allocating the cost of the natural resource to expense over the period in which the resource produces revenue.

Depletion for Financial Statement Purposes

Depletion of the cost of natural resources for financial statement preparation is called *cost depletion*. It is similar to the units-of-output method of depreciation. The formula is:

$$\frac{\text{Cost of natural resource}}{\text{Estimated units of the resource}} = \text{Depletion per unit}$$

A business purchased a clay pit for $80,000. The clay pit is estimated to contain 500,000 tons of extractable clay suitable for making bricks. The depletion cost for each ton of clay is $0.16 ($80,000 ÷ 500,000 tons). During the first year, the business extracted 30,000 tons of clay. The depletion is $4,800 (30,000 × $0.16). The adjusting entry to record depletion follows:

	Dec.	31	Depletion Expense	4,800.00	
			Accumulated Depletion		4,800.00
			To record the extraction of		
			30,000 tons of clay		

After the first year, the natural resource appears on the balance sheet as follows. The net book value of the natural resource is $75,200.

Property, Plant, and Equipment	
Clay Deposits	$80,000
Less Accumulated Depletion	4,800
Net Clay Deposits	$75,200

Oil and gas production and mining operations use long-lived assets such as oil pumps and mining equipment. These assets are depreciated, usually using the units-of-output method.

Depletion for Federal Income Tax Purposes

>> 18-6 OBJECTIVE
Compute and record depletion of natural resources.

Depletion for federal income tax purposes is the larger of cost depletion or percentage depletion. Cost depletion for tax purposes is computed in the same way as it is for financial statement preparation. However, the amount of cost depletion may be different because the cost (the numerator) for financial purposes may be different from the cost for tax purposes. If percentage depletion is taken on the tax return, the amount taken in any year will reduce the cost on which cost depletion is based in future years.

Percentage depletion for a property is calculated by multiplying the gross income from the sale of the natural resource by a percentage. The percentage depends on the specific natural resource.

In 20X1, a mining company has sales of $1,800,000 for ore produced from a mine. For tax purposes, the book value (capitalized costs, less depletion taken in prior years) of the minerals at the beginning of the year was $16,000. The allowable percentage depletion rate for the minerals produced is 15 percent. The company will deduct $270,000 on its federal income tax return ($1,800,000 × 0.15 = $270,000). In future years, there will be no allowable *cost depletion*, but *percentage depletion* may continue to be taken even though the book value for tax purposes is zero.

Impairment of Property, Plant, and Equipment

>> 18-7 OBJECTIVE
Recognize asset impairment and understand the general concepts of accounting for impairment.

Relying on the historical cost concept and the going concern assumption, many accountants have assumed that if a long-term asset continues to be used in income production, the asset will generate future cash revenues, and the value of those revenues will exceed the book value of the asset. However, in the late 1980s and early 1990s, many businesses recorded "write-offs" of assets when their values declined substantially.

Because of concern over situations in which doubt exists as to whether the asset's use will generate adequate cash flows to recover the book value of assets, in 2001 the Financial Accounting Standards Board issued Financial Accounting Standard (FAS) 144, "Accounting for Impairment of Long-Lived Assets." These guidelines can be found in the recently developed Accounting Standards Update (ASU) 360-10, which lay out generally accepted accounting principles for recording impairment of property, plant, and equipment when it appears that the carrying amount of the assets may not be recoverable. Stated simply, **impairment** exists when book value exceeds the "fair value" of the asset.

The procedures and measurement techniques for recording impairment are quite complex and are beyond the scope of this textbook, but a brief summary of measuring and recording impairment will provide you with a basic understanding when you encounter circumstances suggesting that impairment may exist.

The three steps in the process of determining an impairment loss are:

Step 1: *Review circumstances that suggest impairment may have occurred.* ASU 360-10 gives examples of events and changes in circumstance that suggest impairment *may have* occurred:

  a. A significant decrease in the market value of an asset.
  b. A significant change in the extent of use or way in which the asset is used.
  c. A significant adverse change in the legal environment or in the manner in which an asset is used.
  d. A forecast suggesting continuing losses associated with the asset. There are, however, many other economic and technical factors that may suggest assets should be analyzed for possible impairment, for example, increased competition, new technical developments, a forecast of decreased demand for the products, and so forth.

Turner Disposal Company has operated a facility to separate liquids and gaseous products from a stream of crude oil from wells. Present book value of the facility is $792,000. Revenues from the facility have decreased by approximately 14 percent during each of the last two years. *This suggests that impairment may have occurred.*

Step 2: *Apply the recoverability test.* If circumstances suggest that impairment may have occurred, the **recoverability test** should be applied to determine whether impairment does exist. The recoverability test is a comparison of the asset's carrying value (net book value) with the estimated net cash flows from future use of the asset, including eventual disposition of the asset. If the estimated net future cash flows are less than the asset's book value, impairment has occurred.

Obviously, in most cases it is not possible to estimate future net cash flows that are expected to be generated by a single item of equipment, such as a computer used in the office, a display rack used in a retail store, or a piece of machinery in a factory. ASU 360-10 states that in making impairment calculations, the unit of measurement is not a single asset, but the smallest unit of the business for which net cash flows can be determined from the assets used.

Turner made a projection of future cash inflows from services and cash outflows from expenses over the expected remaining life of the facilities and estimates that future net cash

MANAGERIAL IMPLICATIONS <<

PROPERTY, PLANT, AND EQUIPMENT

- Property, plant, and equipment often represent the largest cash investment by the owners of a business.
- Managers are responsible for establishing strong internal controls over property, plant, and equipment.
- Managers should understand the different depreciation methods and how they impact the financial statements and income tax returns of the business.
- Management should ensure that procedures are in place to monitor repairs, power consumed, and other operating costs to make sure that assets are functioning efficiently.
- Managers must understand the methods used to record asset sales and trade-ins because the different methods have different results that impact the financial statements of the business.

THINKING CRITICALLY

How does the choice of depreciation method impact the financial statements?

flows from its operations will total $690,000. These future cash flows are less than the asset's $792,000 book value, so impairment does exist.

Step 3: *Compute the amount of the impairment.* The amount of impairment is the amount by which the asset's book value exceeds its market value. There may be instances in which the market value of an asset can be determined by quoted prices in the markets. However, these quotations may be scarce for many assets, so market value must be determined by other means. The usual methodology is to compute the "discounted value" (present value) of the stream of future net cash flows from use of the assets, calculated in step 2. Essentially, the present value of the estimated future cash flows is the amount that it would be necessary to invest today in order to earn a specific rate of return on the investment, considering the cash flows expected to be received each year during the future life of the asset. If the market value, or present value, is less than the net book value of the asset, impairment exists and should be recorded in the amount of the excess of book value over market value.

In step 2, above, Turner estimated that future cash flows were only $690,000 from an asset with a book value of $792,000. Turner then applied to the future cash stream a discount factor based on its expected rate of return on an asset of this type. In applying the discount rate, Turner estimated that the company would be willing to pay $540,000 for the asset today. That is its market value to the firm. Turner records impairment by debiting ***Loss from Impairment of Separation Equipment*** for $252,000 and crediting ***Separation Equipment*** for that amount.

Once an impairment write-down of an asset has been made, the amount charged off is not reinstated even if the market value subsequently increases—the conservatism constraint and the realization principle in effect.

In the year following Turner's write-down of the separation equipment in the preceding example, the price of oil and gas increased dramatically, and as a result the value of the processing facility increased to $858,000. However, this increase in value is not recognized in the accounts.

Intangible Assets

In addition to property, plant, and equipment, many businesses have intangible assets. **Intangible assets** are assets that lack a physical substance. The major types of intangible assets are patents, copyrights, franchises, trademarks, brand names, organizational costs, computer software, and goodwill. With the exception of computer software, intangible assets usually do not have any physical attributes.

Classifying Intangible Assets

A **patent** is an exclusive right given by the U.S. Patent and Trademark Office to manufacture and sell an invention for a period of 20 years from the date the patent is granted. A patent may not be renewed; however, a new patent may be obtained if significant improvements in the original idea can be demonstrated. The right to the patent may be sold, assigned, or otherwise controlled by the owner.

A **copyright** is the exclusive right granted by the federal government to produce, publish, and sell a literary or artistic work for a period equal to the creator's life plus 70 years.

There are two types of **franchises.** The first type is a right granted by a governmental unit for the business to provide a service to the governmental unit (such as cable television). The second type is an exclusive dealership or an exclusive arrangement between a manufacturer and a dealer or distributor.

Trademarks, trade names, and **brand names** are used to build consumer confidence and loyalty. They can be registered with the U.S. Patent and Trademark Office. They can be sold, traded, or otherwise controlled by the owner.

Organizational costs are the costs incurred when organizing a business. Organizational costs include attorneys' fees, accountants' fees, legal filing fees, and other costs of beginning a business.

Computer software consists of written programs that instruct a computer's hardware to do certain tasks. Software can be developed by the company's employees or purchased outside the company. For some firms, computer software is the most important (and most costly) asset owned.

Goodwill represents the value of a business in excess of the value of its identifiable assets. Goodwill is recorded only at the time of the purchase of a business. It usually occurs when a business being purchased has extraordinary earnings or earnings potential.

> For many companies, intangible assets are a very important part of the total assets. For example, in its balance sheet at the end of 2018, Johnson & Johnson reported total assets of $152.95 billion. This total included *Goodwill,* $50.45 billion, and other intangibles of $47.61 billion.

Acquiring Intangible Assets

There are two ways to acquire intangible assets: (1) produce or develop them or (2) purchase them. The general rule is that an intangible asset is recorded in the books of the firm only if it is purchased from another party. Costs to develop intangible assets internally are expensed in the year incurred to the **Research and Development Expense** account. Similarly, costs related to software development by a company are expensed in the year incurred. However, there are special rules if the software is to be sold, leased, or otherwise marketed:

1. Costs are expensed as incurred when creating the software product until technological feasibility is established for the product. *Technological feasibility* is deemed to occur when a detailed program design or a working model of the product has been developed.
2. Costs are capitalized to an asset account once a product is deemed to be technologically feasible.

>> **18-8 OBJECTIVE**
Compute and record amortization and impairment of intangible assets.

Disposition of Capitalized Acquisition Costs of Intangible Assets

For accounting purposes, costs of intangibles that have been acquired for a cost and are identified as being appropriately capitalized are classified into two groups:

1. Those that are determined to have lives that are definite or can be reasonably estimated. The most common of these are patents, copyrights, most franchises, and purchased computer software.
2. Those that do not have definite or reasonably estimable useful lives. These include organization costs, purchased goodwill, trademarks, brand names, and trade names.

Amortization of Cost of Intangibles with Estimable Useful Lives The accounting treatment of costs of intangibles in this category is very similar to depreciation of property, plant, and equipment. The periodic transfer of intangibles' cost to expense is known as **amortization.** The costs are typically amortized on a straight-line basis or on a units-of-production basis.

In January 20X1, Marcus Company purchased for $200,000 a patent that had a remaining life of 10 years. Based on straight-line amortization, Marcus recorded the following entry for amortization at the end of 20X1:

	Dec.	31	Amortization of Patent		20 000 00		
11							11
12			Patent			20 000 00	12
13			To record annual amortization				13
14			of patent				14

An identical entry will be made at the end of 20X2 so that the balance remaining in the *Patent* account on January 1, 20X3, will be $160,000. Suppose in 20X3 it is estimated that the patent will be of benefit only through the year 20X6. Based on this estimate, the patent amortization for each year 20X3 to 20X6 will be $40,000 ($160,000 ÷ 4 years).

Impairment of Cost of Intangibles with Indefinite Useful Lives

When intangibles that do not have estimable lives have been purchased, an assessment must be made each year to estimate the value of the intangible. If the estimate is less than the existing book value, impairment must be recorded in the same way that impairment of property, plant, and equipment is recorded. Here, the concept of conservatism comes into play.

Fifteen years ago, Marcus Company purchased from another business a "brand name" for $400,000 and charged it to the intangible asset account **Brand Names.** Because of declining sales of the products covered by the brand and the decrease in profits on sales of the products, Marcus concluded in 20X1 that the brand name was no longer worth $400,000 and that a conservative estimate of its value was $100,000. Based on that, the following entry was made by Marcus:

	Dec.	31	Loss from Impairment of Brand Name		300 000 00	
			Brand Names			300 000 00
			To record impairment of brand name			

A similar assessment should be made each year to see if further impairment should be recorded. However, if the value of the intangible asset increases in years subsequent to recording impairment, the carrying value of the asset *is not increased.*

The annual report for The Coca-Cola Company and Subsidiaries for 2018 contained the following as part of its note explaining its accounting for "Goodwill."

Goodwill

All business combinations are accounted for using the acquisition method. Goodwill is tested for impairment annually, or more frequently if facts and circumstances indicate such assets may be impaired. The Company performs its annual impairment tests, which includes qualitative assessment to determine whether it is more likely than not that the fair value of the goodwill is below its carrying value, as of the first day of the fourth quarter each year, and more often if there are significant changes in business conditions that could result in impairment.

The Company has determined it has one reporting unit, within the Nonalcoholic Beverages reportable segment, for the purpose of assessing goodwill for potential impairment. The Company uses its overall market capitalization as part of the estimate of fair value of the reporting unit in assessing the reasonableness of the Company's internal estimates of fair value.

When a quantitative analysis is considered necessary for the annual impairment analysis of goodwill, the Company develops an estimated fair value for the reporting unit considering three different approaches.

- market value, using the Company's stock price plus outstanding debt;
- discounted cash flow analysis, and
- multiple of earnings before interest, taxes, depreciation, and amortization based upon relevant industry data.

The estimated fair value of the reporting unit is then compared to its carrying amount, including goodwill. If the estimated fair value exceeds the carrying amount, goodwill is not considered impaired. If the carrying amount, including goodwill, exceeds its estimated fair value, any excess of the carrying value of goodwill of the reporting unit over its fair value is recorded as an impairment.

To the extent the actual and projected cash flows decline in the future or if market conditions significantly deteriorate, the Company may be required to perform an interim impairment analysis that could result in an impairment of goodwill.

Source: From the 2018 Annual Report on Form 10-K. https://cocacolabottlingcoconsolidated.gcs-web.com/static-files/b29c43af-6d84-4bb9-82fb-7a7976e48c22

Internal Control of Property, Plant, and Equipment

The internal control of property, plant, and equipment involves physical safeguards to prevent theft or misuse. The following are standard internal control procedures for fixed assets:

- Authorize and justify the purchase of all long-lived assets.
- Assign and, if possible, engrave an identification number on each asset.
- Maintain an asset register listing all capital assets, their costs, acquisition dates, location, and any other useful information.
- Assign responsibility for safekeeping, maintaining, and operating each asset to a specific person.
- Take a physical inventory periodically. Compare the physical inventory with the asset register and investigate any differences.
- Establish procedures to authorize asset retirement, sale, or other disposition.

The internal control of intangible assets consists primarily of the safe storage of documents and protection of the storage location. Businesses need to be alert to copyright and trademark infringements. Legal action is required when an infringement of an intangible asset occurs.

Section 3 Review

1. Impairment exists when:
   a. book value is less than the fair value of the asset.
   b. book value is more than the fair value of the asset.
   c. book value is equal to the fair value of the asset.
   d. None of the above are correct.

2. Depletion for federal income tax purposes is:
   a. cost depletion.
   b. percentage.
   c. the larger of cost depletion or percentage.
   d. fair value depletion.

3. Strategic Innovations Company spent $80 million in 20X1 on research and development costs (R&D). Some work was general research seeking basic knowledge about products. Other work was getting several projects started to investigate ways to develop and improve a line of drugs manufactured by the company. Other costs were incurred in the final stages of perfecting new products. How should these costs be accounted for by Strategic Innovations?
   a. capitalized as an asset and amortized over the expected useful life of the research
   b. charged to expense as incurred
   c. capitalized as an asset not subject to amortization
   d. capitalized and expensed against revenue as revenue from the research is realized

4. Intangible assets include all the following except:
   a. patents.
   b. copyrights.
   c. franchises.
   d. land.

5. The allocation of the cost of intangible assets over their estimated useful life is called:
   a. depletion.
   b. depreciation.
   c. amortization.
   d. cost recovery.

6. Percentage depletion may continue to be taken even though the book value of the asset for tax purposes is zero.
   a. True
   b. False

7. An oil company paid a landowner $30,000 for the mineral rights underlying his property. The well was drilled and equipped at a cost of $900,000. It is estimated that 300,000 barrels of oil will be produced from the property. How should these costs be treated in the accounting records?
   a. The cost of the mineral rights should be capitalized and depleted over the estimated units of production.
   b. The drilling equipment should be capitalized and depreciated over its estimated useful life.
   c. Both a and b are correct.
   d. Only b is correct.

8. Goodwill represents the value of the business in excess of the value of its identifiable assets and should only be recorded at the time of the purchase of a business.
   a. True
   b. False

REVIEW Chapter Summary

Property, plant, and equipment are those tangible assets used in carrying out the company's business operations. In this chapter, you have learned how to record transactions for the purchase, use, and disposition of these assets. You have also studied the accounting methods required to record the acquisition of intangible assets such as copyrights and patents, as well as the costs of amortization.

Learning Objectives

18-1 Determine the amount to record as an asset's cost.

The cost of an asset is its net purchase price, plus costs of transportation, installation, and all other costs necessary to put the asset into normal operation.

18-2 Compute and record depreciation of property, plant, and equipment by commonly used methods.

Costs of a tangible asset should be charged to expense over its useful life through systematic depreciation charges. Depreciation is recorded by a debit to *Depreciation Expense* and a credit to *Accumulated Depreciation.* Four widely used methods of computing depreciation for financial accounting purposes are the:

- straight-line method,
- declining-balance method,
- sum-of-the-years'-digits method,
- units-of-production method.

18-3 Apply the Modified Accelerated Cost Recovery System (MACRS) for federal income tax purposes.

Under the federal income tax laws, new assets must be depreciated under the Modified Accelerated Cost Recovery System (MACRS), with minor exceptions. Under MACRS, each type of asset is assigned to a MACRS class. Each class is assigned a different depreciable life.

18-4 Record sales of plant and equipment.

Property, plant, and equipment are disposed of in various ways; most commonly, they are sold or scrapped. At an asset's sale, its depreciation is brought up to date. Gain or loss at the time of disposal is computed by comparing the asset's net book value with the proceeds, if any, received on its disposal. For financial accounting purposes, a gain or loss may be recorded from the sale, retirement, or scrapping of an asset.

18-5 Record asset trade-ins using financial accounting rules and income tax requirements.

If a business trades old equipment when purchasing new equipment, two transactions must be recorded. The depreciation on the used equipment must be brought up to date. Then, the trade and purchase are recorded. Both gains and losses are recognized under financial accounting rules. Using the income tax method, no gain or loss is recorded on the trade-in of an asset on a new similar asset.

18-6 Compute and record depletion of natural resources.

The costs of natural resources such as mineral deposits are charged to expense on a per-unit-of-production basis for financial accounting and reporting purposes. Special rules apply for income tax purposes.

18-7 Recognize asset impairment and understand the general concepts of accounting for impairment.

If an asset's expected future net cash flows are less than the asset's book value, impairment may need to be recognized. The amount of impairment is the amount by which the book value exceeds the asset's fair value—usually defined as the discounted value of the future net cash flows from its use.

18-8 Compute and record amortization and impairment of intangible assets.

Except for software, intangibles have no physical characteristics. If they are bought from outside parties, intangibles are recorded at cost. Costs incurred by firms that produce their own intangible assets are not capitalized but are charged to *Research and Development Expense* in the year incurred. Costs of intangibles with identifiable lives are amortized. Costs of those with indefinite lives are charged to expense through impairment tests.

18-9 Define the accounting terms new to this chapter.

Glossary

Accelerated method of depreciation (p. 627) A method of depreciating an asset's cost that allocates greater amounts of depreciation to an asset's early years of useful life

Amortization (p. 644) The process of periodically transferring the acquisition cost of intangible assets with estimated useful lives to an expense account

Brand name (p. 643) *See* Trade name

Capitalized costs (p. 624) All costs recorded as part of an asset's costs

Computer software (p. 644) An intangible asset; written programs that instruct a computer's hardware to do certain tasks

Copyright (p. 643) An intangible asset; an exclusive right granted by the federal government to produce, publish, and sell a literary or artistic work for a period equal to the creator's life plus 70 years

Declining-balance method (p. 627) An accelerated method of depreciation in which an asset's book value at the beginning of a year is multiplied by a constant percentage (such as 125%, 150%, or 200%) to determine depreciation for the year

Depletion (p. 640) Allocating the cost of a natural resource to expense over the period in which the resource produces revenue

Double-declining-balance (DDB) method (p. 627) A method of depreciation that uses a rate equal to twice the straight-line rate and applies that rate to the book value of the asset at the beginning of the year

Franchise (p. 643) An intangible asset; a right to exclusive dealership granted by a governmental unit or a business entity

Gain (p. 633) The disposition of an asset for more than its book value

Goodwill (p. 644) An intangible asset; the value of a business in excess of the net value of its identifiable assets

Impairment (p. 641) A situation that occurs when the asset is determined to have a fair market value less than its book value

Income tax method (p. 638) A method of recording the trade-in of an asset for income tax purposes. It does not permit a gain or loss to be recognized on the transaction

Intangible assets (p. 643) Assets that lack a physical substance, such as goodwill, patents, copyrights, and computer software, although software has, in a sense, a physical attribute

Loss (p. 633) The disposition of an asset for less than its book value

Net book value (p. 626) The cost of an asset minus its accumulated depreciation, depletion, or amortization, also known as book value

Net salvage value (p. 626) The salvage value of an asset less any costs to remove or sell the asset

Patent (p. 643) An intangible asset; an exclusive right given by the U.S. Patent and Trademark Office to manufacture and sell an invention for a period of 20 years from the date the patent is granted

Real property (p. 624) Assets such as land, land improvements, buildings, and other structures attached to the land

Recoverability test (p. 642) Test for possible impairment that compares the asset's net book value with the estimated net cash flows from future use of the asset

Residual value (p. 626) The estimate of the amount that could be obtained from the sale or disposition of an asset at the end of its useful life; also called salvage or scrap value

Scrap value (p. 626) *See* Residual value

Sum-of-the-years'-digits method (p. 628) A method of depreciating asset costs by allocating as expense each year a fractional part of the asset's depreciable cost, based on the sum of the digits of the number of years in the asset's useful life

Tangible personal property (p. 624) Assets such as machinery, equipment, furniture, and fixtures that can be removed and used elsewhere

Trade name (p. 643) An intangible asset; an exclusive business name registered with the U.S. Patent and Trademark Office; also called brand name

Trademark (p. 643) An intangible asset; an exclusive business symbol registered with the U.S. Patent and Trademark Office

Units-of-output method (p. 629) *See* Units-of-production method

Units-of-production method (p. 629) A method of depreciating asset cost at the same rate for each unit produced during each period

Comprehensive Self Review

1. Under what circumstances would the unit-of-production depreciation method be the logical choice from the different methods available?
2. What generally accepted accounting principle or convention supports the writing down of impaired assets to their fair market values?
3. What is the denominator of the fraction used in the calculation of annual depreciation using the sum-of-the-years'-digits method of depreciation for an asset with a useful life of 10 years?
4. How does real property differ from personal property?
5. Distinguish between the legal life and the economic life of an intangible asset. Which is used in computing amortization if amortization is appropriate?
6. An asset with a cost of $60,000 and accumulated depreciation of $54,600 is retired and sold as junk for $1,600. How much gain or loss is recorded on the retirement?

(Answers to Comprehensive Self Review are at the end of the chapter.)

Discussion Questions

1. What account is debited and what account is credited to record depreciation on trucks?
2. Explain how the sum-of-the-years'-digits method would be applied to an asset with a life of six years.
3. Is MACRS used for federal income tax rules acceptable under GAAP?
4. Which method will give you a higher amount of depreciation expense in the later years of an asset's life, straight-line or declining-balance? Explain.
5. What is the basic test for determining whether impairment does, in fact, exist?
6. Under what circumstances is the units-of-production method of depreciation especially desirable?
7. What information related to the company's property, plant, and equipment must be presented in the financial statements and in the notes to the financial statements?
8. Name three or more events, developments, or situations that indicate impairment of property, plant, and equipment may exist.
9. Which of these, if any, is not "real property"?
    a. land
    b. a building
    c. a motor home being used as an office
    d. pavement for a parking lot
10. What is meant by "capitalized costs"?
11. A company purchased some land on which an old building is located. The building has to be torn down to enable construction of a new building. Which, if any, of the following costs related to the old building should be capitalized as part of the land cost?
    a. purchase price of the property
    b. permit fee for tearing down the old building
    c. cost of tearing down the building in excess of salvage proceeds
    d. costs of hauling off debris of old building

12. Explain how straight-line depreciation is computed.
13. What is meant by the term "personal property"?
14. Name two accelerated depreciation methods.
15. Which, if any, of the depreciation methods discussed in this chapter ignore(s) salvage value?
16. Explain how double-declining-balance depreciation is computed on an asset with a life of six years.
17. What is the name of the process by which costs of a natural resource deposit are removed from the asset account as the resources are produced?
18. Explain how to measure the gain or loss when an old asset is traded in on a new one.
19. What are the requirements for recording an intangible asset such as goodwill?
20. Are gains and losses on trade-in transactions recognized and recorded under GAAP?
21. What accounting treatment is given to most research costs?
22. What are the two categories of intangible assets for the purposes of disposing of their capitalized costs?
23. What are the rules for determining the amount of cost in each category of intangibles in Question 22 to be removed from the asset account during each accounting period?
24. How is the amount of impairment to be recorded determined?

APPLICATIONS

Exercises

Exercise 18.1
Objective 18-1

▶ **Determining the elements that make up the cost of an asset.**

The following costs were incurred by Euro Auto Parts in connection with the construction of a retail store building:

Cost of land, including $7,500 of legal costs	$175,000
Cost to demolish old building	10,325
Costs of grading land for building site	6,500
Costs related to building construction	525,000
Legal costs relating to building permits	9,500
Costs of paving parking lot	35,000

1. What is the capitalized cost of the land?
2. What is the capitalized cost of the new building?

Exercise 18.2
Objective 18-1

▶ **Determining the elements that make up the cost of an asset.**

The South Pacific Shipping Company incurred the costs below related to a new packing machine:

Invoice price of packing machine	$75,000
Cash discount for prompt payment	3,925
Transportation costs	2,880
Installation costs	1,575

What is the capitalized cost of the new packing machine?

Recording depreciation.

For the year ending December 31, 20X1, Peterson Manufacturing Company had depreciation totaling $42,000 on its office equipment. Give the general journal entry to record the adjusting entry.

◀ **Exercise 18.3**
Objective 18-2

Computing depreciation under various methods.

Atkins Company acquired an asset on January 2, 20X1, at a cost of $142,000. The asset's useful life is four years and its salvage value is $32,000. Compute the depreciation expense for each of the first two years, using the straight-line method, the double-declining-balance method, and the sum-of-the-years'-digits method.

◀ **Exercise 18.4**
Objective 18-2

Computing depreciation under the units-of-production method.

On January 12, 20X1, Harris Company purchased a machine to mold components for one of its products. Total cost of the machine was $480,000. It is expected to produce 450,000 units and to have a salvage value of $30,000. The company used the units-of-production method of depreciation.

a. In 20X1, it produced 52,000 units. Compute the depreciation expense for 20X1.
b. During 20X2, 60,000 units were produced. Compute the depreciation expense for 20X2.

◀ **Exercise 18.5**
Objective 18-2

Applying Modified Accelerated Cost Recovery System (MACRS) under federal income tax rules.

On January 20, 20X1, Starksville Transport Company purchased a new lightweight truck for $90,000.

1. Into which MACRS "class" is this asset classified?
2. What would be the amount of cost recovery on the truck in 20X1 and in 20X2?

◀ **Exercise 18.6**
Objective 18-3

Recording the sale of plant and equipment.

Paxton Company owns a truck that cost $112,000. Depreciation totaling $76,000 had been taken on the truck up to January 8, 20X1, when it was sold for $34,300.

1. Give the journal entry to record the sale.
2. Assume, instead, that the truck is sold for $38,200. Give the journal entry to record the sale.

◀ **Exercise 18.7**
Objective 18-4

Recording asset trade-ins using financial accounting rules.

At the beginning of the year four years ago, Cedar Valley Company purchased construction equipment for $715,000, with a useful life of six years and estimated salvage value of $100,000. The company uses the straight-line method of depreciation. On July 3, 20X1, this equipment was traded for new similar construction equipment that has a value of $800,000. The company paid $582,000 cash and was given a trade-in allowance of $218,000 for the old equipment.

1. Give the general journal entry needed on July 3, 20X1, to record the trade-in. (Assume that the entry to bring depreciation up to date has been made.)
2. Assume the same facts as stated above, except that Cedar Valley paid cash of $514,750 on the trade-in and was given an allowance of $285,250 for the old equipment. Give the journal entry to record the trade-in.

◀ **Exercise 18.8**
Objective 18-5

Reporting asset trade-ins using federal income tax requirements.

(Refer to the truck purchased by Starksville Transport Company, Exercise 18.6.)
At the beginning of the year, it became obvious that the truck purchased the year before was too small to handle many of Starksville's jobs. On January 2, 20X2, Starksville traded in the old truck on a new, larger lightweight truck. Its sale price (and fair market value) was $120,000. The dealer gave Starksville a trade-in allowance of $60,000 for the old truck and Starksville paid the balance of $60,000 in cash.

1. For tax purposes, how much gain or loss is recognized on the trade-in?
2. For tax purposes, what is the basis (the cost) to be recorded for the new truck?

◀ **Exercise 18.9**
Objective 18-5

Exercise 18.10
Objective 18-6

▶ **Computing depletion of mineral property cost.**

Heath Mining Company acquired a mine in 20X1. Capitalized costs of the minerals were $5,460,000. The company mined 200,000 tons of ore in 20X1 and on December 31, 20X1, it is estimated that 2,200,000 tons of ore remained in the ground.

Compute the amount of depletion expense for 20X1.

Exercise 18.11
Objective 18-7

▶ **Recognize asset impairment and understand the general concepts of accounting for impairment.**

a. Orison Milling Company operates, on a contract basis, equipment that grinds and mixes grains used as animal feed. In September 20X1 the book value of the equipment was $144,000. Because of declining processing fees, the company's chief financial officer became concerned that the asset might be impaired. An analysis of expected future cash flows from use of the asset resulted in an estimate of $143,000 of future cash flows. Further study led to the company's finding several almost identical processors that ranged in price from $99,000 to $101,000. The CFO decided that the asset was impaired and should be "written down" to $99,000. Do you agree?

b. What account would be debited and what account would be credited to record impairment? What would be the amount of the impairment recorded?

Exercise 18.12
Objective 18-8

▶ **Computing and recording amortization and impairment of intangible assets.**

On December 31, 20X1, Warren Company's *Intangible Assets* account reflects two assets:

1. *Goodwill,* $145,000. This amount was recorded in December 20X0 as part of the cost of acquiring an existing business. It represents the excess of the total purchase price over the value of net identifiable assets. Warren has studied carefully the operations and concluded that the fair value of goodwill on December 31, 20X1, is $110,000 and that benefits should exist for at least another 10 years.

2. *Patent,* $299,000. The patent was purchased on January 20X0 for $322,000, when it had a remaining legal life of 14 years. On December 31, 20X0, $23,000 of cost was amortized. On December 31, 20X1, Warren estimates that the patent will be useful for only another 9 years. However, it is estimated that the patent still has a value to the company of over $310,000.

For each of the intangibles—goodwill and patent—explain what entry, if any, is necessary at the end of 20X1 to adjust the accounts.

PROBLEMS

Problem Set A

Problem 18.1A
Objective 18-1

▶ **Determining the cost to be capitalized for acquisition of assets.**

On January 6, 20X1, Turner Company purchased a site for a new manufacturing plant for $7,200,000. At a cost of $45,880, it razed an existing facility (fair market value $600,000) and received $32,000 from its salvage. The company also paid $15,200 in attorney fees, $5,250 in inspection fees, and $3,675 for a permit to raze the facility. After the facility was torn down, the following costs were incurred: $139,300 for fill dirt for the site, $86,000 for leveling the site, $291,000 for paving sidewalks and curbs, and $12,560,000 for building costs of the new facility. The parking area was paved at a cost of $285,900.

INSTRUCTIONS

Compute the capitalized costs of (1) the manufacturing plant, (2) the land, and (3) the land improvements.

Analyze: Unfortunately, Turner's new building was not completed on schedule, but the company had to vacate the old building. As a result, the business was shut down for two months. During this period, the company reported a net loss of $690,000. The president suggests that the loss should be capitalized as part of the cost of the new building. What is your recommendation?

Using different depreciation methods and comparing the results.

◄ **Problem 18.2A**
Objective 18-2

On January 4, 20X1, Wilson Company purchased new equipment for $310,000 that had a useful life of four years and a salvage value of $40,000.

INSTRUCTIONS

Prepare a schedule showing the annual depreciation and end-of-year accumulated depreciation for the first three years of the asset's life under (1) the straight-line method, (2) the sum-of-the-years'-digits method, and (3) the double-declining-balance method.

Analyze: If the sum-of-the-years'-digits method is used to compute depreciation, what would be the book value of the asset at the end of 20X2?

Using the straight-line and units-of-output methods of depreciation.

◄ **Problem 18.3A**
Objective 18-2

On January 5, 20X1, Sampson Company purchased equipment for $325,000 that had an estimated useful life of five years or 150,000 units of product. The estimated salvage value was $25,000. Actual production data for the first three years were 20X1—26,000 units; 20X2—37,000 units; and 20X3—32,000 units.

INSTRUCTIONS

Compute each year's depreciation and the end-of-year accumulated depreciation for the first three years under (1) the straight-line method and (2) the units-of-output method.

Analyze: Would the total depreciation taken over the five-year life depend on which of the two methods is used? Why?

Computing depreciation and MACRS on assets.

◄ **Problem 18.4A**
Objectives 18-2, 18-3

On January 12, 20X1, Zolle Company purchased a computer (cost, $7,500; expected life, five years; estimated salvage value, $1,500) and a lightweight van for delivery purposes (cost, $36,000; estimated life, seven years; estimated salvage value, $8,000). For financial accounting purposes, the company uses straight-line depreciation on all assets.

INSTRUCTIONS

1. Compute depreciation of the computer cost for financial accounting purposes for 20X1 and 20X2.
2. Compute cost recovery of the computer cost for income tax purposes for 20X1 and 20X2.
3. Compute depreciation of the van cost for financial accounting purposes for 20X1 and 20X2.
4. Compute cost recovery of the van cost for income tax purposes for 20X1 and 20X2.

Analyze: What objectives or principles account for the differences between the financial accounting depreciation rules and the income tax cost recovery rules?

Recording asset trade-ins and sales.

◄ **Problem 18.5A**
Objectives 18-2, 18-4, 18-5

The transactions listed below occurred at Jenson Company during 20X1:

DATE	TRANSACTIONS
Mar. 25	Exchanged a printer (**Office Equipment**) that had an original cost of $13,600 when purchased on January 4th, two years ago. The useful life of the old asset was originally estimated at five years and the salvage value at $600. The new printer had a price and market value of $22,400. Jarred gave up the old machine and paid $11,200 cash. The new printer is estimated to have a useful life of five years and a salvage value of $1,400.
July 19	Exchanged a truck (**Vehicles**) for a new one that had a sales price, and fair value, of $89,600. Received a trade-in allowance of $23,000 on the old truck and paid cash of $66,600. The old truck had been purchased for $75,520 on May 27th, three years earlier. The life of the old truck was originally estimated at four years and the salvage value at $13,600. The life of the new truck is estimated to be five years and it is estimated to have a salvage value of $19,600.
Aug. 18	Sold a truck that was purchased on January 5th, two years ago, for an original purchase price of $22,960. It had an estimated life of four years and an estimated salvage value of $4,000. Sales price is as indicated in Instructions, below.

INSTRUCTIONS

Note: In following these instructions, assume that straight-line depreciation is used and that depreciation was last recorded on December 31, 20X0. Compute depreciation to the nearest whole dollar.

1. Give the entries in general journal form to record the two exchange transactions.
2. Give the entries in general journal form to record the sale of the truck, assuming:
   a. The sales price was $11,000.
   b. The sales price was $8,500.

Analyze: What was the book value of the truck sold on August 18?

Problem 18.6A
Objectives 18-4, 18-5

▶ **Recording asset sales and trade-ins.**

James Company purchased four identical machines on January 10, 20X1, paying $5,500 for each. The useful life of each machine is expected to be five years, with a salvage value of $700 each. The company uses the straight-line method of depreciation. Selected transactions involving the machines follow. The accounts for recording these transactions are also given.

INSTRUCTIONS
Record the transactions in general journal form. Round all calculations to the nearest whole dollar.

ACCOUNTS

101	Cash
141	Machinery
142	Accumulated Depreciation—Machinery
495	Gain on Sale of Machinery
541	Depreciation Expense—Machinery
595	Loss on Sale of Machinery
597	Loss on Stolen Machinery

DATE	TRANSACTIONS FOR 20X1
Jan. 10	Paid $5,500, in cash, for each of four machines.
Dec. 31	Recorded depreciation for the year on the four machines.

DATE	TRANSACTIONS FOR 20X2
Apr. 3	Machine 1 was stolen; no insurance was carried.
Dec. 31	Recorded depreciation for the year for the three remaining machines.

DATE	TRANSACTIONS FOR 20X3
Sept. 18	Sold machine 2 for $3,200 cash.
Dec. 31	Recorded depreciation for the year on the two remaining machines.

DATE	TRANSACTIONS FOR 20X4
June 4	Machine 3 was traded in for a similar machine (no. 5) with a $6,580 list price and fair market value. A trade-in allowance of $2,510 was received. The balance was paid in cash. The new machine has an estimated life of five years and salvage value of $700.
Aug. 29	Machine 4 was traded in for a similar machine (no. 6) with an $8,200 list price and fair market value. A trade-in allowance of $1,390 was received. The balance was paid in cash. The new machine has an estimated life of five years, with salvage value of $700.
Dec. 31	Record depreciation on the two new machines.

Analyze: What is the balance of the *Accumulated Depreciation* account on December 31, 20X4?

Compute and record depletion of natural resources.

◀ **Problem 18.7A**

Objective 18-6

Kingston Mining Company had total depletable capitalized costs of $828,000 for a mine acquired in early 20X1. It was estimated that the mine contained 920,000 tons of recoverable ore when production began. During 20X1, 46,500 tons were mined, and 174,800 tons were mined in 20X2.

INSTRUCTIONS

1. Compute the depletion expense in 20X1 and 20X2 for financial accounting purposes. What accounts will be debited and credited to record the depletion?
2. **a.** In 20X1, 46,500 tons of ore were sold for $4,600,000. For tax purposes, operating expenses of the mine were $600,000. The taxpayer may deduct either cost depletion or percentage depletion, which for the type ore produced is 8 percent of production sold from the mine. (Assume, however, that percentage depletion is limited to the amount of net income from the property.) What would be the amount of percentage depletion allowable in 20X1?
   b. What would be the amount of cost depletion allowable for tax purposes in 20X1, assuming that capitalized mineral costs are the same for tax purposes as for financial accounting purposes?

c. What will be the amount of depletion based on cost that the company could deduct on its tax return in 20X2 if it deducts percentage depletion in 20X1?

d. Suppose that in the first three years of the mine's life, the company took percentage depletion totaling $820,000. In the fifth year of the mine's life, production proceeds were $5,300,000. How much percentage depletion could the company deduct in the fifth year?

Analyze: What explanation do you think might be given for the deviation of income tax rules from basic accounting principles in the determination of depletion of costs of minerals?

Problem 18.8A

Objective 18-7

▶ **Recording impairment of property, plant, and equipment.**

Hendrix Realty Company owns a number of large office buildings in several cities in the United States. One of the buildings is 16 years old and has had a large number of vacant office suites for several years. The building's book value is $26.4 million. The company has examined carefully its future cash flows and has determined that it is highly unlikely that the company can recover the building's book value from future cash flows. Further study in November 20X1 has resulted in three estimates of the market value of the building. All of the estimates of value are approximately $16.6 million.

INSTRUCTIONS

1. Should Hendrix record impairment of the building? Why?
2. If impairment should be recorded, what is the amount of impairment?
3. What accounting entry would be necessary based on the above facts?
4. If impairment is recorded in 20X1 and subsequently the value of the building increases in 20X2 so that the market value exceeds the book value, should the book value of the building be increased at that time?

Analyze: How could the company use its estimates of cash flows to arrive at a "market value" of the building?

Problem 18.9A

Objective 18-8

▶ **Recording intangible asset acquisition, amortization, and impairment.**

Selected accounts of the Johnson Company are listed below. On January 1, 20X1, the only intangible asset in the company's accounts was *Goodwill.* This was recorded seven years ago when the company acquired another company and paid $150,000 more than the fair market value of the net identifiable tangible assets acquired. For two years, the company amortized the costs on the basis of a 40-year life, charging a total of $7,500 ($3,750 each year) to an account called *Amortization Expense—Goodwill.* However, no amortization of goodwill has been recorded in the last six years. Transactions and events that took place at the company during 20X1 are given below.

INSTRUCTIONS

1. Record the transactions for 20X1 in general journal form.
2. Record amortization of the intangible assets, where appropriate, for the year ended December 31, 20X1.
3. Record impairment of assets, where appropriate, on December 31, 20X1.

ACCOUNTS

Cash

Computer Software

Patents

Product Formulas

Goodwill

Amortization Expense—Patents

Amortization Expense—Computer Software

Amortization Expense—Product Formulas

Impairment of Intangibles

TRANSACTIONS AND OTHER INFORMATION

a. On May 10, 20X1, the company paid $94,500 to purchase a product formula. The formula is expected to have a useful life of seven years.

b. On July 5, the company paid $333,000 for a patent having a useful life of nine years.

c. On September 22, the company purchased a unique computer program for $104,000. This program has an estimated useful life of four years.

d. During the year, the company recorded various cash expenditures of $110,000 for labor and supplies used in its research department. (Date entry December 31.)

e. At the end of 20X1, the company reviewed the goodwill shown in the accounts. Based on the profitability of activities acquired in purchasing the other business, the owners of the business think the goodwill has a value of $115,000 and should be of benefit for many more years.

Analyze: Based on the transactions above, what is the total net book value of Johnson Company's intangible assets on December 31, 20X1?

Problem Set B

Determining the costs to be capitalized for acquisition of an asset.

◀ **Problem 18.1B**
Objective 18-1

On July 5, 20X1, Piney Woods Company purchased a site for its new headquarters for $320,000. At a cost of $25,000, it razed two existing houses, with a total appraised value of $52,700, and received $13,100 from salvage. The firm also paid $7,500 in attorney's fees, $1,250 in inspection fees, and $550 for a permit to raze the houses. After the houses were razed, the firm incurred these costs:

- $25,000 for fill dirt for the site
- $18,000 for leveling the site
- $42,000 for paving sidewalks and curbs
- $53,550 for paving a parking lot
- $1,897,500 for construction costs of new building

INSTRUCTIONS

Compute the capitalized costs of (1) the land, (2) the building, and (3) the land improvements.

Analyze: What net effect did these transactions have on the total owner's equity?

Using different depreciation methods and comparing the results.

◀ **Problem 18.2B**
Objective 18-2

On January 5, 20X1, Terrell Company purchased a new $400,000 machine with a five-year useful life and an estimated salvage value of $30,000.

INSTRUCTIONS

Prepare a schedule showing the annual depreciation and accumulated depreciation for each of the first three years of the asset's life under (1) the straight-line method, (2) the sum-of-the-years'-digits method, and (3) the double-declining-balance method.

Analyze: If the double-declining-balance method is used, what would be the book value of the machine at the end of 20X3?

Using various methods to compute depreciation.

◀ **Problem 18.3B**
Objective 18-2

Havana Company purchased a carton fabrication unit for $247,500 on January 8, 20X1. The machine's useful life is estimated as 3,000,000 units of product or eight years, and its salvage value is estimated at $22,500. The number of cartons fabricated in each year, 20X1 to 20X3, is as follows:

Year	Cartons Fabricated
20X1	160,000
20X2	168,400
20X3	236,000

INSTRUCTIONS

Compute the depreciation expense and accumulated depreciation at year-end for each of the three years under (1) the straight-line method and (2) the units-of-production method.

Analyze: If the units-of-output method were used, what would be the book value of the machine at the end of 20X3?

Problem 18.4B ▶ **Computing depreciation and MACRS on assets.**

Objectives 18-2, 18-3

On January 3, 20X1, Richardson Company purchased a computer (cost, $20,000; expected life, four years; estimated salvage value, $4,000) and an eight-passenger van (cost, $78,000; estimated life, eight years; estimated salvage value, $14,000). For financial accounting purposes, the company has always used straight-line depreciation on all assets.

INSTRUCTIONS

1. Compute depreciation of the computer's cost for financial accounting purposes for 20X1 and 20X2.
2. Compute MACRS cost recovery of the computer's cost for income tax purposes for 20X1 and 20X2.
3. Compute depreciation of the van's cost for financial accounting purposes for 20X1 and 20X2.
4. Compute MACRS cost recovery of the van's cost for income tax purposes for 20X1 and 20X2.

Analyze: The owner suggests that to avoid duplication of work, the company should use the amount of cost recovery taken on the tax return for each asset as the amount to be used for depreciation in financial statements. Do you agree? Why?

Problem 18.5B ▶ **Recording asset trade-ins and sales.**

Objectives 18-2, 18-4, 18-5

The following transactions occurred at Wilson Company during 20X1:

DATE	TRANSACTIONS
Apr. 2	Traded in a copy machine (**Office Equipment**) that had been purchased for $10,400 on December 29th, four years ago. Straight-line depreciation of the old copier has been based on an estimated useful life of five years, with salvage value of $1,600. The new copier had a purchase price and value of $24,000. Wilson received a trade-in allowance of $7,000 on the old machine and paid cash of $17,000. The new copier has a useful life of five years and an estimated salvage value of $1,200.
July 8	Exchanged a delivery truck (**Vehicles**) for a new one with a list price of $22,000, estimated useful life of five years, and salvage value of $4,200. A trade-in allowance of $5,000 was received on the old truck, which had been purchased on July 1st, three years ago for $16,500. Depreciation on the old truck has been based on an estimated $2,500 salvage value and a five-year life.
Sept. 23	Sold a refrigeration unit (**Store Equipment**) for cash (see Instruction 2). The unit was purchased on January 3rd, three years ago, for $64,000 and was depreciated on the straight-line basis, using an estimated life of six years and a salvage value of $4,000.

INSTRUCTIONS

Note: In each case, assume that straight-line depreciation is used and that depreciation was last recorded on December 31, 20X0. Compute depreciation to the nearest whole dollar.

1. Record in general journal form the two trade-in transactions on April 2 and July 8.
2. Record the sale of the refrigeration unit, assuming:

   a. the sales price was $27,000.

   b. the sales price was $20,400.

Analyze: What accounting concepts underlie the accounting treatments for the transactions of April 2 and July 8?

Recording asset sales and trade-ins.

◀ **Problem 18.6B**
Objectives 18-2, 18-4, 18-5

Freedom Company purchased four identical machines on January 4, 20X1, paying $9,000 for each machine. The useful life of each machine is expected to be five years, with no salvage value expected. The company uses the straight-line method of depreciation. Selected transactions involving the machines are listed below. The necessary accounts for recording these transactions are also given.

INSTRUCTIONS

Record the transactions in general journal form. Use the following accounts, as necessary.

ACCOUNTS

101	Cash	541	Depreciation Expense—Machinery
141	Machinery	595	Loss on Sale of Machinery
142	Accumulated Depreciation—Machinery	596	Loss on Trade-in of Machinery
495	Gain on Sale of Machinery	597	Fire Loss on Machinery

DATE		TRANSACTIONS FOR 20X1
Jan.	4	Paid $9,000 each for four machines.
Dec.	31	Recorded depreciation for the year on the four machines.

DATE		TRANSACTIONS FOR 20X2
Mar.	31	Machine 1 was destroyed by fire; no insurance was carried.
Dec.	31	Recorded depreciation for the year for the three remaining machines.

DATE		TRANSACTIONS FOR 20X3
Oct.	2	Sold machine 2 for $4,400 cash.
Dec.	31	Recorded depreciation for the year on the two remaining machines.

DATE		TRANSACTIONS FOR 20X4
May	28	Traded machine 3 for a similar machine (no. 5) with an $8,800 price and fair market value. A trade-in allowance of $2,800 was received. The balance of $6,000 was paid in cash.
Sept.	3	Traded in machine 4 for a similar machine (no. 6) with a $9,200 list price and fair value. A trade-in allowance of $2,000 was received. The balance was paid in cash.
Sept.	3	Assume that the company somehow has adopted a policy of recording trade-in transactions using the rules required for federal income tax purposes—even though the cost of assets and the depreciation are determined under financial accounting rules as you have computed them previously in this problem. Give the entry that would be recorded on September 3 to record the trade-in of machine 4 on machine 6, using the facts given.

Analyze: What is the difference between the financial accounting entries and tax entries for the trade-in of machine 4?

Problem 18.7B
Objective 18-6

▶ **Compute and record depletion of natural resources.**

Campuzano Company acquired a mineral property and drilled an oil well in 20X1. Capitalized costs subject to depletion totaled $800,000. When the well began producing in late 20X1, it was estimated that one million barrels of oil could ultimately be produced from the property. In 20X1, 5,000 barrels were produced and sold for $180,000. Operating costs for the property were $160,800. Sixty thousand barrels were produced and sold for $2,600,000 in 20X2 and operating costs that year were $330,000.

INSTRUCTIONS

1. Compute the depletion expense in 20X1 and 20X2 for financial accounting purposes. What accounts will be debited and credited to record the depletion?

2. Assume that capitalized costs and operating expenses were the same for financial accounting and tax purposes. The taxpayer may deduct either cost depletion or percentage depletion. The percentage depletion for oil and gas production is 15 percent of gross income from the property, but limited to 100 percent of net income from the property. Assume that all of the oil produced is eligible for percentage depletion.

   a. What would be the amount of cost depletion allowable for tax purposes in 20X1?

   b. What will be the amount of depletion that the company could deduct on its tax return in 20X1?

   c. What amount of cost depletion could the company deduct on its tax return in 20X2 (round to two places)?

   d. What would be the amount, if any, of percentage depletion deductible in 20X2?

   e. Suppose that in the first four years of the property's life, the company deducted depletion totaling $798,800 on the tax returns. No additional depletable costs were capitalized. In the fifth year of the property's life, proceeds of $4,800,000 were received from the oil produced, and operating expenses of $900,000 were incurred. What amount, if any, of percentage depletion may be deducted on the company's tax return in that year?

Analyze: Would the company be entitled to percentage depletion in the sixth and future years in which there was gross income that exceeded the operating expenses?

Problem 18.8B
Objective 18-7

▶ **Recognize and record impairment of property, plant, and equipment.**

Liberty National Airlines is a small commercial airline operating in the United States. Because of poor economic conditions in the airline industry in 20X1, Liberty National has eliminated some routes and reduced the frequency of flights on all other routes. As a result, the airline has indefinitely stored 8 of its 20 aircraft. The company continues to lose money and sees no time in the foreseeable future that the parked aircraft will be operated again. The company's public accountant has told the airline officials that it must assess whether the parked planes (and perhaps some of those flying routes) should be assessed for impairment. The parked planes have a combined book value of $96 million.

Company officials have researched the problem and found that there is an abundance of identical or similar planes that could be purchased for approximately $9 million each. Several of these similar planes have been recently sold and the $9 million value for each has been accepted by company officials as being a good estimate of the going sales price and of their fair value. It has been impossible for company officials to estimate future cash flows, or if there will be any future cash flows from those planes.

INSTRUCTIONS

Answer the following questions:

1. Should Liberty National Airlines record impairment of the parked planes? Why or why not?
2. If impairment should be recorded, what is the amount of impairment?
3. What accounting entry would be necessary based on the above facts?
4. If impairment is recorded in 20X1 and subsequently the value of the planes increases before they are sold, with the result that market value exceeds the book value, should the value of the planes be increased at that time?

Analyze: What steps can you suggest the company take in considering whether the planes that are still flying also may be impaired?

Recording intangible asset acquisition, amortization, and impairment.

◄ **Problem 18.9B**
Objective 18-8

Selected accounts of the Mayo Medical Labs are listed below. Also given are some transactions and events that took place at the company during 20X1.

INSTRUCTIONS

1. Record in general journal form the transactions for 20X1 described.
2. Record amortization of the intangible assets for the year ended December 31, 20X1.
3. Indicate what steps should be taken, if any, to properly account for the balance of $1,200,000 in the *Goodwill* account on December 31. The following accounts related to intangible assets are found in Mayo's general ledger:

ACCOUNTS

Cash	Research and Development Expense
Patents	Amortization of Patents
Computer Software	Amortization of Computer Software
Goodwill	Impairment of Intangibles

DATE	TRANSACTIONS AND INFORMATION
April 10	Purchased for cash of $840,000 a patent related to a chemical compound. It has a legal life of 12 years remaining but is expected to be used for only 8 years because of new patents for similar products being developed.
Sept. 1	Purchased a computer software program for $72,000 in cash from a computer software supply firm. The software program is to be used in the company's inventory control system and has an estimated useful life of seven years.
Dec. 31	(Date of journal entry, reflecting summary for year.) During the year, made cash expenditures of $8,000,000 for research and development costs related to a new electronic medical procedure being developed. Researchers have worked on the project for 10 months of the year and think the project will result in a valuable patent.
Dec. 31	The company examined the balance of $3,800,000 in the *Goodwill* account. This balance arose from purchase of another business two years earlier and represents the amount paid for the acquired business in excess of the value of the net identifiable assets acquired. The examination concluded that the activities acquired have continued to be very profitable and that there is no reason to record impairment on the $3,800,000 balance.

Analyze: Suppose that the examination of goodwill had revealed that the benefits (future profits) resulting from the acquisition two years ago are decreasing. Based on the estimated value of the excess of the future profits over the value of the net assets acquired, the value of goodwill is estimated to be currently only $2,600,000. What accounting entry, if any, should be made to record this fact?

Critical Thinking Problem 18.1

Depreciation Expense Company Practices

In a review of the annual reports of Pierce Wholesale Company and International Distributors, you note that Pierce Wholesale uses straight-line depreciation and International Distributors uses the declining-balance method.

1. Are these companies violating the generally accepted accounting principle of consistency by using different depreciation methods?

2. If you examined the federal income tax returns of these companies, would you expect the deductions, similar to depreciation taken on their income tax returns, to be the same as the depreciation expenses shown on their financial statements? Why or why not?

3. Assume that these companies are similar in all respects except for their difference in computing depreciation. Which company would you expect to report the lower net income for the year?

4. Who is responsible for determining the depreciation method used by the company for financial accounting purposes?

Critical Thinking Problem 18.2

Cost Capitalization, Depreciation, MACRS, Impairment

Lawrence's Company operates a real estate abstract, title, and insurance company. Below are selected transactions and events that occurred during the years 20X1 to 20X4. Using those transactions and events, follow the instructions given.

INSTRUCTIONS

1. Give the adjusting entries on December 31, 20X2, to record depreciation expense for the year on all assets.

2. a. Compute the amount of MACRS cost recovery for tax purposes on the furniture and fixtures in (1) 20X2 and (2) 20X3.

   b. What is the MACRS recovery period for the building?

3. Should Lawrence's management be concerned with the possibility of asset impairment at the end of 20X4? Explain.

4. Do you agree with the company's financial manager that depreciation should be reduced in 20X4 because of the decline in business? Explain your answer.

TRANSACTIONS AND EVENTS 20X1 AND 20X2

The company purchased a building site for $225,000 on August 2, 20X1. Preparation for construction began in October. Costs that were incurred other than land in 20X1 and 20X2 were:

a. grading and preparing the site, $10,000.

b. in late June 20X2, paving the sidewalks and parking lot, $18,750 (estimated life 15 years, no salvage value; straight-line depreciation to be used).

c. fencing back of the property, $4,000, erected in same week building was completed (estimated life, 10 years; no salvage value; straight-line depreciation to be used).

d. building construction contract costs $180,000, completed June 25, 20X2 (estimated life, 35 years; salvage value, $5,000; straight-line depreciation to be used).

e. telephone system installed in the last week of June 20X2, $10,000 (estimated life, five years; estimated salvage value, $1,000; sum-of-the-years'-digits depreciation method to be used).

f. furniture and fixtures purchased in late June 20X2, $22,500 (estimated life, 10 years; estimated salvage value, $1,500; double-declining-balance method to be used).

The company opened for business in the new building on July 5, 20X2. During the remainder of 20X2, the business grew at about the pace anticipated by the company's management when the project was planned.

20X3 AND 20X4

1. The business continued to grow at the anticipated pace in 20X3.

2. In June 20X4, a rumor was circulated that a hazardous waste deposit existed on the company's property, but no evidence was presented to support the allegation. In November 20X4, an investigative team from local, state, and federal health services arrived on the scene to conduct a detailed investigation of the property. In the third week of December, they reported having found what had once been a dump site. The investigators took many samples

and sent these to laboratories, then left, stating they would return in the second week of January. They hope to have tentative laboratory reports at the time of their return. The company's attorneys are concerned about the investigation because the company's insurance does not cover losses from this problem and the state law places responsibility on the current owner to clean up the property. Because of the rumors, customers were reluctant to come to the building and business declined dramatically in November and December 20X4.

3. In late December 20X4, the company's executive manager suggested that because of the decline in business the company should reduce its current depreciation charge, resulting in lower depreciation in the next few years, with greater depreciation in subsequent years. The manager thinks his plan is akin to units-of-production depreciation and he expects future business to be greater, resulting in higher depreciation at that time.

BUSINESS CONNECTIONS

Plant Asset Procedures

1. Suggest three key procedures involving internal control of property, plant, and equipment that do not relate specifically to accounting records.
2. Suggest three key procedures involving internal control of property, plant, and equipment that relate to accounting records.
3. Generally accepted accounting principles require that all research and development costs be expensed in the year they are incurred. An officer of the company wants to amortize these costs. What can you say to explain why this accounting requirement exists?
4. Assume that you are the accountant at a fabricating plant. One of the vice presidents has asked you why one of the pieces of equipment used in the plant is shown at its original cost in the asset accounts. Respond to the question.
5. Suppose you are on the controller's staff at a large company. You have suggested assigning responsibility for the company's equipment to specific individuals. One supervisor has objected, saying it is a waste of time. Defend your suggestion to the controller and to the supervisor.

Managerial | FOCUS

Internal Control for Property, Plant, and Equipment

Property, plant, and equipment often represents the largest investment by owners of a business. Owners and managers are responsible for establishing strong internal control over property, plant, and equipment. List and discuss at least six internal control policies and procedures for property, plant, and equipment.

Internal Control and FRAUD PREVENTION

Depreciation Amounts and Method

Refer to The Home Depot, Inc., *Annual Report (for the fiscal year ended February 3, 2019)* in Appendix A.

1. Locate the Notes to Consolidated Financial Statements. Review Note 1, Summary of Significant Accounting Policies. What methods are used to depreciate the company's furniture, fixtures, and equipment? What estimated useful life is assigned to buildings?
2. In the Notes to the Consolidated Financial Statements, what amount was charged to depreciation and capital lease amortization expense, including depreciation expense included in the cost of sales? In the Consolidated Balance Sheet, what net value is reported for Property and Equipment for the fiscal year ended February 3, 2019?

Financial Statement ANALYSIS

Home Depot

Goodwill

Hernandez's Auto Repair Service has been in business for five years. He has developed a great reputation of doing a good job at reasonable prices. His reputation has given him a large, loyal clientele. During those years, Mr. Hernandez has purchased net assets of $160,000, on which he

TEAMWORK

owes $50,000. Hernandez has decided to sell his business and open another one 10 miles away. Rudy Rodriguez has agreed to purchase the business for $210,000. Divide the class into two teams to discuss and compare answers to the following questions: (1) Is it ethical for Mr. Hernandez to accept a larger amount for this business than its value? (2) If so, how would Mr. Rodriguez record this transaction? (3) Is it ethical for Mr. Hernandez to open a new business so close to the old business?

Answers to Comprehensive Self Review

1. When the life of the asset is limited to an estimable number of units of production.
2. The matching principle of matching costs with revenues. The constraint of conservatism plays an important role in applying the matching principle.
3. 55 (10 + 9 + 8 + 7 + 6 + 5 + 4 + 3 + 2 + 1).
4. Real property comprises land and other assets that are affixed permanently to the land. It includes land, land improvements, buildings, and other structures attached to the land. Personal property comprises those assets that are not affixed to the land and are relatively moveable—such as furniture, equipment, and vehicles.
5. Legal life is the time period over which the business or individual has legal rights to utilize whatever rights can be derived from the intangible asset. Intangibles such as copyrights, patents, and most franchises may be used exclusively only for a limited period. The economic life is the period over which the intangible will provide economic benefits to the holder of the right. For example, a patent owned by a business may provide exclusive right to produce a product for another 15 years. This is the legal life. However, new processes being developed may make the existing patent obsolete within three years. Three years is the economic life. In general, intangibles with a legal life are initially amortized over their legal life. However, if it becomes evident that the economic life is shorter than the remaining legal life, the remaining costs to be amortized are recovered over the remaining economic life of the intangible.
6. $3,800 loss ($5,400 book value − $1,600 sales price).

Accounting for Partnerships

Chapter 19

Steve Debenport/Getty Images

www.hvpros.com

Healthcare Venture Professionals, LLC (HVP), is a full-service management company that provides professional leadership and consultative resources to hospitals and physicians. The company is designated as an LLC, or limited liability company. It functions very similarly to a partnership where the partner-owners divide the profits of the business based on their LLC agreement. HVP's agreement, created by its members, is similar to the agreements of other LLCs. It governs the affairs of HVP and provides the procedures for admitting new members, outlines the status of the company upon a member's withdrawal, and outlines the procedures for dissolution of the business.

The founders of HVP, John Smalley and Chuck Owen, seasoned health care executives with 60+ years of combined health care leadership experience, chose to personally fund the company to eliminate undue influences from outside investors. In this way, the company is free to act in the best interest of its clients. All senior-level employees enjoy a degree of ownership and share in the success of HVP not only through higher salaries but also through profit sharing.

The company has been successful working with its clients to develop joint-ventured outpatient centers. More than 200 hospitals or health care systems and thousands of physicians have used their expertise.

thinking critically

Before a partnership agreement is signed by its partners, what are some possible questions that should be answered in the agreement?

LEARNING OBJECTIVES

19-1 Explain the major advantages and disadvantages of a partnership.
19-2 State the important provisions that should be included in every partnership agreement.
19-3 Account for the formation of a partnership.
19-4 Compute and record the division of net income or net loss between partners in accordance with the partnership agreement.
19-5 Prepare a statement of partners' equities.
19-6 Account for the revaluation of assets and liabilities prior to the dissolution of a partnership.
19-7 Account for the sale of a partnership interest.
19-8 Account for the investment of a new partner in an existing partnership.
19-9 Account for the withdrawal of a partner from a partnership.
19-10 Define the accounting terms new to this chapter.

NEW TERMS

articles of partnership
dissolution
distributive share
general partner
limited partner
limited partnership
liquidation
memorandum entry
mutual agency
partnership
partnership agreement
statement of partners' equities
unlimited liability

Section 1

SECTION OBJECTIVES

>> 19-1 Explain the major advantages and disadvantages of a partnership.

WHY IT'S IMPORTANT
Selecting the most advantageous form of business organization contributes to the overall success of a company.

>> 19-2 State the important provisions that should be included in every partnership agreement.

WHY IT'S IMPORTANT
A partnership agreement is a legal document that dictates the operating structure and terms of the business entity.

>> 19-3 Account for the formation of a partnership.

WHY IT'S IMPORTANT
Assets, liabilities, and owners' capital must all be correctly stated from the partnership's start.

TERMS TO LEARN

articles of partnership
general partner
limited partner
limited partnership
memorandum entry
mutual agency
partnership
partnership agreement
unlimited liability

Forming a Partnership

Accounting procedures for a sole proprietorship have been covered in previous chapters. This chapter discusses accounting for partnerships.

The Characteristics of a Partnership

The *Uniform Partnership Act,* adopted by all 50 states, defines a **partnership** as "an association of two or more persons who carry on, as co-owners, a business for profit." The partnership form of organization is widely used in small service, merchandising, and manufacturing businesses. Historically, professionals such as accountants, lawyers, and physicians have formed partnerships to pool their talents and abilities.

> Woolpert LLP began operations in 1911. Charlton Putnam, a surveyor and landscape engineer, joined forces with Edward Deeds and Charles Kettering, inventors of the self-starting automobile ignition system. In 1916, Ralph L. Woolpert, a civil engineer, joined the company as a partner. Throughout the years, the company extended partner status to others who contributed their expertise.

>> **19-1 OBJECTIVE**
Explain the major advantages and disadvantages of a partnership.

Advantages of the Partnership

A partnership has three important advantages. It pools the skills, abilities, and financial resources of two or more individuals. It is easy and inexpensive to form, especially when compared with a corporation. A partnership does not pay income tax. The partners report their shares of the partnership's income or loss on their individual income tax returns.

Disadvantages of the Partnership

Certain characteristics of partnerships are clearly disadvantages. Each partner has **unlimited liability** for the partnership's debts. Thus, a partner's personal assets as well as the partnership's assets can be required in payment of the firm's debts. This characteristic enhances the credit standing of the business, but it can be a danger to the individual partners.

In most states, it is possible for some partners to have limited liability. A **limited partnership** is a partnership with one or more limited partners. **Limited partners** are liable only for their investment in the partnership. State laws generally require that limited partnerships have at least one **general partner,** a partner who has unlimited liability. Limited partners are prohibited from taking an active management role and from having their names in the partnership's name.

The partnership is a **mutual agency;** each partner is empowered to act as an agent for the partnership, binding the firm by those acts so long as they are within the normal scope of the partnership's activities.

A partnership lacks continuity; it has a limited life. When a partner dies or is incapacitated, the partnership is dissolved.

Partnership interest is not freely transferable; other partners must approve the sale of a partner's interest to a new partner. Upon a transfer of interest, the existing partnership is dissolved and a new partnership must be formed.

Partnership Agreements

>> **19-2 OBJECTIVE**
State the important provisions that should be included in every partnership agreement.

It is easy to form a partnership. Two or more partners agree to form the business entity by entering into an oral or written contract. A partnership may be deemed to have been formed without an explicit agreement if the behavior of the parties implies that a partnership exists. An oral agreement is binding on the partners, but a written contract is preferred. To avoid any future misunderstandings, an attorney prepares a legal contract forming a partnership and specifying certain details of the operation, called a **partnership agreement.** This is legally known as the **articles of partnership.** The partnership agreement can be simple, or complex and detailed. Every partnership agreement should contain the:

- names of the partners;
- name, location, and nature of the business;
- starting date of the agreement;
- life of the partnership;
- rights and duties of each partner;
- amount of capital to be contributed by each partner;
- drawings by the partners;
- fiscal year and accounting method;
- method of allocating income or loss to the partners;
- procedures to be followed if the partnership is dissolved or the business is liquidated.

Partnerships dissolve upon a partner's death, incapacity, or withdrawal.

Accounting for the Formation of a Partnership

>> **19-3 OBJECTIVE**
Account for the formation of a partnership.

Partnerships and sole proprietorships use the same types of journals and ledgers as well as asset, liability, revenue, and expense accounts. The only difference is that in a partnership, each partner has a capital account and a drawing account.

There are many ways to form a partnership. Partnerships are often formed when a sole proprietorship "takes in" a partner or partners to continue an existing business. Usually the new partners invest cash, and the sole proprietor contributes noncash assets and liabilities of the existing business. Sometimes two sole proprietors combine their operations into a partnership. Often partners start a completely new business with initial investments of cash.

When noncash assets are transferred to a partnership, they are recorded at their fair market value, as agreed to by the partners, on the transfer date. Liabilities are stated at their correct balances on the transfer date.

> Sometimes two existing companies form a partnership with a new objective or mission in mind. For example, in the early 2000s, America Online, Inc., and Time Warner Cable established a partnership designed to connect computer users to the Internet. The two companies joined together to provide high-speed Internet service in New York and other areas. The cable company furnished physical connections to the Internet, while AOL provided e-mail services and other online content.

Let's look at a partnership formed by Ellen Barret and Jerry Reed. Barret operates Old Army, a small clothing store that sells T-shirts, jeans, and other casual clothing. Reed works in another store selling athletic shoes. To get additional capital and to obtain Reed's talents, Barret offered to make Reed a partner in the business. Barret agreed to transfer the assets (except cash) and the liabilities of Old Army to the new partnership. Reed agreed to invest cash of $28,000 in the business. Figure 19.1 shows the balance sheet of Old Army on December 31, 20X0.

After examining Old Army's assets, Barret and Reed agreed that:

- Net accounts receivable is $19,300.

recall

Allowance Method
Under the allowance method for uncollectible accounts, an estimate is made before actual losses occur.

Accounts receivable on balance sheet	$22,300
Definitely uncollectible	(1,800)
Accounts receivable, adjusted	$20,500
Likely to be uncollectible	(1,200)
Net accounts receivable	$19,300

- The value of merchandise inventory is $105,200.
- The store equipment's value is $3,000 based on an appraisal.

FIGURE 19.1

Balance Sheet for a Sole Proprietor

Old Army
Balance Sheet
December 31, 20X0

Assets		
Cash		2,600.00
Accounts Receivable	22,300.00	
Less Allowance for Doubtful Accounts	750.00	21,550.00
Merchandise Inventory		115,000.00
Store Equipment	10,450.00	
Less Accumulated Depreciation	8,000.00	2,450.00
Total Assets		141,600.00
Liabilities and Owner's Equity		
Liabilities		
Notes Payable—Bank	39,100.00	
Accounts Payable	36,000.00	
Total Liabilities		75,100.00
Owner's Equity		
Ellen Barret, Capital		66,500.00
Total Liabilities and Owner's Equity		141,600.00

- Accrued interest payable on the note payable is $500. This liability was not recorded as of December 31.
- Accounts payable total is $34,700 as the result of settling a dispute with a creditor after the balance sheet was prepared.

Thus, Barret and Reed have agreed that the net assets Barret transferred are $53,200:

Accounts receivable	$ 19,300
Merchandise inventory	105,200
Store equipment	3,000
Notes payable	(39,100)
Interest payable	(500)
Accounts payable	(34,700)
Total	$ 53,200

Memorandum Entry to Record Formation of Partnership

The first entry in the general journal of the new partnership is a **memorandum entry,** which is an informational entry. It indicates the name of the business, the partners' names, and other pertinent information. Note that the memorandum entry references the partnership agreement, which provides information about the capital contributed by each partner and the division of income:

20X1					
Jan.	1	On this date, a partnership was formed			
		between Ellen Barret and Jerry Reed to			
		carry on a retail clothing business under			
		the name of Old Army, according to the terms			
		of the partnership agreement effective this			
		date.			

Investment of Assets and Liabilities by Sole Proprietor

The first journal entry records the transfer of Barret's assets and liabilities to the partnership:

Jan. 1	Accounts Receivable	111	20,500.00	
	Merchandise Inventory	121	105,200.00	
	Store Equipment	131	3,000.00	
	Allowance for Doubtful Accounts	112		1,200.00
	Notes Payable—Bank	201		39,100.00
	Accounts Payable	205		34,700.00
	Interest Payable	215		500.00
	Ellen Barret, Capital	301		53,200.00
	Investment of Barret			

Note that the entry includes *Accounts Receivable* of $20,500 and *Allowance for Doubtful Accounts* of $1,200. All individual customers' balances, except for those that were definitely uncollectible, were transferred to the partnership. Consequently, the *Accounts Receivable* control account agrees with the total of the accounts receivable subsidiary ledger. Note that *Store Equipment* is transferred at fair market value. No accumulated depreciation is transferred. Depreciation on plant and equipment that was recorded by the previous owner is irrelevant. Depreciation will be recorded by the partnership based on the asset's value at the date of transfer.

ABOUT ACCOUNTING

Family Partnerships

Family partnerships are frequently designed to facilitate transfers of property, business interests, and investments between family members in a tax-efficient manner. These partnerships permit family members to pool funds for investment purposes.

Investment of Cash by Partner

The next journal entry records the investment of cash by Reed:

	Jan.	1	Cash	101	28 000 00	
			Jerry Reed, Capital	311		28 000 00
			Investment of cash by Reed			

Subsequent Investments and Permanent Withdrawals

During the life of the partnership, additional investments are recorded in the same manner as the initial investments. When partners make cash withdrawals that are intended to be permanent reductions of capital, the withdrawals are recorded as debits to the partners' capital accounts.

Drawing Accounts

Partners need funds with which to pay their living expenses. Partners can obtain funds by making withdrawals against anticipated income. Each partner has a drawing account to record withdrawals.

The partnership agreement of Old Army specifies that Barret can withdraw up to $2,500 each month and that Reed can withdraw up to $1,900 each month. The withdrawals are recorded in the cash payments journal. The entry is a debit to the partners' drawing accounts and a credit to cash. At the end of 12 months, on December 31, Barret's drawing account has a debit balance of $30,000 ($2,500 × 12), and Reed's drawing account has a debit balance of $22,800 ($1,900 × 12).

Partners sometimes pay their personal bills with partnership funds. This practice is not sound because it leads to confusion between business and personal transactions. If the business pays a partner's personal expense, however, the debit in the cash payments journal is to the partner's drawing account, not an expense account.

It is common for partners to take merchandise from the business for their personal use. The cost of merchandise is debited to the partner's drawing account. The credit is to the **Purchases** account if the periodic inventory method is used and to the **Merchandise Inventory** account if the perpetual inventory method is used. Note that the inventory account is not involved—if the periodic inventory method is used as illustrated in the journal entry below. The beginning inventory in the current period's cost of goods sold should agree with ending inventory of the prior period. Barret withdrew merchandise that cost $180 and had a retail sales price of $230. The transaction is recorded as follows:

	20X1					
	June	14	Ellen Barret, Drawing	302	180 00	
			Purchases	501		180 00
			Cost of merchandise withdrawn			
			by Barret			

---

recall

Separate Entity

The separate entity assumption states that the business is separate from its owners. This explains why personal expenses paid by the business are charged to the partner's drawing account rather than to a business expense account.

Section 1 Review

1. Jackson and Jones, partners in the JJ Grocery Group, frequently withdraw cash for personal living expenses. How should these cash withdrawals be recorded in the records of the partnership?
   a. debit an expense account; credit cash
   b. debit the partner's drawing account; credit cash
   c. debit the partner's capital account; credit cash
   d. debit the revenue account; credit cash

2. All the following are disadvantages of the partnership form of business except:
   a. unlimited liability for the partnership's debt.
   b. each partner is empowered to act as an agent for the partnership.
   c. pooling the skills, abilities, and financial resources of two or more individuals.
   d. limited continuity of life of the partnership.

3. A business owner has agreed to transfer the assets and liabilities of her business to a new partnership. The new partner will invest cash in the new business in return for one-half interest. At what values should assets and liabilities of the old business be recorded in the accounts of the partnership?
   a. fair market value
   b. historical cost
   c. book value
   d. net realizable value

4. If the periodic inventory method is used, a withdrawal of merchandise from the business by one of the partners should be recorded as:
   a. a debit to the partner's drawing account and a credit to *Purchases* for the cost of the merchandise.
   b. a debit to the partner's drawing account and a credit to *Merchandise Inventory* for the cost of the merchandise.
   c. a debit to the partner's drawing account and a credit to *Merchandise Inventory* for the sales price of the merchandise.
   d. some other entry.

5. An investment of cash in the partnership by Carl Smith, a partner in Smith-Kelly Web Services, should be recorded by:
   a. a debit to *Cash* and a credit to *Smith-Kelly, Capital*.
   b. a debit to *Cash* and a credit to *Carl Smith, Capital*.
   c. a debit to *Smith-Kelly, Capital* and a credit to *Cash*.
   d. a debit to *Carl Smith, Capital* and a credit to *Cash*.

6. John Monroe and Sam Hill are combining their businesses to form a new partnership. Monroe invests merchandise inventory valued at $111,000, store equipment with a book value of $1,200 but appraised at $8,200, and accounts receivable of $24,000, of which $1,600 is assumed to be uncollectible. In addition, he is transferring liabilities of $12,000 owed to creditors. After the entry to record his investment is posted, what is the balance in Monroe's partnership capital account?
   a. $124,200
   b. $122,800
   c. $141,600
   d. $129,600

7. Every partnership agreement should contain all the following except:
   a. names of the partners.
   b. name, location, and nature of the business.
   c. method of allocating income or loss to the partners.
   d. rights and duties of each partner.
   e. the last will and testament of each partner.

8. A memorandum entry includes all the following except:
   a. name of the business and the partners' names.
   b. references to the partnership agreement.
   c. a journal entry to record each partner's investment.
   d. a and b are correct.
   e. a, b, and c are all correct.

Section 2

SECTION OBJECTIVES

>> 19-4 Compute and record the division of net income or net loss between partners in accordance with the partnership agreement.

WHY IT'S IMPORTANT
The records must reflect the partnership agreement's allocation of profit and loss.

>> 19-5 Prepare a statement of partners' equities.

WHY IT'S IMPORTANT
The statement of partners' equities summarizes the changes that have occurred in each partner's equity account. The ending balance appears on the balance sheet.

TERMS TO LEARN

distributive share
statement of partners' equities

Allocating Income or Loss

Recall that a partnership does not pay income tax. The net income or net loss "flows through" to the partners, who report their share of the partnership income on their individual tax returns.

>> **19-4 OBJECTIVE**
Compute and record the division of net income or net loss between partners in accordance with the partnership agreement.

Allocating Partnership Income or Loss

At the end of a period, the closing procedures for a partnership are similar to those used for a sole proprietorship:

Step 1: *Close revenue to* **Income Summary.**
Step 2: *Close expenses to* **Income Summary.**
Step 3: *Close* **Income Summary** *to the partners' capital accounts.*
Step 4: *Close each partner's drawing account to the partners' capital account.*

In step 3, the business needs to determine the **distributive share,** which is the amount of net income or net loss allocated to each partner. Distributive share refers solely to the division of net income or net loss among partners, not to cash distributions.

Partners may agree to divide or allocate the income in any manner they desire. Typical considerations for each partner include the:

- amount of time spent in the business;
- skills, expertise, and experience;
- amount of capital invested.

important!

Distribution of Income
Income allocation or division is frequently referred to as the distribution of income. This does not mean that cash is distributed to the partners.

The partnership agreement should clearly and carefully spell out the basis for allocation so that there will be no misunderstanding among the partners. *In the absence of an agreement to the contrary, partners share income and losses equally.* Typical allocations are based on a fixed ratio or on capital account balances. Some agreements call for salary allowances and interest allowances.

Let's examine the end-of-year procedures for the partnership of Barret and Reed. The following T accounts show the capital and drawing accounts for Barret and Reed at the end of the first year of business before the accounts have been closed for the year. Note that the capital accounts reflect the amounts of original investment at this point.

```
           Ellen Barret, Capital      301              Jerry Reed, Capital       311
                              Dec. 31                                     Dec. 31
                              Bal.     53,200                             Bal.    28,000

           Ellen Barret, Drawing      302              Jerry Reed, Drawing       312
   Dec. 31                                      Dec. 31
   Bal.    30,000                                Bal.    22,800
```

To illustrate the most common allocation methods, the allocation of income or loss is shown under four different arrangements.

Agreed-Upon Ratio

Assume that Barret and Reed agreed that net income will be split in the ratio of 3:2 (3 to 2) to Barret and Reed, respectively. Follow these steps to convert the ratios to decimals:

Step 1: *Add the figures given in the ratio.*

Barret	3
Reed	2
Total	5

Step 2: *Express each figure as a fraction of the total.*

Barret's share	3/5
Reed's share	2/5

Step 3: *Convert each fraction into a percentage by dividing the numerator by the denominator.*

Barret's share	3/5 = 0.60, or 60 percent
Reed's share	2/5 = 0.40, or 40 percent

Allocating Net Income Assume that *Income Summary* has a credit balance of $100,000 (net income) after closing the revenue and expense accounts. Net income is allocated as follows:

Barret	$100,000 × 0.60 = $60,000
Reed	$100,000 × 0.40 = $40,000

Step 3 of the closing process is to close *Income Summary* to the partners' capital accounts as follows:

1	20X1					1
2	Dec.	31	Income Summary	399	100 000 00		2
3			Ellen Barret, Capital	301		60 000 00	3
4			Jerry Reed, Capital	311		40 000 00	4
5			To record allocation of net income in				5
6			ratio of 3:2				6

The partners' drawing accounts are then closed to their capital accounts:

1	20X1					1
8	Dec.	31	Ellen Barret, Capital	301	30 000 00		8
9			Ellen Barret, Drawing	302		30 000 00	9
10							10
11		31	Jerry Reed, Capital	311	22 800 00		11
12			Jerry Reed, Drawing	312		22 800 00	12

important!

Income Allocation
Unless the partnership agreement provides otherwise, net income or net loss is allocated equally to the partners.

After posting the closing entries, the T accounts appear as follows:

```
                    Income Summary              399
                Dec. 31          Dec. 31
                Clos.   100,000  Net Inc.  100,000
                                 Bal.            0
```

```
         Ellen Barret, Capital    301                    Jerry Reed, Capital    311
Dec. 31              Dec. 31                  Dec. 31              Dec. 31
Draw.   30,000       Bal.    53,200           Draw.   22,800       Bal.    28,000
                     Dec. 31                                       Dec. 31
                     Net Inc. 60,000                               Net Inc. 40,000
                     Bal.    83,200                                Bal.    45,200
```

```
         Ellen Barret, Drawing    302                    Jerry Reed, Drawing    312
Dec. 31              Dec. 31                  Dec. 31              Dec. 31
Bal.    30,000       Clos.   30,000           Bal.    22,800       Clos.   22,800
Bal.         0                                Bal.         0
```

Allocating Net Loss Assume that *Income Summary* has a debit balance of $30,000 (net loss) after closing revenue and expense accounts. This represents a net loss for the year. The loss is allocated as follows, using their allocation ratio of 3:2:

Barret $30,000 × 0.60 = $18,000
Reed $30,000 × 0.40 = $12,000

Steps 3 and 4 of the closing process are recorded as follows:

20X1					
Dec.	31	Ellen Barret, Capital	301	18 000 00	
		Jerry Reed, Capital	311	12 000 00	
		Income Summary	399		30 000 00
	31	Ellen Barret, Capital	301	30 000 00	
		Ellen Barret, Drawing	302		30 000 00
	31	Jerry Reed, Capital	311	22 800 00	
		Jerry Reed, Drawing	312		22 800 00

Capital Account Balances

Allocating net income or net loss on the basis of capital account balances is quite logical when capital is extremely important in the income-earning process. For example, partnerships that own and rent real estate often allocate income or loss based on capital account balances.

Barret and Reed agreed that net income or net loss will be allocated based on the ratio of capital account balances at the beginning of the year. The beginning balances for Barret and

Reed were $53,200 and $28,000, respectively. Follow the steps below to convert the capital account ratio to decimals:

Step 1: *Add the capital account balances.*

Barret	$53,200
Reed	28,000
Total	$81,200

Step 2: *Express each balance as a fraction and convert it to a decimal.*

Barret	$53,200/$81,200 = 0.65517, or 65.517 percent
Reed	$28,000/$81,200 = 0.34483, or 34.483 percent

Using these percentages, net income of $100,000 would be allocated as follows:

Barret	$100,000 × 0.65517 = $65,517
Reed	$100,000 × 0.34483 = $34,483

Assuming a profit of $100,000 and withdrawals of $30,000 for Barret and $22,800 for Reed, the steps 3 and 4 closing entries are as follows:

20X1					
Dec.	31	Income Summary	399	100,000.00	
		Ellen Barret, Capital	301		65,517.00
		Jerry Reed, Capital	311		34,483.00
	31	Ellen Barret, Capital	301	30,000.00	
		Ellen Barret, Drawing	302		30,000.00
	31	Jerry Reed, Capital	311	22,800.00	
		Jerry Reed, Drawing	312		22,800.00

A net loss would be allocated in the same ratio as net income. *Income Summary* would be credited to close the debit balance to the capital accounts.

Salary Allowances

Salary allowances are intended to reward the partners for the time they spend in the business and for the expertise and talents they bring to it. Barret and Reed agreed that each would work full time in the business. Both partners recognize Barret's long experience in retail trade, her superior skill and ability, and her good reputation and established clientele.

Barret and Reed agreed that each will receive a salary allowance equal to the monthly withdrawals permitted in the partnership agreement. After considering the salary allowance, the balance of net income or net loss will be divided between Barret and Reed in the ratio of 3:2.

Salary allowances are allocations of income. Salary allowances paid in cash to partners are withdrawals. They do not represent salary expense. They do not appear in the expense section of the income statement. Salary allowances are not subject to payroll taxes or withholdings.

When salary allowances are included in the income or loss distribution formula, step 3 of the closing process has two parts:

a. *Record the salary allowances; debit Income Summary and credit the partners' capital accounts.*

b. *Close Income Summary to the partners' capital accounts based on the partnership agreement.*

important!

Salary Withdrawals

A salary withdrawal is a cash payment to a partner and is debited to the partner's drawing account. It does not represent an expense of the partnership.

important!

Partnership Income
Partnership income is not taxed. Instead, partners include their share of the net income or net loss on their individual income tax returns.

Allocating Net Income Assume that the net income of Old Army was $112,800.

Step 3a: Record the salary allowances of $30,000 to Barret and $22,800 to Reed as follows:

	20X1						
1	20X1						1
2	Dec.	31	Income Summary	399	52 800 00		2
3			Ellen Barret, Capital	301		30 000 00	3
4			Jerry Reed, Capital	311		22 800 00	4

After recording the salary allowances, *Income Summary* has a credit balance of $60,000:

```
            Income Summary              399
        Dec. 31            Dec. 31
        Sal. All.  52,800  Net Inc.  112,800
                           Bal.       60,000
```

The balance of *Income Summary* is allocated as follows:

Barret $60,000 × 0.60 = $36,000
Reed $60,000 × 0.40 = $24,000

Step 3b: Record the entry to close the credit balance of *Income Summary* as follows:

	20X1						
1	20X1						1
6	Dec.	31	Income Summary	399	60 000 00		6
7			Ellen Barret, Capital	301		36 000 00	7
8			Jerry Reed, Capital	311		24 000 00	8

The partners' drawing accounts are closed to the capital accounts in the usual manner. Remember that the fact that a partner has or has not withdrawn cash as a salary allowance does not affect the profit or loss allocation.

important!

Withdrawals Do Not Affect Profit Allocation
Even though cash withdrawn from the business by a partner may be called "salary allowance," it is debited to the partner's drawing account. The fact that the salary allowance has, or has not, been withdrawn is irrelevant in allocating net income for the period.

Allocating Net Loss Assume net loss for Old Army is $30,000. Entries to record the loss distribution follow.

Step 3a: Record the salary allowances of $30,000 to Barret and $22,800 to Reed:

	20X1						
1	20X1						1
2	Dec.	31	Income Summary	399	52 800 00		2
3			Ellen Barret, Capital	301		30 000 00	3
4			Jerry Reed, Capital	311		22 800 00	4

After this entry is posted, *Income Summary* has a debit balance of $82,800:

```
              Income Summary            399
        Dec. 31
        Net Loss   30,000
        Dec. 31
        Sal. All.  52,800
        Bal.       82,800
```

The balance of *Income Summary* is allocated as follows:

Barret	$82,800 × 0.60 = $49,680
Reed	$82,800 × 0.40 = $33,120

Step 3b: Record the entry to close *Income Summary* as follows:

1	20X1				1
6	Dec. 31	Ellen Barret, Capital	301	49 680 00	6
7		Jerry Reed, Capital	311	33 120 00	7
8		Income Summary	399		82 800 00	8

The partners' drawing accounts are closed to the capital accounts in the usual way:

1	20X1				1
10	Dec. 31	Ellen Barret, Capital	301	30 000 00	10
11		Ellen Barret, Drawing	302		30 000 00	11
12					12
13	31	Jerry Reed, Capital	311	22 800 00	13
14		Jerry Reed, Drawing	312		22 800 00	14

After the closing entries are posted, the T accounts appear as follows:

```
         Income Summary             399
  Dec. 31                 Dec. 31
  Net Loss    30,000      Clos.    82,800
  Dec. 31
  Sal. All.   52,800
              _____
              82,800
                         Bal.           0
```

```
      Ellen Barret, Capital    301              Jerry Reed, Capital    311
  Dec. 31            Dec. 31                  Dec. 31            Dec. 31
  Net Loss  49,680   Bal.       53,200        Net Loss  33,120   Bal.       28,000
  Dec. 31            Dec. 31                  Dec. 31            Dec. 31
  Draw.     30,000   Sal. All.  30,000        Draw.     22,800   Sal. All.  22,800
            _____              _____                  _____              _____
            79,680              83,200                  55,920              50,800
                     Bal.        3,520                           Bal.        5,120
```

```
      Ellen Barret, Drawing    302              Jerry Reed, Drawing    312
  Dec. 31            Dec. 31                  Dec. 31            Dec. 31
  Bal.      30,000   Clos.      30,000        Bal.      22,800   Clos.      22,800
  Bal.           0                             Bal.           0
```

Salary and Interest Allowances

Assume that Barret and Reed want to reward themselves for their time and skills through salary allowances of $30,000 to Barret and $22,800 to Reed. They also wish to recognize their capital investments by allowing each partner 8 percent interest on his or her capital balance at the start of the period.

The partnership agreement does not specify how the remaining income or loss is to be allocated. Remember that if the partnership agreement is silent on this matter, the remaining net income or net loss is divided equally.

Step 3 of the closing process has three parts:

a. Record the salary allowances.

b. Record the interest allowances. Credit each partner's capital account for the interest allowed, and debit *Income Summary* for the total interest.

c. Close *Income Summary* to the partners' capital accounts. Again, remember that the fact that cash has or has not been paid to the partner for this allowance does not affect these entries.

Allocation When Net Income Is Adequate to Cover Allowances

Assume net income of $100,000.

Step 3a: Record the salary allowances of $30,000 to Barret and $22,800 to Reed as follows:

20X1						
Dec.	31	Income Summary	399	52,800.00		
		Ellen Barret, Capital	301		30,000.00	
		Jerry Reed, Capital	311		22,800.00	

Step 3b: Record the interest allowances. The interest allowed is 8 percent of the beginning capital balance.

Barret $53,200 × 0.08 × 1 year = $4,256
Reed $28,000 × 0.08 × 1 year = $2,240

The journal entry to record the interest allowances is as follows:

20X1						
Dec.	31	Income Summary	399	6,496.00		
		Ellen Barret, Capital	301		4,256.00	
		Jerry Reed, Capital	311		2,240.00	
		To record 8% interest allowance on				
		beginning investments				

After recording the salary and interest allowances, *Income Summary* has a credit balance of $40,704:

Income Summary		399	
Dec. 31 Sal. All.	52,800	Dec. 31 Net Inc.	100,000
Dec. 31 Int. All.	6,496		
	59,296		
		Bal.	40,704

Step 3c: Close *Income Summary* to the partners' capital accounts. The balance is divided equally between Barret and Reed. The entry to close the credit balance of *Income Summary* is as follows:

	20X1				
12	Dec. 31	Income Summary	399	40 704 00	
13		Ellen Barret, Capital	301		20 352 00
14		Jerry Reed, Capital	311		20 352 00

Allocation of Net Loss Assume that Old Army had a $40,000 net loss for the year.

Step 3a: Record the salary allowances of $30,000 to Barret and $22,800 to Reed.

Step 3b: Record the interest allowances of $4,256 to Barret and $2,240 to Reed.

After these steps, *Income Summary* has a debit balance of $99,296:

Income Summary		399
Net Loss Dec. 31	40,000	
Sal. All. Dec. 31	52,800	
Int. All.	6,496	
Bal.	99,296	

The debit balance of $99,296 is divided equally between Barret and Reed.

Step 3c: Record the entry to close *Income Summary.* Debit each partner's capital account $49,648; credit *Income Summary,* $99,296.

After the closing entries are posted, the T accounts appear as follows:

Income Summary			399
Net Loss Dec. 31	40,000	Dec. 31 Closing	99,296
Sal. All. Dec. 31	52,800		
Int. All.	6,496		
	99,296		
		Bal.	0

Ellen Barret, Capital			301
Dec. 31 Net Loss	49,648	Bal.	53,200
		Dec. 31 Sal. All.	30,000
		Dec. 31 Int. All.	4,256
			87,456
		Bal.	37,808

Jerry Reed, Capital			311
Dec. 31 Net Loss	49,648	Bal.	28,000
		Dec. 31 Sal. All.	22,800
		Dec. 31 Int. All.	2,240
			53,040
		Bal.	3,392

The partners' drawing accounts are closed to the capital accounts in the usual manner.

Income Less Than Difference Between Partners' Allocations Assume that Old Army had net income of $3,400.

Step 3a: Record the salary allowances of $30,000 to Barret and $22,800 to Reed.

Step 3b: Record the interest allowances of $4,256 to Barret and $2,240 to Reed.

After recording the salary and interest allowances, *Income Summary* has a debit balance of $55,896. The balance of *Income Summary* is divided equally between Barret and Reed.

Step 3c: Record the entry to close *Income Summary*.

After the closing entries are posted, the T accounts appear as follows:

Income Summary			399
Dec. 31 Sal. All.	52,800	Dec. 31 Net. Inc.	3,400
Dec. 31 Int. All.	6,496	Dec. 31 Closing	55,896
	59,296		59,296
		Bal.	0

Ellen Barret, Capital			301
Dec. 31 Loss	27,948	Dec. 31 Bal.	53,200
		Dec. 31 Sal. All.	30,000
		Dec. 31 Int. All.	4,256
			87,456
		Bal.	59,508

Jerry Reed, Capital			311
Dec. 31 Loss	27,948	Dec. 31 Bal.	28,000
		Dec. 31 Sal. All.	22,800
		Dec. 31 Int. All.	2,240
			53,040
		Bal.	25,092

Notice that at this point, prior to closing the drawing accounts, the capital account balance for Barret increased by $6,308 and for Reed decreased by $2,908. This is due to the relationships between the income-sharing agreements and the amount of net income reported.

	Barret	Reed
Beginning capital balance	$53,200	$28,000
Ending capital balance	59,508	25,092
Difference	$ 6,308	($ 2,908)

Partnership Financial Statements

Once the net income or net loss distribution is complete, the financial statements are prepared.

Income Statement Presentation

With one exception, the income statements for a partnership and a sole proprietorship are identical. On a partnership's income statement, it is customary to show on the bottom of the statement the division of net income or net loss among partners. The salary allowances, interest allowances, and other allocation factors are shown.

Old Army's income statement for the most recent example follows. Revenue and expense details are omitted.

Net Income for Year			$ 3,400

Allocation of Net Income	Barret	Reed	Total
Salary Allowance	$30,000	$22,800	$52,800
Interest Allowance	4,256	2,240	6,496
Balance Equally	(27,948)	(27,948)	(55,896)
Totals	$ 6,308	($ 2,908)	$ 3,400

Balance Sheet Presentation

The balance sheet of a partnership is identical to that of a sole proprietorship, except that the partnership's balance sheet shows the balance of each partner's capital account. The capital account partnership balance sheet appears in the Partners' Equity section.

The **statement of partners' equities** summarizes the changes in the partners' capital accounts during an accounting period. It includes the following:

- beginning capital,
- additional investments,
- share of net income or net loss,
- withdrawals,
- ending capital.

Figure 19.2 shows the statement of partners' equities for Old Army.

>> **19-5 OBJECTIVE**
Prepare a statement of partners' equities.

Old Army
Statement of Partners' Equities
Year Ended December 31, 20X1

	Barret Capital	Reed Capital	Total Capital
Capital Balances, Jan. 1, 20X1	0 00	0 00	0 00
Investment During Year	53 200 00	28 000 00	81 200 00
Net Income (Loss) for Year	6 308 00	(2 908 00)	3 400 00
Totals	59 508 00	25 092 00	84 600 00
Less Withdrawals During Year	30 000 00	22 800 00	52 800 00
Capital Balances, Dec. 31, 20X1	29 508 00	2 292 00	31 800 00

FIGURE 19.2

Statement of Partners' Equities

Section 2 Review

1. Partner income is not taxed. Instead, partners include their share of the net income or net loss on their individual tax return.
   a. True
   b. False

2. In the absence of an agreement to the contrary, how are partnership income and losses allocated among the partners?
   a. based on the ratio of their capital balances
   b. based on the ratio of their withdrawals to total withdrawals
   c. equally
   d. based on the ratio of their salary allowances

3. What two allowances are commonly used in allocating net income or net loss to partners?
   a. salary
   b. interest
   c. withdrawals
   d. both a and b are correct

4. The entry to record the equal distribution of net income between two partners consists of a:
   a. debit to *Income Summary* and a credit to *Cash*.
   b. debit to *Income Summary* and a credit to each partner's drawing account.
   c. debit to each partner's capital account and a credit to *Cash*.
   d. debit to *Income Summary* and a credit to each partner's capital account.

5. The amount that each partner withdraws from a partnership:
   a. is always divided evenly among the partners.
   b. cannot exceed the net income reported by the partnership.
   c. is the base on which federal income taxes are levied on the partnership income.
   d. should be specified in the partnership agreement.

6. Len Thomas and Wilson Wade formed a partnership. Thomas invested $120,000. Wade invested $80,000. Net income for the year is $100,000. If net income is allocated based on the capital account balances at the beginning of the year, what is the income allocation for Thomas and Wade?
   a. $60,000 to Thomas; $40,000 to Wade
   b. $60,000 to Wade; $40,000 to Thomas
   c. $50,000 to Thomas; $50,000 to Wade
   d. $75,000 to Thomas; $25,000 to Wade

7. If both salary and interest allowances are made to the partners, what are the three steps in closing the *Income Summary* account to the partners' capital accounts?
   a. Record salary allowances; record withdrawals; close balance of *Income Summary* to partners' capital accounts.
   b. Record salary allowances; record interest allowances; close balance of *Income Summary* to partners' capital accounts.
   c. Record profit and loss by agreement; record salary allowances; record interest allowances.
   d. Record profit and loss by agreement; record withdrawals; close balance of *Income Summary* to partners' capital accounts.

8. Even though cash withdrawn from the business by a partner may be called "salary allowance," it is debited to the partner's drawing account.
   a. True
   b. False

Section 3

SECTION OBJECTIVES	TERMS TO LEARN
>> 19-6 Account for the revaluation of assets and liabilities prior to the dissolution of a partnership. **WHY IT'S IMPORTANT** The gains or losses must be properly allocated to the partners. **>> 19-7** Account for the sale of a partnership interest. **WHY IT'S IMPORTANT** The capital account of the new partner must be properly stated. **>> 19-8** Account for the investment of a new partner in an existing partnership. **WHY IT'S IMPORTANT** The capital account of the new partner must reflect the interest to be received by the new partner. **>> 19-9** Account for the withdrawal of a partner from a partnership. **WHY IT'S IMPORTANT** The withdrawal of a partner from a business changes the equity ratios and the valuation of the partnership.	dissolution liquidation

Partnership Changes

The partners in an existing business can change. Former partners might withdraw, sell their interests, or die. New partners may be admitted.

Changes in Partners

A partnership has a limited life. Whenever a partner dies or withdraws, or when a new partner is admitted, a dissolution of the old partnership occurs. If the surviving partners continue the business, a new partnership legally exists. **Dissolution** is the legal term for termination of a partnership. It has little impact on the business activities of the partnership. On the other hand, when the business is completely terminated, it is called a **liquidation.** The business ceases to exist, and the partnership agreement is void.

When a partnership is dissolved, two steps are taken:

Step 1: *The accounting records are closed and the net income or net loss on the date of dissolution is recorded and transferred to the partners' capital accounts.*

Step 2: *Assets and liabilities are revalued at fair market value. The partners, including any newly admitted partners, agree on the amounts.*

Recording Revaluation of Assets

The partnership agreement usually provides that when a partnership is dissolved and the business is to be continued as a new partnership, the assets and liabilities are revalued. The revaluation may require the services of a professional appraiser. The revaluation is made because the difference between the fair market value and the book value is a gain or loss resulting from events that occurred during the old partnership. The new partner does not share the gain or loss.

>> 19-6 OBJECTIVE

Account for the revaluation of assets and liabilities prior to the dissolution of a partnership.

Based on the revaluation, the assets and liabilities are written up or down, and the difference between the book and fair market values is allocated to the original partners' capital accounts. The allocation of gains and losses is made in accordance with the formula used for sharing net income or net loss.

The partners of Key Notes Music Store agreed to admit a new partner, effective April 1. The assets and liabilities will be revalued following the close of business on March 31. Figure 19.3 shows the balance sheet of Key Notes after the closing entries are made on March 31 and net income or net loss is transferred to the partners' capital accounts.

The partners agree that:

- ***Allowance for Doubtful Accounts*** should be increased to $4,300.
- ***Value of Merchandise Inventory*** is $79,000.
- ***Land*** is worth $22,000 according to an appraisal.
- Liabilities are properly stated.

The result is a $6,700 net increase in assets:

Merchandise inventory	$9,000
Accounts receivable/Allowance for doubtful accounts	(2,300)
Net increase in assets	$6,700

Assume that the partners share income and losses as follows:

Lee	40 percent
Wilner	40 percent
Flores	20 percent

FIGURE 19.3

Partnership Balance Sheet

important!

Asset Revaluation

When transferred from one partnership to another, assets are revalued to their fair market value. The new value will not necessarily agree with the book value carried by the old firm.

Key Notes Music Store
Balance Sheet
March 31, 20X1

Assets		
Cash		60 000 00
Accounts Receivable	40 000 00	
Less Allowance for Doubtful Accounts	2 000 00	38 000 00
Merchandise Inventory		70 000 00
Land		22 000 00
Total Assets		190 000 00
Liabilities and Partners' Equity		
Liabilities		
Notes Payable—Bank	19 000 00	
Accounts Payable	23 200 00	
Total Liabilities		42 200 00
Partners' Equity		
Tom Lee, Capital	38 300 00	
Joan Wilner, Capital	58 500 00	
Nau Flores, Capital	51 000 00	
Total Partners' Equity		147 800 00
Total Liabilities and Partners' Equity		190 000 00

The gain on revaluation of the assets is allocated as follows:

Lee	$6,700 × 0.40 = $2,680
Wilner	$6,700 × 0.40 = $2,680
Flores	$6,700 × 0.20 = $1,340

Revaluation of the assets is recorded as follows:

	GENERAL JOURNAL			PAGE 4	
DATE	DESCRIPTION	POST. REF.	DEBIT	CREDIT	
20X1					1
April 1	Merchandise Inventory	121	9 000 00		2
	Allowance for Doubtful Accounts	112		2 300 00	3
	Tom Lee, Capital	301		2 680 00	4
	Joan Wilner, Capital	311		2 680 00	5
	Nau Flores, Capital	321		1 340 00	6
	To record revaluation of assets and				7
	allocations of gain to partners.				8

>> **THE BOTTOM LINE**
Revaluation of Assets

Income Statement
No effect on net income

Balance Sheet
Assets ↑ 6,700
Equity ↑ 6,700

After the entry is posted, the capital accounts contain the following balances:

Lee	($38,300 + $2,680)	$ 40,980
Wilner	($58,500 + $2,680)	61,180
Flores	($51,000 + $1,340)	52,340
Total		$154,500

Admission of a New Partner

There are two ways to admit a new partner:

1. The new partner may purchase all or part of the interest of an existing partner, making payment directly to the selling partner. In this case, no cash or other asset is transferred to the partnership.
2. The new partner may invest cash or other assets directly in the existing partnership.

Purchase of an Interest One way to join an existing partnership is to buy a portion of a partner's share of capital. The prospective partner must have the approval of the existing partners. The money or other consideration passes directly from the new partner to the selling partner and does not appear in the accounting records of the partnership.

Suppose Key Notes's books are closed and the assets revalued as described. Lee sells half his interest in the business to Beth Rivera for $32,000. Rivera pays $32,000 directly to Lee. The partnership's records do not reflect this cash transaction. In the partnership's accounting records, the transfer is recorded by a debit to **Tom Lee, Capital** for $20,490 and a credit to **Beth Rivera, Capital** for $20,490. The $20,490 is one-half of Lee's capital account balance after revaluation (0.50 × $40,980). (The other partners would have to agree to this transfer of interest to Rivera.)

Frequently the amount paid by the new partner is not the same as the amount credited to the new partner's capital account. The value of the partner's interest is a matter for bargaining between the two parties. Rivera paid $32,000 in order to obtain a capital account of $20,490. The difference between the two amounts does not affect the partnership's accounting records.

With the admission of the new partner, the current partnership comes to an end and a new partnership is established. The partners should draw up a new partnership agreement.

Investment of Assets by a New Partner A new partner may invest money or other property to obtain admission to the partnership while the existing partners remain as partners in the business. The new partner's investment, share of ownership in capital, and share of the

>> **19-7 OBJECTIVE**
Account for the sale of a partnership interest.

>> **19-8 OBJECTIVE**
Account for the investment of a new partner in an existing partnership.

net income or net loss are agreed upon among the partners and specified in the partnership agreement for the new partnership. The new partner may receive credit for the amount invested or for a higher or lower amount.

New Partner Given Credit for Amount Invested Suppose the four parties involved in Key Notes Music agree that Rivera will receive a one-fourth interest in the capital of the business for cash equal to one-fourth of the total capital in the new partnership. After revaluation, the capital accounts of the three existing partners total $154,500. The investment for Rivera to own one-fourth of the capital of the new partnership is $51,500:

- The three existing partners, whose capital accounts total $154,500 after the revaluation, will own three-fourths of the business. The $154,500 is three-fourths (or 75 percent) of the new partnership capital. Each quarter interest is therefore $51,500.
- The new partnership capital is $206,000 ($51,500 × 4).
- Rivera is purchasing one-fourth (or 25 percent) of the new partnership capital, $51,500.

The entry to record Rivera's investment is as follows:

20X1				
April 1	Cash	101	51 500 00	
	Beth Rivera, Capital	331		51 500 00
	To record investment of Rivera for			
	one-fourth interest in partnership			

New Partner Given Credit for More Than Amount Invested The new partner can be given credit for more capital than the amount invested. This is often done if the new partner brings to the business skills that the existing partners are eager to have. Suppose Rivera agreed to invest $45,500 for a one-fourth interest in the partnership. It takes two steps to record the investment: record the cash investment and adjust the capital account balances.

The cash investment is recorded as a debit to **Cash** for $45,500 and a credit to **Beth Rivera, Capital** for $45,500. After this entry is posted, the capital account balances are $200,000:

Lee	$ 40,980
Wilner	61,180
Flores	52,340
Rivera	45,500
Total	$200,000

According to the capital account balances, Rivera owns 22.75 percent of the partnership ($45,500/$200,000). However, Rivera paid $45,500 to purchase a one-fourth interest in the partnership. Rivera's capital account balance should be $50,000 ($200,000 × 1/4). The $4,500 ($50,000 − $45,500) increase necessary to bring Rivera's account to $50,000 is referred to as a "bonus to the new partner." The $4,500 is credited to Rivera's capital account. The debit is deducted from the original partners' capital accounts on the basis of the former partnership income and loss ratio. The amounts deducted from the original partners' accounts are as follows:

Lee	$4,500 × 0.40 = $1,800
Wilner	$4,500 × 0.40 = $1,800
Flores	$4,500 × 0.20 = $900

The general journal entry to record the bonus is as follows:

20X1				
April 1	Tom Lee, Capital	301	1,800 00	
	Joan Wilner, Capital	311	1,800 00	
	Nau Flores, Capital	321	900 00	
	Beth Rivera, Capital	331		4,500 00
	To record bonus allowed new partner			

The partners' capital accounts after posting the entry for the bonus appear as follows:

Tom Lee, Capital 301

April 1 Rivera bonus	1,800	April 1 Bal.	40,980
		Bal.	39,180

Joan Wilner, Capital 301

April 1 Rivera bonus	1,800	April 1 Bal.	61,180
		Bal.	59,380

Nau Flores, Capital 321

April 1 Rivera bonus	900	April 1 Bal.	52,340
		Bal.	51,440

Beth Rivera, Capital 301

	April 1 Invest.	45,500
	April 1 Bonus	4,500
	Bal.	50,000

New Partner Given Credit for Less Than Amount Invested Suppose that Rivera agreed to invest $45,500 for a one-fifth interest in the capital of the partnership. The $45,500 investment is recorded as a debit to **Cash** for $45,500 and a credit to **Beth Rivera, Capital** for $45,500.

After this entry is posted, the capital account balances are $200,000:

Lee	$ 40,980
Wilner	61,180
Flores	52,340
Rivera	45,500
Total	$200,000

According to the capital account balances at this point, Rivera owns 22.75 percent of the partnership ($45,500/$200,000). However, she paid $45,500 for a one-fifth (or 20 percent) interest in the partnership. Rivera's capital account balance should be $40,000 ($200,000 × 0.20). The $5,500 ($40,000 − $45,500) decrease necessary to bring Rivera's capital account to $40,000 is referred to as "bonus allowed the original partners." The $5,500 is debited to Rivera's capital account and credited to the original partners' capital accounts on the basis of the former partnership income and loss ratio. The amounts credited to the original partners' capital accounts are as follows:

Lee	$5,500 × 0.40 = $2,200
Wilner	$5,500 × 0.40 = $2,200
Flores	$5,500 × 0.20 = $1,100

	20X1						
	April	1	Beth Rivera, Capital	331	5 500 00		
			Tom Lee, Capital	301		2 200 00	
			Joan Wilner, Capital	311		2 200 00	
			Nau Flores, Capital	321		1 100 00	
			To record bonus to original partners				

After this entry is posted, Rivera's capital account balance will be $40,000, or one-fifth of the total partnership capital of $200,000.

>> 19-9 OBJECTIVE

Account for the withdrawal of a partner from a partnership.

Withdrawal of a Partner

The partnership agreement should contain provisions specifying the procedures to be followed for the withdrawal of a partner. The partnership agreement for Key Notes provides that, upon withdrawal of a partner, the assets are to be revalued and the retiring partner is to be paid an amount equal to that partner's capital account after revaluation. Suppose that the partners of Key Notes agree that Nau Flores is to withdraw from the partnership after the close of business on March 31. He is to receive cash in an amount equal to the balance of his capital account after revaluation of the assets.

The revalued assets result in the following capital account balances:

Lee	$ 40,980
Wilner	61,180
Flores	52,340
Total	$154,500

The entry to record the withdrawal of Flores from the partnership is as follows:

	20X1					
	Mar.	31	Nau Flores, Capital	321	52 340 00	
			Cash	101		52 340 00
			To record cash payment made to Flores			
			on withdrawal from partnership			

MANAGERIAL IMPLICATIONS <<

PARTNERSHIP CONSIDERATIONS

- Management and owners need to understand the advantages the partnership form of business offers to sole proprietors who need more capital, managerial assistance, or technical help.
- The partnership does not pay taxes. The partnership's taxable income "flows through" to the individual partners.
- It is essential that individuals who enter into a partnership have a clear understanding of the duties, obligations, rights, and responsibilities of each partner.
- There should be a written partnership agreement drafted by a lawyer and reviewed by the partners' accountants.
- The partnership agreement should be very specific about the income and loss allocation formula.
- Upon dissolution, the partnership assets and liabilities should be revalued.

THINKING CRITICALLY

What are the essential elements of a partnership agreement?

The parties might agree that the withdrawing partner is to receive either more or less than the balance of that partner's capital account at the time of withdrawal. In this event, the withdrawing partner's capital account is debited for the balance of the account:

- If the amount paid is higher than the withdrawing partner's capital account balance, the excess is debited to the capital accounts of the remaining partners according to their income and loss ratio.
- If the amount paid is less than the withdrawing partner's capital account balance, the difference is credited to the remaining partners' capital accounts based on their income and loss ratio.

After the assets of Key Notes are revalued, Flores's capital account balance is $52,340. Flores wishes to withdraw, and the partners agree to pay him $61,340 from partnership funds. The $9,000 ($61,340 − $52,340) bonus paid to the withdrawing partner is divided between the remaining partners according to their income and loss ratio of 40:40 (equally). The general journal entry to record the withdrawal of Flores is as follows:

20X1				
Mar. 31	Nau Flores, Capital	321	52 340 00	
	Tom Lee, Capital	301	4 500 00	
	Joan Wilner, Capital	311	4 500 00	
	Cash	101		61 340 00
	To record cash payment made to Flores			
	on withdrawal from partnership			

Section 3 Review

1. If a new partner invests cash greater than the fractional share of the total capital being purchased, the existing partners' capital accounts will be increased in proportion to the income or loss distribution ratio of the existing partners.
    a. True
    b. False

2. If a withdrawing partner is paid less than his capital account balance, the difference is debited to the retiring partner's capital account and is credited to the existing partners' capital accounts in proportion to the income or loss distribution ratio of the existing partners.
    a. True
    b. False

3. An existing partner sells one-half of his capital interest to a new partner. What is the accounting entry to record this transaction?
    a. Debit the existing partner's capital account for one-half of the balance of that account.
    b. Debit *Cash* and credit the new partner's capital account for the cash payment.
    c. Credit the new partner's capital account for the same amount debited to the existing partner's capital account.
    d. Both a and c are correct.

4. The profit-sharing percentages of partners Jones, Jackson, and Jolly are 40 percent, 40 percent, and 20 percent, respectively. Their capital account balances are $40,000, $30,000, and $20,000, respectively. Jones withdraws from the partnership and receives $36,000 from the partnership in settlement of his withdrawal. As a result of this transaction:
    a. the capital account of Jackson is credited for $2,668.
    b. the capital account of Jackson is debited for $1,000.
    c. the capital account of Jackson is credited for $1,000.
    d. the capital account of Jackson is not affected.

5. When a partner withdraws from the partnership and receives cash in excess of the balance in his capital account, the excess is:
    a. debited to the capital accounts of the remaining partners, allocated equally to those partners.
    b. debited to the capital accounts of the remaining partners, allocated to those partners in proportion to their profit and loss percentages.
    c. credited to the capital accounts of the remaining partners, allocated to those partners in proportion to their profit and loss percentages.
    d. debited to the capital accounts of the remaining partners, allocated to those partners on the basis of the ratio of their capital account balances.

6. James Thomas paid $14,000 to Paul Torres for one-half of his interest in the partnership of Thomas and Torres. Torres's capital account balance prior to the purchase was $100,000. What is the entry required in the partnership's accounts to record this transaction?
   a. Debit *Paul Torres, Capital* for $14,000; credit *James Thomas, Capital* for $14,000.
   b. Debit *Paul Torres, Capital* for $50,000; credit *James Thomas, Capital* for $50,000.
   c. Debit *Paul Torres, Capital* for $100,000; credit *James Thomas, Capital* for $100,000.
   d. No entry is necessary; the transaction is between Torres and Thomas.

7. When transferred from one partnership to another, assets are revalued to their fair market value.
   a. True
   b. False

8. When a partnership is completely terminated, it is called a:
   a. dissolution.
   b. liquidation.
   c. reorganization.
   d. split up.

Accounting for Partnerships CHAPTER 19 691

REVIEW Chapter Summary

Chapter **19**

A partnership is the joining together of two or more persons under a written or oral contract as co-owners of a business. You have learned about the advantages and disadvantages of the partnership form of business. In addition, you have studied the accounting methods and procedures unique to partnerships.

Learning Objectives

19-1 Explain the major advantages and disadvantages of a partnership.

There are advantages to a partnership:
- It is relatively easy and inexpensive to form.
- It permits pooling of skills and resources.
- No income tax is paid on its profits, although partners report their share of income or loss on their tax returns.

There are disadvantages to a partnership:
- Partners have unlimited liability.
- Any partner can bind the other partners.
- The business lacks continuity.
- Ownership rights are not freely transferable.

19-2 State the important provisions that should be included in every partnership agreement.

A written agreement should detail the partnership specifics: amount of initial investment, partners' duties, fiscal year, accounting method, division of gains or losses (including any allowances for salaries and interest), policy for withdrawals, and length of partnership life.

19-3 Account for the formation of a partnership.

Assets and liabilities may be exchanged for a partnership interest:
- Assets are appraised and recorded at the agreed-upon fair market value at the transfer date.
- Each partner's capital account is credited for the amount of the investment.

19-4 Compute and record the division of net income or net loss between partners in accordance with the partnership agreement.

Division of partnership income and losses can be made in any manner. If no agreement has been made, income and losses are divided equally.

19-5 Prepare a statement of partners' equities.

A statement of partners' equities summarizes the changes in the capital accounts during the period.

19-6 Account for the revaluation of assets and liabilities prior to the dissolution of a partnership.

Before a partnership is dissolved, the business assets are revalued and the income or loss allocated according to the original agreement.

19-7 Account for the sale of a partnership interest.

A new partner may purchase a partnership interest from a current partner. The portion of ownership sold is transferred from the existing partner's capital account to the new partner's capital account.

19-8 Account for the investment of a new partner in an existing partnership.

A new partner may invest more or less than the proportionate part of total capital that the new partner will own after the investment:
- If more is invested, a bonus is recorded to the current partners (the new partner's capital account is debited and the current partners' capital accounts are credited).
- If less is invested, a bonus is recorded to the new partner (the new partner's capital account is credited and the current partners' capital accounts are debited).

19-9 Account for the withdrawal of a partner from a partnership.

When a partner withdraws, the assets and liabilities are revalued and the income or loss allocated according to the original agreement. If the amount the retiring partner is paid is different from the capital account balance, the difference is allocated to the remaining partners in accordance with their profit and loss ratios.

19-10 Define the accounting terms new to this chapter.

Glossary

Articles of partnership (p. 667) *See* Partnership agreement

Dissolution (p. 683) The legal term for termination of a partnership

Distributive share (p. 672) The amount of net income or net loss allocated to each partner

General partner (p. 667) A member of a partnership who has unlimited liability

Limited partner (p. 667) A member of a partnership whose liability is limited to his or her investment in the partnership

Limited partnership (p. 667) A partnership having one or more limited partners

Liquidation (p. 683) Termination of a business by distributing all assets and discontinuing the business

Memorandum entry (p. 669) An informational entry in the general journal

Mutual agency (p. 667) The characteristic of a partnership by which each partner is empowered to act as an agent for the partnership, binding the firm by his or her acts

Partnership (p. 666) A business entity owned by two or more people who carry on a business for profit and who are legally responsible for the debts and taxes of the business

Partnership agreement (p. 667) A legal contract forming a partnership and specifying certain details of operation

Statement of partners' equities (p. 681) A financial statement prepared to summarize the changes in the partners' capital accounts during an accounting period

Unlimited liability (p. 667) The implication that a creditor can look to all partners' personal assets as well as the assets of the partnership for payment of the firm's debts

Comprehensive Self Review

1. What nonfinancial information should be considered in forming a partnership?
2. What are the major disadvantages of the partnership form of business enterprise?
3. Explain how one partner might receive a profit allocation even though the partnership has a loss for the period.
4. Explain the difference between the accounting treatment of "salary withdrawals" and "salary allowances" in allocating income or loss.
5. Why are the assets and liabilities revalued prior to a dissolution?

(Answers to Comprehensive Self Review are at the end of the chapter.)

Discussion Questions

1. Explain the use of a drawing account in a partnership.
2. List the steps required to dissolve a partnership.
3. What are typical considerations that affect the way income is allocated among partners?
4. What is the difference between a dissolution and liquidation?
5. Explain how the partnership accounts for the sale by a partner of a portion of his partnership interest to another individual.
6. The two partners in a business often pay personal bills by writing checks on the business bank account. Is this a good business practice? Explain. How should such payments be recorded?
7. What information appears on a statement of partners' equities?
8. List the major advantages of the partnership form of business over a corporation.
9. What are the major disadvantages of the partnership form of business entity?
10. Does a partnership continue to exist after the death of a partner? Explain.

11. Does a partnership pay federal income tax? Explain.
12. Why are assets of an existing sole proprietorship revalued when they are transferred to a partnership?
13. Is *Allowance for Doubtful Accounts* brought forward from the general ledger of a sole proprietorship when the firm's assets and liabilities are being transferred to the partnership? Why?
14. How does the balance sheet of a partnership differ from that of a sole proprietorship?
15. What is the advantage of a limited partnership?
16. Are partners' salaries considered to be expenses of the partnership? Explain.
17. Explain how the net income of a partnership is allocated if it is less than the salary and interest allowances.
18. Explain what the term "mutual agency" means in regard to a partnership.
19. Why should the assets and liabilities of an existing partnership be revalued when a new partner is to be admitted by the investment of cash in the organization?

APPLICATIONS

Exercises

Recording cash investment in a partnership.

In 20X1, Ruby Canti invests cash of $220,000 in a newly formed partnership that will operate The Pro Shop. In return, Canti receives a one-third interest in the capital of the partnership. In general journal form, record Canti's investment in the partnership.

◀ **Exercise 19.1**
Objective 19-3

Recording investment of assets and liabilities in a partnership.

Wade Wilson operates a sole proprietorship business that sells golf equipment. In 20X1, Wilson agrees to transfer his assets and liabilities to a partnership that will operate The Golf Shop. Wilson will own a two-thirds interest in the capital of the partnership. The agreed-upon values of assets and liabilities to be transferred follow:

Total accounts receivable of $130,000 will be transferred and approximately $10,000 of these accounts may be uncollectible

Merchandise inventory, $106,000

Furniture and fixtures, $48,000

Accounts payable, $18,500

Record the receipt of the assets and liabilities by the partnership in the general journal.

◀ **Exercise 19.2**
Objective 19-3

Preparing a balance sheet for a partnership.

On May 1, 20X1, James Dear and Jerold Morgan formed The Wine Shop. The two partners invested cash and other assets and liabilities with the following agreed-upon values:

Dear: Cash, $6,500; Merchandise inventory, $12,500; Equipment, $38,500; Accounts payable, $6,000.

Morgan: Furniture $12,500; Cash, $18,500.

Dear is to own two-thirds of the capital, and Morgan is to own one-third of the capital, but they will split profits and losses equally. Prepare a balance sheet for the partnership just after the assets and liabilities have been transferred to it.

◀ **Exercise 19.3**
Objective 19-3

Computing and recording allocation of net income with salaries and interest allowed.

Alexis Wells and Jessica Harris are partners who share profits and losses in the following manner. Wells receives a salary of $106,000 and Harris receives a salary of $150,000. These amounts were

◀ **Exercise 19.4**
Objective 19-4

paid to the partners and charged to their drawing accounts. Both partners also receive 10 percent interest on their capital balances at the beginning of the year. The balance of any remaining profits or losses is divided equally. The beginning capital accounts for 20X1 were Wells, $104,500, and Harris, $129,500. At the end of the year, the partnership had a net income of $300,000. Compute the amount of net income or loss to be allocated to each partner.

Exercise 19.5
Objective 19-4

▶ **Computing and recording allocation of net income with interest allowed.**

Collins and Allen are partners. Their partnership agreement provides that, in dividing profits, each is to be allocated interest at 10 percent of her beginning capital balance. The balance of net income or loss after the interest allowances is to be split in the ratio of 70:30 to Collins and Allen, respectively. The beginning capital balances were Collins, $130,000, and Allen, $34,000. Net income for the year was $62,500. Compute the amount of net income to be allocated to each partner.

Exercise 19.6
Objective 19-4

▶ **Computing and recording division of net income, with salaries allowed.**

Charles Brown and Robert Huddleston are partners who share profits and losses in the ratio of 70 to 30 percent, respectively. Their partnership agreement provides that each will be paid a yearly salary of $120,000. The salaries were paid to the partners during 20X1 and were charged to the partners' drawing accounts. The *Income Summary* account has a credit balance of $175,800 after revenue and expense accounts are closed at the end of the year. What amount of net income or net loss will be allocated to each?

Exercise 19.7
Objective 19-4

▶ **Computing and recording division of net loss, with no partnership agreement on method of allocation.**

After revenue and expense accounts of The In and Out Stop were closed on December 31, 20X1, *Income Summary* contained a credit balance of $198,200. The drawing accounts of the two partners, Thomas Muir and Kerry Goree, showed debit balances of $80,000 and $184,000, respectively. The partnership agreement is silent on the division of profits and losses. Record the general journal entries to close the *Income Summary* account and the partners' drawing accounts.

Exercise 19.8
Objective 19-4

▶ **Computing and recording division of net income based on fixed ratio.**

The net income for the new partnership known as The Pit Stop for the year ended December 31, 20X1, was $34,000. The partners, Robert Taylor and David Brown, share profits in the ratio of 40 to 60 percent, respectively. Record the general journal entry (or entries) to close the *Income Summary* account.

Exercise 19.9
Objective 19-4

▶ **Computing the division of net income of a partnership.**

The partnership agreement of Emily Adams and Shaun McGowan does not indicate how the profits and losses will be shared. Before dividing the net income, Adams' capital account balance was $80,000, and McGowan's capital balance was $20,000. The net income of their firm for the year that just ended was $52,000. How much income will be allocated to Adams and how much to McGowan?

Exercise 19.10
Objective 19-6

▶ **Recording revaluation of assets prior to dissolution of a partnership.**

Billy Allen and Thomas Klammer are partners who share profits and losses in the ratio of 40:60, respectively. On December 31, 20X1, they decide that Klammer will sell one-half of his interest to Marvel Turner. At that time, the balances of the capital accounts are $260,000 for Allen and $360,000 for Klammer. The partners agree that before the new partner is admitted, certain assets should be revalued. These assets include merchandise inventory carried at $105,800, revalued at $98,900, and a building with a book value of $90,000, revalued at $150,000.

1. Record the revaluations in the general journal.
2. What will the capital balances of the two existing partners be after the revaluation is made?

Exercise 19.11
Objective 19-7

▶ **Recording sale of a part interest.**

Nelson Ellis and Hank Tollis are partners who share profits and losses in the ratio of 40 to 60 percent, respectively. The balances of their capital accounts on December 31, 20X0, are Ellis, $105,000, and Tollis, $115,000. With Tollis's agreement, Ellis sells one-half of his interest in the partnership to Kate Cantu for $80,000 on January 1, 20X1. What will the capital account balances for each of the three partners be after this sale?

Recording withdrawal of a partner.

William, Henderson, and Middleton are partners, sharing profits and losses in the ratio of 40 to 30 to 30 percent, respectively. Their partnership agreement provides that if one of them withdraws from the partnership, the assets and liabilities are to be revalued, the gain or loss allocated to the partners, and the retiring partner paid the balance of his account. Middleton withdraws from the partnership on December 31, 20X1. The capital account balances before recording revaluation are Williams, $250,000; Henderson, $270,000; and Middleton, $240,000. The effect of the revaluation is to increase **Merchandise Inventory** by $52,000 and the **Building** account balance by $30,000. How much cash will be paid to Middleton?

◀ **Exercise 19.12**
Objective 19-9

PROBLEMS

Problem Set A

Accounting for formation of a partnership.

James Walker operates a store that sells computer software. Walker has agreed to enter into a partnership with Robert Tolliver, effective January 1, 20X1. The new firm will be called International Computing. Walker is to transfer all assets and liabilities of his firm to the partnership at the values agreed on. Tolliver will invest cash that is equal to 75 percent of Walker's investment after revaluation. The accounts shown on Walker's books and the agreed-on value of assets and liabilities are shown below.

◀ **Problem 19.1A**
Objective 19-3

		Balances Shown in Walker's Records	Value Agreed to by Partners
Assets Transferred			
Cash		$200,000	$200,000
Accounts Receivable	$131,000		
Allowance for Doubtful Accounts	5,000	126,000	112,000
Merchandise Inventory		360,000	375,000
Furniture and Equipment	140,000		100,000
Accumulated Depreciation	60,000	80,000	
Total Assets		$766,000	$787,000
Liabilities and Owner's Equity Transferred			
Accounts Payable		70,000	70,000
James Walker, Capital		$696,000	$717,000

INSTRUCTIONS

1. Prepare the general journal entries to record the following transactions in the books of the partnership on January 1, 20X1:
   a. Receipt of Walker's investment of assets and liabilities.
   b. Receipt of Tolliver's investment of cash.
2. Prepare a balance sheet for the partnership as of the beginning of its operations on January 1, 20X1.

Analyze: Based on the balance sheet you have prepared, what percentage (to the nearest 1/10 of 1%) of total equity is owned by James Walker?

Accounting for formation of a partnership.

Thomas Richey operates a small shop that sells fishing equipment. His postclosing trial balance on December 31, 20X1, is shown below.

Richey plans to enter into a partnership with Kathryn Price, effective January 1, 20X2. Profits and losses will be shared equally. Richey is to transfer all assets and liabilities of his store to the partnership

◀ **Problem 19.2A**
Objective 19-3

after revaluation as agreed. Price will invest cash equal to Richey's investment after revaluation. The agreed values are **Accounts Receivable** (net), $58,000; **Merchandise Inventory**, $199,600; and **Furniture and Equipment**, $49,200. The partnership will operate as Richey and Price Angler's Outpost.

Richey's Tackle Center
Postclosing Trial Balance
December 31, 20X1

ACCOUNT NAME	DEBIT	CREDIT
Cash	19 000 00	
Accounts Receivable	65 600 00	
Allowance for Doubtful Accounts		10 000 00
Merchandise Inventory	180 000 00	
Furniture and Equipment	116 400 00	
Accumulated Depreciation		92 000 00
Accounts Payable		16 000 00
Capital		263 000 00
Totals	381 000 00	381 000 00

INSTRUCTIONS

1. In general journal form, prepare the entries to record:
   a. The receipt of Richey's investment of assets and liabilities by the partnership.
   b. The receipt of Price's investment of cash.
2. Prepare a balance sheet for Richey and Price Angler's Outpost just after the investments.

Analyze: By what net amount were the net assets of Richey's Tackle Center adjusted before they were transferred to the partnership?

Problem 19.3A
Objective 19-4

Computing and recording the division of net income or loss between partners.

Angie Castillo and Reesa Cameron own The Garden and Lawn Shop. The partnership agreement provides that Castillo can withdraw $10,000 a month and Cameron, $9000 a month in anticipation of profits. The withdrawals, which are not considered to be salaries, were made each month. Net income and net losses are to be allocated 40 percent to Castillo and 60 percent to Cameron. For the year ended December 31, 20X1, the partnership earned a net income of $300,000.

INSTRUCTIONS

1. Prepare general journal entries to:
   a. Close the **Income Summary** account.
   b. Close the partners' drawing accounts.
2. Assume that there was a net loss of $100,000 for the year instead of a profit of $300,000. Give the general journal entries to:
   a. Close the **Income Summary** account.
   b. Close the partners' drawing accounts.

Analyze: Assume the business earned net income of $300,000. If 20X1 was the first year of operation, what balance should be reflected for the **Reesa Cameron, Capital** account at the end of the year if Cameron's beginning capital was $220,000?

Problem 19.4A
Objectives 19-4, 19-5

Computing and recording the division of net income or loss between partners; preparing a statement of partners' equities.

Lewis Wardell and Lewis Lomas own Lewis's Antiques. Their partnership agreement provides for annual salary allowances of $200,000 for Wardell and $180,000 for Lomas, and interest of 10 percent on each partner's invested capital at the beginning of the year. The remainder of the net income or loss is to be distributed 50 percent to Wardell and 50 percent to Lomas. The partners withdraw their salary allowances monthly. On January 1, 20X1, the capital account balances were

Wardell, $600,000, and Lomas, $560,000. On December 15, 20X1, Lomas made a permanent withdrawal of $55,000. The net income for 20X1 was $640,000.

INSTRUCTIONS

1. Prepare the general journal entry on December 15, 20X1, to record the permanent withdrawal by Lomas.
2. Prepare the general journal entries on December 31, 20X1, to:
   a. Record the salary allowances for the year.
   b. Record the interest allowances for the year.
   c. Record the division of the balance of net income.
   d. Close the drawing accounts into the capital accounts, assuming that Wardell and Lomas have withdrawn their full salary allowances.
3. Prepare a schedule showing the division of net income to the partners as it would appear on the income statement for 20X1.
4. Prepare a statement of partners' equities showing the changes that took place in the partners' capital accounts during 20X1.

Analyze: By what percentage did Wardell's capital account increase in fiscal year 20X1?

Accounting for revaluation of assets and liabilities of a partnership, investment of a new partner, and withdrawal of a partner.

◀ **Problem 19.5A**
Objectives 19-6, 19-8, 19-9

The balance sheet of Adams Pharmacy after the revenue, expense, and partners' drawing accounts have been closed on December 31, 20X1, follows:

Adams Pharmacy
Balance Sheet
December 31, 20X1

Assets		
Cash		83 400 00
Accounts Receivable		17 000 00
Merchandise Inventory		435 000 00
Equipment	174 000 00	
Accumulated Depreciation—Equipment	101 000 00	73 000 00
Building	420 000 00	
Accumulated Depreciation—Building	330 000 00	90 000 00
Land		50 000 00
Total Assets		748 400 00
Liabilities and Partners' Equity		
Liabilities		
Accounts Payable		415 200 00
Taxes Payable		23 200 00
Total Liabilities		438 400 00
Partners' Equity		
Larry Adams, Capital	170 000 00	
Hazel Adams, Capital	70 000 00	
Isiah Adams, Capital	70 000 00	
Total Partners' Equity		310 000 00
Total Liabilities and Partners' Equity		748 400 00

On that date, Larry Adams, Hazel Adams, and Isiah Adams agree to admit Vickie Neal to the partnership. The partnership agreement provides that, in case of dissolution of the partnership, all assets and liabilities should be revalued. Profits and losses are shared in the ratio of 50:25:25, to Larry, Hazel, and Isiah, respectively. The agreed-upon values of the assets are as follows:

Accounts receivable	$15,000	Building	$139,000
Merchandise inventory	408,400	Land	103,000
Equipment	73,000		

All liabilities are properly recorded.

INSTRUCTIONS (Round all numbers to the nearest dollar)

1. Prepare the general journal entries to record revaluation of the assets.
2. Prepare the general journal entry (or entries) to record Vickie Neal's investment of $120,000, assuming that she is to receive capital equal to the amount invested.
3. Prepare the general journal entry (or entries) to record Vickie Neal's investment of $120,000, assuming that she is to receive one-fifth of the capital of the partnership.
4. Prepare the general journal entry (or entries) to record Vickie Neal's investment of $120,000, assuming that she is to receive one-third of the capital of the partnership.
5. Assume that after the revaluation had been recorded, the existing partners and Vickie Neal decided that their previous agreement should be canceled and that Vickie Neal should not become a partner. Instead, the partners agreed that Hazel Adams would withdraw from the partnership and be paid cash by the partnership.
    a. Prepare the general journal entry to record the payment to Hazel Adams if she is paid an amount equal to her capital account balance after the revaluation.
    b. Prepare the general journal entry to record the payment to Hazel Adams if she is paid an amount equal to $15,000 less than her capital account balance after revaluation.
    c. Prepare the general journal entry to record the payment to Hazel Adams if she is paid an amount equal to $12,600 more than her capital account balance after revaluation.

Analyze: Assume that only items 1 and 3 have been recorded in the records of the partnership. What is the balance of Isiah Adams's capital account at January 1, 20X2?

Problem 19.6A
Objectives 19-7, 19-8

▶ **Accounting for sale of a partnership interest and investment of a new partner.**

Dexter Thomas and Herman Walker, attorneys, operate a law practice. They would like to expand the expertise of their firm. In anticipation of this, they have agreed to admit Jewell Lorenzo to the partnership on January 1, 20X1. The capital account balances on January 1, 20X1, after revaluation of assets, are Thomas, $340,000, and Walker, $300,000. Net income or net loss is shared equally.

INSTRUCTIONS (Round all numbers to the nearest dollar)

Prepare the entries in general journal form to record the admission of Lorenzo to the partnership on January 1, 20X1, under each of the following independent conditions:

1. Thomas sells one-half of his interest in the partnership to Lorenzo for $276,000 cash.
2. Thomas sells one-half of his interest in the partnership to Lorenzo for $188,000 cash.
3. Lorenzo invests $260,000 in the business for a 25 percent interest in the partnership.
4. Lorenzo invests $268,000 in the business for a 30 percent interest in the partnership.

Analyze: Based only on item 3, what percentage of total equity does each partner own?

Problem Set B

Problem 19.1B
Objective 19-3

▶ **Accounting for the formation of a partnership.**

Teresa Ballard operates the Ballard Broadcast Company. Her postclosing trial balance on December 31, 20X1, is as follows:

Ballard Broadcast Company
Postclosing Trial Balance
December 31, 20X1

ACCOUNT NAME	DEBIT	CREDIT
Cash	52,700.00	
Accounts Receivable	56,000.00	
Allowance for Doubtful Accounts		10,000.00
Merchandise Inventory	362,000.00	
Fixtures and Store Equipment	475,000.00	
Accumulated Depreciation		325,000.00
Accounts Payable		20,800.00
Teresa Ballard, Capital		589,900.00
Totals	945,700.00	945,700.00

Ballard agrees to enter into a partnership with Helena Pittman, effective January 1, 20X2. Profits and losses will be shared equally. Ballard is to transfer the assets and liabilities of her store to the partnership after revaluation as agreed. Pittman will invest cash equal to one-half of Ballard's investment after revaluation. The agreed-upon values are **Accounts Receivable** (net), $42,200; **Merchandise Inventory,** $388,000; and **Fixtures and Store Equipment** (net), $372,000. All liabilities are properly recorded. The partnership will operate as the Ballard-Pittman Broadcast Company.

INSTRUCTIONS

1. In general journal form, prepare the entries to record the following on the books of the partnership:
   a. The receipt of Ballard's investment of assets and liabilities in the partnership.
   b. The receipt of Pittman's investment of cash.
2. Prepare a balance sheet for Ballard-Pittman Broadcast Company for January 1, 20X2.

Analyze: By what net amount was Ballard's equity adjusted before the partnership was formed?

Accounting for formation of a partnership.

◀ **Problem 19.2B**
Objective 19-3

James Grayson operates a store that sells paintings and portraits by local artists. Grayson has agreed to enter into a partnership with Connie Chu, effective January 1, 20X1. The new firm will be called Paintings and Portraits Supply Company. Grayson is to transfer the assets and liabilities of his business to the partnership at the values agreed on. Chu will invest cash that is equal to Grayson's investment after revaluation. The accounts shown on Grayson's books and the agreed-on value of assets and liabilities follow:

		Balances Shown in Grayson's Records	Value Agreed to by Partners
Assets Transferred			
Cash		$ 72,000	$ 72,000
Accounts Receivable	$78,000		
Allowance for Doubtful Accounts	14,000	64,000	54,400
Merchandise Inventory		384,000	344,000
Furniture and Equipment	216,000		95,200
Accumulated Depreciation	164,000	52,000	
Total Assets		$572,000	$565,600
Liabilities and Owner's Equity Transferred			
Accounts Payable		32,000	32,000
James Grayson, Capital		$540,000	$533,600

INSTRUCTIONS

1. Prepare the general journal entries to record the following transactions on the books of the partnership on January 1, 20X1:
   a. Receipt of Grayson's investment of assets and liabilities.
   b. Receipt of Chu's investment of cash.
2. Prepare a balance sheet for the partnership as of the beginning of its operations on January 1, 20X1.

Analyze: If Connie Chu agreed to a cash investment equal to 80 percent of the value of James Grayson's investment, what would the balance of Connie Chu's capital account be after the formation of the partnership?

Problem 19.3B
Objective 19-4

▶ **Computing and recording the division of net income or loss between partners.**

Warren Burggren and Justin Beavers operate a retail furniture store. Under the terms of the partnership agreement, Burggren is authorized to withdraw $9,000 a month and Beavers $7,500 a month. The withdrawals, which are not considered to be salaries, were made each month and charged to the drawing accounts. The partners have agreed that net income or loss is to be allocated 40 percent to Burggren and 60 percent to Beavers. For the year ended December 31, 20X1, the partnership earned a net income of $380,000.

INSTRUCTIONS

1. Prepare general journal entries to:
   a. Close the *Income Summary* account.
   b. Close the partners' drawing accounts.
2. Assume that there had been a net loss of $210,900 instead of net income of $380,000. Prepare the general journal entries to:
   a. Close the *Income Summary* account.
   b. Close the partners' drawing accounts.

Analyze: Justin Beavers's capital account on January 1, 20X1, was $295,600. What is the balance in that account at the end of 20X1, assuming the profit for the year was $380,000?

Problem 19.4B
Objectives 19-4, 19-5

▶ **Computing and recording the division of net income or loss between partners; preparing a statement of partners' equities.**

Alicia Meeks and Charolette Hicks operate Uptown Apartments. Their partnership agreement provides for salaries of $120,000 a year for Meeks and $96,000 for Hicks and for an interest allowance of 10 percent on each partner's invested capital at the beginning of the year. The remainder of the net income or loss is to be distributed equally to the two partners. On January 1, 20X1, the capital account balances were $208,000 for Meeks and $448,000 for Hicks. On July 15, 20X1, Hicks made a permanent withdrawal of capital of $160,000 for a down payment on a yacht. The net income for 20X1 was $385,600.

INSTRUCTIONS

1. Prepare the general journal entry on July 15, 20X1, to record the permanent withdrawal by Hicks.
2. Prepare the general journal entries on December 31, 20X1, to:
   a. Record the salary allowances for the year.
   b. Record the interest allowances for the year.
   c. Record the division of the balance of net income.
   d. Close the drawing accounts into the capital accounts, assuming that the partners had withdrawn only the full amount of their salary allowances.
3. Prepare a schedule showing the division of net income to the partners as it would appear on the income statement for 20X1.
4. Prepare a statement of partners' equities showing the changes that took place in the partners' capital accounts during the year 20X1.

Analyze: Do the facts stated in the problem suggest changes that probably should be made in the provision for interest in allocating income? Explain.

Accounting for revaluation of assets and liabilities of a partnership, investment of a new partner, and withdrawal of a partner.

◀ **Problem 19.5B**
Objectives 19-6, 19-8, 19-9

The balance sheet of The Office Equipment and Supply Shop after the revenue, expense, and partners' drawing accounts have been closed on December 31, 20X1, is provided below.

On that date, Rush, Hatten, and Booker agree to admit Rosie Hinojosa to the partnership. The partnership agreement among Rush, Hatten, and Booker provides that in case of dissolution of the partnership, all assets and liabilities should be revalued. Profits and losses are shared in the ratio of 50:20:30 to Rush, Hatten, and Booker, respectively. The agreed-upon values of the assets are given below:

Accounts receivable	$ 10,040
Merchandise inventory	202,000
Equipment	36,000
Building	58,000
Land	46,200

All liabilities are properly recorded.

The Office Equipment and Supply Shop
Balance Sheet
December 31, 20X1

Assets		
Cash		45,000.00
Accounts Receivable		12,000.00
Merchandise Inventory		210,000.00
Equipment	85,000.00	
Accumulated Depreciation—Equipment	48,000.00	37,000.00
Building	210,000.00	
Accumulated Depreciation—Building	160,000.00	50,000.00
Land		22,000.00
Total Assets		376,000.00
Liabilities and Partners' Equity		
Liabilities		
Accounts Payable		215,000.00
Taxes Payable		16,000.00
Total Liabilities		231,000.00
Partners' Equity		
Helen Rush, Capital	70,000.00	
Billy Hatten, Capital	30,000.00	
Quinton Booker, Capital	45,000.00	
Total Partners' Equity		145,000.00
Total Liabilities and Partners' Equity		376,000.00

INSTRUCTIONS (Round all numbers to the nearest dollar)

1. Prepare the general journal entries to record revaluation of the partnership's assets.
2. Prepare the general journal entry (or entries) to record Hinojosa's investment of $66,000, assuming that she is to receive credit for the amount invested.
3. Prepare the general journal entry (or entries) to record Hinojosa's investment of $66,000, assuming that she is to receive one-fifth of the capital of the entity.

4. Prepare the general journal entry (or entries) to record Hinojosa's investment of $66,000, assuming that she is to receive 45 percent of the capital of the entity.

5. Assume that after the revaluation had been recorded, the existing partners and Hinojosa decided that their previous agreement should be canceled and that Hinojosa should not become a partner. Instead, the partners agreed that Booker would withdraw from the partnership.

   a. Prepare the general journal entry to record the payment to Booker if he is paid an amount equal to his capital account balance after the revaluation.

   b. Prepare the general journal entry to record the payment to Booker if he is paid an amount equal to $6,500 less than his capital account balance after the revaluation.

   c. Prepare the general journal entry to record the payment to Booker if he is paid an amount equal to $9,000 more than his capital account balance after the revaluation.

Analyze: Assume only items 1 and 5(b) occurred. What is the balance of the *Billy Hatten, Capital* account at December 31, 20X1?

Problem 19.6B

Objectives 19-7, 19-8

▶ **Accounting for sale of partnership interest and investment of a new partner.**

Franklin Winston and Haley Thomas are partners in Technology Applications. The balances of their capital accounts on January 2, 20X1, after revaluation of assets were Winston, $240,000, and Thomas, $320,000. Profits and losses are shared in the ratio of 55:45 between Winston and Thomas. The partners agree to admit Wilson Martin to the partnership, effective January 3, 20X1.

INSTRUCTIONS (Round all numbers to the nearest dollar)

Give the entries in general journal form to record the admission of Martin under each of the following independent conditions:

1. Winston sells one-half of his interest in the partnership to Martin for $176,000 in cash.
2. Thomas sells one-half of his interest in the partnership to Martin for $128,000 in cash.
3. Martin invests $240,000 in the business for a one-fourth interest in the partnership.
4. Martin invests $240,000 in the business for a 35 percent interest in the partnership.

Analyze: What percentage of partnership equity is owned by Winston and by Thomas after transaction 4?

Critical Thinking Problem 19.1

New Partnership

Joseph Colgan has operated a successful motorcycle repair business for the past several years. Colgan thinks his business is almost too successful because he has very little time for himself. Colgan and Brianna Jenkins, who is also a motorcycle enthusiast, have had a number of discussions about her joining him in the business. Finally, they agree to form a partnership that will operate under the name CJ Motorcycle Repair Shop. They have asked you to provide assistance, particularly with help in establishing terms for dividing partnership profits and losses.

The partners give you the following information about their plans for the business:

1. Colgan plans to contribute to the partnership the assets of his sole proprietorship. They have been appraised to have a fair market value of $400,000.
2. Jenkins will invest $600,000 in cash.
3. Colgan will work full time in the business, while Jenkins will work part time and continue to attend the class she is taking in pursuit of a college degree.

   Assume that CJ Motorcycle Repair earned a net income of $350,000 during its first year of operation.

INSTRUCTIONS

1. What division of profits and losses would you suggest for Colgan and Jenkins?
2. Using your proposed plan of profit sharing, prepare a schedule showing the distribution of the first year's net income to the partners.

Critical Thinking Problem 19.2

From Sole Proprietor to Partner

For several years, Herschel Anderson had operated Management Consulting Company as its sole proprietor. On January 1, 20X1, he formed a partnership with Richard Harris to operate the company under the name Harris-Anderson Professional Management Consultants. Pertinent terms of the partnership agreement are as follows:

1. Anderson was to transfer to the partnership the accounts receivable, merchandise inventory, furniture and equipment, and all liabilities of the sole proprietorship in return for a partnership interest of 60 percent of the partnership capital. Assets were appraised and transferred to the partnership at the appraised values.

   Balances in the relevant accounts of Anderson's sole proprietorship at the close of business on December 31, 20X0, are shown below:

Accounts Receivable	$134,000 Dr.
Allowance for Doubtful Accounts	8,000 Cr.
Merchandise Inventory	190,000 Dr.
Furniture and Equipment	119,600 Dr.
Allowance for Depreciation—Furniture & Equipment	76,000 Cr.
Accounts Payable	26,000 Cr.

   The two parties agreed to the following:
   - There were unrecorded accounts payable of $4,000.
   - Accounts receivable of $6,000 were definitely uncollectible and should not be transferred to the partnership.
   - The value of **Allowance for Doubtful Accounts** should be $8,400.
   - The appraised value of **Merchandise Inventory** was $175,000.
   - The appraised value of **Furniture and Equipment** was $35,000.

2. In return for a 40 percent interest in partnership capital, Harris invested cash in an amount equal to two-thirds (.667) of Anderson's net investment in the business.
3. Each partner was allowed a salary payable on the 15th day of each month. Anderson's salary was to be $9,000 per month and Harris's salary was to be $8,000 per month.
4. The partners were to be allowed interest of 10 percent of their beginning capital balances.
5. No provision was made for profit division except for the salaries and interest previously discussed.
6. The partnership's revenues for the year 20X1 were $2,250,000, and expenses were $1,800,000. Payments for salary allowances were charged to the partners' drawing accounts.

INSTRUCTIONS (Round numbers to two decimal places)

1. Record the following information in general journal form in the partnership's records:
   a. Receipt of assets and liabilities from Anderson.
   b. Investment of cash by Harris.
   c. Summary of cash withdrawals for salaries by the two partners during the year.
   d. Profit or loss division including salary and interest allowances and the closing balance of the *Income Summary* account determined on an appropriate basis.

2. Record the journal entry to close the partners' drawing accounts into the capital accounts. No other cash was withdrawn.

3. Open general ledger accounts for the partners' capital accounts. The account numbers are: **Herschel Anderson, Capital,** 301, and **Richard Harris, Capital,** 311. Post the journal entries from instructions 1 and 2 to the capital accounts.

4. Prepare a schedule showing the division of net income to the partners as it would appear on the income statement for 20X1.

5. Prepare a statement of partners' equities for the year ended 20X1.

6. On January 1, 20X2, the partners agreed to admit John Amos as a partner. Amos is to invest cash of $120,000 for a one-fourth interest in the capital of the partnership. The three parties agree that the book value of assets and liabilities properly reflects their values. Give the general journal entry to record Amos's investment.

Analyze: What percentage of the total partnership capital after the admission of Amos on January 1, 20X2, is owned by Anderson?

BUSINESS CONNECTIONS

Managerial FOCUS

Forming a Partnership

1. The owner of an accounting practice is considering establishing a partnership with two other persons to carry on the business. What are the major disadvantages of the partnership form of organization that she should consider in making her decision?

2. Your employer is planning to form a partnership with one of his close friends. He explains to you that because he is well acquainted with the prospective partner, there is no need to have a written partnership agreement. He asks your advice. Give him your recommendation and the reasons for it.

3. Your employer is considering investing $50,000 in a partnership. In discussing the advantages and disadvantages of the arrangement, the employer informs you that a friend has told him that his potential loss is limited to the amount invested, $50,000. Is his information regarding this arrangement correct?

4. Two individuals who are forming a partnership ask you how they should divide the income and losses of the business. What factors should you consider in making a recommendation?

5. You work for a partnership. The partnership agreement between the two partners specifies that one partner is allowed a monthly draw of $3,000 and the other a monthly draw of $2,000. The agreement does not mention salary allowances for the partners. At the end of the year, one partner maintains that a drawing is the same as a salary allowance. They ask your opinion. What do you tell them?

6. One of the partners in a partnership that employs you is retiring from the business. Her capital account has a balance of $256,000. She tells you that she expects to receive a check for $256,000 from the partnership. Explain to her the proper procedure for determining the amount she will be paid.

Internal Control and FRAUD PREVENTION

Partnership Agreements and Internal Control

Each partner brings certain personal skills and assets into a partnership. One partner could have the technical knowledge while the other partner has the business knowledge. This partnership agreement would easily be 50/50. However, when there are multiple partners and one brings in time, one talent, and the other physical assets, the partnership agreement becomes complicated.

List the items that should be in the policies and procedures of every partnership agreement in order to maximize internal controls for the partnership and prevent misunderstandings and fraud.

Financial Statement ANALYSIS

Partners' Equity

The following excerpts were taken from the 10-K Annual Report filed by TransMontaigne Partners, L.P., for the year ended December 31, 2018.

Balance Sheets

December 31 (in thousands)	2018	2017
Partners' equity:		
General partner	$ 53,490	$ 53,448
Limited partners and other	286,237	310,769
Total partners' equity	$339,727	$364,217

Consolidated Statements of Income

Year Ended December 31	2018	2017
Net income	$39,475	$48,493
Net income attributable to general partner	15,675	12,705
Net income attributable to limited partners	$23,800	$35,788

Analyze:

1. On December 31, 2018, what percentage of total equity belongs to the general partner of TransMontaigne Partners, L.P.?
2. By what amount has the equity of the limited partners decreased from December 31, 2017, to December 31, 2018?
3. Based on the net earnings allocation reflected on the 2018 income statement, what percentage of earnings is allocated to the general partner? To the limited partners?

Analyze Online: TransMontaigne Partners's website is www.transmontaignepartners.com. Click on *Investors,* then *SEC Filings* and find the most recent 10-K SEC filing for TransMontaigne Partners, L.P.

4. What is the year covered by the 10-K filing?
5. What partners' equity is reported for the general partner?
6. What was the earnings allocation to the general partner? To the limited partners?

Partnership Agreements

TEAMWORK

Each partner brings certain personal skills and assets into a partnership. One partner could have the technical knowledge while the other partner has the business knowledge. This partnership agreement could easily be 50/50. However, when there are multiple partners and one brings in time, one talent, and the other physical assets, the partnership agreement becomes complicated.

In groups of three or four, decide on a partnership business. Determine what the partnership business will provide, how the partnership will allocate income and loss, and any salary arrangements. Decide when and how the partnership is dissolved should it become necessary.

Answers to Comprehensive Self Review

1. Answers may vary but could include:
   - Future plans for the partnership.
   - Potential personality conflicts.
   - Differences in ethical codes of conduct.
2. The disadvantages of a partnership stem from its inherent characteristics; that is, it brings unlimited liability, mutual agency, lack of continuity, and lack of transferability.
3. One partner may receive an interest and/or salary allowance considerably larger than the other partner receives. Allowances must be recorded, even if there is a loss.
4. Salary withdrawals are cash payments to be charged to the partners' drawing accounts. Salary allowances are part of the income or loss allocation and are charged to *Income Summary* and credited to the partners' capital accounts.
5. The value changes represent income or loss that should be shared by the existing partners, not by the new partner.

Chapter 20

Corporations: Formation and Capital Stock Transactions

C Flanigan/WireImage/Getty Images

www.facebook.com

On February 4, 2004, Mark Zuckerberg, along with his Harvard University roommates and four of his fellow students, launched the online social networking service, naming it Facebook. Initially intended as a means for college students to connect, account rules were changed in 2006 to anyone over 12 years old to become a registered user. As of September 2018, Facebook has over 2.3 billion active monthly users.

As initially incorporated, Facebook was a private corporation in that the founders decided who could own stock in the company. In May 2012, Facebook held its initial public offering and sold 180,000,000 shares of Class A common stock at a price of $38 per share. The net proceeds, after deducting the offering expenses, totaled $6.76 billion. Concurrently, shareholders holding the private Facebook stock sold 241,233,615 shares to the public. An additional offering was completed in 2013, resulting in an additional 27,004,761 shares of Class A common stock being sold for net proceeds of approximately $1.48 billion; in addition, existing shareholders sold 42,995,239 shares to the public.

In the company's SEC filing of its Form 10-K for the fiscal year ending December 31, 2017, Facebook reported $84.5 billion of assets, liabilities of $10.2 billion, and stockholders' equity of $74.3 billion. While shareholders are the owners of Facebook, however, they are not usually involved in the day-to-day operations of the company. The shareholders elect the board of directors to set major policies and provide direction for the company. As owners, the shareholders profit from the success of the company through increased stock prices.

thinking critically
Common stockholders typically elect who or what for a corporation?

LEARNING OBJECTIVES

- **20-1** Explain the characteristics of a corporation.
- **20-2** Describe special "hybrid" organizations that have some characteristics of partnerships and some characteristics of corporations.
- **20-3** Describe the different types of stock.
- **20-4** Compute the number of shares of common stock to be issued on the conversion of convertible preferred stock.
- **20-5** Compute dividends payable on stock.
- **20-6** Record the issuance of capital stock at par value.
- **20-7** Prepare a balance sheet for a corporation.
- **20-8** Record organization costs.
- **20-9** Record stock issued at a premium and stock with no par value.
- **20-10** Record transactions for stock subscriptions.
- **20-11** Describe the capital stock records for a corporation.
- **20-12** Define the accounting terms new to this chapter.

NEW TERMS

authorized capital stock
bylaws
callable preferred stock
capital stock ledger
capital stock transfer journal
common stock
convertible preferred stock
corporate charter
cumulative preferred stock
dividends
limited liability company (LLC)
limited liability partnership (LLP)
liquidation value
market value
minute book
noncumulative preferred stock
nonparticipating preferred stock
no-par-value stock
organization costs
par value
participating preferred stock
preemptive right
preference dividend
preferred stock
registrar
shareholder
stated value
stock certificate
stockholders' equity
stockholders' ledger
subchapter S corporation (S corporation)
subscribers' ledger
subscription book
transfer agent

Section 1

SECTION OBJECTIVES	TERMS TO LEARN
>> **20-1** Explain the characteristics of a corporation. **WHY IT'S IMPORTANT** The corporate form of business is widely used in the national and international marketplace. >> **20-2** Describe special "hybrid" organizations that have some characteristics of partnerships and some characteristics of corporations. **WHY IT'S IMPORTANT** "Hybrid" organizations are becoming increasingly popular for the tax advantages and limited liability features they offer.	bylaws corporate charter limited liability company (LLC) limited liability partnership (LLP) shareholder stockholders' equity subchapter S corporation (S corporation)

Forming a Corporation

Previous chapters focused on sole proprietorships and partnerships. Now we consider the third form of business organization, the corporation.

Characteristics of a Corporation

Corporate enterprises account for a majority of business transactions, even though there are more sole proprietorships and partnerships than corporations. Most large national and international businesses use the corporate business form.

In 1818, Chief Justice John Marshall of the U.S. Supreme Court defined the *corporation* as "an artificial being, invisible, intangible, and existing only in contemplation of the law." The corporation is a legal entity, completely separate and apart from its owners. It is created by a **corporate charter** issued by a state government. Because it is a legal entity, a corporation can enter into contracts, can own property, and has almost all of the rights and privileges of a sole proprietorship or a partnership.

Corporations can have few or many owners. A *privately held* corporation is one whose stock is not traded on an organized stock exchange. It may be owned by one or more persons or entities like a private equity investment group. A *publicly held* corporation has many owners and its stock is traded on an organized stock exchange.

A **shareholder** or *stockholder* is a person who owns shares of stock in a corporation and is, thus, one of the owners of the corporation.

>> **20-1 OBJECTIVE**
Explain the characteristics of a corporation.

Advantages of the Corporate Form

The corporate form offers some major advantages:

- *Limited Liability.* Sole proprietors and general partners have unlimited liability; they are personally liable for all debts of the business. Shareholders have no personal liability for the corporation's debts. The corporation's creditors must look to the assets of the business to satisfy their claims, not to the owners' personal property, even in the event of liquidation. It is not unusual, however, for major shareholders of small corporations to give personal guarantees to repay its loans.

- *Restricted Agency.* A shareholder has no right to act on behalf of the business. Instead, the board of directors controls the corporation, and the corporate officers are in direct charge of operations. For example, a person who owns 10,000 shares of Microsoft Corporation

has no greater power to act on behalf of Microsoft than a person who has no ownership interest at all.
- *Continuous Existence.* The death, disability, or withdrawal of a shareholder has no effect on the life of a corporation.
- *Transferability of Ownership Rights.* Generally, shareholders can sell their stock without consulting or obtaining the consent of the other owners. Shareholders are free to shift their investments at any time, provided they can find buyers for their stock. Organized stock markets, such as the New York Stock Exchange, make it easy to sell or buy interests in corporations whose stocks are traded.

  Small companies often sell shares of stock with a contract that gives the corporation or the existing shareholders "the right of first refusal" to repurchase the shares when the shareholder wishes to sell them.
- *Ease of Raising Capital.* A corporation can have an unlimited number of shareholders. Some corporations have more than a million shareholders, making available a vast pool of capital.

Disadvantages of the Corporate Form

Although the advantages of the corporate entity are impressive, the corporate form of operation also has certain disadvantages:

- *Corporate Income Tax.* Corporate profits are subject to federal income tax. Profits distributed to shareholders in the form of dividends are taxed a second time as part of the personal income of the stockholder. The taxation of profits at the corporate level and at the shareholder level is known as *double taxation.*

  State and local governments can also levy income taxes on corporations. In addition, most states require corporations to pay an annual franchise tax for the privilege of carrying on business in the state. In some states, especially those that have no corporate income tax, the franchise tax can be quite burdensome.
- *Governmental Regulation.* Corporations are subject to laws and regulations imposed by the state. In general, the state regulatory bodies exercise closer supervision and control over corporations than they do over sole proprietorships or partnerships. State laws may prohibit corporations from entering into particular types of transactions or from owning specific types of property. Special reports are frequently required of corporations.

Entities Having Attributes of Both Partnerships and Corporations

Some business entities have operational characteristics of partnerships and of corporations. Three of these special entities are subchapter S corporations, limited liability partnerships, and limited liability companies.

Subchapter S Corporations Subchapter S corporations, also known as *S corporations,* are entities formed as corporations that meet the requirements of subchapter S of the Internal Revenue Code to be treated essentially as a partnership so the corporate entity pays no income tax. Instead, shareholders include their share of corporate profits, and any items that require special tax treatment, on their individual income tax returns. Otherwise, S corporations have all the characteristics of regular corporations. The primary advantages of S corporations are that the owners have limited liability and avoid double taxation.

Limited Liability Partnerships The limited liability partnership (LLP) is a general partnership that provides some limited liability for all partners. LLP partners are responsible and have liability for their own actions and the actions of those under their control or supervision. They are not liable for the actions or malfeasance of another partner. LLPs must have more than one owner, so a sole proprietorship cannot be treated as one. In some states, LLPs are for the service professions only, such as law, accounting, medicine, and engineering.

ABOUT ACCOUNTING

Mutual Funds
Mutual funds allow small investors to pool their funds with other small investors. There are many types of mutual funds. Each fund concentrates on a particular type of stock. Index funds invest in indices like the S&P 500, Russell 1000, or NASDAQ Composite. Growth funds invest in companies that are growing quickly. International funds buy stocks from European and Pacific Rim companies. Bond funds invest in the bond market.

>> 20-2 OBJECTIVE
Describe special "hybrid" organizations that have some characteristics of partnerships and some characteristics of corporations.

Except for the limited liability aspect, LLPs generally have the same characteristics, advantages, and disadvantages as any other partnership.

Limited Liability Companies Limited liability companies (LLCs) provide limited liability to the owners, who can elect to have the profits taxed at the LLC level or on their individual income tax returns. LLCs may also own other LLC entities, thus protecting assets of each LLC within each separate entity. The profits and losses can be allocated to the owners other than in proportion to the ownership interests. In most states, one individual can form an LLC. Its ownership interests are not freely transferable; other owners must approve a transfer of ownership interest. When transferring ownership, the existing LLC is terminated and a new one formed. Unlike the limited partners discussed in Chapter 19, LLC owners can take part in policy and operating decisions. LLCs are formed and operate under state laws and regulations. Over recent years, the LLC has become the preferred organizational type of corporation.

Formation of a Corporation

To understand why and how a corporation is formed, place yourself in the shoes of Carlos Allen. Allen is the sole proprietor of Allen's Outdoor Supply Store, a retail business selling camping equipment. Allen wants to expand the variety of equipment he sells and add guidebooks.

To expand his operations, Allen needs more money to remodel the store and buy new fixtures, to acquire more inventory, and to extend more credit to customers. Several of his friends are willing to invest as partners in his business, but Allen has some doubts about this. Although he needs the extra funds, he does not want to share operating control with people who know nothing about the business. Also, he does not wish to go further in debt.

Allen's prospective backers have some doubts, too. They do not mind risking the money they invest, but they do not want to be responsible for the debts of the business. Although they do not mind letting Allen run the business, they do want to have some voice in general policy. They would also like to be assured of a reasonable and regular return on their money.

Allen and his friends consulted an attorney who specializes in business law and taxation. The lawyer suggested that a corporation offers the best solution to their needs. She explained the necessary steps to form a corporation. Requirements differ from state to state, but typically the process is as follows.

One or more persons, the "organizers" or "promoters," apply to a state officer, usually the secretary of state, for a charter permitting the proposed corporation to do business. The state charges a fee for the charter.

When issued, the charter specifies the exact name (must be a unique name in the state), length of life (usually unlimited), rights and duties, and scope of operations of the corporation. Most corporate charters grant the corporation a broad sphere of operation. The charter also sets forth the classes of stock and number of shares in each class that can be issued in exchange for money, property, or services.

Shortly after the charter is issued, the organizers meet to elect an acting board of directors. The corporation proceeds to issue shares of stock to individuals who have paid the full purchase price of the stock. The shareholders then elect permanent directors, usually the same individuals as the acting directors. The directors or shareholders approve the corporation's **bylaws,** which are the guidelines for conducting the corporation's business affairs. The board then selects officers, who hire employees and begin operating the business.

The amount received for the capital stock issued by the corporation appears on the balance sheet. The corporate equivalent of owner's equity is called **stockholders' equity** or shareholders' equity.

Structure of a Corporation

Stockholders can participate in stockholders' meetings, elect a board of directors, and vote on basic corporate policy.

The board of directors formulates general operating policies and is responsible for seeing that the corporation's activities are conducted. The board selects officers and other top management

TABLE 20.1 Flow of Corporate Authority and Responsibility

Stockholders	• Elect directors
Directors	• Make policies
	• Appoint officers
Officers	• Carry out policies
	• Hire managers
Managers	• Oversee and supervise daily operations
Other employees	• Perform assigned tasks

personnel to direct everyday operations. The officers hire managers who hire other employees. Officers and managers make the day-to-day decisions necessary to operate the business.

A corporation's officers include the president, one or more vice presidents, a corporate secretary, and a treasurer. The top accounting official is called the *controller* or *chief financial officer*. Large firms might have several layers of management, including division managers, department heads, and supervisors. The levels depend on the nature and complexity of the operations.

Table 20.1 shows the flow of authority and responsibility in a corporate entity.

Section 1 Review

1. Which level of government is responsible for issuing charters for most corporations?
   a. city government
   b. federal government
   c. county government
   d. state government

2. What is an advantage of the LLC form of business?
   a. It is a corporate entity that avoids federal corporate income tax.
   b. It does not have to register with state government.
   c. It can transfer ownership easier than a corporation.
   d. It can sell additional shares of the LLC without any individual approvals.

3. What is the role of stockholders in running the business of a corporation?
   a. to decide on operating hours of the entity
   b. to elect the board of directors
   c. to appoint a CFO
   d. to sign the tax returns of the corporation

4. The stockholders of a corporation:
   a. have the power to act for the business unless specifically prohibited by the corporate charter.
   b. are generally liable for the debts of the corporation.
   c. can sell their shares of stock without permission from other stockholders.
   d. are forbidden to be employees of the corporation.

5. In a corporate organization, the stockholders:
   a. must pay federal income tax on their proportional shares of profits reported by the corporation.
   b. have the right to surrender preferred stock to the corporation at any time for a payment equal to the par value of the stock.
   c. hire the corporate officers.
   d. are entitled to a proportionate share of dividends declared on their classes of stock.

6. Lucia Torrez and her husband, Juan, are sole shareholders in a corporation they formed to operate their existing chain of five restaurants. Their corporation earned net income of approximately $150,000 in its first year of operations. One of Lucia's friends suggested to her that she and Juan had made a mistake in incorporating and should operate as a sole proprietorship or partnership. What reasons may Lucia use to support their decision to incorporate?
   a. double taxation of income
   b. protection of personal assets and limiting their individual liability
   c. paying dividends to themselves
   d. none of the above

Section 2

SECTION OBJECTIVES	TERMS TO LEARN
>> 20-3 Describe the different types of stock. **WHY IT'S IMPORTANT** Shareholders and others must understand the rights and limitations of each class of stock. **>> 20-4** Compute the number of shares of common stock to be issued on the conversion of convertible preferred stock. **WHY IT'S IMPORTANT** Conversion of stock changes the allocation of stockholders' equity between classes of stock. **>> 20-5** Compute dividends payable on stock. **WHY IT'S IMPORTANT** Dividends are a major benefit of stock ownership.	authorized capital stock callable preferred stock common stock convertible preferred stock cumulative preferred stock dividends liquidation value market value noncumulative preferred stock nonparticipating preferred stock no-par-value stock par value participating preferred stock preemptive right preference dividend preferred stock stated value

Types of Capital Stock

Decisions about the classes of stock to be offered and the number of shares of each class must be made before the charter application is filed.

Capital Stock

The **authorized capital stock** is the number of shares authorized for issue by the corporate charter. Usually the authorized stock is more than the number of shares the corporation plans to issue in the foreseeable future. This gives the corporation flexibility to issue stock in the future without having to amend the corporate charter.

When a corporation *issues* stock, the stock is sold (transferred to stockholders). *Outstanding* stock is stock that has been issued and is still in circulation, meaning it is still in the hands of stockholders.

Capital Stock Values

There are three terms commonly used to describe stock values.

Par Value. **Par value** is an amount assigned by the corporate charter to each share of stock for accounting purposes. It may be any designated amount; it can be $25, $5, or even less than $1 per share. Stock can be issued for more than par value. State laws prohibit the issuance of par-value stock for less than the par value.

Stated Value. State laws permit stock to be issued without par value. This type of stock is called **no-par-value stock.** The value that can be assigned to no-par-value stock by a board of directors for accounting purposes is called the **stated value.**

Market Value. **Market value** is the price per share at which stock is bought and sold. After the corporation issues stock, it can be resold for any price that can be agreed on between the shareholder and purchaser. Usually a stock's market value has little relation to its par or stated value.

Classes of Capital Stock

Each type, or class, of stock has different rights and privileges.

Common Stock If there is only one class of stock, the stock is called **common stock.** Each share of common stock conveys to the owner the same rights and privileges as every other share including the right to:

- attend stockholders' meetings,
- vote in the election of directors and on other matters (each share entitles the owner to one vote),
- receive dividends as declared by the board of directors,
- purchase a proportionate amount of any new stock issued at a later date, referred to as the **preemptive right.**

If a corporation has two or more classes of stock, one class must be common. The other class or classes of stock typically will have certain preferences over the common shares.

> Some corporations have more than one class of preferred stock issued. Typically these shares are issued to help finance specific activities and bear different dividend rates reflecting the differences in economic factors, interest rates prevailing, and relative risks at the time of issuance. Facebook has both Class A and Class B common stock.

>> 20-3 OBJECTIVE
Describe the different types of stock.

Preferred Stock **Preferred stock** has special claims on the corporate profits or, in case of liquidation, on corporate assets. In receiving special preferences, the owners of preferred stock might lose some of their general rights, such as the right to vote. The charter may allow preferred stock shareholders to have voting rights.

Liquidation Preferences on Preferred Stock In case of liquidation, preferred stockholders have a claim on assets before that of common stockholders. A **liquidation value** (usually par value or an amount higher than par value) is assigned to the preferred stock. After the creditors are paid, the preferred stockholders are paid the liquidation value for each share of preferred stock before any assets are distributed to common stockholders. The liquidation value of preferred stock includes any cumulative dividends that have not been paid. (Cumulative dividends are explained later in this chapter.) The liquidation preference on preferred stock is disclosed in the Stockholders' Equity section of the balance sheet.

Assume that a corporation is going out of business. It has paid all of its liabilities. There remains $1,700,000 to distribute to the shareholders. The company has outstanding 25,000 shares of $50 preferred stock, with a liquidation value of $52 per share, and 50,000 shares of $20 par-value common stock. The preferred stockholders will receive $1,300,000 (25,000 shares × $52 per share). The common stockholders will receive what's left, $400,000 ($1,700,000 − $1,300,000).

Convertible Preferred Stock **Convertible preferred stock** is preferred stock that conveys the right to convert that stock to common stock after a specified date or during a period of time. The conversion ratio is the number of shares of common stock that will be issued for each share of preferred stock surrendered. The conversion ratio is indicated on the preferred stock certificate.

Some investors are reluctant to purchase preferred stock because its market price does not increase significantly even if the corporation is quite profitable. The ability to convert preferred stock to common stock can make the preferred stock more attractive to investors. The decision to convert the preferred stock to common stock depends on the market prices, the relative dividends paid on the common and the preferred stock, and the degree of risk involved.

Assume that a corporation has outstanding 100,000 shares of 12 percent, $25 par-value preferred stock that can be converted into common stock. (The term "12 percent" refers to the dividend rate and is discussed below.) The conversion ratio is two shares of common stock for

>> 20-4 OBJECTIVE
Compute the number of shares of common stock to be issued on the conversion of convertible preferred stock.

each share of preferred stock surrendered. The conversion privilege is exercisable on or after January 1, 20X1. A stockholder can convert 400 shares of preferred stock into 800 (400 × 2) shares of common stock.

Callable Preferred Stock **Callable preferred stock** gives the issuing corporation the right to repurchase the preferred shares from the stockholders at a specific price. The call price is usually substantially greater than the original issue price. The rights are effective after some specified date. Callable stock gives the corporation flexibility in controlling its capital structure.

The following example illustrates the call feature. Assume a corporation issued 50,000 shares of 10 percent, $50 par-value preferred stock at $50 per share. The corporation has the right to call any part of the preferred stock any time after December 31, 20X1, for $53 per share. If the corporation has funds available, or if money can be borrowed at substantially less than 10 percent (the required preferred stock dividend rate), the corporation may call the preferred stock and retire it so it is not required to continue paying the dividend.

>> **20-5 OBJECTIVE**
Compute dividends payable on stock.

Dividends on Stock

Dividends are distributions of the profits of a corporation to its shareholders. The right to receive a dividend is one of the major incentives for buying stock. The board of directors declares dividends. The board of directors has complete discretion, subject to certain legal restrictions or contractual restrictions, in deciding whether to declare a dividend and the amount of the dividend. The amount of the dividend depends on the corporation's earnings and on the need to keep profits for use in the business. Dividends are usually paid on a quarterly basis.

Dividends on Preferred Stock

Preferred stock has a priority with respect to dividends. The priority is specified in the corporate charter. Preferred stock bears a basic or stated dividend rate, called the **preference dividend,** that must be paid before dividends can be paid on common stock. The *dividend rate* is expressed in dollars-per-share per year or as a percentage. When the dividend is expressed as a percentage, the dividend amount is par value of the stock multiplied by the percentage. For example, the annual dividend on 5 percent preferred stock with a par value of $100 is $5 per share ($100 × 0.05).

Special dividend rights can improve the market demand for preferred shares of stock:

- **Cumulative preferred stock** conveys to its owners the right to receive the preference dividend for the current year and any prior years in which the preference dividend was not paid before common stockholders receive any dividends (commonly called dividends in arrears).
- **Noncumulative preferred stock** conveys to its owners the stated preference dividend for the current year, but stockholders have no rights to dividends for years in which none were declared.
- **Nonparticipating preferred stock** conveys to its owners the right to only the preference dividend amount specified on the stock certificate.
- **Participating preferred stock** conveys the right not only to the preference dividend amount but also to a share of other dividends paid.

Dividends on Common Stock

Common stock dividends are paid only after preferred dividend requirements have been met. The fewer the dividend privileges enjoyed by preferred stockholders, the higher the dividends that common stockholders can receive, especially in prosperous years.

The amount of dividends paid each year reflects such factors as the company's trend of profits and cash flows, tax laws, availability of cash, plans for future expansion, and so on. Typically, a company avoids decreases in dividend payouts because a decrease often leads to loss of investor confidence and reduced prices for the stock.

Comparison of Dividend Provisions

Let's analyze several dividend plans.

Only Common Stock Issued Suppose that a corporation has only one class of stock—common stock. Assume that 10,000 shares of $50 par-value common stock are authorized, issued, and outstanding:

- *Situation 1.* The board of directors declared a 5 percent dividend for the year. Total dividends are $25,000 (10,000 shares × $50 par × 0.05). (The dividend is usually announced as $2.50 per share.)
- *Situation 2.* The board of directors decides to *pass* the dividend (not declare or pay it).

There is no guarantee that the corporation will pay dividends. The uncertainty of dividends is a risk of owning common stock.

Common and Noncumulative Nonparticipating Preferred Stock Issued Preferred stock reduces the uncertainty of dividends. Assume that a corporation has issued preferred stock and common stock as follows:

Preferred stock, 10% noncumulative, nonparticipating ($50 par value, 1,000 shares)	$ 50,000
Common stock ($20 par value, 10,000 shares)	200,000
Total capital stock	$250,000

- *Situation 1.* The board of directors declares dividends of $20,000. The preferred stockholders get first consideration. They receive the preference dividend of $5,000 (1,000 shares × $50 par × 0.10). There is $15,000 ($20,000 − $5,000) to distribute to the common stockholders. The dividend per share for common stock is $1.50 ($15,000 ÷ 10,000 shares).
- *Situation 2.* The board of directors declares dividends of $10,000. The preferred stockholders receive the preference dividend of $5,000. There is $5,000 ($10,000 − $5,000) to distribute to the common stockholders. The dividend per share of common stock is $0.50 ($5,000 ÷ 10,000 shares).
- *Situation 3.* The board of directors declares dividends of $4,000. The preferred stockholders receive all of it. The portion of the preference dividend not paid this year ($1,000) will never be paid because the stock is noncumulative. The common stockholders receive no dividends.

Common and Cumulative Nonparticipating Preferred Stock Issued When business conditions are poor, preferred stockholders have a better chance of receiving a dividend than do common stockholders. In turn, cumulative preferred stockholders have a better chance of receiving a dividend than do noncumulative preferred stockholders. The dividends not paid on cumulative preferred stock are carried forward as a continuing claim into future periods. These cumulative preferred dividends (dividends in arrears) not previously paid are shown on the balance sheet or in the footnotes to the financial statements.

When dividends are paid, they are paid in the following order:

1. To holders of cumulative preferred stock for prior year dividends (oldest year first) not paid (commonly called dividends in arrears).
2. To preferred stockholders for the preference dividend for the current year.
3. To common stockholders.

Assume that a corporation has issued preferred and common stock as follows:

Preferred stock, 10% cumulative, nonparticipating ($50 par value, 1,000 shares)	$ 50,000
Common stock ($20 par value, 10,000 shares)	200,000
Total capital stock	$250,000

- *Situation 1.* Last year, $2,000 of preferred dividends were not paid. This year the board of directors declared dividends of $9,000. The dividends are distributed as follows:

  1. To cumulative preferred stockholders for prior year dividends $2,000
  2. To preferred stockholders for this year's preference dividend
     (1,000 shares × $50 par value × 0.10) $5,000
  3. To common stockholders ($9,000 − $2,000 − $5,000) $2,000

- *Situation 2.* The board of directors declares dividends of $50,000. In previous years, all preferred dividends were paid. The cumulative preferred stockholders will receive the preference dividend of $5,000. There is $45,000 ($50,000 − $5,000) to distribute to common shareholders. The dividend per share of common stock is $4.50 ($45,000 ÷ 10,000 shares).

Common and Cumulative Participating Preferred Stock Issued When cumulative participating preferred stock is issued, dividend distributions are allocated to preferred and common stock as follows:

1. Preferred stockholders receive any prior year dividends not paid ("in arrears") plus the preference dividend for the current year.
2. A specific rate of dividend is paid to common stockholders, equal to the same percentage rate paid to preferred.
3. The dividends that remain are shared between preferred and common stockholders. The participation terms determine how the dividends are shared. Typically, equal rates are paid on common stock and preferred stock.

Because almost all preferred stock is nonparticipating, this textbook provides examples of nonparticipating preferred stock only.

Table 20.2 summarizes the dividend rights of the different classes of stock.

TABLE 20.2 Dividend Rights of Different Classes of Stock

Type of Stock	Dividend Rights
Noncumulative, nonparticipating preferred stock	• Has right to receive preference dividend each year before any dividend can be paid on common stock • If dividend is passed (not paid) in one year, the amount not paid is not cumulative and does not affect dividend payments in future years
Cumulative preferred stock	• Has right to receive preference dividend each year before any dividend can be paid on common stock • If dividend is passed in one year, the amount not paid carries over and must be paid in subsequent year before any dividend can be paid on common stock
Participating preferred stock	• Has right to receive preference dividend each year before any dividend can be paid on common stock • After preference dividend is paid, any additional dividend up to specified rate or amount is paid to common stockholders • After common shareholders have received the specified dividend, preferred and common stock share in remaining dividends
Common stock	• Receives dividends after preferred stock dividends are paid in accordance with contractual obligation

Capital Stock on the Balance Sheet

Owner's equity for a corporation is known as stockholders' equity. The Stockholders' Equity section of the balance sheet includes the following information for each class of stock: the number of shares authorized and issued, the par value, and any special privileges carried by the stock. The following illustrates a typical balance sheet presentation for a corporation:

Stockholders' Equity

Preferred Stock (10% noncumulative, $100 par value, 5,000 shares authorized)	
At Par Value (500 shares issued)	$ 50,000
Common Stock ($10 par value, 100,000 shares authorized)	
At Par Value (20,000 shares issued)	200,000
Total Stockholders' Equity	$250,000

Section 2 Review

1. Why is preferred stock called "preferred"?
   a. It is stock owned by company founders.
   b. It is listed on the balance sheet above Common Stock.
   c. It is preferred in the distribution of dividends.
   d. It sounds better than common stock.

2. How does cumulative preferred stock work for the investor?
   a. "Cumulative" means the investor is more likely to receive the stated dividend rate before any dividend is paid to common shareholders.
   b. The corporation does not have to pay this dividend.
   c. Preferred shareholders may elect to defer receiving the dividend and allow it to accumulate.
   d. The dividend rate multiplies every year.

3. In what ways, if any, may common stock be preferable to preferred stock?
   a. It receives dividends before preferred stockholders.
   b. It represents ownership in assets after all liabilities are satisfied upon dissolution.
   c. It is entitled to a seat on the board of directors.
   d. It makes the owner eligible to be named CFO.

4. Court Company has outstanding 10,000 shares of 10 percent, $50 par-value, cumulative, nonparticipating preferred stock and 25,000 shares of $20 par-value common stock. No dividends were declared in 20X1. In 20X2, the directors voted to distribute dividends of $48,000. What amount of dividends, if any, will be distributed to holders of preferred stock?
   a. $50
   b. $5
   c. $50,000
   d. $48,000

5. If the preferred shareholders are entitled to receive the preference rate, and in addition to share in any further dividends declared in a year, the stock is known as:
   a. cumulative.
   b. participating.
   c. nonparticipating.
   d. quasi-common.

6. RealTime Company has outstanding 10,000 shares of 8 percent, $50 par-value, cumulative, preferred stock and 20,000 shares of $25 par-value common stock. There are no dividends in arrears on the preferred stock. In the current year, the corporation distributed dividends of $100,000. How much will be distributed to common stockholders?
   a. $60,000
   b. $40,000
   c. $100,000
   d. $25

Section 3

SECTION OBJECTIVES	TERMS TO LEARN
>> 20-6 Record the issuance of capital stock at par value. **WHY IT'S IMPORTANT** Stock sales affect equity.	capital stock ledger capital stock transfer journal minute book organization costs registrar stock certificate stockholders' ledger subscribers' ledger subscription book transfer agent
>> 20-7 Prepare a balance sheet for a corporation. **WHY IT'S IMPORTANT** The balance sheet must show the classes and values of stock.	
>> 20-8 Record organization costs. **WHY IT'S IMPORTANT** The start-up of a corporation involves a variety of costs.	
>> 20-9 Record stock issued at a premium and stock with no par value. **WHY IT'S IMPORTANT** Stockholders' equity must be reported accurately.	
>> 20-10 Record transactions for stock subscriptions. **WHY IT'S IMPORTANT** Stock subscriptions increase assets.	
>> 20-11 Describe the capital stock records for a corporation. **WHY IT'S IMPORTANT** Records are legally required.	

Recording Capital Stock Transactions

In this section, you will learn about the entries necessary to record the issuance of capital stock and the records needed to manage capital stock.

>> **20-6 OBJECTIVE**
Record the issuance of capital stock at par value.

Recording the Issuance of Stock

Stock is issued after the purchaser has paid for it in full with one of the following:
- cash
- noncash assets
- services rendered

Stock Issued at Par Value

Assume that Carlos Allen and his associates determine that their new corporation, Outdoor Supply Center, Inc., will ultimately have capital requirements of $1,800,000. The incorporators decide to issue two classes of stock, preferred and common:

Preferred stock (10%, $100 par value, noncumulative and nonparticipating, 8,000 shares)	$ 800,000
Common stock ($25 par value, 40,000 shares)	1,000,000
Total capital stock	$1,800,000

Allen transferred the noncash assets and the liabilities of his existing business to the new corporation at the close of business on December 31, 20X0. Allen also invested cash for shares of common stock in the new corporation. Allen's friends invested cash for common and preferred stock.

When the corporate charter was received, the accounting records were established. The following memorandum entry provides the details of the authorized capital stock:

20X0					
Dec.	31	Outdoor Supply Center, Inc., was formed to			
		sell camping equipment and supplies and to			
		carry on all necessary and related activities.			
		It is authorized to issue 40,000 shares of			
		$25 par-value common stock and 8,000			
		shares of $100 par-value, 10% preferred			
		stock that is noncumulative			
		and nonparticipating.			

Data relating to each class of stock are entered on ledger sheets:

ACCOUNT: Common Stock ($25 Par Value; 40,000 Shares Authorized)   ACCOUNT NO. 301

DATE	DESCRIPTION	POST. REF.	DEBIT	CREDIT	BALANCE DEBIT	BALANCE CREDIT

ACCOUNT: Preferred Stock (10% Noncumulative, Nonparticipating; $100 Par Value; 8,000 Shares Authorized)   ACCOUNT NO. 311

DATE	DESCRIPTION	POST. REF.	DEBIT	CREDIT	BALANCE DEBIT	BALANCE CREDIT

Stock Issued at Par Value for Cash

When stock is issued for cash equal to the par value of the shares, cash proceeds are credited to the capital stock account. Allen and his colleagues purchased the following number of shares at par value for cash:

	Common Stock Shares	Preferred Stock Shares
Carlos Allen	528	
Karen Wilcox	600	400
Wibb Kamp	400	400
Jill Carrell	200	
Ramon Hill	700	

The receipt of cash was recorded in the cash receipts journal. To simplify the illustration, the entry is shown for Karen Wilcox only in general journal form. Similar entries would be made for other cash purchases of stock.

20X0				
Dec.	31	Cash ($15,000 + $40,000)	55 000 00	
		Common Stock (600 x $25)		15 000 00
		Preferred Stock (400 x $100)		40 000 00
		Issuance of stock to Karen Wilcox:		
		600 shares of common at par ($25 per		
		share) and 400 shares of preferred at		
		par ($100 per share)		

important!

Capital Stock Account
The amount credited to the capital stock account is the par value of the stock issued.

Stock Issued at Par Value for Noncash Assets The following are the assets and liabilities transferred by Allen to the corporation:

Assets	
Accounts receivable	$ 22,500
Allowance for doubtful accounts	(1,500)
Merchandise inventory	40,000
Land	30,000
Building	72,000
Equipment and fixtures	8,000
Total assets	$171,000
Liabilities	
Accounts payable	19,200
Net value of assets transferred	$151,800

Allen and the other shareholders agreed that Allen would be issued 800 shares of the $100 par-value preferred stock, to be recorded at par value ($80,000). In addition, shares of the $25 par-value common stock are to be issued to Allen for the difference between the net value of the noncash assets received by the corporation and the par value of the 800 shares of preferred stock. Thus, 2,872 shares of common stock are also issued:

Net value of assets transferred	$151,800
Par value of preferred stock issued (800 shares × $100 per share)	80,000
Par value of common stock to be issued	$ 71,800

Number of common shares to be issued:
$71,800 ÷ $25 per share = 2,872 shares

The transaction is recorded as follows:

	20X0				
18	Dec.	31 Accounts Receivable		22 500 00	
19		Merchandise Inventory		40 000 00	
20		Land		30 000 00	
21		Building		72 000 00	
22		Equipment and Fixtures		8 000 00	
23		Allowance for Doubtful Accounts			1 500 00
24		Accounts Payable			19 200 00
25		Common Stock (2,872 × $25)			71 800 00
26		Preferred Stock (800 × $100)			80 000 00
27		Issuance of stock in payment for net			
28		noncash assets of Allen,			
29		2,872 shares of $25 par			
30		common stock at $25 per share and			
31		800 shares of $100 par preferred			
32		stock at $100 per share			

> **recall**
>
> **Owner's Investment**
>
> Common and preferred stock are owners' (stockholders') equity accounts. Increases to owners' equity accounts are recorded as credits.

The assets and liability are recorded at fair market value. *Accounts Receivable* and *Allowance for Doubtful Accounts* are recorded separately. The $22,500 balance in the *Accounts Receivable* control account agrees with the total of the accounts receivable subsidiary ledger.

>> **20-7 OBJECTIVE**
> Prepare a balance sheet for a corporation.

Preparing a Balance Sheet for a Corporation Figure 20.1 shows the balance sheet for Outdoor Supply Center, Inc., immediately following the organization of the corporation. The

FIGURE 20.1

Corporate Balance Sheet Prepared after Organization

Outdoor Supply Center, Inc.				
Balance Sheet				
December 31, 20X0				
Assets				
Current Assets				
Cash			140 700 00	
Accounts Receivable	22 500 00			
Less Allowance for Doubtful Accounts	1 500 00		21 000 00	
Merchandise Inventory			40 000 00	
Total Current Assets			201 700 00	
Property, Plant, and Equipment				
Land	30 000 00			
Building	72 000 00			
Equipment and Fixtures	8 000 00			
Total Property, Plant, and Equipment			110 000 00	
Total Assets			311 700 00	
Liabilities and Stockholders' Equity				
Current Liabilities				
Accounts Payable			19 200 00	
Stockholders' Equity				
Preferred Stock (10%, $100 par value, 8,000 shares authorized)				
At Par Value (1,600 shares issued)		160 000 00		
Common Stock ($25 par value, 40,000 shares authorized)				
At Par Value (5,300 shares issued)		132 500 00		
Total Stockholders' Equity			292 500 00	
Total Liabilities and Stockholders' Equity			311 700 00	

balance sheet reflects the acquisition of the assets and liabilities of Allen's Camping Supply Store by the issuance of stock and the issuance of stock for cash.

Recording Organization Costs A variety of costs are incurred when a business is incorporated, including legal fees, attorneys' fees, charter fees paid to the state, and the cost of the organizational meeting of the directors.

Organization costs are incurred to provide benefit over the entire life of the corporation because they are necessary in order for the entity to exist and carry on business. For this reason, in past years, organization costs have been capitalized and amortized over an arbitrary period (typically the period from the U.S. tax code). Some corporations, however, simply record the costs as an intangible asset and do not amortize the costs for financial accounting purposes.

In Chapter 18, the accounting requirements for intangible assets that do not have an identifiable economic or legal life were discussed. Because organization costs have no fixed legal life, these costs would, if capitalized, be an intangible asset requiring it to be amortized over some period (the current tax rule is to amortize the amount over 180 months). Because of

>> **20-8 OBJECTIVE**

Record organization costs.

the difficulty estimating an identifiable life and the additional fact that the amount spent for organization costs is typically immaterial, the practice today is to charge organization costs to expense during the first financial reporting period after the corporation begins activities.

On January 18, Outdoor Supply Center, Inc., paid $2,000 of organization costs to its attorney. The amount includes legal fees, reimbursement for the charter fee, and the cost of drafting and printing the stock certificates. This reimbursement is recorded by a debit to **Organization Expense** and a credit to **Cash.**

>> **20-9 OBJECTIVE**
Record stock issued at a premium and stock with no par value.

Stock Issued at a Premium

If the corporation has the potential for earning very attractive profits, investors are willing to pay more than par value to become stockholders. Likewise, if the preferred stock dividend is more attractive than other investments with similar risk, investors are willing to pay more than par value. The amount received by a corporation that is in excess of the par value is called a *premium*. A premium on preferred stock is credited to an account called **Paid-in Capital in Excess of Par Value—Preferred Stock.**

Suppose that May Newman, a new shareholder, agreed to pay $105 per share for 400 shares of preferred stock of Outdoor Supply Center, Inc. She paid a premium of $5 per share ($105 price – $100 par). The general journal entry for this transaction is:

THE BOTTOM LINE
Purchase of Preferred Stock at a Premium

Income Statement
No effect on net income

Balance Sheet
Assets ↑ 42,000
Equity ↑ 42,000

20X1				
Mar. 2	Cash		42 000 00	
	Preferred Stock			40 000 00
	Paid-in Capital in Excess of Par			
	Value—Preferred Stock			2 000 00
	Issuance of 400 shares for $105			
	per share			

In the Stockholders' Equity section of the balance sheet shown below, the amount of the new account, **Paid-in Capital in Excess of Par Value—Preferred Stock,** is added to the par value of the shares issued to show the total paid in by that class of stockholder. (The account title might also be **Premium on Preferred Stock** or a similar name.)

important!

In Excess of Par
The amount credited to the **Paid-in Capital in Excess of Par Value** account is the price paid by the stockholder minus the par value of the stock multiplied by the number of shares issued.

Stockholders' Equity

Preferred Stock (10%, $100 par value, 8,000 shares authorized)	
At Par Value (2,000 shares issued)	$200,000
Paid-in Capital in Excess of Par Value	2,000
Total Preferred Stockholders' Equity	$202,000

> At the end of its fiscal year ending January 31, 2017, Walmart had authorized 100 million shares of preferred stock with 10 cents par value, of which none had been issued. The company's authorized common stock was 11 billion shares, with par value of $0.10. The company had outstanding approximately 3.0 billion shares of common stock. As a result, its Common Stock account had a balance of $300 million. At the same time, the balance sheet reflected "Capital in Excess of Par Value" of $2.6 billion and Retained Earnings of $85.1 billion.

Issuance of No-Par-Value Stock

No-par-value stock is not assigned a par value in the corporate charter. No-par-value stock has the following theoretical advantages over par-value stock:

- No-par-value stock can be issued at any price. Par-value stock cannot be issued for less than its par value.
- If there is no par value, investors cannot confuse par value and market value.

No-Par-Value Stock without Stated Value Some states require no-par-value stock to be assigned a stated value. Even if it is not required, the board of directors can assign a stated value. If no-par-value stock does not have a stated value, the proceeds from the issue of shares are credited to the *Common Stock* account. For example, suppose that Nature's Best Snacks Corporation is authorized to issue no-par-value common stock. A stated value has not been assigned the shares. On March 4, the corporation issued 1,000 shares for $20 per share, and on March 15, it issued 600 shares for $22 per share. The two stock issues are recorded as follows:

20X1					
Mar.	4	Cash		20 000 00	
		Common Stock			20 000 00
		Issue of 1,000 shares of no-par-value			
		common stock at $20 per share			
	15	Cash		13 200 00	
		Common Stock			13 200 00
		Issue of 600 shares of no-par-value			
		common stock at $22 per share			

No-Par-Value Stock with Stated Value Most no-par-value stock is assigned a stated value by the board of directors. The stated value is treated like par value. If no-par-value common stock with a stated value is issued at a price higher than the stated value, the stated value is credited to the *Common Stock* account. Any excess received over stated value is treated as a premium and credited to *Paid-in Capital in Excess of Stated Value.*

For example, Bakersville Music Corporation is authorized to issue no-par-value common stock. The board of directors assigned $25 as the stated value of the stock. On April 1, the corporation issued 2,400 shares at $26 per share. The stock issuance is recorded as shown:

20X1					
Apr.	1	Cash		62 400 00	
		Common Stock			60 000 00
		Paid-in Capital in Excess of Stated			
		Value			2 400 00
		Issue of 2,400 shares of common			
		stock at $26 per share			

The credit to the *Paid-in Capital in Excess of Stated Value* account is $2,400 [($26 price − $25 stated value) × 2,400 shares]. On the balance sheet, the premium is shown as an addition to the stated value to show the total paid by common stockholders.

Summary of Recording Rules for Par-Value and No-Par-Value Stock

Table 20.3 summarizes the effects on the capital accounts of issuing stock with and without a par value.

MANAGERIAL IMPLICATIONS

CORPORATION CONSIDERATIONS

- New business owners should have a clear idea of the nature of a corporation, its rights and limitations, and how the corporation differs from other forms of business organization.
- Management and stockholders need to realize that the corporation is a separate legal entity apart from its owners and that regardless of changes in ownership, the corporation continues to exist.
- New business owners need to understand the disadvantages of the corporate form of business, including double taxation and government regulation.
- In order to select the most beneficial capital structure, management needs to be familiar with the various classes of stock. Management is responsible for ensuring the following:
  - Assets acquired through the issue of stock are recorded at fair market value so that the corporation's profitability can be properly computed and evaluated.
  - Capital stock issues are properly recorded and tracked.
- Stock subscriptions are in conformity with state laws, and the accounting records fully reflect all information relating to stock subscriptions.
- The corporation has adequate records to comply with legal requirements and to track stockholder transactions.
- Officers act within the limitations set by the board of directors and the shareholders.
- The bylaws and charter provisions of the corporation are carefully followed, and minutes are kept of all meetings of directors and stockholders.
- Management needs to be aware that state laws prohibit the issuance of stock at less than par value.
- Management must be aware that actions of the board of directors, as reported in the corporate minutes, often have accounting effects.

THINKING CRITICALLY
Why must the management and directors of a corporation be fully informed about laws and regulations affecting corporations? How can they find out what they need to know?

TABLE 20.3 Comparison of Rules for Par-Value and No-Par-Value Stock

Par-Value Stock	No-Par-Value Stock	
	Stated Value	No Stated Value
Par value is specified in corporate charter.	Stated value is assigned by directors. Corporate charter indicates that stock is no-par-value stock.	Corporate charter indicates that stock is no-par-value stock.
Stock certificate indicates par value.	Stock certificate generally does not show stated value.	Stock certificate shows that stock is no-par-value stock.
Change in par value requires revision of charter.	Stated value can be changed by directors.	
On issue of stock, par value is credited to capital stock account.	On issue of stock, stated value is credited to capital stock account.	On issue of stock, entire proceeds are credited to capital stock account.

Subscriptions for Capital Stock

Some prospective stockholders want to buy stock but pay for it later. They sign a subscription contract that states the stock price and describes the payment plan. They receive the actual stock (and ownership provisions) when payment is made in full. A stock subscription is recorded as a receivable from the subscriber. The corporation must have stock available to issue when the subscription is paid in full.

>> **20-10 OBJECTIVE**
Record transactions for stock subscriptions.

Receipt of Subscriptions

On May 1, Outdoor Supply Center, Inc., received a subscription from Herman Coles to purchase 400 shares of common stock at $25 per share. Coles is to pay for the stock in full on June 1.

The corporation also received a subscription from Remu Patel to purchase 400 shares of preferred stock at $105 per share. Patel is to pay for the stock in two equal installments, on June 1 and July 1. These subscriptions are recorded as follows:

	20X1					
1	May	1	Subscriptions Receivable—Common	10 000 00		
2			Common Stock Subscribed		10 000 00	
3			Subscription from Herman Coles to buy			
4			400 shares of common stock at par			
5			value of $25 per share			
6						
7		1	Subscriptions Receivable—Preferred	42 000 00		
8			Preferred Stock Subscribed		40 000 00	
9			Paid-in Capital in Excess of Par Value—			
10			Preferred Stock		2 000 00	
11			Subscription from Remu Patel to buy			
12			400 shares of $100 par preferred stock			
13			at $105 per share			

A separate **Subscriptions Receivable** account is used for each class of stock. There are also separate **Stock Subscribed** accounts. When the subscriptions are paid in full, the stock is issued. Until then, the **Stock Subscribed** accounts appear in the Stockholders' Equity section of the balance sheet as additions to the class of stock issued.

For example, immediately after the receipt of Patel's stock subscription, the preferred stock in the Stockholders' Equity section of the balance sheet appears as follows:

Stockholders' Equity

Preferred Stock (10%, $100 par value, 8,000 shares authorized)	
At Par Value (2,000 shares issued)	$200,000
Subscribed (400 shares)	40,000
Paid-in Capital in Excess of Par Value	4,000
Total Preferred Stockholders' Equity	$244,000

Collection of Subscriptions and Issuance of Stock

When Coles pays his $10,000 subscription in full on June 1, the corporation issues 400 shares of common stock to him. The $10,000 is recorded in the cash receipts journal. To simplify the illustration, the transaction is shown in general journal form, followed by an entry to record the issuance of the stock:

	20X1					
1	June	1	Cash	10 000 00		
2			Subscriptions Receivable—Common		10 000 00	
3			Received Herman Coles's subscription			
4			in full			
5						
6		1	Common Stock Subscribed	10 000 00		
7			Common Stock		10 000 00	
8			Issued 400 shares of common stock to			
9			Herman Coles			

important!

Stock Subscriptions

Subscriptions receivable accounts are presented in the Asset section. Stock subscribed accounts are presented in the Stockholders' Equity section of the balance sheet.

When these entries are posted, the *Subscriptions Receivable—Common* and *Common Stock Subscribed* accounts are closed. Both *Cash* and *Common Stock* are increased by $10,000:

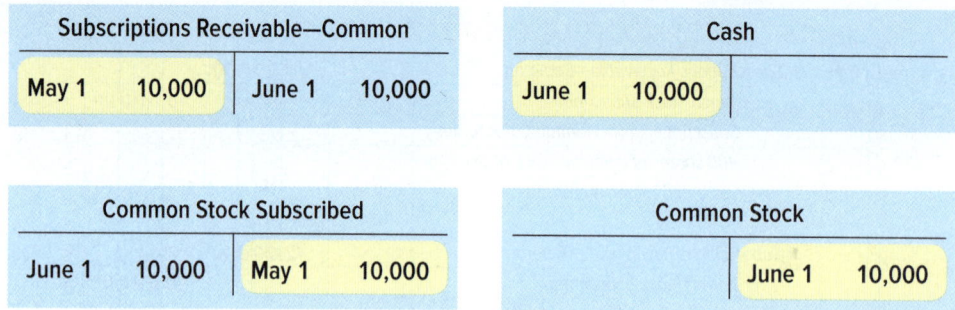

Patel paid his preferred stock subscription in two monthly installments of $21,000 each. The company debits each payment to *Cash* and credits *Subscriptions Receivable—Preferred*.

After Patel makes the second payment, the corporation issues the stock to him. The collection of the final installment and the issuance of the stock are recorded in the general journal as shown:

	20X1			
	July	1	Cash	21,000.00	
			Subscriptions Receivable—Preferred		21,000.00
			Receipt of final installment from		
			Remu Patel on his stock subscription		
		1	Preferred Stock Subscribed	40,000.00	
			Preferred Stock		40,000.00
			Issuance of 400 shares of preferred		
			stock to Remu Patel		

This stock subscription transaction resulted in a $42,000 increase in *Cash,* a $40,000 increase in *Preferred Stock,* and a $2,000 increase in *Paid-in Capital in Excess of Par Value—Preferred Stock:*

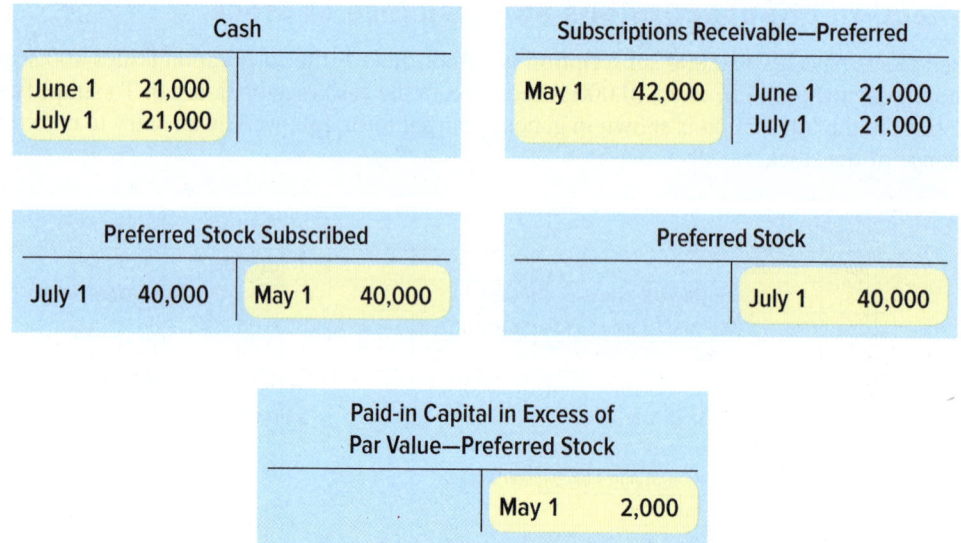

Special Corporation Records and Agents

Corporations keep detailed records of stockholders' equity. They maintain special corporate records such as:

- minutes of meetings of stockholders and directors,
- corporate bylaws,
- stock certificate books,
- stock ledgers,
- stock transfer records.

>> 20-11 OBJECTIVE
Describe the capital stock records for a corporation.

Minute Book

A **minute book** keeps accurate and complete records of all meetings of stockholders and directors. The minute book formally reports actions taken, directives issued, directors elected, officers elected, and other matters.

Stock Certificate Books

Capital stock is usually issued by a corporation in the form of a **stock certificate.** A separate series of stock certificates is prepared for each class of stock. A corporation that expects to issue few stock certificates can have them prepared in books. Each certificate is numbered consecutively and attached to a stub from which it is separated at the time of issuance. The certificate indicates the:

- name of the corporation,
- name of the stockholder to whom the certificate was issued,
- class of stock,
- number of shares.

Certificates are valid when they are properly signed by corporate officers and have the corporate seal affixed to them.

Figure 20.2 shows a common stock certificate for The McGraw-Hill Companies, Inc. Certificates for preferred stock are similar to those for common stock and include the details of the preferred stock.

Capital Stock Ledger It is essential for corporations to keep accurate records of the shares of stock issued and the names and addresses of the stockholders. This information is needed to mail dividend checks and official notices about stockholders' meetings and votes.

To keep the required information, corporations set up a **capital stock ledger,** or **stockholders' ledger,** for each class of stock issued. There is a sheet for each stockholder with the following information:

- stockholder's name and address,
- dates of transactions affecting stock holdings,
- certificate numbers,
- number of shares for each transaction.

The balance shows the number of shares held. The ledger sheets can also include a record of dividends. For each class of stock, the stockholders' ledger is a subsidiary to the capital stock account. The total shares shown in the stockholders' ledger must agree with the number of shares in the capital stock account for that class.

After the corporation issues stock, new stockholders purchase shares from existing stockholders. The process is as follows:

- The buyer pays the seller.
- The seller surrenders the stock certificate to the corporation.
- The corporation issues a new certificate to the buyer.

FIGURE 20.2

Stock Certificate

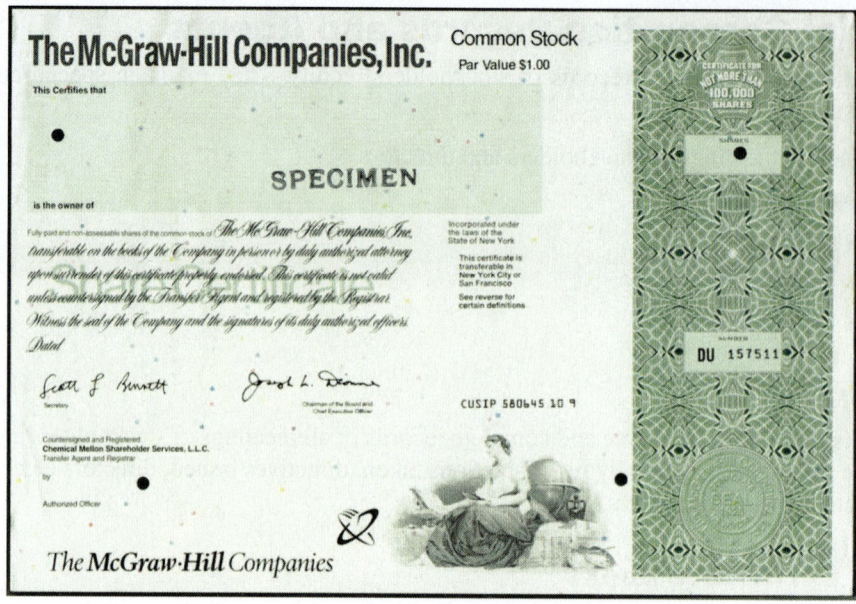

The **capital stock transfer journal** is a record of stock transfers used for posting to the stockholders' ledger. There is a capital stock transfer journal for each class of stock issued by the corporation.

Records of Stock Subscriptions

The corporation tracks stock subscriptions using the subscription book and the subscribers' ledger. The **subscription book**:

- is a listing of the stock subscriptions received,
- shows the names and addresses of the subscribers,
- shows the number of shares subscribed,
- contains the amounts and times of payment.

A subscription book can contain the actual stock subscription contracts.

The **subscribers' ledger** contains an account receivable for each stock subscriber. The account is debited for the total subscription and credited when the subscriber makes payments. The subscribers' ledger is a subsidiary ledger. The balances of the individual subscriber accounts must agree with the *Subscriptions Receivable* control account in the general ledger.

Summary of Stock Control Accounts and Subsidiary Ledgers

Table 20.4 shows the relationship between control accounts and subsidiary ledgers for corporate stock recordkeeping.

> **recall**
>
> **Subsidiary Ledgers**
> The total of the individual accounts must agree with the control account in the general ledger.

Special Agents

Corporations whose stock is widely held and actively traded do not keep their own stockholder records. Instead, they turn the responsibility over to a transfer agent and a registrar. The **transfer agent** receives the stock certificates surrendered. A bank that serves as a transfer agent is often chosen for its proximity to the stock exchange or market where the corporation's stock is expected to trade. The same bank may also be appointed registrar.

An assignment form on the certificate indicates to whom a new certificate should be issued. The agent:

- cancels the old certificates,
- issues the new ones,

TABLE 20.4

Relationship Between Control Accounts and Subsidiary Stock Ledgers

Control Account	Subsidiary Ledgers
Common Stock	Common Stockholders' Ledger Contains an account for each owner of common stock and shows shares bought or transferred and the balance of shares owned
Preferred Stock	Preferred Stockholders' Ledger Contains an account for each owner of preferred stock and shows shares bought or transferred and the balance of shares owned
Subscriptions Receivable—Common Stock	Subscribers' Ledger—Common Contains the account receivable for each subscriber to common stock
Subscriptions Receivable—Preferred Stock	Subscribers' Ledger—Preferred Contains an account receivable for each subscriber to preferred stock

- makes the necessary entries in the capital stock ledger,
- prepares lists of stockholders who should receive dividend payments and notices.

The agent might also prepare and mail the dividend checks.

The **registrar** accounts for all the stock issued by the corporation and makes sure that the corporation does not issue more shares than are authorized. The registrar receives from the transfer agent all the canceled certificates and all the new certificates issued. The registrar must countersign the new certificates before they are valid.

Section 3 Review

1. Which of the following accurately describes stated value?
   a. the amount received by a corporation in excess of the par value upon the sale of stock
   b. the current market value of a share of stock
   c. an amount assigned to no-par-value stock by the board of directors
   d. total organization costs incurred by a corporation

2. What is *not* an advantage of issuing no-par-value common stock?
   a. It can credit *Common Stock* for any amount.
   b. It produces a small value of stockholders' equity.
   c. The company has a wider available market for selling stock.
   d. The company never has to deal with paid-in capital in excess of a par amount.

3. What are organization costs?
   a. attorneys' and other fees related to preparing to file for the corporate charter and other start-up costs
   b. salaries paid to owners
   c. rental expenses for company property when starting
   d. costs of preparing tax returns

4. Duck Company receives a subscription to 1,000 shares of its $25 par-value common stock for $31 per share. What accounts are debited and credited, and for what amounts?
   a. Debit *Cash,* $31,000; credit *Common Stock,* $31,000.
   b. Debit *Cash,* $6,000; credit *Paid-in Capital in Excess of Par,* $6,000.
   c. Debit *Subscriptions Receivable,* $25,000; credit *Common Stock Subscribed,* $25,000.
   d. Debit *Subscriptions Receivable,* $31,000; credit *Common Stock Subscribed,* $25,000; credit *Paid-in Capital in Excess of Par,* $6,000.

5. Which, if any, of the following statements is generally true? The stated value of no-par common stock is:
   a. specified in the corporate charter.
   b. shown on the stock certificate.
   c. can be changed by the board of directors.
   d. credited to the *Common Stock* account when issued, and any excess of issue price over stated value is credited to *Paid-in Capital in Excess of Stated Value.*

Chapter 20 Review — Chapter Summary

In this chapter, you have learned about the basic characteristics of a corporation and the accounting procedures unique to its formation, operations, and shareholder transactions. You have learned about capital stock transactions, dividend declarations, and reporting of stockholders' equity on the balance sheet.

Learning Objectives

20-1 Explain the characteristics of a corporation.

A corporation is organized under state law to carry on activities permitted by its charter:

- Ownership is indicated by shares of stock.
- Stockholders owning voting stock elect a board of directors.
- The board selects officers to run the business.
- The corporate charter specifies the types and amounts of capital stock authorized.
- The bylaws guide the firm's general operation, which must be consistent with charter provisions.
- The corporation is subject to federal income tax.

20-2 Describe special "hybrid" organizations that have some characteristics of partnerships and some characteristics of corporations.

A corporation formed as an S corporation is taxed as a partnership. The limited liability partnership and limited liability company avoid federal corporate income tax and also provide limited liability.

20-3 Describe the different types of stock.

If a corporation issues only one type of stock, it is called *common stock*. Common stockholders vote on corporate matters and receive dividends as declared by the board of directors.

Corporations can issue a second class of stock that carries special preferences, called *preferred stock*. Preferred stockholders are often given priority in the distribution of dividends. Liquidation value is often assigned to preferred stock; this stock class may be convertible to common stock.

20-4 Compute the number of shares of common stock to be issued on the conversion of convertible preferred stock.

Convertible preferred stock gives its owners the right to convert their shares into common stock after a specified date by using the stated conversion ratio.

20-5 Compute dividends payable on stock.

The board of directors declares dividends based on corporate earnings. Dividends are first allocated to preferred stockholders, then to common stockholders.

20-6 Record the issuance of capital stock at par value.

The entire amount of stock issued in return for a cash investment is credited to the appropriate capital stock account. Noncash assets traded for capital stock are recorded at their fair market value.

20-7 Prepare a balance sheet for a corporation.

The Stockholders' Equity section identifies the classes, values, and number of stock authorized and issued.

20-8 Record organization costs.

Organization costs are charged to expense when incurred.

20-9 Record stock issued at a premium and stock with no par value.

A premium on stock is recorded in a *Paid-in Capital in Excess of Par Value* account. Stock without a par value is called *no-par-value stock*. A few states require it to be assigned a stated value, similar to par value for accounting purposes.

20-10 Record transactions for stock subscriptions.

Stock can be subscribed, then paid for and issued later. It is recorded in a subsidiary ledger with a separate account receivable for each subscriber. Individual accounts receivable are controlled by a *Subscriptions Receivable* account in the general ledger.

20-11 Describe the capital stock records for a corporation.

Corporate records must include minute books, stockholders' ledgers, stock certificate books, and stock transfer records.

20-12 Define the accounting terms new to this chapter.

Glossary

Authorized capital stock (p. 712) The number of shares authorized for issue by the corporate charter

Bylaws (p. 710) The guidelines for conducting a corporation's business affairs

Callable preferred stock (p. 714) Stock that gives the issuing corporation the right to repurchase the preferred shares from the stockholders at a specific price

Capital stock ledger (p. 727) A subsidiary ledger that contains a record of each stockholder's purchases, transfers, and current balance of shares owned; also called stockholders' ledger

Capital stock transfer journal (p. 728) A record of stock transfers used for posting to the stockholders' ledger

Common stock (p. 713) The general class of stock issued when no other class of stock is authorized; each share carries the same rights and privileges as every other share. Even if preferred stock is issued, common stock will also be issued

Convertible preferred stock (p. 713) Preferred stock that conveys the right to convert that stock to common stock after a specified date or during a period of time

Corporate charter (p. 708) A document issued by a state government that establishes a corporation

Cumulative preferred stock (p. 714) Stock that conveys to its owners the right to receive the preference dividend for the current year and any prior years in which the preference dividend was not paid before common stockholders receive any dividends

Dividends (p. 714) Distributions of the profits of a corporation to its shareholders

Limited liability company (LLC) (p. 710) Provides limited liability to the owners, who can elect to have the profits taxed at the LLC level or on their individual tax returns

Limited liability partnership (LLP) (p. 709) A partnership that provides some limited liability for all partners

Liquidation value (p. 713) Value of assets to be applied to preferred stock, usually par value or an amount in excess of par value, if the corporation is liquidated

Market value (p. 712) The price per share at which stock is bought and sold

Minute book (p. 727) A book in which accurate and complete records of all meetings of stockholders and directors are kept

Noncumulative preferred stock (p. 714) Stock that conveys to its owners the stated preference dividend for the current year but no rights to dividends for years in which none were declared

Nonparticipating preferred stock (p. 714) Stock that conveys to its owners the right to only the preference dividend amount specified on the stock certificate

No-par-value stock (p. 712) Stock that is not assigned a par value in the corporate charter

Organization costs (p. 721) The costs associated with establishing a corporation

Par value (p. 712) An amount assigned by the corporate charter to each share of stock for accounting purposes

Participating preferred stock (p. 714) Stock that conveys the right not only to the preference dividend amount but also to a share of other dividends paid

Preemptive right (p. 713) A shareholder's right to purchase a proportionate amount of any new stock issued at a later date

Preference dividend (p. 714) A basic or stated dividend rate for preferred stock that must be paid before dividends can be paid on common stock

Preferred stock (p. 713) A class of stock that has special claims on the corporate profits or, in case of liquidation, on corporate assets

Registrar (p. 729) A person or institution in charge of the issuance and transfer of a corporation's stock

Shareholder (p. 708) A person who owns shares of stock in a corporation; also called a stockholder

Stated value (p. 712) The value that can be assigned to no-par-value stock by a board of directors for accounting purposes

Stock certificate (p. 727) The form by which capital stock is issued; the certificate indicates the name of the corporation, the name of the stockholder to whom the certificate was issued, the class of stock, and the number of shares

Stockholders' equity (p. 710) The corporate equivalent of owners' equity; also called shareholders' equity

Stockholders' ledger (p. 727) *See* Capital stock ledger

Subchapter S corporation (S corporation) (p. 709) An entity formed as a corporation that meets the requirements of subchapter S of the Internal Revenue Code to be treated essentially as a partnership, so that the corporation pays no income tax

Subscribers' ledger (p. 728) A subsidiary ledger that contains an account receivable for each stock subscriber

Subscription book (p. 728) A list of the stock subscriptions received

Transfer agent (p. 728) A person or institution that handles all stock transfers and transfer records for a corporation

Comprehensive Self Review

1. How are the *Stock Subscribed* accounts reported in the financial statements?
2. What does market value of a stock mean?
3. What information is found in the subscribers' ledger?
4. What are the duties of the corporation's registrar?
5. What is the special right conveyed to holders of convertible preferred stock?
6. What is callable preferred stock?
7. What is the special benefit of a limited liability partnership?
8. What is the "preemptive right" of a shareholder?

(Answers to Comprehensive Self Review are at the end of the chapter.)

Discussion Questions

1. Why would a new corporation issue no-par stock with a stated value, rather than par-value stock?
2. Selling stock on a subscription basis involves considerable recordkeeping. Why does a corporation sell its shares in this way?
3. How are the members of a corporation's board of directors selected?
4. What is the purpose of the minute book?
5. What is the role of the transfer agent?
6. What is meant by the "par value of stock"?
7. What does the term "restricted agency" mean?
8. Who makes the day-to-day decisions necessary for a corporation to operate?
9. Describe the flow of authority and responsibility in a corporate entity.
10. What is a stock subscription?
11. What are organization costs?
12. What role does the registrar of a corporation serve?
13. How are organization costs accounted for?
14. What is the control account for the individual shareholder accounts in the common stockholders' ledger?

15. What is participating preferred stock?
16. What is cumulative preferred stock?
17. When common stock without a par value or a stated value is issued, what amount is credited to the capital stock account when the stock is issued?
18. What is convertible preferred stock?
19. What is the difference between the *Common Stock Subscribed* account and the *Subscriptions Receivable—Common Stock* account?
20. Where is the usual place for organizers of a new corporation to acquire a corporate charter?
21. What are the corporation's bylaws?
22. If there is only one class of stock, what is it called?
23. What are some benefits of a subchapter S corporation?
24. How does par value differ from stated value?

APPLICATIONS

Exercises

Computing dividends payable.

Exercise 20.1
Objective 20-5

Florida Corporation has only one class of stock. There are 200,000 shares outstanding. During 20X1, the corporation's net income after taxes was $800,000. The policy of the corporation is to declare dividends equal to 20 percent of its net income. Black owns 500 shares of the stock. How much will Black receive as a dividend on these shares?

Computing dividends payable.

Exercise 20.2
Objective 20-5

SFC has outstanding 50,000 shares of noncumulative, 5 percent, $100 par-value preferred stock and 100,000 shares of no-par-value common stock.

1. During 20X1, the corporation distributed dividends of $250,000. What amount will be paid on each share of preferred stock? What amount will be paid on each share of common stock?
2. During 20X2, the corporation distributed dividends of $750,000. How much will be paid on each share of preferred stock? How much will be paid on each share of common stock?

Computing dividends payable.

Exercise 20.3
Objective 20-5

CBoxCorporation has outstanding 110,000 shares of 12 percent, $80 par-value cumulative preferred stock and 500,000 shares of no-par-value common stock.

1. During 20X1, the corporation distributed dividends of $792,000. What amount will be paid on each share of preferred stock? What amount will be paid on each share of common stock?
2. During 20X2, the corporation distributed dividends of $1,720,000. What amount will be paid on each share of preferred stock? What amount will be paid on each share of common stock?

Converting preferred stock.

Exercise 20.4
Objective 20-5

Daily Corporation has outstanding 50,000 shares of $30 par-value preferred stock, issued at an average price of $37 a share. The preferred stock is convertible into common stock at the rate of three shares of common stock for each share of preferred stock. Neil Thomas owns 900 shares of the preferred stock. During the current year, he decides to convert 600 shares into common stock. How many shares of common stock will he receive?

Issuing stock for assets.

Exercise 20.5
Objective 20-6

Juan Joseph, the owner of a sole proprietorship, is planning to incorporate his business. His capital account has a balance of $480,000 after revaluation of the assets. His cash account totals $80,000. He will receive 8 percent, $100 par-value preferred stock with a total par value equal to the cash transferred. The balance of his capital is to be exchanged for shares of $50 par-value common stock with a total par value equal to the remaining capital. How many shares of preferred stock should be issued to Joseph? How many shares of common stock should be issued to him?

Exercise 20.6
Objective 20-8

▶ **Accounting for organization costs.**

Alway Company, a newly organized corporation, received a bill from its lawyers for $10,000 for time spent in organizing the company.

1. How should these costs be treated in the financial reports?
2. How should they be treated for federal income tax purposes?

Exercise 20.7
Objective 20-6

▶ **Issuing stock at par value for cash.**

On January 2, 20X1, Cotton Inc. issued 50,000 shares of $10 par-value common stock and 10,000 shares of 5 percent, $100 par-value preferred stock for cash at par value. Prepare the entry in general journal form to record the issuance of the stock.

Exercise 20.8
Objective 20-9

▶ **Issuing par-value stock at a premium.**

On January 2, 20X1, BYU Corporation issued 5,000 shares of its $10 par-value common stock for cash at $12 a share. Prepare the entry in general journal form to record the issuance of the stock.

Exercise 20.9
Objective 20-9

▶ **Issuing no-par stock for cash.**

On January 2, 20X1, AC Company issued 50,000 shares of its no-par-value common stock ($50 stated value) for cash at $51 a share. Give the entry in general journal form to record the issuance of the stock.

Exercise 20.10
Objective 20-10

▶ **Transactions for stock subscriptions.**

On May 1, 20X1, TONI Inc. received a subscription from Angel Paz for 700 shares of its $1 par-value common stock at a price of $28 a share.

Paz made a payment of $14.00 per share on the stock at the time of the subscription. Give the entries in general journal form to record receipt of the subscription and the cash payment.

Prepare entries on June 1, 20X1, to record payment of the balance of Paz's subscription and issuance of the stock.

PROBLEMS

Problem Set A

Problem 20.1A
Objective 20-5

▶ **Computing dividends payable.**

Red Hot Company issued and has outstanding 100,000 shares of $10 par-value common stock and 5,000 shares of $50 par-value 6 percent preferred stock. The board of directors votes to distribute $10,000 as dividends in 20X1, $20,000 in 20X2, and $100,000 in 20X3.

INSTRUCTIONS

Compute the total dividend and the dividend for each share paid to preferred stockholders and common stockholders each year under the following assumed situations:

Case A: The preferred stock is nonparticipating and noncumulative.
Case B: The preferred stock is cumulative and nonparticipating.

Analyze: If a stockholder owned 350 shares of cumulative preferred stock in 20X1, 20X2, and 20X3, what total dividends should be paid to this stockholder in the fiscal year 20X3, assuming Case B?

Problem 20.2A
Objective 20-5

▶ **Computing dividends payable.**

This problem consists of two parts.

PART I

A portion of the Stockholders' Equity section of CMH Corporation's balance sheet as of December 31, 20X3, appears below. Dividends have not been paid for the years 20X1 and 20X2. There has been no change in the number of shares of stock issued and outstanding during these years. Assume that the board of directors of CMH Corporation declares a dividend of $50,000 after completing operations for the year 20X3.

Stockholders' Equity

Preferred Stock (10% cumulative, $50 par value, 10,000 shares authorized)	
At Par Value (2,000 shares issued)	$100,000
Common Stock (no-par value, with stated value of $5, 50,000 shares authorized)	
At Stated Value (30,000 shares issued)	150,000

INSTRUCTIONS (calculate 20X3 amounts)

1. Compute the total amount of the dividend to be distributed to preferred stockholders.
2. Compute the amount of the dividend to be paid on each share of preferred stock.
3. Compute the total amount of the dividend available to be distributed to common stockholders.
4. Compute the amount of the dividend to be paid on each share of common stock.
5. Compute the amount of dividends in arrears (if any) that preferred stockholders may expect from future declarations of dividends.

PART II

Use the information given in Part I to solve this part of the problem. Assume that the board of directors of CMH Corporation has declared a dividend of $100,000 instead of $50,000 after operations for 20X3 are completed.

INSTRUCTIONS (calculate 20X3 amounts)

1. Compute the total amount of the dividend to be distributed to preferred stockholders.
2. Compute the amount of the dividend to be paid on each share of preferred stock.
3. Compute the total amount of the dividend available to be distributed to common stockholders.
4. Compute the amount of the dividend to be paid on each share of common stock.
5. Compute the amount of dividends in arrears (if any) that preferred stockholders may expect from future declarations of dividends.

Analyze: Assume only Part I has transpired. If, in 20X2, the board of directors declared a dividend of $60,000, what amount would be paid to preferred stockholders?

Issuing stock for cash and noncash assets at par.

◀ **Problem 20.3A**
Objective 20-6

Jone Nelson and Helen Giddings are equal partners in N&G Appliance Center, which sells appliances and operates an appliance repair service. Nelson and Giddings have decided to incorporate the business. The new corporation will be known as N&G Appliance Center, Inc.

The corporation is authorized to issue 4,000 shares of $100 par-value, 10 percent preferred stock that is noncumulative and nonparticipating, and 100,000 shares of no-par-value common stock with a stated value of $20 per share. It is mutually agreed that the accounting records of N&G Appliance Center will be closed on December 31, 20X1, and that certain assets will be revalued. N&G Appliance Center, Inc., will then take over all assets and assume all liabilities of the partnership. In payment for the business, the corporation will issue 400 shares of preferred stock to Nelson and 400 shares of preferred stock to Giddings, plus a sufficient number of shares of common stock to each partner to equal the balance of the partners' capital accounts. After the partners have recorded the revaluation of their assets immediately prior to the dissolution of their partnership and withdrawn the amounts of cash agreed on, the trial balance of N&G Appliance Center as of December 31, 20X1, appears below.

INSTRUCTIONS

1. In the corporation's general journal, record a memorandum entry describing the corporation's formation on December 31, 20X1.
2. Record general journal entries as of December 31 to show the takeover of the assets and liabilities of the partnership and the issuance of stock in payment to Nelson and Giddings. Use the same account titles that the partnership used for assets and liabilities. Also use two new accounts: **Common Stock** and **Preferred Stock**.

N&G Appliance
Trial Balance
December 31, 20X1

ACCOUNT NAME	DEBIT	CREDIT
Cash	13,240 00	
Accounts Receivable	55,400 00	
Allowance for Doubtful Accounts		3,740 00
Merchandise Inventory	460,600 00	
Parts Inventory	40,200 00	
Land	90,000 00	
Building	553,280 00	
Accumulated Depreciation—Building		74,480 00
Furniture and Equipment	98,400 00	
Accumulated Depreciation—Furn. and Equip.		7,900 00
Accounts Payable		55,000 00
Jone Nelson, Capital		585,000 00
Helen Giddings, Capital		585,000 00
Totals	1,311,120 00	1,311,120 00

Analyze: What percentage of authorized common stock has been issued as of January 1, 20X2?

Problem 20.4A

Objectives 20-6, 20-7, 20-10

Issuing stock at par and no-par value and preparing a balance sheet.

Cold Corp., a new corporation, took over the assets and liabilities of Trey Cold on January 2, 20X1. The assets and liabilities, after appropriate revaluation by Cold, are as follows (amounts in parentheses are credits; other amounts are debits):

Cash	$ 70,000
Accounts Receivable	215,000
Allowance for Doubtful Accounts	(25,000)
Merchandise Inventory	175,000
Accounts Payable	(25,000)
Accrued Expenses Payable	(10,000)

The corporation is authorized to issue 500,000 shares of $10 par-value common stock and 500,000 shares of $10 par-value preferred stock. The preferred stock bears a stated yearly dividend rate of $1 per share. The transactions that follow were entered into at the time the corporation was formed.

INSTRUCTIONS

1. Make general journal entries to record the transactions.
2. Prepare the opening balance sheet as of January 2, 20X1, for Cold Corp.

DATE	TRANSACTIONS
Jan. 2	The corporation issued 40,000 shares of common stock to Trey Cold for his equity in the sole proprietorship business, and the corporation took over Cold's assets and liabilities.
2	Issued 3,000 shares of preferred stock at par to Harriet Cold, Trey's wife, for cash.
2	Issued 4,000 shares of common stock to Carol Kennedy. She paid $40,000 in cash for the stock.
2	Issued 2,000 shares of preferred stock to James Walker. He paid $20,000 in cash for the stock.

Analyze: What is the current ratio for the corporation at January 2, 20X1?

Issuing stock at par and at a premium, preparing Stockholders' Equity section of balance sheet, and recording stock subscriptions.

◀ **Problem 20.5A**
Objectives 20-6, 20-7, 20-9, 20-11

Stove Inc. was organized on March 1, 20X1, to operate a delivery service. The firm is authorized to issue 75,000 shares of no-par-value common stock with a stated value of $100 per share and 30,000 shares of $100 par-value, 8 percent preferred stock that is nonparticipating and noncumulative. Selected transactions that took place during March 20X1 follow.

INSTRUCTIONS

1. Set up the following general ledger accounts:

101	Cash	305	Paid-in Capital in Excess of Stated Value—Common
114	Subscriptions Receivable—Common Stock		
115	Subscriptions Receivable—Preferred Stock	311	Preferred Stock
301	Common Stock	312	Preferred Stock Subscribed
302	Common Stock Subscribed	315	Paid-in Capital in Excess of Par Value—Preferred

   Record in general journal form the transactions listed below, and post them to the general ledger accounts.

2. Prepare the Stockholders' Equity section of a balance sheet for Stove Inc. as of March 31, 20X1.

DATE	TRANSACTIONS
March 1	The corporation received its charter. (Make a memorandum entry.)
1	Issued 650 shares of common stock for cash at $100 per share to Jerri Harris.
3	Issued 400 shares of preferred stock for cash at par value to Gloria Amos.
5	Issued 400 shares of common stock for cash at $107 to Carolyn Reed.
5	Received a subscription for 450 shares of common stock at $106 per share from Joan Patterson, payable in two installments due in 10 and 20 days.
14	Received a subscription for 300 shares of preferred stock at $109 per share from Robert Tolliver, payable in two installments due in 15 and 30 days.
20	Received payment of a stock subscription installment due from Joan Patterson (one-half of the purchase price—see March 5 transaction).
29	Received payment of a stock subscription installment due from Robert Tolliver (one-half the purchase price—see March 14 transaction).
30	Received the balance due on the stock subscription of March 5 from Joan Patterson; issued the stock.

Analyze: What percentage of total stockholders' equity is held by common stockholders?

Problem Set B

Problem 20.1B
Objective 20-5

▶ **Computing dividends payable.**

Cancell Corporation issued and has outstanding 50,000 shares of $5 par-value common stock and 10,000 shares of $100 par-value, 5 percent preferred stock. The board of directors votes to distribute $40,000 as dividends in 20X1, $90,000 in 20X2, and $120,000 in 20X3.

INSTRUCTIONS

Compute the total dividend and the dividend for each share to be paid to preferred stockholders and common stockholders each year under the following assumed situations:

Case A: The preferred stock is nonparticipating and noncumulative.
Case B: The preferred stock is cumulative and nonparticipating.

Analyze: If a stockholder owned 1,600 shares of preferred stock throughout 20X1–20X3, what total dividends did he receive for Case B?

Problem 20.2B
Objective 20-5

▶ **Computing dividends payable.**

This problem consists of two parts.

PART I

A portion of the Stockholders' Equity section of LTB Corporation's balance sheet as of December 31, 20X1, appears below. Dividends have not been paid for the year 20X0. There has been no change in the number of shares of stock issued and outstanding during 20X0 or 20X1. Assume that the board of directors of the corporation declared a dividend of $250,000 after completing operations for the year 20X1.

Stockholders' Equity

Preferred Stock (6% cumulative, $100 par value,
   50,000 shares authorized)
   At Par Value (25,000 shares issued) $2,500,000

Common Stock ($20 par value, 300,000 shares authorized)
   At Par Value (150,000 shares issued)   3,000,000

INSTRUCTIONS (calculate 20X1 amounts)

1. Compute the total amount of the dividend to be distributed to preferred stockholders.
2. Compute the amount of the dividend to be paid on each share of preferred stock.
3. Compute the total amount of the dividend available to be distributed to common stockholders.
4. Compute the amount of the dividend to be paid on each share of common stock.
5. Compute the amount of dividends in arrears (if any) that preferred stockholders can expect from future declarations of dividends.

PART II

Assume that after operations for 20X1 were completed, the board of directors declares a dividend of $500,000 instead of $250,000. Use the information given in Part I to answer Questions 1 through 5 above under these new assumptions.

Analyze: In regard to Part I, if dividends of $360,000 were declared in 20X2, what per-share amount would be paid to preferred stockholders?

Problem 20.3B
Objective 20-6

▶ **Issuing stock at par for cash and noncash assets.**

Laura Cisneros and Kay Osborn are equal partners in Creative Toys Nook. Cisneros and Osborn have decided to form Toy Chest Corporation to take over the operation of Creative Toys Nook on December 31, 20X1. The corporation is authorized to issue 8,000 shares of no-par-value common stock with a stated value of $25 per share and 2,000 shares of $50 par-value, 12 percent preferred stock that is noncumulative and nonparticipating. Certain assets are revalued so that the accounts will reflect current values. Cisneros and Osborn will each receive 250 shares of Toy Chest Corporation preferred stock at par value ($50) and sufficient no-par-value shares of common stock at stated value ($25) to cover the partners' adjusted net investment in the partnership.

The trial balance shown below was prepared after the firm's accounting records were closed at the end of its fiscal year on December 31, 20X1, and the assets were revalued as agreed on.

INSTRUCTIONS

1. In the corporation's general journal, record a memorandum entry describing its formation on December 31, 20X1.
2. Make general journal entries as of December 31 to show the takeover of the assets and liabilities of the partnership and the issuance of stock in payment to Laura Cisneros and Kay Osborn. Use the same account names that the partnership used for assets and liabilities. Also use the following new account titles: **Common Stock** and **Preferred Stock**.

Creative Toys Nook
Adjusted Trial Balance
December 31, 20X1

ACCOUNT NAME	DEBIT	CREDIT
Cash	6 960 00	
Accounts Receivable	26 540 00	
Allowance for Doubtful Accounts		650 00
Merchandise Inventory	102 000 00	
Furniture and Equipment	45 800 00	
Accumulated Depreciation—Equipment		2 200 00
Accounts Payable		30 450 00
Laura Cisneros, Capital		74 000 00
Kay Osborn, Capital		74 000 00
Totals	181 300 00	181 300 00

Analyze: After the corporation's formation, what is the fundamental accounting equation for Toy Chest Corporation?

Issuing stock at par for cash and noncash assets, issuing stock at a premium, and preparing corporate balance sheet.

◀ **Problem 20.4B**
Objectives 20-6, 20-7, 20-9

Travel Inc., a new corporation, took over the assets and liabilities of Worldwide Travel Agency, owned by Roma James, on June 1, 20X1. The assets and liabilities assumed, after appropriate revaluation by Worldwide Travel Agency, are as follows (amounts in parentheses are credits; others are debits):

Cash	$ 50,000
Accounts Receivable	130,000
Allowance for Doubtful Accounts	(25,000)
Merchandise Inventory	95,000
Accounts Payable	(35,000)
Accrued Expenses Payable	(10,000)

The corporation is authorized to issue 100,000 shares of no-par-value common stock with a stated value of $10 per share and 20,000 shares of $100 par-value preferred stock. The preferred stock bears a dividend of $5 per share per year. The transactions entered into at the time the corporation was formed follow.

INSTRUCTIONS

1. Prepare the general journal entries to record the transactions.
2. Prepare the opening balance sheet as of June 1, 20X1, for Travel Inc.

DATE		TRANSACTIONS
June	1	The corporation issued to Roma James common stock with a stated value equal to her net equity in the sole proprietorship business, and the corporation took over James's assets and liabilities.
	1	Issued 2,000 shares of common stock to Ned Turner for $20,000 cash.
	1	Issued 2,000 shares of preferred stock to Charles Suz. He paid $100,000 in cash for the stock.

Analyze: What is the amount of total stockholders' equity at end of day June 1, 20X1?

Problem 20.5B
Objectives 20-6, 20-7, 20-9, 20-11

Issuing stock at par, issuing stock at a premium, preparing Stockholders' Equity section of balance sheet, and recording stock subscriptions.

PSquared Inc. was organized on January 2, 20X1, to operate a chain of pet supply stores. The firm is authorized to issue 50,000 shares of $10 par-value common stock and 18,000 shares of $50 par-value, 8 percent preferred stock. The preferred stock is noncumulative and nonparticipating. Selected transactions that took place during January 20X1 are given below.

INSTRUCTIONS

1. Set up the following general ledger accounts:

101	Cash		305	Paid-in Capital in Excess of Par Value—Common
114	Subscriptions Receivable—Common Stock		311	Preferred Stock
115	Subscriptions Receivable—Preferred Stock		312	Preferred Stock Subscribed
301	Common Stock		315	Paid-in Capital in Excess of Par Value—Preferred
302	Common Stock Subscribed			

   Record the transactions listed below in general journal form and post them to the general ledger accounts.

2. Prepare the Stockholders' Equity section of a balance sheet for PSquared Inc. as of January 31, 20X1.

DATE		TRANSACTIONS
Jan.	2	The corporation received its corporate charter. (Make a memorandum entry.)
	3	Issued 3,000 shares of common stock for cash at $10 per share to Alice Young.
	3	Issued 1,500 shares of preferred stock for cash at $50 per share to Marcia Greene.
	10	Issued 200 shares of common stock for cash at $14 per share to Mark Merki.
	12	Received a subscription for 500 shares of common stock at $12 per share from Nora Barnett, payable in two installments due in 5 and 15 days.
	14	Received a subscription for 500 shares of preferred stock at $54 per share from Sun Wu, payable in two installments due in 10 and 20 days.
	17	Received payment of a stock subscription installment due from Nora Barnett (one-half of purchase price—see January 12 transaction).
	24	Received payment of a stock subscription installment due from Sun Wu (one-half of purchase price—see January 14 transaction).
	27	Received the balance due from Nora Barnett; issued the stock.

Analyze: What percentage of authorized common stock has been issued at January 27, 20X1?

Critical Thinking Problem 20.1

Understanding Stockholders' Equity

Just after its formation on September 1, 20X1, the ledger accounts of Ducks, Inc., contained the following balances:

Accrued Expenses Payable	$ 4,000
Accounts Payable	7,000
Accounts Receivable	53,000
Allowance for Doubtful Accounts	4,000
Building	300,000
Cash	32,000
Common Stock ($20 par)	400,000
Common Stock Subscribed	40,000
Furniture and Fixtures	55,000
Merchandise Inventory	79,000
Notes Payable—Short Term	5,000
Paid-in Capital in Excess of Par Value—Common	44,000
Paid-in Capital in Excess of Par Value—Preferred	5,000
Preferred Stock (10%, $50 par)	50,000
Preferred Stock Subscribed (10%, $50 par)	25,000
Subscriptions Receivable—Common Stock	40,000
Subscriptions Receivable—Preferred Stock	25,000

The corporation is authorized to issue 100,000 shares of $20 par-value common stock and 20,000 shares of 10 percent, $50 par-value preferred stock (noncumulative and nonparticipating).

INSTRUCTIONS

1. Answer the following questions:
   a. How many shares of common stock are outstanding?
   b. How many shares of common stock are subscribed?
   c. How many shares of preferred stock are outstanding?
   d. How many shares of preferred stock are subscribed?
   e. At what average price has common stock been subscribed or issued?
   f. Assume that no dividends are paid in the first year of the corporation's existence. What are the rights of the preferred stockholders?
   g. Assuming that all of the **Paid-in Capital in Excess of Par Value—Common** was applicable to the shares of common stock that have been subscribed but not yet issued, what was the subscription price per share of the common stock subscribed?

2. Prepare a classified balance sheet for the corporation just after its formation on September 1, 20X1.

Analyze: What is the current ratio for the corporation at September 1, 20X1?

Critical Thinking Problem 20.2

Interpreting the Balance Sheet

The Stockholders' Equity section of the FT Company balance sheet at the close of the current year follows:

Stockholders' Equity

Preferred Stock (6%, $100 par value, 100,000 shares authorized)	
At Par Value (60,000 shares issued)	$ 6,000,000
Paid-in Capital in Excess of Par Value	120,000
Common Stock (no-par value, stated value of $1; 2,000,000 shares authorized)	
At Stated Value	1,500,000
Paid-in Capital in Excess of Stated Value	3,000,000
Retained Earnings	5,600,000
Total Stockholders' Equity	$16,220,000

1. What is the amount of the annual dividend on the preferred stock? Per share? In total?
2. How many shares of common stock have been issued?
3. What was the average price paid by the stockholders for the preferred stock?
4. What was the average price paid by the stockholders for the common stock?
5. How many shares of common stock are currently outstanding (held by stockholders)?
6. If total dividends of $2,550,000 were paid to stockholders in the current year, how much was paid to the common stockholders in total? Per share? Assume that no preferred dividends are in arrears.

BUSINESS CONNECTIONS

Managerial FOCUS

Forming a Corporation

1. Anna Claire and Baker are establishing a new restaurant and discussing whether to organize as a partnership or a corporation. What are some of the most important characteristics of these two types of organizations that they should weigh in making the decision?
2. Anna Claire and Baker are considering organizing as a subchapter S corporation. What are the advantages and disadvantages they should consider?
3. Anna Claire and Baker are considering whether to issue preferred stock or to borrow funds on a long-term basis for additional cash for the corporation. Suggest some factors they should consider. How can they make the preferred stock more attractive to investors?
4. A group of individuals is planning to form a corporation. Explain in general terms the usual steps necessary to do this.
5. Why should the management of a corporation be concerned about the realistic valuation of assets transferred to the firm?

Internal Control and FRAUD PREVENTION

Stock Option

Vice president Eli Gold consults the board of directors in regard to the issuance of stock and negotiates an initial public offering price per share. As a bonus at the end of each fiscal year, he receives stock options. Within weeks of negotiating the highest price possible, Gold sells his stock. Is this an ethical action?

Balance Sheet

The information below was compiled from The Home Depot, Inc., balance sheet and footnotes in the 2018 Form 10-K *(for the fiscal year ended February 3, 2019).* Use it to answer the following questions:

(in millions)	February 3, 2019	January 28, 2018
Stockholders' Equity		
Common stock, par value $0.05; authorized: 10,000 shares; issued: 1,782 shares at February 3, 2019 and 1,780 shares at January 28, 2018; outstanding: 1,105 shares at February 3, 2019 and 1,158 shares at January 28, 2018.	89	89

Financial Statement ANALYSIS

Home Depot

Analyze:

1. What percentage of common stock authorized has been issued at February 3, 2019?
2. What journal entry was made on the books of The Home Depot, Inc., when the company authorized the 10 billion shares?
3. If all of the common stock that The Home Depot, Inc., authorized was issued at par, how much additional capital would be raised?

Analyze Online: Log on to The Home Depot, Inc., website at www.homedepot.com. Locate the most recent annual report or SEC Form 10-K.

4. How many shares of common stock have been issued?
5. Have any shares of preferred stock been authorized? If so, how many?
6. What is the current market price for a share of The Home Depot, Inc., stock?

Corporation Details

Divide into teams of three or four students to decide on a new corporation. Determine a name and a product or service this corporation will provide. Develop a stock certificate for your corporation. How many shares will you ask to be authorized by the state? What will be the par value? Will these shares be preferred, common, or both? How much will you accept as a price per share for the initial public offering (IPO)?

TEAMWORK

Answers to Comprehensive Self Review

1. As Stockholders' Equity.
2. What stock is being sold at in the market. Sometimes market value is defined as what buyers are willing to pay for the shares.
3. It is a control account for stock subscribed, containing an account receivable from each subscriber. The balance of this account agrees with *Subscriptions Receivable* on the balance sheet.
4. The registrar accounts for all stock issued by the corporation, for transfers of shares, for cancellation of shares, and for handling certificates or other records of stock issued.
5. To convert the preferred shares into common shares under predetermined conditions and exchange rates.
6. Callable preferred stock is preferred stock that can be called and retired at the option of the corporation within specified terms, including price and time.
7. As the name suggests, it frees the partners from some of the liability of a partner. Primarily, it provides relief from liability for actions of other partners but holds the partner liable for his or her own actions and those of employees supervised by that partner.
8. The preemptive right of the shareholder is to be able to purchase a proportionate part of new shares issued by the corporation.

Corporate Earnings and Capital Transactions

Chapter 21

Ken Wolter/Shutterstock

urbn.com

One of today's most chic retailers appealing to the younger set is Urban Outfitters. Born from the dreams of a couple of college entrepreneurs, Dick Hayne and Scott Belair, this enterprise originated in a small, secondhand retail store located near the University of Pennsylvania.

This corporation operates fundamentally two segments—retail and wholesale segments. Four brands are housed in the retail segment: Urban Outfitters, Anthropologie (including Anthropologie, Bhldn, and Terrain), Free People, and Vetri Family restaurant chain. The common thread of these enterprises is to offer a totally unique retail shopping/dining experience! Always wanting to be on the leading edge, URBN began in the late 1990s actively investing in and pursuing the e-commerce platform for sales with great results.

URBN had its initial public offering in 1993. For the fiscal year ended January 31, 2018, it had net sales of approximately $3.6 billion. Net income of $108 million yielded a net income per share of common stock of $0.97.

thinking critically

What financial and nonfinancial factors would be important in deciding whether to purchase stock in a company that is going public?

LEARNING OBJECTIVES

21-1 Estimate the federal corporate income tax and prepare related journal entries.
21-2 Complete a worksheet for a corporation.
21-3 Record corporate adjusting and closing entries.
21-4 Prepare an income statement for a corporation.
21-5 Record the declaration and payment of cash dividends.
21-6 Record the declaration and issuance of stock dividends.
21-7 Record stock splits.
21-8 Record appropriations of retained earnings.
21-9 Record a corporation's receipt of donated assets.
21-10 Record treasury stock transactions.
21-11 Prepare financial statements for a corporation.
21-12 Define the accounting terms new to this chapter.

NEW TERMS

appropriation of retained earnings
book value (stock)
Common Stock Dividend Distributable account
declaration date
deferred income taxes
donated capital
paid-in capital
payment date
record date
retained earnings
statement of retained earnings
statement of stockholders' equity
stock dividend
stock split
stockholders of record
treasury stock

Section 1

SECTION OBJECTIVES	TERM TO LEARN
>> 21-1 Estimate the federal corporate income tax and prepare related journal entries. **WHY IT'S IMPORTANT** Corporations are required to pay federal, state, and local income taxes.	deferred income taxes
>> 21-2 Complete a worksheet for a corporation. **WHY IT'S IMPORTANT** The worksheet is a tool used to prepare financial statements.	
>> 21-3 Record corporate adjusting and closing entries. **WHY IT'S IMPORTANT** Adjusting and closing entries ensure that revenues are matched with expenses and prepare temporary accounts for the next period.	
>> 21-4 Prepare an income statement for a corporation. **WHY IT'S IMPORTANT** Corporations must report accurate financial results.	

Accounting for Corporate Earnings

Chapter 21 will continue Chapter 20's focus on transactions that are unique to the corporate form. We will look at transactions that affect the statement of retained earnings and the Stockholders' Equity section of the balance sheet.

Corporate Income Tax

One of the disadvantages of the corporate form of business is that corporations must pay income taxes on their profits. Taxable income can be calculated differently for federal, state, and local purposes; however, the procedures to record these taxes are identical. For the sake of simplicity, we will cover federal taxes only and assume that taxable income and financial reporting income are identical. In reality, the two are often different because of special tax provisions.

>> **21-1 OBJECTIVE**
Estimate the federal corporate income tax and prepare related journal entries.

Federal Income Tax Rates

In 2017, Congress enacted the most dramatic change in the federal taxation of corporations in U.S. history, reducing the federal corporate rate of tax on taxable income to a flat rate of 21%. The long history of marginal rates is eliminated, making calculation of federal income tax for corporations relatively simple.

Quarterly Tax Estimates

Corporations estimate their income taxes for the year and make estimated tax payments four times during the year. To avoid a possible penalty, the tax deposits at the end of the year should be equal to or higher than the tax liability for the year. For calendar-year corporations, the estimated tax payments are due on April 15, June 15, September 15, and December 15. To record an estimated tax payment, debit **Income Tax Expense** and credit **Cash.**

Just4U, Inc., estimated its tax liability for 20X1 to be $20,000. During the year, it made four tax deposits of $5,000 ($20,000 ÷ 4). The journal entry to record the first deposit (April 15) is as follows:

	20X1				
	Apr.	15	Income Tax Expense	5 000 00	
			Cash		5 000 00
			Quarterly income tax deposit		

Each quarterly deposit would have a similar journal entry to record the payment. At the end of the year, the **Income Tax Expense** account has a balance of $20,000.

Year-End Adjustment of Tax Liability

At the end of the year, the tentative tax expense for the year is computed. Usually there is a difference between the tentative tax expense and the tax deposits made during the year. An adjustment is recorded to reconcile the difference.

At the end of 20X1, Just4U, Inc., computed its tentative tax expense as $23,100. The corporation had underpaid its taxes by $3,100:

Tax liability for the year	$23,100
Quarterly payments	20,000
Additional tax due	$ 3,100

recall

S Corporations
S corporations do not pay federal taxes on corporate profits. Instead, corporate income is passed through and taxed on the shareholders' individual tax returns.

The amount owed is recorded in the **Income Tax Payable** account, a liability:

	20X1		Adjusting Entries		
	Dec.	31	Income Tax Expense	3 100 00	
			Income Tax Payable		3 100 00
			Estimate of additional tax due		

Let's consider another possibility. Suppose that Just4U, Inc., computed its tentative tax expense as $19,600. In this case, the corporation would have overpaid its taxes by $400:

Tax liability for the year	$19,600
Quarterly payments	20,000
Overpaid tax	$ (400)

The overpayment would be recorded in a receivable account as follows:

	20X1				
	Dec.	31	Income Tax Refund Receivable	400 00	
			Income Tax Expense		400 00
			Estimate of tax overpayment		

Note that the adjustment is made at the time the worksheet is completed and the financial statements are prepared. Because the tax return is complex and differences exist between *taxable income* and *financial income*, this computation can also be described as an estimate. The tentative tax expense computed at the end of the year usually differs from the actual tax expense shown on the tax return. The difference is recorded in the **Income Tax Expense** account.

When the tax return was prepared, the actual tax for the year was $24,000. Just4U, Inc., sent a check for $4,000 to the Internal Revenue Service for the difference between the tax for the year and the tax deposits ($24,000 − $20,000):

20X2				
Mar. 15	Income Tax Payable		3 100 00	
	Income Tax Expense		900 00	
	Cash			4 000 00
	Pay balance of federal income tax			

This entry reduces to zero the **Income Tax Payable** account. It debits **Income Tax Expense** and records the check sent to the Internal Revenue Service. Notice that the difference between the tentative tax expense and the actual tax expense, $900, is recorded in the year following the tax year. This violates the matching principle. It does not match income tax expense to taxable income. However, these differences are usually minor and do not result in a material misstatement of income.

Reporting Income Tax Expense on the Income Statement

There are two ways to show income tax expense on the income statement:

1. As a deduction at the bottom of the income statement, after Net Income before Income Tax. To see this presentation, refer to Figure 21.3.
2. As an operating expense, to emphasize that taxes represent a cost of doing business.

Deferred Income Taxes

Usually net income reported on the financial statements does not match taxable income reported on the tax return because tax laws do not always follow generally accepted accounting principles.

- Income can be included in taxable income this year and appear on the financial statements in later years, or vice versa.
- Income can be included on the financial statements but never appear in taxable income.
- Expenses can be included in taxable income this year and appear on the financial statements in later years, or vice versa.
- Expenses can be included on the financial statements and never be deducted from taxable income.

Accountants use the concept of deferred income taxes to match income tax on the financial statements to the related net income.

Deferred income taxes represent the amount of taxes that will be payable (or beneficial) in the future as a result of the difference between taxable income and income for financial statement purposes in the current and past years. Let's use depreciation to illustrate the concept.

Suppose that this year tax depreciation (MACRS) is higher than depreciation on the financial statements (straight-line). In the future, then, tax depreciation should be less than depreciation on the financial statements. As a result, in the future, when taxable income is higher because depreciation is lower, the company will owe more taxes than would be paid on the net income reported for financial accounting purposes. Those future taxes really apply to the income reported on the financial statement in prior years.

Each year, the accountant estimates the amount of future taxes that will be paid as a result of the MACRS depreciation taken in this and prior years. An adjustment for the future taxes is made to **Tax Expense** and to the liability account **Deferred Income Tax Liability**.

Sometimes the cumulative taxable income is higher than that reported on the financial statements. This gives rise to a *deferred tax asset* because some of the taxes that have been paid apply to future financial statement income. Deferred taxes are complex and are not covered in this text. This book assumes that income on the income statement and on the tax return is the same. Therefore, the deferred tax adjustment is not necessary.

Completing the Corporate Worksheet

The worksheets for a corporation and a sole proprietorship are almost identical. The major difference is the income tax adjustment. Figure 21.1 shows the worksheet for Just4U, Inc., for 20X1. This worksheet omits the Adjusted Trial Balance columns. It is common for the experienced accountant to enter the adjusted amounts directly in the Income Statement and Balance Sheet sections. However, when the Adjusted Trial Balance section is omitted, errors in adding and subtracting adjustments are more difficult to detect.

Study the worksheet carefully as you follow the steps to complete the worksheet for Just4U, Inc.:

Step 1: *Enter the trial balance in the Trial Balance section.* To simplify the example, control accounts for general expenses and selling expenses are used instead of individual expense accounts. There are a few unfamiliar accounts on the worksheet; they will be explained later.

Step 2: *Enter the adjustments (except the adjustment to income tax expense) in the Adjustments section of the worksheet.*

Step 3: *Extend the balances of all income and expense amounts (except income tax expense) to the Income Statement section of the worksheet.* Total the Debit and Credit columns of the Income Statement section. Write the totals on a separate paper. The difference between the totals represents the income or loss before income taxes. At this point, the Income Statement columns of the worksheet contain the following information:

>> 21-2 OBJECTIVE
Complete a worksheet for a corporation.

	Income Statement	
	Debit	Credit
Sales		$1,300,000
Purchases	$850,000	
Selling Expenses	200,000	
General and Administrative Expenses	190,000	
Income Summary	200,000	250,000
Totals	$1,440,000	$1,550,000

The difference between the Credit and Debit column totals is $110,000 ($1,550,000 − $1,440,000). This is income before income tax (commonly referred to as taxable income).

Step 4: *Compute income tax based on income before tax.* Assume there is no difference between financial and taxable income. Using the 21% corporate tax rate, the federal income tax is $110,000 × .21 = $23,100.

Just4U, Inc., made tax deposits of $20,000. The difference between the tax deposits and the total tax is $3,100 ($23,100 − $20,000). An adjustment is made to debit **Income Tax Expense** for $3,100 and to credit **Income Tax Payable** for $3,100.

Step 5: *Total the columns in the Adjustments section.* Extend the balance of **Income Tax Expense** to the Debit column of the Income Statement section of the worksheet.

Step 6: *Total the Debit and Credit columns of the Income Statement section.* The difference between the totals is net income after tax.

Step 7: *Extend the adjusted balances of the asset, liability, and stockholders' equity accounts to the Balance Sheet columns.* Enter net income after income tax to the Credit column of the Balance Sheet section. Complete the worksheet in the usual manner.

recall
Worksheet
Asset, liability, and equity accounts are extended to the Balance Sheet columns. Revenue and expense accounts are extended to the Income Statement columns.

FIGURE 21.1 A Completed, Eight-Column Worksheet

Just4U, Inc
Worksheet
Year Ended December 31, 20X1

#	ACCOUNT NAME	TRIAL BALANCE DEBIT	TRIAL BALANCE CREDIT	ADJUSTMENTS DEBIT	ADJUSTMENTS CREDIT
1	Cash	70,750.00			
2	Accounts Receivable	60,000.00			
3	Allowance for Doubtful Accounts		2,500.00		(c) 900.00
4	Merchandise Inventory	200,000.00		(b) 250,000.00	(a) 200,000.00
5	Prepaid Insurance	5,000.00			(d) 2,500.00
6	Land	92,000.00			
7	Buildings	120,000.00			
8	Accumulated Depreciation—Building		4,000.00		(e) 4,000.00
9	Equipment and Fixtures	72,000.00			
10	Accumulated Depreciation—Equipment and Fixtures		6,000.00		(f) 6,000.00
11	Accounts Payable		37,200.00		
12	Dividends Payable—Preferred		10,000.00		
13	Dividends Payable—Common		16,000.00		
14	Accrued Expenses Payable				(g) 3,500.00
15	Income Tax Payable				(h) 3,100.00
16	Preferred Stock—10%, $100 Par		200,000.00		
17	Paid-in Cap. in Excess of Par—Preferred		12,000.00		
18	Common Stock, $50 Par		200,000.00		
19	Paid-in Cap. in Excess of Par—Common		4,400.00		
20	Common Stock Dividend Distributable		20,000.00		
21	Retained Earnings		50,750.00		
22	Sales		1,300,000.00		
23	Purchases	850,000.00			
24	Selling Expenses (control)	195,600.00		(c) 900.00	
25				(d) 500.00	
26				(e) 1,000.00	
27				(f) 2,000.00	
28	General and Admin. Expenses (control)	177,500.00		(d) 2,000.00	
29				(e) 3,000.00	
30				(f) 4,000.00	
31				(g) 3,500.00	
32	Income Tax Expense	20,000.00		(h) 3,100.00	
33	Income Summary			(a) 200,000.00	(b) 250,000.00
34	Totals	1,862,850.00	1,862,850.00	470,000.00	470,000.00
35	Net Income after Income Tax Expense				

INCOME STATEMENT		BALANCE SHEET		
DEBIT	CREDIT	DEBIT	CREDIT	
		70 750 00		1
		60 000 00		2
			3 400 00	3
		250 000 00		4
		2 500 00		5
		92 000 00		6
		120 000 00		7
			8 000 00	8
		72 000 00		9
			12 000 00	10
			37 200 00	11
			10 000 00	12
			16 000 00	13
			3 500 00	14
			3 100 00	15
			200 000 00	16
			12 000 00	17
			200 000 00	18
			4 400 00	19
			20 000 00	20
			50 750 00	21
	1,300 000 00			22
850 000 00				23
200 000 00				24
				25
				26
				27
190 000 00				28
				29
				30
				31
23 100 00				32
200 000 00	250 000 00			33
1,463 100 00	1,550 000 00		580 350 00	34
86 900 00			86 900 00	35
1,550 000 00	1,550 000 00	667 250 00	667 250 00	36

21-3 OBJECTIVE
Record corporate adjusting and closing entries.

Adjusting and Closing Entries

The closing process for a corporation is similar to that of a sole proprietorship. First close revenue to *Income Summary.* Then close expenses to *Income Summary.* Finally, close *Income Summary* (net income or net loss) to *Retained Earnings.* The *Retained Earnings* account accumulates the profits and losses of the business.

Figure 21.2 shows the adjusting and closing entries for Just4U, Inc. Compare the journal entries to the worksheet to see how the journal entries are prepared.

21-4 OBJECTIVE
Prepare an income statement for a corporation.

The Corporate Income Statement

After the worksheet is complete, the financial statements are prepared. The income statements of a sole proprietorship and a corporation are similar. The major difference is income taxes. The corporate income statement contains a deduction for income tax expense.

FIGURE 21.2

Adjusting and Closing Entries

GENERAL JOURNAL — PAGE 38

DATE	DESCRIPTION	POST. REF.	DEBIT	CREDIT
20X1				
	Adjusting Entries			
	(Entry a)			
Dec. 31	Income Summary		200 000 00	
	Merchandise Inventory			200 000 00
	(Entry b)			
31	Merchandise Inventory		250 000 00	
	Income Summary			250 000 00
	(Entry c)			
31	Selling Expenses (control)		900 00	
	Allowance for Doubtful Accounts			900 00
	(Entry d)			
31	Selling Expenses (control)		500 00	
	General and Admin. Expenses (control)		2 000 00	
	Prepaid Insurance			2 500 00
	(Entry e)			
31	Selling Expenses (control)		1 000 00	
	General and Admin. Expenses (control)		3 000 00	
	Accumulated Depreciation—Buildings			4 000 00
	(Entry f)			
31	Selling Expenses (control)		2 000 00	
	General and Admin. Expenses (control)		4 000 00	
	Accum. Depr.—Equip. and Fixtures			6 000 00
	(Entry g)			
31	General and Admin. Expenses (control)		3 500 00	
	Accrued Expenses Payable			3 500 00
	(Entry h)			
31	Income Tax Expense		3 100 00	
	Income Tax Payable			3 100 00

(continued)

FIGURE 21.2 (continued)

		GENERAL JOURNAL			PAGE 39	
	DATE	DESCRIPTION	POST. REF.	DEBIT	CREDIT	
1	20X1					1
2		Closing Entries				2
3	Dec. 31	Sales		1,300 0 0 0 00		3
4		Income Summary			1,300 0 0 0 00	4
5						5
6	31	Income Summary		1,263 1 0 0 00		6
7		Purchases			850 0 0 0 00	7
8		Selling Expenses (control)			200 0 0 0 00	8
9		Gen. and Admin. Expenses (control)			190 0 0 0 00	9
10		Income Tax Expense			23 1 0 0 00	10
11						11
12	31	Income Summary		86 9 0 0 00		12
13		Retained Earnings			86 9 0 0 00	13
14		Close Income Summary				14

FIGURE 21.3

Corporate Income Statement

Just4U, Inc.
Income Statement
Year Ended December 31, 20X1

Sales		1,300 0 0 0 00
Cost of Goods Sold		
Inventory, January 1, 20X1	200 0 0 0 00	
Purchases	850 0 0 0 00	
Goods Available for Sale	1,050 0 0 0 00	
Less Inventory, December 31, 20X1	250 0 0 0 00	
Costs of Goods Sold		800 0 0 0 00
Gross Profit on Sales		500 0 0 0 00
Expenses		
Selling Expenses	200 0 0 0 00	
General and Administrative Expenses	190 0 0 0 00	390 0 0 0 00
Net Income before Income Tax		110 0 0 0 00
Income Tax Expense		23 1 0 0 00
Net Income after Income Tax		86 9 0 0 00

Figure 21.3 shows the income statement for Just4U, Inc., for 20X1. It is prepared from the information on the worksheet in Figure 21.1. Note that income tax expense is deducted from the Net Income before Income Tax line to arrive at Net Income after Income Tax.

Variations in Income Statement Presentation

Corporations use a variety of formats for the income statement. Some common variations are summarized as follows:

- Some corporations include cost of goods sold with the operating expenses. They do not show gross profit on sales. This text uses the traditional income statement with a separate Gross Profit section.

- Some corporations show income tax expense as an operating expense rather than as a deduction from net income before income tax. This presentation can be used to emphasize that income taxes are a cost of doing business like any other expense.

Section 1 Review

1. Where does the corporate income tax appear in the income statement?
   a. below Net Income before Income Tax
   b. added to Cost of Goods Sold section
   c. last line on the Income Statement
   d. not required to be displayed/disclosed

2. At what point in preparing the corporate end-of-year worksheet does the accountant enter the adjustment for income taxes?
   a. at the beginning preparation
   b. ignore the adjustment in preparation
   c. at the beginning of the last month of the fiscal year
   d. near the end of preparation

3. What does the account *Retained Earnings* represent?
   a. the amount of cash retained by the business
   b. the amount of net earnings that have not been distributed as dividends
   c. the original investment in the business by stockholders
   d. the amount of income subject to corporate taxation

4. How do the adjusting entries for the beginning and ending inventories for a corporation differ, if at all, from those for a sole proprietorship?
   a. There is no difference.
   b. A sole proprietorship does not have this adjusting entry.
   c. Corporations do not have this adjusting entry.
   d. The sole proprietorship adjusting entry is the reverse of the corporate entry.

5. Name some reasons why the taxable income of a corporation is likely not to be the same as its financial statement net income.
   a. Depreciation Expense on the tax return is typically greater than Depreciation Expense for financial statements.
   b. Accounts Payable are usually different.
   c. Net assets are usually larger on the tax return.
   d. Sales amounts differ because of Internet sales.

Section 2

SECTION OBJECTIVES	TERMS TO LEARN
>> 21-5 Record the declaration and payment of cash dividends. **WHY IT'S IMPORTANT** Corporate profits are distributed to stockholders through cash dividends. >> 21-6 Record the declaration and issuance of stock dividends. **WHY IT'S IMPORTANT** Corporations may declare and issue stock dividends to reward their shareholders. >> 21-7 Record stock splits. **WHY IT'S IMPORTANT** Corporations use stock splits to lower market share prices in an effort to attract new investors. >> 21-8 Record appropriations of retained earnings. **WHY IT'S IMPORTANT** One way to identify specific future transactions and related cash requirements is by appropriating retained earnings.	appropriation of retained earnings book value (stock) *Common Stock Dividend Distributable* account declaration date paid-in capital payment date record date retained earnings stock dividend stock split stockholders of record

Accounting for Retained Earnings

The fundamental accounting equation for corporations can be restated as Assets = Liabilities + (Paid-in Capital + Retained Earnings).

Paid-in capital (or contributed capital) represents the amount of capital acquired from capital stock transactions.

Retained earnings represents the cumulative profits and losses of the corporation not distributed as dividends. Dividends reduce retained earnings.

Retained Earnings

There are legal and financial distinctions between paid-in capital and retained earnings. This is why profits and losses are accumulated in retained earnings, separate from the capital paid in by the stockholders.

It is important to remember that retained earnings does not represent a cash fund. Retained earnings are reinvested in inventory, plant and equipment, and various other types of assets. A corporation can have a large cash balance but no retained earnings. Conversely, it can have a large balance in the *Retained Earnings* account but no cash.

Cash Dividends

Stockholders receive a share of the profits of the corporation through cash dividends. Most corporations pay dividends quarterly. In some corporations, the board of directors establishes a policy of making regular cash dividends at the same or an increasing amount. A regular dividend policy tends to make a stock more attractive to investors and may help avoid sharp fluctuations in the stock's market price. Many corporations, however, retain their earnings to finance growth and do not pay cash dividends. This is especially true in the first several years of a corporation's existence.

Dividend Policy Before declaring a dividend, the board of directors considers two issues: legality and financial feasibility.

1. *Legality.* State laws differ, but in general the corporation must have retained earnings in order to declare dividends. These laws are intended to protect the corporation's creditors. The restriction prevents an *impairment of capital.* Capital is impaired when dividends are paid that reduce total stockholders' equity to less than the paid-in capital accounts, which may result from paying excessive dividends.
2. *Financial Feasibility.* The corporation must have the cash to pay the dividend. The board of directors does not declare dividends that lead to a cash shortage or other financial difficulties, even though there may be a large balance in Retained Earnings.

>> **21-5 OBJECTIVE**
Record the declaration and payment of cash dividends.

Dates Relevant to Dividends Three dates are involved in declaring and paying dividends:

- The **declaration date** is the date on which the board of directors declares the dividend. The dividend declaration is recorded in the corporation's minute book. Once a dividend is declared, the firm has a liability to the stockholders for the amount of the declared dividend.
- The **record date** is the date used to determine who will receive the dividend. The capital stock ledger is used to prepare a list of the **stockholders of record,** that is, the stockholders who will receive the declared dividend. This does not require a journal entry.
- The **payment date** is the date on which the dividend is paid.

important!

Journal Entries for Dividends

A journal entry is recorded on the date of declaration and the date of payment. A journal entry is not made on the date of record.

Declaration of a Cash Dividend Just4U's board of directors met on November 28, 20X1, and declared cash dividends of $5 per share on preferred stock and $4 per share on common stock. The dividends are payable on January 15 to stockholders of record on December 31. On the declaration date, the firm had outstanding 2,000 shares of preferred stock and 4,000 shares of common stock. The dividend declaration is recorded as shown below:

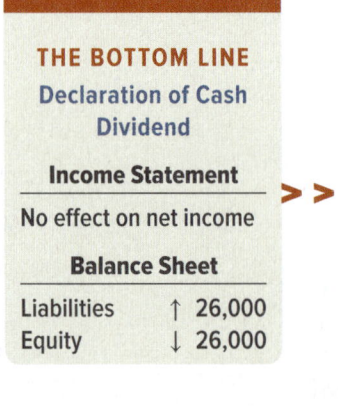

THE BOTTOM LINE

Declaration of Cash Dividend

Income Statement
No effect on net income

Balance Sheet
Liabilities ↑ 26,000
Equity ↓ 26,000

20X1				
Nov. 28	Retained Earnings		10 000 00	
	Dividends Payable—Preferred			10 000 00
	Dividend declaration of $5			
	per share on 2,000 shares,			
	payable Jan. 15 to holders			
	of record Dec. 31			
28	Retained Earnings		16 000 00	
	Dividends Payable—Common			16 000 00
	Dividend declaration of $4			
	per share on 4,000 shares,			
	payable on Jan. 15 to			
	holders of record Dec. 31			

Dividends payable appear on the balance sheet as a current liability. An example is shown in the balance sheet presented later in this chapter (Figure 21.5).

Payment of a Cash Dividend The capital stock ledger is used to prepare a list of the stockholders and the number of shares owned on the record date. The list is used to determine the dividend due each shareholder. On January 15, 20X2, the payment date, the dividend checks are issued to the stockholders on the list. The payment is recorded as follows:

	20X2					
1	20X2					1
2	Jan.	15	Dividends Payable—Preferred	10 000 00		2
3			Dividends Payable—Common	16 000 00		3
4			Cash		26 000 00	4
5			Payment of cash dividends			5

Stock Dividends

A corporation may have retained earnings but be short of cash and unable to pay a cash dividend. Or the board of directors may want to transfer part of retained earnings to a paid-in capital account. In these cases, the board of directors may declare a stock dividend. A **stock dividend** is a distribution of the corporation's own stock on a pro rata basis that results in conversion of a portion of the firm's retained earnings to permanent capital.

Suppose that, on November 30, 20X1, the board of directors of Just4U, Inc., declared a stock dividend payable the following January 20 to common stockholders of record on December 28. The stock dividend is for one new share of common stock for each 10 shares held. On the declaration date, there were 4,000 shares outstanding, so 400 (4,000 ÷ 10) additional shares will be issued.

When a stock dividend is declared, the total amount charged to the *Retained Earnings* account is the estimated fair value of the shares to be issued. Assume that each share of Just4u, Inc.'s stock is expected to have a fair value of $57. A total of $22,800 (400 shares × $57 expected fair value) is debited to *Retained Earnings*. The par value of the shares, $20,000 (400 shares × $50 par), is credited to **Common Stock Dividend Distributable,** an equity account used to record par or stated value of shares to be issued as the result of the declaration of a stock dividend. The excess of the fair value over the par value, $2,800 ($22,800 − $20,000), is credited to *Paid-in Capital in Excess of Par Value—Common Stock* or to *Paid-in Capital from Common Stock Dividends.* Let's see how the declaration of a stock dividend is recorded:

	20X1					
1	20X1					1
2	Nov.	30	Retained Earnings	22 800 00		2
3			Common Stock Dividend Distributable		20 000 00	3
4			Paid-in Capital in Excess of Par			4
5			Value—Common Stock		2 800 00	5
6			Declaration of 10% stock dividend,			6
7			distributable on Jan. 20 to holders			7
8			of record on Dec. 28			8

The **Common Stock Dividend Distributable** account appears on the balance sheet in the Stockholders' Equity section as a part of paid-in capital. One possible balance sheet presentation follows:

Common Stock ($50 par value, 10,000 shares authorized)	
Issued and outstanding, 4,000 shares	$200,000
Distributable as stock dividend, 400 shares	20,000
Paid-in Capital in Excess of Par	2,800
	$222,800

On December 28, a list is made of the stockholders' names, number of shares owned, and number of new shares to issue. For example, Sandra Fee owns 400 shares of common stock. She will receive 40 (400 ÷ 10) new shares as a stock dividend. On January 20, the 400 shares are distributed. This issuance of stock is recorded as follows:

	20X2					
1	20X2					1
2	Jan.	20	Common Stock Dividend Distributable	20 000 00		2
3			Common Stock		20 000 00	3
4			Distribution of stock dividend			4

<< THE BOTTOM LINE
Payment of Cash Dividend

Income Statement
No effect on net income

Balance Sheet
Assets ↓ 26,000
Liabilities ↓ 26,000
No effect on equity

>> 21-6 OBJECTIVE
Record the declaration and issuance of stock dividends.

THE BOTTOM LINE
Declaration of Cash Dividend

Income Statement <<
No effect on net income

Balance Sheet
No effect on equity

important!
Fair value is a concept addressed under GAAP that calls for a process to be followed in determining what the fair value of an equity (or other item) may actually be. This discussion is most appropriate in an auditing or advanced accounting text.

> **important!**
>
> **Stock Dividends**
>
> A stock dividend does not change the total stockholders' equity, nor does it change the percentage of ownership of any stockholder.

Book value for each share of stock is the total equity applicable to the class of stock divided by the number of shares outstanding. The total book value is the same before and after a stock dividend, but each shareholder owns more shares of stock with a proportionately smaller book value per share.

Before the stock dividend, Fee owned 400 shares, or 10 percent (400 ÷ 4,000 shares), of the stock of the corporation. After the stock dividend, Fee still owned 10 percent (440 ÷ 4,400 shares) of the corporation's stock:

	Fee	Total
Shares before	400	4,000
Stock dividend	40	400
Shares after	440	4,400

In theory, a stock dividend should result in a proportionate reduction in each share's value. Sometimes the market price declines less than it should in theory because a lower price per share can result in a wider market for the shares and because investors associate stock dividends with successful corporations. Thus, after a stock dividend, the total market value of a stockholder's shares can increase slightly.

>> 21-7 OBJECTIVE
Record stock splits.

Stock Splits

A **stock split** occurs when a corporation issues two or more shares of new stock to replace each share outstanding without making any changes in the capital accounts. Stock splits are often declared when the stock is relatively difficult to sell because the market price is too high. If par-value stock is split, the corporation's charter is amended to reduce the par value.

Fish Corporation is authorized to issue 500,000 shares of no-par-value stock, with a stated value of $75 per share. There are 40,000 shares issued and outstanding. On November 2, the market price of the stock is $300 per share. The board of directors believes that if the price of the stock were lower, the shares would have a wider market. Accordingly, the board declared a 3-for-1 split and reduced the stated value to $25 ($75 ÷ 3) per share. Two additional shares will be issued for each share outstanding. The shares will be issued on November 30 to holders of record on November 15. A stockholder who owned one share of stock with a stated value of $75 before the split will own three shares of stock with a stated value of $25 per share after the split. Stockholders realize no income from the stock split, and the corporation's capital balances are not affected.

Theoretically, the market price will decrease to one-third of the original market value, or to $100 per share ($300 × 1/3). If the price per share does not decrease to its theoretical level, the total market value of a stockholder's shares will be higher.

On the date of declaration of the stock split, a memorandum notation is made in the general journal of Fish Corporation:

> **ABOUT ACCOUNTING**
>
> **Stock Splits**
>
> Many companies have had spectacular numbers of stock splits. Two of the most commonly cited corporations with many stock splits are McDonald's and Microsoft.

	20X1				
1	Nov.	2	On this date the board of directors declared a		1
2			3-for-1 stock split and reduced the stated value of		2
3			common stock from $75 to $25 per share. Total		3
4			outstanding shares will be 120,000		4

On November 30, a similar memorandum entry is made in the general journal to note issuance of the new shares.

An entry is made in the **Common Stock** account in the general ledger to indicate that the stated value is now $25 per share and 120,000 shares are outstanding. The stockholders' records are changed to reflect the number of shares now held by each stockholder.

>> 21-8 OBJECTIVE
Record appropriations of retained earnings.

Appropriations of Retained Earnings

Most corporations pay out only a portion of retained earnings as dividends. They restrict dividend payments in order to reinvest in plant assets or working capital. Sometimes dividends are restricted by contract, such as the requirements of a bond issue. A footnote to the financial statements can be used to indicate how management's plans or contractual obligations will affect (restrict) the dividends. A more formal way for the board of directors to show an intention to restrict dividends is to make an **appropriation of retained earnings** by resolution. Dividends cannot be declared from appropriated retained earnings.

Just4U, Inc.'s directors foresee the need to build a $200,000 retail shop within the next five years. They want to notify the stockholders that the new retail facility will be built and that dividends will be restricted. A resolution is passed at a board meeting on October 5, 20X2, to transfer $50,000 from *Retained Earnings* to a *Retained Earnings Appropriated for Retail Center Construction* account. The resolution is recorded in the minutes and the general journal entry is recorded. Similar appropriations and entries are made in each of the next three years.

The balance sheet presentation shows appropriated and unappropriated retained earnings. Assume that *Retained Earnings* had a balance of $154,600 before the first appropriation. The following is the balance sheet presentation immediately after the appropriation. Notice that total retained earnings stays the same, but it now has two parts:

Retained Earnings
   Appropriated
      Appropriated for Retail Center Construction $ 50,000
   Unappropriated   104,600
   Total Retained Earnings $154,600

			Debit	Credit
20X2				
Oct.	5	Retained Earnings	50 000 00	
		Retained Earnings Appropriated for		
		Retail Center Construction		50 000 00
		Appropriation made by board of		
		directors on Oct. 5		

> **THE BOTTOM LINE**
> **Appropriation of Retained Earnings**
>
> **Income Statement**
> No effect on net income
>
> **Balance Sheet**
> No effect on equity

Remember that retained earnings does not represent cash, nor does appropriating retained earnings provide cash. The appropriation simply restricts the amount of retained earnings available for dividends, thus making it more likely that cash will be available to build the retail center.

Assume that in six years cash was available and the retail center construction project was completed at a cost of $252,000, which is $52,000 more than appropriated. The accounting records reflect an increase to *Building* of $252,000 and a decrease to *Cash* of $252,000. The balance of the *Retained Earnings Appropriated for Retail Center Construction* account ($200,000 at this point in time) has not been affected. When the purpose for which retained earnings was appropriated has been attained, the board can direct that the balance be transferred back to *Retained Earnings,* as follows:

			Debit	Credit
20X8				
Feb.	7	Retained Earnings Appropriated for		
		Retail Center Construction	200 000 00	
		Retained Earnings		200 000 00
		Closing out balance of appropriation		
		account at end of project		

Section 2 Review

1. Which of the following is not one of the three dates related to a cash dividend declaration and issue?
   a. declaration date
   b. anniversary date
   c. payment date
   d. date of record

2. How does the general journal entry for a stock split differ from one for a stock dividend?
   a. Stock splits require a debit to *Retained Earnings* for the face amount of stock.
   b. Stock splits require a debit to *Retained Earnings* for the market value of stock.
   c. Stock splits require a credit to the stock account on the date of declaration for the par value of the stock.
   d. A stock split does not require a journal entry except a memorandum entry.

3. Does an appropriation of retained earnings include a transfer of cash to a restricted account?
   a. no, never
   b. yes, at the date of the board of director decision
   c. yes, at the time of funding the appropriation
   d. not until board action is taken

4. Which of the following will decrease total stockholders' equity?
   a. stock dividend
   b. stock split
   c. cash dividend
   d. appropriation of retained earnings

5. The balance of an appropriated retained earnings account is reduced:
   a. as expenses are accrued.
   b. as payments are made.
   c. when the board of directors passes a resolution to return the amount to unappropriated retained earnings.
   d. when net income is known for the year.

6. On April 20, the board of directors of Auto Corporation declared a 15 percent stock dividend payable on June 1 to stockholders of record on May 15. The stock is expected to trade at $35 per share. On the declaration date, there are 4,000 shares outstanding. The par value of the shares is $30. What amount is credited to the *Paid-in Capital in Excess of Par Value—Common Stock* account?
   a. $12,000
   b. $3,000
   c. $21,000
   d. $20,000

Section 3

SECTION OBJECTIVES	TERMS TO LEARN
>> 21-9 Record a corporation's receipt of donated assets. **WHY IT'S IMPORTANT** Corporations may receive donated property as an incentive to locate in a community. >> 21-10 Record treasury stock transactions. **WHY IT'S IMPORTANT** The impact of treasury stock purchases must be made clear to statement users. >> 21-11 Prepare financial statements for a corporation. **WHY IT'S IMPORTANT** Shareholders, analysts, and management use financial statements issued by corporations.	donated capital statement of retained earnings statement of stockholders' equity treasury stock

Other Capital Transactions and Financial Statements

Many other transactions affect the stockholders' equity. Two types of transactions that occur often are donations of capital and purchase of treasury stock.

Other Capital Transactions

Two transactions that affect stockholders' equity include the donation of assets to a corporation and a corporation's purchase of its own stock.

Donations of Capital

Property can be given to a corporation. This often occurs when a community that wishes to attract new industry gives a corporation land or a building for a plant site. **Donated capital** is capital resulting from the receipt of gifts by a corporation. An asset received as a gift is recorded in the accounting records at the asset's appraised value or fair value based on similar properties. The credit is to **Donated Capital**, a paid-in capital account. This account may also be labeled **Paid-in Capital from Donations**. The following general journal entry indicates how a gift of a plant site valued at $150,000 is recorded:

>> **21-9 OBJECTIVE**
Record a corporation's receipt of donated assets.

1	20X1			
2	Jan. 2	Land	150 000 00	
3		Donated Capital		150 000 00
4		Appraised value of plant site donated		
5		by city		

On the balance sheet, the **Donated Capital** account is shown as a new category under paid-in capital, following the preferred and common stock accounts.

Treasury Stock

Treasury stock is a corporation's own capital stock that has been issued and reacquired. To be considered treasury stock, the stock must have been previously paid for in full and issued to a stockholder. Any class or type of stock can be reacquired as treasury stock. No dividends, voting rights, or liquidation preferences apply to treasury stock.

Stockholders may benefit when the corporation repurchases common stock because there are fewer shares of outstanding stock to share the profits and dividends. If preferred stock is reacquired, the dividends on the stock are no longer payable, thus increasing the dividends available to owners of common stock.

Corporations purchase their own stock for many reasons:

- The corporation has extra cash, and the board of directors thinks that the corporation's own stock is a better investment than other potential investments.
- The corporation wishes to transfer treasury stock to officers and key employees in connection with incentive plans. If unissued shares instead of treasury stock were used, it would be necessary to ask stockholders to give up their preemptive rights. However, preemptive rights do not apply to treasury stock.
- The corporation wants to create a demand for the stock and thus increase its market value.
- In privately held corporations with few owners, the board of directors can vote to purchase the shares of a stockholder who needs cash or wishes to retire.

> As the U.S. economy improved during 2017–2018, reaching record levels of GDP, many major corporations began systematic buyback programs of their common stock.

>> **21-10 OBJECTIVE**
Record treasury stock transactions.

Recording the Purchase of Treasury Stock When treasury stock is purchased, the *Treasury Stock* account is debited for the entire amount paid. There is a separate treasury stock account for each class of stock. For example, assume that in 20X3, Just4U, Inc., repurchased 500 shares of $50 par preferred stock for $52 per share. The transaction is recorded as follows:

20X3					
Jan.	10	Treasury Stock—Preferred		26 000 00	
		Cash			26 000 00
		Purchased 500 shares of treasury stock			

Appropriation of Retained Earnings for Treasury Stock The purchase of treasury stock reflects a payment to a shareholder and thus reduces capital. Stockholder withdrawals could be disguised as treasury stock purchases. In order to protect creditors, some states require that retained earnings be appropriated in an amount equal to the cost of treasury stock. If a corporation does not have retained earnings with a value higher than the purchase price, it cannot purchase treasury stock. If Just4U, Inc., is required to appropriate retained earnings equal to the cost of treasury stock, the following entry would be made:

20X3					
Jan.	10	Retained Earnings		26 000 00	
		Retained Earnings Appropriated—			
		Treasury Stock			26 000 00
		To appropriate retained earnings equal			
		to purchase price of preferred treasury			
		stock			

On the balance sheet, treasury stock is deducted from the sum of all items in the Stockholders' Equity section. To see how treasury stock and retained earnings appropriated for treasury stock appear on the balance sheet, refer to Figure 21.5.

ABOUT ACCOUNTING

Initial Public Offerings

An initial public offering (IPO) is a company's first sale of stock to the public.

Not all companies are prepared for the rigorous scrutiny thrust upon public entities, according to a study conducted by Ernst & Young (EY). Twenty-eight percent of executives surveyed would have made additional preparations for their IPOs.

MANAGERIAL IMPLICATIONS

CAPITAL TRANSACTIONS

- In order to make prudent decisions, managers need to understand how net income is calculated.
- The board of directors needs to develop a dividend policy that gives appropriate consideration to legal restrictions and to financial feasibility.
- Stock dividends offer an opportunity to make distributions to shareholders while limiting the distribution of cash.
- Stock dividends provide a means for transforming a part of retained earnings into paid-in capital.
- Both stock dividends and stock splits reduce the price per share of the company's stock, which may make the stock more marketable.
- Prudent managers inform stockholders about restrictions on dividends by appropriating retained earnings.
- Treasury stock purchases can enhance the value of the stock held by other shareholders.
- Treasury stock can be used to offer stock incentives to officers and key employees and to obtain stock for employee stock-purchase plans.

THINKING CRITICALLY
What factors should be considered before a company declares a cash dividend?

Financial Statements for a Corporation

Four financial statements are usually prepared for a corporation:

- income statement,
- statement of retained earnings,
- balance sheet,
- statement of cash flows.

Figure 21.3 shows the income statement for 20X1 of Just4U, Inc. Let's move ahead a couple of years to 20X3 and examine the statement of retained earnings and the balance sheet. These statements will reflect some of the transactions that you have studied in this chapter. The statement of cash flows is explained in Chapter 24.

>> 21-11 OBJECTIVE
Prepare financial statements for a corporation.

The Statement of Retained Earnings

The **statement of retained earnings** shows all changes that have occurred in retained earnings during the period. The statement shows the beginning balance, the changes, and the ending balance for the unappropriated and appropriated *Retained Earnings* accounts. Because of the importance of retained earnings to the corporation and the stockholders, a statement of retained earnings should be presented as part of the financial statements.

Figure 21.4 shows the 20X3 statement of retained earnings of Just4U, Inc. The unappropriated retained earnings are:

- increased by net income,
- decreased by dividends and appropriations.

Just4U, Inc., has two appropriation accounts—one for retail center construction and another for treasury stock.

Some corporations combine the statement of retained earnings with the income statement. In the combined statement of income and retained earnings, the beginning balance of *Retained Earnings* is added to the net income after taxes for the period. All other amounts are shown in the same way they are shown on the separate statement of retained earnings.

The Securities and Exchange Commission requires publicly held corporations to disclose the reasons for major changes in equity. Corporations find that the most convenient way to make

FIGURE 21.4 Statement of Retained Earnings

Just4U, Inc.
Statement of Retained Earnings
December 31, 20X3

Unappropriated Retained Earnings			
Balance, January 1, 20X3	254 042 00		
Add Net Income after Taxes for 20X3	72 600 00	326 642 00	
Deductions			
Dividends on Preferred Stock	15 000 00		
Dividends on Common Stock	17 600 00		
Transfer to Appropriation for Retail Center Construction	50 000 00		
Transfer to Appropriation for Treasury Stock	26 000 00	108 600 00	
Total Unappropriated Retained Earnings, December 31, 20X3			218 042 00
Appropriated Retained Earnings			
Appropriated for Retail Center Construction			
Balance, January 1, 20X3	50 000 00		
Add Appropriation for the Year	50 000 00		
Balance, December 31, 20X3		100 000 00	
Appropriated for Treasury Stock			
Balance, January 1, 20X3	–0–		
Add Appropriation for the Year	26 000 00		
Balance, December 31, 20X3		26 000 00	
Total Appropriated Retained Earnings, December 31, 20X3			126 000 00
Total Retained Earnings, December 31, 20X3			344 042 00

the required disclosures is to prepare a **statement of stockholders' equity** (often referred to as an *analysis of changes in stockholders' equity*). It provides an analysis reconciling the beginning and ending balance of each of the stockholders' equity accounts. There is, however, no specified form for the statement, and various types of schedules are used.

The Corporate Balance Sheet

Figure 21.5 shows the balance sheet of Just4U, Inc. Because the statement of retained earnings shows changes in each account, only the ending balances of each appropriated retained earnings account and of the unappropriated retained earnings account are shown on the balance sheet. Note that

- income tax payable and dividends payable appear in the Current Liabilities section,
- treasury stock is subtracted from the Stockholders' Equity section.

FIGURE 21.5 An End-of-Year Balance Sheet

Just4U, Inc.
Balance Sheet
December 31, 20X3

Assets			
Current Assets			
Cash		168 084 00	
Accounts Receivable	245 000 00		
Allowance for Doubtful Accounts	8 600 00	236 400 00	
Merchandise Inventory		169 458 00	
Prepaid Insurance		12 000 00	
Total Current Assets			585 942 00
Property, Plant, and Equipment			
Land		92 000 00	
Buildings	120 000 00		
Accumulated Depreciation—Buildings	12 000 00	108 000 00	
Equipment and Fixtures	72 000 00		
Accumulated Depreciation—Equipment and Fixtures	18 000 00	54 000 00	
Total Property, Plant, and Equipment			254 000 00
Total Assets			839 942 00

Liabilities and Stockholders' Equity			
Current Liabilities			
Accounts Payable		68 000 00	
Dividends Payable—Preferred		7 500 00	
Dividends Payable—Common		4 400 00	
Accrued Expenses Payable		3 200 00	
Income Tax Payable		2 400 00	
Total Current Liabilities			85 500 00
Stockholders' Equity			
Paid-in Capital			
Preferred Stock (10%, $100 par value, 10,000 shares authorized)			
Issued 2,000 shares (of which 500 shares are held as treasury stock)	200 000 00		
Paid-in Capital in Excess of Par Value—Preferred Stock	12 000 00	212 000 00	
Common Stock ($50 par value, 20,000 shares authorized)			
Issued and Outstanding, 4,400 shares	220 000 00		
Paid-in Capital in Excess of Par Value—Common Stock	4 400 00	224 400 00	
Total Paid-in Capital		436 400 00	
Retained Earnings			
Appropriated			
For Treasury Stock Purchase	26 000 00		
For Retail Center Construction	100 000 00		
Total Appropriated		126 000 00	
Unappropriated		218 042 00	
Total Retained Earnings		344 042 00	
Less Treasury Stock, Preferred (500 shares at cost)		26 000 00	
Total Stockholders' Equity			754 442 00
Total Liabilities and Stockholders' Equity			839 942 00

Section 3 Review

1. **How does donated capital arise?**
   a. when a corporation receives the gift of an asset
   b. when an asset is purchased
   c. when a loan closes and funds are made available to buy an asset
   d. when a corporation trades property

2. **Why would a corporation purchase its own stock as treasury stock?**
   a. when the stock selling price has gotten very high
   b. when the corporation wants to reduce total stockholders' equity
   c. when the corporation has issued more stock than authorized
   d. when the corporation has a large line of credit available

3. **Where should treasury stock be shown on the balance sheet?**
   a. Asset section
   b. Liability section
   c. addition to stockholders' equity
   d. subtraction from stockholders' equity

4. **Treasury stock is shown on the balance sheet as:**
   a. a deduction from the sum of all other items in the Stockholders' Equity section.
   b. an asset.
   c. an addition to common stock in the Stockholders' Equity section.
   d. an addition to the total of all other Stockholders' Equity accounts.

5. **Which of the following would not be found on the statement of retained earnings?**
   a. dividends on preferred stock
   b. appropriation for treasury stock
   c. appropriation for construction of an office building
   d. the cash payment made when the corporation completes construction of a building for which an appropriation of retained earnings had been made

6. **The balance for *Retained Earnings* on December 1 is $300,000. During December, dividends of $15,000 on common stock and $10,000 on preferred stock were declared. Neither dividend was paid in December. An *Appropriation for Building Expansion* account with a balance of $100,000 was closed and the balance transferred back to *Retained Earnings*. Net income after taxes is $90,000. What is the balance of unappropriated retained earnings on December 31?**
   a. $465,000
   b. $565,000
   c. $490,000
   d. $165,000

REVIEW Chapter Summary

Chapter 21

A corporation has two major classifications of corporate capital: paid-in capital from capital stock transactions and retained earnings from its profits and losses. In this chapter, you learned also to account for corporate income taxes and to record capital transactions affecting stockholders' equity: dividends, stock splits, appropriation of retained earnings, and treasury stock.

Learning Objectives

21-1 Estimate the federal corporate income tax and prepare related journal entries.

Debit *Income Tax Expense* and credit *Cash*. Amounts owed or overpaid are recorded as adjustments.

21-2 Complete a worksheet for a corporation.

Enter the trial balance in the Trial Balance section and the adjustments, except income tax expense, in the Adjustments section. Extend balances of all income and expense amounts except income tax expense to the Income Statement section; total its Debit and Credit columns. The difference is the income or loss before income taxes; compute income tax based on it. After entering the income tax adjustment, total the columns in the Adjustments section. Extend Income Tax Expense to the Debit column of the Income Statement section. Total the Debit and Credit columns of the Income Statement section; the difference is net income after tax. Extend the adjusted balances of the asset, liability, and stockholders' equity accounts to the Balance Sheet columns. Enter net income after income tax to the Credit column of the Balance Sheet section. Complete the worksheet in the usual manner.

21-3 Record corporate adjusting and closing entries.

Close revenues and expenses to the *Income Summary* account; close *Income Summary* to *Retained Earnings*.

21-4 Prepare an income statement for a corporation.

The corporation income statement is similar to that of a sole proprietorship, except for the inclusion of an income tax expense deduction.

21-5 Record the declaration and payment of cash dividends.

Recording cash dividends involves the following: on the declaration date, debit *Retained Earnings* and credit *Dividends Payable*. No journal entry is made on the record date. On the payment date, record the outgoing cash and the reduction of the *Dividends Payable* liability established on the declaration date.

21-6 Record the declaration and issuance of stock dividends.

Issuance of stock dividends above the par-value price involves a debit to *Retained Earnings*, a credit to *Common Stock Dividend Distributable*, and a credit to *Paid-in Capital in Excess of Par Value*. Upon distribution, *Common Stock Dividend Distributable* is debited and *Common Stock* is credited.

21-7 Record stock splits.

A memorandum entry records stock splits on the date of declaration, and another is made on the date of issuance.

21-8 Record appropriations of retained earnings.

Debit *Retained Earnings;* credit the *Appropriated Retained Earnings* account for the appropriation amount.

21-9 Record a corporation's receipt of donated assets.

Property given to a corporation is recorded at appraised or fair value and is credited to *Donated Capital*.

21-10 Record treasury stock transactions.

Treasury stock purchase is recorded as a debit to *Treasury Stock* and a credit to *Cash*.

21-11 Prepare financial statements for a corporation.

The major corporation financial statements discussed in this chapter are the income statement, statement of retained earnings, and balance sheet.

21-12 Define the accounting terms new to this chapter.

Glossary

Appropriation of retained earnings (p. 759) A formal declaration of an intention to restrict dividends

Book value (stock) (p. 758) The total equity applicable to a class of stock divided by the number of shares outstanding

Common Stock Dividend Distributable account (p. 757) Equity account used to record par, or stated, value of shares to be issued as the result of the declaration of a stock dividend

Declaration date (p. 756) The date on which the board of directors declares a dividend

Deferred income taxes (p. 748) The amount of income taxes that will be payable or an amount that may benefit the corporation in the future as a result of the difference between the current year's taxable income and financial statement net income

Donated capital (p. 761) Capital resulting from the receipt of gifts by a corporation

Paid-in capital (p. 755) Capital acquired from capital stock transactions (also known as contributed capital)

Payment date (p. 756) The date that dividends are paid

Record date (p. 756) The date on which the specific stockholders to receive a dividend are determined

Retained earnings (p. 755) The cumulative profits and losses of the corporation not distributed as dividends

Statement of retained earnings (p. 763) A financial statement that shows all changes that have occurred in retained earnings during the period

Statement of stockholders' equity (p. 764) A financial statement that provides an analysis reconciling the beginning and ending balance of each of the stockholders' equity accounts

Stock dividend (p. 757) Distribution of the corporation's own stock on a pro rata basis that results in conversion of a portion of the firm's retained earnings to permanent capital

Stock split (p. 758) When a corporation issues two or more shares of new stock to replace each share outstanding without making any changes in the capital accounts

Stockholders of record (p. 756) Stockholders in whose name shares are held on date of record and who will receive a declared dividend

Treasury stock (p. 761) A corporation's own capital stock that has been issued and reacquired; the stock must have been previously paid in full and issued to a stockholder

Comprehensive Self Review

1. What effect does a common stock dividend have on an individual shareholder's share of ownership in a corporation?
2. What is the difference between treasury stock and unissued stock?
3. Does an appropriation of retained earnings assure a cash balance? Explain.
4. How is treasury stock shown on the balance sheet?
5. What is the purpose of the statement of retained earnings of a corporation?
6. What is meant by "donated capital"?

(Answers to Comprehensive Self Review are at the end of the chapter.)

Discussion Questions

1. How is income tax expense classified in the corporation's income statement?
2. What causes "deferred income taxes" to arise? How are balances in "deferred income taxes" accounts disposed of?
3. Explain the three dates related to declaration and payment of a cash dividend. On which of these dates must journal entries be made?
4. Compare the effects on stockholders' equity of a cash dividend and a stock dividend.
5. When a stock dividend is declared, what journal entry is made? How is the amount of the dividend determined or measured?
6. How is the *Common Stock Dividend Distributable* account classified in the financial statements?
7. What effect does a stock split have on retained earnings? Explain.
8. What effect does an appropriation have on total retained earnings?
9. Several years ago a corporation made an appropriation of retained earnings because of a building project. The building project was completed in the current year. What accounting entry will probably be made with respect to the appropriation?
10. As an inducement for Paul Company to locate in Townville, the local chamber of commerce gave the corporation a tract of land with an appraised value of $250,000. How should the gift be accounted for by Paul?
11. At what amount is treasury stock shown on the balance sheet? How is it classified on the balance sheet?
12. What information is shown on the statement of retained earnings?
13. What is the purpose of the statement of stockholders' equity?

APPLICATIONS

Exercises

Estimating corporation income tax.

◄ **Exercise 21.1**
Objective 21-1

After all revenue and expense accounts, other than *Income Tax Expense,* have been extended to the Income Statement section of the worksheet of US Trucks, Inc., the net income is determined to be $305,000. Using the corporate tax rate given in this chapter, compute the corporation's federal income taxes payable. (Assume that the firm's taxable income is the same as its income for financial accounting purposes.)

Recording journal entries related to taxes.

◄ **Exercise 21.2**
Objective 21-1

A corporation has paid estimated income taxes of $50,000 during the year 20X1. At the end of the year, the corporation's tax bill is computed to be $52,000. Give the general journal entry to adjust the *Income Tax Expense* account.

Recording closing of Income Summary.

◄ **Exercise 21.3**
Objective 21-3

In each of the following situations, what is the amount of profit or loss? In each situation, what accounts will be debited and credited, and for what amount, in the journal entry to close the *Income Summary* account?

  a. The total of the Debit column in the Income Statement section of the worksheet was $650,000 and the total of the Credit column in that section was $518,000.
  b. The total in the Debit column of the Income Statement section was $704,000 and the total of the Credit column was $764,000.
  c. The total of the Debit column in the Balance Sheet section of the worksheet was $426,000 and the total of the Credit column in that section was $391,825.

Exercise 21.4
Objective 21-3

▶ **Recording closing of Income Summary.**

After the revenue and expense accounts were closed into *Income Summary* on December 31, 20X1, the *Income Summary* account showed a net loss for the year of $50,000. Prepare the general journal entry to close the *Income Summary* account.

Exercise 21.5
Objective 21-5

▶ **Recording cash dividends.**

On October 15, 20X1, the board of directors of Trump Inc. declared a cash dividend of $1 per share on its 100,000 outstanding shares of common stock. The dividend is payable on November 15 to stockholders of record on October 30. Give any general journal entries necessary on October 15, October 30, and November 15, 20X1.

Exercise 21.6
Objective 21-6

▶ **Recording a stock dividend.**

ACH Company had outstanding 100,000 shares of $5 par-value common stock on August 13, 20X1. On that date, it declared a 10 percent common stock dividend distributable on September 15 to stockholders of record on September 1. The estimated fair value of the shares at the time of the declaration was $30 per share. Give any general journal entries necessary on August 13, September 1, and September 15, 20X1.

Exercise 21.7
Objective 21-7

▶ **Recording a stock split.**

TNCO Corporation had outstanding 100,000 shares of no-par-value common stock, with a stated value of $12, on December 1, 20X1. The directors voted to split the stock on a 2-for-1 basis, issuing one new share to stockholders for each share presently owned. The estimated fair value of the new share will be $6. Give any general journal entry required on December 1.

Exercise 21.8
Objective 21-8

▶ **Recording appropriation of retained earnings.**

On December 31, 20X1, the board of directors of NoCal Corporation voted to appropriate $100,000 of retained earnings each year for five years to establish a reserve for contingencies. Give the general journal entry on December 31, 20X1, to record the appropriation.

Exercise 21.9
Objective 21-8

▶ **Closing appropriation of retained earnings.**

Because of fears about the outcome of several lawsuits in progress during the past five years, Falcon Corporation had appropriated retained earnings of $250,000, and transferred that amount from the *Retained Earnings* account to *Retained Earnings Appropriated for Contingencies*. In October 20X1, the lawsuits were settled, and Falcon Corporation paid $150,000 to settle them. The board of directors breathed a sigh of relief and on November 1, 20X1, passed a resolution that the appropriation was no longer needed. Prepare the necessary journal entry on November 1 to close the appropriation account.

Exercise 21.10
Objective 21-9

▶ **Recording receipt of property as gift.**

The city of Springfield contributed to Orange Corporation a tract of land on which to build a plant. When the contribution was made on April 1, 20X1, the land's appraised value was $350,000. Give the general journal entry, if any, necessary to record the receipt of the contribution.

Exercise 21.11
Objective 21-10

▶ **Purchasing treasury stock.**

On March 31, 20X1, Alpha Corporation had outstanding 100,000 shares of 5 percent preferred stock with a par value of $100. The stock was originally issued for $110 per share. On that date, the corporation repurchased 10,000 shares of the preferred stock, paying cash of $112 per share for the stock. Give the general journal entry to record repurchase of the treasury stock.

Exercise 21.12
Objective 21-11

▶ **Preparing Stockholders' Equity section of balance sheet.**

The following are selected accounts from the general ledger of the First Company on December 31, 20X1. Show how the corporation's Stockholders' Equity section would appear on the December 31, 20X1, balance sheet.

Common Stock, $1 par, authorized 100,000 shares, issued and outstanding 50,000 shares	$ 50,000
Paid-in Capital in Excess of Par Value—Common	100,000
Retained Earnings	125,000

PROBLEMS

Problem Set A

Recording federal income tax transactions and cash dividend transactions.

◀ **Problem 21.1A**
Objectives 21-1, 21-5

Selected transactions of Oceanic Corporation during 20X1 follow. Record them in the general journal.

DATE		TRANSACTIONS
Mar.	15	Filed the federal income tax return for 20X0 (the prior year's). The total tax for the year was $120,000. During 20X0, quarterly deposits of estimated tax totaling $110,000 had been made. The additional tax of $10,000 was paid with the return. On December 31, 20X0, the accountant had estimated the total tax for 20X0 to be $105,000 and had recorded a liability of $5,000 for federal income tax payable.
Apr.	15	Paid first quarterly installment of $35,000 on 20X1 estimated federal income tax.
May	3	Declared dividend of $0.10 per share on the 50,000 shares of common stock outstanding. The dividend is payable on June 2 to stockholders of record as of May 20, 20X1.
June	2	Paid dividend declared on May 3.
	15	Paid second quarterly installment of $35,000 on 20X1 estimated federal income tax.
Sept.	15	Paid third quarterly installment of $35,000 on 20X1 estimated federal income tax.
Nov.	2	Declared dividend of $0.10 per share on 50,000 shares of common stock outstanding. The dividend is payable on December 2 to holders of record on November 20.
Dec.	2	Paid dividend declared on November 2.
	15	Paid fourth quarterly installment of $35,000 on 20X1 estimated income tax.
	31	Total income tax for 20X1 was $150,000. Record as an adjustment the difference between this amount and the total quarterly deposits.

Analyze: What annual per share dividend was paid to common stockholders in 20X1?

Completing a corporate worksheet, recording adjusting and closing entries, preparing an income statement and balance sheet.

◀ **Problem 21.2A**
Objectives 21-2, 21-3, 21-4, 21-11

Bruin Corporation has been authorized to issue 5,000 shares of 12 percent noncumulative, nonparticipating preferred stock with a par value of $100 per share and 200,000 shares of common stock with a par value of $10 per share. As of December 31, 20X1, 2,600 shares of preferred stock and 19,000 shares of common stock had been issued. A condensed trial balance as of December 31, 20X1, is provided below.

INSTRUCTIONS

1. Enter the December 31, 20X1, trial balance on an eight-column worksheet. Provide three lines for the **Selling Expenses** control account and three lines for the **General Expenses** control account. Total and rule the Trial Balance columns.
2. Record the following transactions in general journal form, using page number 6:
   a. Ending merchandise inventory is $115,000. Close the beginning inventory and set up the ending inventory.
   b. Depreciation of buildings is $14,500 ($11,000 is selling expense; $3,500 is general expense).
   c. Depreciation of equipment is $27,000 ($18,000 is selling expense; $9,000 is general expense).
   d. Accrued expenses are $10,000 ($7,000 is selling expense; $3,000 is general expense).

e. The balance in *Allowance for Doubtful Accounts* is adequate.

f. The $49,300 balance in *Income Tax Expense* represents the quarterly tax deposits. Adjust the *Income Tax Expense* account using the following procedure:

(1) Extend the adjusted income and expense items to the Income Statement columns and compute the net income before taxes.

(2) Assume that the federal corporate income tax is $49,375. Ignore state and local income taxes.

3. Complete the worksheet as shown in the text.
4. Prepare a condensed income statement for the year.
5. Prepare a balance sheet as of December 31, 20X1. The balance of *Retained Earnings* on January 1, 20X1, was $171,300. All dividends for the year were declared on December 5, 20X1, and are payable January 4, 20X2.
6. Journalize the adjusting and closing entries on December 31. Explanations are not required.

Bruin Corporation
Trial Balance (Condensed)
December 31, 20X1

ACCOUNT NAME	DEBIT	CREDIT
Cash	48,470.00	
Accounts Receivable	150,800.00	
Allowance for Doubtful Accounts		3,000.00
Income Tax Refund Receivable		
Inventory	101,000.00	
Land	110,000.00	
Buildings	348,000.00	
Accumulated Depreciation—Buildings		43,500.00
Equipment	270,000.00	
Accumulated Depreciation—Equipment		27,000.00
Accounts Payable		149,720.00
Dividends Payable—Preferred		31,200.00
Dividends Payable—Common		17,100.00
Accrued Expenses Payable		
Income Tax Payable		
Preferred Stock, 12%		260,000.00
Paid-in Capital in Excess of Par Value—Preferred		26,000.00
Common Stock		190,000.00
Retained Earnings		123,000.00
Sales (Net)		1,150,550.00
Purchases	700,000.00	
Selling Expenses Control	164,800.00	
General Expenses Control	78,700.00	
Amortization of Organization Costs		
Income Tax Expense	49,300.00	
Income Summary		
Totals	2,021,070.00	2,021,070.00

Analyze: Assume that dividends were declared in equal amounts over the four quarters of 20X1. What percentage of Bruin Corporation's annual income before tax was spent on dividends to stockholders? Round to one decimal place.

Recording cash dividends, stock dividends, and appropriation of retained earnings; preparing statement of retained earnings.

◀ **Problem 21.3A**

Objectives 21-5, 21-6, 21-8, 21-11

The stockholders' equity accounts of Genisus Corporation on January 1, 20X1, contained the following balances:

Preferred Stock (10%, $100 par value, 10,000 shares authorized)		
Issued and Outstanding, 2,000 Shares	$200,000	
Paid-in Capital in Excess of Par Value—Preferred	2,000	$202,000
Common Stock ($20 par value, 100,000 shares authorized)		
Issued and Outstanding, 20,000 Shares		400,000
Retained Earnings		325,000
Total Stockholders' Equity		$927,000

Transactions affecting stockholders' equity during 20X1 follow.

INSTRUCTIONS

1. Set up a ledger account (381) for *Retained Earnings* and record the January 1, 20X1, balance.
2. Record the transactions in general journal form and post them to the *Retained Earnings* account only. Use the account titles in the chapter.
3. Prepare a statement of retained earnings for the year 20X1.

DATE		TRANSACTIONS
June	15	Declared a semiannual dividend of 5 percent on preferred stock, payable on July 15 to stockholders of record on June 30.
July	15	Paid the dividend on preferred stock.
Dec.	15	Declared a semiannual dividend of 5 percent on preferred stock, payable on January 15, 20X2, to stockholders of record on December 31, 20X1, and a cash dividend of $2 per share on common stock, payable on January 15, 20X2, to stockholders of record on December 31, 20X1. Make separate entries.
	15	Declared a 10 percent common stock dividend to common stockholders of record on December 31, 20X1. The new shares are to be issued on January 15, 20X2. A fair value price of $25 per share is expected for the new shares of common stock.
Dec.	31	Created an "appropriation of retained earnings for contingencies" of $75,000 because of the poor economic outlook.
	31	The *Income Summary* account contained a debit balance of $25,000. The board had anticipated a net loss for the year and no quarterly deposits of estimated income taxes were made, so income taxes may be ignored.

Analyze: If Genisus Corporation had not declared cash or stock dividends for common stockholders, what balance would be found in the unappropriated *Retained Earnings* account at December 31, 20X1?

Problem 21.4A

Objectives 21-5, 21-7, 21-8, 21-9, 21-11

Recording cash dividends, stock splits, appropriations of retained earnings, and donated assets; preparing the Stockholders' Equity section of the balance sheet.

The Stockholders' Equity section of the balance sheet of Serious Corporation on January 1, 20X1, is shown below; selected transactions for the year follow:

Stockholders' Equity

Preferred Stock (10% cumulative, $10 par value, 200,000 shares authorized)		
Issued and Outstanding, 9,000 Shares	$90,000	
Paid-in Capital in Excess of Par Value	9,000	$ 99,000
Common Stock (no-par value, $50 stated value, 300,000 shares authorized)		
Issued and Outstanding, 3,000 Shares	150,000	
Paid-in Capital in Excess of Stated Value	6,000	156,000
Total Paid-in Capital		$255,000
Retained Earnings		140,000
Total Stockholders' Equity		$395,000

INSTRUCTIONS

1. Open the stockholders' equity accounts in the general ledger and enter the beginning balances. In addition to the accounts listed, open the following accounts:

    Donated Capital
    Treasury Stock—Preferred
    Retained Earnings—Appropriated for Treasury Stock

2. Record the transactions in general journal form.
3. Post the transactions to the stockholders' equity accounts.
4. Prepare the Stockholders' Equity section of the balance sheet.

DATE		TRANSACTIONS
Feb.	15	Repurchased 4,100 shares of the outstanding preferred stock for $45,100 in cash. The stock is to be held as treasury stock. State law requires that an amount of retained earnings equal to the cost of treasury stock held must be appropriated. Record the purchase and the appropriation of retained earnings.
Mar.	4	Declared a 2-for-1 stock split of common stock. Each shareholder will own twice as many shares as originally owned. Stated value is reduced to $25 per share. Date of record is March 15. Date of issue of new shares is April 1.
April	1	Issued new shares called for by split.
June	17	Declared semiannual dividend of 5 percent on preferred stock, to be paid on July 12 to holders of record on June 30.
July	12	Paid cash dividend on preferred stock.
Sept.	25	Purchased 600 shares of outstanding preferred stock at $10 per share to be held as treasury stock. Record appropriated retained earnings equal to cost of the treasury stock.
Dec.	15	Declared semiannual cash dividend of 5 percent on preferred stock to be paid on January 12 to holders of record on December 30.

DATE	21.4A (cont.) TRANSACTIONS
15	Declared cash dividend of $1.40 per share on common stock to be paid on January 12 to holders of record on December 30.
15	Accepted title to a tract of land with an appraised value of $160,000 from the City of Greenville. The tract is to be used as a building site for the corporation's new factory.
31	Had net income after taxes for the year of $80,000. Give the entry to close the *Income Summary* account.

Analyze: If Serious Corporation had not repurchased preferred stock to place in treasury, what total stockholders' equity would be reported on December 31, 20X1?

Problem Set B

Recording federal income tax and cash dividend transactions.

Selected transactions of Orange Corporation during 20X1 are given below. Record them in the general journal.

◀ **Problem 21.1B**
Objectives 21-1, 21-5

DATE		TRANSACTIONS
Mar.	15	Filed the federal tax return for 20X0 (the prior year). The total tax for the year was $190,000. Estimated tax deposits of $175,000 had been made during 20X0, and on December 31, 20X0, the accountant had accrued an additional liability of $10,000. Paid the tax due of $15,000.
Apr.	15	Paid first quarterly installment of $50,000 on 20X1 estimated federal income tax.
May	30	Declared dividend of $0.05 per share on the 25,000 shares of common stock outstanding. The dividend is payable on June 30 to holders of record on June 15.
June	15	Paid second quarterly installment of $50,000 on 20X1 estimated federal income tax.
	30	Paid the dividend declared on May 30.
Sept.	15	Paid third quarterly installment of $50,000 on 20X1 estimated federal income tax.
Oct.	30	Declared cash dividend of $0.05 per share on the 25,000 shares of common stock outstanding. The dividend is payable on December 1 to holders of record on November 15.
Dec.	1	Paid dividend declared on October 30.
	15	Paid fourth quarterly installment of $50,000 on 20X1 estimated federal income tax.
	31	In completing the worksheet at the end of the year, the accountant estimated that the total income tax for 20X1 was $195,000. The difference between this amount and the quarterly deposits is to be recorded as an adjustment.

Analyze: If the dividends declared on October 30 were to be paid on January 15, what balance would be reflected in the *Dividends Payable* account on December 31, 20X1?

Completing a corporate worksheet; recording adjusting and closing entries; preparing an income statement and balance sheet.

Jackson Corp. has been authorized to issue 10,000 shares of 10 percent noncumulative, nonparticipating preferred stock with a par value of $100 per share and 10,000 shares of common stock with a stated value of $100 per share. As of December 31, 20X1, 800 shares of preferred stock and 800 shares of common stock have been issued and are outstanding. Dividends are paid quarterly on the preferred stock. A condensed trial balance as of December 31, 20X1, is shown below.

◀ **Problem 21.2B**
Objectives 21-2, 21-3, 21-4, 21-11

INSTRUCTIONS

1. Enter the December 31 trial balance on an eight-column worksheet. Provide four lines for the **Selling Expenses** control account and three lines for the **General Expenses** control account. Total and rule the Trial Balance columns.
2. Enter the necessary adjustments on the worksheet, based on the following data for December 31:
   a. Ending merchandise inventory is $78,000. Close the beginning inventory and set up the ending inventory.
   b. **Allowance for Doubtful Accounts** should be adjusted to a balance of $1,300 (debit **Selling Expenses**).
   c. Depreciation of buildings is $4,000 ($3,600 is selling expense; $400 is general expense).
   d. Depreciation of equipment is $6,000 ($2,000 is selling expense; $4,000 is general expense).
   e. Accrued expenses are $3,800 ($1,200 is selling expense; $2,600 is general expense).
   f. The $16,000 balance in **Income Tax Expense** represents the quarterly tax deposits. Adjust the **Income Tax Expense** account using the following procedure:
      (1) Extend the adjusted income and expense items to the Income Statement columns. Using this data, compute the net income before income taxes.
      (2) Assume the federal corporate income tax for the year is $18,401. Ignore state and local income taxes.

Jackson Corp
Trial Balance (Condensed)
December 31, 20X1

ACCOUNT NAME	DEBIT	CREDIT
Cash	40 000 00	
Accounts Receivable	52 800 00	
Allowance for Doubtful Accounts		700 00
Merchandise Inventory	74 920 00	
Land	60 000 00	
Buildings	88 000 00	
Accumulated Depreciation—Buildings		8 000 00
Equipment	78 000 00	
Accumulated Depreciation—Equipment		12 000 00
Accounts Payable		31 450 00
Dividends Payable—Preferred		2 400 00
Accrued Expenses Payable		
Income Tax Payable		
Preferred Stock, 10%		80 000 00
Paid-in Capital in Excess of Par Value—Preferred		6 000 00
Common Stock		80 000 00
Retained Earnings		89 170 00
Sales (Net)		445 000 00
Purchases	220 000 00	
Selling Expenses Control	85 000 00	
General Expenses Control	40 000 00	
Income Tax Expense	16 000 00	
Income Summary		
Totals	754 720 00	754 720 00

3. Complete the worksheet as shown in the text.
4. Prepare a condensed income statement for the year.
5. Prepare a balance sheet as of December 31, 20X1. The balance of *Retained Earnings* on January 1, 20X1, was $89,170. The only dividends declared during the year were dividends on preferred stock.
6. Journalize the adjusting and closing entries on December 31, 20X1. Descriptions are not required.

Analyze: Assume that dividends were declared in equal amounts over the four quarters of fiscal 20X1. What percentage of Jackson Corp.'s annual income before tax was spent on dividends to stockholders?

Recording cash dividends, stock dividends, and appropriations of retained earnings; preparing statement of retained earnings.

◀ **Problem 21.3B**
Objectives 21-5, 21-6, 21-8, 21-11

The stockholders' equity accounts of CAH Inc. on January 1, 20X1, contained the following balances:

Preferred Stock (5%, $100 par value, 2,000 shares authorized)		
Issued and Outstanding, 1,000 shares		$100,000
Common Stock (no-par, $5 stated value, 100,000 shares authorized)		
Issued and Outstanding, 10,000 shares	$50,000	
Paid-in Capital in Excess of Stated Value	10,000	60,000
Retained Earnings		120,000
Total Stockholders' Equity		$280,000

The transactions affecting stockholders' equity during 20X1 are given below. The worksheet at the end of 20X1 showed a net loss of $5,000.

INSTRUCTIONS

1. Set up a ledger account (381) for *Retained Earnings* and record the January 1, 20X1, balance.
2. Record the following transactions in general journal form using page 6. Use the account titles used in the text. No descriptions are required. Post these entries to the *Retained Earnings* account only.
3. Prepare a statement of retained earnings for the year 20X1.

DATE		TRANSACTIONS
June	15	Declared a semiannual 2.5 percent cash dividend on preferred stock and a cash dividend of $1.00 per share on common stock. Both are payable July 15 to stockholders of record on July 1. (Make a compound entry.)
July	15	Paid the cash dividends.
Sept.	15	Declared a 5 percent common stock dividend to be distributed on October 12 to common stockholders of record on October 1. The stock is expected to have an expected fair trading value of $7 per share.
Oct.	12	Distributed the common stock dividend.
Dec.	15	Declared a semiannual 2.5 percent cash dividend on preferred stock and a cash dividend of $0.50 per share on common stock. Both dividends are payable January 15 to stockholders of record on December 31. (Make a compound entry.)
	15	Directed that retained earnings of $10,000 be appropriated each year for the next four years to purchase a new computer system. Title the account *Retained Earnings Appropriated for Equipment Acquisition.* Record the appropriation for 20X1.
	31	Closed the debit balance of $5,000 in *Income Summary.*

Analyze: What balances should be reflected in the *Dividends Payable—Preferred* account on December 31, 20X1?

Problem 21.4B

Objectives 21-5, 21-7, 21-8, 21-9, 21-11

Recording cash dividends, stock splits, appropriation of retained earnings, and donated assets; preparing the Stockholders' Equity section of the balance sheet.

The Stockholders' Equity section of Austin Corporation's balance sheet on January 1, 20X1, follows, along with selected transactions for the year:

Stockholders' Equity

Preferred Stock (6%, $50 par value, 10,000 shares authorized)		
Issued and Outstanding, 1,000 Shares	$50,000	
Paid-in Capital in Excess of Par Value	3,500	$ 53,500
Common Stock (no-par value, $20 stated value, 20,000 shares authorized)		
Issued and Outstanding, 4,000 Shares	$80,000	
Paid-in Capital in Excess of Stated Value	3,000	83,000
Retained Earnings		165,500
Total Stockholders' Equity		$302,000

INSTRUCTIONS

1. Set up general ledger accounts for the stockholders' equity items and enter the given balances. In addition to the accounts listed, open the accounts **Donated Capital, Treasury Stock—Preferred,** and **Retained Earnings Appropriated for Treasury Stock.** Use the following General Ledger Account numbers: **301,** 6% Preferred Stock, $50 Par; **305,** Paid-in Capital in Excess of Par Value—Preferred; **311,** Common Stock, no par, Stated Value $10; **315,** Paid-in Capital in Excess of Stated Value—Common Stock; **371,** Donated Capital; **372,** Treasury Stock-Preferred; **381,** Retained Earnings; **382,** Retained Earnings Appropriated for Treasury Stock.
2. Record the transactions listed below in general journal form.
3. Post general journal entries only to the stockholders' equity accounts.
4. Prepare the Stockholders' Equity section of the balance sheet as of December 31, 20X1.

DATE		TRANSACTIONS
Feb.	1	Reacquired 100 shares of preferred stock at $52 per share and set up an appropriation of retained earnings equal to cost of treasury stock purchased, as required by law.
Mar.	1	Declared a 2-for-1 split of common stock and reduced the stated value to $10.00 per share. Date of record is March 20. Date of issue is April 1.
Apr.	1	Issued new shares of common stock called for by split.
June	20	Declared a cash dividend of 3 percent on preferred stock outstanding, payable July 10 to holders of record on July 1.
July	10	Paid cash dividends on preferred stock.
Nov.	10	Purchased 200 shares of the corporation's own preferred stock to be held as treasury stock, paying $53 per share. Appropriated retained earnings equal to cost of the shares.
Dec.	17	Declared the semiannual cash dividends of 3 percent on preferred stock and $1 per share on common stock. Both are payable to stockholders of record on December 28 and are payable on January 8. Make separate entries.
	24	Received land valued at $100,000 as a gift from a neighboring city for agreeing to build a new factory.
	31	The *Income Summary* account had a credit balance of $50,000 after income tax. Give the entry to close the account.

Analyze: As of December 31, what percent of total authorized preferred stock is held in treasury?

Critical Thinking Problem 21.1

Stockholders' Equity

The Stockholders' Equity section of the balance sheets for Ztop Corporation on December 31, 20X0, and December 31, 20X1, along with other selected account balances on the two dates is provided below. (Certain information is missing from the statements.)

In 20X1 (the current year), the following transactions affecting equity occurred:

a. Additional shares of common stock were issued in July. No other common stock was issued during the year.
b. A cash dividend of $1 per share was declared and paid on common stock in December.
c. The Treasury Stock—Preferred was purchased at par in January.
d. Additional preferred stock was issued for cash in July.
e. The yearly cash dividend of $0.50 per share was declared and paid on preferred stock outstanding as of December 3, 20X1.

INSTRUCTIONS

Answer the following questions about transactions in 20X1:

1. How many shares of preferred stock were outstanding at year-end?
2. How many common stock shares were outstanding at year-end?
3. How many shares of preferred stock were purchased as treasury stock?
4. How many shares of preferred stock were issued for cash?
5. What was the sales price per share of the preferred stock issued?
6. What was the total cash dividend on preferred stock?
7. What was the total cash dividend on common stock?

	20X1	20X0
Stockholders' Equity		
Paid-in Capital		
Preferred Stock (5 percent, $10 par, authorized 20,000 shares)		
Issued	$ 80,000	$ 60,000
Paid-in Capital in Excess of Par Value—Preferred	2,000	–0–
Common Stock ($10 par value, 500,000 shares authorized)		
Issued	750,000	500,000
Paid-in Capital in Excess of Par Value—Common	25,000	
Total Paid-in Capital	$ 857,000	$ 560,000
Retained Earnings		
Appropriated for Plant Expansion	$ 100,000	$ 100,000
Appropriated for Treasury Stock	40,000	–0–
Unappropriated	640,000	600,000
Total Retained Earnings	$ 780,000	$ 700,000
	$1,637,000	$1,260,000
Less Treasury Stock—Preferred	5,000	–0–
Total Stockholders' Equity	$1,642,000	$1,260,000

Analyze: What is the yearly dividend reduction because of the treasury stock purchase?

Critical Thinking Problem 21.2

Individual Investor

EZLife Inc. has the following stockholders' equity on June 30, 20X1:

Common Stock, $15 par (200,000 shares issued)	$3,000,000
Paid-in Capital in Excess of Par	2,000,000
Retained Earnings	4,000,000
Total Stockholders' Equity	$9,000,000

For the past three years, EZLife Inc. has paid dividends of $1.60 per share. On July 1, 20X1, the board declared a 20 percent stock dividend instead of the $1.60 cash dividend. Before the end of the year and after the stock dividend distribution, however, the board declared a cash dividend of $1.33 per share.

In June 20X1, before the stock dividend was declared, Beth Jones purchased 12,000 shares of EZLife Inc. stock for $60 per share. Now she is concerned because she purchased the stock expecting a $1.60 per-share dividend, only to learn that the dividend has been reduced to $1.33 per share.

Answer the following questions concerning this investment:

1. What could have caused EZLife's board of directors to declare a stock dividend rather than a cash dividend in July?
2. How did the book value of Jones's stock prior to the stock dividend compare with its book value after the stock dividend?
3. Why does the market value of the stock ($60) when Jones purchased her shares differ from its book value at that time?
4. How does the total amount of cash dividends on Jones's stock differ between the $1.60 per share on her original holdings and the $1.33 per share on her holdings after the stock dividend?
5. Assume the market price of the stock fell to $50 after the stock dividend was distributed. Does this drop represent a loss to Jones?
6. What do you think would have happened to the market price of the stock if the board had not reduced the amount of the cash dividend per share of stock?

BUSINESS CONNECTIONS

Shareholders' Equity

Managerial FOCUS

1. Three individuals are planning to form a new business. What are the five major types of entities that they can use to operate their business?
2. Assume that you are the controller of a corporation. Some members of the board of directors have asked you how the firm can have a large balance in the **Retained Earnings** account but no cash with which to pay dividends. Explain.
3. A corporation's balance sheet shows **Retained Earnings Appropriated for Plant Expansion** with a balance of $2,000,000. Does this mean that the corporation has set aside $2,000,000 in cash to expand its plant? Why would management want to establish such an account?
4. Trump Corporation's $50 par-value stock has a market price of $250 per share. As a result of the high price per share, finding buyers for stock that existing shareholders wish to sell has become difficult. Suggest a way for management to resolve this problem.
5. Why would the management of a corporation consider using corporate funds to purchase the firms' own outstanding stock?
6. The president of a corporation suggests to the controller that one way to convert retained earnings into permanent capital is to have a stock split. What explanation should the controller give the president?

Corporate Incentives

A small community called Fairview needs to increase jobs in the community. Fairview has some public land that could be developed. The city could sell this land to a private individual for $200,000. The city council decided, however, to make arrangements with a national chain "superstore" to receive the land free if they would build a store in their community. The superstore must first hire from the people who live in Fairview to receive this free land. Is it ethical for the City Council to propose this gift? How would the superstore record this transaction?

Statement of Shareholders' Equity

Refer to the 2018 Form 10-K *(for the fiscal year ended February 3, 2019)* for The Home Depot, Inc. Based on the data presented in the consolidated statements of earnings, answer the following:

1. What approximate income tax rate does the company pay?
2. Did the company record an accrual for current income tax payable for the year ended February 3, 2019? If so, on which statement did you locate this information?

Dividends to Declare

The board of directors has the responsibility to determine the dollar amount of dividends to be given to investors. As a group of three or four students acting as the board of directors, determine the amount of dividends to declare for your investors given the following information: (1) 100,000 shares outstanding, (2) $249,000 in net income, (3) $1,500,000 proposed future expansion, (4) $900,000 balance in *Retained Earnings*. Should the board approve a dividend in stock, cash, or a combination of both? Justify your answer.

Answers to Comprehensive Self Review

1. The shareholder's ownership percentage is unaffected by a common stock dividend.
2. Treasury stock is stock that has been issued, paid for, and reacquired. Unissued stock meets none of those requirements for treasury stock.
3. The appropriation account merely restricts the payment of dividends to the amount of retained earnings in excess of the appropriations. Retained earnings—and the appropriation—have nothing to do with cash.
4. On the balance sheet, treasury stock is deducted from the total of all other stockholders' equity.
5. The statement of retained earnings is to show all changes in retained earnings that have occurred during the period.
6. Donated capital represents the value of assets that have been donated to, or contributed to, the corporation. Usually such contributions are to be used for some specified purpose.

Long-Term Bonds

Chapter 22

www.kraftheinzcompany.com

Two food products are very familiar to most children in the United States—Kraft macaroni and Heinz ketchup! In 2015, Heinz completed a merger with Kraft Foods Group, Inc., and became known as Kraft Heinz Company, becoming what is today's number 5 ranked food and beverage company in the world. To accomplish this merger, all the long-term debt of Kraft was assumed by the newly formed company, increasing this category of debt from about $13 billion in 2014 to more than $25 billion in 2015. Additional long-term debt acquired since 2015 shows the company obligated in excess of $48.5 billion, according to the December 31, 2017, financial statements filed with the company's annual 10-K.

This debt has varying due dates and interest rates ranging from 1.5 percent to 7.125 percent.

When a company like Kraft Heinz decides to borrow to finance its operations, it needs to consider many issues, including, but not limited to: Can it repay the debt? What interest should it pay the holder of the debt? and, of course, What will it do with the money raised?

thinking critically

What are some other sources of long-term financing that could be used by a firm if selling bonds is not a possibility?

Jon Rehg/Shutterstock

LEARNING OBJECTIVES

- **22-1** Name and define the various types of bonds.
- **22-2** Explain the advantages and disadvantages of using bonds as a method of financing.
- **22-3** Record the issuance of bonds.
- **22-4** Record the payment of interest on bonds.
- **22-5** Record the accrual of interest on bonds.
- **22-6** Compute and record the periodic amortization of a bond premium.
- **22-7** Compute and record the periodic amortization of a bond discount.
- **22-8** Record the transactions of a bond sinking fund investment.
- **22-9** Record an increase or decrease in retained earnings appropriated for bond retirement.
- **22-10** Record retirement of bonds payable.
- **22-11** Define the accounting terms new to this chapter.

NEW TERMS

bond indenture
bond issue costs
bond retirement
bond sinking fund investment
bonds payable
call price
callable bonds
carrying value of bonds
collateral trust bonds
convertible bonds
coupon bonds
debentures
discount on bonds payable
face interest rate
leveraging
market interest rate
mortgage loan
premium on bonds payable
registered bonds
secured bonds
serial bonds
straight-line amortization
trading on the equity

Section 1

SECTION OBJECTIVES

>> **22-1** Name and define the various types of bonds.

WHY IT'S IMPORTANT
Corporations frequently issue bonds to raise capital.

>> **22-2** Explain the advantages and disadvantages of using bonds as a method of financing.

WHY IT'S IMPORTANT
The use of bonds as a method of financing carries certain financial obligations and tax implications.

TERMS TO LEARN

bond indenture
bonds payable
call price
callable bonds
collateral trust bonds
convertible bonds
coupon bonds
debentures
face interest rate
leveraging
market interest rate
mortgage loan
registered bonds
secured bonds
serial bonds
trading on the equity

Financing Through Bonds

There are two primary ways for corporations to raise funds. They may sell stock, or they may borrow money (go into debt) by signing a note payable (short-term or long-term).

A long-term note may be secured by a mortgage on specific assets such as land, buildings, or equipment. A **mortgage loan** is a long-term debt created when a note is given as part of the purchase price of land or buildings.

Corporations that need long-term funds often obtain those funds by issuing bonds payable. **Bonds payable** are long-term debt instruments (contracts) that are written promises to repay the principal at a future date along with periodic interest payments to the investors over the life of the bond. Interest is paid at a fixed rate and may be paid annually, semiannually, or quarterly. Bonds are similar to notes payable, but the contract is more formal. Bonds may be easily transferred from one owner (the bondholder or investor) to another.

>> **22-1 OBJECTIVE**
Name and define the various types of bonds.

Types of Bonds

Bonds are classified by the following characteristics:

- Bonds can be secured by collateral (something having value), or they can be unsecured.
- Bonds can be registered or unregistered.
- Bonds can all mature on the same date, or portions can mature over a period of several years. *Mature* means to fall due or to become payable.

Secured and Unsecured Bonds

Secured bonds have property pledged to secure the claims of the bondholders. **Collateral trust bonds** involve the pledge of securities, such as stocks or bonds of other companies. A bond contract, known as a **bond indenture,** is prepared. A trustee, frequently an investment banker, is named to protect the bondholders' interests. If the bonds are not paid when due, the trustee takes legal steps to sell the pledged property and pay off the bonds.

Bonds are identified according to the nature of the property pledged and the year of maturity. Examples are as follows:

- First Mortgage 7 percent Real Estate Bonds Payable, 2029
- Collateral Trust 5 percent Bonds Payable, 2024

Unsecured bonds backed only by a corporation's general credit are called **debentures.** They involve no pledge of specific property. However, the bondholders do have some protection in case of liquidation. The claims of creditors, including bondholders, rank above those of stockholders. Creditors must be paid in full before stockholders can receive anything.

Registered and Unregistered Bonds

Registered bonds are bonds issued to a party whose name is listed in the corporation's records. Ownership is transferred by completing an assignment form and having the change of ownership entered in the corporation's records. Interest is paid by check to each registered bondholder. The corporation maintains a detailed subsidiary ledger, similar to the stockholders' ledger, for registered bonds. At all times, the corporation knows who owns the bonds and who is entitled to receive interest payments.

Some bonds do not require that the names of the owners be registered. These bonds are known as **coupon bonds.** The bonds have coupons attached for each interest payment. The coupons are, in effect, checks payable to the bearer. No record of the owner's identity is kept by the corporation. On or after each interest date, the bondholder detaches the coupon from the bond and presents it to a bank for payment. Coupon bonds are often referred to as *bearer bonds* because the bearer is assumed to be the owner. Coupon bonds are rarely issued because the IRS requires corporations to report the name, tax identification number, and interest received by each bondholder. State and local governments continue to issue coupon bonds because the interest is not subject to federal income tax.

> **ABOUT ACCOUNTING**
> **Accounting Textbooks**
> Benjamin Workman published *The American Accountant,* the earliest known accounting textbook, in 1769.

Single-Maturity and Serial-Maturity Bonds

Most bonds in an issue mature on the same day. However, **serial bonds** are payable over a period of years. For example, a corporation might issue serial bonds totaling $10 million, dated January 1, 2022, with $2,000,000 maturing each year for five years, beginning on January 1, 2032. The corporation might find it easier to retire bonds on a serial basis rather than to have all $10 million due on the same date.

Other Characteristics of Bonds Payable

Bonds are issued in various denominations. The denomination specified on the contract is called the *face value.* The typical face value is $1,000 or $10,000.

Convertible bonds give the owner the right to convert the bonds into common stock under specified conditions. For example, an indenture can give the holder of a 20-year, $1,000 bond the right to convert the bond into 50 shares of the corporation's common stock at any time. When the price of the stock reaches $20 or more ($1,000 bond ÷ 50 shares of stock), the bondholder is likely to convert it into stock.

Bonds are frequently callable. **Callable bonds** allow the issuing corporation to require the holders to surrender the bonds for payment before their maturity date. Call provisions are clearly stated on the bond. The **call price** is the amount the corporation must pay for the bond when it is called. Usually the call price is slightly above the face value. If the market interest rate declines below the face interest rate on the bonds, or if the corporation has excess cash, it might call all or part of the bonds and retire them.

Market interest rate refers to the interest rate a corporation is willing to pay and investors are willing to accept at the current time. **Face interest rate** refers to the contractual interest rate specified on the bond. Market interest rate changes constantly. Face interest rate of a bond does not change.

For example, assume that on October 1, 2022, CAH Incorporated issues 20-year bonds with a face value of $100,000. The bonds mature on October 1, 2042. Under the terms of the indenture,

> **recall**
> **Face Value**
> The term *face value* also applies to notes payable and notes receivable. It is sometimes known as *face amount.*

CAH can call the bonds at any time after October 1, 2032, at a call price of 103 (103 percent of face value). The bonds are called by CAH on October 1, 2033. Johnson, an owner of bonds with a face value of $30,000, must surrender the bonds and will be paid $30,900 ($30,000 × 1.03).

>> 22-2 OBJECTIVE

Explain the advantages and disadvantages of using bonds as a method of financing.

Stock versus Bonds as a Financing Method

Corporations raise funds through various combinations of common stock, preferred stock, and bonds. Management considers several factors when deciding whether to issue stock or bonds. Table 22.1 shows some factors to consider when comparing capital stock and bonds.

When deciding whether to issue bonds, a company needs to determine whether the rate of return on the assets acquired with the bond proceeds is higher than the interest rate paid on the bonds. Suppose that a newly formed corporation issued both common stock and bonds payable to provide total capital of $500,000. The owners invest $300,000 for common stock and borrow $200,000 by issuing bonds. The bonds pay 10 percent interest per year. The corporation's income before interest and taxes is $70,000. Assume a corporate income tax rate of 20 percent. Let's compute the rate of profit on the stockholders' investment.

Amount available to stockholders:

Net income before bond interest expense	$ 70,000
Bond interest expense ($200,000 × 0.10)	(20,000)
Net income before income taxes	$ 50,000
Income tax expense ($50,000 × 0.20)	(10,000)
Net income after taxes	$ 40,000

The stockholders invested $300,000 in the business, and the net income is $40,000. The stockholders earned 13.3 percent ($40,000 ÷ $300,000) profit on their equity. Let's see what happens if the owners invest $500,000 in common stock. Because there is no bond payable, there is no interest expense:

Net income before taxes	$ 70,000
Income tax expense ($70,000 × 0.20)	(14,000)
Net income after income taxes	$ 56,000

The stockholders invested $500,000, and net income is $56,000. The stockholders earned 11.2 percent ($56,000 ÷ $500,000) on their equity. With financing coming 100 percent from

TABLE 22.1

Stock and Bonds Compared

Capital Stock	Bonds Payable
Capital stock is permanent capital. There is no debt to be repaid.	Bonds payable are debt. When the bonds fall due, the debt must be repaid.
Because the stock is permanent capital, it is classified as stockholders' equity	Because the bonds represent debt, they are classified as long-term liabilities.
Dividends are not legally required on common stock. The requirements on preferred stock depend on the contract.	Interest must be paid on the bonds.
Dividends are not deductible for income tax purposes.	Interest is deducted in arriving at the taxable income.
Preference dividends on preferred stock are usually slightly higher than interest rates on bonds because there is more risk associated with preferred stock.	Interest rates on bonds are slightly lower than dividends on preferred stock.

capital stock, the net income available to the stockholders is higher ($56,000 versus $40,000), but the rate of profit on equity is lower (11.2 percent versus 13.3 percent).

The increase in the rate of profit on stockholders' equity when bonds are used is due to the fact that the company's profits are higher than the face rate of interest (10 percent) on the bonds. Using borrowed funds to earn a profit higher than the interest that must be paid on the borrowing is called **trading on the equity,** or **leveraging.** In lean years, such financing can be dangerous from the stockholders' standpoint. The bond interest expense might leave little or nothing for dividends to the stockholders. Moreover, even when the firm operates at a loss, the interest must be paid in full to the bondholders. In addition, the principal amount of the debt must also be paid when the bonds mature.

For example, if the income before interest and taxes had been only $12,000, the use of bonds payable would result in the corporation having a net loss:

Net income before bond interest expense	$ 12,000
Bond interest expense ($200,000 × 0.10)	(20,000)
Net loss	$ (8,000)

Section 1 Review

1. What is a convertible bond?
   a. a bond that may be converted to stock
   b. a form of stockholder equity
   c. a bond that may change its interest payments
   d. a bond that may change its maturity date

2. All of the following have characteristics of registered bonds except:
   a. the bond owner's name is recorded.
   b. payments are made to the registered bond owner.
   c. the bond owner may transfer ownership.
   d. a coupon must be presented to receive the interest payment.

3. Why would a corporation issue callable bonds?
   a. to limit the number of shareholders
   b. fluctuating interest rates
   c. desire to limit liabilities in the future
   d. all of the above

4. Bonds that are payable over a period of years are called:
   a. callable bonds.
   b. serial bonds.
   c. bearer bonds.
   d. coupon bonds.

5. Bonds backed only by the general credit of the corporation are called:
   a. secured bonds.
   b. collateral trust bonds.
   c. registered bonds.
   d. debentures.

6. A small corporation is considering a bond issue. The amount of stockholders' equity is $250,000. The corporation projects income before bond interest and taxes of $60,000. The corporate income tax rate is 20 percent. If $125,000 of bonds is issued at 10 percent, what is the rate of profit on stockholders' equity?
   a. 11%
   b. 18.2%
   c. 15.2%
   d. 17.5%

Section 2

SECTION OBJECTIVES

>> **22-3** Record the issuance of bonds.

WHY IT'S IMPORTANT
The issuance of bonds creates a long-term liability that needs to be reflected in the accounting records of the issuer.

>> **22-4** Record the payment of interest on bonds.

WHY IT'S IMPORTANT
Bondholders receive interest from the bond issuer as stated in the debt instrument.

>> **22-5** Record the accrual of interest on bonds.

WHY IT'S IMPORTANT
At year-end, expenses that have not been recorded are accrued to conform to the matching principle.

>> **22-6** Compute and record the periodic amortization of a bond premium.

WHY IT'S IMPORTANT
Bond premiums reduce the overall interest expense.

>> **22-7** Compute and record the periodic amortization of a bond discount.

WHY IT'S IMPORTANT
Issuing a bond at less than face value increases total interest expense.

TERMS TO LEARN

bond issue costs
carrying value of bonds
discount on bonds payable
premium on bonds payable
straight-line amortization

Bond Issue and Interest

The board of directors of AGA Inc. authorized the issue of 300 registered, unsecured bonds that will mature in 10 years. The face value of each bond is $1,000. The face interest rate is 10 percent. Interest will be paid on April 1 and October 1 of each year. Interest on each bond is $100 per year ($1,000 × 0.10). Because interest is paid semiannually, each interest payment is $50 ($100 ÷ 2). Some of the authorized bonds will be sold immediately. The remainder will be held for future needs.

>> **22-3 OBJECTIVE**
Record the issuance of bonds.

Bonds Issued at Face Value

On April 1, 2022, the issue date, AGA sells 50 bonds at face value for $50,000 ($1,000 × 50). The journal entry follows:

GENERAL JOURNAL PAGE _____

	DATE		DESCRIPTION	POST. REF.	DEBIT	CREDIT	
1	2022						1
2	Apr.	1	Cash		50 000 00		2
3			10% Bonds Payable, 2032			50 000 00	3
4			Issued bonds at face value				4
5							5

After the entry is posted, the ledger account for the bonds appears as follows:

ACCOUNT	10% Bonds Payable, 2032 (Authorized $300,000; Interest April 1, October 1)				ACCOUNT NO. 261	
					BALANCE	
DATE	DESCRIPTION	POST. REF.	DEBIT	CREDIT	DEBIT	CREDIT
2022						
Apr. 1		J4		50 000 00		50 000 00

> **important!**
>
> A buyer of bonds that are purchased on dates other than interest payment dates must include, in the purchase transaction for the bonds, the amount of interest due from the last payment through the date of the bond purchase.

Notice that the amount of bonds authorized is recorded as a memorandum on the ledger account form. On the balance sheet, the bonds payable appear as long-term liabilities. (Bonds that mature within one year from the balance sheet date appear as current liabilities.) There are three ways to report bonds on the balance sheet.

1. Show the face value of the bonds authorized, unissued, and issued:

    Long-Term Liabilities

    10% Bonds Payable, Due April 1, 2032

Authorized	$300,000	
Less Unissued	250,000	
Issued		$50,000

2. Show the face value of the bonds authorized as a parenthetical note:

    Long-Term Liabilities

    10% Bonds Payable, Due April 1, 2032 .... $50,000
    (Bonds with a face value of $300,000 are authorized, of which $250,000 are unissued)

3. Show the face value of the bonds issued. Provide details about the bonds in a note to the financial statements.

Payment of Interest

On October 1, 2022, the first interest payment is due: 10 percent interest on $50,000 for six months. The interest is $2,500 ($50,000 × 0.10 × 1/2). The journal entry to record the payment is as follows:

	DATE	DESCRIPTION	POST. REF.	DEBIT	CREDIT	
1	2022					1
2	Oct. 1	Bond Interest Expense		2 500 00		2
3		Cash			2 500 00	3
4		Paid semiannual bond				4
5		interest				5
6						6

>> **22-4 OBJECTIVE**
Record the payment of interest on bonds.

Corporations with many bondholders open a separate checking account for bond interest payments. A separate account makes it easier to reconcile the bank account and to keep records of interest checks that have not yet been presented for payment.

recall

Interest Formula
$I = Prt$ (Principal times interest rate times time of debt)

22-5 OBJECTIVE
Record the accrual of interest on bonds.

Accrual of Interest

On December 31, 2022, at the end of the fiscal year, three months (October, November, and December) of bond interest is owed but will not be paid until April 1, 2023. The accrued interest is $1,250 ($50,000 × 0.10 × 3/12). The adjusting entry is as follows:

	2022		Adjusting Entries			
26	Dec.	31	Bond Interest Expense		1 250 00	
27			Bond Interest Payable			1 250 00
28			Accrued interest for three months			

When the adjusting entry has been posted, the **Bond Interest Expense** account has a balance of $3,750, the correct amount of interest for the nine months the bonds have been outstanding. **Bond Interest Expense** usually appears in the Other Expenses (nonoperating expenses) section of the income statement:

ACCOUNT **Bond Interest Expense**   ACCOUNT NO. **692**

DATE		DESCRIPTION	POST. REF.	DEBIT	CREDIT	BALANCE DEBIT	BALANCE CREDIT
2022							
Oct.	1		J10	2 500 00		2 500 00	
Dec.	31	Adjusting	J12	1 250 00		3 750 00	

recall

Reversing Entries

The adjusting entry to record accrued interest is reversed on the first day of the following period. Remember also that reversing entries are not required, but companies must be consistent from year to year.

Entries for Second-Year Interest

Assuming that the same bonds remain outstanding during all of the second year, 2023, the following entries would be required. AGA utilizes reversing entries:

- **January 1:** Reverse the accrued interest payable entry for $1,250 made on December 31:
  Debit **Bond Interest Payable** for $1,250.
    Credit **Bond Interest Expense** for $1,250.
- **April 1:** Record the payment of interest for six months:
  Debit **Bond Interest Expense** for $2,500.
    Credit **Cash** for $2,500.
- **October 1:** Record the payment of interest for six months:
  Debit **Bond Interest Expense** for $2,500.
    Credit **Cash** for $2,500.
- **December 31:** Record accrued interest for three months:
  Debit **Bond Interest Expense** for $1,250.
    Credit **Bond Interest Payable** for $1,250.

After these entries have been posted, the **Bond Interest Expense** account appears as below. Notice that on December 31, 2023, the balance in the **Bond Interest Expense** account is $5,000. This is the annual interest on the bonds ($50,000 × 0.10):

ACCOUNT **Bond Interest Expense**   ACCOUNT NO. **692**

DATE		DESCRIPTION	POST. REF.	DEBIT	CREDIT	BALANCE DEBIT	BALANCE CREDIT
2023							
Jan.	1	Reversing	J1		1 250 00		1 250 00
Apr.	1		J4	2 500 00		1 250 00	
Oct.	1		J10	2 500 00		3 750 00	
Dec.	31	Adjusting	J12	1 250 00		5 000 00	

Bonds Issued at a Premium

Two years after the first bonds were sold, AGA issues another 50 bonds. The market interest rate is about 9.5 percent. The face interest rate on the bonds remains at 10 percent. Bondholders will be attracted by the bond interest rate, which is higher than the market rate. They will be willing to pay more than the face value ($1,000) for each bond in order to earn 10 percent interest.

On April 1, 2024, $50,000 of bonds are sold at 104.8. Bond prices are quoted in terms of percent of face value. Each bond was issued for $1,048 ($1,000 × 1.048), yielding cash of $52,400 ($1,048 × 50). The issue price in excess of face value is $2,400 ($52,400 − $50,000). The excess of the price paid over the face value of a bond is called a **premium on bonds payable.** Investors are willing to pay a premium because the face interest rate is higher than the market interest at the time the bonds are issued. This transaction is recorded in general journal form as follows:

	2024				
	Apr.	1	Cash	52 400 00	
			10% Bonds Payable, 2032		50 000 00
			Premium on Bonds Payable		2 400 00
			Issued bonds at 104.8		

important!
Bond Prices
If the face interest rate on bonds is higher than the market interest rate, the bonds will sell at a premium.

THE BOTTOM LINE
Issue Bonds at Premium

Income Statement
No effect on net income

Balance Sheet
Assets ↑ 52,400
Liabilities ↑ 52,400
No effect on equity

Amortization of Bond Premium

The issuing corporation writes off, or amortizes, the premium paid by the bond purchasers over the period from the issue date to the maturity date. Amortizing the premium reduces bond interest expense shown on the income statement. In this case, the bonds are 10-year bonds sold two years after their authorization date. That leaves eight years over which to amortize the premium.

There are two ways to compute the amortization: straight-line amortization and effective interest method. The effective interest method is covered in intermediate accounting courses. This text uses the **straight-line amortization** method, which amortizes an equal amount of the premium each interest payment date. The amortization for AGA is $300 per year ($2,400 ÷ 8 years), or $150 each bond interest payment date.

On October 1, 2024, AGA records the semiannual interest on the $100,000 of bonds outstanding. The bond interest paid is $5,000 ($100,000 × 0.10 × 6/12). AGA also records amortization of the premium received on $50,000 of the bonds. The amortization is $150 each payment date. Notice how the amortization of the *Premium on Bonds Payable* reduces the amount of *Bond Interest Expense*:

>> **22-6 OBJECTIVE**
Compute and record the periodic amortization of a bond premium.

	2024				
	Oct.	1	Bond Interest Expense	5 000 00	
			Cash		5 000 00
			Payment of semiannual interest		
			on $100,000 of bonds		
		1	Premium on Bonds Payable	150 00	
			Bond Interest Expense		150 00
			Amortization on $50,000 of		
			bonds sold at premium		

Adjusting and Reversing Entries

On December 31, 2024, an adjusting entry is made for three months of accrued interest on the entire $100,000 of bonds outstanding. The accrued interest is $2,500 ($100,000 × 0.10 × 3/12). An adjustment is also made for the amortization of bond premium at $75 for three months (3/12 × $300 annual amortization). Bond interest expense is $2,425, the interest accrued less the amount of the bond premium ($2,500 − $75). The adjustment is recorded as shown and is reversed on January 1, 2024:

	2024		Adjusting Entries			
30	Dec.	31	Bond Interest Expense	2 425 00		30
31			Premium on Bonds Payable	75 00		31
32			Bond Interest Payable		2 500 00	32
33			Accrue interest and amortize			33
34			premium for three months			34

Bonds Issued at a Discount

AGA issues another 50 bonds on April 1, 2025. The market interest rate is 11 percent. The bonds' interest rate remains fixed at 10 percent. Investors will pay less than face value for a bond that pays interest at a lower rate than the market rate. The **discount on bonds payable** is the excess of the face value over the price received for a bond.

AGA Inc. sells 50 bonds at 97.76. Each bond is issued for $977.60 ($1,000 × 0.9776), yielding cash of $48,880 ($50,000 × 0.9776). The excess of the face value over the issue price is $1,120 ($50,000 − $48,880). The $1,120 is the discount. The entry to record issuance of the bond is shown in general journal form as follows:

	2025					
1						1
2	Apr.	1	Cash	48 880 00		2
3			Discount on Bonds Payable	1 120 00		3
4			10% Bonds Payable, 2032		50 000 00	4
5			Issued bonds at 97.76			5
6						6

important!

Bond Prices

If the face interest rate on bonds is lower than the market interest rate, the bonds will sell at a discount.

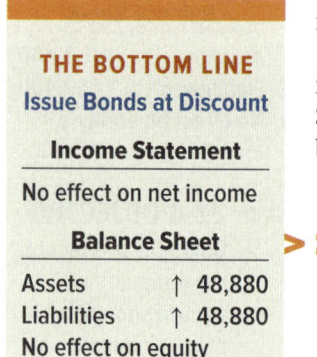

THE BOTTOM LINE

Issue Bonds at Discount

Income Statement

No effect on net income

Balance Sheet

Assets ↑ 48,880
Liabilities ↑ 48,880
No effect on equity

>> **22-7 OBJECTIVE**

Compute and record the periodic amortization of a bond discount.

Amortization of Bond Discount

The issuing corporation amortizes the discount over the period from the issue date to the maturity date. Amortizing the discount increases the bond interest expense shown on the income statement. The bonds are 10-year bonds sold three years after the authorization date. That leaves seven years over which to amortize the discount. On a straight-line basis, the amortization is $160 per year, or $80 per interest payment date.

On October 1, 2025, AGA Inc. records the semiannual interest on the $150,000 of bonds outstanding. The bond interest paid is $7,500 ($150,000 × 0.10 × 6/12). The company records the amortization of the premium for six months ($150). It records the amortization of the discount for six months ($80). The bond interest expense is $7,430, the interest paid ($7,500) less the amortized premium ($150) plus the amortized discount ($80). Notice how the discount increases the actual cost of borrowing. The journal entry to record the interest payment and the amortization of the premium and the discount follows:

	2025					
1						1
2	Oct.	1	Bond Interest Expense	7 430 00		2
3			Premium on Bonds Payable	150 00		3
4			Discount on Bonds Payable		80 00	4
5			Cash		7 500 00	5
6			Interest payment and amortization			6
7			of premium and discount for			7
8			six months			8

Adjusting and Reversing Entries

On December 31, 2025, an adjusting entry is made to accrue interest on the bonds for the three-month period. The accrued interest is $3,750 ($150,000 × 0.10 × 3/12). An adjustment is made for the bond discount for three months ($40) and for the bond premium for three months ($75). Bond interest expense is $3,715, the interest accrued plus the discount less the premium ($3,750 + $40 − $75). The adjusting entry is recorded as follows. It is reversed on January 1, 2026:

	2025		Adjusting Entries			
26	Dec.	31	Bond Interest Expense	3,715.00		
27			Premium on Bonds Payable	75.00		
28			Discount on Bonds Payable		40.00	
29			Bond Interest Payable		3,750.00	
30			Accrue interest on $150,000 of bonds,			
31			amortize premium on $50,000 of			
32			bonds, and amortize discount on			
33			$50,000 of bonds for three months			

Balance Sheet Presentation of Bond Premium and Discount

The *Premium on Bonds Payable* account has a normal credit balance. It is shown as an addition to the face value of bonds payable on the balance sheet. The *Discount on Bonds Payable* account has a normal debit balance; it is subtracted from the face value of bonds payable on the balance sheet. When there are both a discount and a premium on a bond issue, the two are combined and shown on the balance sheet as a single figure. For example, on December 31, 2025, AGA has a net premium on bonds payable of $875 as follows:

Discount	$1,120	
Amortization taken	(120)	
Unamortized discount		$ 1,000
Premium	$2,400	
Amortization taken	(525)	
Unamortized premium		(1,875)
Net unamortized premium		$ 875

On December 31, 2025, AGA reports bonds payable on the balance sheet as follows:

Long-Term Liabilities

10% Bonds Payable, Due April 1, 2032 (authorized $200,000 face value, less $50,000 face value unissued)	$150,000
Net Premium on Bonds Payable	875
Net Liability	$150,875

The book value, or the **carrying value of bonds,** is the balance of the *Bonds Payable* account plus the *Premium on Bonds Payable* account minus the *Discount on Bonds Payable* account:

    Bonds payable
+   Premium on bonds
−   Discount on bonds
    Carrying value or book value

Accounting for Bond Issue Costs

Bond issue costs are costs incurred in issuing bonds, including items such as legal and accounting fees and printing costs. Bond issue costs reduce the proceeds of borrowing. These costs should be shown as a deferred charge in the long-term asset category of the balance sheet. That cost would be allocated over the life of the bonds.

recall

Book Value
The term *book value* (or net book value) can apply to assets or liabilities. The book value of property, plant, and equipment is the original cost minus the accumulated depreciation.

Section 2 Review

1. How are bond discounts shown on the balance sheet?
   a. added to *Bonds Payable*
   b. subtracted from *Bonds Payable*
   c. line added to *Retained Earnings*
   d. subtracted from *Stockholders' Equity*

2. What is the straight-line method for amortizing bond discount or premium?
   a. The same amount of amortization is taken each period.
   b. An increasing amount of amortization is recorded each period.
   c. A decreasing amount of amortization is taken each period.
   d. A large amount of amortization is taken in the first year, followed by the same amount in the remainder of the years.

3. Why is amortization of a bond premium offset against interest expense?
   a. because the bondholder paid less than the face value of the bond
   b. because the bondholder paid more than the face value of the bond
   c. because interest rates rose after the bond was purchased
   d. because interest rates dropped after the bond was purchased

4. The entry to record the issuance of bonds includes a:
   a. debit to *Bonds Payable.*
   b. credit to *Bonds Payable.*
   c. credit to *Bond Interest Payable.*
   d. debit to *Bond Interest Payable.*

5. If bonds are issued for a price below their face value, the bond discount is:
   a. debited to expense on the date the bonds are issued.
   b. amortized over the life of the bond issue.
   c. shown as an addition to bonds payable in the Long-Term Liabilities section of the balance sheet.
   d. shown as a deduction to bonds payable in the Current Liabilities section of the balance sheet.

6. Ten-year bonds, dated January 1, 2022, with a face value of $100,000 are issued at 101 on January 1, 2022. How much premium will be amortized on the interest payment date, July 1, 2022?
   a. $50
   b. $100
   c. $25
   d. $1,000

Section 3

SECTION OBJECTIVES	TERMS TO LEARN
>> 22-8 Record the transactions of a bond sinking fund investment. **WHY IT'S IMPORTANT** Companies make plans to ensure that the required funds are available to pay off bonds on their maturity date. >> 22-9 Record an increase or decrease in retained earnings appropriated for bond retirement. **WHY IT'S IMPORTANT** Retained earnings are often restricted for specific expenditures. >> 22-10 Record retirement of bonds payable. **WHY IT'S IMPORTANT** Upon retirement of a bond, total long-term debt is adjusted to reflect the payment of the liability.	bond retirement bond sinking fund investment

Bond Retirement

Bond retirement occurs when a bond is paid and the liability is removed from the company's balance sheet. When AGA's bond issue matures, the corporation has to pay bondholders the face amount of their outstanding bonds, a total of $150,000, in cash.

Accumulating Funds to Retire Bonds

In order to ensure that the cash is available, the corporation established a bond sinking fund investment account. A **bond sinking fund investment** is a fund established to accumulate assets to pay off bonds when they mature. Some bond contracts require bond sinking funds.

Bond Sinking Fund Investment

AGA Inc. decides to accumulate $30,000 per year in the bond sinking fund for each of the last five years that the bonds are outstanding. The net earnings of the fund will reduce the amount that the corporation has to add each year. Suppose that the bond sinking fund investment account is started on April 1, 2027, by making a $30,000 cash deposit. The $30,000 is immediately invested. During the year, $1,800 is earned on the sinking fund investments. Expenses of $40 are incurred in operating the bond sinking fund. Net earnings for the year are $1,760. The following year only $28,240 ($30,000 − $1,760) needs to be added to the fund. This procedure is repeated each year, so that at the end of the fifth year the fund will have the $150,000 needed to retire the bonds.

>> **22-8 OBJECTIVE**
Record the transactions of a bond sinking fund investment.

The following journal entries are for the first transfer of cash to the fund, net earnings for the first year, second transfer of cash to the fund, and retirement of the bonds at the end of the fifth year:

Date		Description	Debit	Credit
2027				
Apr.	1	Bond Sinking Fund Investment	30 000 00	
		Cash		30 000 00
		First annual installment in bond sinking fund		
2028				
Apr.	1	Bond Sinking Fund Investment	1 760 00	
		Income from Sinking Fund Investment		1 760 00
		Net income earned by bond sinking fund for year		
2028				
Apr.	1	Bond Sinking Fund Investment	28 240 00	
		Cash		28 240 00
		Second annual installment in bond sinking fund ($30,000 less $1,760 income earned for year)		
2032				
Apr.	1	10% Bonds Payable, 2032	150 000 00	
		Bond Sinking Fund Investment		150 000 00
		Retirement of bonds		

This illustration assumes that an outside trustee managed the sinking fund investment account and made the necessary entries to record the fund transactions. If the corporation handled the bond sinking fund itself, additional entries would be required to show the investment of the fund's cash, the receipt of earnings, and the payment of fund expenses.

Other procedures may be used to finance the sinking fund investment. For example, an assumption may be made about the rate of earnings of the fund. A constant amount would be contributed each period, which when added to the earnings would equal the required balance. If earnings differ from the rate assumed, the contributions would be adjusted.

The bond sinking fund is reported under the heading "Investments" in the Assets section of the balance sheet. Investments are usually shown before property, plant, and equipment.

>> **22-9 OBJECTIVE**

Record an increase or decrease in retained earnings appropriated for bond retirement.

Retained Earnings Appropriated for Bond Retirement

To protect bondholders and to restrict dividends, the bond contract might require that retained earnings are appropriated while the bonds are outstanding. Even if the bond contract does not require an appropriation, retained earnings may be appropriated by order of the board of directors.

Suppose that the board of directors of AGA Inc. decided to appropriate $30,000 of retained earnings during each of the last five years the bonds are outstanding. When the bonds are retired, the balance in the appropriated retained earnings account is returned to the *Retained Earnings* account. The *Retained Earnings Appropriated for Bond Retirement* account appears on the balance sheet under the heading "Appropriated Retained Earnings." The following entry shows an annual appropriation of retained earnings. Five such entries would be made.

MANAGERIAL IMPLICATIONS

RAISING CASH

- A critical management task is to ensure that cash is available to the company when it is needed.
- Managers need to know the advantages and disadvantages of raising cash through the sale of bonds and stock.
- Managers need to have a thorough understanding of bond characteristics, including the differences between registered versus bearer bonds and secured versus debenture bonds. They also need to understand convertible bonds and callable bonds.
- Bond sinking fund investments and the appropriation of retained earnings are tools that management can use to ensure that the funds are available to retire the bonds.
- Call provisions and early retirement of bonds allow for flexible financing and can reduce financing costs.

THINKING CRITICALLY
What factors would you consider in choosing between stock financing and bond financing?

The next entry shows the appropriation being returned to retained earnings after the bonds are retired:

2027					
Apr.	1	Retained Earnings		30 000 00	
		Retained Earnings Appropriated for			
		Bond Retirement			30 000 00
		Annual appropriation			
2032					
Apr.	1	Retained Earnings Appropriated for			
		Bond Retirement		150 000 00	
		Retained Earnings			150 000 00
		Close appropriation account			
		upon retirement of bonds			

important!

Bond Retirement
The fact that retained earnings are appropriated for bond retirement does not mean that a bond retirement fund has been funded with cash.

Retirement of Bonds

Bonds payable are usually retired at the maturity date, but some or all of the bonds can be retired prior to that date.

>> 22-10 OBJECTIVE
Record retirement of bonds payable.

Retirement on Due Date

If there had been no bond sinking fund, AGA Inc. would have recorded the retirement on the maturity date by debiting *10% Bonds Payable, 2032,* and crediting **Cash.**

Early Retirement

A corporation may retire bonds early because it has surplus cash, or interest rates have decreased or are expected to decrease. The corporation may purchase the bonds on the open market or, if they are callable, it may require the holders to surrender their bonds for cash.

When bonds are retired prior to maturity, the bondholders are paid the agreed-upon price for the bonds plus the accrued interest to the date of purchase. There are two steps to record the retirement of bonds:

Step 1. *Amortize the discount or premium on the bonds up to the date of retirement.*

Step 2. *Remove the book value, and record the gain or loss.*

    a. Remove the book value of the bonds.

    b. Record interest up to the date of retirement.

    c. Record the cash payment for the repurchase price and interest.

    d. Record the gain or loss (book value minus the repurchase price).

> **important!**
>
> **Gain or Loss**
>
> The gain or loss on the retirement of bonds is the book value of the bonds minus the repurchase price.

Assume that AGA Inc. decides to retire (call) the April 1, 2025, issue of $50,000 of bonds that were sold at a discount. Remember that these bonds were sold at 97.76, resulting in a debit to **Discount on Bonds Payable** for $1,120 with seven years remaining before the bonds' due date. The amortization of the discount was taken at $160 per year, or $80 each time the bond interest was paid. The company has decided to retire these bonds on April 1, 2026.

On December 31, 2025, after adjusting entries, the related account balances of this bond issue are:

Bonds Payable		$50,000
Discount on Bonds Payable	$1,120	
Amortization of Discount on Bonds Payable through December 31, 2025	120	1,000
Net Carrying Value of Bonds		$49,000

Please remember that AGA has three bond issues and is retiring only those bonds that were issued at a discount. In this early retirement illustration, let's assume that AGA does not use reversing entries.

On April 1, 2026, the corporation repurchases and retires the $50,000 of bonds. They are purchased at 101:

Step 1. *Amortize the premium or discount on the bonds up to the date of retirement.* Remember that you previously calculated the amount of amortization of the discount would be $80 each interest payment date. Also recall that on December 31 you made an adjusting entry recording the interest expense and amortization of the discount for three months (or one-half an interest payment period).

GENERAL JOURNAL   PAGE _____

DATE	DESCRIPTION	POST. REF.	DEBIT	CREDIT
2026				
Apr. 1	Bond Interest Expense		40 00	
	Discount on Bonds Payable			40 00
	Amortization of discount for three months			
	on bonds to be retired			

Step 2. *Remove the book value of the bonds, and record the gain or loss on the repurchase of the bonds:*

    a. Remove the book value of the bonds:

Bonds being retired	$50,000
Discount on retired bonds ($1,000 − $40)	960
Net book value of bonds	$49,040

b. Record bond interest expense up to the date of bond retirement.

$50,000 \times 0.10 \times 3/12 = \$1,250$

Recall that you already recorded three months of interest when you made the adjusting entry on December 31, 2025.

c. Record the cash payment for the repurchase of the bonds.

$50,000 \times 1.01 = \$50,500$

d. Record the gain or loss (net book value of bonds minus repurchase price).

($50,000 − $960) − $50,500 = ($1,460) loss

GENERAL JOURNAL

DATE		DESCRIPTION	POST. REF.	DEBIT	CREDIT
2026					
Apr.	1	Bond Interest Expense		1 250 00	
		Bond Interest Payable		1 250 00	
		Cash			2 500 00
Apr.	1	Bonds Payable		50 000 00	
		Loss on Early Retirement of Bonds		1 460 00	
		Discount on Bonds Payable			960 00
		Cash			50 500 00

A gain or loss on early retirement of bonds will be reflected on the company's income statement, obviously affecting net income.

Section 3 Review

1. What is a bond sinking fund investment?
   a. an investment that is decreasing in value
   b. a liability
   c. an asset
   d. part of *Bonds Payable* (contra account)

2. Why would a corporation purchase its own bonds and retire them?
   a. reduce number of shareholders
   b. reduce expenses for the company
   c. reduce cash on hand
   d. increase corporate debt

3. How is gain on early retirement of bonds shown on the income statement?
   a. not shown on the income statement
   b. increases net income
   c. reduces net income
   d. reduces *Retained Earnings*

4. The entry to record income earned by a bond sinking fund investment includes a credit to:
   a. *Bonds Payable.*
   b. *Bond Sinking Fund Investment.*
   c. *Income from Sinking Fund Investment.*
   d. *Interest Income.*

5. The entry to record retirement of a bond includes a debit to:
   a. *Discount on Bonds Payable.*
   b. *Retained Earnings.*
   c. *Bonds Payable.*
   d. *Retained Earnings Appropriated for Bond Retirement.*

6. What is the entry to record $300,000 of bonds that were retired at maturity? There was no bond sinking fund.
   a. Debit *Cash* $300,000; credit *Bonds Payable* $300,000.
   b. Debit *Bond Sinking Fund* $300,000; credit *Cash* $300,000.
   c. Debit *Bonds Payable* $300,000; credit *Bond Sinking Fund* $300,000.
   d. Debit *Bonds Payable* $300,000; credit *Cash* $300,000.

22 Chapter REVIEW Chapter Summary

Corporations often use bonds to acquire funds. In this chapter, you have reviewed the types of bonds frequently issued by corporations and have learned how to record a variety of bond transactions.

Learning Objectives

22-1 Name and define the various types of bonds.
- Bonds may be secured by the pledge of specific assets as security, or they may be unsecured.
- Some bonds are registered; owners are listed in corporation records. Other bonds are bearer bonds with interest coupons attached.
- Convertible bonds can be converted into common stock by the bondholder.
- Callable bonds may be recalled before their maturity date.

22-2 Explain the advantages and disadvantages of using bonds as a method of financing.
- Businesses that choose to raise capital using bonds may deduct bond interest charges when computing taxable income.
- Bonds payable are debts. The face amount of the bond must be repaid at maturity. Interest must also be paid on the bonds.

22-3 Record the issuance of bonds.

Bonds may be issued at face value, at a premium, or at a discount.
- If the bond's face interest rate exceeds the market interest rate when the bonds are issued, the bonds are issued at a premium.
- If the market interest rate exceeds the face interest rate on the bonds, the bonds are issued at a discount.

22-4 Record the payment of interest on bonds.

A bond bears interest that is usually payable annually or semiannually at a specified rate. The amount of interest is calculated and recorded as a debit to *Bond Interest Expense* and a credit to *Cash*.

22-5 Record the accrual of interest on bonds.

When bond interest dates do not coincide with the fiscal year-end, an adjustment is made for accrued bond interest at the end of the year. The adjustment may be reversed at the beginning of the next year.

22-6 Compute and record the periodic amortization of a bond premium.

The corporation writes off, or amortizes, a bond premium over the period from the issue date through the maturity date. The amortization is treated as a reduction of interest expense for that period.

22-7 Compute and record the periodic amortization of a bond discount.

A bond discount is amortized over the period that begins on the date the bonds are issued and ends on the date of maturity. The amortization is treated as an increase to interest expense for that period.

22-8 Record the transactions of a bond sinking fund investment.

A bond sinking fund accumulates cash to pay the bonds at maturity. The cash in the sinking fund is invested, earning interest to reduce the amount that the corporation will have to add in subsequent years. The establishment of the fund is recorded with a debit to *Bond Sinking Fund Investment* and a credit to *Cash*.

22-9 Record an increase or decrease in retained earnings appropriated for bond retirement.

An appropriation of retained earnings for bond retirement may be established and increased by debits to *Retained Earnings* and credits to *Retained Earnings Appropriated for Bond Retirement*. An appropriation shows that some retained earnings are not available for dividends; they are needed to pay off the bonds.

22-10 Record retirement of bonds payable.

Bonds are retired at maturity or, under certain circumstances, retired prior to maturity. The difference between the book value and the repurchase price is a gain or loss on retirement of bonds.

22-11 Define the accounting terms new to this chapter.

Glossary

Bond indenture (p. 784) A bond contract

Bond issue costs (p. 793) Costs incurred in issuing bonds, such as legal and accounting fees and printing costs

Bond retirement (p. 795) When a bond is paid and the liability is removed from the company's balance sheet

Bond sinking fund investment (p. 795) A fund established to accumulate assets to pay off bonds when they mature

Bonds payable (p. 784) Long-term debt instruments that are written promises to repay the principal at a future date; interest is due at a fixed rate payable over the life of the bond

Call price (p. 785) The amount the corporation must pay for the bond when it is called

Callable bonds (p. 785) Bonds that allow the issuing corporation to require the holder to surrender the bonds for payment before their maturity date

Carrying value of bonds (p. 793) The balance of the *Bonds Payable* account plus the *Premium on Bonds Payable* account minus the *Discount on Bonds Payable* account; also called *book value of bonds*

Collateral trust bonds (p. 784) Bonds secured by the pledge of securities, such as stocks or bonds of other companies

Convertible bonds (p. 785) Bonds that give the owner the right to convert the bonds into common stock under specified conditions

Coupon bonds (p. 785) Unregistered bonds that have coupons attached for each interest payment; also called *bearer bonds*

Debentures (p. 785) Unsecured bonds backed only by a corporation's general credit

Discount on bonds payable (p. 792) The excess of the face value over the price received by the corporation for a bond

Face interest rate (p. 785) The contractual interest rate specified on the bond

Leveraging (p. 787) Using borrowed funds to earn a profit greater than the interest that must be paid on the borrowing

Market interest rate (p. 785) The interest rate a corporation is willing to pay and investors are willing to accept at the current time

Mortgage loan (p. 784) A long-term debt created when a note is given as part of the purchase price for land or buildings

Premium on bonds payable (p. 791) The excess of the price paid over the face value of a bond

Registered bonds (p. 785) Bonds issued to a party whose name is listed in the corporation's records

Secured bonds (p. 784) Bonds for which property is pledged to secure the claims of bondholders

Serial bonds (p. 785) Bonds issued at one time but payable over a period of years

Straight-line amortization (p. 791) Amortizing the premium or discount on bonds payable in equal amounts each month over the life of the bond

Trading on the equity (p. 787) *See* Leveraging

Comprehensive Self Review

1. Generally, would an investor want secured bonds or debenture bonds? Why?
2. Name two disadvantages of raising capital through the issue of bonds payable rather than through the issue of preferred stock.
3. What factor would cause bonds to be sold at a premium?

4. Why does a corporation use an account such as *Appropriation of Retained Earnings* for bond retirement?

5. What entry, or entries, will be made when bonds are retired at maturity?

(Answers to Comprehensive Self Review are at the end of the chapter.)

Discussion Questions

1. What is a collateral trust bond?
2. What is a bond indenture?
3. How is the *Bonds Payable* account classified on the balance sheet?
4. Are authorized, unissued bonds shown on the balance sheet? If so, where?
5. Why might a company use a special bank account for paying bond interest?
6. In a bond indenture dated January 1, 2022, Pink Company authorized the issuance of $500,000 face value, 10 percent, 20-year bonds payable. No bonds were issued until July 1, 2023, when bonds with a face value of $200,000 were issued. At that time, the market rate of interest on similar debt was 9 percent. Would the issue price of the bonds be more than or less than face value? Explain.
7. Why is a bond premium or discount amortized as part of the adjustment process at the end of the year?
8. Why is the year-end adjusting entry for amortization of a bond premium or discount reversed at the start of the new year?
9. How are the legal costs and other costs related to issuing bonds accounted for?
10. What is a bond sinking fund?
11. What is the relationship between a bond sinking fund and an appropriation of retained earnings for bond retirement? Explain.
12. Explain the accounting treatment necessary when bonds are retired before maturity.

APPLICATIONS

Exercises

Exercises 22.1 through 22.3. First Corp issued $500,000 of its 5 percent bonds payable on April 1, 2022. The bonds were issued at face value. Interest is payable semiannually on October 1 and April 1.

Exercise 22.1

Objective 22-3

▶ **Issuing bonds.**

Give the general journal entry to record the April 1, 2022, bond issue.

Exercise 22.2

Objective 22-4

▶ **Paying interest on bonds payable.**

Give the entry in general journal form to record the interest payment on October 1, 2022.

Exercise 22.3

Objective 22-5

▶ **Accruing interest on bonds.**

Give the entry to accrue bond interest on First's bonds payable on December 31, 2022.

Exercises 22.4 through 22.6. Jon Inc. was authorized to issue $1,000,000 of 6 percent bonds. On April 1, 2022, the corporation issued bonds with a face value of $500,000 at a price of 102.0. The bonds mature 10 years from the date of issue. Interest is payable semiannually on October 1 and April 1.

Recording issuance of bonds.

◀ **Exercise 22.4**
Objective 22-3

Give the general journal entry to record the April 1, 2022, bond issue.

Computing amortization of premium on bonds.

◀ **Exercise 22.5**
Objective 22-6

Using the data given above, what amount of premium will be amortized by Jon Inc. on October 1, 2022, using straight-line amortization? Give the general journal entry to record this amortization.

Recording adjusting entry for bond interest and premium.

◀ **Exercise 22.6**
Objectives 22-5, 22-6

Using the data given above, give the adjusting entry that would be made by Jon Inc. on December 31, 2022, to record accrued interest and to amortize the premium.

Recording transactions of a bond sinking fund investment.

◀ **Exercise 22.7**
Objective 22-8

Give the general journal entries to record the following transactions:
a. On December 31, 2021, Blue Co. established a bond sinking fund investment by depositing $25,000 with the fund trustee.
b. On December 31, 2022, Blue Co. recorded $2,000 net income from its bond sinking fund investment for the year.
c. On December 31, 2022, Blue Co. made a deposit of $23,000 into the bond sinking fund investment.

Appropriating retained earnings for bond retirement.

◀ **Exercise 22.8**
Objective 22-9

Record the appropriation of $75,000 of retained earnings on December 31, 2022, by Dawn Inc. to establish an appropriation for bond retirement.

Retiring bonds before maturity.

◀ **Exercise 22.9**
Objective 22-10

On April 1, 2022, Dave's Deli issued $70,000 of its 9 percent bonds, maturing 10 years later. Interest is payable semiannually on April 1 and October 1. The issue price was 94.0. Dave's has decided to retire the bonds on August 1, 2025, three years and four months after the bonds were initially issued. The bonds were repurchased at 99. After recording the accrued interest expense payable through August 1, 2025, the balance in the *Discount on Bonds Payable* account is $2,800. Give the general journal entry to record the repurchase and retirement of the bonds.

PROBLEMS

Problem Set A

Issuing bonds; bond interest transactions.

◀ **Problem 22.1A**
Objectives 22-3, 22-4, 22-5

The board of directors of ALL Services Inc. authorized the issuance of $500,000 face value, 20-year, 5 percent bonds dated April 1, 2022, and maturing on April 1, 2042. Interest is payable semiannually on April 1 and October 1. ALL uses the calendar year as its fiscal year. The bond transactions that occurred in 2022 and 2023 follow.

INSTRUCTIONS

Record the transactions in general journal form. Use the account names given in the chapter. Round to the nearest dollar.

DATE		TRANSACTIONS FOR 2022
Apr.	1	Issued $300,000 of bonds at face value.
Oct.	1	Paid the semiannual interest on the bonds issued.
Dec.	31	Recorded the adjusting entry for the accrued bond interest.
	31	Closed the **Bond Interest Expense** account to the **Income Summary** account.

DATE		TRANSACTIONS FOR 2023
Jan.	1	Reversed the adjusting entry made on December 31, 2022.
Apr.	1	Issued $100,000 of bonds at face value.
	1	Paid the interest for six months on the bonds previously issued.
Oct.	1	Paid the interest for six months on the outstanding bonds.
Dec.	31	Recorded the adjusting entry for the accrued bond interest.
	31	Closed the **Bond Interest Expense** account to the **Income Summary** account.

Analyze: Based on the transactions given, what is the balance in the **Bonds Payable** account on December 31, 2022?

Problem 22.2A ▶ **Issuing bonds; bond interest transactions and amortization of discount.**

Objectives 22-3, 22-4, 22-5, 22-7

The board of directors of Calmont, LLC, authorized the issuance of $600,000 face value, 20-year, 6 percent bonds, dated March 1, 2022, and maturing on March 1, 2042. Interest is payable semiannually on September 1 and March 1.

INSTRUCTIONS

1. Record the following transactions in general journal form. Use the account names given in the chapter. (Round to the nearest dollar.)
2. Prepare the Long-Term Liabilities section of the corporation's balance sheet on December 31, 2022.

DATE		TRANSACTIONS FOR 2022
June	1	Issued bonds with a face value of $500,000 at 97.63 plus accrued interest from March 1. (When bonds are issued between interest payment dates, the accrued interest is paid to the corporation by the purchaser. Credit **Bond Interest Expense**.)
Sept.	1	Paid the semiannual bond interest and amortized the discount for three months. (Make two entries. Use the straight-line method to compute the amortization.)
Dec.	31	Recorded an adjusting entry to accrue the interest and to amortize the discount. (Make one entry.)
	31	Closed the **Bond Interest Expense** account to the **Income Summary** account.

DATE		TRANSACTIONS FOR 2023
Jan.	1	Reversed the adjusting entry made on December 31, 2022.
Mar.	1	Paid the semiannual bond interest and amortized the discount on the outstanding bonds.

Analyze: What is the balance of the *Discount on Bonds Payable* account on December 31, 2022?

Issuing bonds; recording interest transactions and amortization of premium.

◀ **Problem 22.3A**

Objectives 22-3, 22-4, 22-5, 22-6

The board of directors of Watch Shop, Inc., authorized the issuance of $1,000,000 face value, 10-year, 5 percent bonds dated April 1, 2022, and maturing on April 1, 2032. Interest is payable semiannually on April 1 and October 1.

INSTRUCTIONS

1. Record the transactions below in general journal form. Use the account names given in the chapter.
2. Prepare the Long-Term Liabilities section of the corporation's balance sheet on December 31, 2022.

DATE		TRANSACTIONS FOR 2022
Apr.	1	Issued $500,000 face value bonds at 102.
Oct.	1	Paid the semiannual interest on the outstanding bonds and amortized the bond premium. (Make two entries. Use the straight-line method to compute the amortization.)
Dec.	31	Recorded the adjusting entry for accrued interest and amortization of the bond premium for three months. (Make one entry.)
	31	Closed the *Bond Interest Expense* account to the *Income Summary* account.

DATE		TRANSACTIONS FOR 2023
Jan.	1	Reversed the adjusting entry made on December 31, 2022.

Analyze: If the reversing entry was not recorded, what entry would be required when the interest expense is paid in April 2023?

Recording bond sinking fund transactions, retained earnings appropriated for bond retirement, and retirement of bonds.

◀ **Problem 22.4A**

Objectives 22-8, 22-9, 22-10

TNCal Company has outstanding $500,000 of its 6 percent bonds payable, dated January 1, 2022, and maturing on January 1, 2042, 20 years later. The corporation is required under the bond contract to transfer $25,000 to a sinking fund each year. The directors have also voted to restrict retained earnings by transferring $25,000 each year on January 1 over the life of the bond issue to a *Retained Earnings Appropriated for Bond Retirement* account.

INSTRUCTIONS

1. Prepare entries in general journal form to record the January 1, 2022, issuance of bonds at face value, the establishment of the *Bond Sinking Fund Investment* account, and the appropriation of retained earnings.
2. Show how the *Bond Sinking Fund Investment* account and the *Retained Earnings Appropriated for Bond Retirement* account would be presented on the balance sheet as of

December 31, 2026. (Assume that the ending balance of the *Bond Sinking Fund Investment* was $125,000 and the *Retained Earnings—Unappropriated* account was $320,210.)

3. Assuming that the *Bond Sinking Fund Investment* account had a balance of $500,000 on January 1, 2042, give the entry in general journal form to record the retirement of the bonds and remove the appropriation for retained earnings.

Analyze: What percentage of total retained earnings has been appropriated for bond retirement on December 31, 2026?

Problem 22.5A
Objective 22-10

▶ **Retiring bonds payable prior to maturity.**

On May 1, 2022, Star Inc. issued $600,000 face value, 10 percent bonds at 98.6. The bonds are dated May 1, 2022, and mature 10 years later. The discount is amortized on each interest payment date. The interest is payable semiannually on May 1 and November 1. On May 1, 2024, after paying the semiannual interest, the corporation purchased the outstanding bonds from the bondholders and retired them. The purchase price was 98.9.

INSTRUCTION

Give the entry in general journal form to record the repurchase and retirement of the bonds. (Use the *Loss on Early Retirement of Bonds* account.)

Analyze: If Star Inc. did not purchase the outstanding bonds, what total bond interest expense would have been incurred over the life of the bonds?

Problem Set B

Problem 22.1B
Objectives 22-3, 22-4, 22-5, 22-6

▶ **Issuing bonds; bond interest transactions.**

The board of directors of Bow Products, Inc., authorized the issuance of $1,000,000 face value, 5 percent bonds dated April 1, 2022. The bonds will mature on April 1, 2032. The interest is payable semiannually on April 1 and October 1. The bond transactions that occurred in 2022 and 2023 are shown below.

INSTRUCTIONS

Record the transactions below in general journal form. Use the account names given in the chapter.

DATE		TRANSACTIONS FOR 2022
April	1	Issued $600,000 of bonds at face value.
Oct.	1	Paid the semiannual bond interest on the outstanding bonds.
Dec.	31	Recorded the adjusting entry to accrue the interest on the bonds issued.
	31	Closed the *Bond Interest Expense* account to the *Income Summary* account.

DATE		TRANSACTIONS FOR 2023
Jan.	1	Reversed the adjusting entry of December 31, 2022.
April	1	Paid the semiannual bond interest.
Oct.	1	Paid the semiannual bond interest.
	1	Issued $400,000 of bonds at face value.
Dec.	31	Recorded the adjusting entry to accrue the interest on all bonds issued.
	31	Closed the *Bond Interest Expense* account to the *Income Summary* account.

Analyze: What total bond interest would have been reported on the income statement for the year ended December 31, 2022?

Issuing bonds; bond interest transactions and amortization of discount.

◀ **Problem 22.2B**

Objectives 22-3, 22-4, 22-5, 22-7

The board of directors of CAR Corporation authorized the issuance of $1,000,000 face value, 6 percent bonds. The bonds mature 10 years from their issue date of March 1, 2022. The interest is payable semiannually on March 1 and September 1. Because the funds were not immediately needed, no bonds were issued until July 1, 2022. Round to the nearest dollar.

INSTRUCTIONS

1. Record the following transactions in general journal form. Use the account names given in the chapter.
2. Prepare the Long-Term Liabilities section of the corporation's balance sheet on December 31, 2022.

DATE		TRANSACTIONS FOR 2022
July	1	Issued $500,000 of bonds at 97.68 plus accrued interest from March 1. (When bonds are issued between interest payment dates, the accrued interest is paid to the corporation by the purchaser. Credit **Bond Interest Expense**.)
Sept.	1	Paid the semiannual bond interest.
	1	Amortized the discount on the bonds issued.
Dec.	31	Recorded the adjusting entry to accrue the interest on the bonds issued and to amortize the discount for four months. (Make one entry.)
	31	Closed the **Bond Interest Expense** account.

DATE		TRANSACTIONS FOR 2023
Jan.	1	Reversed the adjusting entry of December 31, 2022.
Mar.	1	Paid the semiannual bond interest and amortized the discount on the bonds issued.

Analyze: What is the balance of the **Bond Interest Expense** account at December 31, 2022, prior to closing?

Issuing bonds; recording interest transactions and amortization of premium.

◀ **Problem 22.3B**

Objectives 22-3, 22-4, 22-5

The board of directors of Amora Company authorized issuance of $1,000,000 of 6 percent bonds. Each bond has a face value of $10,000. The interest is payable semiannually on February 1 and August 1. The bonds are dated February 1, 2022, and mature 10 years later.

INSTRUCTIONS

1. Record the transactions below in general journal form. Use the account names given in the chapter. (Round your numbers to the nearest whole dollar.)
2. Prepare the Long-Term Liabilities section of the corporation's balance sheet on December 31, 2022.

DATE		TRANSACTIONS FOR 2022
Feb.	1	Issued $500,000 of bonds at 105.
Aug.	1	Paid the semiannual interest on the bonds issued and recorded the amortization of the premium.
Dec.	31	Recorded the adjusting entry to accrue interest on the bonds issued and to amortize the premium for five months. Round to the nearest whole dollar.
	31	Recorded the closing entry for **Bond Interest Expense**.

DATE		TRANSACTIONS FOR 2023
Jan.	1	Reversed the adjusting entry of December 31, 2022.

Analyze: If the reversing entry had not been recorded in January 2023, how would the payment of bond interest be recorded in February 2023?

Problem 22.4B
Objectives 22-8, 22-9, 22-10

Recording bond sinking fund transactions, retained earnings appropriated for bond retirement, and retirement of bonds.

TV Products, Inc., has outstanding $400,000 face value, 5 percent bonds payable dated January 1, 2022, and maturing 10 years later. The corporation is required under the bond contract to transfer $36,000 each year to a sinking fund. The directors have also voted to restrict retained earnings by transferring $40,000 each year to a *Retained Earnings Appropriated for Bond Retirement* account.

INSTRUCTIONS

1. Prepare entries in general journal form to record the 2022 transactions.
2. Prepare the partial balance sheet for December 31, 2031, showing the presentation of the *Bond Sinking Fund Investment* and the *Retained Earnings Appropriated for Bond Retirement* (assume *Retained Earnings—Unappropriated* has a balance of $325,000).
3. Prepare the journal entries to retire the bonds and remove the appropriation of retained earnings on January 1, 2032.

DATE		TRANSACTIONS FOR 2022
Jan.	1	Sold the bonds at 100.
	1	Made the annual bond sinking fund investment deposit.
Dec.	31	Recorded the annual appropriation of retained earnings.
	31	The bond sinking fund trustee reported a net income of $2,500 on the sinking fund investments for the year. (Assume this amount is earned each year within the bond sinking fund.)

On December 31, 2031, the balance in the *Bond Sinking Fund Investment* account is $400,000. The balance in the *Retained Earnings Appropriated for Bond Retirement* account is also $400,000.

Analyze: What percentage of total retained earnings had been allocated for bond retirement at December 31, 2031?

Problem 22.5B
Objective 22-10

Retiring bonds payable prior to maturity.

On April 1, 2022, Big Sky Corporation issued $400,000 face value, 10 percent bonds at 99.16. The bonds were dated April 1, 2022, and will mature in 10 years. The discount is to be amortized on each interest payment date. The interest is payable semiannually on April 1 and October 1. On October 1, 2025, after paying the semiannual bond interest, the corporation decided to retire the bonds. The bondholders were paid 98.5.

INSTRUCTION

Give the entry in general journal form to record the repurchase and retirement of the bonds. (Use the *Gain on Early Retirement of Bonds* account.)

Analyze: If the bond had been retired on the original due date, what credit would have been made to the *Cash* account?

Critical Thinking Problem 22.1

Financing Decision

On December 31, 2022, the equity accounts of Book Creations, Inc., contained the following balances:

Common stock ($10 par, 100,000 shares authorized) 50,000 shares issued and outstanding	$500,000
Retained earnings	$500,000

For the year 2022, the corporation had net income before income taxes of $200,000, income taxes of $42,000, and net income after taxes of $158,000. The corporation's tax rate is 21 percent.

An expansion of the existing plant at a cost of $500,000 is planned. The corporation's president, who owns 60 percent of the corporation's common stock, estimates that the expansion would result in an increased net income of approximately $200,000 before interest and taxes. The financial vice president forecasts that the increase would be only $100,000. Round all calculations to the nearest dollar.

Management is considering two possibilities for financing:

a. Issuance of 40,000 additional shares of common stock for $15 per share.

b. Issuance of $500,000 face amount, 10-year, 6 percent bonds payable, secured by a mortgage lien on the plant.

Assume that profits from existing operations will remain the same.

INSTRUCTIONS

1. Assume that the president's estimate of net income from the new plant is correct. Prepare a two-column table for each of the proposed financing plans. Show the following items: (a) total net income before interest and tax; (b) total bond interest; (c) total income tax; (d) total income after tax; (e) present income after tax; (f) increase or decrease in total income after bond interest and tax; (g) present earnings per share of common stock (compute earnings per share by dividing the net income after taxes by the number of shares of common stock outstanding); (h) estimated earnings per share of common stock.

2. Construct a similar table, assuming the financial vice president's estimate of earnings is correct.

3. Write a brief comment on the results of your analysis.

Analyze: Assume the company issued 40,000 shares of common stock and net income before taxes was $350,000. Would shareholders have realized an increase or decrease in earnings per share over fiscal 2022?

Critical Thinking Problem 22.2

Early Retirement

On December 31, 2022, Express, Inc., has $1,000,000 of 6 percent, 10-year bonds outstanding. These bonds were issued on January 1, 2016, at par value. Interest rates have dropped to 5 percent, and the president of the company is considering buying back the outstanding 6 percent bonds and issuing new 10-year bonds with a 3 percent interest rate.

1. How much money would Express save in interest payments if new, 3 percent bonds were issued?

2. Under what circumstances would this action be advantageous for Express?

BUSINESS CONNECTIONS

Managerial FOCUS

Financing Through Bonds

1. What would cause corporate management to obtain cash by issuing bonds instead of selling stock?
2. Which type of bonds would give management greater flexibility in formulating and controlling a corporation's financial affairs?
3. In what situations would management be wise to issue additional common stock rather than bonds to meet long-term capital needs?
4. Why would management repurchase and retire a corporation's bonds prior to their maturity?
5. SBH Corporation's board of directors is considering authorization of a new bond issue. The controller notes that the bonds are callable at 101.6 at any time beginning five years after the date of the bond contract. What does this mean? What is the advantage of such a provision?

Internal Control and FRAUD PREVENTION

Conflict of Interest

Lorenzo White is the president of the Water Filter Company. As president, he is in control of the issuance of stocks and bonds. Three years ago when the company needed cash, White purchased from the company a $100,000, 4 percent, 10-year unsecured bond. The interest rate has begun to increase. White suggests that the company refinance the bonds to extend the life of the bonds, even though the interest rate has increased to 7 percent. Is this a conflict of interest? Why or why not?

Financial Statement ANALYSIS

Home Depot

Bond Financing Agreements

Refer to the 2018 Form 10-K *(for the fiscal year ended February 3, 2019)* for The Home Depot, Inc.

Analyze:

1. Locate the Notes to Consolidated Financial Statements. The Selected Financial Data presents a detailed list of earnings, selected balance sheet items, cash flow data, and financial ratios. What is the total debt to equity ratio for 2018?
2. Over the past three years, is The Home Depot, Inc., in a better or worse financial situation in regard to the long-term debt?

TEAMWORK

Sell Stocks or Bonds

DanceTime Inc. is a corporate dance studio. It is a popular investment with investors between the ages of 20 and 30. DanceTime has a dilemma. It needs money to expand its business to cash in on its popularity. However, management is not sure whether to sell stock in the company or to sell corporate bonds. The company has $100,000 in liabilities and 1,000,000 authorized shares of common stock, of which 100,000 shares are issued. It has a bid of $1,000,000 to build the additional location. Divide your class into groups with each group representing the board of directors. Discuss whether the company should sell stock or bonds. What price would it need to get for each share? How much should it sell in bonds? What bond characteristics would be the best for the company?

Answers to Comprehensive Self Review

1. Secured bonds are bonds that have specific assets pledged as security. If the corporation does not pay the principal and interest, the bondholders may take possession of the assets. Debenture bonds have no specific assets pledged to secure payment. So, the secured bond is a more attractive investment.
2. Two disadvantages are (a) interest must be paid and (b) the face amount must be repaid at maturity.
3. Bonds sell at a premium when the face interest rate is greater than the market rate of interest on similar investments on the date of the sale.
4. The appropriation is intended to protect the bondholders. It clearly indicates that dividends are being restricted because of a future need to pay off the bonds.
5. When bonds are retired at maturity, **Bonds Payable** is debited and **Cash** (or **Bond Sinking Fund Investment**) is credited. If the company has **Retained Earnings Appropriated** for the bonds, that account should be closed and returned to **Retained Earnings Unappropriated**.

Mini-Practice Set 3

Corporation Accounting Cycle

The Purple Company

This project will give you an opportunity to apply your knowledge of accounting principles and procedures to a corporation. You will handle the accounting work of The Purple Company for 2022.

INTRODUCTION

The chart of accounts and account balances of The Purple Company on January 1, 2022, are shown below. The company *does not* use reversing entries.

INSTRUCTIONS

Round all computations to the nearest whole dollar.

1. Open the general ledger accounts and enter the balances for January 1, 2022. Obtain the necessary figures from the trial balance.
2. Analyze the transactions below and record them in the general journal. Use 1 as the number of the first journal page.
3. Post the journal entries to the general ledger accounts.
4. Prepare a worksheet for the year ended December 31, 2022.
5. Prepare a summary income statement for the year ended December 31, 2022.
6. Prepare a statement of retained earnings for the year ended December 31, 2022.
7. Prepare a balance sheet as of December 31, 2022.
8. Journalize and post the adjusting entries as of December 31, 2022.
9. Journalize and post the closing entries as of December 31, 2022.

Analyze: Assume that the firm declared and issued a 3:1 stock split of common stock in 2022. What is the effect on total par value?

The Purple Company
Chart of Accounts/Account Balances on January 1, 2022

Account Number	Account Name	Debit	Credit
101	Cash	$176,000	
103	Accounts Receivable	170,000	
104	Allowance for Doubtful Accounts		$ 5,000
105	Subscriptions Receivable—Common Stock		
121	Interest Receivable		
131	Merchandise Inventory	150,000	
141	Land	85,000	
151	Buildings	225,000	
152	Accumulated Depreciation—Buildings		22,500
161	Furniture and Equipment	70,000	
162	Accumulated Depreciation—Furniture and Equipment		14,000
202	Accounts Payable		75,000
203	Interest Payable		2,500
205	Estimated Income Taxes Payable		17,000
206	Dividends Payable—Preferred Stock		
207	Dividends Payable—Common Stock		
211	10-year, 10% Bonds Payable		100,000
212	Premium on Bonds Payable		2,625
301	5% Preferred Stock ($100 par, 10,000 shares authorized)		100,000
302	Paid-In Capital in Excess of Par—Preferred Stock		10,000
303	Common Stock ($10 par, 100,000 shares authorized)		200,000
304	Paid-in Capital in Excess of Par—Common Stock		25,000
305	Common Stock Subscribed		
306	Common Stock Dividend Distributable		
311	Retained Earnings Appropriated		100,000
312	Retained Earnings Unappropriated		202,375
343	Treasury Stock—Preferred		
399	Income Summary		
401	Sales		
501	Purchases		
601	Operating Expenses		
701	Interest Income		
711	Gain on Early Retirement of Bonds Payable		
751	Interest Expense		
801	Income Tax Expense		
	Totals	$876,000	$876,000

DATE		TRANSACTIONS FOR 2022
Jan.	5	Issued 1,000 shares of 5 percent $100 par preferred stock for $101 per share. (The corporation has been authorized to issue 10,000 shares of preferred stock.)
	15	Paid estimated income taxes of $17,000 accrued at the end of 2021.
Apr.	1	Paid semiannual bond interest on the 10-year, 10 percent bonds payable and amortized the premium for the period since December 31, 2021. (The interest and premium were recorded as of December 31, 2021; the entry was not reversed.) The bonds were issued on October 1, 2020, at a price of 103, and they mature on October 1, 2030. Use straight-line amortization.
July	1	The board of directors declared a cash dividend of $0.10 per share on the common stock. The dividend is payable on July 26 to stockholders of record as of July 15.
	26	Paid the cash dividend on the common stock.
Aug.	12	A purchaser of 600 shares of preferred stock issued on January 5 asked the corporation to repurchase the shares. The corporation repurchased the stock for $102 per share. The stock is to be held by the corporation until it can be resold to another purchaser.
Oct.	1	Paid the semiannual bond interest and recorded amortization of the bond premium.
Dec.	1	Because of its good cash position and current bond prices, The Purple Company repurchased and retired $20,000 par value of the 10 percent bonds that it has outstanding. The repurchase price was 98, plus accrued interest.
	15	The company's board of directors declared a cash dividend of $5 per share on the outstanding preferred stock. This dividend is payable on January 10 to stockholders of record as of December 31.
	15	The board of directors also declared a 10 percent stock dividend on the outstanding common stock. The new shares are to be distributed on January 10 to stockholders of record as of December 31. At the time the dividend was declared, the common stock had a fair market value of $15 per share.
	30	Received a subscription for 500 shares of The Purple Company's common stock at $12 per share from the company's president. Received cash equal to one-half the purchase price on the date of subscription. The balance of the purchase price is to be paid on January 15, 2023. (The subscriber will not be entitled to the stock dividend previously declared on the outstanding shares of common stock.)
	30	Because the management of Purple foresees the need to expand a warehouse the firm owns, the board of directors has restricted future dividend payments. Record the appropriation of $100,000 of retained earnings for plant expansion.

Journalize the following summary transactions using December 31, 2022, as the record date:

	SUMMARY OPERATING TRANSACTIONS FOR 2022
1.	Total sales of merchandise for the year were $2,800,000. All sales were on credit.
2.	Total collections on accounts receivable during the year were $2,810,000.
3.	Total purchases of merchandise for the year were $1,880,000. All purchases were on credit.
4.	Total operating expenses incurred during the year were $650,000. (Debit **Operating Expenses** and credit **Accounts Payable**.)
5.	Total cash payments on accounts payable during the year were $2,335,000.
6.	Total accounts receivable charged off as uncollectible during the year were $10,000. (The Orange Company uses the allowance method to record uncollectible accounts.)

Data for Year-End Adjustments

1. The balance of *Allowance for Doubtful Accounts* should be adjusted to equal 3 percent of the balance of *Accounts Receivable*. (Debit *Operating Expenses*.)
2. Depreciation on the buildings should be recorded. (Debit *Operating Expenses*.) The firm uses the straight-line method and an estimated life of 20 years to compute this adjustment.
3. Depreciation on furniture and equipment should be recorded. The firm uses the straight-line method and an estimated life of 10 years to compute this adjustment. (Debit *Operating Expenses*.)
4. Accrued interest on the outstanding bonds payable of The Purple Company should be recorded and the premium amortized.
5. The ending merchandise inventory is $130,000.

Other Data

Estimated federal income taxes are to be recorded using the tax rate of 21%. Round your amount to the nearest dollar.

Financial Statement Analysis

Chapter 23

Abigail McCann/Shutterstock

www.cvs.com

CVS Health Corporation (CVS) was started by brothers Stanley and Sidney Goldstein and Ralph Hoagland as a single store in Lowell, Massachusetts, in 1963. Since that time CVS has expanded to more than 9,800 retail locations throughout the United States, Puerto Rico, and Brazil. This extraordinary growth has fueled overall sales, with CVS reporting Net Revenues of nearly $185 billion within its 2017 annual report. How though does an investor determine if this indicates that CVS is a good investment? To make an educated decision, a potential investor must analyze financial results over multiple years, both for CVS as well as for its competitors.

A financial statement analysis of the 2017 annual report for CVS indicates an increase in Net Revenues of 4.1% over the prior year, and an increase in Cash Dividends per Common Share of 17.6%. These figures sound favorable, but to create a more complete picture of the company's performance, an investor should also examine financial ratios. One such metric is the Current Ratio (Current Assets/Current Liabilities), which, based on 2017 annual report data, decreased from 1.18 in 2016 to 1.02 in 2017. This indicates that the company's ability to satisfy short-term liabilities has weakened over the past year. Another widely used metric is Basic Earnings per Share, which, per the CVS 2017 annual report, has increased from 4.93 in 2016 to 6.47 in 2017, indicating that CVS was more profitable in 2017 on a per share basis. While evaluating the financial performance of a company can be a complex process, a thorough financial statement analysis helps to focus an investor on key elements of the financial statements, such as those outlined above.

thinking critically

How can studying and comparing how a company performed from one year to the next help potential investors decide whether to invest in a company?

LEARNING OBJECTIVES

- **23-1** Use vertical analysis techniques to analyze a comparative income statement and balance sheet.
- **23-2** Use horizontal analysis techniques to analyze a comparative income statement and balance sheet.
- **23-3** Use trend analysis to evaluate financial statements.
- **23-4** Interpret the results of the statement analyses by comparison with industry averages.
- **23-5** Compute and interpret financial ratios that measure profitability, operating results, and efficiency.
- **23-6** Compute and interpret financial ratios that measure financial strength.
- **23-7** Compute and interpret financial ratios that measure liquidity.
- **23-8** Recognize shortcomings in financial statement analysis.
- **23-9** Define the accounting terms new to this chapter.

NEW TERMS

accounts receivable turnover
acid-test ratio
asset turnover
average collection period
common-size statements
comparative statements
horizontal analysis
industry averages
leveraged buyout
price-earnings ratio
quick assets
ratio analysis
return on common stockholders' equity
total equities
trend analysis
vertical analysis

Section 1

SECTION OBJECTIVES	TERMS TO LEARN
>> 23-1 Use vertical analysis techniques to analyze a comparative income statement and balance sheet. **WHY IT'S IMPORTANT** Analysis techniques reveal the financial strengths and weaknesses of a business.	common-size statements comparative statements horizontal analysis ratio analysis vertical analysis

Vertical Analysis

Owners, managers, creditors, and other parties use financial statements to gather the information needed to make business decisions.

The Phases of Statement Analysis

The two phases of financial statement analysis are (1) compute differences, percentages, and ratios and (2) interpret the results.

The Computation Phase

The first step in financial statement analysis is the *computation phase*. Three basic types of calculations are used:

- **Vertical analysis** is the relationship of each item on a financial statement to some base amount on the statement. On the income statement, each item is expressed as a percentage of net sales. On the balance sheet, each item is expressed as a percentage of total assets or total liabilities and stockholders' equity.
- **Horizontal analysis** is the percentage change for individual items in the financial statements from year to year.
- **Ratio analysis** is the relationship between various items in the financial statements. Ratio analysis can involve items on the same statement or items on different statements. Ratio analysis is a form of analytical review.

The Interpretation Phase

The second step in statement analysis, the *interpretation phase,* is the more difficult and important step. Financial statement interpretation requires an understanding of financial statements and knowledge of the operations of the business and its industry. In the interpretation phase, the analyst develops an understanding of the significance of the percentages and ratios computed. Analysts compare the ratios for the current year to prior years' ratios, budgeted ratios, and industry averages.

>> **23-1 OBJECTIVE**
Use vertical analysis techniques to analyze a comparative income statement and balance sheet.

Vertical Analysis of Financial Statements

Let's learn the techniques of vertical analysis of financial statements using comparative financial statements. **Comparative statements** are financial statements presented side by side for

FIGURE 23.1 Comparative Income Statement—Vertical Analysis

Direct Sales, Inc.
Comparative Income Statement (Vertical Analysis)
Years Ended December 31, 2022 and 2021

	Amounts 2022	Amounts 2021	Percent of Net Sales* 2022	Percent of Net Sales* 2021
Revenue				
Sales	3,104,450	2,825,625	104.6	104.7
Less Sales Returns and Allowances	135,450	125,625	4.6	4.7
Net Sales	2,969,000	2,700,000	100.0	100.0
Cost of Goods Sold				
Merchandise Inventory, January 1	225,000	215,000	7.6	8.0
Purchases (Net)	1,706,500	1,565,721	57.5	58.0
Freight In	26,000	19,000	0.9	0.7
Total Merchandise Available for Sale	1,957,500	1,799,721	66.0	66.7
Less Merchandise Inventory, December 31	205,000	225,000	6.9	8.3
Cost of Goods Sold	1,752,500	1,574,721	59.0	58.4
Gross Profit	1,216,500	1,125,279	41.0	41.7
Operating Expenses				
Selling Expenses	526,425	496,750	17.7	18.4
General and Administrative Expenses	605,000	599,300	20.4	22.2
Total Operating Expenses	1,131,425	1,096,050	38.1	40.6
Net Income from Operations	85,075	29,229	2.9	1.1
Other Income				
Gain on Sale of Equipment	4,000	15,000	0.1	0.6
Interest Income	1,800	1,700	0.1	0.1
Total Other Income	5,800	16,700	0.2	0.7
Other Expenses				
Bond Interest Expense	9,500	9,500	0.3	0.4
Other Interest Expense	2,000	2,500	0.1	0.1
Total Other Expenses	11,500	12,000	0.4	0.4
Income before Income Taxes	79,375	33,929	2.7	1.3
Income Tax Expense	23,812	10,179	0.8	0.4
Net Income after Income Taxes	55,563	23,750	1.9	0.9

*Rounded, percentages may not add up as expected.

two or more years. Figure 23.1 shows the comparative income statement of Direct Sales, Inc., for the years 2021 and 2022.

Vertical Analysis of the Income Statement

Notice the income statement heading. The third line indicates the periods covered by the statement. The more recent year, 2022, is in the left column. The income statement is in condensed form. In actual practice, separate schedules of the detailed Selling Expenses and General and Administrative Expenses are provided with the financial statements.

Vertical analysis of the income statement expresses each item as a percentage of the *net sales* figure. In each column, the net sales figure is used as the base, or 100 percent. Every amount in the column is expressed as a percentage of net sales. To compute an item's percentage of net

ABOUT ACCOUNTING

NYSE

The New York Stock Exchange (NYSE) is the world's largest stock exchange by market capitalization of $30.1 trillion in February 2018. NYSE is owned by Intercontinental Exchange (ICE).

---

important!

Rounding

In statement analysis, it is customary to compute percentages to the nearest one-tenth of a percent. This procedure is followed in this chapter.

---

important!

Percentages

In common-size statements, percentages (of net sales on the income statement and of total assets on the balance sheet) are shown instead of dollar amounts.

---

sales, divide the amount of that item by the amount of net sales. For example, in 2022 the cost of goods sold is 59.0 percent of net sales:

$$\frac{\text{Cost of goods sold}}{\text{Net sales}} = \frac{\$1{,}752{,}500}{\$2{,}969{,}000} = 0.5903 = 59.03 \text{ percent}$$
(rounded to 59.0 percent)

In making these types of computations, it is customary to carry the division one place further than needed and then round off. The usual practice is to round percentages to the nearest one-tenth of a percent. The computation in the example is made to the fourth decimal (0.5903). That decimal fraction is converted to a percentage by moving the decimal point two places to the right (59.03 percent). The percentage is then rounded to the nearest one-tenth of a percent; hence, 59.03 is rounded to 59.0.

In Figure 23.1, note that gross sales are more than 100 percent ($3,104,450 ÷ $2,969,000 = 104.6 percent in 2022). That is because of **Sales Returns and Allowances,** which are 4.6 percent of net sales.

The percentages may be added and subtracted, giving informative subtotals and totals. Because of rounding, the individual percentages may not add up to 100 percent. In this case, one or more percentages are adjusted slightly until the total equals 100 percent. If the difference is more than a small amount, it is probable that an error has been made, and all the computations should be checked before adjusting any of the amounts.

Financial statements with items expressed as percentages of a base amount are called **common-size statements.** The last two columns in the comparative income statement are referred to as a *comparative common-size statement.*

Percentages obtained by vertical analysis of the income statement are useful when compared with the company's percentages for prior years. It is helpful to make comparisons with several years to detect trends, but even year-to-year comparisons are useful. For example, the comparative income statement of Direct Sales, Inc., shows gross profit on sales of 41.7 percent in 2021 and 41.0 percent in 2022. A comparison with the industry average might be helpful. For example, suppose that trade association publications reveal that the average gross profit for the industry is 51.7 percent. Direct Sales, Inc.'s gross profit on sales compares unfavorably to the industry average. This could be attributed to peculiarities of its operations, local competition, or other factors. However, it indicates the need for further examination.

Vertical Analysis of the Balance Sheet

Vertical analysis of the balance sheet expresses each item as a percentage either of total assets or of total liabilities and stockholders' equity.

Figure 23.2 shows a comparative balance sheet for Direct Sales, Inc., with the vertical analysis results. The pair of columns on the right shows each item as a percentage of total assets for each year. The more recent year is on the left. On December 31, 2022, the cash balance was $115,231 and the total assets were $555,711. Thus, the cash balance is 20.7 percent of total assets in 2022:

$$\frac{\text{Cash}}{\text{Total assets}} = \frac{\$115{,}231}{\$555{,}711} = 0.2074 = 20.7 \text{ percent}$$

In rounding off, it might be necessary to adjust one or more of the figures to obtain an even 100 percent for each total, if desired.

Vertical analysis percentages of the balance sheet are very useful when they are compared with the percentages of the same company for previous years and with those of other companies in the same industry. Changes in the percentages might reveal situations that need investigation. For example, the comparative balance sheet of Direct Sales, Inc., shows that cash has increased from 15.5 percent of total assets in 2021 to 20.7 percent of total assets in 2022. The accountant may suggest that this increase be studied.

FIGURE 23.2 Comparative Balance Sheet—Vertical Analysis

Direct Sales, Inc.
Comparative Balance Sheet (Vertical Analysis)
December 31, 2022 and 2021

	Amounts on December 31		Percent of Total Assets	
	2022	2021	2022	2021
Assets				
Current Assets				
Cash	115,231	80,773	20.7	15.5
Accounts Receivable	102,000	73,500	18.4	14.1
Merchandise Inventory	205,000	225,000	36.9	43.3
Prepaid Expenses	1,200	1,500	0.2	0.3
Supplies	500	250	0.1	0.0
Total Current Assets	423,931	381,023	76.3	73.2
Property, Plant, and Equipment				
Land	80,000	80,000	14.4	15.4
Building and Store Equipment	71,800	77,800	12.9	15.0
Less Accumulated Depreciation—Building and Store Equipment	28,520	23,340	5.1	4.5
Net Book Value—Building and Store Equipment	43,280	54,460	7.8	10.5
Office Equipment	10,500	6,000	1.9	1.2
Less Accumulated Depreciation—Office Equipment	2,000	1,500	0.4	0.3
Net Book Value—Office Equipment	8,500	4,500	1.5	0.9
Total Property, Plant, and Equipment	131,780	138,960	23.7	26.7
Total Assets	555,711	519,983	100.0	100.0
Liabilities and Stockholders' Equity				
Current Liabilities				
Accounts Payable	71,000	84,500	12.8	16.3
Sales Tax Payable	2,900	2,500	0.5	0.5
Payroll Taxes Payable	1,145	1,025	0.2	0.2
Interest Payable	860	215	0.2	0.0
Total Current Liabilities	75,905	88,240	13.7	17.0
Long-Term Liabilities				
10% Bonds Payable, 2031	100,000	100,000	18.0	19.2
Premium on Bonds Payable	3,500	4,000	0.6	0.8
Mortgage Payable	60,000	65,000	10.8	12.5
Total Long-Term Liabilities	163,500	169,000	29.4	32.5
Total Liabilities	239,405	257,240	43.1	49.5
Stockholders' Equity				
Preferred Stock ($100 par, 8%, 500 shares authorized, issued and outstanding)	50,000	50,000	9.0	9.6
Common Stock ($1 par, 25,000 shares authorized)				
Issued and outstanding: 7,000 shares in 2021; 8,000 shares in 2022	8,000	7,000	1.4	1.3
Paid-in Capital—Common Stock	4,500	3,500	0.8	0.7
Retained Earnings				
Retained Earnings—Unappropriated	253,806	202,243	45.7	38.9
Total Retained Earnings	253,806	202,243	45.7	38.9
Total Stockholders' Equity	316,306	262,743	56.9	50.5
Total Liabilities and Stockholders' Equity	555,711	519,983	100.0	100.0

Section 1 Review

1. How does the computation phase of statement analysis differ from the interpretation phase?
   a. The computation phase involves estimates.
   b. The interpretation phase takes foreign currency amounts and interprets those to dollar amounts.
   c. Basic math computations are used in statement analysis.
   d. The computation phase is only done every five years.

2. What is a common-size statement?
   a. a statement that does not contain dollar amounts but only displays percentages
   b. a statement that averages the company's past five years of data
   c. a statement based on U.S. dollars
   d. all the above

3. What item serves as the base for the percentage calculations in a vertical analysis of the income statement?
   a. Total Sales
   b. Net Sales
   c. Net Income
   d. Gross Profit

4. Which of the following is true of vertical analysis?
   a. Each item on the balance sheet is expressed as a percentage of total liabilities.
   b. Each item in the income statement is divided by net sales.
   c. Each item in the income statement is expressed as a percentage of net income.
   d. The amount of increase or decrease for each item in the income statement is divided by net sales.

5. In a vertical analysis of a balance sheet, each item is expressed as a percentage of:
   a. total assets or total liabilities.
   b. total assets or total stockholders' equity.
   c. total assets or total liabilities and stockholders' equity.
   d. total liabilities or total stockholders' equity.

6. Net sales for 2022 were $1,200,000. Net income after income taxes for 2022 was $60,000. Compute the percentage of net income after taxes (based on net sales) for 2022.
   a. 5.0%
   b. 50%
   c. 0.5%
   d. 105%

Section 2

SECTION OBJECTIVES	TERMS TO LEARN
>> 23-2 Use horizontal analysis techniques to analyze a comparative income statement and balance sheet. **WHY IT'S IMPORTANT** Analysis techniques help managers pinpoint operational or procedural problems that require investigation. **>> 23-3** Use trend analysis to evaluate financial statements. **WHY IT'S IMPORTANT** Review of several years of financial data can reveal performance trends. **>> 23-4** Interpret the results of the statement analyses by comparison with industry averages. **WHY IT'S IMPORTANT** Global competition requires businesses to remain in touch with industry trends and financial conditions.	industry averages trend analysis

Horizontal Analysis

In this section, you will learn the second type of basic calculation, horizontal analysis.

Horizontal Analysis of Financial Statements

Financial statements for two or more periods may be evaluated by means of horizontal analysis. Horizontal analysis compares the items on each line to determine the change in dollar amounts. A percentage change can be shown by using the earlier figure as the base.

Horizontal Analysis of the Income Statement

Let's learn the techniques of horizontal analysis using the comparative income statement. Figure 23.3 shows the comparative income statement of Direct Sales, Inc., for 2021 and 2022.

Each amount for 2022 is compared to the corresponding amount for 2021. The increase or decrease of the change and the percentage of change are shown in the right two columns. Look at the sales figures. The gross sales for 2022 are higher than those for 2021. The increase is $278,825:

>> **23-2 OBJECTIVE**
Use horizontal analysis techniques to analyze a comparative income statement and balance sheet.

Sales for 2022	$ 3,104,450
Sales for 2021	−2,825,625
Increase	$ 278,825

To find the percentage of increase, divide the increase by the amount for the base year. The base year is always the earlier year. The percentage of increase for gross sales is 9.9 percent:

$$\frac{\text{Increase in sales}}{\text{Sales for base year}} = \frac{\$278{,}825}{\$2{,}825{,}625} = 9.9 \text{ percent}$$

If the amount for the most recent year is less than that for the base year, the percentage decrease is calculated in the same manner. For example, ending merchandise inventory decreased by $20,000 for 2022. Divide the decrease by the base year amount:

$$\frac{\text{Amount of decrease}}{\text{Amount in base year}} = \frac{(\$20{,}000)}{\$225{,}000} = (8.9) \text{ percent}$$

FIGURE 23.3 Comparative Income Statement—Horizontal Analysis

Direct Sales, Inc.
Comparative Income Statement (Horizontal Analysis)
Years Ended December 31, 2022 and 2021

	Amounts 2022	Amounts 2021	Increase or (Decrease) Amount	Percent*
Revenue				
Sales	3,104,450	2,825,625	278,825	9.9
Less Sales Returns and Allowances	135,450	125,625	9,825	7.8
Net Sales	2,969,000	2,700,000	269,000	10.0
Cost of Goods Sold				
Merchandise Inventory, January 1	225,000	215,000	10,000	4.7
Purchases (Net)	1,706,500	1,565,721	140,779	9.0
Freight In	26,000	19,000	7,000	36.8
Total Merchandise Available for Sale	1,957,500	1,799,721	157,779	8.8
Less Merchandise Inventory, December 31	205,000	225,000	(20,000)	(8.9)
Cost of Goods Sold	1,752,500	1,574,721	177,779	11.3
Gross Profit	1,216,500	1,125,279	91,221	8.1
Operating Expenses				
Selling Expenses	526,425	496,750	29,675	6.0
General and Administrative Expenses	605,000	599,300	5,700	1.0
Total Operating Expenses	1,131,425	1,096,050	35,375	3.2
Net Income from Operations	85,075	29,229	55,846	191.1
Other Income				
Gain on Sale of Equipment	4,000	15,000	(11,000)	(73.3)
Interest Income	1,800	1,700	100	5.9
Total Other Income	5,800	16,700	(10,900)	(65.3)
Other Expenses				
Bond Interest Expense	9,500	9,500	0	0.0
Other Interest Expense	2,000	2,500	(500)	(20.0)
Total Other Expenses	11,500	12,000	(500)	(4.2)
Net Income before Income Taxes	79,375	33,929	45,446	133.9
Income Tax Expense	23,812	10,179	13,633	133.9
Net Income after Income Taxes	55,563	23,750	31,813	133.9

*Rounded

A decrease can be expressed by using a negative sign before the number, italics, or parentheses.

All the amounts in the right two columns on the comparative statement are computed in the same manner. If the amount of change is zero, there is no percentage of change. When there is no amount for the base period, no percentage change is computed.

Interpretation of the Percentages The amounts of increase or decrease can be added or subtracted in the column and will give correct subtotals at each point. However, the percentages cannot be added or subtracted. Each percentage relates only to the line on which it appears.

Some important changes shown in the comparative income statement for Direct Sales, Inc., include the following:

- Gross sales increased 9.9 percent.
- Cost of goods sold increased 11.3 percent.

important!

Base Year

In preparing horizontal percentage analyses, the earlier year is used as the base for computing the percentage of change.

- Gross profit on sales increased 8.1 percent.
- Total operating expenses increased 3.2 percent.
- Net income from operations increased 191.1 percent.
- Income tax expense increased 133.9 percent.
- Net income after income taxes increased 133.9 percent.

Horizontal analysis is especially useful in identifying items that need further investigation. For example, the increase in net sales was 10.0 percent, but the increase in cost of goods sold was 11.3 percent. An alert manager would want to determine the reasons for the increase in cost of goods sold.

Management would also be interested in learning why freight increased 36.8 percent during 2022 while purchases increased only 9.0 percent.

Keep in mind that percentages of increase or decrease can be misleading when small amounts are involved. For example, total other income decreased 65.3 percent. However, in terms of actual dollars, the amount is relatively small, from $16,700 to $5,800. On the other hand, a small percentage change is important for items involving large dollar amounts.

The process of interpretation is easier if some basis of comparison is available, such as a company budget or industry averages. Significant changes need to be investigated in detail and the reasons evaluated.

important!

Adding It Up
In horizontal analysis, the amounts in the Increase or (Decrease) column can be added or subtracted vertically, but the percentages cannot be.

Horizontal Analysis of the Balance Sheet

A firm's balance sheets for two or more periods can be presented in comparative form to permit a detailed horizontal analysis. Figure 23.4 shows a comparative balance sheet for Direct Sales, Inc., for December 31 of 2021 and 2022.

The calculations are the same as those for a horizontal analysis of income statements. The amounts are compared line by line. For example, for accounts receivable, the difference is an increase of $28,500 ($102,000 − $73,500). The percentage of change is 38.8 percent. It is determined by dividing the amount of the change by the base year (2021) amount: $28,500 ÷ $73,500 = 38.78, or 38.8 percent.

Trend Analysis of Financial Statements

>> **23-3 OBJECTIVE**
Use trend analysis to evaluate financial statements.

Comparing ratio and percentage relationships of the current year with those of the immediately preceding year is a normal and helpful procedure. However, comparisons between only two years could be misleading and might not be adequate to indicate long-term trends. A better technique is **trend analysis,** which compares selected ratios and percentages over a period of time. Often the time period is five years.

Let's look at one trend. The percentage of gross profit to net sales decreased from 41.7 percent in 2021 to 41.0 percent in 2022 (Figure 23.1). A higher gross profit percentage is desirable, so the decrease is unfavorable. A comparison with the several prior years follows:

	2018	2019	2020	2021	2022
Net sales	$2,055,600	$2,223,240	$2,587,500	$2,700,000	$2,969,000
Cost of goods sold	1,059,900	1,234,560	1,495,642	1,574,721	1,752,500
Gross profit on sales	$ 995,700	$ 988,680	$1,091,858	$1,125,279	$1,216,500
Percentage of gross profit to net sales	48.4	44.5	42.2	41.7	41.0

In looking at the data over five years, it is clear that the decrease in percentage from 2018 to 2022 is significant. It calls for the attention of management. Management must obtain other facts, talk with employees, and observe other trends before arriving at a solution to the problem.

FIGURE 23.4 A Comparative Balance Sheet—Horizontal Analysis

Direct Sales, Inc.
Comparative Balance Sheet (Horizontal Analysis)
December 31, 2022 and 2021

	Amounts 2022	Amounts 2021	Increase or (Decrease) Amount	Percent*
Assets				
Current Assets				
Cash	115,231	80,773	34,458	42.7
Accounts Receivable	102,000	73,500	28,500	38.8
Merchandise Inventory	205,000	225,000	(20,000)	(8.9)
Prepaid Expenses	1,200	1,500	(300)	(20.0)
Supplies	500	250	250	100.0
Total Current Assets	423,931	381,023	42,908	11.3
Property, Plant, and Equipment				
Land	80,000	80,000	0	0.0
Building and Store Equipment	71,800	77,800	(6,000)	(7.7)
Less Accumulated Depreciation—Building and Store Equipment	28,520	23,340	5,180	22.2
Net Book Value—Building and Store Equipment	43,280	54,460	(11,180)	(20.5)
Office Equipment	10,500	6,000	4,500	75.0
Less Accumulated Depreciation—Office Equipment	2,000	1,500	500	33.3
Net Book Value—Office Equipment	8,500	4,500	4,000	88.9
Total Property, Plant, and Equipment	131,780	138,960	(7,180)	(5.2)
Total Assets	555,711	519,983	35,728	6.9
Liabilities and Stockholders' Equity				
Current Liabilities				
Accounts Payable	71,000	84,500	(13,500)	(16.0)
Sales Tax Payable	2,900	2,500	400	16.0
Payroll Taxes Payable	1,145	1,025	120	11.7
Interest Payable	860	215	645	300.0
Total Current Liabilities	75,905	88,240	(12,335)	(14.0)
Long-Term Liabilities				
10% Bonds Payable, 2031	100,000	100,000	0	0.0
Premium on Bonds Payable	3,500	4,000	(500)	(12.5)
Mortgage Payable	60,000	65,000	(5,000)	(7.7)
Total Long-Term Liabilities	163,500	169,000	(5,500)	(3.3)
Total Liabilities	239,405	257,240	(17,835)	(6.9)
Stockholders' Equity				
Preferred Stock ($100 par, 8%, 500 shares authorized, issued and outstanding)	50,000	50,000	0	0.0
Common Stock ($1 par, 25,000 shares authorized) Issued and outstanding: 7,000 shares in 2021; 8,000 shares in 2022	8,000	7,000	1,000	14.3
Paid-in Capital—Common Stock	4,500	3,500	1,000	28.6
Retained Earnings				
Retained Earnings—Unappropriated	253,806	202,243	51,563	25.5
Total Retained Earnings	253,806	202,243	51,563	25.5
Total Stockholders' Equity	316,306	262,743	53,563	20.4
Total Liabilities and Stockholders' Equity	555,711	519,983	35,728	6.9

*Rounded

MANAGERIAL IMPLICATIONS

COMPARATIVE STATEMENTS

- Statement analysis is extremely important to managers in detecting areas of strength and weakness in a business.
- Comparison of current data with the data of prior years indicates favorable and unfavorable trends.
- Managers compare percentages from year to year and with industry averages in order to detect variations that require prompt investigation.
- Management must consider certain factors when using industry averages.

THINKING CRITICALLY

What type of financial statement analysis would you use to assess profitability of a company for the last five years?

Trend analysis makes it possible to ask questions about all aspects of operations of the company. The accountant makes the most valuable contribution to the success of the business when analyzing operating data.

Comparison with Industry Averages

Trade associations survey their members to obtain financial and other data. The financial ratios and percentages that reflect averages for similar companies are called **industry averages.** These data are converted to a uniform presentation, usually in common-size statements arranged by company size (based on sales volume or total assets). Income statement items are expressed as a percentage of net sales and balance sheet items as a percentage of total assets. Common-size statements can be presented for one year or for several years. Individual companies compare their results to industry averages.

Let's look at an example of how the management of Direct Sales, Inc., might evaluate the corporation in comparison with others in the same industry. Table 23.1 shows highly condensed data from its income statement as well as the data provided by the trade association for companies with the same general sales level. Note that income tax expense has been omitted. Because companies included in the trade averages are sole proprietorships, partnerships, and corporations, it is not appropriate to compare net income after income taxes with entities that do not pay taxes.

You can see why the comparison to industry averages would be of interest to management, owners, and others. The operations of Direct Sales, Inc., are not as efficient or as profitable as those of its competitors. Its rate of gross profit is lower (and on a downward trend) than the industry averages. Its ratio of operating expenses to net sales is higher than that of others in the industry. The end result is that Direct Sales, Inc.'s ratio of income before income tax to sales is much lower than that of its competitors. Based on this comparison, management needs to immediately determine the causes of its poor results.

In comparing to industry averages, keep in mind the following:

- Different businesses keep different types of accounts and do not classify items in the same manner.
- No two businesses are exactly alike. There are differences in the merchandise sold, the type of customers, and the method of financing (owners' equity versus borrowed funds). Some businesses buy fixed assets while others lease all or some of the fixed assets.
- The industry figures could include data from corporations, partnerships, and sole proprietorships. The different business entities might report salary allowances, benefits for owners, and other items in very different ways.

Despite these problems, common-size statements provided by trade associations or commercial financial service companies are important to managers in comparing their operations to those of other firms. They are of special value when comparing data not affected by the factors listed above.

---

recall

Consistency Principle
The consistency principle permits comparisons between years. Using the same methods allows meaningful comparisons.

>> 23-4 OBJECTIVE
Interpret the results of the statement analyses by comparison with industry averages.

TABLE 23.1
Comparison of Trade Data

| | Percentage of Net Sales* | | | |
| | Direct Sales, Inc. | | Industry Average | |
	2022	2021	2022	2021
Revenue				
Sales	104.6	104.7	104.0	103.5
Returns and Allowances	4.6	4.7	4.0	3.5
Net Sales	100.0	100.0	100.0	100.0
Cost of Goods Sold	59.0	58.3	50.5	47.0
Gross Profit on Sales	41.0	41.7	49.5	53.0
Operating Expenses				
Selling Expenses	17.7	18.4	18.2	20.1
General Expenses	20.4	22.2	19.5	22.0
Total Operating Expenses	38.1	40.6*	37.7	42.1
Operating Income	2.9	1.1	11.8	10.9
Other Income and Expenses				
Other Income	0.2	0.6	0.9	1.2
Other Expenses	(0.4)	(0.4)	(0.5)	(0.1)
Net Other Income or (Exp.)	(0.2)	0.2	0.4	1.1
Income before Income Tax	2.7	1.3	12.2	12.0

*Rounded

Section 2 Review

1. In horizontal analysis of the balance sheet, how is the percentage of change determined?
   a. base year and current year amounts added and the total divided by 2
   b. base year amount divided by current year amount
   c. current year minus base year divided by base year
   d. current year divided by total assets

2. In the same industry, when comparing an established company and a newer one, which company would have a higher percentage of net property, plant, and equipment to total assets and why?
   a. new company because it has not taken significant depreciation
   b. established company because it has purchased more PP&E over time
   c. new company because it has higher credit limits available
   d. All the above are possible answers.

3. Why is comparison with industry averages helpful when analyzing financial statements?
   a. Companies want to be average.
   b. It serves as a baseline for comparison with similar companies of larger/smaller size.
   c. Management bonuses are based on averages.
   d. It is helpful in evaluating sales campaigns.

4. If a comparative balance sheet shows the amount and percentage of decrease in merchandise inventory from one year to the next, the firm used:
   a. horizontal analysis.
   b. vertical analysis.
   c. common-size analysis.
   d. trend analysis.

5. If current assets are $200,000 and total assets are $500,000, the percentage of current assets to total assets is:
   a. 15 percent.
   b. 5 percent.
   c. 40 percent.
   d. 3 percent.

6. Total selling expenses for 2022 were $749,100. Net sales for 2022 were $3,300,000. What are total selling expenses as a percentage of net sales?
   a. 4.6%
   b. 21.2%
   c. 2.3%
   d. 22.7%

Section 3

SECTION OBJECTIVES	TERMS TO LEARN
>> 23-5 Compute and interpret financial ratios that measure profitability, operating results, and efficiency. **WHY IT'S IMPORTANT** Various factors, in combination with the measurement of net income, contribute to the overall prosperity of a company. **>> 23-6** Compute and interpret financial ratios that measure financial strength. **WHY IT'S IMPORTANT** The long-term viability of a business depends on effective use of equity and earnings. **>> 23-7** Compute and interpret financial ratios that measure liquidity. **WHY IT'S IMPORTANT** To establish financial credibility, a business needs to demonstrate its ability to pay its debts when due. **>> 23-8** Recognize shortcomings in financial statement analysis. **WHY IT'S IMPORTANT** The analysis of financial statements, without considering different accounting processes or operational procedures, could lead to improper conclusions.	accounts receivable turnover acid-test ratio asset turnover average collection period leveraged buyout price-earnings ratio quick assets return on common stockholders' equity total equities

Ratios

>> **23-5 OBJECTIVE**
Compute and interpret financial ratios that measure profitability, operating results, and efficiency.

Ratio analysis is used to assess a company's profitability, financial strength, and liquidity. Ratio analysis investigates a relationship between two items either as a ratio (2 to 1 or 2:1) or as a rate (percentage).

Financial ratios have three classifications:

1. Profitability, operating results, and efficiency
2. Financial strength
3. Liquidity

The financial statements of Direct Sales, Inc., will be used to illustrate ratio analysis. You will need to refer to Figures 23.3 and 23.4 while studying this section.

Profitability is measured by net income. However, a dollar amount of net income is not a sufficient yardstick. Net income of $150,000 might be excellent for a small firm but unsatisfactory for a large corporation. A number of ratios are used to determine the adequacy of a company's profit.

Profitability Ratios
Rate of Return on Sales

The rate of return on sales is a measure of managerial efficiency and profitability. It is computed as follows:

$$\frac{\text{Net income after taxes}}{\text{Net sales}} = \text{Rate of return on net sales}$$

important!

Rate of Return on Sales
The rate of return on sales measures what part of each sales dollar remains as net income. It measures operating efficiency and profitability.

Some companies use income before taxes to calculate the percentage because income taxes depend on factors not related to sales. Direct Sales, Inc., uses net income after income taxes to calculate the rate.

The rate of return on net sales at Direct Sales, Inc., was 1.9 percent for 2022, compared to 0.9 percent in 2021 as sales increased significantly in 2022:

2022	2021
$\dfrac{\$55{,}563}{\$2{,}969{,}000} = 1.9\%$	$\dfrac{\$23{,}750}{\$2{,}700{,}000} = 0.9\%$

The higher the rate of return on net sales, the more satisfactory are the business operations. Management should look for and investigate unfavorable trends.

Rate of Return on Common Stockholders' Equity

Corporations are expected to earn a profit for their shareholders. Preferred shareholders are entitled to the dividends provided for in the preferred stock contract. The remainder of the earnings is available to common shareholders. **Return on common stockholders' equity** is a key measure of how well the corporation is making a profit for its shareholders. It is computed as follows:

$$\dfrac{\text{Income available to common stockholders}}{\text{Common stockholders' equity}} = \text{Return on common stockholders' equity}$$

Step 1. *Compute income available to common stockholders.* Income available to common stockholders is net income after taxes reduced by any preferred dividend requirements. Direct Sales, Inc., has a $4,000 dividend requirement for preferred stock (500 shares at $100 par value at 8 percent). Subtract $4,000 from net income after taxes to determine the income available for common stockholders:

	2022	2021
Net income after income taxes	$55,563	$23,750
Less dividend requirements on preferred stock	4,000	4,000
Income available to common stockholders	$51,563	$19,750

Step 2. *Compute the common stockholders' equity.* There are many ways to compute common stockholders' equity: end-of-year balance, average of the beginning and ending balances, average based on quarterly balances, or average based on monthly balances. Direct Sales, Inc., uses the end-of-year balance of total common stockholders' equity:

	2022	2021
Total stockholders' equity	$316,306	$262,743
Less preferred stock equity	50,000	50,000
Common stockholders' equity	$266,306	$212,743

Step 3. *Divide the income available to common stockholders by the common stockholders' equity:*

2022	2021
$\dfrac{\$51{,}563}{\$266{,}306} = 19.4\%$	$\dfrac{\$19{,}750}{\$212{,}743} = 9.3\%$

The increase in the 2022 rate of return on common stockholders' equity is caused primarily by the increase in net income. As net income increases, you should expect this ratio to improve. As a common stock shareholder, you would want to monitor this ratio yearly.

ABOUT ACCOUNTING

Stock Sales

From the creation of the NYSE in 1783 until 1997, stock prices were offered in increments of one-eighth of one dollar, or 12.5 cents. This changed in 1997 to one-sixteenth of a dollar, or 6.25 cents. In 2001, the stock market switched to the decimal system.

Earnings per Share of Common Stock

Earnings per share of common stock measures the profit accruing to each share of common stock owned. It is computed as follows:

$$\frac{\text{Income available to common stockholders}}{\text{Average number of shares of common stock outstanding during year}} = \text{Earnings per share}$$

Step 1. *Compute income available to common stockholders.* Subtract the dividend requirements on preferred stock from the income after income tax:

	2022	2021
Net income after income taxes	$55,563	$23,750
Less dividend requirements on preferred stock	4,000	4,000
Income available to common stockholders	$51,563	$19,750

Step 2. *Determine the average number of shares of common stock outstanding during the year.* An analysis of the common stock account reveals that 7,000 shares were outstanding throughout 2021 and most of 2022. On October 2, 2022, 1,000 additional shares were issued. *The weighted average number of shares outstanding* for 2022 was 7,250, calculated as follows:

$$7{,}000 \text{ shares} \times \frac{12 \text{ months}}{12 \text{ months}} = 7{,}000 \text{ shares}$$

$$1{,}000 \text{ shares} \times \frac{3 \text{ months}}{12 \text{ months}} = 250 \text{ shares}$$

$$\text{Weighted average number of shares} = 7{,}250 \text{ shares}$$

Step 3. *Divide the income available to common stockholders by the average number of shares of common stock outstanding:*

2022	2021
$\frac{\$51{,}563}{7{,}250 \text{ shares}} = \$7.11$	$\frac{\$19{,}750}{7{,}000 \text{ shares}} = \$2.82$

Earnings per share were $7.11 in 2022 and $2.82 in 2021. The large increase in net income caused earnings per share to increase significantly even though there were more shares of stock outstanding in 2022.

Analysts, stockholders, and creditors watch the earnings per share measurement very closely. Comparing earnings per share for the same company for several years could show a trend.

Price-Earnings Ratio

The **price-earnings ratio** compares the market value of common stock with the earnings per share of that stock. It is computed as follows:

$$\frac{\text{Market price per share of common stock}}{\text{Earnings per share of common stock}} = \text{Price-earnings ratio}$$

If a corporation's common stock sells for $144 per share and its earnings are $12 per share, the price-earnings ratio is 12 to 1 ($144 ÷ $12).

The price-earnings ratio is an indicator of the attractiveness of the stock as an investment at its present market value. The amount investors are willing to pay for stock is based on expectations for the future. The price-earnings ratio is not computed for privately held companies because there is no readily available market value for the shares.

important!

Price-Earnings Ratio
The price-earnings ratio depends in large part on expectations of future profitability, which cause stock prices to increase or decrease.

Yield on Common Stock

For a publicly held corporation, the relationship between the dividends received by the stockholders and the market value of each share is important. The yield on common stock is computed as follows:

$$\frac{\text{Cash dividend per share}}{\text{Market price per share}} = \text{Yield on common stock}$$

For example, if the price of a share of common stock is $60 and the corporation is paying an annual dividend of $6, the yield is 10 percent ($6 ÷ $60).

Rate of Return on Total Assets

The rate of return on total assets measures the rate of return on the assets used by a company. This rate helps the analyst to judge managerial performance, measure the effectiveness of the assets used, and evaluate proposed capital expenditures. The rate is computed as follows:

$$\frac{\text{Income before interest expense and income taxes}}{\text{Total assets}} = \text{Rate of return on total assets}$$

Income before interest and taxes is used to measure how effectively management utilized the assets, regardless of how the assets were financed. If nonoperating revenue amounts (such as dividend and interest income) are large, they should not be included in income. This ensures that only income from normal business operations is considered. For Direct Sales, Inc., income is computed by adding interest expense to income before income taxes.

	2022	2021
Income before income taxes	$79,375	$33,929
Interest expense	11,500	12,000
Income before interest and taxes	$90,875	$45,929

Analysts might average the assets at the beginning and end of the year, average the assets monthly, use the beginning assets, or use the ending assets. Direct Sales, Inc., uses year-end total assets.

The rate of return on total assets for Direct Sales, Inc., is as follows:

$$\textbf{2022} \qquad \qquad \textbf{2021}$$
$$\frac{\$90,875}{\$555,711} = 16.4\% \qquad \frac{\$45,929}{\$519,983} = 8.8\%$$

The results are meaningful only if compared with rates of prior years and with the industry average.

Asset Turnover

> **important!**
>
> **Asset Turnover**
>
> A low asset turnover compared to the industry average shows that the business uses more assets to generate the same sales volume as its competitors.

The ratio of net sales to total assets measures the effective use of assets in making sales. This ratio is usually called **asset turnover.** It is computed as follows:

$$\frac{\text{Net sales}}{\text{Total assets}} = \text{Asset turnover}$$

Assets that are not used in producing sales, primarily investments, are excluded. Assets may be measured as end-of-year totals, average of beginning and ending totals, or average of monthly totals. Direct Sales, Inc., uses net sales and total assets at the end of the year.

2022	2021
$\dfrac{\$2{,}969{,}000}{\$555{,}711} = 5.3 \text{ to } 1$	$\dfrac{\$2{,}700{,}000}{\$519{,}983} = 5.2 \text{ to } 1$

The higher the asset turnover, the more effectively the assets of the company are being used. The trend of this ratio is important because it indicates whether asset growth is accompanied by corresponding sales growth. If sales increase proportionately more than total assets, the ratio increases, which is a favorable indicator.

Financial Strength Ratios

Number of Times Bond Interest Earned

>> **23-6 OBJECTIVE**
Compute and interpret financial ratios that measure financial strength.

A corporation's bondholders and stockholders want to know if net income is sufficient to cover the required bond interest payments. Times bond interest earned measures this. It is computed as follows:

$$\frac{\text{Income before bond interest and income taxes}}{\text{Bond interest cash requirement}} = \text{Times bond interest earned}$$

Step 1. *Compute the income before bond interest and income taxes.* To compute the income amount, add the bond interest expense to income before income taxes. For Direct Sales, Inc., bond interest expense was $9,500 in 2021 and $9,500 in 2022 (interest paid on the bonds minus the amortization of bond premium). Direct Sales, Inc., uses the straight-line method to amortize the premium on bonds payable. The amount is computed as follows:

	2022	2021
Income before income tax	$79,375	$33,929
Add bond interest expense	9,500	9,500
Available for bond interest	$88,875	$43,429

recall

Bond Premium
The excess of the price paid over the face value of a bond is known as bond premium.

Step 2: *Compute the cash required to pay bond interest.* The cash interest for bonds outstanding at the end of each year is computed as follows:

$$2022: \$100{,}000 \times 0.10 = \$10{,}000$$
$$2021: \$100{,}000 \times 0.10 = \$10{,}000$$

Step 3: *Compute the ratio.*

2022	2021
$\dfrac{\$88{,}875}{\$10{,}000} = 8.9 \text{ times}$	$\dfrac{\$43{,}429}{\$10{,}000} = 4.3 \text{ times}$

Direct Sales, Inc.'s income easily covers required bond payments.

Ratio of Stockholders' Equity to Total Equities

The sum of a corporation's liabilities and stockholders' equity is referred to as its **total equities.** The ratio of stockholders' equity to total equities measures the portion of total capital provided by the stockholders. It indicates the protection afforded creditors against possible losses. The more capital provided by the stockholders, the greater the protection to creditors. The ratio of stockholders' equity to total equities is computed as follows:

$$\frac{\text{Stockholders' equity}}{\text{Total equities}} = \text{Ratio of stockholders' equities to total equities}$$

The ratios for Direct Sales, Inc., follow:

2022	2021
$\dfrac{\$316{,}306}{\$555{,}711} = 0.57 \text{ to } 1$	$\dfrac{\$262{,}743}{\$519{,}983} = 0.51 \text{ to } 1$

In 2022, the stockholders of Direct Sales, Inc., provided 57 cents of each dollar of total equities compared to 51 cents in 2021. This ratio varies widely from industry to industry. A comparison with the industry average is important in determining a desirable ratio for a particular business.

Ratio of Stockholders' Equity to Total Liabilities

The ratio of stockholders' equity to total liabilities is known as the *ratio of owned capital to borrowed capital.* It is computed as follows:

$$\frac{\text{Stockholders' equity}}{\text{Total liabilities}} = \text{Ratio of stockholders' equity to total liabilities}$$

The ratios for Direct Sales, Inc., follow:

2022	2021
$\dfrac{\$316{,}306}{\$239{,}405} = 1.32 \text{ to } 1$	$\dfrac{\$262{,}743}{\$257{,}240} = 1.02 \text{ to } 1$

This ratio reveals a significant improvement in 2022. In 2021, stockholders provided slightly more than $1 of equity for each dollar of liability. In 2022, they provided $1.32 of equity for each dollar of debt.

In a **leveraged buyout,** the purchasers of a business buy the corporation's stock by having the acquired corporation incur debt to pay the sellers. The result is that the debt created by the purchase is a debt of the corporation. That debt is structured in such a way that the acquired entity's cash flow is adequate to pay the debt. The balance sheets of these corporations would reflect a very low ratio of stockholders' equity to total liabilities.

Book Value per Share of Stock

Book value per share measures the financial strength underlying each share of stock. It is frequently reported in financial publications. It represents the amount that each share would receive in case of liquidation if the assets were sold for book value.

When there is one class of stock outstanding, the book value of each share is total stockholders' equity divided by the number of shares outstanding. If more than one class of stock is outstanding, the rights of the various classes of stock are considered. The book value of preferred stock is computed first. Then the remaining balance of stockholders' equity is divided by the number of common shares. Special treatment is given to dividends in arrears on cumulative preferred stock. In case of liquidation, the owner of a share of preferred stock will receive its par value.

$$\frac{\text{Common stockholders' equity}}{\text{Number of common shares outstanding}} = \text{Book value per share of common stock}$$

Follow these steps to compute the book value per share of stock for Direct Sales, Inc.:

Step 1: *Compute the claims of preferred stockholders.* There are no cumulative dividends or special liquidation provisions for the preferred stock of Direct Sales, Inc. Therefore, the book value is the same as the par value, $100 per share. There were 500 shares of preferred stock outstanding during 2021 and 2022, so the claims of the preferred stockholders for both years are $50,000 (500 shares at $100 par value).

---

important!

Stockholders' Equity
A low ratio of stockholders' equity to total liabilities can be risky. The corporation might not be able to make interest and principal payments on its debts.

important!

Book Value per Share
Book value and fair market value often are quite different. Book value per share does not indicate how much the stockholder would receive if the assets were sold and the corporation liquidated.

Step 2. *Deduct the claims of preferred stockholders from total stockholders' equity to compute the claims of common stockholders.* The common stockholders are entitled to the difference between the total stockholders' equity and the portion assigned to the preferred stock.

	2022	2021
Stockholders' equity	$316,306	$262,743
Less preferred stock equity	50,000	50,000
To common stockholders	$266,306	$212,743

Step 3: *Divide the total claims of common stockholders by the number of shares of common stock outstanding.* Direct Sales, Inc., had 8,000 shares of common stock outstanding on December 31, 2022, and 7,000 shares outstanding on December 31, 2021. The book value of each share is computed as follows:

$$\text{2022} \quad \frac{\$266{,}306}{8{,}000 \text{ shares}} = \$33.29 \qquad \text{2021} \quad \frac{\$212{,}743}{7{,}000 \text{ shares}} = \$30.39$$

The book value of Direct Sales, Inc.'s common stock increased from $30.39 to $33.29 per share.

Liquidity Ratios
Working Capital

Liquidity measures the ability of a business to pay its debts when due. Many businesses fail because they cannot pay their debts, even though they are profitable and have long-term financial strength. Working capital is a measure of the ability of a company to meet its current obligations. It represents the margin of security afforded short-term creditors. Working capital, sometimes called *net working capital,* is computed as follows:

$$\text{Current assets} - \text{Current liabilities} = \text{Working capital}$$

In 2022, Direct Sales, Inc.'s working capital increased by $55,243. This is a significant change that needs to be investigated.

	2022	2021	Increase or (Decrease)
Current assets	$423,931	$381,023	$42,908
Current liabilities	75,905	88,240	(12,335)
Working capital	$348,026	$292,783	$55,243

Current Ratio

Working capital is a very important measure of liquidity. The current ratio is another way to evaluate liquidity. The current ratio measures the ability of a business to pay its current debts using current assets. The current ratio is computed as follows:

$$\frac{\text{Current assets}}{\text{Current liabilities}} = \text{Current ratio}$$

>> **23-7 OBJECTIVE**
Compute and interpret financial ratios that measure liquidity.

important!

Whenever a business has long-term debt, please remember that the current year's payments (12 months) represent a current liability. For simplicity, we have not included a Current Portion of Long-Term Debt liability within the Current Liabilities section of Liabilities.

recall

Current Assets

Assets are considered current if they will be converted to cash or used within one year.

In 2022, Direct Sales, Inc., had $5.59 of current assets for each dollar of current liabilities.

$$\text{2022} \qquad \text{2021}$$
$$\frac{\$423,931}{\$75,905} = 5.59:1 \qquad \frac{\$381,023}{\$88,240} = 4.32:1$$

The current ratio varies widely among industries and even from company to company within an industry. A popular guideline is that a current ratio of at least 2 to 1 is desirable in retail and manufacturing businesses. This guideline is not applicable, however, to all businesses.

From the viewpoint of a short-term creditor, the higher the current ratio, the greater the amount of protection afforded. However, the current ratio can be too high. A very high current ratio indicates that excess current assets are on hand and are not earning income. A high current ratio could be caused by large sums of money tied up in accounts receivable that might be uncollectible. A high current ratio could also be caused by obsolete inventory or an inventory level higher than required to conduct normal operations.

Acid-Test Ratio

Although the current ratio measures a company's ability to cover current liabilities using current assets, it is not a measure of immediate liquidity. A considerable period of time might be necessary to sell the inventory and convert it into cash in the normal course of business. The **acid-test ratio** measures immediate liquidity. This ratio uses **quick assets,** which are cash, receivables, and marketable securities.

$$\frac{\text{Cash + Receivables + Marketable securities}}{\text{Current liabilities}} = \text{Acid-test ratio}$$

Direct Sales, Inc.'s acid-test ratios follow:

$$\text{2022} \qquad \text{2021}$$
$$\frac{\$115,231 + \$102,000}{\$75,905} = 2.86:1 \qquad \frac{\$80,773 + \$73,500}{\$88,240} = 1.75:1$$

The acid-test ratio shows that in 2022, Direct Sales, Inc., had $2.86 of quick assets for each dollar of current liabilities. In 2021, the acid-test ratio was 1.75. This dramatic increase should be investigated.

Acid-test ratios vary widely from industry to industry. A general guideline is that the acid-test ratio should be at least 1 to 1. The due dates of current liabilities, composition of quick assets, and various operating factors are considered when evaluating the adequacy of the ratio. Comparisons with the industry average and with the company's ratio in prior years can be helpful.

important!

Inventory Turnover

A high inventory turnover indicates tight control over the level of inventory on hand.

Inventory Turnover

It is important that a business sell its inventory rapidly so that excess working capital is not tied up in merchandise. Inventory turnover measures the number of times the inventory is replaced during the period. The higher the turnover, the shorter the time between the purchase and sale of the inventory. Inventory turnover is computed as follows:

$$\frac{\text{Cost of goods sold}}{\text{Average merchandise inventory}} = \text{Inventory turnover}$$

Ideally, average inventory is computed using month-end balances. However, these amounts are not available to analysts outside the business. Therefore, year-end balances are often used, but they might not be typical of the inventory levels during the year. Inventory is often at its lowest level at year-end.

To compute the inventory turnover for Direct Sales, Inc., follow these steps:

Step 1. *Compute the average inventory.*

	2022	2021
Inventory, Jan. 1	$225,000	$215,000
Inventory, Dec. 31	205,000	225,000
Totals	$430,000	$440,000
	÷2	÷2
Average inventory	$215,000	$220,000

Step 2. *Divide the cost of goods sold by the average inventory.*

2022: $\dfrac{\$1,752,500}{\$215,000} = 8.15$ times

2021: $\dfrac{\$1,574,721}{\$220,000} = 7.16$ times

The inventory turnover ratio varies widely by industry. Inventory turnover for a bakery is almost daily. A vendor of construction equipment might turn inventory just twice a year. A business must compare its inventory turnover with prior years and with the industry average.

Accounts Receivable Turnover

A company should collect accounts and notes receivable promptly. This minimizes the amount of working capital tied up in receivables and reduces the likelihood that accounts will become uncollectible. The **accounts receivable turnover** is a measure of the reasonableness of the accounts outstanding. This measurement uses net credit sales, which includes notes receivable from sales transactions. The accounts receivable turnover is computed as follows:

$$\dfrac{\text{Net credit sales}}{\text{Average receivables}} = \text{Accounts receivable turnover}$$

It is desirable to use monthly balances to compute the average receivables. However, because these amounts are not available to analysts outside the business, year-end balances are often used. Outside analysts normally use net sales because they cannot determine net credit sales. For Direct Sales, Inc., accounts receivable on January 1, 2021, were $71,500. Net credit sales were $2,969,000 in 2022 and $2,700,000 in 2021.

Step 1: *Compute average accounts receivable.*

	2022	2021
Accounts receivable, Jan. 1	$ 73,500	$ 71,500
Accounts receivable, Dec. 31	102,000	73,500
Totals	$175,500	$145,000
	÷2	÷2
Average accounts receivable	$ 87,750	$ 72,500

Step 2: *Divide net credit sales by average accounts receivable.*

2022: $\dfrac{\$2,969,000}{\$87,750} = 33.8$ times

2021: $\dfrac{\$2,700,000}{\$72,500} = 37.2$ times

The accounts receivable turnover can be used to determine the **average collection period** of accounts receivable, or *number of days' sales in receivables*. The average collection period is computed as follows:

$$\dfrac{365 \text{ days}}{\text{Accounts receivable turnover}}$$

2022: $\dfrac{365}{33.8} = 10.8$ days

2021: $\dfrac{365}{37.2} = 9.8$ days

MANAGERIAL IMPLICATIONS

INTERPRETING FINANCIAL STATEMENTS

- It is important that managers understand the relationships among the items on the financial statements. Understanding these relationships will help management run the business effectively.
- Managers use statement analysis to identify areas of operations that are weak and need attention.
- It is essential that management know how to compute and interpret financial ratios. For example, a low inventory turnover compared with the industry average might reflect obsolete goods, excess merchandise, poor purchasing procedures, or other operating inefficiencies.
- Effective managers recognize the key role the accountant plays in financial statement analysis and interpretation. Accountants understand what each line on the financial statements represents and can assist management in analyzing and understanding accounting reports.

THINKING CRITICALLY
Which ratios will best measure the company's ability to meet current obligations?

Direct Sales, Inc., collected accounts receivable in 2022 in about 11 days and about 10 days in 2021. Businesses want a short collection period on accounts receivable. The credit terms for customers of Direct Sales, Inc., are net 15 days. For both years, the collection period for Direct Sales, Inc., is much less than the guideline, so it appears they are doing a fine job with collections on credit sales.

Other Ratios

The number of ratios that could be developed from financial statements is almost limitless. Analysts use their preferred ratios. Financial analysts use many more ratios than those presented in this chapter. Depending on the industry, some ratios are more important than others. The ratios in this chapter are those most often used by accountants.

>> **23-8 OBJECTIVE**
Recognize shortcomings in financial statement analysis.

Some Precautionary Notes on Statement Analysis

There are limits to the benefits of financial statement analysis. Financial statements use book values. Book value depends on accounting procedures and policies. Different accounting policies and procedures make it difficult to compare financial results across companies. One firm, for example, might record a purchase as an asset and another firm could record it as an expense. Businesses also have many choices regarding depreciation methods, useful lives, and salvage value.

Another limitation of financial statement analysis is that financial statements are prepared assuming that the dollar is a stable monetary unit; this is far from correct. The amounts reported do not necessarily represent dollars with today's purchasing power.

Finally, it is difficult to compare financial results of businesses that use different financing methods, classify expenses differently, have different policies for paying owner-employees, and operate as different types of business entities. Financial statement analysis is useful only if these limitations are clearly understood.

recall

Cost Basis Principle
Accounts reflect historical costs, not current market values. This must be considered when analyzing financial statements. Book value rarely reflects fair market value.

Summary of Ratios

This chapter examined many ratios that are commonly used by analysts to evaluate a business. A summary of the ratios is shown in Table 23.2.

TABLE 23.2 Summary of Ratios Used in Statement Analysis

Ratio	Equation	Performance Measured
Ratios That Measure Profitability, Operating Results, and Efficiency		
Rate of return on net sales	$\dfrac{\text{Net income after taxes}}{\text{Net sales}}$	Percentage of each sales dollar that reflects net income
Rate of return on common stockholders' equity	$\dfrac{\text{Income available to common stockholders}}{\text{Common stockholders' equity}}$	Rate of return on book value of common stock
Earnings per share of common stock	$\dfrac{\text{Income available to common stockholders}}{\text{Average number of shares of common stock outstanding during year}}$	Income accruing on each share of common stock
Price-earnings ratio	$\dfrac{\text{Market price per share of common stock}}{\text{Earnings per share of common stock}}$	Value of a share of common stock compared with income accruing to that share
Yield on common stock	$\dfrac{\text{Cash dividend per share}}{\text{Market price per share}}$	Cash income (dividend) from a share of common stock as a percentage of the market value of the share
Rate of return on total assets	$\dfrac{\text{Income before interest expense and income taxes}}{\text{Total assets}}$	Effectiveness of management in utilizing assets, regardless of how they were financed
Asset turnover	$\dfrac{\text{Net sales}}{\text{Total assets}}$	Effectiveness of management in using assets to generate sales
Ratios That Measure Financial Strength		
Number of times bond interest earned	$\dfrac{\text{Income before bond interest and income taxes}}{\text{Bond interest cash requirement}}$	Security afforded bondholders
Ratio of stockholders' equity to total equities	$\dfrac{\text{Stockholders' equity}}{\text{Total equities}}$	Portion of assets provided by stockholders and therefore security afforded creditors
Ratio of stockholders' equity to total liabilities	$\dfrac{\text{Stockholders' equity}}{\text{Total liabilities}}$	Owners' capital compared with liabilities; measures security afforded creditors
Book value per share of common stock	$\dfrac{\text{Common stockholders' equity}}{\text{Number of common shares outstanding}}$	Amount owner of each share would receive if assets were sold for their book value and the corporation was liquidated
Ratios That Measure Liquidity		
Working capital	Current assets − Current liabilities	Dollar amount of security provided short-term creditors
Current ratio	$\dfrac{\text{Current assets}}{\text{Current liabilities}}$	Ability of business to pay current debts using current assets
Acid-test ratio	$\dfrac{\text{Cash + Receivables + Marketable securities}}{\text{Current liabilities}}$	Immediate liquidity or short-run debt-paying ability
Inventory turnover	$\dfrac{\text{Cost of goods sold}}{\text{Average merchandise inventory}}$	Effectiveness of control of inventory for sales volume
Accounts receivable turnover	$\dfrac{\text{Net credit sales}}{\text{Average receivables}}$	Efficiency with which sales on account are collected
Average collection period	$\dfrac{\text{365 days}}{\text{Accounts receivable turnover}}$	Average number of days required to collect sales on account

Section 3 Review

1. What does book value per share measure?
   a. current selling price of stock
   b. amount shareholder would receive if assets sold for book value and the company was liquidated
   c. net assets
   d. total equity

2. Which of the following is a measurement often used in evaluating profitability?
   a. ratio of Stockholders' Equity to Total Liabilities
   b. Current Ratio
   c. Book Value of Common Stock
   d. Earnings per Share of Common Stock

3. Why is it useful to know the inventory turnover for a company?
   a. to evaluate website effectiveness
   b. to determine amount of warehouse storage needed
   c. to determine warehouse hourly wages
   d. to judge effectiveness of CEO

4. The price-earnings ratio for common stock is computed using:
   a. par value.
   b. market value.
   c. book value.
   d. stated value.

5. The average collection period is determined by dividing:
   a. 365 days by the accounts receivable turnover.
   b. net credit sales by 365 days.
   c. net credit sales by average receivables.
   d. beginning accounts receivable by ending accounts receivable.

6. A corporation's stock is selling at $40 per share, and its earnings are $8 per share. The corporation is paying an annual dividend of $4.00. What is the price-earnings ratio?
   a. 5.0
   b. 50.0
   c. 320.0
   d. 32.0

REVIEW Chapter Summary

Financial statement analysis involves computation and interpretation. Computation includes the calculation of percentages and ratios. Interpretation means comparing one set of figures with another (prior statements, budgets, or industrial averages) and determining the financial implications of those comparisons. The comparative statement is a convenient form for the presentation of figures for analysis and appraisal.

Learning Objectives

23-1 Use vertical analysis techniques to analyze a comparative income statement and balance sheet.

Vertical analysis expresses each item as a percentage of a base amount on the statement.

- Net sales are the base for all income statement items. To compute an item's percentage of net sales, divide the amount of that item by the amount of net sales.

$$\text{Example: } \frac{\text{Total operating expenses}}{\text{Net sales}}$$

- Total assets (or total liabilities plus owner's equity) are the base for vertical analysis items on a balance sheet. Each figure is expressed as a percentage of the base.

$$\text{Example: } \frac{\text{Cash}}{\text{Total assets}}$$

It is customary to carry the percentage computed to one decimal place further than needed and then to round it off. The usual practice is to round percentages to the nearest one-tenth of a percent.

23-2 Use horizontal analysis techniques to analyze a comparative income statement and balance sheet.

Horizontal analysis compares items from one year to the next. The amount of change and the percentage change are computed.

- Changes to items such as gross sales, cost of goods sold, operating expenses, and net income can be studied on the income statement.

$$\text{Example: } \frac{\text{Increase in total operating expenses}}{\text{Total operating expenses for base year}}$$

- A firm's balance sheets for two or more periods can be presented in comparative form to permit a comparison of items from year to year.

$$\text{Example: } \frac{\text{Increase in cash}}{\text{Cash in base year}}$$

23-3 Use trend analysis to evaluate financial statements.

Comparing ratio and percentage relationships of the current year with only those of the previous year can be misleading and is not adequate to indicate long-term trends.

Using data from five or more years, trend analysis compares selected ratios and percentages to analyze operations.

Trend analysis often omits income tax expense because the companies' forms of business could be different (that is, sole proprietorships, partnerships, corporations).

23-4 Interpret the results of the statement analyses by comparison with industry averages.

Companies often compare financial statements with industry averages to determine how the company's operations stack up against other businesses in the industry. In order to make these comparisons, similar classification structures must be in place.

Varied operational procedures and accounting treatments can create inconsistency in data presentation:

- Different businesses keep different types of accounts and do not classify items in a consistent manner.
- No two businesses are exactly alike in terms of merchandise, customers, financing, asset acquisition, and other areas.
- Industry averages might include data from sole proprietorships, partnerships, and corporations. This creates inconsistency in presentation of financial information.

23-5 Compute and interpret financial ratios that measure profitability, operating results, and efficiency.

Net income and other factors are used to evaluate profitability, operating results, and business efficiencies. Analysts review the sales of the company in relation to net income, the nature of operations, how assets are used to earn income for the business, and how successful the company has been in rewarding its stockholders.

Measures of profitability, operating results, and efficiency include:

Learning Objectives (continued)

- rate of return on net sales,
- rate of return on common stockholders' equity,
- earnings per share of common stock,
- price-earnings ratio,
- yield on common stock,
- rate of return on total assets,
- asset turnover.

23-6 Compute and interpret financial ratios that measure financial strength.

The ability to satisfy long-term debt obligations and to deliver adequate dividend returns to stockholders offers key indications of a company's overall financial strength. Comparison of a company's long-term liabilities to the book value of its property, plant, and equipment can reveal the level of security afforded to long-term creditors. In addition, measurements of book value indicate the financial strength underlying each share of stock.

Measures of financial strength include:

- number of times bond interest earned,
- ratio of stockholders' equity to total equities,
- ratio of stockholders' equity to total liabilities,
- book value per share of common stock.

23-7 Compute and interpret financial ratios that measure liquidity.

A company's ability to pay its currently maturing debts is of critical importance to short-term creditors, long-term creditors, and stockholders. Current assets such as cash, inventories, and accounts receivable are measured against items such as current liabilities and credit sales to establish the liquidity of the business.

Measures of liquidity include:

- working capital,
- current ratio,
- acid-test ratio,
- inventory turnover,
- accounts receivable turnover, and
- average collection period.

23-8 Recognize shortcomings in financial statement analysis.

The benefits of analysis are limited by a number of significant issues:

- Different companies use different accounting methods. No two companies are exactly the same: there are different mixes of products sold, different organizational structures, and different types of entities.
- Financial statements reflect historical costs, rather than current market values.
- Financial statements are prepared assuming that the dollar is a stable monetary unit.

23-9 Define the accounting terms new to this chapter.

Glossary

Accounts receivable turnover (p. 835) A measure of the speed with which sales on account are collected; the ratio of net credit sales to average receivables

Acid-test ratio (p. 834) A measure of immediate liquidity; the ratio of quick assets to current liabilities

Asset turnover (p. 830) A measure of the effective use of assets in making sales; the ratio of net sales to total assets

Average collection period (p. 835) The ratio of 365 days to the accounts receivable turnover; also called the *number of days' sales in receivables*

Common-size statements (p. 818) Financial statements with items expressed as percentages of a base amount

Comparative statements (p. 816) Financial statements presented side by side for two or more years

Horizontal analysis (p. 816) Computing the percentage change for individual items in the financial statements from year to year

Industry averages (p. 825) Financial ratios and percentages reflecting averages for similar companies

Leveraged buyout (p. 832) Purchasing a business by acquiring the stock and obligating the business to pay the debt incurred

Price-earnings ratio (p. 829) The ratio of the current market value of common stock to earnings per share of that stock

Quick assets (p. 834) Cash, receivables, and marketable securities

Ratio analysis (p. 816) Computing the relationship between various items in the financial statements

Return on common stockholders' equity (p. 828) A measure of how well the corporation is making a profit for its shareholders; the ratio of net income available for common stockholders to common stockholders' equity

Total equities (p. 831) The sum of a corporation's liabilities and stockholders' equity

Trend analysis (p. 823) Comparing selected ratios and percentages over a period of time

Vertical analysis (p. 816) Computing the relationship between each item on a financial statement to some base amount on the statement

Comprehensive Self Review

1. What is the difference between vertical analysis and horizontal analysis?
2. What does the current ratio tell you?
3. In general, would it be preferable in a retail store to have a higher or lower inventory turnover? Explain.
4. Name several factors that may cause misleading results when comparing percentage figures of a specific company to industry averages.
5. Explain how to compute book value per share of common stock.

(Answers to Comprehensive Self Review are at the end of the chapter.)

Discussion Questions

1. What are common-size statements?
2. Why would a short-term creditor be interested in the analysis of a company's income statement?
3. If a company's net sales and its cost of goods sold both increase by 12 percent from 2021 to 2022, would gross profit on sales also increase by 12 percent?
4. What is meant by vertical analysis of the income statement?
5. In a vertical analysis of the balance sheet, what is the base for comparing each item on the statement?
6. Which is more important: a larger change in percentage or a large change in dollar amount?
7. What does the rate of net income on stockholders' equity tell stockholders?
8. What is the procedure for measuring earnings per share of common stock?
9. How does the acid-test ratio differ from the current ratio?
10. How is inventory turnover computed?
11. What does the accounts receivable turnover measure?
12. As a rule of thumb, what is the minimum desired current ratio?

APPLICATIONS

Exercises

Use the comparative income statement and the comparative balance sheet for ACRH, Inc., to solve Exercises 23.1 through 23.12.

ACRH, Inc.
Comparative Income Statement
Years Ended December 31, 2022 and 2021

	Amounts	
	2022	2021
Sales	1,850,000	1,700,000
Less Sales Returns and Allowances	55,500	51,000
Net Sales	1,794,500	1,649,000
Cost of Goods Sold	1,345,875	1,236,750
Gross Profit on Sales	448,625	412,250
Selling Expenses	215,000	200,000
General Expenses	210,000	190,000
Total Expenses	425,000	390,000
Net Income before Income Taxes	23,625	22,250
Income Tax Expense	4,961	4,672
Net Income after Income Taxes	18,664	17,578

Exercise 23.1
Objective 23-1

▶ **Vertical analysis of income statement.**
Using the comparative income statement, prepare a vertical analysis of all items from sales through gross profit on sales for the years shown.

Exercise 23.2
Objective 23-1

▶ **Vertical analysis of balance sheet.**
Prepare a vertical analysis of all asset items on the comparative balance sheet for these years.

Exercise 23.3
Objective 23-2

▶ **Horizontal analysis of income statement.**
Using the comparative income statement, prepare a horizontal analysis of all items on the income statement for years displayed.

Exercise 23.4
Objective 23-2

▶ **Horizontal analysis of balance sheet.**
Prepare a horizontal analysis of all items on the comparative balance sheet for the years shown.

Exercise 23.5
Objective 23-1

▶ **Rate of return on sales.**
Calculate the rate of net income on sales for these two years.

Exercise 23.6
Objective 23-1

▶ **Rate of return on stockholders' equity.**
Compute the rate of net income on stockholders' equity for 2022 and 2021. Retained earnings on January 1, 2021, was $69,160.

Exercise 23.7
Objective 23-1

▶ **Rate of return on assets.**
Compute the rate of net income before income taxes on total assets for each of these two years. Base your calculation on total ending assets each year.

Exercise 23.8
Objective 23-1

▶ **Earnings per share.**
Calculate the earnings per share of common stock for each year.

ACRH, Inc.
Comparative Balance Sheet
December 31, 2022 and 2021

	2022	2021
Assets		
Current Assets		
Cash	123,923	112,250
Accounts Receivable (Net)	113,400	107,000
Inventory	55,705	60,800
Total Current Assets	293,028	280,050
Property, Plant, and Equipment		
Buildings (Net)	157,600	175,100
Equipment (Net)	65,950	63,850
Land	56,000	56,000
Total Property, Plant, and Equipment	279,550	294,950
Total Assets	572,578	575,000
Liabilities and Stockholders' Equity		
Liabilities		
Current Liabilities		
Accounts Payable	155,000	160,000
Other Current Liabilities	40,000	45,000
Total Current Liabilities	195,000	205,000
Long-Term Liabilities		
Bonds Payable	65,000	75,000
Total Long-Term Liabilities	65,000	75,000
Total Liabilities	260,000	280,000
Stockholders' Equity		
Common Stock ($1 par)	200,000	200,000
Retained Earnings	112,578	95,000
Total Stockholders' Equity	312,578	295,000
Total Liabilities and Stockholders' Equity	572,578	575,000

◀ **Exercise 23.9**
Objective 23-5

Price-earnings ratio.

Calculate the price-earnings ratio for the two years displayed. The common stock selling price at year-end 2022 was $2.00 and for 2021 was $1.60.

◀ **Exercise 23.10**
Objective 23-7

Current ratio.

Calculate the current ratio for each year.

◀ **Exercise 23.11**
Objective 23-3

Inventory turnover.

Using the data for the two years, calculate the inventory turnover for each year. The beginning inventory for year 2021 was $59,000.

◀ **Exercise 23.12**
Objective 23-3

Accounts receivable turnover.

Compute the accounts receivable turnover on December 31, 2022, for ACRH, Inc. Assume that all sales were credit sales.

PROBLEMS

Problem Set A

Problem 23.1A ▶ **Horizontal and vertical analysis of income statement and balance sheet.**

Objectives 23-1, 23-2

The firm's comparative income statement and balance sheet for the years 2022 and 2021 follow:

Meeting Pointe, Inc.
Comparative Income Statement
For Years Ended December 31, 2022 and 2021

	Amounts 2022	Amounts 2021
Revenue		
Sales	679 000	605 000
Less Sales Returns and Allowances	3 500	2 500
Net Sales	675 500	602 500
Cost of Goods Sold		
Merchandise Inventory, January 1	19 000	26 000
Net Purchases	149 800	150 000
Total Merchandise Available for Sale	168 800	176 000
Less Merchandise Inventory, December 31	29 500	19 000
Cost of Goods Sold	139 300	157 000
Gross Profit on Sales	536 200	445 500
Operating Expenses		
Selling Expenses		
Sales Salaries Expenses	140 000	100 000
Payroll Tax Expense—Selling	14 000	10 000
Other Selling Expenses	7 500	5 500
Total Selling Expenses	161 500	115 500
General and Administrative Expenses		
Officers' Salaries Expense	85 000	75 000
Payroll Tax Expense—Administrative	8 500	4 500
Depreciation Expense	5 000	5 000
Other General and Administrative Expenses	1 500	1 000
Total General and Administrative Expenses	100 000	85 000
Total Operating Expenses	261 500	201 000
Net Income before Income Taxes	274 700	244 500
Income Tax Expense	57 687	51 345
Net Income after Income Taxes	217 013	193 155

Meeting Pointe, Inc.
Comparative Balance Sheet
December 31, 2022 and 2021

	Amounts 2022	Amounts 2021
Assets		
Current Assets		
Cash	19,782.8	8,975.0
Accounts Receivable	21,000.0	14,350.0
Merchandise Inventory	2,950.0	1,900.0
Prepaid Expenses	100.0	80.0
Supplies	50.0	70.0
Total Current Assets	43,882.8	25,375.0
Property, Plant, and Equipment		
Land	5,500.0	5,500.0
Building and Store Equipment	5,000.0	5,000.0
Less Accumulated Depreciation–Bldg & Store Equipment	(1,500.0)	(1,000.0)
Net Book Value–Building and Store Equipment	3,500.0	4,000.0
Total Property, Plant, and Equipment	9,000.0	9,500.0
Total Assets	52,882.8	34,875.0
Liabilities and Stockholders' Equity		
Current Liabilities		
Accounts Payable	9,600	33,405
Sales Tax Payable	3,200	5,770
Payroll Taxes Payable	915	875
Interest Payable	600	1,200
Total Current Liabilities	14,315	41,250
Long-Term Liabilities		
Mortgage Payable	68,000	78,000
Total Long-Term Liabilities	68,000	78,000
Total Liabilities	82,315	119,250
Stockholders' Equity		
Common Stock ($1 par, 10,000 shares authorized, 2,000 shares issued and outstanding)	2,000	2,000
Paid-in Capital—Common Stock	5,000	5,000
Retained Earnings	439,513	222,500
Total Stockholders' Equity	446,513	229,500
Total Liabilities and Stockholders' Equity	528,828	348,750

INSTRUCTIONS

1. Prepare both a horizontal and a vertical analysis of the statements. Carry all calculations to two decimal places, and then round to one decimal place. (Leave all vertical analysis percentages unadjusted in this problem.)

2. Make written comments about any of the results that seem worthy of investigation.

Analyze: Based on your analysis, which expense category experienced the greatest percentage change?

Problem 23.2A
Objectives 23-5, 23-6, 23-7

CONTINUING >>> Problem

Computing financial ratios.

PART I

Using the financial statements for Meeting Pointe, Inc. from Problem 23.1A, calculate the following financial ratios for 2021 and 2022. Round percentages to nearest 0.1 percent; round to whole numbers those ratios expressed as a number times 1 (as current ratio may be 3:1). Comment on any ratio that merits additional consideration.

1. Current ratio
2. Acid-test ratio
3. Inventory turnover
4. Return on sales
5. Earnings per share of common stock
6. Book value per share of common stock
7. Return on total assets
8. Ratio of stockholders' equity to total equities
9. Rate of return on stockholders' equity
10. Asset turnover

Assume all sales are credit sales.

PART II

Selected ratios for other common-size companies in the same industry as Meeting Pointe, Inc. follow. Using these data and the ratios you computed in Part I, write brief comments on areas you feel are strengths or weaknesses, or require further observation for this company.

1. Rate of return on stockholders' equity, 45.0 percent
2. Stockholders' equity to total equities, 0.6 to 1 (or 60 percent)
3. Asset turnover, 2.5 to 1
4. Merchandise inventory turnover, 4.5 times

Analyze: Meeting Pointe, Inc. experienced a 17.7 percent increase in net income after taxes from 2021 to 2022. What return on sales can be anticipated if net sales and net income after taxes increase by 5 percent in 2023?

Problem 23.3A
Objectives 23-5, 23-6, 23-7

Compute and interpret ratios.

Below you will find the condensed financial statements for Koko Inc. and Suz Inc. for 2022.

INSTRUCTIONS

1. Compute the following ratios for each company (please round to 2 decimal places for these calculations):
   a. Rate of return on net sales
   b. Rate of return on total assets at year-end
   c. Rate of return on stockholders' equity at year-end
   d. Earnings per share of common stock
   e. Ratio of stockholders' equity to total equities
   f. Current ratio
   g. Asset turnover
   h. Book value per share of common stock

2. Comment on any similarities or differences in the two companies' ratios. When possible, comment on the cause for these differences.

3. From the investor's point of view, is one company more at risk than the other?

4. Would you grant a five-year loan to either company? Explain.

Income Statements
Year Ended December 31, 2022

	Koko Inc.	Suz Inc.
Sales (Net)	920 000	700 000
Cost of Goods Sold	580 000	360 000
Gross Profit	340 000	340 000
Operating Expenses	200 000	135 000
Net Income from Operations	140 000	205 000
Interest Expense	10 000	0
Net Income before Income Tax	130 000	205 000
Income Tax Expense	32 500	51 250
Net Income after Income Tax	97 500	153 750

Balance Sheets
December 31, 2022

	Koko Inc.	Suz Inc.
Assets		
Current Assets	135 000	114 900
Property, Plant, and Equipment (Net)	235 000	206 000
Total Assets	370 000	320 900
Liabilities and Stockholders' Equity		
Liabilities		
Current Liabilities	108 500	89 800
Long-Term Liabilities (Bonds Payable)	110 000	0
Total Liabilities	218 500	89 800
Stockholders' Equity		
Common Stock ($10 Par Value)	30 000	30 000
Retained Earnings	121 500	201 100
Total Stockholders' Equity	151 500	231 100
Total Liabilities and Stockholders' Equity	370 000	320 900

Analyze: Assume that Suz Inc. believes that it can cut the cost of goods sold by 5 percent in 2023 while keeping net sales and operating expenses at 2022 levels. If the company met this goal, discuss the potential implications to the rate of return on sales and earnings per share. Assume a tax rate of 25 percent.

Problem Set B

Problem 23.1B
Objectives 23-1, 23-2

▶ **Horizontal and vertical analysis of income statement and balance sheet.**

Chevy Hill, Inc., sells vintage clothes. The firm's comparative income statement and balance sheet for the years 2021 and 2022 follow:

Chevy Hill, Inc.
Comparative Income Statement
For Years Ended December 31, 2022 and 2021

	Amounts 2022	Amounts 2021
Revenue		
Sales	825,000	745,000
Less Sales Returns and Allowances	4,900	5,000
Net Sales	820,100	740,000
Cost of Goods Sold		
Merchandise Inventory, January 1	40,000	45,000
Net Purchases	310,000	300,000
Total Merchandise Available for Sale	350,000	345,000
Less Merchandise Inventory, December 31	29,500	40,000
Cost of Goods Sold	320,500	305,000
Gross Profit on Sales	499,600	435,000
Operating Expenses		
Selling Expenses		
Sales Salaries Expenses	210,000	180,000
Payroll Tax Expense—Selling	21,000	18,000
Other Selling Expenses	12,000	10,000
Total Selling Expenses	243,000	208,000
General and Administrative Expenses		
Officers' Salaries Expense	130,000	125,000
Payroll Tax Expense—Administrative	13,000	12,500
Depreciation Expense	5,000	5,000
Other General and Administrative Expenses	2,500	1,000
Total General and Administrative Expenses	150,500	143,500
Total Operating Expenses	393,500	351,500
Net Income Before Income Taxes	106,100	83,500
Income Tax Expense	22,281	17,535
Net Income After Income Taxes	83,819	65,965

Chevy Hill, Inc.
Comparative Balance Sheet
December 31, 2022 and 2021

	Amounts	
	2022	2021
Assets		
Current Assets		
Cash	109,039	89,750
Accounts Receivable	99,500	58,000
Merchandise Inventory	29,500	40,000
Prepaid Expenses	1,000	800
Supplies	500	700
Total Current Assets	239,539	189,250
Property, Plant, and Equipment		
Land	55,000	55,000
Building and Store Equipment	50,000	50,000
Less Accumulated Depreciation—Bldg & Store Equip.	(15,000)	(10,000)
Net Book Value—Building and Store Equipment	35,000	40,000
Total Property, Plant, and Equipment	90,000	95,000
Total Assets	329,539	284,250
Liabilities and Stockholders' Equity		
Current Liabilities		
Accounts Payable	9,600	35,000
Sales Tax Payable	3,200	5,770
Payroll Taxes Payable	915	875
Interest Payable	600	1,200
Total Current Liabilities	14,315	42,845
Long-Term Liabilities		
Mortgage Payable	68,000	78,000
Total Long-Term Liabilities	68,000	78,000
Total Liabilities	82,315	120,845
Stockholders' Equity		
Common Stock ($1 par, 10,000 shares authorized, 2,000 shares issued and outstanding)	2,000	2,000
Paid-in Capital—Common Stock	5,000	5,000
Retained Earnings	240,224	156,405
Total Stockholders' Equity	247,224	163,405
Total Liabilities and Stockholders' Equity	329,539	284,250

INSTRUCTIONS

1. Prepare both a horizontal and a vertical analysis of the two statements. Round all calculations to one decimal place. (Leave all vertical analysis percentages unadjusted in this problem.)
2. Make written comments about any of the results that seem worthy of investigation.

Analyze: If Chevy Hill, Inc., experiences the same growth in net sales in 2023 as was reported in 2022, what net sales can be projected?

Problem 23.2B ▶ Computing financial ratios.
Objectives 23-1, 23-2, 23-3

CONTINUING >>> Problem

PART I

Using the data from Problem 23.1B, Chevy Hill, Inc., calculate the following financial ratios. Comment on any ratio that merits further consideration. Inventory on December 31, 2021, was $40,000. Please round percentages to nearest 0.1 percent.

1. Current ratio
2. Acid-test ratio
3. Inventory turnover
4. Return on sales
5. Earnings per share of common stock
6. Book value per share of common stock
7. Return on total assets
8. Ratio of stockholders' equity to total equities
9. Ratio of stockholders' equity to total liabilities
10. Rate of return on ending stockholders' equity
11. The dividend yield per share of common stock. Assume a dividend of $1.00 per share was paid in 2019 and $0.50 per share was paid in 2021. The market value per share of common stock in 2022 was $2.50 and in 2021 was $1.50.

PART II

Selected industry ratios are given below. Compare the ratios of Chevy Hill, Inc., with these ratios.

1. Rate of return on sales, 8 percent
2. Return on total assets, 10 percent
3. Merchandise inventory turnover, 6 times
4. Current ratio, 2.5 to 1

Analyze: Based on the analysis you have performed, do you see a trend that could affect the company's stock in the next fiscal year?

Compute and interpret various ratios.

Condensed financial statements for Alpha Corp. and Omega Corp. for 2022 follow:

◀ **Problem 23.3B**

Objectives 23-1, 23-2, 23-3

Income Statements
Year Ended December 31, 2022

	Alpha Corp.	Omega Corp.
Sales (Net)	2,700,000	2,500,000
Costs of Goods Sold	1,593,000	1,300,000
Gross Profit on Sales	1,107,000	1,200,000
Operating Expenses	837,000	915,000
Net Income from Operations	270,000	285,000
Interest Expense	25,000	15,000
Net Income before Income Tax	245,000	270,000
Income Tax Expense	61,250	67,500
Net Income after Income Tax	183,750	202,500

Balance Sheets
December 31, 2022

	Alpha Corp.	Omega Corp.
Assets		
Current Assets	558,600	526,600
Property, Plant, and Equipment (Net)	817,000	750,000
Total Assets	1,375,600	1,276,600
Liabilities and Stockholders' Equity		
Liabilities		
Current Liabilities	315,000	205,500
Long-Term Liabilities (Bonds Payable)	250,000	150,000
Total Liabilities	565,000	355,500
Stockholders' Equity		
Common Stock ($10 Par Value)	500,000	500,000
Retained Earnings	310,600	421,100
Total Stockholders' Equity	810,600	921,100
Total Liabilities and Stockholders' Equity	1,375,600	1,276,600

INSTRUCTIONS

1. Compute the following ratios for each company (rounding to 2 decimal places when appropriate):
    a. Rate of return on net sales
    b. Rate of return on total assets at end of year
    c. Rate of return on stockholders' equity at end of year
    d. Earnings per share of common stock
    e. Ratio of stockholders' equity to total equities
    f. Current ratio
    g. Asset turnover
    h. Book value per share of common stock

2. Comment on the similarities and differences in the ratios computed for the two companies, pointing out the major factor that causes differences.
3. In which corporation would stock ownership be riskier? Explain.
4. Would you consider the extension of short-term credit to Alpha Corp. or Omega Corp. riskier? Explain.

Analyze: What percentage of net sales was expended for operating expenses by Alpha Corp.? By Omega Corp.?

Critical Thinking Problem 23.1

Company Improvements

Doors, Inc.'s condensed income statement and balance sheet for the years 2022 and 2021 follow.

INSTRUCTIONS

Using the following additional information, fill in the missing values:

1. Accounts Receivable increased 50 percent from 2021 to 2022.
2. There were no new purchases of land, property, or equipment in 2022.
3. Accounts Payable decreased 40 percent from 2021 to 2022.
4. No new shares of common stock were issued in 2022.
5. The company paid out cash dividends of $43,048 in 2022.
6. The inventory turnover ratio for 2022 was 6 times.
7. The asset turnover ratio in 2022 was 2.1 times and in 2021 was 2.0 times.
8. The earnings per share in 2022 was $44.624 and in 2021 was $26.00.
9. The effective income tax rate in both years was 20 percent.

Analyze: Assume that the management of Doors, Inc. had been given a directive by the board of directors to improve the company's current ratio in 2022. Did the company improve its standing in this regard from the prior year?

Doors, Inc. Condensed Comparative Income Statement For Years Ending December 31, 2022 and 2021		
	Amounts	
	2022	2021
Sales	?	?
Less Cost of Goods Sold	?	120,000
Gross Profit	?	?
Operating Expenses	115,000	100,000
Net Income before Income Tax	?	?
Income Tax Expense	?	?
Net Income after Income Tax	?	?

Doors, Inc.
Comparative Balance Sheet
December 31, 2022 and 2021

	Amounts	
	2022	2021
Assets		
Current Assets		
Cash	54,600	35,500
Accounts Receivable	?	22,000
Merchandise Inventory	26,000	20,000
Total Current Assets	?	77,500
Property, Plant, and Equipment		
Land	20,000	?
Equipment	50,000	?
Less Accumulated Depreciation	(10,000)	?
Total Property, Plant, and Equipment	?	65,000
Total Assets	?	142,500
Liabilities and Stockholders' Equity		
Current Liabilities		
Accounts Payable	21,000	?
Accrued Expenses	?	?
Total Current Liabilities	24,900	40,000
Stockholders' Equity		
Common Stock ($1 par, 10,000 shares authorized)	2,000	?
Paid-in Capital in Excess of Par—Common Stock	500	?
Retained Earnings	?	100,000
Total Stockholders' Equity	?	?
Total Liabilities and Stockholders' Equity	?	?

Critical Thinking Problem 23.2

Filling in the Blanks

Charles Allen, the accountant for Sue Bee Inc., was asked to make a presentation to the board of directors concerning the corporation's year-end financial position. While flying to the meeting on Saturday morning, Allen checked the papers in his briefcase and realized he had left the revised income statement on his desk back at the office and did not have a copy in his e-mail. Because he knew there was no one at the office to send him the document, he examined the rest of the material in his briefcase to see what information was available.

From memory, Allen recalled that net income after income taxes for the year was $400,000. From some notes he had made for the presentation, he knew that the corporation's gross profit on sales was 40 percent and net income as a percentage of net sales was 10 percent. The income tax rate for the corporation is 25 percent. Allen also remembered that the selling and administrative expenses were the same amount. With this information, he was able to reconstruct the income statement for the corporation before the plane reached its destination.

INSTRUCTIONS

Using the same information given above, prepare an income statement for Sue Bee Inc. for the current year. To get started, first list the major headings for a condensed income statement. Then, starting with the net income figure, work to fill in the dollar amounts based on the percentage relationships given.

BUSINESS CONNECTIONS

Managerial FOCUS

Statement Analysis

1. Suppose that a vertical analysis of the income statement shows an item to be 18 percent of net sales. How would this information be used in order to make it meaningful? With what would it be compared?
2. In 2022, the cost of goods sold was 66 percent of net sales. For 2021, the same item was 63 percent, and for 2020 it was 60 percent. What recommendations would you make about items or activities that should be investigated further?
3. In deciding whether an increase in accounts receivable during the current year is desirable or undesirable, what factors should management consider?
4. Management is concerned that over a three-year period a company's balance sheets show that the total stockholders' equity has changed from 55 percent to 50 percent to 45 percent of total equities. What factors might explain this trend?
5. A company's income statements reveal that its net income after taxes has been 4.5 percent of net sales for each of the past three years. During that time, the industry average has been about 7 percent. What types of questions would management want answered in seeking an explanation for this difference?
6. A company's net sales increased by 35 percent from one year to the next year. During that period, selling expenses increased by 41 percent. Is this desirable? Explain.

Internal Control and FRAUD PREVENTION

Timing of Adjusting Entry

The timing of adjusting entries can alter the analysis of a company. As the full-charge bookkeeper, it is your job to ensure that the adjusting entries are entered on a timely basis. You have noticed that the adjusting entry to transfer the current year's portion from *Mortgage Payable—Long Term* to *Mortgage Payable—Current* has not been entered. You mention it to your controller and are told not to record this adjusting entry. The company is applying for a loan from the bank and the controller found out that the loan officer looks only at the current assets and current liabilities. You are further told that, if anyone questions the lack of the adjusting entry, apologize for the error and record it immediately. Is this ethical for you and the company's controller? Provide justification for your decision.

Financial Statement ANALYSIS

Performance Analysis

Refer to the 2018 Form 10-K *(for the fiscal year ended February 3, 2019)* for The Home Depot, Inc.

1. Locate the consolidated statements of earnings. Using vertical analysis, what is the cost of goods sold expressed as a percentage of net sales for the year ended February 3, 2019? If the industry average for this percentage is 70 percent, is The Home Depot, Inc., performing better than the industry average or worse? Why?
2. Locate the consolidated balance sheets. Using horizontal analysis, by what dollar amount and percentage have total assets decreased from fiscal year 2017 to 2018?

TEAMWORK

Vertical Analysis

Vertical analysis of comparative financial statements can indicate the success or failure of a business. As a loan officer for a bank, you must choose the company that will receive a $50,000 loan. To help make the decision, perform a vertical analysis of the two companies shown in the table below. In groups of two, decide who should receive the loan. Explain why you consider your company better able to repay the loan. Defend your decision to the class.

	My Store	Your Store
Cash	$ 30,000	$ 30,000
Accounts Receivable	2,000	3,500
Total Current Assets	40,000	50,000
Total Assets	100,000	100,000
Current Liabilities	20,000	50,000
Total Liabilities	50,000	70,000
Common Stock	20,000	20,000
Retained Earnings	30,000	10,000
Total Stockholders' Equity	50,000	30,000
Net Sales	10,000	7,000
Cost of Sales	7,000	3,500
Operating Expenses	2,000	1,500
Net Income	1,000	2,000

Answers to Comprehensive Self Review

1. Vertical analysis refers to a comparison of items on an individual financial statement, using one number as the base. The income statement uses net sales as 100 percent, while the balance sheet uses total assets or total liabilities and stockholders' equity as 100 percent. Each item on the statement is compared to the base. Horizontal analysis refers to a comparison of data for the current period with data of a prior period for the financial statement.
2. It tells you the general ability of a business to pay its short-term debts on time. It is computed by dividing current assets by current liabilities.
3. A higher inventory turnover number would probably indicate that assets are being used more effectively in generating sales in a retail business.
4. Different accounting methods, different types of entities, different ages of assets, and different financing methods can impair comparability.
5. The value is determined by dividing the common stockholders' equity (total stockholders' equity minus the book value of preferred stock) by the number of shares of common stock outstanding.

Mini-Practice Set 4

Financial Analysis and Decision Making

Home Suppliers, Inc.

This project will give you an opportunity to evaluate financial statements and to make decisions based on the information presented in the financial statements of Home Suppliers, Inc.

INTRODUCTION

Home Suppliers, Inc. sells a variety of consumer products. Its comparative income statement and balance sheet for the years 2022 and 2021 are presented on the following pages. The Retained Earnings balance on January 1, 2021, was $188,442. Also, Preferred Stockholder cash dividends of $5,000 were paid each year as was $50,000 in dividends paid to Common Stockholders each year.

INSTRUCTIONS

1. Prepare a horizontal and a vertical analysis of the statements. Round all dollar calculations to the nearest whole dollar. Percentage calculations should be rounded to one decimal place (e.g., 11.2%). Remember that some vertical addition of percentages may not equal 100 percent due to rounding.

2. Calculate the following ratios for each year:
    a. The rate of return on net sales.
    b. The rate of return on common stockholders' equity. Preferred dividends are $5,000 for both years. (Remember that dividend requirements on preferred stock must be deducted from net income after taxes to obtain income available to common stockholders.)
    c. The earnings per share of common stock, assuming that the preferred stock is nonparticipating, noncumulative, and has no liquidation value. The number of outstanding shares of common stock remained constant at 100,000 throughout all of 2021 and 2022.
    d. The price-earnings ratio on common stock. The market values were $4.00 in 2021 and $3.00 in 2022.
    e. The rate of return on total assets.
    f. The ratio of stockholders' equity to total liabilities.
    g. The current ratio.
    h. The acid-test ratio.
    i. The merchandise inventory turnover. Inventory was $75,000 at January 1, 2021.
    j. The accounts receivable turnover. Credit sales were $1,400,000 for 2022 and $1,300,000 for 2021. The beginning accounts receivable balance for 2021 was $123,500.

Home Suppliers, Inc.
Comparative Income Statement
Years Ended December 31, 2022 and 2021

	Amounts 2022	Amounts 2021
Revenue		
Sales	1 898 00 0	1 642 000
Less: Sales Returns and Allowances	(2 950)	(2 200)
Net Sales	1 868 500	1 620 000
Cost of Goods Sold		
Merchandise Inventory, January 1	76 000	75 000
Purchases	945 650	800 000
Freight In	9 500	7 500
Less: Purchases Discounts	(10 000)	(8 250)
Purchases Returns and Allowances	(8 250)	(5 000)
Total Merchandise Available for Sale	1 012 900	869 250
Less Merchandise Inventory, December 31	(78 000)	(76 000)
Cost of Goods Sold	934 900	793 250
Gross Profit on Sales	933 600	826 750
Operating Expenses		
Selling Expenses		
Advertising	25 000	21 000
Sales Salaries	200 000	175 000
Payroll Taxes Sales	20 000	17 500
Supplies Expense	11 825	9 650
Miscellaneous Selling Expenses	9 575	7 950
Insurance Expense	7 700	7 500
Total Selling Expenses	274 100	238 600
Administrative Expenses		
Officers' Salaries	350 000	300 000
Office Employees	137 500	125 000
Payroll Taxes Office Employees	4 8750	42 500
Office Supplies	12 250	10 000
Insurance Expense—Administrative	8 000	7 500
Uncollectible Accounts Expense	9 000	8 000
Legal and Accounting	18 000	15 000
Depreciation Expense—Building	15 000	15 000
Depreciation Expense—Furniture	12 000	10 000
Utilities Expense	18 400	16 750
Total Administrative Expenses	628 900	549 750
Total Operating Expenses	903 000	788 350
Net Income from Operations	30 600	38 400
Other Income		
Interest and Dividends	4 675	4 500
Total Other Income	4 675	4 500
Other Expenses		
Bond Interest Expense	6 930	6 930
Interest Expense	6 320	6 070
Total Other Expenses	13 250	13 000
Net Other Expenses	8 575	8 500
Net Income Before Taxes	22 025	29 900
Income Tax Expense	7 709	10 465
Net Income After Taxes	14 316	19 435

Home Suppliers, Inc.
Comparative Balance Sheet
December 31, 2022 and 2021

	2022	2021
Assets		
Current Assets		
Cash	38,157	61,942
Accounts Receivable	90,000	121,500
Merchandise Inventory	78,000	76,000
Prepaid Insurance	600	600
Supplies	975	1,000
Total Current Assets	207,732	261,042
Property, Plant, and Equipment		
Land	105,000	105,000
Building	300,000	300,000
Less: Accumulated Depreciation—Building	(45,000)	(30,000)
Furniture	60,000	50,000
Less: Accumulated Depreciation—Furniture	(22,000)	(10,000)
Total Property, Plant, and Equipment	398,000	415,000
Other Assets		
Marketable Securities (Long-Term)	40,000	40,000
Total Assets	645,732	716,042
Liabilities and Stockholders' Equity		
Current Liabilities		
Accounts Payable	119,500	125,000
Notes Payable	45,000	60,000
Bond Interest Payable	500	500
Income Taxes Payable	7,709	10,465
Sales Salaries Payable	10,000	14,000
Other Payables	5,200	7,500
Total Current Liabilities	187,909	217,465
Long-Term Liabilities		
10% Bonds Payable, due January 1, 2028	70,000	70,000
Premium on Bonds Payable	630	700
Total Long-Term Liabilities	70,630	70,700
Total Liabilities	258,539	288,165
Stockholders' Equity		
5% Preferred Stock ($100 par, 1,000 shares authorized/outstanding)	100,000	100,000
Common Stock ($1 par, 500,000 shares authorized, 100,000 shares outstanding)	100,000	100,000
Paid-in Capital in Excess of Par—Common Stock	50,000	50,000
Total Paid-in Capital	250,000	250,000
Retained Earnings		
Retained Earnings—Unappropriated	112,193	152,877
Retained Earnings—Appropriated	25,000	25,000
Total Retained Earnings	137,193	177,877
Total Stockholders' Equity	387,193	427,877
Total Liabilities and Stockholders' Equity	645,732	716,042

The Statement of Cash Flows

Chapter 24

AFP/Getty Images

www.apple.com

One of the most recognizable brands in the world is Apple Inc. In the company's 2018 10-K, sales revenue of over $265 billion was reported. With a highly skilled workforce and pressure from product demand, the company must have available cash. And they do! In fiscal 2018, the company generated over $77 billion in operating cash flow.

The company's unique approach to design and creative advertising campaigns has generated a distinctive identity and significant brand loyalty for the Apple line of products. During FY 2018, Apple reported sales of more than 217 million iPhones! In addition to product sales, since their App Store opened in 2008, the company's incredible developer community has created an app for doing almost everything imaginable, from accounting homework apps to a zombie survival guide app. The App Store is only one component of Apple's service sector, which also includes Internet services (iOS) and licensing.

As the company continues to evolve, it uses its surplus of cash to generously reward its shareholders and continue its aggressive stock repurchase program. In fact, Apple is among the largest dividend payers in the world, with recent annual dividend payments of $10 billion!

thinking critically

If a company is low on cash, how does this affect the business?

LEARNING OBJECTIVES

24-1 Distinguish between operating, investing, and financing activities.
24-2 Compute cash flows from operating activities.
24-3 Compute cash flows from investing activities.
24-4 Compute cash flows from financing activities.
24-5 Prepare a statement of cash flows.
24-6 Define the accounting terms new to this chapter.

NEW TERMS

cash equivalents
direct method
financing activities
indirect method
investing activities
operating activities
operating assets and liabilities
schedule of operating expenses
statement of cash flows

Section 1

SECTION OBJECTIVES	TERMS TO LEARN
24.1 Distinguish between operating, investing, and financing activities. **WHY IT'S IMPORTANT** When forecasting the cash needs of a business, accountants need to understand how cash and cash equivalents are generated, as well as how the business uses its cash.	cash equivalents financing activities investing activities operating activities statement of cash flows

Sources and Uses of Cash

Corporations issue four financial statements: income statement, balance sheet, statement of retained earnings or stockholders' equity, and statement of cash flows.

The Importance of a Statement of Cash Flows

The **statement of cash flows** provides information about the cash receipts and cash payments of a business. Creditors, including bondholders, noteholders, and suppliers of goods and services, review the statement of cash flows to determine how the firm will pay interest and principal on debts. Investors examine the statement of cash flows to determine if the corporation will have the cash to pay dividends. Management is also interested in cash flows. The firm needs cash to pay employees and suppliers and to meet other obligations. Analyzing past cash flows is helpful because they indicate the sources and uses of cash in the future.

The Meaning of Cash

On the statement of cash flows, the term *cash* includes cash and cash equivalents. As you know, cash consists of coin, currency, and bank accounts. **Cash equivalents** are easily convertible into known amounts of cash. They include certificates of deposit (CDs), U.S. Treasury bills, and money market funds. A short-term investment is a cash equivalent if it matures within three months from the date the business acquired it. Suppose a certificate of deposit acquired by a corporation on September 1, 2021, matures on March 1, 2022. The CD is not classified as a cash equivalent on the December 31, 2021, balance sheet because the maturity date is more than three months from the date the certificate was acquired.

>> **24-1 OBJECTIVE**
Distinguish between operating, investing, and financing activities.

Sources and Uses of Cash

Cash inflows are called *sources of cash*. *Cash outflows* are called *uses of cash*. Sources and uses of cash are classified under three headings on the statement of cash flows:

- **Cash Flows from Operating Activities. Operating activities** are routine business operations. Cash inflows from operating activities include the sale of merchandise or services for cash, collection of accounts receivable created by the sale of merchandise or services, and miscellaneous sources, such as interest income. Cash outflows from operations commonly result from paying operating expenses when they are incurred, paying accounts payable for merchandise purchased on account, and paying accounts payable for operating expenses incurred but not immediately paid.

- **Cash Flows from Investing Activities. Investing activities** involve the acquisition (cash outflow) or disposal (cash inflow) of long-term assets, including land, buildings, equipment, and investments in bonds and other securities.

- **Cash Flows from Financing Activities. Financing activities** involve transactions that provide cash to the business to carry on its activities. Cash inflows from financing activities include issuing bonds and capital stock for cash, borrowing cash by signing notes payable, and reselling treasury stock. Cash outflows from financing activities include paying notes or bonds payable, purchasing treasury stock, and paying cash dividends.

Table 24.1 summarizes sources (inflows) and uses (outflows) of cash.

TABLE 24.1 Sources and Uses of Cash in a Corporation

	Sources of Cash	Uses of Cash
Operating Activities	Sale of merchandise Sale of services Interest income Dividend income Miscellaneous income	Pay for merchandise Pay taxes Pay salaries and wages Pay interest expense Pay for other expenses
Investing Activities	Sale of land, buildings, or equipment Principal payments collected on receivable(s) for long-term assets Sale of investment in bonds or other securities	Pay for the purchase of land, buildings, or equipment Pay for the purchase of investments in bonds or other securities
Financing Activities	Issuance of common stock Issuance of preferred stock Issuance of bonds payable Borrowing through signing a note payable Resale of treasury stock	Pay cash dividends on common stock Pay cash dividends on preferred stock Repay bond indebtedness Repay notes payable or other borrowing Purchase treasury stock

Section 1 Review

1. Which of the following are cash equivalents?
   a. bitcoins
   b. letter of credit from bank
   c. certificate of deposit
   d. all the above
2. What is an example of an investing activity?
   a. issuing a bond payable
   b. selling a building the company owns
   c. purchasing a new cell phone
   d. selling your services to clients
3. Where is short-term borrowing reported on the cash flow statement?
   a. operating activities
   b. investing activities
   c. financing activities
   d. not reported on cash flow statement
4. Investing activities include:
   a. purchases of merchandise for cash.
   b. purchases of plant and equipment for cash.
   c. purchases of prepaid expense items such as supplies and insurance for cash.
   d. issuance of common stock.
5. An example of a financing activity is the:
   a. sale of merchandise for cash.
   b. issuance of stock for cash.
   c. sale of used equipment for cash.
   d. collection of debts acquired from the sale of long-term assets.
6. Indicate where transactions recording taxes expense are reported on the cash flow statement.
   a. operating activities
   b. financing activities
   c. investing activities
   d. shown in footnote, not in a section

Section 2

SECTION OBJECTIVES	TERMS TO LEARN
>> 24.2 Compute cash flows from operating activities. **WHY IT'S IMPORTANT** The income statement reports net income on an accrual basis. It does not report actual cash flows. To identify cash flows from operating activities, the financial statement reader needs to review the statement of cash flows.	operating assets and liabilities schedule of operating expenses

Cash Flows from Operating Activities

To prepare the statement of cash flows, you need the income statement, schedule of operating expenses, the statement of retained earnings, and a comparative balance sheet. The **schedule of operating expenses** is a supplemental schedule showing the selling and general and administrative expenses in greater detail.

Let's use the financial statements for Web Products, Co., to explain the statement of cash flows. These statements appear in Figures 24.1 through 24.4.

FIGURE 24.1

Income Statement

Web Products, Co.
Income Statement
Year Ended December 31, 2022

Revenue		
Sales	3,104,450	
Less Sales Returns and Allowances	135,450	
Net Sales		2,969,000
Cost of Goods Sold		
Merchandise Inventory, January 1	225,000	
Purchases (Net)	1,706,500	
Freight In	26,000	
Total Merchandise Available for Sale	1,957,500	
Less Merchandise Inventory, December 31	205,000	
Cost of Goods Sold		1,752,500
Gross Profit		1,216,500
Operating Expenses		
Selling Expenses	526,425	
General and Administrative Expenses	605,000	
Total Operating Expenses		1,131,425
Net Income from Operations		85,075
Other Income		
Gain on Sale of Equipment	4,000	
Interest Income	1,800	
Total Other Income		5,800
Other Expenses		
Bond Interest Expense	9,500	
Other Interest Expense	2,000	
Total Other Expenses		11,500
Net Income Before Income Taxes		79,375
Income Tax Expense		23,812
Net Income After Income Taxes		55,563

FIGURE 24.2 Schedule of Operating Expenses

Web Products, Co.
Schedule of Operating Expenses
Year Ended December 31, 2022

Selling Expenses		
Advertising	22,800	
Depreciation	7,180	
Employee Fringe Benefits	30,000	
Freight Out and Deliveries	16,000	
Insurance	3,000	
Miscellaneous	2,070	
Other Taxes	3,000	
Payroll Taxes—Sales Staff	30,000	
Rent	12,000	
Repairs and Maintenance	5,000	
Sales Commissions	164,500	
Sales Salaries	175,000	
Sales Supplies	22,500	
Travel and Entertainment	26,875	
Utilities	6,500	
Total Selling Expenses		526,425
General and Administrative Expenses		
Officers' Salaries	350,000	
Office Employees' Salaries	150,000	
Payroll Taxes—Administrative Staff	35,000	
Office Supplies	6,500	
Postage, Copying, and Miscellaneous	7,000	
Uncollectible Accounts Expense	16,500	
Rent or Lease Expense	8,750	
Depreciation	500	
Other Taxes	16,500	
Utilities	14,250	
Total General and Administrative Expenses		605,000
Total Operating Expenses		1,131,425

FIGURE 24.3 Comparative Statement of Retained Earnings

Web Products, Co.
Comparative Statement of Retained Earnings
Years Ended December 31, 2022 and 2021

	Amounts		Increase or Decrease
	2022	2021	
Balance, January 1	202,243	164,993	37,250
Additions			
Net Income After Taxes	55,563	41,250	14,313
Total	257,806	206,243	51,563
Deductions			
Dividends, Preferred	4,000	4,000	0
Total Deductions	4,000	4,000	0
Balance, December 31	253,806	202,243	51,563

FIGURE 24.4 Comparative Balance Sheet

Web Products, Co.
Comparative Balance Sheet
December 31, 2022 and 2021

	Amounts 2022	Amounts 2021	Increase or (Decrease) Amount
Assets			
Current Assets			
Cash	115,231	80,773	34,458
Accounts Receivable	102,000	73,500	28,500
Merchandise Inventory	205,000	225,000	(20,000)
Prepaid Expenses	1,200	1,500	(300)
Supplies	500	250	250
Total Current Assets	423,931	381,023	42,908
Property, Plant, and Equipment			
Land	80,000	80,000	0
Building and Store Equipment	71,800	77,800	(6,000)
Less Accumulated Depreciation—Building and Store Equipment	28,520	23,340	5,180
Net Book Value—Building and Store Equipment	43,280	54,460	(11,180)
Office Equipment	10,500	6,000	4,500
Less Accumulated Depreciation—Office Equipment	2,000	1,500	500
Net Book Value—Office Equipment	8,500	4,500	4,000
Total Property, Plant, and Equipment	131,780	138,960	(7,180)
Total Assets	555,711	519,983	35,728
Liabilities and Stockholders' Equity			
Current Liabilities			
Accounts Payable	71,000	84,500	(13,500)
Sales Tax Payable	2,900	2,500	400
Payroll Taxes Payable	1,145	1,025	120
Interest Payable	860	215	645
Total Current Liabilities	75,905	88,240	(12,335)
Long-Term Liabilities			
10% Bonds Payable, 2031	100,000	100,000	0
Premium on Bonds Payable	3,500	4,000	(500)
Mortgage Payable	60,000	65,000	(5,000)
Total Long-Term Liabilities	163,500	169,000	(5,500)
Total Liabilities	239,405	257,240	(17,835)
Stockholders' Equity			
Preferred Stock ($100 par, 8%, 500 shares authorized, issued and outstanding)	50,000	50,000	0
Common Stock ($1 par, 25,000 shares authorized Issued and outstanding: 7,000 shares in 2021; 8,000 shares in 2022)	8,000	7,000	1,000
Paid-in Capital—Common Stock	4,500	3,500	1,000
Retained Earnings			
Retained Earnings—Unappropriated	253,806	202,243	51,563
Total Retained Earnings	253,806	202,243	51,563
Total Stockholders' Equity	316,306	262,743	53,563
Total Liabilities and Stockholders' Equity	555,711	519,983	35,728

Statement of Cash Flows

The statement of cash flows reconciles the beginning and ending cash balances. It ties together the income statement and the changes in the noncash items on the balance sheet and on the statement of retained earnings.

Figure 24.4 shows the comparative balance sheet for Web Products, Co. There are no cash equivalents on the balance sheet. In 2022, the beginning cash balance was $80,773; the ending cash balance was $115,231. Cash increased by $34,458. The statement of cash flows shows the factors that caused the increase in cash.

There are two ways to prepare the statement of cash flows: the direct method and the indirect method. Web Products, Co., uses the indirect method. The direct method will be described later in this chapter. The indirect method treats net income as the primary source of cash from operating activities and adjusts net income for changes in noncash items.

The accrual basis of accounting is used when recording transactions and preparing the balance sheet and the income statement. Net income shown on the income statement includes both cash and noncash transactions. On the statement of cash flows, net income is adjusted for the noncash items.

Figure 24.5 shows the statement of cash flows for Web Products, Co. Let's examine it and learn how to prepare the statement of cash flows. Throughout this chapter, you will need to refer to the financial statements and reports for Web Products, Co.

recall

Accrual Basis
Under the accrual basis of accounting, revenues are recorded when earned and expenses are recorded when owed, not necessarily when the cash is received or paid.

Cash Flows from Operating Activities

The first section of the statement of cash flows shows net cash provided by operating activities. For Web Products, Co., $37,958 was provided by operating activities. Because cash flows from operating activities are closely related to net income, the starting point for the analysis of the cash flows from operating activities is the net income after income taxes, taken from the income statement in Figure 24.1. The Cash Flows from Operating Activities section of the cash flows statement explains why the net cash flows from operations differ from the net income after taxes, which is $55,563, in this period. There were several income and expense items reported on the income statement that did not involve cash inflows or outflows during that period. Let's analyze those items.

>> **24-2 OBJECTIVE**
Compute cash flows from operating activities.

Expense and Income Items Involving Long-Term Assets and Liabilities

Some items on the income statement result from adjustments related to long-term assets or long-term liabilities. They do not involve cash inflows or outflows in the current year. These adjustments are added to or subtracted from net income.

Depreciation Expense The acquisition of property, plant, and equipment is reported in the Cash Flows from Investing Activities section of the statement of cash flows in the year acquired. Depreciation, depletion, and amortization of assets do not involve a cash outlay in the year the expense is recorded. Instead, these expenses represent a reduction in the net asset value. Figure 24.2 shows depreciation expense of $7,680 (sum of $7,180 recorded as selling expenses and $500 recorded as general and administrative expenses). The depreciation expense was recorded as follows:

important!

Depreciation Expense
The depreciation expense on the income statement is not a cash outflow; therefore, it is added back to net income on the statement of cash flows.

2022					
Dec.	31	Depreciation Expense (Selling)	7 180 00		
		Depreciation Expense (General)	500 00		
		Accumulated Depreciation		7 680 00	

Note that the depreciation expense did not involve a cash outflow. Net income was reduced by a noncash expense. To obtain cash flows from operating activities, the depreciation expense is added back to net income.

FIGURE 24.5

Statement of Cash Flows

Web Products, Co.
Statement of Cash Flows
Year Ended December 31, 2022

Cash Flows from Operating Activities		
Net income after taxes (per income statement)		55,563
Adjustments to reconcile net income to net cash provided by operating activities		
Depreciation Expense	7,680	
Amortization of premium on bonds payable	(500)	
Gain on sale of equipment	(4,000)	
Changes in noncash current assets and current liabilities		
Increase in Accounts Receivable	(28,500)	
Decrease in Merchandise Inventory	20,000	
Decrease in Prepaid Expenses	300	
Increase in Supplies	(250)	
Decrease in Accounts Payable	(13,500)	
Increase in Sales Tax Payable	400	
Increase in Payroll Taxes Payable	120	
Increase in Interest Payable	645	
Total Adjustments		(17,605)
Net Cash Provided by Operating Activities		37,958
Cash Flows from Investing Activities		
Proceeds from sale of equipment	8,000	
Purchase of Office Equipment	(4,500)	
Net Cash Provided by Investing Activities		3,500
Cash Flows from Financing Activities		
Payment of Mortgage Payable principal	(5,000)	
Proceeds from issue of Common Stock	2,000	
Payment of dividends on Preferred Stock	(4,000)	
Net Cash used in Financing Activities		(7,000)
Net Increase in Cash and Cash Equivalents		34,458
Cash and Cash Equivalents, January 1, 2022		80,773
Cash and Cash Equivalents, December 31, 2022		115,231

Note: During the year, cash payments for income taxes was $23,812 and cash payments for interest was $10,855.

---

important!

Bond Interest Expense

The bond interest expense on the income statement is less than the actual cash outflow; therefore, on the statement of cash flows, the difference is subtracted from net income.

Amortization of Premium on Bonds Payable The income statement shows bond interest expense of $9,500. This is not the actual cash outflow for interest. It reflects the cash paid minus $500 of bond premium amortization. The bond interest expense was recorded as follows:

11	Bond Interest Expense	9,500 00		11
12	Premium on Bonds Payable	500 00		12
13	Cash		10,000 00	13

The amount of bond interest expense reported on the income statement understates the actual cash outflow by $500. To obtain cash flows from operating activities, the amortization of the bond premium is deducted from net income.

Gain or Loss on Sale of Equipment The income statement shows a gain of $4,000 on the sale of equipment. The equipment was sold for $8,000 cash. Thus, the proceeds from the sale of the equipment were shown as a cash inflow from investing activities. At the time of sale, the following entry was made:

21	Cash	8 000 00		21
22	Accumulated Depreciation—Equipment	2 000 00		22
23	Equipment		6 000 00	23
24	Gain on Sale of Equipment		4 000 00	24

The sale of the equipment is not a part of the routine operating activities of the business. The gain of $4,000 is a part of the $8,000 in cash received from the asset sale. As we see, the entire $8,000 was included in cash inflows from investing activities. It is therefore necessary to remove (deduct) the $4,000 of gain on sale of equipment from the net income figure in arriving at the net cash inflow provided by operations. A loss on sale of long-term assets would be added to net income.

Income and Expense Items Involving Changes in Current Assets and Current Liabilities

Current assets and current liabilities are often referred to as **operating assets and liabilities.** Usually, changes in current assets and current liabilities are related to routine business operations and are reflected in net income. Assume that all the changes in the current assets and current liabilities of Web Products, Co., resulted from routine operating activities.

Increases in Current Assets Current assets include accounts receivable, merchandise inventory, and prepaid expenses. Increases in current assets are deducted from net income to arrive at cash flows from operating activities. Look at the following examples. The comparative balance sheet for Web Products, Co., Figure 24.4, shows that several current assets increased during the year.

Increase in Accounts Receivable Figure 24.4 shows that *Accounts Receivable* increased by $28,500. This means that more sales on account were recorded than collected. The sales were included in net income, but the cash has not been received. To obtain cash flows from operating activities, the increase in accounts receivable is subtracted from net income.

> Amazon.com reported net income during 2017 of approximately $3 billion. During the same period, cash provided by operating activities was $18.4 billion and the balance sheet reported cash and cash equivalents of over $20.5 billion. Net sales during the same period were approximately $177 billion, an increase of $42 billion over 2016.

Increase in Supplies Figure 24.4 shows that *Supplies* increased by $250. This means that more supplies were paid for than were used. Net income does not reflect all cash paid for supplies. To obtain cash flows from operating activities, the increase in supplies is subtracted from net income.

Decreases in Current Assets Decreases in noncash current assets are added to net income to arrive at cash flows from operating activities. The following examples will illustrate why this rule applies.

Decrease in Prepaid Expenses Figure 24.4 shows that *Prepaid Expenses* decreased by $300. This means that more was charged to expenses than was paid for prepaid expenses in arriving at net income for the year. In other words, net income reflects the use of prepaid expenses. To obtain cash flows from operating activities, the decrease in prepaid expenses is added to net income.

Decrease in Merchandise Inventory Figure 24.4 shows that *Merchandise Inventory* decreased by $20,000. This means that more inventory was sold than was purchased. The sale of the inventory was reflected in net income as cost of goods sold, but cash was not paid to replace the inventory. Net income reflects higher costs than actual cash outflows. To obtain cash flows from operating activities, a decrease in inventory is added to net income.

Increases in Current Liabilities Current liabilities include accounts payable, sales tax payable, payroll taxes payable, and interest payable. Increases in current liabilities are added to net income to obtain the cash flows from operating activities. Look over the following situations:

Increase in Sales Tax Payable Figure 24.4 shows that *Sales Tax Payable* increased by $400. This means that more sales tax was owed than was paid during the year. To obtain cash flows from operating activities, the increase in sales tax payable is added to net income.

Increase in Payroll Taxes Payable Figure 24.4 shows that *Payroll Taxes Payable* increased by $120. This means that more payroll taxes were owed than were paid. To obtain cash flow from operating activities, the increase in payroll taxes payable is added to net income.

Increase in Interest Payable Figure 24.4 shows that *Interest Payable* increased by $645. This means that more interest was recorded as expense than was paid in cash. To obtain cash flows from operating activities, the increase in interest payable is added to net income.

Decreases in Current Liabilities Decreases in current liabilities are subtracted from net income. An illustration using *Accounts Payable* will show why this rule exists.

Decrease in Accounts Payable Figure 24.4 shows that *Accounts Payable* decreased $13,500. This means more cash was paid on account than purchases were recorded on account. The cash was paid out but was not reflected in net income. To obtain cash flows from operating activities, the decrease in accounts payable is subtracted from net income.

Summary of Effects of Changes in Current Assets and Current Liabilities Let's summarize how net income is adjusted for changes in current assets and current liabilities when computing cash flows from operating activities.

	Add to Net Income	Deduct from Net Income
Increase in current asset		X
Decrease in current asset	X	
Increase in current liability	X	
Decrease in current liability		X

Figure 24.5 shows all items considered when computing net cash provided by operating activities. During the year, operating activities for Web Products, Co., provided $37,958 of cash.

Effect of Net Loss on Cash Flows from Operations

If the income statement reflects a net loss, the first line of the statement of cash flows is the net loss. All adjustments for changes in current assets and current liabilities are made to the net loss figure.

Section 2 Review

1. How is the loss from the sale of a building handled when computing net cash provided by operating activities?
   a. not reported in the operating section
   b. added in operating activities
   c. subtracted in operating activities
   d. reported in a note to the statement, not within the statement

2. The income statement shows depreciation expense of $25,000. How is the expense handled when computing net cash provided by operating activities?
   a. added in cash provided by operating activities
   b. subtracted from cash provided by operating activities
   c. can ignore; it is included in the net income amount
   d. reported in a note to the statement, not within the statement

3. During the year, the notes payable account increased from $45,000 to $50,000. How, if at all, is this reflected when computing net income from operations?
   a. not reported in the operating section
   b. added in operating activities
   c. subtracted in operating activities
   d. added in cash flows from financing

4. The net cash provided by operating activities is affected by:
   a. the issue of bonds payable for cash.
   b. a purchase of land for cash.
   c. the sale of stock for cash.
   d. a change in merchandise inventory.

5. To determine the net cash provided by operating activities, an increase in prepaid assets should be:
   a. not included in the calculation.
   b. deducted from net income.
   c. added to net cash flow.
   d. added to net income.

6. The net loss for the year was $15,000. Depreciation expense was $4,000. *Merchandise Inventory* decreased by $3,000. *Accounts Receivable* decreased by $5,000. *Accounts Payable* decreased by $2,500. *Income Tax Payable* decreased by $5,000. Calculate the net cash provided or used by operating activities for the year.
   a. $10,500 cash used
   b. $10,500 cash provided
   c. $14,500 cash used
   d. $10,000 cash used

Section 3

SECTION OBJECTIVES	TERMS TO LEARN
>> 24-3 Compute cash flows from investing activities. **WHY IT'S IMPORTANT** Cash flows from the acquisition or disposal of assets are reported separately from cash flows from operating activities. **>> 24-4** Compute cash flows from financing activities. **WHY IT'S IMPORTANT** Transactions such as selling stock, securing loans, or repaying notes impact the cash balance of a business. **>> 24-5** Prepare a statement of cash flows. **WHY IT'S IMPORTANT** Investors, managers, and creditors want to know the reasons for changes in a company's cash position.	direct method indirect method

Cash Flows from Investing and Financing Activities

Investing and financing activities can produce both cash outflows and cash inflows.

Cash Flows from Investing Activities

Investing activities are transactions involving the acquisition or disposal of assets that are not consumed in routine operations within one year.

Cash Outflows from Investing Activities

The most common cash outflows from investing activities are cash payments for purchases of property, plant, and equipment and for purchases of the stocks and bonds of other corporations.

Figure 24.4 shows that the *Office Equipment* account increased by $4,500 during 2022. The increase resulted from the purchase of office equipment for $4,500 in cash. This is a cash outflow from investing activities. It is reported on the statement of cash flows in Figure 24.5.

>> **24-3 OBJECTIVE**
Compute cash flows from investing activities.

Cash Inflows from Investing Activities

Most cash inflows from investing activities reflect the sale of land, buildings, equipment, or investments in securities of other corporations. Payments of principal received on mortgages or notes held by the company in connection with the sale of plant and equipment are classified as cash inflows from investing activities.

In 2022, Web Products, Co., had one cash inflow from investing activities. The corporation sold store equipment for $8,000 in cash.

Sales price (cash inflow)		$8,000
Asset cost	$6,000	
Accumulated depreciation	(2,000)	(4,000)
Gain on sale		$4,000

The statement of cash flows shows the $8,000 received from the sale of the store equipment as a cash inflow from investing activities. Recall that the gain was subtracted from net income in the Cash Flows from Operating Activities section.

At this point, it is possible to reconcile the changes in the long-term asset accounts. The net change of $6,000 (decrease) in the **Building and Store Equipment** account is reconciled as follows:

Building and store equipment, Dec. 31, 2021	$77,800
Add Purchases during 2022	–0–
Less Cost of equipment sold during 2022	6,000
Building and store equipment, Dec. 31, 2022	$71,800

The increase in accumulated depreciation can be reconciled to the depreciation expense for the year as follows:

Accumulated Depreciation

	Building & Store Equip.		Office Equip.		Total
2022	$28,520	+	$2,000	=	$30,520
2021	(23,340)	+	(1,500)	=	(24,840)
Increase	$ 5,180	+	$ 500	=	$ 5,680
Accumulated depreciation on equipment sold					2,000
Depreciation expense for 2022					$ 7,680

The Cash Flows from Investing Activities section of the statement of cash flows for Web Products, Co., shows that $3,500 cash was provided by investing activities during 2022.

Cash Flows from Financing Activities

Financing activities include debt and equity transactions.

Cash Inflows from Financing Activities

Cash inflows from financing activities include amounts received from the original issue of preferred stock or common stock, the resale of treasury stock, and the issue of bonds and notes payable.

Proceeds of Cash Investments by Stockholders Figure 24.4 shows that the *Common Stock* account increased by $1,000 and the *Paid-in Capital—Common Stock* account increased by $1,000. During 2022, Web Products, Co., issued 1,000 shares of common stock for $2.00 per share. This resulted in a cash inflow of $2,000 (1,000 × $2.00) as reported on the statement of cash flows.

Proceeds of Short-Term and Long-Term Borrowing Figure 24.4 shows that Web Products, Co., did not seek additional cash from short-term or long-term note payable during 2022. If the company had obtained cash from borrowing, it would have been reported in the financing activities section of the cash flow statement as noted in Table 24.1.

During 2022, bond premium of $500 was amortized. Remember that the amortized premium was included in the Cash Flows from Operating Activities section. The change of $500 in *Premium on Bonds Payable* is reconciled as follows:

Premium on bonds payable, Dec. 31, 2021	$4,000
Add Premium on bonds sold in 2022	0
Less Premium amortized in 2022	(500)
Premium on bonds payable, Dec. 31, 2022	$3,500

---

important!

Investing Activities
Investing activities are transactions that involve the acquisition or disposal of assets that will not be used up or consumed in routine operations in a short time.

ABOUT ACCOUNTING

Managing Cash
Large companies actively manage their own corporate cash. Smaller businesses often place their cash in money market funds due to the limited time and resources available for cash management.

>> 24-4 OBJECTIVE
Compute cash flows from financing activities.

recall

Treasury Stock
Treasury stock is a corporation's own capital stock that has been issued, fully paid for, and reacquired by the corporation.

recall

Bonds Issued at a Premium
On the day that bonds are issued, if the market rate of interest is lower than the face rate of interest, the bonds will sell at a premium.

Cash Outflows from Financing Activities

Cash outflows from financing activities result from the repayment of debt obligations such as bonds payable, notes payable, and mortgages; the purchase of treasury stock; and the retirement of preferred stock. The payment of cash dividends is classified as a cash outflow from financing activities. Interest expense, however, is classified as an outflow of cash from operating activities.

Payment of Mortgage Payable Figure 24.4 shows a decrease of $5,000 in the *Mortgage Payable* account during 2022. This decrease is a result of $5,000 of principal payments. These payments are shown on the statement of cash flows as a cash outflow from financing activities.

During 2022, Web Products, Co., did not acquire cash through short-term borrowing, nor did it repay any short-term loans. However, if it had, these short-term transactions might not appear on the balance sheet. For example, the corporation could have borrowed $10,000 by signing a three-month note payable on March 1, 2022, and repaid the note on June 1, 2022. The note would not appear on the December 31, 2022, balance sheet. However, the note would represent both an inflow and an outflow of cash. The note would be reported in the Cash Flows from Financing Activities section of the statement of cash flows.

Payment of Cash Dividends Figure 24.3 indicates that during the year Web Products, Co., paid cash dividends of $4,000 on preferred stock. This amount is included as a part of cash flows from financing activities.

The statement of cash flows shows that in 2022 cash of $7,000 was used by the financing activities of Web Products, Co.

>> **24-5 OBJECTIVE**
Prepare a statement of cash flows.

ABOUT **ACCOUNTING**
While the FASB prefers the direct method, most businesses continue to use the indirect method for preparing the statement of cash flows.

Preparing a Statement of Cash Flows

The cash flows from the three types of business activities—operating, investing, and financing—are combined to arrive at the net change in cash and cash equivalents for the year. The net change is then combined with the beginning balance of cash and cash equivalents to reconcile to the ending balance of cash and cash equivalents. Figure 24.5 shows that the net change in the cash and cash equivalents was an increase of $34,458. The cash balance was $80,773 on January 1, 2022, and $115,231 on December 31, 2022. These are the same amounts reported on the comparative balance sheet in Figure 24.4.

Direct and Indirect Methods of Preparing the Statement of Cash Flows

There are two methods of preparing the statement of cash flows: the indirect and direct methods. Figure 24.5 was prepared using the **indirect method.** Under this method, in the Cash Flows from Operating Activities section, net income is treated as the primary source of cash and is adjusted for changes in current assets and liabilities associated with net income, noncash transactions, and other items. Most corporations use the indirect method.

The Financial Accounting Standards Board allows the indirect or direct method. Under the **direct method,** all revenue and expenses reported on the income statement appear in the operating section of the statement of cash flows and show the cash received or paid out for each type of transaction. Under the direct method, a corporation reports cash flows from operating activities in two major classes: gross cash receipts and gross cash payments. The FASB suggests the following classifications for reporting cash inflows and outflows:

- cash collected from customers
- interest and dividends received
- cash paid to employees and other suppliers of goods or services, including suppliers of insurance and advertising
- interest paid
- income taxes paid

MANAGERIAL IMPLICATIONS

CASH FLOW

- Management needs to ensure that cash is available to meet operating expenses and to pay debts promptly.
- Management analyzes the statement of cash flows to evaluate the operations of the company, plan future operations, forecast cash needs, arrange proper financing, and plan dividend payments.
- Management uses the statement of cash flows to determine how well the company will be able to meet its maturing obligations.
- Management analyzes past cash flows in order to make plans that will keep the company solvent and profitable.

THINKING CRITICALLY

If the only financial statement available to you is the cash flow statement, could you evaluate the business as a potential investment?

The cash flows from investing activities and cash flows from financing activities are the same in both direct and indirect methods.

Corporations that use the direct method are encouraged to provide additional meaningful information about operating cash receipts and cash payments if feasible. The direct method is not commonly used because of the many additional disclosures and schedules that must accompany the direct method.

When the statement of cash flows is based on the direct method, it must be accompanied by a reconciliation of net income to the net cash provided by operating activities. This reconciliation shows the same information as the Cash Flows from Operating Activities section of the statement of cash flows prepared using the indirect method. The additional work is another reason that many corporations avoid the direct method of preparing the statement of cash flows. Intermediate accounting textbooks provide detailed information about the direct method.

Disclosures Required in the Statement of Cash Flows

Various disclosures are added to the statement of cash flows. If the indirect method of presentation is used, the amount of interest and income taxes paid during the period are reported in notes accompanying the statement. The note at the bottom of Figure 24.5 shows that cash payments were $23,813 for income taxes and $11,355 for interest.

In order to provide complete information to statement readers, information about noncash investing and financing activities is disclosed on the statement of cash flows. Examples of financing and investing activities not affecting cash flows include issuing bonds payable for land and converting bonds payable into common stock.

important!

Disclosures
If the indirect method is used, the interest and income taxes paid during the period are separately disclosed.

> The Hasbro, Inc., consolidated statements of cash flows for the fiscal year ended December 31, 2017, reported net cash provided by operating activities of $724 million. Net income during the same period was approximately $397 million!

Section 3 Review

1. During the year, equipment was sold for $80,000, and a $5,000 gain was recorded. How is this transaction reported on the statement of cash flows?
   a. inflow of $80,000 from investing; reduce cash $5,000 from operating
   b. only an inflow of cash of $80,000 from investing
   c. inflow of $80,000 from investing; increase cash from operating by $5,000
   d. inflow of $80,000 from investing; reduce cash $5,000 from financing

2. During the year, a corporation issued $250,000 of bonds payable in return for land with a fair market value of $250,000. How is this reported on the statement of cash flows?
   a. no requirement to report on cash flow statement
   b. disclosed by a note to the statement using $250,000 as the value of a capital asset obtained by issuing a bond payable for the same amount
   c. cash inflow of $250,000 from financing; $250,000 cash outflow for investing
   d. cash inflow of $250,000 from operating; $250,000 cash outflow for financing

3. On the statement of cash flows, how is the payment of a cash dividend reported?
   a. cash outflow from investing
   b. cash outflow from financing
   c. cash outflow from operating
   d. not reported on the cash flow statement

4. Most corporations prepare the statement of cash flows using the:
   a. accrual method.
   b. indirect method.
   c. direct method.
   d. equivalent method.

5. The purchase of equipment for cash is shown on the statement of cash flows as a(n):
   a. increase in Cash Flows from Financing Activities.
   b. decrease in Cash Flows from Investing Activities.
   c. decrease in Cash Flows from Financing Activities.
   d. increase in Cash Flows from Investing Activities.

6. A truck that originally cost $40,000 was sold for $10,000 cash. Accumulated depreciation up to the date of the sale was $36,000. A $6,000 gain was reported on the income statement. What is the effect on the statement of cash flows?
   a. cash inflow of $40,000 from sale of truck in investing; $36,000 depreciation added to cash from operating; gain ignored
   b. $4,000 added to cash from operating; $6,000 subtracted from cash from operating; $10,000 inflow from sale added to cash from investing
   c. $4,000 depreciation added to cash from operating; $10,000 added to cash from operating; $40,000 subtracted from cash from financing
   d. $10,000 increase in cash from investing; $6,000 gain subtracted from cash from operating (net income)

REVIEW Chapter Summary

Chapter 24

In previous chapters, you learned about the three major financial statements prepared for corporations—the income statement, the balance sheet, and the statement of retained earnings. In addition, some corporations prepare a statement of stockholders' equity. The annually published financial statements should also include a statement of cash flows showing the sources and uses of cash.

Learning Objectives

24-1 Distinguish between operating, investing, and financing activities.

The corporation's activities are divided into three categories on the statement of cash flows: operating, investing, and financing. Cash inflows and outflows from transactions for each type of activity are shown, along with the net cash inflow or outflow:

- Cash flows from operating activities involve routine business operations: selling merchandise for cash, collecting accounts receivable, paying expenses when incurred, and paying accounts payable.
- Investing activities are transactions that involve the acquisition of assets or disposal of assets such as land, equipment, or buildings.
- Financing activities involve transactions such as issuing stocks or bonds, paying a note or bond payable, and paying cash dividends.

24-2 Compute cash flows from operating activities.

The first section of the statement of cash flows involves operating activities—buying, selling, and administrative activities. This section begins with the net income amount from the income statement:

- To arrive at the net cash flow provided by operating activities, the net income amount is adjusted for noncash items used to calculate net income.
- The most common items added to net income are (1) depreciation, (2) losses on sales of assets, (3) amortization of bond discount, (4) decreases in current assets, and (5) increases in current liabilities.
- The most common items deducted from net income are (1) gains on sales of assets, (2) amortization of bond premium, (3) increases in current assets, and (4) decreases in current liabilities.

24-3 Compute cash flows from investing activities.

The second section of the statement discloses investing activities:

- Cash inflows from investing often result from cash sales of property, plant, and equipment and cash sales of the stocks and bonds of other corporations held as investments.
- Cash outflows come from cash purchases of plant and equipment and cash purchases of the stocks and bonds of other corporations.

24-4 Compute cash flows from financing activities.

The third section of the statement concerns financing activities. These activities may reflect transactions between a corporation and its stockholders:

- Cash inflows often result from the issuing of common or preferred stock or selling treasury stock.
- Typical cash outflows are dividend payments and the purchase of treasury stock.
- Cash inflows result from issuing bonds payable for cash and from borrowing money by issuing or discounting notes payable. Cash outflows result when notes payable or bonds payable are repaid. However, interest paid on debt is seen as resulting from an operating activity.

24-5 Prepare a statement of cash flows.

There are two statement preparation methods—direct and indirect:

- Most corporations use the indirect method because the statement is easier to prepare when this method is used.
- The Financial Accounting Standards Board allows either method.
- Some major transactions that do not involve cash should be disclosed in notes to the statement of cash flows.

24-6 Define the accounting terms new to this chapter.

Glossary

Cash equivalents (p. 860) Assets that are easily convertible into known amounts of cash

Direct method (p. 872) A means of reporting sources and uses of cash under which all revenue and expenses reported on the income statement appear in the operating section of the statement of cash flows and show the cash received or paid out for each type of transaction

Financing activities (p. 860) Transactions with those who provide cash to the business to carry on its activities

Indirect method (p. 872) A means of reporting cash generated from operating activities by treating net income as the primary source of cash in the operating section of the statement of cash flows and adjusting that amount for changes in current assets and liabilities associated with net income, noncash transactions, and other items

Investing activities (p. 860) Transactions that involve the acquisition or disposal of long-term assets

Operating activities (p. 860) Routine business transactions—selling goods or services and incurring expenses

Operating assets and liabilities (p. 867) Current assets and current liabilities

Schedule of operating expenses (p. 862) A schedule that supplements the income statement, showing the selling and general and administrative expenses in greater detail

Statement of cash flows (p. 860) A financial statement that provides information about the cash receipts and cash payments of a business

Comprehensive Self Review

1. What are the three types of activities for which cash flows must be shown in a statement of cash flows?
2. Name some financing activities.
3. During the year, accounts payable increased from $35,000 to $50,000. How, if at all, would this change be reflected in computing cash flows from operations?
4. Where on the statement of cash flows should cash payments of interest be shown?
5. Where on the statement of cash flows should a loss on the sale of equipment be shown?

(Answers to Comprehensive Self Review are at the end of the chapter.)

Discussion Questions

1. What is the purpose of the statement of cash flows?
2. Where is information obtained for preparing the statement of cash flows?
3. Give two examples of cash inflows from investing activities.
4. Give two examples of cash outflows from investing activities.
5. Give two examples of cash outflows from financing activities.
6. Give two examples of cash inflows from financing activities.
7. What are cash and cash equivalents?

8. Is an investment in a corporate bond maturing 180 days after the purchase date a cash equivalent? Explain.

9. A corporation's income statement shows a gain of $8,000 on the sale of plant and equipment. In computing the net cash provided by operating activities, how would this $8,000 be treated?

10. A corporation's income statement shows bond interest expense of $16,500. Amortization of the discount on the bonds during the year was $1,500. What is the amount of cash outflow for bond interest expense?

11. Explain the difference between the direct method and the indirect method of preparing the statement of cash flows.

12. On January 1, 2022, the balance of the *Accounts Payable* account was $31,000. On December 31, 2022, the balance was $41,000. How, if at all, would this change be reflected in the statement of cash flows?

13. Why are cash equivalents included on the statement of cash flows?

14. Why must noncash investing and financing activities be disclosed on the statement of cash flows?

15. Identify in which of the three types of activities on the statement of cash flows the following transactions appear. Indicate whether each is a cash inflow or outflow:

    a. Cash dividends paid.
    b. Cash interest payment received.
    c. Cash on notes receivable collected.
    d. Cash interest paid.
    e. Cash received from customers.
    f. Cash proceeds from issuing stock.

APPLICATIONS

Exercises

Effects of transactions on cash flows.

Exercise 24.1
Objective 24-1

What effect would each of the following transactions have on the statement of cash flows?

1. The sum of $16,000 in cash was received from the sale of used office equipment that originally cost $25,000. Depreciation of $12,000 had been taken on the asset up to the date of the sale. The resulting $3,000 gain was shown on the income statement.

2. The sum of $50,000 in cash was received from the sale of investments in the stock of another corporation. The stock had a book value of $55,000. The $5,000 loss on the sale was shown on the income statement.

Cash flows from operating activities.

Exercise 24.2
Objective 24-2

The following data are summarized from the income statement of More, Inc., for the year ended December 31, 2022. Using these data and ignoring changes in current assets, current liabilities, and income taxes, prepare a schedule of cash flows from operating activities for the year. (Use Figure 24.5 as a model for this schedule.)

More, Inc.
Income Statement
Year Ended December 31, 2022

Sales			700 000 00
Cost of Goods Sold			330 000 00
Gross Profit on Sales			370 000 00
Operating Expenses			
Depreciation	20 500 00		
Other Selling Expenses	160 000 00		
Other Administrative Expenses	92 500 00	273 000 00	
Net Income from Operations		97 000 00	
Bond Interest Expense			
Cash Interest	20 000 00		
Amortization of Discount on Bonds Payable	3 000 00	23 000 00	
Net Income for Year		74 000 00	

Exercise 24.3
Objective 24-2

▶ **Cash flows from operating activities.**

The current assets and current liabilities of Titan Company on December 31, 2022 and 2021, are as follows. The corporation's net income for 2022 was $50,000. Included in its expenses was depreciation of $12,000. Prepare a schedule of the cash flows from operating activities for 2022. (Use Figure 24.5 as a model for this schedule.)

	Dec. 31, 2022	Dec. 31, 2021
Cash	$ 83,500	$75,000
Accounts Receivable	100,000	95,000
Prepaid Expenses	14,000	16,100
Merchandise Inventory	75,000	90,000
Accounts Payable	60,400	51,000
Notes Payable (Borrowing)	45,000	53,000

Exercise 24.4
Objective 24-2

▶ **Cash flows from operating activities.**

The income statement of Eastwood, Inc., showed net income of $80,000 for 2022. The firm's beginning inventory was $50,000 and its ending inventory was $54,000. Accounts payable were $44,000 on January 1 and $39,000 on December 31. Compute the net cash provided by the firm's operating activities during the year.

Exercise 24.5
Objective 24-2

▶ **Cash flows from operating activities.**

The following information is taken from the income statement of Nashville Inc. for 2022:

Sales		$950,000
Cost of Goods Sold		600,000
Gross Profit on Sales		350,000
Operating Expenses		
Depreciation	$ 20,000	
Other Operating Expenses	180,000	200,000
Net Income from Operations		$150,000

Additional information relating to account balances at the beginning and end of the year appears below:

	Jan. 1, 2022	Dec. 31, 2021
Accounts Receivable	$56,000	$50,000
Merchandise Inventory	74,000	78,000
Accrued Liabilities	5,000	2,500
Accounts Payable	38,000	29,000

Determine the cash flows from operations for 2022.

Cash flows from investing activities.

◀ **Exercise 24.6**
Objective 24-3

The following transactions occurred at E Brainerd Inc. during 2022. Use this information to compute the company's net cash flow from investing activities.

1. The company issued 100,000 shares of its own $1 par-value common stock for land with a fair market value of $100,000.

2. The company gave its president a loan of $50,000 and obtained a 5 percent note receivable, dated December 22, 2022, and maturing two years later.

3. The company sold a used truck for $10,000 in cash. The original cost of the truck was $54,000. Depreciation of $44,000 had been deducted.

Cash flows from investing activities.

◀ **Exercise 24.7**
Objective 24-3

The following transactions occurred at Signal Company in 2022. Use this information to compute the company's net cash flow from investing activities.

1. The company purchased a new building for $450,000. A down payment of $50,000 was made. The balance is due in four equal annual installments (plus interest) beginning July 1, 2023.

2. The company bought 1,000 shares of its own common stock for $25,000.

3. The company purchased as an investment $60,000 par value of Lakeside Company's 8 percent bonds, maturing in five years. The purchase price was $57,000.

Cash flows from financing activities.

◀ **Exercise 24.8**
Objective 24-4

The following transactions occurred at John Inc. in 2022. Use this information to compute the company's net cash flow from financing activities for the year.

1. Holders of $200,000 par-value 3 percent bonds surrendered the bonds for redemption and were paid $205,000 in cash. The unamortized discount on these bonds as of the date of redemption was $2,000.

2. Cash interest of $3,600 was paid on bonds during the year. The bond discount amortized was $400.

3. Cash dividends of $20,000 were paid on common stock during the year.

Cash flows from financing activities.

◀ **Exercise 24.9**
Objective 24-4

The following transactions occurred at Peter's Second Company in 2022. Use this information to compute the company's net cash flow from financing activities for the year.

1. The company reacquired as treasury stock 30,000 shares of its outstanding common stock, paying a total of $90,000 for the shares.

2. On November 30, the company borrowed $200,000 from the bank, signing a 90-day, 8 percent note payable.

PROBLEMS

Problem Set A

Problem 24.1A

Objectives 24-1, 24-2, 24-3, 24-4, 24-5

▶ **Prepare a statement of cash flows.**

A comparative balance sheet for Stokely, Inc., on December 31, 2022 and 2021, follows. Additional information about the firm's financial activities during 2022 is also given below.

INSTRUCTIONS

Prepare a statement of cash flows for 2022. Additional information for the year follows:

a. Had net income of $100,000.
b. Recorded $20,000 in depreciation.
c. Issued bonds payable with a par value of $50,000 at par and received cash.
d. Received $30,000 in cash for the issue of an additional 30,000 shares of $1 par value common stock.
e. Purchased equipment for $50,000 in cash.

Stokely, Inc.
Comparative Balance Sheet
December 31, 2022 and 2021

Assets	2022	2021
Cash	149,900	73,500
Accounts Receivable (Net)	130,600	80,600
Merchandise Inventory	47,600	44,000
Property, Plant, and Equipment	250,000	200,000
Less Accumulated Depreciation	(40,000)	(20,000)
Total Assets	538,100	378,100
Liabilities and Stockholders' Equity		
Liabilities		
Accounts Payable	57,000	77,000
Bonds Payable	160,000	110,000
Total Liabilities	217,000	187,000
Stockholders' Equity		
Common Stock ($1 par, 100,000 shares authorized, 60,000 shares issued in 2021 and 30,000 shares issued in 2022)	90,000	60,000
Retained Earnings	231,000	131,100
Total Stockholders' Equity	321,100	191,100
Total Liabilities and Stockholders' Equity	538,100	378,100

Analyze: Explain why a decrease in accounts payable is considered an adjustment to cash flows from operating activities.

Problem 24.2A

Objectives 24-1, 24-2, 24-3, 24-4, 24-5

▶ **Prepare a statement of cash flows.**

Postclosing trial balance data and other financial data for KB Company as of December 31, 2022 and 2021, follow.

INSTRUCTIONS

Prepare a statement of cash flows for 2022. Additional information for the year follows:

a. Sold common stock for $50,000 in cash.
b. Had net income of $75,000 after income taxes.
c. Sold bonds payable for $50,000 cash at par value.
d. Completed a major addition to the building for $100,000 in cash.
e. Bought additional land for $35,000 in cash.
f. Paid common stock dividends of $25,000 in cash.
g. Amortized intangible assets for $500.
h. The short-term note payable resulted from operating activities, not borrowing or financing activities.

KB Company
Postclosing Trial Balance
December 31, 2022 and 2021

Account Name	2022 Debit	2022 Credit	2021 Debit	2021 Credit
Cash	88 200 00		85 400 00	
Accounts Receivable (Net)	91 500 00		86 000 00	
Merchandise Inventory	62 750 00		66 450 00	
Prepaid Expenses	2 700 00		2 100 00	
Land	75 000 00		40 000 00	
Plant and Equipment	215 000 00		115 000 00	
Accumulated Depreciation—Plant and Equipment		18 500 00		11 500 00
Intangible Assets	5 600 00		6 100 00	
Notes Payable—Short Term		6 000 00		10 000 00
Accounts Payable		25 750 00		31 750 00
Payroll Taxes Payable		2 700 00		2 500 00
Income Taxes Payable		1 500 00		3 000 00
Mortgage Payable, 2029		129 000 00		135 000 00
7% Bonds Payable, 2024		50 000 00		0
Common Stock $1 par		100 000 00		50 000 00
Retained Earnings		207 300 00		157 300 00
Totals	540 750 00	540 750 00	401 050 00	401 050 00

Analyze: Were activities related to operations, investing, or financing responsible for the largest net inflow of cash?

Preparing a statement of cash flows.

◀ **Problem 24.3A**
Objectives 24-1, 24-2, 24-3, 24-4, 24-5

The condensed income statement and comparative balance sheet of The Donald Inc. as of December 31, 2022 and 2021, are provided below. Other financial data are also given.

INSTRUCTIONS

Prepare a statement of cash flows for The Donald Inc. for 2022. Additional information for the year that is pertinent to its preparation follows:

a. No items of property, plant, and equipment were disposed of during the year.
b. Paid cash for the additions to property, plant, and equipment during the year.
c. Paid $10,000 in dividends on the common stock in cash during the year.
d. Issued common stock at par value for cash.
e. Paid cash to retire the long-term note payable.

The Donald Inc.
Condensed Income Statement
Year Ended December 31, 2022

Revenues	700 000
Costs and Expenses	
Cost of Goods Sold	430 000
Salaries Expense	126 000
Depreciation Expense	16 000
Advertising Expense	15 900
Utilities Expense	19 000
Total Costs and Expenses	606 900
Net Income Before Income Taxes	93 100
Income Taxes Expense	19 600
Net Income After Income Taxes	73 500

The Donald Inc.
Comparative Balance Sheet
December 31, 2022 and 2021

Assets	2022	2021
Cash	122 800	82 000
Accounts Receivable (Net)	57 150	53 000
Merchandise Inventory	50 000	55 500
Prepaid Advertising	9 000	11 500
Property, Plant, and Equipment	135 000	110 000
Less Accumulated Depreciation	(27 000)	(11 000)
Total Assets	346 950	301 000
Liabilities and Stockholders' Equity		
Liabilities		
Accounts Payable	51 450	80 500
Salaries Payable	5 500	4 000
Unearned Revenues	4 500	6 000
Income Taxes Payable	7 500	6 000
Note Payable—2024	0	40 000
Total Liabilities	68 950	136 500
Stockholders' Equity		
Common Stock ($2 par)	110 000	60 000
Retained Earnings	168 000	104 500
Total Stockholders' Equity	278 000	164 500
Total Liabilities and Stockholders' Equity	346 950	301 000

Analyze: If The Donald Inc. had written off an uncollectible account receivable of $5,500 during this fiscal period, what adjustment, if any, would be required on the statement of cash flows?

Problem 24.4A ▶ Prepare a statement of cash flows.

Objectives 24-1, 24-2, 24-3, 24-4, 24-5

The comparative balance sheet for Short Company as of December 31, 2022 and 2021, is shown below, followed by the condensed income statement.

INSTRUCTIONS

Prepare a statement of cash flows for 2022. Additional information for the year follows:

a. Acquired land at a cost of $80,000; paid one-half of the purchase price in cash and issued common stock for the balance.

b. Sold used equipment for $30,000 in cash. The original cost was $50,000; depreciation of $15,000 had been taken. The remaining change in the **Property, Plant, and Equipment** account represents a purchase of equipment for cash. Total depreciation expense for the year was $10,000.

c. Issued bonds payable at par value for cash.

d. Sold bond investments costing $20,000 at no gain or loss during the year.

e. Paid $25,000 in cash dividends on the common stock.

Short Company
Comparative Balance Sheet
December 31, 2022 and 2021

Assets	2022	2021
Cash	12,287.5	59,750
Accounts Receivable (Net)	87,000	67,750
Merchandise Inventory	84,150	75,000
Prepaid Rent	6,500	5,000
Land	110,000	30,000
Property, Plant, and Equipment	194,000	229,000
Less Accumulated Depreciation—PPE	(17,900)	(22,900)
Investment in TVA Bonds	40,000	60,000
Total Assets	626,625	503,600

Liabilities and Stockholders' Equity		
Liabilities		
Accounts Payable	67,300	88,100
Income Taxes Payable	9,750	10,500
Bonds Payable	160,000	110,000
Total Liabilities	237,050	208,600
Stockholders' Equity		
Common Stock	125,000	85,000
Retained Earnings	264,575	210,000
Total Stockholders' Equity	389,575	295,000
Total Liabilities and Stockholders' Equity	626,625	503,600

Short Company
Condensed Income Statement
Year Ended December 31, 2022

Revenues		819,000
Costs and Expenses		
Cost of Goods Sold	478,250	
Depreciation Expense	10,000	
Selling and Administrative Expenses	200,150	
Interest Expense	19,500	
Loss on Sale of Equipment	5,000	
Income Taxes Expense	26,525	
Total Costs and Expenses		739,425
Net Income After Income Taxes		79,575

Analyze: By what percentage did *Cash* increase from January 1 to December 31?

Problem Set B

Problem 24.1B
Objectives 24-1, 24-2, 24-3, 24-4, 24-5

▶ **Prepare a statement of cash flows.**

A comparative balance sheet for U&ME Corporation as of December 31, 2022 and 2021, is given below.

INSTRUCTIONS

Use these data to prepare a statement of cash flows for 2022. Additional information for the year follows:

a. Had net income of $25,100.
b. Paid $25,000 cash for new store equipment.
c. Sold used machinery for $8,000 cash. The original cost was $30,000, and the accumulated depreciation was $26,000; included the gain of $4,000 in net income.
d. Paid cash dividends of $10,000.
e. Recorded $15,000 in depreciation.

U&ME Corporation
Comparative Balance Sheet
December 31, 2022 and 2021

Assets	2022	2021
Cash	51,600	49,500
Accounts Receivable (Net)	84,000	60,000
Merchandise Inventory	46,000	34,000
Property, Plant, and Equipment	145,000	150,000
Less Accumulated Depreciation	(34,000)	(45,000)
Total Assets	292,600	248,500

Liabilities and Stockholders' Equity	2022	2021
Liabilities		
Accounts Payable	50,000	46,000
Total Liabilities	50,000	46,000
Stockholders' Equity		
Common Stock ($1 par, 500,000 shares authorized: 50,000 shares issued in 2021 and 75,000 shares issued in 2022)	75,000	50,000
Retained Earnings	167,600	152,500
Total Stockholders' Equity	242,600	202,500
Total Liabilities and Stockholders' Equity	292,600	248,500

Analyze: Name the events that were the largest outflow of cash during fiscal 2022.

Problem 24.2B
Objectives 24-1, 24-2, 24-3, 24-4, 24-5

▶ **Prepare a statement of cash flows.**

Postclosing trial balance data and other financial data for Char, Inc., as of December 31, 2022 and 2021, follow.

INSTRUCTIONS

Prepare a statement of cash flows for 2022. Additional information for the year follows:

a. Sold an unused lot for $25,000 in cash; it originally cost $15,000.

b. Constructed a new building for $150,000, of which $20,000 was paid in cash and $130,000 is a long-term mortgage payable.

c. Issued $20,000 of 5 percent bonds payable, maturing in 2024, for cash at par.

d. Sold common stock at par for $25,000 in cash.

e. Had net income of $50,000 after income taxes.

f. Paid common stock dividends of $25,000 in cash.

g. Amortized organization costs of $500.

h. The short-term note payable resulted from operating activities, not financing.

Char, Inc.
Postclosing Trial Balance
December 31, 2022 and 2021

Account Name	2022 Debit	2022 Credit	2021 Debit	2021 Credit
Cash	9 3 8 5 0		5 2 5 0 0	
Accounts Receivable (Net)	6 0 7 5 0		4 5 7 5 0	
Merchandise Inventory	6 5 0 0 0		5 5 0 0 0	
Prepaid Expenses	2 5 0 0		1 0 0 0	
Land	3 4 0 0 0		4 9 0 0 0	
Plant and Equipment	2 7 5 0 0 0		1 2 5 0 0 0	
Accumulated Depreciation—Plant and Equipment		2 4 7 5 0		1 0 0 0 0
Organization Costs	4 5 0 0		5 0 0 0	
Notes Payable—Short Term		0		7 5 0 0
Accounts Payable		3 2 2 5 0		3 6 2 5 0
Payroll Taxes Payable		2 6 0 0		2 5 0 0
Income Taxes Payable		1 0 0 0		2 0 0 0
Mortgage Payable, 2026		2 0 5 0 0 0		7 5 0 0 0
5% Bonds Payable, 2024		2 0 0 0 0		0
Common Stock, $1 par		7 5 0 0 0		5 0 0 0 0
Retained Earnings		1 7 5 0 0 0		1 5 0 0 0 0
Totals	5 3 5 6 0 0	5 3 5 6 0 0	3 3 3 2 5 0	3 3 3 2 5 0

Analyze: Did operating, investing, or financing activities generate the greatest net inflow of cash?

◀ Problem 24.3B
Objectives 24-1, 24-2, 24-3, 24-4, 24-5

Prepare a statement of cash flows.

Lee Corporation's comparative balance sheet as of December 31, 2022 and 2021, and 2022 condensed income statement appear below.

INSTRUCTIONS
Prepare a statement of cash flows for 2022. Additional information for the year follows:

a. Depreciation totaling $10,000 is included in expenses.

b. Sold land for $35,000 in cash; the land, which is included in plant and equipment, had a cost of $35,000.

c. Acquired a building with a fair market value of $100,000 by issuing common stock.

d. Purchased equipment for $35,000 in cash.

e. Paid dividends of $50,000.

Lee Corporation
Comparative Balance Sheet
December 31, 2022 and 2021

Assets	2022	2021
Cash	99,200	90,000
Accounts Receivable (Net)	65,650	70,000
Merchandise Inventory	50,000	64,000
Prepaid Advertising	8,000	10,000
Property, Plant, and Equipment	300,000	200,000
Less Accumulated Depreciation	(20,000)	(10,000)
Total Assets	502,850	424,000
Liabilities and Stockholders' Equity		
Liabilities		
Accounts Payable	64,500	95,000
Income Taxes Payable	6,000	25,000
Notes Payable—2024	25,000	40,000
Total Liabilities	95,500	160,000
Stockholders' Equity		
Common Stock ($1 par)	200,000	100,000
Retained Earnings	207,350	164,000
Total Stockholders' Equity	407,350	264,000
Total Liabilities and Stockholders' Equity	502,850	424,000

Lee Corporation
Condensed Income Statement
Year Ended December 31, 2022

Revenues		775,000
Costs and Expenses		
Cost of Goods Sold	385,000	
Expenses	296,650	
Net Income		93,350

Analyze: If the company had purchased equipment on credit instead of using cash, what would the cash balance have been at year-end?

Problem 24.4B

Objectives 24-1, 24-2, 24-3, 24-4, 24-5

Prepare a statement of cash flows.

The comparative balance sheet for MP, Inc., as of December 31, 2022 and 2021, is shown below, followed by the condensed income statement for 2022.

INSTRUCTIONS

Prepare a statement of cash flows for 2022. Other financial data for the year follow:

a. Sold used equipment for $32,000 in cash that originally cost $37,000; accumulated depreciation was $8,000. The remainder of the change in **Equipment** represents equipment purchased for cash.

b. Issued short-term notes payable with a par value of $50,000. Retired bonds payable at maturity.

c. Paid cash dividends of $20,000.

d. Issued common stock at par value for cash.

MP, Inc.
Comparative Balance Sheet
December 31, 2022 and 2021

Assets	2022	2021
Cash	124,010	101,500
Accounts Receivable (Net)	88,650	66,250
Merchandise Inventory	89,000	75,000
Prepaid Advertising	5,500	3,500
Land	75,000	75,000
Property, Plant, and Equipment	241,400	219,000
Less Accumulated Depreciation—Property, Plant, and Equipment	(34,600)	(21,900)
Total Assets	588,960	427,000

Liabilities and Stockholders' Equity	2022	2021
Liabilities		
Accounts Payable	61,300	68,500
Notes Payable—Short Term	50,000	0
Income Taxes Payable	10,250	8,500
Bonds Payable	0	50,000
Total Liabilities	121,550	127,000
Stockholders' Equity		
Common Stock	150,000	100,000
Retained Earnings	317,410	200,000
Total Stockholders' Equity	467,410	300,000
Total Liabilities and Stockholders' Equity	588,960	427,000

MP, Inc.
Condensed Income Statement
Year Ended December 31, 2022

Revenues (including gain on sale of equipment)		925,600
Costs and Expenses		
Cost of Goods Sold	501,600	
Depreciation Expense	20,700	
Selling and Administrative Expenses	195,000	
Interest Expense	12,000	
Income Taxes Expense	58,890	
Total Costs and Expenses		788,190
Net Income After Income Taxes		137,410

Analyze: Was the amount of net cash provided by operating activities sufficient to cover the cash that the company required for financing activities? Explain.

Critical Thinking Problem 24.1

Transactions

Charles Alan, the bookkeeper for Roswell Company, asks for your help in identifying whether the following transactions should be reported on the corporation's statement of cash flows. Prepare a list for Alan indicating whether or not each transaction should be reported on the statement. If the transaction should appear on the statement, indicate whether it should be classified as a financing activity, an investing activity, or an operating activity. If the transaction should not be part of the statement of cash flows, explain why not.

1. Prepaid six months of rent on office space at the end of the year.
2. Paid (utility bills) vendors amounts due on accounts payable.
3. Issued common stock for cash.
4. Collected an accounts receivable from a customer.
5. Paid cash dividends on common stock.
6. Purchased common stock of another company as investment for cash.
7. Borrowed cash, signing a 90-day note that was repaid before the end of the year.
8. Paid state and federal income taxes due.
9. Issued long-term bonds due in 10 years for cash.
10. Used proceeds from bond issue to purchase new computer system.
11. Received principal payments on note receivable held in connection with sale of building last year.
12. Distributed a stock dividend on common stock.

Critical Thinking Problem 24.2

Adjustments

Knotting Company was formed and began business on January 1, 2022, when J. T. Wood transferred merchandise inventory with a value of $60,000, cash of $55,000, accounts receivable of $60,000, and accounts payable of $35,000. Common stock with a par value of $5 per share was issued to Mr. Wood. The company's common stock was recorded at par.

Knotting Company's statement of cash flows for 2022 is shown below:

Knotting Company
Statement of Cash Flows
Year Ended December 31, 2022

Cash Flow from Operations			
Net Income			50 000
Adjustments			
Depreciation of building	5 000		
Depreciation of equipment	6 000		
Increase in accounts receivable	(15 000)		
Increase in inventory	(8 000)		
Increase in prepaid insurance	(800)		
Increase in accounts payable	17 000		
Increase in income tax payable	2 500	6 700	
Net cash flow provided by operations			56 700
Cash Flow from Investing Activities			
Purchase of land	(30 000)		
Purchase of building	(25 000)		
Purchase of equipment	(60 000)		
Net cash used in investing activities			(115 000)
Cash Flow from Financing Activities			
Issuance of common stock at $5/share	5 000		
Borrowing at bank by issuance of note payable	40 000		
Net cash provided by financing activities			45 000
Net decrease in cash balance			(13 300)
Cash balance, January 1, 2022			55 000
Cash balance, December 31, 2022			41 700

Note: A building was acquired at a cost of $250,000. Cash of $25,000 was paid, and a mortgage of $225,000 was given for the balance.

INSTRUCTIONS

Based on the data supplied, prepare the December 31, 2022, balance sheet for the corporation.

Analyze: Describe four adjusting entries that were made by Knotting Company in fiscal 2022.

BUSINESS CONNECTIONS

Using All Statements

Managerial FOCUS

1. How can the statement of cash flows help management arrange for proper financing?
2. A corporation's income statement shows a net income of $10,000 after income taxes for the year. Its statement of cash flows shows that its cash balance increased by $150,000: net cash outflow from operating activities, $100,000; net cash inflow from financing activities, $50,000; and net cash inflow from investing activities, $200,000. The president of the corporation has commented, "Even though the company's profit is small, it is clear, based on our positive cash flow, that we are doing quite well." Do you agree with this comment? Why or why not?
3. A member of a corporation's board of directors commented that because the statement of cash flows and the income statement are so similar, there is no need to prepare the income statement. Respond.
4. Assume that you are an accountant preparing the statement of cash flows for the year. Should the cash proceeds of $100,000 from a short-term note payable discounted in June of this year be included in the statement? The note was repaid in October. Would it be preferable to simply ignore both the loan and the repayment because it might confuse management to show both? Explain.
5. A potential customer has applied for an open-account credit line with a manufacturing firm. Explain how the potential customer's statement of cash flows would help to evaluate its short-term debt-paying ability.

Delay Payment of Bonds

Internal Control and FRAUD PREVENTION

Marie Corporation has a cash flow problem. It has bonds due before the end of the fiscal year. It will need to sell more bonds to pay the bonds due. Ann, the controller, understands that many investors consider the cash flow statement to be the key statement that indicates the company's future value. She has decided to delay the payment of the bonds until after the end of the fiscal year. This will show a higher balance in cash because the bonds will not be paid. There will be no indication in the financial statements that she has defaulted on the bonds. It is Ann's plan to issue additional bonds after the close of the fiscal year to pay off the current bonds. However, she will need to record the interest paid in the current fiscal year. Are Ann's actions acceptable accounting practices?

Statement of Cash Flows

Financial Statement ANALYSIS

Home Depot

Refer to the 2018 Form 10-K *(for the fiscal year ended February 3, 2019)* for The Home Depot, Inc.

1. Locate the consolidated statements of cash flows for the year ended February 3, 2019. What net cash was (1) provided by operations? (2) used in investing activities? (3) used by financing activities?
2. Is the most significant source of cash generated from the company's operating, investing, or financing activities?

Cash Flow Information

TEAMWORK

As a team of four students, obtain the cash flow statements from two companies. Each group of two students should explain their company's cash flow statements to the other two students. The explanation should include the following: (1) Has cash increased or decreased? (2) What is the main source of cash? (3) What are the principal uses of cash? (4) Is the company's business expanding or contracting? (5) Has more common stock been sold? (6) Is the company paying down debt or getting further into debt? (7) Has treasury stock been purchased?

Answers to Comprehensive Self Review

1. Operating, investing, and financing activities are shown in a statement of cash flows.
2. Financing activities are transactions that provide or use cash through selling stock, issuing bonds, or paying cash dividends.
3. The increase in accounts payable must be added to net income to arrive at cash flow from operations.
4. In a note to the statement of cash flows.
5. In the operating activities section as an addition to net income.

Chapter 25

Departmentalized Profit and Cost Centers

www.spglobal.com

McGraw-Hill Financial (created in May 2013) rebranded itself as S&P Global Inc. in April 2016. It operates some of the most successful and well-known brands in business and finance. The company is built on the values of fairness, integrity, and transparency with a mission to promote sustainable growth in the global capital, commodity, and corporate markets by providing customers with essential intelligence (i.e., information and knowledge) coupled with superior customer service.

The company provides its clients with information necessary to manage risk and identify opportunities to grow. S&P Global divisions include S&P Global Ratings, S&P Global Market Intelligence, S&P Dow Jones Indices, S&P Global Platts, and CRISIL, an S&P Global company. Each of these divisions provides specialized financial services to its customers, and each division is responsible for its own operations and profits as separate business segments within S&P Global Inc.

For the fiscal year 2017, the now rebranded S&P Global reported revenue of $6.1 billion with approximately 20,000 employees. While the revenue is reported for the company as a whole, each business division maintains detailed records of its individual revenues and expenses, and managers of each division are responsible for that business unit's financial performance. Some expenses may not be controllable by the division manager, such as depreciation or rent expense. However, some costs are controllable at the division level, such as wages expense, and the manager will be responsible for justifying a controllable cost that is considered too high.

gary yim/Shutterstock

thinking critically

What types of costs do you think can be controlled by the officers and managers of the S&P Global Ratings division?

LEARNING OBJECTIVES

- **25-1** Explain profit centers and cost centers.
- **25-2** Prepare the Gross Profit section of a departmental income statement.
- **25-3** Explain and identify direct and indirect departmental expenses.
- **25-4** Choose the basis for allocation of indirect expenses and compute the amounts to be allocated to each department.
- **25-5** Prepare a departmental income statement showing the contribution margin and operating income for each department.
- **25-6** Use a departmental income statement in making decisions such as whether a department should be closed.
- **25-7** Define the accounting terms new to this chapter.

NEW TERMS

break-even point (BEP)
contribution margin
cost center
departmental income statement
direct expenses
indirect expenses
managerial accounting
profit center
responsibility accounting
semidirect expenses
transfer price

Section 1

SECTION OBJECTIVES	TERMS TO LEARN
25-1 Explain profit centers and cost centers. **WHY IT'S IMPORTANT** Different business segments contribute to a firm's financial success in varying degrees. **25-2** Prepare the Gross Profit section of a departmental income statement. **WHY IT'S IMPORTANT** Operating results are evaluated for each segment of the business. **25-3** Explain and identify direct and indirect departmental expenses. **WHY IT'S IMPORTANT** Some operating expenses relate directly to a specific department; others benefit all company operations. **25-4** Choose the basis for allocation of indirect expenses and compute the amounts to be allocated to each department. **WHY IT'S IMPORTANT** Indirect and semidirect expenses benefit all company operations and are assigned using a logical method.	cost center direct expenses indirect expenses managerial accounting profit center responsibility accounting semidirect expenses transfer price

Profit and Cost Centers and Departmental Accounting

In previous chapters, you have studied financial statements that report the results of transactions that happened in the past. This chapter shows how management can use financial data for forward-looking analysis and decision making, not just historical reporting.

Managerial Accounting

Managerial accounting is the branch of accounting that provides financial information about business segments, activities, or products. Managerial accounting supplies information about the profit made on an order or the profitability of a specific department. Management uses this information to make decisions such as when to replace a machine or whether to discontinue a product, or to determine the selling price for a new product.

> In accordance with GAAP, Ford Motor Company publishes information on revenues, net income, and assets for two primary segments: Automotive and Financial Services.

Profit Centers and Cost Centers

>> **25-1 OBJECTIVE**
Explain profit centers and cost centers.

Managerial accounting is concerned with segments of a business. The segments are often called *centers*. Accounting information is accumulated and analyzed separately for each center. There are two types of centers: cost centers and profit centers. A **cost center** is a business segment that incurs costs but does not produce revenue. A **profit center** is a business segment that produces revenue.

> Ford Motor Company reports its Automotive sector to show four primary segments: (1) Ford North America, (2) Ford South America, (3) Ford Europe, and (4) Ford Asia Pacific and Africa. Segment selection is based upon the organizational structure that Ford uses to evaluate performance and make decisions on resource allocation, as well as availability and materiality of separate financial results consistent with that structure.

Cost centers do not directly earn revenue. Cost centers often provide services to other segments of the business. The emphasis in accounting for cost centers is on cost control. Typical cost centers include the accounting department, information systems department, maintenance department, storeroom, research laboratory, and purchasing department. A common practice today is to charge back to profit centers the business support provided by these types of "back office" services.

Profit centers are revenue-producing segments that sell products or services to customers outside the business. For example, a clothing store might have separate profit centers for the coat, dress, suit, and shoe departments. Sales and costs are accumulated for each department. A "profit" is computed for the department.

Sometimes it is convenient to think of a segment of a company as a profit center even though it does not sell products or services to outside customers. For example, the segment of an oil company that produces crude oil from the ground can be treated as a profit center even though the oil it produces is transferred to the company's refinery. The revenue from the segment's activities is the **transfer price** of its product—the price at which the segment's goods are transferred to another segment of the company.

Responsibility Accounting

Responsibility accounting allows management to evaluate the performance of each segment of the business and assign responsibility for its financial results. Internal accounting reports provide detailed data for each cost and profit center so that management can determine how efficiently the individual segments are functioning.

important!

Responsibility Accounting
Responsibility accounting provides information that helps in evaluating each segment of a business and assigning responsibility for results.

Departmentalized Operations

When a business has more than one type of sales or service activity, it is important to know what each activity is contributing to the income or loss of the business. Let's learn how accountants gather revenue and expenses for the different activities by studying the system used by First Avenue, a business that sells upscale clothing and shoes. Income taxes will be ignored in the following illustration.

Gross Profit Section of a Departmental Income Statement

>> **25-2 OBJECTIVE**
Prepare the Gross Profit section of a departmental income statement.

To calculate gross profit by department, First Avenue gathers data by department for each transaction.

Departmental Accounts in the General Ledger Businesses that prepare departmental financial statements maintain general ledger accounts for sales, purchases, merchandise inventory, and some operating expenses. For example, First Avenue has two sales departments, clothing and shoes. The sales accounts are *Sales—Clothing* and *Sales—Shoes*.

FIGURE 25.1 Departmental Sales Journal

SALES JOURNAL							**PAGE 1**
DATE	SALES SLIP NO.	CUSTOMER'S NAME	POST. REF.	ACCOUNTS RECEIVABLE DEBIT	SALES TAX PAYABLE CREDIT	SALES— CLOTHING CREDIT	SALES— SHOES CREDIT
20X1 Jan. 2	1005	Sullivan Morgan	✓	212 00	12 00	200 00	
3	1006	Rob Cortez	✓	477 00	27 00	300 00	150 00
3	1007	Billy Williams	✓	190 80	10 80	115 00	65 00
31		Totals		9 540 00	540 00	6 200 00	2 800 00
				(111)	(231)	(401)	(402)

important!

Sales Journal
When the sales account is departmentalized, the sales journal records transactions by department.

recall

Posting
Postings are made daily from the sales journal to the individual accounts receivable subsidiary ledger accounts.

Recording Sales and Purchases by Departments Figure 25.1 shows the sales journal for First Avenue. Notice that there are two sales columns, one for clothing and one for shoes. Sales are recorded in the usual manner except that the sales amounts are divided between the sales columns. For example, Rob Cortez purchased $300 of clothing and $150 of shoes. These amounts are reported in separate columns. The sales tax rate is 6 percent.

The departmental sales journal is posted in the usual manner. Transactions are posted daily in the accounts receivable subsidiary ledger. The sales journal column totals are posted to the general ledger at month-end. Similarly, the voucher register and the sales returns and allowances journal have separate columns for the two departments.

Merchandise Inventories Merchandise inventory is counted by department so that the departmental cost of goods sold can be computed.

A Sample Gross Profit Section Figure 25.2 shows the Gross Profit section of the departmental income statement for First Avenue.

FIGURE 25.2 Departmental Income Statement (Partial)

	Clothing	Shoes	Total
First Avenue			
Income Statement (Partial)			
Year Ended December 31, 20X1			
Operating Revenue			
Sales	5 437 50	1 812 50	7 250 00
Less Sales Returns and Allowances	41 25	13 75	55 00
Net Sales	5 396 25	1 798 75	7 195 00
Cost of Goods Sold			
Merchandise Inventory, January 1, 20X1	350 00	150 00	500 00
Purchases	2 250 00	480 00	2 730 00
Freight In	42 00	5 00	47 00
Delivered Cost of Purchases	2 292 00	485 00	2 777 00
Less Purchases Returns and Allowances	35 00	3 50	38 50
Purchases Discounts	40 00	4 00	44 00
Total Deductions	75 00	7 50	82 50
Net Delivered Cost of Purchases	2 217 00	477 50	2 694 50
Total Merchandise Available for Sale	2 567 00	627 50	3 194 50
Less Merchandise Inventory, December 31, 20X1	360 00	95 00	455 00
Cost of Goods Sold	2 207 00	532 50	2 739 50
Gross Profit	3 189 25	1 266 25	4 455 50

Operating Expenses Section of a Departmental Income Statement

There are two types of operating expenses: direct expenses and indirect (or semidirect) expenses.

Direct Expenses Direct expenses are identified directly with a department and are recorded by department. At First Avenue, sales clerks work in only one department, so it is easy to record salary expenses. Advertising costs, store supplies, cash short or over, and delivery expenses are also recorded by department.

Figure 25.3 shows the direct expenses for First Avenue.

Indirect and Semidirect Expenses Not all operating costs are direct expenses. Semidirect expenses cannot be directly assigned to a department, but they are closely related to departmental activities. Semidirect expenses are allocated among the departments at the end of the accounting period. Semidirect expenses include depreciation on store equipment and the cost of insurance for equipment and inventory.

Indirect expenses are operating expenses that cannot be readily identified and are not closely related to activity within a department. At the end of the accounting period, indirect expenses are allocated to the departments. Examples of indirect expenses are postage and stationery.

The accountant for First Avenue treats semidirect and indirect expenses as indirect expenses as follows:

Indirect Expenses	
Insurance expense	$ 25,000
Rent expense	36,000
Utilities expense	11,000
Office salaries expense	50,000
Other office expenses	1,800
Uncollectible accounts expense	2,000
Depreciation expense—furniture and fixtures	1,000
Depreciation expense—office equipment	500
Total indirect expenses	$127,300

Allocating Semidirect and Indirect Expense Items After the worksheet has been completed, the accountant allocates indirect expenses to the departments. The accountant tries to find some logical relationship between the departments and each type of expense. Let's see

>> **25-3 OBJECTIVE**
Explain and identify direct and indirect departmental expenses.

ABOUT ACCOUNTING

Stress
Job stress has been estimated to cost American businesses $300 billion per year. A recent survey reported that stress accounts for half of the U.S. work days lost due to absenteeism. Want to be a tax preparer in early April?

>> **25-4 OBJECTIVE**
Choose the basis for allocation of indirect expenses and compute the amounts to be allocated to each department.

FIGURE 25.3 Schedule of Direct Departmental Expenses

<table>
<tr><th colspan="4">First Avenue
Schedule of Direct Departmental Expenses
Year Ended December 31, 20X1</th></tr>
<tr><th></th><th>Clothing</th><th>Shoes</th><th>Total</th></tr>
<tr><td>Sales Salaries Expense</td><td>102 500</td><td>42 500</td><td>145 000</td></tr>
<tr><td>Advertising Expense</td><td>18 000</td><td>10 000</td><td>28 000</td></tr>
<tr><td>Store Supplies Expense</td><td>500</td><td>150</td><td>650</td></tr>
<tr><td>Cash Short or Over</td><td>65</td><td>25</td><td>90</td></tr>
<tr><td>Delivery Expense</td><td>500</td><td>250</td><td>750</td></tr>
<tr><td>Total Direct Expenses</td><td>121 565</td><td>52 925</td><td>174 490</td></tr>
</table>

TABLE 25.1

Allocation of Insurance Expense

Asset Item	Clothing Department	Shoes Department	Percent		Total Insurance Expense		Amount Allocated to Each Department
Merchandise inventory	$35,000	$15,000					
Furniture and fixtures	7,000	3,000					
Total clothing	$42,000	$18,000	70	×	$25,000	=	$17,500
Total shoes	18,000		30	×	25,000	=	7,500
Combined Totals	$60,000		100				$25,000

how the accountant allocates the indirect costs for First Avenue. The allocated costs appear in Figure 25.4, the departmental income statement for First Avenue, which appears in Section 2 of this chapter. Notice that the allocated expenses are rounded to the nearest dollar.

Insurance Expense Insurance premiums total $25,000. They are allocated based on the cost of the furniture, fixtures, and inventory used in the department's operations. As of December 31, First Avenue's total of these items was $42,000 in the clothing department and $18,000 in the shoes department. The accountant allocates $17,500 of insurance expense to the clothing department and $7,500 to the shoes department, as shown in Table 25.1.

Rent Expense Rent expense was $36,000. It is allocated based on square footage. The accountant allocates $28,800 to the clothing department and $7,200 to the shoes department.

Department	Basis: Square Feet	Percent		Rent Expense		Allocation
Clothing	2,400	80	×	$36,000	=	$28,800
Shoes	600	20	×	36,000	=	7,200
Total	3,000	100				$36,000

recall

Matching

Indirect expenses are allocated to departments to match the expenses to the revenue earned by the departments.

Utilities Expense Utilities expense was $11,000. It is allocated based on square footage. The accountant allocates $8,800 ($11,000 × 0.80) to the clothing department and $2,200 ($11,000 × 0.20) to the shoes department.

Office Salaries Expense Office salaries expense was $50,000. It is allocated based on total sales for each department. The accountant allocates $37,500 to the clothing department and $12,500 to the shoes department as shown:

Department	Basis: Total Sales	Percent		Office Salaries Expense		Allocation
Clothing	$543,750	75	×	$50,000	=	$37,500
Shoes	181,250	25	×	50,000	=	12,500
Total	$725,000	100				$50,000

Other Office Expenses Other office expenses, including postage and stationery, totaled $1,800. They are allocated based on total sales for each department. The accountant allocates $1,350 ($1,800 × 0.75) to the clothing department and $450 ($1,800 × 0.25) to the shoes department.

Uncollectible Accounts Expense As a result of the aging of the accounts receivable balance on December 31, an adjustment of $2,000 was recorded as an expense for uncollectible accounts. The uncollectible accounts expense is allocated on the basis of credit sales, preferably on net credit sales. Sometimes it takes too much time to distinguish between returns from cash and credit sales, so gross sales on account are used to make the allocation. The accountant for First Avenue uses gross credit sales. Credit sales for each department of First Avenue are presented in the calculations below. Based on those calculations, the accountant allocates uncollectible accounts expenses of $1,500 to the clothing department and $500 to the shoes department:

> **important!**
>
> **Uncollectible Accounts Expense**
>
> If feasible, the estimated expense for uncollectible accounts is allocated based on net credit sales.

Department	Basis: Credit Sales	Percent		Uncollectible Accounts Expense		Allocation
Clothing	$300,000	75	×	$2,000	=	$1,500
Shoes	100,000	25	×	2,000	=	500
Total	$400,000	100				$2,000

Depreciation Expense—Furniture and Fixtures

The assets used to compute depreciation for furniture and fixtures are identified with specific departments. Depreciation is computed at 10 percent per year. First Avenue uses $7,000 of furniture and fixtures in the clothing department and $3,000 in the shoes department. The accountant allocates $700 ($7,000 × 0.10) of depreciation to the clothing department and $300 ($3,000 × 0.10) to the shoes department.

Depreciation Expense—Office Equipment

Depreciation on the office equipment was $500. It is allocated according to total sales by department—the same basis used to allocate office salaries. The accountant allocates $375 ($500 × 0.75) to the clothing department and $125 ($500 × 0.25) to the shoes department.

Nondepartmentalized Expenses Revenue and expenses that do not apply to operations are not allocated to the departments. Generally, all items that appear in the Other Income and Other Expenses section of the income statement are treated as nondepartmental items. For example, interest income and interest expense are not allocated to departments because they relate to the financing of the business, rather than to its operating activities.

Other income and expense accounts that are not allocated to the departments at First Avenue are *Miscellaneous Income* for $775 and *Interest Expense* for $750.

Section 1 Review

1. What is the primary goal of responsibility accounting?
   a. to see how most accurately to record transactions
   b. to make determining income tax expense easy
   c. to allow management to evaluate the operating performance of each business segment
   d. to make indirect cost allocation easier

2. What distinguishes a profit center from a cost center?
   a. Profit centers have revenues and expenses.
   b. Profit centers have personnel costs.
   c. Cost centers are on the second floor.
   d. Profit centers are the most important operations in the business.

3. What is a logical basis for allocating tangible property tax expense to departments?
   a. on the basis of total numbers of tangible property items
   b. pro-rata based on number of business sites the company operates
   c. based only on new tangible property purchases this year
   d. based on the ratio of property classifications to the total value of tangible property owned

4. If a segment of a business is considered a profit center:
   a. it incurs costs but does not have revenues.
   b. no expenses can be allocated to the segment.

c. both revenue and costs are accumulated for the segment.

d. it must sell products or services to customers outside the business.

5. In a store with several sales departments, departmentalized accounts are used for:

a. sales only.

b. purchases and expense items only.

c. sales, purchases, and merchandise inventory.

d. sales and other income items only.

6. Department A had total sales of $250,000 and Department B had total sales of $50,000. Office salaries expense of $30,000 is allocated on the basis of total sales. How much would be allocated to Department B? (Round to the nearest whole percent.)

a. $15,000 (50% × $30,000)

b. $24,900 (83% × $30,000)

c. $5,100 (17% × $30,000)

d. $20,100 (67% × $30,000)

Section 2

SECTION OBJECTIVES

>> **25-5** Prepare a departmental income statement showing the contribution margin and operating income for each department.

WHY IT'S IMPORTANT
Individual departments need to cover their direct expenses and contribute toward increasing the income of the business.

>> **25-6** Use a departmental income statement in making decisions such as whether a department should be closed.

WHY IT'S IMPORTANT
The viability of business segments can be evaluated based on departmental income statements.

TERMS TO LEARN

break-even point (BEP)
contribution margin
departmental income statement

Departmental Income Statements

The balance sheet is prepared in the same manner whether or not a business has departmentalized operations. The income statement for a departmentalized firm, however, is expanded to highlight the individual departments' financial information.

Preparing the Departmental Income Statement

A **departmental income statement** shows each department's contribution margin and net income from operations after all expenses are allocated. Figure 25.4 shows the departmental income statement for First Avenue. Notice the amount labeled "Contribution Margin." It appears between "Total Direct Expenses" and "Indirect Expenses." **Contribution margin** is gross profit on sales minus direct expenses. It is the amount that the department has earned beyond its direct costs. The contribution margin is available to cover the semidirect and indirect expenses of running the business. A department that has a positive contribution margin is contributing toward increasing the net income (or decreasing the net loss) of the business.

>> **25-5 OBJECTIVE**
Prepare a departmental income statement showing the contribution margin and operating income for each department.

Departmental Income

Income from operations by department is used to make many business decisions. However, there are limitations to using departmental operating income. For example, it is difficult to determine each department's fair share of semidirect and indirect expenses. Another limitation is that if a particular department were eliminated, many of the indirect expenses allocated to it would not be eliminated. They would have to be absorbed by the remaining departments. When making decisions, knowledgeable managers rely more on contribution margin per department than on income from operations.

>> **25-6 OBJECTIVE**
Use a departmental income statement in making decisions such as whether a department should be closed.

Contribution Margin

Departments with a positive contribution margin help to pay the semidirect and indirect costs of the business. As already mentioned, many of the indirect costs allocated to an eliminated department may have to be absorbed by the remaining departments. Departments with a negative contribution margin reduce the net income (or increase the net loss) of the business as a whole. The business would be more profitable if the department with the negative contribution margin was eliminated.

FIGURE 25.4 Departmental Income Statement

First Avenue
Income Statement (Partial)
Year Ended December 31, 20X1

	Clothing	Shoes	Total
Operating Revenue			
Sales	543 750	181 250	725 000
Less Sales Returns and Allowances	4 125	1 375	5 500
Net Sales	539 625	179 875	719 500
Cost of Goods Sold			
Merchandise Inventory, January 1, 20X1	35 000	15 000	50 000
Purchases	225 000	48 000	273 000
Freight In	4 200	500	4 700
Delivered Cost of Purchases	229 200	48 500	277 700
Less Purchases Returns and Allowances	3 500	350	3 850
Purchases Discounts	4 000	400	4 400
Total Deductions	7 500	750	8 250
Net Delivered Cost of Purchases	221 700	47 750	269 450
Total Merchandise Available for Sale	256 700	62 750	319 450
Less Merchandise Inventory, December 31, 20X1	36 000	9 500	45 500
Cost of Goods Sold	220 700	53 250	273 950
Gross Profit	318 925	126 625	445 550
Operating Expenses			
Direct Expenses			
Sales Salaries Expense	102 500	42 500	145 000
Advertising Expense	18 000	10 000	28 000
Store Supplies Expense	500	150	650
Cash Short or Over	65	25	90
Delivery Expense	500	250	750
Total Direct Expenses	121 565	52 925	174 490
Contribution Margin	197 360	73 700	271 060
Indirect Expenses			
Insurance Expense	17 500	7 500	25 000
Rent Expense	28 800	7 200	36 000
Utilities Expense	8 800	2 200	11 000
Office Salaries Expense	37 500	12 500	50 000
Other Office Expenses	1 350	450	1 800
Uncollectible Accounts Expense	1 500	500	2 000
Depreciation Expense—Furniture and Fixtures	700	300	1 000
Depreciation Expense—Office Equipment	375	125	500
Total Indirect Expenses	96 525	30 775	127 300
Net Income from Operations	100 835	42 925	143 760
Other Income			
Miscellaneous Income			775
Other Expenses			
Interest Expense			750
Net Other Expenses/Income			25
Net Income before Income Taxes			143 785

MANAGERIAL IMPLICATIONS

DEPARTMENTAL INCOME STATEMENTS

- Departmentalized income statements illustrate which departments are most profitable and which are losing money or have low profit margins. Once alerted, department managers can take steps to improve the profit picture.
- Profitable departments may be expanded. Less profitable departments may undergo policy changes or may be closed.
- Departmentalized income statements help managers evaluate and control the operations of each unit.
- The contribution margin is very important in making managerial decisions. The contribution margin is gross profit minus direct expenses. It indicates how much each department contributes toward the indirect expenses and income for the business.
- Decisions to retain, eliminate, expand, or contract a segment of the business are based on the analysis of the contribution margin of the department or product.
- Departmental income is, at best, an estimate. It should be used with great care when making decisions.
- Managers need to consider that many of the indirect expenses would not be eliminated by the decision to do away with a department.

THINKING CRITICALLY

Should a business base a manager's bonus on gross profit, contribution margin, or net income from operations of a department?

As can readily be seen, the concept of contribution margin is important to business owners and managers because it provides them with valuable assistance in making decisions. Unfortunately, contribution margin figures are not provided in traditional financial reports.

Break-Even Point

A business is said to "break even" when total revenues equal total expenses. Obviously, businesses exist to make a profit, not just break even, but it is very important for management to know the **break-even point (BEP).** While this chapter focuses just on operating expenses, you will learn more about fixed and variable expenses in a later chapter. Simply put, a fixed expense is one that does not change with the volume of unit sales of the business. Other expenses would be variable or semivariable. The break-even point is when the contribution margin equals fixed expenses.

A simple example will illustrate. Let's say a business has fixed monthly expenses of $1,500 for rent, $500 for utilities, and $4,000 for salaries. The average selling price of the business's product is $29 and the average variable costs of obtaining the product are $9, making the contribution margin equal to $20 ($29 − $9). Dividing the fixed monthly expenses of $6,000 ($1,500 + $500 + $4,000) by the contribution margin of $20 gives you a break-even point of 300 units. In other words, the business must sell 300 units to break even for the month.

Section 2 Review

1. Define *contribution margin*.
   a. fixed costs minus variable costs
   b. net sales minus direct expenses
   c. net sales minus variable costs
   d. gross sales minus cost of goods sold

2. What is the difference between direct departmental expenses and indirect expenses?
   a. Indirect expenses benefit all departments and have only personnel costs.
   b. Direct expenses are easily identifiable and traceable to benefit only one department.
   c. Direct expenses will include salaries while indirect expenses will not.
   d. Indirect expenses are primarily noncash items.

3. How does the accountant choose a basis for allocating indirect expenses to sales departments?
   a. Basis is determined on the date an invoice is received.
   b. Basis is equal amounts to all departments.
   c. The best basis is a ratio of department net sales to total net sales
   d. Basis is a ratio of net income of a department to total net income of a business.

4. A department probably would be considered for elimination if it had a:
   a. positive contribution margin and income from operations.
   b. negative contribution margin and a loss from operations.
   c. positive contribution margin and a loss from operations.
   d. positive contribution margin and no income tax expense.

5. Department A had gross profit of $30,000, total direct expenses of $15,000, and total indirect expenses of $6,000. What is its contribution margin?
   a. $24,000
   b. $15,000
   c. $6,000
   d. $14,000

6. A department had a contribution margin of $18,000 and a loss from operations of $5,000. If the department is eliminated, the indirect expenses allocated to it will still be incurred. If the department is eliminated, how will net income for the business be affected?
   a. $18,000 lower
   b. $5,000 lower
   c. $5,000 higher
   d. $13,000 lower

REVIEW Chapter Summary

Chapter 25

The basic financial statements summarize the financial operations and position of the business as a whole, but they do not provide all of the accounting information necessary in running a business. Additional information needed about individual segments and activities of the business is provided by managerial accounting. In this chapter, you have learned how departmental financial reports are prepared and how they contribute to business decision making.

Learning Objectives

25-1 Explain profit centers and cost centers.

Managerial accounting provides information about the operating centers of a business:

- Some operating centers are called *profit centers* because they generate both revenues and expenses.
- Other operating centers are called *cost centers* because they incur expenses in providing services but do not produce revenues.

Many retail stores refer to profit and cost centers as departments:

- Separate accounts for sales, inventory, and other elements of the cost of goods sold are established because separate information is needed for each department.
- Departmental accounts can be established in the ledger with a column for each department.
- The sales journal, voucher register, and other records of original entry gather transaction data by department.

25-2 Prepare the Gross Profit section of a departmental income statement.

To determine departmental gross profit, the following figures for each department must be determined:

- gross sales
- sales returns and allowances
- sales discounts
- purchases
- purchases returns and allowances
- beginning and ending inventories

25-3 Explain and identify direct and indirect departmental expenses.

Operating expenses that can be identified directly with a specific department are considered direct expenses. Other expenses must be allocated to departments on some predetermined basis at the end of the accounting period:

- Expenses that are allocated on a logical basis closely related to use are sometimes referred to as *semidirect expenses*.
- Expenses that must be allocated on a more arbitrary basis are called *indirect expenses*.
- Many accountants refer to both types as indirect expenses.

25-4 Choose the basis for allocation of indirect expenses and compute the amounts to be allocated to each department.

When selecting the basis for making the allocation of expenses, the accountant chooses a basis that:

- relates the department and the expense in a logical manner and
- can be measured for each department.

25-5 Prepare a departmental income statement showing the contribution margin and operating income for each department.

The departmental income statement shows the contribution margin of each department as well as a final net income figure after allocation of all expenses.

25-6 Use a departmental income statement in making decisions such as whether a department should be closed.

The departmental income statement helps managers assess the profitability of a department. Departments with low profit margins or other operational weaknesses can be identified.

25-7 Define the accounting terms new to this chapter.

Glossary

Break-even point (BEP) (p. 901) The sales volume when total revenue equals total expenses

Contribution margin (p. 899) Gross profit on sales minus direct expenses; revenues minus variable costs

Cost center (p. 893) A business segment that incurs costs but does not produce revenue

Departmental income statement (p. 899) Income statement that shows each department's contribution margin and net income from operations after all expenses are allocated

Direct expenses (p. 895) Operating expenses that are identified directly with a department and are recorded by department

Indirect expenses (p. 895) Operating expenses that cannot be readily identified and are not closely related to activity within a department

Managerial accounting (p. 892) Accounting work carried on by an accountant employed by a single business in industry; the branch of accounting that provides financial information about business segments, activities, or products

Profit center (p. 893) A business segment that produces revenue

Responsibility accounting (p. 893) The process that allows management to evaluate the performance of each segment of the business and assign responsibility for its financial results

Semidirect expenses (p. 895) Operating expenses that cannot be directly assigned to a department but are closely related to departmental activities

Transfer price (p. 893) The price at which one segment's goods are transferred to another segment of the company

Comprehensive Self Review

1. What are the logical profit centers in a retail store?
2. How can a nonselling business segment be called a profit center?
3. Compare the recording process for direct and indirect expenses.
4. Why are indirect expenses allocated to departments?
5. Give the steps in determining a department's contribution margin.

(Answers to Comprehensive Self Review are at the end of the chapter.)

Discussion Questions

1. How does managerial accounting differ from financial accounting?
2. Why does managerial accounting focus on the future?
3. Briefly define *responsibility accounting*.
4. Is departmental accounting a form of responsibility accounting? Explain.
5. Why would a retail operation departmentalize its records?
6. How is contribution margin computed?
7. How does a departmentalized income statement differ from one that is not departmentalized?
8. Explain the difference between semidirect and indirect expenses.
9. Suggest a logical basis for allocating these indirect expenses: housekeeping services; office equipment repairs; general institutional advertising.
10. Why is interest expense not allocated to departments?

APPLICATIONS

Exercises

Information for Exercises 25.1 through 25.3

Selected financial data, as of year end, December 31, for Courtney's Cuties, a children's retail store, follows. Round all calculations to the nearest percentage point and nearest dollar.

Credit sales
- Women's clothing, $1,000,000
- Men's clothing, $300,000

Total sales
- Women's clothing, $1,200,000
- Men's clothing, $400,000

Sales returns and allowances
- Women's clothing
  - Credit sales, $50,000
  - Cash sales, $500
- Men's clothing
  - Credit sales, $10,000
  - Cash sales, $2,000

Book value of inventory and equipment
- Women's clothing, $200,000
- Men's clothing, $50,000

◀ Exercise 25.1
Objective 25-4

Computing the amount of indirect expense to be allocated to a department.

The company insurance expense for the year totaled $25,000 and is to be allocated on the basis of the book value of the inventory and equipment in each department. Compute the amount to be allocated to each department.

◀ Exercise 25.2
Objective 25-4

Computing the amount of indirect expense to be allocated to a department.

The total office expense for the year was $120,000. Compute the amount to be allocated to each department using total sales as the basis for the allocation.

◀ Exercise 25.3
Objective 25-4

Computing the amount of indirect expense to be allocated to a department.

The uncollectible accounts expense is estimated to be 1 percent of net credit sales. Compute the amount to be allocated to each department.

◀ Exercise 25.4
Objective 25-5

Preparing a departmental income statement showing contribution margin and net income for each department.

Data related to the income and expenses of the TNCO Inc. year ending December 31, 20X1, follow:

Allocated indirect expenses		
Outside department		$44,500
Inside department		35,500
Interest income		$400
Gross profit		
Outside department		$300,500
Inside department		205,000
Direct expenses		
Outside department		$145,500
Inside department		85,000

Prepare a partial departmental income statement showing the contribution margin and net income of each department.

Exercise 25.5
Objective 25-6

▶ **Using departmental income statements in making decisions.**

Data from the departmental income statement of Numbers, Inc. for the year ended December 31, 20X1, is given below. Assuming that a department's direct expenses can be eliminated if it is closed, what factors should management consider when deciding whether to close Department 1?

Numbers, Inc.
Income Statement (Partial)
For Year Ended December 31, 20X1

	Department 1	Department 2	Total
Net Sales	400000	700000	1100000
Cost of Goods Sold	280000	420000	700000
Gross Profit on Sales	120000	280000	400000
Direct Expenses	74000	117000	191000
Contribution Margin	46000	163000	209000
Indirect Expenses	55000	88000	143000
Net Income (Loss)	(9000)	75000	66000

Exercise 25.6
Objective 25-5

▶ **Preparing a departmental income statement showing contribution margin and net income of departments.**

Using the data given in Exercise 25.5, prepare an income statement for the company if Department 1 is closed.

Exercise 25.7
Objective 25-6

▶ **Using a departmental income statement in making decisions.**

Using the data given in Exercise 25.5, would you recommend closing Department 1? Why or why not?

Exercise 25.8
Objective 25-6

▶ **Calculating the break-even point.**

Quik Gift Company sells a product for $59. It costs $19 to obtain the product. The company has a total of $80,000 of fixed expenses. What is the break-even point?

PROBLEMS

Problem Set A

Allocating indirect expenses to departments and preparing a departmental income statement.

Problem 25.1A
Objectives 25-4, 25-5

Selected information from the adjusted trial balance of 4Feet Co. as of December 31, 20X1, follows:

	Department A	Department B	Total
Merchandise Inventory, January 1	$ 45,000	$ 15,000	$ 60,000
Merchandise Inventory, December 31	50,000	12,000	62,000
Sales	623,000	303,000	926,000
Sales Returns and Allowances	5,000	3,000	8,000
Purchases	350,000	100,000	450,000
Freight In	500	400	900
Purchases Returns and Allowances	2,000	600	2,600
Sales Salaries Expense	110,000	60,000	170,000
Advertising Expense	16,000	6,000	22,000
Store Supplies Expense	760	50	810
Cash Short or Over	40	80	120
Insurance Expense			15,000
Rent Expense			50,000
Utilities Expense			10,000
Office Salaries Expense			50,000
Other Office Expense			2,000
Uncollectible Accounts Expense			4,500
Depreciation Expense—Furniture and Fixtures			6,000
Depreciation Expense—Office Equipment			500
Interest Income			300
Interest Expense			600

INSTRUCTIONS

Prepare a departmental income statement for the year ended December 31, 20X1. The bases for allocating indirect expenses are given below. (**Note:** Because allocations are not precise, round each allocated amount to the nearest whole percent and dollar.) Show all allocations in a neat and orderly form.

1. *Insurance Expense:* in proportion to the total of the furniture and fixtures (the gross assets before depreciation) and the ending inventory in the departments. These totals are as follows:

	Department A	$180,000
	Department B	120,000
	Total	$300,000

2. **Rent Expense** and **Utilities Expense:** on the basis of floor space occupied, as follows:

Department A	6,000 square feet
Department B	4,000 square feet
Total	10,000 square feet

3. **Office Salaries Expense, Other Office Expenses,** and **Depreciation Expense—Office Equipment:** on the basis of the gross sales in each department.
4. **Uncollectible Accounts Expense:** on the basis of net sales in each department.
5. **Depreciation Expense—Furniture and Fixtures:** in proportion to cost of furniture and fixtures in each department. These costs are as follows. (Round to nearest dollar.)

Department A	$ 60,000
Department B	40,000
Total	$100,000

Analyze: Which department reports the higher return on net sales?

Problem 25.2A
Objectives 25-5, 25-6

Preparing a departmental income statement and using the statement in making a business decision.

The Lawn Shop sells plants, fertilizers, and other garden products. The store has three departments: plants, chemicals, and tools. Certain information about the revenues and expenses of the departments for the year ended December 31, 20X1, follows. Indirect expenses have been allocated on bases similar to those discussed and illustrated in the text:

	Plants	Chemicals	Tools
Allocated Indirect Expenses	$ 9,000	$ 1,000	$ 3,000
Direct Expenses	50,000	3,000	15,000
Cost of Goods Sold	118,200	5,900	35,970
Sales	198,500	14,750	59,950
Sales Returns and Allowances	1,500	750	6,950

INSTRUCTIONS

1. Prepare a departmental income statement showing the contribution margin and the net profit for each department.
2. Based solely on accounting information, would you recommend that any departments be closed? Explain.
3. What information, other than accounting data, would you suggest the owners consider in deciding whether to close any departments?

Analyze: If the indirect expenses had been allocated on the basis of net sales, what conclusions would you draw about the viability of each department? Explain.

Problem Set B

Allocating indirect expenses and preparing a departmental income statement.

◄ **Problem 25.1B**
Objectives 25-4, 25-5

Selected information from the adjusted trial balance of Woo Books, LLC, as of December 31, 20X1, is shown below:

	Collectors	Contemporary	Total
Merchandise Inventory, January 1	$ 40,000	$ 20,000	$ 60,000
Merchandise Inventory, December 31	40,000	18,000	58,000
Sales	545,000	305,000	850,000
Sales Returns and Allowances	5,000	5,000	10,000
Purchases	300,000	150,000	450,000
Freight In	1,000	500	1,500
Purchases Returns and Allowances	1,000	500	1,500
Sales Salaries Expense	110,000	40,000	150,000
Advertising Expense	15,000	5,000	20,000
Store Supplies Expense	250	250	500
Cash Short or Over	40	60	100
Insurance Expense			20,000
Rent Expense			50,000
Utilities Expense			13,000
Office Salaries Expense			60,000
Other Office Expense			2,000
Uncollectible Accounts Expense			6,000
Depreciation Expense—Furniture and Fixtures			10,000
Depreciation Expense—Office Equipment			5,000
Interest Income			200

INSTRUCTIONS

Prepare a departmental income statement for the year ended December 31, 20X1. The bases for allocating indirect expenses are given below. (**Note:** Because allocations are not precise, round each allocated amount to the nearest whole percent and dollar.) Show all allocations in a neat and orderly form.

1. **Insurance Expense:** in proportion to the total of the furniture and fixtures (the gross assets before depreciation) and the ending inventory in the departments. These totals are as follows:

Collectors	$ 70,000
Contemporary	30,000
Total	$100,000

2. *Rent Expense* and *Utilities Expense:* on the basis of floor space occupied, as follows:

Collectors	2,000 square feet
Contemporary	3,000 square feet
Total	5,000 square feet

3. *Office Salaries Expense, Other Office Expenses,* and *Depreciation Expense—Office Equipment:* on the basis of the gross sales in each department.
4. *Uncollectible Accounts Expense:* on the basis of net sales in each department.
5. *Depreciation Expense—Furniture and Fixtures:* in proportion to cost of furniture and fixtures in each department. These costs are as follows:

Collectors	$ 6,000
Contemporary	4,000
Total	$10,000

Analyze: To what degree does Contemporary contribute to the overall net income of the business? Express your answer as a percentage.

Problem 25.2B
Objectives 25-5, 25-6

▶ **Preparing a departmental income statement and using the statement in making a business decision.**

Solutions Inc. has three departments: printing, supplies, and cards. Certain information about the revenues and expenses of the departments for the year ending December 31, 20X1, is given below. Indirect expenses have been allocated on bases similar to those discussed and illustrated in the text:

	Printing	Supplies	Cards	Total
Allocated Indirect Expenses	$ 7,000	$ 15,000	$ 3,000	$ 25,000
Direct Expenses	40,000	9,500	8,500	58,000
Cost of Goods Sold	86,100	120,250	11,970	218,320
Sales	145,000	185,000	19,950	349,950
Sales Returns and Allowances	1,500	1,500	500	3,500

INSTRUCTIONS

1. Prepare a departmental income statement showing the contribution margin and the net profit for each department.
2. Based solely on accounting information, would you recommend that any departments be closed? Explain.
3. What information, other than accounting data, would you suggest the owners consider in deciding whether to close any departments?

Analyze: What increase in gross profit would be required to ensure that the Cards Department would be able to cover its indirect expenses? Assume that all other figures remained steady.

Critical Thinking Problem 25.1

Departmental Closure

Home Gifts has three sales departments: dishes, clothing, and paper products. The store's condensed income statement for the year ended December 31, 20X1, is shown below:

Home Gifts
Condensed Income Statement
Year Ended December 31, 20X1

	Dishes	Clothing	Paper Products
Sales	300,000	100,000	70,000
Cost of Goods Sold	80,000	45,000	32,000
Gross Profit	220,000	55,000	38,000
Operating Expenses			
Direct Expenses	50,000	15,000	10,000
Indirect Expenses	20,000	9,000	4,000
Total Operating Expenses	70,000	24,000	14,000
Net Income	150,000	31,000	24,000

The proprietor asked the auditor if the Clothing and/or Paper Products departments should be closed. In the opinion of both the owner and the auditor, if the Clothing department is closed, the total indirect expenses could possibly be reduced to $20,000. If only the Paper Products department is closed, the indirect expenses could possibly be reduced to a total of $25,000. In the opinion of the owner, if the Paper Products department is closed, a loss of $10,000 in sales could be lost by the Dishes department. This loss in sales would reduce the Dishes Cost of Goods Sold by $4,000. She also thinks that closing the Paper Products department would have no effect on sales of the Clothing department.

INSTRUCTIONS

1. Based on the preceding information, what would the estimated total profit or loss be if the Paper Goods department were closed?
2. What would the estimated total profit or loss be if the Clothing department were closed?
3. What advice would you give the proprietor?

Analyze: What is the current contribution margin for each department?

Critical Thinking Problem 25.2

Indirect Costs

At the last staff meeting of the Beach Shop, the question of how expenses are allocated to each department was raised. Because year-end bonuses are awarded to the managers on the basis of departmental net income from operations, the discussion was lively.

Susie Shark, manager of the repair department, said that each department should be charged only with the expenses directly related to the department. She indicated that while managers can influence the sales and direct expenses in their departments, they have little control over many of the indirect expenses such as depreciation, office salaries, and taxes.

Betty Brandon, manager of the new boat sales department, argued that all expenses—direct and indirect—should be allocated. "After all," she said, "all the revenue is allocated to each department, so why not allocate all the expenses? The store could not operate if it did not incur the indirect expenses." She also stated that many of the indirect expenses, such as insurance and cleaning services, could be allocated on a meaningful basis.

INSTRUCTIONS

Evaluate these comments.

BUSINESS CONNECTIONS

Managerial FOCUS

Departmental Accounting

1. Is the identification of purchases returns and allowances by department valuable to managerial control? Explain.
2. If one department consistently has a comparatively large amount of cash short in its operations, what management action might be appropriate?
3. Why is it better for managers to use contribution margin analysis rather than net income analysis when deciding whether to retain, expand, or contract operations?
4. How does a firm's accountant determine the reasonable basis to be used in allocating a specific indirect expense? Should management be concerned about the basis used?
5. The management of a store with three sales departments plans to install a bonus system for department managers. Do you think the bonus system should be based on each department's contribution margin or on the department's net income after allocating all administrative expenses? Explain.

Internal Control and FRAUD PREVENTION

Assigning Indirect Costs

Allocation of indirect costs to various departments can alter the departmental profit. Stop Company manufactures plates for drum brakes. To make the brake plate, three departments are required: stamping, plating, and packaging. At Stop, each department manager is eligible for a bonus based on departmental profit. You are the manager of the stamping department. Top management has given you the responsibility of assigning the indirect costs to each department. Stamping has higher material costs, whereas plating has higher labor costs. You decide that it would be best to have the indirect costs evenly distributed to each department. Is this a correct decision? Should you have the authority to make this decision?

Financial Statement ANALYSIS

Segment Reporting

Refer to the *2018 Annual Report (for the fiscal year ended February 3, 2019)* for The Home Depot, Inc., in Appendix A, particularly the Selected Financial Data.

In the Other Key Metrics presentation, what was the comparable sales increase percentage in FY 2018? Does the data indicate a trend?

TEAMWORK

Direct and Indirect Costs

Select a food product your group can produce; for example, tortilla chips, ice cream, cookies, or pretzels. List the steps to produce this product. Determine the direct and indirect materials and labor needed in its production. Present your findings to the class. How are the costs similar and dissimilar?

Answers to Comprehensive Self Review

1. Departments that sell similar items to customers outside the business.
2. Some cost centers render services or make products that are transferred to other centers in the same company. In such cases, a hypothetical revenue, or transfer price, is attributed to the goods or services transferred. This price permits measuring a "profit" for the center.
3. Direct expenses are usually charged when incurred. Indirect expenses are allocated at the end of the fiscal period.
4. Indirect expenses are allocated to departments in an attempt to measure the profitability of each department.
5. Subtract the department's direct expenses from its gross profit.

Accounting for Manufacturing Activities

Chapter 26

Monty Rakusen/Getty Images

www.ford.com

In early 2019, two of the world's largest vehicle manufacturers announced an agreement to work collaboratively to boost global competitiveness and better serve each company's large customer base. Ford Motor Company and Volkswagen AG agreed to deliver medium-sized trucks globally and commercial vans for the European market.

Additionally, they have agreed to work together developing electric and other technologies to meet future demands from customers. VW's electric initiative will be produced in the United States at its Chattanooga, Tennessee, manufacturing facility.

The company CEOs' (Volkswagen—Dr. Herbert Diess and Ford—Jim Hackett) vision of new vehicle architectures will place both companies in global leadership roles with alternatives to petroleum-based fuels in the truck and commercial van markets. Together, the companies sold approximately 1.2 million light commercial vehicles in 2018. They expect to introduce these newly designed trucks and vans as soon as 2022.

thinking critically
What are some of the materials that manufacturers use to produce one of its cars or trucks?

LEARNING OBJECTIVES

- **26-1** Prepare a statement of cost of goods manufactured.
- **26-2** Explain the basic components of manufacturing cost.
- **26-3** Prepare an income statement for a manufacturing business.
- **26-4** Prepare a balance sheet for a manufacturing business.
- **26-5** Prepare a worksheet for a manufacturing business.
- **26-6** Record the end-of-period adjusting entries for a manufacturing business.
- **26-7** Record closing entries for a manufacturing business.
- **26-8** Record reversing entries for a manufacturing business.
- **26-9** Define the accounting terms new to this chapter.

NEW TERMS

direct labor
direct materials
finished goods inventory
indirect labor
indirect materials and supplies
manufacturing overhead
Manufacturing Summary account
raw materials
statement of cost of goods manufactured
work in process

Section 1

SECTION OBJECTIVES	TERMS TO LEARN
>> 26-1 Prepare a statement of cost of goods manufactured. **WHY IT'S IMPORTANT** Manufacturing businesses carefully track production costs to maximize profits. **>> 26-2** Explain the basic components of manufacturing cost. **WHY IT'S IMPORTANT** Manufacturing costs consist of many elements such as labor, materials, and manufacturing overhead. **>> 26-3** Prepare an income statement for a manufacturing business. **WHY IT'S IMPORTANT** The income statement for a manufacturing business differs slightly from the merchandising income statement. **>> 26-4** Prepare a balance sheet for a manufacturing business. **WHY IT'S IMPORTANT** The balance sheet for a manufacturer shows inventory accounts for raw material, work in process, and finished goods.	direct labor direct materials finished goods inventory indirect labor indirect materials and supplies manufacturing overhead raw materials statement of cost of goods manufactured work in process

Accounting for Manufacturing Costs

Merchandising businesses purchase merchandise to be resold in the same condition and form but at a profit. Manufacturing businesses purchase and convert raw materials into finished goods to be sold at a profit.

>> **26-1 OBJECTIVE**
Prepare a statement of cost of goods manufactured.

Cost of Goods Manufactured

The difference between merchandising and manufacturing businesses is reflected in the income statements of the two types of businesses. You can see the similarities and differences by examining the partial income statements that follow for Snow Company and The Pink Manufacturing Company. Note that the major difference is that a manufacturing business uses "Cost of Goods Manufactured" instead of "Purchases." Both companies utilize a periodic system of inventory.

Snow Company		
Partial Income Statement		
Year Ended December 31, 20X1		
Revenue		
Sales (Net)		690 000 00
Cost of Goods Sold		
Merchandise Inventory, Jan. 1	30 000 00	
Purchases (Net)	327 506 00	
Goods Available for Sale	357 506 00	
Less Merchandise Inventory, Dec. 31	29 000 00	
Cost of Goods Sold		328 506 00
Gross Profit on Sales		361 494 00

The Pink Manufacturing Company
Partial Income Statement
Year Ended December 31, 20X1

Revenue			
Sales (Net)		690 000 00	
Cost of Goods Sold			
Finished Goods Inventory, Jan. 1	30 000 00		
Cost of Goods Manufactured	327 506 00		
Total Goods Available for Sale	357 506 00		
Less Finished Goods Inventory, Dec. 31	29 000 00		
Cost of Goods Sold		328 506 00	
Gross Profit on Sales		361 494 00	

Let's look more closely at the components that make up the cost of goods manufactured in the financial statements of a manufacturing concern. We will examine the accounts and financial statements of The Pink Manufacturing Company, a producer of trailers. Its manufacturing process involves the acquisition and use of raw materials such as steel, lumber, rivets, screws, nails, and paint. These materials are cut, shaped, assembled, painted, and polished in the factory and emerge as finished products ready for sale.

Statement of Cost of Goods Manufactured

The **statement of cost of goods manufactured** shows details of the cost of goods completed for a manufacturing business. This statement supports the Cost of Goods Sold figure shown on the income statement. Figure 26.1 shows the statement of cost of goods manufactured for The Pink Manufacturing Company.

Components of Manufacturing Cost

The components of manufacturing cost are the raw materials used **(1)**, the direct labor **(2)**, and the manufacturing overhead **(3)**. The numbers in parentheses refer to amounts in Figure 26.1.

Raw Materials A major component of manufacturing cost is **raw materials**—the materials placed into production. Let's examine how data about the cost of raw materials appears on the statement of cost of goods manufactured. The beginning inventory of raw materials, $25,000, is added to net purchases of raw materials, $165,000. Net purchases is materials purchases minus purchases discounts ($168,000 − $3,000). The result is total materials available, $190,000. The ending raw materials inventory, $24,000, is subtracted to determine the raw materials used, $166,000.

In this section, all references to materials (raw materials, materials purchases, and materials available) relate to direct materials. **Direct materials** are all identifiable items that go into a product and become part of it. For example, the direct materials in a trailer include the metal, rivets, screws, and paint.

Indirect materials and supplies are used in manufacturing a product, typically are of an insignificant dollar amount, and do not become part of the product. Indirect materials appear in the Manufacturing Overhead section of the statement. Indirect materials include sandpaper, steel wool, cleaning materials, and lubricants. Some businesses treat insignificant direct materials, such as glue, as indirect materials.

Direct Labor **Direct labor** costs are the costs of the personnel who work directly on the product being manufactured. Direct labor includes workers who cut and shape the metals, assemble the pieces into trailers, and finish or paint them. On the statement of cost of goods manufactured, direct labor is $98,500. This amount is obtained from the *Direct Labor* account.

Indirect labor costs are the costs of personnel who support production but are not directly involved in the manufacture of a product, such as supervisory, repair and maintenance, and

---

ABOUT
ACCOUNTING

Benchmarking
Benchmarking involves evaluating another company's business processes and adopting them to incorporate best practices to improve performance, search for innovative ideas, and gain a competitive advantage. The goal of benchmarking is to learn from others, adapt, implement, and improve.

>> **26-2 OBJECTIVE**
Explain the basic components of manufacturing cost.

FIGURE 26.1

Statement of Cost of Goods Manufactured

The Pink Manufacturing Company
Statement of Cost of Goods Manufactured
Year Ended December 31, 20X1

Work in Process Inventory, Jan. 1			**(5)**	1 600 000
Raw Materials				
Raw Materials Inventory, Jan. 1		2 500 000		
Materials Purchases	16 800 000			
Less Purchases Discounts	300 000			
Net Purchases		16 500 000		
Total Materials Available		19 000 000		
Less Raw Materials Inventory, Dec. 31		2 400 000		
Raw Materials Used		**(1)** 16 600 000		
Direct Labor		**(2)** 9 850 000		
Manufacturing Overhead				
Indirect Labor	450 000			
Payroll Taxes—Factory	980 600			
Utilities—Factory	900 000			
Repairs and Maintenance—Factory	500 000			
Indirect Materials and Supplies	720 000			
Depreciation—Factory Building	750 000			
Depreciation—Factory Equipment	500 000			
Insurance—Factory	350 000			
Property Taxes—Factory	750 000			
Total Manufacturing Overhead		**(3)** 5 900 600		
Total Manufacturing Cost			**(4)** 32 350 600	
Total Work in Process for Year			33 950 600	
Less Work in Process Inventory, Dec. 31			**(6)** 1 200 000	
Cost of Goods Manufactured			**(7)** 32 750 600	

janitorial staff. Supervisors are included in indirect labor because although they ensure that the work is done properly, they do not work directly on the product. Indirect labor is included in the Manufacturing Overhead section of the statement.

Manufacturing Overhead **Manufacturing overhead** includes all manufacturing costs that are not classified as direct materials or direct labor. In addition to indirect materials and supplies and indirect labor, manufacturing overhead includes utilities, depreciation, repair and maintenance, insurance, and property taxes for factory buildings and equipment. Manufacturing overhead also includes payroll taxes on factory wages.

> The Boeing Company is the United States' largest manufacturing exporter. Boeing is producing the Boeing 787-10 Dreamliner, the 737 MAX, and the 777XI to compete with Europe's Airbus. Another innovation for many air passengers is the Connexion by Boeing® that features areas in the aircraft that function like an office for business travelers. Only by controlling costs can a larger manufacturer, like Boeing, begin new business ventures.

Work in Process

On the statement of cost of goods manufactured, the total manufacturing cost **(4)** includes all raw materials used, all direct labor costs incurred, and all manufacturing overhead applicable to the current production period. However, it does not represent the total cost of goods manufactured because some products that were finished this period were started in the previous period. **Work in process** refers to partially completed units in the production process. At the end of each period, an estimate is made of the costs of raw materials, direct labor, and manufacturing overhead for the work in process. For The Pink Manufacturing Company, the beginning inventory of work in process was $16,000 **(5)** and the ending inventory of work in process was $12,000 **(6)**. The numbers in parentheses refer to amounts in Figure 26.1.

On the statement of cost of goods manufactured, the beginning work in process is added to total manufacturing cost. The result is total work in process for the year. The ending work in process is subtracted from the total work in process for the year to arrive at the cost of goods manufactured **(7)**.

Income Statement for a Manufacturing Concern

Notice that the cost of goods manufactured from Figure 26.1 is used to calculate the cost of goods sold in the income statement. The income statement for The Pink Manufacturing Company appears in Figure 26.2. An effective income tax rate of 25 percent is assumed throughout these illustrations.

The cost of goods sold can differ from the cost of goods manufactured because of changes in the level of **finished goods inventory.** Some finished goods that are sold in the current period were made in previous periods. Some products made during the current period will be sold in later periods. In order to prepare the income statement, a count is made of the finished goods inventory at the end of each period.

In Figure 26.2, the beginning finished goods inventory, $30,000, is added to the cost of goods manufactured, $327,506. The result is the total finished goods available for sale, $357,506. The ending finished goods inventory, $29,000, is subtracted, and the difference represents the cost of goods sold, $328,506.

Balance Sheet for a Manufacturing Concern

Figure 26.3 shows the balance sheet for a manufacturing business. Notice that it includes three inventory categories: raw materials, work in process, and finished goods.

>> **26-3 OBJECTIVE**
Prepare an income statement for a manufacturing business.

important!

Income Statement
In the income statement of a manufacturing company, the line item "Cost of Goods Manufactured" replaces "Purchases."

>> **26-4 OBJECTIVE**
Prepare a balance sheet for a manufacturing business.

FIGURE 26.2
Income Statement for a Manufacturing Concern

important!

Cost of Goods Sold
The cost of goods sold may differ from the cost of goods manufactured because of beginning and ending inventories of finished goods.

The Pink Manufacturing Company
Income Statement
Year Ended December 31, 20X1

Revenue			
Sales		695 000 00	
Less Sales Returns and Allowances		5 000 00	
Net Sales		690 000 00	
Cost of Goods Sold			
Finished Goods Inventory, Jan. 1	30 000 00		
Cost of Goods Manufactured	327 506 00		
Total Goods Available for Sale	357 506 00		
Less Finished Goods Inventory, Dec. 31	29 000 00		
Cost of Goods Sold		328 506 00	
Gross Profit on Sales		361 494 00	
Operating Expenses			
Selling Expenses (Control)	100 000 00		
Administrative Expenses (Control)	92 880 00		
Total Operating Expenses		192 880 00	
Net Income before Income Taxes		168 614 00	
Income Tax Expense		42 154 00	
Net Income after Income Taxes		126 460 00	

FIGURE 26.3 Balance Sheet for a Manufacturing Concern

The Pink Manufacturing Company
Balance Sheet
December 31, 20X1

Assets			
Current Assets			
Cash			4 0 0 0 0 0
Accounts Receivable		6 5 5 0 0 0	
Less Allowance for Doubtful Accounts		1 8 8 0 0 0	6 3 6 2 0 0 0
Inventories			
Raw Materials		2 4 0 0 0 0 0	
Work in Process		1 2 0 0 0 0 0	
Finished Goods		2 9 0 0 0 0 0	6 5 0 0 0 0 0
Prepaid Expenses			
Prepaid Insurance		2 0 0 0 0 0	
Supplies on Hand		8 0 0 0 0	2 8 0 0 0 0
Total Current Assets			1 7 1 4 2 0 0 0
Property, Plant, and Equipment			
Land		5 0 0 0 0 0 0	
Factory Building	1 5 0 0 0 0 0 0		
Accumulated Depreciation—Factory Building	2 2 5 0 0 0 0	1 2 7 5 0 0 0 0	
Factory Equipment	1 0 0 0 0 0 0 0		
Accumulated Depreciation—Factory Equipment	2 5 0 0 0 0 0	7 5 0 0 0 0 0	
Office Equipment	1 0 0 0 0 0 0		
Accumulated Depreciation—Office Equipment	6 0 0 0 0 0	4 0 0 0 0 0	
Total Property, Plant, and Equipment			2 5 6 5 0 0 0 0
Total Assets			4 2 7 9 2 0 0 0
Liabilities and Stockholders' Equity			
Current Liabilities			
Accounts Payable			3 0 0 0 0 0 0
Salaries and Wages Payable			4 0 0 0 0 0
Income Tax Payable			2 1 5 4 0 0
Social Security Tax Payable			2 4 8 0 0
Medicare Tax Payable			5 8 0 0
Total Liabilities			3 6 4 6 0 0 0
Stockholders' Equity			
Common Stock $1 par value (200,000 shares authorized, 100,000 issued and outstanding)	1 0 0 0 0 0 0 0		
Paid-in Capital in Excess of Par Value	5 0 0 0 0 0 0		
Total Paid-in Capital		1 5 0 0 0 0 0 0	
Retained Earnings		2 4 1 4 6 0 0 0	
Total Stockholders' Equity			3 9 1 4 6 0 0 0
Total Liabilities and Stockholders' Equity			4 2 7 9 2 0 0 0

Importance of Inventory in Manufacturing Business

Managing Inventory Chapter 17 discussed the importance of the valuation of inventory. Many businesses actually count the number of each type of goods on hand, then multiply the number of units obtained during the count by the appropriate cost per unit. This is referred to as the process of taking a *physical inventory*. It is generally performed only at the end of a period.

Managers of manufacturing businesses, however, need reliable information about inventory more frequently, sometimes on a daily basis. The procedure used to obtain this information is known as keeping a *perpetual inventory*. Additions to and deletions from all inventory accounts, such as finished goods, work in process, and materials, are recorded as they occur. Although this requires additional bookkeeping, many managers justify this cost because it enables them to aggressively control costs. Perpetual inventory records are customarily verified by taking a physical count at least once a year.

Section 1 Review

1. What does work in process represent?
   a. inventory that is partially completed
   b. inventory shipped to customers
   c. raw materials used
   d. inventory returned

2. What are direct materials?
   a. sandpaper and other like-kind items of minor cost used in production
   b. finished goods
   c. identifiable items that become part of a product
   d. the item that costs the most used in making a product

3. How does the cost of goods manufactured relate to the income statement?
   a. does not relate to the income statement
   b. reduces cost of goods sold
   c. increases cost of goods sold
   d. increases finished goods

4. The components of total manufacturing cost are:
   a. raw materials used, direct labor, and manufacturing overhead.
   b. manufacturing overhead and administrative expenses.
   c. selling expenses, administrative expenses, and manufacturing overhead.
   d. cost of goods manufactured, cost of goods sold, and work in process.

5. Indirect labor for a manufacturing business includes the wages of:
   a. employees who assemble the product.
   b. factory repair and maintenance employees.
   c. employees who finish and paint the product.
   d. employees who sell the product.

6. What is the cost of goods manufactured if beginning work in process was $30,000, ending work in process was $30,000, raw materials used were $60,000, direct labor was $50,000, and manufacturing overhead was $20,000?
   a. $130,000
   b. $160,000
   c. $110,000
   d. $190,000

Section 2

SECTION OBJECTIVES	TERMS TO LEARN
>> 26-5 Prepare a worksheet for a manufacturing business. **WHY IT'S IMPORTANT** There are accounts on the worksheet that are specific to manufacturing businesses. **>> 26-6** Record the end-of-period adjusting entries for a manufacturing business. **WHY IT'S IMPORTANT** Adjusting entries are made in the same way for merchandising and manufacturing businesses. **>> 26-7** Record closing entries for a manufacturing business. **WHY IT'S IMPORTANT** All manufacturing and operating costs are closed at the end of the period. **>> 26-8** Record reversing entries for a manufacturing business. **WHY IT'S IMPORTANT** Reversing entries save time and help to reduce errors.	*Manufacturing Summary* account

Completing the Accounting Cycle

The worksheet for a manufacturing business has a section to facilitate the preparation of the statement of cost of goods manufactured. Refer to Figure 26.4 as we complete the worksheet for The Pink Manufacturing Company.

>> **26-5 OBJECTIVE**
Prepare a worksheet for a manufacturing business.

The Worksheet and Financial Statements

After all transactions have been journalized and posted, the worksheet is completed. The first step is to enter the trial balance.

Entering the Trial Balance on the Worksheet

Notice that there are several accounts unique to manufacturing businesses. There are three inventory accounts: *Raw Materials Inventory, Work in Process Inventory,* and *Finished Goods Inventory.* There is a *Direct Labor* account as well as various manufacturing overhead accounts that appear on the statement of cost of goods manufactured.

The *Manufacturing Summary account* is similar to the *Income Summary* account. All of the accounts that appear on the statement of cost of goods manufactured are closed to *Manufacturing Summary.* Then the balance of *Manufacturing Summary,* which represents the cost of goods manufactured, is closed to *Income Summary.*

Entering Adjusting Entries on the Worksheet

Notice that there are some adjustments that pertain to manufacturing operations only. Carefully trace each adjustment. For the sake of simplicity, selling and administrative expenses are recorded in the control accounts.

Ending Inventories

Six adjustments are made for inventory: *Raw Materials Inventory* **(a)** and **(b)**, *Work in Process Inventory* **(c)** and **(d)**, and *Finished Goods Inventory* **(e)** and **(f)**. The inventory accounts are credited for beginning inventory amounts and debited for the ending inventory amounts. For *Raw Materials Inventory* and *Work in Process Inventory*, the adjustment is made to *Manufacturing Summary*. For *Finished Goods Inventory*, the adjustment is made to *Income Summary*.

Uncollectible Accounts

Entry **(g)** is made to record the uncollectible accounts expense, which is estimated to be 0.2 percent of net sales, or $1,380 (0.002 × $690,000).

Expired Insurance

Entry **(h)** records insurance expired during the year. Expired insurance includes $3,500 on assets related to manufacturing (equipment, buildings, and inventories) and $500 on office equipment.

Supplies on Hand

Entry **(i)** records the adjustment for supplies on hand. In this example, when manufacturing supplies are purchased, they are debited to the *Indirect Materials and Supplies* account, a manufacturing overhead expense account. Manufacturing companies follow this procedure because most of the supplies are consumed in a short time. Supplies used in selling and in administrative activities are debited to the *Selling Expenses Control* and *Administrative Expenses Control* accounts.

At the end of December, there was $800 of factory supplies on hand. Adjustment **(i)** debits the asset account *Supplies on Hand* for $800 and credits the overhead account *Indirect Materials and Supplies* for $800. The cost of the sales and office supplies on hand is deemed immaterial.

> **important!**
> **Manufacturing Summary**
> All items that appear on the statement of cost of goods manufactured are transferred to the *Manufacturing Summary* account.

Depreciation

Entry **(j)** records the adjustment for depreciation on assets for the year: $7,500 on the factory building, $5,000 on the factory equipment, and $1,000 on the office equipment.

Accrued Salaries and Wages

On December 31, accrued wages are $3,500 for direct labor and $500 for indirect labor. These accruals are recorded by entry **(k)**.

Payroll Taxes on Accrued Payroll

Entry **(l)** records payroll taxes on the $4,000 accrued wages of factory workers at the end of the year. All of the workers have earned the maximum amount subject to federal and state unemployment taxes. Therefore, the accrual is for $248 (0.062 × $4,000) of social security tax and $58 (0.0145 × $4,000) of Medicare tax.

> **recall**
> **Accruals**
> Adjustments are made for items that relate to the current period but that have not been paid for and do not yet appear in the accounts.

Income Tax Payable

The federal income tax is estimated to be 25 percent of the taxable income. Based on the worksheet, the estimated taxable income is $168,614, and the estimated income tax (rounded to the nearest dollar) for the year is $42,154 ($168,614 × 0.25). During the year, $40,000 of estimated tax payments were made. As a result, $2,154 ($42,154 − $40,000) of additional taxes are accrued on December 31. The accrual is recorded on the worksheet as entry **(m)**.

FIGURE 26.4 Worksheet for a Manufacturing Concern

The Pink Manufacturing Company
Worksheet
Year Ended December 31, 20X1

#	ACCOUNT NAME	TRIAL BALANCE DEBIT	TRIAL BALANCE CREDIT	ADJUSTMENTS DEBIT	ADJUSTMENTS CREDIT	ADJUSTED TRIAL BALANCE DEBIT	ADJUSTED TRIAL BALANCE CREDIT
1	Cash	4 000 00				4 000 00	
2	Accounts Receivable	6 550 00				6 550 00	
3	Allowance for Doubtful Accounts		500 00		(g) 1 380 00		1 880 00
4	Raw Materials Inventory	2 500 00		(b) 2 400 00	(a) 2 500 00	2 400 00	
5	Work in Process Inventory	1 600 00		(d) 1 200 00	(c) 1 600 00	1 200 00	
6	Finished Goods Inventory	3 000 00		(f) 2 900 00	(e) 3 000 00	2 900 00	
7	Prepaid Insurance	600 00			(h) 400 00	200 00	
8	Supplies on Hand			(i) 800 00		800 00	
9	Land	5 000 00				5 000 00	
10	Factory Building	15 000 00				15 000 00	
11	Accum. Depr.—Building		1 500 00		(j) 750 00		2 250 00
12	Factory Equipment	10 000 00				10 000 00	
13	Accum. Depr.—Factory Equipment		2 000 00		(j) 500 00		2 500 00
14	Office Equipment	1 000 00				1 000 00	
15	Accum. Depr.—Office Equipment		500 00		(j) 100 00		600 00
16	Accounts Payable		3 000 00				3 000 00
17	Salaries and Wages Payable				(k) 400 00		400 00
18	Income Tax Payable				(m) 2 154 00		2 154 00
19	Social Security Tax Payable				(l) 248 00		248 00
20	Medicare Tax Payable				(l) 58 00		58 00
21	Common Stock, $1 par		10 000 00				10 000 00
22	Paid-in Cap. in Exc. of par Value		5 000 00				5 000 00
23	Retained Earnings		11 500 00				11 500 00
24	Sales		69 500 00				69 500 00
25	Sales Returns and Allowances	500 00				500 00	
26	Materials Purchases	16 800 00				16 800 00	
27	Purchases Discounts		300 00				300 00
28	Direct Labor	9 500 00		(k) 350 00		9 850 00	
29	Indirect Labor	400 00		(k) 50 00		450 00	
30	Payroll Taxes—Factory	950 00		(l) 306 00		9 806 00*	
31	Utilities—Factory	900 00				900 00	
32	Repairs & Maintenance—Factory	500 00				500 00	
33	Indirect Materials and Supplies	800 00			(i) 800 00	720 00	
34	Depreciation—Factory Building			(j) 750 00		750 00	
35	Depreciation—Factory Equipment			(j) 500 00		500 00	
36	Insurance—Factory			(h) 350 00		350 00	
37	Property Taxes—Factory	750 00				750 00	
38	Selling Expense (Control)	10 000 00				10 000 00	
39	Administrative Expense (Control)	9 000 00		(g) 1 380 00		9 288 00	
40				(h) 50 00			
41				(j) 100 00			
42	Income Tax Expense	4 000 00		(m) 2 154 00		4 215 40*	
43	Manufacturing Summary			(a) 2 500 00	(b) 2 400 00	2 500 00	2 400 00
44				(c) 1 600 00	(d) 1 200 00	1 600 00	1 200 00
45	Income Summary			(e) 3 000 00	(f) 2 900 00	3 000 00	2 900 00
46		103 350 00	103 350 00	16 214 00	16 214 00	111 984 00	111 984 00
47	Cost of Goods Manufactured						
48							
49	Net Income						
50	Totals						

FIGURE 26.4 Worksheet for a Manufacturing Concern (concluded)

COST OF GOODS MANUFACTURED		INCOME STATEMENT		BALANCE SHEET		
DEBIT	CREDIT	DEBIT	CREDIT	DEBIT	CREDIT	
				40 000 00		1
				6 550 00		2
					1 880 00	3
				2 400 00		4
				1 200 00		5
				2 900 00		6
				200 00		7
				80 00		8
				5 000 00		9
				15 000 00		10
					2 250 00	11
				10 000 00		12
					2 500 00	13
				1 000 00		14
					600 00	15
					3 000 00	16
					400 00	17
					2 154 00	18
					248 00	19
					58 00	20
					10 000 00	21
					5 000 00	22
					11 500 00	23
			6 950 00			24
		500 00				25
168 000 00						26
	300 00					27
9 850 00						28
450 00						29
9 806 00						30
900 00						31
500 00						32
720 00						33
750 00						34
500 00						35
350 00						36
750 00						37
		1 000 00 00				38
		9 288 00				39
						40
						41
		4 215 40 0				42
2 500 00	2 400 00					43
1 600 00	1 200 00					44
		3 000 00	2 900 00			45
366 506 00	3 900 00					46
	327 506 00	327 506 00				47
366 506 00	366 506 00	597 540 00	724 000 00	483 300 00	356 840 00	48
		126 460 00			126 460 00	49
		724 000 00	724 000 00	483 300 00	483 300 00	50

Preparing the Adjusted Trial Balance on the Worksheet

Note that for the inventory accounts, both the debit and credit amounts are entered in the *Manufacturing Summary* and *Income Summary* accounts because these amounts appear on the cost of goods manufactured statement and on the income statement.

Some accountants omit the Adjusted Trial Balance columns to reduce the number of columns in the worksheet. If these columns are omitted, the adjusted balances are extended to the appropriate statement columns.

Completing the Financial Statement Columns

Accounts that appear on the statement of cost of goods manufactured are extended to the Cost of Goods Manufactured columns. Accounts that appear on the income statement are transferred to the Income Statement columns. Accounts that appear on the balance sheet are extended to the Balance Sheet columns.

In the Cost of Goods Manufactured section, total debits are $366,506 and total credits are $39,000. The difference is $327,506, which is the cost of goods manufactured. The $327,506 is entered in the Credit column of the Cost of Goods Manufactured section and the Debit column of the Income Statement section.

Preparing the Financial Statements

The financial statements and the statement of cost of goods manufactured are prepared from the worksheet.

Completing the Accounting Cycle

Once the financial statements have been prepared, the accountant completes the steps in the accounting cycle: adjusting entries, closing entries, postclosing trial balance, and interpretation of the financial information.

>> **26-6 OBJECTIVE**
Record the end-of-period adjusting entries for a manufacturing business.

Recording and Posting Adjusting Entries

Figure 26.5 shows how the adjustments recorded on the worksheet are journalized. For the sake of brevity, journal entry explanations have been omitted.

FIGURE 26.5

Adjusting Entries

GENERAL JOURNAL PAGE _____

DATE	DESCRIPTION	POST. REF.	DEBIT	CREDIT
20X1	Adjusting Entries			
	(Adjustment a)			
Dec. 31	Manufacturing Summary		25 000 00	
	Raw Materials Inventory			25 000 00
	(Adjustment b)			
31	Raw Materials Inventory		24 000 00	
	Manufacturing Summary			24 000 00
	(Adjustment c)			
31	Manufacturing Summary		16 000 00	
	Work in Process Inventory			16 000 00
	(Adjustment d)			
31	Work in Process Inventory		12 000 00	
	Manufacturing Summary			12 000 00

18		(Adjustment e)											18
19	31	Income Summary	30	0	0	0	00						19
20		Finished Goods Inventory						30	0	0	0	00	20
21													21
22		(Adjustment f)											22
23	31	Finished Goods Inventory	29	0	0	0	00						23
24		Income Summary						29	0	0	0	00	24
25													25
26		(Adjustment g)											26
27	31	Uncollectible Accounts Expense	1	3	8	0	00						27
28		Allowance for Doubtful Accounts						1	3	8	0	00	28
29													29
30		(Adjustment h)											30
31	31	Insurance—Factory	3	5	0	0	00						31
32		Administrative Expense (Control)		5	0	0	00						32
33		Prepaid Insurance						4	0	0	0	00	33
34													34
35		(Adjustment i)											35
36	31	Supplies on Hand		8	0	0	00						36
37		Indirect Materials and Supplies							8	0	0	00	37

1		(Adjustment j)											1
2	31	Depreciation—Factory Building	7	5	0	0	00						2
3		Depreciation—Factory Equipment	5	0	0	0	00						3
4		Administrative Expense (Control)	1	0	0	0	00						4
5		Accumulated Depr.—Factory Building						7	5	0	0	00	5
6		Accumulated Depr.—Factory Equipment						5	0	0	0	00	6
7		Accumulated Depr.—Office Equipment						1	0	0	0	00	7
8													8
9		(Adjustment k)											9
10	31	Direct Labor	3	5	0	0	00						10
11		Indirect Labor		5	0	0	00						11
12		Salaries and Wages Payable						4	0	0	0	00	12
13													13
14		(Adjustment l)											14
15	31	Payroll Taxes—Factory		3	0	6	00						15
16		Social Security Tax Payable							2	4	8	00	16
17		Medicare Tax Payable								5	8	00	17
18													18
19		(Adjustment m)											19
20	31	Income Tax Expense	2	1	5	4	00						20
21		Income Tax Payable						2	1	5	4	00	21

Recording Closing Entries

>> **26-7 OBJECTIVE**
Record closing entries for a manufacturing business.

The closing entries of a manufacturing business are done in three steps.

Closing Accounts to Manufacturing Summary Refer to the Cost of Goods Manufactured section of the worksheet (Figure 26.4). From the Credit column, close the *Purchases Discounts* account to *Manufacturing Summary*:

1			Closing Entries									1
2	20X1											2
3	Dec.	31	Purchases Discounts	3	0	0	00					3
4			Manufacturing Summary					3	0	0	00	4
5												5

MANAGERIAL IMPLICATIONS

MANUFACTURING COSTS

- Managers of manufacturing concerns must have reliable accounting data in order to plan and control operations.
- In manufacturing businesses, managers need timely information to control the costs incurred in the production of goods.
- The cost of goods manufactured statement provides detailed information about the individual cost elements and the total cost of manufacturing. Managers use this information to evaluate past performance and to guide future operations.
- The worksheet is an efficient way to summarize and classify information so that financial statements can be prepared easily and quickly.
- Reversing entries save time and help to prevent errors in the new period.

THINKING CRITICALLY

Why does a manufacturing business have multiple inventory accounts?

From the Debit column, close the manufacturing costs to **Manufacturing Summary**. After these entries have been posted, the balance in the **Manufacturing Summary** account is a debit of $327,506:

	Dec.	31	Manufacturing Summary	325,506.00	
6			Materials Purchases		168,000.00
7			Direct Labor		98,500.00
8			Indirect Labor		4,500.00
9			Payroll Taxes—Factory		9,806.00
10			Utilities—Factory		9,000.00
11			Repairs and Maintenance—Factory		5,000.00
12			Indirect Materials and Supplies		7,200.00
13			Depreciation—Factory Building		7,500.00
14			Depreciation—Factory Equipment		5,000.00
15			Insurance—Factory		3,500.00
16			Property Taxes—Factory		7,500.00

ACCOUNT Manufacturing Summary **ACCOUNT NO.** 398

DATE		DESCRIPTION	POST. REF.	DEBIT	CREDIT	BALANCE DEBIT	BALANCE CREDIT
20X1							
Dec.	31	Adj. a		25,000.00		25,000.00	
	31	Adj. b			24,000.00	1,000.00	
	31	Adj. c		16,000.00		17,000.00	
	31	Adj. d			12,000.00	5,000.00	
	31	Closing			3,000.00	2,000.00	
	31	Closing		325,506.00		327,506.00	

Closing Revenue and Expense Accounts into Income Summary The entries to close the revenue and expense accounts into *Income Summary* are almost identical to those for a merchandising concern. An additional account, *Manufacturing Summary*, is closed into *Income Summary:*

17	Dec.	31	Sales	695 000 00		17
18			Income Summary		695 000 00	18
19						19
20		31	Income Summary	567 540 00		20
21			Sales Returns and Allowances		5 000 00	21
22			Selling Expense (Control)		100 000 00	22
23			Administrative Expense (Control)		92 880 00	23
24			Income Tax Expense		42 154 00	24
25			Manufacturing Summary		327 506 00	25

Closing Income Summary At this point, all revenue and expense accounts are closed. The balance in the *Income Summary* account, $126,460, represents the net income after income taxes:

ACCOUNT Income Summary   ACCOUNT NO. 399

DATE	DESCRIPTION	POST. REF.	DEBIT	CREDIT	BALANCE DEBIT	BALANCE CREDIT
20X1						
Dec. 31	Adj. e		30 000 00		30 000 00	
31	Adj. f			29 000 00	1 000 00	
31	Closing			695 000 00		694 000 00
31	Closing		567 540 00			126 460 00

The balance of the *Income Summary* account is closed to *Retained Earnings:*

27	Dec.	31	Income Summary	126 460 00		27
28			Retained Earnings		126 460 00	28

Preparing the Postclosing Trial Balance

After adjusting and closing entries have been posted to the ledger accounts, a postclosing trial balance is prepared to prove that the adjusting and closing entries were posted correctly. The ledger account balances should match those listed in the Balance Sheet section of the worksheet.

Recording the Reversing Entries

Reversing entries may be made for adjustments for accruals. Reversing entries are also made for expenditures initially debited to expense accounts and then adjusted at the end of the year. Remember that reversing entries are optional, not required by GAAP.

>> **26-8 OBJECTIVE**
Record reversing entries for a manufacturing business.

Section 2 Review

1. What is the difference between the worksheet for a manufacturing and a merchandising business?
   a. A merchandising business has only finished goods inventory.
   b. A manufacturing business has only one inventory—work in process.
   c. Only the merchandising business computes a cost of goods sold.
   d. A manufacturing business has two inventory accounts.
2. What is the additional column heading on the worksheet of a manufacturing business?
   a. Cost of Goods Sold
   b. Cost of Goods Manufactured
   c. Cost of Goods Available for Sale
   d. Ending Inventory Balances
3. To what account is the *Manufacturing Summary* account closed?
   a. *Finished Goods*
   b. *Cost of Goods Sold*
   c. *Purchases*
   d. *Income Summary*

4. On the completed worksheet of a manufacturing business, the accounts related to materials purchases, direct labor, and factory overhead appear in the:
   a. Cost of Goods Sold section.
   b. Income Statement section.
   c. Cost of Goods Manufactured section.
   d. Balance Sheet section.

5. On the completed worksheet of a manufacturing business, the accounts related to raw materials inventory, work in process inventory, and finished goods inventory appear in the:
   a. Cost of Goods Manufactured section.
   b. Balance Sheet section.
   c. Cost of Goods Sold section.
   d. Income Statement section.

6. What is the journal entry to adjust for accrued wages of $5,000 for direct labor and $500 for indirect labor?
   a. Debit *Direct Labor* $5,000; debit *Indirect Labor* $500; credit *Salaries and Wages Payable* $5,500.
   b. Debit *Work in Process* $5,000; debit *Manufacturing Overhead* $500; credit *Cash* $5,500.
   c. Debit *Direct Labor* $5,500; credit *Income Summary* $5,500.
   d. Debit *Direct Labor* $5,000; debit *Indirect Labor* $500; credit *Cash* $5,500.

REVIEW Chapter Summary

Chapter 26

A manufacturing company purchases raw materials that it converts into finished goods to be sold at a profit. You have learned the differences in the preparation of financial statements for a manufacturer and a merchandiser. A different set of accounts is required to classify the costs associated with manufacturing processes.

Learning Objectives

26-1 Prepare a statement of cost of goods manufactured.

A statement of cost of goods manufactured is prepared to show the results of the manufacturing activities and to support the income statement.

26-2 Explain the basic components of manufacturing cost.

Manufacturing costs are recorded in three categories:

- Raw materials are those materials placed into production and used to create finished goods. Raw materials include direct materials and indirect materials.
- Direct labor costs are costs of personnel who work directly on the product as it is manufactured.
- Manufacturing overhead includes costs of manufacturing operations that are not classified as direct labor or direct materials. Examples are insurance, property taxes, and utilities.

26-3 Prepare an income statement for a manufacturing business.

One major difference distinguishes the format of an income statement of a manufacturing business from that of a merchandising company.

The cost of goods manufactured is included on the income statement as part of Cost of Goods Sold, corresponding to the merchandise purchases on the income statement of a merchandising business.

26-4 Prepare a balance sheet for a manufacturing business.

The balance sheet of a manufacturing business is similar to that of a merchandising business. The only new accounts required are inventory accounts for raw materials, work in process, and finished goods. The *Finished Goods Inventory* account corresponds to the *Merchandise Inventory* account of a merchandising business.

26-5 Prepare a worksheet for a manufacturing business.

The worksheet for a manufacturing business is similar to one for a merchandising firm, but it has an added pair of columns in which to record the figures from the cost of goods manufactured statement:

- The worksheet gives the data used for the statement of cost of goods manufactured, the income statement, and the balance sheet.
- To prepare a statement of retained earnings, accountants analyze the *Retained Earnings* account in the general ledger for the details.

26-6 Record the end-of-period adjusting entries for a manufacturing business.

Adjustments for inventories, expired insurance, and accruals or deferrals are entered on the worksheet and then recorded and posted in the accounting records.

26-7 Record closing entries for a manufacturing business.

All accounts relating to the cost of goods manufactured are closed to *Manufacturing Summary*:

- The *Manufacturing Summary* account final balance—the cost of goods manufactured—is closed to the *Income Summary* account.
- All items in the Income Statement section of the worksheet are closed to *Income Summary*.
- The final closing entry transfers net income after income taxes to the *Retained Earnings* account.

26-8 Record reversing entries for a manufacturing business.

After the accounting records are adjusted and closed, a postclosing trial balance is prepared. At each new period, certain adjusting entries are reversed if the business uses reversing entries.

26-9 Define the accounting terms new to this chapter.

Glossary

Direct labor (p. 915) The costs attributable to personnel who work directly on the product being manufactured

Direct materials (p. 915) All items that go into a product and become a part of it

Finished goods inventory (p. 917) The cost of completed products ready for sale; corresponds to the *Merchandise Inventory* account of a merchandising business

Indirect labor (p. 915) Costs attributable to personnel who support production but are not directly involved in the manufacture of a product; for example, supervisory, repair and maintenance, and janitorial staff

Indirect materials and supplies (p. 915) Materials used in manufacturing a product that may not become a part of the product and are not a significant material cost factor

Manufacturing overhead (p. 916) All manufacturing costs that are not classified as direct materials or direct labor

Manufacturing Summary **account** (p. 920) The account to which all items on the statement of cost of goods manufactured are closed; similar to the *Income Summary* account

Raw materials (p. 915) The materials placed into production

Statement of cost of goods manufactured (p. 915) A financial report showing details of the cost of goods completed for a manufacturing business

Work in process (p. 917) Partially completed units in the production process

Comprehensive Self Review

1. What is direct labor cost?
2. What are indirect materials?
3. Explain how the following items are handled on the worksheet:
   a. beginning and ending inventories of raw materials.
   b. beginning and ending inventories of work in process.
   c. beginning and ending inventories of finished goods.
4. Does the *Manufacturing Summary* account have a balance during the fiscal period? Explain.
5. What entries are reversed at the beginning of the accounting period?

(Answers to Comprehensive Self Review are at the end of the chapter.)

Discussion Questions

1. How do the accounting problems of a manufacturing business differ from those of a merchandising business?
2. Name the three inventory accounts found in the chart of accounts of a manufacturing business and explain each one.
3. What is the relationship between the cost of goods manufactured and the income statement?
4. What procedure is used on the statement of cost of goods manufactured to arrive at the cost of raw materials used?
5. What is indirect labor?
6. It is possible that one company might consider an item, such as glue, as one of its direct materials, while another company with identical manufacturing processes might classify the item as one of its indirect materials. Why?
7. How would the wages of the employee who issues materials from the factory storeroom be classified?

8. What is manufacturing overhead?
9. Why does the figure for total manufacturing cost not equal the cost of goods manufactured?
10. How is the work in process inventory determined?
11. Give some examples of manufacturing overhead items.
12. What is the source of the information for preparing the journal entry to close manufacturing cost accounts to the *Manufacturing Summary* account?
13. Are the financial statements prepared after the closing entries have been posted? Explain.
14. Is the statement of cost of goods manufactured prepared before or after the income statement? Explain.
15. Describe the flow of costs through the inventory accounts of a manufacturing firm.
16. Give three examples not given in the chapter of indirect labor for a manufacturing firm.
17. How is the cost of goods sold determined for a manufacturing business?
18. Explain how a manufacturing business records reversing entries and why the reversing entries are made.

APPLICATIONS

Exercises

Cost of goods manufactured statement (partial).

◀ **Exercise 26.1**
Objective 26-1

The following selected items appeared in the Adjustments columns of the worksheet for Red Inc. on December 31, 20X1. From this information, prepare the section of the statement of cost of goods manufactured relating to the cost of raw materials used:

	Debit	Credit
Finished Goods Inventory	$ 50,000	$55,000
Work in Process Inventory	75,000	78,000
Raw Materials Inventory	40,000	45,000
Materials Purchases	800,000	
Purchases Returns and Allowances		8,000
Freight In (on Materials Purchases)	10,000	

Adjusting entries.

◀ **Exercise 26.2**
Objective 26-6

Using the data given in Exercise 26.1, prepare the general journal entry to record adjustments for inventory accounts.

Components of manufacturing cost.

◀ **Exercise 26.3**
Objective 26-2

WFC Company's beginning raw materials inventory was $85,000. Its net purchases for the period were $795,000, and its ending raw materials inventory was $75,000. What was its cost of raw materials used?

Components of manufacturing cost.

◀ **Exercise 26.4**
Objective 26-2

Cat Company's total manufacturing cost for the year was $1,500,000. Its manufacturing overhead was $300,000, and its cost of raw materials used was $900,000. What was its direct labor cost for the year?

Exercise 26.5

Objective 26-2

▶ **Components of manufacturing cost.**

Which of the following items would not appear on the statement of cost of goods manufactured?

1. Advertising expense
2. Depreciation of factory equipment
3. Direct labor

Exercise 26.6

Objective 26-2

▶ **Components of manufacturing cost.**

Which of the following items would appear on the statement of cost of goods manufactured?

1. Work in process inventory
2. Finished goods inventory
3. Raw materials inventory

Exercise 26.7

Objective 26-2

▶ **Components of manufacturing cost.**

Which of the following items would not be included in the Manufacturing Overhead section of the statement of cost of goods manufactured?

1. Payroll taxes on wages of plant security guards
2. Insurance costs for factory
3. Freight-in charges on purchases of raw materials

Exercise 26.8

Objective 26-2

▶ **Components of manufacturing cost.**

Which of the following items would be included in the Manufacturing Overhead section of the statement of cost of goods manufactured?

1. Direct labor
2. Raw materials used
3. Indirect materials and supplies
4. Repairs to factory building
5. Depreciation of factory equipment
6. Office supplies expense
7. Advertising expense

Exercise 26.9

Objective 26-5

▶ **Worksheet for a manufacturing business.**

Which of the following account balances would not be extended to the Cost of Goods Manufactured section of the worksheet?

1. Insurance on finished goods
2. Payroll taxes on outside sales salaries
3. Salary of factory shift supervisor
4. Insurance on raw materials in factory storeroom
5. Salary of accounts receivable clerk
6. Utilities for factory
7. Payroll taxes on factory wages
8. Insurance on factory equipment
9. Freight out
10. Salary of factory material handler

Adjusting, closing, and reversing entries.

Information about certain account balances in the trial balance of Vol Corp. on December 31, 20X1, follows:

a. Balance in *Raw Materials Inventory* account that reflects the beginning balance, December 31, 20X0, $52,000; physical count on December 31, 20X1, that reflects the ending balance, $50,000

b. Balance in *Prepaid Insurance* account, $22,500; insurance expired, $18,000

c. Balance in *Direct Labor* account, $100,000; accrued direct labor, $7,000

d. Balance in *Factory Supplies on Hand* account, $8,500; physical count shows supplies on hand, $600

Record the following in the general journal:

1. Adjusting entries required
2. Closing entries required
3. Reversing entries on January 1, 20X2

◀ **Exercise 26.10**
Objectives 26-6, 26-7, 26-8

PROLEMS

Problem Set A

Preparing a statement of cost of goods manufactured and an income statement.

SuSu Manufacturing Company makes water heaters. Selected account balances on December 31, 20X1, the end of its fiscal year, are given below. Data about the beginning and ending inventories are also given.

◀ **Problem 26.1A**
Objectives 26-1, 26-3

INSTRUCTIONS

1. Prepare a statement of cost of goods manufactured for 20X1.
2. Prepare an income statement for 20X1.

Accounts	Balances
Sales	$1,106,500
Sales Returns and Allowances	6,500
Materials Purchases	215,000
Direct Labor	250,000
Indirect Labor	40,000
Payroll Taxes—Factory	29,000
Utilities—Factory	20,500
Repairs and Maintenance—Factory	5,000
Indirect Materials and Supplies	5,000
Depreciation—Factory Building	6,000
Depreciation—Factory Equipment	5,000
Insurance—Factory	20,000

Accounts	Balances
Property Taxes—Factory	9,000
Sales Salaries Expense	150,000
Payroll Taxes Expense—Selling	15,000
Delivery Expense	9,000
Advertising Expense	10,000
Miscellaneous Selling Expenses	26,000
Officers' Salaries Expense	180,000
Office Salaries Expense	50,000
Payroll Taxes Expense—Administrative	23,000
Other Administrative Expenses	4,000
Income Tax Expense	4,095

Inventory Data	Jan. 1, 20X1	Dec. 31, 20X1
Finished Goods Inventory	$32,000	$30,000
Work in Process Inventory	45,000	40,000
Raw Materials Inventory	23,000	21,000

Analyze: For every dollar earned in net sales, what portion was spent on manufacturing costs?

Problem 26.2A
Objectives 26-1, 26-3, 26-4, 26-5, 26-6, 26-7, 26-8

▶ **Preparing a statement of cost of goods manufactured, an income statement, a statement of retained earnings, and a balance sheet; completing the worksheet; recording adjusting, closing, and reversing entries.**

RealTime Inc. manufactures parts for computers. The Trial Balance section of its worksheet and other year-end data follow.

INSTRUCTIONS

1. Prepare a 12-column manufacturing worksheet for the year ended December 31, 20X1. Enter the trial balance in the first two columns.
2. Using the data given, enter the adjustments. Then complete the worksheet. Label all inventory adjustments as (a).
3. Prepare a statement of cost of goods manufactured.
4. Prepare an income statement.
5. Prepare a statement of retained earnings. Additional data needed is as follows:
    a. Balance of *Retained Earnings* on January 1 was $603,300.
    b. Dividends declared and paid on common stock during the year amounted to $110,000.
    c. There were no changes in any other stockholders' equity accounts.
6. Prepare a balance sheet as of December 31, 20X1. There are 110,000 shares of $1 par common stock outstanding, out of the 110,000 shares authorized.
7. Record the adjusting entries shown on the worksheet in general journal form. For each journal entry, use the letter that identifies the adjustment on the worksheet. Make a separate entry for each inventory adjustment. Do not give explanations.
8. Prepare the closing entries for all accounts involved in the cost of goods manufactured.
9. Prepare the closing entries for all revenue and expense accounts and the *Manufacturing Summary* account.
10. Prepare the closing entry to close the *Income Summary* account.
11. Journalize the reversing entries. Date the entries January 1, 20X2.

YEAR-END DATA

a. Physical inventories taken on December 31, 20X1, show $31,000 of raw materials on hand and $45,000 of finished goods on hand. The work in process inventory is estimated to be $48,000 on the same date.
b. It is estimated that 2 percent of the outstanding accounts receivable might not be collectible.
c. Of the prepaid insurance, $4,900 covering the factory building and equipment has expired.
d. A physical inventory discloses $4,400 of factory supplies on hand at the end of the period.
e. Depreciation expense for the year is as follows: $9,800 on the factory building, $9,800 on the factory machines, and $3,000 on the office furniture. (Make a compound entry.)
f. Payroll accruals at the end of the period include $3,500 of direct labor and $500 of indirect labor.
g. Payroll taxes on accrued wages are social security, 6.2 percent, and Medicare tax, 1.45 percent.
h. Use an income tax rate of 25 percent. (Round to nearest dollar).

RealTime Inc.
Trial Balance
December 31, 20X1

ACCOUNT NAME	DEBIT	CREDIT
Cash	6 000 00	
Accounts Receivable	7 600 00	
Allowance for Doubtful Accounts		100 00
Raw Materials Inventory	3 500 00	
Work in Process Inventory	5 000 00	
Finished Goods Inventory	5 200 00	
Prepaid Insurance	700 00	
Factory Supplies	500 00	
Land	6 000 00	
Factory Building	30 000 00	
Accumulated Depreciation—Factory Building		1 960 00
Factory Machines	15 000 00	
Accumulated Depreciation—Factory Machines		1 960 00
Office Furniture and Equipment	3 000 00	
Accumulated Depreciation—Office Furniture and Equipment		600 00
Accounts Payable		8 600 00
Salaries and Wages Payable		
Income Tax Payable		
Social Security Tax Payable		
Medicare Tax Payable		
Employee Income Tax Payable		
Common Stock		11 000 00
Retained Earnings		4 933 00
Sales		100 550 00
Sales Returns and Allowances	650 00	
Materials Purchases	26 200 00	
Purchases Returns and Allowances		300 00
Freight In	1 100 00	
Direct Labor	19 100 00	
Indirect Labor	3 000 00	
Payroll Taxes Expenses—Factory	3 060 00	
Utilities—Factory	900 00	
Repairs and Maintenance—Factory	340 00	
Indirect Materials and Supplies	300 00	
Depreciation—Factory Building		
Depreciation—Factory Machines		
Insurance—Factory		
Property Taxes—Factory	700 00	
Sales Salaries Expense	9 500 00	
Payroll Taxes Expense—Sales	950 00	
Delivery Expense	600 00	
Advertising Expense	600 00	
Uncollectible Accounts Expense		
Miscellaneous Selling Expense	750 00	
Officers' Salaries Expense	15 500 00	
Office Salaries Expense	5 000 00	
Payroll Taxes Expense—Administrative	1 950 00	
Depreciation Expense—Office Furniture and Equipment		
Other Administrative Expenses	600 00	
Income Tax Expense	1 100 00	
Totals	174 400 00	174 400 00

Analyze: Assume that the industry standard for direct labor costs is 20 percent of cost of goods manufactured. How is RealTime Inc. performing as compared to this industry standard? Explain.

Problem Set B

Problem 26.1B
Objectives 26-1, 26-3

▶ **Preparing a statement of cost of goods manufactured and an income statement.**

Tebow Manufacturing Company makes camping equipment. Selected account balances (listed alphabetically) for this firm on December 31, 20X1, the end of its fiscal year, are given below. Data about the beginning and ending inventories is also shown.

INSTRUCTIONS

1. Prepare a statement of cost of goods manufactured for 20X1.
2. Prepare an income statement for 20X1.

Accounts	Balances
Depreciation—Factory Assets	$ 5,000
Depreciation Expense—Office Assets	3,000
Direct Labor	210,000
Freight In	5,000
Income Tax Expense	80,220
Indirect Labor	20,000
Indirect Materials and Supplies	7,000
Insurance—Factory	12,000
Materials Purchases	350,000
Office Salaries Expense	50,000
Officers' Salaries Expense	180,000
Other Administrative Expenses	1,800
Other Selling Expenses	15,000
Payroll Taxes Expense—Administration	20,000
Payroll Taxes Expense—Factory	20,000
Payroll Taxes Expense—Sales Salaries	9,000
Property Taxes—Office	2,000
Property Taxes—Factory	8,000
Purchases Returns and Allowances	4,000
Repairs and Maintenance—Factory	3,200
Repairs and Maintenance—Office	1,000
Sales	1,400,000
Sales Returns and Allowances	8,000
Sales Salaries Expense	100,000

Inventory Data	Jan. 1, 20X1	Dec. 31, 20X1
Finished Goods Inventory	$25,000	$30,000
Work in Process Inventory	30,000	32,000
Raw Materials Inventory	20,000	21,000

Analyze: What percentage of cost of goods manufactured did the company spend on raw materials used? On direct labor costs? On overhead costs?

Preparing a statement of cost of goods manufactured, an income statement, a statement of retained earnings, and a balance sheet; completing the worksheet; recording adjusting, closing, and reversing entries.

◀ **Problem 26.2B**

Objectives 26-1, 26-3, 26-4, 26-5, 26-6, 26-7, 26-8

Holding Inc. makes shipping containers. The Trial Balance section of its worksheet and other year-end data follow.

INSTRUCTIONS

1. Prepare a 12-column manufacturing worksheet for the fiscal year ended December 31, 20X1. Enter the trial balance in the first two columns.
2. Using the data given, enter the adjustments and complete the worksheet. Label all inventory adjustments as (a).
3. Prepare a statement of cost of goods manufactured.
4. Prepare an income statement.
5. Prepare a statement of retained earnings. Additional data follows:
    a. Balance of *Retained Earnings,* January 1, was $185,000.
    b. Dividends declared and paid on common stock during the year were $10,000.
6. Prepare a balance sheet as of December 31, 20X1. Common Stock, $1 par, was authorized for 100,000 shares and 50,000 shares were outstanding.
7. Record the adjusting entries shown on the worksheet in general journal form. For each journal entry, use the letter that identifies the adjustment on the worksheet. Make a separate entry for each inventory adjustment. Do not give explanations.
8. Prepare the closing entries for all accounts involved in the cost of goods manufactured.
9. Prepare the closing entries for all revenue and expense accounts and the *Manufacturing Summary* account.
10. Prepare the closing entry to close the *Income Summary* account.
11. Journalize the reversing entries. Date the entries January 1, 20X2.

YEAR-END DATA

a. Ending inventories: finished goods, $25,000; work in process, $36,000; and raw materials, $21,000.
b. Estimated uncollectible accounts: increase *Allowance for Uncollectible Accounts* to 4 percent of *Accounts Receivable.*
c. Expired insurance, $2,000; debit the *Insurance—Factory* account for the amount of the necessary adjustment.
d. Factory supplies on hand, $1,000.
e. Depreciation for the year: on factory building, $15,000; on factory machinery, $5,000; and on office equipment, $2,000.
f. Accrued factory wages: direct labor, $1,800; indirect labor, $200.
g. Accrued payroll taxes: social security, $124; Medicare tax, $29.
h. Total income tax expense for the year, $34,212.

Analyze: Assume that the industry standard for direct labor costs in its manufacturing industry is 31 percent of costs of goods manufactured. How does this company compare to others in regard to this standard? Explain.

Holding Inc.
Trial Balance
December 31, 20X1

ACCOUNT NAME	DEBIT	CREDIT
Cash	5 000 00	
Accounts Receivable	6 000 00	
Allowance for Doubtful Accounts		200 00
Raw Materials Inventory	3 000 00	
Work in Process Inventory	4 000 00	
Finished Goods Inventory	2 600 00	
Prepaid Insurance	240 00	
Factory Supplies	500 00	
Land	8 000 00	
Factory Building	15 000 00	
Accumulated Depreciation—Factory Building		6 000 00
Factory Machines	5 000 00	
Accumulated Depreciation—Factory Machines		2 000 00
Office Furniture and Equipment	2 000 00	
Accumulated Depreciation—Office Furniture and Equipment		800 00
Accounts Payable		4 600 00
Salaries and Wages Payable		
Income Tax Payable		
Social Security Tax Payable		
Medicare Tax Payable		
Employee Income Tax Payable		
Common Stock		5 000 00
Retained Earnings		17 500 00
Sales		110 650 00
Sales Returns and Allowances	1 650 00	
Materials Purchases	30 000 00	
Purchases Returns and Allowances		500 00
Freight In	900 00	
Direct Labor	16 000 00	
Indirect Labor	2 500 00	
Payroll Taxes—Factory	1 850 00	
Utilities—Factory	3 000 00	
Repairs and Maintenance—Factory	500 00	
Indirect Materials and Supplies	400 00	
Depreciation—Factory Building		
Depreciation—Factory Machines		
Insurance—Factory		
Property Taxes—Factory	600 00	
Sales Salaries Expense	10 000 00	
Payroll Taxes Expense—Sales	1 000 00	
Delivery Expense	750 00	
Advertising Expense	200 00	
Uncollectible Accounts Expense		
Miscellaneous Selling Expense	650 00	
Officers' Salaries Expense	18 000 00	
Office Salaries Expense	4 000 00	
Payroll Taxes Expense—Administrative	2 200 00	
Depreciation Expense—Office Furniture and Equipment		
Other Administrative Expenses	1 100 00	
Income Tax Expense	1 600 00	
Manufacturing Summary		
Income Summary		
Totals	147 250 00	147 250 00

Critical Thinking Problem 26.1

Incomplete Records

In January 20X1, Kate Kasal started Warmers, a business manufacturing ladies' scarves. Kasal was so busy with the manufacturing side of the business that she did not take time to set up detailed accounting records; the business checkbook was her only record of accounting transactions. When cash came in, she deposited the receipts in the bank, and when invoices were due, she wrote checks to pay them. Now it is the end of the year and Kasal would like to know how the business did during its first year of operation.

She asks for your help in summarizing the first year's operations. A review of the checkbook yields the following information:

- Raw materials purchases paid for totaled $105,000.
- Wages paid to employees totaled $70,000, with payroll taxes relating to their wages of $7,000.
- Factory supplies cost $2,000.
- Utility bills paid totaled $2,200.
- Repairs to factory equipment were $800.
- Rent of $16,000 was paid on the factory building.

Discussions with the owner disclose that $2,000 of raw materials have been received and used in the manufacturing process but have not yet been paid because the invoice for the purchase is not due until next year. Kasal has determined depreciation on the factory equipment for the year to be $1,000. An inventory taken on the last day of the year showed $3,000 of raw materials on hand, $4,500 of scarves partially completed, and $3,500 of finished scarves waiting to be sold.

INSTRUCTIONS

Prepare a statement of cost of goods manufactured for 20X1 for Warmers.

Critical Thinking Problem 26.2

Inventories

Certain information about the statement of cost of goods manufactured and the income statement for the year ended December 31, 20X1, for Paul's Production, Inc., is given below:

Beginning inventory of finished goods, 105 percent of ending inventory	
Work in process inventory, January 1, 95 percent of ending inventory	
Net income	$130,000
Raw materials inventory, January 1	25,000
Direct labor costs	100,000
Manufacturing overhead, 120 percent of direct labor costs	
Work in process inventory, December 31	22,000
Finished goods inventory, December 31	35,000
Raw materials inventory, December 31	27,000
Net purchases of raw material	179,000
Net sales	650,000

INSTRUCTIONS

Prepare a statement of cost of goods manufactured and an income statement for the year.

Analyze: Did total inventories for the business increase or decrease during the year? By what amount?

BUSINESS CONNECTIONS

Manufacturing Concerns

Managerial FOCUS

1. Why do managers need special manufacturing records and a separate statement reporting the costs involved in producing goods?
2. How can an inventory be taken if work in process items are in varying stages of completion at the end of the accounting period?
3. Why might management want to separate direct and indirect labor costs?
4. Why should the statement of cost of goods manufactured not be used alone to measure efficiency and control costs?
5. In this chapter, we said that the value of sales supplies and office supplies on hand at period-end is considered too small to justify an adjusting entry. If this omission were questioned (arguing that the accounting records should show everything), what would you say?

Hiding Returns

Internal Control and FRAUD PREVENTION

Pellosi is the manager of a company that produces toasters. He has instructed his production department to replace a steel handle shaft with a plastic shaft. This will save the company $1 per toaster. Since making this change, the toasters are being returned in great quantities because of handle breakage. Pellosi tries to hide his poor decision. He instructs the accountant to ignore the returned items and put them back into inventory so they can be resold. Manufacturing was told to install new plastic handles and place the toasters into finished goods. What effect does Pellosi's action have on the Cost of Goods Sold section? Is it ethical? What could be the eventual result of his actions?

Vendor Allowances

Financial Statement ANALYSIS

Home Depot

Refer to the *2018 Annual Report (for the fiscal year ended February 3, 2019)* for The Home Depot, Inc., in Appendix A.

In the Notes to Consolidated Financial Statements, find the paragraph Vendor Allowances.

1. Describe how the vendor allowance is recorded and reflected in the financial statements.
2. Do all vendors qualify for a vendor allowance?

Cost Flowchart

TEAMWORK

The costs for items manufactured are collected in work in process and then sent to finished goods when the items are complete. When the items are sold, the costs are taken out of finished goods and put into cost of goods sold. As a group, select a product to be manufactured, such as a skateboard. Determine the direct costs to make this product. Assume the indirect costs are equal to the direct labor costs. Show the class how the costs for your product will move from work in process to finished goods to cost of goods sold.

Answers to Comprehensive Self Review

1. The cost of those employees who are working directly on the product being manufactured.
2. Materials that are insignificant in cost or relatively minor in the total cost of materials.
3. The balances of the beginning inventories of raw materials and work in process are entered in the Adjustments columns as credits to the two inventory accounts and debits to the *Manufacturing Summary* account. The ending inventories of raw materials and work in process are entered in the Adjustments columns as debits to the inventory accounts and credits to the *Manufacturing Summary* account. The beginning inventory of finished goods is credited to *Finished Goods Inventory* and debited to *Income Summary.* The ending inventory of finished goods is debited to *Finished Goods Inventory* and credited to *Income Summary.*
4. No, the account is used only during the closing process.
5. The adjusting entries for accrued expenses and accrued income.

Job Order Cost Accounting

Chapter 27

www.bayliner.com

Gary Blakeley/Shutterstock

There are few things more relaxing and beautiful than floating effortlessly in your own boat on the open water with the warm sun caressing your face and the wind softly ruffling your hair. This is the dream of many that has made Bayliner the world's largest manufacturer of recreational boats. But as you are lounging on the deck as your boat gently rocks in the rippling water, rarely do you stop to ponder what materials and how many labor hours were used to construct your floating paradise.

Bayliner was established in 1957 by Orin Edson and now operates as a division of Brunswick Corporation. Bayliner offers 33 different boat models that can be purchased either from its global network of worldwide dealers or custom ordered on its website. Each boat manufactured, whether premade for a dealer's showroom or custom ordered, has different features and specifications, and, as such, each boat that is crafted requires its own recordkeeping of costs. Bayliner needs to know the cost of each boat made to be able to accurately determine the sales price; the higher the cost to manufacture, the higher the sales price.

This job order cost accounting system provides Bayliner with the cost data relative to each individual boat, including materials costs, direct labor costs, and overhead costs, enabling it to assess the profit earned on each unit. The more accurately Bayliner tracks the cost of each boat, the more accurate and reliable the sales and profit data will be.

thinking critically
What types of raw materials inventories do you think Bayliner holds?

LEARNING OBJECTIVES

- **27-1** Explain how a job order cost accounting system operates.
- **27-2** Journalize the purchase and issuance of direct and indirect materials.
- **27-3** Maintain perpetual inventory records.
- **27-4** Record labor costs incurred and charge labor into production.
- **27-5** Compute overhead rates and apply overhead to jobs.
- **27-6** Compute overapplied or underapplied overhead and report it in the financial statements.
- **27-7** Maintain job order cost sheets.
- **27-8** Record the cost of jobs completed and the cost of goods sold under a perpetual inventory system.
- **27-9** Define the accounting terms new to this chapter.

NEW TERMS

finished goods subsidiary ledger
job order
job order cost accounting
job order cost sheet
just-in-time system
manufacturing overhead ledger
materials requisition
overapplied overhead
overhead application rate
perpetual inventory system
process cost accounting
production order
raw materials ledger record
raw materials subsidiary ledger
standard costs
time ticket
underapplied overhead
work in process subsidiary ledger

Section 1

SECTION OBJECTIVES	TERMS TO LEARN
>> 27-1 Explain how a job order cost accounting system operates. **WHY IT'S IMPORTANT** Manufacturing businesses choose the accounting system best suited to provide detailed information about production costs.	job order job order cost accounting just-in-time system perpetual inventory system process cost accounting production order standard costs

Cost Accounting

The statement of cost of goods manufactured provides information on manufacturing costs. However, it cannot be used to determine the cost of each unit produced and does not help in controlling costs during the accounting period. In this and subsequent chapters, you will learn how to calculate the cost of producing items and track manufacturing costs.

>> **27-1 OBJECTIVE**
Explain how a job order cost accounting system operates.

Types of Cost Accounting Systems

There are two principal cost accounting systems:

- job order cost accounting system
- process cost accounting system

This chapter covers the job order cost accounting system. Chapter 28 introduces process cost accounting.

Standard cost accounting is described in Chapter 29. Standard cost accounting may be used with either the job order cost system or the process cost system.

Job Order Cost Accounting

important!

Job Order Cost Accounting
Under a job order cost accounting system, unit costs are determined for products manufactured for each job order.

The job order cost accounting system is used by businesses that produce special orders or produce more than one product in batches. Businesses that use job order cost accounting systems include custom drapery manufacturers, machine tool plants, and furniture manufacturers.

Under the **job order cost accounting** system, each "batch" of goods is produced under a **production order,** which is also known as a **job order.** Unit costs are determined for each production order. To calculate the cost per unit, divide the manufacturing costs for each order by the number of units produced.

Process Cost Accounting

important!

Process Cost Accounting
Under the process cost accounting system, the unit cost of a product is computed by adding the unit costs from each producing department.

The **process cost accounting** system is used when standard products are manufactured using a continuous process. Businesses that use process cost accounting systems include cement plants, flour mills, and manufacturers of cake mixes.

Under the process cost accounting system, the cost of a unit of product is the sum of the unit costs in each department through which the product passes while it is being manufactured.

Standard Cost Accounting

Standard costs are a measure of what costs should be in an efficient operation. Managers can compare actual costs with standard costs to determine manufacturing efficiency. Standard cost accounting systems can be used with a job order cost accounting system or a process cost accounting system.

Cost Flows in a Job Order Cost System

ELI Manufacturing Inc. makes several types of work tables. Customers order various tables in different quantities. ELI does not have a continuous manufacturing process; it produces the tables in batches. The business uses the job order cost system, which is designed to facilitate recording costs related to the following four manufacturing operations:

- Procurement (Purchasing)—obtaining materials, labor, and services necessary for the manufacturing process.
- Production—using materials, labor, and services on the factory floor.
- Warehousing—handling and storing finished goods.
- Selling—removing finished goods from the storeroom to fill orders.

Figure 27.1 summarizes the flow of costs through a job order cost accounting system.

To understand how *Raw Materials Inventory, Work in Process Inventory,* and *Finished Goods Inventory* fit into the flow of costs shown in Figure 27.1, you need to comprehend the perpetual inventory system.

The Perpetual Inventory System

The use of a **perpetual inventory system** tracks the inventories on hand at all times. The following are typical procedures for the three types of inventory in a manufacturing concern:

Raw Materials Inventory Throughout the accounting period, raw materials and manufacturing supplies are recorded in the *Raw Materials Inventory* account. Purchases of raw materials and manufacturing supplies increase the *Raw Materials Inventory* account. The costs of materials used in production reduce the *Raw Materials Inventory* account. Direct materials used in production increase the *Work in Process Inventory* account. The costs of indirect materials and supplies used in production increase the *Manufacturing Overhead* account.

ABOUT ACCOUNTING

Survey of Manufacturers Private industry and trade associations use results from the U.S. Census Bureau's Annual Survey of Manufacturers to plan operations, analyze markets, and make investment and production decisions.

FIGURE 27.1

Flow of Costs through Four Phases of Manufacturing

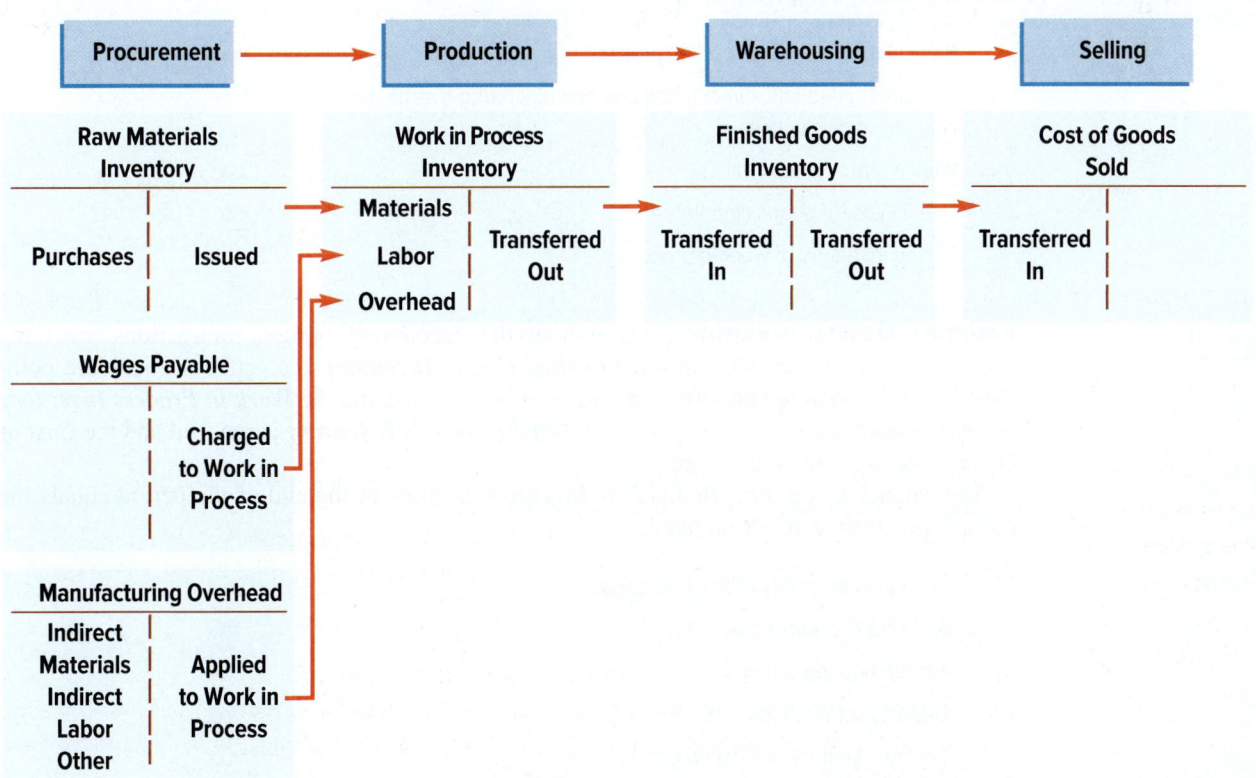

recall

Cost Accounting System
In a manufacturing firm, managers must understand the costs of producing goods.

At the end of the accounting period, the balance of the *Raw Materials Inventory* account reflects the cost of materials and supplies on hand:

Beginning inventory of raw materials	xxx
Add purchases during period	xxx
Total available for use	xxx
Deduct materials used during period	xxx
Ending inventory of raw materials	xxx

At least once a year, a physical inventory count is taken to check the accuracy of the recorded inventory. In the event of a difference, the *Raw Materials Inventory* account is adjusted to agree with the physical inventory count.

> As a global leader in RFID (radio frequency identification), Avery Dennison's track-and-trace technologies can help accelerate inventory process speeds, prevent losses, and improve efficiencies throughout the stages of customers' supply chains. Health care facilities, factories, libraries, airlines, retailers, and document management services are just a few of the industries that have enhanced the effectiveness of their operations with RFID solutions.

Work in Process Inventory Throughout the accounting period, transactions involving production are recorded in the *Work in Process Inventory* account. All manufacturing costs placed into production during the accounting period are recorded in *Work in Process Inventory*. *Work in Process Inventory* is increased when direct materials are issued for production and for direct labor and manufacturing overhead charged into production. As production is completed, the manufacturing costs reduce *Work in Process Inventory* and increase *Finished Goods Inventory*. See Figure 27.1 for the flow of costs into and out of *Work in Process Inventory*.

The balance in the *Work in Process Inventory* account at the end of the period reflects the cost of partially completed units:

Beginning inventory of work in process	xxx
Add direct materials, direct labor, and manufacturing overhead charged to production	xxx
Work in process subtotal	xxx
Deduct cost of goods completed	xxx
Ending inventory of work in process	xxx

Finished Goods Inventory Throughout the accounting period, transactions involving finished goods are recorded in the *Finished Goods Inventory* account. As goods are completed, the *Finished Goods Inventory* account is increased and the *Work in Process Inventory* account is decreased. As goods are sold, *Finished Goods Inventory* is reduced and the *Cost of Goods Sold* account is increased.

The balance of the *Finished Goods Inventory* account at the end of the period equals the cost of the finished goods on hand:

Beginning inventory of finished goods	xxx
Add cost of goods manufactured	xxx
Finished goods subtotal	xxx
Deduct cost of goods sold	xxx
Ending inventory of finished goods	xxx

At least once a year, a physical inventory count of all inventories is taken to check the accuracy of the recorded inventory.

Just-In-Time Inventory Systems

Many manufacturing companies attempt to eliminate raw materials inventory by using the **just-in-time system,** in which raw materials are ordered so they arrive just in time to be placed into production. When the goods arrive, they are moved immediately to the factory floor and the *Work in Process Inventory* account is increased. No entry is made in the *Raw Materials Inventory* account; in fact, there might not be a *Raw Materials Inventory* account in those industrial settings.

The advantages of a just-in-time system are that it reduces the amount of working capital tied up in inventory, the space necessary for inventory storage, and the costs associated with storeroom personnel, insurance, and recordkeeping.

Just-in-time systems are risky unless the source of supply is highly dependable. Late deliveries or damaged materials could cause an interruption in supply that could halt manufacturing operations, resulting in a delay of delivery of the finished products to the buyers.

Section 1 Review

1. When is a job order cost accounting system used?
   a. in a business that makes only one product at a time
   b. by a business that makes many products at the same time
   c. by a retail business
   d. by professional athletic teams

2. Why are physical inventory counts made when a perpetual inventory system is used?
   a. same as last year principle requires it
   b. it verifies inventory numbers recorded
   c. SEC recommends it
   d. CFO typically has doubts about the purchasing department

3. What is a standard cost?
   a. actual cost of production
   b. estimated cost of production
   c. cost of production in an efficiently run business
   d. budgeted cost of production

4. Job order cost accounting is appropriate:
   a. only when a company orders materials just in time to be placed into production.
   b. when there are continuous operations on standard types of products.
   c. when a company produces more than one product in batches rather than on a continuous basis.
   d. only for goods produced on special order.

5. A standard cost system can be used:
   a. with either the job order cost system or the process cost system.
   b. only with the process cost system.
   c. only with the job order cost system.
   d. in place of the job order cost system.

6. The beginning balance of *Work in Process Inventory* was $40,000. During the year, direct materials of $200,000, direct labor of $100,000, and manufacturing overhead of $20,000 were charged to production. The ending inventory of work in process is $30,000. What is the cost of goods completed?
   a. $340,000
   b. $390,000
   c. $310,000
   d. $330,000

Section 2

SECTION OBJECTIVES

>> 27-2 Journalize the purchase and issuance of direct and indirect materials.
   WHY IT'S IMPORTANT
   Raw materials must be accounted for.

>> 27-3 Maintain perpetual inventory records.
   WHY IT'S IMPORTANT
   Physical counts are compared to inventory records.

>> 27-4 Record labor costs incurred and charge labor into production.
   WHY IT'S IMPORTANT
   Labor costs are often substantial.

>> 27-5 Compute overhead rates and apply overhead to jobs.
   WHY IT'S IMPORTANT
   Businesses apply overhead to specific production jobs.

>> 27-6 Compute overapplied or underapplied overhead and report it in the financial statements.
   WHY IT'S IMPORTANT
   Financial statements reflect a period's costs.

TERMS TO LEARN

finished goods subsidiary ledger
manufacturing overhead ledger
materials requisition
overapplied overhead
overhead application rate
raw materials ledger record
raw materials subsidiary ledger
time ticket
underapplied overhead
work in process subsidiary ledger

Job Order Cost Accounting System

Examples of companies that use the job order cost accounting system are toy manufacturers, automobile manufacturers, and computer manufacturers.

A Job Order Cost Accounting System

The job order cost accounting system has procedures to record the costs incurred, the costs of items placed into production, and the transfer of products to finished goods.

Perpetual Inventory Accounts

The job order cost system uses three inventory accounts: *Raw Materials Inventory, Work in Process Inventory,* and *Finished Goods Inventory.* Each inventory account has a related subsidiary account. The **raw materials subsidiary ledger** contains a record for each of the different types of raw materials and manufacturing supplies used by the firm.

The **work in process subsidiary ledger** includes a job order cost sheet for each job in production. The **finished goods subsidiary ledger** contains a record for each of the different types of finished products.

Accounting for Materials

The *Raw Materials Inventory* account reflects all of the transactions related to raw materials and supplies.

Purchases of Materials Purchases of raw materials and supplies are debited to the *Raw Materials Inventory* account. When a company uses a voucher register system, a special column is typically set up for Raw Materials Debit. All material purchases would be debited to that column. For simplicity, the raw material purchases are shown below as they would be entered in a general journal:

	20X1					
1						1
2	Jun.	30	Raw Materials Inventory	15 000 00		2
3			Accounts Payable		15 000 00	3
4			Cost of materials and supplies			4
5			purchased during June			5

important!

Perpetual Inventory System
When a cost accounting system is used, perpetual inventory records are kept for raw materials, work in process, and finished goods.

Raw Materials Ledger For internal control purposes, all purchases are made using prenumbered purchase orders. When the materials and supplies are received, they are checked and counted or weighed. They are sent to the storeroom with a report showing what was received. Before the invoice is approved for payment, a copy of the receiving report is compared with the supplier's invoice and with the purchase order. Prices and quantities are entered in each item's **raw materials ledger record.**

Figure 27.2 shows a raw materials ledger record. This record is for BRC02, a brace. It shows no balance for material BRC02 at the beginning of the month. On June 4, 200 braces were purchased on Purchase Order PO-3 for $1 each. After this transaction, the 200 units are reflected in the Balance section of the record.

Materials Requisition Materials or supplies are issued by the storeroom only upon presentation of a materials requisition signed by an authorized employee. The **materials requisition** describes the item and quantity needed and shows the job or purpose. Jobs are identified by a job order number, which is assigned when production on the job begins. The raw materials ledger clerk prices the items listed on the materials requisition. The storeroom clerk uses the materials requisition to record materials issued on the individual raw materials ledger records.

Figure 27.3 illustrates a requisition for ELI Manufacturing Inc. issuing 100 units of material BRC02 on June 8.

Now look at the second entry on the raw materials ledger record in Figure 27.2. This entry on Requisition R-24 shows the issuance of 100 braces. The braces cost $1 each. After this transaction, 100 units are on hand at a cost of $1 per brace.

At the end of the month, the raw materials ledger clerk at ELI Manufacturing Inc. summarized all issued material requisitions. The summary classified the direct materials costs by jobs

>> 27-2 OBJECTIVE
Journalize the purchase and issuance of direct and indirect materials.

>> 27-3 OBJECTIVE
Maintain perpetual inventory records.

FIGURE 27.2
Raw Materials Ledger Record

RAW MATERIALS LEDGER RECORD
(FIFO Cost Method)

ITEM: Brace   NUMBER: BRC02

DATE		REF.	RECEIVED			ISSUED			BALANCE		
			UNITS	PRICE	AMOUNT	UNITS	PRICE	AMOUNT	UNITS	PRICE	AMOUNT
20X1		Bal									0
Jun.	4	PO-3	200	1 00	200 00				200	1 00	200 00
	8	R-24				100	1 00	100 00	100	1 00	100 00
	12	PO-14	150	1 10	165 00				100	1 00	
									150	1 10	265 00
	17	R-51				100	1 00				
						50	1 10	155 00	100	1 10	110 00
	24	PO-32	100	1 15	115 00				100	1 10	
									100	1 15	225 00
	29	R-90				100	1 10	110 00	100	1 15	115 00

FIGURE 27.3

Materials Requisition Form

MATERIALS REQUISITION   No. R-24

Charged to Account No. **122**
Job No. **J-5**   Date: **June 8, 20X1**

Quantity	Description	Unit Cost	Total Cost
100	Braces BRC02	1 00	100 00

Authorized by: *J. Sinclair*
Issued by: *E. Layden*
Received by: *T. Santos*

> **recall**
>
> **Subsidiary Records**
>
> The job order cost sheet is a subsidiary record showing all manufacturing costs charged to a specific job. The subsidiary record supports the **Work in Process Inventory** account.

> **recall**
>
> Methods for determining costs of inventory:
> - First-in, first-out (FIFO)
> - Last-in, first-out (LIFO)
> - Average cost of similar items during a specified period (average cost)

and listed the supplies and indirect materials issued. The summary is the basis for entries on the job order cost sheets and for a journal entry to record materials issued. The journal entry has a debit to **Work in Process Inventory** for $28,000 of direct materials placed into production, a debit to **Manufacturing Overhead** for $2,000 of indirect materials and supplies issued, and a credit to **Raw Materials Inventory** for the $30,000. The journal entry to record materials and supplies issued is as follows:

20X1					
Jun.	30	Work in Process Inventory		28 000 00	
		Manufacturing Overhead		2 000 00	
		Raw Materials Inventory			30 000 00
		Cost of materials and supplies			
		issued during month			

Cost Basis In Chapter 17, you learned that there are different methods for determining the cost of inventory including FIFO, LIFO, and average cost methods. In conformity with the consistency principle, each business chooses a cost method and follows it. ELI Manufacturing Inc. uses the FIFO method for raw materials. Figure 27.2 shows how the FIFO method is applied to purchases and requisitions of BRC02 braces. The entry on June 12 reflects the purchase of an additional 150 units at a cost of $1.10 per unit. After this transaction, there are 250 units on hand. The units are identified with specific purchases. There are 100 units from the purchase of June 4, at a cost of $1.00 per unit, and 150 units from the purchase of June 12, at a cost of $1.10 per unit. The entry on June 17 reflects the issuance of 150 units. Under the FIFO method, the units issued are assumed to be:

100 units from the purchase of June 4	
100 units × $1.00 per unit	$100.00
50 units from the purchase of June 12	
50 units × $1.10 per unit	55.00
Total 150 units	$155.00

It is assumed that all units purchased on the June 4 order were issued. The 100 units on hand come from the June 12 purchase. The balance of BRC02 after the June 17 issuance is 100 units at $110 (100 × $1.10).

Accounting for Labor

Factory labor costs are identified as direct labor, which is recorded in **Work in Process Inventory,** or as indirect labor, which is recorded in **Manufacturing Overhead.** The factory labor costs incurred during June follow:

Payroll Period		Direct Labor	Indirect Labor	Total
June	8	$ 3,000	$ 800	$ 3,800
	15	2,000	300	2,300
	22	2,500	200	2,700
	29	2,500	200	2,700
Totals		$10,000	$1,500	$11,500

>> **27-4 OBJECTIVE**
Record labor costs incurred and charge labor into production.

The entry to record the payroll data in general journal form follows:

	20X1				
Jun.	30	Work in Process Inv. (Direct Labor)	10 000 00		
		Manufacturing Overhead (Indirect Labor)	1 500 00		
		Social Security Tax Payable		713 00	
		Medicare Tax Payable		166 75	
		Employee Income Tax Payable		1 200 00	
		Salaries and Wages Payable		9 420 25	
		Total labor costs for June			

important!

Work in Process Inventory
The balance in the **Work in Process Inventory** account at the end of the period reflects the cost of work still incomplete at that time.

Employees record the time they enter and leave the plant. Workers complete a separate **time ticket** for each job indicating the job performed and the starting and stopping time. If the worker is idle for part of the day, an "idle time" time ticket is prepared so that the cost of idle time can be charged appropriately. This process today is paperless in most larger manufacturing concerns.

Usually, idle time is charged to manufacturing overhead. If, however, the idle time is due solely to the specifications or peculiarities of a particular job, the idle time costs are charged to that job. Figure 27.4 shows a manual time ticket.

A cost clerk computes the total time shown on the time ticket and applies the worker's rate to obtain the cost of the labor. Labor time tickets are sorted by job and summarized at the end of each payroll period for entry on individual job order cost sheets. The total charged to all the cost sheets must agree with the direct labor debited to **Work in Process Inventory.**

Many factories use automated systems for recording the time spent by an employee on each task. Each employee has an identification card. When starting and completing work on

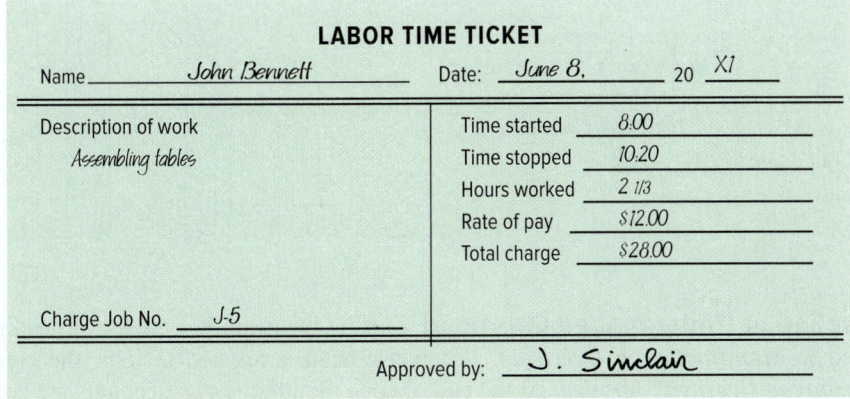

FIGURE 27.4

Labor Time Ticket

27-5 OBJECTIVE
Compute overhead rates and apply overhead to jobs.

Accounting for Manufacturing Overhead

Manufacturing overhead includes all manufacturing costs except direct materials and direct labor. Common overhead items are indirect labor, indirect materials, depreciation of factory buildings and equipment, insurance, utilities, property taxes, repairs and maintenance, and payroll taxes on factory labor. There are different ways to enter overhead costs in the accounting records. ELI Manufacturing Inc. uses an account called **Manufacturing Overhead.** A subsidiary ledger, the **manufacturing overhead ledger,** contains a record for each overhead item. The overhead costs incurred are debited to the control account, and the details are posted to the appropriate subsidiary ledger accounts.

We have already seen that ELI incurred indirect materials costs (supplies) of $2,000 and indirect labor costs of $1,500. These amounts were debited to **Manufacturing Overhead** (see entries under "Materials Requisition" and "Accounting for Labor"). In addition to indirect materials and indirect labor, the company incurred overhead costs of $3,500. The entry to record these additional overhead costs in general journal form follows:

	Jun.	30	Manufacturing Overhead		3 500 00	
			Accounts Payable and other accounts			3 500 00
			Overhead costs for June			

Basing Overhead Application on Direct Labor Costs Several methods are used to apply overhead to specific jobs, including those based on direct labor costs or direct labor hours. ELI Manufacturing Inc.'s accountant estimates overhead and direct labor costs for the coming year. Estimated total overhead is divided by estimated total direct labor costs. The result is a predetermined **overhead application rate.** Using summaries of labor time tickets, direct labor is recorded for each job. At the same time, the direct labor costs are multiplied by the overhead rate. The result is the amount of overhead to record for each job.

ELI Manufacturing Inc. calculated an overhead rate of 75 percent of direct labor costs as follows:

$$\frac{\text{Estimated overhead costs}}{\text{Estimated direct labor costs}} = \frac{\$90{,}000}{\$120{,}000} = 75 \text{ percent}$$

In June, direct labor costs charged to jobs totaled $10,000. The overhead applied to jobs was $7,500 ($10,000 × 0.75). This is recorded in general journal form as follows:

	Jun.	30	Work in Process Inventory		7 500 00	
			Manufacturing Overhead Applied			7 500 00
			Overhead applied to jobs in June at			
			75% of direct labor costs			

27-6 OBJECTIVE
Compute overapplied or underapplied overhead and report it in the financial statements.

Overapplied or Underapplied Overhead During the year, the actual overhead incurred is debited to **Manufacturing Overhead.** When overhead is applied to jobs, the credit is to **Manufacturing Overhead Applied.** At the end of each month, the two accounts are compared:

- If the total debits in *Manufacturing Overhead* are higher than the total credits in *Manufacturing Overhead Applied,* there is **underapplied overhead.**
- If the total debits in *Manufacturing Overhead* are less than the total credits in *Manufacturing Overhead Applied,* there is **overapplied overhead.**

In June, overhead was overapplied by $500:

Manufacturing Overhead (debits)		
Indirect materials and supplies	$2,000	
Indirect labor	1,500	
Other overhead costs	3,500	
Total charged to manufacturing overhead		$7,000
Manufacturing Overhead Applied (credits)		−7,500
Overapplied overhead in June		$ 500

During the year, underapplied or overapplied overhead occurs, in part, because the application rate is an average based on estimates for the year, and fluctuations happen from month to month.

At the end of the year, the *Manufacturing Overhead Applied* account is closed into the *Manufacturing Overhead* account. The balance in the *Manufacturing Overhead* account represents the underapplied or overapplied overhead for the year, which is closed to the *Cost of Goods Sold* account. The overapplied or underapplied amount appears as an adjustment to the Cost of Goods Sold amount on the income statement.

Overapplied manufacturing overhead means that too much cost was included in Cost of Goods Sold. Therefore, Cost of Goods Sold must be reduced! The opposite is true for underapplied manufacturing overhead.

Section 2 Review

1. When direct materials are issued from the storeroom, are any entries made in the subsidiary records?
   a. Increase raw material item record.
   b. Decrease raw material item record.
   c. No entry is needed.
   d. Cost of direct labor is added into raw material subsidiary item.

2. What entry is made for indirect materials issued from the storeroom?
   a. Debit *Raw Materials;* credit *Work in Process.*
   b. Debit *Work in Process;* credit *Raw Materials.*
   c. Debit *Manufacturing Overhead;* credit *Raw Materials.*
   d. Debit *Work in Process;* credit *Purchases.*

3. What is underapplied overhead?
   a. Less than actual overhead was applied.
   b. More than actual overhead was applied.
   c. Labor overtime costs were not accurately recorded.
   d. Direct material costs were less than standard.

4. The entry to record the application of overhead to jobs consists of a:
   a. debit to *Manufacturing Overhead Applied* and a credit to *Manufacturing Overhead.*
   b. debit to *Manufacturing Overhead* and a credit to *Manufacturing Overhead Applied.*
   c. debit to *Work in Process Inventory* and a credit to *Manufacturing Overhead Applied.*
   d. debit to *Manufacturing Overhead Applied* and a credit to *Work in Process Inventory.*

5. At the end of the year, any underapplied overhead is shown as an adjustment to:
   a. *Cost of Goods Sold.*
   b. *Manufacturing Overhead.*
   c. *Raw Materials Inventory.*
   d. *Manufacturing Overhead Applied.*

6. A firm applies overhead based on direct labor hours. The firm estimates direct labor hours of 5,000 and overhead costs of $30,000. What is the overhead application rate?
   a. $5 per direct labor hour
   b. $6 per direct labor hour
   c. $150 per direct labor hour
   d. $30 per direct labor hour

Section 3

SECTION OBJECTIVES	TERM TO LEARN
>> 27-7 Maintain job order cost sheets. **WHY IT'S IMPORTANT** The job order cost sheet shows all manufacturing costs for a specific job. >> 27-8 Record the cost of jobs completed and the cost of goods sold under a perpetual inventory system. **WHY IT'S IMPORTANT** Manufacturing records need to reflect all the costs of a manufactured product.	job order cost sheet

Accounting for Job Orders

Each new job started in production is assigned a number for identification and reference. A job order cost sheet is also set up at this time.

>> **27-7 OBJECTIVE**
Maintain job order cost sheets.

The Job Order Cost Sheet

A **job order cost sheet** is a record of all manufacturing costs charged to a specific job. It is set up when a job starts production. The cost sheets for all jobs currently in production constitute the subsidiary ledger for the *Work in Process Inventory* account.

Figure 27.5 shows the job order cost sheet for job J-8. The job was started and completed during the month of June. The information at the top of the sheet shows the job number and the product being manufactured, the start and completion dates, and the number of units ordered and produced:

- Direct materials used are entered weekly in the Materials section from summaries of materials requisitions.
- Direct labor costs are entered weekly in the Labor section from summaries of the labor time tickets.

FIGURE 27.5

Job Order Cost Sheet

JOB ORDER COST SHEET

For Stock __X__ Job No. __J-8__ Date __June 15, 20X1__
Customer's Name _____ Started __June 8, 20X1__
Address _____ Completed __June 15, 20X1__
Item __Slang Tables__ Quantity __25__ (ordered) __25__ (completed)

MATERIALS		LABOR		OVERHEAD APPLIED			SUMMARY	
Date	Amount	Date	Amount	Date	Rate	Amount	Item	Amount
June 8	150 00	June 8	150 50	June 8	75%	112 88	Materials	250 00
15	100 00	15	75 00	15	75%	56 25	Labor	225 50
							Overhead	169 13
							Total	644 63
							Unit Cost	25 785
							Comments:	
Totals	250 00		225 50			169 13		

- Overhead is computed using the predetermined overhead application rate (75 percent of direct labor costs). Overhead is entered in the Overhead Applied section.
- When the job has been completed, the costs are totaled in the Summary section. The unit cost is determined by dividing the total cost by the number of units produced.

Accounting for Work Completed

As each job is completed, the units are transferred to finished goods. The job order cost sheet contains the quantity, unit cost, and total cost needed to post to the inventory record in the finished goods subsidiary ledger. The finished goods ledger record is similar to the raw materials ledger record shown in Figure 27.2.

At the end of the month, a summary of completed jobs is prepared and an entry is made to transfer the total cost from the *Work in Process Inventory* account to the *Finished Goods Inventory* account:

>> **27-8 OBJECTIVE**
Record the cost of jobs completed and the cost of goods sold under a perpetual inventory system.

	20X1				
	Jun.	30	Finished Goods Inventory	30 500 00	
			Work in Process Inventory		30 500 00
			Cost of jobs completed during June		

Accounting for Cost of Goods Sold

As goods are sold, sales invoices are prepared for the customers. The cost of each order is entered on the office copy of the invoice; the cost information comes from the finished goods ledger. Entries are made in the finished goods ledger to record the quantities and costs of units sold. At month-end, the total cost of goods sold is determined from a summary of the information entered on the invoice copies:

	Jun.	30	Cost of Goods Sold	40 000 00	
			Finished Goods Inventory		40 000 00
			Cost of goods sold during June		

	Jun.	30	Accounts Receivable	70 000 00	
			Sales		70 000 00
			Sales for June		

MANAGERIAL IMPLICATIONS

JOB ORDER COST SYSTEM

- The job order cost system keeps managers informed of the cost of manufacturing specific orders or batches of goods. It permits the computation of the cost per unit of product.
- The use of an overhead application rate helps to develop a consistent unit cost from month to month because the effects of unusual expenses or variations in monthly volume of output are averaged over the entire year.
- Unit costs help management to evaluate and maintain efficiency.
- Perpetual inventory procedures are useful tools for inventory control because they help keep management informed about inventory balances.

THINKING CRITICALLY
When is it appropriate to use a job order cost accounting system?

On the June income statement, the *Cost of Goods Sold* account and adjustment for underapplied or overapplied overhead appear as follows:

Sales		$70,000
Cost of Goods Sold (per ledger account)	$40,000	
Subtract Overapplied Manufacturing Overhead	− 500	
Cost of Goods Sold (adjusted)		39,500
Gross Profit on Sales		$30,500

Instead of showing overapplied or underapplied overhead on the income statement, the accountant might prefer to show actual manufacturing costs on the statement of cost of goods manufactured.

Summary of Cost Flow Through Inventory Accounts

The flow of costs during June is illustrated in the following three perpetual inventory accounts and the *Cost of Goods Sold* account. ELI Manufacturing Inc. had inventories of raw materials and finished goods on June 1 but no beginning inventory of work in process.

ACCOUNT Raw Materials Inventory   **ACCOUNT NO.** 121

DATE	DESCRIPTION	POST. REF.	DEBIT	CREDIT	BALANCE DEBIT	BALANCE CREDIT
20X1						
Jun. 1	Balance	✓			22,500.00	
30		J1	15,000.00		37,500.00	
30		J1		30,000.00	7,500.00	

ACCOUNT Work in Process Inventory   **ACCOUNT NO.** 122

DATE	DESCRIPTION	POST. REF.	DEBIT	CREDIT	BALANCE DEBIT	BALANCE CREDIT
20X1						
Jun. 30	Materials	J1	28,000.00		28,000.00	
30	Labor	J1	10,000.00		38,000.00	
30	Overhead Applied	J1	7,500.00		45,500.00	
30	To Finished Goods	J1		30,500.00	15,000.00	

ACCOUNT Finished Goods Inventory   **ACCOUNT NO.** 126

DATE	DESCRIPTION	POST. REF.	DEBIT	CREDIT	BALANCE DEBIT	BALANCE CREDIT
20X1						
Jun. 1	Balance	✓			20,000.00	
30		J1	30,500.00		50,500.00	
30		J1		40,000.00	10,500.00	

ACCOUNT Cost of Goods Sold   **ACCOUNT NO.** 560

DATE	DESCRIPTION	POST. REF.	DEBIT	CREDIT	BALANCE DEBIT	BALANCE CREDIT
20X1						
Jun. 30		J1	40,000.00		40,000.00	

Section 3 Review

1. What is an overhead application rate?
   a. average cost of actual direct labor
   b. actual direct material costs
   c. estimated amount of overhead costs in an efficient operation applied to work in process
   d. estimated amounts of administrative costs to be applied to work in process

2. Which of the following is not recorded on the job order cost sheets?
   a. material costs
   b. labor costs
   c. overhead actual costs
   d. overhead applied costs

3. Under the perpetual inventory system, which of the following journal entries are made for sales and/or cost of goods sold?
   a. Debit *Cost of Goods Sold;* credit *Finished Goods.*
   b. Debit *Cost of Goods Sold;* credit *Raw Materials.*
   c. Debit *Finished Goods;* credit *Sales.*
   d. Debit *Accounts Receivable;* credit *Inventory.*

4. The entry to transfer work in process to finished goods is a:
   a. debit to *Finished Goods Inventory* and a credit to *Cost of Goods Sold.*
   b. debit to *Cost of Goods Sold* and a credit to *Finished Goods Inventory.*
   c. debit to *Work in Process Inventory* and a credit to *Finished Goods Inventory.*
   d. debit to *Finished Goods Inventory* and a credit to *Work in Process Inventory.*

5. The entry to record cost of goods sold at the end of the month is a:
   a. debit to *Work in Process Inventory* and a credit to *Finished Goods Inventory.*
   b. debit to *Cost of Goods Sold* and a credit to *Finished Goods Inventory.*
   c. debit to *Finished Goods Inventory* and a credit to *Cost of Goods Sold.*
   d. debit to *Finished Goods Inventory* and a credit to *Work in Process Inventory.*

6. During the year, sales were $300,000. The unadjusted balance of *Cost of Goods Sold* was $225,000. Overapplied manufacturing overhead was $5,000. What is the gross profit on sales?
   a. $300,000
   b. $80,000
   c. $220,000
   d. $180,000

Chapter 27 REVIEW   Chapter Summary

Manufacturing companies use accounting systems that best supply detailed information about the costs of production. The job order cost system, as you learned in this chapter, provides records of costs identified to specific job orders.

Learning Objectives

27-1 Explain how a job order cost accounting system operates.

Under the job order cost accounting system, each batch of goods is produced under a production order called a job order. The job order cost system requires that inventory accounts and related subsidiary ledgers are set up for *Raw Materials, Work in Process,* and *Finished Goods:*

- The raw materials ledger is a subsidiary ledger to the *Raw Materials Inventory* account and contains a separate ledger record for each item of raw material.
- A job cost sheet is a subsidiary ledger for *Work in Process Inventory* in the general ledger.
- The finished goods ledger is a subsidiary ledger to the *Finished Goods Inventory* account and has a record for each type of item.

27-2 Journalize the purchase and issuance of direct and indirect materials.

The account *Raw Materials Inventory* reflects all transactions related to materials and supplies:

- Purchases of raw materials are debited to the *Raw Materials Inventory* account.
- Raw materials are issued by a written requisition that shows the number of the job involved; that job is charged with the proper cost. A requisition for indirect materials or supplies is charged to the proper overhead account.

27-3 Maintain perpetual inventory records.

Materials or supplies are issued by the storeroom only upon presentation of a materials requisition describing the item and quantity needed and the job or purpose for which it is needed:

- Costs of materials placed into production are debited to *Work in Process Inventory.*
- Costs of indirect materials and supplies used are debited to *Manufacturing Overhead.*
- The total of indirect and direct materials is credited to *Raw Materials Inventory.*

27-4 Record labor costs incurred and charge labor into production.

Factory labor costs are identified as either direct labor or indirect labor. Time tickets are used for charging direct labor to specific jobs.

27-5 Compute overhead rates and apply overhead to jobs.

Manufacturing overhead is assigned to jobs based on a rate that is commonly related to direct labor costs or to direct labor hours.

27-6 Compute overapplied or underapplied overhead and report it in the financial statements.

To apply overhead to jobs, debit *Work in Process Inventory* and credit *Manufacturing Overhead Applied.* Compute the overapplied or underapplied overhead by comparing total credits recorded in *Manufacturing Overhead Applied* with total debits recorded in *Manufacturing Overhead* for the month:

- Underapplied or overapplied overhead is carried forward from month to month.
- Net underapplied or overapplied overhead is closed out each year, usually as an adjustment to *Cost of Goods Sold* on the income statement.

27-7 Maintain job order cost sheets.

The job order cost sheet shows all manufacturing costs for a specific job.

27-8 Record the cost of jobs completed and the cost of goods sold under a perpetual inventory system.

As a job is done, the cost sheet gives data needed for transferring costs from *Work in Process Inventory* to *Finished Goods Inventory:*

- Record an order's cost on the sales invoice office copy.
- Summarize the cost of goods sold each month from the invoices.
- Record the transfer entry in the general journal.

27-9 Define the accounting terms new to this chapter.

Glossary

Finished goods subsidiary ledger (p. 946) A ledger containing a record for each of the different types of finished products

Job order (p. 942) A specific order for a specific batch of manufactured items

Job order cost accounting (p. 942) A cost accounting system that determines the unit cost of manufactured items for each separate production order

Job order cost sheet (p. 952) A record of all manufacturing costs charged to a specific job

Just-in-time system (p. 945) An inventory system in which raw materials are ordered so they arrive just in time to be placed into production

Manufacturing overhead ledger (p. 950) A subsidiary ledger that contains a record for each overhead item

Materials requisition (p. 947) A form that describes the item and quantity needed and shows the job or purpose

Overapplied overhead (p. 951) The result of applied overhead exceeding the actual overhead costs

Overhead application rate (p. 950) The rate at which the estimated cost of overhead is charged to each job

Perpetual inventory system (p. 943) An inventory system that tracks the inventories on hand at all times

Process cost accounting (p. 942) A cost accounting system whereby unit costs of manufactured items are determined by totaling unit costs in each production department

Production order (p. 942) *See* Job order

Raw materials ledger record (p. 947) A record showing details of receipts and issues for a type of raw material

Raw materials subsidiary ledger (p. 946) A ledger containing the raw materials ledger records

Standard costs (p. 942) A measure of what costs should be in an efficient operation

Time ticket (p. 949) Form used to record hours worked and jobs performed

Underapplied overhead (p. 951) The result of actual overhead costs exceeding applied overhead

Work in process subsidiary ledger (p. 946) A ledger containing the job order cost sheets

Comprehensive Self Review

1. How is a cost accounting system used?
2. What is a process cost accounting system?
3. Why is a perpetual inventory system used with a job order cost accounting system?
4. What would you find on a raw materials ledger record?
5. How is underapplied or overapplied manufacturing overhead disposed of at the end of the year?

(Answers to Comprehensive Self Review are at the end of the chapter.)

Discussion Questions

1. What is a perpetual inventory?
2. What information does a job order cost sheet contain?
3. When direct materials are issued from the storeroom, what entries are made in the subsidiary records?
4. What is a materials requisition?

5. What does the *Raw Materials Inventory* account show?
6. What entry is made for indirect materials issued from the storeroom?
7. What is idle time? How is the cost of idle time usually accounted for?
8. Name the sources of postings to the job order cost sheet.
9. What account is debited and what account is credited when manufacturing overhead is applied?
10. Name five common manufacturing overhead costs.
11. Why is an overhead application rate used?
12. What account is debited and what account is credited when completed goods are transferred from the factory floor to the finished goods storeroom?
13. What is a time ticket? What is its relationship to an order cost sheet?
14. Name three types of businesses that would use a job order cost accounting system.
15. Discuss how costs flow through the *Raw Materials Inventory, Work in Process Inventory,* and *Finished Goods Inventory* accounts to cost of goods sold.
16. Describe a just-in-time inventory system, including its advantages and disadvantages, if any.

APPLICATIONS

Exercises

The following data is for Exercises 27.1 through 27.4.
During July 20X1, White Co. purchased and issued the following materials and supplies. Use July 31 as the date for all entries:

Purchases		Issues from Storeroom	
Materials	$100,000	Direct materials	$60,000
Manufacturing supplies	6,000	Manufacturing supplies	4,500

Exercise 27.1
Objective 27-2

▶ **Journalizing purchase of materials.**

Give the entry in general journal form to record the cost of the materials purchased.

Exercise 27.2
Objective 27-2

▶ **Journalizing purchase of indirect materials.**

Give the entry in general journal form to record the cost of the manufacturing supplies purchased.

Exercise 27.3
Objective 27-2

▶ **Journalizing the assignment of indirect materials into production.**

Give the entry in general journal form to record the issuance of the manufacturing supplies into production.

Exercise 27.4
Objective 27-2

▶ **Journalizing the assignment of direct materials into production.**

Give the entry in general journal form to record the issuance of the direct materials into production.

Exercise 27.5
Objective 27-4

▶ **Recording labor costs incurred.**

A payroll summary prepared at ELI Manufacturing Company showed the following figures for January 20X1:

Direct labor costs incurred	$50,000.00
Indirect labor costs incurred	14,000.00
Social security tax withheld	3,968.00
Medicare tax withheld	928.00
Income tax withheld	16,000.00

Give the January 31 entry in general journal form to record the labor costs incurred.

Computing overhead rate.
◀ **Exercise 27.6**
Objective 27-5

IAM Co. estimates the following manufacturing overhead costs for 20X1:

Estimated direct labor hours	60,000 hours
Estimated direct labor costs	$900,000
Estimated overhead costs	$270,000

What is the overhead application rate based on direct labor costs?

Applying manufacturing overhead.
◀ **Exercise 27.7**
Objective 27-5

CHAR Co.'s direct labor costs were $100,000 for May 20X1. Assuming that the company applies overhead at the rate of 65 percent of direct labor costs, give the general journal entry for May summarizing the overhead applied for the month.

Applying overhead and cost of job.
◀ **Exercise 27.8**
Objective 27-5

During 20X1, Truck Manufacturing Company began and completed Job 1203. Costs entered on the job cost sheet for this job were $50,000 for materials and $10,000 for direct labor:

1. Assuming that overhead is applied at 65 percent of direct labor costs, compute the amount of overhead that should be applied to this job.
2. Compute the total cost of Job 1203.

Computing overapplied or underapplied overhead.
◀ **Exercise 27.9**
Objective 27-6

For the year 20X1, WolfT Inc. had actual overhead costs of $90,000, and its applied overhead was $85,000:

1. Did the firm have overapplied or underapplied overhead for the year?
2. What was the amount of overapplied or underapplied overhead?

Recording cost of goods completed and cost of goods sold.
◀ **Exercise 27.10**
Objective 27-8

The records of HHI Inc. for 20X1 show that it completed goods costing $160,000 and that it sold goods costing $209,000 for the year. Give the entries in general journal form on December 31, 20X1, to record the cost of goods completed and the cost of goods sold for the year.

PROBLEMS

Problem Set A

Recording purchase and issuance of direct and indirect materials, recording labor costs, applying overhead, computing overapplied or underapplied overhead, recording cost of jobs completed, and adjusting cost of goods sold.
◀ **Problem 27.1A**
Objectives 27-2,
27-4, 27-5,
27-6, 27-8

In April 20X1, TN Trailers Inc. had the following cost data:

COST DATA

a. Raw materials costing $100,000 were purchased.
b. Raw materials costing $90,000 were used: direct materials, $85,000; indirect materials $5,000.
c. Factory wages of $55,000 were incurred: direct labor, $50,000; indirect labor, $5,000. Social security tax deductions were $3,410; Medicare tax deductions were $798; federal income tax deductions were $8,250.
d. Other overhead costs of $25,000 were incurred. (Credit **Accounts Payable**.)

e. Estimated manufacturing overhead costs were applied to jobs in production at the rate of 75 percent of direct labor costs.

f. Finished goods costing $130,000 were transferred from production to the warehouse.

g. The cost of goods sold was $100,000.

h. Sales on account for the month were $225,000.

INSTRUCTIONS

1. Prepare general journal entries (using the last day of the month) to record each item of cost data given. Use the account titles listed in your textbook.

2. Compute the amount of overapplied or underapplied overhead for the month.

3. Prepare a partial income statement for April. Adjust the *Cost of Goods Sold* for any overapplied or underapplied overhead.

Analyze: Based on the partial income statement you have prepared, what portion of each sales dollar is realized as gross profit?

Problem 27.2A
Objectives 27-5, 27-6, 27-7, 27-8

▶ **Maintaining job order cost sheets, applying overhead to jobs, computing overapplied or underapplied overhead, recording cost of jobs completed, and adjusting cost of goods sold.**

Kitchen Inc. builds kitchen cabinets. On January 1, 20X2, one job (D42) was in progress. The order is from Dallas Apartment Corporation and was begun on December 21, 20X1. Costs accumulated to date on that job are materials, $1,040; labor, $1,500; and overhead, $900. During January, the following costs were incurred in production work on Job D42 and on Jobs J01 and J02, which were started on January 5, 20X2:

	Materials	Labor	Overhead	Quantity
Job D42	$ 600	$ 600	$ 360	5
Job J01	2,600	3,000	1,800	8
Job J02	4,600	4,000	2,400	5

Job J01 is being manufactured for Luxery Cabinets and Job J02 is for stock.

Manufacturing overhead is applied at the rate of 60 percent of direct labor costs. During January, actual manufacturing overhead costs of $4,910 were incurred. Job D42 was completed on January 19 and was delivered to the customer. The sales price was $10,000.

INSTRUCTIONS

1. Prepare job order cost sheets for the three jobs. Enter the beginning balances applicable to Job D42.

2. Post the costs of the materials and labor for January to the job order cost sheets.

3. Enter the overhead amounts that should be applied to the three jobs worked on during the month on the job cost sheets.

4. Give the entry in general journal form to transfer the cost of the job completed from work in process to finished goods.

5. Compute the amount of underapplied or overapplied overhead for January. Give the entry in general journal form to transfer your result to Cost of Goods Sold.

Analyze: If Kitchen Inc. sold the five cabinets referenced in Job D42 to Dallas Apartment Corporation for a new total invoice price of $10,350, what gross profit amount was realized on the job? Assume that no overapplication or underapplication of overhead occurred on this job.

Problem Set B

◀ **Problem 27.1B**
Objectives 27-2,
27-4, 27-5
27-6, 27-8

Recording purchase and issuance of direct and indirect materials, recording labor costs, applying overhead, computing overapplied or underapplied overhead, recording cost of jobs completed, and adjusting cost of goods sold.

In June 20X1, Red Fab, Inc., had the following cost data:

COST DATA

a. Raw materials costing $150,000 were purchased.

b. Raw materials costing $105,000 were used: direct materials, $100,000; indirect materials, $5,000.

c. Factory wages of $100,000 were incurred: direct labor, $95,000; indirect labor, $5,000. Social security tax deductions were $6,200, Medicare tax deductions were $1,450, and income tax deductions were $15,000.

d. Other overhead costs amounting to $20,000 were incurred. (Credit **Accounts Payable**.)

e. Estimated manufacturing overhead costs were applied to jobs in production at the rate of 50 percent of direct labor costs.

f. Finished goods costing $200,000 were transferred to the warehouse.

g. Goods costing $175,000 were sold and billed to customers for $350,000.

INSTRUCTIONS

1. Prepare general journal entries to record each item of cost data given. Use the account titles in the textbook.
2. Compute the amount of overapplied or underapplied overhead for the month.
3. Prepare a partial income statement for the month of June. Adjust the cost of goods sold for any overapplied or underapplied overhead.

Analyze: What percentage of raw materials purchased during the month of June was used?

◀ **Problem 27.2B**
Objectives 27-5,
27-6, 27-7, 27-8

Maintaining job order cost sheets, applying overhead to jobs, computing overapplied or underapplied overhead, recording cost of jobs completed, and adjusting cost of goods sold.

Custom Cabinet Company builds kitchen cabinets. On November 1, 20X1, two jobs, Job 045 and Job 048, were in progress. The order is from Grace Apartments and was begun on October 5, 20X1. The accumulated costs for each job are detailed as follows:

	Job 045	Job 048
Materials	$17,000	$12,000
Labor	12,000	6,000
Overhead	6,000	3,000

During November, Job N01 was begun. Following are the November costs incurred for each of the three jobs:

	Materials	Labor	Overhead	Quantity
Job 045	$3,000	$3,000	$1,500	10
Job 048	6,000	6,000	3,000	10
Job N01	6,000	2,000	1,000	5

Manufacturing overhead is applied at the rate of 50 percent of direct labor costs. During November, actual manufacturing overhead costs of $5,400 were incurred. Job 045 was completed on November 20 and was delivered to the customer. The sales price was $75,000.

INSTRUCTIONS

1. Prepare job order cost sheets for the three jobs. Enter the beginning balances applicable to Jobs 045 and 048.
2. Post the costs of the materials and labor for November to the job order cost sheets.
3. Post the overhead amounts that should be applied to the three jobs worked on during the month on the job cost sheets.
4. Give the entry in general journal form to transfer the cost of the job completed from work in process to finished goods.
5. Compute the amount of underapplied or overapplied overhead for November. Give the journal entry to transfer your result to Cost of Goods Sold.

Analyze: What adjusted cost of goods sold should be reported for November manufacturing activities?

Critical Thinking Problem 27.1

Reaching Goals

John Manufacturing Company manufactures one product that has several model styles. All materials are added at the beginning of production. Manufacturing overhead is applied as a percentage of direct labor cost. On January 1, 20X1, one job, DE31, was in process, with the following accumulated costs:

Materials	$10,000
Direct labor	5,000
Manufacturing overhead	1,000
Total	$16,000

The beginning finished goods inventory for John Manufacturing Company on January 1, 20X1, was $30,000.

The following additional data is given for the month of January:

Total labor costs incurred	$40,000
Total cost of completed Job DE31	21,000
Total materials costs incurred	23,000

In addition, Job JA01 was begun and completed during the month. Its costs included materials of $10,000 and labor of $4,000. Job JA02 was begun during the month and was in process at the end of the month. During the month, sales were $100,000, and the gross profit rate was 40 percent.

INSTRUCTIONS

1. For Jobs DE31, JA01, and JA02, calculate the cost of materials, labor, and overhead for the month of January to find the total cost of each job.
2. Prepare a schedule of cost of goods sold for the month of January.

Analyze: On January 1, 20X1, John Manufacturing Company established a goal to hold raw materials costs at or below 48 percent of total job costs. Based on your computations, has the company attained this goal? Explain.

Critical Thinking Problem 27.2

Gross Profit

The job order cost sheets for Nash Inc. show the following information about special orders for June and July of the current year:

Job Number	Manufacturing Costs June	Manufacturing Costs July	Status of Job
JU–688	$15,000		Sold, 7/3
JU–689	4,500		Completed, 6/27
JU–690	1,900	$3,850	Completed, 7/8
JU–691	1,500	4,500	Sold, 7/10
JU–692	300	3,200	Sold, 7/16
JL–701		5,000	Sold, 7/22
JL–702		7,000	Completed, 7/20
JL–703		6,000	In process, 7/31
JL–704		800	In process, 7/31

The company prices its jobs to make a 50 percent gross profit on sales. Operating expenses for July totaled $7,500, and the company's income tax rate is 15 percent of net income before income taxes.

INSTRUCTIONS

1. From this data, compute the following:
   a. Work in Process Inventory, July 1
   b. Finished Goods Inventory, July 1
   c. Cost of Goods Sold for July
   d. Work in Process Inventory, July 31
   e. Finished Goods Inventory, July 31
   f. Sales for July
2. Prepare a condensed income statement for Nash Inc. for the month of July.

BUSINESS CONNECTIONS

Cost Accounting Controls

1. Assume that you are an accountant for a manufacturing firm. At the end of one year, there is a large overapplied overhead amount. How would you explain to management why this balance might exist?
2. The president of a fairly large manufacturing company suggests that it would be more efficient to discontinue the job of storeroom clerk and to let factory workers enter the storeroom and select their own materials. Comment on this suggestion.
3. Why should management insist that a physical inventory be taken once a year even though perpetual inventory records are kept?
4. From an administrative standpoint, why is direct labor cost a simple basis to use for the application of manufacturing overhead?
5. In general, would managers prefer to see overapplied or underapplied overhead? Why?

Managerial FOCUS

Internal Control and FRAUD PREVENTION

Travel Costs

The costs for a supervisor are included in indirect costs. The supervisor's travel is included in the indirect costs. Susie is a supervisor for a sewing department at a clothing manufacturing company. As a supervisor, she makes $70,000 per year. Lately, Susie has been traveling to conferences and recruiting employees. She has completed her own travel reports with copies of her receipts, not originals. Terry, Susie's administrative assistant, noticed that Susie has submitted a travel report for days she was in the office. Terry then reviews all of Susie's travel reports. Terry's investigation revealed that Susie had been in the office on at least half of the dates listed on the travel reports. What should Terry do? What effect does this fraud have on the company?

Financial Statement ANALYSIS — Home Depot

Gift Card Revenues

Refer to The Home Depot, Inc., *2018 Annual Report (for the fiscal year ended February 3, 2019)* in Appendix A.

Under the paragraph Fiscal 2018 and Subsequent Periods, from Notes to Consolidated Financial Statements, read how the company treats gift card revenues.

1. Identify where the liability for unredeemed gift cards is reported on the financial statements.
2. What was the account balance at FY 2018 year-end, and how does that compare with year-end for FY 2017?

TEAMWORK

Job Cost Record Design

Keeping track of materials that are provided by each vendor and the employees working on each job is an important process to maintain the high quality of your product. Job cost records can accumulate this information if properly designed. In a group, design a job cost record for a selected product making sure to include an area to collect the information needed to monitor materials and labor. Share your job cost record design with the class.

Answers to Comprehensive Self Review

1. To determine the cost of each manufactured unit and help managers monitor cost behavior and control costs.
2. One in which the total cost of a unit of product is found by adding the unit costs in each department through which the product passes during the manufacturing process.
3. Because the firm must always know the costs of the inventory being used at each stage of production.
4. The quantities and costs of items purchased and issued and the balance on hand.
5. It is closed, usually into *Cost of Goods Sold.*

Process Cost Accounting

Chapter 28

Bloomberg/Getty Images

www.conocophillips.com

Every time we fill up our car at the gas station, the cost of a gallon of gas is different. We don't have much say in the price we pay, but the price is linked to how much each gallon costs to produce.

Per its 2017 annual report, ConocoPhillips is the world's largest independent exploration and production company, with operations and activities in 17 countries. It explores for, produces, transports, and markets crude oil, bitumen, natural gas, liquefied natural gas (LNG), and natural gas liquids on a worldwide basis.

Its oil refineries are more than just a complicated maze of steel towers and pipes. Each is actually a factory that takes crude oil and turns it into gasoline and hundreds of other products necessary for our modern society to function.

How is a gallon of gas produced? Actually, there are three basic steps common to all refining operations: First, the *separation process* separates crude oil into various chemical components. Next, the *conversion process* goes a step further by breaking these chemicals down into molecules called hydrocarbons. Lastly, the *treatment process* combines and transforms hydrocarbon molecules, and other chemicals called additives, to create a host of new products.

Large refineries are complex operations that run 365 days a year, employ as many as 2,000 people, and may occupy as much land as several hundred football fields. At any point in time, some oil may be in the separation, conversion, or treatment process, and Conoco's technicians keep track of how much is completed in each of these areas on a daily basis before it is moved to the next process.

The costs incurred in each of these three processes contribute to the end price of the gas we buy at our local gas station.

thinking critically

How do you think ConocoPhillips estimates ending work in process inventory in its petroleum plants?

LEARNING OBJECTIVES	NEW TERMS	
28-1 Compute equivalent units of production with no beginning work in process inventory.	average method of process costing	equivalent production process cost accounting system
28-2 Prepare a cost of production report with no beginning work in process inventory.	cost of production report	
28-3 Compute the unit cost of manufacturing under the process cost accounting system.		
28-4 Record costs incurred and the flow of costs as products move through the manufacturing process and are sold.		
28-5 Compute equivalent production and prepare a cost of production report with a beginning work in process inventory.		
28-6 Define the accounting terms new to this chapter.		

Section 1

SECTION OBJECTIVES

>> **28-1** Compute equivalent units of production with no beginning work in process inventory.

WHY IT'S IMPORTANT
Manufacturers estimate units completed based on labor, materials, and overhead costs.

>> **28-2** Prepare a cost of production report with no beginning work in process inventory.

WHY IT'S IMPORTANT
Tracking production costs can help identify manufacturing inefficiencies or cost overruns.

>> **28-3** Compute the unit cost of manufacturing under the process cost accounting system.

WHY IT'S IMPORTANT
Unit costs help management set prices.

>> **28-4** Record costs incurred and the flow of costs as products move through the manufacturing process and are sold.

WHY IT'S IMPORTANT
Cumulative product costs are tracked and categorized at every point in the manufacturing process.

TERMS TO LEARN

cost of production report
equivalent production
process cost accounting system

Process Cost Accounting System

A process cost accounting system is used in operations when a single product is manufactured and production is continuous. Examples of companies that use process cost accounting systems include oil refineries, cement producers, and paint manufacturers.

The Process Cost Accounting System

In a **process cost accounting system,** costs are accumulated for each process or department and then transferred on to the next process or department. The flow of costs is similar to that shown in Figure 27.1. There are *Raw Materials Inventory* and *Finished Goods Inventory* accounts. However, job order cost sheets are not needed because products are not made in batches or by order; instead they are produced continuously. There is a separate *Work in Process* account for each department. Materials, labor, and overhead costs are identified with each department and charged to the departmental *Work in Process* accounts. At the end of the month, each departmental *Work in Process* account reflects the materials, labor, and overhead costs incurred by the department.

The process cost accounting system is like an average cost system. Total manufacturing costs are divided by the number of units worked on to obtain a cost per unit of product. As products are physically transferred from one department to the next, the related costs are also transferred.

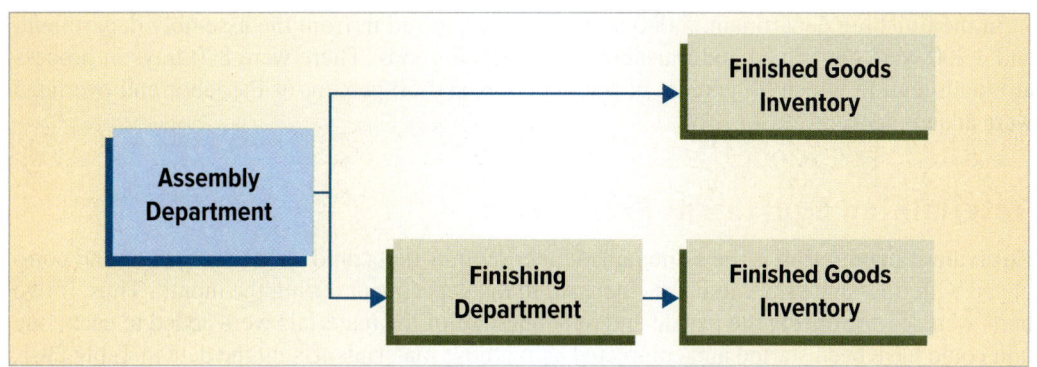

FIGURE 28.1

Flow of Goods in a Factory Operation

MAG Manufacturing Company has two production departments: assembly and finishing. All products begin in the assembly department. Trays that are to be sold in an unpainted state are moved directly to the finished goods storeroom and are recorded in the **Finished Goods Inventory** account. Other trays are moved to the finishing department. This flow of goods is shown in Figure 28.1.

Analyzing Process Cost Data

Let's study the process cost accounting system used by MAG Manufacturing Company. All transactions involving materials, labor, and overhead are recorded by department. The service department costs are allocated as overhead to the departments that benefit from the services. For each department, there is a record of products started, completed, and in process. The stage of completion of the ending work in process is estimated. Table 28.1 summarizes the production data for June.

In the assembly department, 6,000 units were started in production, 5,000 were transferred to the finishing department, and 500 were transferred to finished goods for sale as unpainted trays. At the end of the month, there were 500 trays in process in the assembly department. For the trays in process, all the required materials were issued, and 70 percent of the labor and overhead was added.

recall

Work in Process

Work in process refers to products that have started but have not completed the production process.

TABLE 28.1

Departmental Cost Data for June 20X1

	Assembly Department	Finishing Department
Costs		
Materials	$24,000.00	$ 5,000.00
Labor	25,000.00	16,000.00
Manufacturing overhead	12,400.00	7,800.00
Total costs	$61,400.00	$28,800.00
Quantities		
Started in production	6,000	0
Transferred in from prior department	0	5,000
Transferred out to next department	5,000	0
Transferred out to finished goods	500	4,200
Work in process—ending	500	800
Stages of Completion—Ending Work in Process		
Materials	100%	90%
Labor	70	50
Manufacturing overhead	70	50

important!

Unit Cost

Under the process cost system, unit costs are calculated by dividing all departmental manufacturing costs by the production for the period.

In the finishing department, 5,000 units were transferred in from the assembly department, and 4,200 were completed and transferred to finished goods. There were 800 trays in process at month-end, to which 90 percent of the materials and 50 percent of the labor and overhead were added.

Determining Equivalent Production

>> **28-1 OBJECTIVE**
Compute equivalent units of production with no beginning work in process inventory.

Equivalent production is the estimated number of units that could have been started and completed with the same effort and costs incurred in the department during the month. Thus, if two units were started during the period and only one-half of the materials were added to each, one unit could have been started and completed using those materials. Using the data in Table 28.1, let's calculate June's equivalent production.

Calculating Equivalent Units for Assembly Department

Separate equivalent unit computations are made for the materials, labor, and overhead. Table 28.2 shows how to compute the equivalent units of production for the assembly department. For materials, the equivalent units of production are 6,000 units (5,500 + 500). All the materials were issued for the 5,500 units transferred out and for the 500 trays in process.

For labor and manufacturing overhead, the equivalent units of production are 5,850 (5,500 + 350). All the labor and overhead were applied to the units transferred out. Of the 500 trays in ending work in process, 70 percent of the labor and overhead was applied. This is the equivalent of 350 (500 × 0.7) completed units.

important!

Equivalent Production
In computing equivalent production, accountants frequently consider labor and overhead to be at the same stage of production.

TABLE 28.2

Computation of Equivalent Production, Assembly Department

Materials		
Units transferred out:		
To next department: 100% × 5,000 units	5,000	
To finished goods: 100% × 500 units	500	
Total transferred out		5,500
Work in process: 100% × 500 units		500
Equivalent units of production for materials		6,000
Labor and Manufacturing Overhead		
Units transferred out:		
To next department: 100% × 5,000 units	5,000	
To finished goods: 100% × 500 units	500	
Total transferred out		5,500
Work in process: 70% × 500 units		350
Equivalent units of production for labor and overhead		5,850

recall

Manufacturing Overhead
Manufacturing overhead is all of the manufacturing costs not classified as direct materials or direct labor. Manufacturing overhead includes utilities, depreciation, maintenance, taxes, and insurance for the factory building and payroll taxes for factory wages.

Calculating Equivalent Units for Finishing Department

Table 28.3 shows the equivalent units of production for the finishing department. For materials, the equivalent units are 4,920 (4,200 + 720). All the materials were issued for the 4,200 units transferred out. For the 800 trays in process, 90 percent of the materials were issued. The ending work in process for materials is 720 (800 × 0.9) equivalent units.

For labor and manufacturing overhead, the equivalent units of production are 4,600 (4,200 + 400). All the labor and overhead were applied to the units transferred out. Of the 800 trays in ending work in process, 50 percent of the labor and overhead was applied. This is the equivalent of 400 (800 × 0.5) completed units.

TABLE 28.3 Computation of Equivalent Production, Finishing Department

Materials		
Units transferred out:		
To finished goods: 100% × 4,200 units	4,200	
Total transferred out		4,200
Work in process: 90% × 800 units		720
Equivalent units of production for materials		4,920
Labor and Manufacturing Overhead		
Units transferred out:		
To finished goods: 100% × 4,200 units	4,200	
Total transferred out		4,200
Work in process: 50% × 800 units		400
Equivalent units of production for labor and overhead		4,600

Preparing the Cost of Production Report

The **cost of production report** summarizes all costs charged to each department and shows the costs assigned to the goods transferred out of the department and to the goods still in process. It has separate sections to summarize quantities and costs. Each section has two parts that reconcile the total *to be accounted for* with the total *accounted for*.

Calculating Costs for the Assembly Department

Table 28.4 shows the cost of production report for the assembly department. The Quantity Schedule shows the units to be accounted for (a) and explains what happened to these units (b). The first part of the Cost Schedule (c) shows the total and unit costs of each element and the cumulative cost total. The unit cost is the total cost divided by the equivalent units. The unit cost for the assembly department totals $10.39.

The second part of the Cost Schedule (d) shows the cost of units completed and transferred out, $57,145. It lists the cost of the ending work in process by element, which is computed by multiplying the equivalent units by the cost per unit. For example, the ending work in process for materials is $2,000 (500 equivalent units × $4). The total work in process is the sum of the three elements plus an adjustment for rounding, $4,255. Note that the costs to account for (cumulative cost total) equal the total costs accounted for.

It is customary to round unit costs to the nearest cent. Often an adjustment is required due to rounding. The accountant for MAG Manufacturing Company adjusts the ending work in process inventory to ensure that the cumulative cost total equals the total costs accounted for. In subsequent periods, the rounding adjustment is added to, or subtracted from, manufacturing overhead in work in process.

Calculating Costs for the Finishing Department

Table 28.5 shows the cost of production report for the finishing department. In the Quantity Schedule (a), the quantity to be accounted for consists of units transferred in from the assembly department. These units are accounted for (b) as transferred to finished goods or still in process.

In the Cost Schedule (c), there is a new item. The cost of units transferred in from the assembly department is $51,950 for 5,000 units. Costs in the finishing department are listed next, in total and per unit. The total department costs are $28,800 and the cumulative cost total is $80,750 ($51,950 + $28,800). The unit cost from the assembly department was $10.39. The unit cost for the finishing department is $6.20. The cumulative unit cost is $16.59 ($10.39 + $6.20).

The second part of the Cost Schedule (d) shows the cost of units completed and transferred out, $69,678 (4,200 units × $16.59). In addition, it lists the cost of the ending work in process

>> **28-2 OBJECTIVE**
Prepare a cost of production report with no beginning work in process inventory.

>> **28-3 OBJECTIVE**
Compute the unit cost of manufacturing under the process cost accounting system.

important!

Costs Accounted For
The total costs accounted for must equal the cumulative cost total for the department.

important!

Work in Process
If there is no beginning inventory of work in process, the total cost to be accounted for is the total of (1) costs transferred in from the prior department and (2) costs incurred in the current department.

TABLE 28.4 Cost of Production Report, June 20X1, Assembly Department

Quantity Schedule	Units
(a) Quantity to be accounted for:	
Started in production	6,000
Total to be accounted for	6,000
(b) Quantity accounted for:	
Transferred out to next department	5,000
Transferred out to finished goods	500
Work in process—ending	500
Total accounted for	6,000

Cost Schedule	Total Cost		E.P. Units*		Unit Cost
(c) Costs to be accounted for:					
Costs in current department					
Materials	$24,000.00	÷	6,000	=	$ 4.00
Labor	25,000.00	÷	5,850	=	4.27
Manufacturing overhead	12,400.00	÷	5,850	=	2.12
Cumulative cost total	$61,400.00				$10.39
(d) Costs accounted for:					
Transferred out to next department	$51,950.00	=	5,000	×	$10.39
Transferred out to finished goods	5,195.00	=	500	×	10.39
Total costs transferred out	$57,145.00				
Work in process—ending					
Materials	$ 2,000.00	=	500	×	4.00
Labor	1,494.50	=	350	×	4.27
Manufacturing overhead	742.00	=	350	×	2.12
Rounding adjustment	18.50				
Total work in process—ending	$ 4,255.00				
Total costs accounted for	$61,400.00				

*Equivalent Production Units or Equivalent Units of Production

by element, which is computed by multiplying the equivalent units by the cost per unit. For example, the ending work in process for labor is $1,392 (400 × $3.48). The total work in process is $11,072. It includes the costs from the prior department ($8,312) and the sum of the three cost elements minus the rounding adjustment. Note that the costs to be accounted for equal the total costs accounted for.

>> **28-4 OBJECTIVE**
Record costs incurred and the flow of costs as products move through the manufacturing process and are sold.

Recording Cost Flows

The flow of costs in the accounting records follows the flow of production. Let's look at the journal entries that summarize June's operations.

TABLE 28.5 Cost of Production Report, June 20X1, Finishing Department

Quantity Schedule		Units		
(a) Quantity to be accounted for:				
Transferred in from prior department		5,000		
Total to be accounted for		5,000		
(b) Quantity accounted for:				
Transferred out to finished goods		4,200		
Work in process—ending		800		
Total accounted for		5,000		
Cost Schedule	**Total Cost**		**E.P. Units***	**Unit Cost**
(c) Costs to be accounted for:				
Costs in prior department	$51,950.00	÷	5,000	= $10.39
Costs in current department				
Materials	$ 5,000.00	÷	4,920	= $ 1.02
Labor	16,000.00	÷	4,600	= 3.48
Manufacturing overhead	7,800.00	÷	4,600	= 1.70
Total current department costs	$28,800.00			$ 6.20
Cumulative cost total	$80,750.00			$16.59
(d) Costs accounted for:				
Transferred out to finished goods	$69,678.00	=	4,200	× $16.59
Work in process—ending				
Costs in prior department	8,312.00	=	800	× 10.39
Cost in current department				
Materials	734.40	=	720	× 1.02
Labor	1,392.00	=	400	× 3.48
Manufacturing overhead	680.00	=	400	× 1.70
Rounding adjustment	−46.40			
Total work in process	$11,072.00			
Total costs accounted for	$80,750.00			

*Equivalent Production Units or Equivalent Units of Production

Charging Costs to Work in Process

Departmental **Work in Process** accounts are debited for direct materials issued to production as follows:

20X1				
June 30	Work in Process—Assembly Department	24,000.00		
	Work in Process—Finishing Department	5,000.00		
	Raw Materials Inventory		29,000.00	
	Allocation of materials to production			

Departmental **Work in Process** accounts are debited for direct labor; various liability accounts are credited:

	20X1				
	June	30	Work in Process—Assembly Department	25 000 00	
			Work in Process—Finishing Department	16 000 00	
			Social Security Tax Payable		2 542 00
			Medicare Tax Payable		594 50
			Employee Income Tax Payable		6 150 00
			Salaries and Wages Payable		31 713 50
			Salaries and wages for June		

important!

Costs Charged to the Department

The total of (1) the cost of products transferred out of a department and (2) the cost of ending work in process in the department must equal the cumulative cost total.

When manufacturing overhead costs are incurred, they are debited to the *Manufacturing Overhead* control account. At the same time, they are entered in manufacturing overhead subsidiary ledger sheets for each department. At the end of the month, the overhead costs of all service departments are allocated to the producing departments. After this allocation, the total of the overhead ledger sheets for the departments equals the total manufacturing overhead costs incurred during the month. This total also equals the balance in the *Manufacturing Overhead* control account. The *Manufacturing Overhead* control account is closed into the departmental *Work in Process* accounts.

Manufacturing overhead for June was $20,200—$12,400 for the assembly department and $7,800 for the finishing department. The following entry charges the overhead to production:

	20X1				
	June	30	Work in Process—Assembly Department	12 400 00	
			Work in Process—Finishing Department	7 800 00	
			Manufacturing Overhead		20 200 00
			Charge overhead to work in process		

Recording Transfers of Products out of Departments The cost of production reports show the cost of goods transferred from the assembly department to the finishing department and to finished goods inventory, Table 28.4, and from the finishing department to finished goods inventory, Table 28.5. Based on these reports, a journal entry is made to transfer the costs:

	20X1				
	June	30	Work in Process—Finishing Department	51 950 00	
			Finished Goods Inventory	5 195 00	
			Work in Process—Assembly Department		57 145 00
			Cost of goods transferred out of		
			assembly department in June		
		30	Finished Goods Inventory	69 678 00	
			Work in Process—Finishing Department		69 678 00
			Cost of goods completed in June		

After the above entries are posted, the departmental *Work in Process* accounts appear as follows. Note that ending balances agree with the amounts shown on the departmental cost of production reports:

ACCOUNT Work in Process—Assembly Department   ACCOUNT NO. 122

DATE	DESCRIPTION	POST. REF.	DEBIT	CREDIT	BALANCE DEBIT	BALANCE CREDIT
20X1						
June 30	Materials	J1	24 000 00		24 000 00	
30	Labor	J1	25 000 00		49 000 00	
30	Overhead	J1	12 400 00		61 400 00	
30	Transferred Out	J1		57 145 00	4 255 00	

ACCOUNT Work in Process—Finishing Department   ACCOUNT NO. 123

DATE	DESCRIPTION	POST. REF.	DEBIT	CREDIT	BALANCE DEBIT	BALANCE CREDIT
20X1						
June 30	Materials	J1	5 000 00		5 000 00	
30	Labor	J1	16 000 00		21 000 00	
30	Overhead	J1	7 800 00		28 800 00	
30	Prior Dept.	J1	51 950 00		80 750 00	
30	Transferred Out	J1		69 678 00	11 072 00	

Recording Sale of Finished Goods The final step is to record the sale of finished goods. Assume that June sales were $125,000 and the cost of the goods sold was $66,360. Note that it takes two journal entries, one to record the sales and another to record the cost of goods sold:

1	20X1				1
2	June 30	Accounts Receivable		125 000 00	2
3		Sales			125 000 00	3
4		Record sales on credit for June				4
5						5
6	30	Cost of Goods Sold		66 360 00		6
7		Finished Goods			66 360 00	7
8		Cost of goods sold in June				8

After the sales and cost of goods sold are posted, the *Finished Goods Inventory* and *Cost of Goods Sold* ledger accounts appear as follows:

ACCOUNT Finished Goods Inventory   ACCOUNT NO. 126

DATE	DESCRIPTION	POST. REF.	DEBIT	CREDIT	BALANCE DEBIT	BALANCE CREDIT
20X1						
June 30		J1	5 195 00		5 195 00	
30		J1	69 678 00		74 873 00	
30		J1		66 360 00	8 513 00	

ACCOUNT Cost of Goods Sold   ACCOUNT NO. 560

DATE	DESCRIPTION	POST. REF.	DEBIT	CREDIT	BALANCE DEBIT	BALANCE CREDIT
20X1						
June 30		J1	66 360 00		66 360 00	

Section 1 Review

1. What information is not found in the Quantity Schedule section of the cost of production report?
   a. units started into production
   b. total units to account for
   c. cost of units started this period
   d. units transferred to the next department

2. What journal entry is made to record the transfer of goods from the final producing department to the finished goods inventory?
   a. Debit *Raw Materials*; credit *Finished Goods Inventory*.
   b. Debit *Work in Process Inventory*; credit *Raw Materials Inventory*.
   c. Debit *Cost of Goods Sold*; credit *Work in Process Inventory*.
   d. Debit *Finished Good Inventory*; credit *Work in Process Inventory*.

3. Some of the units processed in a department are sold without further processing. Others are transferred to a second department for further processing. How will this reflect on the cost of production report?
   a. They are reported on separate lines in the Quantity Schedule and Cost Schedule.
   b. They are shown only in the Quantity Schedule.
   c. They are shown only in the Cost Schedule.
   d. Only the costs transferred to *Finished Goods Inventory* are reported in the Cost Schedule.

4. Goods are transferred from the cleaning department to the mixing department. The costs transferred in April totaled $85,000. The journal entry to record the transfer is to:
   a. debit *Cost of Goods Sold* for $85,000 and credit *Work in Process—Cleaning* for $85,000.
   b. debit *Work in Process—Cleaning* for $85,000 and credit *Work in Process—Mixing* for $85,000.
   c. debit *Work in Process—Mixing* for $85,000 and credit *Work in Process—Cleaning* for $85,000.
   d. debit *Cost of Goods Sold* for $85,000 and credit *Work in Process—Mixing* for $85,000.

5. Materials issued to production are recorded by:
   a. debiting *Raw Materials Inventory* and crediting the departmental *Finished Goods* account.
   b. debiting *Raw Materials Inventory* and crediting the departmental *Work in Process* account.
   c. debiting the departmental *Work in Process* account and crediting *Raw Materials Inventory*.
   d. debiting the departmental *Finished Goods* account and crediting *Raw Materials Inventory*.

6. Compute the equivalent units of production for the finishing department assuming materials, labor, and manufacturing overhead are at the same stage of completion. The 400 units in ending work in process are 60 percent complete. There were 2,000 units transferred out.
   a. 2,100
   b. 2,000
   c. 2,240
   d. 2,400

Section 2

SECTION OBJECTIVES	TERM TO LEARN
>> 28-5 Compute equivalent production and prepare a cost of production report with a beginning work in process inventory. **WHY IT'S IMPORTANT** Inventories that are carried from one period to the next need to be included in cost of production computations.	average method of process costing

Work in Process Inventory

There was no beginning work in process for MAG Manufacturing Company in June.

The Beginning Work in Process Inventory

Table 28.6 shows the production and cost data for June. It includes beginning work in process by department and by cost element. Notice that manufacturing overhead in beginning work in process is adjusted for rounding. For the assembly department at the end of June, manufacturing overhead in ending work in process was $742.00, and the rounding adjustment was $18.50 (see Table 28.4). In July, the beginning work in process for manufacturing overhead was $760.50 ($742.00 + $18.50).

Determining Equivalent Production

Table 28.7 summarizes the equivalent units of production for July.

>> **28-5 OBJECTIVE**
Compute equivalent production and prepare a cost of production report with a beginning work in process inventory.

Preparing the Cost of Production Report

Table 28.8 shows the June cost of production report for both departments. MAG Manufacturing Company uses the **average method of process costing,** which combines the cost of beginning inventory for each cost element with the costs of the current period.

Quantity Schedule The Quantity Schedule section combines the beginning inventory of work in process plus the units started in production or received from the prior department during the period. The result is the total to be accounted for (a). These units are either transferred out or remain in process at the end of the period (b).

Cost Schedule In the Cost Schedule for the assembly department, there are costs for the beginning work in process (c), (d), and (e). To determine the unit costs, the accountant adds the beginning inventory and the current period costs (f), (g), and (h) and divides the result by the equivalent units:

	Materials	Labor	Overhead
Beginning	$ 2,000.00	$ 1,494.50	$ 760.50
Current	19,000.00	25,500.00	12,500.00
Total	$21,000.00	$26,994.50	$13,260.50
Equivalent units	6,500	6,320	6,320
Cost per unit	$ 3.23	$ 4.27	$ 2.10

The total unit cost for the assembly department is $9.60.

TABLE 28.6

Departmental Production and Cost Data for July 20X1

	Assembly Department	Finishing Department
Costs		
Work in process—beginning:		
Costs in prior department		$ 8,312.00
Costs in current department		
Materials	$ 2,000.00	734.40
Labor	1,494.50	1,392.00
Manufacturing overhead*	760.50	633.60
Costs transferred in from prior department		52,800.00
Current department costs:		
Materials	19,000.00	7,900.00
Labor	25,500.00	17,000.00
Manufacturing overhead	12,500.00	8,600.00
Total costs	$61,255.00	$97,372.00
Quantities		
Work in process—beginning	500	800
Started in production	6,000	
Transferred in from prior department		5,500
Transferred out to next department	5,500	
Transferred out to finished goods	400	5,900
Work in process—ending	600	400
Stage of completion—Ending Work in Process		
Materials	100%	80%
Labor	70	50
Manufacturing overhead	70	50

*Rounding adjustment included in overhead.

The total cost transferred out is the quantity transferred to the finishing department (i) and to finished goods inventory (j) multiplied by the total unit cost. The ending work in process inventory (k) is the equivalent production units for each cost element multiplied by the unit cost. There is a rounding adjustment of $1.60:

Assembly Department—Ending Work in Process:

	Materials	Labor	Overhead
Equivalent units	600	420	420
Unit cost	× $3.23	× $4.27	× $2.10
Total	$1,938.00	$1,793.40	$882.00

For the finishing department, there are two costs from the prior department: the prior department costs ($8,312) and the cost transferred in ($52,800). The total cost ($61,112) is divided by the total units (6,300) to get an average unit cost of $9.70.

Assembly Department

Materials
  Units transferred out:
    To next department   5,500
    To finished goods   400   5,900
  Work in process—ending: 100% × 600 units   600
  Equivalent units for materials   6,500

Labor and manufacturing overhead
  Units transferred out:
    To next department   5,500
    To finished goods   400   5,900
  Work in process—ending: 70% × 600 units   420
  Equivalent units for labor and overhead   6,320

Finishing Department

Prior department costs: 100% × 6,300 units   6,300

Materials
  Units transferred out: 5,900
  Work in process—80% × 400 units   320
  Equivalent units for materials   6,220

Labor and overhead
  Units transferred out: 5,900
  Work in process—50% × 400 units   200
  Equivalent units for labor and overhead   6,100

TABLE 28.7

Computation of Equivalent Units of Production for July 20X1

Department unit costs are computed in the same manner as they were for the assembly department:

	Materials	Labor	Overhead
Beginning	$ 734.40	$ 1,392.00	$ 633.60
Current	7,900.00	17,000.00	8,600.00
Total	$8,634.40	$18,392.00	$9,233.60
Equivalent units	6,220	6,100	6,100
Cost per unit	$1.39	$3.02	$1.51

The unit cost for the current department is $5.92. The total unit cost for the finishing department is $15.62. The total cost transferred out is the quantity transferred to finished goods (j) multiplied by the total unit cost. The ending work in process inventory (k) is the equivalent production units for units transferred in and for each cost element multiplied by the unit cost. There is a $16.80 rounding adjustment:

Finishing Department—Ending Work in Process:

	Transferred In	Materials	Labor	Overhead
Equivalent units	400	320	200	200
Unit cost	× $9.70	× $1.39	× $3.02	× $1.51
Total	$3,880.00	$444.80	$604.00	$302.00

TABLE 28.8 Cost of Production Report, July 20X1

	Assembly Department			Finishing Department	
Quantity Schedule	Units			Units	
(a) Quantity to be accounted for					
Work in process—beginning	500			800	
Started in production	6,000			–0–	
Transferred in from prior department	–0–			5,500	
Total to be accounted for	6,500			6,300	
(b) Quantity accounted for					
Transferred out to next department	5,500				
Transferred out to finished goods	400			5,900	
Work in process—ending	600			400	
Total accounted for	6,500			6,300	
Cost Schedule	Total Cost	Unit Cost		Total Cost	Unit Cost
Costs to be accounted for					
Costs in prior department					
Work in process—beginning				$ 8,312.00	
Transfers in—current month				52,800.00	
Total prior department cost				$61,112.00	$ 9.70
Costs in current department					
Work in process—beginning					
(c) Materials	$ 2,000.00			$ 734.40	
(d) Labor	1,494.50			1,392.00	
(e) Manufacturing overhead*	760.50			633.60	
Current period costs					
(f) Materials	19,000.00	$3.23		7,900.00	$ 1.39
(g) Labor	25,500.00	4.27		17,000.00	3.02
(h) Manufacturing overhead	12,500.00	2.10		8,600.00	1.51
Total current department cost	$61,255.00	$9.60		$36,260.00	$ 5.92
Cumulative total cost	$61,255.00	$9.60		$97,372.00	$15.62
Costs accounted for					
(i) Transferred out to next department	$52,800.00	$9.60		–0–	
(j) Transferred out to finished goods	3,840.00	9.60		92,158.00	$15.62
Total costs transferred out	$56,640.00			$92,158.00	
(k) Work in process—ending					
Costs in prior department					
Transferred in				$ 3,880.00	9.70
Costs in current department					
Materials	$ 1,938.00	3.23		444.80	1.39
Labor	1,793.40	4.27		604.00	3.02
Manufacturing overhead	882.00	2.10		302.00	1.51
Rounding adjustment	1.60			(16.80)	
Total work in process	$ 4,615.00			$ 5,214.00	
Total costs accounted for	$61,255.00			$97,372.00	

*Rounding adjustment included in overhead.

Recording Cost Flows

Entries to summarize the July costs and transfers, and the departmental **Work in Process** accounts after the entries are posted, appear as follows. The July beginning balances of the **Work in Process** accounts are the same as the ending balances for June. Balances in the accounts at the end of July correspond to the amounts on the July cost of production report. The two entries to record the sale of finished goods are not shown but would be recorded as described in Section 1 of this chapter:

	20X1				
	July	31	Work in Process—Assembly Department	19,000.00	
			Work in Process—Finishing Department	7,900.00	
			Raw Materials Inventory		26,900.00
			Charge materials to production		
		31	Work in Process—Assembly Department	25,500.00	
			Work in Process—Finishing Department	17,000.00	
			Social Security Tax Payable		2,635.00
			Medicare Tax Payable		616.25
			Employee Income Tax Payable		6,375.00
			Salaries and Wages Payable		32,873.75
			Salaries and wages for month		
		31	Work in Process—Assembly Department	12,500.00	
			Work in Process—Finishing Department	8,600.00	
			Manufacturing Overhead		21,100.00
			Charge overhead to work in process		
		31	Work in Process—Finishing Department	52,800.00	
			Finished Goods Inventory	3,840.00	
			Work in Process—Assembly Department		56,640.00
			Cost of goods transferred out of		
			assembly department in July		
		31	Finished Goods Inventory	92,158.00	
			Work in Process—Finishing Department		92,158.00
			Cost of goods completed in July		
			and transferred out		

ACCOUNT Work in Process—Assembly Department   ACCOUNT NO. 122

DATE		DESCRIPTION	POST. REF.	DEBIT	CREDIT	BALANCE DEBIT	BALANCE CREDIT
20X1							
July	1	Balance				4,255.00	
	31	Materials	J1	19,000.00		23,255.00	
	31	Labor	J1	25,500.00		48,755.00	
	31	Overhead	J1	12,500.00		61,255.00	
	31	Trans. Out	J1		56,640.00	4,615.00	

ACCOUNT Work in Process—Finishing Department   ACCOUNT NO. 123

DATE		DESCRIPTION	POST. REF.	DEBIT	CREDIT	BALANCE DEBIT	BALANCE CREDIT
20X1							
July	1	Balance				11,072.00	
	31	Materials	J1	7,900.00		18,972.00	
	31	Labor	J1	17,000.00		35,972.00	
	31	Overhead	J1	8,600.00		44,572.00	
	31	Prior Dept.	J1	52,800.00		97,372.00	
	31	Trans. Out	J1		92,158.00	5,214.00	

MANAGERIAL IMPLICATIONS

PROCESS COST ACCOUNTING

- Managers need accurate, up-to-date cost data to set prices, evaluate efficiency, and make operating decisions.
- Manufacturing firms should rely on a cost accountant to develop an accounting system that will yield the required data accurately and swiftly.
- The process cost accounting system provides a unit manufacturing cost for products that are manufactured on a continuous basis.
- The average cost method of handling beginning inventories of work in process simplifies calculation of the costs per unit.

THINKING CRITICALLY

Think of some manufacturing plants near you and name any that you think would use a process cost accounting system.

Section 2 Review

1. How is the unit cost of labor calculated when there is beginning work in process inventory?
   a. Beginning cost of labor is ignored.
   b. Current period unit labor cost is applied to beginning units.
   c. Beginning cost of labor is added to current period labor cost and total is divided by equivalent units of labor.
   d. Beginning cost of labor is divided by the number of beginning units in production to get beginning labor cost per unit.

2. What is the difference between cost of production reports with and without beginning work in process inventory?
   a. Reports with beginning work in process require all quantities and costs to be reported to present accurate per unit costs.
   b. Reports with beginning work in process will ignore associated costs and units.
   c. Beginning work in process totals are only accounted for in the Quantity Schedule.
   d. Unit costs will ignore any beginning work in process costs.

3. In the cost of production report, how are the costs transferred in from a prior department handled?
   a. reported out to *Finished Goods Inventory*
   b. must be treated as a "cost to be accounted for"
   c. ignored in computing the unit cost
   d. reported out to *Cost of Goods Sold* immediately

4. The source of the cost data in a cost of production report is:
   a. *Raw Materials* accounts.
   b. *Work in Process* accounts.
   c. job order costs sheets.
   d. the prior period income statement.

5. March sales are $100,000 and cost of goods sold is $65,000. What is the entry to *Finished Goods Inventory*?
   a. $65,000 debit
   b. $65,000 credit
   c. $35,000 debit
   d. $100,000 credit

6. Compute the unit cost for materials when beginning work in process is $965, current period costs are $12,835, and equivalent units for the department are 4,000.
   a. $3.45
   b. $3.21
   c. $0.24
   d. $34.50

REVIEW Chapter Summary

The process cost accounting system is commonly used when only one product is manufactured in a department and production is on a continuous basis rather than in batches or by specific job. In this chapter, you have reviewed the procedures for process cost accounting systems and how they differ from a job order cost accounting system.

Learning Objectives

28-1 Compute equivalent units of production with no beginning work in process inventory.

The equivalent production unit technique is used to convert ending work in process to equivalent finished production. Separate computations must be made for the three elements of production (materials, labor, and overhead) whenever the states of completion of the three elements in the work in process inventory are different.

28-2 Prepare a cost of production report with no beginning work in process inventory.

The cost of production report summarizes all costs charged to each department during the month and shows how these costs are assigned to the goods transferred out of the department and those still in process:

- The equivalent production unit technique is used to convert ending work in process to equivalent finished production.
- Then the costs for each equivalent unit of materials, labor, and overhead are computed.
- The value of goods transferred out of the department, as well as of work in process inventories, is determined on the basis of the equivalent units of production for each cost element.
- The costs of the goods transferred from one department to another are charged to the receiving department and removed from the *Work in Process* account of the first department.

28-3 Compute the unit cost of manufacturing under the process cost accounting system.

The unit cost to manufacture a product is computed by dividing the total cost of each production element by the appropriate equivalent production units.

28-4 Record costs incurred and the flow of costs as products move through the manufacturing process and are sold.

- A *Work in Process* inventory account is set up for each producing department.
- Direct materials costs and direct labor costs are charged to the departmental *Work in Process* accounts.
- Overhead costs incurred are charged to the *Manufacturing Overhead* control account.
- Each producing and service department has a cost sheet in the subsidiary ledger.
- At the end of each month, the costs of the service departments are allocated to the producing departments.

28-5 Compute equivalent production and prepare a cost of production report with a beginning work in process inventory.

If there is a beginning work in process inventory, the same basic process cost accounting procedures are followed to prepare a cost of production report:

- Under the average cost system, the cost of each element in the beginning work in process is added to the cost of that element during the month.
- Equivalent units of production are computed for each element just as when there was no beginning inventory of work in process.
- The total cost of an element divided by the equivalent units of production for the element yields the unit cost for the element.
- Cost of product transferred out of the department and cost of ending work in process are then computed in the usual manner.

28-6 Define the accounting terms new to this chapter.

Glossary

Average method of process costing (p. 975) A method of costing that combines the cost of beginning inventory for each cost element with the costs during the current period

Cost of production report (p. 969) Summarizes all costs charged to each department and shows the costs assigned to the goods transferred out of the department and to the goods still in process

Equivalent production (p. 968) The estimated number of units that could have been started and completed with the same effort and costs incurred in the department during the same time period

Process cost accounting system (p. 966) A method of accounting in which costs are accumulated for each process or department and then transferred on to the next process or department

Comprehensive Self Review

1. Explain the flow of costs in the accounting records.
2. What is the source of the information in the Costs to Be Accounted For section of a cost of production report?
3. A company uses the process cost accounting system. It has two service departments. How will the costs of the service departments enter into the cost of an equivalent unit for the producing departments?
4. What is the purpose of the cost of production report?
5. Why can a process cost accounting system be referred to as an average cost system?

(Answers to Comprehensive Self Review are at the end of the chapter.)

Discussion Questions

1. Why are job order cost sheets not used in the process cost accounting system?
2. What are equivalent units of production?
3. In a cost of production report, what items are found in the Costs to Be Accounted For section?
4. How is the ending work in process inventory computed in a process cost accounting system?
5. Will the same equivalent units always be used for materials, labor, and overhead? Explain.
6. Will the amount shown as a department's ending inventory of work in process on the cost of production report agree with the work in process for the department in the general ledger after adjusting and closing entries have been posted? Explain.
7. Why is it not necessary to use an overhead application rate when the process cost accounting system is employed?
8. Why might the process cost accounting system be unsatisfactory when several different products are being manufactured in the same department?
9. How does accounting for the raw materials inventory and the finished goods inventory differ under the process cost accounting system and the job order cost accounting system?
10. Explain what is meant by "the average method" of accounting for beginning work in process inventories in a process cost system.
11. Explain how to compute the equivalent production for labor when there is a beginning work in process inventory for the period, assuming that the average cost method is used.

APPLICATIONS

Exercises

Data for Exercises 28.1 through 28.3.
Information about production in the fabricating department of the AGAM Company for March 20X1 follows:

Beginning inventory	–0–
Transferred in from prior department	20,000 units
Transferred out to next department	16,000 units
Ending inventory, work in process	4,000 units
Stage of completion of ending work in process:	
Prior department costs	100%
Materials	90%
Labor and overhead	60%

Computing equivalent production for prior department costs with no beginning inventory. ◀ **Exercise 28.1** Objective 28-1

Compute the equivalent units of production for the prior department costs for the month.

Computing equivalent production for materials with no beginning inventory. ◀ **Exercise 28.2** Objective 28-1

Compute the equivalent units of production for materials for the month.

Computing equivalent production for labor and overhead with no beginning inventory. ◀ **Exercise 28.3** Objective 28-1

Compute the equivalent units of production for labor and overhead for the month.

Computing equivalent production for materials and unit cost of materials with no beginning work in process. ◀ **Exercise 28.4** Objectives 28-1, 28-3

On April 1, 20X1, the assembly department of Ros Inc. had no beginning work in process. During the month, production was started on 10,000 units. The total cost of materials was $60,000. All materials were placed in production at the start of the manufacturing process in the department. During the month, 8,000 units were transferred to the next department and 2,000 units were still in process at the end of the month.

1. What is the cost per equivalent unit for materials?
2. What is the cost of materials in the goods transferred to the next department?
3. What is the cost of materials in the ending work in process inventory?

Data for Exercises 28.5 and 28.6.
The cutting department is the first department of BrakeParts Co. On April 1, 20X1, the beginning inventory in this department consisted of 700 units. Costs for the beginning work in process were as follows:

Materials (100% complete)	$7,000
Labor (60% complete)	5,000
Overhead (60% complete)	4,000

During April 20X1, 2,900 units were started into production with the following costs:

Materials	$34,400
Labor	17,000
Overhead	17,228

The number of units completed and sent to the finishing department was 3,000. The ending inventory of 600 units was 100 percent complete with regard to materials, 70 percent complete with regard to labor and overhead.

Exercise 28.5
Objectives 28-3, 28-5

▶ **Computing equivalent production for materials and cost per equivalent unit with beginning work in process.**

1. Compute the equivalent production for materials for BrakeParts Co. for the month.
2. Compute the cost per equivalent unit for materials for April.
3. Compute the cost of materials in the work transferred out of the department during the month.
4. Compute the month-end cost of materials in the ending work in process.

Exercise 28.6
Objectives 28-3, 28-5

▶ **Computing equivalent production for overhead and cost per equivalent unit with beginning work in process.**

1. Compute the equivalent production for overhead for the month.
2. Compute the cost per equivalent unit for overhead for April.
3. Compute the cost of overhead in the goods transferred out.
4. Compute the cost of overhead in the ending work in process inventory.

Data for Exercises 28.7 through 28.9.
At SanAn Corporation, production is started in the fab department. The work is then transferred to the finishing department, where goods are completed and then transferred to the finished goods storeroom. Data about the company's costs during September 20X1 follows:

Material costs placed into production	
Fab department	$ 78,000.00
Finishing department	7,000.00
Direct labor costs	
Fab department	122,000.00
Finishing department	18,000.00
Taxes withheld from employees' earnings	
Social security tax withheld	8,680.00
Medicare tax withheld	2,030.00
Federal income tax withheld	21,000.00
Overhead costs	
Fab department	48,800.00
Finishing department	7,200.00

During the month, products costing $200,000 were transferred from the fab department to the finishing department; goods costing $225,000 were transferred from the finishing department to finished goods inventory; and goods that cost $185,000 were sold on account for $310,000.

Exercise 28.7
Objective 28-4

▶ **Recording costs incurred in production.**

Give the journal entries on September 30 to summarize the following:

1. Materials placed into production

2. Labor costs charged into production
3. Overhead costs charged into production

Recording transfer of product between departments and from work in process to finished goods.

◀ **Exercise 28.8**
Objective 28-4

Give the general journal entries on September 30 to record the following:

1. Transfer of product from the fab department to the finishing department
2. Transfer of finished goods from the finishing department to finished goods inventory

Recording cost of goods completed.

◀ **Exercise 28.9**
Objective 28-4

Give general journal entries to record the following events during September:

1. Sale of goods
2. Cost of goods sold

PROBLEMS

Problem Set A

Computing equivalent production with no beginning work in process.

◀ **Problem 28.1A**
Objective 28-1

RedTek, Inc., manufactures a single type of garden cart. The monthly production report for May 20X1 follows:

RedTek, Inc. Monthly Production Report for May 20X1			
	Molding Department	Assembly Department	Completion Department
Quantities			
Started in production—current month	10,000	–0–	–0–
Transferred in from prior department	–0–	8,000	7,100
Transferred out to next department	8,000	7,100	–0–
Transferred out to finished goods	–0–	–0–	6,600
Work in process—ending	2,000	900	500
Stage of Completion—Ending Work in Process			
Materials	100%	100%	100%
Labor	80	80	90
Overhead	80	80	90

INSTRUCTIONS

Prepare the equivalent production computations for each department.

Analyze: Which department's ending work in process inventory is at the lowest stage of completion in regard to labor and overhead for the month?

Computing equivalent production, preparing a cost of production report, computing unit costs, and recording flow of cost through manufacturing process and sale.

◀ **Problem 28.2A**
Objectives 28-1, 28-2, 28-3, 28-4

KAT Games Inc. has two producing departments—fabricating and assembly. The following data is from the firm's records for the month of April 20X1. There were no beginning inventories.

INSTRUCTIONS

1. In general journal form, record the flow of costs that follow. Date all entries April 30, 20X1:
   a. The issuance of materials to each department
   b. The monthly payroll withholdings for the producing departments: social security, $3,925.00; Medicare, $918.00; federal income tax, $9,495
   c. The distribution of manufacturing overhead to each department
2. Prepare equivalent production computations for each department.
3. Prepare a cost of production report for each department.
4. Record the following in general journal form:
   a. The transfer of goods from the fabricating department to the assembly department
   b. The transfer of completed goods from the assembly department to the finished goods storeroom
   c. Sales on credit for $152,100; these goods cost $106,500 to manufacture

	Fabricating Department	Assembly Department
Costs		
Materials	$ 60,000.00	$10,000.00
Labor	46,980.00	16,320.00
Manufacturing overhead	24,940.00	11,040.00
Total costs	$131,920.00	$37,360.00
Quantities		
Started in production	6,000	–0–
Transferred in from prior department	–0–	5,000
Transferred out to next department	5,000	–0–
Transferred out to finished goods	–0–	4,600
Work in process—ending	1,000	400
Stage of Completion—Ending Work in Process		
Materials	100%	100%
Labor	80	50
Manufacturing overhead	80	50

Analyze: What was the balance of the *Work in Process* account for the fabricating department at the end of the month?

Problem 28.3A
Objective 28-5

Computing equivalent production and preparing a cost of production report with a beginning work in process.

MP Corporation adds all materials at the beginning of production. On August 1, 20X1, 2,500 gallons of its product were in production in the first department. During the month of August, 7,500 gallons were put into production. On August 31, 2,000 gallons were still in production. The ending inventory is estimated to be 60 percent complete as to labor and overhead. Cost data for the month follows:

	Materials	Labor	Overhead
Beginning inventory of work in process	$ 9,500	$ 6,000	$ 3,600
Added during August	54,000	34,000	13,600

INSTRUCTIONS

Prepare a cost of production report for the month of August, assuming that the average cost method is used.

Analyze: How many gallons of product will be held as beginning inventory of work in process on September 1 for the first department? What is the total cost for this quantity of product?

Problem Set B

Computing equivalent production with no beginning work in process.

◀ **Problem 28.1B**
Objective 28-1

C8K Company manufactures plastic hats. The monthly production report for October 20X1 follows:

C8K Company Monthly Production Report for October 20X1			
	Molding Department	Assembly Department	Finishing Department
Quantities			
Started in production—current month	9,000	–0–	–0–
Transferred in from prior department	–0–	7,000	6,800
Transferred out to next department	7,000	6,800	–0–
Transferred out to finished goods	–0–	–0–	5,500
Work in process—ending	2,000	200	1,300
Stage of Completion—Ending Work in Process			
Materials	100%	100%	100%
Labor	80	60	50
Overhead	80	60	50

INSTRUCTIONS

Prepare the equivalent production computations for each department.

Analyze: What portion of materials was added in October in the assembly department's ending work in process inventory?

Computing equivalent production, preparing a cost of production report, computing unit costs, and recording flow of costs through manufacturing process and sale.

◀ **Problem 28.2B**
Objectives 28-1, 28-2, 28-3, 28-4

H20 Inc. has two producing departments—fabricating and assembly. The data below is from the firm's records for the month of July 20X1. There were no beginning inventories.

INSTRUCTIONS

1. In general journal form, record the flow of costs that follow. Date all entries July 31, 20X1:
   a. The issuance of materials to each department
   b. The producing department's monthly payroll taxes withheld: social security, $4,770.28; Medicare, $1,115.62; federal income tax, $11,541.00
   c. The distribution of manufacturing overhead to each department
2. Prepare equivalent production computations for each department.
3. Prepare a cost of production report for each department.

4. Record the following in general journal form:

   a. The transfer of goods from fabricating to assembly

   b. The transfer of completed goods from the assembly department to the finished goods storeroom

   c. Sales on credit for $270,000; cost of goods sold, $125,000

	Fabricating Department	Assembly Department
Costs		
Materials	$ 52,500.00	$10,000.00
Labor	37,440.00	39,500.00
Manufacturing overhead	18,720.00	19,750.00
Total costs	$108,660.00	$69,250.00
Quantities		
Started in production	21,000	–0–
Transferred in from prior department	–0–	20,000
Transferred out to next department	20,000	–0–
Transferred out to finished goods		19,500
Work in process—ending	1,000	500
Stage of completion—Ending Work in Process		
Materials	100%	100%
Labor	80	50
Manufacturing overhead	80	50

Analyze: What is the balance of the *Work in Process* account for the fabricating department on July 31?

Problem 28.3B
Objective 28-5

▶ **Computing equivalent production and preparing a cost of production report when there is beginning work in process.**

TX Chemical Company manufactures a pharmaceutical chemical. All materials are put into process at the beginning of production. On April 1, 20X1, 3,000 pounds of the product were in process in the first department. During the month of April, 57,000 pounds were put into production. On April 30, 4,000 pounds were still in production. The ending inventory is estimated to be complete as to materials and 60 percent complete as to labor and overhead. Cost data for the month is as follows:

	Materials	Labor	Overhead
Beginning inventory of work in process	$ 9,500	$ 6,000	$ 2,400
Added during April	65,000	28,000	11,200

INSTRUCTIONS

Compute equivalent production, and prepare a cost of production report for the month of April, assuming that the average cost method is used.

Analyze: What total production cost is attributable to products transferred from the first department to the next department?

Critical Thinking Problem 28.1

Red Manufacturing, Inc.

Selected data about the operations of the mixing department, the first department of Red Manufacturing, Inc., for November 20X1 follows.

At the beginning of the month, there were 1,000 units in process with total costs of $48,000. Included in the total was $38,000 of material costs. The labor and overhead costs in the beginning work in process were equal.

During the month, 20,000 units were transferred to the next department at a per unit cost of $31.80. Included in this amount was a per unit cost of $8.40 for labor. Materials added to production this month were $277,000.

At the end of the month, the 1,000 units in process were 100 percent complete with material costs and 50 percent complete with labor and overhead costs.

INSTRUCTIONS

1. Compute the equivalent units of production for the month.
2. Prepare a cost of production report for the department for the month.

Analyze: What percentage of total department costs is attributable to materials costs in the mixing department?

Critical Thinking Problem 28.2

Cost Flows

Sticky Inc. makes candy. The continuous production operation starts in the mixing department, where the chocolate, sugar, water, and other ingredients are blended. It then moves to the second department (cooking), where the ingredient mix is heated and poured into molds. Finally, in the last department (cooling and packaging), the product is packed 24 boxes to a container. The containers are sealed, ready for shipping to supermarkets around the country. Prepare a diagram to show the flow of costs through Sticky Inc.'s perpetual inventory accounts. Indicate with arrows the direction of the cost flow through the accounts.

BUSINESS CONNECTIONS

Accurate Cost Accounting

1. The directors of the firm where you work have asked you to explain whether the job order cost accounting system or the process cost accounting system provides the more accurate costs for each unit of product. What will you tell them?
2. What are the benefits of perpetual inventories to management?
3. How would managers use the cost of labor for each equivalent unit to help control costs?
4. Why would a comparison of the cost per equivalent unit of each cost element (materials, labor, and overhead) for the current month with that of the preceding month be useful to management?
5. A manager in the company where you work asks why it is necessary to convert production to equivalent units when determining the cost of each unit of product produced under the process cost accounting system. Explain.

Percentage Complete

The percentage complete for the beginning and ending inventory is an important figure to determine the cost of the work in process inventory and the finished goods inventory. If the ending finished goods inventory is overstated, so is the net income. Charlotte works for The Paint Palace. She knows

that the beginning inventory is last month's ending inventory. She has decided to help the business by overstating the ending inventory percentage complete. Has Charlotte violated any ethical area of accounting or committed a fraudulent act?

Long-Term Debt

Financial Statement ANALYSIS

Home Depot

Refer to The Home Depot, Inc., *2018 Annual Report (for the fiscal year ended February 3, 2019)* in Appendix A.

Look over the Consolidated Balance Sheets and the Consolidated Statements of Cash Flows for information related to the company's long-term debt.

1. Did the company incur more debt or pay off long-term debt in the past year?
2. How did the cash payments for long-term debt for FY 2018 compare with fiscal years 2017 and 2016?

Process or Job Costing

TEAMWORK

The manufacturing of concrete includes three processes: (1) crushing the gravel with water, (2) burning the wet gravel in a rotary kiln, and (3) grinding the mix while adding gypsum. Discuss why the process costing approach would be the best approach. Could the job cost approach be used?

Answers to Comprehensive Self Review

1. Direct costs are charged to the departmental **Work in Process** accounts. Overhead costs are charged to the **Manufacturing Overhead** control account, and then allocated to departmental overhead sheets for each department. At the end of the month, the costs of the service departments are allocated to the producing department. Finally, the **Manufacturing Overhead** control account is closed into the departmental **Work in Process** accounts.

2. The current month's costs to be accounted for in the cost of production report are taken from the departmental **Work in Process** accounts. The details of beginning inventory of work in process can be determined from the cost of production report of the prior month.

3. At the end of the month, the costs of service departments are allocated to the overhead of the producing departments.

4. It summarizes all costs charged to each department during the month and shows how these costs are assigned to the goods transferred out of the department and those still in process.

5. All costs for each manufacturing element (materials, labor, and overhead) incurred during the month are added together and divided by the equivalent units of production for that element during the month. Costs incurred for each element are, in a sense, averaged.

Controlling Manufacturing Costs: Standard Costs

Chapter **29**

SAJJAD HUSSAIN/Getty images

www.harleydavidson.com

The year 2018 was the 115th anniversary of the Harley-Davidson Company (HD). For several years, the iconic American motorcycle brand with a cult-like following has concentrated on selling an experience, and the bike just happens to be a fundamental part of that experience.

According to the Motorcycle Industry Council, HD's cruiser and touring categories of motorcycles accounted for approximately 50.7% of total new 2017 retail unit motorcycle registrations in the United States in the large engine (601 cc and higher) motorcycle category.

After you finalize the design and choose the other options and accessories you want, Harley-Davidson will build your dream bike for you. HD has a flexible manufacturing process designed to help ensure it is well-positioned to meet customer demand in a timely and cost-effective manner. HD believes this flexible manufacturing capability allows the company to increase the production of motorcycles ahead of and during the peak retail selling season to more closely correlate the timing of production and wholesale shipments to the retail selling season. As their motorcycles are first mass-produced, then customized, HD probably employs a mix of process cost and job order accounting systems to track the material costs as well as the amount of labor budgeted for your specific design.

HD's revenues in its motorcycle segment fell by 6.8% in 2017 from the preceding year due to lower unit sales. As its traditional customer base, middle-aged men, ages, the company must find a way to attract younger riders and women as customers. According to Chief Marketing Officer Heather Malenshek, HD addresses this goal through "Innovation in design, innovation in technology, and innovation in performance (which) will inspire Harley-Davidson fans and a new generation of riders to share the wide-open freedom of motorcycling." Harley-Davidson's plans to increase sales include a plan to produce and market a new electric motorcycle, the launch of their new Softail models, and increased outreach to the international motorcycle community.

thinking critically

How do you think Harley-Davidson accountants budget for the changing levels of production at the plants the company operates?

LEARNING OBJECTIVES

29-1 Explain how fixed, variable, and semivariable costs change as the level of manufacturing activity changes.

29-2 Use the high-low point method to determine the fixed and variable components of a semivariable cost.

29-3 Prepare a fixed budget for manufacturing costs.

29-4 Develop a flexible budget for manufacturing costs.

29-5 Develop standard costs per unit of product.

29-6 Compute the standard costs of products manufactured during the period and determine cost variances between actual costs and standard costs.

29-7 Compute the amounts and analyze the nature of variances from standard for raw materials, labor, and manufacturing overhead.

29-8 Define the accounting terms new to this chapter.

NEW TERMS

budget
budget performance report
cost variance
fixed budget
fixed costs
flexible budget
high-low point method
labor efficiency variance
labor rate variance
labor time variance
manufacturing cost budget
materials price variance
materials quantity variance
materials usage variance
relevant range of activity
semivariable costs
standard cost card
variable costs
variance analysis

Section 1

SECTION OBJECTIVES

>> **29-1** Explain how fixed, variable, and semivariable costs change as the level of manufacturing activity changes.

WHY IT'S IMPORTANT
Planning for varying levels of activity helps managers anticipate costs.

>> **29-2** Use the high-low point method to determine the fixed and variable components of a semivariable cost.

WHY IT'S IMPORTANT
To measure efficiency, it is necessary to separate costs into their components.

>> **29-3** Prepare a fixed budget for manufacturing costs.

WHY IT'S IMPORTANT
Accountants must estimate costs for an expected level of activity.

>> **29-4** Develop a flexible budget for manufacturing costs.

WHY IT'S IMPORTANT
Production levels can fluctuate.

TERMS TO LEARN

budget
budget performance report
fixed budget
fixed costs
flexible budget
high-low point method
manufacturing cost budget
relevant range of activity
semivariable costs
variable costs

Cost Behavior and the Budget

To control costs and make effective decisions, managers need information on the *variability of costs*—how costs change as the volume of output changes. In this chapter, you will learn how cost variability is measured. You will also learn how to use cost behavior to develop budgets and standard costs.

>> **29-1 OBJECTIVE**
Explain how fixed, variable, and semi-variable costs change as the level of manufacturing activity changes.

Cost Behavior

Manufacturing costs can be classified as variable, fixed, and semivariable. It is essential to understand these terms in order to analyze costs.

Variable Costs

Variable costs are costs that vary *in total* in direct proportion to changes in the level of activity. Direct materials and direct labor are examples of variable costs. If direct materials cost $5 for one unit, then the materials cost for 1,000 units is $5,000 (1,000 × $5) and for 5,000 units is $25,000 (5,000 × $5). If direct labor cost is $5 per unit of product, the total labor cost for manufacturing 1,000 units is $5,000 (1,000 × $5) and for 4,000 units is $20,000 (4,000 × $5).

Note that the term *variable* refers to the *total* cost. The cost *per unit* of material or labor does not change as output changes, but the total cost of material or labor changes.

Fixed Costs

Fixed costs are costs that do not change *in total* as the level of activity changes. For example, the salary of the production vice president does not vary from month to month based on the number of units produced.

Note that although fixed costs do not change in total as the level of activity changes, the cost per unit does change. For example, if factory supervisory salaries are $10,000 for the month, the cost per unit is $5.00 if 2,000 units are produced ($10,000 ÷ 2,000) and $4.00 if 2,500 units are produced ($10,000 ÷ 2,500).

Semivariable Costs

Semivariable costs, also called *mixed costs,* are costs that vary with, but not in direct proportion to, the volume of activity. A semivariable cost contains a fixed element that does not change because of changes in the level of activity. It also contains a variable component that does vary with changes in activity.

Utilities are an example of a semivariable cost. Lighting, heating, and cooling are necessary to operate the factory regardless of how many units are produced. The fixed portion of these costs ensures basic service. However, the electricity used to operate machines will vary in proportion to the level of production.

To prepare budgets, measure efficiency, develop expected costs, and analyze the differences between actual costs and expected costs, it is necessary to separate semivariable costs into their fixed and variable components. The **high-low point method** is a simple method to determine the fixed and variable components of a semivariable cost.

Let's examine how the Manufacturing Company uses the high-low point method.

>> **29-2 OBJECTIVE**
Use the high-low point method to determine the fixed and variable components of a semivariable cost.

1. Determine the production and cost data for the months of highest and lowest production during the past year. The data for the Manufacturing Company follows. The month of July had the highest production level. January had the lowest production level.

Month	Direct Labor Hours	Utilities Costs
January	1,600	$1,900
February	2,160	2,360
March	2,600	2,750
April	2,800	3,000
May	2,950	3,050
June	2,700	3,000
July	3,200	3,500
August	2,040	2,240
September	2,120	2,320
October	2,200	2,400
November	2,060	2,260
December	1,750	1,950

important!

Fixed Costs
As the volume of output increases, the fixed cost per unit of output decreases.

2. Compute the difference in direct labor hours in the months of highest and lowest production. Also compute the difference in utilities costs.

Month	Direct Labor Hours	Utilities Costs
July	3,200	$3,500
January	1,600	1,900
Difference	1,600	$1,600

3. Compute the variable cost per direct labor hour by dividing the difference in utilities costs by the difference in direct labor hours. The variable cost per direct labor hour is $1 ($1,600 ÷ 1,600 hours).

4. Compute the fixed cost for a month by deducting the variable cost from the total cost for either the highest or lowest production month (in this case, either July or January). The variable cost is the cost per direct labor hour, computed in step 3, multiplied by the number of hours of direct labor worked during the month selected. For example, using the month of July, the total variable costs are $3,200 (3,200 hours × $1 per hour).

Total cost	$3,500
Less variable costs	3,200
Fixed costs	$ 300

The major advantage of using the high-low point method is its simplicity. The results could be misleading, however, if the highest and lowest months are not representative of the other months. For this reason, some accountants also compute fixed costs using the second highest and second lowest months. They compare the results of the two calculations to ensure that they are consistent. If the results are not similar, the accountant might need to use other methods to separate fixed and variable costs; these methods are covered in cost accounting textbooks.

>> 29-3 OBJECTIVE

Prepare a fixed budget for manufacturing costs.

Preparation of the Fixed Budget

A **budget** is an operating plan expressed in monetary units. Well-run companies prepare detailed budgets for each year and for each month within the year. The **manufacturing cost budget** is a budget for each manufacturing cost for the budget period.

The management of the Manufacturing Company plans to produce various products during August. The budgets for direct materials and direct labor are relatively easy to compute. The unit costs of materials and unit costs of labor are multiplied by the number of units to be produced.

For example, suppose that 500 toy cars are to be produced and each car requires $1.50 of direct materials. The budgeted direct material cost for toy cars is $750.00 (500 × $1.50).

Computations are also made for all other products to be manufactured. The expected materials costs for each product are added to arrive at the materials budget for the period. Similar computations are made for direct labor costs.

The budget for manufacturing overhead costs is more complex. It is necessary to identify the cost behavior of each manufacturing overhead item as fixed, variable, or semivariable. The accountant for the Manufacturing Company used the high-low point method to determine the cost behavior of each item as shown below:

	Fixed Costs per Months	Variable Costs per Direct Labor Hour
Supervision and clerical wages	$6,000	$–0–
Other indirect labor		2.00
Payroll taxes and fringe benefits	600	1.50
Manufacturing supplies	200	0.50
Depreciation	1,500	
Utilities	300	1.00
Insurance and taxes	400	–0–
Total	$9,000	$5.00

Figure 29.1 shows the budget of manufacturing costs for the Manufacturing Company for August. It is called a **fixed budget** because it shows only one level of activity—1,000 direct labor hours. Management expects that $30,000 of direct materials will be used and that 1,000 direct labor hours will be worked at $15 per hour.

Fixed overhead costs include supervision and clerical wages, depreciation, and insurance and taxes. There is one budgeted variable overhead cost—other indirect labor. It is calculated by multiplying the budgeted direct labor hours by the variable cost per hour (1,000 hours × $2).

FIGURE 29.1

Fixed Budget of Manufacturing Costs

Manufacturing Company
Budget of Manufacturing Costs
Month Ended August 31, 20X1

Direct materials		30 000 00
Direct labor		15 000 00
Manufacturing overhead		
Supervision and clerical wages	6 000 00	
Other indirect labor (1,000 × $2)	2 000 00	
Payroll taxes and fringe benefits		
[$600 + (1,000 × $1.50)]	2 100 00	
Manufacturing supplies		
[$200 + (1,000 × $0.50)]	700 00	
Depreciation	1 500 00	
Utilities [$300 + (1,000 × $1.00)]	1 300 00	
Insurance and taxes	400 00	
Total manufacturing overhead		14 000 00
Total manufacturing cost		59 000 00

There are three semivariable overhead costs: payroll taxes and fringe benefits, manufacturing supplies, and utilities. The budgeted overhead for utilities includes $300 as a fixed cost and $1,000 as a variable cost. The budgeted variable cost for utilities is 1,000 direct labor hours multiplied by the variable cost per hour of $1.00 (1,000 × $1.00). The budgeted amounts for payroll taxes and fringe benefits and manufacturing supplies are calculated in a similar manner.

Budgets serve many purposes. One key purpose is to provide a basis for measuring performance. Management needs to know how well manufacturing costs are being controlled. As soon as actual manufacturing costs have been accumulated and reported for the month, the accountant prepares a **budget performance report,** which compares actual costs and budgeted costs. Figure 29.2 shows the budget performance report for the Manufacturing Company for August.

The budget performance report shows that there are numerous differences between the budgeted amounts and the actual costs incurred. In some cases, actual costs exceeded the amounts budgeted, while in others the actual costs were less than budgeted costs. Management needs to determine why costs were over or under budget.

FIGURE 29.2

Budget Performance Report

Manufacturing Company
Budget Performance Report
Month of August 20X1

	Budget	Actual	(Over) Under
Direct materials	30 000	29 000	1 000
Direct labor	15 000	14 500	500
Manufacturing overhead			
Supervision and clerical wages	6 000	5 000	1 000
Other indirect labor	2 000	2 150	(1 5 0)
Payroll taxes and fringe benefits	2 100	2 200	(1 0 0)
Manufacturing supplies	700	350	350
Depreciation	1 500	1 600	(1 0 0)
Utilities	1 300	550	750
Insurance and taxes	400	500	(1 0 0)
Total manufacturing overhead	14 000	12 350	1 650
Total manufacturing cost	59 000	55 850	3 150

One of the first considerations is to determine how many hours were worked during the month. Was the actual number more or less than the hours budgeted? If the actual hours worked is close to the hours budgeted, then the fixed budget is a meaningful way to evaluate manufacturing performance. However, if the number of hours worked is materially more or less than the budgeted hours, the fixed budget is not the best tool to use to measure efficiency and cost control.

The fixed budget is based on 1,000 direct labor hours. Direct labor was budgeted at $15,000. Suppose that in August only 960 direct labor hours were worked. When management compares the actual labor costs of $14,500 to the budgeted labor costs of $15,000, the difference appears favorable. The company was under budget by $500. Actually, the difference is not favorable. Direct labor should have been $14,400 (960 hours × $15). At the level of 960 direct labor hours, the company spent $100 more than it should have ($14,500 − $14,400).

In order to provide management with a more useful tool for estimating and controlling manufacturing overhead costs, companies often prepare a budget that takes into account different levels of activity.

>> **29-4 OBJECTIVE**
Develop a flexible budget for manufacturing costs.

Preparation of the Flexible Budget

A **flexible budget** shows the budgeted costs at various levels of activity. Flexible budgets are particularly useful when the level of activity fluctuates from month to month. The flexible budget usually shows fixed and variable costs separately. The different levels of activity are called the **relevant range of activity.** For example, separate budgets might be prepared for the expected activity level as well as levels of 90 percent, 95 percent, 105 percent, and 110 percent of the expected activity level.

Figure 29.3 shows the flexible budget for the Manufacturing Company for August. It has columns for the expected level of activity (1,000 direct labor hours), for 95 percent of expected activity (950 direct labor hours), and for 105 percent of expected activity (1,050 direct labor hours).

A flexible budget prepared for several activity levels is helpful for planning purposes. In addition, it allows management to see whether manufacturing overhead costs are being controlled. For example, management can compare overhead expenses at an actual activity level of 960 hours with the flexible budget for 950 hours. This will provide a reasonable indication of how well costs are being controlled. For a more precise measure of efficiency and cost control, however, a flexible budget can be prepared for the actual activity level.

important!

Budget Performance Report
Efficiency and cost control can be evaluated by comparing actual overhead costs with the budget for the actual level of operations.

FIGURE 29.3

Flexible Budget of Manufacturing Costs

Manufacturing Company
Budget of Manufacturing Costs
Month of August 20X1

	Activity Level		
Number of direct labor hours	950	1 000	1 050
Percent of expected activity	95	100	105
Variable costs			
Other indirect labor	1 900	2 000	2 100
Payroll taxes and fringe benefits	1 425	1 500	1 575
Manufacturing supplies	475	500	525
Utilities	950	1 000	1 050
Total variable costs	4 750	5 000	5 250
Fixed costs			
Supervision and clerical wages	6 000	6 000	6 000
Payroll taxes and fringe benefits	600	600	600
Manufacturing supplies	200	200	200
Depreciation	1 500	1 500	1 500
Utilities	300	300	300
Insurance and taxes	400	400	400
Total fixed costs	9 000	9 000	9 000
Total manufacturing overhead	13 750	14 000	14 250

FIGURE 29.4 Budget Performance Report for August

Manufacturing Company
Manufacturing Overhead Budget Performance Report
Month Ended August 31, 20X1

	Budget for 960 hours	Actual	(Over) Under
Supervision and clerical wages	6 0 0 0	6 1 0 0	(1 0 0)
Other indirect labor (960 × $2)	1 9 2 0	2 0 0 0	(8 0)
Payroll taxes and fringe benefits [$600 + (960 × $1.50)]	2 0 4 0	1 8 5 0	1 9 0
Manufacturing supplies [$200 + (960 × $0.50)]	6 8 0	6 0 0	8 0
Depreciation	1 5 0 0	1 4 5 0	5 0
Utilities [$300 + (960 × $1.00)]	1 2 6 0	1 1 0 0	1 6 0
Insurance and taxes	4 0 0	4 5 0	(5 0)
Total manufacturing overhead	13 8 0 0	13 5 5 0	2 5 0

Figure 29.4 shows a flexible overhead budget for an actual activity of 960 hours in August. Note that the various actual costs are both over and under the budgeted costs, although no single amount is significant.

Section 1 Review

1. Which of the following is not true concerning cost behavior?
   a. Fixed costs do not change in total as the level of activity changes.
   b. Variable costs change in total as the level of activity changes.
   c. Fixed costs per unit change as the level of activity changes.
   d. Variable costs per unit change as the level of activity changes.

2. Which of the following is true concerning semivariable (mixed) costs?
   a. Semivariable costs contain both fixed and variable costs.
   b. Semivariable costs do not change in total as the level of activity changes.
   c. The salary of the vice president of finance is a good example of a semivariable cost.
   d. Semivariable costs per unit do not change as the level of activity changes.

3. A flexible budget contains:
   a. fixed, variable, and semivariable costs.
   b. variable costs only.
   c. semivariable costs only.
   d. fixed costs only.

4. The salary of the factory supervisor is an example of a:
   a. variable cost.
   b. semivariable cost.
   c. fixed cost.
   d. mixed cost.

5. Pavilion Company is using the high-low method to determine the fixed and variable components of its utilities expense, a semivariable cost. Pavilion Company believes direct labor hours is the best activity to measure the cost. In its low month, there were 1,600 direct labor hours and utilities expense was $8,000. In its high month, there were 3,600 direct labor hours and utilities expense was $12,000. Using the high-low method, what is the variable cost per direct labor hour, rounded to the nearest cent?
   a. $0.77
   b. $2.00
   c. $3.33
   d. $5.00

6. Pavilion Company is using the high-low method to determine the fixed and variable components of its utilities expense, a semivariable cost. Pavilion Company believes direct labor hours is the best activity to measure the cost. In its low month, there were 1,600 direct labor hours and utilities expense was $8,000. In its high month, there were 3,600 direct labor hours and utilities expense was $12,000. Using the high-low method, what is the fixed cost per month, rounded to the nearest whole dollar?
   a. $0
   b. $9,231
   c. $4,000
   d. $4,800

Section 2

SECTION OBJECTIVES	TERMS TO LEARN
>> 29-5 Develop standard costs per unit of product. **WHY IT'S IMPORTANT** Manufacturing businesses need a measurement that indicates per-unit costs based on a normal, efficient operating period. >> 29-6 Compute the standard costs of products manufactured during the period and determine cost variances between actual costs and standard costs. **WHY IT'S IMPORTANT** Standard costs help managers assess efficiencies and costs. >> 29-7 Compute the amounts and analyze the nature of variances from standard for raw materials, labor, and manufacturing overhead. **WHY IT'S IMPORTANT** Labor, materials, or overhead variances help managers pinpoint inefficiencies in the manufacturing process.	cost variance labor efficiency variance labor rate variance labor time variance materials price variance materials quantity variance materials usage variance standard cost card variance analysis

Standard Costs as a Control Tool

Recall that standard costs reflect what costs *should be* per unit manufactured under normal, efficient operating conditions. If standard costs are used to measure the efficiency and effectiveness of operations, the standards should be achievable. If they are set artificially high and cannot be attained, workers might become discouraged and demoralized, and they could make little or no attempt to achieve the standards.

There are two ways to handle standard costs. Some companies actually enter standard costs in the accounts. This procedure is discussed in cost accounting textbooks. Other companies record actual costs in the accounting system but compare these actual costs with standards in order to measure efficiency and to control manufacturing costs. This is the method used by the Manufacturing Company.

Developing Standard Costs

To develop the standard cost of a specific unit of product, standards are set for each cost element, including materials, labor, and overhead.

Developing Raw Materials Standards

The *standard quantity* is the number of units of each type of raw material required to manufacture one unit of finished product. Engineers usually determine the standard quantity, although it is sometimes based on past experience in manufacturing the product. The *standard cost* is the cost of each unit of raw material required to make the product. The purchasing department determines standard cost. The *raw material standard* is the standard quantity of each raw material multiplied by its standard cost.

Developing Direct Labor Standards

The standard quantity is the number of hours of each type of labor needed to manufacture one unit of finished product. Industrial engineers usually determine the standard quantity by making time and motion studies. Sometimes the standard quantity is based on past experience in making the product. The standard cost is the cost of each type of labor used to make the product. The human resources department and union contracts provide wage rate information used in setting the standard cost. The *direct labor standard* is the standard quantity of each type of labor multiplied by its standard cost.

Developing Manufacturing Overhead Standards

The *standard overhead cost* per unit of product is usually based on the overhead application rate used to assign overhead costs to products. The overhead application rate can be based on direct labor cost, direct labor hours, or some other measure.

If the overhead application rate is based on direct labor hours, the standard overhead cost per unit is the standard labor *hours* for each finished unit multiplied by the overhead application rate. If the overhead application rate is based on direct labor costs, the standard overhead cost per unit is the standard labor *cost* for each finished unit multiplied by the overhead application rate.

Manufacturing Company uses a job order cost accounting system. Prior to the start of each year, the accountant prepares a manufacturing overhead budget for the year. This year's budget is based on a projection that 20,000 direct labor hours will be worked during the year:

Budgeted manufacturing overhead		
Fixed manufacturing overhead		$108,000
Variable manufacturing overhead, 20,000 hours × $5.00 per hour		100,000
Total budgeted manufacturing overhead		$208,000

The manufacturing overhead application rate is based on direct labor hours. Using the budgeted manufacturing costs of $208,000 and the expectation that 20,000 direct labor hours will be used, the overhead application rate is computed as $10.40 per direct labor hour:

$$\frac{\text{Estimated overhead costs}}{\text{Estimated direct labor hours}} = \frac{\$208,000}{20,000} = \$10.40 \text{ per hour}$$

Using Standard Costs

Most well-managed manufacturing companies use standard costs to evaluate efficiency.

Preparing a Standard Cost Card

Standard costs are measured on a per-unit basis. A standard cost card helps facilitate the comparison of actual costs to standard costs. The **standard cost card** shows the per-unit standard costs for materials, labor, and overhead.

Figure 29.5 shows the standard cost card for product BA 25, a toy car. Each toy car requires $1.65 in direct materials and one-tenth hour of direct labor. Manufacturing overhead rate is applied at $1.04 per toy car (1/10 hour × $10.40).

---

recall

Job Order Cost System
In a job order cost system, unit costs are determined for each production order.

recall

Process Cost System
In a process cost system, unit costs are determined by totaling the cost per unit in each production department.

recall

Overhead Application Rate
The overhead application rate is the rate at which overhead is applied to each job.

ABOUT ACCOUNTING

Inventory Costing Policies
McCormick & Company, Inc., a manufacturer of cooking spices and seasonings, described its accounting policies for inventories as follows in its annual report for the fiscal year ended November 30, 2017: "Inventories are stated at the lower of cost or market. Cost is determined using standard or average costs which approximate the first-in, first-out costing method."

McCormick & Company, Inc.

>> 29-5 OBJECTIVE
Develop standard costs per unit of product.

FIGURE 29.5
Standard Cost Card

STANDARD COST CARD

Item: Toy Car—Product BA 25

Materials
    Base material: 1 pound @ $1.50/lb. $1.50
    Finishing material: 3 ounces @ $0.05/oz.   0.15
    Total materials $1.65

Labor
    1/10 hour @ $15/hour $1.50

Manufacturing Overhead
    1/10 hour @ $10.40/hr. $1.04

Total Standard Cost per Unit $4.19

>> **29-6 OBJECTIVE**
Compute the standard costs of products manufactured during the period and determine cost variances between actual costs and standard costs.

Comparing Actual and Standard Costs

The following is from the job order cost sheet for Job Order A16, for the manufacture of 1,000 decorated cars:

Job A16
Product: Toy Car BA 25
Number of units manufactured: 1,000
Manufacturing costs:

Materials	
Base material: 990 pounds × $1.52 per pound	$1,504.80
Finishing material: 3,060 ounces × $0.045 per ounce	137.70
Total materials	$1,642.50
Direct labor: 110 hours × $15.20 per hour	1,672.00
Manufacturing overhead: 110 hours × $10.40 per hour	1,144.00
Total manufacturing costs	$4,458.50

Using the standard cost card and the job order cost sheet, the accountant can compare the actual costs to the standard costs for Job A16. The **cost variance** is the difference between the total standard cost and the total actual cost. The cost variance is $268.50; the actual cost is $268.50 more than the standard cost:

Standard cost of 1,000 units: 1,000 units × $4.19 per unit	$4,190.00
Manufacturing costs charged to job	4,458.50
Unfavorable variance	$ (268.50)

Because the actual cost is more than the standard cost of the job, the variance is unfavorable. When the actual cost is less than the standard cost, the variance is favorable.

>> **29-7 OBJECTIVE**
Compute the amounts and analyze the nature of variances from standard for raw materials, labor, and manufacturing overhead.

Analyzing Variances Between Standard and Actual Costs

The total variance helps measure how well costs were controlled. It is also useful to compute the variances between actual and standard cost for each cost element—materials, labor, and overhead.

Analyzing Materials Variances

The following is a summary of the materials costs for Job A16. The left side shows the standard costs and the right side shows the actual costs:

	\multicolumn{3}{c	}{Standard}	\multicolumn{3}{c	}{Actual}	Favorable (Unfavor.) Variance
	Quantity	Unit Cost	Total Cost	Quantity	Unit Cost	Total Cost	
Base material	1,000	$1.50	$1,500.00	990	$1.52	$1,504.80	$ (4.80)
Finishing material	3,000	0.05	150.00	3,060	0.045	137.70	12.30
Totals			$1,650.00			$1,642.50	$ 7.50

Variance analysis explains the difference between standard cost and actual cost. The **materials quantity variance** (also called **materials usage variance**) is the cost of the actual quantity of raw materials used on a job minus the standard cost of the raw materials allowable for the units produced. The **materials price variance** is the actual cost of the raw materials used on a job minus the standard cost of the materials used.

Determining Materials Quantity Variance The materials quantity variance is the difference between the actual quantity used and the standard quantity allowed multiplied by the standard cost of the material. The following are the quantity variances for the materials used on Job A16:

Base Material

Standard quantity (1,000 units × 1 lb./unit)	1,000 pounds
Actual quantity	990 pounds
Base material under standard	10 pounds
Times standard price per pound	$ 1.50
Favorable quantity variance	$15.00

Because the actual quantity of base material used was less than the standard quantity allowed for the job, the quantity variance for base material is favorable.

Finishing Material

Actual quantity	3,060 ounces
Standard quantity (1,000 units × 3 oz./unit)	3,000 ounces
Excess finishing material used	60 ounces
Times standard price per ounce	$ 0.05
Unfavorable quantity variance	$(3.00)

Because the actual quantity of finishing material exceeded the standard quantity allowed for the job, the quantity variance for finishing material is unfavorable.

The materials quantity variance measures how well the production manager and factory employees are controlling material waste. Unfavorable quantity variances often result because of defective materials or inexperienced workers.

Determining Materials Price Variance The materials price variance is the difference between the actual price and the standard cost multiplied by the actual quantity used. The following are the price variances for the materials used on Job A16:

Base Material

Actual price per pound	$ 1.52
Standard price per pound	1.50
Excess of actual over standard price	$ 0.02
Times actual number of pounds consumed	990
Unfavorable materials price variance	$(19.80)

Because the actual price for the base material was more than the standard price, the price variance for base materials is unfavorable.

Finishing Material	
Actual price per ounce	$0.045
Standard price per ounce	0.050
Excess of standard over actual price	$0.005
Times actual number of ounces consumed	3,060
Favorable materials price variance	$15.30

Because the actual price of finishing material was less than the standard price, the price variance is favorable.

The purchasing department is usually responsible for the price variance. There is little that the manufacturing department can do to control the prices paid for raw materials.

Summary of Materials Variance The materials variances for Job A16 are summarized as follows:

	Favorable or (Unfavorable) Variance	
Base material		
Quantity variance	$15.00	
Price variance	(19.80)	$(4.80)
Finishing material		
Quantity variance	$ (3.00)	
Price variance	15.30	12.30
Total material variance		$7.50

Analyzing Labor Variance The total labor variance for Job A16 is $172.00 (unfavorable), calculated as follows:

Actual labor costs, 110 hours × $15.20 per hour	$1,672.00
Standard labor costs, 1,000 units × 1/10 hour per unit × $15 per hour	1,500.00
Unfavorable labor variance	$ (172.00)

The total labor variance is divided into the labor time (or efficiency) variance and the labor rate variance.

Determining Labor Time Variance The **labor time variance** (or **labor efficiency variance**) is the difference between the actual hours worked and the standard labor hours allowed for the job multiplied by the standard cost per hour:

Actual hours worked	110
Standard hours allowed (1,000 units × 1/10 hour per unit)	100
Excess of actual over standard hours	10
Times standard rate per hour	$ 15.00
Unfavorable labor time variance	$(150.00)

Because more hours were worked than the number of hours allowed by the standard, the labor time variance is unfavorable.

The production manager is usually responsible for the labor time variances. Part of the time variance might be attributed to the human resources department, which hires factory employees.

Determining Labor Rate Variance The **labor rate variance** is the difference between the actual labor rate per hour and the standard labor rate per hour multiplied by the actual number of hours worked on the job:

Actual rate per hour	$ 15.20
Standard rate per hour	15.00
Excess of actual over standard rate	$ 0.20
Times actual number of hours worked	110
Unfavorable labor rate variance	$(22.00)

Usually the human resources department is responsible for the labor rate variance. However, operating decisions also affect the labor rate variance, including whether to work overtime at one and one-half the normal rate or how to assign workers to jobs. In addition, labor market conditions and wage scales set in union contracts may make it difficult to hire workers at the standard rates.

Summary of Direct Labor Variance Analysis The total direct labor variance is summarized as follows:

Labor time variance, unfavorable	$(150.00)
Labor rate variance, unfavorable	(22.00)
Total labor variance, unfavorable	$(172.00)

Analyzing Manufacturing Overhead Variance Recall that under the cost system described for the Manufacturing Company, manufacturing overhead is applied to jobs on the basis of a predetermined manufacturing overhead rate. As illustrated in this chapter, manufacturing overhead is applied at $10.40 per direct labor hour (based on a standard of 20,000 direct labor hours for the year). This $10.40 rate includes $5.40 for fixed manufacturing overhead and $5.00 for variable manufacturing overhead.

The calculation of the manufacturing overhead variance is beyond the scope of this text and is included in most cost accounting courses. However, for illustrative purposes, a brief discussion and monthly summary of overhead variances follows.

> *ABOUT*
> **ACCOUNTING**
>
> **Injuries**
> Many companies have invested heavily in workplace injury and illness prevention programs in order to increase worker safety and reduce workers' compensation insurance costs. According to the California Occupational Safety and Health Department, employee training is one of the most important elements of any injury and illness prevention program. It allows employees to learn their jobs properly, brings new ideas into the workplace, reinforces existing ideas and practices, and puts the program into action.
>
> State of California

MANAGERIAL IMPLICATIONS

COST BEHAVIOR

- Management needs to understand cost behavior in order to make decisions and to plan for the future.
- Budgets help in planning and controlling manufacturing costs. Fixed budgets are useful, but flexible budgets allow management to evaluate cost containment for the level of production activity.
- Standard costs reflect what costs should be when based on efficient, yet attainable, operating conditions.
- Management analyzes the difference between actual and standard costs to determine what factors caused the variances:
  - The materials price variance is the responsibility of the purchasing department.
- The materials quantity variance is the responsibility of factory management.
- The labor rate variance is the responsibility of the human resources department.
- The labor time variance is the responsibility of factory management.

THINKING CRITICALLY
What can factory management do to minimize the labor time variance?

In computing the variance analysis for manufacturing overhead, the accountant will calculate two primary variances: (1) flexible budget or controllable variance (difference between the actual overhead costs incurred and the flexible budgeted amount for overhead applied based on standard hours for units produced) and (2) production volume or uncontrollable variance (difference between the flexible budgeted amount for overhead applied based on standard hours for units produced and the total standard overhead costs). A cost accounting course will teach you how to calculate all the variances related to manufacturing overhead.

Analysis of Monthly Overhead Variances Because of the nature (fixed and variable components) of overhead, businesses are unable to determine the actual overhead costs related to individual jobs. Usually overhead is analyzed based on the total actual overhead and the total standard overhead for the products manufactured during a period of time.

The following is a summary of the production and cost data in August for the Manufacturing Company. The company had a $104 unfavorable total overhead variance.

Total standard hours for goods manufactured		100
Total actual hours required for work completed		110
Manufacturing overhead applied to products:		
100 hours × $10.40 per hour		$1,040
Actual manufacturing overhead costs incurred:		
Fixed costs (110 hours × $5.00)	$550	
Variable costs (110 hours × $5.40)	594	
Total		1,144
Total overhead variance, unfavorable		$ (104)

The variance is unfavorable because actual costs were greater than allowed costs for the quantity produced. A common cause for such a variance is a production level that is different from the level used to calculate the predetermined overhead application rate.

Section 2 Review

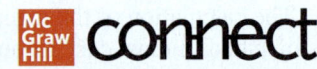

1. The standard quantity of materials for a product was 49 pounds per unit at a standard price of $20 per pound. The actual price per pound of materials was $14.00, and the actual quantity used was 57 pounds. Which of the following is true?
   a. The price variance is $342.00 favorable.
   b. The quantity variance is $294.00 favorable.
   c. The quantity variance is $112.00 unfavorable.
   d. The price variance is $274.00 unfavorable.

2. Costless Corporation produces only one product. The standard material cost for that product is 6 gallons at $11.50 per gallon. During August, the company made 9,400 units of product and used 25,750 gallons. The actual price for materials was $10.50 per gallon. Which of the following is true?
   a. The materials quantity variance is $378,225 unfavorable.
   b. The materials quantity variance is $352,475 favorable.
   c. The materials quantity variance is $25,750 unfavorable.
   d. The materials quantity variance is $378,225 favorable.

3. Office Supplies Manufacturing has established direct labor standards of 1.5 hours at $30.25 per hour for a product it makes. During July, the company made 11,300 units of that product. Direct labor used was 12,600 hours, and workers were paid $34.25 per hour. Which of the following is true?
   a. The labor rate variance was $50,400 favorable.
   b. The labor rate variance was $39,325 favorable.
   c. The labor rate variance was $39,325 unfavorable.
   d. The labor rate variance was $50,400 unfavorable.

4. Metcalf Manufacturing Company has established direct labor standards of 1.0 hour at $15.25 per hour for a product it makes. During December, the company made 5,500 units of that product. Direct labor used was 5,400 hours, and workers were paid $16.25 per hour. Which of the following is true?
   a. The labor efficiency variance is $5,400 favorable.
   b. The labor efficiency variance is $5,400 unfavorable.
   c. The labor efficiency variance is $1,525 favorable.
   d. The labor efficiency variance is $1,525 unfavorable.

5. Better Housewares, Inc., budgets its variable manufacturing overhead at a rate of $10 per unit (.5 hour at $20 per hour) for a product it makes. In February, the company made 12,000 units of that product. Actual direct labor hours used were 6,100, and actual variable overhead costs were $58,000. The overhead spending variance in February is:

   a. $2,000 unfavorable.
   b. $1,000 unfavorable.
   c. $1,000 favorable.
   d. $2,000 favorable.

6. The price variance is the difference between the actual price and the standard price multiplied by:

   a. unused capacity.
   b. the actual quantity.
   c. the difference between the actual quantity and the standard quantity.
   d. the standard quantity.

7. Which variance is controllable by the production manager?

   a. materials price variance
   b. labor rate variance
   c. labor time variance
   d. standard variance

Chapter 29 Review — Chapter Summary

To control costs and make effective business decisions, management also needs information based on the variability of manufacturing costs. In this chapter, you have learned how cost variability is measured and how budgets are developed and evaluated for manufacturing entities.

Learning Objectives

29-1 Explain how fixed, variable, and semivariable costs change as the level of manufacturing activity changes.

Accountants must understand cost variability—how costs behave as the volume of manufacturing activity increases or decreases:

- Total variable costs vary in direct proportion to activity level. The per-unit variable cost remains constant.
- Fixed costs remain relatively constant within the range of activity level at which the factory is likely to operate.
- Semivariable costs vary to some extent with changes in the volume of activity, but not in direct proportion. An element of these costs is fixed, while another element is variable.

29-2 Use the high-low point method to determine the fixed and variable components of a semivariable cost.

The high-low method compares the activity and the cost of the highest month of activity in a year with the activity and cost of the lowest month of activity. The difference in cost is divided by the difference in activity to measure the variable cost per unit of activity.

29-3 Prepare a fixed budget for manufacturing costs.

A budget is important for planning manufacturing activities and for controlling costs. A fixed budget shows the anticipated costs for a period—a month, a quarter, or a year—for one level of production:

- At the end of the period, actual results are compared with the budget and differences are noted and investigated.
- If the production volume is significantly different from the volume assumed in preparing the budget, the budgeted figures for variable and semivariable costs will not be meaningful.

29-4 Develop a flexible budget for manufacturing costs.

Flexible budgets show what the budgeted costs should be at several levels within the relevant range of activity. Actual results can then be compared with more meaningful budgeted amounts.

29-5 Develop standard costs per unit of product.

Standard costs help businesses control and evaluate manufacturing efficiency. Costs of efficient, yet attainable, levels of performance are set for each element of materials, labor, and overhead. A standard cost card for each product details cost.

29-6 Compute the standard costs of products manufactured during the period and determine cost variances between actual costs and standard costs.

The difference between the total standard cost and the total actual cost is called the cost variance. At the end of the period, actual costs related to the product are compared with the standard costs allowed for each unit. Variances between standard costs and actual costs are analyzed.

29-7 Compute the amounts and analyze the nature of variances from standard for raw materials, labor, and manufacturing overhead.

- The total variance between the actual cost and standard cost of material is separated into two components: a materials quantity variance and a materials price variance.
- Similarly, the total labor cost variance is separated into two components: a labor time variance and a labor rate variance.
- Manufacturing overhead variances cannot be easily computed on a per-job or per-unit basis, especially under the job order cost accounting system. Instead, manufacturing overhead is applied to jobs using a predetermined rate often based on direct labor hours.

29-8 Define the accounting terms new to this chapter.

Glossary

Budget (p. 994) An operating plan expressed in monetary units

Budget performance report (p. 995) A comparison of actual costs and budgeted costs

Cost variance (p. 1000) The difference between the total standard cost and the total actual cost

Fixed budget (p. 994) A budget representing only one level of activity

Fixed costs (p. 992) Costs that do not change in total as the level of activity changes

Flexible budget (p. 996) A budget that shows the budgeted costs at various levels of activity

High-low point method (p. 993) A method to determine the fixed and variable components of a semivariable cost

Labor efficiency variance (p. 1002) See Labor time variance

Labor rate variance (p. 1003) The difference between the actual labor rate per hour and the standard labor rate per hour multiplied by the actual number of hours worked on the job

Labor time variance (p. 1002) The difference between the actual hours worked and the standard labor hours allowed for the job multiplied by the standard cost per hour

Manufacturing cost budget (p. 994) A budget made for each manufacturing cost

Materials price variance (p. 1001) The difference between the actual price and the standard cost for materials multiplied by the actual quantity of materials used

Materials quantity variance (p. 1001) The difference between the actual quantity used and the quantity of materials allowed multiplied by the standard cost of the materials

Materials usage variance (p. 1001) See Materials quantity variance

Relevant range of activity (p. 996) The different levels of activity at which a factory is expected to operate

Semivariable costs (p. 993) Costs that vary with, but not in direct proportion to, the volume of activity

Standard cost card (p. 999) A form that shows the per-unit standard costs for materials, labor, and overhead

Variable costs (p. 992) Costs that vary in total in direct proportion to changes in the level of activity

Variance analysis (p. 1001) Explains the difference between standard cost and actual cost

Comprehensive Self Review

1. What is the primary characteristic of a fixed cost?
2. What does the following statement mean? A variable cost remains fixed per unit.
3. Is there a weakness in using a fixed budget as a cost control tool?
4. What is a flexible budget?
5. When will a job be charged more overhead than the standard allowed for the units produced?

(Answers to Comprehensive Self Review are at the end of the chapter.)

Discussion Questions

1. Define the term "fixed cost."
2. What are semivariable costs?

3. Explain how variable costs per unit change as the level of activity changes.
4. Briefly explain the high-low point method for analyzing semivariable costs.
5. What is the relevant range of activity as used in budgeting?
6. What is a budget?
7. What is included in a budget performance report?
8. What is a flexible budget?
9. What is the advantage of using a flexible budget?
10. What are standard costs?
11. How are standards set for materials?
12. Explain how to compute the quantity variance for materials.
13. What does the price variance for materials show?
14. Which manager would more likely be responsible for materials quantity variances?
15. What are the possible causes of unfavorable materials variances?
16. Who provides information about wage rates in setting labor standards?
17. What two variances make up the total labor variance?
18. What are the possible causes of labor variances?
19. What are the possible causes of overhead variances?

APPLICATIONS

Exercises

Exercise 29.1
Objective 29-2

▶ **Using the high-low point method.**

Alpha Company's records show the following data for the four quarters of 20X1:

Quarter	Direct Labor Hours	Utilities Cost
First	11,700	$5,429
Second	13,700	6,580
Third	18,400	7,908
Fourth	12,700	5,545

Compute the fixed and variable elements of utilities cost, using the high-low point method.

Exercise 29.2
Objective 29-4

▶ **Developing a flexible budget for overhead.**

In Woodinville Power Corporation's factory, fixed indirect labor costs are $6,300 per month. Variable indirect labor costs are $1.40 per direct labor hour. The budget for the month of May 20X1 calls for employment of 16,500 direct labor hours. Compute the flexible budget amounts for indirect labor costs at the following levels of activity: 100 percent of budget, 95 percent of budget, and 105 percent of budget.

Exercise 29.3
Objective 29-5

▶ **Developing standard costs per unit of product.**

In preparing the standard cost for each unit of QS500, the company's only product, the accountant for Total Earth Solvents Corporation has developed the following data for the year 20X1:

Total budgeted production, 23,000 units

Raw material:

Two units of raw material are required for each unit of finished goods.

The cost of each unit of raw material is $13.

Labor:

Three hours of direct labor are required for each unit of finished goods.

The labor rate per hour is $20.00.

Manufacturing overhead:

Overhead is 20 percent of direct labor.

Compute the standard cost per unit of product, showing the standard cost of materials, labor, and overhead.

Data for Exercises 29.4 through 29.11. Please round your answers to the nearest dollar.
The standard cost card for a unit of Product AX at the Cleaning Chemicals Corp. shows the following standard cost information:

Materials: 2 gallons at $12 per gallon	$ 24
Labor: 5 hours at $20 per hour	100
Overhead: 80% of direct labor	80
Total	$204

During the month of October 20X1, Job O-3 was completed. It was the only job worked on during October. Six thousand units were produced from the job. The actual costs were as shown below:

Materials: 12,200 gallons at $12.10 per gallon	$ 147,620
Labor: 30,100 hours at $20.10 per hour	605,010
Actual overhead	484,008
Total	$1,236,638

Computing total variance between standard costs and actual costs. ◀ **Exercise 29.4**
Calculate the total variance between the actual cost and the standard cost for the month. **Objective 29-6**

Computing total variance for materials. ◀ **Exercise 29.5**
Calculate the total variance for materials for the month. **Objective 29-7**

Computing quantity variance for materials. ◀ **Exercise 29.6**
Calculate the quantity variance for materials for the month. **Objective 29-7**

Computing price variance for materials. ◀ **Exercise 29.7**
Calculate the price variance for materials for the month. **Objective 29-7**

Computing total variance for labor. ◀ **Exercise 29.8**
Calculate the total variance for labor for the month. **Objective 29-7**

Computing quantity variance for labor. ◀ **Exercise 29.9**
Calculate the quantity variance for labor for the month. **Objective 29-7**

Computing rate variance for labor. ◀ **Exercise 29.10**
Calculate the rate variance for labor for the month. **Objective 29-7**

Computing total overhead variance. ◀ **Exercise 29.11**
Calculate the total variance for overhead for the month. **Objective 29-7**

PROBLEMS

Problem Set A

Problem 29.1A
Objective 29-2

▶ **Analyzing semivariable costs using the high-low point method.**

The accountant of Saturn Health Products, LLC, has compiled the following information about the direct labor hours and the indirect labor costs for each month of 20X1:

Month	Direct Labor Hours	Indirect Labor Costs
January	1,700	$6,890
February	1,520	6,460
March	2,250	7,410
April	2,400	7,630
May	3,150	8,820
June	3,000	8,490
July	3,050	8,660
August	2,800	8,370
September	2,560	8,020
October	2,700	8,220
November	2,590	8,070
December	2,000	7,200

INSTRUCTIONS

1. Compute the monthly fixed costs (rounded to the nearest whole dollar) and the variable costs per hour (rounded to the nearest whole cent) using the high-low point method. Use the highest-cost month in calculating fixed costs.
2. Compute the estimated total indirect labor cost if 2,600 hours of direct labor are employed during a month.

Analyze: Refer to your Instruction 1 answer. What percentage of total costs for May is attributable to variable costs?

Problem 29.2A
Objective 29-3

▶ **Preparing a flexible overhead budget and an overhead performance report.**

The accountant for C. Breit Products, Inc., has analyzed the manufacturing overhead costs for the company's assembly department. The fixed and variable costs follow:

	Variable Cost Element per Hour	Monthly Fixed Cost Element
Indirect labor	$2.00	$1,900
Payroll taxes	0.35	200
Indirect materials	0.25	200
Utilities	0.50	300
Depreciation	—	1,500
Taxes and insurance	—	1,000
Maintenance	0.35	300

INSTRUCTIONS

1. Prepare a flexible budget for the department for the month of May 20X1, assuming that the expected production is for 3,500 direct labor hours. Show costs for production levels of 90 percent and 110 percent of the expected production level of 3,500 hours.
2. Assume that during the month of May, actual production was 3,000 hours. Actual costs for the month were as follows:

Indirect labor	$7,850
Payroll taxes	1,035
Indirect materials	980
Utilities	1,860
Depreciation	1,500
Taxes and insurance	985
Maintenance	1,320

Prepare a departmental monthly overhead performance report comparing actual costs with the budget allowance for the total number of hours worked. Round amounts to the nearest dollar.

Analyze: If C. Breit Products, Inc., operates at the expected production level of 3,500 direct labor hours, what total manufacturing overhead cost is projected per direct labor hour?

Analyzing materials variances.

◀ **Problem 29.3A**
Objective 29-7

West Texas Chemical Company manufactures a product called Kylon, which requires three raw materials. Production is in batches of 1,000 gallons of finished product. The firm uses standard costs as a control device. Its standard costs for materials for each batch of Kylon have been established as follows:

Material	Quantity	Standard Cost per Gallon	Standard Cost per Batch
Starter	720 gal.	$2.20	$1,584.00
Acid	190 gal.	6.00	1,140.00
Activator	90 gal.	15.00	1,350.00
Total standard cost	1,000 gal.		$4,074.00

The output is packaged in 50-gallon drums. During the month of June 20X1, 200 drums of Kylon were produced. There was no beginning or ending inventory of work in process. The materials actually used during June are listed below:

Material	Quantity	Cost per Gallon
Starter	7,270 gal.	$ 2.00
Acid	1,940 gal.	6.60
Activator	630 gal.	19.50

INSTRUCTIONS

1. Compute the total variance between the actual cost of the materials used during June and the standard cost of the materials. Also compute the total variance for each type of material.
2. Analyze the variances for each type of material for the month.

Analyze: Which raw materials were obtained at a price that was lower than standard cost?

Problem 29.4A
Objective 29-7

▶ **Analyzing material and labor variances.**

Zack Manufacturing Company makes a product that is processed through two departments: cutting and final. All materials are added in the first department. During the month of March 20X1, the company made 6,000 units of the product. Standard costs and actual costs for materials and labor are given below:

STANDARD COSTS

Raw materials

Framing: 11 square feet at $0.30 per square foot	$ 3.30
Filler: 14 pounds at $0.19 per pound	2.66
Standard materials cost per unit	$ 5.96

Direct labor

Cutting dept.: 1.4 hours at $15.00 per hour	$ 21.00
Final dept.: 0.6 hour at $22.00 per hour	13.20
Standard direct labor cost per unit	$ 34.20

ACTUAL COSTS

Raw materials

Framing: 62,700 square feet at $0.31 per square foot	$ 19,437.00
Filler: 84,800 pounds at $0.17 per pound	14,416.00
Total actual materials cost	$ 33,853.00

Direct labor

Cutting dept.: 8,200 hours at $15.30 per hour	$125,460.00
Final dept.: 3,960 hours at $21.80 per hour	86,328.00
Total actual direct labor cost	$211,788.00

INSTRUCTIONS

1. Prepare a comparison of the actual cost of materials with the standard cost of materials for the 6,000 units of product. Then prepare an analysis of the materials variances.
2. Prepare a comparison of the actual cost of labor with the standard cost of labor for the 6,000 units of product. Then prepare an analysis of the labor variances.

Analyze: What total variance in labor was reported by the final department?

Problem Set B

Problem 29.1B
Objective 29-2

▶ **Analyzing semivariable costs using the high-low point method.**

The accountant for BioSafe Products, Inc., has compiled the following information about the direct labor hours and utility costs for each month of 20X1:

Month	Direct Labor Hours	Utility Costs
January	2,550	$2,250
February	2,695	2,295
March	3,280	2,630
April	3,745	2,885
May	4,410	3,575

Month	Direct Labor Hours	Utility Costs
June	4,190	3,185
July	4,288	3,300
August	3,810	3,010
September	3,679	2,895
October	3,452	2,895
November	3,018	2,840
December	2,400	2,200

INSTRUCTIONS

1. Compute the monthly fixed costs (rounded to nearest whole dollar) and the variable costs per hour (rounded to nearest whole cent) using the high-low point method. Use the highest-cost month in calculating fixed costs.
2. Compute the estimated total indirect labor cost if 3,500 hours of direct labor are employed during the month.

Analyze: Refer to your Instruction 1 answer. What approximate percentage of total costs is attributable to fixed costs?

Preparing a flexible overhead budget and an overhead performance report. ◀ Problem 29.2B

Midwest Manufacturing Company makes a single product that requires one hour of labor for each unit. The budgeted output for 20X1 is 36,000 units. Fixed and variable overhead cost data are as follows:

Objective 29-3

	Variable Element per Hour	Yearly Fixed Cost Element
Indirect labor	$0.75	$20,000
Payroll taxes	0.25	1,500
Indirect materials	0.25	1,800
Utilities	0.35	2,400
Depreciation	—	20,000
Taxes and insurance	—	5,250
Maintenance	0.30	2,400

INSTRUCTIONS

1. Prepare a flexible budget for Midwest Manufacturing for the year 20X1. The flexible budget should show costs for production levels of 90 percent, 100 percent, and 110 percent of the expected production level of 36,000 units (36,000 hours).
2. Assume that during the year 20X1, actual production was 35,500 hours. Actual costs for the year were as follows:

Indirect labor	$46,600
Payroll taxes	10,350
Indirect materials	11,050
Utilities	15,200
Depreciation	20,000
Taxes and insurance	5,175
Maintenance	12,750

Prepare a yearly overhead performance report comparing actual costs with the budget allowance for the number of hours worked.

Analyze: If Midwest Manufacturing Company operates at the expected production level of 36,000 direct labor hours, what total manufacturing overhead cost can be projected per direct labor hour? (Round to nearest cent.)

Problem 29.3B
Objective 29-7

Analyzing materials variances.

Organic Manufacturing Co. manufactures the product Orgex, which requires three raw materials. Production is in batches of 2,500 pounds of materials. Any waste is thrown away. The firm uses standard costs as a control device. Its standard costs for materials are as follows:

Material	Quantity	Standard Cost per Pound	Standard Cost per Batch
Natural resins	2,200 lb.	$0.65	$1,430
Vegetable tint	100 lb.	0.22	22
Hardener	200 lb.	0.65	130
Totals	2,500 lb.		$1,582

During the month of July 20X1, 25,000 pounds of Orgex were produced. There was no beginning or ending inventory of work in process. The materials actually used during July are listed below:

Material	Quantity	Total Cost
Natural resins	22,100 lb.	$13,923
Vegetable tint	1,150 lb.	230
Hardener	2,050 lb.	1,353

INSTRUCTIONS

1. Compute the total variance between the actual cost of the materials used during July and the standard cost of the materials. Also compute the total variance for each type of material.
2. Analyze the variances for each type of material for the month.

Analyze: Which raw materials were obtained at lower-than-standard unit costs?

Problem 29.4B
Objective 29-7

Analyzing material and labor variances.

Milano Leather Goods, Inc., makes one product that is processed through two departments: cutting and accessory. All materials are added in the first department. During the month of January 20X1, 8,000 units of the product were made. Standard costs and actual costs for materials and labor are given as follows:

STANDARD COSTS

Raw materials
- Raw material: 4 units at $4.75 per unit .... $ 19.00
- Accessory sets: 4 sets at $0.50 per unit 2.00
- Standard materials cost per unit .... $ 21.00

Direct labor
- Cutting dept.: 1/10 hour at $12.00 per hour .... $ 1.20
- Accessory dept.: 1/4 hour at $16.00 per hour 4.00
- Standard direct labor cost per unit .... $ 5.20

ACTUAL COSTS

Raw materials

Raw material: 32,600 units at $4.72 per unit	$153,872.00
Accessory sets: 32,050 sets at $0.52 per unit	16,666.00
Total actual materials cost	$170,538.00

Direct labor

Cutting dept.: 830 hours at $12.10 per hour	$ 10,043.00
Accessory dept.: 2,050 hours at $16.10 per hour	33,005.00
Total actual direct labor cost	$ 43,048.00

INSTRUCTIONS

1. Prepare a comparison of the actual cost of materials with the standard cost of materials for the 8,000 units of product. Then prepare an analysis of the materials variances.
2. Prepare a comparison of the actual cost of labor with the standard cost of labor for the 8,000 units of product. Then prepare an analysis of the labor variances.

Analyze: Is the greatest portion of the total accessory set materials variance attributable to quantity or to price?

Critical Thinking Problem 29.1

Costs Incurred

Tess Company manufactures one product. Standard costs for each unit of the product follow:

Materials: 5 gallons at $1.15	$ 5.75
Direct labor: 1 hour at $18	18.00
Manufacturing overhead: 0.5 hour at $18	9.00
Total standard costs per unit	$32.75

During the month of June 20X1, 1,000 units of product were manufactured. At the end of the month, the following data was available:

a. The total materials variance was $38 favorable.
b. The materials quantity variance was $115 unfavorable.
c. The labor rate variance was $1,050 unfavorable.
d. Actual hours worked amounted to 1,050.

INSTRUCTIONS

Answer the following questions. Show all computations.

1. What was the actual total materials cost?
2. How many units of raw material were used?
3. What was the amount of materials price variance?
4. What was the actual labor rate per hour?
5. What was the actual labor cost for the month?
6. What was the amount of labor time variance?

Analyze: What was the cost incurred per gallon of raw materials? (Round to the nearest cent.)

Critical Thinking Problem 29.2

Recreating Data

New Millennium Industries, a manufacturer of sports shoes, uses a standard cost system. When Michelle Nicole, the cost accountant for the company, started to analyze the labor variances for May, she discovered that some of the data had inadvertently been destroyed.

From a review of the data available, Michelle learns that the labor time variance for May was $7,272 favorable and that the standard labor rate was $24 per hour. A cost-of-living adjustment in the workers' hourly rate caused an unfavorable labor price variance of $0.40 per hour. Total standard labor hours for May's output of shoes was 12,000 hours.

Determine the actual number of labor hours worked in May.

BUSINESS CONNECTIONS

Managerial | FOCUS

Controlling Costs

1. How would the distinction between fixed and variable costs help management in forecasting cash needs for the business?
2. Explain how a flexible budget can be used by management to help control costs.
3. Briefly explain to management the reasons why variances between actual and standard costs of materials might exist.
4. The accountant for JRH Corporation has noticed that historically, when there have been favorable labor rate variances, there have been unfavorable labor time variances. What factors could explain this phenomenon?
5. In a large company, the overall wage structure is determined by the personnel department. However, the manager of each producing department has limited control over the rates paid to individual workers. Who would be responsible for labor rate variances?
6. Explain how determination of standard costs enables managers to pinpoint responsibility for inefficient performance.

Internal Control and FRAUD PREVENTION

Evaluating Standards

The budget uses cost standards that are developed by management. These standards determine if a product is being produced according to the business plan. If the product is using more materials than planned, it will cause net income to decrease from planned net income. If labor hours used are more but the budgeted labor pay rate is less than planned, the net income could increase from the planned net income.

Shelly is an accountant who determines the standards to be used for materials and labor. Shelly feels she understands payroll rates in the job market much better than the payroll department. She has set a labor time standard higher than what has been suggested by management. Her attitude is that the company needs more lower-paid workers, and by increasing the time standard, the labor time variance will be favorable. She believes this will strengthen her argument that workers are overpaid.

At the end of the month, the total labor costs have a favorable variance, primarily due to a high labor time variance. Is Shelly unethical in her actions? What could happen because of her actions?

Financial Statement ANALYSIS

Home Depot

Revenues and Service Revenues

Refer to The Home Depot, Inc., *2018 Annual Report (for the fiscal year ended February 3, 2019)* in Appendix A.

In Note 1 of the Notes to Consolidated Financial Statements, review the Fiscal 2018 and Subsequent Periods paragraph. The company calls attention to three sources of revenue that are outside of normal building product sales.

1. Name the three sources of revenue discussed in these notes.
2. Define gift card breakage income. Explain whether this figure is significant in comparison to the figures reported on the Consolidated Statements of Earnings.

TEAMWORK

Standard Costs Development

Your company makes crayons. Determine the materials and labor you would need to make a box of 10 crayons. Next, determine the amount of materials per box and the labor hours per box. Next, determine the cost per ounce of each material and the cost per hour for each worker. These are your standards. Your company has an order from Vans Supermarkets for 10,000 boxes. Using the standards you have developed, calculate the standard cost for materials and labor. Compare your group standards to the other groups. What are the differences? Can you see how different groups can develop standards differently?

Answers to Comprehensive Self Review

1. It remains constant in total during the period and does not change merely because the level of activity changes.
2. A variable cost is one whose total varies in direct proportion to the level of activity, yet the cost per unit of activity remains the same within the usual range of activity level.
3. Yes, if the level of production activity is substantially different from the level anticipated in the fixed budget, the actual and budgeted costs will not be related to comparable bases.
4. A flexible budget is a budget showing expected costs at more than one level of activity.
5. When actual hours worked exceed the standard hours allowed (assuming that the overhead application rate is based on direct labor hours) and the business is allocating overhead on each job.

Cost-Revenue Analysis for Decision Making

Chapter 30

www.lowes.com

Ken Wolter/Shutterstock

Lowe's Companies, Inc. (Lowe's) is the world's second-largest retailer of home improvement products. Lowe's was incorporated in 1952 and operated 1,839 stores in the United States (including both Lowe's and Orchard Supply Hardware locations), 303 stores in Canada, and 10 stores in Mexico in 2017. As the company continually strives to improve profitability, it undertook a strategic reassessment of its business during 2018. This examination led to a number of difficult decisions, including the closure of some of the above-mentioned retail locations, that are designed to benefit the company as it moves forward.

This strategic reassessment led to the decision to discontinue all operations in Mexico, close 20 Lowe's stores and all Orchard Supply Hardware stores in the United States, close 31 locations in Canada, and exit a number of businesses such as Alacrity Renovation Services and Iris Smart Home. To make these decisions, Lowe's examined the profitability of each segment independently and determined they were not contributing sufficiently to the overall profit of the company. Lowe's pursued this reassessment to "build a sustainable foundation to position the company for long-term success." The decision to close stores and discontinue other business segments should allow the company to focus on improving execution in online and retail locations.

thinking critically

What do you think are the critical questions a company like Lowe's asks before making the decision to close one of its stores?

LEARNING OBJECTIVES

30-1 Explain the basic steps in the decision-making process.

30-2 Prepare income statements using the absorption costing and direct costing methods.

30-3 Using the contribution margin approach, analyze the profits of segments of a business.

30-4 Determine relevant cost and revenue data for decision-making purposes.

30-5 Apply an appropriate decision process in three situations:
   a. Pricing products in special cases.
   b. Deciding whether to purchase new equipment.
   c. Deciding whether to make or to buy a part.

30-6 Define the accounting terms new to this chapter.

NEW TERMS

absorption costing
capacity
common costs
contribution margin
controllable fixed costs
differential cost
direct costing
manufacturing margin
marginal income
opportunity cost
sunk cost
variable costing

Section 1

SECTION OBJECTIVES	TERMS TO LEARN
>> 30-1 Explain the basic steps in the decision-making process. **WHY IT'S IMPORTANT** Decisions require data about feasible alternatives. **>> 30-2** Prepare income statements using the absorption costing and direct costing methods. **WHY IT'S IMPORTANT** How costs are treated must be considered when decisions are made. **>> 30-3** Using the contribution approach, analyze the profits of segments of a business. **WHY IT'S IMPORTANT** A business needs to assess the performance of its segments. **>> 30-4** Determine relevant cost and revenue data for decision-making purposes. **WHY IT'S IMPORTANT** Decision makers need to identify relevant from nonrelevant data.	absorption costing common costs contribution margin controllable fixed costs differential cost direct costing manufacturing margin marginal income opportunity cost sunk cost variable costing

The Decision Process

Accountants play a key role in a company's decision-making processes. They gather, analyze, and present large amounts of financial information to decision makers.

>> **30-1 OBJECTIVE**
Explain the basic steps in the decision-making process.

Exploring the Decision Process

The decision-making process involves the following six steps:

Step 1. *Define the problem.*
Step 2. *Identify workable alternatives.*
Step 3. *Determine relevant cost and revenue data.*
Step 4. *Evaluate the cost and revenue data.*
Step 5. *Consider appropriate nonfinancial factors.*
Step 6. *Make a decision.*

>> **30-2 OBJECTIVE**
Prepare income statements using the absorption costing and direct costing methods.

Direct Costing Versus Absorption Costing

Recall that some costs are *fixed;* they do not vary in total during a period, even though the volume of goods manufactured or sold might be higher or lower than anticipated. Examples of fixed costs are depreciation of equipment, rent on the building, and salaries and related expenses for employees. *Variable costs* vary in total directly with the volume of manufacturing or sales activity. Variable costs include sales commissions, delivery expenses, and the loss from uncollectible accounts. *Semivariable costs* have characteristics of both fixed and variable costs. Utilities expense is an example of a semivariable cost.

Under **absorption costing,** all manufacturing costs, including fixed manufacturing costs, are included in the cost of goods manufactured. The value of the ending inventory includes direct material, direct labor, variable manufacturing overhead, and fixed manufacturing overhead costs. Under **direct costing,** which is also known as **variable costing,** only variable costs are included in the cost of goods manufactured. Fixed manufacturing costs are charged to expense in the period incurred. Accountants who support direct costing contend that fixed costs are not dependent on the quantity of goods produced, so they should not be allocated to specific units manufactured. They believe that fixed costs relate to the capacity to produce goods, not to the actual goods produced. Additionally, absorption costing is required by GAAP for financial reporting and the IRS for income tax reporting.

Direct costing is widely used when making business decisions; however, **direct costing is not acceptable either for GAAP financial reporting purposes** or for tax reporting to the IRS.

Absorption Costing
Let's use White Manufacturing Corporation to illustrate the difference between absorption and direct costing. The manufacturing costs are separated into fixed and variable elements as follows:

Beginning inventory of finished goods	–0–
Units produced (no work-in-process inventories)	10,000
Units sold	9,000
Units in ending inventory of finished goods	1,000
Sales price for each unit	$50
Variable manufacturing costs per unit—materials, labor, and variable manufacturing overhead	$15
Variable selling and administrative expenses per unit sold	$5
Fixed manufacturing costs	$70,000
Fixed selling and administrative expenses	$100,000

Figure 30.1 is a condensed income statement using absorption costing. It includes the cost of goods manufactured.

Direct Costing
Figure 30.2 is a condensed income statement using direct costing. Note these differences in direct costing:

- Only variable manufacturing costs are included in the cost of goods manufactured and in the finished goods inventory.
- The **manufacturing margin** is sales minus the variable cost of goods sold.

ABOUT ACCOUNTING

Problem Solving

General problem-solving skills might not be sufficient to meet the demands of a global economy. Accountants must develop a quick sense of assessing relevant costs in decision making.

White Manufacturing Corporation
Partial Income Statement
Year Ended December 31, 20X1

Sales (9,000 units @ $50)		450,000
Cost of goods sold		
Variable manufacturing costs (10,000 units @ $15)	150,000	
Fixed manufacturing costs	70,000	
Total cost of goods manufactured		
($220,000/10,000 units = $22 per unit)	220,000	
Less finished goods ending inventory (1,000 units @ $22)	22,000	
Cost of goods sold		198,000
Gross profit on sales		252,000
Selling and administrative expenses		
Variable expenses (9,000 units @ $5)	45,000	
Fixed expenses	100,000	
Total selling and administrative expenses		145,000
Net income before taxes		107,000

FIGURE 30.1

Income Statement Using Absorption Costing

FIGURE 30.2

Income Statement Using Direct Costing

White Manufacturing Corporation
Income Statement
Year Ended December 31, 20X1

Sales (9,000 units @ $50)		450 000 00
Cost of Goods Sold		
Variable manufacturing costs		
(10,000 units @ $15)	150 000 00	
Less finished goods inventory		
(1,000 units @ $15)	15 000 00	
Cost of goods sold		135 000 00
Manufacturing margin		315 000 00
Variable selling and administrative expenses		
(9,000 units @ $5)		45 000 00
Marginal income on sales		270 000 00
Fixed costs and expenses		
Fixed manufacturing costs	70 000 00	
Fixed selling and administrative expenses	100 000 00	170 000 00
Net income before taxes		100 000 00

important!

Direct Costing

Under direct costing, all fixed manufacturing overhead costs are charged to expense in the period incurred.

- The **marginal income** on sales is the manufacturing margin minus variable operating expenses. This is also known as the contribution margin.
- The net income is the marginal income on sales minus fixed manufacturing costs and fixed selling and administrative expenses.
- If there is a change in the inventory level, income under absorption costing will be different from income under direct costing.

The statement in Figure 30.2 illustrates only one of several different arrangements that might be used.

When absorption costing is used, a portion of the fixed manufacturing overhead is included in finished goods inventory and is not expensed in the current period. Under absorption costing, if the number of units in ending inventory increases, the amount of fixed overhead in finished goods inventory increases and the amount of fixed overhead expensed in the current period decreases. In contrast, under direct costing all fixed overhead is expensed in the current period. Under direct costing, an increase in finished goods inventory does not affect the amount of fixed costs expensed.

When finished goods inventory increases, net income under absorption costing is higher than that under direct costing. This is the case in Figures 30.1 and 30.2. Finished goods inventory increased by 1,000 units, and net income under absorption costing is $7,000 higher than net income under direct costing. When the finished goods inventory level decreases, net income under absorption costing is less than net income under direct costing.

>> **30-3 OBJECTIVE**

Using the contribution margin approach, analyze the profits of segments of a business.

The Concept of Contribution Margin

Contribution margin is revenues minus variable costs. Most decisions concerning segments of a business, such as branch stores, divisions, and products, also involve an analysis of the contribution margin because it avoids arbitrary allocations of common costs. **Common costs** are costs not directly traceable to a specific segment of a business. The profitability of a segment is judged by its contribution margin; that is, the amount contributed toward covering the common costs of the business and producing a profit.

Under the contribution margin approach, the contribution margin is calculated for the business segment. Then the controllable fixed costs of the segment are deducted to determine the segment's contribution to the overall profit of the business. **Controllable fixed costs** are costs that the segment manager can control. Common costs are not allocated to specific segments when computing the segment margin. They are deducted from the total of all segment contributions to determine the company's profit.

The contribution margin approach allows managers to make sound decisions about adding, keeping, or eliminating a segment of the business. If a segment produces a positive contribution margin, it is helping to cover total fixed costs and to provide a profit for the business. Management would consider eliminating any segment with a negative contribution margin. Plans for adding a new segment would include a contribution margin analysis. Management would favorably consider segments with a projected positive contribution margin.

The Concept of Relevant Costs

A **sunk cost** is a cost that has already been incurred. When making decisions, sunk costs are irrelevant. Relevant costs are future or expected costs that will change as a result of a decision. For example, when deciding whether to replace a machine, the original cost of the existing machine is irrelevant. The cost of the new machine is relevant. When deciding whether to close a warehouse, a relevant cost is the salaries of the warehouse personnel. The nonrefundable prepaid rent on the warehouse is irrelevant because it has been paid and cannot be recovered.

>> **30-4 OBJECTIVE**
Determine relevant cost and revenue data for decision-making purposes.

The Concept of Differential Costs

Decision making involves comparing two or more alternatives. A **differential cost** is the difference in cost between one alternative and another. For example, the difference in cost between using a hand-operated press and an automated press is a *differential cost*. While the term *incremental cost* is often used interchangeably with differential cost, incremental cost actually means only an *increase* in cost from one alternative to another. For example, if it costs $40,000 to produce 20 units and $45,000 to produce 30 units, the incremental cost of producing the additional 10 units is $5,000 ($45,000 − $40,000).

The Concept of Opportunity Cost

Opportunity cost is the potential earnings or benefits that are given up because a certain course of action is taken. For example, assume management is deciding between purchasing equipment or investing in securities. The opportunity cost of the decision to purchase the equipment is the amount of interest or dividends that would be received from the securities, if the securities had been purchased rather than the equipment.

Section 1 Review

1. Which of the following is not true concerning absorption costing?
   a. It is required by GAAP for financial reporting purposes.
   b. It is required by the IRS for income tax reporting.
   c. All manufacturing costs, except fixed factory overhead, are included in the cost of finished goods inventory.
   d. All manufacturing costs are included in the cost of finished goods inventory.

2. Which of the following costs are included in the cost of finished goods inventory using direct costing?
   a. direct materials
   b. direct labor
   c. variable factory overhead
   d. all of these

3. Northwood Company reported net sales of $500,000, variable cost of goods sold of $200,000, variable selling and administrative expenses of $85,000, fixed manufacturing costs of $105,000, and fixed selling and administrative expenses of $80,000. The contribution margin is:
   a. $30,000.
   b. $215,000.
   c. $615,000.
   d. $200,000.

4. Northwood Company reported net sales of $500,000, variable cost of goods sold of $200,000, variable selling and administrative expenses of $85,000, fixed manufacturing costs of $105,000, and fixed selling and administrative expenses of $80,000. The net income is:
   a. $30,000.
   b. $215,000.
   c. $110,000.
   d. $135,000.

5. Southwest Inc. would like to exchange an old piece of equipment for a new one. Which of the following is relevant to the decision?
   a. the cost of the old piece of equipment
   b. the book value of the old piece of equipment
   c. the repair costs incurred on the old piece of equipment
   d. the cost of the new equipment

6. When direct costing is used, cost of goods sold reflects:
   a. all manufacturing costs.
   b. variable manufacturing costs only.
   c. variable manufacturing costs and variable selling and administrative expenses.
   d. both variable and fixed manufacturing costs.

7. The potential earnings or benefits given up as a result of a certain course of action is a(n):
   a. opportunity cost.
   b. differential cost.
   c. incremental cost.
   d. sunk cost.

Section 2

SECTION OBJECTIVES	TERM TO LEARN
30-5 Apply an appropriate decision process in three situations: a. Pricing products in special cases. b. Deciding whether to purchase new equipment. c. Deciding whether to make or to buy a part. **WHY IT'S IMPORTANT** Differential revenues and costs are analyzed when choosing among alternatives.	capacity

Cost-Revenue Analysis

In many different situations, managers analyze costs and revenues in order to make decisions. Three common cost-revenue analysis situations will be discussed in this section: (1) product pricing in special situations, (2) purchasing new equipment, and (3) making or buying a part.

> News Media Alliance (https://www.newsmediaalliance.org/) provides comprehensive data covering critical financial areas for print and media companies. Most industry trade organizations report similar data useful for management decision making.

Product Pricing in Special Situations

Direct costing is often useful in setting prices and considering offers to buy products in special circumstances. For example, White Manufacturing Corporation received an offer from an overseas customer to purchase 1,000 units at $25 per unit. The units would incur the usual manufacturing and selling and administrative costs. In addition, there would be a shipping cost of $1 per unit. The company has adequate manufacturing capacity to take the special order without endangering its regular production or its ability to take care of existing customers. **Capacity** in this sense refers to a facility's power to produce or use.

>> **30-5 OBJECTIVE**
> a. Apply an appropriate decision process in pricing products in special cases.

> According to the Federal Reserve, the rate of capacity utilization for total industry in the United States was approximately 78.5 percent in November 2018.

Management reviewed the information shown in Figure 30.1 and computed the following average unit cost under absorption costing:

Manufacturing costs ($220,000 ÷ 10,000 units)	$22.00
Selling and administrative expenses ($145,000 ÷ 9,000 units)	16.11
Total average cost per unit	$38.11

Management also reviewed the information shown in Figure 30.2 to determine the costs under direct costing. The additional shipping expense of $1 per unit was also considered.

Variable manufacturing costs	$15
Variable selling and administrative expenses	5
Variable costs per unit	$20
Additional shipping cost	1
Total variable cost per unit	$21

The difference between the costs ($38.11 and $21) is due to fixed costs, and in this situation the fixed costs are irrelevant. The fixed costs will be incurred whether or not the order is accepted. The incremental cost of making the additional 1,000 units is $21 per unit. Based on this analysis, the company would make a profit of $4 ($25 − $21) per unit if the order were accepted.

Management needs to consider carefully all relevant factors when analyzing special pricing situations. For example, management would not accept the special order if the company did not have sufficient capacity or if the special order jeopardized sales to existing customers. Also, management would need to ensure that the company does not violate federal laws that prohibit price differentials.

>> **30-5 OBJECTIVE**

b. Apply an appropriate decision process in deciding whether to purchase new equipment.

Purchasing New Equipment

The management of JAMES Industries, Inc., is considering the purchase of a new machine that will improve worker productivity. The machine costs $50,000 and has an estimated useful life of 10 years, with no anticipated salvage value. Table 30.1 shows the relevant data for the two alternatives.

Table 30.2 shows the analysis. The left two columns reflect the net income under each alternative. The differential cost data are in the right column. This analysis indicates that if JAMES Industries, Inc., were to purchase the machine, its net income would increase by $5,000 each year. Before making the final decision, however, management needs to consider employee morale and the quality of the product that the new machine will make.

>> **30-5 OBJECTIVE**

c. Apply an appropriate decision process in deciding whether to make or to buy a part.

Making or Buying a Part

JAMES Industries, Inc., purchases a part for $15 per unit. The company uses 24,000 of these parts each year. Management has determined that the part could be made in the company's molding department.

The molding department has a capacity of 20,000 direct labor hours per year. For several years, it has operated at 15,000 direct labor hours per year. For the molding department, the direct labor costs are $16 per hour and variable manufacturing overhead costs are $8 per hour. Annual fixed costs for the department total $75,000. The estimated cost of materials is $7 for each part. Four parts can be produced per hour.

Table 30.3 shows the analysis of the data. If JAMES Industries, Inc., decides to manufacture the part, it will realize a savings of $2 per part, which is a $48,000 savings per year.

TABLE 30.1

Cost and Revenue Data Needed for an Analysis of the Effects of Purchasing a New Machine

	If Machine Is Not Purchased	If Machine Is Purchased
Annual sales (units)	10,000	10,000
Sales price (per unit)	$ 45	$ 45
Cost of machine		$50,000
Other cost data:		
Materials (per unit)	$ 15	$ 15
Labor (per unit)	10	9
Variable overhead (per unit)	3	3
Fixed overhead (per year)	$19,000	$24,000*

*Includes $5,000 per year for additional depreciation for new machine.

TABLE 30.2

Analysis of the Effects of Purchasing a New Machine (based on annual income)

	If Machine Is Not Purchased	If Machine Is Purchased	Differential If Purchased
Annual sales	$450,000	$450,000	
Variable costs:			
Materials	$150,000	$150,000	
Labor	100,000	90,000	$(10,000)
Manufacturing overhead	30,000	30,000	
Total variable costs	$280,000	$270,000	
Contribution margin	$170,000	$180,000	10,000
Fixed costs	19,000	24,000	5,000
Net income	$151,000	$156,000	$ 5,000

Notice that the fixed manufacturing overhead costs are not considered because they remain the same whether the part is purchased or made.

Every day, managers must consider decisions similar to those covered in this chapter. Accountants who understand cost-revenue analysis can assist management to consider the appropriate factors to enable them to reach logical decisions that will increase the company's profitability.

In addition to the factors covered in this chapter, accountants also consider the impact of income taxes and the timing of cash receipts and expenditures. These elements have significant impact on the company's profitability.

TABLE 30.3

Analysis of the Effects of Making or Buying a Part

Cost to purchase part		$ 15.00
Cost to manufacture part:		
Variable costs only		
Materials	$7.00	
Labor (1/4 hour @ $16 per hour)	4.00	
Manufacturing overhead (1/4 hour @ $8 per hour)	2.00	13.00
Differential cost (savings per unit if part is manufactured)		$ 2.00
Number of parts per year		24,000
Total annual savings		$48,000

MANAGERIAL IMPLICATIONS <<

USING COST REVENUE ANALYSIS TO MAKE DECISIONS

- Accountants gather and analyze data so that managers have the necessary information to make effective decisions between alternative courses of action.
- When making decisions, managers are concerned about future costs and revenues.
- Managers use cost-revenue analysis to evaluate the financial effects of decisions before they are made.

- It is critical that managers understand cost analysis and related concepts including sunk costs, relevant costs, differential costs, opportunity costs, and contribution margin.
- Managers focus on the differential revenues and differential costs for each course of action.
- Usually, sunk costs are irrelevant in making decisions.

THINKING CRITICALLY

Why should sunk costs be ignored when making decisions?

Section 2 Review

1. Chase Corp. is currently operating at 80% capacity, producing 5,000 units. Per-unit cost information is shown in the table below.

	Per Unit
Sales price	$34
Direct material	2
Direct labor	3
Variable overhead	4
Fixed overhead	5

   Chase Corp. has been approached by a foreign customer wanting to purchase 100 units of product at a discount. The fixed overhead cost per unit of $5 will be incurred whether or not the special order is accepted. What is the minimum per-unit sales price that management would accept for this order if the company wishes to increase current profits?

   a. any amount over $34 per unit
   b. any amount over $20 per unit
   c. any amount over $14 per unit
   d. any amount over $9 per unit

2. State Co. produces 10,000 units of product annually. The cost per unit of product is direct materials, $8; direct labor, $24; variable manufacturing overhead, $24. Additionally, the company incurs $160,000 of fixed manufacturing costs annually. City Incorporated, an outside supplier, offers to provide State with all the units it needs at $60 per unit. The fixed manufacturing costs will not change whether State produces the units itself or purchases them from City. State should:

   a. buy from City because the relevant cost per unit to make it is $72.
   b. produce the units themselves because the relevant cost per unit to make it is $56.
   c. buy from City because the relevant cost per unit to make it is $48.
   d. produce the units themselves because the relevant cost per unit to make it is $48.

3. Which of the following are usually considered irrelevant in making decisions?

   a. variable production costs
   b. differential costs
   c. sunk costs
   d. opportunity costs

4. Contribution margin is calculated by deducting:

   a. controllable fixed costs from revenue.
   b. variable costs from revenue.
   c. variable costs and controllable fixed costs from revenue.
   d. variable costs and common costs from revenue.

5. In deciding whether to purchase a new machine, which of the following is not relevant?

   a. depreciation
   b. labor cost savings
   c. savings in materials used
   d. cost of the old machine

6. Green Company can purchase a new machine for $100,000. The new machine will have a five-year life with no salvage value. The machine should reduce labor costs by $22,000 per year. Green Company would have to scrap its existing machine, receiving no cash. The existing machine has a book value of $15,000. Should Green purchase the new machine?

   a. yes, as the decreased labor costs are greater than the cost of the new machine
   b. no, as the decreased labor costs are less than the cost of the new machine plus the book value of the existing machine
   c. no, as the decreased labor costs are less than the cost of the new machine
   d. yes, as the decreased labor costs are greater than the cost of the new machine plus the book value of the existing machine

REVIEW   Chapter Summary

To make decisions, management constantly requires financial data, which must be gathered and analyzed by the accountant. In this chapter, you have learned how to evaluate data when cost and revenue considerations are involved.

Learning Objectives

30-1 Explain the basic steps in the decision-making process.

Managers use financial information not only to help identify a problem but also to help reach decisions for solving the problem. The decision-making process involves the following steps:

- Define the problem.
- Identify workable alternatives.
- Determine relevant cost and revenue data.
- Evaluate the cost and revenue data.
- Consider appropriate nonfinancial factors.
- Make a decision.

30-2 Prepare income statements using the absorption costing and direct costing methods.

- In direct costing, only the variable manufacturing costs are considered as part of the cost of goods manufactured. The cost of goods sold, based solely on variable costs, is subtracted from net sales to arrive at the manufacturing margin.
- Variable selling and administrative expenses are deducted from the manufacturing margin to obtain the marginal income on sales.
- Fixed manufacturing costs and fixed operating expenses are subtracted from the marginal income on sales to obtain the net income for the period.

30-3 Using the contribution margin approach, analyze the profits of segments of a business.

The contribution margin measures the excess of revenues over variable costs. If a segment produces a positive contribution margin, it is helping to meet companywide common expenses.

30-4 Determine relevant cost and revenue data for decision-making purposes.

- Relevant costs for making decisions are usually future costs.
- Sunk costs are historical costs and are therefore generally not relevant to business decisions.
- Determining differential costs—the differences in cost between various alternatives—is important in decision making.
- Often the contribution approach is used in evaluating the data that results from the analysis.

30-5 Apply an appropriate decision process in three situations:

a. **Pricing products in special cases.**
   Direct costing is often useful in setting prices, especially when special offers from potential customers to buy the company's product are being considered.

b. **Deciding whether to purchase new equipment.**
   Accountants gather relevant data to compare the proposed purchase of a new machine versus continuing to use the old machine, estimating net income under each alternative and calculating the difference.

c. **Deciding whether to make or to buy a part.**
   When comparing alternatives to make or buy a part, data can be analyzed on the basis of unit cost or annual total costs. Fixed manufacturing costs are not considered when making this analysis because these costs remain the same whether the part is made or bought.

30-6 Define the accounting terms new to this chapter.

Glossary

Absorption costing (p. 1020) The accounting procedure whereby all manufacturing costs, including fixed costs, are included in the cost of goods manufactured

Capacity (p. 1025) A facility's ability to produce or use

Common costs (p. 1022) Costs not directly traceable to a specific segment of a business

Contribution margin (p. 1022) Revenues minus variable costs

Controllable fixed costs (p. 1023) Costs that the segment manager can control

Differential cost (p. 1023) The difference in cost between one alternative and another

Direct costing (p. 1021) The accounting procedure whereby only variable costs are included in the cost of goods manufactured, and fixed manufacturing costs are written off as expenses in the period in which they are incurred

Manufacturing margin (p. 1021) Sales minus the variable cost of goods sold

Marginal income (p. 1022) The manufacturing margin minus variable operating expenses

Opportunity cost (p. 1023) Potential earnings or benefits that are given up because a certain course of action is taken

Sunk cost (p. 1023) A cost that has been incurred and will not change as a result of a decision

Variable costing (p. 1021) See Direct costing

Comprehensive Self Review

1. What are relevant costs?
2. Why are sunk costs ignored in most managerial decisions?
3. Should management automatically reject an offer by a potential customer to purchase some of the company's product at a price that is less than the company's total cost to manufacture the product? Explain.
4. Give some reasons why a company might decide to purchase a part from an outside supplier that is used in its finished product rather than manufacture the part.
5. Briefly define incremental costs.

(Answers to Comprehensive Self Review are at the end of the chapter.)

Discussion Questions

1. Which of the following items are subtracted from net sales to arrive at contribution margin?
   a. fixed administrative expenses
   b. variable administrative expenses
   c. fixed manufacturing costs
   d. variable cost of goods sold
   e. fixed selling expenses
   f. variable selling expenses
2. Briefly describe absorption costing.
3. What is the fundamental difference between direct costing and absorption costing?
4. Is absorption costing or direct costing more useful in making decisions? Why?
5. What is the manufacturing margin?
6. Explain the meaning of marginal income on sales.

7. What are sunk costs?
8. What is a differential cost?
9. Explain opportunity costs.
10. Suggest some nonmeasurable data that might be considered in deciding to replace existing equipment with new equipment.
11. Suppose that a company is considering the purchase of new equipment. The old equipment will be sold when the new equipment is acquired. How should the proceeds from the sale of the old equipment be considered in the analysis of the effects of the purchase?
12. Why might management be reluctant to accept a special order for its products at less than the normal price even though such an order would be legal and profitable?
13. Why might employee morale be a factor in deciding whether to replace existing equipment with new equipment?
14. Why do the analyses presented in this chapter focus on future costs rather than on past costs? Explain.

APPLICATIONS

Exercises

Data for Exercises 30.1 and 30.2.
Starmont Manufacturing Co. divided all of its costs and expenses into fixed and variable components. Data for the company's first year of operations follows. Ignore income taxes.

Beginning inventory of finished goods	–0–
Units produced (no work in process)	16,000
Units sold	13,000
Units in ending inventory of finished goods	3,000
Sales price	$215 per unit
Variable manufacturing costs	$80 for each unit manufactured
Variable selling and administrative expenses	$40 per unit sold
Fixed manufacturing costs for year	$160,000
Fixed selling and administrative expenses for year	$380,000

Using the absorption method.

Using the absorption method, calculate the following:

1. Cost of goods manufactured for the year.
2. The value of the ending inventory of finished goods.
3. The cost of goods sold for the year.
4. Net income for the year.

◀ **Exercise 30.1**
Objective 30-2

Using direct costing.

Using the direct costing method, calculate the following:

1. Ending inventory of finished goods.
2. Manufacturing margin for the year.
3. Net income for the year.

◀ **Exercise 30.2**
Objective 30-2

Exercise 30.3
Objective 30-4

▶ **Identifying relevant costs.**

Memphis Company is considering replacing its existing wrapping system with new equipment. The existing system has a book value of $125,000 and a remaining useful life of two years. The new wrapping system would cost $300,000 and have a useful life of five years with an estimated salvage value of $50,000. The annual production of 10,000 units would not change. It would, however, reduce direct labor costs by $6 per unit. Other fixed costs would increase by $50,000 per year.

Of the information just given, which items are relevant to the decision to replace the equipment?

Exercise 30.4
Objectives 30-4, 30-5a

▶ **Determining relevant costs and making a pricing decision.**

Wisconsin Manufacturing has an opportunity to export 2,500 units of its product to a foreign country. The current selling price is $176, but the special order will be sold at a unit price of $110. This special order will not affect its current sales, all of which are domestic. Freight and shipping costs of $12 per unit would be incurred on the foreign order. Current variable manufacturing costs are $48 per unit manufactured, and variable selling and administrative costs are $35 per unit sold. Included in variable selling expenses is a sales commission of $5 per unit, which would not apply to the foreign order. Fixed manufacturing costs are $188,000 per year and fixed selling and administrative expenses are $165,000 per year.

The company now manufactures and sells 6,000 units per year. What is the effect on profits if the special order is taken? Show all calculations.

Exercise 30.5
Objectives 30-3, 30-4, 30-5a

▶ **Selecting relevant data, determining contribution margin of segment, and making a pricing decision.**

The standard cost sheet for the leading product made by Queen Corporation shows the following data:

Direct materials	$ 52
Direct labor (3 hours at $23/hour)	69
Manufacturing overhead:	
Variable costs (3 hours at $23/hour)	69
Fixed costs (3 hours at $20/hour)	60
Total standard cost	$250

The product normally sells for $317. The company is presently operating slightly over 70 percent of capacity.

1. A chain of discount stores has offered to purchase 4,800 units of the product for $237 per unit. Shipping costs would be $3 per unit. Special packaging would be needed and would cost an additional $2 per unit. There would be no other variable selling or administrative expenses. Should the order be accepted? (Show all calculations.)

2. Ignoring all factors except those given, what is the least amount that Queen Corporation could profitably accept for a special order of 4,800 units?

Exercise 30.6
Objectives 30-4, 30-5b

▶ **Selecting relevant data and deciding whether to purchase equipment.**

Santa Clara Microelectronics is considering the purchase of a new factory machine at a cost of $195,000. The machine would perform a function that is now being performed by hand. The new machine would have a life of 10 years, would produce 16,500 units a year (the current output), and would have no salvage value. Direct labor costs would be reduced by $1.00 per unit, and variable overhead costs would also be reduced by $1.00 per unit. Fixed costs other than depreciation would increase by $2,900 per year.

Should the machine be purchased? What is the impact of the decision on annual net income?

Data for Exercises 30.7 and 30.8.

Harbor Corporation is manufacturing a part that is used in its finished product. The costs for each unit of the part follow:

Direct materials		$ 34
Direct labor		35
Manufacturing overhead:		
Variable costs	$25	
Fixed costs	8	33
Total cost		$102

The fixed overhead is based on $800,000 of fixed costs to manufacture 100,000 parts per year. If the part is not manufactured, fixed costs will be reduced by approximately $400,000 per year.

Selecting relevant data, determining contribution margin of a segment, and deciding whether to make or to buy a part. ◀ **Exercise 30.7**
Objectives 30-3, 30-4, 30-5c

Instead of making the part, Harbor has an opportunity to purchase the part from an outside company for $89 per unit. Should the company accept the offer, or should it continue to manufacture the part?

Selecting relevant data, determining contribution margin of a segment, and deciding whether to make or buy a part. ◀ **Exercise 30.8**
Objectives 30-3, 30-4, 30-5c

What is the most that Harbor should pay to an outside vendor to buy the part?

PROBLEMS

Problem Set A

Preparing income statements based on absorption costing and direct costing. ◀ **Problem 30.1A**
Objective 30-2

The following data pertains to the operations of Alpha Corporation for the year ended December 31, 20X1, its first year of operations. Alpha Corporation makes computer equipment. Round ending inventory computations to the nearest dollar.

DATA FOR 20X1

Sales	3,650 units @ $149/unit
Variable manufacturing costs	3,900 units @ $56/unit
Variable selling and administrative expenses	$5/unit
Fixed manufacturing costs	$99,100
Fixed selling and administrative expenses	$60,000
Finished goods inventory, December 31, 20X1	250 units

INSTRUCTIONS

1. Prepare an income statement for the year using the absorption costing approach.
2. Prepare an income statement for the year using the direct costing approach.
3. Explain the reason for the difference between the net income or loss computed under the two methods.

Analyze: Assume that Alpha Corporation's manufacturing managers believe that only those costs that contribute directly to product production should be assigned to cost of goods manufactured. Which costing method would these managers prefer?

Problem 30.2A
Objectives 30-2, 30-3, 30-4, 30-5a

▶ **Preparing an income statement based on direct costing, choosing relevant data, determining contribution margin of a segment, and making a pricing decision.**

Texas Controls Inc. began operations in 20X1 to manufacture a single product. There are no ending work-in-process inventories. Relevant data for the year follow:

OPERATING DATA FOR 20X1

Quantities:

Beginning inventories, finished goods	–0–
Units produced during the year	6,900
Units sold during the year	6,000

Costs:

Direct materials ($34 per unit)	$234,600
Direct labor ($32 per unit)	220,800
Variable factory overhead ($20 per unit)	138,000
Fixed factory overhead	66,000
Variable selling and administrative expenses ($19 per unit)	114,000
Fixed selling and administrative expenses	85,000
Selling price for each unit	141

INSTRUCTIONS

1. Prepare an income statement for 20X1 using direct costing.
2. Assume that the company has an opportunity to sell 900 units of the product in a foreign country for $116 per unit. No fixed or variable selling and administrative expenses would be incurred in connection with these units except shipping costs of $18 per unit and miscellaneous administrative expenses of $3 per unit. The company has idle capacity, and the order would not affect present markets. Would it be profitable for the company to accept the order? Show all computations.

Analyze: What percentage of the foreign sales order would be realized as marginal income?

Problem 30.3A
Objectives 30-3, 30-4, 30-5b

▶ **Choosing relevant data, determining contribution margin of a segment, and deciding whether to purchase equipment.**

Prince Corporation makes a single product that it sells to retail stores. The firm's finishing department uses hand labor to perform its work on all products. A proposal has been made by the company's vice president to acquire machinery that will perform most of the functions of this department. The finishing department has consistently produced 41,000 units a year, and that is the estimated production for the foreseeable future. A summary of the manufacturing costs of the department follows:

Direct materials	$102,500
Direct labor	768,750
Manufacturing overhead:	
Variable costs	153,750
Fixed costs	102,500

The machinery being considered will cost $906,000 and have an estimated useful life of six years, with no salvage value. The machinery will cause the following changes in costs:

a. Direct labor will decrease by $8.10 per unit.
b. Direct materials will not change.
c. Variable manufacturing overhead will decrease by $1.30 per unit.
d. Fixed manufacturing overhead will increase by $41,000 per year.

INSTRUCTIONS

1. Prepare an analysis showing the effect on annual net income of purchasing the equipment.
2. What other factors should be considered in making the decision?

Analyze: Assume that the use of the new machinery will increase the number of imperfect products produced by 2 percent of total production. These imperfect products must be reprocessed at a cost of $10 per unit, increasing variable manufacturing costs. What net annual increase or decrease in costs can be projected?

Choosing relevant data and deciding whether to make or buy a part.

◀ **Problem 30.4A**
Objectives 30-4, 30-5c

OZ Innovations, Inc., is currently manufacturing a part that goes into its main product. Each year 5,000 of these parts are used. Cost data for the past year that relates to the 5,000 parts are given below. Fixed costs are allocated on the basis of direct labor hours. An outside company has offered to supply the part for $48.00 per unit, plus a shipping charge of $5.00 per unit. The plant now used by OZ Innovations, Inc., to manufacture the part would not be used to capacity within the foreseeable future if the part is purchased outside.

Variable costs:	
Direct materials	$150,000
Direct labor	100,000
Variable overhead costs	10,000
Fixed overhead costs	25,000

INSTRUCTIONS

1. Prepare an analysis comparing the unit cost of manufacturing the part with the unit cost of purchasing it.
2. What other factors are important in making the decision to accept or reject the offer?

Analyze: What is the highest cost that the company should consider paying for the part in an outside purchase?

Problem Set B

Preparing income statements based on absorption costing and direct costing.

◀ **Problem 30.1B**
Objective 30-2

The following data pertains to the operations of Eastern Industries for the year ended December 31, 20X1, its first year of operations. Eastern Industries makes kitchen appliances. Round ending inventory computations to the nearest dollar.

DATA FOR 20X1

Sales	3,700 units @ $67/unit
Variable manufacturing costs	4,000 units @ $32/unit
Variable selling and administrative costs	$4/unit
Fixed manufacturing costs	$52,000
Fixed selling and administrative expenses	$25,000
Finished goods inventory, December 31, 20X1	300 units

INSTRUCTIONS

1. Prepare an income statement for the year using the absorption costing approach.
2. Prepare an income statement for the year using the direct costing approach.
3. Explain the reason for the difference between the net income or loss computed by the two different methods.

Analyze: Under the absorption costing method, what percentage of cost of goods sold is attributable to fixed manufacturing costs?

Problem 30.2B
Objectives 30-2, 30-3, 30-4, 30-5a

▶ **Preparing an income statement based on direct costing, choosing relevant data, determining contribution margin of a segment, and making a pricing decision.**

Pitt Corporation began operations in 20X1 to manufacture a single product. Relevant data for the year follow. There are no work-in-process inventories.

OPERATING DATA FOR 20X1

Quantities:	
Beginning inventories, finished goods	–0–
Units produced during the year	5,000
Units sold during the year	4,800
Costs:	
Direct materials ($26 per unit)	$130,000
Direct labor ($24 per unit)	120,000
Variable factory overhead ($10 per unit)	50,000
Fixed factory overhead	125,000
Variable selling and administrative expenses ($7 per unit)	33,600
Fixed selling and administrative expenses	75,000
Selling price for each unit	125

INSTRUCTIONS

1. Prepare an income statement for 20X1 using direct costing.

2. Assume that the company has an opportunity to sell 1,000 units of the product in a foreign country for $79 per unit. No fixed or variable selling and administrative expenses would be incurred in connection with these units except a $7 shipping and handling cost per unit. The company has idle capacity, and the order would not affect present markets. Would it be profitable for the company to accept the order? Show all computations.

Analyze: If Pitt Corporation had used the absorption costing method, would the value of ending inventories be higher or lower than that reflected in the statement you prepared? Explain.

Problem 30.3B
Objectives 30-3, 30-4, 30-5b

▶ **Choosing relevant data, determining contribution margin of a segment, and deciding whether to purchase equipment.**

Washington Architectural Manufacturing makes architectural wood products, such as crown molding, onlays, and panels, which it sells to commercial builders. The firm's finishing department is not mechanized. Employees use hand tools to finish the product. The factory superintendent has proposed that the firm acquire an electric-powered machine to perform some of the finishing functions. Presently, 6,000 units per year are manufactured and sold. A summary of the manufacturing costs of the finishing department follows:

Direct materials	$ 90,000
Direct labor	105,000
Manufacturing overhead:	
Variable costs	15,000
Fixed costs	22,500

The machine being considered will cost $90,000 and have a useful life of five years, with no salvage value. The machine will cause the following changes in costs:

a. Direct labor will decrease by $18,000.
b. Indirect materials will decrease by $1.75 per unit.
c. No change in direct materials.
d. Fixed manufacturing overhead will decrease by $15,000 per year before considering depreciation on the new machine.

INSTRUCTIONS

1. Prepare an analysis showing the effect on net income of purchasing the equipment.
2. What other factors should be considered in making the decision?

Analyze: What direct labor costs are incurred per unit for the current manual process?

Choosing relevant data and deciding whether to make or buy a part.

◄ **Problem 30.4B**
Objectives 30-4, 30-5c

HiTech Computer Company is currently manufacturing a part that goes into its main product. Each year, 2,000 of these parts are used. Cost data for the past year that relate to the 2.000 parts are given below. Fixed costs are allocated on the basis of direct labor hours. An outside company has offered to supply the part at $105 per unit, plus a shipping charge of $4 per unit. The plant capacity now used by HiTech Computer Company to manufacture the part would not be used in the foreseeable future if the part is purchased outside.

Variable costs:	
Direct materials	$180,000
Direct labor	38,000
Variable overhead	10,000
Fixed overhead costs	30,000

INSTRUCTIONS

1. Prepare an analysis comparing the unit cost of manufacturing the part with the unit cost of purchasing it.
2. What other factors are important in making the decision to accept or reject the offer?

Analyze: If HiTech Computer Company could negotiate a $1 reduction in shipping charge per unit from the outside supplier, what is the per-unit difference between the cost to make and the cost to purchase?

Critical Thinking Problem 30.1

New Line of Business

Healthy Hair Inc. makes and distributes hair products to retail stores, beauty salons, and barber shops. Early in 20X1, officers of the company decided to develop and market a line of shampoos and hair conditioners under their own private brand. They contracted with another company to manufacture and package the products. After the end of the first year, however, officers of Healthy

Hair Inc. became quite concerned over the profitability of the new line. An analysis of operations is shown below:

	Fixed Cost per Month	Percent of Selling Price per Unit
Average cost of products		25%
Average cost of containers and packaging		10
Average freight in		2
Average delivery costs		5
Sales commissions		10
Advertising expenses:		
Variable		9
Fixed	$1,500	
Warehousing costs:		
Variable		2
Fixed	$1,400	
Other costs:		
Variable		12
Fixed	$500	

An analysis of the fourth quarter 20X1 showed sales of $8,000 for the quarter. Several officers in the company have suggested that the line of products should be discontinued.

INSTRUCTIONS

1. Based on the information above, what is the amount of income or loss for the fourth quarter?
2. Based on the information above only, should the venture be discontinued? The fixed costs are allocated costs and will not be eliminated by discontinuing the venture.
3. What questions, other than those related to the information given above, should be asked by the officers to arrive at a decision on whether or not to discontinue the product line?
4. What sales volume would be necessary to pay all variable costs and cover the allocated fixed costs?

Analyze: Assume that the sales staff has been asked to forfeit half of its sales commissions for the fourth quarter of 20X1. What effect do you think this measure would have on the company's income for the period?

Critical Thinking Problem 30.2

Making Decisions

The cost accountant for Bruin Manufacturing, Inc., has prepared the following analysis of the profitability of each of the firm's three products. All fixed costs are allocated costs and are not related to specific products.

	Item 101	Item 102	Item 103	Total
Sales	$60,000.00	$64,000.00	$87,500.00	$211,500.00
Cost of goods sold	28,400.00	32,800.00	65,500.00	126,700.00
Gross profit	$31,600.00	$31,200.00	$22,000.00	$ 84,800.00
Operating expenses	12,200.00	11,000.00	25,000.00	48,200.00
Net income (loss)	$19,400.00	$20,200.00	$(3,000.00)	$ 36,600.00
Units sold	1,200	1,600	2,500	
Sales price per unit	$50	$40	$35	
Variable cost of goods sold per unit	$22	$18	$23	
Variable operating expenses per unit	$6	$5	$7	

Management has been considering several options concerning the company's product mix to reduce or eliminate the loss on Item 103. The company's president has asked you to prepare an analysis of the effects on the company's net income before taxes for each of the following proposals. Consider each proposal independently; no changes would occur in the other products.

PROPOSALS

1. Discontinue Item 103.
2. Increase the sales price of Item 103 to $40. Marketing analysis indicates that the increase in price will cause a decrease in sales of Item 103 to 1,000 units.
3. Discontinue Item 103 and use the resulting plant capacity to produce a new product, Item 104. The department's marketing studies estimate that 1,500 units could be sold at $35 each. The variable costs and expenses per unit of Item 104 are estimated to be $11 per unit manufacturing cost and $8 per unit for operating expenses.

BUSINESS CONNECTIONS

Decision Making

1. The vice president of the manufacturing company for which you are the accountant has suggested to the president that all prices should be established on the basis of direct costing. Respond to this suggestion.
2. Assume that the company where you are employed has a substantial amount of unused plant capacity. A foreign company has offered to purchase a large quantity of your company's product, but at a price of 12 percent less than the product's normal selling price. What types of information are needed to arrive at a decision about whether to accept the order?
3. Suppose that your company is considering the purchase of a new machine to use in its production process. The cost of the machine is $295,000. If the purchase is made, an old machine currently used will be scrapped. It has no net salvage value because the cost to remove it equals its market value. The old machine has a book value of $150,000, and management is reluctant to take the loss that would result if this machine is scrapped. Discuss the types of information that management would need to make a decision about purchasing the new asset. Give special attention to the problem of the old asset's book value.
4. Suppose that your company has been manufacturing a part used in its finished product. The total manufacturing cost of the part is $35. An outside supplier has offered to provide the part for $32. Describe the measurable data that management would need in making a decision about whether to accept the supplier's offer.

Managerial FOCUS

Internal Control and FRAUD PREVENTION

Eliminating a Region

Brad's employer, an eastern-based firm, is going through tough times. Downsizing is the only way to keep the company from going bankrupt.

Brad has been given the assignment to eliminate an unprofitable region. His analysis has shown that the southwest region has a positive contribution margin but a net loss due to fixed costs. The western region has a positive contribution margin and a net loss. The eastern region has a positive contribution margin and a net income. The northeastern region has a positive contribution margin but a net loss. Brad further discovers that the net losses of the western and southwestern regions are due to fixed costs. Further investigation finds that the fixed costs can be separated into regional costs and corporate costs.

In Brad's investigation, the eastern region, though having all the costs of a corporate office, has lower fixed costs, making it a profitable region. Brad finds that Joe Black, the manager of the eastern region, has decided to allocate all the corporate office expenses to the other three divisions to make his region appear more profitable. More analysis indicates that if the corporate offices are allocated evenly to all four regions, the eastern region would have a net loss and the other regions would have a small net income.

What should Brad do? Should Joe have the ability to allocate costs to other regions?

Financial Statement ANALYSIS

Home Depot

Analyzing Financial Data

Refer to The Home Depot, Inc., *2018 Annual Report (for the fiscal year ended February 3, 2019)* in Appendix A.

Locate the Selected Financial Data. Review the information for the following data points:

a. Inventory turnover

b. Number of stores

c. Sales per square foot

d. Average ticket ($)

1. For each of the above data points, calculate the increase or decrease from fiscal 2014 to fiscal 2018.

2. What was the percentage change in average ticket ($) from fiscal 2017 to fiscal 2018?

TEAMWORK

Choosing a Machine

Knowing the right questions to ask and information to obtain is important in making the correct decision. Your company has just decided to purchase a new machine. This machine will double production, decrease the material waste, and increase profits by 20 percent. However, it is double the size of the old one and takes twice as many workers to run. Your group has been given the task to decide whether to purchase this machine or stay with the current old machine. What questions would you need to ask to make your decision?

Answers to Comprehensive Self Review

1. Future or expected costs that will be incurred as a result of a specific decision.

2. Because they have already been incurred and will not change as a result of the decision being considered.

3. Acceptance of an order for less than total cost may be considered if the company has idle capacity, the price exceeds variable costs, the pricing would be legal, and the special order would not interfere with existing business.

4. It may be cheaper to purchase a part than to manufacture it, purchase may be necessary in order to assure supply, there may be a need to purchase one part in order to get favorable terms on other parts or supplies, and it may simplify the hiring of personnel or the handling of raw materials.

5. Incremental costs are the increases in total costs from one alternative to another.

Appendix A

Appendix A highlights key elements of the 2018 Home Depot Annual Report, including the financial statements, key notes to the financial statements, and attestations of both Home Depot management and an independent accounting firm. These real-world elements have been selected to provide the student with context surrounding concepts introduced throughout the textbook. The importance of internal controls, the requirement that financial statements be presented fairly and accurately, and various accounting policies selected by Home Depot are all discussed within this appendix. Furthermore, this appendix can be used to answer many of the *Financial Statement Analysis* questions found within the *Business Connections* section at the end of each chapter. Consistent reference to Appendix A will serve to reinforce the material presented within each of the chapters of the textbook.

The Home Depot 2018 Financial Statements (for the fiscal year ended February 3, 2019)

Management's Responsibility for Financial Statements	A-1
Report of Independent Registered Public Accounting Firm	A-2
Consolidated Balance Sheets	A-3
Consolidated Statements of Earnings	A-4
Consolidated Statements of Comprehensive Income	A-4
Consolidated Statements of Stockholders' Equity	A-5
Consolidated Statements of Cash Flows	A-6
Notes to Consolidated Financial Statements—Note 1, Summary of Significant Accounting Policies	A-7–A-12
Five-Year Summary of Financial and Operating Results	A-12

Item 9A. Controls and Procedures.

Disclosure Controls and Procedures

We maintain disclosure controls and procedures as defined in Rule 13a-15(e) under the Exchange Act that are designed to ensure that information required to be disclosed in our Exchange Act reports is recorded, processed, summarized, and reported within the time periods specified in the SEC's rules and forms, and that such information is accumulated and communicated to our management, including our Chief Executive Officer and Chief Financial Officer, as appropriate, to allow timely decisions regarding required disclosure.

Management, with the participation of our Chief Executive Officer and Chief Financial Officer, has evaluated the effectiveness of our disclosure controls and procedures as of the end of the period covered by this report. Based on that evaluation, our Chief Executive Officer and Chief Financial Officer have concluded that, as of the end of the period covered by this report, our disclosure controls and procedures were effective.

Changes in Internal Control Over Financial Reporting

There have not been any changes in our internal control over financial reporting during the fiscal quarter ended February 3, 2019 that have materially affected, or are reasonably likely to materially affect, our internal control over financial reporting.

Management's Report on Internal Control Over Financial Reporting

Our management is responsible for establishing and maintaining adequate internal control over financial reporting, as such term is defined in Rule 13a-15(f) promulgated under the Exchange Act. Under the supervision and with the participation of our management, including our Chief Executive Officer and Chief Financial Officer, we conducted an evaluation of the effectiveness of our internal control over financial reporting as of February 3, 2019 based on the framework in *Internal Control – Integrated Framework (2013)* issued by the Committee of Sponsoring Organizations of the Treadway Commission. Based on our evaluation, our management concluded that our internal control over financial reporting was effective as of February 3, 2019 in providing reasonable assurance regarding the reliability of financial reporting and the preparation of financial statements for external purposes in accordance with GAAP. The effectiveness of our internal control over financial reporting as of February 3, 2019 has been audited by KPMG LLP, an independent registered public accounting firm, as stated in their report which is included herein.

/s/ CRAIG A. MENEAR	/s/ CAROL B. TOMÉ
Craig A. Menear	Carol B. Tomé
Chairman, Chief Executive Officer and President	Chief Financial Officer and Executive Vice President – Corporate Services

Report of Independent Registered Public Accounting Firm

The Stockholders and Board of Directors
The Home Depot, Inc.:

Opinion on Internal Control Over Financial Reporting

We have audited The Home Depot, Inc. and Subsidiaries' internal control over financial reporting as of February 3, 2019, based on criteria established in *Internal Control - Integrated Framework (2013)* issued by the Committee of Sponsoring Organizations of the Treadway Commission. In our opinion, the Company maintained, in all material respects, effective internal control over financial reporting as of February 3, 2019, based on criteria established in *Internal Control - Integrated Framework (2013)* issued by the Committee of Sponsoring Organizations of the Treadway Commission.

We also have audited, in accordance with the standards of the Public Company Accounting Oversight Board (United States) ("PCAOB"), the Consolidated Balance Sheets of The Home Depot, Inc. and Subsidiaries as of February 3, 2019 and January 28, 2018, and the related Consolidated Statements of Earnings, Comprehensive Income, Stockholders' Equity, and Cash Flows for each of the fiscal years in the three-year period ended February 3, 2019, and the related notes (collectively, the "Consolidated Financial Statements"), and our report dated March 28, 2019 expressed an unqualified opinion on those Consolidated Financial Statements.

Basis for Opinion

The Company's management is responsible for maintaining effective internal control over financial reporting and for its assessment of the effectiveness of internal control over financial reporting, included in the accompanying Report on Internal Control Over Financial Reporting. Our responsibility is to express an opinion on the Company's internal control over financial reporting based on our audit. We are a public accounting firm registered with the PCAOB and are required to be independent with respect to the Company in accordance with the U.S. federal securities laws and the applicable rules and regulations of the Securities and Exchange Commission and the PCAOB.

We conducted our audit in accordance with the standards of the PCAOB. Those standards require that we plan and perform the audit to obtain reasonable assurance about whether effective internal control over financial reporting was maintained in all material respects. Our audit of internal control over financial reporting included obtaining an understanding of internal control over financial reporting, assessing the risk that a material weakness exists, and testing and evaluating the design and operating effectiveness of internal control based on the assessed risk. Our audit also included performing such other procedures as we considered necessary in the circumstances. We believe that our audit provides a reasonable basis for our opinion.

Definition and Limitations of Internal Control Over Financial Reporting

A company's internal control over financial reporting is a process designed to provide reasonable assurance regarding the reliability of financial reporting and the preparation of financial statements for external purposes in accordance with generally accepted accounting principles. A company's internal control over financial reporting includes those policies and procedures that (1) pertain to the maintenance of records that, in reasonable detail, accurately and fairly reflect the transactions and dispositions of the assets of the company; (2) provide reasonable assurance that transactions are recorded as necessary to permit preparation of financial statements in accordance with U.S. generally accepted accounting principles, and that receipts and expenditures of the company are being made only in accordance with authorizations of management and directors of the company; and (3) provide reasonable assurance regarding prevention or timely detection of unauthorized acquisition, use, or disposition of the company's assets that could have a material effect on the financial statements.

Because of its inherent limitations, internal control over financial reporting may not prevent or detect misstatements. Also, projections of any evaluation of effectiveness to future periods are subject to the risk that controls may become inadequate because of changes in conditions, or that the degree of compliance with the policies or procedures may deteriorate.

/s/ KPMG LLP

Atlanta, Georgia
March 28, 2019

Report of Independent Registered Public Accounting Firm

The Stockholders and Board of Directors
The Home Depot, Inc.:

Opinion on the Consolidated Financial Statements

We have audited the accompanying Consolidated Balance Sheets of The Home Depot, Inc. and Subsidiaries as of February 3, 2019 and January 28, 2018, and the related Consolidated Statements of Earnings, Comprehensive Income, Stockholders' Equity, and Cash Flows for each of the fiscal years in the three-year period ended February 3, 2019, and the related notes (collectively, the "Consolidated Financial Statements"). In our opinion, the Consolidated Financial Statements present fairly, in all material respects, the financial position of The Home Depot, Inc. and Subsidiaries as of February 3, 2019 and January 28, 2018, and the results of their operations and their cash flows for each of the fiscal years in the three-year period ended February 3, 2019, in conformity with U.S. generally accepted accounting principles.

We also have audited, in accordance with the standards of the Public Company Accounting Oversight Board (United States) ("PCAOB"), The Home Depot, Inc.'s internal control over financial reporting as of February 3, 2019, based on criteria established in *Internal Control - Integrated Framework (2013)* issued by the Committee of Sponsoring Organizations of the Treadway Commission, and our report dated March 28, 2019 expressed an unqualified opinion on the effectiveness of the Company's internal control over financial reporting.

Basis for Opinion

These Consolidated Financial Statements are the responsibility of the Company's management. Our responsibility is to express an opinion on these Consolidated Financial Statements based on our audits. We are a public accounting firm registered with the PCAOB and are required to be independent with respect to the Company in accordance with the U.S. federal securities laws and the applicable rules and regulations of the Securities and Exchange Commission and the PCAOB.

We conducted our audits in accordance with the standards of the PCAOB. Those standards require that we plan and perform the audit to obtain reasonable assurance about whether the Consolidated Financial Statements are free of material misstatement, whether due to error or fraud. Our audits included performing procedures to assess the risks of material misstatement of the Consolidated Financial Statements, whether due to error or fraud, and performing procedures that respond to those risks. Such procedures included examining, on a test basis, evidence regarding the amounts and disclosures in the Consolidated Financial Statements. Our audits also included evaluating the accounting principles used and significant estimates made by management, as well as evaluating the overall presentation of the Consolidated Financial Statements. We believe that our audits provide a reasonable basis for our opinion.

/s/ KPMG LLP

We have served as the Company's auditor since 1979.

Atlanta, Georgia
March 28, 2019

THE HOME DEPOT, INC.
CONSOLIDATED BALANCE SHEETS

in millions, except per share data	February 3, 2019	January 28, 2018
Assets		
Current assets:		
Cash and cash equivalents	$ 1,778	$ 3,595
Receivables, net	1,936	1,952
Merchandise inventories	13,925	12,748
Other current assets	890	638
Total current assets	18,529	18,933
Net property and equipment	22,375	22,075
Goodwill	2,252	2,275
Other assets	847	1,246
Total assets	$ 44,003	$ 44,529
Liabilities and Stockholders' Equity		
Current liabilities:		
Short-term debt	$ 1,339	$ 1,559
Accounts payable	7,755	7,244
Accrued salaries and related expenses	1,506	1,640
Sales taxes payable	656	520
Deferred revenue	1,782	1,805
Income taxes payable	11	54
Current installments of long-term debt	1,056	1,202
Other accrued expenses	2,611	2,170
Total current liabilities	16,716	16,194
Long-term debt, excluding current installments	26,807	24,267
Deferred income taxes	491	440
Other long-term liabilities	1,867	2,174
Total liabilities	45,881	43,075
Common stock, par value $0.05; authorized: 10,000 shares; issued: 1,782 at February 3, 2019 and 1,780 shares at January 28, 2018; outstanding: 1,105 shares at February 3, 2019 and 1,158 shares at January 28, 2018	89	89
Paid-in capital	10,578	10,192
Retained earnings	46,423	39,935
Accumulated other comprehensive loss	(772)	(566)
Treasury stock, at cost, 677 shares at February 3, 2019 and 622 shares at January 28, 2018	(58,196)	(48,196)
Total stockholders' (deficit) equity	(1,878)	1,454
Total liabilities and stockholders' equity	$ 44,003	$ 44,529

See accompanying notes to consolidated financial statements.

THE HOME DEPOT, INC.
CONSOLIDATED STATEMENTS OF EARNINGS

in millions, except per share data	Fiscal 2018	Fiscal 2017	Fiscal 2016
Net sales	$ 108,203	$ 100,904	$ 94,595
Cost of sales	71,043	66,548	62,282
Gross profit	37,160	34,356	32,313
Operating expenses:			
Selling, general and administrative	19,513	17,864	17,132
Depreciation and amortization	1,870	1,811	1,754
Impairment loss	247	—	—
Total operating expenses	21,630	19,675	18,886
Operating income	15,530	14,681	13,427
Interest and other (income) expense:			
Interest and investment income	(93)	(74)	(36)
Interest expense	1,051	1,057	972
Other	16	—	—
Interest and other, net	974	983	936
Earnings before provision for income taxes	14,556	13,698	12,491
Provision for income taxes	3,435	5,068	4,534
Net earnings	$ 11,121	$ 8,630	$ 7,957
Basic weighted average common shares	1,137	1,178	1,229
Basic earnings per share	$ 9.78	$ 7.33	$ 6.47
Diluted weighted average common shares	1,143	1,184	1,234
Diluted earnings per share	$ 9.73	$ 7.29	$ 6.45

Fiscal 2018 includes 53 weeks. Fiscal 2017 and fiscal 2016 include 52 weeks.
See accompanying notes to consolidated financial statements.

THE HOME DEPOT, INC.
CONSOLIDATED STATEMENTS OF COMPREHENSIVE INCOME

in millions	Fiscal 2018	Fiscal 2017	Fiscal 2016
Net earnings	$ 11,121	$ 8,630	$ 7,957
Other comprehensive (loss) income:			
Foreign currency translation adjustments	(267)	311	(3)
Cash flow hedges, net of tax	53	(1)	34
Other	8	(9)	—
Total other comprehensive (loss) income	(206)	301	31
Comprehensive income	$ 10,915	$ 8,931	$ 7,988

Fiscal 2018 includes 53 weeks. Fiscal 2017 and fiscal 2016 include 52 weeks.
See accompanying notes to consolidated financial statements.

THE HOME DEPOT, INC.
CONSOLIDATED STATEMENTS OF STOCKHOLDERS' EQUITY

in millions	Fiscal 2018	Fiscal 2017	Fiscal 2016
Common Stock:			
Balance at beginning of year	$ 89	$ 88	$ 88
Shares issued under employee stock plans	—	1	—
Balance at end of year	89	89	88
Paid-in Capital:			
Balance at beginning of year	10,192	9,787	9,347
Shares issued under employee stock plans	104	132	76
Tax effect of stock-based compensation	—	—	97
Stock-based compensation expense	282	273	267
Balance at end of year	10,578	10,192	9,787
Retained Earnings:			
Balance at beginning of year	39,935	35,519	30,973
Cumulative effect of accounting change	75	—	—
Net earnings	11,121	8,630	7,957
Cash dividends	(4,704)	(4,212)	(3,404)
Other	(4)	(2)	(7)
Balance at end of year	46,423	39,935	35,519
Accumulated Other Comprehensive Income (Loss):			
Balance at beginning of year	(566)	(867)	(898)
Foreign currency translation adjustments	(267)	311	(3)
Cash flow hedges, net of tax	53	(1)	34
Other	8	(9)	—
Balance at end of year	(772)	(566)	(867)
Treasury Stock:			
Balance at beginning of year	(48,196)	(40,194)	(33,194)
Repurchases of common stock	(10,000)	(8,002)	(7,000)
Balance at end of year	(58,196)	(48,196)	(40,194)
Total stockholders' (deficit) equity	$ (1,878)	$ 1,454	$ 4,333

Fiscal 2018 includes 53 weeks. Fiscal 2017 and fiscal 2016 include 52 weeks.
See accompanying notes to consolidated financial statements.

THE HOME DEPOT, INC.
CONSOLIDATED STATEMENTS OF CASH FLOWS

in millions	Fiscal 2018	Fiscal 2017	Fiscal 2016
Cash Flows from Operating Activities:			
Net earnings	$ 11,121	$ 8,630	$ 7,957
Reconciliation of net earnings to net cash provided by operating activities:			
Depreciation and amortization	2,152	2,062	1,973
Stock-based compensation expense	282	273	267
Impairment loss	247	—	—
Changes in receivables, net	33	139	(138)
Changes in merchandise inventories	(1,244)	(84)	(769)
Changes in other current assets	(257)	(10)	(48)
Changes in accounts payable and accrued expenses	743	352	446
Changes in deferred revenue	80	128	99
Changes in income taxes payable	(42)	29	109
Changes in deferred income taxes	26	92	(117)
Other operating activities	(103)	420	4
Net cash provided by operating activities	13,038	12,031	9,783
Cash Flows from Investing Activities:			
Capital expenditures, net of non-cash capital expenditures	(2,442)	(1,897)	(1,621)
Payments for businesses acquired, net	(21)	(374)	—
Proceeds from sales of property and equipment	33	47	38
Other investing activities	14	(4)	—
Net cash used in investing activities	(2,416)	(2,228)	(1,583)
Cash Flows from Financing Activities:			
(Repayments of) proceeds from short-term debt, net	(220)	850	360
Proceeds from long-term debt, net of discounts	3,466	2,991	4,959
Repayments of long-term debt	(1,209)	(543)	(3,045)
Repurchases of common stock	(9,963)	(8,000)	(6,880)
Proceeds from sales of common stock	236	255	218
Cash dividends	(4,704)	(4,212)	(3,404)
Other financing activities	(26)	(211)	(78)
Net cash used in financing activities	(12,420)	(8,870)	(7,870)
Change in cash and cash equivalents	(1,798)	933	330
Effect of exchange rate changes on cash and cash equivalents	(19)	124	(8)
Cash and cash equivalents at beginning of year	3,595	2,538	2,216
Cash and cash equivalents at end of year	$ 1,778	$ 3,595	$ 2,538
Supplemental Disclosures:			
Cash paid for income taxes	$ 3,774	$ 4,732	$ 4,623
Cash paid for interest, net of interest capitalized	1,035	991	924
Non-cash capital expenditures	248	150	179

Fiscal 2018 includes 53 weeks. Fiscal 2017 and fiscal 2016 include 52 weeks.
See accompanying notes to consolidated financial statements.

THE HOME DEPOT, INC.
NOTES TO CONSOLIDATED FINANCIAL STATEMENTS

1. SUMMARY OF SIGNIFICANT ACCOUNTING POLICIES

Business

The Home Depot, Inc., together with its subsidiaries (the "Company," "Home Depot," "we," "our" or "us"), is a home improvement retailer that sells a wide assortment of building materials, home improvement products, lawn and garden products, and décor items and provides a number of services, in stores and online. We operate in the U.S. (including the Commonwealth of Puerto Rico and the territories of the U.S. Virgin Islands and Guam), Canada, and Mexico.

Consolidation and Presentation

Our consolidated financial statements include our accounts and those of our wholly-owned subsidiaries. All significant intercompany transactions have been eliminated in consolidation. Certain amounts in prior fiscal years have been reclassified to conform with the presentation adopted in the current fiscal year. Our fiscal year is a 52- or 53-week period ending on the Sunday nearest to January 31. Fiscal 2018 includes 53 weeks compared to fiscal 2017 and fiscal 2016, both of which include 52 weeks.

Use of Estimates

We have made a number of estimates and assumptions relating to the reporting of assets and liabilities, the disclosure of contingent assets and liabilities, and reported amounts of revenues and expenses in preparing these financial statements in conformity with GAAP. Actual results could differ from these estimates.

Cash Equivalents

We consider all highly liquid investments purchased with original maturities of three months or less to be cash equivalents. Our cash equivalents are carried at fair market value and consist primarily of money market funds.

Receivables

The components of receivables, net, follow.

in millions	February 3, 2019		January 28, 2018
Card receivables	$	696	$	734
Rebate receivables		660		609
Customer receivables		284		261
Other receivables		296		348
Receivables, net	$	1,936	$	1,952

Card receivables consist of payments due from financial institutions for the settlement of credit card and debit card transactions. Rebate receivables represent amounts due from vendors for volume and co-op advertising rebates. Receivables due from customers relate to credit extended directly to certain customers in the ordinary course of business. The valuation reserve related to accounts receivable was not material to our consolidated financial statements at the end of fiscal 2018 or fiscal 2017.

Merchandise Inventories

The majority of our merchandise inventories are stated at the lower of cost (first-in, first-out) or market, as determined by the retail inventory method. As the inventory retail value is adjusted regularly to reflect market conditions, the inventory valued using the retail method approximates the lower of cost or market. Certain subsidiaries, including retail operations in Canada and Mexico, and distribution centers, record merchandise inventories at the lower of cost or net realizable value, as determined by a cost method. These merchandise inventories represent approximately 29% of the total merchandise inventories balance. We evaluate the inventory valued using a cost method at the end of each quarter to ensure that it is carried at the lower of cost or net realizable value. The valuation allowance for merchandise inventories valued under a cost method was not material to our consolidated financial statements at the end of fiscal 2018 or fiscal 2017.

Independent physical inventory counts or cycle counts are taken on a regular basis in each store and distribution center to ensure that amounts reflected in merchandise inventories are properly stated. Shrink (or in the case of excess inventory, "swell") is the difference between the recorded amount of inventory and the physical inventory. We calculate shrink based on actual inventory losses occurring as a result of physical inventory counts during each fiscal period and estimated inventory losses occurring between physical inventory counts. The estimate for shrink occurring in the interim period between physical inventory counts is calculated on a store-specific basis based on recent shrink results and current trends in the business.

Property and Equipment, including Capitalized Lease Assets

Buildings, furniture, fixtures, and equipment are recorded at cost and depreciated using the straight-line method over their estimated useful lives. Leasehold improvements are amortized using the straight-line method over the original term of the lease or the useful life of the improvement, whichever is shorter. The estimated useful lives of our property and equipment follow.

	Life
Buildings	5 – 45 years
Furniture, fixtures and equipment	2 – 20 years
Leasehold improvements	5 – 45 years

We capitalize certain costs related to the acquisition and development of software and amortize these costs using the straight-line method over the estimated useful life of the software, which is three to six years. Certain development costs not meeting the criteria for capitalization are expensed as incurred.

We evaluate our long-lived assets each quarter for indicators of potential impairment. Indicators of impairment include current period losses combined with a history of losses, our decision to relocate or close a store or other location before the end of its previously estimated useful life, or when changes in other circumstances indicate the carrying amount of an asset may not be recoverable. The evaluation for long-lived assets is performed at the lowest level of identifiable cash flows, which is generally the individual store level. The assets of a store with indicators of impairment are evaluated for recoverability by comparing its undiscounted future cash flows with its carrying value. If the carrying value is greater than the undiscounted future cash flows, we then measure the asset's fair value to determine whether an impairment loss should be recognized. If the resulting fair value is less than the carrying value, an impairment loss is recognized for the difference between the carrying value and the estimated fair value. Impairment losses on property and equipment are recorded as a component of SG&A. When a leased location closes, we also recognize, in SG&A, the net present value of future lease obligations less estimated sublease income. Impairments and lease obligation costs on closings and relocations were not material to our consolidated financial statements in fiscal 2018, fiscal 2017, or fiscal 2016.

Leases

We categorize leases at their inception as either operating or capital leases. Lease agreements include certain retail locations, office space, warehouse and distribution space, equipment, and vehicles. Most of these leases are operating leases. However, certain retail locations and equipment are leased under capital leases. Short-term and long-term obligations for capital leases are included in the applicable long-term debt category based on maturity. We expense rent related to operating leases on a straight-line basis over the lease term, which commences on the date we have the right to control the property. The cumulative expense recognized on a straight-line basis in excess of the cumulative payments is included in other accrued expenses and other long-term liabilities. Total rent expense for fiscal 2018, fiscal 2017, and fiscal 2016 is net of an immaterial amount of sublease income.

Goodwill

Goodwill represents the excess of purchase price over the fair value of net assets acquired. We do not amortize goodwill, but assess the recoverability of goodwill in the third quarter of each fiscal year, or more often if indicators warrant, by determining whether the fair value of each reporting unit supports its carrying value. Each fiscal year, we may assess qualitative factors to determine whether it is more likely than not that the fair value of each reporting unit is less than its carrying amount as a basis for determining whether it is necessary to complete quantitative impairment assessments, with a quantitative assessment completed at least once every three years. We completed our last quantitative assessment in fiscal 2016.

In fiscal 2018, we completed our annual assessment of the recoverability of goodwill for the U.S., Canada, and Mexico reporting units. We performed qualitative assessments, concluding that the fair value of the reporting units substantially exceeded the respective reporting unit's carrying value, including goodwill. As a result, there were no impairment charges related to goodwill for fiscal 2018, fiscal 2017, or fiscal 2016.

Changes in the carrying amount of our goodwill follow.

in millions	Fiscal 2018	Fiscal 2017	Fiscal 2016
Goodwill, balance at beginning of year	$ 2,275	$ 2,093	$ 2,102
Acquisitions [1]	4	164	—
Disposition	(15)	—	—
Other [2]	(12)	18	(9)
Goodwill, balance at end of year	$ 2,252	$ 2,275	$ 2,093

(1) Includes purchase price allocation adjustments.
(2) Primarily reflects the impact of foreign currency translation.

Other Intangible Assets

We amortize the cost of other finite-lived intangible assets over their estimated useful lives, which range up to 12 years. Intangible assets with indefinite lives are tested in the third quarter of each fiscal year for impairment, or more often if indicators warrant. Intangible assets other than goodwill are included in other assets.

In January 2019, we recognized a pretax impairment loss of $247 million for certain trade names as a result of a shift in strategy for our MRO business. Our remaining finite-lived and indefinite-lived intangibles were not material at February 3, 2019.

Debt

We record any premiums or discounts associated with an issuance of long-term debt as a direct addition or deduction to the carrying value of the related senior notes. We also record debt issuance costs associated with an issuance of long-term debt as a direct deduction to the carrying value of the related senior notes. Premium, discount, and debt issuance costs are amortized over the term of the respective notes using the effective interest rate method.

Derivatives

We use derivative financial instruments in the management of our interest rate exposure on long-term debt and our exposure to foreign currency fluctuations. For derivatives that are designated as hedges, changes in their fair values that are considered effective are either accounted for in earnings or recognized in other comprehensive income or loss until the hedged item is recognized in earnings, depending on the nature of the hedge. Any ineffective portion of a derivative's change in fair value is immediately recognized in earnings. Financial instruments that do not qualify for hedge accounting are recorded at fair value with unrealized gains or losses reported in earnings. All qualifying derivative financial instruments are recognized at their fair values in either assets or liabilities at the balance sheet date and are reported on a gross basis. The fair values of our derivative financial instruments are discussed in Note 4 and Note 7.

Insurance

We are self-insured for certain losses related to general liability (including product liability), workers' compensation, employee group medical, and automobile claims. We recognize the expected ultimate cost for claims incurred (undiscounted) at the balance sheet date as a liability. The expected ultimate cost for claims incurred is estimated based upon analysis of historical data and actuarial estimates. We also maintain network security and privacy liability insurance coverage to limit our exposure to losses such as those that may be caused by a significant compromise or breach of our data security. Insurance-related expenses are included in SG&A.

Treasury Stock

Treasury stock is reflected as a reduction of stockholders' equity at cost. We use the weighted-average purchase cost to determine the cost of treasury stock that is reissued, if any.

Net Sales

On January 29, 2018, we adopted ASU No. 2014-09 using the modified retrospective transition method which requires that we recognize revenue differently pre- and post-adoption. See "—Recently Adopted Accounting Pronouncements—ASU No. 2014-09" below for more information.

Fiscal 2018 and Subsequent Periods. We recognize revenue, net of expected returns and sales tax, at the time the customer takes possession of merchandise or when a service is performed. The liability for sales returns, including the impact to gross profit, is estimated based on historical return levels and recognized at the transaction price. We also recognize a return asset, and corresponding adjustment to cost of sales, for our right to recover the goods returned by the customer, measured at the former carrying amount of the goods, less any expected recovery cost. At each financial reporting date, we assess our estimates of expected returns, refund liabilities, and return assets.

Net sales include services revenue generated through a variety of installation, home maintenance, and professional service programs. In these programs, the customer selects and purchases material for a project, and we provide or arrange for professional installation. These programs are offered through our stores and in-home sales programs. Under certain programs, when we provide or arrange for the installation of a project and the subcontractor provides material as part of the installation, both the material and labor are included in services revenue. We recognize this revenue when the service for the customer is complete, which is not materially different from recognizing the revenue over the service period as the substantial majority of our services are completed within one week.

For product sold in stores or online, payment is typically due at the point of sale. For services, payment in full is due upon completion of the job. When we receive payment from customers before the customer has taken possession of the merchandise or the service has been performed, the amount received is recorded as deferred revenue until the sale or service is complete. Such performance obligations are part of contracts with expected original durations of three months or less. We further record deferred revenue for the sale of gift cards and recognize the associated revenue upon the redemption of those gift cards in net sales. Gift card breakage income, which is our estimate of the non-redeemed gift card balance, was immaterial in fiscal 2018.

We also have agreements with third-party service providers who directly extend credit to customers and manage our PLCC program. Deferred interest charges incurred for our deferred financing programs offered to these customers, interchange fees charged to us for their use of the cards, and any profit sharing with the third-party service providers are included in net sales.

Fiscal 2017 and Fiscal 2016. We recognize revenue, net of estimated returns and sales tax, at the time the customer takes possession of merchandise or when a service is performed. The liability for sales returns, including the impact to gross profit, is estimated based on historical return levels.

Net sales include services revenue generated through a variety of installation, home maintenance, and professional service programs. In these programs, the customer selects and purchases material for a project, and we provide or arrange professional installation. These programs are offered through our stores and in-home sales programs. Under certain programs, when we provide or arrange the installation of a project and the subcontractor provides material as part of the installation, both the material and labor are included in services revenue. We recognize this revenue when the service for the customer is complete.

When we receive payment from customers before the customer has taken possession of the merchandise or the service has been performed, the amount received is recorded as deferred revenue until the sale or service is complete. We also record deferred revenue for the sale of gift cards and recognize this revenue upon the redemption of gift cards in net sales. Gift card breakage income, which is our estimate of the non-redeemed gift card balance, was immaterial in fiscal 2017 and fiscal 2016.

Cost of Sales

Cost of sales includes the actual cost of merchandise sold and services performed; the cost of transportation of merchandise from vendors to our distribution network, stores, or customers; shipping and handling costs from our stores or distribution network to customers; and the operating cost and depreciation of our sourcing and distribution network and online fulfillment centers. In fiscal 2017 and fiscal 2016, cost of sales also included cost of deferred interest programs offered through our PLCC programs.

Cost of Credit

We have agreements with third-party service providers who directly extend credit to customers, manage our PLCC program, and own the related receivables. We have evaluated the third-party entities holding the receivables under the program and concluded that they should not be consolidated. The agreement with the primary third-party service provider for our PLCC program expires in 2028, with us having the option, but no obligation, to purchase the receivables at the end of the agreement. The deferred interest charges we incur for our deferred financing programs offered to our customers are included in net sales in fiscal 2018 and subsequent periods and in cost of sales in fiscal 2017 and fiscal 2016. The interchange fees charged to us for our customers' use of the cards and any profit sharing with the third-party service providers are included in net sales in fiscal 2018 and subsequent periods and in SG&A in fiscal 2017 and fiscal 2016. The sum of the deferred interest charges, interchange fees, and any profit sharing is referred to as the cost of credit of the PLCC program.

Vendor Allowances

Vendor allowances primarily consist of volume rebates that are earned as a result of attaining certain purchase levels and co-op advertising allowances for the promotion of vendors' products that are typically based on guaranteed minimum amounts with additional amounts being earned for attaining certain purchase levels. These vendor allowances are accrued as earned, with those allowances received as a result of attaining certain purchase levels accrued over the incentive period based on estimates of purchases. Volume rebates and certain co-op advertising allowances earned are initially recorded as a reduction in merchandise inventories and a subsequent reduction in cost of sales when the related product is sold.

Certain other co-op advertising allowances that are reimbursements of specific, incremental, and identifiable costs incurred to promote vendors' products are recorded as an offset against advertising expense in SG&A. The co-op advertising allowances recorded as an offset to advertising expense follow.

in millions	Fiscal 2018	Fiscal 2017	Fiscal 2016
Specific, incremental, and identifiable co-op advertising allowances	$ 235	$ 198	$ 166

Advertising Expense

Television and radio advertising production costs, along with media placement costs, are expensed when the advertisement first appears. Certain co-op advertising allowances are recorded as an offset against advertising expense. Gross advertising expense included in SG&A follows.

in millions	Fiscal 2018	Fiscal 2017	Fiscal 2016
Gross advertising expense	$ 1,156	$ 995	$ 955

Stock-Based Compensation

We are currently authorized to issue incentive and nonqualified stock options, stock appreciation rights, restricted stock, restricted stock units, performance shares, performance units, and deferred shares to certain of our associates, officers, and directors under certain stock incentive plans. We measure and recognize compensation expense for all share-based payment awards made to associates and directors based on estimated fair values. The value of the portion of the award that is ultimately expected to vest is recognized as stock-based compensation expense over the requisite service period or as restrictions lapse. Additional information on our stock-based payment awards is included in Note 8.

Income Taxes

Income taxes are accounted for under the asset and liability method. We provide for federal, state, and foreign income taxes currently payable, as well as for those deferred due to timing differences between reporting income and expenses for financial statement purposes versus tax purposes. Deferred tax assets and liabilities are recognized for the future tax consequences attributable to temporary differences between the financial statement carrying amounts of existing assets and liabilities and their respective tax bases. Deferred tax assets and liabilities are measured using enacted income tax rates expected to apply to taxable income in the years in which those temporary differences are expected to be recovered or settled. The effect of a change in income tax rates is recognized as income or expense in the period that includes the enactment date.

We recognize the effect of income tax positions only if those positions are more likely than not of being sustained. Recognized income tax positions are measured at the largest amount that is greater than 50% likely of being realized. Changes in recognition or measurement are reflected in the period in which the change in judgment occurs.

We file a consolidated U.S. federal income tax return which includes certain eligible subsidiaries. Non-U.S. subsidiaries and certain U.S. subsidiaries, which are consolidated for financial reporting purposes, are not eligible to be included in our consolidated U.S. federal income tax return. Separate provisions for income taxes have been determined for these entities. For unremitted earnings of our non-U.S. subsidiaries, we are required to make an assertion regarding reinvestment or repatriation for tax purposes. For any earnings that we do not make a permanent reinvestment assertion, we recognize a provision for deferred income taxes. For earnings where we have made a permanent reinvestment assertion, no provision is recognized. See Note 5 for further discussion.

Comprehensive Income

Comprehensive income includes net earnings adjusted for certain gains and losses that are excluded from net earnings under GAAP, which consists primarily of foreign currency translation adjustments.

Foreign Currency Translation

Assets and liabilities denominated in a foreign currency are translated into U.S. dollars at the current rate of exchange on the last day of the reporting period. Revenues and expenses are translated using average exchange rates for the period and equity transactions are translated using the actual rate on the day of the transaction.

Reclassifications

Certain prior period amounts have been reclassified to conform to the current period's financial statement presentation. See "Recently Adopted Accounting Pronouncements" below for a discussion of our adoption of new accounting standards.

Recently Adopted Accounting Pronouncements

ASU No. 2016-16. In October 2016, the FASB issued ASU No. 2016-16, "Income Taxes (Topic 740): Intra-Entity Transfers of Assets Other Than Inventory," which requires an entity to recognize the income tax consequences of an intercompany transfer of assets other than inventory when the transfer occurs. An entity will continue to recognize the income tax consequences of an intercompany transfer of inventory when the inventory is sold to a third party.

On January 29, 2018, we adopted ASU No. 2016-16 using the modified retrospective transition method with no impact on our consolidated financial statements. We expect the impact of the adoption to be immaterial to our financial position, results of operations, and cash flows on an ongoing basis.

ASU No. 2014-09. In May 2014, the FASB issued a new standard related to revenue recognition. Under ASU No. 2014-09, "Revenue from Contracts with Customers (Topic 606)," revenue is recognized when a customer obtains control of promised goods or services in an amount that reflects the consideration the entity expects to receive in exchange for those goods or services. In addition, the standard requires disclosure of the nature, amount, timing, and uncertainty of revenue and cash flows arising from contracts with customers. On January 29, 2018, we adopted ASU No. 2014-09 using the modified retrospective transition method.

In preparation for implementation of the standard, we finalized key accounting assessments and then implemented internal controls and updated processes to appropriately recognize and present the associated financial information. Based on these efforts, we determined that the adoption of ASU No. 2014-09 changes the presentation of (i) certain expenses and cost reimbursements associated with our PLCC program (now recognized in net sales), (ii) certain expenses related to the sale of gift cards to customers (now recognized in operating expense), and (iii) gift card breakage income (now recognized in net sales). We also have changed our recognition of gift card breakage income to be recognized proportionately as redemption occurs, rather than based on historical redemption patterns.

In addition, the adoption of ASU No. 2014-09 requires that we recognize our sales return allowance on a gross basis rather than as a net liability. As such, we now recognize (i) a return asset for the right to recover the goods returned by the customer, measured at the former carrying amount of the goods, less any expected recovery costs (recorded as an increase to other current assets) and (ii) a return liability for the amount of expected returns (recorded as an increase to other accrued expenses and a decrease to receivables, net).

We applied ASU No. 2014-09 only to contracts that were not completed prior to fiscal 2018. The cumulative effect of initially applying ASU No. 2014-09 was a $99 million reduction to deferred revenue, a $24 million increase to deferred income taxes (included in other long-term liabilities), and a $75 million increase to the opening balance of retained earnings as of January 29, 2018. The comparative prior period information continues to be reported under the accounting standards in effect during those periods. We expect the impact of the adoption to be immaterial to our financial position, results of operations, and cash flows on an ongoing basis.

Excluding the effect of the opening balance sheet adjustment noted above, the impact of the adoption of ASU No. 2014-09 on our consolidated balance sheet as of February 3, 2019 follows.

in millions	As Reported	ASU No. 2014-09 Impact	Excluding ASU No. 2014-09 Impact
Receivables, net	$ 1,936	$ (40)	$ 1,976
Other current assets	890	256	634
Other accrued expenses	2,611	216	2,395

The impact of the adoption of ASU No. 2014-09 on our consolidated statements of earnings for fiscal 2018 follows.

in millions	As Reported	ASU No. 2014-09 Impact	Excluding ASU No. 2014-09 Impact
Net sales	$ 108,203	$ 216	$ 107,987
Cost of sales	71,043	(382)	71,425
Gross profit	37,160	598	36,562
Selling, general and administrative	19,513	598	18,915

Recently Issued Accounting Pronouncements

ASU No. 2018-15. In August 2018, the FASB issued ASU No. 2018-15, "Intangibles – Goodwill and Other – Internal-Use Software (Subtopic 350-40): Customer's Accounting for Implementation Costs Incurred in a Cloud Computing Arrangement That is a Service Contract," which aligns the requirements for capitalizing implementation costs incurred in a hosting arrangement with the requirements for capitalizing implementation costs incurred to develop or obtain internal-use software. ASU No. 2018-15 is effective for us in the first quarter of fiscal 2020 and early adoption is permitted. We are evaluating the effect that ASU No. 2018-15 will have on our consolidated financial statements and related disclosures.

ASU No. 2018-02. In February 2018, the FASB issued ASU No. 2018-02, "Income Statement – Reporting Comprehensive Income (Topic 220): Reclassification of Certain Tax Effects from Accumulated Other Comprehensive Income," which allows for an optional reclassification from accumulated other comprehensive income to retained earnings for stranded tax effects as a result of the Tax Act. ASU No. 2018-02 is effective for us in the first quarter of fiscal 2019 and early adoption is permitted. Two transition methods are available: at the beginning of the period of adoption, or retrospective to each period in which the income tax effects of the Tax Act related to items remaining in accumulated other comprehensive income are recognized. We will adopt this standard in the first quarter of 2019, applying the adjustment at the beginning of the period of adoption. We have evaluated the effect that ASU No. 2018-02 will have on our consolidated financial statements and related disclosures and noted no material impact.

ASU No. 2017-12. In August 2017, the FASB issued ASU No. 2017-12, "Derivatives and Hedging (Topic 815): Targeted Improvements to Accounting for Hedging Activities," which amends the hedge accounting recognition and presentation requirements. ASU No. 2017-12 eliminates the concept of recognizing periodic hedge ineffectiveness for cash flow and net investment hedges and allows an entity to apply the shortcut method to partial-term fair value hedges of interest rate risk. ASU No. 2017-12 is effective for us in the first quarter of fiscal 2019. Early adoption is permitted in any interim period after issuance of this update. We have evaluated the effect that ASU No. 2017-12 will have on our consolidated financial statements and related disclosures and noted no material impact.

ASU No. 2017-04. In January 2017, the FASB issued ASU No. 2017-04, "Intangibles–Goodwill and Other (Topic 350): Simplifying the Test for Goodwill Impairment," which simplifies how an entity is required to test goodwill for impairment. The amendments in ASU No. 2017-04 require goodwill impairment to be measured using the difference between the carrying amount and the fair value of the reporting unit and require the loss recognized to not exceed the total amount of goodwill allocated to that reporting unit. ASU No. 2017-04 should be applied on a prospective basis and is effective for our annual goodwill impairment tests beginning in the first quarter of fiscal 2020. Early adoption is permitted. We have evaluated the effect that ASU No. 2017-04 will have on our consolidated financial statements and related disclosures and noted no material impact.

ASU No. 2016-02. In February 2016, the FASB issued ASU No. 2016-02, "Leases (Topic 842)," which establishes a right-of-use model and requires an entity that is a lessee to recognize the right-of-use assets and liabilities arising from leases on its balance sheet. ASU No. 2016-02 also requires disclosures about the amount, timing, and uncertainty of cash flows arising from leases. Leases will be classified as finance or operating, with classification affecting the pattern and classification of expense recognition in the income statement. This new standard is effective for us on February 4, 2019 (the "effective date").

ASU No. 2016-02 was subsequently amended by ASU No. 2018-01, "Land Easement Practical Expedient for Transition to Topic 842"; ASU No. 2018-10, "Codification Improvements to Topic 842"; and ASU No. 2018-11, "Targeted Improvements". ASU 2016-02 and relevant updates require a modified retrospective transition, with the cumulative effect of transition, including initial recognition of lease assets and liabilities for existing operating leases as of (i) the effective date or (ii) the beginning of the earliest comparative period presented. These updates also provide a number of practical expedients for transition and implementation that will be elected.

We will adopt this standard using the modified retrospective method with a cumulative-effect adjustment to the opening balance of retained earnings as of the effective date. We plan to elect the package of practical expedients in transition, which permits us to not reassess our prior conclusions pertaining to lease identification, lease classification, and initial direct costs on leases that commenced prior to our adoption of the new standard. We do not expect to elect the use-of-hindsight or land easements transition practical expedients. Additionally, we will elect ongoing practical expedients including the option to not recognize right-of-use assets and lease liabilities related to leases with an original term of twelve months or less.

We believe that ASU 2016-02 will have a material impact on our consolidated balance sheet as a result of the requirement to recognize right-of-use assets and lease liabilities for our operating leases upon adoption. We estimate total assets and liabilities will increase approximately $6 billion upon adoption. This estimate may change as the implementation is finalized as a result of changes to our lease portfolio prior to adoption. We do not believe that there will be a material impact to our results of operations, stockholders' equity, or cash flows upon adoption of ASU No. 2016-02.

We reviewed and selected a new lease accounting system and are currently accumulating and processing lease data into the system. We are continuing to evaluate our internal control framework, including implementing changes to our processes, controls, and systems in connection therewith, to determine any necessary changes upon adoption of ASU 2016-02.

Recent accounting pronouncements pending adoption not discussed above are either not applicable or are not expected to have a material impact on us.

THE HOME DEPOT, INC.
SELECTED FINANCIAL DATA

amounts in millions, except per share data or where noted	Fiscal 2018	Fiscal 2017	Fiscal 2016	Fiscal 2015	Fiscal 2014
STATEMENT OF EARNINGS DATA					
Net sales	$ 108,203	$ 100,904	$ 94,595	$ 88,519	$ 83,176
Net sales increase (%)	7.2	6.7	6.9	6.4	5.5
Earnings before provision for income taxes ($)	14,556	13,698	12,491	11,021	9,976
Net earnings ($)	11,121	8,630	7,957	7,009	6,345
Net earnings increase (%)	28.9	8.5	13.5	10.5	17.8
Diluted earnings per share ($)	9.73	7.29	6.45	5.46	4.71
Diluted earnings per share increase (%)	33.5	13.0	18.1	15.9	25.3
Diluted weighted average number of common shares	1,143	1,184	1,234	1,283	1,346
Gross profit – % of sales	34.3	34.0	34.2	34.2	34.1
Total operating expenses – % of sales	20.0	19.5	20.0	20.9	21.5
Net earnings – % of sales	10.3	8.6	8.4	7.9	7.6
BALANCE SHEET DATA AND FINANCIAL RATIOS					
Total assets	$ 44,003	$ 44,529	$ 42,966	$ 41,973	$ 39,449
Working capital ($)	1,813	2,739	3,591	3,960	3,589
Merchandise inventories ($)	13,925	12,748	12,549	11,809	11,079
Net property and equipment ($) [1]	22,375	22,075	21,914	22,191	22,720
Long-term debt, excluding current installments ($)	26,807	24,267	22,349	20,789	16,786
Stockholders' (deficit) equity ($)	(1,878)	1,454	4,333	6,316	9,322
Total debt-to-equity (%)	(1,550.0)	1,858.9	544.7	335.9	183.6
Inventory turnover	5.1x	5.1x	4.9x	4.9x	4.7x
STATEMENT OF CASH FLOWS DATA					
Depreciation and amortization	$ 2,152	$ 2,062	$ 1,973	$ 1,863	$ 1,786
Capital expenditures ($)	2,442	1,897	1,621	1,503	1,442
OTHER KEY METRICS					
Return on invested capital (%)	44.8	34.2	31.4	28.1	25.0
Cash dividends per share ($)	4.12	3.56	2.76	2.36	1.88
Number of stores	2,287	2,284	2,278	2,274	2,269
Square footage at fiscal year-end	238	237	237	237	236
Comparable sales increase (%) [2]	5.2	6.8	5.6	5.6	5.3
Sales per square foot ($) [3]	446.86	417.02	390.78	370.55	352.22
Customer transactions [3]	1,621	1,579	1,544	1,501	1,442
Average ticket ($) [3]	65.74	63.06	60.35	58.77	57.87
Number of associates at fiscal year-end (in thousands)	413	413	406	385	371

Note: Fiscal 2018 includes 53 weeks. All other fiscal periods disclosed include 52 weeks. This information should be read in conjunction with MD&A and our consolidated financial statements and related notes.

(1) Includes capital leases.
(2) The calculations for fiscal 2017, fiscal 2016, fiscal 2015, and fiscal 2014 do not include results for Interline, which was acquired in fiscal 2015.
(3) These amounts do not include the results for Interline, which was acquired in fiscal 2015.

Appendix B

Combined Journal

Most small businesses have just a few employees and can devote only a limited amount of time to the preparation of accounting records. To serve the needs of these businesses, accountants have developed certain types of record systems that have special time-saving and labor-saving features but still produce all the necessary financial information for management. One example of such a system is the combined journal discussed in this appendix.

Small firms play an important role in our economy today. In fact, almost one-half of the businesses in the United States are classified as small entities. Despite their limited size, these businesses need good accounting systems that can produce accurate and timely information.

Systems Involving the Combined Journal

The **combined journal,** also called the *combination journal,* provides the cornerstone for a simple yet effective accounting system in many small firms. As its name indicates, this journal combines features of the general journal and the special journals in a single record.

If a small business has enough transactions to make the general journal difficult to use but too few transactions to make it worthwhile to set up special journals, the combined journal offers a solution. It has many of the advantages of special journals but provides the simplicity of a single journal. Like the special journals, the combined journal contains separate money columns for the accounts used most often to record a firm's transactions. This speeds up the initial entry of transactions and permits summary postings at the end of the month. Most transactions can be recorded on a single line, and the need to write account names is minimized.

Other Accounts columns allow the recording of transactions that do not fit into any of the special columns. These columns are also used for entries that would normally appear in the general journal, such as adjusting and closing entries.

Some small firms just use a combined journal and a general ledger in their accounting systems. Others need one or more subsidiary ledgers in addition to the general ledger.

Designing a Combined Journal

To function effectively, a combined journal must be designed to meet the specific needs of a firm. For a new business, the accountant first studies the proposed operations and develops an appropriate chart of accounts. Then the accountant decides which accounts are likely to be used often enough in recording daily transactions to justify special columns in the combined journal.

Consider the combined journal shown in Figure B.1, which belongs to Quality Lawn Care and Landscaping Services, a small business that provides lawn and landscaping services. In designing this journal before the firm opened, the accountant established a Cash section with Debit and Credit columns because it was known that the business would constantly be receiving cash from customers and paying out cash for expenses and other obligations. Debit and Credit columns were also set up in the Accounts Receivable and Accounts Payable sections because the firm planned to offer credit to qualified customers and would make credit purchases of supplies and other items.

After further analysis it was realized that the business would have numerous entries for the sale of services, the payment of employee salaries, and the purchase of supplies. Therefore, columns were established for recording credits to **Sales,** debits to **Salaries Expense,** and debits to **Supplies.** Finally, a column was set up for an Other Accounts section to take care of transactions that cannot be entered in the special columns.

FIGURE B.1 Combined Journal

COMBINED JOURNAL

	DATE	CK. NO.	DESCRIPTION	POST. REF.	CASH DEBIT	CASH CREDIT	ACCOUNTS RECEIVABLE DEBIT	ACCOUNTS RECEIVABLE CREDIT
1	20X1							
2	Jan. 3	711	Rent for month			1050 00		
3	5		Treschell Seymore	✓			250 00	
4	6		C & M Garden Supply	✓				
5	7		Cash sales		2300 00			
6	7	712	Payroll			780 00		
7	10		Annie McGowan	✓	150 00			150 00
8	12		The Greenery	✓				
9	13		Allen Clark	✓	440 00			440 00
10	14		Cash sales		2770 00			
11	14	713	Payroll			780 00		
12	17		Jessica Savage	✓			175 00	
13	18		Lawn and Garden Supply	✓				
14	19	714	Telephone service			201 00		
15	20		Ned Jones	✓	125 00			125 00
16	20		Starlene Neal	✓			110 00	
17	21		Cash sales		2540 00			
18	21	715	Payroll	✓		780 00		
19	24		Lawn and Garden Supply	✓				
20	25		Jeraldine Wells	✓			225 00	
21	26	716	Ace Garden Supply			460 00		
22	28		Cash sales		2200 00			
23	28	717	Payroll			780 00		
24	30		Note issued for purchase					
25			of landscape equipment					
26	31		Juanda Fischer	✓			98 00	
27	31		Totals		10525 00	4831 00	858 00	715 00
28					(101)	(101)	(111)	(111)

Recording Transactions in the Combined Journal

The combined journal shown in Figure B.1 contains the January 20X1 transactions of Quality Lawn Care and Landscaping Services. Notice that most of these transactions require only a single line and involve the use of just the special columns. The entries for major types of transactions are explained in the following paragraphs.

Payment of Expenses During January, Quality Lawn Care and Landscaping Services issued checks to pay three kinds of expenses: rent, telephone service, and employee salaries. Notice how the payment of the monthly rent on January 3 was recorded in the combined journal. Because there is no special column for rent expense, the debit part of this entry appears in the Other Accounts section. The offsetting credit appears in the Cash Credit column. The payment of the monthly telephone bill on January 19 was recorded in a similar manner. However, when employee salaries were paid on January 7, 14, 21, and 28, both parts of the entries could be made in special columns. Because the firm has a weekly payroll period, a separate column in the combined journal was set up for debits to Salaries Expense.

PAGE 1

ACCOUNTS PAYABLE DEBIT	ACCOUNTS PAYABLE CREDIT	SALES CREDIT	SUPPLIES DEBIT	SALARIES EXPENSE DEBIT	ACCOUNT TITLE	POST REF.	OTHER ACCOUNTS DEBIT	OTHER ACCOUNTS CREDIT	
									1
					Rent Expense	511	1050 00		2
		250 00							3
	450 00		450 00						4
		2300 00							5
				780 00					6
									7
	225 00		225 00						8
									9
		2770 00							10
				780 00					11
		175 00							12
	1200 00				Equipment	131	1200 00		13
					Telephone Exp.	514	201 00		14
									15
		110 00							16
		2540 00							17
				780 00					18
	290 00		290 00						19
		225 00							20
460 00									21
		2200 00							22
				780 00					23
					Equipment	131	8500 00		24
					Notes Payable	201		8500 00	25
		98 00							26
460 00	2165 00	10668 00	965 00	3120 00			10951 00	8500 00	27
(202)	(202)	(401)	(121)	(517)			(X)	(X)	28

Sales on Credit On January 5, 17, 20, 25, and 31, Quality Lawn Care and Landscaping Services sold services on credit. The necessary entries were made in two special columns of the combined journal: the Accounts Receivable Debit column and the Sales Credit column.

Cash Sales Entries for the firm's weekly cash sales were recorded on January 7, 14, 21, and 28. Again, special columns were used: the Cash Debit column and the Sales Credit column.

Cash Received on Account When Quality Lawn Care and Landscaping Services collected cash on account from credit customers on January 10, 13, and 20, the transactions were entered in the Cash Debit column and the Accounts Receivable Credit column.

Purchases of Supplies on Credit Because the firm's combined journal includes a Supplies Debit column and an Accounts Payable Credit column, all purchases of supplies on credit can be recorded in special columns. Refer to the entries made on January 6, 12, and 24.

Purchases of Equipment on Credit On January 18, Quality Lawn Care and Landscaping Services bought some store equipment on credit. Because there is no special column for equipment, the debit part of the entry was made in the Other Accounts section. The offsetting credit appears in the Accounts Payable Credit column.

Payments on Account Any payments made on account to creditors are recorded in two special columns: Accounts Payable Debit and Cash Credit, as shown in the entry of January 26.

Issuance of a Promissory Note On January 30, the business purchased new cleaning equipment and issued a promissory note to the seller. Notice that both the debit to *Equipment* and the credit to *Notes Payable* had to be recorded in the Other Accounts section.

Posting from the Combined Journal

One of the advantages of the combined journal is that it simplifies the posting process. All amounts in the special columns can be posted to the general ledger on a summary basis at the end of the month. Only the figures that appear in the Other Accounts section require individual postings to the general ledger during the month. Of course, if the firm has subsidiary ledgers, individual postings must also be made to these ledgers.

Daily Postings The procedures followed at Quality Lawn Care and Landscaping Services will illustrate the techniques used to post from the combined journal. Each day any entries appearing in the Other Accounts section are posted to the proper accounts in the general ledger. For example, refer to the combined journal shown in Figure B.1. The five amounts listed in the Other Accounts Debit and Credit columns were posted individually during the month. The account numbers recorded in the Posting Reference column of the Other Accounts section show that the postings have been made.

Because Quality Lawn Care and Landscaping Services has subsidiary ledgers for accounts receivable and accounts payable, individual postings were also made on a daily basis to these ledgers. As each amount was posted, a check mark was placed in the Posting Reference column of the combined journal.

End-of-Month Postings At the end of the month, the combined journal is totaled, proved, and ruled. Then the totals of the special columns are posted to the general ledger. Proving the combined journal involves a comparison of the column totals to make sure that the debits and credits are equal. The following procedure is used:

Proof of Combined Journal	
	Debits
Cash Debit Column	10,525
Accounts Receivable Debit Column	858
Accounts Payable Debit Column	460
Supplies Debit Column	965
Salaries Expense Debit Column	3,120
Other Accounts Debit Column	10,951
	26,879
	Credits
Cash Credit Column	4,831
Accounts Receivable Credit Column	715
Accounts Payable Credit Column	2,165
Sales Credit Column	10,668
Other Accounts Credit Column	8,500
	26,879

After the combined journal is proved, all column totals except those in the Other Accounts section are posted to the appropriate general ledger accounts. As each total is posted, the account number is entered beneath the column in the journal. Notice that an X is used to indicate that the column totals in the Other Accounts section are not posted because the individual amounts were posted on a daily basis.

Typical Uses of the Combined Journal

The combined journal is used most often in small professional offices and small service businesses. It is less suitable for merchandising businesses but is sometimes used in firms of this type if they are very small and have only a limited number of transactions.

Professional Offices   The combined journal can be ideal to record the transactions that occur in a professional office, such as the office of a doctor, lawyer, accountant, or architect. However, special journals are more efficient if transactions become very numerous or are too varied.

Service Businesses   The use of the combined journal to record the transactions of Quality Lawn Care and Landscaping Services has already been illustrated. The combined journal may be advantageous for a small service business, provided that the volume of transactions does not become excessive and the nature of the transactions does not become too complex.

Merchandising Businesses   The combined journal can be used by a merchandising business, but only if the firm is quite small and has a limited number and variety of transactions involving few accounts. However, even for a small merchandising business, the use of special journals might prove more advantageous.

Disadvantages of the Combined Journal

If the variety of transactions is so great that many different accounts are required, the combined journal will not work well. Either the business will have to set up so many columns that the journal will become unwieldy, or it will be necessary to record so many transactions in the Other Accounts columns that little efficiency will result. As a general rule, if the transactions of a business are numerous enough to merit the use of special journals, any attempt to substitute the combined journal is a mistake. Remember that each special journal can be designed for maximum efficiency in recording transactions.

Glossary

Absorption costing The accounting procedure whereby all manufacturing costs, including fixed costs, are included in the cost of goods manufactured

Accelerated method of depreciation A method of depreciating an asset's cost that allocates greater amounts of depreciation to an asset's early years of useful life

Account balance The difference between the amounts recorded on the two sides of an account

Account form balance sheet A balance sheet that lists assets on the left and liabilities and owner's equity on the right (*see also* Report form balance sheet)

Accounting The process by which financial information about a business is recorded, classified, summarized, interpreted, and communicated to owners, managers, and other interested parties

Accounting cycle A series of steps performed during each accounting period to classify, record, and summarize data for a business and to produce needed financial information

Accounting Standards Codification The source of authoritative U.S. GAAP

Accounting Standards Update Changes to Accounting Standards Codification are communicated through Accounting Standards Update covering approximately 90 topics

Accounting system A process designed to accumulate, classify, and summarize financial data

Accounts Written records of the assets, liabilities, and owner's equity of a business

Accounts payable Amounts a business must pay in the future

Accounts payable ledger A subsidiary ledger that contains a separate account for each creditor

Accounts receivable Claims for future collection from customers

Accounts receivable ledger A subsidiary ledger that contains credit customer accounts

Accounts receivable turnover A measure of the speed with which sales on account are collected; the ratio of net credit sales to average receivables

Accrual basis A system of accounting by which all revenues and expenses are matched and reported on financial statements for the applicable period, regardless of when the cash related to the transaction is received or paid

Accrued expenses Expense items that relate to the current period but have not yet been paid and do not yet appear in the accounting records

Accrued income Income that has been earned but not yet received and recorded

Acid-test ratio A measure of immediate liquidity; the ratio of quick assets to current liabilities

Adjusting entries Journal entries made to update accounts for items that were not recorded during the accounting period

Adjustments *See* Adjusting entries

Aging the accounts receivable Classifying accounts receivable balances according to how long they have been outstanding

Allowance method A method of recording uncollectible accounts that estimates losses from uncollectible accounts and charges them to expense in the period when the sales are recorded

Amortization The process of periodically transferring the acquisition cost of intangible assets with estimated useful lives to an expense account

Appropriation of retained earnings A formal declaration of an intention to restrict dividends

Articles of partnership *See* Partnership agreement

Asset turnover A measure of the effective use of assets in making sales; the ratio of net sales to total assets

Assets Property owned by a business

Audit trail A chain of references that makes it possible to trace information, locate errors, and prevent fraud

Auditing The review of financial statements to assess their fairness and adherence to generally accepted accounting principles

Auditor's report An independent accountant's review of a firm's financial statements

Authorized capital stock The number of shares authorized for issue by the corporate charter

Average collection period The ratio of 365 days to the accounts receivable turnover; also called the *number of days' sales in receivables*

Average cost method A method of inventory costing using the average cost of units of an item available for sale during the period to arrive at cost of the ending inventory

Average method of process costing A method of costing that combines the cost of beginning inventory for each cost element with the costs during the current period

Average number of days in inventory The average number of days for merchandise inventory to be sold after it is purchased

Balance ledger form A ledger account form that shows the balance of the account after each entry is posted

Balance sheet A formal report of a business's financial condition on a certain date; reports the assets, liabilities, and owner's equity of the business

Bank draft A check written by a bank that orders another bank to pay the stated amount to a specific party

Bank reconciliation statement A statement that accounts for all differences between the balance on the bank statement and the book balance of cash

Banker's year A 360-day period used to calculate interest on a note

Bill of lading A business document that lists goods accepted for transportation

Blank endorsement A signature of the payee written on the back of the check that transfers ownership of the check without specifying to whom or for what purpose

Bond indenture A bond contract

Bond issue costs Costs incurred in issuing bonds, such as legal and accounting fees and printing costs

Bond retirement When a bond is paid and the liability is removed from the company's balance sheet

Bond sinking fund investment A fund established to accumulate assets to pay off bonds when they mature

Bonding The process by which employees are investigated by an insurance company that will insure the business against losses through employee theft or mishandling of funds

Bonds payable Long-term debt instruments that are written promises to repay the principal at a future date; interest is due at a fixed rate payable over the life of the bond

Book value That portion of an asset's original cost that has not yet been depreciated

Book value (stock) The total equity applicable to a class of stock divided by the number of shares outstanding

Brand name *See* Trade name

Break even A point at which revenue equals expenses

Break-even point (BEP) The sales volume when total revenue equals total expenses

Budget An operating plan expressed in monetary units

Budget performance report A comparison of actual costs and budgeted costs

Business transaction A financial event that changes the resources of a firm

Bylaws The guidelines for conducting a corporation's business affairs

Call price The amount the corporation must pay for the bond when it is called

Callable bonds Bonds that allow the issuing corporation to require the holder to surrender the bonds for payment before their maturity date

Callable preferred stock Stock that gives the issuing corporation the right to repurchase the preferred shares from the stockholders at a specific price

Canceled check A check paid by the bank on which it was drawn

Capacity A facility's ability to produce or use

Capital Financial investment in a business; equity

Capital stock ledger A subsidiary ledger that contains a record of each stockholder's purchases, transfers, and current balance of shares owned; also called stockholders' ledger

Capital stock transfer journal A record of stock transfers used for posting to the stockholders' ledger

Capitalized costs All costs recorded as part of an asset's costs

Carrying value of bonds The balance of the *Bonds Payable* account plus the *Premium on Bonds Payable* account minus the *Discount on Bonds Payable* account; also called *book value of bonds*

Cash In accounting, currency, coins, checks, money orders, and funds on deposit in a bank

Cash discount A discount offered by suppliers for payment received within a specified period of time

Cash equivalents Assets that are easily convertible into known amounts of cash

Cash payments journal A special journal used to record transactions involving the payment of cash

Cash receipts journal A special journal used to record and post transactions involving the receipt of cash

Cash register proof A verification that the amount of currency and coins in a cash register agrees with the amount shown on the cash register audit tape

***Cash Short or Over* account** An account used to record any discrepancies between the amount of currency and coins in the cash register and the amount shown on the audit tape

Cashier's check A draft on the issuing bank's own funds

Certified Bookkeeper (CB) A designation that assures an individual possesses the level of knowledge and skill needed to carry out all key functions through the adjusted trial balance, including payroll

Certified public accountant (CPA) An independent accountant who provides accounting services to the public for a fee

Charge-account sales Sales made through the use of open-account credit or one of various types of credit cards

Chart of accounts A list of the accounts used by a business to record its financial transactions

Check A written order signed by an authorized person instructing a bank to pay a specific sum of money to a designated person or business

Chronological order Organized in the order in which the events occur

Classification A means of identifying each account as an asset, liability, or owner's equity

Classified financial statement A format by which revenues and expenses on the income statement, and assets and liabilities on the balance sheet, are divided into groups of similar accounts and a subtotal is given for each group

Closing entries Journal entries that transfer the results of operations (net income or net loss) to owner's equity and reduce the revenue, expense, and drawing account balances to zero

Collateral trust bonds Bonds secured by the pledge of securities, such as stocks or bonds of other companies

Combined journal A journal that combines features of the general journal and the special journals in a single record

Commercial draft A note issued by one party that orders another party to pay a specified sum on a specified date

Commission basis A method of paying employees according to a percentage of net sales

Common costs Costs not directly traceable to a specific segment of a business

Common stock The general class of stock issued when no other class of stock is authorized; each share carries the same rights and privileges as every other share. Even if preferred stock is issued, common stock will also be issued

***Common Stock Dividend Distributable* account** Equity account used to record par, or stated, value of shares to be issued as the result of the declaration of a stock dividend

Common-size statements Financial statements with items expressed as percentages of a base amount

Comparative statements Financial statements presented side by side for two or more years

Compensation record *See* Individual earnings record

Compound entry A journal entry with more than one debit or credit

Computer software An intangible asset; written programs that instruct a computer's hardware to do certain tasks

Conceptual framework A basic framework developed by the FASB to provide conceptual guidelines for financial statements. The most important features are statements of qualitative features of statements, basic assumptions underlying statements, basic accounting principles, and modifying constraints

Condensed income statement An income statement summarizing detailed income statement accounts into a few lines of information

Conservatism The concept that revenue and assets should be understated rather than overstated if GAAP allows alternatives. Similarly, expenses and liabilities should be overstated rather than understated

Contingent liability An item that can become a liability if certain things happen

Contra account An account with a normal balance that is opposite that of a related account

Contra asset account An asset account with a credit balance, which is contrary to the normal balance of an asset account

Contra revenue account An account with a debit balance, which is contrary to the normal balance for a revenue account

Contribution margin Gross profit on sales minus direct expenses

Control account An account that links a subsidiary ledger and the general ledger since its balance summarizes the balances of the accounts in the subsidiary ledger

Controllable fixed costs Costs that the segment manager can control

Convertible bonds Bonds that give the owner the right to convert the bonds into common stock under specified conditions

Convertible preferred stock Preferred stock that conveys the right to convert that stock to common stock after a specified date or during a period of time

Copyright An intangible asset; an exclusive right granted by the federal government to produce, publish, and sell a literary or artistic work for a period equal to the creator's life plus 70 years

Corporate charter A document issued by a state government that establishes a corporation

Corporation A publicly or privately owned business entity that is separate from its owners and has a legal right to own property and do business in its own name; stockholders are not responsible for the debts or taxes of the business

Correcting entry A journal entry made to correct an erroneous entry

Cost center A business segment that incurs costs but does not produce revenue

Cost of goods sold The actual cost to the business of the merchandise sold to customers

Cost of production report Summarizes all costs charged to each department and shows the costs assigned to the goods transferred out of the department and to the goods still in process

Cost variance The difference between the total standard cost and the total actual cost

Cost-benefit test If accounting concepts suggest a particular accounting treatment for an item, but it appears that the theoretically correct treatment would require an unreasonable amount of work, the accountant may analyze the benefits and costs of the preferred treatment to see if the benefit gained from its adoption is justified by the cost

Coupon bonds Unregistered bonds that have coupons attached for each interest payment; also called *bearer bonds*

Credit An entry on the right side of an account

Credit memorandum (accounts receivable) A note verifying that a customer's account is being reduced by the amount of a sales return or sales allowance plus any sales tax that may have been involved

Credit memorandum (banking) A form that explains any addition, other than a deposit, to a checking account

Creditor One to whom money is owed

Cumulative preferred stock Stock that conveys to its owners the right to receive the preference dividend for the current year and any prior years in which the preference dividend was not paid before common stockholders receive any dividends

Current assets Assets consisting of cash, items that normally will be converted into cash within one year, and items that will be used up within one year

Current liabilities Debts that must be paid or otherwise satisfied within one year

Current ratio A relationship between current assets and current liabilities that provides a measure of a firm's ability to pay its current debts (current ratio = current assets ÷ current liabilities)

Debentures Unsecured bonds backed only by a corporation's general credit

Debit An entry on the left side of an account

Debit memorandum A form that explains any deduction, other than a check or other electronic payment transaction, from a checking account

Declaration date The date on which the board of directors declares a dividend

Declining-balance method An accelerated method of depreciation in which an asset's book value at the beginning of a year is multiplied by a constant percentage (such as 125%, 150%, or 200%) to determine depreciation for the year

Deferred expenses *See* Prepaid expenses

Deferred income *See* Unearned income

Deferred income taxes The amount of income taxes that will be payable or an amount that may benefit the corporation in the future as a result of the difference between the current year's taxable income and financial statement net income

Departmental income statement Income statement that shows each department's contribution margin and net income from operations after all expenses are allocated

Depletion Allocating the cost of a natural resource to expense over the period in which the resource produces revenue

Deposit in transit A deposit that is recorded in the cash receipts journal but that reaches the bank too late to be shown on the monthly bank statement

Deposit slip A form prepared to record the deposit of cash or checks to a bank account

Depreciation Allocation of the cost of a long-term asset to operations during its expected useful life

Differential cost The difference in cost between one alternative and another

Direct charge-off method A method of recording uncollectible account losses as they occur

Direct costing The accounting procedure whereby only variable costs are included in the cost of goods manufactured, and fixed manufacturing costs are written off as expenses in the period in which they are incurred

Direct expenses Operating expenses that are identified directly with a department and are recorded by department

Direct labor The costs attributable to personnel who work directly on the product being manufactured

Direct materials All items that go into a product and become a part of it

Direct method A means of reporting sources and uses of cash under which all revenue and expenses reported on the income statement appear in the operating section of the statement of cash flows and show the cash received or paid out for each type of transaction

Discount on bonds payable The excess of the face value over the price received by the corporation for a bond

Discount on credit card sales A fee charged by the credit card companies for processing sales made with credit cards.

Discounting Deducting the interest from the principal on a note payable or receivable in advance

Discussion memorandum An explanation of a topic under consideration by the Financial Accounting Standards Board

Dishonored (NSF) check A check returned to the depositor unpaid because of insufficient funds in the drawer's account; also called an NSF check

Dissolution The legal term for termination of a partnership

Distributive share The amount of net income or net loss allocated to each partner

Dividends Distributions of the profits of a corporation to its shareholders

Donated capital Capital resulting from the receipt of gifts by a corporation

Double-declining-balance (DDB) method A method of depreciation that uses a rate equal to twice the straight-line rate and applies that rate to the book value of the asset at the beginning of the year

Double-entry system An accounting system that involves recording the effects of each transaction as debits and credits

Draft A written order that requires one party (a person or business) to pay a stated sum of money to another party

Drawee The bank on which a check is written

Drawer The person or firm issuing a check

Drawing account A special type of owner's equity account set up to record the owner's withdrawal of cash from the business

Economic entity A business or organization whose major purpose is to produce a profit for its owners

Electronic funds transfer (EFT) An electronic transfer of money from one account to another

Employee A person who is hired by and works under the control and direction of the employer

Employee's Withholding Allowance Certificate, Form W-4 A form used to claim exemption (withholding) allowances

Employer's Annual Federal Unemployment Tax Return, Form 940 Preprinted government form used by the employer to report unemployment taxes for the calendar year

Employer's Quarterly Federal Tax Return, Form 941 Preprinted government form used by the employer to report payroll tax information relating to social security, Medicare, and employee income tax withholding to the Internal Revenue Service

Endorsement A written authorization that transfers ownership of a check

Entity Anything having its own separate identity, such as an individual, a town, a university, or a business

Equity An owner's financial interest in a business

Equivalent production The estimated number of units that could have been started and completed with the same effort and costs incurred in the department during the same time period

Exempt employees Salaried employees who hold supervisory or managerial positions who are not subject to the maximum hour and overtime pay provisions of the Wage and Hour Law

Expense An outflow of cash, use of other assets, or incurring of a liability

Experience rating system A system that rewards an employer for maintaining steady employment conditions by reducing the firm's state unemployment tax rate

Exposure draft A proposed solution to a problem being considered by the Financial Accounting Standards Board

Face interest rate The contractual interest rate specified on the bond

Face value An amount of money indicated to be paid, exclusive of interest or discounts

Fair market value The current worth of an asset or the price the asset would bring if sold on the open market

Federal unemployment taxes (FUTA) Taxes levied by the federal government against employers to benefit unemployed workers

Financial statements Periodic reports of a firm's financial position or operating results

Financing activities Transactions with those who provide cash to the business to carry on its activities

Finished goods inventory The cost of completed products ready for sale; corresponds to the *Merchandise Inventory* account of a merchandising business

Finished goods subsidiary ledger A ledger containing a record for each of the different types of finished products

First-in, first-out (FIFO) method A method of inventory costing that assumes the oldest merchandise is sold first

Fixed budget A budget representing only one level of activity

Fixed costs Costs that do not change in total as the level of activity changes

Flexible budget A budget that shows the budgeted costs at various levels of activity

Footing A small pencil figure written at the base of an amount column showing the sum of the entries in the column

Franchise An intangible asset; a right to exclusive dealership granted by a governmental unit or a business entity

Fraud Intentional or reckless acts that result in the confiscation of a firm's assets or the misrepresentation of the firm's accounting data

***Freight In* account** An account showing transportation charges for items purchased

Full disclosure principle The requirement that all information that might affect the user's interpretation of the profitability and financial condition of a business be disclosed in the financial statements or in notes to the statements

Full endorsement A signature transferring a check to a specific person, firm, or bank

Fundamental accounting equation The relationship between assets and liabilities plus owner's equity

Gain The disposition of an asset for more than its book value

General journal A financial record for entering all types of business transactions; a record of original entry

General ledger A permanent, classified record of all accounts used in a firm's operation; a record of final entry

General partner A member of a partnership who has unlimited liability

Generally accepted accounting principles (GAAP) Accounting standards developed and applied by professional accountants

Going concern assumption The assumption that a firm will continue to operate indefinitely

Goodwill An intangible asset; the value of a business in excess of the net value of its identifiable assets

Governmental accounting Accounting work performed for a federal, state, or local governmental unit

Gross profit The difference between net sales and the cost of goods sold (gross profit = net sales − cost of goods sold)

Gross profit method A method of estimating inventory cost based on the assumption that the rate of gross profit on sales and the ratio of cost of goods sold to net sales are relatively constant from period to period

Gross profit percentage The amount of gross profit from each dollar of sales (gross profit percentage = gross profit ÷ net sales)

High-low point method A method to determine the fixed and variable components of a semivariable cost

Historical cost basis principle The principle that requires assets and services to be recorded at their cost at the time they are acquired and that, generally, long-term assets remain at historical costs in the asset accounts

Horizontal analysis Computing the percentage change for individual items in the financial statements from year to year

Hourly rate basis A method of paying employees according to a stated rate per hour

Impairment A situation that occurs when the asset is determined to have a fair market value less than its book value

Income statement A formal report of business operations covering a specific period of time; also called a profit and loss statement or a statement of income and expenses

Income Summary **account** A special owner's equity account that is used only in the closing process to summarize the results of operations

Income tax method A method of recording the trade-in of an asset for income tax purposes. It does not permit a gain or loss to be recognized on the transaction

Independent contractor One who is paid by a company to carry out a specific task or job but is not under the direct supervision or control of the company

Indirect expenses Operating expenses that cannot be readily identified and are not closely related to activity within a department

Indirect labor Costs attributable to personnel who support production but are not directly involved in the manufacture of a product; for example, supervisory, repair and maintenance, and janitorial staff

Indirect materials and supplies Materials used in manufacturing a product that may not become a part of the product and are not a significant material cost factor

Indirect method A means of reporting cash generated from operating activities by treating net income as the primary source of cash in the operating section of the statement of cash flows and adjusting that amount for changes in current assets and liabilities associated with net income, noncash transactions, and other items

Individual earnings record An employee record that contains information needed to compute earnings and complete tax reports

Industry averages Financial ratios and percentages reflecting averages for similar companies

Industry practice constraint In a few limited cases, unusual operating characteristics of an industry, usually based on risk, for which special accounting principles and procedures have been developed. These may not conform completely with GAAP for other industries

Intangible assets Assets that lack a physical substance, such as goodwill, patents, copyrights, and computer software, although software has, in a sense, a physical attribute

Interest The fee charged for the use of money

Internal control A company's policies and procedures to safeguard assets, ensure reliability of accounting data, and promote compliance with management policies and applicable laws

International accounting The study of accounting principles used by different countries

Interpret To understand and explain the meaning and importance of something (such as financial statements)

Inventory sheet A form used to list the quantity and type of goods a firm has in stock

Inventory turnover The number of times inventory is purchased and sold during the accounting period (inventory turnover = cost of goods sold ÷ average inventory)

Investing activities Transactions that involve the acquisition or disposal of long-term assets

Invoice A customer billing for merchandise bought on credit

Job order A specific order for a specific batch of manufactured items

Job order cost accounting A cost accounting system that determines the unit cost of manufactured items for each separate production order

Job order cost sheet A record of all manufacturing costs charged to a specific job

Journal The record of original entry

Journalizing Recording transactions in a journal

Just-in-time system An inventory system in which raw materials are ordered so they arrive just in time to be placed into production

Labor efficiency variance *See* Labor time variance

Labor rate variance The difference between the actual labor rate per hour and the standard labor rate per hour multiplied by the actual number of hours worked on the job

Labor time variance The difference between the actual hours worked and the standard labor hours allowed for the job multiplied by the standard cost per hour

Last-in, first-out (LIFO) method A method of inventory costing that assumes that the most recently purchased merchandise is sold first

Ledger The record of final entry

Leveraged buyout Purchasing a business by acquiring the stock and obligating the business to pay the debt incurred

Leveraging Using borrowed funds to earn a profit greater than the interest that must be paid on the borrowing

Liabilities Debts or obligations of a business

Limited liability company (LLC) Provides limited liability to the owners, who can elect to have the profits taxed at the LLC level or on their individual tax returns

Limited liability partnership (LLP) A partnership that provides some limited liability for all partners

Limited partner A member of a partnership whose liability is limited to his or her investment in the partnership

Limited partnership A partnership having one or more limited partners

Liquidation Termination of a business by distributing all assets and discontinuing the business

Liquidation value Value of assets to be applied to preferred stock, usually par value or an amount in excess of par value, if the corporation is liquidated

Liquidity The ease with which an item can be converted into cash; the ability of a business to pay its debts when due

List price An established retail price

Long-term liabilities Debts of a business that are due more than one year in the future

Loss The disposition of an asset for less than its book value

Lower of cost or net realizable value rule The principle by which inventory is reported at either its original cost or its net realizable value, whichever is lower

Management advisory services Services designed to help clients improve their information systems or their business performance

Managerial accounting Accounting work carried on by an accountant employed by a single business in industry; the branch of accounting that provides financial information about business segments, activities, or products

Manufacturing business A business that sells goods that it has produced

Manufacturing cost budget A budget made for each manufacturing cost

Manufacturing margin Sales minus the variable cost of goods sold

Manufacturing overhead All manufacturing costs that are not classified as direct materials or direct labor

Manufacturing overhead ledger A subsidiary ledger that contains a record for each overhead item

Manufacturing Summary **account** The account to which all items on the statement of cost of goods manufactured are closed; similar to the *Income Summary* account

Marginal income The manufacturing margin minus variable operating expenses

Markdown Price reduction below the original markon

Market interest rate The interest rate a corporation is willing to pay and investors are willing to accept at the current time

Market value The price per share at which stock is bought and sold

Markon The difference between the cost and the initial retail price of merchandise

Markup A price increase above the original markon

Matching principle The concept that revenue and the costs incurred in earning the revenue should be matched in the appropriate accounting periods

Materiality constraint The significance of an item in relation to a particular situation or set of facts

Materials price variance The difference between the actual price and the standard cost for materials multiplied by the actual quantity of materials used

Materials quantity variance The difference between the actual quantity used and the quantity of materials allowed multiplied by the standard cost of the materials

Materials requisition A form that describes the item and quantity needed and shows the job or purpose

Materials usage variance *See* Materials quantity variance

Maturity value The total amount (principal plus interest) payable when a note comes due

Medicare tax A tax levied on employees and employers to provide medical care for the employee and the employee's spouse after each has reached age 65

Memorandum entry An informational entry in the general journal

Merchandise inventory The stock of goods a merchandising business keeps on hand

Merchandising business A business that sells goods purchased for resale

Merit rating system *See* Experience rating system

Minute book A book in which accurate and complete records of all meetings of stockholders and directors are kept

Monetary unit assumption It is assumed that only those items and events that can be measured in monetary terms are included in the financial statements. An inherent part of this assumption is that the monetary unit is stable. Thus, assets purchased one year may be combined in the accounts with those purchased in other years even though the dollars used in each year actually may have different purchasing power

Mortgage loan A long-term debt created when a note is given as part of the purchase price for land or buildings

Multiple-step income statement A type of income statement on which several subtotals are computed before the net income is calculated

Mutual agency The characteristic of a partnership by which each partner is empowered to act as an agent for the partnership, binding the firm by his or her acts

Negotiable A financial instrument whose ownership can be transferred to another person or business

Negotiable instrument A financial document containing a promise or order to pay that meets all requirements of the Uniform Commercial Code in order to be transferable to another party

Net book value The cost of an asset minus its accumulated depreciation, depletion, or amortization, also known as book value

Net income The result of an excess of revenue over expenses

Net income line The worksheet line immediately following the column totals on which net income (or net loss) is recorded in two places: the Income Statement section and the Balance Sheet section

Net loss The result of an excess of expenses over revenue

Net price The list price less all trade discounts

Net realizable value The estimated selling price of an inventory item in the ordinary course of business, less reasonably predictable costs of completion, disposal, and transportation

Net sales The difference between the balance in the *Sales* account and the balance in the *Sales Returns and Allowances* account

Net salvage value The salvage value of an asset less any costs to remove or sell the asset

Neutrality concept The concept that information in financial statements cannot be selected or presented in a way to favor one set of interested parties over another

No-par-value stock Stock that is not assigned a par value in the corporate charter

Noncumulative preferred stock Stock that conveys to its owners the stated preference dividend for the current year but no rights to dividends for years in which none were declared

Nonparticipating preferred stock Stock that conveys to its owners the right to only the preference dividend amount specified on the stock certificate

Normal balance The increase side of an account

Note payable A liability representing a written promise by the maker of the note (the debtor) to pay another party (the creditor) a specified amount at a specified future date

Note receivable An asset representing a written promise by another party (the debtor) to pay the note holder (the creditor) a specified amount at a specified future date

On account An arrangement to allow payment at a later date; also called a charge account or open-account credit

Open-account credit A system that allows the sale of services or goods with the understanding that payment will be made at a later date

Operating activities Routine business transactions—selling goods or services and incurring expenses

Operating assets and liabilities Current assets and current liabilities

Opportunity cost Potential earnings or benefits that are given up because a certain course of action is taken

Organization costs The costs associated with establishing a corporation

Outstanding checks Checks that have been recorded in the cash payments journal but have not yet been paid by the bank

Overapplied overhead The result of applied overhead exceeding the actual overhead costs

Overhead application rate The rate at which the estimated cost of overhead is charged to each job

Owner's equity The financial interest of the owner of a business; also called proprietorship or net worth

Paid-in capital Capital acquired from capital stock transactions (also known as contributed capital)

Par value An amount assigned by the corporate charter to each share of stock for accounting purposes

Participating preferred stock Stock that conveys the right not only to the preference dividend amount but also to a share of other dividends paid

Partnership A business entity owned by two or more people who carry on a business for profit and who are legally responsible for the debts and taxes of the business

Partnership agreement A legal contract forming a partnership and specifying certain details of operation

Patent An intangible asset; an exclusive right given by the U.S. Patent and Trademark Office to manufacture and sell an invention for a period of 20 years from the date the patent is granted

Payee The person or firm to whom a check is payable

Payment date The date that dividends are paid

Payroll register A record of payroll information for each employee for the pay period

Periodic inventory Inventory based on a periodic count of goods on hand

Periodic inventory system An inventory system in which the merchandise inventory balance is only updated when a physical inventory is taken

Periodicity of income assumption The concept that economic activities of an entity can be divided logically and identified with specific time periods, such as the year or quarter

Permanent account An account that is kept open from one accounting period to the next

Perpetual inventory Inventory based on a running total of number of units

Perpetual inventory system An inventory system that tracks the inventories on hand at all times

Petty cash analysis sheet A form used to record transactions involving petty cash

Petty cash fund A special-purpose fund used to handle payments involving small amounts of money

Petty cash voucher A form used to record the payments made from a petty cash fund

Physical inventory An actual count of the number of units of each type of good on hand

Piece-rate basis A method of paying employees according to the number of units produced

Plant and equipment Property that will be used in the business for longer than one year

Postclosing trial balance A statement that is prepared to prove the equality of total debits and credits after the closing process is completed

Postdated check A check dated some time in the future

Posting Transferring data from a journal to a ledger

Preemptive right A shareholder's right to purchase a proportionate amount of any new stock issued at a later date

Preference dividend A basic or stated dividend rate for preferred stock that must be paid before dividends can be paid on common stock

Preferred stock A class of stock that has special claims on the corporate profits or, in case of liquidation, on corporate assets

Premium on bonds payable The excess of the price paid over the face value of a bond

Prepaid expenses Expense items acquired, recorded, and paid for in advance of their use

Price-earnings ratio The ratio of the current market value of common stock to earnings per share of that stock

Principal The amount shown on the face of a note

Private sector This is the nongovernmental sector of society; in an accounting context, it is the business sector, which is represented in developing accounting principles by the Financial Accounting Standards Board (FASB)

Process cost accounting A cost accounting system whereby unit costs of manufactured items are determined by totaling unit costs in each production department

Process cost accounting system A method of accounting in which costs are accumulated for each process or department and then transferred on to the next process or department

Production order *See* Job order

Profit center A business segment that produces revenue

Promissory note A written promise to pay a specified amount of money on a specific date

Property, plant, and equipment Long-term assets that are used in the operation of a business and that are subject to depreciation (except for land, which is not depreciated)

Public accountants Members of firms that perform accounting services for other companies

Public sector The government sector, which is represented in developing accounting principles by the Securities and Exchange Commission (SEC)

Purchase allowance A price reduction from the amount originally billed

Purchase invoice A bill received for goods purchased

Purchase order An order to the supplier of goods specifying items needed, quantity, price, and credit terms

Purchase requisition A list sent to the purchasing department showing the items to be ordered

Purchase return Return of unsatisfactory goods

Purchases **account** An account used to record cost of goods bought for resale during a period

Purchases discount A cash discount offered to customers for payment within a specified period

Purchases journal A special journal used to record the purchase of goods on credit

Qualitative characteristics Traits necessary for credible financial statements: relevance (confirmatory and predictive value), faithful representation (completeness, neutrality, and freedom from error), comparability, timeliness, verifiability, and understandability

Quick assets Cash, receivables, and marketable securities

Ratio analysis Computing the relationship between various items in the financial statements

Raw materials The materials placed into production

Raw materials ledger record A record showing details of receipts and issues for a type of raw material

Raw materials subsidiary ledger A ledger containing the raw materials ledger records

Real property Assets such as land, land improvements, buildings, and other structures attached to the land

Realization The concept that revenue occurs when goods or services, merchandise, or other assets are exchanged for cash or claims to cash

Receiving report A form showing quantity and condition of goods received

Record date The date on which the specific stockholders to receive a dividend are determined

Recoverability test Test for possible impairment that compares the asset's net book value with the estimated net cash flows from future use of the asset

Registered bonds Bonds issued to a party whose name is listed in the corporation's records

Registrar A person or institution in charge of the issuance and transfer of a corporation's stock

Relevant range of activity The different levels of activity at which a factory is expected to operate

Report form balance sheet A balance sheet that lists the asset accounts first, followed by liabilities and owner's equity

Residual value The estimate of the amount that could be obtained from the sale or disposition of an asset at the end of its useful life; also called salvage or scrap value

Responsibility accounting The process that allows management to evaluate the performance of each segment of the business and assign responsibility for its financial results

Restrictive endorsement A signature that transfers a check to a specific party for a stated purpose

Retail business A business that sells directly to individual consumers

Retail method A method of estimating inventory cost by applying the ratio of cost to selling price in the current accounting period to the retail price of the inventory

Retained earnings The cumulative profits and losses of the corporation not distributed as dividends

Return on common stockholders' equity A measure of how well the corporation is making a profit for its shareholders; the ratio of net income available for common stockholders to common stockholders' equity

Revenue An inflow of money or other assets that results from the sales of goods or services or from the use of money or property; also called income

Revenue recognition principle Revenue is recognized when it has been earned and realized

Reversing entries Journal entries made to reverse the effect of certain adjusting entries involving accrued income or accrued expenses to avoid problems in recording future payments or receipts of cash in a new accounting period

Salary basis A method of paying employees according to an agreed-upon amount for each week or month

Sales allowance A reduction in the price originally charged to customers for goods or services

Sales discount A cash discount offered by the supplier for payment within a specified period

Sales invoice A supplier's billing document

Sales journal A special journal used to record sales of merchandise on credit

Sales return A firm's acceptance of a return of goods from a customer

Sales Returns and Allowances A contra revenue account where sales returns and sales allowances are recorded; sales returns and allowances are subtracted from sales to determine net sales

Salvage value An estimate of the amount that could be received by selling or disposing of an asset at the end of its useful life

Schedule of accounts payable A list of all balances owed to creditors

Schedule of accounts receivable A listing of all balances of the accounts in the accounts receivable subsidiary ledger

Schedule of operating expenses A schedule that supplements the income statement, showing the selling and general and administrative expenses in greater detail

Scrap value *See* Residual value

Secured bonds Bonds for which property is pledged to secure the claims of bondholders

Semidirect expenses Operating expenses that cannot be directly assigned to a department but are closely related to departmental activities

Semivariable costs Costs that vary with, but not in direct proportion to, the volume of activity

Separate entity assumption The concept that a business is separate from its owners; the concept of keeping a firm's financial records separate from the owner's personal financial records

Serial bonds Bonds issued at one time but payable over a period of years

Service business A business that sells services

Service charge A fee charged by a bank to cover the costs of maintaining accounts and providing services

Shareholder A person who owns shares of stock in a corporation; also called a stockholder

Sight draft A commercial draft that is payable on presentation

Single-step income statement A type of income statement where only one computation is needed to determine the net income (total revenue − total expenses = net income)

Slide An accounting error involving a misplaced decimal point

Social entity A nonprofit organization, such as a city, public school, or public hospital

Social security (FICA or OASDI) tax A tax imposed by the Federal Insurance Contributions Act and collected on employee earnings to provide retirement and disability benefits

Social Security Act A federal act providing certain benefits for employees and their families; officially the Federal Insurance Contributions Act

Sole proprietorship A business entity owned by one person, who is legally responsible for the debts and taxes of the business

Special journal A journal used to record only one type of transaction

Specific identification method A method of inventory costing based on the actual cost of each item of merchandise

Standard cost card A form that shows the per-unit standard costs for materials, labor, and overhead

Standard costs A measure of what costs should be in an efficient operation

State unemployment taxes (SUTA) Taxes levied by a state government against employers to benefit unemployed workers

Stated value The value that can be assigned to no-par-value stock by a board of directors for accounting purposes

Statement of account A form sent to a firm's customers showing transactions during the month and the balance owed

Statement of cash flows A financial statement that provides information about the cash receipts and cash payments of a business

Statement of cost of goods manufactured A financial report showing details of the cost of goods completed for a manufacturing business

Statement of owner's equity A formal report of changes that occurred in the owner's financial interest during a reporting period

Statement of partners' equities A financial statement prepared to summarize the changes in the partners' capital accounts during an accounting period

Statement of retained earnings A financial statement that shows all changes that have occurred in retained earnings during the period

Statement of stockholders' equity A financial statement that provides an analysis reconciling the beginning and ending balance of each of the stockholders' equity accounts

Statements of Financial Accounting Standards Accounting principles established by the Financial Accounting Standards Board

Stock Certificates that represent ownership of a corporation

Stock certificate The form by which capital stock is issued; the certificate indicates the name of the corporation, the name of the stockholder to whom the certificate was issued, the class of stock, and the number of shares

Stock dividend Distribution of the corporation's own stock on a pro rata basis that results in conversion of a portion of the firm's retained earnings to permanent capital

Stock split When a corporation issues two or more shares of new stock to replace each share outstanding without making any changes in the capital accounts

Stockholders The owners of a corporation; also called shareholders

Stockholders of record Stockholders in whose name shares are held on date of record and who will receive a declared dividend

Stockholders' equity The corporate equivalent of owners' equity; also called shareholders' equity

Stockholders' ledger *See* Capital stock ledger

Straight-line amortization Amortizing the premium or discount on bonds payable in equal amounts each month over the life of the bond

Straight-line depreciation Allocation of an asset's cost in equal amounts to each accounting period of the asset's useful life

Subchapter S corporation (S corporation) An entity formed as a corporation that meets the requirements of subchapter S of the Internal Revenue Code to be treated essentially as a partnership, so that the corporation pays no income tax

Subscribers' ledger A subsidiary ledger that contains an account receivable for each stock subscriber

Subscription book A list of the stock subscriptions received

Subsidiary ledger A ledger dedicated to accounts of a single type and showing details to support a general ledger account

Sum-of-the-years'-digits method A method of depreciating asset costs by allocating as expense each year a fractional part of the asset's depreciable cost, based on the sum of the digits of the number of years in the asset's useful life

Sunk cost A cost that has been incurred and will not change as a result of a decision

T account A type of account, resembling a T, used to analyze the effects of a business transaction

Tangible personal property Assets such as machinery, equipment, furniture, and fixtures that can be removed and used elsewhere

Tax accounting A service that involves tax compliance and tax planning

Tax-exempt wages Earnings in excess of the base amount set by the Social Security Act

Temporary account An account whose balance is transferred to another account at the end of an accounting period

Time and a half Rate of pay for an employee's work in excess of 40 hours a week

Time draft A commercial draft that is payable during a specified period of time

Time ticket Form used to record hours worked and jobs performed

Total equities The sum of a corporation's liabilities and stockholders' equity

Trade acceptance A form of commercial time draft used in transactions involving the sale of goods

Trade discount A reduction from list price

Trade name An intangible asset; an exclusive business name registered with the U.S. Patent and Trademark Office; also called brand name

Trademark An intangible asset; an exclusive business symbol registered with the U.S. Patent and Trademark Office

Trading on the equity *See* Leveraging

Transfer agent A person or institution that handles all stock transfers and transfer records for a corporation

Transfer price The price at which one segment's goods are transferred to another segment of the company

Transmittal of Wage and Tax Statements, Form W-3 Preprinted government form submitted with Forms W-2 to the Social Security Administration

Transparency Information provided in the financial statements and notes accompanying them should provide a clear and accurate picture of the financial affairs of the company. The key to this idea is that of disclosure

Transportation In **account** *See Freight In* account

Transposition An accounting error involving misplaced digits in a number

Treasury stock A corporation's own capital stock that has been issued and reacquired; the stock must have been previously paid in full and issued to a stockholder

Trend analysis Comparing selected ratios and percentages over a period of time

Trial balance A statement to test the accuracy of total debits and credits after transactions have been recorded

Underapplied overhead The result of actual overhead costs exceeding applied overhead

Unearned income Income received before it is earned

Unemployment insurance program A program that provides unemployment compensation through a tax levied on employers

Units-of-output method *See* Units-of-production method

Units-of-production method A method of depreciating asset cost at the same rate for each unit produced during each period

Unlimited liability The implication that a creditor can look to all partners' personal assets as well as the assets of the partnership for payment of the firm's debts

Updated account balances The amounts entered in the Adjusted Trial Balance section of the worksheet

Valuation account An account, such as *Allowance for Doubtful Accounts,* whose balance is revalued or reappraised in light of reasonable expectations

Variable costing *See* Direct costing

Variable costs Costs that vary in total in direct proportion to changes in the level of activity

Variance analysis Explains the difference between standard cost and actual cost

Vertical analysis Computing the relationship between each item on a financial statement to some base amount on the statement

Wage and Tax Statement, Form W-2 Preprinted government form that contains information about an employee's earnings and tax withholdings for the year

Wage-bracket table method A simple method to determine the amount of federal income tax to be withheld using a table provided by the government

Weighted average method *See* Average cost method

Wholesale business A business that manufactures goods for or distributes goods to retail businesses or large consumers such as hotels and hospitals

Withdrawals Funds taken from the business by the owner for personal use

Withholding statement *See* Wage and Tax Statement, Form W-2

Work in process Partially completed units in the production process

Work in process subsidiary ledger A ledger containing the job order cost sheets

Workers' compensation insurance Insurance that protects employees against losses from job-related injuries or illnesses, or compensates their families if death occurs in the course of the employment

Working capital The measure of the ability of a company to meet its current obligations; the excess of current assets over current liabilities

Worksheet A form used to gather all data needed at the end of an accounting period to prepare financial statements

Index

Key terms and page numbers where defined in the text are in **bold.**

A

AAA (American Accounting Association), 13, 515
Absorption costing, 1020
   direct costing *versus,* 1020–1022
Accelerated methods of depreciation, 627–629
Account balances, 62, 434
Account form balance sheet, 138
Accounting, 2
   accrual basis of, 420, 476, 865
   business entities, 10–12
   careers in, 3–5
   definition of, 2–3
   financial information, need for, 2
   financial information, users of, 5–8
Accounting and auditing guidelines (AcSEC of AICPA), 515
Accounting assumptions; *see* International Accounting Standards Board (IASB)
Accounting careers; *see* Careers in accounting
Accounting conceptual framework; *see* International Accounting Standards Board (IASB)
Accounting cycle, 92, 178
   flow of data through accounting system, 179, 481
   for manufacturing activities, 924–927
   review of, 479–481
   steps in, 178–180
Accounting equation, 31; *see also* Fundamental accounting equation
Accounting information, 175–179; *see also* Accounting cycle; Financial statements; Postclosing trial balance
Accounting principles; *see* Generally accepted accounting principles (GAAP)
Accounting Standards Codification (FASB), 13
Accounting Standards Executive Committee (AcSEC), of AICPA, 515
Accounting Standards Update (Update, FASB), 13
Accounting Standard Update (ASU) 2014-09, Revenue from Contracts with Customers (Topic 606), 523–524
Accounting systems, 2, 40, 105
Accounts, 56; *see also* T accounts
Accounts payable, 26; *see also* Purchases
   accounts payable ledger for, 252–253, 291–292
   cost of purchases in, 257
   internal control of purchases in, 258
   as liability account, 59
   purchase returns and allowances, 253–255
   schedule of, 255–257
Accounts payable ledger, 252–253, 291–292
Accounts receivable, 32; *see also* Merchandising; Sales; Uncollectible accounts
   accounts receivable ledger for, 205–206
   accounts receivable turnover ratio, 835–836
   cash increases from, 867
   collections from, 67
   internal control of, 559
   overview, 32–33
   sales returns and allowances, 206–211
   schedule of, 211–212
Accounts receivable ledger, 205–206
Accounts receivable turnover, 474–475
Accrual basis, 420, 476, 865
Accrued expenses, adjustments for, **425**–427
Accrued income, 429
Accrued interest on notes payable, 427
Accrued interest on notes receivable, 429
Accrued payroll, 921
Accrued payroll taxes, 426
Accrued salaries, 425–426, 921
Accrued wages, 921
Accumulated depreciation, 425
Accumulated depreciation account, 130–131
Acid-test ratio, 834
Actual costs, standard costs *versus,* 1000–1004
Adelphia Communications Corporation, 7
Adjusted trial balance section of worksheets
   completing, 133–134
   general ledger accounts listed in, 140–142
   preparing, 431–434
Adjusting entries, 127
   accrual basis of accounting, 420
   for accrued expenses, 425–427
   for accrued income, 429
   for corporate earnings, 752
   for depreciation, 130–131, 424–425
   for expired rent, 129–130
   journalizing and posting, 467–470
   for loss from uncollectible accounts, 423–424
   for merchandise inventory, 421–423
   for prepaid expenses, 427–428
   recording and posting, 924–925
   for tax liability, 747–748
   for unearned income, 429–430
   on worksheets, 127–131, 147–148, 920
Adjustments; *see* Adjusting entries
Adobe Systems, Inc., 88, 179
ADP, Inc., 353
Affordable Care Act, 387
Agents of corporations, 708–709, 727–729
Aging the accounts receivable, 551–552
Agreed-upon ratio, in partnerships, **673**
AICPA (American Institute of Certified Public Accountants), 13, 479, 511–515
Alacrity Renovation Services, 1019
Allowance for Doubtful Accounts, 423–424

Allowance method, 547
    aging accounts receivable under, 551–552
    collecting previously written-off accounts under, 554
    estimated expense recording under, 548–549
    overview, 546–547
    as percentage of net credit sales, 549–550
    as percentage of total accounts receivable, 550–551
    writing off customers' accounts under, 552–553
    year-end provision for, 549
Allstate, Inc., 98
Alternative method for prepaid expenses, 428
Amazon.com, Inc., 423, 474, 545, 867
American Accountant, The (Workman), 785
American Accounting Association (AAA), 13, 515
American Airlines Group, 23
American Eagle Outfitters, Inc., 20, 37
American Express, 218
American Institute of Certified Public Accountants (AICPA), 13, 479, 511–515
American Institute of Professional Bookkeepers, 193
American Production and Inventory Control Society (APICS), 610
America Online, Inc., 668
Amortization, 644
    of bond discount, 792
    of bond premium, 791
    cash flows from, 866
    overview, 644–645
Analysis of financial statements; *see* Financial statements, analysis of
Annual percentage rate (APR), 583
Annual reports, 88; *see also* Home Depot, Inc.
Annual Survey of Manufacturers (U.S. Census Bureau), 943
APICS (American Production and Inventory Control Society), 610
Apple, Inc., 859
Appropriations of retained earnings, 758–759
APR (annual percentage rate), 583
Arthur Andersen LLC, 7, 479
Articles of partnership, 667
Assembly-line manufacturing process, 385
Asset Advisors consultants, 625
Assets, 29
    current, 465
    disposition methods for, 633–638
    liquidity ratios using, 833–836
    long-term, 139, 465
    operating, 867–868
    quick, 834
    rate of return on total, 830
    reevaluation of, 683–685
    T accounts for, 56–61
Asset turnover, 830–831
Association of Certified Fraud Examiners, 258
AT&T, Inc., 55
Auditing, 5
Auditor's reports, 14
Audit trail, 93, 123
Authorized capital stock, 712; *see also* **Corporations**
Automated teller machines (ATMs), 281
Average collection period, 474–475, **835**–836

Average cost basis for inventory, 948
Average cost method of costing inventory, **601**–603, 965–966
Average method of process costing, 975, 980
Average number of days in inventory, 474–475
Avery Dennison, Inc., 944

B

Bad debt losses, 558
Balance ledger form, 101
Balances; *see also* Adjusted trial balance section of worksheets
    account, 62–63
    trial, 72–73
Balance sheet, 29
    bonds on, 793
    capital on, 717
    classified, 463–465
    for corporations, 720–721, 764–765
    information on, 38
    for manufacturing activities, 917–919
    for partnerships, 681
    preparing, 39–40
    as statement of financial position, 29
    worksheets for, 134–139, 143, 145–147, 434–436
Bank credit cards, 217–218, 316–317
Bank drafts, 588
Banker's year, 577
Banking procedures
    deposit slip preparation, 299–300
    endorsing checks, 299
    financial record adjustments, 304–306
    internal control of, 306
    online, 307–308
    postdated checks, 300–301
    reconciling bank statements, 301–304, 303
    writing checks, 298–299
Bank of America, 575
Banks, financial information used by, 6, 8
Bayliner.com, 942
Bearer bonds, 785
Bed Bath & Beyond, 243
Belair, Scott, 745
Bell, Alexander Graham, 55
Benchmarking, 915
Ben & Jerry's Homemade Ice Cream, Inc., 27
BEP (break-even point), 36–37, **901**
Best Buy, Inc., 211, 610
Bezos, Jeff, 545
Bill of lading, 589
Blank endorsement, 299
Bloch, Henry, 349
Bloch, Leon, 349
Bloch, Richard, 349
Boeing, William, 91
Boeing Company, 91, 139, 916
Bond indenture, 784
Bonding, 295
Bond issue costs, 793
Bond retirement, 795
    bond sinking fund retirement, 795–796

on due date, 797
early retirement, 797–799
retained earnings appropriated for, 796–797
Bonds
on balance sheet, 793
carrying value of, 793
discounted value issuance of, 792–793
face value issuance of, 788–790
issue cost accounting, 793
number of times bond interest earned ratio, 831
premium on bonds payable, 866
premium value issuance of, 791–792
retained earnings to retire, 796–797
retirement process, 797–799
sinking fund to retire, 795–796
stock *versus*, 786–787
types of, 784–786
Bond sinking fund investment, 795–796
Bonds payable, 784
Bookkeeping, historical, 27
Book value, 131
in asset sales, 634–636
balance sheet reporting of, 137
of common stock dividend, 758
per share of stock, 832–833
Borrowing, short- and long-term, 871
Brand names, 643
Break-even, 36
Break-even point (BEP), 36–37, **901**
British Airways, 23
Brunswick Corporation, 942
Budget performance report, 995–997
Budgets, 994–997, 1003
Bush, George W., 6
Business classifications, 198
Business credit cards, 217
Business entities, 10–12
Businesses, starting, 24–25
Business transactions, 23–54, **24**; *see also* T accounts
accounting equation for, 31–36
on balance sheet, 38–40
example of, 23
on income statement, 36–37
property and financial interest, 24–29
on statement of owner's equity, 37–38
Buyback programs for common stock, 762
Bylaws, 710

C

California Occupational Safety and Health Department, 1003
Callable bonds, 785
Callable preferred stock, 714
Call price, 785
Canadian Airlines, 23
Canceled checks, 302
Capacity, 1025
Capital, 25; *see also* Corporate earnings; Retained earnings
on balance sheet, 717
in closing process, 171–174
corporate ease of raising, 709

donations of, 761
owned capital to borrowed capital ratio, 832
paid-in, 755
stock as, 712–714, 724–726
treasury stock, 761–763
working capital ratio, 833
Capital account balances in partnerships, 674–675
Capitalized costs, 624, 644
Capital stock
of corporations, 712–714
par value of, 712, 718–720, 724
subscriptions for corporate, 724–726
Capital stock ledger, 727
Capital stock transfer journal, 728
Careers in accounting, 3–5
Carnival Cruise Lines, 165
Carrying value of bonds, 793
Cash, 280
combined journal recording of, B-3
managerial implications of, 305
posting payments of, 253–254
purchasing with, 25–27, 58–60
received on account, 206, 282
recording investments of, 57
services sold for, 65–66
Cash discounts, 248–249, 282, 315–316
Cash dividends from retained earnings, 755–757
Cash equivalents, 860
Cash flows
from financing activities, 871–872
from investing activities, 870–871
from operating activities, 865–868
schedule of operating expenses, 862–864
sources and uses of, 860–861
statement of cash flows, 865, 872–873
Cashier's check, 588
Cash payments
internal control over, 295–296
petty cash funds, 293–295
Cash payments journal, 287–292
Cash receipts
internal control over, 295
journal for, 280–286
transactions as, 280
Cash register proof, 281
Cash short or over **account, 282**
Caterpillar, Inc., 29, 587
Cathay Pacific Airways, 23
Certified Bookkeepers (CB), 3
Certified public accountants (CPAs), 3, 5
Charge accounts, 26
Charge-account sales, 217
Chart of accounts, 73–74
Checks, 298
canceled, 302
dishonored, 302
endorsing, 299
outstanding, 303
paying employees by, 367–368
postdated, 300–301
writing, 298–299

Chemical Bank, 281
Chronological order, 92
Classification, 56
Classifications of businesses, 198
Classifications of property, plant, and equipment, 624
Classified balance sheet, 463–465
Classified financial statements, 460
Classified income statement, 460–463
Closely held corporations, 11
Closing entries, 470
    for corporate earnings, 752
    journalizing and posting, 470–472
    recording, 925–926
Closing process
    in accounting cycle, 178–180
    financial statement interpretation, 176–177
    income summary account in, 166–167
    postclosing trial balance preparation, 175–176
    transfer drawing account balance to capital, 171–174
    transfer expense account balances, 168–170
    transfer net income or net loss to owner's equity, 170–171
    transfer revenue account balances, 167–168
CNA Financial Corporation, 98
Coca-Cola Company, Inc., 460, 549, 602, 645
Cohen, Ben, 27
Collateral trust bonds, 784
Collecting previously written-off accounts, 554
Combined journal, B-1
    designing, B-1–B-2
    disadvantages of, B-5
    posting from, B-4–B-5
    transaction recording in, B-2–B-4
    uses for, B-5
Commercial drafts, 588–589
Commission basis, 356
Common costs, 1022
Common-size statements, 818
Common stock, 713
    dividends on, 714–716
    earnings per share of, 829
    yield on, 830
Common Stock Dividend Distributable account, **757**
Common stockholders' equity, 828
Comparability, as qualitative characteristic of financial reports, 520
Comparative financial statements, 816–817, 821
Compensation record, 368
Completeness, as qualitative characteristic of financial reports, 520
Compound entries, 98–100
Computer software, 644
Conceptual Framework for Financial Reporting (FASB), 518–519
Conceptual framework project (FASB and IASB), **514**, 516, 518–519, 547
Condensed income statement, 463

Confirmatory value, as qualitative characteristic of financial reports, 520
Conoco, Inc., 130
ConocoPhillips, 965
Conservatism, 526
Consistency principle, 603, 825
Contingent liability, 585
Continuous existence of corporations, 709
Contra accounts, 130, 255
Contra asset accounts, 130, 548
Contra revenue accounts, 207
Contribution margin, 899, 1022–1023, 1027
Control accounts, 211, 253
Controllable fixed costs, 1023
Convertible bonds, 785
Convertible preferred stock, 713–714
Copyrights, 643
Corporate and Auditing Accountability, Responsibility, and Transparency Act, 543
Corporate charter, 708
Corporate earnings; *see also* Capital; Retained earnings
    adjusting and closing entries for, 752
    corporate income tax, 746–749
    income statement for, 752–753
    worksheets for, 749–751
Corporations, 11–12; *see also* Corporate earnings; Retained earnings
    balance sheet for, 764–765
    capital stock of, 712–714
    characteristics of, 13, 708–710
    dividends on stock of, 714–717
    forming, 710
    recording stock issuance, 718–724
    special records and agents of, 727–729
    structure of, 710–711
    Subchapter S, 12, 709
    subscriptions for capital stock of, 724–726
Correcting entry, 105–106
Cost accounting; *see* Job order cost accounting; Process cost accounting; Standard cost accounting
Cost basis for inventory, 948
Cost-benefit test, 525–526
Cost centers, 893; *see also* Profit and cost centers
Cost flows
    in job order cost accounting, 943–945
    in process cost accounting, 970–973, 979
    through inventory accounts, 954
Costing; *see* Inventory
Cost of goods manufactured, 914–915, 917
Cost of goods sold, 246
    accounting for, 953–954
    in closing entries, 471
    cost of goods manufactured *versus*, 917
    on income statement, 462
    in specific-identification inventory costing, 601
Cost of production report, 969–970, 975–978
Cost recovery, 630–631; *see also* Depreciation
Cost-revenue analysis, 1019–1040
    contribution margin, 1022–1023
    differential costs, 1023

direct *versus* absorption costing, 1020–1022
equipment purchases, 1026
opportunity costs, 1023
parts production or purchases, 1026–1027
product pricing in special situations, 1025–1026
relevant costs, 1023
Costs
capitalized, 624
cost behavior, 992–994, 1003
of purchases, 257
Cost schedule, in cost of product report, 975–977
Cost variance, 1000
Coupon bonds, 785
CPAs (certified public accountants), 3, 5
Credit, 70
combined journal recording of, B-3
credit and debit rules, 70–72
managerial implications of sales on, 223
managing, 558
merchandise inventory as basis for, 610
in net income determination, 136, 147
posting credit sales, 206
purchases on, 58–59
sales on, 549–550
services sold for, 66–67
in wholesale business sales, 214–215
Credit balances, 471
Credit card companies, 218–219
Credit cards, 217–219
Credit memorandum (accounts receivable), 206
Credit memorandum (banking), 302
Credit memos, 240
Creditors, 10
buying from and paying, 26–28
recording payments to, 60–61
of sole proprietorships, 10–11
Credit policies, in merchandising, 216–219, 223
Crundwell, Rita, 306
CSX Corporation, 193–194
Cumulative preferred stock, 714–716
Current assets, 465
Current liabilities, 465, 867–868
Current ratio, 473–475, 833–834
Customers, financial information used by, 7–8
CVS Health Corporation, 815
Cycle counts of inventory, 610

D

Data analysis of process cost, 967–968
DDB (double-declining-balance) method of depreciation, 627–629
Debentures, 785
Debit cards, 289
Debit memorandum, 302
Debits, 70
credit and debit rules, 70–72
debit balances, 471
in net income determination, 136, 147
Decision making; *see* Cost-revenue analysis
Declaration date, 756

Declining-balance method, 627
Deductions from wages, 359–362
Deeds, Edward, 666
Deferred expenses, 427–428
Deferred income, 429–430
Deferred income tax, 748–749
Delinquent invoices, 558
Deloitte & Touche, 3
Departmental income statement, 899–901
Departmentalized operations, 893–897
DePaul University, 209
Depletion, 640–641
Deposits in transit, 303
Deposit slip, 299–300
Depreciation, 130
adjusting for, 130–131, 424–425
cash flows from, 865–866
of property, plant, and equipment, 625–630
as worksheet entries, 921
Diess, Herbert, 913
Differential costs, 1023, 1027
Diners Club, 218
Direct charge-off method, 547, 556–558
Direct costing, 1020–1022
Direct deposit, paying employees by, 366, 368
Direct expenses, 895
Direct labor, 915
overhead application rate based on cost of, 950
standard costs of, 999
Direct materials, 915
Direct method of statement of cash flow preparation, 872–873
Discarding, asset disposition by, 633–634
Discounts
cash, 248–249, 282, 315–316
on notes payable, 579–580
on notes receivable, 584–587
purchase, 248, 312
sales, 248
trade, 214–215, 312–313
Discounts on bonds payable, 792–793
Discounts on credit card sales, 217–218
Discussion memorandum (FASB), 13
Dishonored checks, 302
Disposition methods for property, plant, and equipment, 633–638
Dissolution, 683
Distributive share, in partnerships, **672**
Dividends, 714
cash, 872
of cash from retained earnings, 755–757
stock, 757–758
on stock, 714–717
taxation of, 709
Dole Food Company, 602
Donate capital, 761
Double-declining-balance (DDB) method of depreciation, 627–629
Double-entry system, 70–72
Double taxation, 12, 709

Drafts, 588
    bank, 588
    commercial, 588–589
    internal control of, 589–590
    sight, 588
    time, 589
Drawee of checks, **298**
Drawer of checks, **298**
Drawing accounts, 472
    balance transferred to capital, 171–174, 472
    description of, 69–70
    in partnerships, 670
Dun & Bradstreet, 216
DuPont, Inc., 163

E

Early retirement of bonds, 797–798
Earnings; see Payroll; Taxes
Earnings in excess of base amount, for SUTA, 398–399
Earnings per share of common stock, 829
Economic entity, 10
Edson, Orin, 942
Electronic Federal Tax Payment System (EFTPS), 358, 386, 399
Electronic funds transfer (EFT), 307
Employees, 350
    federal earnings and withholding laws, 350–351
    financial information used by, 7–8
    fraud by, 258
    hourly, 356–362
    paying, 366–368
    records of, 353–354
    salaries of, 34, 362–364
    segregation of duties of, 122
    total earnings of, 355–356
Employee's Withholding Allowance Certificate (Form W-4), 358–359
Employers, payroll taxes and insurance paid by, 352–353
Employer's Annual Federal Unemployment Tax Return (Form 940), 399–402
Employer's Quarterly Federal Tax Return (Form 941), 390–394
Endorsement, 299
Enhancing qualitative characteristics of financial reports, 520–521
Enron Corporation, scandals of, 7, 479, 513
Entity, 10
Equipment; see also Property, plant, and equipment
    on balance sheet, 465
    cost-revenue analysis for purchase of, 1026
    gains and losses on sales of, 867
Equity, 25
Equivalent production determination, **968**–969, 975, 977
Ernst & Young, 3
Estimated annual premium in advance, for workers' compensation insurance, 400, 403
Estimated tax payments, corporate quarterly, 746–747
Estimation of inventory cost, 607–609
Ethics, profitability of, 209
European Union, 515
Exempt employees, 362
Expense accounts, 65–69
Expenses, 32
    accrual basis recognition of, 420
    cash payments for, 287–288
    in closing process, 168–170
    combined journal recording of, B-2–B-3
    from current assets and liabilities, 867–868
    on departmental income statement, 895–897
    operating, 462
    prepaid, 128
    schedule of operating expenses, 862–864
    uncollectible accounts, allowance for, 548–549
    utilities, 34–35
Experience rating system, 397–398
Expired insurance, 921
Exposure drafts, 13

F

Facebook.com, 707, 713
Face interest rate, 785
Face value, 785
    bonds issued at, 788–790
    of notes payable, 577
Fair Labor Standards Act (FSLA) of 1938, 351, 355
Fair market value, 38
Faithful representation, as qualitative characteristic of financial reports, 520
Family partnerships, 669
Federal Bureau of Investigation (FBI), 5
Federal Communications Commission, 6
Federal employee earnings and withholding laws, 350–351
Federal income tax, 351, 358, 369; see also Income tax
Federal Insurance Contributions Act (FICA), 351
Federal Reserve, 1025
Federal unemployment taxes (FUTA), 352–353
Federal withholding laws, 350–351; see also Income tax
FICA (Federal Insurance Contributions Act), 351
FIFO (first-in, first-out) inventory costing method, 602–604, 948
Financial Accounting Standards Board (FASB); see also Generally accepted accounting principles (GAAP); International Accounting Standards Board (IASB)
    on accounting for impairment of long-lived assets, 641
    allowance method for uncollectible accounts and, 547
    conceptual framework of, 513–514
    GAAP development by, 13
    on lower of cost or net realizable value rule for inventory (ASU 2015-11), 605–606
    overview, 511
Financial Accounting Standards Board Accounting Standards Codification, 514
Financial information
    managerial implications of, 14
    need for, 2
    users of, 5–8
Financial records, banking procedures to adjust, 304–306

Index

Financial statements, 3, 459–510; *see also* Business transactions; Generally accepted accounting principles (GAAP); International Accounting Standards Board (IASB)
   accounting cycle review, 479–481
   adjusting entries, journalizing and posting, 467–470
   adjustment effects on, 435
   balance sheet for corporations, 764–765
   classified balance sheet, 463–465
   classified income statement, 460–463
   closing entries, journalizing and posting, 470–472
   from closing process, 176–177
   interpreting, 473–475
   managerial implications of, 180
   postclosing trial balance, 472–473
   preparing, 924
   reversing entries, journalizing and posting, 475–479
   statement of owner's equity, 463
   statement of retained earnings, 763–764
   T accounts and, 72–73
Financial statements, analysis of
   financial strength ratios, 831–833, 837
   horizontal analysis of balance sheet, 823
   horizontal analysis of income statement, 821–823
   industry averages in, 825–826
   liquidity ratios, 833–836
   phases of, 816
   profitability ratios, 827–831
   summary of ratios, 836–837
   trend analysis of, 823–825
   vertical analysis of balance sheet, 818–819
   vertical analysis of income statement, 816–818
Financial strength ratios, 831–833, 837
Financing activities
   cash flows from, 871–872
   merchandise inventory as basis for, 610
   overview, 860–861
   stock *versus* bonds for, 786–787
Finished goods inventory, 917, 944–945, 953
Finished goods subsidiary ledger, 946
First-in, first-out (FIFO) method, 602, 948
Fixed assets, 625; *see also* Property, plant, and equipment
Fixed budget, 994–996
Fixed costs, 992–993, 996, 1020, **1023**
Flexible budget, 996–997
Footing, 62
Ford, Henry, 385
Ford Motor Company, 385, 892–893, 913
Form 940, Employer's Annual Federal Unemployment Tax Return, 399–402
Form 941, Employer's Quarterly Federal Tax Return, 390–394
Form 1065, U.S. Return of Partnership Income, 12
Form 1120, U.S. Return of Corporation Income, 12
Form 1120S, U.S. Income Tax Return for an S Corporation, 12
Form W-2, Wage and Tax Statement, 394–395
Form W-3, Transmittal of Wage and Tax Statements, 395–396
Form W-4, Federal Income Tax Withholding, 358
Fortune 500, 625
Franchises, 643, 709

Fraud, 5–6
   on Certified Bookkeeper exam, 193
   segregation of duties for, 122
   in small businesses, 258
Freedom from error, as qualitative characteristic of financial reports, 520
Freight charges, 245, 289, 310–311
***Freight In* account, 246**
FSLA (Fair Labor Standards Act) of 1938, 351, 355
Full disclosure principle, of FASB, **524**–525
Full endorsement of checks, **299**
Fundamental accounting equation, 31
   owner withdrawal impact on, 35
   receivables collection in, 33
   revenue and expenses in, 32
   salaries paid in, 34
   services sold for cash in, 32
   services sold for credit in, 32–33
   transaction impact on, 35–36
   utilities expenses paid in, 34–35
Fundamental qualitative characteristics of financial reports, 519
FUTA (federal unemployment taxes), 352–353

G

GAAP (generally accepted accounting principles); *see* Generally accepted accounting principles (GAAP)
Gains, 633
   in asset disposition, 633
   in asset trade-in, 636–637
   on bond retirement, 798–799
   on equipment sales, 867
Gap, Inc., 473
General journal, 92–93; *see also* General ledger
   compound entries in, 98–100
   correcting entries to, 105–106
   recording transactions in, 93–98
   for sales returns and allowances, 208
General ledger, 101; *see also* General journal
   account forms for, 101–102
   control accounts to subsidiary ledgers, 211
   correcting entries to, 105–106
   posting purchases in, 249–250
   posting to, 101–105
Generally accepted accounting principles (GAAP), 12–14; *see also* International Accounting Standards Board (IASB)
   development of, 512–516
   direct costing not acceptable under, 1021
   impact of, 526–527
   users and uses of, 516–517
General partners, 667
Global Study on Occupational Fraud and Abuse of 2018 (Association of Certified Fraud Examiners), 258
Going concern, 521
Goldstein, Sidney, 815
Goldstein, Stanley, 815
Goodwill, 644–645
Governmental accounting, 5
Government regulation of corporations, 709

Greenfield, Jerry, 27
Gross pay, 356
Gross profit, 462, 893–894
Gross profit method of inventory valuation, **607**–608
Gross profit percentage, 473, 475

H

Hackett, Jim, 913
Harley-Davidson Company, 991
Harvard University, 707
Hasbro, Inc., 628, 873
Hayne, Dick, 745
HBO, Inc., 55
Healthcare Venture Professionals, LLC (HVP), 665
Heinz, Inc., 783
High-low point method, 993
Historical cost basis principle of FASB, **522**–523
Hoagland, Ralph, 815
Home Depot, Inc.
  balance sheet of, 598
  cash as percentage of total assets of, 347–348
  cash sources of, 889
  common stock of, 743
  Consolidated Balance Sheets, A-3
  Consolidated Statements of Cash Flows, A-6
  Consolidated Statements of Comprehensive Income, A-4
  Consolidated Statements of Earnings, A-4
  Consolidated Statements of Stockholders' Equity, A-5
  cost of goods sold by, 276
  depreciation methods of, 663
  Disclosure Controls and Procedures, A-1
  employee retirement plans of, 417–418
  Five-Year Summary of Financial and Operating Results, A-12
  income tax paid by, 781
  inventory of, 600, 609–610, 621–622
  long-term debt of, 810, 990
  Notes to Consolidated Financial Statements: Note 1, Summary of Significant Accounting Policies, A-7–A-12
  operating expenses of, 170
  products offered by, 244, 276
  profitability ratio results for, 505, 543
  qualitative characteristics of financial statements of, 543
  Report of Independent Registered Public Accounting Firm, A-2
  revenue sources of, 964, 1016
  sales of, 168, 170, 240–241
  Selected Financial Data, 1040
  trend analysis of, 912
  vendor allowance of, 940
  vertical and horizontal analysis of, 854
Homeland Security, 5
Horizontal analysis, 816
  of balance sheet, 823
  of income statement, 821–823
Hourly rate basis, 355
  federal income tax withheld, 358–361
  gross pay computation for, 356–357
  hours worked computation for, 356
  Medicare tax withheld, 357
  social security tax withheld, 357
  state and local tax withheld, 359
  total earnings computation for, 355–356
  withholding not required by law, 360–362
H&R Block, 349

I

IASB (International Accounting Standards Board); *see* International Accounting Standards Board (IASB)
IASC (International Accounting Standards Committee), 13
ICE (Intercontinental Exchange), 818
Identity theft, 308
IFRS (International Financial Reporting Standards), 515–516
Impairment, 641
  of intangible assets with indefinite useful lives, 645
  of property, plant, and equipment, 641–643
Income
  from current assets and liabilities, 867–868
  partnership allocation of, 672–674
Income statement, 36–37, 39
  classified, 460–463
  condensed, 463
  for corporate earnings, 752–753
  departmental, 899–901
  income tax expense reported on, 748
  for manufacturing activities, 917
  of partnerships, 681
  worksheets for preparation of, 134–137, 143, 145–146, 434–436
Income summary **account, 166**–167, 421, 471–472, 920
Income tax
  corporate, 709, 746–749
  for cost recovery of property, plant, and equipment, 630–631
  for depletion, 641
  direct charge-off method for uncollectible accounts accounting required for, 547
  federal, 351, 358, 369
  payable, 921
  for trade-in transactions, 638
Income tax method, 638
Independent contractors, 350
Indirect expenses, 895–897
Indirect labor, 915–916
Indirect materials and supplies, 915
Indirect method, 872–873
Individual earnings records, 368
Industry averages, 825–826
Industry practice, 526
Initial public offering (IPO), 707, 745
Injury and illness prevention programs, 1003
Insurance
  employer-paid, 352–353
  prepaid, 428
  workers' compensation, 353
  as worksheet entries, 921
Intangible assets, 643–645
Intercontinental Exchange (ICE), 818
Interest, 577
  accrual of, 790

on bonds, 789–790
face rate of, 785
market rate of, 785
on notes payable, 427–428, 577, 579, 580
on notes receivable, 429, 583
number of times bond interest earned ratio, 831
partnership allowances for, 678–680
on promissory notes, 289–290
Interest-bearing note receivable discounted, 586–587
Internal control, 5–6
   of accounts receivable, 559
   of banking procedures, 306
   of cash payments, 295–296
   of cash receipts, 295
   on Certified Bookkeeper exam, 193
   of drafts, 589–590
   of inventory, 610
   journal entries to conceal theft, 162
   of notes payable, 589–590
   of notes receivable, 589–590
   of payroll operations, 404
   of petty cash fund, 294–295
   of property, plant, and equipment, 646
   of purchases, 258
   segregation of duties for, 122
Internal Revenue Code, 12
Internal Revenue Service (IRS)
   accountants in, 5
   direct costing not acceptable for tax reporting to, 1021
   employee guidelines of, 350
   financial information used by, 6, 8
   W-2 form of, 394–395
International accounting, 13
International Accounting Standards Board (IASB); see also
       Financial Accounting Standards Board (FASB);
       Generally accepted accounting principles (GAAP)
   assumptions of, 521–522
   general principles of, 522–525
   modifying constraints of, 525–526
   overview, 13, 518–519
   purpose of, 515–516
   qualitative characteristics of financial reports, 519–521
International Accounting Standards Committee (IASC), 13
International Financial Reporting Standards (IFRS),
       515–516
*International Financial Reporting Standards (IFRS) 15,
       Revenue from Contracts with Customers,* 523–524
International Financial Reporting Standards Foundation, 515
Interpreting financial statements, 176
Inventory; *see also* Perpetual inventory system
   adjustments to merchandise, 421–423
   average cost method of costing, 601–602
   cost flow through accounts for, 954
   costing methods comparison, 603–604
   ending, 921
   finished goods, 917
   first-in, first-out method of costing, 602
   gross profit method of valuation for, 607–608
   internal control of, 610
   inventory turnover ratio, 834–835
   just-in-time inventory systems, 945

   last-in, first-out method of costing, 602–603
   lower of cost or net realizable value rule for, 605–607
   managing, 918–919
   merchandise, 198
   perpetual inventory accounts, 946
   perpetual inventory system, 943–945
   retail method of valuation for, 608–610
   RFID control of, 610
   specific identification method of costing, 601
   valuation of, 600
   work in process, beginning, 975
Inventory sheet, 421
Inventory turnover, 474–475
Investing activities, 860–861
   of assets in partnerships, 685–688
   of cash, 282
   cash flows from, 870–871
   financial information used in, 6–8
Invoices, 215
   delinquent, 558
   in purchasing procedures, 244–245
IPO (initial public offering), 707, 745
Iris Smart Home, 1019
IRS (Internal Revenue Service); *see* Internal Revenue
       Service (IRS)
Issuance of stock, 718–724
Issue costs of bonds, 793

J

Javelin Strategy, 308
JetBlue Airways Corporation, 427
Job order cost accounting, 941–964, 942
   cost flows in, 943–945
   cost flow through inventory accounts, 954
   job order cost sheet, 952–954
   labor, accounting for, 949–950
   manufacturing overhead, accounting for, 950–951
   materials, accounting for, 946–948
   perpetual inventory accounts in, 946
Job order cost sheet, 952–954
Job order cost system, unit costs in, 999
Job orders, 942
Job stress, 895
Johnson & Johnson, Inc., 644
Journalizing, 92
Journalizing and posting
   adjusting entries, 467–470
   closing entries, 470–472
   description of, 92
   internal controls in, 162
   reversing entries, 475–479
   worksheets and, 147–148
Journals, 92; *see also* General journal
   for cash payments, 287–292
   for cash receipts, 280–286
   combined, B-1–B-5
   for purchases, 245–250
   for sales, 199–204
   for sales returns and allowances, 208
   special, 198–199

JPMorgan Chase & Co., 279, 575
Just-in-time inventory systems, 945

K

Kettering, Charles, 666
Keurig Dr Pepper (KDP), 623, 626
KPMG International Cooperative, 3, 125
Kraft Foods Group, Inc., 783
Kraft Heinz, Inc., 783

L

Labor
    accounting for, 949–950
    overhead application rate based on direct, 950
    standard costs of direct, 999
Labor efficiency variance, 1002–1003
Labor rate variance, 1003
Labor time tickets, in job cost accounting, 949
Labor time variance, 1002
Land and building costs, 625; see also Property, plant, and equipment
Last-in, first-out (LIFO) cost basis for inventory, **602**–604, 948
Ledgers, 101
    accounts payable, 252–253, 291–292
    accounts receivable, 205–206, 284–286
    posting payroll to, 369–370
    subsidiary, 198–199
Left-right rules, in T accounts, 57–61
Leveraged buyouts, 832
Leveraging, 787
Liabilities, 29
    current, 465
    long-term, 465
    operating, 867–868
    T accounts for, 56–61
LIFO (last-in, first-out) cost basis for inventory, **602**–604, 948
Limited liability, of corporations, 708
Limited liability companies (LLCs), 12, 710
Limited Liability Partnership Act, 11
Limited liability partnerships (LLPs), 11, 709–710
Limited partners, 667
Limited partnerships, 667
Lindbergh, Charles, 23
Liquidation, 683
Liquidation value on preferred stock, **713**
Liquidity, 465
Liquidity ratios, 833–837
List price, 214
Long-term assets
    expenses and income items involving, 865–867
    impairment of, 641–643
    as net amount, 139
    plant and equipment as, **465**
Long-term liabilities, 465, 865–867
Lookback period, for deposit schedules, 387
Losses, 633
    in asset disposition, 633
    in asset trade-in, 637–638
    bad debt, 558
    on bond retirement, 798–799
    on equipment sales, 867
    partnership allocation of, 674
    from uncollectible accounts, 423–424
Lower of cost or net realizable value rule, 605–607
Lowe's Companies, Inc., 1019

M

MACRS (Modified Accelerated Cost Recovery System), 630–631
Macy's, Inc., 512
Magnetic ink character recognition (MICR), 299–300
Malenshek, Heather, 991
Management advisory services, 5
Managerial accounting, 5, 892–893
Managerial implications
    accounting for purchases, 259
    accounting systems, 40, 105
    adjustment impact on financial statements, 435
    capital transactions, 763
    cash, 305, 797
    cash flow, 873
    comparative statements, 825
    corporations, 724
    cost behavior, 1003
    cost revenue analysis in decision making, 1027
    credit, 223, 558
    departmental income statements, 901
    financial information, 14
    financial statements, 72, 180, 480, 527
    inventory, 608
    job order cost system, 953
    laws and controls, 368
    manufacturing costs, 926
    negotiable instruments, 589
    partnerships, 688
    payroll taxes, 403
    process cost accounting, 980
    property, plant, and equipment, 642
    worksheets, 149
Managers, financial information used by, 5–6
Manufacturing activities, 913–940
    accounting cycle completion for, 924–927
    Annual Survey of Manufacturers (U.S. Census Bureau), 943
    balance sheet for, 917–919
    cost of goods manufactured, 914–915
    income statement for, 917
    statement of cost of goods manufactured, 915–917
    worksheet for financial statements for, 920–924
Manufacturing business, 198
Manufacturing cost budget, 994
Manufacturing margin, 1021–1022
Manufacturing overhead, 916
    accounting for, 950–951
    idle time charged to, 949
    standard costs of, 999
Manufacturing overhead ledger, 950

Manufacturing overhead variance, **1003**–1004
Manufacturing Summary account, **920**
Marginal income, 1022
Markdowns, 609
Market interest rate, 785
Market value, 137
Market Value Added (MVA), 209
Market value of stock, 712
Markon, 608
Markups, 609
Marshall, John, 708
MasterCard credit cards, 217
Matching principle, of FASB, **524**
Materiality, 525
Materials, accounting for, 946–948
Materials price variance, 1001–1002
Materials quantity variance, 1001
Materials requisition, 947–948
Materials usage variance, 1001
Maturity date
    discounted noninterest-bearing note receivable at, 585–586
    of interest-bearing note receivable, 587
    note receivable not collected at, 584
    of notes payable, 577–578
    of notes receivable, 584
Maturity value, 577
McCormick, Willoughby M., 197
McCormick & Company, Inc., 197, 456–457, 504, 573, 999
McGraw-Hill Companies, Inc., 728
McGraw-Hill Financial, 891
Medicare taxes, 351
    accrued salaries subject to, 426
    employee share of, 351
    employer share of, 352
    hourly employee withholding of, 357
    in payroll register, 387–389
Memorandum entry, 669
Merchandise inventory, 198; *see also* Inventory
Merchandising business, 198; *see also* Accounts payable; Accounts receivable; Purchases; Sales
    cash payments in, 289
    combined journal use by, B-5
    credit policies, 216–219
    inventory in, 198
    sales taxes, 220–224
    wholesale business credit sales, 214–215
Merit rating system, 397
Merrill Lynch, 575
MICR (magnetic ink character recognition), 299–300
Microsoft Corporation, 424, 474, 553, 708–709
Minute book, 727
Modified Accelerated Cost Recovery System (MACRS), 630–631
Modifying constraints, 525–526
Monetary unit assumption, of FASB conceptual framework, **521**–522
Mortgage loan, 784
Mortgages payable, 872
Motorcycle Industry Council, 991
Multiple-step income statement, 460–463

Mutual agency, 667
MVA (Market Value Added), 209

N

NASDAQ Global Select Marker, 23
NationsBank, 575
Natural resources, depletion of, 640–641
Negotiable, 298
Negotiable instruments, 576–577, 589
Net book value, 626
Net credit sales, 549–550
Net income, 36–37
    calculating, 434–436
    as debit and credit difference, 136
    from operations, 463
    transferred to owner's equity in closing process, 170–171
    worksheets to determine, 144
Net income line, 436
Net losses, 36–37
    calculating, 434–436
    in cash flows from operations, 868
    from operations, 463
    transferred to owner's equity in closing process, 170–171
    worksheets to determine, 144
Net price, 214
Net realizable value (NRV) of inventory, **605**
Net sales, 209–211
Net salvage value, 626
Neutrality, as qualitative characteristic of financial reports, **520**
News Media Alliance, 1025
New York Stock Exchange (NYSE), 216, 515, 818, 828
Noncumulative preferred stock, 714–716
Nondepartmentalized expenses, 897
Noninterest-bearing notes receivable, 582–583
Noninterest-bearing notes receivable discounted, 584–586
Nonparticipating preferred stock, 714–716
No-par-value stock, 712, 722–724
Normal balance of accounts, **62**
Notes payable, 578
    accrued interest on, 427
    combined journal recording of, B-3–B-4
    interest on, 577
    internal control of, 589–590
    maturity date of, 577–578
    as negotiable instruments, 576–577
    prepaid interest on, 428
    recording issuance of, 578
    recording issuance of discounted, 579
    recording payment and interest of, 579
    recording payment of discounted, 580
    register for, 580
    renewing or making partial payment on, 579
    reporting, 580
Notes receivable, 582
    accounting for partial collection of, 583–584
    accrued interest on, 429
    discounting, 584–587
    interest-bearing, 583
    internal control of, 589–590

Notes receivable—*Cont.*
noninterest-bearing, 582–583
not collected at maturity, 584
received at time of sale, 584
register for, 587
reporting, 587–588
NRV (net realizable value), 605
Number of times bond interest earned, 831
NYSE (New York Stock Exchange), 216, 515, 818, 828

O

Old Age and Survivors, Disability Insurance, and Supplemental Security Income (OASDI) programs, 391
On account, 26
Oneworld global airline alliance, 23
Online banking, 307–308
Open-account credit, 26, 217
Operating activities, 860–861
cash flows from, 865–868
Operating assets and liabilities, 867–868
Operating expenses, 462, **895**–896
Operating revenue, 460–462
Operations, departmentalized, 893–897
Opportunity costs, 1023, 1027
Orchard Supply Hardware, 1019
Order, purchase, 244
Organization costs of corporations, **721**–722
Outstanding checks, 303
Overapplied overhead, 950–951
Overhead; *see* Manufacturing overhead
Overhead application rate, 950, 953, 999
Overtime rate of pay, 351
Owen, Chuck, 665
Owned capital to borrowed capital ratio, 832
Owners, financial information used by, 5–6
Owner's equity, 29
on balance sheet, 465
net income or net loss transferred to, 170–171
statement of, 37–39, 137, 145–146
T accounts for, 56–61

P

Pacioli, Luca, 27
Paid-in capital, 755
Participating preferred stock, 714, 716
Partnership agreements, 667
Partnerships, 11, 666–667
accounting for formation of, 667–670
allocating income in, 672–674
allocating losses in, 674
balance sheet of, 681
capital account balances in, 674–675
changes in partners in, 683–689
characteristics of, 13
entities with attributes of corporations and, 709–710
income statement of, 681
interest allowances in, 678–680
salary allowances in, 675–680
Subchapter S corporations treated as, 12

Parts production or purchases, 1026–1027
Par value of capital stock, 712, 718–720, 724
Patents, 643
Payee, 298
Payment date of dividends, **756**
Payments Source, Inc., 281
Payroll computations and records, 349–383
employee definition, 350
employee records, 353–354
employee total earnings computation, 355–356
employer's payroll taxes and insurance, 352–353
example of, 369–370
federal employee earnings and withholding laws, 350–351
hourly employees' pay, 356–362
individual earnings records, 368
paying employees, 366–368
recording, 365–366
salaried employees' pay, 362–364
state and local taxes, 352
Payroll register, 362–364
Payroll taxes and deposits, 385–418
accrued, 426
Employer's Quarterly Federal Tax Return (Form 941), 390–394
internal control of, 404
overview, 386–387
Social Security and Medicare, 387–389
Transmittal of Wage and Tax Statements (Form W-3), 395–396
unemployment insurance program, 396–404
Wage and Tax Statement (Form W-2), 394–395
withheld taxes, recording payment of, 389–390
as worksheet entries, 921
PCAOB (Public Company Accounting Oversight Board), 513
Peat, William Barclay, 125
Percentage depletion, 641
Percentage of net credit sales, 549–550
Percentage of total accounts receivable, 550–551
Percentages, in common-size statements, 818, 822
Periodic inventory, 600
Periodic inventory system, 198
Periodicity of income assumption, 522
Permanent accounts, 74–75
Perpetual inventory accounts in job order cost accounting, 946
Perpetual inventory system, 198
advantages of, 600
for finished goods inventory, 944–945
in job order cost system, 943, 953
merchandise inventory adjustment and, 423
purchasing transactions in, 310–313
sales transactions in, 313–317
for work in process inventory, 944
Petty cash analysis sheet, 293
Petty cash funds, 280, 293–295
Petty cash voucher, 293
Physical inventory, 600, 610
Piece-rate basis, 356
Plant and equipment, 465; *see also* Property, plant, and equipment

Index

Point-of-sale cash registers and scanners, 600
Postclosing trial balance, 175–176, 472–473
Postdated checks, 300–301
Posting, 101
   to accounts payable ledger, 291–292
   to accounts receivable ledger, 284–286
   from cash payments journal, 290–291
   cash payments on account, 253–254
   from cash receipts journal, 283–284
   from combined journal, B-4–B-5
   credit purchases, 253
   credit sales, 206
   to general ledger, 101–105
   payroll to ledgers, 369–370
   purchases in general ledger, 249–250
   purchases returns or allowances, 255
   from sales journal, 202–203
   sales returns and allowances, 208–209
Practice bulletins (AcSEC of AICPA), 515
Predictive value, as qualitative characteristic of financial reports, 520
Preemptive right, 713
Preference dividends, 714
Preferred stock, 713
Premium, stock issued at, 722
Premium on bonds payable, 791–793, 831, 866
Prepaid expenses, 128
   adjustments for, 427–428
   common, 128
   decrease in, 867–868
   depreciation adjustments as, 130–131
   expired rent as, 129–130
Prepaid rent, recording, 61, 129
Price, 214, 1025–1026
Price-earnings ratio, 829
PricewaterhouseCoopers, 3
Principal, 577
Privately owned corporations, 11
Private sector, 512
Process cost accounting, 942, 965–990
   cost flows recording, 970–973, 979
   cost of production report preparation, 969–970, 975–978
   equivalent production determination, 968–969, 975, 977
   process cost data analysis in, 967–968
   work in process inventory, beginning, 975
Production orders, 942
Product pricing in special situations, 1025–1026
Professional offices, combined journal use by, B-5
Profitability ratios, 827–831, 837
Profit and cost centers
   departmental income statement, 899–901
   departmentalized operations, 893–897
   managerial accounting, 892–893
   responsibility accounting, 893
Profit center, 893
Promissory notes, 282; see also Notes payable
   collection of, 282–283, 289–290
   combined journal recording of, B-3–B-4
   interest and maturity date of, 577
   payment of, 289–290

Property, plant, and equipment, 424
   on balance sheet, 465
   classifications of, 624
   cost-revenue analysis for, 1026
   depletion of, 640–641
   depreciation of, 424–425, 625–630
   disposition methods for, 633–638
   federal income tax requirements for cost recovery of, 630–631
   impairment of, 641–643
   intangible assets, 643–645
   internal control of, 646
Property and financial interest, in business transactions, 24–29
Property equals financial interest equation, 27
Property taxes, 427
Public accountants, 3
Public Accounting Reform and Investor Protection Act, 543
Public Company Accounting Oversight Board, 7
Public Company Accounting Reform and Investor Protection Act of 2002, 6–7
Publicly owned corporations, 11
Public sector, 512
Purchase allowance, 253, 311
Purchase discounts, 248, 312
Purchase invoice, 244
Purchase order, 244
Purchase requisition, 244–245
Purchase return, 253–255
Purchases; see also Accounts payable
   combined journal recording of, B-3–B-4
   cost of, 257
   on credit, 58–59
   discounts applied to, 248
   equipment, 25–27, 289, 1026
   freight charges for, 245
   general ledger posting of, 249–250
   of interest in partnerships, 685
   internal control of, 258
   managerial implications of accounting for, 259
   in perpetual inventory system, 310–313
   procedures for, 244–245
   returns and allowances for, 253–255, 311–312
   supplies, 27, 59–60, 289
Purchases **account, 246**
Purchases journal, 246–250
Putnam, Charles, 666

Q

Qantas Airlines, 23
Qualitative characteristics of financial reports, 519–521
Quantity schedule, in cost of product report, 975
Quick assets, 834

R

Radio frequency identification (RFID), for control of inventory, 610, 944

Rate of return
　on common stockholders' equity, 828
　on sales, 827–828
　on total assets, 830
Ratio analysis, 816, 837
　of financial strength, 831–833
　of liquidity, 833–836
　of profitability, 827–831
Raw materials, 915, 998
Raw materials inventory, 943–944
Raw materials ledger record, 947
Raw materials subsidiary ledger, 946–947
Realization of revenue, of FASB, **523**
Real property, 624
Receiving report, 244
Reconciling bank statements, 301–304
Record date of dividends, **756**
Recoverability test, 642
Refunds, cash, 282, 289
Registered bonds, 785
Registrars for corporations, **729**
Regulatory agencies, 6–8, 515
Relevance, as qualitative characteristic of financial reports, 519–520
Relevant costs, 1023, 1027
Relevant range of activity, 996
Rent, prepaid, 61, 129
Renting facilities, 28–29
Report form balance sheet, 138
Requisition, purchase, 244–245
Residual value, 626
Responsibility accounting, 893
Restricted agency, of corporations, 708–709
Restrictive endorsement, 299
Retail business, 198
Retail method of inventory valuation, **608**–610
Retained earnings, 755; see also Capital
　appropriations of, 758–759
　cash dividends from, 755–757
　to retire bonds, 796–797
　stock dividends from, 757–758
　stock splits and, 758
　for treasury stock, 762
Retiring bonds, 795–799
Return on common stockholders' equity, 828
Returns and allowances
　for purchases, 253–255, 311–312
　for sales, 206–211, 315
Revenue, 32
　accounts for, 65–69, 471
　accrual basis recognition of, 420
　in closing process, 168–170
　from contracts with customers, 523–524
Revenue recognition principle of FASB, **523**
Reversing entries, 475
　of accrued interest on bonds, 790–793
　journalizing and posting, 475–479
　recording, 927
RFID (radio frequency identification), 610, 944
Rounding, in statement analysis, 818

S

Salaries
　accrued, on worksheet, 921
　expense of, 34, 67–68
　partnerships allowances for, 675–680
Salaries payable as accrued liability, 420, 425–426, 476–477
Salary basis, 356
　pay determination for, 362
　payroll register for, 362–364
Sales; see also Accounts receivable; Merchandising
　asset disposition by, 634–636
　cash, 281–282
　combined journal recording of, B-3
　of finished goods, 973
　gross profit on, 462
　journals for, 199–204, 206
　marginal income on, 1022
　in perpetual inventory system, 313–317
　rate of return on, 827–828
　special journals and subsidiary ledgers for, 198–199
Sales allowance, 206, 315
Sales discounts, 248
Sales invoice, 218, **244**
Sales journal, 215
Sales return, 206, 315
Sales returns and allowances **account, 206**–207
　business transaction for, 207
　credit memorandum for, 206–207
　net sales after, 209–211
　posting, 208–209
　recording, 208
Sales taxes
　cash sales and, 281–282
　payable, 314
　preparing tax return for, 220–223
　sales account recording of, 223–224
Salvage value, 130, 626, 628
Sam's Club, 599
Sarbanes-Oxley (SOX) Act of 2002, 6–7, 162, 479, 513–514, 516–517, 543
Schedule of accounts payable, 255–257
Schedule of accounts receivable, 211–212
Schedule of operating expenses, 862–864
Scrapping, asset disposition by, 633–634
Scrap value, 626
Secured bonds, 784
Securities and Exchange Commission (SEC)
　accountants in, 5
　comparative financial statement requirements of, 464
　developments in, 513
　on Financial Accounting Standards Board (FASB) standards, 13, 511
　financial information used by, 6–7
　GAAP and, 12
　improper professional conduct of accountants defined by, 479
　on Sarbanes-Oxley Act requirements, 517
Securities Exchange Act of 1934, 6, 513
Segregation of duties, 122

Semidirect expenses, 895–897
Semivariable costs, 993–994, 1020
Separate economic entity assumption, 521
Separate entity assumption, 11
Separate payroll accounts, 367–368
Serial bonds, 785
Service business, 32–33, **198**, B-5
Service charges, 302
Shareholder, 12, **708**
Short or over, cash, 282
Shrink of inventory, 610
Sight draft, 588
Single-maturity bonds, 785
Single-step income statement, 460
Single trade discounts, 214–215
Sinking fund investment to retire bonds, 795–796
Slide errors, **73**
Smalley, John, 665
Smith, Gordon, 279
Social entities, 10
Social Security Act, 351, 357
Social Security Administration, 389, 391
Social security (FICA or OASDI) taxes, 351
    accrued salaries subject to, 426
    employee share of, 351
    employer share of, 352, 387–389
    withholdings for hourly employees of, 357
Sole proprietorships, 10–11
    assets and liabilities investment of, 669
    characteristics of, 13
Southwest Airlines Co., 52–53, 366
Special journals, 198–199
Specific identification method of costing inventory, **601,** 603
S&P Global, Inc., 891
Standard cost accounting, 991–1018
    actual *versus* standard costs, 1000–1004
    cost behavior, 992–994
    direct labor standard costs, 999
    fixed budget preparation, 994–996
    flexible budget preparation, 996–997
    manufacturing overhead standard costs, 999
    overview, 942
    raw materials standard costs, 998
    standard cost card, 999–1000
Standard cost card, 999–1000
Standard costs, 942
Starbucks, Inc., 419
State and local taxes, 352
Stated value of stock, 712
Statement of account, 282
Statement of cash flows, 865
    disclosures required in, 873
    indirect and direct preparation methods for, 872–873
Statement of cost of goods manufactured, 915–917, 926
Statement of financial position, 29
Statement of owner's equity, 37–39
    for balance sheet preparation, 463
    worksheets and, 137, 145–146
Statement of partners' equities, 681

Statement of retained earnings, 763–764
Statement of stockholders' equity, 764
Statements of Financial Accounting Concepts (FASB), 514
Statements of Financial Accounting Standards (FASB), **13,** 514
Statements of position (SOPs, AcSEC of AICPA), 515
State sales tax return, 220–223
State unemployment taxes (SUTA), 353, 397–398
Stock, 11
    bonds *versus,* 786–787
    book value per share of stock, 832–833
    corporate capital, 712–714
    dividends on, 714–717
    earnings per share of common, 829
    recording issuance of, 718–724
    sales of, 828
    subscriptions for corporate capital, 724–726
Stock certificates, 727–728
Stock control accounts, 728–729
Stock dividends, 757–758
Stockholders, 12
    in corporations, **708**
    proceeds of cash investments by, 871
Stockholders' equity, 710, 832
Stockholders' ledger, 727–728
Stockholders of record, 756
Stock splits, 758
Straight-line amortization, 791
Straight-line depreciation, 130, 626–627, 629, 631
Stress, on job, 895
Subchapter S corporations, 12, **709**
Subscribers' ledger, 728
Subscription book for stock subscriptions, **728**
Subsidiary ledgers, 198–199
    control accounts and, 253
    in perpetual inventory system, 317
    for stock, 728–729
Sum-of-the-years'-digits method of depreciation, 628–629
Sunk costs, 1023, 1027
Suppliers, financial information used by, 6, 8
Supplies, 427, 867
Swell of inventory, 610

T

T accounts, 55–89, **56;** *see also* Business transactions
    account balances, 62–63
    for asset, liability, and owner's equity, 56–61
    chart of accounts, 73–74
    debit and credit rules, 70–72
    drawing accounts, 69–70
    example of, 55
    financial statements, 73
    permanent and temporary accounts, 74–75
    revenue and expense accounts, 65–69
    trial balances, 72–73
Tangible personal property, 624–625
Target Stores, Inc., 610
Tax accounting, 5, 515

Taxes
    federal income, 351, 358, 369
    Federal Insurance Contributions Act (FICA), 351–352
    federal unemployment taxes (FUTA), 352–353
    Medicare, 351–352, 357, 387–389
    OASDI, 351
    payment of, 289
    payroll, 352–353, 426, 921
    property, 427
    sales, 220–224, 281–282, 314
    social security, 351–352, 357, 387–389
    state and local, 352
    state unemployment taxes (SUTA), 353
    withheld, recording payment of, 389–390
Tax-exempt wages, 357
Tax Foundation, 220
Temporary T accounts, 74–75
Time and a half (overtime rate of pay), **351**
Time draft, 589
Timeliness, as qualitative characteristic of financial reports, 520
Time tickets, in job cost accounting, **949**
Time Warner, Inc., 55, 668
Total equities, 831–832
Total net realizable value of inventory, 606
Trade acceptances, 589
Trade discounts, 214, 312–313
Trade-in, disposal by, 636
Trademarks, 643
Trade names, 643
Trading on the equity, 787
Transactions, combined journal recording of, B-2–B-4
Transferability of ownership rights, in corporations, 709
Transfer agents for corporations, **728**–729
Transfer price, 893
Transmittal of Wage and Tax Statements (Form W-3), 395–396
TransMontaigne Partners, L. P., 704–705
Transparency, 525
Transportation charges, 246
Transportation In account, **246**
Transposition errors, **73,** 135
Treasury stock, 761–763
Trend analysis, 823–825
Trial balance, 72
    adjusted, 141–142, 431–434
    errors in, 73
    postclosing, 175–176, 472–473, 927
    preparation of, 72
    as worksheet entry, 920, 924
    worksheet section for, 126–127, 139–140
Turner Broadcasting, 55

U

Uber, Inc., 1
UCC (Uniform Commercial Code), 576, 589
Uncollectible accounts; *see also* Accounts receivable
    adjustments to, 423–424
    allowance method of accounting for, applying, 547–554
    allowance method of accounting for, overview, 546–547
    at Amazon.com, 545
    definition of, 216
    direct charge-off method of accounting for, applying, 556–558
    direct charge-off method of accounting for, overview, 547
    expenses for, 423
    losses from, 423
    as worksheet entries, 921
Underapplied overhead, 950–951
Understandability, as qualitative characteristic of financial reports, 521
Unearned income, adjustments for, **429**–430
Unemployment insurance program, 397–404
Uniform Commercial Code (UCC), 576, 589
Uniform CPA Examination, 3
Unions, financial information used by, 7–8
Unit costs, 967
United Business Company, 349
Units-of-output method of depreciation, 629–630
Units-of-production method of depreciation, 629–630
University of Pennsylvania, 745
Unlimited liability, 667
Unsecured bonds (debentures), 785
Updated account balances, 434
Urban Outfitters, Inc., 745
US Airways Group, 23
U.S. Census Bureau, 943
U.S. Department of Defense, 610
U.S. Patent and Trademark Office, 643
U.S. Supreme Court, 7, 708
Utilities expense, 34, 68–69

V

Valuation account, 547
Valuation of inventory, 600
Variable costing; *see* Direct costing
Variable costs, 992, 996, 1020
Variance analysis, 1000–1004
Verifiability, as qualitative characteristic of financial reports, 520
Verschoor, Curtis, 209
Vertical analysis, 816
    of balance sheet, 818–819
    of income statement, 816–818
Visa credit cards, 217
Vitamin Shoppe, Inc., 459
Volkswagen AGF, 913
Voucher system, for internal control, 258, 293

W

Wage and Hour Law method, 356
Wage and Tax Statement (Form W-2), 394–395
Wage-bracket table method, 358–361
Wages accrued, 921
Walmart Stores, Inc., 122–123, 246, 356, 610, 722
Warehouse expenses, 462
Weighted average method of inventory costing, **601**
Whistle-blowers, protection for, 7
Wholesale business, 214–215
William Barclay Peat & Company, 125

Withdrawals, 35
Withheld taxes, recording payment of, 389–390
Withholding statement (Form W-2), **394**
Woolpert, Ralph L., 666
Woolpert LLP, 666
Workers' compensation insurance, 353, 400–404
Working capital, 473, 475
Working capital ratio, 833
Work in process, 916–917
    beginning inventory for, 975
    costs charged to, 971–972
    inventory for, 944, 949
Work in process subsidiary ledger, 946, 948
Workman, Benjamin, 785
Workplace injury and illness prevention programs, 1003
Worksheets, 126–163
    adjusted trial balance section of, 133–134, 141–142, 431–434
    adjustments section of, 127–131
    balance sheet prepared from, 137–139, 145–147
    balance sheet section of, 434–436
    for corporate earnings, 749–751
    income statement and balance sheet sections of, 134–136, 143
    income statement prepared from, 136–137, 145–146
    income statement section of, 434–436
    journalizing and posting adjusting entries from, 147–148
    managerial implications of, 149
    for manufacturing activities, 920–924, 926
    net income and net loss determined from, 144
    statement of owner's equity prepared from, 137, 145–146
    trial balance section of, 126–127, 139–140
WorldCom, Inc., 7, 162, 513
Writing checks, 298–299
Writing off customers' uncollectible accounts, 552–553

Y

Yield on common stock, 830

Z

Zuckerberg, Mark, 707

SAMPLE GENERAL LEDGER ACCOUNTS

Account Name	Classification	Permanent or Temporary	Normal Balance
INCOME STATEMENT			
Fees Income	Revenue	Temporary	Credit
Sales	Revenue	Temporary	Credit
Sales Discounts	Contra Revenue	Temporary	Debit
Sales Returns and Allowances	Contra Revenue	Temporary	Debit
Purchases	Cost of Goods Sold	Temporary	Debit
Freight In	Cost of Goods Sold	Temporary	Debit
Purchases Discounts	Contra Cost of Goods Sold	Temporary	Credit
Purchases Returns and Allowances	Contra Cost of Goods Sold	Temporary	Credit
Direct Labor	Cost of Goods Manufactured	Temporary	Debit
Indirect Labor	Cost of Goods Manufactured	Temporary	Debit
Indirect Materials and Supplies	Cost of Goods Manufactured	Temporary	Debit
Payroll Taxes—Factory	Cost of Goods Manufactured	Temporary	Debit
Repairs and Maintenance—Factory	Cost of Goods Manufactured	Temporary	Debit
Depreciation—Factory	Cost of Goods Manufactured	Temporary	Debit
Insurance—Factory	Cost of Goods Manufactured	Temporary	Debit
Property Taxes—Factory	Cost of Goods Manufactured	Temporary	Debit
Advertising Expense	Operating Expense	Temporary	Debit
Amortization	Operating Expense	Temporary	Debit
Bank Fees Expense	Operating Expense	Temporary	Debit
Cash Short or Over	Operating Expense	Temporary	Debit
Delivery Expense	Operating Expense	Temporary	Debit
Depreciation Expense	Operating Expense	Temporary	Debit
Insurance Expense	Operating Expense	Temporary	Debit
Payroll Taxes Expense	Operating Expense	Temporary	Debit
Property Tax Expense	Operating Expense	Temporary	Debit
Rent Expense	Operating Expense	Temporary	Debit
Research and Development Expense	Operating Expense	Temporary	Debit
Salaries Expense	Operating Expense	Temporary	Debit
Supplies Expense	Operating Expense	Temporary	Debit
Telephone Expense	Operating Expense	Temporary	Debit
Uncollectible Accounts Expense	Operating Expense	Temporary	Debit
Utilities Expense	Operating Expense	Temporary	Debit
Workers' Compensation Insurance Expense	Operating Expense	Temporary	Debit
Gain/Loss on Sale of Assets	Other Income/Expense	Temporary	—
Interest Income/Expense	Other Income/Expense	Temporary	—
Miscellaneous Income/Expense	Other Income/Expense	Temporary	—
Income Tax Expense	Other Expense	Temporary	Debit
STATEMENT OF OWNER'S EQUITY			
*(Owner's Name), Capital	Owner's Equity	Permanent	Credit
(Owner's Name), Drawing	Owner's Equity	Temporary	Debit
STATEMENT OF PARTNERS' EQUITY			
*(Partner's Name), Capital	Partners' Equity	Permanent	Credit
(Partner's Name), Drawing	Partners' Equity	Temporary	Debit
STATEMENT OF RETAINED EARNINGS			
*Retained Earnings—Appropriated	Stockholders' Equity	Permanent	Credit
*Retained Earnings	Stockholders' Equity	Permanent	Credit

*Account also appears on the balance sheet.

SAMPLE GENERAL LEDGER ACCOUNTS

Account Name	Classification	Permanent or Temporary	Normal Balance
BALANCE SHEET			
Cash	Current Asset	Permanent	Debit
Petty Cash Fund	Current Asset	Permanent	Debit
Notes Receivable	Current Asset	Permanent	Debit
Notes Receivable—Discounted	Contra Current Asset	Permanent	Credit
Accounts Receivable	Current Asset	Permanent	Debit
Allowance for Doubtful Accounts	Contra Current Asset	Permanent	Credit
Interest Receivable	Current Asset	Permanent	Debit
Stock Subscriptions Receivable	Current Asset	Permanent	Debit
Prepaid Expenses	Current Asset	Permanent	Debit
Merchandise Inventory	Current Asset	Permanent	Debit
Raw Materials Inventory	Current Asset	Permanent	Debit
Work in Process Inventory	Current Asset	Permanent	Debit
Finished Goods Inventory	Current Asset	Permanent	Debit
Building	Property, Plant & Equipment	Permanent	Debit
Equipment	Property, Plant & Equipment	Permanent	Debit
Land	Property, Plant & Equipment	Permanent	Debit
Land Improvements	Property, Plant & Equipment	Permanent	Debit
Accumulated Depreciation	Contra Property, Plant & Equipment	Permanent	Credit
Goodwill	Intangible Asset	Permanent	Debit
Organization Costs	Intangible Asset	Permanent	Debit
Patent	Intangible Asset	Permanent	Debit
Notes Payable	Current Liability	Permanent	Credit
Accounts Payable	Current Liability	Permanent	Credit
Dividends Payable—Preferred	Current Liability	Permanent	Credit
Dividends Payable—Common	Current Liability	Permanent	Credit
Salaries Payable	Current Liability	Permanent	Credit
Social Security Tax Payable	Current Liability	Permanent	Credit
Medicare Tax Payable	Current Liability	Permanent	Credit
Employee Income Tax Payable	Current Liability	Permanent	Credit
Federal Unemployment Tax Payable	Current Liability	Permanent	Credit
State Unemployment Tax Payable	Current Liability	Permanent	Credit
Health Insurance Premiums Payable	Current Liability	Permanent	Credit
Workers' Compensation Insurance Payable	Current Liability	Permanent	Credit
Interest Payable	Current Liability	Permanent	Credit
Sales Tax Payable	Current Liability	Permanent	Credit
Income Tax Payable	Current Liability	Permanent	Credit
Accrued Expenses Payable	Current Liability	Temporary	Credit
Unearned Income	Current Liability	Permanent	Credit
Bonds Payable	Long-Term Liability	Permanent	Credit
Premium on Bonds Payable	Long-Term Liability	Permanent	Credit
Discount on Bonds Payable	Contra Long-Term Liability	Permanent	Debit
(Owner's Name), Capital	Owner's Equity	Permanent	Credit
(Partner's Name), Capital	Partners' Equity	Permanent	Credit
Preferred Stock	Stockholders' Equity	Permanent	Credit
Preferred Stock Subscribed	Stockholders' Equity	Permanent	Credit
Paid-in Capital in Excess of Par—Preferred	Stockholders' Equity	Permanent	Credit
Common Stock	Stockholders' Equity	Permanent	Credit
Common Stock Dividend Distributable	Stockholders' Equity	Permanent	Credit
Common Stock Subscribed	Stockholders' Equity	Permanent	Credit
Paid-in Capital in Excess of Par—Common	Stockholders' Equity	Permanent	Credit
Donated Capital	Stockholders' Equity	Permanent	Credit
Retained Earnings—Appropriated	Stockholders' Equity	Permanent	Credit
Retained Earnings	Stockholders' Equity	Permanent	Credit
Treasury Stock	Contra Stockholders' Equity	Permanent	Debit

RULES OF DEBIT AND CREDIT

PERMANENT ACCOUNTS

Assets	
Debit **+** **Increase** **Normal Balance**	Credit – Decrease

Examples: Cash
Accounts Receivable
Building
Equipment

Contra Assets	
Debit – Decrease	**Credit** **+** **Increase** **Normal Balance**

Examples: Allowance for Doubtful Accounts
Accumulated Depreciation—Building

Liabilities	
Debit – Decrease	**Credit** **+** **Increase** **Normal Balance**

Examples: Accounts Payable
Notes Payable
Bonds Payable

Contra Liabilities	
Debit **+** **Increase** **Normal Balance**	Credit – Decrease

Example: Discount on Bonds Payable

Equity	
Debit – Decrease	**Credit** **+** **Increase** **Normal Balance**

Examples: Linda Carter, Capital *(Sole Proprietorship)*
Ted West, Capital *(Partnership)*
Capital Stock *(Corporation)*
Retained Earnings *(Corporation)*

RULES OF DEBIT AND CREDIT

TEMPORARY ACCOUNTS

Withdrawals
(Sole Proprietorship/Partnership)

Debit	Credit
+	−
Increase	Decrease
Normal Balance	

Example: Linda Carter, Withdrawals

Revenue

Debit	Credit
−	+
Decrease	Increase
	Normal Balance

Examples: Fees Income
Sales

Contra Revenue

Debit	Credit
+	−
Increase	Decrease
Normal Balance	

Examples: Sales Discounts
Sales Returns and Allowances

Cost of Goods Sold

Debit	Credit
+	−
Increase	Decrease
Normal Balance	

Examples: Purchases
Freight In

Contra Cost of Goods Sold

Debit	Credit
−	+
Decrease	Increase
	Normal Balance

Examples: Purchases Discounts
Purchases Returns and Allowances

Expenses

Debit	Credit
+	−
Increase	Decrease
Normal Balance	

Examples: Advertising Expense
Utilities Expense
Rent Expense